Encyclopedia of Knowledge Management

David G. Schwartz
Bar–Ilan University, Israel

IDEA GROUP REFERENCE
Hershey · London · Melbourne · Singapore

Acquisitions Editor:	Renée Davies
Development Editor:	Kristin Roth
Senior Managing Editor:	Amanda Appicello
Managing Editor:	Jennifer Neidig
Copy Editors:	Maria Boyer, Amanda O'Brien and Shanelle Ramelb
Typesetters:	Diane Huskinson, Sara Reed and Larissa Zearfoss
Support Staff:	Michelle Potter
Cover Design:	Lisa Tosheff
Printed at:	Yurchak Printing Inc.

Published in the United States of America by
Idea Group Reference (an imprint of Idea Group Inc.)
701 E. Chocolate Avenue, Suite 200
Hershey PA 17033
Tel: 717-533-8845
Fax: 717-533-8661
E-mail: cust@idea-group.com
Web site: http://www.idea-group-ref.com

and in the United Kingdom by
Idea Group Reference (an imprint of Idea Group Inc.)
3 Henrietta Street
Covent Garden
London WC2E 8LU
Tel: 44 20 7240 0856
Fax: 44 20 7379 3313
Web site: http://www.eurospan.co.uk

Library of Congress Cataloging-in-Publication Data

Encyclopedia of knowledge management / David Schwartz, Editor.
    p. cm.
  Summary: "This encyclopedia is a research reference work documenting the past, present, and possible future directions of knowledge management"--Provided by publisher.
  Includes bibliographical references and index.
  ISBN 1-59140-573-4 (hc) -- ISBN 1-59140-574-2 (ebook)
  1. Knowledge management. 2. Information resources management. 3. Information networks--Management. 4. Organizational learning. I. Schwartz, David G.
  HD30.2.E53 2006
  658.4'038--dc22
                    2005013818

British Cataloguing in Publication Data
A Cataloguing in Publication record for this book is available from the British Library.

All work contributed to this encyclopedia is new, previously-unpublished material. Each article is assigned to at least 2-3 expert reviewers and is subject to a blind, peer review by these reviewers. The views expressed in this encyclopedia are those of the authors, but not necessarily of the publisher.

Editorial Advisory Board

List of Contributors

Contents

Table of Contents

Table of Contents

Contents
by Category

Theoretical Aspects of Knowledge Management

Philosophical Underpinnings

Types of Knowledge

Knowledge Management Models

Effects of Knowledge Management

Processes of Knowledge Management

Creation

Discovery

Gathering

Calibration

Modeling

Integration

Organizational and Social Aspects of Knowledge Management

Organizational Learning

Managerial Aspects of Knowledge Management

Knowledge Management Strategies

Knowledge Management Systems

Managing the Knowledge Environment

Technological Aspects of Knowledge Management

Representation

Artificial Intelligence in Knowledge Management

Table of Contents by Category

Application-Specific Knowledge Management

Healthcare in Knowledge Management

Safety Critical Systems

Customer Knowledge Management

Engineering Design

Professional Services Knowledge Management

Mathematical Knowledge

Military Knowledge

Dedication

No function of man has so much permanence as virtuous activities - these are thought to be more durable even than knowledge of the sciences - and of these themselves the most valuable are more durable because those who are happy spend their life most readily and most continuously in these; for this seems to be the reason why we do not forget them. The attribute in question, then, will belong to the happy man, and he will be happy throughout his life; for always, or by preference to everything else, he will be engaged in virtuous action and contemplation, and he will bear the chances of life most nobly and altogether decorously, if he is 'truly good' and 'foursquare beyond reproach'.

–Aristotle, Nicomachean Ethics, Book 1, 10

Grant me the strength, time and opportunity always to correct what I have acquired, always to extend its domain; for knowledge is immense and the spirit of man can extend indefinitely to enrich itself daily with new requirements.

–Oath of Maimonides, 1135-1204

I dedicate this volume to my parents
Phil and Faygie Schwartz
and in honor of my father's 70th birthday.
A man who is a student of the teachings of both
Aristotle and Maimonides, and lives life guided by the
virtues inspired by those great teachers.

Foreword

A whole encyclopedia devoted to knowledge management (KM)! Who would have thought this possible a few decades back when the subject was first developed? What a great distance we have all traveled since then. Back then if someone would have predicted such a venture I'm sure much laughter would have ensued. I, myself, would have been astounded. And yet, here we are with just such a venture. I think it can be safely stated that when a field of study reaches a point when such a product is produced, it has truly arrived and can no longer be thought of as a fad or management fashion. We have reached just this point.

It might be of value to readers of this foreword to stop for a moment and consider where knowledge management came from—intellectually and in practice and how it evolved from a collection of disparate insights and models from several disciplines into a reasonably coherent subject that can have an entire encyclopedia be devoted to it.

In the realm of theory there were several social science disciplines that were the foundation of the subject, economics may have been the most important of these. Economists had been looking at the subject of knowledge as long ago as Adam Smith in the 18th century—the division of labor being, after all, a knowledge-based concept. The great Victorian economist, Alfred Marshall, wrote about knowledge often being the basis for firm location and clustering. More recently economists during World War II began measuring how long it took to build a combat plane, and then how long it took to build the second and third plane. This early focus on learning-by-doing proved to have a significant influence on subsequent knowledge studies. The contemporary emphasis on evolutionary economics, behavioral economics, and the economics of information, have all emphasized the role of knowledge as has many areas of development economics.

Sociology, too, offered many insights. The current fascination of networks and knowledge derives from sociological tools developed in the past forty years. The interest in communities of practice is strongly influenced by sociological analysis and methods. Trust, too, falls into the category of sociology and is proving a very durable way of understanding why knowledge is effective (or not) in organizations and nations. In fact, the whole movement that emphasizes knowledge as a social phenomenon is a function of much social theory and analysis.

Philosophy has given us at least two critical thinkers for us to digest and reflect on, Michael Polanyi (originally a chemist) and Gilbert Ryle. It can even be argued that Aristotle and Plato play behind the field roles that still influence what we say about knowledge.

The fields of computer science have given us much to think and work with. Artificial intelligence may not have lived up to all its hype, but it had a very strong role in stimulating thought on what knowledge can and can not be modeled that is still being debated. There are also some applications that can truly said to be knowledge-based. The same can be said for expert systems. Cognitive science, especially when it is applied to system thinking, has also proven to be a powerful stimulant with great potential for understanding and modeling knowledge.

Of course, management and business scholars have often taken the lead in the field, synthesizing some of the work mentioned above, as well as developing theories, cases, approaches, proscriptions that can be applied fairly easily by actual knowledge practitioners at work. Often this work was influenced in turn by several earlier management trends, especially information management, the quality movement, and re-engineering. The need for business schools to develop cases for teaching the growing number of KM classes has also spurred practical research into how the theory looks and works out when actually implemented in an organization.

Reviewing the contents of this encyclopedia, I am struck by the diverse and eclectic nature of the field as well as how much convergence and coherence has emerged in such a short time. This volume manages to deal with virtually every aspect of the field without becoming some huge unwieldy black box of a thing focused on data, information, knowledge and everything else under the sun. It is fascinating to see just how much agreement there exists amongst researchers and practitioners as to what KM is, what are its component pieces and core processes, and what are the drivers and mechanisms that make it work.

There is no doubt in my mind that knowledge will only grow in the coming decades as a source of wealth throughout the world economy. The various forms of knowledge—from an individual speculating at her desk to a patent or embedded practice—will gain in value and subsequently gain in management attention and focus. More and more organizations and countries are focusing on knowledge as bedrock of their policy. This volume should provide all of these pioneers with an essential reference source for ideas as to what needs to be addressed and what we have learned about the subject over the past few decades.

Laurence Prusak
Distinguished Scholar, Babson College, USA

Preface:Knowledge Management as a Layered Multi–Disciplinary Pursuit

WHY AN ENCYCLOPEDIA OF KNOWLEDGE MANAGEMENT—AND WHY NOW?

Albert Einstein once said, "Whoever undertakes to set himself up as a judge of truth and knowledge is shipwrecked by the laughter of the Gods." Fortunately Einstein did not extend that fate to those who limit their judgmental activities to the *management* of knowledge.

But an encyclopedia? The very term brings to mind images of heavy dusty tomes documenting centuries of study. So when Mehdi Khosrow-Pour of IGI approached me with the idea for an encyclopedia of knowledge management (KM), my initial reaction was one of skepticism. Would it not be presumptuous, I thought, to take a field as young as knowledge management and compile an encyclopedia?

Then I took a good look at what has been going on in KM-related research over the past two decades. Over 15 peer-reviewed research journals with major aspects of KM as a primary focus (Table 1) producing over 500 articles per annum as well as major annual conferences such as KMEurope (http://www.kmeurope.com) and smaller events covering everything from practical aspects of knowledge management (http://www.dke.univie.ac.at/pakm2004/) to the knowledge and argument visualization (http://www.graphicslink.demon.co.uk/IV05/).

Table 1. KM-focused research journals

#	Journal Title	Publisher
1	Data and Knowledge Engineering	Elsevier Science
2	Data Mining and Knowledge Discovery	Springer-Verlag
3	IEEE Transactions on Knowledge and Data Engineering	IEEE Computer Society
4	Int. J. of Intellectual Property Management	Inderscience Publishers
5	Int. J. of Knowledge and Learning	Inderscience Publishers
6	Int. J. of Knowledge Management	Idea Group Publishing
7	Int. J. of Knowledge Management Studies	Inderscience Publishers
8	Int. J. of Learning and Intellectual Capital	Inderscience Publishers
9	Int. J. of Software Engineering and Knowledge Engineering	World Scientific
10	Journal of Information and Knowledge Management	World Scientific
11	Journal of Intellectual Capital	Emerald Publishers
12	Journal of Knowledge Acquisition	Academic Press
13	Journal of Knowledge Management	Emerald Publishers
14	Knowledge and Information Systems	Springer-Verlag
15	Knowledge, Technology, and Policy	Transaction Publishers
16	Knowledge-Based Systems	Elsevier Science
17	Organizational Learning	Sage Publications
18	The Knowledge Engineering Review	Cambridge University Press

Burden's (2000) KM bibliography, which encompasses both research and industry/trade publications, cites over 900 books and a whopping 8,000 articles devoted to the field. In Rollett's (2003) KM bibliography we are treated to over 1,000 academic research articles on KM.

During the period this volume was being compiled at least two new peer-reviewed KM research journals were announced:

- *International Journal of Knowledge Management Studies* (Inderscience Publishers)
- *International Journal of Knowledge Management* (Idea Group Publishing)

All this, *in addition* to the established list of more general information systems and information science journals and conference venues that serve as a forum knowledge management research. And of course an abundance of industry magazines and newsletters dedicated to the understanding, development, and adoption of organizational knowledge management have been established.

It became clear that not only is there a need to create an authoritative repository of knowledge management concepts, issues, and techniques; but an even stronger compelling need to create a logical structure that maps out the field of knowledge management across its diverse disciplines.

THE SIGNIFICANCE OF ARTICLES IN THE VOLUME

How does this differ from a traditional encyclopedia? Every scientific and intellectual pursuit presents a spectrum of knowledge ranging from the speculative to the experimental to the proven to the well-established. An encyclopedia traditionally presents definitive articles that describe well-established and accepted concepts or events. While we have avoided the speculative extreme, this volume does include a number of entries that may be closer to the 'experimental' end of the spectrum than the 'well-established' end. The need to do so is driven by the youth of the discipline and the desire to not only document the established, but to provide a resource for those who are pursuing the experimental and speculative.

Alavi and Leidner, in their oft-cited *Review of Knowledge Management and Knowledge Management Systems* (2001) bring three pointed conclusions to the fore:

There is no single clear approach to the development of knowledge management systems—it is a multi-faceted endeavor.

Knowledge management is a dynamic, continuous organizational phenomenon of interdependent processes with varying scope and changing characteristics.

Information technology can be used to extend knowledge management beyond traditional storage and retrieval of coded knowledge.

Not only does this encyclopedia reinforce those conclusions, it relishes and thrives in the complexity and diversity to which they allude. The systems and technology perspective is but one of many that have been dealt with in this volume. While we do not wish to lose focus on our main goal of managing knowledge in organizations, in order to better achieve that goal it is necessary to look at areas of study as diverse as epistemology and anthropology in order to map the future directions of knowledge management.

With that goal in mind, a wide net was cast in the Call for Papers in an attempt to attract researchers from many relevant disciples. The resulting articles that appear in this volume were selected through a double-blind review process followed by one or more rounds of revision prior to acceptance. Treatment of certain topics is not exclusive according to a given school or approach, and you will find a number of topics tackled from different perspectives with differing approaches. A field as dynamic as KM needs discussion, disagreement, contradiction—and of course wherever possible, consensus. But we must not sacrifice any of the former on the altar of the latter.

To that end, each author has provided a list of key terms and definitions deemed essential to the topic of his or her article. Rather than aggregate and filter these terms to produce a single "encyclopedic" definition, we have preferred instead to let the authors stand by their definition and allow each reader to interpret and understand each article according to the specific terminological twist taken by its author(s). The comprehensive Index of Key Terms provided at the back of this volume provides pointers to each concept and term in its multiple incarnations.

VOLUME STRUCTURE

The *Encyclopedia of Knowledge Management* is divided into six logical categories:

1. Theoretical Aspects of Knowledge Management
2. Processes of Knowledge Management
3. Organizational and Social Aspects of Knowledge Management
4. Managerial Aspects of Knowledge Management
5. Technological Aspects of Knowledge Management
6. Application-Specific Knowledge Management

The Table of Contents by Category will help you find articles based on this logical section structure.

Within each of the six major categories are one or more articles on each of the topics that comprise that category—often multiple articles on different aspects of a given topic.

Even though the articles appear in alphabetical order based on the title of the article, the Table of Contents by Category gives our readers a content-oriented logical map to this publication.

PEELING BACK THE LAYERS

The first five sections are the result of what I would characterize as a *layered approach* to the discipline of knowledge management. It is this layered view, as shown in Figure 1 that I have sought to reinforce with this encyclopedic volume.

Consider the view presented in Figure 1 giving a holistic view of knowledge management and its foundations. The central core of philosophies (the middle) must inform our choice of practical knowledge management processes (the first ring). These processes must be implemented and adapted to address managerial, social and organizational needs (the second ring). Finally the implementation of KM process to meet our organizational needs must be supported by and implemented through a set of relevant information technologies (the outer ring).

The primary processes that make up knowledge management in practice should ideally derive from the core theories. Figure 1 illustrates a number of the philosophers whose theories of knowledge, economics, and business form the core of knowledge management. Understanding these philosophies is fundamental to our common endeavor. Without grounding our processes in their theoretical soil we run the very real risk of simply cobbling together processes on an opportunistic basis. We must, in a disciplined manner, turn to our theoretical core in determining the essential processes of KM. In cases where experience begets a process that has yet to be identified with a core theory one must not belittle the need to eventually discover that grounding. At the end of the day this is what will help distinguish fad from enduring science.

The layer of processes presents one view of the different stages, activities, and cycles that comprise knowledge management. Processes need to be pragmatic, in terms of our ability to implement them, comprehensive so that we can achieve end-to-end solutions, replicable and generalizable so they can be applied across a wide range of organizations.

That is not to say that these processes should be devoid of organizational context. On the contrary, it is the function of the third layer, that of organizational, social and managerial considerations, to mold, combine, and innovate using the KM processes in order to meet their well-defined theory-driven goals.

Encasing all is the outer ring—that of the enabling technologies that so often seem to be driving KM rather than facilitating it. Figure 1 is, of course, representative rather than exhaustive. Additional technologies and new applications of existing technologies will continue to expand this layer.

Being driven by technology is not necessarily negative. Consider how the development of the electron microscope led to the discovery of a plethora of atomic and elemental behaviors. The observation of these behaviors led to the development of new theories upon which those discoveries were validated and new discoveries predicated. So too the

Figure 1. Layer upon layer of knowledge management

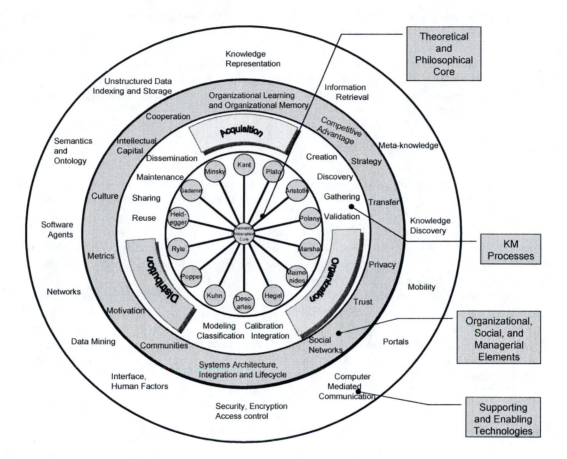

computing, storage, and communications technologies available today are enabling the implementation and study of new types of knowledge representation, sharing, communications, and interactions.

As the theoreticians among us deepen their understanding of the many diverse technologies that have a positive impact on KM, they can experimentally apply those technologies more effectively and in innovative ways. As the technologists among us are enriched with a solid theoretical foundation they can focus their efforts on the most promising application areas and most difficult theoretical challenges. And our social scientists provide us with lenses through which we can view both theory and technology, and perhaps build the bridge between theory and praxis. Everyone benefits from a richer more constructive research and development environment.

HOW TO USE THIS BOOK

As a Research Reference

The primary purpose of this volume is to serve as a research reference work. To that end extensive indexing has been undertaken to allow the reader quick access to primary and secondary entries related to keywords and topics. The six logical sections and the list of topics provided for each section will enable the reader to locate and delve deeply into any given area of knowledge management from their desired perspective.

As a Course Reference

The sheer comprehensiveness combined with the logical structure of this volume also lends itself towards use as a reference for knowledge management courses.

Selecting two to three articles from each of the six section results in many possible study sequences for a comprehensive introductory course in knowledge management. Alternatively, the first five logical sections of this volume can be used individually as the curricular foundation for courses in: knowledge management theory, designing KM processes, organizational KM, managing KM, and technologies for knowledge management respectively.

CONCLUSION

The need for an *Encyclopedia of Knowledge Management* is driven by the tremendous growth and diversity that has become associated with knowledge management. Whether treated as an emerging discipline (Jennex & Croadsell, 2005; Schwartz, 2005), or a possibly recycled concept (Spiegler, 2000), knowledge management will continue to make its mark on organizations of all forms and sizes. The need to help organizations manage their knowledge has been extolled in nearly two decade's worth of management literature. In order to truly understand and appreciate what goes into making knowledge management work, we need to approach it from theoretical, procedural, social, managerial and technical perspectives. The layered approach can help us achieve those objectives.

The process of editing this encyclopedia has been enlightening. Most enjoyable has been the interaction with the authors, some of whom have appeared from the most unexpected of places, and others who have come forward from established bastions of knowledge management research.

It is my sincere hope that this volume serves not only as a reference to KM researchers, both novice and veteran, but also as a resource for those coming from the hundreds of disciplines and organizations upon which knowledge management has, should, and will have an everlasting impact.

REFERENCES

Alavi, M., & Leidner, D.E. (2001). Knowledge management and knowledge management systems: Conceptual foundations and research issues. *MIS Quarterly, 1*(25), 107-136.

Burden, P.R. (2000). Knowledge management: The bibliography. Information Today Inc. Retrieved November 2004, from *http://domin.dom.edu/faculty/SRIKANT/lis88001/kmbib.html*

Jennex, M.E., & Croasdell, D. (2005). Is knowledge management a discipline? *International Journal of Knowledge Management, 1*(1).

Rollett, H. (2003). Knowledge management bibliography. Retrieved November 2004, from *http://www2. iicm.edu/ herwig/kmbib.html*

Schwartz, D.G. (2005). The emerging discipline of knowledge management. *International Journal of Knowledge Management, 2*(1).

Spiegler, I. (2000). Knowledge management: A new idea or a recycled concept? *Communications of the Association for Information Systems, 14*(3).

David G. Schwartz
Bar-Ilan University, Israel

Acknowledgments

First and foremost, I would like to acknowledge the efforts of the more than 160 researchers from over 20 countries whose work appears in this encyclopedia. Without your hard work, responsiveness in the review and revision process, attention to detail, and of course your daily research endeavors, this volume could never have taken shape. I have thoroughly enjoyed my interactions with you, the debates over terminology, clarity of thought and discourse, big picture vs. small picture, KM philosophy, and hundreds of other points that arose during the review process. In the cases in which authors have worked with me to split their initial contributions into multiple articles in order to preserve the necessary granularity and clarity of the volume, I thank you for your openness and willingness to revisit, restructure, and rethink your writings.

I thank our huge team of reviewers comprised of all the authors whose work appears in this volume and well as many others too numerous to list. I thank you all for taking part in the Herculean review effort.

The highly professional team at Idea Group Inc. deserves a special note of thanks. Dr. Mehdi Khosrow-Pour, whose vision for a comprehensive set of encyclopedias covering all aspects of information technology and management, conceived the *Encyclopedia of Knowledge Management* and saw the need and potential for this volume. Jan Travers and Renée Davies have, through their professionalism, support and encouragement, made the editorial and production process as smooth as could have been hoped for.

To my editorial advisory board (EAB)—I thank you thrice, for it is a threefold contribution that you have brought to this volume. First, by helping conceptualize a high level map of the knowledge management landscape, we were able to compose a call for papers that encouraged all forms, schools, types, approaches, and levels of KM researchers to propose a diverse superset of articles from which the final volume developed. Second, by having access to the "social networks" of some of the preeminent knowledge management and information systems researchers in the world, we were able to generate a phenomenal high quality response to the CFP. Finally, I thank you for helping to fine-tune the article line-up, making sure the gaps were filled and the presentations cohesive and coherent.

Thanks to my colleague and friend Dov Te'eni who, in addition to his editorial advisory board participation, helped me before this project was even announced—to clarify the need, conceptualization, and direction of what an encyclopedia of knowledge management should be, and has provided encouragement and valued advice throughout.

Thanks to EAB member Pat Molholt and the faculty and staff of Columbia University's Office of Scholarly Resources and Department of Biomedical Informatics for hosting me during part of my sabbatical and providing me with a welcoming environment in which to advance my work on the encyclopedia.

To my dear wife Ronit, thank you for putting up with the long hours, extra pressure, and nighttime writing sessions. Thank you for standing beside me with your confidence, love, and support throughout this long and oftentimes overwhelming project. To my children, Ariel, Noam, Tal, Batya, and Moriah, I hope some day you will have occasion to read this—well, at least the preface—and get an idea of what sort of things your dad has been busy with.

David G. Schwartz
Jerusalem, Israel
March 2005

About the Editor

David G. Schwartz, PhD, is head of the Information Systems Division and a senior lecturer at the Bar-Ilan University Graduate School of Business Administration, Israel. He serves as editor of the internationally acclaimed journal *Internet Research* (Emerald Group Publishing) and currently serves on the editorial boards of the *International Journal of Knowledge Management Studies* (Inderscience Publishers) and the *International Journal of Knowledge Management* (Idea Group Publishing).

Dr. Schwartz has published extensively on many aspects of software and information technology and his writings have been included in leading publications such as *IEEE Intelligent Systems, International Journal of Human-Computer Studies, IEEE Transactions on Professional Communications, Kybernetes,* and the *Journal of Organizational Behavior.* His books include *Cooperating Heterogeneous Systems* (Kluwer, 1995) and the co-edited *Internet-Based Knowledge Management and Organizational Memory* (Idea Group Publishing, 2000). Dr. Schwartz's research interest in knowledge management ranges from its epistemological roots through to enabling technologies, drawing heavily from his background in artificial intelligence. Other research areas in which he is active include computer mediated communications, distributed artificial intelligence, and Internet-based systems.

In addition to his research activities, Dr. Schwartz is a partner of Apropos IT Ventures, a Venture Capital Fund focused on early stage Israeli information technology. Dr. Schwartz received a PhD from Case Western Reserve University; an MBA from McMaster University; and a BSc from the University of Toronto, Canada.

Anti-Foundational Knowledge Management

Tom Butler
University College Cork, Ireland

INTRODUCTION

Under the influence of Enlightenment epistemological thought, the social sciences have exhibited a distinct tendency to prefer deterministic[1] explanations of social phenomena. In the sociology of knowledge, for example, "foundational" researchers seek to arrive at objective knowledge of social phenomena through the application of "social scientific methodolog[ies] based on the eternal truths of human nature, purged of historical and cultural prejudices" and which also ignore the subjective *intrusions* of social actors (Hekman, 1986, p. 5). This article argues that "foundationalist" perspectives heavily influence theory and praxis in knowledge management. "Foundationalist" thinking is particularly evident in the posited role of IT in creating, capturing, and diffusing knowledge in social and organisational contexts. In order to address what many would consider to be a deficiency in such thinking, a constructivist "antifoundationalist" perspective is presented that considers socially constructed knowledge as being simultaneously "situated" and "distributed" and which recognizes its role in shaping social action within "communities-of-practice." In ontological terms, the constructivist "antifoundational" paradigm posits that realities are constructed from multiple, intangible mental constructions that are socially and experientially based, local and specific in nature, and which are dependent on their form and content on the individual persons or groups holding the constructions (see Guba & Lincoln, 1994; Bruner, 1990). One of the central assumptions of this paradigm is that there exist multiple realities with differences among them that cannot be resolved through rational processes or increased data. Insights drawn from this short article are addressed to academics and practitioners in order to illustrate the considerable difficulties inherent in representing individual knowledge and of the viability of isolating, capturing, and managing knowledge in organisational contexts with or without the use of IT.

BACKGROUND: WHAT KNOWLEDGE IS AND WHAT IT IS NOT?

The point of departure for the present treatise on the concept of "knowledge" is a definition that is in good standing within the IS field and which is congruent with extant perspectives across the social sciences (e.g., Grant, 1996). In their book *Working Knowledge,* Davenport and Prusak (1998) posit that:

Knowledge is a fluid mix of framed experience, values, contextual information, and expert insight that provides a framework for evaluating and incorporating new experiences and information. It originates and is applied in the minds of knowers. In organisations, it often becomes embedded not only in documents and repositories but also in organisational routines, processes, practices, and norms. (p. 3)

While this definition is, on the surface, all-embracing and without contradiction it does, however, possess certain weaknesses that can only be illustrated by a consideration of taken-for-granted issues of ontology. This involves a description of the relationships that exist between the individual and his social world; that is between the knowing social actor and the social groupings and contexts in which he or she participates and exists, and in which knowledge is socially constructed. In terms of the present analysis, this task begins with a brief consideration of the constructivist, "antifoundational" philosophies of Martin Heidegger and Hans Georg Gadamer in order to sketch out the ontological basis of knowledge. This undertaking is particularly timely given the recent emphasis on knowledge management, which is described "[as] an integrated, systematic approach to identifying, managing, and sharing all of an enterprise's information assets, including databases, documents, policies, and procedures, as well as previously unarticulated expertise and experience held by individual workers."[2] Whereas the ability of organisations to identify, manage, and share, databases, documents, and codified procedures using IT is not in question, identifying, managing, and sharing tacit knowledge using IT is questionable, as the following treatise on knowledge illustrates.

An Anti-Foundational Perspective on Knowledge

In response to the question "What is knowledge and what is it not?" we argue that knowledge cannot ever become "embedded...in documents and repositories [and] also in organisational routines, processes, practices, and norms." Why? Precisely because it is impossible to isolate and represent objectively "a fluid mix of framed experience, values, contextual information, and expert insight." Certainly, as Bruner (1990) points out, a social actor's knowledge resides not only in his head, but also in the notes, underlined book passages, manuals, and guides he consults, and in the computer-based data he has access to. This is, in many respects, a shorthand description by Bruner. Social actors use such sources because of their inability to recall every source of data they have interpreted and laid down in memory (see Goleman, 1996)—hence they are considered sources of personal information only for the actor who has painstakingly sought out, collated, and put into context the data contained in each personal artefact. Accordingly, contextual, temporally based data makes the transition to knowledge only when an actor interprets (or subsequently reinterprets) them in order to inform his or her understanding of some phenomenon or other. This is a fairly straightforward task for the individual who has, over time, constructed a personal database of the type described. However, others who access the personal "notes, underlined passages, manuals, etc." that constitute such databases may interpret their content differently and not come to the same understanding, as they may not have the same pre-existing ground of understanding and knowledge of the phenomenon in question as the original author[3]. All this is indicative of the "situated" and "distributed" and "temporal" nature of knowledge[4] (hence the origins of Hermeneutics in biblical studies and philosophy): But how does it relate to the social context and ground of knowledge?

As part of the interpretive process that characterizes all understanding, meaning is attributed to data within the context of the actor's constantly evolving "lived experience" and under the sway of a "tradition" (Gadamer, 1975). Heidegger (1976) and Gadamer (1975) illustrate that the "lived experience" of social actors arises out of the web of encounters and dialogues that characterize individual existence or "Being-in-the-world." The concept of "lived experience" describes the relation-

ship between social actors and other beings that populate the tradition or culture in which they are embedded (in a Heideggerian sense, the term "beings" refers not only to other humans but all social phenomena). In delineating the constitution of "lived experience," Heidegger (1976) points out that social actors are "thrown" into a "life-world" where their existence has, from the outset, been "tuned" or "situated" to be a specific existence with other beings, within a specific "tradition," and with a specific history. However, in order to cope with their "throwness" social actors come ready equipped with a "fore-knowledge" or, in Gadamerian terms, a "prejudice"-laden "effective-historical consciousness," that enables them to interpret, make sense of, and partake in their social world. "Fore-knowledge" is, in many ways, knowledge of the "ready-to-hand" (Zuhanden) that constitutes an actor's "life world." Thus, the "ready-to-hand" possess a degree of familiarity that effectively sees them dissolved into the unreflective background of the actor's daily existence. If, however, something happens that results in a "breakdown" in understanding, social phenomena become the object of "theoretical" reasoning and acquire the ontological status of being "present-at-hand" (i.e., a Vorhanden) until the "breakdown" has been repaired. As Gadamer illustrates, social actors must give recognition to the influence that "effective-historical consciousness" exerts if they are to work out their "prejudices."

The process of "working out" prejudices and of repairing breakdowns in understanding is governed by what Gadamer called the hermeneutic "circle of understanding." Here, the "whole" that constitutes a phenomenon is apprehended by the cyclical interpretation of its constituent "parts" as they relate to each other and to the "whole." In so doing, an actor interprets relevant data as "present-at-hand" using a form of question and answer called the dialectic (Socratic, Hegelian, and Analytic-Reductionist—see Butler, 1998). Thus, the actor's understanding of constituent "parts" will be consolidated, and in so doing the horizons or perspectives of interpreter and interpreted will gradually fuse. Thus, in repairing breakdowns, a "fusion of horizons" (of understanding) takes place between interpreter and interpreted.

The pivotal role of language in the interpretive process of understanding has been noted by Gadamer (1975). Accordingly, Bruner (1990) argues that institutional contexts are socially constructed through the narratives of constituent actors. Thus, over time and through highly complex and ill-defined social processes constituted by a polyphonic dialectic, there evolves a shared understanding that constitutes a culture and tradition. In addition, it is clear from Gadamer (1975) that the authoritative impulse to conform, as indicated by the existence of Heidegger's "das Man," is testimony to the resilience of a shared "world view" among actors in institutional contexts and the unwillingness to accept "new" knowledge (e.g., Leonard-Barton, 1995; Pfeffer & Sutton, 2000). This brief ontological view of knowledge has profound implications for those who examine the nature of knowledge and its diffusion in institutional contexts, as will be seen in the following subsection.

IT AND THE SOCIAL CONSTRUCTION OF KNOWLEDGE

If the key to understanding social action lies in explicating the influence of shared "weltanschauungen," "lived experience," and "tradition," as socially embedded institutional knowledge, then the representation of such knowledge must be the goal of all who propose to manage it. However, the impossibility of this task is underlined by Dreyfus (1998), who cites Husserl's exasperation at trying to give a detailed account of the experience of the everyday lives of social actors. Husserl (1960) termed social actors' representations of their experiential knowledge the *noema*. However, after devoting his life's work to its delineation, he concluded in the face of the noema's "huge concreteness" that the "tremendous complication" in its representation made it an impossible task (Husserl, 1969, p. 244 and p. 246). Significantly, Minsky (1981) commented on the enormity of attempting to represent commonsense experiential knowledge using computer-based systems. This point is underscored by Bruner (1990) who argues that:

Information processing cannot deal with anything beyond well-defined and arbitrary entries that can enter into specific relationships that are strictly governed by a program of elementary operations. (p. 5)

Thus, in Bruner's *Acts of Meaning*, the message is clear: The experiential knowledge and skills of social actors cannot readily, if ever, be embedded in IT (see Boland, 1987). However, this is not surprising as Dreyfus (1998) notes that philosophers from Socrates to Husserl have wrestled with the problem of knowledge representation without much success. Nevertheless, additional arguments are now adduced to convince the skeptical.

The socially constructed nature of knowledge is described by Berger and Luckmann (1967) who posit that:

The primary knowledge about institutional order is knowledge on the pretheoretical level. It is the sum total of 'what everyone knows' about a social world, an assemblage of maxims, morals, proverbial nuggets

of wisdom, values and beliefs, myths, and so forth, the theoretical integration of which requires considerable intellectual fortitude in itself, as the long line of heroic integrators from Homer to the latest sociological system-builders testify. (p. 65)

This point is indicative of the nature of institutional and organisational reality. For example, it indicates why there exists a high degree of rigidity in and immutability of the social stock of knowledge, especially if beliefs are strongly held, or of a religious nature[5]. This is why "das Man" exerts such a strong influence in fostering resistance to the acceptance of new knowledge and understanding and why those who articulate it often receive the opprobrium of "true believers."

Berger and Luckmann's insights also are congruent with the perspectives of Heidegger and Gadamer articulated previously. Hence, pretheoretical knowledge, as the articulated (present-at-hand) and unarticulated (ready-to-hand) components of Aristotelian phronesis (experiential "self-knowledge") and techne ("skills-based" knowledge), plays a formative role in establishing canonical modes of behaviour (habitualised social action or organisational routines, if you will) and in the transmission of social behaviours among actor networks (Gadamer, 1975; Dunne, 1993). To underscore the points made here, Dreyfus (1998) turns to Heidegger to argue that "the everyday context which forms the background of communications is not a belief system or a set of rules or principles...but is rather a set of social skills, a kind of know-how, any aspect of which makes sense only on the rest of the shared social background" (p. 285). What then of the IS researchers and practitioners who assume that it is possible to describe and codify social contexts as objective facts and who therefore consider unproblematic the transfer of knowledge in organisations? Dreyfus (ibid.) again draws on Heidegger to reject the notion that "the shared world presupposed in communication could be represented as an explicit and formalized set of facts" (p. 283). All this implies that social knowledge cannot be objectified and exist outside the "heads" of knowers (or the social relationships in which knowledge is constructed and maintained); furthermore, it renders fruitless any attempt to codify it objectively. It also casts doubt on those who speak authoritatively about knowledge transfer mechanisms and who ignore the social contexts that gives rise to such knowledge.

The Aristotelian Perspective on Knowledge

In Book 6 of *Nicomachean Ethics*, Aristotle focuses on practical and technical reason—*phronesis* and *techne.* The importance and relevance of this work to any treatment of knowledge is underscored by Dunne (1993). Hence, an understanding of phronesis and techne is essential to the present project as it brings into sharp focus the situated nature of individual knowledge and, as Gadamer (1975) illustrates, adds to the ontological description already offered. To begin, it must be noted that in reading the *Ethics* in the context of the *Metaphysics* one is led to conclude that both phronesis and techne are, ultimately, forms of practical knowledge. However, in the *Ethics* Aristotle distinguishes between *praxis* and *poiesis.* The conduct of social affairs in a thoughtful and competent manner Aristotle refers to as *praxis.* This involves the application of *phronesis,* that is, a social actor's experientially based "self-knowledge." *Poiesis,* on the other hand, Aristotle involves the activities of "making" or "production." Here *techne* is the kind of knowledge possessed by the expert craftsmen and involves the understanding and application of the principles governing the production of social phenomena—both tangible and intangible. It is important to note that Dunne (1993) in his extensive treatment of the topic interprets phronesis as being practical knowledge and techne as being skills-based knowledge. However, he (ibid.) states, in regard to poiesis and praxis, that: "To these two specifically different modes of activity, techne and phronesis correspond, respectively, as two rational powers which give us two quite distinct modes of practical knowledge" (p. 244). Thus, a social actor's "self-knowledge" or "practical wisdom" (phronesis) is a synthesis of his temporal experience of social phenomena with an ability to perform practical actions in relation to such phenomena. According to Gadamer's (1975) interpretation of Aristotle's phronesis, experiential or "self-knowledge" cannot be learned or forgotten; it is ethical and moral in character and, as such, it is the supreme influence on an individual's actions. It is clear that skill-based knowledge (techne) and theoretical knowledge (as theoria, sophia, or episteme) are informed by the "self-knowledge" (phronesis) of relevant social actors. In so doing, self-knowledge embraces, as Gadamer indicates, both the means and ends of social action. Because of its unique constitution, self-knowledge does not often lend itself to linguistic expression. The same could be said of techne, which provides the expert or craftsman with an understanding of the why and the wherefore, the how, and with-what of the production process. Thus, techne, in providing a rational plan of action, also embraces both the means and ends of production activities.

FUTURE TRENDS: IMPLICATIONS OF *PHRONESIS* AND *TECHNE* FOR KNOWLEDGE MANAGEMENT

This article argues that an understanding of phronesis and techne as the two primordial components of individual practical knowledge is vital for researchers and practitioners who involved in creating knowledge management systems (KMS), yet studies on information systems development and the field of knowledge management pay scant attention to the ontological ground of knowledge. Consider the assertion by Checkland and Holwell (1998) that "the core concern of the IS field [is] the orderly provision of data and information within an organisational using IT" (p. 39)—clearly this involves the development of IS and their use.

So what of the posited role for IT in the management of knowledge? Can phronesis and techne be embedded in IT? And can such systems account for all contingencies in their application? As Orr (1990) illustrated in his study of photocopier repair technicians, the attempted codification of a fairly well defined techne proved a failure; here phronesis proved the more influential of the two types of individual knowledge. Why? Because of the contextual nature of the Heideggerian breakdowns encountered and the experiential knowledge of the repairmen, some of which was vicariously acquired through the Brunerian narratives they engaged in while constructing their "community of knowing." How then can IT capture adequately the experiential and interpretive nature of the phronesis required for this type of problem-solving? As Dreyfus (1998) concludes, the answer to this question is "It cannot."

Consider also the IT-enabled techne of processing a business transaction. It is evident that the experiential knowledge of the business person managing the transaction plays a major role in dictating the questions posed and details taken in efficiently executing a transaction, irrespective of the routines and activities embedded in an IT-based business information system. Why? Because information systems are "closed" in the sense that they cannot ever capture all aspects of a business problem domain. In different spheres of organizational activity, the data required to resolve a breakdown might be of a more comprehensive nature (e.g., a report or narrative aimed at informing task-based problem-solving) while targeting a problem-solving techne. In this scenario, the context-dependent experiential knowledge of both the author and the recipient(s) will be of special import and will depend on the actors' unarticulated, shared social background. If, for example, the author and recipient belong to a particular socially constructed "community-of-practice" (Brown & Duguid, 1991), then each will participate in a shared tradition with similar phronetic and technic backgrounds. However, even with this shared background, Boland and Tenkasi (1995) indicate that the support available from conventional systems will be limited to well-defined user needs. Echoing Boland and Tenkasi (1995), McDermott (1999) argues that the important "technical challenge is to design human and information systems that not only make information available, but help community members think together" (p. 116); However, McDermott (1999) cautions that "[t]he great trap in knowledge management is using information management tools and concepts to design knowledge management systems" (p. 104).

Given all that has been said here, it is doubtful that the futuristic "electronic communication forums" suggested by Boland and Tenkasi (1995) will be anymore successful than their data processing predecessors in supporting knowledge transfer and management within "communities of knowing," despite shared phronetic and technic backgrounds. Echoing Dunne (1993), practical knowledge (as phronesis and techne) is a fruit that can grow on the fertile soil of individual experience; however, experience of the world occurs within a web of social relationships, and individual knowledge develops within the historical context of a tradition under the influence of significant others. But what are the implications in this for the IS field?

Consider, for example, that extant perspectives on IT capabilities chiefly operate from resource-based view of the firm[6], which, with certain exceptions, is chiefly positivist in its orientation and focuses on the outcomes of the application of capabilities rather than the process by which they come into being (Butler & Murphy, 1999; cf. Wade & Hulland, 2004). It is clear from the literature that the resultant applications of this theory of the firm are not sensitive to the type of ontological issues described herein and, accordingly, fail to capture the social and historical nature of knowledge in institutional contexts. On this point, future studies on the development and application of IT capabilities should, we believe, take an interpretive stance and focus on how phronesis and techne are developed and applied in institutional contexts and not just on outcomes of their application.

CONCLUSION

This article joins calls within the IS field for a reassessment of its position on the important topic of knowledge (see Galliers & Newell, 2001). True, the fundamental ideas presented herein are not new, but the manner of their presentation and argument is. In any event, given the recent feeding frenzy on the topic of knowledge and the unquestioning acceptance of the nostrums proposed by some of those championing the cause, a timely injection of commonsense is called for. To recap, this article's main argument is that knowledge of social phenomena, which is enmeshed in a web of social relationships and contexts, defies objectification and cannot be comprehensively and unambiguously represented due to the uncertainty that arises from interpretations that are informed by divergent "worldviews" and different "horizons of understanding." Institutional knowledge does not therefore exist as an objective phenomenon outside of the heads of the knowers and their "communities-of-practice," where it exists primarily in the intersubjective understandings of social actors.

Having illustrated why knowledge cannot be represented objectively, a question is raised as to the status of information. Following a constructivist logic, Introna (1997) points out that information is "hermeneutic understanding" and is acquired through an interpretive process by an "already-knowing" individual. Hence, if information also is abstract and ambiguous in its depiction, data is all that can be represented, stored, transferred, and manipulated by IT. It must be emphasized that the primary mode of informing is the narrative: Narratives serve to define the canonical, and help construct and maintain institutionalised patterns of behaviour. Nevertheless, narratives, written or oral, consist of data, not knowledge or information—hence, the need for dialogue and dialectic. Therefore, if information technology is to be utilized to give voice to organizational narratives, then it must be recognized that it will be a conduit for data only. And, because gaps in comprehension will always exist, no matter how sophisticated the technology and its power of representation, IT must enable a dialectic to take place between social actors and the phenomena they wish to understand. These points are reflected in the capabilities of the latest generation of Internet/Intranet-enabled knowledge management tools[7]. Although the vendors of such products argue that they are capturing the knowledge of customers, employees, and domain experts, the inputs to and outputs from such applications tend to be well-defined and constitute significant abstractions from the phronesis and techne of social actors (again in the form of data). Hence, considerable interpretation is required, and while knowledge base inference engines are limited in this respect (Butler, 2003), human beings are well adapted to this process, even though their interpretations of phenomena rarely concur with those of other actors, except in situations where the data in question is well delimited. That such systems are of limited value in helping social actors communicate and repair the break-downs they encounter is not at issue; they do not, however, help social actors manage knowledge in organisations.

REFERENCES

Aristotle (1945). *Nicomachean ethics*. Translated by H. Rackham. Cambridge, MA: Harvard University Press.

Berger, P., & Luckmann, T. (1967). *The social construction of reality: A treatise in the sociology of knowledge*. Garden City, NY: Doubleday and Company, Inc.

Boland, R.J. (1987). The in-formation of information systems. In R.J. Boland and R.A. Hirschheim (Eds.), *Critical issues in information systems research* (pp. 362-379). Chichester, UK: John Wiley.

Boland, R.J., & Tenkasi, R.V. (1995). Perspective making and perspective taking in communities of knowing. *Organization Science*, 6(4), 350-372.

Brown, J.S., & Duguid, P. (1991). Organisational learning and communities of practice: Toward a unified view of working, learning and innovation. *Organisation Science*, 2, 40-57.

Bruner, J. (1990) *Acts of meaning*. Cambridge, MA: Harvard University Press.

Butler, T. (1998). Towards a Hermeneutic method for interpretive research in information systems. *Journal of Information Technology*, 13(4), 285-300.

Butler, T. (2003). From data to knowledge and back again: Understanding the limitations of KMS. *Knowledge and Process Management: The Journal of Corporate Transformation*, 10(4), 144-155.

Butler T., & Murphy, C. (1999, December 13-15). Shaping information and communication technologies infrastructures in the newspaper industry: Cases on the role of IT competencies. In Prabuddha De & J. I. DeGross (Eds.), *The Proceedings of the 20th International Conference on Information Systems* (pp. 364-377). Charlotte, NC.

Checkland, P., & Holwell S. (1998). *Information, systems and information systems: Making sense of the field*. Chichester, UK: John Wiley & Sons.

Conway, S., & Sligar, C. (2002). *Unlocking knowledge assets*. Redmond, WA: Microsoft Press.

Davenport, T.H., & Prusak, L. (1998). *Working knowledge: How organisations manage what they know*. Boston: Harvard Business School Press.

Dreyfus, H.L. (1998). Why we do not have to worry about speaking the language of the computer. *Information Technology and People, 11*(4), 281-289.

Dunne, J. (1993). *Back to the rough ground: 'Phronesis' and 'techne' in modern philosophy and in Aristotle*. Notre Dame, IN: University of Notre Dame Press.

Gadamer, H.G. (1975). *Truth and method*. New York: The Seabury Press.

Galliers, R.D., & Newell, S. (2001, June 27-29). Back to the future: From knowledge management to data management. In *Global Co-Operation in the New Millennium, The 9th European Conference on Information Systems* (pp. 609-615). Bled, Slovenia.

Goleman D.P. (1996). *Vital lies simple truths: The psychology of self-deception*. New York: Touchstone Books.

Grant, R.M. (1996). Toward a knowledge-based theory of the firm. *Strategic Management Journal, 17*, Winter Special Issue, 109-122.

Guba, E.G., & Lincoln, Y.S. (1994) Competing paradigms in qualitative research. In N. K. Denzin & Y. S. Lincoln (Eds.), *Handbook of qualitative research* (pp. 105-117). Thousand Oaks, CA: Sage Publications Inc.

Hayek, F.A. (1945). The use of knowledge in society. *American Economic Review, 35*, 519-532.

Heidegger, M. (1976). *Being and time*. New York: Harper and Row.

Hekman, S. (1986). *Hermeneutics and the sociology of knowledge*. Cambridge, UK: Polity Press.

Husserl, E. (1960). *Cartesian meditations*. The Hague: M.Nijhoff.

Husserl, E. (1960). *Formal and transcendental logic*. The Hague: M.Nijhoff.

Husserl, E. (1969). *The crisis of European sciences*. Evanston, IL: Northwestern University Press.

Introna, L.D. (1997). *Management, information and power: A narrative for the involved manager.* London: MacMillan Press Ltd.

Leonard Barton, D. (1995). *Wellsprings of knowledge: Building and sustaining the sources of innovation.* Boston: Harvard Business School Press.

Minsky, M. (1981). A framework for representing knowledge. In J. Hagueland (Ed.), *Mind design.* Cambridge, MA: The MIT Press.

Orr, J.E. (1990). Sharing knowledge, celebrating identity: War stories and community memory in a service culture. In D. Middleton and D. Edwards (Eds.), *Collective remembering: Memory in society* (pp. 168-189). London: Sage Publications Ltd.

Pfeffer, J., & Sutton, R.I. (2000). *The knowing doing gap: How smart companies turn knowledge into action.* Boston: Harvard Business School Press.

Teece, D.J. (2001). Strategies for managing knowledge assets: The role of firm structure and industrial context. In I. Nonaka and D.J. Teece, (Eds.), *Managing industrial knowledge: Creation, transfer and utilization* (pp. 125-144). London: Sage Publications Ltd.

Wade, M., & Hulland, J. (2004). The resource-based view and information systems research: Review, extension and suggestions for future research. *MIS Quarterly, 28*(1), 107-142.

KEY TERMS

Das Man: According to Gadamer (1975), "Tradition" influences a social actor's attitudes and behaviour through authority; such authority is transmitted through time and history via cultural mechanisms. Heidegger (1976) argues that it is the quiet authority of "das Man" (roughly translated as "the they" or "the anyone") which provides reassurance in the face of existential turbulence.

Effective-Historical Consciousness: In order to deal with the problems caused by prejudice and the authority of tradition, Gadamer argues that a "historical consciousness" is vital if misunderstood prejudices are to be understood for what they are. Prejudices need to be isolated; that is, their validity needs to be suspended. This, Gadamer (1975) argues, is to be accomplished through the structure of a question: "The essence of the question is the opening up, and keeping open, of possibilities" (p. 266). It is here that the dialectic comes into play. However, another concept, that of "effective-historical consciousness," requires attention. Basically, effective-historical consciousness is the acknowledgement of the fact that the effect of historical events through "lived experience" influences our interpretation, and hence understanding, of phenomena. The experience of effective-historical understanding is achieved when, in questioning phenomena that are "present-at-hand," one opens oneself up to tradition and to what the phenomenon has to say, in order to allow its meaning to become evident.

Fusion of Horizons: A "horizon," for Gadamer (1975), is simply "the range of vision that includes everything that can be seen from a particular vantage point" (p. 269). Horizons have definite boundaries, and although definable, they are not static. It is the existence of "historical consciousness" which keeps the horizon in motion; "Tradition," as the horizon of the past, is constantly in motion with the advance of time. In the "working out" of prejudices—that is, in interpreting and endeavouring to understand some social phenomenon—two horizons are fused: The "fusion of horizons" is therefore the culmination of the act of understanding between interpreter and interpreted, between researcher and researched.

"Ready-to-Hand" vs. "Present-at-Hand": In the everyday nature of a social actor's existence, the phenomena that constitute his or her "life-world" are (Zuhanden) and, as such, are not the object of reflection; the reason for this is that they possess a degree of familiarity that effectively sees them dissolved into an actor's daily existence. From an actor's perspective, such phenomena appear to be perfectly understood, not requiring interpretation as to their ontological status. If, however, an event occurs that constitutes a breakdown in understanding, and that challenges the actor's conception of the phenomenon by putting it in a different light, or, indeed, uncovers its ontological status as a phenomenon for the first time, then it will require interpretation so that it may be comprehended. As a consequence of such breakdowns, a phenomenon thus becomes the object of "theoretical" reasoning and acquires the ontological status of being "present-at-hand" (i.e., a Vorhanden).

Reductionist/Analytical Dialectic: In subjecting social phenomena to a structural analysis, Ricoeur (1981) argues that "we proceed from naïve interpretations to critical interpretations, from surface interpretations to depth interpretations" (p. 220). In probing beneath the surface of social phenomena, a reductionist/analytical dialectic is employed; this involves the Aristotelian method of division or repeated logical analysis of genera into species or, in hermeneutic terms, of deconstructing the "whole" into its component "parts."

It is through the identification and analysis of these parts and their reconstitution into the "whole" that the structural model of the reductionist/analytic dialectic proceeds. In the social sciences, this approach allows phenomena to be explained in structural terms such that they may be understood.

The Hegelian Dialectic: The Hegelian dialectic comes into play when a particular interpretation or thesis is worked out with a competing interpretation or antithesis so as to arrive at a newer, fuller, and more informed interpretation or understanding—the Hegelian synthesis or Gadamarian "fusion of horizons" results. The Hegelian dialectic involves an interpretive synthesis of expectation or "pre-understanding" with "objective" observations in order to make sense of a phenomenon and thus attain an understanding of it.

The Hermeneutic "Circle of Understanding": Understanding has a circular structure. Gadamer (1975) points out that the whole that is a phenomenon is comprised of the "parts" or "details" that constitute it; there is, as Gadamer illustrates, a formal relationship between these parts (component phenomena), the whole (as constituted by its component phenomena), and what he terms the "subjective reflex" that an actor adopts toward a phenomenon—that is, the intuitive anticipation of the "whole" and its subsequent articulation in the parts. Gadamer goes on to stress that the means of apprehending this relationship possesses a circular structure—the hermeneutic "circle of understanding." However, the understanding attained in working out this relationship, in negotiating the "circle," is not in any way perfect; rather, a temporally based understanding is realized—the so-called "fusion of horizons." Commencing with one's "pre-understanding" or prejudice, the interpretation of a phenomenon (the hermeneutic "whole") begins by the examination of its component phenomena (the parts). However, understanding the component phenomena can only begin when their relationships to the whole have been determined—the determination of these contextual relationships is itself guided by an expectation of meaning arising from the preceding context (i.e., derived from one's "Tradition"-influenced "prejudice"). Cycling through the "circle of understanding" continues until the breakdown is repaired and the phenomenon achieves the status of "ready-to-hand." It must be noted that because new questions might arise or "facts" emerge over time, further movements through the circle are necessary.

The Socratic Dialectic: Gadamer (1975) argues that the "logical structure of openness" is to be found in the model of the Platonic dialogue or, to be more accurate, in the Socratic dialectic of question and answer. In order to effect a "fusion of horizons" between the horizon of the interpreter and the object of his interpretation, a dialogue takes place between the individual and the phenomenon of interest. However, the interpreter must be aware of his or her prejudices and recognise that this knowledge is not absolute but incomplete—he or she must be "open" to the phenomenon.

Tradition and Prejudice: Gadamer (1975) significantly broadens the concept of Heideggerian "pre-understanding" and "historicality" by introducing the concept of "Tradition"; Gadamer, for example, illustrates that "Tradition" shapes an actor's pre-understanding, or as Gadamer puts it, his or her prejudices. Here, the concept of "lived experience" (Erlebnis) describes the relationship between actors and the tradition in which they are embedded; as such, it provides the contexts for their understanding and contributes to the formation of their prejudices. For Gadamer (ibid.) "a prejudice is a provisional legal verdict before the final verdict is reached" (p. 240). A "prejudice" may be true or false, accurate or inaccurate—hence, we might say that there exists legitimate and illegitimate, visible and invisible prejudice. But, as with the "working out" of Heideggerian "pre-understanding," "critical reasoning" is required to distinguish between legitimate and illegitimate prejudice.

ENDNOTES

1. The Enlightenment is generally characterized by Rationalism, Empiricism, Determinism, and an emphasis on logic (for a basic overview see http://www.philosopher.org.uk/enl.htm). Tarnas (1991) highlights the influence of deterministic thinking and argues man's "belief in his own rational and volitional freedom" was attenuated by the "principles of determinism—Cartesian, Newtonian, Darwinian, Marxist, Freudian, behaviorist, genetic, neurophysiological, [and] sociobiological" (p. 332).

2. Army Knowledge Online—An Intelligent Approach to Mission Success, U.S. Department of the Army, Washington, D.C., 1999.

3. The author has some considerable experience in this area in his former capacity as a telecommunications engineer and member of a tightly knit "community-of-practice" in which knowledge sharing was critical to the community's organisational function.

4. Antifoundationalists recognise that knowledge is socially constructed and therefore distributed among social actors in "communities-of-practice."

5. Remember the neo-Platonic definition of knowledge as 'justified true belief' and Nonaka and Takeuchi's (1995) argument that "knowledge, unlike information, is about beliefs and commitment" (p. 58).

A

[6]   The resource-based view considers knowledge as an intangible firm specific asset (see Teece, 2001; Conway & Sligar, 2002).

[7]   ServiceWare Inc.'s Enterprise, Microsoft's Sharepoint, PricewaterhouseCoopers' Knowledge Direct, and KnowledgeCurve tools and KM tools found in Siemens Learning Valley are examples of KM technologies.

Aristotelian View of Knowledge Management

David G. Schwartz
Bar-Ilan University, Israel

INTRODUCTION

Defining and understanding knowledge is a rather broad and open-ended pursuit. We can narrow it considerably by stating that we are interested in defining and understanding knowledge as it pertains to knowledge management (KM) rather than tackling the entire realm of epistemology. This article takes the theory of knowledge espoused by Aristotle and views it through the lens of knowledge management.

The writings of Aristotle have proven to be fertile ground for uncovering the foundations of knowledge management. Snowden (2006) points to Aristotle's three types of rhetorical proof as a basis for incorporating narrative in knowledge management. Buchholz (2006) traces the roots of ontological philosophy forming the basis of current KM ontology efforts back to Aristotle's work. Butler (2006), in his antifoundational perspective on KM, following Dunne (1993), argues that Aristotle's phrónésis and téchné need to be at the core of knowledge-management efforts, and while they cannot be directly applied to IT applications, they must be among the elements upon which knowledge management is based.

It is instructive to seek theoretical foundations for our treatment of knowledge in organizational settings and knowledge-management systems. By doing so we increase the likelihood that our solutions are complete and that we have considered all relevant forms of knowledge that we may desire to manage. Rather than start with modern differentiators of knowledge such as tacit vs. explicit (Nonaka & Takeuchi, 1995), descriptive vs. procedural (Holsapple & Winston, 1996), local vs. global (Novins & Armstrong, 1997), and declarative vs. procedural (Minsky, 1975), we will take a step back to first principles.

Aristotle (n.d.), in his *Nicomachean Ethics*, presents five virtues of thought that can be mapped to levels of knowledge.

- **Epistémé:** Factual or scientific knowledge
- **Téchné:** Skills-based technical and action-oriented knowledge
- **Phrónésis:** Experiential self-knowledge or practical wisdom based on experience
- **Noûs:** Intuition
- **Sophía:** Theoretical knowledge of universal truths or first principles

Other learned traditions and cultures give us similar and related elements, such as the Talmudic philosophical tradition (Luzzatto, 1988; Maimonides, 1966) and Eastern religion and philosophy (Gier, 2004).

As a starting point, we are concerned with the processes shown in the first ring of Figure 1.

1. Knowledge that can be acquired in an organizational setting
    a. creation
    b. discovery
    c. gathering
    d. validation
2. Knowledge that can be organized, categorized, and stored
    a. modeling
    b. classification
    c. calibration
    d. integration
3. Knowledge that can be distributed to some point of action
    a. sharing
    b. reuse
    c. maintenance
    d. dissemination

Without the abilities to acquire, represent, store, retrieve, and apply knowledge in a way that positively affects the operation of our organizations, we are not engaging in knowledge management. Conversely, any form of knowledge to which the aforementioned cannot be applied, while of theoretical importance and interest, cannot be managed. True, as argued by Butler (2003, 2006), the knowledge foundations defined by Aristotle might not be transparently converted into IT-based systems, but that should not prevent us from designing our KM systems and processes to support those knowledge foundations to the greatest extent possible.

Consider the view presented in Figure 1 giving a holistic view of knowledge management and its foundations. The central core of philosophies (the middle) must inform our choice of practical knowledge-management processes (the first ring). These processes must be implemented and adapted to address managerial, social, and organizational needs (the second ring). Finally,

Figure 1. *Layer upon layer of knowledge management*

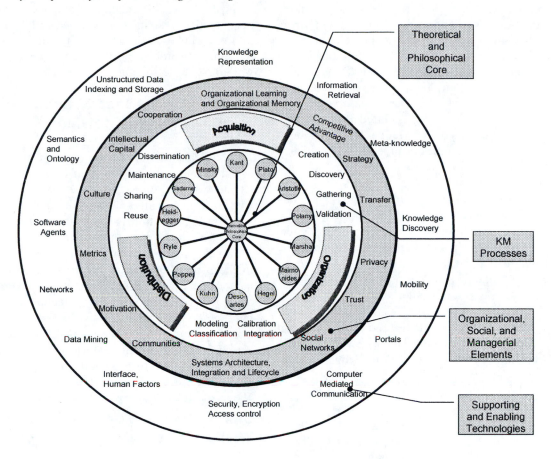

the implementation of KM processes to meet our organizational needs must be supported by and implemented through a set of relevant information technologies (the outer ring).

But how do we get from the central core to the first ring? In this article we will examine the definition and understanding of knowledge as a meeting between the Aristotelian classification and the requirements of practical knowledge-management processes.

BACKGROUND

The KM-process ring of Figure 1 shows the three bases of acquisition, organization, and distribution (Schwartz, Divitini, & Brasethvik, 2000), and it is but one of many viable characterizations of process-oriented knowledge management. It represents an emphasis on praxis, taking as a starting point the question, What do we need to do with knowledge in order to make it viable for an organization to use, reuse, and manage it as a tangible resource, and apply it toward specific actions?

By taking this perspective, we avoid to a certain extent the knowledge-information-data (KID) debate regarding the granularity of knowledge. We argue that the distinction between data, information, and knowledge can be conveniently ignored: not treated as irrelevant for a philosophical debate, mind-body discussion, or a metalevel, object-level analysis, but not essential to the fundamental mission of knowledge management.

Arguing that information technologies process data and not information or knowledge, Galliers and Newell (2003) seek to refocus the KM-IT effort on the better management of data. They suggest that since an IT system cannot deal with the fundamental elements of truth and knowledge, it can be counterproductive to create IT-centric knowledge-management initiatives. Holsapple (2002) provides an excellent introduction to different aspects of knowledge and its attributes, including perspectives based on representational issues, knowledge states, production, and the KID debate as well.

Knowledge management, however, does not need to get bogged down in the KID debate. What it does need is to become knowledge centric. Becoming knowledge centric does not necessitate a resolution to the KID debate.

Rather, it means that the field of knowledge management could benefit from taking cues from its philosophical lineage—the theories of knowledge—and not only from the praxis that has driven KM over the past two decades. The heavily practice-oriented roots of organizational knowledge management (Davenport & Prusak, 1998; Senge, 1990) have largely developed independent of any relationship to a theory of knowledge. The necessary KM processes have not evolved from any declared need to find an applied outlet for theories of knowledge. While that in no way invalidates KM processes or practice, it does leave open a very broad question as to how knowledge management relates to its epistemological roots.

Aydede's (1998) analysis of different possible interpretations of Aristotle's epistémé and noûs provides some intellectual breathing room to shape our own interpretation of those concepts in directions most amenable to knowledge management.

Hanley (1998) helps provide insights into the applicability of Aristotle to knowledge management by presenting the work of Heidegger, who takes the basic Aristotelian approach to knowledge and presents it from an applied pragmatic view. While Hanley's work does not explicitly consider the discipline of knowledge management, the perspectives drawn from Heidegger's interpretation of Aristotle will appear familiar to knowledge-management researchers.

Let us begin by examining each level of knowledge as envisioned by Aristotle, and see how each relates to certain elements of knowledge management.

AN ARISTOTELIAN VIEW OF MANAGING ORGANIZATIONAL KNOWLEDGE

The Aristotelian virtues are not hierarchical in nature. They are presented as discrete forms of knowledge intended to cover all possible acts of knowing.

Epistémé: Factual or Scientific Knowledge

Epistémé may be the most controversial element of knowledge for knowledge management. It is pure knowledge, such as that of mathematics or logic. Attempting to pin down epistémé is the essence of the knowledge-information-data debate that we discussed, and chose to dismiss, earlier. As scientific knowledge, epistémé is most relevant to our pursuit, and it encompasses knowledge of cause and effect, and deduction (Parry, 2003). A stated goal of information technology is to represent those facts and relationships known as epistémé in digital form, and leverage that

representation in different applications as declarative knowledge. In addition, data-mining techniques seek to help identify epistémé that is buried within an organization and bring it to the surface. In parallel, IT seeks to do the same for procedural knowledge, which maps very well to Aristotle's téchné.

Téchné: Skills-Based Technical and Action-Oriented Knowledge

Téchné deals with things that change rather than the constant relationships found in epistémé. Harnessing téchné is at once one of the most challenging and most fruitful of knowledge-management pursuits. To begin with, an organization is the primary place where one would find the bearer of téchné relevant to that organization, and it is precisely that knowledge that we seek to encapsulate and reuse. Téchné reflects the dynamic nature of knowledge. Furthermore, and perhaps most difficult in practice, it is the téchné that artificial intelligence and decision-support systems seek to automate. So, from that perspective, Aristotle has given us a clearly defined and delimited type of knowledge that can be addressed by information technologies.

Phrónésis: Experiential Self-Knowledge or Practical Wisdom Based on Experience

Phrónésis is practical knowledge dealing with action and getting things done. In Aristotle's view, phrónésis is acquired through hands-on training and experiencing the actions being learned. From a learning-through-action perspective, phrónésis differs from téchné in terms of the way each type of knowledge can be shared. The Aristotelian view would be that téchné can be taught from practitioner to student, whereas phrónésis can only be shared through actual mutual experience. In terms of the value of knowledge, Sveiby's (1997) focus on the knowledge-action value chain can find relevant roots in phrónésis. In terms of knowledge management, phrónésis leads us in the direction of simulation, rich media, e-learning, and other forms of the experiential presentation of knowledge or immersion in a virtual environment in which the experience yielding phrónésis can be achieved.

Noûs: Intuition

Noûs is perhaps the least understood of all elements necessary for knowledge management. Noûs not only embodies the intuitive side of knowledge, it also subsumes a large part of what we have come to refer to as tacit knowledge (although clearly there can be tacit knowledge of téchné and phrónésis). Noûs is not restricted to knowledge of first principles, but is viewed by Aristotle as a manner in which one can become aware of first principles. Observing the relationship between noûs and tacit knowledge, we note that there are two fundamental approaches to dealing with tacit knowledge in knowledge management. The first approach is to attempt to externalize the tacit knowledge through interventions and representation methods in order to create explicit knowledge. This, in essence, is attempting to transform the noûs into the epistémé. The second approach is to recognize that the tacit will and should remain tacit, but that the goal of knowledge management is to enable the organization to identify and reach the owner of the tacit—the bearer of the noûs—in an efficient and effective manner. This leads us to employ information technologies to support organizational communications, forums, communities, relationship networks, and the abundance of Internet-enabled interactions that have developed over the past decade.

Another interpretation of noûs is that it emerges from our familiarity with phrónésis and téchné. In other words, by nurturing our support for phrónésis and téchné, we strengthen our ability to exhibit noûs. Butler (personal communication, 2005), based on Bruner's observation (1962, p. 18) that "the act that produces effective surprise...[is] the hallmark of the creative enterprise," suggests that noûs can come about as a result of the processes in which phrónésis and téchné are applied to repairing breakdowns (and to a certain extent epistémé as well). In other words, what we know and how we intuit noûs comes about in part from our reflections on téchné and phrónésis. Therefore, it would appear that support for the noûs within knowledge management may in fact be derived from our treatment of these two contributing types of knowledge.

Sophia: Theoretical Knowledge of Universal Truths or First Principles

We argue that sophía, representing the universal and necessary characteristics of knowledge, has little place in understanding knowledge specific to organizational knowledge management. While universal and necessary truths are surely important to any analysis and treatment of knowledge, they are firmly in the domain of the philosophical and theoretical. Scientific discovery (which we may wish to manage postdiscovery), argumentation, and proof of theorems are all in the realm of the sophía, but still not within the knowledge-management mandate.

DISCUSSION

The first step in bridging the gap between Aristotle's theory of knowledge and knowledge management is to envision how each Aristotelian virtue can be addressed in each phase of knowledge management. Table 1 illustrates.

We can see that the acquisition, organization, and distribution process demands of knowledge management will differ for each of Aristotle's types of knowledge. By understanding this categorization of knowledge, we can achieve greater clarity of thought in our attempts to develop knowledge-management processes for application in organizational settings.

Finally, we can take the analysis one step further by considering which of the 12 specified processes of knowledge management can be reasonably performed on each type of knowledge, as shown in Table 2.

Consider the noûs, for example. We would argue that while noûs cannot be acquired by an IT-based KM system, it can in fact be discovered, modeled, and classified through the use of social network-mapping tools. True, from a philosophical purist perspective, the noûs itself will always remain within its bearer; however, the sharing and dissemination of knowledge within an organization considers both knowledge and metaknowledge. Having a digital representation of where noûs can be found and how it might be applied is as important for some aspects of knowledge management as building a lessons-learned database is for others. Thus, the values for noûs shown in Table 2 relate to a metalevel reference to the noûs.

Knowledge of the types téchné and phrónésis, while they cannot be created through KM processes, can indeed be discovered, gathered for storage by representational systems, organized, and distributed. While phrónésis and téchné may be the core constituents of practical knowledge (Butler & Murphy, 2006), we can enhance noûs within the organization by increasing accessibility to téchné and phrónésis, leveraging the relationship between these different types of knowledge discussed earlier. Here there would seem to be an important role to be played by metaknowledge describing the téchné and phrónésis within the organization to create some form of organizational noûs, which may effectuate to some degree Heidegger's hermeneutical circle (Sampaio, 1998) or Gadamer's (1975) circle of understanding.

With epistémé we can go a step further and utilize data mining, text mining, neural networks, information resource discovery, and other advanced pattern-recognition technologies to create new knowledge based on the patterns of data that exist within our extensive organizational information systems.

Table 1. Mapping Aristotle's knowledge virtues to knowledge management stages

	Acquisition	**Organization**	**Distribution**
Epistémé	By gathering facts and relationships known about the organizational knowledge domain and its human participants	Knowledge bases, databases, data warehouses, documents, and diagrams	Enabled and enhanced by information technologies and computer-mediated communications
Téchné	Through interaction, interviews, and discussions with practitioners who have exhibited acquired téchné	Extensive cross-referencing of skills and activities across the organization	Potentially replicated and implemented through information technologies, artificial intelligence, and decision-support systems.
Phrónésis	By recording lessons learned and case studies in the ongoing organizational experience	Case books, project retrospectives, and narratives	Stored, replicated, and delivered through rich media-based computer technologies
Noûs	By determining paths to those people who have exhibited relevant noûs within the organization By increasing support for phrónésis and téchné	Social networks guided by metaknowledge describing participants and their capabilities	The network through which noûs is uncovered is enabled by computer-mediated communications, forums, and online communities.
Sophía	Not a goal of knowledge management	Not a goal of knowledge management	Not a goal of knowledge management

FUTURE DIRECTIONS

For knowledge management to advance, it must continue to explore different theories of knowledge and how those theories will affect both the representation and use of knowledge in organizations.

Viewing knowledge as something that we want to manage forces us to narrow down the realm of epistemology to something we can handle in an applied manner. The analysis shown in this article can also be fruitfully applied to other philosophies of knowledge that differ from the Aristotelian view.

The choice of processes presented in Table 2 is by no means definitive: There are many KM frameworks and models proposing equally attractive alternative sets of processes. However, we should seek the broadest possible matching or coverage between our proposed KM processes and the core knowledge virtues. Subjecting a model of KM processes to some form of "Aristotle test" can help us evaluate the completeness of that model.

Table 2. Mapping Aristotle's knowledge virtues to KM processes

Process	*Noûs*	*Epistémé*	*Téchné*	*Phrónésis*	*Sophía*
Acquisition					
creation	no	yes	no	no	n/a
discovery	yes	yes	yes	yes	n/a
gathering	no	yes	yes	yes	n/a
validation	no	yes	yes	yes	n/a
Organization					
modeling	yes	yes	yes	yes	n/a
classification	yes	yes	yes	yes	n/a
calibration	yes	yes	yes	yes	n/a
integration	yes	yes	yes	yes	n/a
Distribution					
sharing	yes	yes	yes	yes	n/a
reuse	no	yes	yes	yes	n/a
maintenance	no	yes	yes	yes	n/a
dissemination	yes	yes	yes	yes	n/a

CONCLUSION

Understanding and defining knowledge can lead us to an open-ended philosophical debate, or it can lead us to a pragmatic characterization aimed at enabling the organizational goals of knowledge management. By choosing the latter, we are able to focus on those elements of knowledge that truly make a difference in practice: in this case, a mapping of the Aristotelian view to managing knowledge in organizations.

Knowledge can be debated at an epistemological and theological level as seen from Aristotle down to Heidegger and beyond. It can be debated at an implementation and representational level as seen in the ongoing knowledge-information-data discussions. We need to understand and appreciate both debates if we are to engage in the management of knowledge, but we should not let the lack of resolution in either debate hinder our advancement. The pragmatic, process-oriented view of defining and understanding knowledge is what we need to embrace, while the insights from both knowledge debates will continue to inform our activities and enrich our understanding. Examining the philosophical bases of knowledge will enable us to move outward from the philosophical core of Figure 1, to relevant KM processes that can then be moderated by and applied to organizational settings.

Each type of knowledge has different applied value and different challenges in acquisition, organization, and distribution. Aristotle's five core intellectual virtues or types of knowledge can even today serve as a base from which we launch our knowledge-management initiatives, and understanding them will help guide us.

REFERENCES

Aristotle. (n.d.). *Nicomachean ethics: Book VI* (W. D. Ross, Trans.). Retrieved November 2004, from *http://classics.mit.edu/Aristotle/nicomachaen.html*

Aristotle. (1934). *Metaphysics* (H. Rackham, Trans.). Retrieved November 2004, from *http://www.perseus.tufts.edu/*

Aydede, M. (1998). Aristotle on Episteme and Nous: The posterior analytics. *Southern Journal of Philosophy, 36*(1).

Bruner, J. S. (1962). *On knowing: Essays for the left hand.* Cambridge, MA: Harvard University Press.

Buchholz, W. (2006). Ontology. In D. G. Schwartz (Ed.), *Encyclopedia of knowledge management* (pp. 694-702). Hershey, PA: Idea Group Reference.

Butler, T. (1998). Towards a hermeneutic method for interpretive research in information systems. *Journal of Information Technology, 13*(4), 285-300.

Butler, T. (2005). Personal e-mail correspondence with the author.

Butler, T. (2006). An antifoundational perspective on knowledge management. In D. G. Schwartz (Ed.), *Encyclopedia of knowledge management* (pp. 1-9). Hershey, PA: Idea Group Reference.

Butler, T., & Murphy, C. (2006). Work and knowledge. In D. G. Schwartz (Ed.), *Encyclopedia of knowledge management* (pp. 884-891). Hershey, PA: Idea Group Reference.

Davenport, T., & Prusak, L. (1998). *Working knowledge: How organizations manage what they know.* Boston: Harvard Business School Press.

Dunne, J. (1993). *Back to the rough ground: "Phronesis" and "techne" in modern philosophy and in Aristotle.* Notre Dame, IN: University of Notre Dame Press.

Gadamer, H. G. (1975). *Truth and method.* New York: The Seabury Press.

Galliers & Newell. (2003). Back to the future: From knowledge management to the management of information and data. *Information Systems and E-Business Management, 1*(1).

Gier, N. F. (2004). The Buddha and Aristotle compared. In *The virtue of non-violence: From Gautama to Gandhi.* Albany: State University of New York Press.

Hanley, C. (1998). Theory and praxis in Aristotle and Heidegger. *Proceedings of the 20th World Congress of Philosophy*, Boston. Retrieved November 2004, from *http://www.bu.edu/wcp/Papers/Acti/ActiHanl.htm*

Holsapple, C. (2002). Knowledge and its attributes. In C. Holsapple (Ed.), *Handbook on knowledge management: Vol. 1. Knowledge matters.* Springer.

Holsapple, C., & Winston, A. (1996). *Decision support systems: A knowledge based approach.* West Publishing.

Luzzatto, M. H. (1988). *The ways of reason.* Feldheim Publishers.

Maimonides. (1966). *Maimonides' Arabic treatise on logic.* American Academy for Jewish Research.

Marvin, M. (1975). A framework for representing knowledge. In P. Winston (Ed.), *The psychology of computer vision.* McGraw-Hill.

Nonaka, I., & Takeuchi, T. (1995). *The knowledge creating company*. New York: Oxford University Press.

Novins, P., & Armstrong, R. (1997). Choosing your spots for knowledge management: A blueprint for change. *Perspectives on Business Innovation: Managing Organizational Knowledge, 1*.

Parry, R. (2003). *Episteme* and *techne*. In E. N. Zalta (Ed.), The Stanford encyclopedia of philosophy (summer 2003 ed.). Retrieved November 2004, from *http:// plato.stanford.edu/archives/sum2003/entries/epistemetechne/*

Sampaio, R. (1998). The hermeneutic conception of culture. *Proceedings of the 20th World Congress of Philosophy*, Boston.

Schwartz, D. G. (2005). The emerging discipline of knowledge management. *International Journal of Knowledge Management, 1*(2), 1-11.

Schwartz, D. G., Divitini, M., & Brasethvik, T. (2000). *Internet-based organizational memory and knowledge management*. Hershey, PA: Idea Group Publishing.

Senge, P. M. (1990). *The fifth discipline: Five practices of the learning organization*. New York: Doubleday.

Snowden, D. (2006). Narrative. In D. G. Schwartz (Ed.), *Encyclopedia of knowledge management* (pp. 678-682). Hershey, PA: Idea Group Reference.

Sveiby, K. E. (1997). *The new organizational wealth: Managing & measuring knowledge based assets*. San Francisco: Berrett-Koehler Publishers.

KEY TERMS

Epistémé: Aristotle's term for factual or scientific knowledge. Epistémé deals with real unchanging objects and what we can know about those objects, their characteristics, and their interrelationships. Covering self-evident, axiomatic principles and what can be logically derived from them, epistémé is central to a deductive system of reasoning. It is united with noûs to form sophía.

Knowledge Information Data (KID) Debate: A discussion (alternatively, the data-information-knowledge debate) that pervades the knowledge-management literature and attempts to determine at what point, if any, data becomes information, and information becomes knowledge.

Noûs: Aristotle's term for intuition. Noûs does not follow particular rules of construction or deduction. It is viewed as the human ability to comprehend fundamental principles without demonstration or proof. It may emerge from téchné and phrónésis, and is united with epistémé to form sophía.

Phrónésis: Aristotle's term for experiential self-knowledge or practical wisdom based on experience. The end result, or realization of phrónésis, is action or praxis. Phrónésis should determine the correct means to achieve a particular action.

Sophía: Aristotle's term for theoretical knowledge of universal truths or first principles. Sophía is viewed as the highest level of knowledge. The end result, or realization of Sophía, is not to be found in action, but rather in theory, which can be developed by understanding and applying the elements of epistémé and noûs.

Téchné: Aristotle's term for skills-based technical and action-oriented knowledge: how to perform a specific task. The end result, or realization of téchné, is the production of something.

Biological and Information Systems Approaches

Barry E. Atkinson
Monash University, Australia

Frada Burstein
Monash University, Australia

INTRODUCTION

Knowledge of past activities, discoveries, and events is applied by businesses to support everyday operations in much the same manner that human beings use their personal memories. But the true nature of organizational memory (OM) remains obscure, and information-systems practitioners have no clear definitional model of what they are working toward and have been unable to build a convincing organizational memory system (Olfman, 1998).

Having apparently reached a dead end, OM studies have been subsumed into knowledge management (KM) research as a subsidiary field. OM research is currently focused on the faculties of an organization that are capable of storing knowledge perceived or experienced beyond the duration of the actual event. Researchers and practitioners in the field use a definitional frameworks and models of organizational memory derived from flawed models of aggregate human behavior used in earlier sociological studies (Frost, 1942; Wilson, 1998). Models derived from earlier sociological studies rarely consider the exact nature and sources of commonplace thinking and memory use, and focus on highly visible and significant behavior and activities. Rapid theoretical and technological advances made in psychology research, brought about by the advent of sophisticated technological aids, have disparaged and largely disproved many of the naive systemic models of human cognition developed by earlier social scientists (Dominowski & Bourne, 1994; Sternberg, 1994) and were incorporated into information-systems sciences in the early years.

Before we consign the hope of deeper knowledge of business memory to the "too hard basket," it might be fruitful to examine an alternative path to understanding the nature of organizational memory and its application: The impersonal and generalized models of business activity (and cognitive operations) inherited from social sciences have not proved fertile, but the individual and personal models of memory and cognition found in biological and related sciences offer some promise in light of recent advances.

BACKGROUND

The human mind has always been, and always will be, an area of great interest to the layperson and scientist alike (Luria, 1973). The sheer volume, and constancy, of research attention it receives has inevitably resulted in a plethora of knowledge that enlightens us about various aspects of the human mind, but, on the other hand, it has tended to add a complexity to our view of human cognitive functioning. The modeling theory and conceptual analysis techniques, however, offer a means whereby the complexity and controversies of a topic can be isolated or marginalized in the interest of building a clear overall picture of a concept or phenomenon (Dubin, 1969). This can be particularly valuable in a field of study like human cognition where scholarly research has branched into many unreconciled and introverted schools of thought.

While many gaps still exist in our knowledge of exactly how humans think and remember (Baddeley, 1998), and the mind is shrouded in scientific (and nonscientific) controversy and beliefs, many incontrovertible aspects and fundamental elements of biological memory offer a path to a less controversial understanding of what organizational memory might be.

Biological studies offer some clues as to the purpose memory has been put to and the structure of memory elements (Carlson, 1994). Anthropology offers an indication of how simple behaviors dependent on memory have evolved over time into sophisticated activities of modern man (Hallpike, 1979). Studies of the psychology of memory provide an increasingly vivid breakdown of what happens when people remember (Carter, 1998). Specialist research into cognitive subelements such as consciousness (Dennett, 1991), emotion (Dimasio, 2000), language (Jackendoff, 1992), and perception (Sowa, 1984) offer insight into the essential nature of human ideas and at the same time provide a means for isolating many of the complexities involved in understanding the relationship between thinking and memory. Some of the more interesting ideas that can be gleaned from these research fields in respect to memory phenomena, and which could stabilize and enrich our current model of organization-centered memory, are presented here.

A BIOLOGICAL MODEL OF MEMORY

Organizational Self

Deutsch's (1966) central idea in his influential model of organizational cognition is an "organizational self," which, like a personal human self, has a central role in focusing and directing all organizational behavior. This idea was studiously avoided in subsequent OM research (Stein, 1995) probably because such a concept is problematic in the context of the shifting (and often private) constitutional and motivational elements that focus and direct modern collective business behavior: Deutsch's example was a formally constituted government authority whose purpose and goals were published and generally unchanging.

KM and OM researchers have recognized the efficacy of personalizing organizational knowledge (e.g., Spender, 1995; Tuomi, 1999), but not the power of one integral element—a person—as an organizing device. Dimasio's (2000) work describes how an individual biological body informs all that organism's cognitive function and provides a single point of reference for all its cognitive artifacts.

The critical nature of an executive intervention in the component processes of memory might be a fruitful area for further organizational memory systems studies in view of Dimasio's (2000) work. An executive that guides organizational behavior is not a new concept (see Corbett, 1997; Middleton, 2002), but its potential as a unifying element in organizational cognitive behavior is not fully appreciated.

Ubiquity of Memory Application in Everyday Operations

Memory function is a faculty inherited by humans from organisms of a much lower order of complexity (Monod, 1971/1997), and the advanced nature of human cognitive achievement owes much more to an ability to con-

sciously hold more than one idea at a time (which lower organisms seem unable to do) than it does to any sophistication in the fundamental cognitive equipment used to perceive and remember (Dennett, 1991).

Human memory supports seemingly simple operations as well as complex ones, and in order for an organism to operate independently from moment to moment and across space, such services must somehow be ever present. What we pursue in organizational memory studies is not necessarily a complex and mysterious set of functions and artifacts, but rather a collection of well-tested and refined things that interact seamlessly with one another to deliberately preserve past experiences and make them available to support subsequent and increasingly sophisticated actions. Pilot studies carried out by the authors to test a biological model of memory in an organizational setting suggest that memory of past organizational events may be applied to many seemingly minor, but possibly essential, organizational activities given little attention in the current OM and KM research literature.

OM practitioners recognize the need to support access to organizational memory via e-mail and the Internet (Schwartz, Divitini, & Brasethvik, 2000), but neither the support nor the process is recognized as worthy of attention at an organizational policy level. Often we identify the office culture, traditional business practices, conscientious employees, and common sense as coordinators and directors of a relationship between organizational behavior and the organization's best interests without investigating organizational memory, which underpins them. Many seemingly inconsequential business behaviors are the foundational support for ensuring the best interests of the organization in critical day-to-day operations.

Biological memory offers constant and continual support for its owners' endeavors; similar support might be offered to a wider variety of organizational memory applications if they were recognized as such.

Memory Ownership

The unifying element in organic memory systems is the self: a personal prototype that provides an impetus and steers the various component operations, giving them a fundamental associative fulcrum (Dimasio, 2000)—a fulcrum that might provide the key to the efficiency and power we admire in memory systems.

With this in mind, it is easier to appreciate the significance of the personal nature of memory. Each memory system is inextricably bound to an individual owner with its own individual history, individual interests, individual desires, and individual goals, preserving its individual perceptions for its individual use. This perspective also illustrates that knowledge objects that have not passed through the owner's cognitive processes cannot be added to the memory store.

Organizational memories, if they are to be real memories and not simply information, must be consciously collected and laid down in the store of memories by the organization itself. Having acquired and laid down the memories by its own hand, the organization is best placed to know the contents of its stores and where a particular memory is likely to be found. Just because a document or idea relates to the past events or activities of an organization, it does not mean that it is accessible for application by the organization in subsequent deliberations or activities (see Wilson, 1997; Yates, 1990).

Information-systems and information-management theorists and practitioners generally recognize the value of information ordering (Simon, 1957), but the relationship between the individual who orders and stores the information and the individual who uses it may be underappreciated.

The biological phenomenon *memory* does not accord with established concepts of systems and mechanics: The input plus the process may not fully describe the product, and vice versa; what goes into memory may not come out; and the cause or stimulus might not result in any discernable effect (Haberlandt, 1997). Many independent functions might provide services to memory operation while appearing to provide diverse and valuable services in their own right (Chomsky, 1968).

Many established and familiar organizational information and knowledge operations and devices might actually serve essential organizational memory functions. OM researchers risk misidentifying (or ignoring altogether) memory components by taking a systemic view of memory. The relationship between a linking and directing executive and such tasks as the archiving and summarization of documents, and document search operations might not be fully appreciated, and the potential in the relationship for ensuring the best interests of the organization might be overlooked.

Memory psychologist Baddeley (1998) and cognitive scientist Ashcraft (1994) detail a number of sustaining functions and operations supporting memory:

- separate short-term and long-term memory stores and functions, immediate postperception memory stores and functions, and separate autobiographical (sequenced) remembrance stores and functions
- an attention system to monitor prospective sources of memories, and a sensory-perception system to search a stimulus for cues and provide raw material for the subsequent creation of memories

- percept construction systems to associate new experiences to previous knowledge
- an encoding process that transcribes sensory perception into proprietary physiochemical neural matter that matches the structure of those previously stored

The concept of divisions of organizational memory faculties is an interesting one given the diversity of OM support functions previously identified by KM, OM, and information-management researchers. Maier (2002) provides a survey of diverse KM tools and systems. Middleton (2002) describes a history of information-management tools and strategies. These comprehensive lists of technological solutions illustrate the diversity of applications that attempt to operationalise OM functions without an overriding coordination by the particular organization. They can be utilized as guides to OM developers when implementing OM solutions. However, this will require a level of integration across applications to ensure that the knowledge objects are all robustly related to an organizational self.

Focusing attention on prospective sources of valuable information is not a new idea, but its dependence on direction and preexisting contents of information stores is not readily appreciated. In order to attend to the most appropriate sources in the biological world, memory owners must give some thought to who and what are the most potentially valuable sources (Bergson, 1907/1975, 1896/1996). Constant monitoring of the environment to discover other better sources of knowledge are readily appreciated everyday tasks of living things (Sternberg, 1994).

Memory Percepts

Hallpike's (1979) investigation into the anthropology of cognition discovers many simple and universal cognitive operations in primitive, and comparatively unsophisticated, societies. More complex and powerful cognitive operations, familiar in modern Western cultures and clearly the product of enlightened public education systems, are possible because of remembered algorithms, strategies, formulas, and models (made up of a finite set of rules or operations that are unambiguous) rather than from ambiguous reflection, contemplation, or remembrance of past events and facts. Moreover, many of these strategies and models have been deliberately refined to allow a lighter cognitive load: That is, we remember the source of information in lieu of carrying the information itself (*aides memoires*).

19

Current models of organizational memory used in information-systems sciences presume a file, book, or document prototype for memory artifacts (see Ackerman, 1994; Walsh & Ungson, 1990) rather than a discrete fact or formula, or discrete pictorial or aural representation. Neither is the source of information recognized as having a value equal to that of a whole document or complete file.

Biological memories are based on percepts created in response to an eternal stimulus and can best be compared to the concept of an idea (Baddeley, 1998). Memory artifacts themselves are not unitary but comprise a network of component mental elements, which together can evoke a memory. The current concept of a whole file, a complete document, or a work practice as a unit of organizational memory is unhelpful to OM researchers: Storing whole files, archiving complete documents, and articulating a tacit work practice are expensive and time consuming, and maybe storing, preserving, and articulating underlying ideas might be more cost effective in the long run.

Memory Encoding

The biological model of memory encoding describes the recording of responses to sensory stimuli in a series of mental artifacts (Baddeley, 1998) richer than the mere articulation in language of an idea or perception. Chomsky (1968) and Jackenoff (1992) have illustrated how the flexibility of biological memories (they can be rearranged, reinterpreted, reused, colored, and decomposed ad infinitum) may derive from their insubstantiality beyond the confinement of concrete or specific language representation.

While language is clearly a primary method whereby ideas can be organized, categorized, associated, and communicated, OM theorists' current view of organizational memories as communicable and substantial language-based informational artifacts (Walsh & Ungson, 1991; Yates, 1990) appears restrictive. Memories put into words are a transfiguration carried out more for communication with others than for the preservation of memories themselves, and it necessarily alters the totality of the idea to accord with a set of commonly shared word concepts and categories. Polanyi's (1964) often misconstrued notion of tacit knowledge was a description of many kinds of knowledge artifacts (remembrances) that are inexpressible in words for one reason or another. OM and KM theorists might consider his work was a call not necessarily to articulate tacit knowledge into words, but to consider inexpressible ideas as equally relevant and often more powerful than those expressed in language.

FUTURE TRENDS

The nature and composition of organizational memory remains obscure, while theoretical models derived from outmoded psychology, common sense, and social theory continue to provide a framework for research.

In contrast, the phenomenological model of human memory (and simpler biological memory systems) offers an easily appreciated and robust representation of the totality of the processes, components, and functions that make up memory systems generally.

While it is generally recognized that organizational memory exists, researchers have been unable to make unequivocal discovery of it (Walsh & Ungson, 1991). It appears to be applied in modern business activity, but the mechanism whereby organizations apply it remains obscure.

Organizational learning studies, organizational memory research, and information-systems and information-management theories all offer credible and effective explanations of aspects of organizational cognitive operations, but they are without a consilience of the various terminologies and conflicting theories across the different research disciplines. The model of human memory promises to provide that if we can reconcile the personal aspect of the human organism to the collective and shared superpersonal nature of the organization. Maturana (1970) offers some constructive ideas toward this reconciliation in his description of unity. He suggests that if we distinguish the behavior of an organizational agent, which is applied primarily in the service of a particular organization, from its private behavior, it becomes easier to distinguish between organizational memory and private memory. From that point, a differentiation of aspects of agent behavior might lead to an insight about what constitutes organizational-memory-directed behavior and what does not.

CONCLUSION

The model of memory offered by biological studies is a rich one. Many aspects have not been touched here, but remain to be discovered by researchers provided they have a flexible but robust definitional framework to base their investigations on. Biological sciences indicate to us that memory is applied in the seemingly trivial activities of everyday life, and that many of those seemingly commonplace activities support more profound actions. While our current usage of organizational memory might be supported in respect to major decisions and activities, we might question how well it is supported in more mundane, and quite possibly critical, tasks.

By reconciling the concepts of organizational memory systems research to the familiar model of biological human memory, theorists might offer a reconciliation of many information-systems and information-management concepts based on the idea that the knowledge management they are working toward involves the same common objects.

REFERENCES[1]

Ackerman, M. S. (1994). Definitional and conceptual issues in organizational and group memories. *Proceedings of the 27th Hawaii International Conference of Systems Sciences (HICSS 1994)* (pp. 199-200).

Argyris, C., & Schön, D. A. (1996). *Organizational learning II.* Reading, MA: Addison-Wesley Publishing Company.

Ashcraft, M. H. (1994). *Human memory and cognition* (2nd Ed.). New York: Harper Collins College Publishers.

Baddeley, A. (1998). *Human memory: Theory and practice* (Rev. Ed.). Needham Heights, MA: Allyn and Bacon.

Bannon, L. J., & Kuutti, K. (1996). Shifting perspectives on organizational memory: From storage to active remembering. *Proceedings of the 29th Annual Hawaii International Conference on System Sciences (HICSS 1996)* (pp. 156-167).

Bergson, H. (1975). *Creative evolution* (A. Mitchell, Trans.). Westport, CT: Greenwood Publishing. (Original work published 1907).

Bergson, H. (1996). *Matter and memory.* New York: Zone Books. (Original work published 1896).

Bloom, F. E., & Lazerson, A. (1988). *Brain, mind and behavior* (2nd Ed.). New York: W. H. Freeman & Co.

Broad, C. D. (1925). *The mind and its place in nature.* London: Keagan Paul, Trench, Trubner & Co. Ltd.

Brown, D. E. (1991). *Human universals.* New York: McGraw-Hill, Inc.

Carlson, N. R. (1994). *The physiology of behavior.* Boston: Allyn & Bacon.

Carter, R. (1998). *Mapping the mind.* London: Weidenfeld & Nicholson.

Checkland, P. (1981). *Systems thinking, systems practice.* Chichester, UK: John Wiley & Sons.

Chomsky, N. (1968). *Language and mind.* New York: Harcourt Brace Jovanovich, Inc.

Corbett, J. M. (1997). Towards a sociological model of organizational memory. *Proceedings of the 30th Annual Hawaii International Conference on System Sciences (HICSS 1997)* (pp. 252-261).

Cotterill, R. (1998). *Enchanted looms: Conscious networks in brains and computers.* Cambridge, MA: Cambridge University Press.

Dennett, D. C. (1991). *Consciousness explained.* Little, Brown & Company.

Deutsch, K. (1966). *The nerves of government.* New York: The Free Press.

Dimasio, A. (2000). *The feeling of what happens: Body, emotion and the meaning of consciousness.* London: Heinemann.

Dimasio, A. R. (1999). *The feeling of what happens: Body, emotion and the making of consciousness.* London: Heinemann.

Dominowski, R. L., & Bourne, L. E., Jr. (1994). History of research on thinking and problem solving. In R. J. Sternberg (Ed.), *Thinking and problem solving* (Handbook of perception and cognition series). San Diego: Academic Press.

Dubin, R. (1969). *Theory building* (Rev. ed.). New York: The Free Press.

Frost, S. E. (1942). *Basic teachings of the great philosophers.* New York: Doubleday.

Gorry, G. A., & Scott Morton, M. S. (1971). A framework for management information systems. *Sloan Management Review, 13*(1), 55-70.

Haberlandt, K. (1997). *Cognitive psychology.* Boston: Allyn and Bacon.

Hallpike, C. R. (1979). *The foundations of primitive thought.* Oxford, UK: Clarendon Press

Hedberg, B. (1981). How organizations learn and unlearn. In P. C. Nystrom & W. H. Starbuck (Eds.), *Handbook of organizational design.* London: Oxford University Press.

Jackenoff, R. (1992). *Languages of the mind.* Cambridge, MA: The MIT Press.

Jackenoff, R. (1993). *Patterns in the mind: Language and human nature.* New York: Simon & Schuster.

Krippendorff, K. (1975). Some principles of information storage and retrieval in society. In *General systems* (Vol. 20).

Lackoff, G. (1987). *Women, fire and dangerous things: What categories reveal about the mind.* Chicago: University of Chicago Press.

Langer, E. J. (1983). *The psychology of control.* Beverly Hills, CA: Sage.

Levitt, B., & March, J. G. (1988). Organizational learning. *Annual Review of Sociology, 14,* 319-340.

Luria, A. R. (1973). *The working brain: An introduction to neuropsychology.* London: Penguin Books.

Maier, R. (2002). *Knowledge management systems: Information, communication technologies for knowledge management.* Berlin, Germany: Springer Verlag.

Maturana, H. R. (1970). The biology of cognition. In H. R. Maturana & F. J. Varela (Eds.), *Autopoiesis and cognition: The realization of the living.* Dordrecht, The Netherlands: D. Reidel.

Meltzer, M. L. (1983). Poor memory: A case report. *Journal of Clinical Psychology, 39,* 3-10.

Middleton, M. (2002). *Information management: A consolidation of operations analysis and strategy.* Wagga Wagga, New South Wales: CIS Charles Sturt University.

Monod, J. (1997). *Chance and necessity: On the natural philosophy of modern biology* (A. Wainhouse, Trans.). London: Penguin Books. (Original work published 1971).

Morrison, J., & Olfman, L. (1997). Organizational memory. *Proceedings of the 30th Annual Hawaii International Conference on System Sciences (HICSS 1997).*

Norman, D. A. (Ed.). (1970). *Models of human memory.* New York: Academic Press.

Norman, D. A. (1993). *Things that make us smart: Defending human attributes in the age of the machine.* Reading, MA: Perseus Books.

O'Hear, A. (1997). *Beyond evolution: Human nature and the limits of evolutionary explanation.* Oxford, UK: Clarendon Press.

Olfman, L. (1998). *Organizational memory systems: Are they real? A virtual conference transcript.* Retrieved March 18, 2002, from *http://www2.cis.temple.edu/isworld/vmc/april98/olfman/default.htm*

Pinker, S. (1994). *The language instinct: The new science of language and mind.* London: Penguin Books.

Pinker, S. (1997). *How the mind works.* London: Penguin Books.

Polanyi, M. (1964). *Personal knowledge: Towards a post critical philosophy.* New York: Harper & Row.

Rose, S. (1993). *The making of memory.* New York: Bantam Books.

Salton, G., & McGill, M. J. (1983). *Introduction to modern information retrieval.* New York: McGraw-Hill Inc.

Schwartz, D. G., Divitini, M., & Brasethvik, T. (Eds.). (2000). *Internet-based organizational memory and knowledge management.* Hershey, PA: Idea Group Publishing.

Simon, H. A. (1957). *Models of man: Social and rational.* New York: John Wiley.

Sowa, J. F. (1984). *Conceptual structures: Information processing in mind and machine.* Reading, MA: Addison-Wesley Publishing Company.

Spender, J.-C. (1995). Organizational knowledge, learning and memory: Three concepts in search of a theory. *Journal of Organizational Change and Management, 9*(1), 63-78.

Stein, E. W. (1989). *Organizational memory: Socio-technical framework and empirical research.* PhD dissertation, University of Pennsylvania.

Stein, E. W. (1995). Organizational memory: Review of concepts and recommendations for management. *International Journal of Information Management, 15*(2), 17-32.

Stein, E. W., & Zwass, V. (1995). Actualizing organizational memory with information systems. *Information Systems Research, 6*(2), 85-117.

Sternberg, R. J. (Ed.). (1994). *Thinking and problem solving: Handbook of perception and cognition.* San Diego: Academic Press, Inc.

Tulving, E. (1983). *Elements of episodic memory.* London: Oxford University Press.

Tuomi, I. (1995). Abstraction and history: From institutional amnesia to organizational memory. *Proceedings of the 28th Annual Hawaii International Conference on System Sciences* (pp. 303-312).

Tuomi, I. (1999). *Data is more than knowledge: Implications of the reversed knowledge hierarchy for knowledge management and organizational memory.*

Walsh, J. P., & Ungson, G. R. (1991). Organizational memory. *Academy of Management Review, 16*(1), 57-91.

Washburn, S. L., & Shirek, J. (1967). Human evolution. In J. Hirsch (Ed.), *Behavior-genetic analysis.* New York: McGraw-Hill Book Company.

Wilson, E. O. (1998). *Consilience: The unity of knowledge.* London: Little, Brown and Company (UK).

Wilson, F. A. (1997). The brain and the firm: Perspectives on the networked organization and the cognitive metaphor. *Proceedings of the Pacific Asia Conference of Information Systems* (pp. 581-587).

Wilson, R. A., & Keil, F. C. (1999). *The MIT encyclopedia of the cognitive sciences.* Cambridge, MA: The MIT Press.

Yates, J. (1990). For the record: The embodiment of organizational memory, 1850-1920. In *Business and economic history* (2nd series, Vol. 19, pp. 172-182).

KEY TERMS

Aides Memoires: Aids to the memory or mental artifacts that indicate the sources of information rather than the information itself.

Autobiographical Memory: That aspect of memory systems that allows the perception of the historic order in which experiential remembrances are stored in long-term memory.

Biological Model: A construct developed from the observation of biophysical processes of living things.

Cognition: The collection of mental processes and activities used in perceiving, remembering, thinking, and understanding, and the act of using those processes.

Consilience: The reconciliation of all knowledge with the historical and scientific observations of biology, chemistry, and physics in the belief that the findings of those sciences offer a more robust foundation for the proper investigation of all phenomena.

Encoding: To input or take into memory, to convert to a usable mental form, or to store into memory.

Memory Ownership: The proprietorship of memory faculties or the possession of a set of memories.

Organism: An independent living entity.

Percept: A mental artifact (in the form of a network of connected neurons) that allows some mental representation of a directly, or indirectly, experienced thing. Also, it is the "self" mental model of an organism generated by remembrances of experiential perceptions made by the organism previously. Dimasio (2000) characterizes the self as a prototype used to test new perceptions against the perceived current state of the organism, and subsequently to generate percepts enriched by data as to how an idea or event affects the organism itself.

Sensory Memory: A system, independent of memory in the beginning, that consists of a series of stages where sensory signals are transformed into sensory percepts.

Short-Term Memory (STM): The memory component where current and recently attended information is held. It is sometimes loosely equated with attention and consciousness (Baddeley, 1998).

Ubiquity (of Memory): The capacity of being everywhere at all times.

ENDNOTE

[1] Not all of these sources are explicitly referenced in the text, but they are still listed here as relevant bibliographical material for the purposes of completeness.

Capability Maturity

Alfs T. Berztiss
University of Pittsburgh, USA

INTRODUCTION

The dependence of any organization on knowledge management is clearly understood. Actually, we should distinguish between knowledge management (KM) and knowledge engineering (KE): KM is to define and support organizational structure, allocate personnel to tasks, and monitor knowledge engineering activities; KE is concerned with technical matters, such as tools for knowledge acquisition, knowledge representation, and data mining. We shall use the designation KMKE for knowledge management and knowledge engineering collectively. KM is a very young area—the three articles termed "classic works" in Morey, Maybury, and Thuraisingham (2000) date from 1990, 1995, and 1996, respectively. We could regard 1991 as the start of institutionalized KM. This is when the Skandia AFS insurance company appointed a director of intellectual capital. KE has a longer history—expert systems have been in place for many years. Because of its recent origin, KMKE is characterized by rapid change. To deal with the change, we need to come to a good understanding of the nature of KMKE.

One of the lasting contributions of the business reengineering movement is the view that an enterprise is to be regarded as a set of well-defined processes (Davenport, 1993; Berztiss, 1996). This implies that KMKE also should be a process. Implementation of a process has two aspects: there is need for a procedural definition, and for an understanding of the resources and capabilities needed to implement the procedures and manage the process. Here, we will not be considering the procedures. Our purpose is to set up a model that identifies the capabilities needed to define, implement, and maintain the KMKE process.

The Background section of this article introduces capability models. In the Focus section, we define a capability model for KMKE in general terms and look at the management and engineering sides of this model. Then, we look into the future and offer a conclusion.

BACKGROUND: CAPABILITY MATURITY AND SOFTWARE

One area that has had long experience with processes is software engineering, and we turn to it for guidance on how to construct a capability model for KMKE. The software Capability Maturity Model (CMM-SW) was introduced by Humphrey (1989) and elaborated by a team of researchers at the Software Engineering Institute (1995). A later development is CMMI, which stands for CMM Integration. This is a suite of models where CMMI-SW (CMMI Product Team, 2002) is the model for software development. We shall be guided by the original model for two main reasons: First, there is greater familiarity with CMM-SW than with CMMI; second, the original CMM-SW has inspired a number of models that address the specific capabilities needed for specialized applications. Thus, there are CMMs for reuse (Davis, 1993), formal specification (Fraser & Vaishnavi, 1997), maintenance (Kajko-Mattson, 2001), an initial version for KM (Berztiss, 2002a), e-commerce (Berztiss, 2002b), and data quality management (Berztiss, 2004). An investigation of how to adapt CMM-SW for such nontraditional projects as product-line development, database development, and schedule-driven development also has been undertaken (Johnson & Brodman, 2000). Considerable evidence exists on the effectiveness of CMM-SW and CMMI for improving quality and reducing costs (Goldenson & Gibson, 2003).

The CMM-SW has five maturity levels. Level 1 is the base from which an organization moves upward by satisfying a set of requirements expressed as key process areas (KPAs). This level structure with the total of 18 KPAs is shown in Table 1. All KPAs of Level 2 relate to management, those of Level 3 to management and engineering, and those of Levels 4 and 5 relate primarily to engineering.

In CMM-SW, the definition of a KPA starts with a statement of it "goals," a "commitment to perform," which is essentially a policy statement committing the

Table 1. Key process areas of CMM-SW

Level 3	Level 5
Organizational process focus Organizational process definition Training program Integrated software management Software product engineering Intergroup coordination Peer reviews	Defect prevention Technology change management Process change management
Level 2	Level 4
Requirements management Software project planning Software project tracking and oversight Software subcontractor management Software quality assurance Software configuration management	Quantitative process management Software quality management

organization to the satisfaction of these goals, and an "ability to perform" statement, which lists the resources that have to be allocated. Next comes a list of activities that need to be performed in order to achieve the goals of the KPA. This can be regarded as a requirements statement that tells what is to be done without going into details of how the activities are to be performed. In addition, there is an indication of what process measurements are to be made and to what review procedures the activities of a KPA are to be subjected. Both measurements and reviews are important for any CMM. Only by measuring can we tell what does and what does not work, and what is the precise effect of a particular action. The review procedures ensure that the activities are in fact being performed.

FOCUS: A CAPABILITY MODEL FOR KMKE

Considering that the CMM-SW book (SEI, 1995) is about 450 pages, the outline of the CMM-KMKE we present here is very sketchy. The most we can do is define a set of KPAs and assign them to maturity levels. In designing CMM-KMKE, we were guided by our earlier work on the dimensions of the knowledge management process (Berztiss, 2001). Other influences have been the four "success statements" of Smith and Farquhar (2000):

- The organization knows what it knows and uses it, and knows what it needs to know and learns it.
- For any project, for any customer, the project team delivers the knowledge of the overall organization.

- The organization delivers the right information, to the right people, at the right time, with the tools they need to use it.
- The perspective of the employees is aligned with that of the customers.

Reinhardt's (2000) key questions of knowledge management were another source of inspiration. The KPAs of CMM-KMKE are intended to establish capabilities required to answer his questions:

- How can relevant organizational knowledge be identified and new knowledge be created and utilized?
- How can a system of knowledge creation and utilization be designed and organized?
- What measures provide management with information about the quality of the knowledge management process?
- What methods and tools support the implementation of knowledge management?

Table 2 shows the KPAs of CMM-KMKE. We have deviated somewhat from the underlying philosophy of CMM-SW. There, Levels 2 and 3 have a management bias, and Levels 4 and 5 have primarily an engineering orientation. The levels of CMM-KMKE are interleaved: Levels 2 and 4 emphasize KM, Levels 3 and 5 have more to do with the KE aspect. In this way, capability maturity can be achieved for both management and engineering of the knowledge process in parallel. However, it is essential to have in place knowledge requirements management, which is a Level 2 KPA, before any of the Level 3 KPAs are implemented. This KPA establishes what the organization aims to achieve, that is, it draws a

Table 2. Key process areas of CMM-KMKE

Level 4	Level 5
Integrated KMKE process External knowledge acquisition Qualitative cost-benefit analysis	Technology change management Quantitative cost-benefit analysis
Level 2	Level 3
Knowledge requirements management Internal knowledge acquisition Uncertainty awareness Training	Knowledge representation Knowledge engineering techniques User access and profiling

road map for all the knowledge-related activities of the organization.

Management-Oriented Levels of the CMM-KMKE

We would need a book, written by a sizable team of experts in knowledge management and knowledge engineering to define the CMM-KMKE in detail. However, by listing a few of the activities for each KPA, we hope at least to suggest the nature and purpose of the KPA. The outlines of the KPAs follow closely their descriptions first presented in Berztiss (2002a).

- **Knowledge requirements management (Level 2):** The purpose of KMKE has to be clearly understood by the entire organization. The very first step is to set up a KMKE group (K-group) that is to determine the knowledge needs of the organization and to work toward the satisfaction of these needs by institutionalization of KMKE practices. In a smaller organization, the "group" can be a single person. By institutionalization, we mean that the practices are to be documented. A major purpose of a CMM is the distribution of capabilities throughout an organization so that the organization is no longer dependent on single individuals for particular capabilities. The knowledge needs can be expressed as requirements, that is, statements of *what* is needed without the details of *how* the needs are to be satisfied. Considerable literature exists on requirements gathering and management for software (for a brief summary, see Berztiss, 2002c). An important part of requirements determination is the identification of stakeholders, who in the KMKE context include gatherers and organizers of knowledge, experts on privacy laws, and people who will benefit from the knowledge.
- **Internal knowledge acquisition (Level 2):** We distinguish between internal and external knowl-

edge. The former resides in an organization itself, in the form of databases and data warehouses, and, most importantly, the skills of people. External knowledge is gathered via personal contacts and communication media. After the knowledge requirements have been determined, the K-group is to establish a systematic approach to how the requirements are to be satisfied. This means that sources of internal knowledge are to be identified, information gathered from these sources is to be codified, and access to this information is to be facilitated. Abecker, Bernardi, Hinkelmann, Kühn, and Sintek (1998) give an overview of an artificial intelligence approach to the setting up of an organizational memory; Rus and Lindvall (2002) survey the role of KM in software engineering—they provide a very useful list of relevant Web addresses.

- **Uncertainty awareness (Level 2):** All knowledge is subject to uncertainty to a greater or lesser degree. To begin with, at least the K-group has to understand the issues relating to this. Specifically, it should establish guidelines on how to assign degrees of uncertainty to particular items of knowledge. Klir and Yuan (1995) is still the most useful text on uncertainty in general; see Berztiss (2002d) for a more recent survey.
- **Training (Level 2):** The institutionalization of a training program is another priority task for the K-group. Initially, everybody in the organization is to be informed about the purposes of KMKE and how the KMKE processes will affect them. Specialized training needs will become apparent as the KMKE program develops, particularly with respect to KE techniques.
- **Integrated KMKE process (Level 4):** In order to arrive at an integration of KM and KE, there has to be a thorough understanding of both of them at a state-of-the-practice level, and the organization must make full use of KM techniques. By integration, we mean that KE is being applied to KM itself—KM is to manage the KMKE process, and KE is to look after improvements of this process.
- **External knowledge acquisition (Level 4):** Organizations do not operate in isolation. They are embedded in an environment—the environment is the context for the operation. It is customary to denote the context as $<w, t>$, where w is a slice of the "world" at time t. As the context changes over time, an organization has to recognize the changes and has to respond to them. This, of course, has to happen even at Level 1, but this KPA requires that a thorough analysis is undertaken to determine how much of w is relevant, and how this relevant

component is to influence the operation of the enterprise.

- **Qualitative cost-benefit analysis (Level 4):** We should be able to measure the cost of the KMKE process, and we also should be aware of improvements (or the lack of them) in the operation of an organization. But it is difficult to discern cause-effect relationships, that is, to determine that this or that benefit arises from a particular expenditure of resources. The goal of this KPA is to identify cause-effect relationships. Some techniques for this have been developed (Pearl, 2000).

Engineering-Oriented Levels of the CMM-KMKE

- **Knowledge representation (Level 3):** Various representations of knowledge have been studied, particularly in the context of artificial intelligence (Markman, 1999). For example, Bayesian networks are used to facilitate inferences (Pearl, 2000). A recent trend is the use of ontologies to organize knowledge. There are numerous definitions of ontology. A useful one can be found in a survey by Kalfoglou (2002): An ontology is an explicit representation of a shared understanding of the important concepts in some domain of interest.

- **Knowledge engineering techniques (Level 3):** These techniques have been developed for extracting knowledge from different representations, but there is no sharp division between knowledge representation and KE techniques. For example, a Bayesian network represents knowledge, but the setting up of the network is a KE technique. Specialized KE techniques include the design of data warehouses, data mining, data filtering, and the management of uncertainty. Note that uncertainty management differs from the Level 2 KPA of uncertainty awareness: To manage uncertainty means that attempts are made to estimate uncertainty quantitatively by, for example, statistical techniques.

- **User access and profiling (Level 3):** Experience shows that there can be strong resistance to the introduction of KMKE (Kay & Cecez-Kecmanovic, 2000). A common cause of this resistance is that users have to go through complex access procedures and extensive searches to arrive at items of knowledge they are looking for. Moreover, personnel may be unaware of the existence of knowledge useful to them. User profiles that reflect their interests allow the matching of knowledge needs and knowledge availability.

- **Quantitative cost-benefit analysis (Level 5):** The advance from qualitative to quantitative cost-benefit analysis requires extensive measurements relating to the KMKE process. Only experience will tell what should be measured, which measurements contribute to cost-benefit analysis in particular instances of benefits, and how a cause-effect relation is to be expressed in quantitative terms.

- **Technological change management (Level 5):** This is where a transition is made from state-of-the-practice to state-of-the-art. New developments arise constantly. For example, data mining, defined as the analysis of data sets to find unsuspected relationships and to summarize the data in novel ways (Hand et al., 2001), is extending to data mining on the Web. Mining of time series data is one example. Another development is the real-time analysis of streaming data, for example, from cash registers. The K-group must monitor research developments and be ready to introduce new techniques after a careful cost-benefit analysis.

A LOOK TO THE FUTURE

Much remains to be done in the KMKE area, and we cannot expect quick results. Within an organization, even with the best will, the upper levels of a CMM can take a long time to reach. The practices of the KPAs of these levels require reference to measurements relating to the effectiveness of the processes of knowledge gathering, knowledge representation, and knowledge use. In more general terms, the biggest challenge arises from the relative intractability of knowledge. To quote Davenport (1997), "Knowledge *can* be embedded in machines, but it is tough to categorize and retrieve effectively" (p. 10). We have to find better ways to deal with this aspect of knowledge, which Polanyi (1958) has called personal knowledge.

Most of today's knowledge workers are not particularly knowledgeable in theoretical areas. This will have to change. Data mining cannot be undertaken without statistical skills, and the study of causality is based on probabilities. Increasingly, knowledge workers will have to get accustomed to find out about new developments on the Web. As late as April 2004, the primary source of information about CMMI was the Web. On the other hand, the Web contributes to a managerial information overload (Farhoomand & Drury, 2002). The situation will not improve unless more effective filters based on user profiles are developed.

Under CMM-SW, an organization develops a generic software development process, and this process is adapted to the special needs and circumstances of a software project. The purpose of CMM-KMKE is to define capabilities that will make an organization more effective on its projects, but the knowledge process does not have the same project-dependence as the software process. Still, different organizations may have different needs. Kankanhalli, Tanudidjaja, Sutano, and Tan (2003) classify organizations as being service-based or product-based, and, orthogonally, as operating in a low-volatility or a high-volatility context. Thus, there are four types of organizations, and their KMKE needs will differ. The CMM-KMKE as outlined here is sufficiently general to meet the needs of all four types of organizations.

CONCLUSION

CMMs have provided various application areas with road maps for improvement. The effectiveness of CMM-SW, from which these CMMs derive, is well documented. A comparatively new area, such as knowledge management, can derive greatest benefit from a CMM because a new area is very much in need of guidance based on what has worked elsewhere. The most that has been possible here is to sketch an outline of a CMM-KMKE. Still, the outline should help identify the more critical capabilities needed for effective knowledge management.

REFERENCES

Abecker, A., Bernardi, A., Hinkelmann, K., Kühn, O., & Sintek, M. (1998). Toward a technology for organizational memories. *IEEE Intelligent Systems 13*(3), 40-48.

Berztiss, A.T. (1996). *Software methods* for *business reengineering*. New York: Springer.

Berztiss, A.T. (2001). Dimensions of the knowledge management process. In *Proceedings of the 12th International Workshop on Database and Expert Systems Applications (DEXA'01)* (pp. 437-441). Los Alamitos, CA: IEEE CS Press.

Berztiss, A.T. (2002a). Capability maturity for knowledge management. In *Proceedings of the 13th International Workshop on Database and Expert Systems Applications (DEXA'02)* (pp.162-166). Los Alamitos, CA: IEEE CS Press.

Berztiss, A.T. (2002b). Capabilities for e-commerce. In *Proceedings of the 13th International Workshop on Database and Expert Systems Applications (DEXA'02)* (pp. 875-879). Los Alamitos, CA: IEEE CS Press.

Berztiss, A.T. (2002d). Uncertainty management. In S.K. Chang (Ed.), *Handbook of software engineering and knowledge engineering* (Vol. 2, pp. 389-418). Singapore: World Scientific.

Berztiss, A.T. (2004). Models for data quality management. In *Proceedings of CAiSE'04 Workshops* (Vol. 2, pp. 37-48). Faculty of Computer Science and Information Technology, Riga Technical University.

CMMI Product Team (2002). Capability Maturity Model Integration, Version 1.1 (CMMI-SW, V1.1) Staged Representation. CMU/SEI-2002-TR-029. Retrieved from *www.cmu.edu/sei*

Davenport, T.H. (1993). *Process innovation: Reengineering work through technology.* Cambridge, MA: Harvard Business School Press.

Davenport, T.H. (1997). *Information Ecology.* New York: Oxford University Press.

Davis, T. (1993). The reuse capability model: A basis for improving an organization's reuse capabilities. In *Advances in software reuse* (pp. 126-133). Los Alamitos, CA: IEEE CS Press.

Farhoomand, A.F., & Drury, D.H. (2002). Managerial information overload. *Communications of the Association for Computing Machinery, 45*(10), 127-131.

Fraser, M.D., & Vaishnavi, V.K. (1997). A formal specifications maturity model. *Communications of the Association for Computing Machinery, 40*(12), 95-103.

Goldenson, D.R., & Gibson, D.L. (2003). Demonstrating the impact and benefits of CMMI: An update and preliminary results. CMU/SEI-2003-SR-009. Retrieved from *www.cmu.edu/sei*

Humphrey, W.S. (1989). *Managing the software process.* Englewood Cliffs, NJ: Addison-Wesley.

Johnson, D.L., & Brodman, J.G. (2000). Applying CMM project planning practices to diverse environments. *IEEE Software, 17*(4), 40-47.

Kajko-Mattson, M. (2001). *Corrective maintenance maturity model: Problem management.* Doctoral dissertation: Department of Computer and System Sciences, Stockholm University/Royal Institute of Technology.

Kalfoglou, Y. (2002). Exploring ontologies. In S.K. Chang (Ed.), *Handbook of software engineering and knowledge engineering* (Vol. 1, pp. 863-887). Singapore: World Scientific.

Kankanhalli, A., Tanudidjaja, F., Sutano, J., & Tan, B.C.Y. (2003). The role of IT in successful knowledge management initiatives. *Communications of the Association for Computing Machinery, 46*(9), 69-73.

Kay, R., & Cecez-Kecmanovic, D. (2000). When knowledge becomes information: A case of mistaken identity. In *Proceedings of the 11th International Workshop on Database and Expert Systems Applications (DEXA'00)* (pp. 1128-1133). Los Alamitos, CA: IEEE CS Press.

Klir, G.J., & Yuan, B. (1995). *Fuzzy sets and fuzzy logic: Theory and applications.* Englewood Cliffs, NJ: Prentice Hall.

Markman, B. (1999). *Knowledge representation.* Mahwah, NJ: Lawrence Erlbaum.

Morey, D., Maybury, M., & Thuraisingham, B. (Eds.). (2000). *Knowledge management: Classic and contemporary works.* Cambridge, MA: MIT Press.

Pearl, J. (2000). *Causality: Models, reasoning, and inference.* Cambridge, MA: Cambridge University Press.

Polanyi, M. (1958). *Personal knowledge.* London: Routledge & Kegan Paul.

Reinhardt, R. (2000). *Knowledge management: Linking theory with practice.* In Morey et al. (2000), (pp. 187-221).

Rus, I., & Lindvall, M. (2002). Knowledge management in software engineering. *IEEE Software, 19*(3), 26-38.

Smith, R.G., & Farquhar, A. (2000). The road ahead for knowledge management, an AI perspective. *AI Magazine, 21*(4), 17-40.

Software Engineering Institute (1995). *The capability maturity model: Guidelines for improving the software process.* Reading, MA: Addison-Wesley.

KEY TERMS

Capability: Any method, tool, or piece of knowledge that supports the achievement of a goal.

CMM-KMKE: A capability maturity model, based on the CMM, for knowledge management and knowledge engineering.

CMM: The Capability Maturity Model (also known as CMM-SW), developed at the Software Engineering Institute of Carnegie-Mellon University, which helps a software development organization to identify its strengths and weaknesses and provides a well-defined plan for improvement.

CMMI: A suite of models that update and upgrade the CMM.

Key Process Area: A set of activities that define a specific capability area; the CMM has 18 Key Process Areas.

Maturity Level: A level of the CMM reached by the attainment of a clearly defined set of capabilities, expressed as *key process areas*.

Process: A set of linked activities that collectively realize an objective or policy goal.

Communities of Practice

Elayne Coakes
University of Westminster, UK

Steve Clarke
The University of Hull, Uk

INTRODUCTION

This article looks at the concept of communities of practice (CoPs) in the workplace. The theories surrounding these types of communities are still very new and in the process of development. The practice and the importance of these communities for knowledge transfer are also still to be explored as to the best methods for establishing such communities and how to support and encourage them. Below we discuss the background and main threads of theory that are under development. This is very much a short introduction to the concept. Further discussions can be found in Coakes (2004), Coakes and Clarke (in press), and Lehaney, Clarke, Coakes, and Jack (2003).

BACKGROUND

Communities of practice are becoming increasingly important in many organisations. As the APQC (2004) says:

CoPs are becoming the core knowledge strategy for global organizations. As groups of people who come together to share and learn from one another face-to-face and virtually, communities of practice are held together by a common interest in a body of knowledge and are driven by a desire and need to share problems, experiences, insights, templates, tools, and best practices.

To define a community of practice, it is worth considering the words of Etienne Wenger (2001), who is considered one of the foremost experts in this field. He says:

[C]ommunities of practice are a specific kind of community. They are focused on a domain of knowledge and over time accumulate expertise in this domain. They develop their shared practice by interacting around problems, solutions, and insights, and building a common store of knowledge.

The initial concept of communities of practice came out of work by Jean Lave and Etienne Wenger (1991) relating to situated learning in the workplace and other communities with related interests. Thus, such communities are an aggregation of people who are bound (in their specific context) to accomplish tasks or engage in sense-making activities (Brown & Duguid, 1991; Lave & Wenger). Learning, to Lave and Wenger, was the transformation of practice in situated possibilities. Newcomers to a group learn from the old participants, bearing in mind that practices will change over time and place due to changes in circumstances. In addition, intergenerational relationships will affect the learning situation: There may well be a fear from the older group members in transferring knowledge to the younger, implying a loss of power and importance, or a fear from the new or younger group members of demonstrating ignorance. So, the social process of knowledge acquisition affects the practice of knowledge sharing and the desire for knowledge sharing.

The context or domain for these communities is related to the subject matter around which they are formed. Within this domain, communities interact, learn, and build relationships in order that they may practice their skills through tools, frameworks, idea sharing, artefacts, or documents.

In the forthcoming *Encyclopedia of Communities of Practice in Information and Knowledge Management* (Coakes & Clarke, 2006), a number of particular issues are covered in a multilayered form. Here we see that such communities are governed by internal, informal, and unspoken rules dominated by specialised language development. We also see that there are issues in measuring the output and value of such communities for an organisation, that strategy needs to be developed uniquely for each community as well as for the organisation in general, and that how or even whether to reward participants is a matter of some debate. The psychology of participants and the difficulties with creating a shared meaning within a community can be explored through philosophy and psychology as well as organisational studies, and we find that many perspectives are available to understand communities and their actions. This being the case, many fields of study have a view on how and why communities work and how and why people should or could participate in this work.

FOCUS ON COMMUNITIES

If we accept that the role of CoPs in the business environment is to share knowledge and improve the way the organisation does business whether in the public or private sector, and that they are community workplaces where people can share ideas, mentor each other, and tap into interests (APQC, 2002), each CoP can be a focus of learning and competence for the organisation. Much of the organisation's work can be facilitated or conversely frustrated through these communities depending on how permissive or permitted they are. Organisational culture, it would seem, plays a great part in communities and how they operate. The members of a community need to trust the other members before they are willing to share their experience and understanding.

The bonds that tie communities together are both social and professional, and while they can be fostered and supported by organisations, they are not formed by them. Convincing people to participate in communities requires an ongoing commitment from the leaders within an organisation to permit communities to self-organise and collaborate as they see fit with suitable encouragement and support. Education plays a part in this encouragement, but so too does enthusiasm from amongst the community's members, which will come from seeing the benefits to their own self-knowledge and development as well as a business value. Overregulation or understructuring can lead to a stale community or a community that fails to develop and thus eventually fails. In addition, due to the voluntary nature of membership in such a community, some are affected when they become too prominent in an organisation and may disappear from view (Gongla & Rizzuto, 2004). This can happen in a number of ways. The community may apparently disappear while continuing to operate under the organisational surface, not wishing to become too obvious to the formal organisational structure or be bound by its requirements. Other CoPs stop operating, merge with other communities, or redefine themselves. CoPs that become formal organisational structures because their work becomes necessary to organisational functioning lose much of what makes them a CoP and transform into project teams, and so forth.

Vestal (2003) suggests that there are four main types of communities:

- innovation communities that are cross-functional to work out new solutions utilising existing knowledge
- helping communities that solve problems
- best-practice communities that attain, validate, and disseminate information
- knowledge-stewarding communities that connect people, and collect and organise information and knowledge across the organisation

Each of these community types will require different amounts, levels, and functionality of support. However, it is unwise for any business to rely on CoPs performing these tasks continuously or to a set standard as their voluntary nature means that outside control should not, or cannot, be exercised directly or they may cease to comply with the tasks at hand.

BUILDING A COMMUNITY

Communities are easy to destroy but difficult to construct. Membership, and choice, in a community needs to be voluntary otherwise members may not participate in the knowledge sharing, which is their raison d'etre.

McDermott (1999) concludes that there are four challenges when building communities. These four are the design of the human and information systems to help the community members think together and interact, the development of communities such that they will share their knowledge, the creation of an organisational environment that values such knowledge, and each community member being open and willing to share.

CoPs differ from traditional team-working approaches in that they are most likely to be cross-functional and multiskilled. They therefore align themselves closely to the sociotechnical ideals of inclusivity and having fluid boundaries. CoP members will be drawn from those who wish to involve themselves and who desire to share knowledge and learn from others about a specific topic, wherever in an organisation (and in some cases, outside the organisation, too) they may be located. Functional position is irrelevant; topic knowledge or interest is all that is necessary to join a CoP. The diversity of a CoP's population may encourage creativity and problem solving, and linkages to external communities will also enhance their activities. CoPs are the legitimate places for learning through participation. They additionally provide an identity for the participator in terms of social position and knowledge attributes and ownership. CoPs will have a shared domain and domain language, and some members may become apprentices as they are acculturated into this domain and knowledge development. It is also important when establishing CoPs to think about the embedded habits, assumptions, and work practices or cultural norms that exist in the organisation. Communication and how, where, and when people communicate are extremely important in relation to information sharing.

Communities (Brown as cited in Ruggles & Holtshouse, 1999) are also the places that provide us with different perspectives and lenses through which to view the world. Successful communities maintain a clear purpose and active leadership (McDermott, 2004), and support innovation and staff creativity through collaboration and collective solutions. CoPs also provide members with the ability to self-start and search for information and support as required (Heald, 2004), including extended expertise, that is, expertise outside their immediate work environment.

FUTURE TRENDS

The evidence from the workplace is that ICT-supported strategies for CoP development are better than ICT-led strategies (Kling & Courtright, 2003), and that the sociotechnical approach is valid for CoP development. ICT has different roles to play as knowledge-management systems are established and evolve in organisations: It moves from being the underlying infrastructure to the linking mechanism to the support mechanism (Pan & Leidner, 2003). Yet, without an understanding of the underlying work practices and organisational, social, and cultural aspects, ICT support will not match the specific elements that make this organisational culture unique and thus will be ineffective. As Nick Milton ("In the Know: Expert Perspectives. What is the best software supplier for communities of Practice?" 2004) of Knoco argues:

The best software to use is the one the community is most familiar with and is most prepared to use. Ideally one they are already using on a routine basis....why not let the community make the decision?...they can do much of their business through email alone. Do they really need anything further?

In addition, in the same article (a collection of comments from an online community), Giles Grant of BNFI argues, "IT should only be an enabler for sharing and collaboration. It isn't the community; the community is the people."

The future of CoPs, it would seem therefore, is an interesting one. There is increasing evidence that they

are being formalised into organisational structures with budgets, resources, and tasks, thus becoming more like project teams with an aim and a strategy. As such, those who saw them as a means of social support and informal tacit knowledge sharing may choose to go underground as discussed above, and the value of such groups to an organisation may be lost.

CONCLUSION

Thus we see from the discussion above some of the issues that surround CoPs and their establishment in the workplace. Too close to the formal structure, and the community will transform into a project team and thus lose the learning and voluntary nature of participation that is so important. Too far from the formal structure, and the community may not work toward an organisational goal. There is little agreement about how to support CoPs through technology or through organisational means. However, there is much evidence that communities are best left to self-organise and self-manage, and that any organisational outcomes are a benefit and not an expectation.

This article is but a brief summary of some of the more salient points relating to CoPs. It cannot cover all the issues and indeed is not intended to do so. It is instead intended to indicate to the reader the issues and potential areas of study that are related to current thinking.

REFERENCES

APQC. (2002). *Communities of practice.* Houston, TX: Author.

APQC. (2004). Retrieved February 12, 2004, from *http://www.apqc.org/portal/apqc/site/generic?path=/site/km/communities.jhtml*

Brown, J. S., & Duguid, P. (1991). Organisational learning and communities of practice: Towards a unified view of working, learning and organisation. *Organisation Science, 2*(1), S40-S57.

Coakes, E. (2004). Knowledge management: A primer. *Communications of the Association of Information Systems, 14,* 406-489, Article 21.

Coakes, E., & Clarke, S. (in press). *Encyclopedia of communities of practice in information and knowledge management.* Hershey, PA: Idea Group Reference.

Gongla, P., & Rizzuto, C. R. (2004). Where did that community go? Communities of practice that disappear. In P. Hildreth & C. Kimble (Eds.), *Knowledge networks: Innovation through communities of practice* (pp. 295-307). Hershey, PA: Idea Group Publishing.

Heald, B. (2004). Convincing your staff on CoPs: What's in it for them? *KMOnline, 7*(2), 3.

In the know: Expert perspectives. What is the best software supplier for communities of practice? (2004). *KMOnline, 7*(2), 4.

Kling, R., & Courtright, C. (2003). Group behaviour and learning in electronic forums: A sociotechnical approach. *Information Society, 19*(3), 221-235.

Land, F. F. (2000). Evaluation in a socio-technical context. In *LSE working papers.* London.

Lave, J., & Wenger, E. (1991). *Situated learning: Legitimate peripheral participation.* Cambridge: Cambridge University Press.

Lehaney, B., Clarke, S., Coakes, E., & Jack, G. (2003). *Beyond knowledge management.* Hershey, PA: IRM Press.

McDermott, R. (1999). Why information technology inspired but cannot deliver knowledge management. *California Management Review, 41*(4), 103-117.

McDermott, R. (2004). How to avoid a mid-life crisis in your CoPs. *KMOnline, 7*, 2.

Pan, S. L., & Leidner, D. E. (2003). Bridging communities of practice with information technology in pursuit of global knowledge sharing. *Journal of Strategic Information Systems, 12*, 71-88.

Ruggles, R., & Holtshouse, D. (1999). *The knowledge advantage: 14 visionaries define marketplace success in the new economy.* Oxford: Capstone.

Vestal, W. (2003). Ten traits for a successful community of practice. *Knowledge Management Review, 5*(6), 6.

Wenger, E. (2001). Retrieved April 2004, from *http://www.ewenger.com/tech*

KEY TERMS

C

Community of Practice: A group of individuals that may be colocated or distributed, are motivated by a common set of interests, and are willing to develop and share tacit and explicit knowledge.

Domain: Scope or range of a subject or sphere of knowledge.

Domain Language: The language, including specific technical terms, phrases, and shortcuts or abbreviations of speech, that is unique and specific to the sphere of knowledge.

Sociotechnical: *Socio* is derived from *socius*, Latin for *associate* or *companion*, here meaning society and technology, that is, a solution produced by technological means. *Technical* is derived from *technologia*, Greek for *systematic treatment*.

Sociotechnical thinking is a part of social theory and of philosophy. Its original emphasis was on organisational design and change management. The term sociotechnical means a task-design approach that is intended to optimise both the application and development of technology and the application and development of human knowledge and skill. The underlying philosophy of sociotechnical approaches is based essentially on two ideas focusing on the individual and the organisation. The first is the humanistic-welfare paradigm, involving the redesign of work for autonomy, self-actualisation, the use of self-regulating teams, individual empowerment, and thus stress reduction. In this view, the design of work systems is performed to improve the welfare of employees. The second (and perhaps contradictory) philosophy is the managerial paradigm, focusing on improving the performance of the organisation

Competitive Advantage of Knowledge Management

Gabriel Cepeda-Carrión
University of Seville, Spain

INTRODUCTION

Knowledge management has been proposed as a fundamental strategic process and the only sustainable competitive advantage for firms (Grant, 1996; Davenport, 1998). A key to understanding the success and failure of knowledge management efforts within organizations is the ability to identify the relevant knowledge to manage and to extract value out of this knowledge. In the last decade past research has focused heavily on defining what knowledge is and on using different typologies (e.g., tacit vs. explicit knowledge, individual vs. collective) to characterize the different types of knowledge available to firms (e.g., Polanyi, 1967; Spender, 1996). In addition, researchers have described the processes through which knowledge is created, developed, retained, and transferred in firms (e.g., Argote, 1999; Nonaka & Takeuchi, 1995), and the role played by leadership (Bryant, 2003; Vera & Crossan, 2004) and decision-making styles (Kalling, 2003) in influencing these processes. Unfortunately, despite the growing interest in knowledge management, little specific has been said about the mechanisms firms use to identify key knowledge areas and to gain competitive advantage out of knowledge management investments. The recognition of the important knowledge resources for a firm is critical, because the effectiveness of knowledge and learning can only be assessed on the basis of its utility in guiding behavior relative to the firm's relevant domain (Crossan, Lane, & White, 1999; Cepeda, Galán, & Leal, 2004; Zack, 1999). Knowledge for the sake of knowledge is not useful to firms.

We define knowledge management as the formalized, integrated approach of managing an enterprise's articulated and tacit knowledge assets. Knowledge assets include systems, documents, policies, and procedures, as well as unarticulated expertise and experience across the individuals, groups, organizational, and inter-organizational domains. We discuss how a knowledge management infrastructure enables the generation, acquisition, use, and transfer of knowledge, and most importantly, the identification of the critical knowledge areas for a firm. Moreover, we argue that competitive advantage consists of two dimensions: the value created to the customer and the ability to differentiate (through cost, innovation, or both) from competitors. The framework describes specific mechanisms through which knowledge management contributes to these two processes. Building on a resource-based view of the firm (Barney, 1991, 1995, 2001) and the knowledge management and organizational learning literatures (Grant, 1996; Hall, 1992, 1993; Spender, 1996), we develop a framework to address how critical knowledge areas can enable competitive advantage sources through customer approach and competitor approach.

This article integrates knowledge management and strategic management fields by taking a fine-grained look at the connection between knowledge resources and competitive advantage. We are explicit about how firms can identify key knowledge areas that impact competitive advantage, and how they can implement market (value creation) and competitor (differential capabilities) mechanisms that are instrumental in obtaining competitive advantage. Our integrative approach provides a fresh perspective on knowledge management from which we generate important insights for management practice. Only relevant and available knowledge impacts competitive advantage, thus top management needs to proactively engage in identifying this knowledge and extracting value out of it.

BACKGROUND

The relevance and importance of knowledge is becoming increasingly critical in business as we transition from an industrial era into an information and knowledge era.

With the arrival of the knowledge and information age as well as the service economy, the importance of effective knowledge and management has been emphasized by several scholars and industry analysts (Quinn, 1992; Toffler, 1990; Nonaka, 1991; Glazer, 1991; Leonard-Barton, 1992; Bohn, 1994; Klein & Prusak, 1994; Winslow & Bramer, 1994; Davis & Botkin, 1994; Peters, 1992). Drucker (1994) argues that the world is witnessing a great transformation, which he calls the "post-capitalist society," in which the basic economic resources will no longer be the traditional production input factors, but that the primary resource for both organizations and the economy will be knowledge.

Organizational knowledge management (KM) as a source of competitive advantage is now widely recognized (Nonaka, 1991; Bohn, 1994; Davis & Botkin, 1994). KM holds key implications for virtually all industries. Research indicates that knowledge and knowledge work has infiltrated deep into the value chain of most businesses (Quinn, 1992). Some of the reasons for this infiltration, such as product differentiation, creating "best in class" capabilities, and setting high entry barriers, provide important insights in the area of organizational knowledge and its impact on core business processes and functions. According to Quinn (1992) the majority of all public and private organizations are rapidly shifting to become repositories and coordinators of knowledge-based activities.

As we transition from an industrial/manufacturing economy to a more service-driven economy, we see the emergence of knowledge-intensive service organizations emerging alongside the more traditional capital-intensive and labor-intensive organizations (Bonora & Revang, 1993). Examples of knowledge-intensive service organizations include consulting, software engineering, law firms, and health care.

Actually, the challenge posed to contemporary businesses, particularly knowledge-intensive firms, is to remain competitive in a highly volatile and competitive knowledge environment in which markets quickly shift, technologies rapidly proliferate, competitors multiply, and products and services become obsolete almost overnight. Increasing customer needs and demands for immediate high value at low cost mandates the harnessing of knowledge coupled with the flexibility to meet changing needs. Achieving this goal in the information age requires the implementation of different strategies from those that were effective in the industrial age. For traditional organizations, it is no longer adequate to only achieve production and manufacturing efficiency. Knowledge-intensive firms, as well as traditional organizations, now increasingly compete because of knowledge and information. As a result, the issue of ownership and control of knowledge as a source of power in business has also become increasingly important. Both industry and academia are looking for approaches and methods to capture, organize, and leverage knowledge for increased competitiveness.

A set of publications (Stewart, 1994; Sveiby & Risling, 1987; Sveiby, 1990; Starbuck, 1990) indicates that several organizations are learning how to capture, manage, store, and leverage knowledge, and are making significant investments in KM. In this way, increasingly, firms are implementing KM, which is not surprising, since several types of firms, such as consulting and law firms, have the primary business of the application of their knowledge. Some authors include the idea of demonstrating accrued knowledge and experience in their area of service to customers, thereby retaining current customers and gaining new business by quickly delivering high-value solutions at low cost (faster, better, cheaper than their competitors). To leverage knowledge and intellectual capital in a more cost- and time-efficient manner, the firms develop employee competencies by sharing leading practices in their service areas, and capture and preserve knowledge that may be lost as a result of individuals leaving the firm.

A review of literature in the area of knowledge and information management reveals that many scholars have highlighted the importance of knowledge and information management.

MAIN FOCUS OF THE ARTICLE

An Organizing Framework Linking KM and Sustainable Competitive Advantage

Knowledge and Competitive Advantage

Knowledge activities in organizations have increased in significance over the past few years (Davenport & Klahr, 1998). In fact, knowledge has been proposed as the primary source of wealth creation (Cole, 1998), and knowledge protection has been suggested as critical to generate and preserve competitive advantage (Porter-Liebeskind, 1996). Davenport and Prusak (1998) also note that the only sustainable competitive advantage a firm has comes from what it collectively knows, how efficiently it uses what it knows, and how readily it acquires new knowledge.

Our conceptual development builds on the resource-based view (RBV) of the firm, an influential theoretical framework for understanding the creation and sustainability of competitive advantage (Barney, 1991; Nelson, 1991; Peteraf, 1993; Teece, Pisano, & Shuen, 1997). In this perspective, firms are conceptualized as bundles of resources. Resources are heterogeneously distributed across firms; resource differences might persist over time (Amit & Schoemaker, 1993). Resources are defined as all assets, capabilities, organizational processes, or firm attributes which are controlled by a firm, and which enable it to conceive of and implement strategies that improve its efficiency and effectiveness (Barney, 1991; Daft, 1983). When the resources are valuable, rare, inimitable, and non-substitutable (VRIS), firms can achieve sustainable competitive advantage by implementing strategies that leverage their resources in unique ways (Dierickx & Cool, 1989; Barney, 1991; Grant, 1996; Amit & Schoemaker, 1993).

One of the few resources that can pass the VRIS test is knowledge. Consequently, several authors have argued for a knowledge-based view (KBV) of the firm as a specialized case of RBV (Conner, 1991; Conner & Prahalad, 1996; Ghoshal & Moran, 1996; Grant, 1996b). KBV presents firms as social communities (Kogut & Zander, 1992) with the primary role of integrating the specialist knowledge resident in individuals into goods and services, so that organizational capabilities are the manifestation of this knowledge integration (Grant, 1996). Knowledge is embedded in multiple entities within the firm, such as the organizational culture, routines, policies, systems, and documents, as well as individuals and teams (Crossan et al., 1999; Nelson & Winter, 1982; Grant, 1996; Spender, 1996). Knowledge shapes the firm's core competences (Prahalad &Hamel, 1990) and therefore determines value creation (Grant, 1996). Furthermore, tacit knowledge, social knowledge, and complex knowledge are difficult to imitate (Leonard & Sensiper, 1998; Helfat & Raubitschek, 2000; McEvily & Chakravarthy, 2002). Hence, competences based on these types of knowledge cannot be easily duplicated by competitors, and strategies based on these competences are likely to lead to sustainable competitive advantage.

A contentious aspect of knowledge is its definitional domain. Researchers have engaged in a passionate debate about what knowledge is and what forms or types of it are available (Collins, 1993; Drucker, 1994). Knowledge has been defined as information whose validity is established through test of proof (Porter-Liebskind, 1996), and as relevant and actionable information based at least partially on experience (Leonard & Sensiper, 1998). While the positivist view ("knowledge as justified true belief") is the predominant one in Western culture and a generally accepted assumption in organizational theory (Nonaka & Takeuchi, 1995), it has been increasingly complemented by authors arguing that knowledge cannot be conceived independently from action (Blackler, 1995; Cook & Brown, 1999; Polanyi, 1967). These views shift the notion of knowledge as a commodity that people acquire to the study of knowing as something that they do.

For the purpose of this article, we define knowledge as familiarity with or understanding of a phenomenon. Knowledge can be contained in subjects such as individuals, groups, and organizations, and in objects such as systems, products, and processes. We view knowledge as a higher form of information, which is elevated by the specific nature and purpose of the organization to provide an opportunity that the firm can exploit for its advantage (Beckett, Wainwright, & Bance, 2000). Hence, the challenge for many firms is to identify that knowledge, which is relevant to their goals and strategies.

Figure 1 shows interrelationships between knowledge management infrastructure, critical knowledge areas, and various elements leading to sustainable competitive advantage. These relationships between these

Figure 1. Critical knowledge areas, value creation, capability differentials, sustainable competitive advantage, and infrastructure elements (people, process, technology)

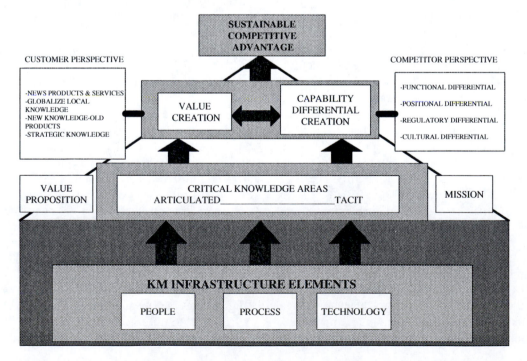

elements ensure the leading and enhancing sustainable competitive advantage. In the next sections, we discuss the factors that influence the identification of critical knowledge areas and the mechanisms through which critical knowledge areas have an impact on competitive advantage.

Identifying Critical Knowledge Areas

Critical knowledge areas are specific bodies of knowledge or key resource capabilities that are unique to an enterprise and reside at the core of their business (Thompsen, Ibarra, & Center, 1997). Given that "the most important context for guiding knowledge management is the firm's strategy" (Zack, 1999, p. 125), every strategic position is linked to some set of intellectual resources and capabilities. In order to implement knowledge management processes (e.g., data analysis and information communication) that support a firm's strategy, managers need to consider several issues. First, they need to assess what the firm must do to compete and what the firm can actually do (strategic gap) (Zack, 1999). Second, they should establish what the firm must know to compete and what the firm actually knows (knowledge gap) (Zack, 1999). Third, organizations need to recognize what their knowledge management infrastructure needs to be and what it currently is. While the first two issues focus on linking knowledge management efforts to strategic goals, the third point acknowledges that knowledge is a path-dependent resource (Teece et al., 1997) and that future knowledge configurations will be constrained by previous investments in a knowledge infrastructure. In the next sections we describe in further detail the role of two tangible components of a firm's strategy—its mission and value proposition—and that of the existing knowledge management infrastructure in helping organizational members to identify the firm's critical knowledge areas.

- **Business mission:** The starting point for business strategy is some underlying idea of why the business exists; this is typically comprised in a firm's mission, which includes a statement of the company's purpose and overarching goal (Grant, 2002). Some mission statements, such as that of Skandia, are explicit about the role of knowledge. For example, "Skandia creates unique skills around the world that allow us to provide the best financial solutions for our customers and enduring value for our shareholders. We build special relationships, engage the energy of our employees, and transfer knowledge with pride." If a statement of corporate purpose embodies or embraces knowledge, it becomes a "knowledge business vision" (Earl, 2001). Otherwise, when a business mission, such as that of

America Online ("To build a global medium as central to people's lives as the telephone or television…and even more valuable") is not explicit about knowledge, the question firms need to answer is, what is the contribution that knowledge can make to the attainment of the firm's purpose?

Because a mission defines the basic functions the firm has decided to perform in society, it provides organizational members with initial strategic guidelines about the knowledge they require (Bailey & Clark, 2000; Beckett et al., 2000). The firm's goals and purpose create a roadmap that helps the company to define its core activities and the knowledge creation and knowledge sharing processes that will support those activities. For example, in an in-depth case study at a European Innovation and Technology Center, Cepeda et al. (2004) showed that the preparation of a mission statement—one that emphasized the promotion of innovation and research activities among companies in the industry—helped the firm to guide its knowledge management efforts. Given that their mission was the promotion of innovation efforts, organizational members identified knowledge areas such as training and development and industry social networks as critical for their success.

- **Value proposition:** A business' value proposition is a statement of the fundamental benefits it has chosen to offer in the marketplace; it answers the question: How does the business intend to attract customers? (Crossan, Fry, & Killing, 2002). A value proposition communicates to employees what the business is trying to do for its customers and, by inference, the requirements of their particular role. It represents the attributes that firms provide, through their products and services, to achieve satisfaction and build loyalty with their targeted customers (Thompsen, 1999). The choice of a value proposition is perhaps the most obvious way in which a business attempts to differentiate itself from competition (Crossan et al., 2002). For example, Microsoft and Harley-Davidson have a product-leadership value proposition; they offer one-of-a-kind products and services, state-of-the-art features, and innovative solutions that customers often cannot get anywhere else. In contrast, firms such as IBM and Nordstrom have a customer-relationship value proposition, choosing to focus on the quality of their relationships with clients and offering them "complete solutions." A third case is that of Wal-Mart and Southwest Airlines, which have an operational-excellence value proposition. These firms opt to excel at attributes such as price, quality, on-time delivery, selection, and availability that their rivals cannot match.

To deliver a value proposition, a business needs to make choices about the core activities it intends to perform and the knowledge needed to perform those activities (Furlong, 2000). Furthermore, by comparing the value proposition to the current performance of the company, performance gaps can be detected (Earl, 2001). There could be quality problems, customer service issues, or a deficit in product innovation efforts. Analyzing the gap between the current and the desired value proposition is a way of discovering the critical knowledge needed. From this perspective, knowledge management supports strategy when it enables the firm to implement solutions based on the unique needs of the client.

- **Knowledge management infrastructure:** To implement knowledge management successfully, it is important to understand the infrastructure required to support the acquisition, generation, transfer, and storage of tacit and explicit knowledge resources. Knowledge management involves the coordination and integration of multiple knowledge-based activities, structures, systems, processes, and individuals with diverse roles in the organization. These elements are frequently grouped into three categories—people, processes, and technology—and constitute what scholars call a knowledge management infrastructure (Gold, 2001; Muzumdar, 1997). While knowledge management solutions are a rising phenomenon, many firms manage knowledge in an implicit way and have elements of a knowledge infrastructure without calling it so. For example, Volvo has extensive databases and core experts in lifecycle analysis; Sony has training cells on product disassembly and ensures knowledge sharing with designers; BMW design teams have permanent members from the recycling function to ensure lessons from previous experiences be incorporated into product design. The existence of implicit or explicit knowledge management elements (people, processes, and technology) creates awareness about the importance of knowledge and facilitates the identification of critical knowledge areas (Thompsen, 1999; Muzumdar, 1997; Cepeda et al., 2004). Furthermore, an existing knowledge infrastructure affects the identification of critical knowledge areas because knowledge resources are path dependent, which is to say that "a firm's previous investments and its repertoire of routines (its 'history') constrain its future behavior" (Teece et al., 1997, p. 522). Resources are specific to a firm, embedded in their routines or assets, and accumulated over time (Dierickx & Cool, 1989). Consequently, an existing

knowledge infrastructure (people, processes, and technology) may constrain the process of identifying critical knowledge areas. Independent of the firm's strategy, the current infrastructure elements might create boundaries and mental models within which managers will evaluate their knowledge needs. In this circumstance, it may appear faster and easier to develop a new strategy that leverages the current knowledge management infrastructure than it would be to create a new knowledge infrastructure to leverage the desired strategy.

Relationship Between Critical Knowledge Area and Competitive Advantage

Having discussed factors that facilitate the identification of the critical knowledge areas that support a firm's strategy, we now discuss two processes that mediate the impact of critical knowledge areas on competitive advantage: value-creation ways and capability differentials. Value-creation ways address how knowledge contributes to competitive advantage through the satisfaction of customer needs (customer perspective). In contrast, capability differentials address how knowledge contributes to competitive advantage through differentiation from competitors (competitor perspective).

- **Value-creation ways:** An emphasis on customer value and value creation is an intangible asset that has been posited to positively influence business performance and competitive advantage (Narver & Slater, 1990; Deshpandé et al., 1993; McNaughton, Osborne, & Imrie, 2002). The ultimate test of value creation is whether customers are willing to pay for a firm's products and services under conditions of wide competitive choices available to them (Rastogi, 2003).

  Knowledge is at the origin of most improvements in customer value (Novo, 2001; Rowley, 2002). Companies create value by instilling knowledge in products and services (Rastogi, 2003), by applying new knowledge to old problems (and in the process displacing existing knowledge), and by synthesizing discrete kinds of existing knowledge (Hamel, 2000). Another way to create value to customers is by globalizing deeply embedded local knowledge (Hamel, 2000). This implies transferring knowledge in the form of products that are easily moved worldwide, but also the more subtle effort of transferring knowledge in the form of services. In addition, firms create value by converting knowledge to strategic knowledge and enhancing shareholder wealth (Hamel, 1996, 2000). Because organizations grow or decline as their value-creation possibilities expand or contract, the richer, wider, and more varied the knowledge resources, the larger the value-creation opportunities open to the enterprise (Rastogi, 2003). Thus, a firm's capacity for sustained and superior value-creating ability may lie in the richness of its knowledge.

- **Capability differentials:** Coyne (1986) identifies the sources of sustainable competitive advantage as being four types of capability differentials, which Hall (1992, 1993) labels functional capabilities, cultural capabilities, positional capabilities, and regulatory capabilities. While functional and cultural capabilities involve competences and processes such as advertising and manufacturing, positional and regulatory capabilities refer to assets that the firm owns such as brands and reputation. By including assets and processes, the notion of capability differentials encompasses the concepts of resources and capabilities as described by RBV (Barney, 1991) and the dynamic capabilities perspectives (Teece et al, 1997; Eisenhardt & Martin, 2000). Because knowledge is the cornerstone of resources and capabilities, competitive advantage depends on the speed at which organizations can generate, capture, and disseminate knowledge, and use it to develop new resources and capabilities that competitors cannot easily imitate (Sharkie, 2003).

Zack (1999) stresses the importance of concentrating on the development of unique and valuable capabilities, rather than exclusively focusing attention on the production of products and services. A concentration of products and services can provide, at best, short-term advantages because, as Schumpeter (1934) argues, organizations that engage in invention, innovation, and imitation in a continual basis render current products and services obsolete. Long and Vickers-Koch (1995) also argue that organizations that wish to improve their performance need to develop underlying skills and expertise, and channel them into process improvements. These skills and expertise include capability differentials such as know-how of employees, suppliers, and distributors (functional); learning ability and quality perception (cultural); reputation and networks (positional); and contracts, licenses, and trade secrets (regulatory). The building up of these internal capabilities results in sustainable competitive advantage because of the difficulty in imitating competences that are based on knowledge, skills, and attitudes; built into processes; and developed over time in a particular organizational context (Long & Vickers-Koch, 1995; Quinn, 1992).

FUTURE TRENDS

On the basis of the issues in this article, specific recommendations are made for further research.

- Multiple case studies are recommended to establish the basis for cross-case analysis and the potential for even more compelling evidence and conclusions. Multiple case studies also provide greater probabilities for external validity and generalizability of the theory.
- A quantitative study is also recommended. Such a study could be designed to establish baseline strategic decisions, measures, and competitive comparisons. Other procedures could be designed to isolate specific decisions that incorporate deliberation of the critical knowledge area and to track the relative measurable impact upon the business results and competitive position of an enterprise.
- Additional research is recommended to establish financial valuation measures for a critical knowledge area and the creation of a theoretical foundation for a business formula to identify a measurable return on critical knowledge.

To summarize, the results of these recommendations would be expected to build upon the theoretical foundation. This additional research would extend and enrich this framework.

CONCLUSION

Several conclusions are derived from the description of this framework. These are presented as follows.

The eventual isolation of a unique body of knowledge, the identity of a critical knowledge area can create a new perspective on the enterprise and how it contributes value to its customers. The framework can support management's intent in creating and using a business planning framework of competitive analysis, strategy formation, and identification of critical success factors for decision making and measurement. Such a business framework is designed to create a managerial mindset that is predisposed to focus upon certain factors. The practitioners could find this predisposition as a source of difficulty in reframing their perspective of the organization. These conclusions align with the research of Penrose (1959), Mahoney (1995), Leonard (1998), and Thompsen (1999) on the impact of mental models on the identification and selection of key resource-capabilities that can serve in the best interest of the firm.

A critical knowledge area can be considered as another critical success factor and important for management decision making and the formation of competitive strategy. By examining the connections between the critical knowledge area and the points of competitive differentiation (differential capabilities and value creation ways), specific actions can be identified to leverage those points and enhance competitive advantage. A critical knowledge area can be a unifying factor in the development of an integrated strategy for enhancing competitive advantage. It can also be used to align infrastructure, policies, practices, systems, and processes to achieve fulfillment of competitive strategies.

Consistent deployment of a critical knowledge area is expected to produce positive impact on business results and relative competitive position. The development of benchmarking data and subsequent measurement are required to confirm such results. These findings and conclusions build on the research of Hall (1993) and Kamoche (1996), which concluded that resource-capabilities have important implications in management practice.

To summarize, the described framework could be aligned with the theoretical proposition that the identification of key resource-capabilities, or critical knowledge areas, in a firm can serve as an important and practical foundation for management decision making and enhancing competitive advantage.

The identification of key resource-capabilities or a critical knowledge area is an essential step in defining competitive forces and determining strategy. A critical knowledge area is another critical success factor that can be used in conducting situational and competitive analysis, formulating differentiating strategies, making strategic decisions, and aligning the organization infrastructure for strategy fulfillment.

The consideration of a critical knowledge area in management deliberations in a variety of scenarios can enhance competitive advantage and the potential for positive business results. The structure of an organization, its processes, systems, policies, and practices can be examined and adjusted to achieve greater leverage with the critical knowledge area. Some of these processes and systems include: acquisition/generation, store/retrieval, transfer, application, and protection.

A critical knowledge area can also used as a benchmarking measure for comparison of practices. Asset valuation and ownership policies can be more intentionally applied to the critical knowledge area. All of these are examples that demonstrate ways in which the identification and measurement of a critical knowledge area can impact management decision making and contribute to the economic value of a firm.

REFERENCES

Amit, R., & Schoemaker P.J. (1993). Strategic assets and organizational rent. *Strategic Management Journal, 14,* 33-46.

Argote, L. (1999). *Organizational learning: Creating, retaining and transferring knowledge*. Boston: Kluwer Academic.

Bailey, C., & Clarke, M. (2000). How do managers use knowledge about knowledge management? *Journal of Knowledge Management, 4*(3).

Barney, J.B. (1991). Firm resources and sustained competitive advantage. *Journal of Management, 17,* 99-120.

Barney, J.B. (1995). Looking inside for competitive advantage. *Academy of Management Executive, 9,* 49-61.

Barney, J.B. (2001). Is the resource-based "view" a useful perspective for strategic management research? Yes. *Academy of Management Review, 26,* 41-56.

Beckett, A.J., Wainwright, E.R.C., & Bance, D. (2000). Knowledge management: Strategy or software? *Management Decision, 38*(9), 601-606.

Blackler, F. (1995). Knowledge, knowledge work and organizations: An overview and interpretation. *Organization Studies, 16*(6), 1021-1046.

Bohn, R. (1994). Measuring and managing technological knowledge. *Sloan Management Review, 36,* 61-72.

Bonora, E., & Revang, O. (1993). A framework for analysing the storage and protection of knowledge in organizations: Strategic implications and structural arrangements. *Implementing strategic processes: Change, learning and cooperation* (pp.190-212). Cambridge: Basil Blackwell.

Bryant, S.E. (2003). The role of transformational and transactional leadership in creating, sharing and exploiting organizational knowledge. *Journal of Leadership & Organizational Studies, 9,* 32-42.

Cepeda, G., Galán, J.L., & Leal, A. (2004). Identifying a key knowledge area in the professional services: A case study. *Journal of Knowledge Management, 8*(6), 131-150.

Cole, R. (1998). Introduction. *California Management Review, 40*(3), 15-21.

Collins, H. (1993). The structure of knowledge. *Social Research, 60,* 95-116.

Conner, K.R. (1991). A historical comparison of resource-based theory and five schools of thought within industrial organization economics: Do we have a new theory of the firm. *Journal of Management, 17,* 121-154.

Conner, K.R., & Prahalad, C.K. (1996). A resource-based theory of the firm: Knowledge versus opportunism. *Organization Science, 7*(5), 477-501.

Cook, S., & Brown, J. (1999). Bridging epistemologies: The generative dance between organizational knowledge and organization knowing. *Organization Science, 10*(4), 381-400.

Coyne, K.P. (1986). Sustainable competitive advantage—what it is and what it isn't. *Business Horizons,* 54-61.

Crossan, M., Fry, J.N., & Killing, J.P. (2002). *Strategic analysis and action* (5th ed.). Toronto: Prentice-Hall Canada.

Crossan, M.W., Lane, H.W., & White, R.E. (1999). An organizational learning framework. From intuition to institution. *Academy of Management Review, 24,* 522-537.

Daft, R.L. (1983). Learning the craft of organizational research. *Academy of Management Review, 8*(4), 539-547.

Davenport, T., & Klahr, P. (1998). Managing customer support knowledge. *California Management Review, 40,* 195-208.

Davenport, T., & Prusak, L. (1998). *Working knowledge: How organizations manage what they know.* Boston: Harvard Business School Press.

Davenport, T.H. (1998). *Some principles of knowledge management.* Retrieved March 23, 2003, from *http://www.bus.utexas.edu/kman/kmprin.htm*

Davis, S., & Botkin, J. (1994). The coming of knowledge-based business. *Harvard Business Review,* (September-October), 165-170.

Deshpande, R., Farley, J.U., & Webster, F. (1993). Corporate culture, customer orientation, and innovativeness in Japanese firms: A quadrad analysis. *Journal of Marketing,* 57, 23-37.

Dierickx, I., & Cool, K. (1989). Asset stock accumulation and sustainability of competitive advantage. *Management Science, 35,* 1504-1511.

Drucker, P.F. (1994). *Post-capitalist society.* New York: Harper Business.

Eisenhardt, K.M., & Martin, J. (2000). Dynamic capabilities: What are they? *Strategic Management Journal, 21,* 1105-1121.

Furlong, G. (2000). *Knowledge management and the competitive edge.* Working Paper University of Greenwich, UK.

Ghoshal, S., & Moran, P., (1995). Bad for practice: A critique of the transaction cost theory. *Academy of Management Review, 21,* 13-47.

Glazer, R. (1991). Marketing in an information intensive environment: Strategic importance of knowledge as an asset. *Journal of Marketing, 55,* 1-19.

Gold, A.H. (2001). *Towards a theory of organizational knowledge management capabilities.* UMI Dissertations, University of North Caroline at Chapel Hill, USA.

Grant, R.M. (1996). Toward a knowledge-based view of the firm. *Strategic Management Journal, 17,* 109-122.

Grant, R.M. (2002). *Contemporary strategy analysis* (4th ed.). Oxford, UK: Blackwell.

Hall, R. (1992). Strategic analysis and intangible resources. *Strategic Management Journal, 13,* 135-144.

Hall, R. (1993). A framework linking intangible resources and capabilities to sustainable competitive advantage. *Strategic Management Journal, 14,* 607-618.

Hamel, G. (1996). Keynote speech. *Proceedings of the Strategic Management Society Conference,* University of Arizona Tech, Phoenix, AZ.

Hamel, G. (2000). Knowledge strategy. *Executive Excellence, 17,* 7.

Helfat, C.E., & Raubitschek, R.S. (2000). Product sequencing: Co-evolution of knowledge, capabilities and products. *Strategic Management Journal, 21*(10-11), 961-979.

Kalling, T. (2003). Organization-internal transfer of knowledge and the role of motivation: A qualitative case study. *Knowledge and Process Management, 10,* 115-126.

Kamoche, K. (1986). Strategic human resource management within a resource-capability view of the firm. *Journal of Management Studies, 33,* 213-233.

Kelly, D., & Amburguey, T.L. (1991). Organizational inertia and momentum: A dynamic model of strategic change. *Academy of Management Journal, 34,* 591-612.

Klein, D., & Prusak, L. (1994). *Characterizing intellectual capital.* CBI Working Paper. Boston: Ernst and Young.

Kogut, B., & Zander, U. (1992). Knowledge of the firm, combinative capabilities, and the replication of technology. *Organization Science, 3*(3), 383-397.

C

Law, K., Wong, C., & Mobley, W. (1998). Toward a taxonomy of multidimensional constructs. *Academy of Management Review, 23,* 741-753.

Leonard-Barton, D. (1992). Core capabilities and core rigidities: A paradox in managing new product development. *Strategic Management Journal, 13,* 111-126.

Leonard, D., & Sensiper, S. (1998). The role of tacit knowledge in group innovation. *California Management Review, 40,* 112-132.

Leonard-Barton, D. (1995). *Wellsprings of knowledge: Building and sustaining the source of innovation.* Boston: Harvard Business School Press.

Long, K., & Vickers-Koch, M. (1995). Using core capabilities to create competitive advantage. *Organizational Dynamics, 24*(1), 6-22.

Mahoney, J.T. (1995). The management of resources and the resource of management. *Journal of Business Research, 33,* 91-101.

McEvily, S., & Chakravarthy, B. (2002). The persistence of knowledge-based advantage: An empirical test for product performance and technological knowledge. *Strategic Management Journal, 23,* 285-305.

McNaughton, R.B., Osborne, P., & Imrie, B. (2002). Market-oriented value creation in service firms. *European Journal of Marketing, 36*(9), 990-1012.

Muzumdar, M. (1998). *Organizational knowledge management frameworks and a case study.* UMI dissertation, Kent State University, USA.

Narver, J.C., & Slater, S. (1990). The effect of market orientation on business profitability. *Journal of Marketing, 54,* 20-35.

Nelson, R.R. (1991). Why do firms differ, and how does it matter? *Strategic Management Journal, 12*(Special Issue), 61-74.

Nelson, R.R., & Winter, S.G. (1982). *An evolutionary theory of economic change.* Cambridge: Harvard University Press

Nonaka, I. (1991). The knowledge creating company. *Harvard Business Review,* (November-December), 96-104.

Nonaka, I., & Takeuchi, H. (1995) *The knowledge creating company: How Japanese companies create the dynamics of innovation.* New York: Oxford University Press.

Novo, J. (2001). *The source of customer value—customer knowledge.* Retrieved from *www.crm-forunm.com*

Penrose, E.T. (1959). *The theory of the growth of the firm.* Oxford: Basil Blackwell.

Peteraf, M.A. (1993). The cornerstones of competitive advantage: A resource-based view. *Strategic Management Journal, 14,* 179-191.

Peters, T. (1992). *Liberation management: Necessary disorganization for the nanosecond nineties.* New York: Ballantine Books.

Polanyi, M. (1967). *The tacit dimension.* London: Routledge and Kegan Paul.

Porter-Liebeskind, J. (1996). Knowledge, strategy, and the theory of the firm. *Strategic Management Journal, 17*(Special Issue), 93-107.

Prahalad, C.K., & Hamel, G. (1990). The core competence of the corporation. *Harvard Business Review, 40*(3), 79-91.

Quinn, J.B. (1992). *Intelligent enterprise: A knowledge and service based paradigm for industry.* New York: Maxwell Macmillan.

Rastogi, P.N. (2003). The nature and role of IC: Rethinking the process of value creation and sustained enterprise growth. *Journal of Intellectual Capital, 4*(2), 227-248.

Rowley, J.E. (2002). Reflections on customer knowledge management in e-business. *Qualitative Market Research: An International Journal, 5*(4), 268-280.

Schumpeter J. (1934). *The theory of economic development: An inquiry into profit, capital, credit, interest, and the business cycle.* London; Oxford; New York: Oxford University Press (reprint 1974).

Sharkie, R. (2003). Knowledge creation and its place in the development of sustainable competitive advantage. *Journal of Knowledge Management, 7*(1), 20-31.

Spender, J.C. (1996). Making knowledge the basis of a dynamic theory of the firm. *Strategic Management Journal, 17,* 45-62.

Starbuck, W.H. (1990). Knowledge-intensive firms: Learning to survive in strange environments. In L. Lindamark (ed.), *Kunskap som kritisk resurs, en artikel sampling om Kunskapsforetag* (pp. 10-20). Handelshigskolan I Umea: Umea University.

Stewart, T.A. (1994). Your company's most valuable asset: Intellectual capital. *Fortune, 3,* 68-74.

Sveiby, K.E. (1990). *The new organizational wealth: Managing and measuring knowledge-based assets.* San Francisco: Berrett-Koehler.

Sveiby, K.E., & Risling, A. (1987). *Kunnskapsbedriften-arhundrets storste lederut fordring?* Kunskapsforetag, Cappelen, Oslo: Liber Forlag.

Teece, D.J., Pisano, G., & Shuen, A. (1997). Dynamic capabilities and strategic management. *Strategic Management Journal, 18,* 509-533.

Thompsen, J., Ibarra, R., & Center, J. (1997). Extending critical knowledge areas: Learn, innovate, propagate. In D.F. Kocaoglu, & T.R. Anderson (Eds.), *Innovation in technology management: The key to global leadership.* Portland International Press.

Thompsen, J.A. (1999). *A case study of identifying and measuring critical knowledge areas as key resources-capabilities of an enterprise.* UMI Dissertation, Walden University.

Toffler, A. (1990). *Powershift: Knowledge, wealth and violence at the edge of the 21st century.* New York: Bantam Books.

Vera, D., & Crossan, M. (2004). Strategic leadership and organizational learning. *Academy of Management Review, 29,* 222-240.

Winslow, C.D., & Bramer, W.L. (1994). *Future work: Putting knowledge to work in the knowledge economy.* New York: The Free Press.

Zack, M. (1999). Developing a knowledge strategy. *California Management Review, 41,* 125-145.

KEY TERMS

Business Mission: A basic role or function that a firm performs in a specific environment.

Capability Differentials: Resource and competence configurations, that is to say, configuration ways to reach competitive advantage sources.

Competitive Advantage: A positive, relative position held by a firm as compared with competitors within a market or industry. There are two types of competitive advantage: cost leadership and differentiation.

Critical Knowledge Areas: Specific bodies of knowledge, or key resource-capabilities, that are unique to a firm and reside at the core of the business mission and value proposition to its customers.

Knowledge: Refers to familiarity with something or the understanding of a phenomenon. This implies that it can be contained in individuals, groups, organizations, systems, products, processes, and so forth.

Knowledge Management Infrastructure: To successfully implement knowledge management, it is important to understand the infrastructure required to support the acquisition, generation, transfer, and storage of tacit and explicit knowledge resources. Knowledge management involves the coordination and integration of multiple knowledge-based activities, structures, systems, processes, and individuals with diverse roles in the organization. These elements are frequently grouped into three categories—people, processes, and technology.

Value Creation Ways: Knowledge creates value when it is incorporated into products and services by, for example, applying it to old products or by developing new products and services. Knowledge in this context does not merely imply know-what, know-why, and know-how; it more importantly implies a firm's ability to produce and deliver customer-valued outcomes. The test of value creation is whether customers are willing to pay for a firm's products and services under conditions of wide competitive choices open or available to them. Other modes are: creation value by globalizing deeply embedded local knowledge and converting knowledge to strategic knowledge to create shareholder wealth. These two value creation ways focus on a firm's employees and investors.

Value Proposition: Attributes that supplying enterprises provide, through their products and services, to achieve satisfaction and build loyalty with their targeted customers.

Competitive Intelligence Gathering

Kevin R. Parker
Idaho State University, USA

Philip S. Nitse
Idaho State University, USA

INTRODUCTION

Knowledge management (KM) is the process through which organizational performance is improved through better management of corporate knowledge. Its goal is to improve the management of internal knowledge processes so that all information required for corporate decisions can be made available and efficiently used. Competitive intelligence (CI) is a process for gathering usable knowledge about the external business environment and turning it into the intelligence required for tactical or strategic decisions. The two are strongly connected because gathered CI has no long-term value unless an effective KM process is in place to turn the information into something usable. Although most information collected during a CI investigation is used in immediate decision making, it must be integrated into the internal knowledge systems to provide a long-term resource when companies attempt to detect trends or adapt to changes in their environments (Aware, 2004).

Both KM and CI systems are designed to enhance the information resources of an enterprise, but often target different information types and sources. While CI is concerned with gathering information from the external environment to enable the company to gain competitive advantage (Williams, 2002), most investigation into KM has focused on capturing the knowledge stored within the minds of individual employees (Nidumolu, Subramani, & Aldrich, 2001). Bagshaw (2000), Johnson (2000), Rubenfeld (2001), and Williams (2002) all focus on the use of KM for collecting, managing, and sharing internally generated knowledge.

Restricting the focus to internal data severely limits the potential of KM systems. The vast wealth of knowledge outside the traditional boundaries of the company may prove just as useful to organizations seeking a competitive advantage (Gold, Malhotra, & Segars, 2001). Fortunately, some studies indicate an awareness of the value of external information. Abramson (1999) notes that KM enables companies to create and systematically use the very best internal and external knowledge that they can obtain. Grzanka (1999) notes that KM provides a methodology to leverage and manage all knowledge, whether external or internal. Other researchers take it a step further and recognize the synergies between KM and CI. Johnson (1999) states that KM and CI are two parts of the same whole because both are designed to apply enterprise knowledge of the internal and external environment for long-term competitive advantage. KM and CI "have similar goals and are natural extensions of one another (e.g., manage information overload and timely/targeted information delivery, provide tools for data analysis, identify subject matter experts, enable collaboration)" (Meta Group, 1998). Davenport (1999) even goes so far as to take the stance that CI can be viewed as a branch or subset of KM.

A major difference between KM and CI is the much broader scope of KM compared to the more clearly focused CI: rather than applying knowledge to the entire firm and its complete set of objectives, CI focuses on defending the firm from competitive threats, while at the same time proactively working to acquire market share from competitors (Johnson, 1999). Further, while KM often falls under the purview of the information technology department, more often than not CI activities are found within strategic planning, marketing, or sales (Fuld, 1998).

While it is difficult to simplify the relationship between CI and KM (Johnson, 1999), it is important to note that the two approaches complement each other. The goal of both disciplines is to evaluate current business decisions, locate and deliver appropriate knowledge from the environment, and ultimately help to give it meaning so that decision makers better understand the options available to them (Johnson, 1999). The synergies between KM and CI indicate that greater convergence between the two approaches is inevitable.

BACKGROUND

Each organization has associated with it a particular context pertaining to such issues as customer attitudes, competitors' actions, regulatory patterns, and technological trends. Environmental scanning tools collect information from the environment to assist in developing strategies that help the organization formulate responses to that environment.

Environmental scanning was first defined by Aguilar (1967) as the process of gathering information about events and relationships in the organization's environment, the knowledge of which assists in planning future courses of action. It entails perceiving and interpreting both the internal and external environment with the objective of making appropriate operational, tactical, and strategic decisions that help insure the success of the firm (Elofson & Konsynski, 1991). Any organization that fails to monitor its environment in order to determine the conditions under which it must operate courts disaster (Mitroff, 1985). Identification of key economic, social, and technological issues that affect the organization, its lifecycle stages, and their relevance to each other helps managers allocate attention and resources to them (McCann & Gomez-Mejia, 1992). Scanning is a fundamental, early step in the chain of perceptions and actions that permit an organization to adapt to its environment (Hambrick, 1981).

Aguilar (1967) stresses the close relationship between strategic planning and scanning, noting that scanning is the acquisition of external strategic information that is useful for making decisions about company strategy and long-term plans. The objectives of environmental scanning vary with the business strategy employed by an organization (Jennings & Lumpkin, 1992). Differentiation strategy is associated with a systematic scanning activity to alert the organization to market opportunities as well as indications of innovations (Miller, 1989). Cost leadership strategy involves scanning for more efficient methods of production as well as innovations made by the competition (Miller, 1989). Reactive strategy is associated with scanning the external environment for problems (Ansoff, 1975), while low-cost strategy directs the scanning effort toward solving specific problems regarding product cost (Hrebiniak & Joyce, 1985). An organization's strategy determines whether environmental scanning is used to search for opportunities or to forewarn of threats (Snyder, 1981). The goals of an organization are continuously evolving, and as they are changing, so too are the pertinent threats and opportunities that must be monitored (Elofson & Konsynski, 1991). Environmental scanning systems are dependent on the identification of pertinent factors, both external and internal, to be scanned.

Many tools can be used to perform environmental scanning, including CI, business intelligence, knowledge acquisition, knowledge discovery, knowledge harvesting, enumerative description, knowledge engineering, information retrieval, document management, and enterprise information portals. This article focuses on the approach most widely used in business, CI.

MAIN FOCUS OF THE ARTICLE

Miller (2001) defines CI as the process of monitoring the competitive environment. This competitive environment includes but is not limited to competitors, customers, suppliers, technology, political and legal arenas, and social and cultural changes. Kahaner (1996) explains that CI is a systematic and ethical program for gathering, analyzing, and managing information about competitors' activities and general business trends that can affect a company's plans, decisions, and operations. Note the distinction of CI as an ethical process, unlike business espionage, which acquires information by illegal means like hacking (Malhotra, 1996). CI enables management to make informed decisions about a wide variety of tactical and strategic issues. Outcomes from a formal CI program should enable strategists to anticipate changes in the company's marketplace and actions of its competitors. CI should also uncover the existence of new competitors, new technologies, products, laws, or regulations that will have an effect on business. CI can help a business learn from the successes and failures of other enterprises, make better mergers and acquisitions, and enter new business arenas. From an internal viewpoint, CI can help a company assess its own business practices from a more open and objective perspective while helping implement new management tools (Kahaner, 1996).

The CI process is becoming even more important as the pace of business both at home and abroad continues to accelerate. CI also helps managers deal with the rapid change in the political, legal, and technical environments (Kahaner, 1996). A key goal of CI is to provide early warnings or timely alerts that allow decision makers to proactively position the company to maintain or gain a competitive advantage. Management must be able to detect changes in the market early enough to place the company in the most strategically advantageous position possible. A key feature of CI is the analysis process, which organizes and interprets raw data to uncover underlying patterns, trends, and interrelationships, thereby converting it into actionable intelligence. Data thus transformed can be applied to the analytical tasks and decision making that form the basis for strategic management (Miller, 2001).

Lackman, Saban, and Lanasa (2000) propose a model of the CI process that consists of several processes, including Identify Users, Assess Intelligence Needs, Identify Sources of Information, Gather Information, Interpret Information, and Communicate Intelligence. In the Interpret Information step, they propose an Intelligence Library that is closely related to KM since the Library serves as a repository for intelligence and secondary data with a user-friendly retrieval system designed to encourage its use. The inputs into the Library could come from CI departments and their activities or from more traditional KM activities designed to capture and disseminate tacit knowledge as explicit knowledge regardless of the organizational structure of the business. This model of CI thus incorporates features of KM.

The classic intelligence cycle has four stages—collection, processing, analysis/production, and dissemination—which is closely mirrored by knowledge management's four-step cycle of capture, transformation, communication, and utilization (Nauth, 1999). Kahaner (1996) describes a four-step CI cycle consisting of planning and direction, collection activities, analysis, and dissemination, while Miller (2001) adds feedback as a fifth step. Planning and direction requires working with decision makers to discover and hone their intelligence needs. Based on the vast array of directions that CI can take as illustrated above, this is one of the most difficult and ill-defined tasks, especially for managers not accustomed to using the CI process. Collection activities involve the legal and ethical gathering of intelligence from various public and private sources, both internal and external to the company. Two major approaches used in information collection are responding to ad hoc requests and continuously monitoring key intelligence areas. Proactive requests can be answered with available data, perhaps in a KM system, while reactive requests require a search process to uncover pertinent intelligence (Breeding, 2000). Several resources can be searched, including pay-for-use services such as Dow Jones, Hoover's Company Data Bank, Standards & Poor's, NewsEdge, as well as free information sources such as company Web sites, SEC's Edgar system, and corporateinformation.com (Breeding, 2000).

There are also specialized databases from third-party vendors (Dialog, Lexus/Nexus), press release and newsfeed collections (WavePhore's Newscast Access or NewsEdge's NewsObjects), product literature, competitor Web sites, archived design specifications, company profiles and financial statements, and numerous other sources that are databased, searchable, and categorized (Johnson, 1998). Monitoring key intelligence areas falls under the purview of environmental scanning. While many of the same information sources can be used, this approach allows critical intelligence to be pushed directly to the desktops of those decision makers who most need it without their having to do any searching through newspapers, Web sites, or other resources on their own, and it heightens awareness about the competition, making users aware of the competition in many of their day-to-day activities (Breeding, 2000). Analysis involves interpreting data and compiling recommended actions. The analysis, like the collection process, is driven by the planning stage to answer specific questions

or concerns that managers are dealing with at the time. These questions or concerns will range from very tactical to very strategic in nature.

Dissemination involves presenting the findings to decision makers. This again is directed by the planning stage where the question of how to disseminate the findings is determined and agreed to prior to the start of the project. It is important to insure that decision makers get the types of reports that they want, rather than what the CI personnel find most interesting. That means that if the decision maker wants a simple, direct-to-the-point report rather than a long, involved presentation, then he/she should get it. Feedback involves soliciting responses from decision makers about the quality, timeliness, and accuracy of the intelligence and their needs for continued intelligence reports. Whether we are contemplating the classic intelligence cycle, the knowledge management cycle, or the competitive intelligence cycle, the cycle is a circular, iterative process. Note that unlike internal knowledge management, CI's focus is on both internal and external events and trends, with a strong focus on competitors' and others' activities and likely intentions.

While all phases of the CI cycle may be equally critical, planning and direction—and the needs identification process involved therein—are pivotal. No information-gathering approach can be successful unless it is provided with an adequate specification of the variables that need to be monitored. A great deal of research has been devoted to studying *how* to look for information, while overlooking the equally vital issue of *what* information to look for. A recent review of software marketed toward the online intelligence community clearly illustrates that the ability of most software to determine *what* information to gather is clearly deficient (Fuld, 2001).

Many tools for gathering intelligence are profile based, designed to sift information through a profile of intelligence needs (Berghel, 1997). These profiles are often made up of a set of topics that describe specific interests (Foltz & Dumais, 1992), and are developed early in the CI cycle and modified throughout the course of the intelligence operations. Each topic can be expressed in terms of a keyword or concept. The primary weakness of this type of approach is its reliance on the completeness and accuracy of a one-dimensional or single-class profile. If the profile is insufficient in any way, the effectiveness of the filtering process is seriously diminished. For example, if the profile is too narrow in scope or omits critical intelligence topics, the competitive intelligence process will overlook much of the pertinent available information, leaving managers unaware of vital facts. Thus, decision makers may consistently make crucial decisions based on faulty information. If, on the other hand, the profile is too broad or general, the intelligence gathering process may be capturing irrelevant information, overwhelming the decision makers and convincing them that the CI process is ineffective. In short, the profile of information needs is the pivotal element in determining how well the CI process performs.

Needs identification requires a structured approach that takes into account multiple dimensions, or classes. Such an approach helps to insure that the process of identifying an organization's intelligence needs considers each of the categories that make up those needs. Stadnyk and Kass (1992) propose the development of knowledge bases of description categories over which individual models of interests can be defined. Herring (1999) proposes the concept of Key Intelligence Topics (KITs) to help identify intelligence requirements by considering strategic decisions, early-warning topics, and key players. Based on Herring's prior work with both the government and Motorola, the KITs process helps management to identify and define critical intelligence needs. CI programs often operate under the direction of upper management, which generally delineates the objectives or needs that CI must attempt to meet.

However, CI activity should not be restricted to the upper management level because it can assist all organizational levels. Further, CI needs vary by company and by project. Therefore, an analysis of the information needs of an enterprise requires consideration of the types of information required by decision makers at all levels of management. Many management models, including Anthony's Managerial Pyramid (1965), represent organizations as having various levels of decision making—operational control, tactical control, and strategic planning—each of which has different information needs.

The multi-class interest profile (M-CLIP), first proposed in 2001 (Parker & Nitse, 2001), addresses these shortcomings. It provides a strategically aligned framework based on the various types of information needs in order to insure that key items within each critical intelligence area are accounted for. Thorough needs identification guided by a structured, multi-dimensional framework increases the likelihood of a successful CI effort. The classes that make up the M-CLIP were derived by taking into consideration such information-intensive activities as project management, strategic planning, competitive analysis, and environmental analysis, and then acknowledging the correlation between the information needs of those activities and the decision-making levels described in the Managerial Pyramid. The project class consists of interest areas intended to target the information necessary for the execution of current projects, including both long-term activities such as tracking the daily or weekly actions of an overseas competitor, as well as shorter-term specialized projects such as the investigation of a possible acquisition or alliance prospect. The enterprise class includes internal and external interest areas, such as technological factors, investment issues, corporate news, operating expenses, and so forth, that are necessary for tactical decision making. The industry class targets information needs that stem from the type of industry or organization performing the investigation and helps the CI process supply intelligence related to the general external environment of the company.

The M-CLIP spans all decision-making levels and provides a structured, expanded set of intelligence topics. The M-CLIP system also provides specialized templates to aid in the identification of critical intelligence needs, an expansion mechanism to help insure that no key concepts are overlooked, and an adaptive mechanism to handle the removal of unproductive topics automatically.

A complete set of intelligence topics encompasses a wide spectrum of corporate interests, thus providing the means to access a greater percentage of relevant online information. A more complete information set makes the analysis and dissemination efforts more likely to succeed, insuring that the CI process provides decision makers with a more complete set of information, enabling them to assess domestic and international issues in an efficient, accurate, and timely manner.

FUTURE TRENDS

As noted above, the KM and CI functions complement each other. There is a great deal of overlap between the two, and KM systems will become more robust as KM workers recognize the benefits of adjusting their focus to include not only internal, but also external sources of information. At the same time, CI efforts will benefit by making greater use of KM. One statistic indicates that as much as 80% of the competitive knowledge that a firm requires to compete successfully is already present somewhere within the company and can be gathered by probing internal sources (Johnson, 2001). Competitive intelligence should be an integral part of knowledge management, and vice versa. Knowledge management can be improved by actively gathering competitive intelligence, and competitive intelligence can be improved by accessing the internal information gathered by knowledge management. The convergence of these two disciplines can be realized only when strategic planners are able to define more completely the relationships between CI and KM, and their specific role in delivering decision support (Johnson, 1998).

CONCLUSION

Effective CI requires an effective KM process. Without KM, gathered CI information is useful for only a brief period. CI data is highly time sensitive and is often useless unless acted upon immediately (Johnson, 1998). However, if CI is integrated into the internal knowledge processes, it will begin to have some long-term value to a firm (Aware, 2004). This integration will enable companies to detect trends and markets in which competitors act, as well as to identify latent and parallel competitors. This intelligence can then be of long-term use to decision makers at all levels (Johnson, 1998).

One measure of organizational effectiveness is the creation and continuance of a measurable competitive advantage (Gupta & McDaniel, 2002). KM and CI share that common goal, and a convergence of these two approaches will enable organizations to use the synergies between the two to take advantage of changes in both the internal and external environment.

REFERENCES

Abramson, G. (1999). On the KM midway. *CIO Enterprise Magazine.* Retrieved March 2003, from *http://www.cio.com/archive/enterprise/ 051599_cons.html*

Aguilar, F.J. (1967). *Scanning the business environment.* New York: Macmillan.

Ansoff, H.I. (1975). Managing strategic surprise by response to weak signals. *California Management Review, 18*(2), 21-31.

Anthony, R. (1965). *Planning and control systems: A framework for analysis.* Boston: Harvard University Press.

Aware. (2004). Knowledge management and competitive intelligence. Retrieved September 21, 2004, from *http://www.marketing-intelligence.co.uk/help/Q&A/question21.htm*

Bagshaw, M. (2000). Why knowledge management is here to stay. *Industrial and Commercial Training, 32*(5), 179-183.

Berghel, H. (1997). Cyberspace 2000: Dealing with information overload. *Communications of the ACM, 40*(2), 19-24.

Breeding, B. (2000). CI and KM convergence: A case study at Shell Services International. *Competitive Intelligence Review, 11*(4) 12-24.

Davenport, T.H. (1999). Knowledge management, round two. *CIO Magazine.* Retrieved May 2001 from *http://www.cio.com/archive/ 110199_think_content.html*

Elofson, G., & Konsynski, B. (1991). Delegation technologies: Environmental scanning with intelligent agents. *Journal of Management Information Systems, 8*(1), 37-62.

Foltz, P., & Dumais, S. (1992). Personalized information delivery: An analysis of information-filtering methods. *Communications of the ACM, 35*(12), 51-60.

Fuld, L. (1998). Ask the expert: Role of IT strategy and knowledge management in competitive intelligence. *CIO Magazine.* Retrieved May 2002, from *http://www2.cio.com/ask/expert/1998/questions/question246.html?CATEGORY=18&NAME=Knowledge%20Management*

Fuld, L. (2001). Intelligence software: Reality or still virtual reality? *Competitive Intelligence Magazine,* 22-27.

Gold, A.H., Malhotra, A., & Segars, A.H. (2001). Knowledge management: An organizational capabilities perspective. *Journal of Management Information Systems, 18*(1), 185-214.

Grzanka, L. (1999). Competitive intelligence. *Knowledge Management, 2*(4), 42-50.

Gupta, A., & McDaniel, J. (2002). Creating competitive advantage by effectively managing knowledge: A framework for knowledge management. *Journal of Knowledge Management Practice, 3.*

Hambrick, D.C. (1981). Specialization of environmental scanning activities among upper level executives. *Journal of Management Studies, 18*(3), 299-320.

Herring, J.P. (1999). Key intelligence topics: A process to identify and define intelligence needs. *Competitive Intelligence Review, 10*(2), 4-14.

Hrebiniak, L.L., & Joyce, W.F. (1985). Organizational adaptation: Strategic choice and environmental determinism. *Administrative Science Quarterly, 30*(3), 336-349.

Jennings, D.F., & Lumpkin, J.R. (1992). Insights between environmental scanning activities and Porter's generic strategies: An empirical analysis. *Journal of Management, 18*(4), 791-803.

Johnson, A. (2001). On predicting the future: Competitive intelligence as a knowledge management discipline. Retrieved September 20, 2004, from *http://www.aurorawdc.com/kmworld1.htm*

Johnson, A.R. (1998). An introduction to knowledge management as a framework for competitive intelligence. *Proceedings of the International Knowledge Management Executive Summit,* San Diego, CA. Retrieved September 20, 2004, from *http://www.aurorawdc.com/ekma.htm*

Johnson, A.R. (1999). Your say: Competitive intelligence and knowledge management—two parts of the same whole. *Knowledge Management Magazine, 3*(3).

Johnson, A.R. (2000). Competitive intelligence and competitor analysis as knowledge management applications. In J.W. Cortada & J.A. Woods (Eds.), *The knowledge management yearbook 2000-2001* (pp. 85-97). Woburn, MA: Butterworth-Heinemann.

Kahaner, L. (1996). *Competitive intelligence: How to gather, analyze, and use information to move your business to the top.* New York: Simon & Schuster.

Lackman, C.L., Saban, K., & Lanasa, J.M. (2000). Organizing the competitive intelligence function: A benchmarking study. *Competitive Intelligence Review, 11*(1), 17-27.

Malhotra, Y. (1996). Competitive intelligence programs: An overview. Retrieved September 20, 2004, from *http://www.kmbook.com/ciover.htm*

McCann, J.E., & Gomez-Mejia, L. (1992). Going 'on line' in the environmental scanning process. *IEEE Transactions on Engineering Management, 39*(4), 394-399.

Meta Group, Inc. (1998). Applying knowledge management to competitive intelligence. Retrieved May 2001 from *http://www2.metagroup.com/products/insights/aims_6_res.htm*

Miller, D. (1989). Matching strategies and strategy making: Process, content, and performance. *Human Relations, 42*(3), 241-260.

Miller, S.H. (2001). Competitive intelligence: An overview. Retrieved September 23, 2004, from *http://www.scip.org/Library/overview.pdf*

Mitroff, I.I. (1985). Two fables for those who believe in rationality. *Technological Forecasting and Social Change, 28,* 195-202.

Nauth, K.K. (1999). In from the cold. Retrieved September 23, 2004, from *http://www.topsecretnet.com/knowmag.htm*

Nidumolu, S.R., Subramani, M., & Aldrich, A. (2001). Situated learning and the situated knowledge web: Exploring the ground beneath knowledge management. *Journal of Management Information Systems, 18*(1), 115-150.

Parker, K.R., & Nitse, P.S. (2001). Improving competitive intelligence gathering for knowledge management systems. *Proceedings of the 2001 International Symposium on Information Systems and Engineering ISE'2001 Workshop: Knowledge Management Systems: Concepts, Technologies and Applications* (pp. 122-128), Las Vegas, NV.

Rubenfeld, J. (2001). Knowledge management for life: Make the world a better place. *Ubiquity, 2*(41).

Snyder, N.H. (1981). Environmental volatility, scanning intensity, and organizational performance. *Journal of Contemporary Business, 10*(2), 5-17.

Stadnyk, I., & Kass, R. (1992). Modeling users' interests in information filters. *Communications of the ACM, 35*(12), 49-50.

Williams, R. (2002). Applying KM lessons to competitive intelligence: Creating a user-driven competitive intelligence culture. Retrieved March 2003 from *http://old.apqc.org/free/articles/dispArticle.cfm?ProductID=1493*

KEY TERMS

Competitive Intelligence: A systematic and ethical program for gathering, analyzing, and managing environmental information that can affect a company's plans, decisions, and operations (http://www.scip.org/ci/).

Environmental Scanning: The systematic gathering of information in order to reduce the randomness of the information flow into the organization, and to provide early warnings of changing conditions in both the external and internal environment.

Intelligence Needs: The topics that an organization must monitor in order to stay competitive.

Key Intelligence Topics (KITs): A process for identifying intelligence requirements by considering strategic decisions, early-warning topics, and key players.

M-CLIP: A structured, expanded profile of information needs, used in conjunction with specialized templates to aid in the identification of critical intelligence needs, an expansion mechanism to help insure that no key concepts are overlooked, and an adaptive mechanism to remove ineffective topics.

Needs Identification: The process of determining which topics an organization must monitor in order to attain or maintain a competitive advantage.

Profile/User Profile: A set of keywords or concepts describing a user or organization's intelligence needs through which profile-based intelligence-gathering tools filter information.

Computational Experimentation

Mark E. Nissen
Naval Postgraduate School, USA

Raymond E. Levitt
Stanford University, USA

INTRODUCTION

Systematic development of new *knowledge* is as important in the developing field of *knowledge management* (KM) as in other social science and technological domains. Careful research is essential for the development of new knowledge in a systematic manner (e.g., avoiding the process of trial and error). The problem is, throughout the era of modern science, a chasm has persisted between laboratory and field research that impedes knowledge development about knowledge management.

This article combines and builds upon recent results to describe a research approach that bridges the chasm between laboratory and field methods in KM: *computational experimentation*. As implied by the name, computational experiments are conducted via computer simulation. But such experiments can go beyond most simulations (e.g., incorporating experimental controls, benefiting from external *model validation*). And they can offer simultaneously benefits of laboratory methods (e.g., internal validity, lack of confounding) and field-work (e.g., external validity, generalizability). Further, computational experiments can be conducted at a fraction of the cost and time associated with either laboratory experiments or field studies. And they provide a window to view the kinds of meta-knowledge that are important for understanding knowledge management. Thus, computational experimentation offers potential to mitigate many limitations of both laboratory and field methods and to enhance KM research. We discuss computational modeling and simulation as a complementary method to bridge the chasm between laboratory and field methods—not as a replacement for either of these methods.

BACKGROUND

To appreciate the power of computational experimentation, we draw heavily from Nissen and Buettner (2004) in this section, and outline the key relative advantages and disadvantages of laboratory and field methods. To begin, the laboratory provides unparalleled opportunity for controlled experimentation. Through experimentation the researcher can manipulate only a few variables of interest at a time and can minimize the confounding associated with the myriad factors affecting complex systems and processes in the field (Box, Hunter, & Hunter, 1978; Johnson & Wichern, 1992). However, limitations of laboratory experimentation are known well (Campbell & Stanley, 1973) and are particularly severe in the KM domain. In KM experimentation such limitations center on problems with external validity. Laboratory conditions can seldom replicate the complexity, scope, and scale of the physical organizations and systems of interest for research. KM experiments also include problems with generalizability. Many experiments utilize samples of convenience (esp. university students) instead of working professionals. This practice calls into question how closely the associated experimental results are representative of KM behavior in operational organizations.

Alternatively, field research provides unparalleled opportunity for realism (Denzin & Lincoln, 1994). The researcher in the field can study full-scale artifacts in operational environments (Yin, 1994) and can minimize the abstraction away from working people, systems, and organizations (Glaser & Strauss, 1967). However, limitations of field research are known well also (Campbell & Stanley, 1973) and are particularly severe in the KM domain also. In KM field research such limitations center on problems with internal validity. Field research affords little opportunity for controlled experimentation (cf. Cook & Campbell, 1979). Also, confounding results often from the myriad influences on complex systems and organizations that cannot be isolated in the field. This practice makes it difficult to identify and trace the causes of differential behaviors—better as well as worse—in KM. In addition, field research can be very expensive, particularly to support researchers' efforts to enhance internal validity and ameliorate confounding. And many research designs for fieldwork (e.g., case study, ethnography, natural experiment) require considerable time for planning and analysis.

As implied by the name, computational experiments are conducted via computer simulation. As such, they

Figure 1. Bridge method (Adapted from: Nissen and Buettner, 2004)

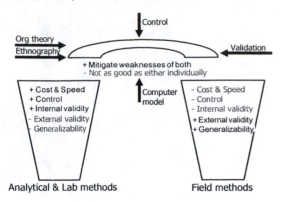

offer all of the cost and time advantages of computational analysis (see Law & Kelton, 1991). But computational experiments go beyond most simulations. Rigorous experimental designs are employed to capture the benefits of laboratory experimentation. The variables affecting physical systems and organizations in the field can be isolated and examined under controlled conditions. This also addresses the internal validity and confounding limitations of field research. Yet computational experiments can be conducted at a fraction of the cost and time required to set up and run experiments with human subjects in the laboratory. Further, through external validation, computational models can emulate key qualitative and quantitative behaviors of the physical systems and organizations they represent with "good" fidelity (e.g., good enough to have confidence that results of computational experiments will track those of physical experiments in the laboratory or field). This mitigates the problems of external validity and generalizability noted above.

Figure 1 illustrates the essential elements of computational experimentation as a research method. The top of the figure includes a shape to depict the bridge metaphor associated with this method. It spans a wide gap between laboratory and field methods. From the left side of this "bridge," two arrows represent inputs to describe the behaviors of computational models. Organization theory, which is predicated upon many thousands of studies over the last half century, provides the basis for most such behaviors. Behaviors pertaining to organizational factors such as centralization, division of labor, task interdependence, function, *coordination*, formalization, technology, and information processing are captured from organization theory. Where extant theory does not address a behavior of interest (e.g., knowledge flows) well, ethnographic and similar immersive field studies (Bernard, 1998) are conducted

to understand the associated organizational behaviors. Because organization theory attempts to be general, and is not based on any single organization, the associated behaviors have broad applicability across organizations in practice. This provides in part for the generalizability attainable through the method of computational experimentation.

From the bottom of the "bridge," an arrow represents the use of computer models to represent organizations and emulate their key behaviors. Some variety exists in terms of specific implementations. But most computer models adhere to standards, norms, and conventions associated with the field of Computational Organization Theory (COT; see Carley & Prietula, 1994). The central goal is to develop computer models that emulate the key behaviors of organizations and to use such models to examine alternate methods of organization and coordination. As such COT shares a focus on many factors of importance in knowledge management.

From the right side of the "bridge" in the figure, one arrow represents a requirement in our approach for model validation. Through validation, the organizational behaviors emulated by computer models are examined and compared with those of operational organizations in the field. We view this as an essential step. It provides confidence that the behaviors emulated by the computer model have sufficient fidelity to mirror faithfully the behaviors of the operational organizations they represent. This provides in part for the external validity attainable through the method of computational experimentation.

It is important to note, not all COT models are subjected to such validation. Many researchers use computational models to conduct theorem-proving studies. Such studies are valuable in their own right to demonstrate various aspects of organization theory (e.g., see Carley, 1999). But without thorough validation of representation and usefulness (Thomsen, Levitt, Kunz, Nass, & Fridsma, 1999), such researchers have difficulty making claims that the theoretical insights derived from their models mirror the behavior of organizations in the field. Hence comprehensive validation represents an important characteristic to distinguish computational experimentation as the research method described specifically in this article from COT in general.

Finally, from the top of the "bridge," an arrow represents the use of experimental controls in research. Following the same rich set of experimental designs available to laboratory researchers, computational experimentation as a research method can be used to control for myriad factors and manipulate just one or a few variables at a time to examine causality. Further, the same experimental design and setup can be replicated any number of times, for instance using Monte Carlo techniques or other computational approaches to introduce variation. This provides for the internal validity attainable through the method of computational experimentation. Combining these "bridge" inputs together—organization theory and ethnography, computer models, validation, and control—the method of computational experimentation can be understood in terms of, and indeed inherits, the various properties of its constituent elements.

COMPUTATIONAL EXPERIMENTATION IN KM

In this section, we draw heavily from Nissen and Levitt (2004) to summarize our approach to computational experimentation in KM. We begin by highlighting key aspects of our research on agent-based modeling and then illustrate its KM application through an example of technological development.

Virtual Design Team Research

The *Virtual Design Team* (VDT) Research Program (VDT, 2004) reflects the planned accumulation of collaborative research over two decades to develop rich, theory-based models of organizational processes. Using an agent-based representation (Cohen, 1992; Kunz, Levitt, & Jin, 1998), micro-level organizational behaviors have been researched and formalized to reflect well-accepted organization theory (Levitt et al., 1999). Extensive empirical validation projects (e.g., Christiansen, 1993; Thomsen, 1998) have demonstrated representational fidelity and have shown how the emulated behaviors of VDT computational models correspond closely with a diversity of enterprise processes in practice.

The development and evolution of VDT has been described in considerable detail elsewhere (e.g., Jin & Levitt, 1996; VDT, 2004), so we do not repeat such discussion here. The VDT modeling environment has been developed directly from Galbraith's (1977) information processing view of organizations. This information processing view has two key implications (Jin & Levitt, 1996). The first is ontological: we model knowledge work through interactions of *tasks* to be performed, *actors* communicating with one another and performing tasks, and an *organization structure* that defines actors' roles and that constrains their behaviors. In essence this amounts to overlaying the task structure on the organization structure and to developing computational agents with various capabilities to emulate the behaviors of organizational actors performing work.

The VDT modeling environment benefits from extensive fieldwork in many diverse enterprise domains (e.g.,

power plant construction and offshore drilling, see Christiansen, 1993; aerospace, see Thomsen, 1998; software development, see, Nogueira 2000; healthcare, see Cheng & Levitt, 2001). Through the process of "backcasting"—predicting known organizational outcomes using only information that was available at the beginning of a project—VDT models of operational enterprises in practice have demonstrated dozens of times that emulated organizational behaviors and results correspond qualitatively and quantitatively to their actual counterparts in the field (Kunz et al., 1998). Thus the VDT modeling environment has been validated repeatedly and longitudinally as representative of both organization theory and enterprises in practice. This gives us considerable confidence in its results.

Moreover, VDT is designed specifically to model the kinds of knowledge work and information processing tasks that comprise the bulk of KM processes. In this sense, the computational model is imbued with meta-knowledge in terms of the constructs and relationships that are important to KM. In particular, building upon emerging *knowledge-flow theory* (e.g., see Nissen, 2002)—which describes the dynamics of how knowledge "moves" between various people, organizations, locations, and points in time—we are extending VDT methods and tools to reproduce increasingly fine-grained behaviors of knowledge in motion. This includes knowledge-flow processes and tools such as direct experience, formal training, transactive memory, mentoring, and simulation, in addition to commonplace KM approaches such as Web portals, knowledge maps, and communities of practice.

VDT Knowledge Management Model

Here we employ the VDT modeling environment to represent work processes associated with a high-level technology development project. The key KM question of interest here is: To what extent should the organization focus on developing specialist knowledge within its two functional areas of design and manufacturing vs. promoting generalist knowledge across functional areas? Figure 2 presents a screenshot delineating two primary tasks (i.e., design and manufacturing), each performed by a corresponding organizational unit (i.e., design actor and manufacturing actor). The two milestone markers ("Start" and "Finish") shown in the figure are used in VDT to denote progress, but such markers neither represent tasks nor entail effort. The tree structure shown in the top left of the figure displays several of the different ontological elements of the VDT model (e.g., tasks, positions, milestones). The table shown in the bottom left displays numerous program-level parameters (e.g., team experience, centralization, for-

Figure 2. VDT baseline product development model

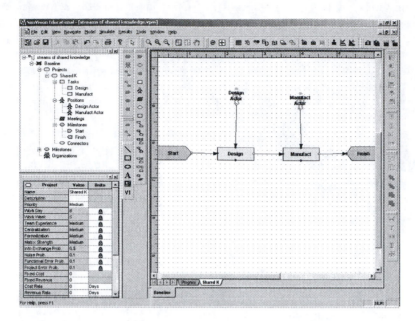

malization), which are all set to empirically determined "normal" values for product development work. Values for such parameters are held constant (i.e., controlled) across simulations of alternate cases and scenarios.

To set up a computational experiment, this model is parameterized to reflect "medium" specialist knowledge and "medium" cross-functional knowledge. The null hypothesis is: varying the relative levels of specialist and cross-functional knowledge has negligible impact on project performance. To test this null, we conduct a full-factorial experiment, with knowledge levels at both "low" and "high" levels for all combinations of specialist and cross-functional settings. Examining each case individually provides us with precise control over which factors can vary and hence excellent insight into causality. Examining exhaustively all combinations of specialist and cross-functional knowledge levels provides us with insight into the entire design space associated with these KM variables of interest. Using consistently the output measure *project duration* enables us to employ a common metric to assess relative performance. These benefits all accrue from our experimental methods and controls. Moreover, using empirically determined and validated "normal" settings to depict the behavior of a representative technology project provides us with confidence that results of our simulations bear resemblance to those of operational organizational projects in the field. This benefit accrues from employing the general and validated modeling environment VDT.

Computational results for the product development model are summarized in Table 1. The values listed in the table reflect simulated project duration and are expressed in workdays. For instance, notice the result in the table's center (highlighted in bold print for emphasis): a project staffed with actors possessing medium levels of manufacturing specialist knowledge (z) and medium levels of cross-functional knowledge (h) is projected by the model to require 216 workdays to complete. This reflects a nominal 200 days of work specified (i.e., work volume), along with 16 days of additional problem solving (e.g., internal communication, delay, and exception handling associated with noise, uncertainty, and errors). The additional 16 days' problem-solving time reflects empirically determined relationships between model parameters (e.g., levels of z and h) and organizational performance.

Table 1 reports full-factorial results of nine simulation runs, with both the z (i.e., specialist knowledge) and

Table 1. Computational model results

Parameter	Low z	Medium z	High z
High h	226	178	141
Medium h	264	**216**	178
Low h	310	264	226

Project Duration in workdays

h (i.e., cross-functional) parameters varying across three levels: low, medium, and high. Notice the simulation results vary in understandable ways across the three levels of both specialist and cross-functional knowledge. For instance, holding the parameter h constant at the medium level of cross-functional knowledge, performance in terms of project duration ranges from 264 days when specialist knowledge is low, to 178 days when specialist knowledge is high. This indicates the marginal product of such knowledge is positive (i.e., consistent with classical microeconomic theory). This same monotonic relationship is evident at the other levels of cross-functional knowledge (i.e., low h, high h) as well. Likewise, holding the parameter z constant at the medium level of specialist knowledge, performance in terms of project duration ranges symmetrically from 264 days when cross-functional knowledge is low, to 178 days when cross-functional knowledge is high. This is also consistent with classical microeconomic theory and is evident too at the other levels of specialist knowledge (i.e., low z, high z).

The symmetry reflected in the results of Table 1 corresponds to the microeconomic case of *perfect knowledge substitution*: specialist and cross-functional knowledge can be substituted—unit for unit—to maintain performance at some arbitrary level (e.g., along an isoquant). For instance, from the table, where specialist knowledge (z) is low, but cross-functional knowledge (h) is medium, performance (264 workdays) is the same as where specialist knowledge (z) is medium (i.e., one unit higher), but cross-functional knowledge (h) is low (i.e., one unit lower). Other instances of such substitutability can be identified readily through different combinations of knowledge types z and h (e.g., low z, high h <—> high z, low h [226 days]; high z, medium h <—> medium z, high h [178 days]). With this our computational model indicates that specialist and cross-functional knowledge represent substitutes for one another. It is important to note here, this result reflecting perfect substitution reflects an *emergent property* of the computational model, not an explicit behavior—that is, nowhere in the development of the VDT environment or this computational project model do we specify behaviors of perfect substitution. Rather, the nature of interactions between VDT actors, tasks, organizations, and environmental settings lead dynamically to this result. In a sense this provides some additional validation of VDT (i.e., from classical microeconomics) behaviors.

Clearly this relatively simple computational experiment excludes several factors and aspects of the world that would complicate the analysis and alter the symmetry of results. For instance, we model the design and manufacturing tasks as sequential, with little interaction and no rework. However, few contemporary technology development projects separate design and manufacturing so cleanly. Designers today are required to understand an organization's manufacturing capabilities, and manufacturers today need to understand the limitations of design. In the case, the coordination requirements associated with concurrency between design and manufacturing functional tasks would skew our results in terms of substitution between specialist and generalist knowledge. Similarly, few contemporary technology development projects are devoid of rework between design and manufacturing tasks. Indeed, a key aspect of concurrency in fast-track projects involves multiple prototypes that are developed, evaluated, and reworked through successive iterations and refinements.

In the case, the rework requirements associated with iterative prototyping would also skew our results in terms of substitution between specialist and generalist knowledge. Other complications (e.g., inclusion of marketing and service organizations, differential pay scales, different rates of change pertaining to specialist and generalist knowledge, different learning rates among actors in the various organizations, different KM technologies in place) can be modeled and simulated as well—one at a time—using experimental controls. Through such computational experimentation, researchers and managers alike can learn much about how knowledge flows in a modeled project organization. Such knowledge can be used to help researchers focus on the most sensitive variables to study in future laboratory and field experiments. It can also be instrumental directly in enhancing the organization's KM projects.

FUTURE TRENDS

The kind of computational experimentation illustrated in the simple example above represents only a modest beginning to what can be accomplished over time by exploiting these new tools and techniques. For instance, as the theoretical basis of KM continues to develop and accumulate, an increasing number of knowledge-specific micro-behaviors can be represented and incorporated into modeling environments such as VDT. This will enable increasingly fine-grained and complex analyses to be conducted, with computational experimentation used to differentiate between closely matched KM alternatives (e.g., competing organizational designs, process flows, personnel systems, technological architectures). In complementary fashion, as computational models become increasingly sophisticated and based on KM theory, using such models through experimentation will enable new KM knowledge to develop and accumulate at an ever faster rate. Hence in a mutually reinforcing manner, KM theory can inform and improve upon computational experimentation, while computational experiments can inform and accelerate the development of KM theory.

Moreover, as computer technology continues to advance, larger and more complex computational experiments can be conducted in less time. As the approach of computational experimentation diffuses through the research and management communities, it may become increasingly routine to employ this technique in everyday settings (Schrage, 1999). Today, the designs of airplanes, bridges, and computers are accomplished principally via computational modeling and analysis. Tomorrow, such modeling and analysis may become indispensable to designing organizations, work processes, personnel systems, and information technologies (Levitt, 2004). Before any KM project reaches a stage of prototyping, much less organizational implementation, it will have undergone extensive computational analysis. Thus, the approach of computational experimentation that we illustrate in this article offers potential to become a mainstay of KM research and practice.

CONCLUSION

Systematic development of new knowledge in the developing field of knowledge management (KM) is impeded by a chasm between laboratory and field research methods. This article describes computational experimentation as a research approach that bridges this chasm and hence offers potential for understanding KM better. Examining a high-level project model, we illustrate how the VDT modeling environment can be employed for computational experimentation through a full-factorial design. And we indicate how this approach can be extended to examine large, complex, and detailed organizations and projects, in addition to adding increasingly sophisticated and analytically demanding factors to the models.

More than simply simulating organizational behaviors, computational experimentation can facilitate the development of knowledge about knowledge management. In time we may find such experimentation used to design KM projects and associated organizations in a manner similar to the use of computational models for the design of complex physical artifacts such as airplanes, bridges, and computers. Should this vision obtain, the KM researcher, manager, and practitioner alike will all be well versed in—and indeed critically dependent upon—computational experimentation. The research described in this article represents a substantial step toward such vision.

REFERENCES

Bernard, H.R. (1998). *Handbook of methods in cultural anthropology.* Walnut Creek, CA: Altamira Press.

Box, G.E.P., Hunter, W.G., & Hunter, J.S. (1978). *Statistics for experimenters: An introduction to design, data analysis and model building.* New York: John Wiley & Sons.

Campbell, D.T., & Stanley, J.C. (1973). *Experimental and quasi-experimental designs for research.* Chicago: Rand McNally.

Carley, K.M. (1999). On generating hypothesis using computer simulations. *Systems Engineering, 2*(2).

Carley, K.M., & Prietula, M.J. (Eds.). (1994). *Computational organization theory.* Hillsdale, NJ: Lawrence Erlbaum.

Cheng, C.H.F., & Levitt, R.E. (2001, November 3-7). Contextually changing behavior in medical organizations. *Proceedings of the 2001 Annual Symposium of the American Medical Informatics Association,* Washington, DC.

Christiansen, T.R. (1993). *Modeling efficiency and effectiveness of coordination in engineering design teams.* PhD Dissertation, Department of Civil and Environmental Engineering, Stanford University.

Cohen, G.P. (1992). *The virtual design team: An object-oriented model of information sharing in project teams.* PhD Dissertation, Department of Civil Engineering, Stanford University.

Cook, T.D., & Campbell, D.T. (1979). *Quasi-experimentation: Design and analysis issues for field settings.* Boston: Houghton Mifflin.

Denzin, N.K., & Lincoln, Y.S. (Eds.). (1994). *Handbook of qualitative research* (pp. 500-515). Thousand Oaks, CA: Sage Publications.

Galbraith, J.R. (1977). *Organization design.* Reading, MA: Addison-Wesley.

Glaser, B.G., & Strauss, A.L. (1967). *The discovery of grounded theory: Strategies for qualitative research.* New York: Aldine de Gruyter.

Jin, Y., & Levitt, R.E. (1996). The virtual design team: A computational model of project organizations. *Computational and Mathematical Organization Theory, 2*(3), 171-195.

Johnson, R.A., & Wichern, D.W. (1992). *Applied multivariate statistical analysis* (3rd ed.). Englewood Cliffs, NJ: Prentice-Hall.

Kunz, J.C., Levitt, R.E., & Jin, Y. (1998). The Virtual Design Team: A computational simulation model of project organizations. *Communications of the ACM, 41*(11), 84-92.

Law, A.M., & Kelton, D. (1991). *Simulation modeling and analysis* (2nd ed.). New York: McGraw-Hill.

Levitt, R. (2004). Computational modeling and simulation come of age. *Journal of Computational and Mathematical Organization Theory.*

Levitt, R.E., Thomsen, J., Christiansen, T.R., Junz, J.C., Jin, Y., & Nass, C. (1999). Simulating project work processes and organizations: Toward a micro-contingency theory of organizational design. *Management Science, 45*(11), 1479-1495.

Nissen, M.E. (2002). An extended model of knowledge-flow dynamics. *Communications of the AIS, 8,* 251-266.

Nissen, M.E., & Buettner, R.R. (2004, June). Computational experimentation: bridging the chasm between laboratory and field research in KM. *Proceedings of the Knowledge Management Research and Technology Symposium,* San Diego, CA.

Nissen, M.E., & Levitt, R.E. (2004, January). Agent-based modeling of knowledge flows: Illustration from the domain of information systems design. *Proceedings of the Hawaii International Conference on System Sciences,* Waikoloa, HI.

Nogueira, J.C. (2000). *A formal model for risk assessment in software projects.* PhD Dissertation, Department of Computer Science, Naval Postgraduate School, USA.

Schrage, M. (1999). *Serious play: How the world's best companies simulate to innovate.* Cambridge, MA: Harvard Business School Press.

Thomsen, J. (1998). *The Virtual Team Alliance (VTA): Modeling the effects of goal incongruency in semi-routine, fast-paced project organizations.* PhD Dissertation, Department of Civil and Environmental Engineering, Stanford University, USA.

Thomsen, J., Levitt, R.E., Kunz, J.C., Nass, C.I., & Fridsma, D.B. (1999). A trajectory for validating computational emulation models of organizations. *Journal of Computational & Mathematical Organization Theory, 5*(4), 385-401.

VDT. (2004). Retrieved from *http://www.stanford.edu/group/CIFE/VDT/*

Yin, R.K. (1994). *Case study research: Design and methods* (2nd ed.). Thousand Oaks, CA: Sage Publications.

KEY TERMS

Computational Experimentation: The use of validated, theory-driven computer models with experimental methods to assess systematically behaviors associated with alternate organizational designs.

Coordination: The activity and effort associated with the information processing tasks of an organization.

Knowledge-Flow Theory: An emerging basis of theory describing the dynamics of how knowledge "moves" between various people, organizations, locations, and points in time.

Knowledge: In this article *knowledge* is operationalized as the ability to enable action in the organization (e.g., good decisions, appropriate behaviors, useful work). As such it complements *information*, which provides the context for and meaning of action (e.g., criteria for decisions, motivations for actions, specifications for work), as well as *data*, which supply details associated with action (e.g., facts, observations, measurements).

Knowledge Management: The use of knowledge (i.e., which enables direct action) for capitalization (e.g., competitive advantage, organization, productivity).

Knowledge Substitution: The degree to which one kind of knowledge (e.g., specialist design knowledge) can be substituted for another (e.g., generalist technology development knowledge) without affecting organizational performance.

Model Validation: Iterative testing and refinement of computational models to ensure the behaviors of such models mirror faithfully those of the operational organizations in practice that they represent.

Virtual Design Team: A stream of research focused on developing computational methods and tools to enable the design of organizations in a manner similar to how complex physical artifacts such as airplanes, bridges, and computers are designed (i.e., via computer models).

Coopetition

Claudia Loebbecke
Department of Media Management, University of Cologne, Germany

Albert Angehrn
Centre for Advanced Learning Technologies (CALT), INSEAD, France

INTRODUCTION

Behind the emerging digital façade, companies have started to operate in a distributed fashion. The intricate connectivity among these firms implies the exchange of valuable resources like knowledge and information. Such cooperation or collaboration is what enables organizations and individuals to make decisions collectively, learn from one another, communicate effectively, and thus create knowledge (Brown & Duguid, 1991; Huber, 1991; McDonald, 1995; von Krogh & Roos, 1995).

However, cooperating organizations often simultaneously compete (coopetition). While reciprocal knowledge sharing may enhance the total and individual added value, inter-firm knowledge sharing may also affect the uniqueness and thus competitive contribution of a firm's knowledge repository. Opportunistic behavior of counterparts may erode anticipated benefits of cooperation and result in unevenly distributed value.

The inherent balancing act between cooperation and competition requires designing and implementing specific management processes to enable economic value maximization for participating individuals and firms. The value-driven balancing act is becoming increasingly relevant in business practice.

This article introduces the scientific literature on Knowledge Management Under Coopetition and then describes the concept of Coopetitive Learning and Knowledge Exchange Networks (CoLKENs), their components, and their generic structure. It reviews CoLKEN fundamentals and components, and suggests a CoLKEN taxonomy. Key research questions are followed by generalized key insights from studying CoLKENs as the setting for Knowledge Management Under Coopetition. The article then examines the levers for managing CoLKENs, and closes with future trends and brief conclusions.

BACKGROUND

The following literature review provides broad definitions and discussions relevant to knowledge management under coopetition.

Fundamental Components of Knowledge Management Under Coopetition

Knowledge is a complex concept and difficult to define, and when seen from a management perspective, it exhibits unique properties that are distinctly different from the ones of traditional corporate resources, such as land, labor, and capital. Intellectual resources are not naturally scarce (Suchmann, 1989); knowledge may increase in value the more it is used, with investment in knowledge and knowledge-creating capabilities characterized by increasing returns (Teece, 1998). These properties tend to make knowledge less amenable to management (Polanyi, 1966; Hedlund, 1994; Nonaka, 1994; Boisot, 1995).

Who are appropriate knowledge agents for Knowledge Management Under Coopetition? Who is intellectually capable, the organization or its individual employees? Does knowledge reside at individual and organizational levels? Among others, Drucker (1993) and Grant (1996) stress the predominant importance of individuals. Others (Nonaka & Takeuchi, 1995; Spender, 1996; Boisot, 1998; Lane & Lubatkin, 1998; Matusik & Hill, 1998; Crossan, Lane, & White, 1999; Inkpen, 2000) consider organizational cognition or organizations as cognitive entities a suitable unit of analysis. In the organization science literature, organizational learning is a central tenet (Huber, 1991; Simon, 1991; Argyris & Schön, 1996) and is believed to lead to competitive advantage (Senge, 1990; Moingeon & Edmondson, 1996). It is closely intertwined with inter-organizational learning (e.g., Larsson, Bengtsson, Henriksson, & Sparks, 1998), as the learning entities in both concepts positively affect each other (Doz & Hamel, 1998; Child, 2001; Holmquist, 2003).

Knowledge networks are commonly defined as formally set up mechanisms, structures, and behavioral patterns that connect knowledge agents who were not previously connected because of functional, hierarchical, or legal boundaries between organizations. Inter-organizational knowledge networks (e.g., Mowery, Oxley, & Silverman, 1996; Klein, 1996) provide the setting for Knowledge Management Under Coopetition.

Theoretical Underpinnings of Knowledge Management Under Coopetition

The "resource-based view of the firm," along with its conceptual predecessor, the "industrial organization view," and its extension, the "knowledge-based view of the firm," have shed light on the question of why firms cooperate to learn from one another, share capabilities and knowledge, while—at the same time—manage knowledge as a valuable resource in the competitive environment.

Until the 1980s, competitive thinking—reflected in the "industrial organization view"—has generally been seen focusing on companies' environments (e.g., Porter, 1980; Spender, 1996; Teece, Pisano, & Shuen, 1997). As such, it stands for an outward focus. Since the mid-1980s, the so-called "resource-based approach" (Wernerfelt, 1984; Rumelt, 1987; Prahalad & Hamel, 1990) has partially built on Penrose's conception of the firm as a "collection of productive resources, both human and material" (Penrose, 1959, p. 31). The resource-based approach builds on two basic assumptions: (a) the firm's ultimate objective is to achieve sustained, above normal returns; and (b) a set of resources and their combination transformed into competencies and capabilities are a precondition for sustained superior returns (Rugman & Verbeke, 2002). These resources are to be firm-specific (i.e., imperfectly mobile), valuable to customers, non-substitutable, difficult to imitate, and differently available to firms. Companies are seen as heterogeneous with respect to their resource and capability endowments (Teece et al., 1997). Assets such as knowledge are not readily tradable; they cannot equilibrate through factor input markets. Hence, critical resources can typically not be acquired via the market and consequently need to be developed internally. Competitive advantage is associated primarily with heterogeneous resource endowments of firms (Wernerfelt, 1984; Prahalad & Hamel, 1990; Hamel, 1991; Barney, 1991).

Recent extensions of the knowledge-based perspective (Grant, 1996) are centered around its application to a "network of firms," rather than an individual firm (Hamel, 1991; Prahalad & Ramaswamy, 2000; Dyer & Nobeoka, 2000; Gulati, Nohria, & Zaheer, 2000; Doz, Santos, & Williamson, 2001; Grant & Baden-Fuller, 2004). As developed in the "relational view of the firm," firms ought to look at inter-organizational networks as a source of sustainable competitive advantage (Liebeskind, Olivier, Zucker, & Brewer, 1996; Powell, Kogut, & Smith-Doerr, 1996; Powell, 1998; Dyer & Singh, 1998).

Different scholars hold different views on what criteria need to be applied to differentiate critical from non-critical resources. Barney (1991) proposes "value creation for the company," "rarity compared to competition," "imitability," and "substitutability." Prahalad and Hamel (1990) distinguish "core competencies" from "non-core competencies" by outlining core competencies as being suitable for application in many different markets, creating a significant contribution to customer value, and being difficult for competitors to imitate.

To specify resources that accommodate these criteria is equally controversial (Priem & Butler, 2001a, 2001b; Rugman & Verbeke, 2002). The literature offers a plethora of phrases such as "firm resources" (Barney, 1991, 2001), "invisible assets" (Itami, 1987), or "dynamic capabilities" (Teece et al., 1997).

Roos and Roos (1996) or Drucker (1993) proclaim that knowledge, whether referred to as invisible assets (Itami, 1987), absorptive capacity (Cohen & Levinthal, 1990), core competencies (Prahalad &, Hamel, 1990), core capabilities (Kogut &, Zander, 1996), or organizational knowledge (Nonaka &, Takeuchi, 1995), can be seen as the only—or at least an important resource—that fulfils the foregoing criteria. Teece (1998) even argues that the essence of a firm is its ability to create, transfer, assemble, integrate, and exploit knowledge assets.

These lines of thought match the traditional analysis that both Ricardian and monopoly rent theorists derive in large part from intangible assets, with organizational learning and knowledge being among the most crucial ones (Penrose, 1959; Liebeskind, 1996; McGaughey, 2002). By stressing the outstanding importance of knowledge, they have given birth to the knowledge-based perspective as a special form of the resource-based one.

COOPETITIVE LEARNING AND KNOWLEDGE EXCHANGE NETWORKS (CoLKENs) AS THE SETTING FOR KNOWLEDGE MANAGEMENT UNDER COOPETITION

As outlined above, knowledge management has been increasingly considered as a key managerial function necessary for achieving competitive advantage (Tsang, 2002). Economic thinking leaves no doubt that scarcity is a precondition for property and thus commercial value of any resource. Consequently, it puts a question mark on generously sharing knowledge in an economic context. Thus, inter-organizational knowledge-sharing processes revolve around a formidable balancing act between borrowing knowledge assets from partners, while protecting one's own assets (Loebbecke, van Fenema, & Powell, 1999). The challenge is to share enough skills to learn and create advantage vis-à-vis companies outside the network, while preventing an unwanted transfer of core competencies to a partner (Hamel, Doz, & Prahalad, 1989). This challenge is exacerbated when some members in the network are competitors. In such constellations, the danger of becoming "hollowed out" by "predatory" partners (Hamel et al., 1989; Kogut & Zander, 1996) seems particularly evident, suggesting that appropriate steps be taken to ensure mutually beneficial sharing. Nevertheless, many of the skills that migrate between companies are not covered in the formal terms of a knowledge exchange (Loebbecke & van Fenema, 2000). Often, what gets traded—that is, what is learned—is determined by day-to-day interactions between engineers, marketers, and product developers (Hamel et al., 1989).

CoLKEN Fundamental Statements and Components

Following the above insights, a CoLKEN Construct (see Figure 1) is built based on seven fundamental statements (see also Loebbecke & Angehrn, 2003a):

1. Knowledge assets have their foundation not only in data and in information, but also in collaborative learning processes.
2. Both the individual employee as well as the organization should be seen as knowledge agents capable of owning and processing knowledge.
3. Knowledge agents exchange knowledge in knowledge networks within and—in the light of ubiquitous

information, communication, and media technologies—increasingly between organizations.

4. The increasing appearance of inter-organizational networks triggers a focus on learning and knowledge exchange processes between organizations during coopetition.
5. Cooperation forms the basis for any knowledge exchange process between organizations as it supports the learning processes through which knowledge is created and acquired, as well as shared and disseminated.
6. In the light of competition, knowledge serves as a critical resource or asset to achieve competitive advantage and above normal rents.
7. Management processes and actively managed strategic interventions (stimuli) in knowledge exchanges allow organizations to create value by significantly impacting the composition, the exploitation and exploitability, as well as the business results of learning, knowledge, and intellectual assets at large.

The three fundamental components, Knowledge, Knowledge Agents, and Knowledge Networks (Statements 1, 2, and 3) lay the foundations for investigating inter-organizational learning and knowledge exchange networks in the context of coopetition (see also 'Background'). The CoLKEN focus is represented as a central platform on which cooperation and competition are performed (Statements 4, 5, and 6). In order to create and

Figure 1. CoLKEN construct

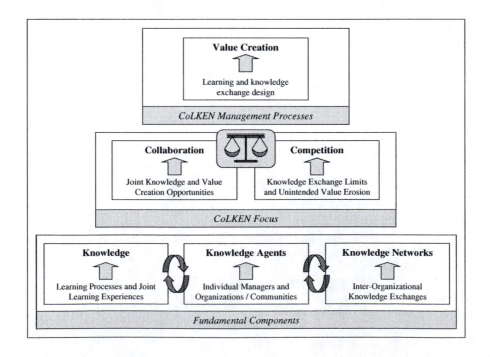

Figure 2. CoLKEN taxonomy

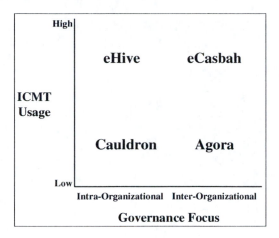

Research Drivers and Key Insights

Research concerning organizational and social aspects of CoLKENs as the setting for Knowledge Management Under Coopetition investigates initiatives ranging from local industry clusters to new forms for organizations with globally distributed knowledge workers operating within Open Source communities. Dominating research drivers are: (1) the motivation for individuals and for companies to participate in the networks (e.g., Argote, McEvily, & Reagans, 2003); (2) issues of leadership, coordination and control strategies, and decision making; (3) the management of collaboration, including knowledge creation, sharing, and management, as well as learning and innovation (e.g., Menon & Pfeffer, 2003); and finally, (4) the management of the competition dimension. These issues ought to be analyzed along the trajectories of who (people), what (topics), and how (processes). Further, various contingencies for inter-organizational knowledge governance based on dominant knowledge types, the assessment of the ease of knowledge sharing and retention, and the direction of knowledge flows (unilateral or bi-directional/reciprocal) play an important role for investigating Knowledge Management Under Coopetition.

Main research insights derived from the above lines of analyses can be summarized as follows:

extract the maximum economic value, the challenge is to balance both aspects by designing and implementing management processes for active strategic interventions in the CoLKEN (Statement 7).

CoLKEN Taxonomy

Possible dimensions for differentiating CoLKENs are information, communication, and media technology (ICMT) usage, governance focus, size, growth pattern, composition, and degree of internal competition. Selecting the first two dimensions, Figure 2 shows a CoLKEN taxonomy (adapted from Loebbecke & Angehrn, 2003b).

A cauldron, the large kettle or boiler used by witches mixing and cooking ingredients without a clear pattern, stands for intra-organizational and low-technology CoLKENs. An agora, the ancient Greek marketplace, represents inter-organizational, low-tech solutions. An e-hive takes the concept of a hive, a container for housing honeybees, to the virtual level. It describes a busy intra-organizational environment without clear pre-arranged patterns of action or movements. An e-casbah, finally, transfers the concept of the older, native section of a north-African city with its busy marketplaces to the e-world, where it represents inter-organizational settings, with learning and knowledge exchanges taking place solely via ICMT infrastructures.

While the basic assumption of coopetition between organizational units requires some degree of 'inter'-organizational networking, the horizontal axis takes into account the more or less overriding legal structures that may emphasize the 'intra'-setting for competing sub-units.

- Individual managers are mostly motivated by opportunities to engage in new forms of collaborative learning and management development. Organizations aim to achieve their objectives through acquisition of knowledge critical to their processes or strategy.

- The dominant form of collaboration and learning is traditional knowledge transfer, that is, contexts in which members do not need to engage too personally or do not need to contribute their knowledge at all. More experiential forms are rare; they emerge primarily in non-critical domains and after having succeeded in helping members to develop more stable relationships and trust (for the impact of different kinds of interventions, see also Cabrera, 2002).

- The competition dimension limits knowledge exchange to pre-defined domains and formats which are perceived by members as non-competitive in terms of not releasing much critical knowledge to potential competitors.

- By better aligning the motivation of their members and 'selecting' them accordingly, CoLKENs could reduce the negative influence of the competition dimension. On the other hand, ambitious growth strategies lead some CoLKENs to operate less selectively when it comes to assessing and aligning the motivation of their members.

Figure 3. Coordination and control mechanisms for knowledge management under coopetition

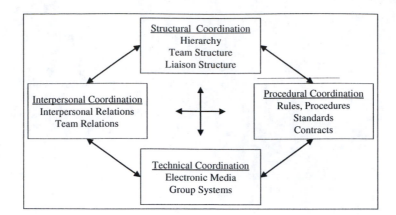

- Appropriate coordination and control mechanisms are crucial for success; structural and interpersonal mechanisms outweigh procedural or technical mechanisms (see Figure 3).

Additionally, for instance, Loebbecke and Angehrn (2003a, 2004), Teigland and Wasko (2003), and Loebbecke and Angehrn (2004) offer contingency-dependent results for various settings of Knowledge Management Under Coopetition.

Levers for Managing CoLKENs

With a significant number of inter-organizational networks failing in some sense (Inkpen & Beamish, 1997; Lam, 1997), there is an established body of literature investigating factors causing such failures together with steps for improvement (Cohen & Levinthal, 1990; Hamel, 1991; Mowery et al., 1996; Powell et al., 1996; Inkpen & Beamish, 1997; Lam, 1997; Dyer & Singh, 1998; Kumar & Nti, 1998; Larsson et al., 1998; Powell, 1998). Possible management levers for dealing with the paradox of simultaneous cooperation and competition have emerged from this literature. The main factors for discussion are: (1) factors influencing the extent of learning and knowledge sharing, (2) factors influencing the stability of the relationship, and (3) factors influencing the ability of CoLKEN partners to collaborate.

As factors influencing the extent of learning and knowledge sharing, Kogut (1988) and Mowery et al. (1996) name alliance contracts and governance structures. For instance, equity joint ventures lead to a higher degree of knowledge sharing than contract-based alliances. Cohen and Levinthal (1990), Dyer and Singh (1998), Kumar and Nti (1998), and Larsson et al. (1998) point to partners' internal capabilities. According to Hamel (1991), Kumar,

and Nti (1998), or Larsson et al. (1998), the amount of learning taking place in the relationship depends on each partner's collaborative strategy.

As the main factor influencing the stability of the relationship, Pfeffer and Salancik (1978) relate to bargaining power. If collaboration provides access to other partners' resources (e.g., knowledge and skills), dependencies caused by resource specificity may change or disappear, and the alliance may be terminated (Inkpen & Beamish, 1997). Hence partners who want to ensure alliance stability should prevent outsiders from learning "all there is to learn," create new knowledge, and consider the track record of their partners.

Finally, factors influencing the ability of network partners to collaborate are discussed. For Dyer and Singh (1998), appropriate management processes and governance structures are crucial for turning membership into a source of competitive advantage. They even suggest protection against: (a) opportunistic behavior in the network, (b) high volume of information exchange, (c) knowledge-sharing routines, and also suggest the development of self-enforcing safeguards (trust and incentives) for sharing. The ability to have influence on the network structure and to occupy an information-rich position shall provide network members with promising entrepreneurial opportunities (Powell et al., 1996).

FUTURE TRENDS

Further research is needed to compare traditional settings for Knowledge Management Under Coopetition, where there is less ICMT usage, with more virtual ones. Additional insights are to be sought as to the actual and potential impact of innovative technologies with regard to managing CoLKENs. One should investigate and assess: (a) the real potential of ICMT for the majority of today's CoLKENs, (b) the ICMT-related challenges the organizations in question are likely to face, as well as (c) the new mindsets and competencies members and managers of such networks will require for taking full advantage of distributed approaches to learning and knowledge management.

CONCLUSION

The fact that motivations and incentives for participation vary, makes Knowledge Management Under Coopetition particularly complex. Here CoLKENs as settings for Knowledge Management Under Coopetition represent opportunities for individual managers to engage in new forms of Knowledge Management Under Coopetition: They provide organizations with opportunities to better achieve their objectives through acquisition of knowledge critical to their processes and strategy, or through collaborative knowledge exchanges and initiatives.

Nevertheless, competitive logic can prevent individuals as well as organizations from taking advantage of constructive Knowledge Management Under Coopetition. The competition dimension influences the design of value-creation processes such as collaborative learning, knowledge exchange, and derived initiatives.

To conclude, innovative forms and settings of Knowledge Management Under Coopetition enable contributors to benefit from their participation in such inter-organizational knowledge management initiatives, whereby members may decisively improve learning efficiency and cooperative acting while taking into account competitive positions. To exploit the opportunities derived from Knowledge Management Under Coopetition to the fullest, appropriate coordination and control mechanisms, as well as a deliberate strategic approach towards Knowledge Management Under Coopetition are indispensable.

REFERENCES

Argote, L., McEvily, B., & Reagans, R. (2003). Managing knowledge in organizations: An integrative framework and review of emerging themes. *Management Science, 49*(4), 571-582.

Argyris, C., & Schön, D. (1996). *Organizational learning II.* Reading, MA: Addison-Wesley.

Barney, J.B. (1991). Types of competition and the theory of strategy: Towards an integrative framework. *Academy of Management Review, 11*(4), 791-800.

Barney, J.B. (2001). Is the resourced-based view a useful perspective for strategic management research? *Academy of Management Review, 26*(1), 41-56.

Boisot, M.H. (1995). *Information space: A framework for learning in organizations, institutions and cultures.* London: Routledge.

Boisot, M.H. (1998). *Knowledge assets: Securing competitive advantage in the information economy.* Oxford: Oxford University Press.

Brown, J.S., & Duguid, P. (1991). Organisational learning and communities-of-practice: Toward a unified view of working, learning and innovation. *Organization Science, 2*(1), 40-55.

Cabrera, Á. (2002). Knowledge-sharing dilemmas. *Organization Studies, 23*(5), 687-711.

Cohen, W.M., & Levinthal, D.A. (1990). Absorptive capacity: A new perspective on learning and innovation. *Administrative Science Quarterly, 35*(1), 128-152.

Crossan, M.H., Lane, H.W., & White, R.E. (1999). An organizational learning framework: From institution to institution. *Academy of Management Review, 24*(3), 522-537.

Child, J. (2001). Learning through strategic alliances. In M. Dierkes, B. Antal, J. Child, & I. Nonaka (Eds.), *Handbook of organizational learning and knowledge* (pp. 657-680). Oxford: University Press.

Doz, Y., Santos, J., & Williamson, P. (2001). *From international to metanational.* Cambridge, MA: Harvard Business School Press.

Doz, Y. & Hamel, G. (1998). *Alliance advantage.* Cambridge, MA: Harvard Business School Press.

Drucker, P. (1993). *The effective executive.* New York: Harper Business.

Dyer, J., & Nobeoka, K. (2000). Creating and managing a high performance knowledge sharing network: The Toyota case. *Strategic Management Journal, 21*(3), 345-367.

Dyer, J.H., & Singh, H. (1998). The relational view: Cooperative strategy and sources of interorganizational competitive advantage. *Academy of Management Review, 23*(4), 660-679.

Grant, R. (1996). Toward a knowledge based theory of the firm. *Strategic Management Journal, 17*(Special Issue), 109-123.

Grant, R., & Baden-Fuller, C. (2004). A knowledge accessing theory of strategic alliances. *Journal of Management Studies, 41*(1), 61-85.

C

Gulati, R., Nohria, N., & Zaheer, A. (2000). Strategic networks. *Strategic Management Journal, 21*(3), 203-215.

Hamel, G. (1991). Competition for competence and inter-partner learning within international strategic alliances. *Strategic Management Journal, 12*(Special Issue), 83-103.

Hamel, G., Doz, Y., & Prahalad, C. (1989). Collaborate with your competitors and win. *Harvard Business Review, 67*(1), 133-139.

Hedlund, G. (1994). A model of knowledge management and the n-form corporation. *Strategic Management Journal, 15*(Special Issue), 73-90.

Holmquist, M. (2003). A dynamic model of intra- and interorganizational learning. *Organization Studies, 24*(1), 95-123.

Huber, G. (1991). Organizational learning: The contributing processes and the literatures. *Organization Science, 2*(1), 88-115.

Inkpen, A., & Beamish, P. (1997). Knowledge, bargaining power, and the instability of international joint ventures. *Academy of Management Review, 22*(1), 177-202.

Inkpen, A.C. (2000). Learning through joint ventures: A framework of knowledge acquisition. *Journal of Management Studies, 37*(7), 1019-1043.

Itami, H. (1987). *Mobilizing invisible assets.* Cambridge, MA: Harvard University Press.

Klein, S. (1996). The configuration of inter-organisational relations. *European Journal of Information Systems, 5*(5), 92-102.

Kogut, B. (1988). Joint ventures: Theoretical and empirical perspectives. *Strategic Management Journal, 9*(4), 319-332.

Kogut, B., & Zander, U. (1996). What firms do? Coordination, identity, and learning. *Organization Science, 7*(5), 502-519.

Kumar, R., & Nti, K.O. (1998). Differential learning and interaction in alliance dynamics: A process and outcome discrepancy model. *Organization Science, 9*(3), 356-367.

Lam, A. (1997). Embedded firms, embedded knowledge: Problems of collaboration and knowledge transfer in global cooperative ventures. *Organization Studies, 18*(6), 973-996.

Lane, P.J., & Lubatkin, M. (1998). Relative absorptive capacity and interorganizational learning. *Strategic Management Journal, 19*(5), 461-477.

Larsson, R., Bengtsson, L., Henriksson, K., & Sparks, J. (1998). The interorganizational learning dilemma: Collective knowledge development in strategic alliances. *Organization Science, 9*(3), 285-305.

Liebeskind, J. (1996). Knowledge, strategy, and the theory of the firm. *Strategic Management Journal, 17*(Special Issue), 93-107.

Liebeskind, J., Oliver, A., Zucker, L. & Brewer, M. (1996). Social networks, learning, and flexibility: Sourcing scientific knowledge in new biotechnology firms. *Organization Science, 7*(4), 428-443.

Loebbecke, C., & Angehrn, A. (2003a). Investigating Coopetitive Learning and Knowledge Exchange Networks (CoLKENs) as emerging concept in management literature and practice. *Proceedings of the 4th Conference on Organizational Knowledge, Learning and Capabilities (OKLC)*, Barcelona, Spain.

Loebbecke, C., & Angehrn, A. (2004, July 1-3). Open source communities reflecting 'Coopetitive Learning and Knowledge Exchange Networks'. *Proceedings of the IFIP International Conference on Decision Support Systems (DSS2004)* (pp. 490-500), Prato, Italy.

Loebbecke, C., van Fenema, P., & Powell, P. (1999). Coopetition and knowledge transfer. *The Data Base for Advances in Information Systems (DATABASE), 30*(2), 14-25.

Loebbecke, C., & van Fenema, P. (2000). Virtual organizations that cooperate and compete: Managing the risks of knowledge exchange. In Y. Malhotra (Ed.), *Knowledge management and virtual organizations* (pp. 162-180). Hershey, PA: Idea Group Publishing.

Loebbecke, C., & Angehrn, A. (2003b, June 18-20). Open source platforms under coopetition: A comparative analysis of SourceForge and 'CodeX' (Xerox) as two 'Coopetitive Learning and Knowledge Exchange Networks' (CoLKENs). *Proceedings of the European Conference of Information Systems (ECIS)*, Naples, Italy.

Matusik, S., & Hill, C. (1998). The utilization of contingent work, knowledge creation, and competitive advantage. *Academy of Management Review, 23*(4), 680-697.

McDonald, S. (1995). Learning to change: An information perspective on learning in the organization. *Organization Science, 6*(2), 557-568.

McGaughey, S. (2002). Strategic interventions in intellectual asset flows. *The Academy of Management Review, 27*(2), 248-274.

Menon, T., & Pfeffer, J. (2003). Valuing internal vs. external knowledge: Explaining the preference for outsiders. *Management Science, 49*(4), 497-514.

Moingeon, B., & Edmondson, A. (1996). *Organisational learning and competitive advantage*. London: Sage Publications.

Mowery, D.C., Oxley, J.E., & Silverman, B.S. (1996). Strategic alliances and interfirm knowledge transfer. *Strategic Management Journal, 17*(Special Issue), 77-91.

Nonaka, I. (1994). A dynamic theory of organizational knowledge creation. *Organization Science, 5*(1), 14-37.

Nonaka, I., & Takeuchi, H. (1995). *The knowledge creating company*. New York: Oxford University Press.

Penrose, E. (1959). *Theory of the growth of the firm*. New York: John Wiley & Sons.

Pfeffer, J., & Salancik, G. (1978). *The external control of organizations: A resource dependence perspective*. New York: Harper & Row.

Polanyi, M. (1966). *The tacit dimension*. London: Routledge & Keegan Paul.

Porter, M. (1980). *Competitive strategy*. New York: The Free Press.

Powell, W. (1998). Learning from collaboration: Knowledge and networks in the biotechnology and pharmaceutical industries. *California Management Review, 40*(3), 228-240.

Powell, W., Kogut, K., & Smith-Doerr, L. (1996). Interorganizational collaboration and the locus of innovation: Networks of learning in biotechnology. *Administrative Science Quarterly, 41*(1), 116-145.

Prahalad, C., & Hamel, G. (1990). The core competence of the corporation. *Harvard Business Review, 68*(3), 79-91.

Prahalad, C., & Ramaswamy, V. (2000). Co-opting customer competence. *Harvard Business Review, 78*(1), 79-87.

Priem, R., & Butler, J. (2001a). Is the resourced-based view a useful perspective for strategic management research? *Academy of Management Review, 26*(1), 22-40.

Priem, R., & Butler, J. (2001b). Tautology in the resource-based view and the implications of externally determined resource value: Further comments. *Academy of Management Review, 26*(1), 57-66.

Roos, J., & Roos, G. (1996). Measuring your company's intellectual performance. *Long Range Planning, 30*(3), 413-426.

Rugman, M., & Verbeke, A. (2002). Edith Penrose's contribution to the resource-based view of strategic management. *Strategic Management Journal, 23*(8), 769-780.

Rumelt, R. (1987). Towards a strategic theory of the firm. In D. Teece (Ed.), *The competitive challenge* (pp. 556-570). Cambridge: Ballinger.

Senge, P. (1990). *The fifth discipline: The art and practice of the learning organization*. London: Sage Publications.

Simon, H. (1991). Bounded rationality and organizational learning. *Organization Science, 2*(1), 125-134.

Spender, J. (1996). Making knowledge the basis of a dynamic theory of the firm. *Strategic Management Journal, 17*(Special Issue), 45-62.

Suchmann, M.C. (1989). Invention and ritual: Notes on the interrelation of magic and intellectual property in preliterate societies. *Columbia Law Review, 89*(6), 1264-1294.

Teece, D. (1998). Capturing value from knowledge assets: The new economy, markets for know-how and intangible assets. *California Management Review, 40*(3), 55-79.

Teece, D., Pisano, G., & Shuen, A. (1997). Dynamic capabilities and strategic management. *Strategic Management Journal, 18*(7), 509-533.

Teigland, R., & Wasko, M. (2003). Integrating knowledge through information trading: Examining the relationship between boundary spanning communication and individual performance. *Decision Sciences, 34*(2), 261-287.

Tsang, E. (2002). Acquiring knowledge by foreign partners from international joint ventures in a transition economy: Learning-by-doing and learning myopia. *Strategic Management Journal, 23*(9), 835-854.

von Krogh, G., & Roos, J. (1995). *Organizational epistemology*. London: MacMillan.

Wernerfelt, B. (1984). A resource-based view of the firm. *Strategic Management Journal, 5*(2), 171-180.

KEY TERMS

CoLKEN: Coopetitive Learning and Knowledge Exchange Network, i.e., a specific setting for inter-organizational knowledge management initiatives focusing on issues related to cooperation-competition-dilemmas and intentional/unintentional knowledge transfer.

CoLKEN Construct: Structure of main CoLKEN components: At the base level are knowledge, knowledge agents, and knowledge networks; at the CoLKEN focus level, we find the balancing act between cooperation and competition, which should lead to value maximization on the top level.

CoLKEN Taxonomy: Depicting groups of CoLKENs by differentiating the overall variety along at least two dimensions. For practical and research purposes, the taxonomy shown in this article differentiates along the dimensions 'ICMT usage' and 'governance focus'.

Coopetition: Simultaneous existence and relevance of cooperation and competition.

Knowledge Agents: Individuals or organizations storing, retrieving, transferring, and applying/exploiting knowledge resources.

Knowledge-Based Perspective: Special form of resource-based perspective stressing the significance of knowledge as a scarce resource and organizational differentiator.

Knowledge Networks: Formally set-up mechanisms, structures, and behavioral patterns that connect knowledge agents who were not previously connected because of functional, hierarchical, or legal boundaries between organizations.

Corporate Semantic Webs

Rose Dieng-Kuntz
INRIA, ACACIA Project, France

INTRODUCTION

An organization is made up of people interacting for common objectives, in a given structure (may be rather formal in the case of a company, an administration, or an institution, or rather informal in the case of an interest community or a practice community), in an internal environment, and with an external environment.

Based on definitions of Grundstein (2004) and O'Leary (1998), we define knowledge management (KM) as the *"management of knowledge resources of an organization in order to ease:*

- *access, sharing, reuse of this knowledge (that can be explicit or tacit, individual or collective), with an objective of capitalization;*
- *creation of new knowledge, with an objective of innovation."*

Among the various approaches for KM, this article focuses on those aimed at knowledge capitalization and sharing. They can rely on the notion of corporate memory (or organizational memory (OM)) that, extending van Heijst's definition (1996), we define as the "explicit and persistent materialization of crucial knowledge and information of an organization in order to ease their access, sharing out and reuse by the members of the organization in their individual and collective tasks" (Dieng-Kuntz et al., 2001).

As such an OM relies on individuals interacting in an organization, with support of software tools, construction and management of a corporate memory require a multidisciplinary approach, taking into account at least three dimensions: (1) *individual* (memory must be compatible with users' cognitive models and their work environment), (2) *organization* (memory must be compatible with culture and strategy of the organization), and (3) *technology* (the chosen software tools must be adapted to the memory objectives and to the environment of future users).

This article will detail a particular approach of OM called the "corporate semantic Webs" approach, proposed by the Acacia team which the author deeply thanks.

BACKGROUND

From Knowledge-Based Systems to Knowledge Management

If the need of KM in enterprises has long been emphasized in management sciences (Grundstein, 2004), this notion started to be studied thoroughly at the beginning of the '90s by artificial intelligence researchers who had previously worked on expert systems and knowledge-based systems (KBSs), and had evolved towards knowledge engineering (KE): Steels (1993) was one of the first researchers in this community to stress the notion of corporate memory in order to promote knowledge growth, knowledge communication, and knowledge preservation in an organization; since 1993, the ISMICK conferences have been dedicated to these topics (Barthès, 1996). In 1996, the KE community emphasized the interest of OMs and its differences with regards to KBS: definitions were proposed (van Heijst, Van der Spek, & Kruizinga, 1996), as well as concrete examples (Dieng et al., 1996). Then several workshops at KAW, ECAI, IJCAI, and AAAI thoroughly studied methods and tools for building and using OMs (Dieng & Matta, 2002).

Ontologies and Knowledge Management

Meanwhile, the KE community was working on *ontologies* (Gruber, 1993). The Banff Knowledge Acquisition workshops (KAW)[1] enabled a better comprehension of foundations of ontologies (Guarino & Giaretta, 1995; Guarino, 1996). Researchers proposed tools for collaborative building of ontologies (Farquhar, Fikes, & Rice, 1996; Domingue, 1998; Tennison & Shadbolt, 1996), as well as concrete, huge ontologies in KM large applications (Swartout et al., 1996; Golebiowska, Dieng, Corby, & Mousseau, 2001). Moreover, some researchers on ontologies emphasized the interest of ontologies for KM (Benjamins, Fensel, & Gómez-Pérez, 1998a; Dieng et al, 2001).

The (KA)² initiative (Benjamins et al., 1998b) was a significant example of collaborative building of an ontology and of semantic annotations by the knowledge acquisition community.

Knowledge Management Based on Ontologies and Documents

The evolution from KBS to KM was based on the idea that a corporate memory could be naturally materialized in a knowledge repository without any reasoning aims; therefore ontologies seemed to be a quite natural way to make the conceptual vocabulary shared by an organization explicit. But this evolution led to recognition that the most frequent knowledge sources that could be integrated in an OM were documents. The need for a link between documents (considered as informal knowledge sources) and knowledge bases/ontologies (expressing formal knowledge) was emphasized by research that associated to a document a knowledge base aimed at making the underlying semantics of the document explicit and at improving information retrieval by reasoning on this knowledge base (Martin, 1997; Euzenat, 1996). The advent of XML led several KM researchers to rely on XML-based formalisms and on the future semantic Web (Rabarijaona, Dieng, Corby, & Ouaddari, 2000; Martin & Eklund, 2000). Shoe (Luke, Spector, Rager, & Hendler, 1997) and Ontobroker (Fensel, Decker, Erdmann, & Studer, 1998) offered an ontology-guided information retrieval approach; community semantic portals were developed using such tools (Staab et al., 2000).

Knowledge Management and the Semantic Web

The interest of the Web for KM and knowledge distribution over the Internet, either through an intranet or through the open Web, was stressed by O'Leary (1997), by the KAW'98 track on "Knowledge Management and Distribution over the Internet,"² as well as some special issues of journals (Dieng, 2000) and books (Schwartz, Divitini, & Brasethvik, 2000).

In 1998, Berners-Lee proposed his vision of the semantic Web:

The Web was designed as an information space, with the goal that it should be useful not only for human-human communication, but also that machines would be able to participate and help. One of the major obstacles to this has been the fact that most information on the Web is designed for human consumption, and...that the structure of the data is not evident to a robot browsing the Web. Leaving aside the artificial intelligence problem of training machines to behave like people, the Semantic Web approach instead develops languages for expressing information in a machine processable form.

He gave a roadmap for evolving "from the Web of today to a Web in which machine reasoning will be ubiquitous and devastatingly powerful" (Berners-Lee, 1998).

Several research communities (database, intelligent systems (Schwartz, 2003), knowledge engineering and knowledge representation, information retrieval, language technologies, distributed artificial intelligence and multi-agent systems, machine learning, Computer-Supported Collaborative Work, etc.) recognized in this ambitious objective a fabulous potential application of their research.

Last, the importance of social networks in which interactions and cooperation could be enhanced through the Web explains the privileged role of the semantic Web as a basis for supporting such networks, in particular with participants distributed geographically.

European Projects on Knowledge Management and the Semantic Web

Several collaborative European or national projects studied semantic Web approaches for KM:

- The C-WEB³ (Community Webs) project (Christophidès, 2000) proposed an infrastructure for Web portals in user communities requiring efficient query answering using various information sources. This infrastructure, aimed at semantic portals, can be seen as an architecture for a community semantic Web.
- The On-to-Knowledge⁴ project (Davies, Fensel, & van Harmelen, 2002) offered languages—such as OIL (Fensel et al., 2000), one precursor of OWL—methods, and tools aimed at applying ontologies to electronically available information for improving KM quality in large, distributed organizations.
- The CoMMA⁵ (Corporate Memory Management through Agents) project (Gandon, Dieng-Kuntz, Corby, & Giboin, 2002) developed an ontology (O'CoMMA), as well as a *multi-agent system* for managing a distributed corporate memory materialized in a corporate semantic Web, some agents having machine learning capabilities.
- The British AKT (Advanced Knowledge Technologies) project (Shadbolt & O'Hara, 2004) relies on an integrated approach, combining artificial intelligence, psychology, linguistics, multimedia, and Internet technology, for developing the next generation of knowledge technologies in order to support

organizational KM, from acquiring and maintaining knowledge, to publishing and sharing it.

- OntoWeb[6] (Ontology-Based Information Exchange for Knowledge Management and Electronic Commerce) network studies thouroughly techniques and methodologies for building and using ontologies in the framework of the semantic Web.

The convergence of all these research topics led to the idea of the corporate semantic Web, which the next section will explain more precisely.

MAIN FOCUS OF THE ARTICLE

The *corporate semantic Web* approach proposed by the Acacia team relies on the analogy between Web resources and corporate memory resources. Intranets or IntraWebs, based on Web technologies, are a widely used means of information diffusion aimed at improving information and knowledge sharing out in enterprises. As the Web users, members of an organization need to access competent persons, to retrieve relevant information in documents, to discover useful services, and to communicate or publish in order to share specific knowledge.

The semantic Web aims at making semantic contents of Web resources understandable, not only by humans, but also by programs, for a better cooperation among humans and machines, according to Berners-Lee's vision (Berners-Lee, Hendler, & Lassila, 2001). The most popular approach consists of making semantic annotations on Web re-

sources explicit, such annotations being represented in the RDF language recommended by W3C.

Our hypothesis is that the social Web constituted by all actors interacting in an organization could be supported by a KM system materialized in an organization-wide web inspired by the World Wide Web. The importance of semantics of the concepts to be handled leads naturally to a corporate semantic Web, inspired by the semantic Web, but at the scale of the organization.

Therefore, we propose to materialize a corporate memory through *a corporate semantic Web* (or organizational semantic Web) consisting of:

- **Resources:** These can be documents (in various formats such as XML, HTML, or even classic formats), but these resources can also correspond to people, services, software, or programs.
- **Ontologies:** Describing the conceptual vocabulary shared by one or several communities in the company.
- **Semantic Annotations on Resources:** Contents of documents, skills of persons, or characteristics of services/software/programs, based on these ontologies, with diffusion on the intranet or the corporate Web.

However, a corporate semantic Web has some specificities with regards to the Semantic Web. The fact that an organization is bounded allows an easier agreement on a corporate policy, an easier creation of ontologies and annotations, an easier verification of validity and

Figure 1. Architecture of a corporate semantic Web

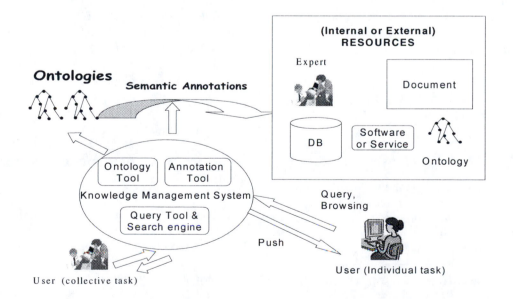

Figure 2. Method of construction of a corporate semantic Web

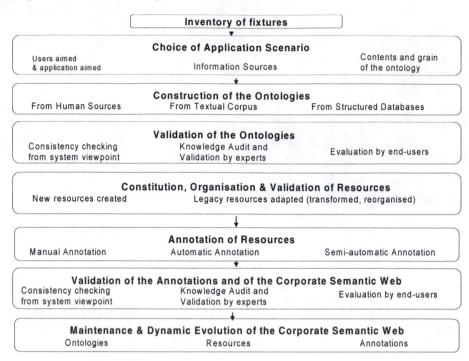

reliability of information sources, a description of more precise user profiles, and a smaller scale for corporate documents and for ontologies. But an organization has security and confidentiality constraints, as well as a need to rely on stable tools or standard languages, compatible with the internal work environment.

Figure 1 shows the architecture of a corporate semantic Web, and Figure 2 summarizes our method for building it. Researchers study how to build, represent, use, and evolve each component of the system and the links among such components. After stressing the actors involved, we will analyze the components of a corporate semantic Web (resources, ontologies, annotations).

COMPONENTS OF A CORPORATE SEMANTIC WEB

The Actors

We distinguish several roles among the involved actors:

- The *knowledge holders* or *authors of resources* (for example, authors of documents, software, or services constituting the memory resources).
- The *end-users*: The objective of annotations is to allow end-users to retrieve resources ("pull") or to

disseminate these resources towards end-users in a proactive way ("push"), in a more precise and relevant way in both cases.
- The *annotators*, who can be either knowledge holders or mediators (such as documentation centers). They must annotate resources in order to ease their retrieval by the future memory users. These annotations must thus take into account, on the one hand, the semantics aimed by the authors, and on the other hand, the users' needs for search for information. Objective annotations correspond to an interpretation common to any user, whereas subjective annotations are related to interpretation by a particular reader. As the annotator cannot guess all possible uses of the resources and all the future users' needs, s/he can collect information about profiles of the intended users and about their work contexts.

Resources in a Corporate Semantic Web

One can regard as resource any human, documentary, or software entity that can possibly be considered as a knowledge source thanks to its interpretation by a human accessing this resource. Resources can be documents with various formats (classic formats or formats dedicated to the Web like XML, HTML), but they can also correspond to people (in the case of a memory aimed at easing access to knowledge holders), services, software, programs, databases (DBs), ontologies, knowledge bases (KB), case bases, and so forth. According to the granularity chosen, the elementary resource enabling access to a knowledge element can consist of an entire document or of an element of document, of a whole database or of a DB record, of a whole KB or of a rule, and so forth, provided that this element is identifiable and can be referred.

Resources can be internal or external to the organization: for example, in a technological watch scenario, the semantic annotations of external resources useful for some employees can be considered as part of the corporate semantic Web.

Ontologies in a Corporate Semantic Web

An ontology is the explicit specification of a conceptualization according to Gruber (1993), or more precisely, according to Borst (1997), the formal specification of a shared conceptualization. We can characterize an ontology by:

- its *root concepts,* indicating the principal semantic axes or points of view considered;
- its *concepts*: each concept can be characterized by the terms enabling to designate it, its informal definition in natural language, its formal definition in intension in the case of a defined concept, its attributes, and its possible relationships with other concepts (parents, brothers, or concepts to which it is connected by a relation);
- the *structure of the ontology*: subsumption link enables the structuring of a concept hierarchy (resp. a relation hierarchy), part-of link enables structuring of a partonomy of concepts;
- possible *relations* between concepts, with the signatures of these relations;
- the *instances of concepts* when they play an ontological part (such as, for example, some constants in a mathematical or physical field: e.g., π, c, g);
- the *axioms* on concepts and relations.

The roles of an ontology in an OM are varied (Gandon, Dieng-Kuntz, Corby & Giboin, 2002):

- The ontology can be a *component of the memory*, a component aimed at being browsed by the end-user: in this case, natural language definitions or explanatory texts understandable for a human user must be associated to concepts and relations of the ontology. Moreover, the ontology contents must

be adapted to users' tasks—at grain level, detail level, visibility level, and so forth.

- The ontology can be a *reference for indexing/ annotating semantically the memory in order to improve resource retrieval or information retrieval in the memory*. In this case, the ontology must include concepts significant for annotation (e.g., *User, Competence, Organization, Document, Task, Project, Domain)*, so as to enable annotation of the resources of the memory (e.g., *This resource is a document of this type, created by someone having this competence in this department of the organization, related to these domain concepts and useful for this type of user in the framework of this task in the context of this project)*, and then reuse these annotations and the ontology in order to make inferences for information retrieval.

- Finally, the ontology can be a *basis for communication and exchange of information among programs or among software agents*. In this case, a formal ontology (with an accurate, non-ambiguous meaning), represented in the formal language of the messages exchanged by these agents, is needed. The content of the ontology must correspond to the needs in messages of the software agents that must be able to handle it formally.

When the OM is materialized in a corporate semantic Web, the situation corresponds to the second case since the ontology must at least be used for semantic annotation of memory resources. However, as we stressed in the previous section, ontologies can also form part of the memory resources, and they can also be annotated semantically.

In the three cases, it is necessary to choose ontology contents (i.e., its domain and its level of granularity), as well as its method of construction and evolution. The following sections will study more thoroughly these two points.

Contents of the Ontology

The applicative objective can help to choose the degree of granularity of the ontology: the contents of an *Automobile* ontology intended to be used by a design engineer working in the drawing office of a car manufacturer will be different from the *Automobile* ontology for an accidentologist analyzing road accidents.

Knowledge on the future users or on applications in which the ontology will be integrated can thus be useful to determine whether it is relevant to integrate a given concept, and can help to choose the adequate width and depth of the ontology.

If the ontology plays the role of a reference for annotating the memory elements semantically, it can be compared with an index on the memory. But, instead of the terms of an index or of a thesaurus, a semantic annotation by the ontology allows to associate to an element of the memory concepts, relations, instances, or particular relations between instances. Moreover these annotations can relate to an elementary resource which can, according to the case, consist of an entire document or of an element of document.

In this case, the criterion to build the ontology will be the answer to the question: *By which concepts/relations/ instances will the annotator need to annotate the resource in order to ease the retrieval of this resource in the most relevant way?*

In the OM scenario, the intended user type or even the use context can be helpful for this purpose:

- In a scenario of *project memory*, concepts allowing description of a project and its organization, its participants, its tasks, problems encountered and possible solutions, lessons learned in the project, and concepts of the project domain will be useful to integrate in the ontology. The SAMOVAR application (Golebiowska, Dieng, Corby & Mousseau, 2001) illustrates such a scenario of project memory. In this scenario—in the context of design of new car—an engineer of a car manufacturer tries to solve a problem encountered on a given part of the vehicle designed, and s/he tries to retrieve in past projects whether the same problem (or a similar one) occurred, which solutions were considered, and which one was adopted for solving it. S/he will then be able either to reuse this solution (perhaps after adapting it) or, if the change of context makes reuse of this solution impossible, to study whether one of the other solutions previously evoked and eliminated would be convenient to be used or adapted.

- In a scenario of *skills management* (Benjamins et al., 2002), the ontology can include the concepts allowing description of various types of competences (technical, organizational, social, or relational skills) and their links with various functions or tasks within the organization.

- In a scenario of *support to a newcomer integration*, the ontology can be based on the needs of a newcomer and on all the actors likely to interact with this newcomer; the ontology can, for example, describe the types of documents having to be consulted by a newcomer or to be used by a mentor/tutor, those describing the organization, and those useful for the Human Resources department. The ontology will be able to also include some concepts of the domain (for example, technical concepts useful for the activity of the newcomer or concepts s/he must learn to master). The CoMMA application (Gandon, Dieng-Kuntz, Corby & Giboin, 2002) illustrates such a scenario.

- In a scenario of *e-learning*, the ontology can rest on the needs of training for acquiring the competences required in the various functions of the company, on the teaching approaches to use, on the profiles of the students, or of the people/companies likely to carry out teaching, on the available e-learning tools, on the possible uses of the Web as exchange medium, on the educational resources. The MEMORAE application (Abel et al., 2004) illustrates this scenario of e-learning.

- In a scenario of *watch (i.e., scientific, strategic, or technological monitoring, business intelligence)*, concepts allowing description of the actors involved in the watch process of the company, as well as concepts on the relevant domain and all those likely to be watch targets, could be included in the ontology (Cao, Dieng-Kuntz, & Fiès, 2004). For example, in a scenario in the pharmacological sector, the watch department analyzes all documents on published patents of their competitors in order to detect new significant trends of research (confirming their own research strategy or to take into account in this strategy).

The ontology creation depends on the modeling choices and rests on several actors: ontologist, experts serving as knowledge sources, experts taking part in the validation. Some modeling choices will also be influenced by the future application and by the future users of the ontology (either those who will consult it directly, or those who will seek resources annotated through it). Thus the ontology must be viewed as the result of a construction process, via a negotiation between several actors: ontologist, experts, and users.

Construction of the Ontology

The ontology construction methodology can be inspired by manual methods of ontology development from experts (Gómez-Pérez, Fernández-López, & Corcho, 2004; Uschold & Gruninger, 1996) or by methods based on corpus analysis (Aussenac, Biébow, & Szulman, 2000; Bachimont, Isaac, & Troncy, 2002).

The construction of the ontology can be manual, semi-automatic from textual corpora, or semi-automatic from a structured database.

Manual Construction

The method of construction of ontologies proposed in Gandon (2002) and Gandon et al. (2002) for building an ontology in the framework of a corporate semantic Web relies on the following phases:

- *collection of data and scenarios,* starting from discussions with some knowledge holders and through manual analysis of documents provided by the company, without use of natural language processing tools;
- *terminological phase,* allowing to determine terms associated with concepts and to solve terminological conflicts (cf., a case where different concepts are designated by the same terms or a case where several terms refer to the same concept);
- *structuring of the ontology,* through specialization links between concepts or relations;
- *validation by experts;*
- *formalization in an ontology representation language* (such as the languages recommended by W3C). According to the expressivity degree needed, one can use RDF(S) (Lassila & Swick, 1999) for basic ontologies, or OWL (Dean & Schreiber, 2004; McGuinness & van Harmelen, 2004) and one of its layers, OWL-Lite, OWL-DL, or Full OWL, for more expressive ontologies.

This method allows development of an ontology by possibly structuring it in several levels:

- a high level including abstract concepts, very reusable but not very usable by end-users in their daily work, and thus needing to be hidden when the end-user browses the ontology;
- an intermediate level comprising concepts useful for the OM scenario and for the domain considered, and thus reusable for these scenarios and similar domains;
- a specific level including concepts specific to the company and thus very useful for end-users, but not very reusable apart from this company.

The O'CoMMA ontology (Gandon, 2002), dedicated to two scenarios of corporate memory (support to integration of a new employee at T-Systems Nova, and support to technological monitoring at CSELT and at CSTB) is thus structured in three such levels.

Semi-Automatic Construction from Textual Sources

The methodology of *ontology construction from texts* proposed by the TIA group[7] and described in Aussenac-Gilles et al. (2000) consists of the following stages:

- *Set up of the textual corpus,* taking into account the aims of the application.
- *Linguistic analysis,* consisting of choosing and applying to this textual corpus the adequate linguistic tools such as: (a) term extractors allowing to propose candidate terms, (b) relation extractors allowing to propose relations between these terms, (c) synonym managers allowing to detect synonym terms, and so forth.
- *Normalization* includes two phases:
  - *Linguistic normalization*: Allows the knowledge engineer to choose among the terms and lexical relations extracted previously, those which will be modeled in the ontology. The knowledge engineer will associate to each term and relation kept, a definition in natural language, if possible close to the text in the corpus. If a term or a relation has several meanings in the domain (i.e., polysemy), the knowledge engineer decides which meanings attested by the corpus will be kept because of their relevance.
  - *Conceptual modeling*: Semantic concepts and relations are then defined in a normalized form using labels of concepts and relations already defined.
- *Formalization* consists of ontology construction and validation. Existing ontologies can help to build the ontology top level and to structure it through main sub-domains. Semantic concepts and relations are then formalized and represented in chosen knowledge representation formalism (for example, description logics or conceptual graphs). If needed, additional concepts (i.e., structuring concepts, not necessarily attested by the textual corpus) can be added to structure the ontology. In a corpus-based approach, the terminological concepts (attested in texts) are distinguished from the other concepts (created by the ontologist in order to gather, factorize information, or structure the ontology). A complete validation can be carried out as soon as the ontology reaches a stable state.

This method was, for example, adapted for a vehicle project memory, within the framework of the SAMOVAR project (Golebiowska, Dieng, Corby & Mousseau, 2001), whose objective was to capitalize knowledge on problems encountered during a vehicle design project.

Semi-Automatic Construction from a Structured Database

One can also start from a structured database to translate it into an ontology represented in a standard representation formalism. The translation algorithm will depend on the database internal format, but the generic idea of building an ontology by decoding a database—the principle of coding of which is known—and to represent this ontology in a standard knowledge representation formalism, is interesting for companies having DBs from which they wish to reconstitute an ontology. This semi-automatic construction of ontologies from DBs is illustrated with the example of the *Life Line* project (Dieng-Kuntz et al., 2004), aimed at developing an organizational semantic Web dedicated to a medical community cooperating in the context of a healthcare network. By using an approach of "reverse engineering" relying on the analysis of its coding principle, Nautilus medical database was decoded to reconstitute a Nautilus ontology represented in RDF(S): the ontology could then be browsed and validated via a semantic search engine, and used for annotating and retrieving documents, and so forth.

Annotations in a Corporate Semantic Web

The construction of annotations relies on the ontology. The choice of grain of resource elements depends on the level to which the user needs to access the OM.

If one compares ontology-based semantic annotation with traditional indexing in information retrieval, their roles are similar, but the hierarchy of concepts, the relations, as well as the presence of axioms, allows several possibilities of reasoning: ontology-guided information retrieval enables retrieval of resources in a more relevant way (Fensel et al., 1998; Dieng et al., 2001; Corby & Faron, 2002; Corby, Dieng-Kuntz, & Faron-Zucker, 2004). An annotation is interpreted as: *"This resource speaks about such concept, speaks about such instance of concept, expresses such relation between such concepts or such instances of concepts."* One could be more precise and indicate the nature of annotation relation: some annotations can be viewed as argumentations, examples, assertions, and so forth.

For the construction of these annotations, one can use manual annotation editors or semi-automatic *annotation tools* such as those described in Handschuh and Staab (2003).

The user can then retrieve resources of the corporate semantic Web, which offers *semantic browsing* or *semantic querying* capabilities, based on resource annotations related to the ontology. There may also be specific annotations on user profiles and centers of interest if the ontology comprises concepts describing types of profiles or of interest centers. Semantic search engines such as Ontobroker (Fensel, Decker, Erdmann & Studer, 1998), WebKB (Martin & Eklund, 2000), or Corese (Corby, Dieng, & Hébert, 2000; Corby & Faron, 2002; Corby, dieng-Kuntz & Faron-Zucker, 2004) are useful to carry out such a search guided by ontologies. The interest of the ontology is to guide reasoning: this reasoning is based either on concept hierarchy or improvement in answers to users' queries. For example, for a request to retrieve patients suffering from a stomach disease, these reasoning capabilities enable a semantic search engine to retrieve a patient who had a surgery for a stomach cancer.

LANGUAGES AND TOOLS USEFUL FOR CREATING CORPORATE SEMANTIC WEBS

For representing semantic annotations of a corporate semantic Web, one can use RDF (Resource Description Format), a language recommended by the W3C for creating metadata for describing Web resources (Lassila & Swick, 1999). For representing ontologies, according to the expressivity level needed, one can use RDF Schema (RDFS) for simple ontologies or, for more complex ontologies, OWL (Ontology Web Language) (Dean & Schreiber, 2004; McGuinness & van Harmelen, 2004)—the ontology representation language recommended by W3C and intended for publishing and sharing ontologies on the Web.

Several tools can support building, use, and maintenance of a corporate semantic Web:

- **Ontology development tools,** enabling creation of a new ontology from scratch or modification of an existing ontology: e.g., Protégé (Noy, Fegerson, & Musen, 2000), KAON (Volz, Oberle, Staab, & Motik, 2003), WebODE (Arpirez et al., 2003).
- **Annotation tools,** enabling manual or semi-automatic semantic annotations on resources (e.g., instances of concepts and of relations)—for example, MnM (Vargas-Vera et al., 2002) or OntoMat-Annotizer (Handschuh, Staab, & Mäedche, 2001).
- **Ontology-guided information retrieval tools,** allowing retrieval of resources using their ontology-based annotations. Examples include semantic search engines such as Ontobroker (Fensel, Decker, Erdmann & Studer, 1998) or Corese (Corby et al.,

2000; Corby & Faron, 2002; Corby et al., 2004), or semantic browsers such as Magpie (Dzbor, Domingue, & Motta, 2003).
- **Multi-agent platforms,** enabling the handling of distributed corporate semantic Webs—for example, tools described in Gandon (2002), and van Elst, Dignum, and Abecker (2003).

The interested reader can find a detailed description of several of such tools in Gomez-Pérez, Fernández-Lopez & Corcho (2004).

FUTURE TRENDS

Research needs to be performed on the construction, management, and evolution of the different elements of a corporate semantic Web. The most important topics seem to be:

- **Maintenance and dynamic evolution of a corporate semantic Web:** More specifically, how do we tackle the problems linked to evolution of ontologies, of resources, and of annotations (Klein, 2004; Stojanovic, 2004)?
- **Validation of knowledge included in a CSW:** Integrity and coherence of the corporate semantic Web (i.e., of the ontology and of the annotations, both after their creation and when they evolve), human validation by experts and evaluation by end-users.
- **Automation in the construction of ontologies and of annotations:** Progress is needed in ontology and annotation learning, using machine learning techniques, statistical or linguistic techniques.
- **Heterogeneity:** Integration of heterogeneous sources in a corporate semantic Web, management of multiple ontologies in a single organization/community or in several organizations/communities, management of multiple, contextual annotations according to multiple viewpoints, building and management of interoperable inter-organizations or inter-communities semantic Webs.
- **Multimedia resources:** Capability to handle multimedia resources and to create semi-automatically semantic annotations on multimedia resources (images, sound, video, etc.).
- **Distribution:** Large, distributed organizations/communities; intelligent agents, peer-to-peer architectures.
- **Semantic Web services:** Since Web services can play the role of resources annotated in a corporate semantic Web, current research on ontology-guided description, discovery, and composition of semantic Web services is useful.

- **Human factors:** Participative design of corporate semantic Webs, taking into account all stakeholders, analysis of social interactions/collaboration through a corporate semantic Web, personalization of interfaces to user, support to such interactions.
- **Human-machine interaction:** Research on ergonomic, intelligent, adaptive interfaces will be crucial for acceptance and usability of organizational semantic Webs.
- **Scalability:** Even if it is less crucial than for the open semantic Web, scalability is required for very large organizations or for watch scenarios in order to be able to handle a huge number of resources, huge ontologies, or huge annotation bases.
- **Reasoning and inference capabilities:** They may help offer a better personalization of interaction with users, according to their profiles.
- **Evaluation of a corporate semantic Web:** Knowledge valuation criteria need to be studied thoroughly (Giboin, Gandon, Corby, & Dieng, 2002; O'Hara & Shadbolt, 2001).

This research will naturally benefit from general research performed by several research communities on the (open) semantic Web, but it needs to be guided by an actual understanding of the KM needs of an organization or a community.

CONCLUSION

This article has illustrated the "corporate semantic Web" approach that enables us to guide information retrieval from corporate memory by ontologies and annotations. This approach can be applied in various scenarios: memory of a team, of a department, or of a project; strategic, scientific, and technological watch; skills management; collaborative work in a community of practice or in a virtual enterprise.

With joint collaboration of all research communities focusing on the semantic Web, of human factor specialists, of researchers in management sciences, instead of being "yet another technology for KM," corporate semantic Webs can be a natural and popular approach for supporting human social Webs dynamically created in (or between) organizations or communities.

REFERENCES

Abel, M.-H., Barry, C., Benayache, A., Chaput, B., Lenne, D., & Moulin, C. (2004). Ontology-based organizational memory for e-learning. *Education Technology & Society, 7*(3).

Arpírez, J.C., Corcho, O., Fernández-Lopez, M., & Gómez-Pérez, A. (2003). WebODE in a nutshell. *AI Magazine, 24*(3), 37-47.

Aussenac-Gilles, N., Biébow, B., & Szulman, S. (2000, October 2-6). Revisiting ontology design: A methodology based on corpus analysis. In R. Dieng & O. Corby (Eds.), Knowledge engineering and knowledge management: Methods, models and tools. *Proceedings of the 12th International Conference* (EKAW'2000) (pp. 172-188), Juan-les-Pins. Berlin: Springer-Verlag (LNAI 1937).

Bachimont, B., Isaac, A., & Troncy, R. (2002, October 1-4). Semantic commitment for designing ontologies: A proposal. In A. Gómez-Pérez & V.R. Benjamins (Eds.), Knowledge engineering and knowledge management. Ontologies and the semantic Web. *Proceedings of the 13th International Conference* (EKAW'2002) (pp. 114-121), Sigüenza, Spain, Berlin: Springer-Verlag (LNAI 2473).

Barthès, J.-P. (1996). ISMICK and knowledge management. In J.F. Schreinemakers (Ed.), *Advances in knowledge management: Organization competence and methodology* (vol. 1, pp. 9-13).

Benjamins, V.R., Fensel, D., & Gómez-Pérez, A. (1998a, October 29-30). Knowledge management through ontologies. In U. Reimer (Ed.), *Proceedings of the 2nd International Conference on Practical Aspects of Knowledge Management* (PAKM'98), Basel, Switzerland.

Benjamins, V.R., Fensel, D., Gómez-Pérez, A., Decker, S., Erdmann, M., Motta, E., & Musen, M. (1998b, April 18-23). Knowledge Annotation Initiative of the Knowledge Acquisition Community (KA)2. *Proceedings of the 11th Workshop on Knowledge Acquisition, Modeling and Management* (KAW'98), Banff, Canada. Retrieved from *http://ksi.cpsc.ucalgary.ca/KAW/KAW98/KAW98Proc.html*

Benjamins, V.R., López Cobo, J.M., Contreras, J., Castillas, J., Blasco, J., de Otto, B., Garcia, J., Blásquez, M., & Dodero, J.M. (2002, October 1-4). Skills management in knowledge-intensive organizations. In A. Gómez-Pérez & V.R. Benjamins (Eds.), Knowledge engineering and knowledge management. Ontologies and the semantic Web. *Proceedings of the 13th International Conference* (EKAW 2002) (pp. 80-95), Sigüenza, Spain. Berlin: Springer-Verlag (LNAI 2473).

Berners-Lee, T. (1998, September). Semantic Web road map. Retrieved from *http://www.w3.org/DesignIssues/Semantic.html*

Berners-Lee, T., Hendler, J., & Lassila, O. (2001). The semantic Web. *Scientific American,* (May 17).

Borst, W.N. (1997). *Construction of engineering ontologies.* Centre for Telematica and Information Technology, University of Twente, Esched, The Netherlands.

Cao, T.-D., Dieng-Kuntz, R., & Fiès, B. (2004, October 6-9). An ontology-guided annotation system for technology monitoring. *Proceedings of the IADIS International Conference* (WWW/Internet 2004), Madrid, Spain.

Christophides, V. (Ed.). (2000, September). *Community Webs (C-Webs): Technological assessment and system architecture.* Deliverable C-WEB-IST-1999-13479-D5.

Corby, O., Dieng, R., & Hébert, C. (2000, August 13-17). A conceptual graph model for W3C resource description framework. In B. Ganter & G.W. Mineau (Eds.), Conceptual structures: Theory, tools, and applications. *Proceedings of ICCS'2000* (pp. 468-482), Darmstadt, Germany. Berlin: Springer-Verlag (LNAI 1867).

Corby, O., Dieng-Kuntz, R., & Faron-Zucker, C. (2004, August 22-27). Querying the semantic Web with the CORESE search engine. In R. Lopez de Mantaras & L. Saitta (Eds.), *Proceedings of the 16th European Conference on Artificial Intelligence* (ECAI'2004) (pp. 705-709). Valencia, Spain. IOS Press.

Corby, O., & Faron, C. (2002, May). CORESE: A corporate semantic Web engine. *Proceedings of the International Workshop on Real World RDF and Semantic Web Applications at the 11th International World Wide Web Conference 2002,* Hawaii. Retrieved from *http://paul.rutgers.edu/~kashyap/workshop.html*

Davies, J., Fensel, D., & van Harmelen, F. (Eds.). (2002). *Towards the semantic Web: Ontology-driven knowledge management.* New York: John Wiley & Sons.

Dean, M., & Schreiber, G. (Eds.). (2004). OWL Web Ontology Language reference. W3C Recommendation, February 10, 2004. Retrieved from *http://www.w3.org/TR/owl-ref/*

Dieng, R. (Ed.). (2000). Special issue of *IEEE Intelligent Systems on Knowledge Management and the Internet.*

Dieng, R., Corby, O., Giboin, A., & Ribière, M. (1999). Methods and tools for corporate knowledge management. *International Journal of Human Computer Studies, 51,* 567-598. Academic Press. Also retrievable from *http://ksi.cpsc.ucalgary.ca/KAW/KAW98/KAW98Proc.html*

Dieng, R., Giboin, A., Amergé, C., Corby, O., Després, S., Alpay, L., Labidi, S., & Lapalut, S. (1996, November 9-14). Building of a corporate memory for traffic accident analysis. *Proceedings of the 10th Knowledge Acquisition for Knowledge-Based Systems Workshop* (KAW'96) (pp.

35.1-35.20), Banff, Canada. Retrieved from *http://ksi.cpsc.ucalgary.ca/KAW/KAW96/KAW96Proc.html*. Also in *AI Magazine* (1998), *19*(4), 80-100.

Dieng-Kuntz, R., Corby, O., Gandon, F., Giboin, A., Golebiowska, J., Matta, N., & Ribière, M. (2001). *Méthodes et outils pour la gestion des connaissances: Une approche pluridisciplinaire pour le knowledge management* (2ⁿᵈ ed.). Dunod.

Dieng-Kuntz, R., Minier, D., Corby, F., Ruzicka, M., Corby, O., Alamarguy, L., & Luong, P.-H. (2004, October). Medical ontology and virtual staff for a health network, In E. Motta et al. (Eds.), Engineering knowledge in the age of the semantic Web. *Proceedings of the 4th International Conference* (EKAW'2004) (pp. 187-202), Whittlebury Hall, UK.

Dieng-Kuntz, R., & Matta, N. (Eds.). (2002). *Knowledge management and organizational memories*. Kluwer Academic Publishers.

Domingue, J. (1998, April 18-23). Tadzebao and WebOnto: Discussing, browsing, and editing ontologies on the Web. *Proceedings of the 11th Workshop on Knowledge Acquisition, Modeling and Management* (KAW'98), Banff, Canada. Retrieved from *http://ksi.cpsc.ucalgary.ca/KAW/KAW98/KAW98Proc.html*

Domingue, J., Motta, E., Buckingham Shum, S., Vargas-Vera, M., Kalfoglou, Y., & Farnes, N. (2001, October 23-24). Supporting ontology driven document enrichment with communities of practice. *Proceedings of the ACM International Conference on Knowledge Capture* (KCAP) (pp. 30-37), Victoria, Australia.

Dzbor, M., Domingue, J., & Motta, E. (2003, October). Magpie: Towards a semantic Web browser. *Proceedings of the 2nd International Semantic Web Conference,* Sanibel Island, FL.

Euzenat, J. (1996, November 9-14). Corporate memory through cooperative creation of knowledge bases and hyper-documents. In B. Gaines & M. Musen (Eds.), *Proceedings of the 10th Knowledge Acquisition for Knowledge-Based Systems Workshop* (KAW'96) (pp. 36.1-36.18), Banff, Canada. Also retrievable from *http://ksi.cpsc.ucalgary.ca/KAW/KAW96/KAW96Proc.html*

Farquhar, A., Fikes, R., & Rice, J. (1996, November 9-14). The Ontolingua server: A tool for collaborative ontology construction. In B. Gaines & M. Musen (Eds.), *Proceedings of the 10th Knowledge Acquisition for Knowledge-Based Systems Workshop* (KAW'96) (pp. 44.1-44.19), Banff, Canada. Also retrievable from *http://ksi.cpsc.ucalgary.ca/KAW/KAW96/KAW96Proc.html*

Fensel, D., Decker, S., Erdmann, M., & Studer, R. (1998, April 18-23). Ontobroker or how to enable intelligent access to the WWW. *Proceedings of the 11th Workshop on Knowledge Acquisition, Modeling and Management* (KAW'98), Banff, Canada. Retrieved from *http://ksi.cpsc.ucalgary.ca/KAW/KAW98/KAW98Proc.html*

Fensel, D., Horrocks, I., van Harmelen, F., Decker, S., Erdmann, M., & Klein, M. (2000). OIL in a nutshell. In R. Dieng & O. Corby (Eds.), *Knowledge engineering and knowledge management: Methods, models and tools* (pp. 1-16). Berlin: Springer-Verlag (LNAI 1937).

Gandon, F. (2002). *Distributed artificial intelligence and knowledge management: Ontologies and multi-agent systems for corporate semantic Webs*. PhD Thesis, UNSA.

Gandon, F., Dieng-Kuntz, R., Corby, O., & Giboin, A. (2002, August 25-30). Semantic Web and multi-agents approach to corporate memory management. *Proceedings of the 17th IFIP World Computer Congress IIP Track* (pp. 103-115), Montréal, Canada.

Giboin, A., Gandon, F., Corby, O., & Dieng, R. (2002, September 30). Assessment of ontology-based tools: Systemizing the scenario approach. *Proceedings of the EKAW'2002 Workshop on Evaluation of Ontology-Based Tools* (EON'2002) (pp. 63-73), Sigüenza (Spain).

Golebiowska, J., Dieng, R., Corby, O., & Mousseau, D. (2001, October 23-24). Building and exploiting ontologies for an automobile project memory. *Proceedings of ACM International Conference on Knowledge Capture* (K-CAP) (pp. 52-59), Victoria, Australia.

Gómez-Pérez, A., Fernández-López, M., & Corcho, O. (2004). *Ontological engineering*. Berlin: Springer-Verlag.

Gruber, T.R. (1993). A translation approach to portable ontology specification. *Knowledge Acquisition, 5*(2), 199-220.

Grundstein, M. (2004). De la capitalisation des connaissances au management des connaissances dans l'entreprise. In I. Boughzala & J.L. Ermine (Eds.), *Management des connaissances en entreprise*. Hermès.

Grunstein, M., & Barthès, J.-P. (1996, October). An industrial view of the process of capitalizing knowledge. In J.F. Schreinemakers (Ed.), Knowledge management: Organization, competence and methodology. *Proceedings of the 4th International Symposium on the Management of Industrial and Corporate Knowledge* (ISMICK'96) (pp. 258-264), Rotterdam, The Netherlands. Ergon.

Guarino, N. (1996, November). Understanding, building, and using ontologies. *Proceedings of the 10th Knowledge Acquisition for Knowledge-Based Systems Work-*

shop (KAW'96), Banff, Canada. Retrieved from *http://ksi.cpsc.ucalgary.ca/KAW/KAW96/KAW96Proc.html*

Guarino, N., & Giaretta, P. (1995). Ontologies and knowledge bases: Towards a terminological clarification. In N. Mars (Ed.), *Towards very large knowledge bases: Knowledge building and knowledge sharing* (pp. 25-32), University of Twente. Enschede, The Netherlands: IOS Press.

Handschuh, S., Staab, S., & Mäedche A. (2001, October 23-24). CREAM—Creating relational metadata with a computer-based, ontology-driven annotation framework. *Proceedings of the ACM International Conference on Knowledge Capture* (KCAP) (pp. 76-83), Victoria, Canada. ACM Press.

Handschuh, S., & Staab, S. (Eds.). (2003). Annotation for the semantic Web. *Frontiers in Artificial Intelligence and Applications, 96.* IOS Press.

Klein, M. (2004). *Change management in distributed ontologies.* PhD Thesis, Vrije Universiteit, The Netherlands.

Lassila, O., & Swick, R.R. (1999). Resource Description Framework (RDF) model and syntax specification. W3C Recommendation, February 22, 1999. Retrieved from *http://www.w3.org/tr/rec-rdf-syntax/*

Luke, S., Spector, L., Rager, D., & Hendler, J.. (1997, February 5-8). Ontology-based Web agents. In W.L. Johnson (Ed.), *Proceedings of the 1st International Conference on Autonomous Agents* (Agents'97) (pp. 59-66), Association for Computing Machinery, New York.

Martin, P. (1997, August 3-8). CGKAT: A knowledge acquisition and retrieval tool using structured documents and ontologies. In D. Lukose, H. Delugach, M. Keeler, L. Searle, & J. Sowa (Eds,), Conceptual structures: Fulfilling Peirce's dream. *Proceedings of the 5th International Conference on Conceptual Structures* (ICCS'97) (pp.581-584), Seattle, Washington. Berlin: Springer-Verlag (LNAI 1257).

Martin, P., & Eklund, P. (2000). Knowledge retrieval and the World Wide Web. *IEEE Intelligent Systems, 15*(3), 18-25.

McGuinness, D.L.,& van Harmelen, F. (Eds). (2004, February 10). OWL Web Ontology Language overview. W3C Recommendation, February 10, 2004. Retrieved from *http://www.w3.org/TR/owl-features/*

Noy, N., Fegerson, B., & Musen, M. (2000, October 2-6). The knowledge model of Protégé-2000. In R. Dieng & O. Corby (Eds.), Knowledge engineering and knowledge management: Methods, models and tools. *Proceedings of*

the 12th *International Conference* (EKAW'2000) (pp. 17-32), Juan-les-Pins. Berlin: Springer-Verlag (LNAI 1937).

O'Hara, K., & Shadbolt, N. (2001, August 5). Issues for an ontology for knowledge valuation. *Proceedings of the IJCAI-01 Workshop on E-Business and the Intelligent Web,* Seattle. Retrievable from *http://www.csd.abdn.ac.uk/~apreece/ebiweb/programme.html*

O'Leary, D.E. (1997). The Internet, intranets and the AI renaissance. *Computer, 30*(1), 71-78.

O'Leary, D.E. (1998). Enterprise knowledge management. *Computer, 31*(3), 54-61.

Rabarijaona, A., Dieng, R., Corby, O., & Ouaddari, R. (2000). Building and searching an XML-based corporate memory. *IEEE Intelligent Systems and their Applications,* Special Issue on Knowledge Management and the Internet (May/June), 56-63.

Schwartz, D.G., Divitini, M., & Brasethvik, T. (Ed.). (2000). *Internet-based organizational memory and knowledge management.* Hershey, PA: Idea Group Publishing.

Schwartz, D.G. (2003). From open IS semantics to the semantic Web: The road ahead. *IEEE Intelligent Systems, 18*(3), 52-58.

Shadboldt, N., & O'Hara, K. (Eds.). (2004). *Advanced knowledge technologies.* Selected Papers, ISBN 85432 8122.

Staab, S., Angele, J., Decker, S., Erdmann, M., Hotho, A., Maedche A., Schnurr H.-P., Studer R., & Sure Y. (2000). Semantic community Web portals. *Computer Networks, 33*(1-6), 473-491.

Steels, L. (1993). Corporate knowledge management. *Proceedings of the International Symposium on the Management of Industrial and Corporate Knowledge* (ISMICK'93) (pp. 9-30), Compiègne, France.

Stojanovic, L. (2004). *Methods and tools for ontology evolution.* PhD Thesis, University of Karlsruhe, Germany.

Tennison, J., & Shadbolt, N.R. (1998, April 18-23). APECKS: A tool to support living ontologies. *Proceedings of the 11th Workshop on Knowledge Acquisition, Modeling and Management* (KAW'98), Banff, Canada. Retrieved from *http://ksi.cpsc.ucalgary.ca/KAW/KAW98/KAW98Proc.html*

Uschold, M., & Gruninger, M. (1996). Ontologies: Principles, methods and applications. *The Knowledge Engineering Review, 11*(2), 93-155.

van Elst, L., Dignum, V., & Abecker, A. (Eds.). (2003, March 24-26). Agent-mediated knowledge management.

Proceedings of the International Symposium of AMKM 2003, Stanford, CA. Berlin: Springer-Verlag (LNCS 2926).

van Heijst, G, Van der Spek, R., & Kruizinga, E. (1996, November). Organizing corporate memories. In B. Gaines & M. Musen (Eds.), *Proceedings of the 10th Knowledge Acquisition for Knowledge-Based Systems Workshop* (KAW'96) (pp. 42.1-42.17), Banff, Canada. Also retrievable from *http://ksi.cpsc.ucalgary.ca/KAW/KAW96/KAW96Proc.html*

Vargas-Vera, M., Motta, E., Domingue, J., Lanzoni, M., Stutt, A., & Ciravegna, F. (2002, October 1-4). MnM: Ontology driven semi-automatic and automatic support for semantic markup. In A. Gómez-Pérez & V.R. Benjamins (Eds.), Knowledge engineering and knowledge management. Ontologies and the semantic Web. *Proceedings of the 13th International Conference* (EKAW'2002) (pp. 379-190), Sigüenza, Spain. Berlin: Springer-Verlag (LNAI 2473).

Volz, R., Oberle, D., Staab, S., & Motik, B. (2003, May 20-24). KAON SERVER—A semantic Web management system. *Alternate Track Proceedings of the 12th International World Wide Web Conference* (WWW2003), Budapest, Hungary.

KEY TERMS

Corporate Semantic Web or Organizational Semantic Web: Semantic Web at the scale of a limited organization (e.g., a company, an institution, a community). It is composed of resources, ontologies, and ontology-based semantic annotations.

Inference: Capability to deduce new knowledge from existing knowledge.

Knowledge Management: Management of activities and processes aimed at amplifying the use and creation of knowledge on an organization with two complementary aims: a "patrimonial" objective and a durable innovation objective; these objectives are underlined by their economic, strategic, organizational, socio-cultural, and technological dimensions (Grundstein, 2004). Also, management of knowledge resources of an organization in order to ease:

- access, sharing, reuse of this knowledge (that can be explicit or tacit, individual or collective), with an objective of capitalization;
- creation of new knowledge, with an objective of innovation (Dieng-Kuntz).

Knowledge Sharing and Reuse: Capability to share knowledge resources among members of an organization and to reuse knowledge underlying such resources. This capability can be extended to privileged partners of the organization (customers, providers, collaborating partners, etc.).

Metadata: Data on data. Semantic Web metadata are data on Web resources and are often called semantic annotations, since they rely on ontologies and aim at representing underlying meaning of these resources or additional information about these resources (even not included in the resource itself).

Ontology: In the KE community, explicit specification of a conceptualization, according to Gruber (1993); formal specification of a shared conceptualization, according to Borst (1997); formal, explicit specification of a shared conceptualization of a domain of interest, according to Handschuh et al. (2001) that thus gathers the definitions of Gruber (1993) and Borst (1997); logical theory that gives an explicit, partial account of a conceptualization (Guarino & Giaretta, 1995). In KM context, ontologies enable description of conceptual vocabulary shared by a community in an organization (Dieng et al., 2001). Ontologies aim to capture consensual knowledge in a generic way, and they may be reused and shared across applications and by groups of people (Gómez Pérez et al., 2004).

Organizational Memory/Corporate Memory: Explicit, disembodied, persistent representation of knowledge and information in an organization» (van Heijst et al., 1996). For example, it may include knowledge on products, production processes, clients, marketing strategies, financial results, plans and strategic goals, and so forth. Also, explicit and persistent materialization of crucial knowledge and information of an organization in order to ease their access, sharing out, and reuse of the members of the organization in their individual and collective tasks (Dieng et al., 2001).

OWL (Ontology Web Language): Ontology representation language recommended by W3C, and intended for publishing and sharing ontologies in the Web. It comprises three layers: OWL Lite, OWL DL, and OWL Full.

Portal: Central entry point and infrastructure for enabling members of an organization/a community to share and exchange information via a Web-based interface. A portal can be internal (intended to the members of the organization) or external (aimed at the organization customers, partners, etc.). A semantic portal relies on an ontology-driven approach for semantic browsing, semantic querying, or semantic integration of the content (such as business content, corporate memory, etc.).

RDF (Resource Description Format): Language recommended by W3C for creating metadata for describing Web resources.

RDF Schema or RDFS: RDF Vocabulary Description Language, which provides the most basic primitives for ontology modeling.

Semantic Annotations: Ontology-based metadata on a Web resource. These may either correspond to the semantics underlying the resource or to information not contained in the resource. Semantic annotations can correspond to instances of concepts or of relations of an ontology. The process of semantic annotation aims to transform a human-understandable content into a machine-understandable content.

Semantic Web: Web where the semantic contents of Web resources are made understandable, not only by humans but also by programs, for a better cooperation among humans and machines (Berners-Lee).

XML: eXtensible Markup Language; meta-language for creating markup languages.

ENDNOTES

[1] http://ksi.cpsc.ucalgary.ca/KAW/

[2] http://ksi.cpsc.ucalgary.ca/KAW/KAW98/KAW98Proc.html

[3] http://cweb.inria.fr

[4] http://www.ontoknowledge.org/

[5] http://www.ii.atos-group.com/sophia/comma/HomePage.htm

[6] http://ontoweb.semanticweb.org/

[7] TIA (Terminologie et Intelligence Artificielle) is a French working group on Terminology and Artificial Intelligence

Creating Knowledge for Business Decision Making

Shiraj Khan
University of South Florida (USF), USA

Auroop R. Ganguly
Oak Ridge National Laboratory, USA

Amar Gupta
University of Arizona, Tucson, USA

INTRODUCTION

Business forecasts and predictive models are rarely perfect. A paraphrase of the Nobel winning physicist Neils Bohr is apt in this context: *Prediction is difficult, especially if it is of the future.* However, executives and managers in enterprises ranging from retail and consumer packaged goods to high tech and semiconductors have to resort to forecasting and planning about the future. Phenomenal growth and spectacular failures are associated with organizations depending on their ability to understand market directions and respond quickly to change. Relatively minor improvements in forecast accuracy and predictive modeling at detailed levels can translate to significant gains for the enterprise through better strategic decisions, continuous performance management, and rapid translation to tactical decisions. The key to these processes is the knowledge-based enterprise, which can effectively utilize information from multiple sources as well as the expertise of skilled human resources, to develop strategies and processes for creating, preserving, and utilizing knowledge. These efforts, spanning revenue-generation endeavors like promotion management or new product launch, to cost-cutting operations like inventory planning or demand management, have significant impacts on the top and bottom lines of an enterprise.

Advances in scalable mathematical model-building, ranging from advanced statistical approaches and data mining (DM) to operations research (OR) and data assimilation, can extract meaningful insights and predictions from large volumes of data. Information technologies and e-business applications can enable a degree of process automation and collaboration within and among enterprises. Enterprises of the new millennium can truly take

Figure 1. "One-number forecasting" for an enterprise

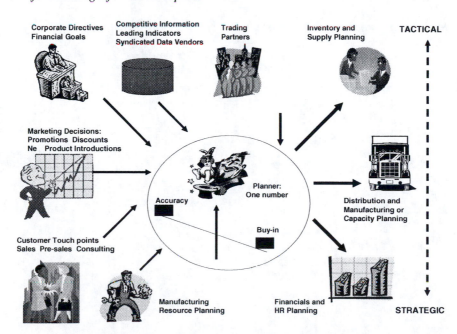

advantage of scalable but cutting-edge data-dictated approaches to understand the past and predict the future, and then focus valuable planner resources on key value drivers or exceptional situations through human-computer interaction, which in turn utilizes tools like online analytical processing (OLAP) and automated or planner-driven decision support systems (DSSs).

Analytic information technologies enable managers of the knowledge-based enterprise to choose the path to new revenues, new markets, good customer service, and competitive advantage over their rivals. The ability to produce "one-number forecasts" that reconcile information from multiple sources and blend disparate points of view is a critical first step for enterprise-scale strategic, operational, and tactical planning (see Figure 1). However, this is a challenging process, especially in recent years owing to short product lifecycles, mass customizations, and dynamic markets, combined with the ever-increasing service expectations of consumers and trading partners on the one hand, versus the need to reduce operating and inventory costs on the other. The need to manage product lifecycles and promotions or pricing decisions, factor in market signals or competitive intelligence, analyze consumer behavior, and achieve buy-in from multiple participants within and across enterprises has fundamentally changed the way the forecast generation process is perceived. Corporate data repositories, collaborative information technologies and processes, syndicated data vendors, and the Internet provide large volumes of historical and real-time information. The challenge is to acquire, manage, analyze, and reconcile the information for knowledge extraction and predictive purposes in an optimal fashion.

BACKGROUND

Data-derived knowledge adds value to a business through products, processes, and better decision making. Davis and Botkin (1994) describe six features of knowledge-based businesses. Manual analysis, evaluation, and interpretation are the most common approaches of creating knowledge from digital data. Volumes of information can grow rapidly, as every communication, interaction, and transaction produces new data. Thus, manual data analysis quickly becomes slow and inexpensive, and is becoming obsolete in applications like retail, telecommunication, health care, marketing, the natural sciences, and engineering. With the advent of analytical information technologies, researchers and engineers have been exploring the possibility of constructing data-dictated models by mining large-scale corporate or scientific data repositories. These approaches combine data management technologies and innovative computational or visualization methods with analytical techniques drawn from the diverse fields of statistics, machine learning, and artificial intelligence (Fayyad & Uthurusamy, 2002; Hand, Mannila, & Smyth, 2001). Many organizations have invested in automated analysis techniques (Ganguly, Gupta & Khan, 2005) to unearth meaningful patters and structures from millions of records with hundreds of attributes. Automated analytical approaches like data mining (DM) and statistics are combined with planner-driven analytic systems like decision support systems (DSSs) and business intelligence (BI) (see Figure 2). These are being integrated with transactions systems, producing insights into how effectively a company does business, responds to or forecasts trends, understands and reacts to market

Figure 2. Examples of technologies used for business planning and forecasting

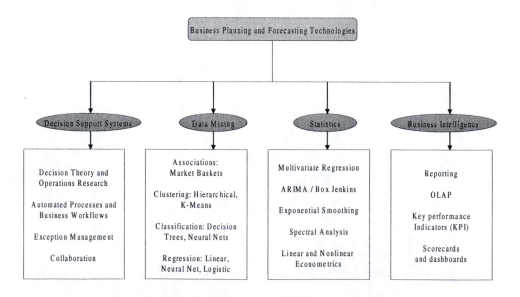

conditions, and develops customer-focused products and services. The knowledge mined from objective data and generated by human experts is encapsulated through adaptive information systems. This knowledge becomes an asset in current business conditions where supply-driven "push" of products and services has yielded to demand-driven "pull" as well as one-on-one or mass customizations. Management scientists (Aviv, 2001; Cachon & Lariviere, 2001; Chen, Drezner, Ryan, & Simchi-Levi, 2000; Lee & Whang, 1998) have theoretically demonstrated the value of collaborative forecasting on the supply chain and modeled the impact of information sharing among trading partners as well propagation of uncertainty (Gilbert, 2005). A research report by the analyst firm Gartner (Peterson, Geishecker, & Eisenfeld, 2003) indicated the opportunity, need, and confusions surrounding the generation of "one-number forecasts," and highlighted the "opportunity for intra-enterprise forecast improvement."

MAIN FOCUS OF THE ARTICLE: TOOLS AND PROCESSES FOR CREATING KNOWLEDGE FOR BUSINESS DECISION MAKING

Data Management

Data warehousing provides an infrastructure to process vast amounts of data, as well as discover and explore important business trends used for knowledge creation and decision making. Inmon (1992) and Kimball (1996) suggested a data warehouse that integrates data from diverse operational databases to aid in the process of decision making. A data warehouse is the first component of a knowledge system where all available information is acquired from online transactional processing (OLTP) sources, cleansed, stored and processed, and made available for use by knowledge creation systems like business planning and forecasting. The information might range from point of sales (POS) data for the retail industry, to income, marital status, location, demographics, and credit history for a financial or a phone company. A few key data warehousing activities include data cleaning or scrub-

Table 1. A taxonomy of data mining tasks (Shaw, Subramaniam, Tan, & Welge, 2001)

Dependency Analysis	*Concept Description*
• Associations • Sequences	• Summarization • Discrimination • Comparison
Class Identification • Mathematical taxonomy • Concept clustering	*Data Visualization* • Pixel oriented • Geometric projection • Graph based
Deviation Detection • Anomalies • Changes	

bing, data transformation, data condensation, data aggregation, data refreshing, data reporting, and metadata synchronization.

Planning and Forecasting Tools

Businesses need to react quickly to evolving market conditions, especially in these days of mass customizations, global competitions, and corporate consolidations. As early as 1999, Forrester Research and Meta Group reported that 30% of firms' data warehouses contained over one trillion characters of data worldwide (Bransten, 1999), and the total sum of data is increasing every hour. Creation of knowledge from this data efficiently through analytical information technologies, and utilizing the knowledge for driving business decisions quickly, is a key requirement.

Data mining (DM) refers to diverse technologies suited for extracting knowledge and insights from vast quantities of data in an efficient manner. Most DM tools use traditional statistical techniques coupled with highly efficient pattern recognition and machine learning algorithms (Breiman, Friedman, Olshen, & Stone, 1984; Ganguly, 2002; Quinlan, 1992). DM methods are used in conjunction with database-centric approaches for knowledge discovery in databases (KDD) (Fayyad, Shapiro, & Smyth, 1996). The type of knowledge created by DM and KDD tasks determines the categories into which these tasks are grouped together (Table 1). Heinrichs and Lim (2003) gave an insight into integrating Web-based DM tools with business models to understand changing customer requirements, monitor product performance, uncover market opportunity, and manage customer relationships in real-time. Web-based software tools help skilled knowledge workers identify and understand their competitors' strategy, thus preparing them to respond to potential competitive threat quickly (Lim, Heinrichs, & Hudspeth, 1999).

The ability to anticipate, react, and adapt to market trends and changes, through appropriate business strategies and implementation, are the characteristics of a successful company. Given the uncertainties inherent in the forecasting planners, some companies rely on the "gut feel" of senior decision makers and executives. However, as business conditions are getting more dynamic, it is becoming more and more important to continuously visualize and monitor the state of business through tools like DSS and BI, and to develop predictive modeling capabilities through tools like DM and KDD, for creating knowledge and insights about the future. Originally, the concept of DSS was provided by Gorry and Mortan (1971), who integrated Simon's description of decision types like unstructured, semi-structured, and structured (Simon, 1960) and Anthony's categories of

Figure 3. A new decision paradigm for DSS (Courtney, 2001)

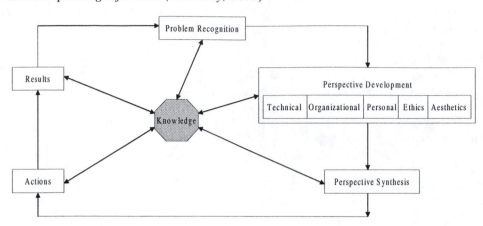

management activities like strategic planning, management control, and operational control (Anthony, 1960). Courtney (2001) described a new paradigm for DSS where a centralized knowledge model is influenced by every step of the process. The model recognizes the problem, creates perspectives to gain insight into the nature of the problem, finds its possible solutions, and continually updates itself. Today, a number of fields like database technologies, management science, operations research, cognitive science, AI, and expert systems (Bonczek, Holsapple, & Whinston, 1981), in addition to software engineering, assist in the design of DSSs. Management science and operations research tools like linear and nonlinear programming, optimization, Monte Carlo simulation, and dynamic programming help to develop mathematical models for use in model-driven DSSs. The use of the Internet and communication technology in DSSs allows organizations to become global and connects suppliers, producers, and customers through collaborative planning, forecasting, and replenishment (CPFR) processes. This helps to achieve full collaboration, develop and share "one-number forecasts" through the extended ("n-tier") supply chain, thus helping in the sales and operations planning (S&OP) process, improving forecasting accuracy, reducing inventory levels, improving customer service levels, designing effective promotions, and maximizing profits through revenue generation and cost cutting.

BI tools like querying or reporting are used to pull information from data stores and present it to end users in the language and structure of a specific business. Key performance indicators (KPIs) are used to monitor critical factors within the business on an ongoing basis. OLAP tools specify fast, consistent, and interactive ways of analyzing multidimensional enterprise data and providing end users analytical navigational activities to gain insights into the knowledge contained in large databases. Drill-down, slice-dice, reach-through, and rotation are the activities of OLAP used for many business applications,

including product performance and profitability, effectiveness of a sales program or a marketing campaign, and sales forecasting.

Planning and Forecasting Processes

Extract, transform, and load (ETL) tools extract data from heterogeneous sources like OLTP systems, syndicated data vendors, public domain sources like the Internet, legacy systems, real-time data repositories maintained by business analysts, decision makers, internal or external collaborators, consultants, and executives for business planning and forecasting (see Figure 4) applications (Gung, Leung, Lin, & Tsai, 2002; Peterson et al., 2003; Wang & Jain, 2003; Yurkiewicz, 2003). The data is crunched and transformed into a standard or desired format and then loaded into a data warehouse or a data mart. The data is further processed inside the data warehouse to make them available for online analysis and decision support. DM and KDD tools access the data from the data warehouse to discover new patterns and fit models to predict future behavior. The results of predictive models are presented and utilized in the form of structured business workflows, interactive formatted data models for visualization, graphic models (Pearl, 1988; Whittaker, 1990), planning cycles, and automated predictive and forecasting outputs which can be used as baselines by business planners and decision makers. DSS and BI tools like OLAP (Hammer, 2003) are utilized to interpret and evaluate predictive and forecasting models for creating knowledge about the future, which in turn helps analysts and decision makers to make strategic and tactical decisions.

Data Mining Technologies and Decision Support Systems

Managers and business planners use DMT to extract meaningful patterns about their business and customers

Figure 4. An overview of the steps involved in business planning and forecasting

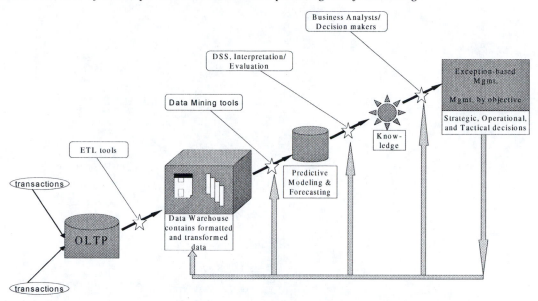

Figure 5. Inter-enterprise DSS in supply chain management

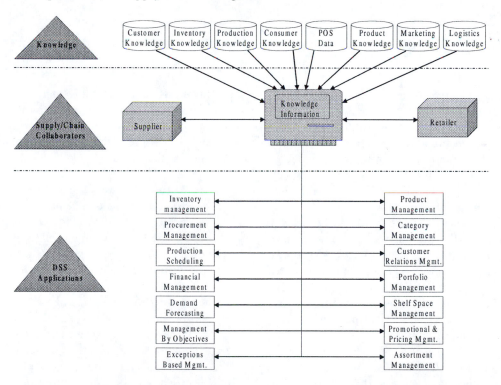

which can be interpreted as useful or interesting knowledge. Machine learning and pattern recognition algorithms, along with statistical methods like classification, clustering, and regression, are used to fit a model to data, to find structure from data, and derive high-level knowledge from the voluminous data present in the data warehouse.

Predictive and forecasting models generated by DM or KDD tools are interpreted and analyzed by business analysts, planners, and executives using DSS and BI tools to understand trends, manage metrics, align organizations against common goals, develop future strategy, and drive action. In this highly competitive world where different manufacturers offer the same category of products,

Figure 6. Intra-enterprise DSS in the CPG company.

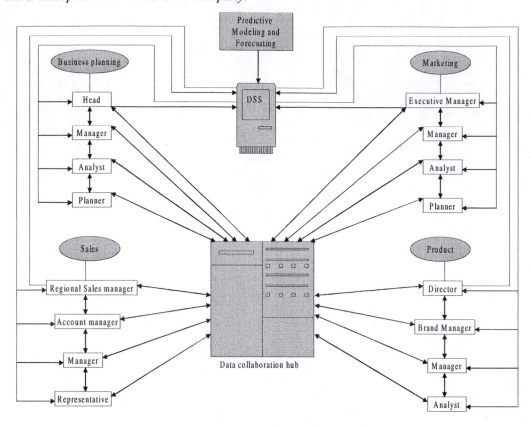

trade promotions and advertisements can result in larger return on investment (ROI) from the perspective of a CPG company if the marginal increase in promotional sales is caused by increase in brand share. There is a need to distinguish these from natural variability in demand (e.g., seasonal, weather, economic, demographic, or other effects), as well as ancillary effects like cannibalization, drag, or pre- and post-sales dips.

A process described in Figure 5 involves a knowledge information system where all partners can access, view, and modify the same data and knowledge to come up with "one number," demand forecasts or a common plan that is shared through the extended enterprise, thus resulting in improvements in forecasting accuracy, shorter lead times, good customer service levels, reduction of inventory levels, and maximum profits.

An intra-enterprise process described in Figure 6 having DSSs used by sales people to understand sales patterns, product people for product lifecycle management, marketing people for managing promotions or introducing new products, and business people for making strategic, operational, and tactical decisions. Each department analyzes and evaluates the information stored in the DSS for creating knowledge about the future and stores this knowledge in the system. A centralized data "collaboration hub" collects every kind of information

from business, marketing, product, and sales so that every department can also access other department's information for its own use. The following activities are performed by different departments to create knowledge about the future:

- **Marketing:** Marketing people want to know: (1) which products need to be promoted, where, when and at what price; (2) which existing products need to be phased out and when; and (3) when and where new products need to be introduced. They might want to interact with sales people to know about historical sales or customer behaviors, product people to know the stage of the product lifecycle, and business people to decide if the promotions would be effective and result in larger ROI or whether to launch a new product. They perform simulations, 'what if' analysis, and scenario planning to ensure the effectiveness of promotions or advertisements. They can create knowledge in terms of the effectiveness of promotions or advertisements on the sales, and determining the best time to phase out existing products and introduce new products.
- **Sales:** The sales people might want to interact with product people to understand the behavior of products, marketing people to know about promotions,

and business people to understand the impact on sales based on their decisions. The knowledge created by them can be sales variability due to seasonality, customer behaviors, and change of sales patterns due to promotions or advertisements.

- **Product:** The product people might need to get POS data from sales to know the stage of the product lifecycle, or interact with marketing and business people to know about promotions and new products. They can create knowledge in terms of the product behaviors at different stages of the product lifecycle.

- **Business:** Business planners and executives (e.g., in a CPG company) analyze the results of predictive models for promotional and baseline demand forecasts to design promotional strategies that maximize profits and ROI. The definition of maximized profits can differ, depending on whether the promotions are designed from longer-term considerations like brand acceptance or shorter-term considerations like the need to sell excess inventory. They get historical sales data or information about new opportunities from the sales department, product information from the product department, and information about market conditions as well as corporate policies like promotions or advertisements from the marketing department to develop future promotional strategy. They need to know if the promotions would result in lifts (e.g., increased demand due to a promotion on a specified product), drag effects (e.g., increase in sales driving the sales of associated product), and cannibalization (e.g., increase in sales reducing the sales of other products). They need to blend the natural variability of demand (e.g., seasonal and cyclical trends) with market information (e.g., competitive landscape, economic drivers, customer forecasts, demography) with direct and indirect promotional impacts. They use BI tools like querying and reporting for pulling and presenting the data relevant for planning, like past sales patterns, seasonal and cyclic patterns, economic indicators, weather patterns, demographics, and sales patterns of competitive products (and competitive promotions, if such information is available), as well as OLAP for viewing multidimensional data to get a better understanding of the information. OLAP-related activities have been described by the OLAP council (1997). Broadly, OLAP tools are well suited for *management by objectives* and *management by exceptions*.

The analysis and evaluation of information through mathematical models and by business analysts and planners produce a wealth of knowledge which can be stored in the system for future use. For example, waterfall accuracy charts can be used to compare forecasts with actual values, as they become available, for continuous evaluation and improvement. Similarly, audit trails and comments entered by planners during manual adjustments can be preserved and mined for evaluation and use in forecasting. The results of prior forecasts and the previous insights of knowledge workers are key building blocks in the process of knowledge creation about the future.

FUTURE TRENDS

The pace of rapid industry consolidations suggests that marketplaces of the future may well be characterized by a few leaders in each vertical, and laggards who run the risk of eventually fading into oblivion. In verticals like retail and CPG where the leaders have probably achieved long-term sustainability, one of the key differentiators between the leaders and the laggards has been the ability to create, retain, and utilize knowledge about the future through forecasting, predictive modeling, and planning efforts. Giants in retail and CPG are known to be superior to their peers in areas like demand forecasting, inventory management, promotion planning, pricing strategies, store and factory placements, as well as product allocations or placement. These leaders have developed the best analytical models, as well as planning and execution systems, in the business, and strive to maintain their superiority. This is indicated by the strong analytical and planning groups in these enterprises, as well as by developments like the use of radio frequency ID (RFID) tags on each product mandated by large retailers. Similar developments are expected in the high-tech industry in the longer term. While innovative newcomers are probably more likely to emerge in these areas even during relatively mature stages, the industry is expected to consolidate around leaders who are not necessarily (or only) the active pioneers and state-of-the-art researchers, but who (also) have the best processes for knowledge creation, retention, and utilization. The advent of globalization will enhance this trend of consolidation around a few large multinationals, who will strive to maintain their superiority by creating knowledge about the future. Mathematical models for extraction of knowledge from vast quantities of information, as well as efficient processes that enable interaction among planners and computers within and among organizations and enterprises, are expected to be ubiquitous in this business scenario. The competition among multinationals to maintain their edge over rivals and innovative challengers may well spawn the age of ubiquitous analytical information technologies, which encapsulates data mining, knowledge discovery, predictive modeling, and decision support.

CONCLUSION

The ability to create, preserve, and utilize knowledge about the future for efficient decision making is a key to competitiveness and survival for a business in this age of globalization, Internet commerce, and rapidly fluctuating economies. Forecasting and predictive modeling is a challenging process and is never perfect. However, even minor improvements can lead to significantly better tactical and strategic decisions, and improve the ability of an enterprise to react quickly to change. The tools, technologies, and processes that enable knowledge creation about the future have been presented in this article. The ability to create knowledge by meaningfully blending data-dictated predictive modeling with the expertise of business planners and executives, as well as retaining and utilizing this knowledge effectively, remains a key requirement for efficient business processes and better decision making, which in turn can make the difference between the leaders and laggards of an industry vertical.

ACKNOWLEDGMENTS

Most of this work was completed while the second author was on a visiting faculty appointment at the University of South Florida, and the third author was a faculty member at the MIT Sloan School of Management. The authors would like to acknowledge the help and support provided by Professor Sunil Saigal of USF.

REFERENCES

Anthony, R.N. (1965). *Planning and control systems: A framework for analysis.* Harvard University Graduate School of Business, MA.

Aviv, Y. (2001). The effect of collaborative forecasting on supply chain performance. *Management Science, 47*(10), 1326-1343.

Bonczek, R.H., Holsapple, C.W., & Whinston, A.B. (1981). *Foundations of decision support systems.* New York: Academic Press.

Bransten, L. (1999). Looking for patterns. *The Wall Street Journal,* (June 21), R16.

Breiman, L., Friedman, J.H., Olshen, R.A., & Stone, C.J. (1984). *Classification and regression trees.* Belmont, CA: AAAI Press.

Cachon, G.P., & Lariviere, M.A. (2001). Contracting to assure supply: How to share demand forecasts in a supply chain. *Management Science, 47*(5), 629-646.

Chen, F., Drezner, Z., Ryan, J.K., & Simchi-Levi, D. (2000). Quantifying the bullwhip effect in a simple supply chain: The impact of forecasting, lead times and information. *Management Science, 46*(3), 436-443.

Courtney, J.F. (2001). Decision making and knowledge management in inquiring organizations: Towards a new decision-making paradigm for DSS. *Decision Support System, 31*(1), 17-38.

Davis, S., & Botkin, J. (1994). The coming of knowledge-based business. *Harvard Business Review,* (September-October), 165-170.

Fayyad, U., Shapiro, G.P., & Smyth, P. (1996). From data mining to knowledge discovery: An overview. *Advances in Knowledge Discovery and Data Mining* (pp. 1-34). AAAI Press and MIT Press.

Fayyad, U., & Uthurusamy, R. (2002). Evolving data mining into solutions for insights. *Communications of the ACM, 45*(8), 28-31.

Ganguly, A.R. (2002). Software review—data mining components. *OR/MS Today,* (October). Institute for Operations Research and the Management Sciences.

Ganguly, A.R., Gupta, A. & Khan, S. (2005). Data mining and decision support for business and science. In J. Wang (Ed.), *Encyclopedia of Data Warehousing and Mining* (pp. 233-238). Hershey, PA: Idea Group Reference.

Gilbert, K. (2005). An ARIMA supply chain model. *Management Science, 51*(2), 305-310.

Gorry, G.A., & Morton, M.S.S. (1971). A framework for management information systems. *Sloan management Review, 13*(1), 50-70.

Gung, R.R., Leung, Y.T., Lin, G.Y., & Tsai, R.Y. (2002). Demand forecasting today. *OR/MS Today,* (December). Institute for Operations Research and the Management Sciences.

Hammer, J. (Ed.). (2003). Advances in online analytical processing. *Data and Knowledge Engineering, 45*(2), 127-256.

Hand, D., Mannila, H., & Smyth, P. (2001). *Principles of data mining.* Cambridge, MA: MIT Press.

Heinrichs, J.H., & Lim, J.S. (2003). Integrating Web-based data mining tools with business models for knowledge management. *Decision Support Systems, 35*, 103-112.

Inmon, W.H. (1992). *Building the data warehouse.* Wellesley, MA: QED Information Sciences.

Kimball, R. (1996). *The data warehouse toolkit.* New York: John Wiley & Sons.

C

Lee, H., & Whang, S. (1998). *Information sharing in a supply chain*. Research Paper No. 1549, Graduate School of Business, Stanford University.

Lim, J.S., Heinrichs, J.H., & Hudspeth, L.J. (1999). *Strategic marketing analysis: Business intelligence tools for knowledge based actions*. Needham Heights, MA: Pearson Custom Publishing.

Pearl, J. (1988). *Probabilistic reasoning in intelligent systems*. San Francisco: Morgan Kaufmann.

Peterson, K., Geishecker, L., & Eisenfeld, B.L. (2003, May 12). *In search of one-number forecasting*. Gartner Group, USA.

Power, D.J. (2002). *Decision support systems: Concepts and resources for managers*. Westport, CT: Quorum Books.

Quinlan, J. (1992). *C4.5: Programs for machine learning*. San Francisco: Morgan Kauffmann.

Shaw, M.J., Subramaniam, C., Tan, G.W., & Welge, M.E. (2001). Knowledge management and data mining for marketing. *Decision Support Systems, 31*, 127-137.

Simon, H.A. (1960). *A new science of management decision*. New York: Harper Brothers.

Wang, G.C.S., & Jain, C.L. (2003). *Regression analysis: Modeling and forecasting*. Institute of Business Forecasting.

Whittaker, J. (1990). *Graphical models in applied multivariate statistics*. New York: John Wiley & Sons.

Yurkiewicz, J. (2003). Forecasting software survey: Predicting which product is right for you. *ORMS Today*, (February). Institute for Operations Research and the Management Sciences.

KEY TERMS

Business Intelligence (BI): Software and set of tools that allow the end users to view and analyze the data and business knowledge through automated analytics or human-computer interaction.

Collaborative Planning, Forecasting, and Replenishment (CPFR): A process where the entire extended supply chain, including manufactures, distributors, and retailers, is using the same information through collaborative process to improve sales and forecast accuracy, reduce inventory levels, and prevent stock outs due to promotions.

Data Mining Technologies (DMTs): Statistical, artificial intelligence, machine learning, or even database-query-based approaches that are capable of extracting meaningful insights or knowledge from large volumes of information.

Data Warehouse: "A subject-oriented, integrated, time-variant, nonvolatile collection of data in support of management's decision-making process" (Inmon, 1992).

Decision Support Systems (DSSs): Holsapple and Whinston specify: "A DSS must have a body of knowledge, a record-keeping capability that can present knowledge on an ad hoc basis in various customized ways as well as in standardized reports for either presentation or for deriving new knowledge, and must be designed to interact directly with a decision maker in such a way that the user has a flexible choice and sequence of knowledge-management activities" (Power, 2002).

Key Performance Indicators (KPIs): Quantifiable measurements that help an organization evaluate how it is progressing towards organizational goals.

Knowledge Creation: This can be divided into both explicit knowledge, which can be formulated in terms of words and numbers and distributed as data, reports, and scientific formulas, and tacit knowledge, which is related to ideas, emotions, intuition, and experience.

One-Number Forecasts: Forecasts that provide an objective and unified view of the future evolution of the enterprise, with buy-in from multiple stakeholders representing the internal organizations of an enterprise as well as its trading partners, and utilized for planning tactical, operational, and strategic planning endeavors.

Online Analytical Processing (OLAP): A type of software and set of tools that enable analysts, managers, and executives to view multidimensional data in the language and structure of business for decision making.

Online Transactional Processing (OLTP): A type of software and set of tools that facilitate real-time processing of transactions for transaction-oriented applications used in many industries including retails, airlines, and banking.

Sales and Operations Planning (S&OP): The process that facilitates integrated demand and supply management among internal departments such as sales, marketing, and manufacturing through effective and efficient sharing of information across the supply chain to enhance business performance.

Customer Knowledge Management

Scott Paquette
University of Toronto, Canada

INTRODUCTION

As companies begin to develop competence in managing internal knowledge and applying it towards achieving organizational goals, they are setting their sights on new sources of knowledge that are not necessarily found within the boundaries of the firm. Customer knowledge management comprises the processes that are concerned with the identification, acquisition, and utilization of knowledge from beyond a firm's external boundary in order to create value for an organization. Companies can utilize this knowledge in many different forms of organizational improvement and change, but it is especially valuable for innovation and the new product development function.

The notion of working with partners to share information was first discussed in 1966 where the possibility of transferring information between a company and its suppliers and customers was identified. Kaufman (1966) describes the advantages to a business that include reduced order costs, reduced delivery time, and increased customer "confidence and goodwill" (p. 148).

Organizations have since been viewed as interpretation systems that must find ways of knowing their environment (Daft & Weick, 1984). Through this environmental learning, a firm's ability to innovate can improve by going beyond a firm's boundaries to expand the knowledge available for creating new and successful products. Some organizations conduct ongoing, active searches of the environment to seek new and vital information. Such organizations become the key innovators within an industry. Other, more passive organizations accept whatever information the environment presents and avoid the processes of testing new ideas and innovation. Marketing literature refers to this concept as *market orientation* (Kohli & Jaworski, 1990; Slater & Narver, 1995).

More recently, many organizations have realized the value of information about their customers through customer relationship management and data mining strategies, and have used this information to tailor their marketing efforts (Berson, Smith, & Thearling, 2003; Blattberg, Getz, & Thomas, 2001; Davenport, Harris, & Kohli, 2001). The idea of using information from suppliers to accurately manage inventory levels within the supply chain (Lin, Huang, & Lin, 2002) also reflects this notion. However, what is missing from these theories and strategies is the realization of the value of knowledge residing *within* customers, and not information *about* customers.

Iansiti and Levien (2004) describe an organization's environment as an ecosystem, where networked organizations rely on the strength of others for survival. Within this ecology, they identify certain "keystone organizations" that "simplify the complex task of connecting network participants to one another or by making the creation of new products by third parties more efficient" (p. 73). This increase in overall ecosystem productivity is accomplished though the incorporation of technological innovations and niche creation through innovative technologies. Through recognizing customer knowledge as a key component to a firm's ability to innovate, and actively searching for sources of knowledge within the business environment, a firm is able to augment its innovation capabilities and position themselves as a keystone organization.

BACKGROUND

In examining the role of external knowledge in an organization's internal processes, *customer* is broadly defined as an organization's stakeholders such as consumers, suppliers, partners, joint ventures and alliances, and competitors. In some cases, a customer may not have a current relationship with the organization, but one is likely to develop in the future. *Knowledge* in this context refers to the model presented by Cook and Brown (1999), where it can be explicit or tacit, and individual or group knowledge. Explicit knowledge is easily codified, transferred, and understood by multiple individuals, where tacit knowledge requires experience and practice in order to flow from one individual to another. Both of these forms of knowledge can reside at the individual level, or be created and transferred between different groups.

Knowledge derived from these relationships through an interactive and mutually beneficial process is referred to as *customer knowledge*. Customer knowledge can be composed of a combination of consumer knowledge, supply chain knowledge, joint venture specific knowledge, and so forth. This knowledge is created within a two-way flow of knowledge which creates value for both parties. It goes beyond information identifying and classifying customers, to knowledge that is resident within the external organization that has been developed through industry and market experience. Examples can be consumer preferences of new product features, newly recognized uses for current products, knowledge derived from joint research and development, design improvements from suppliers intended to reduce the cost of manufacturing, and knowledge regarding trends within the business environment.

An important aspect of customer knowledge is that it is knowledge not owned by the firm, but by others who may or may not be willing to share such knowledge. The processes that a firm employs to manage the identification, acquisition, and internal utilization of customer knowledge are collectively referred to as *customer knowledge management*. It is within these processes that an organization and its customers collectively work together to combine their existing knowledge to create new knowledge. This new knowledge is a key input into a company's ability to innovate, which is reflected in their research and development function. Furthermore, the ability to design and improve new products is also impacted by the level of customer knowledge flows. A depiction of customer knowledge flows is shown in Figure 1.

Many studies have used customer knowledge and customer information interchangeably, causing confusion between the two terms. Blosch (2000) states that understanding "how each customer interacts with business processes is to gain knowledge about that customer" (p. 266). Gibbert, Leibold, and Probst (2002) would describe this only as customer information, as it is knowl-

edge about the customer and is gained without a predetermined close interaction or partnership. Dennis, Marsland, and Cockett (2001) also examine the use of customer information within a retail environment, and look at how data mining can contribute to an organization's understanding of the customer. Once again, the emphasis is on acquiring information about the customer, without interaction or joint knowledge creation.

Davenport et al. (2001) begin to argue that knowledge about the customer is only the first step, and organizations should create processes to better manage the relationships they discover with this information to create profitable interactions. The focus they present remains with learning about the customer's needs through different channels. However, the customer's involvement in the knowledge process is still passive, and not participatory.

Recently, an emphasis on customers as partners in the knowledge creation process has been presented (Sawhney & Prandelli, 2000). Customers co-create knowledge with an organization in order to create value for both parties by sharing knowledge residing within customers in order to create better products. Here, the two entities work together with a shared goal in mind, and the customer becomes an active and key participant in the knowledge creation process. Gibbert et al. (2002) examined a set of organizations that have implemented this idea into their customer relationship strategy, and described the types of CKM they observed.

Figure 1. Summary of customer knowledge

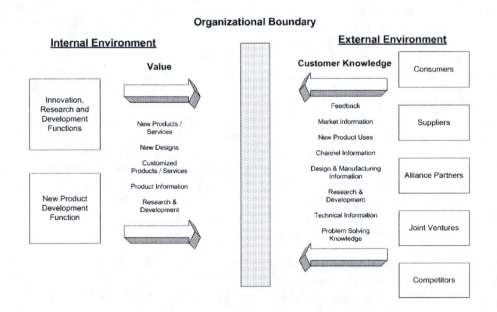

CUSTOMER KNOWLEDGE AND INNOVATION

Henry Chesbrough (2003) states that most innovations fail when brought to the marketplace. However, if companies do not continually innovate, they die. This is in part due to the key role innovation plays in value creation and profitable growth (Prahalad & Ramaswamy, 2003). Innovation creates advantages in the marketplace over competitors, leads to and supports other competitive advantages such as cost savings, and differentiates the organization in the marketplace through the eyes of its customers.

Innovation relies on the creation of new knowledge by the organization, and this is derived from many sources. Companies can identify new and usable knowledge within their employees (Bontis, Crossan, & Hulland, 2002; Leonard & Sensiper, 1998), convert this existing tacit knowledge to easily shared explicit knowledge (Nonaka & Takeuchi, 1995), purchase or acquire knowledge from other organizations, or look to the external environment for new sources of knowledge such as their customers. This is where customer knowledge can significantly contribute to a firm's ability to innovate.

An organization is continually challenged to create new knowledge, and transform this knowledge (i.e., into solutions to problems, new products, etc.) through the integration of knowledge from different sources (Carlile & Rebentisch, 2003). Firms are constantly striving to identify valuable information and disseminate it to the appropriate areas of the organization in order to make informed decisions and create a competitive advantage. More and more, firms are looking beyond external boundaries for new sources of knowledge, and in many cases this points them towards their customers. An organization will be able to stimulate its new product development process and create well-received products if it can collaborate via a knowledge sharing strategy with its customers. A successful knowledge partnership with the most valuable and important customers can not only strengthen these business relationships, but also create a competitive advantage that is difficult for the competition to duplicate.

Customer knowledge can establish a competitive advantage for the organization through increased organizational learning and innovation. The competitive advantage gained through knowledge acquisition can either be temporary, as other competitors will follow and learn the new skills, processes, products, and so forth, or it can be more permanent if the competition is prevented from gaining this knowledge. Customer knowledge can be a barrier to knowledge acquisition for the competition by building a close relationship with the customer that cannot be duplicated. This barrier is strengthened if the customer perceives an intrinsic benefit that cannot be duplicated by other competitors. For example, as Amazon.com learns a customer's buying preferences and is able to offer valuable recommendations, that customer will be reluctant to switch retailers and begin the learning process over. In some cases this is referred to as customer learning (Stewart, 1997), where the two-way exchange of knowledge allows the customer to gain new knowledge and use this to his or her benefit. The knowledge sharing partnership acts both as a facilitator of knowledge transfer and sharing, and a barrier to the competition.

Types of Customer Knowledge

Customers can provide unique knowledge that allows an organization to learn and acquire knowledge to improve its internal operations, including innovation. In turn, the organization provides to the customer knowledge of its products and services which improves the functionality to the customer. This two-way flow of knowledge provides the basis for a competitive advantage through a strong relationship or partnership. Gibbert et al. (2002) discuss the five basic forms of customer knowledge which are prosumerism, team based co-learning, mutual innovation, communities of creation, and joint intellectual property development (Table 1). Each form of customer knowledge originates from a relationship between the organization and a customer source, and can be derived from multiple sources.

The first version of customer knowledge is prosumerism, a term derived from Toffler's (1980) 'prosumer', which describes a customer filling the dual role of consumer and producer. In this instance, knowledge co-production is generated from role patterns and interactivity. For example, Bosch develops engine management systems with Mercedes-Benz who then creates and assembles the finished product, a car. Bosch's customer, Mercedes-Benz, is allowed to share value-creating ideas and facilitates the development of new initiatives and products.

The second form of customer knowledge management is team-based co-learning. This involves intense interactions with the customer to gain their knowledge on processes and systems to facilitate systematic change. A prominent example of this is Amazon.com. By restructuring their organization from being an online book retailer to a seller of many varieties of goods, they accomplished many co-learning interactions with their customers (i.e., suppliers) to design a new value chain. Amazon.com uses this value chain as a competitive advantage against other online retailers, as it allows for quick movement of goods at competitive prices. This strategy has the added value of creating an even closer relationship with their suppliers that other online retailers will not be able to duplicate. A second illustration is Toyota, who has created knowledge-sharing networks

Table 1. Summary of the five forms of customer knowledge

Knowledge Form (Gibbert et al., 2002)	Typical Relationship Form
Prosumerism	Firm—Producer/Manufacturer
Team-Based Co-Learning	Firm—Consumer/Joint Venture
Mutual Innovation	Firm—Supplier/Joint Venture
Communities of Creation	Firm—Consumer/Joint Venture
Joint Intellectual Property	Firm—Consumer

with its suppliers, with the common goal of learning through combining each other's knowledge to create efficiencies in the production process (Dyer & Nobeoka, 2000). Toyota and a supplier will create a team, co-populated with employees from each organization who together study organizational processes and create new customer knowledge.

Mutual innovation was initially identified by von Hippel (1988), who discussed that most product innovations come from the end-users of the product, as they have specific product knowledge derived from use and their own needs. Mutual innovation is more than just asking for future requirements, but constructing knowledge that comes from closely integrated innovation practices. Rider Logistics developed complex and extensive logistical solutions for its customers through close examination of their manufacturing operations and supply chain strategies, then designed services that fit and added value to these processes. This may convert Rider from a basic trucking company towards a logistics solutions provider (Gibbert et al., 2002).

Communities of creation occur when companies organize their customers into groups holding similar expert knowledge and encourage interaction in order to generate new knowledge. These groups are characterized by working together over a long period of time, sharing a common interest, and wanting to create and share valuable knowledge. Unlike traditional communities of practice (Wenger, 1998), these groups span organizational boundaries and develop value for multiple organizations. Microsoft beta testing with customers is an example where groups of targeted customers test products together with the Microsoft product development engineers to jointly create a product that provides value for Microsoft and its participating customer organizations. These communities also form through informal relationships which are capable of producing valuable knowledge.

The final form of CKM is joint intellectual property, which may be the most intense form of cooperation between a company and its customers. Here, the company takes the view that it is owned by its customers and they have ownership in product development. This notion goes beyond normal customer relationships and co-creates new businesses based on customer education and co-development. Skandia Insurance is an example where a company and its valued consumers created new businesses owned by both. They have proven this strategy especially successful in emerging markets where the company initially lacks customer knowledge, yet gains a great deal from its local customers.

Challenges for Customer Knowledge Management

Many of the discussions on internal knowledge transfer deal with the challenges of sharing knowledge at the individual, group, or organizational level. These challenges remain true for sharing customer knowledge across an external boundary. Initially, firms may experience a cultural challenge of perceiving customers as a source of knowledge, not just revenue. This is reflected in the 'not invented here' concept, which demonstrates an organization's unwillingness to accept externally generated ideas. Other companies fear showing internal processes to customers such as suppliers or alliance partners in case a poor perception develops. It is common for heavily brand-based companies who want to control what the customer sees to be afraid of giving away strategic secrets to the marketplace (Gibbert et al., 2002). A further case is resistance to sharing proprietary knowledge with suppliers. Questions of how to control the flow of this knowledge to competitors arise, and the effectiveness of confidentiality agreements are doubted when a firm must reveal or share proprietary technology that is part of a firm's competitive advantage (Ragatz, Handfield et al., 1997).

Besides cultural influences, a firm may not have the competency required to absorb and utilize the external knowledge. Cohen and Levinthal (1990) state that a firm's absorptive capacity, or its ability to absorb new knowledge, is a function of the firm's prior knowledge that allows it to recognize and synthesize new knowledge. Also, information systems may not be able to handle the transfer of knowledge from external sources, as most knowledge sharing support systems are only designed for internal use. Organizations can be quite reluctant to open up these systems, as technical challenges occur without a universal integration and security mechanism that interfaces with both parties' systems. Control of content may be lost, as external knowledge transfer can push the locus of control beyond a firm's boundaries which for some may cause apprehension (Gibbert et al., 2002).

A further obstacle exists when the customer can solely derive innovations from their knowledge and the need for a partner becomes insignificant. Von Hippel (1988) argues that innovators must have a poor ability to gain from their knowledge regarding innovations in order to share this information with others, or else they would capitalize on their knowledge independently and realize higher revenues. Factors such as manufacturing capability, geography, market knowledge, or supply chain requirements can increase an innovator's ability to bring their development to market, and prevent the opportunity for a formalized knowledge sharing alliance.

A key question an organization may ask is how do they know the customer is supplying correct information or that it is representative of the entire market? Although some knowledge sharing partnerships may only be able to encompass the knowledge of one customer, market researchers have techniques to ensure enough customers were consulted to recognize trends or significant findings. However, customer knowledge management still depends on the assumption that an environment exists where useful knowledge can be provided to the company. This may indicate that the potential value to be realized by a customer knowledge management initiative is equal to the ability of the external environment to provide such knowledge, and customer knowledge management may be more effective in some industries over others.

To further this point, companies should realize the limitations of focusing on their current customers and markets, and look beyond their range to products that cannot be foreseen or their value realized by current customers. These new ideas, sometimes called disruptive technologies (Christensen, 2000), go against the axiom of staying close to your customer (Prahalad & Ramaswamy, 2000) and encourage innovators to develop innovative ideas that disrupt a customer's process and patterns to introduce new products that leap the product lifecycle and replace current paradigms and technologies. They may even target new markets that do not exist or satisfy customers' needs today, and therefore cannot be currently used to gain customer knowledge, but possibly will in the future.

FUTURE TRENDS

The concept of customer knowledge is relatively new to the field of knowledge management, yet it continues to develop as more organizations embrace the idea and put it into practice. It is becoming quite common to observe knowledge-sharing agreements between separate firms, and in some cases joint ventures for the specific purpose of creating new knowledge.

As competency in utilizing customer knowledge increases, more companies will conduct new product development through a web of businesses capable of enhancing the process with their unique core competencies. By working as a team, each firm's internal knowledge will contribute to the creation of a new set of shared knowledge. This new knowledge will be the driver for innovative product ideas and advancements. Developing the ability to learn from external organizations will become a key objective in organizational knowledge management strategies. Firms will take the best practices of sharing knowledge over external boundaries, and apply these skills towards improving internal knowledge transfer between different teams, departments, units, and subsidiaries. A cyclical learning cycle of improving knowledge management practices by learning through internal and external knowledge transfer only strengthens a firm's knowledge management abilities.

The definition of customer can be broadened even further to include those entities that may not have a transactional relationship with the firm, yet contain pertinent knowledge of an organization's business environment. Lobby groups, government organizations, legal entities, activist groups such as environmental awareness associations, professional associations, and standards boards all influence the business environment and a firm's ability to operate within it. Each should be considered a valuable source of external knowledge a firm requires to not only understand the environment, but flourish in it (Paquette, 2004). Expanding the range of sources providing customer knowledge will transform this knowledge set into external knowledge management, encompassing all stakeholders' knowledge available to the firm.

CONCLUSION

Facilitating knowledge sharing between internal individuals and groups can be a daunting task for any organization. The challenges of this endeavor multiply when the knowledge sharing involves an external entity possessing knowledge that is not owned by the firm.

However, the benefits of creating social structures, business processes, and technologies to facilitate customer knowledge flows can have a substantial impact on the performance of the organization, and in particular its ability to innovate. By actively involving customers in creating a two-way flow of knowledge that supports innovation, an organization leverages a new source of knowledge which can improve its standing in the marketplace. Determining the correct combination of valuable customer knowledge sources and customer knowledge management forms can create a sustainable competitive advantage through the introduction of products that satisfy a market's latent needs. A firm's acknowledgement of the importance of customer knowledge will encourage the expansion of its current knowledge management practices to beyond the organizational boundary. This creates an improved ability to identify, acquire, and utilize valuable knowledge that an organization requires to be successful.

REFERENCES

Berson, A., Smith, S., & Thearling, K. (2003). Customer acquisition. *Building Data Mining Applications for CRM* (p. 7). New York.

Blattberg, R.C., Getz, G., & Thomas, J.S. (2001). *Customer equity: Building and managing relationships as valuable assets* (1st ed.). Boston: Harvard Business School Press.

Blosch, M. (2000). Customer knowledge. *Knowledge and Process Management, 7*(4), 265-268.

Bontis, N., Crossan, M.M., & Hulland, J. (2002). Managing an organizational learning system by aligning stocks and flows. *Journal of Management Studies, 39*(4).

Carlile, P., & Rebentisch, E.S. (2003). Into the black box: The knowledge transformation cycle. *Management Science, 49*(9), 1180-1195.

Chesbrough, H.W. (2003). *Open innovation: The new imperative for creating and profiting from technology.* Boston: Harvard Business School Press.

Christensen, C.M. (2000). *The innovator's dilemma* (revised ed.). New York: HarperCollins.

Cook, S.D.N., & Brown, J.S. (1999). Bridging epistemologies: The generative dance between organizational knowledge and organizational knowing. *Organization Science, 10*(4), 381-400.

Daft, R.L., & Weick, K.E. (1984). Toward a model of organizations as interpretation systems. *Academy of Management Review, 9*(2), 284-295.

Davenport, T.H., Harris, J.G., & Kohli, A.K. (2001). How do they know their customers so well? *MIT Sloan Management Review,* (Winter), 63-73.

Dennis, C., Marsland, D., & Cockett, T. (2001). Data mining for shopping centers: Customer knowledge management framework. *Journal of Knowledge Management, 5*(4), 368-374.

Dyer, J.H., & Nobeoka, K. (2000). Creating and managing a high-performance knowledge-sharing network: The Toyota case. *Strategic Management Journal, 21*, 345-367.

Gibbert, M., Leibold, M., & Probst, G. (2002). Five styles of customer knowledge management, and how smart companies use them to create value. *European Management Journal, 20*(5), 459-469.

Iansiti, M., & Levien, R. (2004). Strategy as ecology. *Harvard Business Review,* (March), 68-78.

Kaufman, F. (1966). Data systems that cross corporate boundaries. *Harvard Business Review,* (January-February), 141-155.

Kohli, A.K., & Jaworski, B.J. (1990). Market orientation: The construct, research propositions, and managerial implications. *Journal of Marketing, 54*(2), 1-18.

Leonard, D., & Sensiper, S. (1998). The role of tacit knowledge in group innovation. *California Management Review, 40*(3), 112-132.

Lin, F.-R., Huang, S.-H., & Lin, S.-C. (2002). Effects of information sharing on supply chain performance in electronic commerce. *IEEE Transactions on Engineering Management, 49*(3), 258-268.

Nonaka, I., & Takeuchi, H. (1995). *The knowledge creating company.* New York: Oxford University Press.

Paquette, S. (2004, May 14-16). Customer knowledge management systems supporting innovation. *Proceedings of the 9th Annual Great Lakes Information Sciences Conference,* Toronto, Canada.

Prahalad, C.K., & Ramaswamy, V. (2000). Co-opting customer competence. *Harvard Business Review,* 79-87.

Prahalad, C.K., & Ramaswamy, V. (2003). The new frontier of experience innovation. *Sloan Management Review,* (Summer), 12-18.

Ragatz, G.L., Handfield, R.B., & Scannell, T.V. (1997). Success factors for integrating suppliers into new product development. *Journal of Product Innovation Management*, (14), 190-202.

Sawhney, M., & Prandelli, E. (2000). Beyond customer knowledge management: Customers as knowledge co-creators. In Y. Malhtora (Ed.), *Knowledge management and virtual organizations* (pp. 258-281). Hershey, PA: Idea Group Publishing.

Slater, S.F., & Narver, J.C. (1995). Market orientation and the learning organization. *Journal of Marketing, 59*(3), 63-74.

Stewart, T.A. (1997). *Intellectual capital: The new wealth of organizations* (2nd ed., vol. 1). New York: Doubleday.

Toffler, A. (1980). *The third wave.* New York: Morrow.

von Hippel, E. (1988). *The sources of innovation.* New York: Oxford University Press.

Wenger, E. (1998). *Communities of practice: Learning, meaning, and identity.* Cambridge: Cambridge University Press.

KEY TERMS

Communities of Creation: The communities that form when companies organize their customers into groups holding similar expert knowledge and encouraging interaction in order to generate new knowledge. These groups are characterized by working together over a long period of time, sharing a common interest, and wanting to create and share valuable knowledge. Unlike traditional communities of practice, these groups span organizational boundaries and develop value for multiple organizations.

Customer Knowledge: Knowledge derived through relationships from consumers, suppliers, partners, joint ventures and alliances, and competitors. It is knowledge located externally to the firm, and is not owned by the organization. It can be composed of a combination of consumer knowledge, supply chain knowledge, joint venture specific knowledge, and so forth. This knowledge is created within a two-way flow of knowledge which creates value for both parties.

Customer Knowledge Management: The collective processes that a firm employs to mange the identification, acquisition, and internal utilization of customer knowledge. It is within these processes that an organization and its customers work together to combine existing knowledge to create new knowledge. It differs from managing internal knowledge as it must facilitate the flow of knowledge across an external boundary.

Joint Intellectual Property: The result of a company taking the view that it is owned by its customers and they have ownership in product development. This notion goes beyond normal customer relationships and co-creates new businesses based on customer education and co-development. It is probably the most intense form of cooperation between a company and its customers.

Market Orientation: The portion of a company's marketing strategy that continuously collects information and knowledge about customer needs and competitor capabilities. The company must have the ability to scan the environment and acquire information related to its business operations. Also, the internal capability of utilizing this knowledge to create superior value for the customer must also exist in the form of knowledge-based business processes.

Mutual Innovation: The process of two organizations striving for product innovations from the end-users of the product, created from their product knowledge derived from use and their own needs. This goes beyond just asking for future requirements, but constructing knowledge that comes from closely integrated innovation practices.

Prosumerism: The name for an arrangement where a customer fills the dual role of both consumer and producer. Knowledge co-production is generated from role patterns and interactivity, with both parties sharing the traditional responsibilities of a producer and consumer.

Team Based Co-Learning: Where two distinct organizations assemble a cross-organizational team with the purpose of learning from one another. This team utilizes the knowledge contained in each separate organization to create new knowledge beneficial for both. Intense interactions with the customer occur to gain their knowledge on processes and systems to facilitate systematic change.

Data Semantics

Daniel W. Gillman
Bureau of Labor Statistics, USA

INTRODUCTION

Almost every organization, public or private, for profit or non-profit, manages data in some way. Data is a major corporate resource. It is produced, analyzed, stored, and disseminated. And, it is poorly documented.

Descriptions of data are essential for their proper understanding and use by people inside and outside the organization. For instance, systems for disseminating data on the Internet require these descriptions (Census Bureau, n.d.). Either inside or outside the organization, functions of the system support finding the right data for a study, understanding data from a particular source, and comparing data across sources or time (Gillman, Appel, & LaPlant, 1996).

Descriptions of data and other resources are *metadata* (Gillman, 2003). Metadata are part of the corporate memory for the organization, and preserving corporate memory is one of the basic features of knowledge management (King, Marks, & McCoy, 2002). Metadata include the meaning, or semantics, of the data. In some countries, such as the U.S., a large percentage of the population is reaching retirement age. As a result, recording the memories of these workers, including the meaning of data, is increasingly important. Preserving metadata is crucial for understanding data years after the data were created (Gillman et al., 1996).

Traditionally, the metadata for databases and files is developed individually, without reference to similar data in other sources. Even when metadata exist, they are often incomplete or incompatible across systems. As a result, the semantics of the data contained in these databases and files are poorly understood. In addition, the metadata often disappear after the data reach the end of the business lifecycle.

Techniques for documenting data are varied. There are CASE (Computer-Aided Software Engineering) tools such as Oracle Designer® (Oracle, n.d.) or Rational Rose® (IBM, n.d.). These tools produce models of data in databases (Ullman, 1982). The models provide some semantics for the data. For social science data sets, metadata is described in an XML (eXtensible Markup Language) specification (ICPSR, n.d.). For geographic data sets, the U.S. Federal Geographic Data Committee developed a metadata framework, clearinghouse, and supporting software (FGDC, n.d.).

Metadata are data, too. They are structured, semi-structured, or unstructured (Abiteboul, Buneman, & Suciu, 2000), just as data are. Data are structured if one knows both the schema and datatype, semi-structured if one knows one of them, and unstructured otherwise. From the perspective of their content, documents are unstructured or semi-structured data. Their schemas come from presentation frameworks such as HTML (Hyper-Text Mark-up Language) (W3C, 1997) or word processor formats. Documents with the content marked up in XML (W3C, 2004) are semi-structured. When using the full datatyping capability of XML-Schema, the document is structured with respect to the content. However, the colloquial use of the term "document" begins to lose its meaning here.

In describing some resource, the content is more important than the presentation. The content contains the semantics associated with the resource. If the content is structured data, this increases the capability of performing complex queries on it. Retrieving unstructured documents using search engine technology is not as precise.

It turns out there are structured ways to represent the semantics of data. Ontologies (Sowa, 2000) are the newest technique. Traditional database (or registry) models are examples of ontologies. This article describes the constituents of the semantics of data and a technique to manage them using a metadata registry. The process of registration—an approach to control the identification, provenance, and quality of the content—is also described and its benefits discussed.

SEMANTICS OF DATA

Terminology

To begin, we describe some useful constructs from the theory of terminology. These come from several sources (Sager, 1990; ISO, 1999, 2000). We use these constructs to describe the semantics of data. The terms and definitions follow in a list below:

- **Characteristic:** Abstraction of a property of a set of objects.

- **Concept:** Mental constructs, units of thought, or unit of knowledge created by a unique combination of characteristics.
- **Concept system:** Set of concepts structured according to the relations among them.
- **Definition:** Expression of a concept through natural language, which specifies a unique intension and extension.
- **Designation:** Representation of a concept by a sign, which denotes it.
- **Extension:** Set of objects to which a concept refers.
- **General concept:** Concept with two or more objects that correspond to it (e.g., planet, tower).
- **Generic concept:** Concept in a generic relation having the narrower intension.
- **Generic relation:** Relation between two concepts where the intension of one of the concepts includes that of the other concept and at least one additional distinguishing characteristic.
- **Individual concept:** Concept with one object that corresponds to it (e.g., Saturn, Eiffel Tower).
- **Intension:** Sum of characteristics that constitute a concept.
- **Object:** Something conceivable or perceivable.
- **Property:** Attribute used to describe or distinguish an object (e.g., "Dan has blue-gray eyes" means "blue-gray eyes" is the property of Dan associated with the characteristic "eye color" of people.)
- **Specific concept:** Concept in a generic relation having the broader intension.

Designations come in three types: an appellation is a verbal designation of an individual concept; a term is a verbal designation of a general concept; and a symbol is any other designation.

The ancient Greek philosophers began the study of terminology and concept formation in language (Wedberg, 1982), and they discovered a useful relationship between designation, concept, object, and definition which is illustrated in Figure 1 (CEN, 1995).

Figure 1 shows that concepts, designations, objects, and definitions are related but separate constructs. Each plays a role in our understanding (i.e., the semantics of) data.

An important observation is that concepts are human constructions (Lakoff, 2002). No matter how well we define a concept, a complete description is often impossible. Identifying the relevant characteristics is culturally dependent. So, some objects in the extension of a concept fit the characteristics better than other, so-called prototypes.

Framework for Understanding Data

Here, we present a general framework for understanding data. Some terminology comes from the area of statistics. Statisticians view a datum as a designation of a class in a partition of a population of objects, where the partition[1] is defined for some characteristic of the population (Froeschl, Grossmann, & Del Vecchio, 2003). Here, the population is either a general or individual concept, and the objects are the extension of that concept. Four examples illustrate the ideas:

Example 1

- **Population:** Adults age 16 and older in the U.S.
- **Characteristic:** Sex
- **Partition:** {Male, Female}
- **Designations:** 0 for Male 1 for Female

Example 2

- **Population:** The set of adults age 16 and older in the U.S.
- **Characteristic:** Proportion of females
- **Partition:** $\{x \mid 0 <= x <= 1\}$
- **Designations:** Real numbers between 0 and 1, with precision to 3 decimal places

Example 3

- **Population:** Shoe sales
- **Characteristic:** Type of shoe

Figure 1. Illustration of the differences between a referent (an object), a concept, a term (more generally a designation), and a definition in language

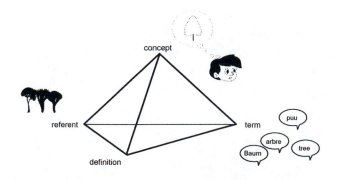

- **Partition:** {Basketball, Business, Casual, Formal, Running, Tennis}
- **Designations:**   Ba for Basketball
    Bu for Business
    C for Casual
    F for Formal
    R for Running
    T for Tennis

Example 4

- **Population:** Stars of the Milky Way Galaxy
- **Characteristic:** Number of known planets
- **Partition:** {n | n >= 0 and n is an integer}
- **Designations:**   0 for no known planets
    1 for one known planet
    etc.

Populations

The idea of a population requires some additional explanation. In one sense, it is a concept represented by a definition or description. In another sense, it is the extension of the concept, the set of objects about which we collect or observe data. We refer to both the concept and its extension as a population.

Also, a population is either an individual concept or a general one. In the ordinary sense, populations are general concepts (see Examples 1, 3, and 4). However, aggregate data requires a population with one object. In Example 2, the characteristic "proportion of females" applies to the entire set of adults age 16 or older in the U.S., not to each person. So, the set consisting of "the set of adults age 16 or older in the U.S." has one element. It is a set whose lone element is a set! But, it is this entirety (an aggregate) that has the characteristic "proportion of females," not the individual people. So, "proportion of females" is not a characteristic of people, "sex" is. Likewise "sex" is not a characteristic of the aggregate, "proportion of females" is.

Every object has an individual concept associated with it. When one thinks of a particular object, the conception of that object is an individual concept. Data associated with a particular object is descriptive of that object. This characterization is necessary but not sufficient to be metadata. Data are only metadata when they are used to describe some object. However, metadata are similar to aggregate data, their populations are individual concepts.

Types of Semantics

Characteristics applied to populations are concepts themselves. So, the characteristic of a population is a concept, and it represents, in part, the contextual semantics of the data (e.g., the sex of U.S. people). The designations denoting the classes of the partition defined for the characteristic represent the symbolic semantics—for example, M is for male and F is for female. Therefore, data have both contextual and symbolic semantics (Gillman, 2003).

The contextual semantics describe, in part, the kinds of objects for which data are collected and the particular characteristic of those objects being measured. The symbolic semantics describe the set of categories, not necessarily finite, representing the meaning of the values that data take.

The set of values that data take has additional descriptions, in particular a computational model for the values, which is called the datatype (ISO, 1995).

Value Domains

As defined above, the set of designations for the classes of a partition determined by a characteristic is called a value domain. In a value domain, a designation is known as a value, the associated class of the partition is described by a concept called the value meaning, and each value and associated value meaning pair is a known as a permissible value (ISO, 2004).

A set of value meanings is called a conceptual domain. It is a concept, and its value meanings are its characteristics. Every value domain is in the extension of some conceptual domain.

Value domains and conceptual domains come in two (non-exclusive) sub-types:

- **Enumerated:** A domain specified by a list of its elements.
- **Non-Enumerated:** A domain specified by a description of its elements.

An enumerated value domain contains a list of all its permissible values. An enumerated conceptual domain contains a list of all its value meanings. Non-enumerated value domains and non-enumerated conceptual domains are specified by descriptions. The non-enumerated value domain description describes precisely which permissible values belong and which do not belong to the value domain. The non-enumerated conceptual domain description describes precisely which value meanings belong and which do not belong to the conceptual domain.

Some value domains contain very similar permissible values from one domain to another. Similarity is based on how much the value meanings overlap. When these similarities occur, the value domains are in the extension of one conceptual domain. The following two examples taken from ISO (2004) illustrate several things:

- Example of non-enumerated value domains and a non-enumerated conceptual domain
- Example of enumerated value domains and an enumerated conceptual domain
- Use of conceptual domains to manage similarities between value domains

Example 5: Similar Non-Enumerated Value Domains

- **Conceptual domain name:** Probabilities
- **Conceptual domain definition:** Real numbers greater than 0 and less than 1
- **Value domain name (1):** Probabilities—2 significant digits
- **Value domain description:** All real numbers greater than 0 and less than 1 represented with 2 digit precision.
- **Precision:** 2 digits to the right of the decimal point
- **Value domain name (2):** Probabilities—5 significant digits
- **Value domain description:** All real numbers greater than 0 and less than 1 represented with 5 digit precision.
- **Precision:** 5 digits to the right of the decimal point

Example 6: Similar Enumerated Value Domains

- **Conceptual domain name:** Marital Status Categories
- **Conceptual domain definition:** Lists of categories for marital status
- **Value domain name (1):** Marital Status Codes (1)
- **Permissible values:** <S, Not married>
  <M, Married>
- **Value domain name (2):** Marital Status Codes (2)

- **Permissible values:** <1, Not married>
  <2, Married>

Data Element Concepts

A data element concept is a concept that contains a population and one of its characteristics. It is the conceptual part of data, that is, independent of the values (i.e., the value domain). The classes (or entities) and attributes in data models approximate populations and characteristics.

A concept may be both a population and a characteristic, depending on its use. For instance, "occupation" is a characteristic of a person. On the other hand, as a population we care about its characteristics, such as physical requirements for a job in that occupation.

Populations and characteristics often are specialized to account for data associated with domains (of populations) or narrower properties. The generic relation is used, and value meanings from enumerated conceptual domains (i.e., classifications) provide the additional characteristics to narrow the concept. Here is an example:

Example 7: Specializing Populations and Characteristics

- **Population:** Persons of the U.S.
- **Classification:** Sex {Male, Female}
- **Specialized Population:** Male Persons of the U.S.
- **Characteristic:** Income
- **Classification:** Income Type {Wages, Retirement, Dividends, Interest, Inheritance, Other}
- **Specialized Characteristic:** Income derived by wages only

Data Elements

Data elements are containers for data, and in some sense, they are indivisible (i.e., elemental). A data element is the association between a data element concept and a value domain. Both data element concepts and value domains may be associated with many data elements.

The term data element is synonymous with the term variable, as it is understood by programmers. Thus, the datatype associated with a data element is important. The data element concept and the value domain provide a semantic model for a data element. The datatype provides a computational model.

METADATA REGISTRIES

Introduction

A database of metadata that supports the functionality of registration is a metadata registry. A metadata registry contains metadata describing data constructs (i.e., data elements, data element concepts, value domains, conceptual domains, populations, characteristics, and value meanings) that retain data semantics.

Of course, the metadata registry contains descriptions of data constructs, not the constructs themselves. This is analogous to the registries maintained by governments to keep track of motor vehicles. A description of each motor vehicle is entered in the registry, but not the vehicle itself.

Metadata Registry Model

The international standard ISO/IEC 11179 (ISO, 2003) contains a metadata registry model for data semantics. It contains two main parts: the conceptual level and the syntactical level. The conceptual level contains the data element concept and conceptual domain. Both are concepts as described above. The syntactical level contains the data element and value domain. Both are containers for data values.

Figure 2 pictorially represents the following facts, some of which were previously mentioned:

- A data element is the association between a data element concept and a value domain.
- Many data elements may share the same data element concept.
- Many data elements may share the same value domain.
- Value domains are not necessarily related to any data element.
- Two value domains that share all the value meanings are conceptually equivalent and share the same conceptual domain.
- Two value domains that share some value meanings are conceptually related and share the same conceptual domain in a concept system containing each of their conceptual domains.
- Many value domains may share the same conceptual domain.
- A data element concept is related to a single conceptual domain, so all the data elements sharing the same data element concept share conceptually related representations.
- In addition to the facts illustrated in the Figure 1, there are two other important facts that need stating:
  - Relationships among data element concepts may be maintained in a metadata registry, which implies that a concept system of data element concepts may be maintained.
  - Relationships among conceptual domains may be maintained in a metadata registry, which

Figure 2. Overview of basic metadata registry model for data semantics (adapted from ISO/IEC 11179)

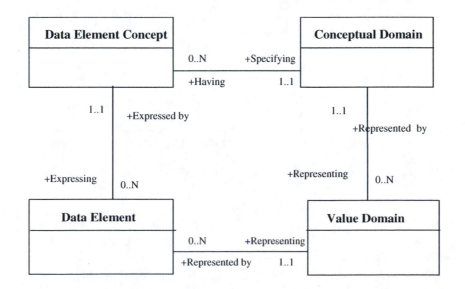

implies that a concept system of conceptual domains may be maintained.

Registration

Registration functions separate a metadata registry from a database of metadata. Registration is the set of rules, operations, and procedures that apply to a metadata registry. The three most important outcomes of registration are the ability to monitor the quality of metadata, provenance (the source of the metadata), and assigning an identifier to each object described.

Registration also requires a set of procedures for managing a registry, submitting metadata for registration of objects, and maintaining subject matter responsibility for metadata already submitted. For actual implementations of a metadata registry, there may be additional requirements.

Each description of a data construct is maintained in a uniform and prescribed manner. Identifiers, quality measures, responsible organizations, names, and definitions are recorded for every data construct.

There are several purposes to monitoring metadata quality. The main purposes are:

- Monitoring adherence to rules for providing metadata
- Monitoring adherence to rules for forming definitions and following naming conventions
- Determining whether a description still has relevance
- Determining the similarity of related data constructs and harmonizing their differences
- Determining whether it is possible to ever get higher quality metadata for some data constructs

Every data construct registered in a metadata registry is assigned a unique identifier. Identifiers are a means to keep track of descriptions for administration purposes, to refer to descriptions by remote users of the registry, and to aid in metadata transfer between registries.

The registration authority is the organization responsible for setting the procedures, administering, and maintaining a registry. The submitting organization is responsible for requesting that a new description be registered in the registry. The steward is responsible for the subject matter content of each registered item. Each of these roles is described in ISO/IEC 11179 (ISO, 2003).

Implementations

Organizations for which data is a major corporate asset or share that data outside the organization have a need to describe the semantics of their data. Many organizations around the world use metadata registries. Some of these exist, and others are under construction. The U.S. Environmental Protection Agency (EPA, n.d.) and the Australian Institute for Health and Welfare (AIHW, n.d.) have functioning metadata registries on the Web. Statistics Canada (Johanis, 2000) and the Australian Bureau of Statistics (Oakley, 2004) are building metadata registries for internal use to support the business lifecycle.

CONCLUSION

This article describes how to manage the semantics of data. It incorporates ideas from statistics that generalize to all data. Data have conceptual and representational components. The conceptual component has contextual and symbolic semantics. The contextual semantics describes the population of objects being described and a characteristic of that population. The symbolic semantics describes the meaning of the categories defined for the characteristic. The representational component includes the values used to represent the categories in the symbolic semantics.

Metadata registries, such as those that conform to the international standard for metadata registries, ISO/IEC 11179, describe and manage data semantics. Many organizations are building metadata registries, and some are available on the Web.

REFERENCES

Aboiteboul, S., Buneman, P., & Suciu, D. (2000). *Data on the Web*. San Francisco: Morgan Kaufman.

AIHW. (n.d.). *Australian Institute for Health and Welfare Knowledge Base*. Retrieved July 2004, from *http://www.aihw.gov.au/knowledgebase*

CEN. (1995). *Medical informatics: Categorical structures of systems of concepts*. Draft. Brussels: European Committee for Standardization.

Census Bureau. (n.d.). *American Fact Finder*. Retrieved July 2004, from *http://factfinder.census.gov/*

EPA. (n.d.) *Environmental Protection Agency Environmental Data Registry*. Retrieved July 2004, from *http://www.epa.gov/edr*

FGDC (Federal Geographic Data Committee). (n.d.). *Content Standard for Digital Geospatial Metadata*. Retrieved July 2004, from *http://www.fgdc.gov/metadata/metadata.html*

Froeschl, K., Grossmann, W., & Del Vecchio, V. (2003). *The concept of statistical metadata. Deliverable #5 for MetaNet Project.* Retrieved July 2004, from *http://www.epros.ed.ac.uk/metanet/deliverables/D5/IST-1999-29093_D5.doc*

Gillman, D. (2003). Metadata registries, data harmonization, and maximizing use of a warehouse. *Proceedings of the Statistical Input Data Warehouse Workshop.* Canberra, Australia: Australian Bureau of Statistics.

Gillman, D., Appel, M., & LaPlant, W. (1996). Design principles for a unified statistical data/metadata system. *Proceedings of the 8th International Conference on Scientific and Statistical Database Management* (pp. 150-155). Los Alamitos, CA: IEEE Computer Society Press.

IBM. (n.d.). *Rational Rose®.* Retrieved July 2004, from *http://www.rational.com*

ICPSR (Inter-University Consortium for Political and Social Research). (n.d.). *Data Documentation Initiative.* Retrieved July 2004, from *http://www.icpsr.umich.edu/ddi*

ISO. (1995). *ISO/IEC 11404: Language independent datatypes.* Geneva: International Organization for Standardization and International Electrotechnical Commission.

ISO. (1999). *ISO 704: Principles and methods of terminology.* Geneva: International Organization for Standardization.

ISO. (2000). *ISO 1087-1: Terminology: Part 1: Vocabulary.* Geneva: International Organization for Standardization.

ISO. (2003). *ISO/IEC 11179: Metadata registries (all parts).* Geneva: International Organization for Standardization and International Electrotechnical Commission.

ISO. (2004). *ISO/IEC TR 20943-3: Procedures for achieving metadata registry content consistency—part 3: Value domains.* Geneva: International Organization for Standardization and International Electrotechnical Commission.

Johanis, P. (2000, November). Statistics Canada's integrated metadatabase: Our experience to date. *Proceedings of the UNECE Workshop on Statistical Metadata,* Washington, DC.

King, W., Marks, P., & McCoy, S. (2002). The most important issues in knowledge management. *Communications of the ACM, 45*(9), 93-97.

Lakoff, G. (2002). *Women, fire, and dangerous things* (reprint ed.). Chicago: University of Chicago Press.

Oakley, G. (2004, February). Using ISO/IEC 11179 to help with metadata management problems. *Proceedings of the Joint UNECE, Eurostat, OECD Workshop on Statistical Metadata,* Geneva.

Oracle Corp. (n.d.). *Oracle Designer®.* Retrieved July 2004 from *http://www.oracle.com*

Sager, J. (1990). *A practical course in terminology processing.* Philadelphia: John Benjamins.

Sowa, J. (2000). *Knowledge representation.* Pacific Grove, CA: Brooks/Cole—Thomson Learning

Ullman, J. (1982). *Principles of database systems* (2nd ed). Rockville, MD: Computer Science Press.

Wedberg, A. (1982). *A history of philosophy—volume 1: Antiquity and the Middle Ages.* Oxford: Clarendon Press.

W3C (World Wide Web Consortium). (1997). *HyperText Markup Language.* HTML 4.0 reference specification. Retrieved July 2004, from *http://www.w3c.org*

W3C. (2004). *Extensible Markup Language.* XML 1.1 Reference Specification. Retrieved July 2004 from *http://www.w3c.org*

KEY TERMS

Characteristic: Abstraction of a property of a set of objects. For example, "Dan has blue-gray eyes" means "blue-gray eyes" is the property of Dan associated with the characteristic "eye color" of people. The term *property* is misused in the ISO/IEC 11179 standard. There, it means the same thing as characteristic.

Concept: Mental constructs, units of thought, or unit of knowledge created by a unique combination of characteristics.

Designation: Representation of a concept by a sign, which denotes it.

Metadata: Data that are used to describe some other resource, including other data. No data are always metadata, but all data may be used as metadata under particular circumstances or context.

Object: Something conceivable or perceivable. This subsumes the object-oriented notion of object.

Partition: Non-empty set of mutually exclusive and exhaustive subsets of some other set. The number of subsets is not necessarily finite.

Property: Attribute used to describe or distinguish an object.

Semantics: Study of meaning. Data semantics is the meaning denoted by some data.

ENDNOTE

[1]   A partition is a non-empty set of mutually exclusive and exhaustive subsets of some other set. The number of subsets is not necessarily finite.

Description Logic–Based Resource Retrieval

D

Simona Colucci
Politecnico di Bari, Italy

Tommaso Di Noia
Politecnico di Bari, Italy

Eugenio Di Sciascio
Politecnico di Bari, Italy

Francesco M. Donini
Universitá della Tuscia, Italy

Marina Mongiello
Politecnico di Bari, Italy

INTRODUCTION

Resource retrieval addresses the problem of finding best matches to a request among available resources, with both the request and the resources described with respect to a shared interpretation of the knowledge domain the resource belongs to. The problem of resource matching and retrieval arises in several scenarios, among them, personnel recruitment and job assignment, dating agencies, but also generic electronic marketplaces, Web services discovery and composition, resource matching in the Grid. All these scenarios share a common purpose: given a request, find among available descriptions those best fulfilling it, or at "worse," when nothing better exists, those that fulfill at least some of the requirements.

Exact, or full, matches are usually rare and the true *matchmaking* process is aimed at providing one or more "promising" matches to be explored. Non-exact matches should take into account both missing information—details that could be positively assessed in a second phase—and conflicting information—details that could leverage negotiation if the proposed match is worth enough pursuing.

Because of its intangibility, it is now a widely shared opinion that knowledge has to be modeled to make unambiguous the interpretation of any information domain. This disambiguation process is usually obtained through an *ontology,* that is, a specification of a representational vocabulary for a shared domain of discourse—definitions of classes, relations, functions, and other objects (Gruber, 1993).

Once a knowledge domain has been modeled, and several different resources have been described using such a model, issues that need to be faced for efficient knowledge management are: What, if any, kind of retrieval is possible on these resources? How could we benefit both of the model and formalisms used to build the model, in order to perform a "smart" search of described resources matching a request? The above questions focus on important aspects of knowledge-based retrieval:

- formalisms used to model a knowledge domain
- retrieval services that fully use the expressiveness of the formalism to infer new knowledge from the model in order to perform a knowledge-based search

Knowledge domain is modeled with a formalism, whose expressiveness is used in the retrieval process to infer not elicited information from the model. In such a context, choosing this formalism strongly affects the complexity, as well as success probability, of the retrieval process.

In recent years *description logics* (DLs) have been investigated by both the academic and industrial world as a formalism for knowledge representation. Modeling an information domain through the formalism of a DL allows one to employ reasoning services provided by DLs to perform a knowledge-based search. Knowledge domains are formalized in ontologies, which resource descriptions refer to. The use of ontologies allows elicited descriptions to be stored so that information can be inferred from them to retrieve a resource.

The remainder of this article is structured as follows: Background work is revised, including DL basics with associated reasoning services and previous approaches to resource retrieval, including non-logic- and logic-based alternatives. Then, we introduce semantic-based resource retrieval, first highlighting new non-standard inference services and then showing how they can be used for "smart" resource retrieval. Finally, we propose some future trends and draw a conclusion.

BACKGROUND

Description Logics Basics

Description, or terminological, logics (Baader, Calvanese, Mc Guinness, Nardi, & Patel-Schneider, 2002; Donini, Lenzerini, Nardi, & Schaerf, 1996) are a family of logic formalisms for knowledge representation. All DLs are endowed of a syntax and a model-theoretic semantics. The basic syntax elements of DLs are: *concept* names, *role* names, *individuals*. Intuitively, concepts stand for sets of objects, and roles link objects belonging to different concepts. Individuals are special named elements of the sets of objects concepts represent.

We give a more formal definition of the outlined basic elements by introducing the concept of semantic *interpretation*.

Definition 1: *A semantic interpretation is a pair $I=(\Delta, \cdot^I)$ made up of a domain Δ and an interpretation function $\cdot^I$, which maps every concept to a subset of Δ, every role to a subset of $\Delta \times \Delta$, and every individual to an element of Δ.*

Usually, a so-called *Unique Name Assumption* (UNA) is made which ensures different individuals to be mapped to different elements of Δ, i.e., $a^I \neq b^I$ for individuals $a \neq b$.

Every DL allows one to combine basic elements using *constructors* to form concept and role *expressions*. Each DL has its distinguished set of constructors, though all of them provide the *conjunction* of concepts, usually denoted as $\sqcap$. Among the distinguishing concept expressions constructors we enumerate disjunction $\sqcup$ of concepts and complement $\neg$ to close concept expressions under Boolean operations.

Role expressions can be obtained by combining roles with concepts using *existential role quantification* and *universal role quantification*. Other constructs may involve counting, as *number restrictions*.

Many other constructs can be defined, increasing the expressive power of the DL, up to n-ary relations (Calvanese, De Giacomo, & Lenzerini, 1998). Nevertheless, it is a well-known result that usually leads to an explosion in computational complexity of inference services (Brachman & Levesque, 1984). Hence, a trade-off is needed between expressivity and expected performance of reasoning services.

Once expressions have been built, they are given semantics by defining the interpretation function over each construct. Concept conjunction is interpreted as set intersection, and the other Boolean connectives also have the usual set-theoretic interpretation. The interpretation of constructs involving quantification on roles needs to make domain elements explicit.

Concept expressions can be used in *inclusion assertions*, and *definitions*, which impose restrictions on possible interpretations according to the knowledge elicited for a given domain. Definitions are useful to give a meaningful name to particular combinations. Sets of such inclusions are called TBox (terminological box). A TBox, which basically amounts to an ontology, represents a formal, shared, and objective *intensional* knowledge on a domain. Individuals can be asserted to belong to a concept using membership assertions in an ABox. An ABox is the *extensional* knowledge of the domain that can be described based on the TBox. The semantics of inclusions and definitions is based on set containment: An interpretation I satisfies an inclusion $C \sqsubseteq D$ if $C^I \sqsubseteq D^I$, and it satisfies a definition $C = D$ when $C^I = D^I$. A *model* of a TBox T is an interpretation satisfying all inclusions and definitions of T. DL-based systems are equipped with reasoning services: logical problems whose solution can make explicit knowledge that was implicit in the assertions.

DL-based systems usually provide at least two basic reasoning services for T:

- **Concept Satisfiability:** Given a TBox T and a concept C, does there exist at least one model of T assigning a non-empty extension to C?
- **Subsumption:** Given a TBox T and two concepts C and D, is C more general than D in any model of T?

The previous services can be seen, from a knowledge management perspective, in a more informal way:

- **Concept Satisfiability:** Given an ontology (T) modeling the domain we are investigating on and a description (C) of a resource referring to the ontology: Is the information modeled in the description consistent with the one in the ontology?
- **Subsumption:** Given an ontology (T) modeling the domain we are investigating on and two resources described by expressions (C, D) referring to the information modeled in the ontology: Is the information about a resource more general than the one related to the other one?

Both Subsumption and Satisfiability are adequate in all those knowledge management contexts where a yes/no answer is enough. For example, given a resource and a request represented respectively by a concept O and a concept R, using Concept Satisfiability we are able to determine whether they are compatible, *that is, O* models information that is not in conflict with the one modeled by R. This task can be performed checking the satisfiability of the concept $O \sqcap R$.

On the other hand, Subsumption can be used to verify, for example, if a resource described by O satisfies a request R, namely, if the relation $O \sqsubseteq R$ holds, then O is more specific than R and it contains at least all the requested features.

For ABoxes, other standard inference services have been defined. Among the various devised, we point out:

- **Instance checking:** An assertion α is entailed by an Abox A, if every interpretation that satisfies A also satisfies α.
- **Retrieval problem:** Given an Abox A and a concept C, find all individuals α such that A entails $C(\alpha)$.
- **Realization problem:** Given an individual α and a set of concepts, find the most specific concept C from the set such that A entails $C(\alpha)$.

Together with standard inference problems, non-standard ones have been proposed and investigated. The *least common subsumer* (*lcs*), *most specific concept* (*msc*), *unification, matching* and *concept rewriting* have been thoroughly presented by Baader et al. (2002). The application field for *lcs* and *msc* is the construction of DL knowledge bases using a bottom-up approach instead of the usual top-down one (Baader & Turhan, 2002). The *unification* and *matching* services are useful for large knowledge bases maintenance, allowing knowledge engineers to catch equivalence or subsumption relationships among concept expressions (Baader & Turhan, 2002). With *concept rewriting* the readability of large concept descriptions can be increased, by using concepts defined in an ontology.

Although the general approach proposed in this article does not depend on a particular DL, it has been fully devised for a particular DL, namely the *ALN* (Attributive Language with Number Restrictions). Constructs allowed in an *ALN* DL are:

- ⊤ Universal Concept: All the objects in the domain
- ⊥ Bottom Concept: The empty set
- **A** Atomic Concepts: All the objects belonging to the set represented by A
- ¬**A** Atomic negation: All the objects not belonging to the set represented by A

- **C⊓D** Intersection: The objects belonging both to C and D
- **∀R.C** Universal restriction: All the objects participating to the R relation whose range are all the objects belonging to C
- **∃R** Unqualified existential restriction: There exists at least one object participating in the relation R. Notice that $\exists R \equiv (\geq 1 R)$
- **(≥ n R) | (≤ n R) | (= n R)** Unqualified number restrictions: Respectively, the minimum, the maximum, and the exact number of objects participating in the relation R. We write (= n R) for $(\geq n R)\sqcap(\leq n R)$

We adopt a simple-TBox, that is, in all the axioms (for both inclusion and definition) the left side is represented by a concept name, and there is only one axiom for each atomic concept.

Ontologies using this logic can be easily modeled using languages for the Semantic Web. These languages have been conceived to allow for representation of machine-understandable, unambiguous, description of Web content through the creation of domain ontologies, and aim at increasing openness and interoperability in the Web environment. The strong relation between DLs and the introduced languages for the Semantic Web also is evident in the definition of the OWL language. In fact, there are three different sub-languages for OWL:

- **OWL-Lite:** It allows class hierarchy and simple constraints on relation between classes.
- **OWL-DL:** Based on description logics theoretical studies, it allows a great expressiveness keeping computational soundness and completeness.
- **OWL-Full:** Using such a language, there is a huge syntactic flexibility and expressiveness. This freedom is paid in terms of no computational guarantee.

The *ALN* DL is basically a subset of OWL-DL.

Approaches to Resource Retrieval

We start with a description of various approaches to resource retrieval, highlighting limitations of non-logical approaches, then discussing the general knowledge representation principles that a logical approach may yield.

Modeling a resource retrieval framework using standard relational database techniques would require to completely align the attributes of the available and requested resources descriptions, in order to evaluate a match. On the other hand, if requests and offers are simple names or terms, the only possible match would be *identity,* resulting in an all-or-nothing approach to the retrieval process. Vague query answering, proposed by Motro (1988), was an initial effort to overcome limitations of relational databases, with the aid of weights attributed to several search variables.

Vector-based techniques taken by classical information retrieval can be used as well, thus, reverting the search for a matching request to similarity between weighted vectors of stemmed terms, as proposed in the COINS matchmaker (Kuokka & Harada, 1996) or in LARKS (Sycara, Klusch, & Lu, 2002). Such a formalization for resource descriptions makes retrieval only probabilistic because descriptions lack a document structure, causing strange situations to ensue. Let us consider for example the following sentences, describing respectively competences required for a job in a company and competences provided by a worker: "engineer, with experience of two years as project manager, not full time employed, available to transfers" and "experienced project manager, full time employed as engineer for two years, not available to transfers."

The former is a simple example in which two descriptions in obvious conflict may be considered an exact match because of the formalism chosen to represent them. A further approach structures resource descriptions as a set of words. This formalization allows one to evaluate not only identity between sets but also some interesting set-based relations between descriptions, such as inclusion, partial overlap, and cardinality of set difference. Modeling resource descriptions as set of words is anyway too much sensible to the choice of words employed to be successfully used: the fixed terminology misses meaning that relate words. Such a problem can be overcome by giving terms a logical and shared meaning through an ontology (Fensel, van Harmelen, Horrocks, McGuinness, & Patel-Schneider, 2001). Nevertheless, set-based approaches have some properties we believe are fundamental in a resource matching and retrieval process. If we are searching for a resource described through a set of words, we also are interested in sets including the one we search, because they completely fulfill the resource to retrieve. Moreover, even if there are characteristics of the retrieved resource not elicited in the description of the searched resource, an exact match is still possible because absent information have not to be considered negative. The two statements may be summarized in the following property:

- **Property 1 [Open-world descriptions]:** The absence of a characteristic in the description of a resource to be retrieved should not be interpreted as a constraint of absence. Instead, it should be considered as a characteristic that could be either refined later or left open if it is irrelevant for the user searching for the resource.

The set-based match evaluation is non-symmetric: If we search for a resource A, whose describing set of words is included in a set characterizing resource B, we may consider B a resource perfectly satisfying the request for A. On the other hand, if we use the description of B for the search, A also may satisfy the request only partially, as some of the terms describing B may be not included in the A set. We formalize this behaviour as follows:

- **Property 2 [Non-symmetric evaluation]:** Given two resource descriptions A and B, a resource retrieval system may give different rankings depending on whether it is searching A using B description as query, or B using A as query.

From now on, we assume that resource descriptions, requested and offered, are expressed in a DL. This approach includes the sets-of-keywords one, since a set of keywords also can be considered as a conjunction of concept names. We also assume that a common ontology is established, as a TBox in DL.

With reference to recent related work on logic-based matching and retrieval of resources, approaches are concentrated on electronic marketplaces, where resources are supplies and demands, and Web services discovery, where resources are e-services to be discovered and composed. Finin, Fritzson, McKay, and McEntire (1994) and Kuokka and Harada (1996) introduced matchmaking based on KQML, as an approach whereby potential producers/consumers could provide descriptions of their products/needs to be later unified by a matchmaker engine to identify potential matches. A rule-based approach using the knowledge interchange format (KIF) (Genesereth, 1991), the SHADE prototype (Kuokka & Harada, 1996), or a free-text comparison (the COINS prototype) (Kuokka & Harada, 1996) were used. Approaches similar to the previous ones were deployed in SIMS (Arens, Knoblock, & Shen, 1996), which used KQML and LOOM as description language and InfoSleuth (Jacobs & Shea, 1995), which adopted KIF and the deductive database language LDL++. LOOM also is at the basis of the matching algorithm addressed by Gil and Ramachandran (2001).

Sycara et al. (2002) and Paolucci, Kawamura, Payne, and Sycara (2002) proposed the LARKS language, specifically designed for agent advertisement. The matching process is a mixture of classical IR analysis of text and semantic match via Q-subsumption. Nevertheless, a basic service of a semantic approach, such as inconsistency check, seems unavailable with this type of match.

First approaches based on standard inference services offered by DL reasoners were proposed by Di Sciascio, Donini, Mongiello, and Piscitelli (2001), Gonzales-Castillo, Trastour, and Bartolini (2001), and Trastour, Bartolini, and Priest (2002). Di Noia, Di Sciascio, Donini, and Mongiello (2003b, 2003c) described and motivated properties that a matchmaker should have in a DL-based framework, and algorithms to classify and rank matches into classes were presented. Matchmaking of Web services, providing a ranking of matches based on this DL-based approach was presented by Colucci, Di Noia, Di Sciascio, Donini, and Mongiello (2003b). An extension to the approach by Paolucci et al. (2002) was proposed by Li and Horrocks (2003) where two new levels for service profiles matching were introduced. Notice that the *intersection satisfiable* level was introduced, whose definition is close to the one of *potential matching* proposed by Di Noia et al. (2003b), but no measure of similarity among intersection satisfiable concepts was given.

Benatallah, Hacid, Rey, and Toumani (2003) proposed an approach to Web services discovery based on the difference operator in DLs (Teege, 1994), followed by a set covering operation optimized using hypergraph techniques.

SEMANTIC-BASED RESOURCE RETRIEVAL

The Need for New Non-Standard Reasoning Services

In all those approaches where no explanation on the obtained results is requested or no belief revision is admitted, Subsumption and Consistency Checking are enough. The following are typical examples of the behaviour the reasoning services would have for resource retrieval:

- **Subsumption:** "Yes, your request is completely satisfied by resourceX"

  resourceX $\sqsubseteq$ request

- **Consistency Checking:** "No, your request is not compatible with resourceX"

  resourceX $\sqcap$ request $\equiv \perp$

Unfortunately, in a semantic-based resource retrieval system a simple yes/no answer cannot be enough; the requester is often interested in explanations especially

when the system returns a negative answer. Some of the questions are:

- *"What should I give up in my request in order to regain satisfiability with the offered resource?"*
- *"How should I contract my request?"*
- *"What should I revise in my request in order to be completely satisfied?"*
- *"What should I abduce in the available resource?"*

Colucci et al. (2003a) and Di Noia et al. (2003a) introduced and defined Concept Abduction—for no-Subsumption explanation—and Concept Contraction—both for un-Consistency Checking explanation and for belief revision suggestion—as new non-standard inference services for DLs. In this subsection, we briefly recall their definitions, explaining their rationale and the need for them in resource retrieval.

Concept Contraction

Starting with the concepts O and R, if the conjunction $O \sqcap R$ is unsatisfiable in the TBox T representing the ontology—*that is,* they are not compatible with each other—we may want to retract requirements in R, G (for *Give up*), to obtain a concept K (for *Keep*) such that $K \sqcap O$ is satisfiable in T. This scenario can be formally depicted as:

Definition 2: *Let L be a DL, O, R, be two concepts in L, and T be a set of axioms in L, where both O and R are satisfiable in T. A Concept Contraction Problem (CCP), identified by* $\langle L,R,O,T \rangle$*, is finding a pair of concepts* $\langle G,K \rangle \in L \times L$ *such that* $T \models R \equiv G \sqcap K$*, and* $K \sqcap O$ *is satisfiable in T. We call K a contraction of R according to O and T.*

We use Q as a symbol for a CCP, and we denote with SOLCCP(Q) the set of all solutions to a CCP Q. We note that there is always the trivial solution $\langle G,K \rangle = \langle R,T \rangle$ to a CCP. This solution corresponds to the most drastic contraction, that gives up everything of R. In our resource retrieval framework, it models the (infrequent) situation in which, in front of some very appealing resource O, incompatible with the requested one, a user just gives up completely his or her specifications R in order to meet O. On the other hand, when $O \sqcap R$ is satisfiable in T, the "best" possible solution is $\langle T,R \rangle$, that is, give up nothing, if possible. Hence, a Concept Contraction problem is an extension of a satisfiable one. Since usually one wants to give up as few things as possible, some minimality in the contraction must be defined (Gärdenfors, 1988). In most cases, a pure logic-based approach could not be sufficient to decide between which beliefs to give up and which to keep. There is the need of modeling and defining some extra-logical information to be taken into account. One approach is to give up minimal information (Colucci et al., 2003a). Another one considers some information more important than other and the information that should be retracted is the least important one, that is negotiable and strict constraints are introduced (Di Noia, Di Sciascio, & Donini, 2004).

Concept Abduction

If the offered resource O and the requested one R are compatible, the partial specifications problem still holds, that is, it could be the case that O—though compatible—does not imply R. Then, it is necessary to assess what should be hypothesized (H) in O in order to completely satisfy R.

Definition 3: Let L be a DL, O, R, be two concepts in L, and T be a set of axioms in L, where both O and R are satisfiable in T. A Concept Abduction Problem (CAP), identified by $\langle L,R,O,T \rangle$, is finding a concept H ∈ L such that $T \vDash O \sqcap H \sqsubseteq R$, and moreover O ⊓ H is satisfiable in T. We call H a hypothesis about O according to R and T.

We use P as a symbol for a CAP, and SOL(P) to denote the set of all solutions to a CAP P. Observe that in the definition, we limit to satisfiable O and R, since R unsatisfiable implies that the CAP has no solution at all, while O unsatisfiable leads to counterintuitive results ($\neg R$ would be a solution in that case). If $O \sqsubseteq R$, then we have H = T as a solution to the related CAP. Hence, Concept Abduction extends subsumption. On the other hand, if $O \equiv T$ then H $\sqsubseteq R$.

Notice that both Concept Abduction and Concept Contraction can be used for, respectively, subsumption and satisfiability explanation. For Concept Contraction, having two concepts not compatible with each other, in the solution $\langle G,K \rangle$ to the CCP $\langle L,R,O,T \rangle$, G represents "why" O and R are not compatible. For Concept Abduction , having R and O such that $T \nvDash O \sqsubseteq R$, the solution H to the CAP $\langle L,R,O,T \rangle$ represents "why" the subsumption relation does not hold. H amounts to *what is specified in R and not in O*.

Expected performances of inference services are obviously of paramount importance to evaluate the feasibility of an approach. We hence provide some insight into complexity issues of the services. We note that since Concept Abduction extends Concept Subsumption w.r.t. a TBox, complexity lower bounds of the latter problem carry over to decision problems related to a CAP.

- **Proposition:** Let P $\langle L,R,O,T \rangle$, be a CAP. If Concept Subsumption w.r.t. a TBox in L is a problem C-hard for a complexity class C, then deciding whether a concept belongs to SOL(P) is C-hard.

As Concept Abduction extends Subsumption, Concept Contraction extends satisfiability—in particular, satisfiability of a conjunction K ⊓ R.

- **Proposition**: Let L be a DL containing $\mathcal{AL}$, and let Concept Satisfiability w.r.t. a TBox in L be a problem C-hard for a complexity class C. Then, deciding whether a pair of concepts is a solution of a CCP Q=$\langle L,R,O,T \rangle$, is C-hard.

Both for Concept Abduction and Concept Contraction, for every single CAP—conversely CCP—there is not only one solution. Different kinds of solution can be classified with respect to different minimality criteria. Colucci et al. (2003a), Di Noia et al. (2003a), and Colucci et al. (2004) present the definition of some minimality criteria and corresponding complexity results.

Approximate Resource Retrieval via Concept Abduction and Concept Contraction

We now show how the previously introduced services can help in an approximate, semantic-based search of resources, fully exploiting their structured description. Let us suppose to have request R and an appealing resource O such that $T \vDash R \sqcap O \equiv \bot$, *that is,* they are incompatible. In order to gain compatibility, a Concept Contraction is needed so that giving up G in R, the remaining K can be satisfied by O. Now, if $T \nvDash O \sqsubseteq K$, the solution H_K to the CAP $\langle L,K,O,T \rangle$ represents what is in K and is not specified in O.

As the O obtained is an approximated match of R, then a measure is needed on how good the approximation is. Given more than one appealing resource, which one is the best approximation? How can it be assigned a numerical score to the approximation, based on K, H and G, in order to rank the resources?

In table 1, we present a simple algorithm to provide answers to the raised issues.

Notice that $H = abduce(O,R,T)$ [rows 3,6] determines H is a solution for the CAP $\langle L,R,O,T \rangle$; $\langle G,K \rangle = contract(O,R,T)$ [row 2] determines $\langle G,K \rangle$ is a solution for the CCP $\langle L,R, O,T \rangle$

Table 1.

---

algorithm *Retrieve(O,R,T, L)*

input O, $R \equiv K \sqcap G$ concepts in L such that both $T \vDash O$ and $T \vDash R$.

output $\langle G, H \rangle$ respectively the part in R that should be given up and the part in O that should be hypothesized in order to find an exact match between O and R.

begin algorithm

1:     **if** $T \vDash R \sqcap O \equiv \bot$ **then**
2:             $\langle G, K \rangle = contract(O,R,T)$;
3:             $H_K = abduce(O,K,T)$;
4:             **return** $\langle G, H_K \rangle$;
5:     **else**
6:             $H = abduce(O,R,T)$;
7:             **return** $\langle \top, H \rangle$;

end algorithm.

The algorithm *retrieve* returns values useful in a retrieval system where explanation of the results is needed and/or a belief revision process is admitted.

[*rows 1-4*] Having a requested resource R and an offered one O, if their descriptions conjunction is not satisfiable w.r.t. the ontology they refer to (i.e., they are not compatible with each other for some concepts in their descriptions), first a contraction on R is performed in order to regain compatibility [*row 2*], and then what is to be hypothesized in O in order to completely satisfy R (its contraction) is computed [*row 3*]. The returned values represent:

- **G:** What is to be given up in the request in order to continue the process, or, in other words, why R is not compatible with O.
- **H_K:** After the contraction of R, the request is represented by K, that is, the portion of R which is compatible with O. H_K represents what is to be hypothesized in O in order to completely satisfy K, or, in other words, why O does not completely satisfy K.

[*rows 5-7*] If the conjunction of R's and O's description is satisfiable w.r.t. the ontology they refer to, then no contraction is needed and only an abductive process is carried out.

The algorithm does not depend on the particular DL adopted. Based on the minimality criteria proposed by Di Noia et al. (2003a), the length $|H|$ of the solution to a CAP for an *ALN* DL can be computed as proposed by Di Noia et al. (2003c). Hence, a relevance ranking score can be computed by an utility function defined as $U(|G|,|K|,|H_K|)$.

The rationale of the *retrieve* algorithm is hereafter presented with the aid of a simple example. Let T, R, O be a set of axioms, a searched resource description, and an available resource description, respectively, defined as follows:

$T = \{$
PC $\sqsubseteq$ Computer $\sqcap \exists$hasOS
HomePC $\sqsubseteq$ PC $\sqcap \forall$hasOS.MS $\sqcap \exists$pointer
HighLevel $\sqsubseteq \exists$cost $\sqcap \forall$cost.Expensive
Expensive $\sqsubseteq \neg$Cheap
MS $\sqsubseteq \neg$Unix
$\}$

$R =$ HomePC $\sqcap \exists$monitor $\sqcap \forall$pointer.$\forall$cost.Cheap
$O =$ PC $\sqcap \exists$pointer $\sqcap \forall$pointer.(Mouse $\sqcap$ HighLevel) $\sqcap \forall$hasOS.Unix

First, we observe that $T \vDash R \sqcap O \equiv \bot$, due to the specifications on both Operating System and cost of the pointer. Hence, the algorithm performs a Concept Contraction solving the CCP $\langle L,R,O,T \rangle$. *A solution for the previous CCP is:*

$\langle G,K \rangle = \langle$ HomePC $\sqcap \forall$pointer.$\forall$cost.Cheap, PC $\sqcap \exists$pointer $\sqcap \exists$monitor$\rangle$

After the contraction operation, the remaining part of R is not yet satisfied by O. That is, $O \sqsubseteq K$ does not hold. To compute what is needed in order to realize the subsumption relation, *retrieve* solves the *CAP* $\langle L,K,O,T \rangle$. A solution for the previous CAP is: $H_K = \exists$monitor

If the searching agent—with the term agent used in its broadest sense—is interested in O, it must give up HomePC $\sqcap \forall$pointer.$\forall$cost.Cheap in its R and ask for further information about $\exists$monitor.

Retrieval performances have been usually evaluated in classical full text information retrieval in terms of precision and recall. Although such measures require large datasets to have any significance, it can be expected that semantic-based retrieval can provide at least a noteworthy improvement in precision, with respect to free-text probabilistic approaches.

FUTURE TRENDS

As the Semantic Web initiative gets momentum, more and more resources described using structured descriptions—based on ontologies—will become available (Schwartz, 2003). Current and future application scenarios of the semantic-based retrieval techniques presented here include: electronic-marketplaces of tangible or intangible goods, skill management systems, mediators for Web service discovery and for grid-based computational resources, and dating and personnel recruitment agencies. The increased availability of semantically annotated descriptions will hence boost the emergence of knowledge-based systems able to take full advantage of these structured descriptions to obtain accurate and efficient retrieval. The framework and services described in this article are general enough to be used in the approximate search and retrieval of a variety of resources, and systems using them can provide—adopting different minimality criteria—logically motivated relevance-based rankings in the retrieval process. The necessary trade-off between expressivity and performance of semantic-based systems is likely to be exploited adopting various approaches. Among them, tableaux-based algorithms (Colucci et al., 2004); careful choice of constructs able to keep complexity tractable, as proposed for example with DL-Lite by Calvanese, De Giacomo, Lenzerini, Rosati, & Vetere (2004), and combined use of DL-based easoners with classical relational databases to face scalability issues when dealing with large numbers of individuals (Horrocks, Li, Turi, & Bechhofer, 2004).

CONCLUSION

We have presented and motivated new DL-based inference services for semantic-based resource retrieval. Currently, our approach is fully devised, and algorithms and a prototype system have been implemented for an *ALN* description logic. Work also is in progress to extend the approach to more expressive DLs, while keeping time performances still acceptable.

REFERENCES

Arens, Y., Knoblock, C.A., & Shen, W. (1996). Query reformulation for dynamic information integration. *Journal of Intelligent Information Systems, 6*, 99-130.

Baader, F., Calvanese, D., Mc Guinness, D., Nardi, D., & Patel-Schneider, P. (Eds.). (2002). *The description logic handbook*. Cambridge, MA: Cambridge University Press.

Baader, F., & Turhan, A. (2002). On the problem of computing small representations of least common subsumers. *KI 2002: Advances in Artificial Intelligence, 25th Annual German Conference on AI*, Vol. 2479 of *Lecture Notes in Computer Science* (pp. 99-113). Berlin: Springer.

Benatallah, B., Hacid, M.-S., Rey, C., & Toumani, F. (2003). Request rewriting-based Web service discovery. *International Semantic Web Conference*, vol. 2870 of *Lecture Notes in Computer Science* (pp. 242-257). Berlin: Springer.

Brachman, R., & Levesque, H. (1984). The tractability of subsumption in frame-based description languages. *Proceedings of the 4th National Conference on Artificial Intelligence (AAAI-84)* (pp. 34-37). Cambridge, MA: Morgan Kaufmann.

Calvanese, D., De Giacomo, G., & Lenzerini, M. (1998). On the decidability of query containment under constraints. *Proceedings of the 17th ACM SIGACT SIGMOD SIGART Symposium on Principles of Database Systems (PODS'98)* (pp. 149-158).

Calvanese, D., De Giacomo, G., Lenzerini, M., Rosati, R., & Vetere, G. (2004). DL-Lite: Practical reasoning for rich Dls. *Proceedings of the 17th International Workshop on Description Logics (DL'04)*, vol. 104 of *CEUR Workshop Proceedings*.

Colucci, S., Di Noia, T., Di Sciascio, E., Donini, F., & Mongiello, M. (2003a). Concept abduction and contraction in description logics. *Proceedings of the 16th International Workshop on Description Logics (DL'03)*, vol. 81 of *CEUR Workshop Proceedings*.

Colucci, S., Di Noia, T., Di Sciascio, E., Donini, F., & Mongiello, M. (2003b). Logic based approach to Web services discovery and matchmaking. *Proceedings of the E-Services Workshop at ICEC'03*.

Colucci, S., Di Noia, T., Di Sciascio, E., Donini, F., & Mongiello, M. (2004). Uniform tableaux-based approach to concept abductiona and contraction in ALN DL. *Proceedings of the 17th International Workshop on Description Logics (DL'04)*, vol. 104 of *CEUR Workshop Proceedings*.

Di Noia, T., Di Sciascio, E., Donini, F., & Mongiello, M. (2003a). Abductive matchmaking using description logics. *Proceedings of the 18th International Joint Conference on Artificial Intelligence (IJCAI 2003)* (pp. 337-342). Morgan Kaufmann.

Di Noia, T., Di Sciascio, E., Donini, F., & Mongiello, M. (2003b). Semantic matchmaking in a P-2-P electronic marketplace. *Proceedings of the Symposium on Applied Computing (SAC'03)* (pp. 582-586). ACM.

Di Noia, T., Di Sciascio, E., Donini, F., & Mongiello, M. (2003c). A system for principled matchmaking in an electronic marketplace. *Proceeding for the International World Wide Web Conference (WWW '03)* (pp. 321-330). ACM.

Di Noia, T., Di Sciascio, E., & Donini, F. (2004). Extending semantic-based matchmaking via concept abduction and contraction. *Proceedings of the 14th International Conference on Knowledge Engineering and Knowledge Management (EKAW 2004)*, vol. 3257 of *Lecture Notes in Computer Science* (pp. 307-320). Springer.

Di Sciascio, E., Donini, F., Mongiello, M., & Piscitelli, G. (2001). A knowledge-based system for person-to-person e-commerce. *Proceedings Workshop on Applications of Description Logics (KI 2001)*, vol. 44 of *CEUR Workshop Proceedings*.

Donini, F. M., Lenzerini, M., Nardi, D., & Schaerf, A. (1996). Reasoning in description logics. In Brewka, G. (Ed.), *Principles of knowledge representation: Studies in logic, language and information* (pp. 193-238). Stanford, CA: CSLI Publications.

Fensel, D., van Harmelen, F., Horrocks, I., McGuinness, D., & Patel-Schneider, P.F. (2001). OIL: An ontology infrastructure for the Semantic Web. *IEEE Intelligent Systems, 16*(2), 38-45.

Finin, T., Fritzson, R., McKay, D., & McEntire, R. (1994). KQML as an agent communication language. *Proceedings of the 3rd International Conference on Information and Knowledge Management (CIKM'94)* (pp. 456-463). ACM.

Gärdenfors, P. (1988). *Knowledge in flux: Modeling the dynamics of epistemic states*. Cambridge, MA: Bradford Books, MIT Press.

Genesereth, M.R. (1991). Knowledge interchange format. *Principles of Knowledge Representation and Reasoning: Proceedings of the 2nd International Conference* (pp. 599-600). Cambridge, MA: Morgan Kaufmann.

Gil, Y., & Ramachandran, S. (2001). PHOSPHORUS: A task based agent matchmaker. *Proceedings for AGENTS '01* (pp. 110-111). ACM.

Gonzales-Castillo, J., Trastour, D., & Bartolini, C. (2001). Description logics for matchmaking of services. *Proceedings of the Workshop on Application of Description Logics (KI 2001)*, vol. 44 of *CEUR Workshop Proceedings*.

Gruber, T. (1993). Toward principles for the design of ontologies used for knowledge sharing. *International Journal of Human-Computer Studies, 43*(5), 907-928.

Horrocks, I., Li, L., Turi, D., & Bechhofer, S. (2004). The instance store: DL reasoning with large numbers of individuals. *Proceedings of the 17th International Workshop on Description Logics (DL'04)*, vol. 104 of *CEUR Workshop Proceedings*.

Jacobs, N., & Shea, R. (1995). Carnot and Infosleuth: Database technology and the Web. *Proceedings of the ACM SIGMOD International Conference on Management of Data* (pp. 443-444). ACM.

Kuokka, D., & Harada, L. (1996). Integrating information via matchmaking. *Journal of Intelligent Information Systems, 6*, 261-279.

Li, L., & Horrocks, I. (2003). A software framework for matchmaking based on Semantic Web technology. *Proceedings of the International World Wide Web Conference (WWW '03)* (pp. 331-339). ACM.

Motro, A. (1988). VAGUE: A user interface to relational databases that permits vague queries. *ACM Transactions on Office Information Systems, 6*(3), 187-214.

Paolucci, M., Kawamura, T., Payne, T., & Sycara, K. (2002). Semantic matching of Web services capabilities. *The Semantic Web—ISWC 2002*, number 2342 in *Lecture Notes in Computer Science* (pp. 333-347). Berlin: Springer-Verlag.

Schwartz, David G., Open IS (2003). Semantics and the Semantic Web: The road ahead. *IEEE Intelligent Systems, 18*(3), 52-58.

Sycara, K., Widoff, S., Klusch, M., & Lu, J. (2002). LARKS: Dynamic matchmaking among heterogeneus software agents in cyberspace. *Autonomous agents and multi-agent systems, 5*, 173-203.

Teege, G. (1994). Making the difference: A subtraction operation for description logics. *Proceedings of the 4th International Conference on the Principles of Knowledge Representation and Reasoning (KR'94)* (pp. 540-550). Cambridge, MA: Morgan Kaufmann.

Trastour, D., Bartolini, C., & Priest, C. (2002). Semantic Web support for the business-to-business e-commerce lifecycle. *Proceedings of the WWW '02* (pp. 89-98). ACM.

KEY TERMS

Belief Revision: It is the process of changing beliefs to reflect the acquisition of new information. A fundamental issue in belief revision is how to decide information to retract in order to maintain consistency, when the addition of a new belief to a theory would make it inconsistent.

Concept Abduction: Non-standard reasoning service provided by DLs. Abduction is a form of non-monotonic reasoning, modeling commonsense reasoning, usually aimed at finding an explanation for some given symptoms or manifestations. Concept Abduction captures the reasoning mechanism—namely, making hypotheses—involved when some constraints required by a resource request R are not specified in a offered resource O—that obviously in later stages of the request/offer interaction might turn out to be fulfilled or not.

Concept Contraction: Non-standard reasoning service provided by DLs. Contraction is the first step in belief revision. Concept Contraction captures the possibility to relax some of the constraints of a requested resource R when they are in conflict with those of an offered resource O—that is, when $O \sqcap R$ is an unsatisfiable concept.

Description Logics: Also known as *terminological logics,* it is a family of logic formalisms for knowledge representation endowed of a syntax and a semantics, which is model theoretic. The basic syntax elements of description logics (DLs) are: *Concept names* standing for sets of objects, *role names* linking objects in different concepts, and *individuals* used for named elements belonging to objects. Basic elements can be combined using constructors to form concept and role *expressions* to be used in *inclusion assertions* and *definitions*, that impose restrictions on possible interpretations according to the knowledge elicited for a given domain. Each DL has its set of constructors.

Matchmaking: The problem of providing satisfactory responses to requests in an open environment. Responses are searched among the available offers, searching the most appropriate to satisfy the request.

Resource Retrieval: A Resource Retrieval model is a 4-tuple $\langle S, r, T, U(s_i, r) \rangle$ where:

- S is a set of descriptions (representations) $s_i \in S$, of the resources belonging to the search space.
- r is the description for the searched resource.
- T is a logic schema representing the knowledge used to define both each $s_i \in S$ and r.
- $U(s_i, r)$ is a utility function $U : S \rightarrow \Re$, assigning a score to the relevance of each retrieved resource with respect to r.

Satisfiability: Standard reasoning service provided by DLs. It checks the consistency of an expression w.r.t. the knowledge elicited for a given domain. More formally, given a TBox T and a concepts C, C is satisfiable w.r.t. T if there exists at least one interpretation satisfying inclusions and definitions of T in which the set of individuals belonging to C may be non-empty.

Subsumption: Standard reasoning service provided by DLs. It is used to check if an expression, formalized in DL, is more specific than another one w.r.t. the knowledge elicited for a given domain. More formally, given a TBox T and two concepts C and D, C *subsumes* D if C is more general than D in any interpretation satisfying inclusions and definitions of T.

Dissemination in Portals

Steven Woods
Boeing Phantom Works, USA

Stephen R. Poteet
Boeing Phantom Works, USA

Anne Kao
Boeing Phantom Works, USA

Lesley Quach
Boeing Phantom Works, USA

INTRODUCTION

While there are many aspects to managing corporate knowledge, one key issue is how to disseminate corporate documents with appropriate context. Upon finding an article on a certain subject, for example the material properties of titanium, a reader is likely to be interested in related articles such as applications of titanium or manufacturing methods for titanium parts. Each related article has the potential to increase the reader's knowledge of the subject. Therefore, organizing documents into categories of interest plays an essential role in discovering and interpreting information. Furthermore, categories can be expected to provide historical context, describing how titanium was used in early designs or initial practices used for the repair of titanium parts.

While most large companies make a practice of cataloging and controlling well-established documents, there is a vast set of *explicit information* that has not traditionally been effectively disseminated. This class of information is less formal and may be exchanged, updated, and otherwise managed at the local level. Such information is usually not controlled at the corporate level or governed by the same organizations established to handle more stable information. Processes to disseminate such information tend to be ad hoc or nonexistent. In this article, we discuss the elements necessary to effectively disseminate informal and explicit information not controlled at the enterprise level. While the main emphasis of the article is to promote a general process for the dissemination of this type of material in large corporations, we will use a specific implementation of this process at the Boeing Company as an illustrative example.

BACKGROUND

Traditionally, the dissemination of corporate knowledge has taken a number of different forms. First, there are the methods of classic library science often as implemented by a formal corporate library staffed by trained librarians (Taylor, 2000). This is used for things that are well established such as textbooks, established how-to knowledge on a subject, published papers on a subject, and so on. Second, it has long been necessary to disseminate official policy and procedure through "Command and Control" processes and associated media. In addition, certain industries also require configuration control processes for special classes of information such as product data, drawings, and manufacturing rejection and acceptance documentation. These are all subject to an authentication process, flowing top-down to intended users. A third, extremely important approach to knowledge maintenance and dissemination has been through mentoring and establishment of departments aligned to technical specialties and communities of interest. These approaches are particularly well suited for *tacit knowledge*. A fourth category of knowledge sharing applies to the communication of explicit knowledge among peers but also includes dissemination to management and other reference groups. This method applies to information that is less formal and frequently ephemeral.

This fourth method is of an entirely more fluid nature and, in some cases, represents the majority of a corporation's explicit knowledge. While it is appropriate for the enterprise to disseminate formal information using traditional, formal means, there is a need to disseminate less formal information as well. This informal knowledge often includes the most current information within a company and without adequate dissemination, corporate decision-making is likely to fall short. In summary, stable and formal information is well handled by existing library or document release systems. Ephemeral, less formal, and generally less controlled content, while important, is currently only shared across the enterprise by a variety of ad hoc means, if at all.

MAIN FOCUS OF THE ARTICLE

This article focuses on how to systematically share this fourth category of informal and uncontrolled knowledge. The ideal for knowledge dissemination is to make sure information of this type can be well integrated into existing formal content, taking advantage of the context that has been created over time by librarians and other formal content management systems. To achieve this, it is necessary to organize this knowledge in a way that is consonant with the information categories of multiple existing systems. This is made possible by using an enterprise *ontology* or some form of controlled system of keywords which can be mapped to existing vocabularies. Portals, and other tools which allow content aggregation and term mapping, enable sharing of this knowledge at a physical level. It provides search and simple navigation across sources, as well as security services to restrict access as needed. A central ontology combined with an interactive text classification tool make dissemination of this knowledge possible at a content level.

In the matter of assigning documents to categories, we emphasize the importance of involving subject matter experts. Traditionally, this is done by librarians who are trained to catalog (categorize) content. However, in the case when authors are widely distributed throughout a complex corporate enterprise, we suggest that text classification software be used by these subject matter experts to facilitate broad knowledge dissemination. The challenge is to provide text classification services which can be used to produce high quality results by users who are not trained in library science.

The essential elements of a distributed dissemination scheme for this type of explicit but informal knowledge are a portal, an ontology, a text classification system, and a publication process. In combination, these four elements allow autonomous subgroups of a corporate entity to interact with common resources and tools to publish their local work in a way that places it within a context comprehensible to an enterprise audience.

Knowledge dissemination, as used here, applies specifically to explicit knowledge captured in documents from many sources. There are a number of frameworks that address the life cycle of explicit knowledge (Bock, 1997; O'Dell, 1998), but here we will follow the steps outlined by Mack (2001). In this framework, the basic tasks in knowledge work are Capture/Extract, Analyze/Organize, Find, Create/Synthesize, and Distribute/Share. In particular, text classification has direct benefit to the Analyze/Organize and Find stages and portal services will be the basis of the Distribute/Share stage. As discussed here, knowledge dissemination applies to the Analyze/Organize, Find, and Distribute/Share stages.

Portals

A portal is used to collect content from many different sources, resulting in a virtual collection available through a single point of access. This aggregation of content is perhaps the key characteristic of all portal products. In addition, a portal provides some capability for metadata management whereby tags and values can be directly replicated from source documents or harmonized within the virtual collection by mapping them to a centralized schema. In addition, a portal may permit the addition of metadata based on characteristics of the source system or based on the decisions made by the group about how ontology terms will be attached to documents. The documents themselves remain in their source system, maintained, refreshed, or deleted by the groups that own them.

Other kinds of information systems besides portals can be useful for knowledge dissemination. However portals, in one form or another, are well suited for publishing a distributed collection based on the intellectual products of many subgroups. Further, because of their flexibility in combining a variety of tools and services, portals can be customized to create a rich knowledge-sharing environment. For example, portals can readily support search and navigation. In addition, they can be extended to support personalization services, which would allow even more focused dissemination.

Thus, portals are a natural element to aid in knowledge dissemination. They can be used to achieve the key goal of achieving awareness (Alavi, 1999; Prusak, 1997). Indeed, creating awareness is a goal of dissemination and is a prerequisite to collaboration or further synthesis.

Ontologies

To produce an organization of corporate documents that can be readily shared, it is essential to have some standard in the form either of a corporate *taxonomy*, a corporate *thesaurus*, or both. What is minimally necessary is simply a list of controlled keywords expressing

Figure 1. The AeroNet ontology contains more than 60,000 concepts used as categories for text classification and subsequent knowledge dissemination. This figure shows a small fragment of the total ontology.

A (tiny) fragment of AeroNet...

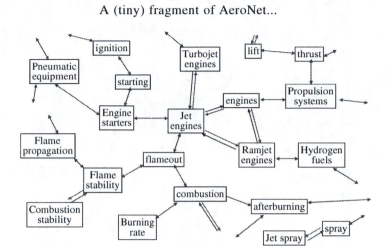

the topics that are important to the enterprise. We refer to the concepts expressed by these keywords as *knowledge categories*. Ideally, there is some kind of structure or organization to the knowledge categories, for example, a *generalization-specialization hierarchy*. Such a specification of the things that can be talked about and their relationships is referred to in artificial intelligence as an *ontology*. There is a strong advantage to organizing documents this way, because it enables much easier and better quality search, and greater use of the knowledge in those documents. In the Boeing case, there were about 60,000 knowledge categories as well as generalization-specialization relationships, synonymy relationships, and more general "is-related-to" relationships, so that the ontology is somewhat richer than a hierarchy (see Figure 1) (Clark, 2000).

This approach benefits most when it can build on an existing cataloging scheme, such as one maintained by an enterprise library system or a professional organization (e.g., the IEEE, Institute of Electrical and Electronics Engineers), or a taxonomy provided by an industrial consortium (e.g., the ATA, or Air Transport Association). The ontology used in the Boeing realization of the approach derives from the corporate thesaurus, a list of controlled keywords sanctioned by the Boeing technical library system, together with the relationships among them. By using a set of controlled keywords created by corporate librarians, not only was an immense amount of time saved in constructing the taxonomy, but the system also was able to leverage off of their collective and accumulated expertise.

However, with some additional effort, categories can be established and applied even when such a resource is

not available or is not sufficiently complete. In this case, one approach is to use text clustering and automatic summarization (Kao, 2004). Text clustering serves to group documents together based on the words they contain. The words with the greatest frequency or strength either throughout or near the center of each cluster can summarize the documents in that cluster. Using this summary, domain experts, knowledge administrators or managers, or librarians can decide which clusters represent important categories to the enterprise and supply standard names for those categories. If desired, they can further subdivide or group the resulting categories giving generalization-specialization relationships, and shared summary words may suggest other relationships. Of course, while this approach will provide more consistency within the enterprise, it will lose the historical context provided by leveraging off of existing ontologies.

Once an ontology is available, the concepts must be attached to documents and used to retrieve those documents. We do not assume that those who are involved in knowledge dissemination, whether as knowledge provider or consumer, have either the training or perspective of librarians. Nevertheless, by allowing participants to interact with a controlled vocabulary in the context of their subject matter of interest and giving them a means to do so easily, the process can improve dissemination of knowledge by grouping topically similar documents together regardless of their original local vocabulary usage. What is required is a tool to aid the author or searcher in finding the appropriate categories, and that is the function of an automatic text classifier.

Figure 2. The Graphical User Interface (GUI) allows users to scan documents and find suggested categories from the AeroNet ontology based on the results of a text classifier.

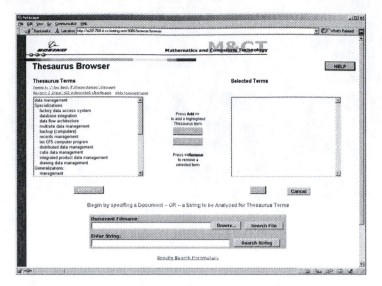

Text Classifier

An automatic text classifier takes a piece of text (e.g., a memo, an abstract, or a longer document), and based on its features (typically the words it contains) determines automatically which of a set of predetermined categories should be assigned to it. There are a number of different approaches, as summarized in Sebastiani (2002), including naïve Bayes (McCallum, 1998), support vector machines (Joachims, 1998), and logistic regression classifiers (Komarek, 2003).

Whichever approach is used, the first step in creating a classifier is to collect a *training sample* of texts that are already associated with the appropriate knowledge categories. Again, if the ontology derives from a set of keywords provided by a corporate library, there is likely a set of documents that have already been assigned these keywords or knowledge categories by the librarians (similarly for other sources of the controlled keywords, be it industrial consortia or professional societies or journals). At the Boeing Company, the abstracts for about 500,000 corporate documents in the technical library were used as the training sample.

If the categories are not a pre-existing set created by librarians or another standard professional body but have been developed as described using a text clustering algorithm, there may still be an easy way to create a training set. If the clustering algorithm generates convex clusters, as does K-means (Hartigan, 1975; Hartigan & Wong, 1979), the central members of the chosen clusters could serve as a training sample for those categories.

A text classifier is then constructed or trained based on the knowledge categories and the training sample of already categorized documents. The text classifier is then made available to both producers and consumers of the documents.

Authors of new documents to be entered into the system can use the text classifier to automatically propose knowledge categories appropriate to their document. In the Boeing implementation of this process, using the Graphical User Interface (GUI) shown in Figures 2 and 3, they first either type in the name and location of their document or browse to enter it into the classifier. The classifier then proposes the most likely knowledge categories ranked in order of likelihood in the box under the "Thesaurus Terms" label (see Figure 2). The authors can either select these terms or use AeroNet, a semantic network of thesaurus keywords developed at the Boeing Company (Clark, 2000), to navigate through the relationships among the categories to find more precise or more general knowledge categories to better describe their document. For example, the knowledge category "data management" might have been returned by the classifier (see Figure 3). By highlighting that and clicking on "EXPAND," AeroNet will bring up specializations like "factory data access system" and "data integration" and generalizations like "management" from which the user can select or use as a starting point for further navigation. If a category was selected incorrectly, they can remove it from the list by highlighting the category of interest and then clicking on the "Remove" button. When the list of selected knowledge categories is finalized, they associate it as metadata

Figure 3. Users can use the GUI to expand terms and then select those that represent the best categories for a given document.

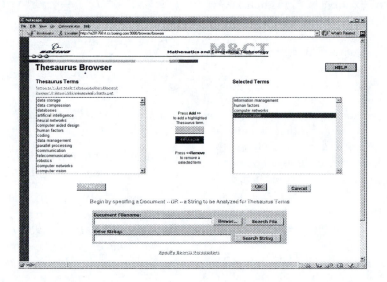

with the document by clicking on the "OK" button. This leads to not only much faster organization of information but also much more consistent quality in the organization of the information.

During the Find phase, the same text classifier can be used to identify information the user is interested in, without requiring the user to know the controlled vocabulary. Users may search for documents in the knowledge management system by entering a natural language query in a similar GUI and then selecting from the knowledge categories suggested to construct a precise query based on the content metadata. This allows the searcher to take advantage of the controlled vocabulary without memorizing it.

Publication Process

A workgroup needs to have a process that uses the classifier and portal for knowledge to be shared outside the group. Minimally, individuals would be required to add metadata to all documents they wish to publish. In addition, the group could use the text classifier on a representative sample of their documents to produce an initial down-selection of knowledge categories appropriate for most documents they are likely to produce.

FUTURE TRENDS

Effective classification and processes for knowledge dissemination have a positive impact on the evolution of

the *Semantic Web* (Berners-Lee, 2001; Schwartz, 2003). The basic idea of the Semantic Web is to make content on the Web machine-sensible with regards to its semantics (what the content is about) and with regards to machine reasoning over (what the content is related to or implies). In achieving semantics it will be important to classify content in terms of one or more ontologies. Tools involving automatic text classification will probably be essential in making this feasible. Using classification based on existing library practices, as an underpinning, to provide these semantics will have the same advantage as mentioned: the meaning assigned to Web content will be more likely consistent with existing catalogs of knowledge. In knowledge dissemination as discussed here, users are able to traverse the relationships in the ontology when choosing terms. However, in the future Semantic Web, reasoning one or more ontologies is expected to occur automatically, at runtime, whenever a query is activated. One function of the Semantic Web will be to improve knowledge dissemination by using software agents to execute queries selectively, taking advantage of both the context of the content and the matching profiles of end users. The different ways that reasoning, and multiple domain ontologies, can be leveraged in the future Semantic Web should substantially extend what is used in current knowledge classification and dissemination. Nonetheless, the four essential elements discussed here will still be crucial. Without effective text classification, reasoning capabilities cannot be expected to provide significant improvements.

CONCLUSION

There is a broad class of explicit but informal knowledge created within almost any enterprise which is not well disseminated by conventional means. Taking advantage of the Web infrastructure, this knowledge can be effectively disseminated using four essential elements: a portal, an ontology, a text classification system, and a publication process. Perhaps most important is a broad, cost-effective means to classify content according to an ontology. We suggest that text classification tools can provide such a means. Given this, portals can be used to disseminate knowledge, subject to appropriate publication processes, according to consistent categories. This provides context that links each new item of content to the information previously collected in library catalogs and published from other content resources.

Further, text classification helps overcome a substantial obstacle to knowledge dissemination within a large enterprise. Users are notoriously reluctant to assign any kind of metadata to documents that they author or maintain. By providing aids to classification, basic users can accomplish cataloging tasks without much training, time, or effort, and are therefore more likely to do it. In the approach outlined, the list of proposed knowledge categories is essentially consistent with the practice of professional librarians. Overall, the quality of the user-selected categories is likely to be much better compared to categories selected without assistance from a large ontology. Consequently, using these four elements, enterprises have at their disposal a means to disseminate a class of information that is likely to aid corporate decision-making and which should qualitatively increase a company's understanding of itself.

REFERENCES

Alavi, M., & Leidner, D. (1999). Knowledge management systems: Issues, challenges and benefits. *Communications of the AIS, 1*(2es), Article 7.

Berners-Lee, B., Hendler, J., & Lassila, O. (2001). The Semantic Web. *Scientific American,* May, 34-43.

Berry, M., Dumais, S., & O'Brien, G. (1995). Using linear algebra for intelligent information retrieval. *SIAM Review, 37*(4), 573-595.

Bock, G. (1997). Knowledge management frameworks. *Patricia Seybold's World Computing Report, 20*(2), February 1997.

Clark, P., Thompson, J., Holmback, H., & Duncan, L. (2000). Exploiting a thesaurus-based semantic net for knowledge-based search. *Proceedings of the 12th Conference on Innovative Applications of AI (AAAI/IAAI'00),* 12, (pp. 988-995).

Hartigan, J.A. (1975). *Clustering algorithms* (97-105). New York: Wiley

Hartigan, J.A., & Wong, M.A. (1979). A k-means clustering algorithm. *Applied Statistics 28,* 100-108.

Joachims, T. (1998). Text categorization with support vector machines: Learning with many relevant features. *Proceedings of ECML-98, 10th Eurpean Conference on Machine Learning,* Chemnitz, Germany (pp. 137-142).

Kao, A., Risch, J., & Poteet, S. (2004). Visualizing text data with TRUST and Starlight. To appear in *Interface 2004 Conference Proceedings.*

Komarek, P. (2003). Fast logistic regression for data mining, text classification and link detection. *Proceedings of NIPS2003, Conference on Neural Information Processing Systems.*

Mack, R., Ravin, Y., & Byrd, R.J. (2001). Knowledge portals and the emerging digital knowledge workplace. *IBM Systems Journal, 40*(4), 925-955.

McCallum, A., & Nigam, K. (1998). A comparison of event models for naïve bayes text classification. *AAAI-98 Workshop on Learning for Text Classification.*

O'Dell, C., Grayson, C. J., & Essaides, N. (1998). If only we knew what we know: *The transformation of internal knowledge and best practice.* New York: Free Press.

Prusak, L.(1997). Introduction to knowledge in organizations. In L. Prusak (Ed.), *Knowledge organizations.* Boston: Butterworth-Heinemann.

Schwartz, D.G. (2003) Open IS semantics and the Semantic Web: The road ahead. *IEEE Intelligent Systems, 3*(18), May/June, 52-58.

Sebastiani, F. (2002). Machine learning in automated text categorization. *ACM Computing Surveys, 34*(1), 1-47.

Taylor, A.G. (2000). *Wynar's introduction to catalog-ng and classification*. Westport, CT: Libraries Unlimited.

KEY TERMS

Explicit Knowledge/Information: Knowledge that is external in the form of documents, graphs, tables, and so forth.

Generalization-Specialization Hierarchy: A set of concepts organized by specialization and generalization relationships into an inverted tree-like structure, such that concepts higher in the tree are broader and encompass the concepts lower in the tree.

Knowledge Categories: Categories used to characterize the topics or areas of knowledge dealt with by documents.

Ontology: The set of the things that can be dealt with in a particular domain, together with their relationships.

Semantic Web: A vision of how the World Wide Web could be more intelligent, based on metatagging the content together with the ability to inference automatically how different Web objects are related to one another.

Tacit Knowledge/Information: Knowledge that is in people's heads and not externalized in documents or any other form.

Taxonomy: Any system of categories used to organize something, including documents, often less comprehensive than a thesaurus.

Thesaurus: Generally, a set of keywords used for indexing and information retrieval; in the Boeing case, various relationships, including synonymy, generalization, specialization, and related-to, also were included.

Training Sample: A set of documents or other pieces of text together with categories that are assigned to them to be used for training an automatic text classifier; there may be exactly one category assigned to each or there may be any number of categories, including zero, assigned to each piece of text.

D

Distributed Knowledge Management

Roberta Cuel
University of Verona, Italy

Paolo Bouquet
University of Trento, Italy

Matteo Bonifacio
University of Trento, Italy

INTRODUCTION

In dynamic markets (characterized by the specialization of work, outsourcing processes, just-in-time and distributed productions, etc.), firms have moved from hierarchical structures to networked models. These are based on both intraorganizational networks among strategic units, divisions, groups, and so on; and interorganizational networks, such as industrial districts and knowledge networks (Hamel & Prahalad, 1990). Production is based on the coordination of a constellation of units, some of which are part of the organization (administration, R&D [research and development], etc.), and others refer to different companies (such as specialized outsourcing production, logistics, etc.). All these units might not totally be controlled by a unique subject, and might grow and differentiate their activities in an autonomous way, coexisting as in a biofunctional system (Maturana & Varela, 1980) and creating unexpected combinations of processes and products (Chandler, 1962).

From a knowledge management (KM) point of view, the need of sharing knowledge among units in a very complex organization, or among networked organizations, increases the importance of introducing new ICT technologies and effective KM systems. For a long time, KM systems and ICT technologies have been proposed and applied as neutral tools whose implementation within the firm does not have any impact on knowledge flows. In particular, for technical reasons, centralized systems (for instance, enterprise knowledge portals [EKPs]) have been developed with the aim of making knowledge sharable and available in a general, objective, context-independent form, avoiding the persistence of noncorrect and nonconsistent information. Opposed to that point of view, studies focused on structuration theories (Giddens, 1984; Orlikowski, 1991) do not consider technology as a neutral asset of organizations. According to these theories, there are strong relationships and interdependencies among human actions, institutional roles (the organizational model de facto), and the technology architecture of KM systems applied within the company. One of the most important results in this area is that ICT technologies and KM systems should be shaped on the processes, practices, and the organizational models in which they are implemented; otherwise, they are bound to failure. As a consequence, in a complex organization composed by a constellation of units that manage in an autonomous way specialized processes, ICT technologies and KM systems must take into account the distributed nature of knowledge, and should allow coordination among autonomous units. In such a scenario, a KM system should satisfy two different needs: supporting the creation of specialized knowledge within a unit, and enabling the coordination of knowledge (and activities through which knowledge is exchanged) among units. These dual needs reflect the tension between the necessity for both highly specialized organization of work and flexible intergroup cooperation within and outside the organizations. This is reflected in the duality between the need for highly articulated local perspectives that make up the communication and knowledge-creation tissue of each community, and the need for sharing cultures and instruments that allow communication across different units (Mark, Gonzalez, Sarini, & Simone, 2002).

The first aim of this article is to describe how, according to structuration theories, a centralized KM system can be replaced or supported by a distributed one, in which the fact of having multiple and specialized "local knowledge bodies" is viewed more as an opportunity to exploit than as a problem to solve. The second aim of this article is to present a specific approach to designing systems for managing knowledge distributed across different units, called distributed knowledge management (DKM), whose principles and main concepts will be introduced and explained in the second part of this article.

BACKGROUND

Even though current KM systems use different technologies, tools, and methodologies (for in-depth discussion, see Davenport & Prusak, 1997; Nonaka & Takeuchi, 1995; Stewart, 2001; Wenger, 1998), most projects eventually lead to the creation of large and homogeneous knowledge repositories, in which corporate knowledge is made explicit and is collected, represented, and organized according to a single, supposedly shared, vision. Such a vision is meant to represent a shared conceptualisation of corporate knowledge, and thus to enable communication and knowledge sharing across the constellation of units composing the entire organization. All these activities are based on the common assumption that raw forms of knowledge, called implicit knowledge by Nonaka and Takeuchi, and tacit knowledge by Polany (1966), can be "cleaned up" from all contextual elements, and that the resulting "objective form" of knowledge can be explicitly represented in an abstract (independent from the original context) and general (applicable to any similar situation) form. This standard architecture of KM systems reflects a traditional view of management, in which managers try to centralize the control on the company processes by allocating and distributing resources and tasks to employees, and monitoring the proper execution of tasks and use of resources. This view of the managerial function leads to an approach to KM where processes of knowledge (resource) production and dissemination (tasks) must be centrally driven (allocated) and controlled (monitored). This condition is met only if knowledge is thought of as an object, which can therefore be kept separate from the people who produce it. Otherwise, as far as knowledge remains embedded within subjective dimensions, it becomes a resource that falls outside the boundaries of managerial control.

The typical outcome of this kind of vision is the creation of an EKP, namely, an interface (Web based) that provides a unique access point to corporate knowledge (Davenport & Prusak, 1997). Such an architecture is generally based on the following:

- technologies like content management tools, text miners, search engines, and so forth, which are used to produce a shared view of the entire collection of corporate documents
- common formats, such as HTML (hypertext markup language), XML (extensible markup language), and PDF (Portable Document Format), which are used to overcome the syntactic heterogeneity of documents from different knowledge sources
- chats and discussion groups, which are used to enable social interactions

Most business operators claim that this traditional approach is the right answer to the needs of managing corporate knowledge. However, many KM systems are deserted by users, who instead continue to produce and share knowledge as they did before, namely, through structures of relations and processes that are quite different from those embedded within the corporate-wide KM system. For instance, workers continue to use nonofficial tools such as shared directories, personalized and local databases, and so on (Bonifacio, Bouquet, & Cuel, 2002; Bonifacio, Bouquet, & Manzardo, 2000). In theory, KM systems are sold as systems that combine and integrate functions for the contextualized handling of both explicit and tacit knowledge throughout the entire organization or part of it. But, in practice, traditional KM systems manage knowledge according to a technology-oriented approach, which considers the cleaned-up and objective knowledge as the good and sharable knowledge (best practices, documentations, etc.) within the firm and among companies. In spite of the declared intention of supporting a subjective and social approach (through community and groupware applications), the way most KM systems are designed embodies an objective view of knowledge and reflects a marginal notion of sociality. In other words, KM systems aim at managing knowledge in an abstract, general, and context-independent form without taking into account the fact that knowledge is dependent on the context of production (the particular viewpoint of the individual), is embedded within subjective dimensions (the daily practice of work), and is not straightforwardly replicable.

Many authors who stressed the subjective nature of knowledge argued also that meanings are not externally given; rather, individuals give meaning to situations through subjective interpretation. Interpretation is subjective since it occurs according to some internal interpretation schema not directly accessible to other individuals. These schemas have been called, for example, mental spaces (Fauconnier, 1985), contexts (Ghidini & Giunchiglia, 2001; McCarthy, 1993), or mental models (Johnson-Laird, 1992). Internal schemas can be made partially accessible to other individuals through language since language is not just a means to communicate information, but also a way of manifesting an interpretation schema. As a consequence, when interpretation schemas are deeply different, people will tend to give a very different meaning to the same facts. Conversely, in order to produce similar interpretations, people need to some extent to share interpretation schemas, or at least to be able to make some conjectures on what the other people's schemas are. For in-depth discussion, see the notions of paradigms in Kuhn (1970), sociotechnical frames in Goffman (1974), and thought worlds in

Dougherty (1992). Since we are talking about organizations, and thus about a collective level, it is relevant to consider that without this intersubjective agreement (or at least believed agreement), communication cannot take place, coordinated action is impossible, and meaning remains connected just at an individual level (Weick, 1993). Thus, this approach leads to some significant consequences.

- Knowledge is intrinsically subjective as the meaning of any statement is always dependent on the context or on the interpreter's schema, which can be either explicit or implicit.
- At a collective level, groups of people can assume they share (or have a reciprocal view on) some part of their intrinsically subjective schemas. These common parts can emerge from participation and reification processes of the community's members, who share (or understand) the others' meanings through practices (Wenger, 1998). In other words, we can say that the intrinsically subjective schema can be shared, or at least coordinated, in the intersubjective agreements of the community's members.

As a result, the notion of knowledge as an absolute concept that refers to an ideal, objective picture of the world leaves the place to a notion of local knowledge, which refers to the different partial interpretations of portions of the world or domains that are generated by individuals and within groups of individuals (e.g., communities) through a process of negotiating interpretations. According to knowledge network theories (see Cross & Parker, 2004; Hildreth & Kimble, 2004), different and specialized actors that coordinate each other move beyond information sharing to the aggregation and creation of new knowledge, and obtain benefits from network communications and engagement strategies. Finally, the network of relationships, the local knowledge developed within a community, the inner motivation that drives people to share knowledge, and the knowledge they produce lead to the creation of an environment that sustains variety and is rich in creativity, namely, one that is innovative. As a consequence, many big organizations now consider communities, their autonomy, and their contextualized and local knowledge as vital components in their organizational KM strategies. Thus, local knowledge appears as the synthesis of both a collection of statements and the schemas that are used to give them meaning. Local knowledge is then a matter that was (and is continuously) socially negotiated by people that have an interest not only in building a common perspective (perspective making for Boland & Tenkasi, 1995, or single-loop learning for Argyris & Schoen, 1978), but

also in understanding how the world looks like from a different perspective (perspective taking for Boland & Tenkasi, or double-loop learning for Argyris & Schoen). Therefore, rather then being a monolithic picture of the world as it is, organizational knowledge appears as a heterogeneous and dynamic system of local knowledge that lives in the interplay between the need of sharing a perspective within a community (to incrementally improve performance) and of meeting different perspectives (to sustain innovation).

MAIN FOCUS OF THE ARTICLE: DISTRIBUTED KNOWLEDGE MANAGEMENT

In this article, we present a new approach to KM called DKM. It provides an original managerial and technological solution to the complementary needs of creating and consolidating (local) knowledge within communities, and of sharing and reproducing knowledge across them. It is based on the assumption that subjectivity and sociality are potential sources of value rather than problems to overcome, and on the idea of modeling organizations as constellations of knowledge nodes (KNs)-this way taking into account autonomous and locally managed knowledge sources-which need to cooperate and negotiate knowledge with others to sustain innovation. Thus, the continuous interplay of multiple instances of local knowledge and the interactions at the boundaries between different communities are critical factors for innovation and for the creation of new knowledge (Brown & Duguid, 1991).

Principles of DKM

DKM is based on two very general principles:

1. **Principle of Autonomy:** Each organizational unit should be granted a high degree of autonomy to manage its local knowledge. Autonomy can be allowed at different levels. We are mainly interested in what we call semantic autonomy, that is, the possibility of choosing the most appropriate conceptualisation of what is locally known (for example, through the creation of their own knowledge maps, contexts, ontologies, etc.).
2. **Principle of Coordination:** Each unit must be enabled to exchange knowledge with other units not through the adoption of a single common interpretation schema (this would be a violation of the first principle), but through a mechanism of projecting what other units know onto its own interpretation schema.

These two principles must support two qualitatively different processes: the autonomous management of knowledge locally produced within a single unit, and the coordination of the different units without a centrally defined view.

If a complex organization can be thought of as a constellation of autonomous units, an important issue is how this socially distributed architecture can be modeled to design an architecturally distributed computer-based system for supporting KM processes. To this end, we introduce the concept of the knowledge Node as the building block of a model for designing DKM systems.

The Definition of Knowledge Node

A KN can be viewed as the reification of organizational units, either formal (e.g., divisions, market sectors) or informal (e.g., interest groups, communities of practice, communities of knowing), that exhibit some degree of semantic autonomy. Each unit, in fact, can cope with KM only if the processes of knowledge (resource) production and dissemination (tasks) can be locally driven (allocated) and controlled (monitored). Moreover, each unit exhibits semantic autonomy through the development of local interpretation schemas (visions of the world). Each KN represents the following:

- **Knowledge Owner:** An entity (individual or collective) that has the capability of managing its own knowledge both from a conceptual and a technological point of view. Notice that most often knowledge owners within an organization are not formally recognized, and thus their semantic autonomy emerges in the creation of artifacts (e.g., databases, Web sites, collections of documents, archives, practices, and so on) that are not necessarily part of the official information system.

- **System of Artifacts:** An important assumption of DKM is that different organizational units tend to (autonomously) develop working tools that suit their internal needs, and that the choice and usage of these tools is a manifestation of their semantic autonomy. This may be for historical reasons (for example, people use old legacy systems that are still effective), but also because different tasks may require the use of different applications and data formats to work out effective procedures and to adopt a specific and often technical language. Examples of local applications are software systems, procedures, and other artifacts, such as relational databases, groupware, and content management tools, and shared directories. Even if technologies and data formats are the same for two or

more KNs, the appropriation (i.e., the local understanding and using of specific uses in a given setting) of each KN can be very different, depending, among other things, on the local interpretation schema.

- **One or More Locally Shared Conceptual Schemata:** It is a special artifact that represents (in an explicit or implicit way) a community's perspective. In simple situations, it can be the category system used to classify documents; in more complex scenarios, it can be an ontology, a collection of guidelines, or a business process. We can say that a schema is the reification of a KN's perspective, and its continuous, autonomous management is a powerful way of keeping a unit's perspective alive and productive.

- **Brokers and Boundary Objects:** They are individuals and objects (Bowker & Star, 1999; Wenger, 1998) legitimated by people to represent and understand (i.e., has direct access to) the locally shared conceptual schema of a KN. Brokers and boundary objects have the main aim of supporting knowledge owners to create and locally manage one or more shared conceptual schemata, and of meeting other brokers or analysing boundary objects that reify and express other local schemata. For instance, a personal agent could be a broker of a KN that knows its locally conceptual schemata and coordinate it with others.

KNs in a Case Study

In the past, we have analysed some complex organizations. A paradigmatic case study is Pizzarotti & C. S. p. A. Its business is focused on construction and prefabricated buildings, and KNs have been unveiled looking at knowledge owners, the systems of artifacts, the locally shared conceptual schemata, and, more importantly, the kind of knowledge that is exchanged within groups and the way in which people negotiate and coordinate knowledge across the whole organization. Through a large number of interviews, we discovered that building yards, registered offices, and cross-organizational communities have their own structures and their own ways of working to solve specific problems that depend on the kind of production and other local environmental factors (e.g., the weather, local customers and suppliers). Then they can be considered KNs. Though the firm does not formally recognize the existence of some of these units, every KN expresses semantic autonomy through specialized systems of artifacts that are used and appropriated in the way that best suits the local needs. For an in-depth description, see Cuel, Bonifacio, and Grosselle (2004).

A Methodology to Unveil Knowledge Nodes within a Complex Organization

In order to develop a KM system based on the DKM approach, an effective methodology of analysis is necessary. This methodology should take into account two relevant aspects, which reflect the two DKM principles.

- identifying the borders of existing KNs within the firm (principle of autonomy)
- identifying the way knowledge is exchanged across the whole organization through negotiation and coordination processes (principle of coordination)

Both aspects are based on social relations within and across communities in the firm, which can be analysed using different methodologies such as social network analysis (SNA) or ethnography. On one hand, SNA and other quantitative methodologies provide a good and general perspective on the organization, and allow the researcher to perceive the real structure of the organizational model by considering the relations among people and groups. They do not allow one to identify the reason why some groups are strategic and others are not. On the other hand, ethnography and other qualitative methodologies are based on the participation of the observer within the firm. The observer tries to achieve a detailed understanding of the circumstances, the strategies, and the power of the few subjects being studied, but cannot determine the significance of what she or he observes without gathering broad statistical information.

In the DKM approach, these two kinds of analysis are not sufficient to unveil KNs since it is difficult to identify the KNs' boundaries and knowledge-exchanging processes. As a matter of fact, individuals belonging to an organizational unit are socially interconnected to achieve different objectives and are often part of two or more units, thus using more than a conceptual schema. Therefore, it seems necessary to develop both quantitative and qualitative analysis in different phases through multiple series of questionnaires, ethnographic interviews (Spradley, 1979), and focus groups. The analysis should be organized in three phases: understanding the main picture of the firm, unveiling KNs and their relations, and validating the first results through focus groups or meetings with experts and workers involved in the organization activity. For an in-depth description, see Cuel (2003).

FUTURE TRENDS

The distributed approach to KM has many important implications, both from a managerial and technological perspective.

Managerial and Organizational Impacts of DKM

From a managerial standpoint, a distributed approach to KM poses fundamental challenges to the traditional model of the managerial function. In particular, managers should abandon the widespread practice of having a unique and homogeneous materialization of knowledge represented as a knowledge-based asset. Managers are requested to change their control processes, imposing strategic directions on innovation processes and enabling knowledge materialization from the ground.

Moreover, even if socially the attitude of sharing knowledge within a group is embedded in worker practices, managers should try to avoid personal or group behaviours of competitiveness and detention of knowledge, and should promote knowledge sharing and coordination across the whole organization. Therefore, managers should work out new roles (for instance, the roles of knowledge manager and broker) that determine new skills for knowledge coordination and negotiation (Argyris & Schoen, 1978; King & Andersen, 2002), and create a culture (using wage incentives, group bonuses, etc.) that allows people to identify themselves within the company as part of a whole and to share knowledge for a common, real gain. People's power should derive more from sharing useful knowledge within the firm and among groups than from owning it.

Technological Impacts of DKM

From a technological standpoint, distributed architectures presuppose the explicit recognition of the distributed nature of knowledge. Distributed architectures should sustain autonomy at different levels: the technological (different groups may use different technologies), the syntactic (different groups may use different information formats), and, most of all, the semantic (different groups may generate different systems of meaning, namely, local schemata). From a group's or a community's perspective, a distributed system supports the exploitation and representation of a community's schemata; this is the layer upon which a community's members produce and negotiate common views. Contexts can be represented as local ontologies (for instance, using Context OWL; Bouquet, Giunchiglia, van Harmelen, Serafini, & Stuckenschmidt, 2003), taxonomies, and, in general, theories through which community members interpret their environment and make sense of organizational events. Although theories conceptualise local events and thoughts, new methodologies and tools are needed for allowing workers (with no knowledge on formal logic or computer science) to create and manage local schemata. These methodologies and tools should allow both the creation of a schemata from scratch (analysing documents, repeated occurrences within databases, etc.) and the chance for management to make sense of processes on concepts through very simple visualization systems.

CONCLUSION

The DKM approach satisfies the managerial needs of creating and consolidating knowledge within each KN and of coordinating it across a constellation of KNs. Therefore, brokers and boundary objects should assume an important role, facilitating coordination processes and allowing communication between KNs, thus increasing innovation opportunities within the organization. As we said, these processes can be facilitated by the creation of a collaborative culture and attitude. Moreover, new organizational roles are needed that allow people to both identify themselves within the firm as part of a whole and to see knowledge sharing as way to achieve a common gain.

The centralized approach is not necessarily in conflict with the decentralized one. Depending on the type of knowledge, the environment, and the structure of the organization, it is beneficial to apply a more centralized (e.g., for secured and general knowledge) or a more decentralized KM approach (e.g., for ad hoc and specific knowledge). In particular, traditional and centralized KM systems, developed according to the technology-driven approach, can be effectively used in an organization in which the environment is stable and the need of efficiency is stronger than the pressure toward innovation. Problems arise when the KM systems create a mismatch between the social process of knowledge creation and sharing (organizational models de facto, processes and practices of KM) and the technological architecture (Camussone & Cuel, 2003). Therefore, two dual processes can be produced by the introduction of a noncoherent KM system: The information systems' architecture will be appropriated or shaped according to the modus operandi of its users (some functionalities of the system will be deserted by users, and others will be shaped on the users' daily work), or the organizational model, processes, and shared practices will change and adapt to the functionalities imposed by the KM system. From this, it follows that a KM system should be designed to be consistent with the distributed social form in which knowledge is created within organizations, finding its right level of centralization and decentralization. As a consequence, the composition of units in the organizational models and the composition of KNs should be compatible, and from this standpoint, they should therefore be analysed or at least planned during the designing phase. Currently, there is not a unique methodology of DKM architecture design, and different types of groups, units, and so forth can be unveiled as KNs. Finally, there are many technology-driven approaches that allow developers to design KM systems, and only few of them take into account organizational features (see Davenport, Long, and Beers, 1998) to analyse how politics, information strategies, behaviours, and culture should be considered for a successful KM system.

REFERENCES

Argyris, C., & Schoen, D. A. (1978). *Organizational learning: A theory of action perspective.* Reading, MA: Addison-Wesley.

Boland, R. J., & Tenkasi, R. V. (1995). Perspective making and perspective taking in communities of knowing. *Organization Science, 6*(4), 350-372.

Bonifacio, M., Bouquet, P., & Cuel, R. (2002). Knowledge nodes: The building blocks of a distributed approach to knowledge management. *Journal for Universal Computer Science, 8*(6), 652-661.

Bonifacio, M., Bouquet, P., & Manzardo, A. (2000). A distributed intelligence paradigm for knowledge management. *Proceedings of AAAI Spring Symposium Series 2000 on Bringing Knowledge to Business Processes.*

Bouquet, P., Giunchiglia, F., van Harmelen, F., Serafini, L., & Stuckenschmidt, H. (2003). C-OWL: Contextualizing ontologies. *Proceedings of the Second International Semantic Web Conference (ISWC2003)*, Sanibel Island, FL.

Bowker, G., & Star, S. L. (1999). *Sorting things out: Classification and its consequences.* Cambridge, MA: MIT Press.

Brown, J. S., & Duguid, P. (1991). Organizational learning and communities of practices: Toward a unified view of working, learning and innovation. *Organization Science, 2*.

Camussone, P. F., & Cuel, R. (2003). Knowledge management e modelli organizzativi: La scelta tra accentramento e distribuzione delle responsabilità. *Proceedings of AIDEA*.

Chandler, A. D. (1962). *Strategy and structure: Chapters in the history of the industrial enterprise.* Cambridge, MA: MIT Press.

Cross, R., & Parker, A. (2004). *The hidden power of social networks: Understanding how work really gets done in organizations.* Boston: HBS Press Book.

Cuel, R. (2003). A knowledge-oriented analysis of organizations. Knowledge nodes: The building blocks of a distributed knowledge management approach. *Proceedings of DCEIS*, (Vol. 10, No. 3). France.

Cuel, R., Bonifacio, M., & Grosselle, M. (2004). Knowledge nodes: The reification of organizational communities. The Pizzarotti case study. *Journal for Universal Computer Science*.

Davenport, T. H., Long, D. W. D., & Beers, M. C. (1998). Successful knowledge management projects. *Sloan Management Review, 39*(2).

Davenport, T. H., & Prusak, L. (1997). *Working knowledge: How organizations manage what they know.* Boston: Harvard Business School Press.

Dougherty, D. (1992). Interpretative barriers to successful product innovation in large firms. *Organization Science, 3*, 179-202.

Fauconnier, G. (1985). *Mental spaces: Aspects of meaning construction in natural language.* Bradford Books, Cambridge, MA: MIT Press.

Ghidini, C., & Giunchiglia, F. (2001). Local models semantics, or contextual reasoning = locality + compatibility. *Artificial Intelligence, 127*(2), 221-259.

Giddens, A. (1984). *The constitution of society.* Berkeley: University of California Press.

Goffman, I. (1974). *Frame analysis.* New York: Harper & Row.

Hamel, C., & Prahalad, G. (1990). The core competences of the corporation. *Harvard Business Review, 68*(3), 79-91.

Hildreth, P., & Kimble, C. (2004). *Knowledge networks: Innovation through communities of practice.* Hershey, PA: IGP.

Johnson-Laird, P. (1992). *Mental models.* Cambridge, MA: Cambridge University Press.

King, N., & Anderson, N. (2002). *Managing innovation and change: A critical guide for organizations.* London: Thomson.

Kuhn, T. S. (1970). *The structure of scientific evolutions.* Chicago: University of Chicago Press.

Mark, G., Gonzalez, V., Sarini, M., & Simone, C. (2002). Reconciling different perspectives: An experiment on technology support. *Proceedings of COOP02* (pp. 23-37).

Maturana, H. R., & Varela, F. J. (1980). *Autopoiesis and cognition: The realization of the living.* Dordrecht, Holland: D. Reidel.

McCarthy, J. (1993). Notes on formalizing context. *Proceedings of the 13th International Joint Conference in Artificial Intelligence (IJCAI'93)* (pp. 555-560).

Nonaka, I., & Takeuchi, H. (1995). *The knowledge creating company.* New York: Oxford University Press.

Orlikowski, W. J. (1991). Integrated information environment or matrix of control? The contradictory implications of information technology. *Accounting, Management, and Information Technology, 1*(1), 9-42.

Polany, M. (1966). *The tacit dimension.* London: Routeledge & Keagan Paul.

Spradley, J. P. (1979). *The ethnographic interview.* New York: Holt, Rinehart, Winston.

Stewart, T. A. (2001). *The wealth of knowledge: Intellectual capital and the twenty-first century organization.* New York: Doubleday.

Weick, E. K. (1993). Collective mind in organizations: Heedful interrelating on flight decks. *Administrative Science Quarterly, 38*.

Wenger, E. (1998). *Communities of practice: Learning, meaning, and identity.* Cambridge, MA: Cambridge University Press.

KEY TERMS

Brokers and Boundary Objects: Individuals or objects (Bowker & Star, 1999) that are legitimated to know and represent (i.e., have direct access to) the locally shared conceptual schema of a knowledge owner.

Distributed Knowledge Management Approach: A knowledge management approach based on the duality of perspective making and taking, the localization and centralization of knowledge, and the autonomy and coordination of organizational units. In this approach, subjectivity and sociality are considered as potential sources of value rather than as problems to overcome.

Distributed Knowledge Management System: A KM system that supports two qualitatively different processes: the autonomous management of knowledge locally produced within a single unit, and the coordination of the different units without centrally defined semantics.

Knowledge Node: A knowledge node can be viewed as the reification of an organizational unit, either formal (e.g., divisions, market sectors) or informal (e.g., interest groups, communities of practice, communities of knowing), that exhibits some degree of semantic autonomy.

Knowledge Owner: An entity (individual or collective) that has the capability of managing its own knowledge from a syntactical, semantic, and technological point of view.

Locally Shared Conceptual Schema: A special artifact that explicitly represents the community's perspective. In simple situations, it can be the system of categorization used to classify documents; in more complex scenarios, it can be an ontology, a collection of guidelines, or a business process.

Principle of Autonomy: Each organizational unit should be granted a high degree of autonomy to manage its local knowledge. Autonomy can be allowed at different levels, the most important of which is the semantic level. Semantic autonomy allows the unit to choose the most appropriate conceptualisation of what is locally known (for example, through the creation of personalized knowledge maps, contexts, ontologies, etc.).

Principle of Coordination: Each unit must be enabled to exchange knowledge with other units, not through the adoption of a single common interpretation schema (this would be a violation of the principle of coordination), but through a mechanism of mapping other units' contexts onto its context from its own perspective (that is, by projecting what other units know onto its own interpretation schema).

System of Artifacts: The system of documents, processes, mental models, and so forth that different organizational units tend to (autonomously) develop while satisfying their internal needs. The choice and usage of these tools is a manifestation of the units' semantic autonomy. This may be for historical reasons (for example, people use old legacy systems that are still effective), but also because different tasks may require the use of different applications and data structures (i.e., text documents, audio, or movies) to work out effective procedures and to adopt a specific and often technical language.

Document Search Practices

Karen L. Corral
Arizona State University, USA

Ryan C. LaBrie
Seattle Pacific University, USA

Robert D. St. Louis
Arizona State University, USA

INTRODUCTION

A large portion of the knowledge of most organizations is contained in electronic documents. For users to get pertinent information from the accumulation of stored documents, they need effective document retrieval systems. Unfortunately, electronic document management has fallen into the same trap that electronic data processing fell into: simply automating what previously was done manually. Paper documents were stored in folders in drawers in file cabinets. Electronic documents are stored in folders in directories on disk drives.

The ability to find a document depends on the logic of the filing system, how familiar the individual is with the filing system, and how familiar the individual is with the problem domain of the item being sought. Some persons (e.g., research librarians) are much better than others at organizing and retrieving documents. Rarely, however, is a manager an expert at either storing or retrieving documents. Unfortunately, many electronic filing systems are set up by managers with little or no training on how to organize a filing system, and few tools, other than the Windows Search command, are available to help managers find documents that have been filed.

The filing systems for libraries and knowledge management systems are more sophisticated than the filing systems of most small offices or individual managers. But even libraries and knowledge management systems predominately rely on keyword searching for retrieval. For example, if one visits the Web site for the *Journal of Management Information Systems* at *http://jmis.bentley.edu/keywords/*, one notes that the only option available for searching (other than browsing the entire collection) is a keyword search.

Keyword searching has improved over the years. Knowledge seekers have benefited enormously from the ability to search remotely, the increased speed with which searches are conducted, and the ability of the search mechanism to identify variations of the keywords. Nevertheless, keyword searches have significant limitations. In particular, keyword searches cannot return all relevant documents nor can they filter out irrelevant documents. This article briefly reviews the difficulties associated with keyword searches, especially as the number of documents increases, and proposes a way to overcome those limitations.

BACKGROUND

In his 1990 seminal article on business process engineering, Hammer (1990) argues that organizations should use computers to redesign—not just automate—existing business processes. With document management systems, the opposite has been done. Documents were stored in file cabinets in offices or on shelves in libraries, and electronic document storage systems adopted the same basic principles.

Paper documents such as memos, white papers, reports, and so forth were filed based on the value of some specific field (e.g., project name). To retrieve a document, a user needed to know the value of the field which was used to organize the documents. Because of the shear mass of paper that quickly accumulated in any office, duplication for the purpose of access through multiple fields was not encouraged. In highly organized filing systems, cross-references were filed for important documents, resulting in the capacity to find some documents from two or three different fields. However, this was done infrequently, was quite time-consuming when it was done, and was difficult to maintain.

The logic of the paper filing system usually was determined by a secretary or office assistant, who also was the person primarily responsible for retrieving the documents. This person generally had significant knowledge of the content of the documents, and therefore the system worked quite well for that individual. Unfortunately, the system did not work as well for others.

Figure 1. Filing cabinet vs. simple computerized system

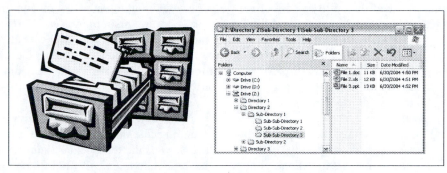

Today, most individuals organize their computer directories in the same manner in which their file cabinets were organized, or even more poorly because they have had little or no training on filing and tend to store all of their folders in the hard drive root directory. While this may be an acceptable strategy for a small set of documents, it is unacceptable when dealing with a large number of documents.

Figure 1 shows the similarity between paper filing systems and simple computerized filing systems. To find a file in the paper system, an individual needs to know which file cabinet to search, which drawer to select, and which folder contains the sought after file. To find a file in the computerized system, an individual follows a very similar strategy. The individual first selects the disk drive to examine, then searches the directory, sub-directory, sub-sub-directory, and so forth, until the file is located. The only advances made to this point are the amount of physical space saved and the ability to use the "find" command.

At the organizational/library level, document management systems require more structure. Generally, documents are organized by hierarchical levels of categories. For example, with the Dewey Decimal system, documents associated with "technology (applied sciences)" are grouped together. Within that category, "management" is separate from "manufacturing" and so on. A major benefit of this method of organization is that once the individual arrives at one document on the topic of interest, other potentially relevant documents are located in close proximity and are easily browsed for relevance. Everyone who has visited a library has located additional relevant books by browsing the library's physical stacks.

Indexes make cross-referencing of materials possible. Though not physically stored together on shelves, documents that are similar with respect to some characteristic (other than the one used to physically store the document) can be referenced together in a card catalogue. Cross-referencing is very important for libraries. An article that describes how regression analysis is used to conduct mass appraisals, for example, should be locatable both by someone who is interested in applications of regression analysis and by someone who wants to understand how the county assessor determines the assessed value of a home using regression analysis. This only can be done with cross-referencing.

Even with cross-referencing, however, the problem remains of needing an entry point for retrieving relevant documents. Not knowing applicable keywords makes a library little more than a jumble of documents. Given the sheer number of documents that are stored, it no longer is possible for one, or a few individuals, to know the content of each document. Librarians are experts at the storage system, but to be useful to the individual they need to understand the subject matter (e.g., a chemical librarian vs. a general librarian). The ability of librarians to keep up with the content of documents is limited by the capacity of human cognition. As the volume of documents increases, the ability of librarians to help individuals diminishes. Further, librarians are limited in their capacity to identify documents from a different area that might be pertinent to the individual. The limitations on human memory prevent any single individual from retaining adequate information to be able to answer questions on a wide variety of subjects.

Current State

Today, more and more documents are being stored electronically. Several factors have contributed to the shift from paper to electronic documents, including the low cost of mass storage devices, the ease with which documents can be scanned and stored, government recognition of electronic signatures, the replacement of desktop computers with notebook computers, and ubiquitous access to the Internet. After more than 30 years of being just around the corner, the paperless office finally is moving from myth to reality. Many organizations provide their employees with notebook computers, and strongly encourage the use of digital documents for sharing information. Unfortunately, those same organizations provide little guidance on how to store or retrieve digital documents, and the ability to effectively retrieve documents has fallen far behind the capability to store documents.

The introduction of electronic document retrieval systems offered an opportunity to address three significant problems associated with the storage of paper documents. First, a large number of documents could be stored in very little space. Second, retrieval time after a document is located became almost zero. And third, anytime, anywhere, access enormously simplified retrieval. Unfortunately, increasing the speed and convenience with which a large number of documents can be retrieved does not help the individual to locate the documents that he or she needs. In fact, it produces a new problem: information overload.

Most document retrieval systems rely on keyword searching as their primary retrieval mechanism. Keyword searches have problems with respect to both locating all of the relevant documents and locating only relevant documents. The problems with respect to locating relevant materials are well documented (Blair, 2002a, 2002b; Gorla & Walker, 1998; LaBrie & St. Louis, 2003). Gorla and Walker (1998) group the problems into the following categories:

- Errors in spelling
- Inconsistencies of abbreviations
- Improper combining of dissimilar terms
- Inconsistent spelling of words
- Inconsistent compounding of words
- Redundant keywords

LaBrie (2004, p. 92) shows that because of these problems keyword searches find only 10% to 30% of the relevant documents in organizational holdings. This is a low percentage as compared to alternative retrieval mechanisms such as visual hierarchies.

Keyword searches also can overwhelm the individual with irrelevant articles. If a keyword insufficiently defines the search scope, many documents will be returned that are not relevant. For example, if a user needs information on the systems development life cycle (SDLC), selecting all documents with the keyword "system" will result in a large number of documents unrelated to the SDLC. This problem is annoying but manageable for small holdings. If 20 documents are returned and only 10% are pertinent, it does not take long to look through the 20 documents to find the two useful ones. However, if the result set size is 5,000 documents, the user will not be able to look through all 5,000 documents.

The scalability of retrieval systems is a serious problem. The Zipf distribution has been shown to apply to natural languages (Blair, 2002). Briefly, the Zipf distri-

bution shows that as the number of documents increases, the number of documents in which a specific term occurs also increases. Further, as the library increases in size, the likelihood of a term being used with different meanings also increases. So not only does the result set size increase, but the percentage of irrelevant documents in the result set also increases.

Increased processing speed makes it possible to scan the full document for a keyword, as opposed to scanning just the keyword field, title, or abstract. This article uses the term "causal modeling" in Figure 2 and its associated text. With full document scanning, a search for documents dealing with causal modeling would return this article, although the content of this article has nothing to do with causal modeling. Blair (2002) labels this phenomenon as "over-description," and defines it as a situation where "some, or many, of the terms that are used to describe the document may misrepresent the intellectual content of the document" (p. 280). Though it is technically possible to perform full document scanning, or have a large set of keywords describing a document, doing so may be counterproductive to the objective of retrieving pertinent documents. Increasing the speed of search mechanisms does not solve the information overload problem.

Cognitive psychologists have been studying human memory capacity for well over 100 years (Ebbinghaus, 1913) and have identified two predominant forms of retrieving information from memory: recall and recognition. Trying to remember the name of someone you met at a conference is recall. Recognition is remembering that person's name when looking at a list of conference attendees. Recognition routinely outperforms recall in retrieval accuracy, especially when context is added by organizing the information hierarchically (Anderson, 1995; Bower, Clark, Lesgold, & Winzenz, 1969; Clark, 1999; Simon, 1962).

Figure 2 is an example of a hierarchical arrangement of keywords. The hierarchy is based on the alphabet and has a four level structure. The root node, or highest level of the hierarchy, is the first letter of any word that has been used in any keyword phrase. The next level represents a unique word that was used in a keyword phrase. The third level identifies the actual keyword phrase provided by the author(s). The fourth and lowest level of this hierarchy is the title of the document that contains the keyword phrase. In an electronic document management system this title would contain a link to the actual document.

In Figure 2, note that all articles with the keyword phrase "user acceptance" are grouped together. Similarly, all articles with the keyword phrase "causal modeling" are grouped together. Although the documents themselves are stored in one location (eliminating

Figure 2. Visual keyword hierarchy

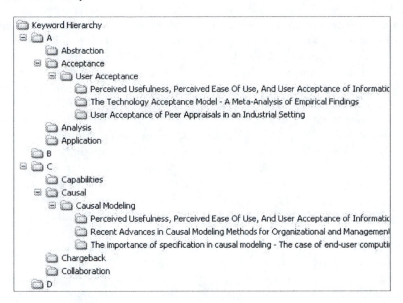

duplicate copies which wastes disk space), links to the articles can be stored in multiple locations. This makes electronic browsing much more effective than physical browsing. As an example, suppose Davis' (1989) article on the technology acceptance model used as its keywords *user acceptance* and *causal modeling*. An individual who is interested in applications of causal modeling, easily finds Davis' article on "Perceived Usefulness, Perceived Ease of Use, and User Acceptance of Information Technology" even though he or she may never have thought to look under "User Acceptance," which is where the article may have been physically stored based on subject.

With existing low cost and pervasive technologies any individual or small office can create the search mechanism shown in Figure 2 (LaBrie & St. Louis, in press). The process to develop such a visual keyword hierarchy is quite simple. Keyword phrases are taken from an article's keywords list when the article is entered into the system. The keyword phrases are broken down into individual words. Trivial words such as "a," "the," and "and," are removed. Individual words are linked to their original keyword phrase and the article with which the keyword is associated. The result is a hierarchy similar to Figure 2 that allows a user to search via any of the words within the keyword phrase. If someone were looking for articles on the "Technology Acceptance Model," they could find them in three different areas of the hierarchy: (1) Under A, Acceptance, Technology Acceptance Model; (2) Under T, Technology, Technology Acceptance Model; or (3) Under M, Model, Technology Acceptance Model.

Hierarchies built on keywords are easily maintained. As new articles with new keywords are added to the holdings, trigger mechanisms can be implemented to dynamically update the hierarchies (LaBrie & St. Louis, in press). These dynamic hierarchies are easily searched because both individual keywords and keyword phrases appear in them. This means the individual does not have to spell the keyword correctly nor recall the exact keyword phrase. The only requirements are that the individual recall the first letter of a relevant keyword (where to enter the hierarchy) and recognize relevant keywords or keyword phrases that appear in the article (browse the hierarchy). This overcomes many of the disadvantages of keyword searches and allows individuals to retrieve documents from their notebook computers or organizational servers as effectively (or more) than documents can be retrieved from a library.

FUTURE TRENDS

The number of stored documents is increasing at an astronomical pace (Ball, 2002). The advances that have occurred with respect to the ease and speed of searching have been equally dramatic. But as the collection of documents grows, the scalability of retrieval systems is adversely affected. As a consequence, both the number of articles and the percent of irrelevant articles in the result set increases. The real challenge now is to filter out the irrelevant documents. A promising approach is to filter articles on the basis of both context and keywords.

To capture the intellectual context of a document requires more than picking out words or phrases from the document. For example, a document that includes the results from a regression analysis that was performed using the SPSS statistical package on data from the assessor's rolls to create mass appraisal values for individual homeowners may be very useful to someone wanting to see an application of regression analysis, but may not be useful to someone wanting to understand how conditional means are calculated by software that enables regression analyses. Using keywords alone, there is no way to distinguish between documents that focus on applying regression analysis and documents that focus on explaining regression analysis. Yet regression analysis is a legitimate keyword for both searches.

One role that the librarian fills is that of a domain expert. The librarian can distinguish between articles that apply regression analysis and articles that explain regression analysis, or even much finer distinctions of word use. Document retrieval systems need a context filtering mechanism that can substitute for the librarian. One reason why librarians are so effective at finding relevant articles is that they understand both the Library of Congress Subject Headings and the Dewey Decimal System. Categorization provides context. If electronic document retrieval systems are going to become as effective as librarians at filtering out irrelevant documents, then they need to use categorization schemes. Presenting the categorization scheme as a visual hierarchy contributes even more to effectiveness because the user can recognize the categories which are appropriate.

Continuing with the example of an article that applies regression analysis vs. an article that explains regression analysis, one lens through which to filter the articles might be "subject of document." The individual, when presented with the initial list of search lenses, would select "subject of document" and then be presented with a list of possible subjects which might include, among others, the subjects "residential property appraisals" and "regression analysis." The individual wanting an explanation of regression analysis would select the "regression analysis" subject and not the "residential property appraisals" subject. Another lens could be "most frequently retrieved," which is similar to one used by Google and other search engines. This presumes that the most useful documents will be retrieved most often. With electronic documents, it is easy to record the number of times a document has been retrieved for a particular subject category.

Applying lenses is different than applying an "and" search on keywords. It is cross-indexing documents by both keywords and the lens categories that are selected. Visual classification hierarchies enable the individual to use recognition-based rather than recall-based search mechanisms to select criteria, and thus enable the individual to see the context of the keyword. This greatly enhances the individual's ability to screen out irrelevant articles. It is important to note that the set of lenses does not have to be the same for every electronic document management system. Rather, a set of search lenses can be designed to fit the needs of the organization. A research lab's document management system, for example, might include a "methodology" lens, while a law office's document management system might not.

Knowledge workers spend a tremendous amount of time culling irrelevant documents. A keyword search can return thousands of documents with only a small fraction of those being relevant to the individual's needs. By adding multiple visual hierarchies as lenses, many of those irrelevant documents can be removed. It takes some time and effort to create and maintain the classification schemes required to add the needed context. However, the amount of time and effort is not Herculean. Allowing users to specify subject headings, and arranging them into visual subject hierarchies using the same technique that is used to construct visual keyword hierarchies (LaBrie & St. Louis, in press), does not require a great deal of effort. Moreover, once established, these new visual classification schemes will greatly facilitate knowledge management. Figure 3 illustrates a situation where four lenses are used: discipline, subject, methodology, and number of hits. In this example, an article would be retrieved only if it were categorized as being in the information systems discipline, had a subject of "user acceptance," used causal modeling as its methodology, and had been retrieved at least 10 times.

CONCLUSION

There is a disconnect between the ability to store documents and the ability to retrieve them. It is extremely easy to save documents. In fact, it is so easy to save documents, and storage space is so inexpensive, that many individuals save all documents that are sent to them, rather than determining which ones might be needed later. Unfortunately, when it comes time to find a document, they frequently fail to do so, or take a long time to do so. The ease with which documents can be stored stands in stark contrast to the difficulty of finding a sought-after document that one knows is stored somewhere in a personal or organizational file.

A solution to this information overload is to add context to the keywords through the application of various classification schemes (subject, author, methodology, etc.). These classification schemes can be maintained and presented to the user in the form of

Figure 3. Examples of lenses

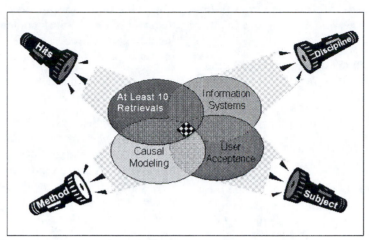

multiple dynamic, visual hierarchies. This approach to document retrieval significantly reduces the numbers of irrelevant articles and therefore reduces information overload. Surprisingly, to combat information overload, "rather than needing less information, we actually may need lots more, specifically information about information, or metadata" (Farhoomand & Drury, 2002). The disconnect between the ability to store documents and the ability to retrieve documents can be resolved. This article explains how simply automating what was done with paper documents created that problem, and how reengineering the process to capture context can resolve the problem.

REFERENCES

Anderson, J.R. (1995). *Cognitive psychology and its implications* (4th Ed.). New York: W.H. Freeman and Company.

Ball, M.K. (2002, March). Knowledge management: Intelligence for today's business world. *KMWorld,* S14-S15.

Blair, D.C. (2002a). The challenge of commercial document retrieval, part I: Major issues, and a framework based on search exhaustivity, determinacy of representation and document collection size. *Information Processing & Management, 38*(2), 273-291.

Blair, D.C. (2002b). The challenge of commercial document retrieval, part II: A strategy for document searching based on identifiable document partitions. *Information Processing & Management, 38*(2), 293-304.

Bower, G.H., Clark, J.C., Lesgold, A.M., & Winzenz, D. (1969). Hierarchical retrieval schemes in recall of cat-egorical word lists. *Journal of Verbal Learning & Verbal Behavior, 8,* 323-343.

Clark, S.E. (1999). Recalling to recognize and recognizing recall. In C. Izawa (Ed.), *On human memory: Evolution, progress, and reflections on the 30th anniversary of the Atkinson-Shiffrin model* (pp. 151-164). Mahwah, NJ: Lawrence Erlbaum Associates.

Davis, F.D. (1989). Perceived usefulness, perceived ease of use, and user acceptance of information technology. *MIS Quarterly, 13*(3), 319-340.

Ebbinghaus, H. (1913). *Memory: A contribution to experimental psychology.* (H.A. Ruger & C.E. Bussenues, Trans.). New York: Teachers College, Columbia University. (Original work published 1885.)

Farhoomand, A.F., & Drury, D.H. (2002). Managerial information overload. *Communications of the ACM, 45*(10), 127-131.

Gorla, N., & Walker, G. (1998). Is the lack of keyword synergism inhibiting maturation in the MIS theory? An exploratory study. *Information Processing & Management, 34*(2-3), 325-339.

Hammer, M. (1990). Reengineering work: Don't automate, obliterate. *Harvard Business Review, 68*(4), 104-113.

LaBrie, R.C. (2004). *The impact of alternative search mechanisms on the effectiveness of knowledge retrieval.* Doctoral dissertaton, Arizona State University.

LaBrie, R.C., & St. Louis, R.D. (2003). Barriers of information retrieval from knowledge management systems: An examination of keyword limitations. *Proceedings of the Americas Conference on Information Systems, Tampa, FL, 9* (pp. 2552-2563).

LaBrie, R.C., & St. Louis, R.D. (in press). Dynamic hierarchies for business intelligence information retrieval. *International Journal of Internet and Enterprise Management.*

Simon, H.A. (1962). The architecture of complexity: Hierarchical systems. *Proceedings of the Philosophical Society, 106* (pp. 467-482).

KEY TERMS

Context Lens: A visual classification scheme for a set of documents that can be dynamically updated. The classification scheme is arranged in a tree hierarchy to facilitate browsing.

Dynamic (Visual) Hierarchy: An alternative mechanism for presenting keywords that is based on a recognition paradigm and can be dynamically updated. Keywords are arranged in a tree hierarchy to facilitate links to keyword phrases and enable browsing.

Electronic Document: A digital object that stores something of use to someone. More general than paper documents, electronic documents can take various forms, including word processing files, spreadsheet files, graphics, audio and video files, and so forth.

Keyword: An attribute of an electronic document used to describe the document.

Keyword Searching: A traditional search mechanism for locating electronic documents based on a specific (keyword) attribute list. Keyword searching is based on a recall paradigm of cognitive retrieval. Keyword searching is currently the most widely used retrieval mechanism, however, it is not without its limitations.

Recall: A form of cognitive retrieval in which the individual must generate a list of possible options.

Recognition: A form of cognitive retrieval in which an individual is given a list of viable options from which to select. Recognition-based search mechanisms have been found to outperform those that are based on recall.

Domain Ontologies

D

Matteo Cristani
University of Verona, Italy

Roberta Cuel
University of Verona, Italy

INTRODUCTION

In conceptual modeling we need to consider a general level of abstraction where the domain of interest is formalized in an independent way with respect to the specific application for which the conceptual modeling process is performed. This leads to an integrated approach that takes into account knowledge about a domain and metaknowledge about a methodology. Indeed, knowledge about a domain is represented by a system of concepts and instances that reify the knowledge that is managed within a domain, and the metaknowledge about a methodology is the description of the knowledge deriving from the method used. For instance, when a technology is used to unveil ontologies within a specific domain, the knowledge about the domain is the resulting ontology, and the metaknowledge about a methodology is the description of the method used to construct the ontology. In this article, a novel method for the creation of both upper level and specific domain ontologies, called the bidirectional method for developing ontologies, is described. In particular, it will guide the developer to obtain ontologies resulting from the combination of both top-down and bottom-up approaches. The first one focuses on conceptual modeling through "armchair" research (philosophical, psychological, sociological aspects) and figures out a formal draft schema. The second approach employs an automatic (or semiautomatic) extraction of categories, taxonomies, partonomies, and dependency graphs in particular from linguistic corpora of documents related to the topics of the domain.

BACKGROUND

Formal ontologies are a popular research topic in several communities, such as knowledge management, knowledge engineering, natural language processing, artificial intelligence (AI), and others (Fensel, 2000). Formal ontology can be defined as the systematic, formal, axiomatic development of the logic of all forms and modes of being (Cocchiarella, 1991). More generally, we employ the term formal ontology to designate an explicit specification of a shared conceptualization that holds in a particular context. In other words, an ontology provides an explicit conceptualization that describes semantics of data, providing a shared and common understanding of a domain (from an AI perspective, see the definitions of Gruber, 1998, and Jasper & Ushold, 1999). Ontologies are used to manage knowledge within and among communities, to manage and organize corporate knowledge bases, and to negotiate meanings among individuals. Moreover, ontologies are used to share knowledge among people, and heterogeneous and widely spread application systems, such as semantic-Web applications (Schwartz, 2003). They are implied in projects, as conceptual models, to enable content-based access on corporate knowledge memories, knowledge bases, or data warehouses. They are employed to allow agents to understand each other when they need to interact, communicate, and negotiate meanings. Finally, they refer to common information and share a common understanding of their structure.

In computer science, knowledge management, knowledge representation, and other fields, several languages and tools exist for helping final users and system developers in creating good and effective ontologies. In particular, various tools help people in manually or semiautomatically creating categories, partonomies, taxonomies, and other organization levels of ontologies. The generally accepted term to designate these tools is ontology editors. Some of them are open source such as Protégé-2000, KAON, and SWOOP, and others are commercial suites for knowledge management based on ontology development, such as tools provided by the onto-Knowledge Project (for an in-depth description, see http://protege.stanford.edu, http://kaon.semantic web.org/, http://www.mindswap.org/2004/SWOOP/, http://www.ontoknowledge.org/index.shtml).

Some Important Methodologies

Behind these tools and techniques, different (domain-independent) approaches and methods are used to develop numerous heterogeneous ontologies. In particular, Ushold's (2000; who proposed codification in a formal language) methodology and methontology, which constructs an ontology in a sequence of intermediate representations finally translated into the actual object (Fernández, Gòmez-Pérez, & Juristo, 1997), are the most representative. Here are short descriptions of some important methodologies:

- One of the first modules of the foundational ontologies library is the descriptive ontology for linguistic cognitive engineering (DOLCE). DOLCE is an ontology of particulars and refers to cognitive artefacts that depend on human perception, cultural imprints, and social conventions. This ontology derives from armchair research in particular, referring to enduring and durable entities from philosophical literature. The main authors' idea is to develop not a monolithic module, but a library of ontologies (WonderWeb Foundation Ontologies Library) that allows agents to understand one another despite enforcing them to interoperate by the adoption of a single ontology (Masolo, Borgo, Gangemi, Guarino, & Oltramari, 2002). Finally, basic functions and relations (according to the methodology introduced by Gangemi, Pisanelli, & Steve, 1998) should be general enough to be applied to multiple domains, be sufficiently intuitive and well studied in the philosophical literature, and hold as soon as their relations are given without mediating additional entities.

- In Gatius and Rodríguez (1996), the authors developed a three-step process (natural-language interface generator [GISE]) to build a domain ontology: the building and maintenance of general linguistic knowledge, a definition of the application in terms of the conceptual ontology, and a definition of the control structure. It includes the metarules for mapping objects in the domain ontology with those in the task ontology, the metarules for mapping the conceptual ontology onto the linguistic ontology, and those for allowing the generation of the specific interface knowledge sources, mainly the grammar and the lexicon.

- One of the most famous ontology-design environments is methontology. It tries to define the necessary activities that people carry out when building an ontology (Fernández et al., 1997). In other words, it is a flow of ontology development for three different processes: management, technology, and support. The ontology-development process is composed of the following steps: project-management activities that include planning, control, and quality assurance; development-oriented activities that include specification, conceptualization, formalization, and implementation; and activities that include knowledge acquisition, evaluation, integration, and documentation.

- The authors Lauser, Wildemann, Poulos, Fisseha, Keizer, and Katz (2002) use the multilingual methontology methodology defined by Fernández et al. (1997), and enrich this one by stressing on specific actions for supporting the creation process for ontology-driven conceptual analysis. The domain ontology is built by using two different knowledge-acquisition approaches: the creation of the core ontology and the derivation of the domain ontology from a thesaurus. The first one is basically comprised of the first three steps of methontology-development activities defining a list of frequent terms and a list of domain-specific documents to analyze. The second one consists of descriptive keywords linked by a basic set of relationships. The goal of this step is to refine an RDFS ontology model to develop a pruned ontology and a list of frequent terms.

- Toronto Virtual Enterprise (TOVE) is a methodology for ontological engineering that allows the developer to build ontology following these steps: scenarios motivation, ontology requirements definitions, terminology specification, formal description requirements, axiom specification, and completeness theorems (Fox & Gruninger, 1994, 1998).

- Ontology Development 101 has been developed by authors involved in these ontology-editing environments: Protégé-2000, Ontolingua, and Chimaera (Noy & McGuinnes, 2001). They propose a very simple guide, based on iterative design, that helps developers to create an ontology using these tools. The sequence of the steps to develop an ontology are to determine the domain and scope of the ontology, consider reusing existing ontologies (e.g., Ontolingua ontology library, DAML ontology library, UNSPSC, RosettaNet, and DMOZ), enumerate important terms in the ontology, define the classes and the class hierarchy, define the properties of class slots, define the facets of the slots, and create instances.

- Ushold's (2000) methodology uses formal language for building ontologies via a purely manual process, identifying purpose and scope, capturing (the identification of key concepts and relationships, and the provision of definitions), and finally coding ontology (committing to the basic terms for ontology), integrating existing ontologies, evaluating, and documenting the ontology processes.

- The On-to-Knowledge (OTK) methodology focuses on application-driven development of ontology during the introduction of ontology-based knowledge-management systems (Fensel, van Harmelen, Klein, & Akkermans, 2000; Lau & Sure, 2002; Sure, Erdmann, Angele, Staab, Studer, & Wenke, 2002). It is based on the following steps: a feasibility study, an impacts and improvements study for the selected target solution, a kickoff phase, a refinement phase, a formalization phase, an evaluation phase, and an application and evolution phase. This methodology stresses the need for ensuring organizational acceptance and the integration of knowledge systems. Then it is based on bottom-up strategies, and gathering insights into the interrelationships between the business task, actors involved, and the use of knowledge for successful performance.

- The authors Izumy and Yamaguchi (2002) have used the business-object ontology to develop an ontology for business coordination. They constructed the business-activity thesaurus by employing WordNet as a general lexical repository. They have constructed the business-object ontology in the following way: by concentrating on the case-study models of e-business and extracting the taxonomy, counting the number of the appearances of each noun concept, comparing the noun hierarchy of WordNet and the taxonomy obtained and adding the number counted for the similar concepts, choosing the main concept with high scores as upper concepts and building upper ontologies by giving all the nouns the formal is-a relation, and merging all the noun hierarchies extracted from the whole process.

Comparing these Methodologies

Although there are relevant differences among the methodologies described above, a number of common points clearly emerge. Many of the methodologies take the domain definition as a starting-point task. From one point of view, it focuses on the acquisition, provides the potential for evaluation, and provides a useful description of the capabilities of the ontology, expressed as the ability to answer well-defined competency questions. On the other side, it seems to provide limitations to the reuse of the ontology and to the possible interactions among ontologies. Besides this, there are two different types of methodology models: the stage-based models (represented, for example, by TOVE) and evolving prototype models (represented by methontology). Both approaches have benefits and drawbacks: The first one seems more appropriate when the purposes and requirements of the ontology are clear, and the second one is more useful when the environment is dynamic and difficult to understand. Finally, both the informal description of the ontology and the formal embodiment in an ontology language are often developed in separate stages, and this separation increases the gap between real-world models and executable systems. There is no one correct way to model a domain; there are always viable alternatives. Most of the time, the best solution depends on the application that the developer has in mind, and the tools that he or she uses to develop the ontology. In particular, we can notice that the need for correspondence between existing methodologies and environments for building ontologies causes these consequences: Conceptual models are implicit in the implementation codes and a reengineering process is usually required to make the conceptual models explicit, ontological commitments and design criteria are implicit in the ontology code, and ontology developer preferences in a given language condition the implementation of the acquired knowledge.

MAIN FOCUS OF THE ARTICLE

In this article, the focus is the necessity for a tenable trade-off between a stable corporate model of knowledge and the dynamism of the very same knowledge in the history of real-world organizations. What is not sufficiently studied in the current literature of ontology methodology, which we believe to be the crucial aspect of this type of investigation from the knowledge-management viewpoint, is the nature of the knowledge of the methodology itself (the metaknowledge of the domain), which is very important for the choices we make in the deployment process of any ontology.

Our discussion focuses on how an explicit representation of the metaknowledge is helpful in knowledge-management practice. To demonstrate this, an analysis of the basic assumptions about ontology creation is provided, the bidirectional method for developing ontologies is described, and finally a knowledge-management viewpoint on ontology creation is presented.

Basic Assumptions on Ontology Creation

As explained above, one of the first steps in ontology creation is the choice of domains and categories that represent, in a neutral way, the real world. In fact, in the real world or in practical applications (e.g., information systems, knowledge-management systems, portals, and other ICT applications), general and universal categories are not widely being used. This is also due to the difficulties in implementing a general ontology within specific domains. Moreover, general and universal categories are very abstract and can lead to heterogeneous interpretations and different conceptualizations. For instance, everyone has a different interpretation and conceptualization of love, trust, or spatial-temporal regions. Besides this, the more a concept is abstract, the more it is difficult to define it. Then, workers very stressed by their daily activities might find it difficult or useless to make their daily used concepts more abstract and decontextualized. Namely, they might prefer to achieve, in short time, an effective agreement on shared spaces in their office than stay days and days talking about space regions.

More often, it is simply too expensive to create complex, complete, and general ontologies. Another important justification of the above-mentioned lack of general and supposedly complete ontologies in real-world applications is that, in the same project or domain, people might use different ontologies composed by several combinations of categories. Indeed, different ontologies might use different categories or systems of categories to describe the same kinds of entities. Even worse, two ontologies may use the same names or systems of categories for different kinds of entities. In fact, when trying to measure the similarity between two ontologies, it is necessary to pursue at both the lexical layer and the conceptual layer (Maedche & Staab, 2002). Therefore, it might be that two entities with different definitions are intended to be the same, but the task of proving that they are indeed the same may be difficult, if not impossible (see Sowa, 2000).

The basic reason for these behaviours is that what we know cannot be viewed simply as a unique picture of the world since it always presupposes some degree of interpretation. Indeed, depending on different interpretation schemas, people (with different perspectives, aims, and world interpretations) may use the same categories with different meanings, or different words to mean the same thing. For example, two groups of people may observe the same phenomenon, but still see different problems, different opportunities, and different challenges. This essential feature of knowledge was studied from different perspectives, and the interpretation schemas have been given various names, for example, paradigms in Kuhn (1979), frames in Goffman (1974), thought worlds in Dougherty (1992), contexts in Ghidini and Giunchiglia (2001), mental spaces in Fauconnier (1985), and cognitive paths in Weick (1979). This view, in which the explicit part of what we know gets its meaning from an (typically implicit, or taken for granted) interpretation schema, leads to some important consequences regarding the adoption and the use of categories and ontologies. An ontology is not a neutral organization of categories, but it is the emergence of some interpretation schema according to which it makes sense to organize and define things. In summary, an ontology is always the result of a sense-making process (conceptual modeling) and represents the point of view (the knowledge representation) of those who took part in that process (see Benerecetti, Bouquet, & Ghidini, 2000, for an in-depth discussion of the dimensions along which any representation, including an ontology, can vary depending on contextual factors).

Moreover, according to a structuration approach (for an in-depth discussion, see, for example, Giddens, 1984; Orlikowski, 1992; Orlikowski & Gash, 1994), technology cannot be considered as a neutral matter with respect to organizational structures and the managing of knowledge. Ontologies can shape knowledge sharing and managing processes, and organizational behaviours can affect the concrete appropriation of technology. Therefore, there is no one correct way to model a domain; there are always viable alternatives. Mainly, the best solution depends on the application that the developer has in mind, the system of artefacts that she or he wants to integrate with the ontology, and the tools that she or he uses to develop the ontology. Indeed, most of the tools only give support for designing and implementing the ontologies, but they do not support all the activities of the ontology life cycle. Besides this, most of the existing methodologies for building ontologies depend on their environments. Therefore, conceptual models are implicit in the implementation codes and a reengineering process is usually required to make the conceptual models explicit. Ontological commitments and design criteria are implicit in the ontology code, and ontology developer preferences, in a given language, condition the implementation of the acquired knowledge (Gruber, 1998).

The Bidirectional Method for Developing Ontologies

The bidirectional method for developing ontologies provides guidelines to assist the ontological engineer in making choices at different levels, from the high-level structure of the ontology to the fine details of whether or not to include distinctions. The bidirectional method for developing ontologies aims at satisfying all the developer needs and merging two different needs: a more adequate representation of the local domain and the very effective development of a top-level ontology. Taking into consideration these aspects, it seems useful to consider that manually constructed ontologies are time consuming, labour intensive, and error prone (Ding & Foo, 2002), but they are necessary to define a domain in which the quality and the general comprehension of the ontology are good. For example, experts might provide the system with a small number of seed words that represent high-level concepts. These concepts can emerge from theoretical ideas and knowledge or from the practice and the experiences of specialized workers. The steps defined by the bidirectional method for developing ontologies shortly are the following:

- **Plan phase:** The goals, amount of resources needed for the ontology development, and bonds (e.g., languages, timing, computational power, type of software used to describe the ontology) are defined. It is important to notice that there is a trade-off between the computational complexity (which is domain independent) and the expressive potential defined by the language.
- **Introspective phase:** The draft schema, such as the general specifications, categories, and relations; its formalization into the chosen formal language; and its demonstration are defined. It is important to notice that this phase is based on references to literature (philosophical, linguistic, psychological, sociological literature) and on armchair research.
- **Bottom-up phase:** The draft terminology is automatically or semiautomatically generated, the description of relations among terms is extracted, and the refinement of draft terminology is handled. The lexical analysis is developed partly in an auto-

mated way (through the extraction of phrases containing seed words in documents, archives, and so on) and partly experienced (through expert discussion; domain experts can help the developer to refine the draft terminology). Notice that this phase is based on a very neat domain knowledge and on semiautomatic ontology generation, which depends, in particular, on data-mining processes, syntax systems of analysis, and so on.

- **Provision of basic axioms:** A set of ontology definitions is obtained through domain-expert interviews or participation.
- **Validation phase:** The set of definitions is tested, validated, and used.

The above-deployed analysis gives to the bidirectional method for developing ontologies the meaning of a metamethodology, namely, a methodology for operating the right choice among different possible methodologies. This is practically useful in ontology constructions within complex organizations. In fact, within big organizations, knowledge is managed according to different perspectives, and specialized knowledge is managed in the way that better suits specific needs. The presented bidirectional method for developing ontologies sustains the creation of very specialized, specific, and different domain ontologies, allowing a high level of flexibility in ontology-construction processes. Moreover, it allows one to manage a complicated ontology commitment that in practice is routed in dynamic contents and in specific methods. Contents and metaknowledge for ontology constructions can be managed and modified only at execution time, namely, at the moment in which the ontology is created. In Figure 1, a schematic analysis of the phases is described. Each

Figure 1. A representation of the bidirectional method for developing ontologies

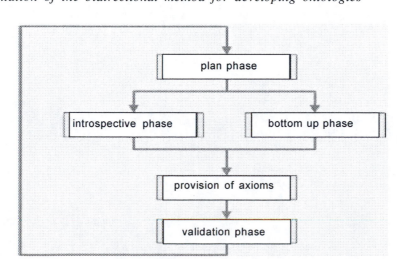

phase is related in terms of the direct dependency on previous phases. The metaknowledge included in the ontology methodology adopted is rendered explicit by the definition of these dependencies. Note that the resulting phase set is minimal with respect to the possible phases in existing methodologies, and that the execution of the phase sequence is cyclic in order to provide a model for reusability.

A Knowledge Management Perspective on Ontology Creation

An ontology is a tool for knowledge management whenever it is used for meaning negotiation. However, a coherent perspective on ontology construction from the knowledge-management point of view is not well defined within the current literature of both artificial intelligence and organizational studies.

The perspective defined here is focused on three fundamental aspects of ontology creation: the widely recognized need for tools to be used in the generation of a shared conceptualization for corporate knowledge management; the generally acknowledged need for methodologies that developers of ontologies can follow in a coherent, systematic, and easy-to-implement way; and the economic value of ontologies as artefacts in the practice of knowledge management.

In particular, using the structuration-theory approach (Giddens, 1984; Orlikowski, 1992; Orlikowski & Gash, 1994), the main features of the bidirectional method should be analyzed, and the most important consequences generated by using a special methodology (the bidirectional method) should be unveiled. In particular, the method facilitates the management of some activities such as controlling the development of knowledge re-

positories in a corporate knowledge-management system, which may include a data warehouse, a corporate Web portal, and intranet tools for accessing distributed data.

The major value of a systematic definition of these aspects is the opportunity for measuring the quality of an ontology from a social and organizational point of view. Though the aim of this investigation is not so far to obtain metrics and evaluation methods for ontologies, we maintain that such a result is going to be shortly available once the methods for building ontologies have been defined.

An important observation is that we have three different situations for ontology development at different levels of difficulty: development from scratch, development as a completion of an existing ontology, and development as a merge (or coordination or alignment) of several ontologies. The three cases require different methodologies, and the methodology we have deployed in this article is valid only for the first case. The other two cases are also interesting extensions of the perspectives of knowledge management we consider as the focus of the article, and they deserve deep analysis. However, we believe that this is possible only when using a flexible methodology for the case from scratch.

FUTURE TRENDS

This article discusses a methodology for building a domain ontology from scratch. The intention of the investigation is to prove that extracting an ontology from a corpus (or from many corpora) is a tenable solution for certain paths, and the opposite way based upon a deep thinking on the topics of the domain is acceptable in other cases. The methodology we propose here is able to help

Figure 2. A description of ontology-creation methodologies

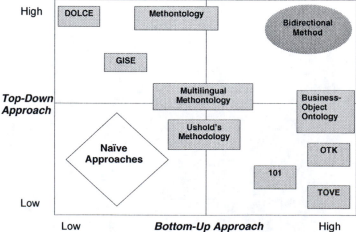

the developer in discriminating between the two cases and provides a general schema for the mentioned purpose.

The investigation on the cases of the development of ontologies as an integration of existing models and as a merge has to be deepened. The other aspects that have to be covered are how this methodology can affect the updating processes, and how it can allow the integration of domain ontologies into an upper level ontology. Finally, the evaluation and measure of ontologies seem interesting issues in order to quantify how much an ontology costs and how one can improve the daily activities of workers. In particular, taking into account organizational and management studies, an ontology should be evaluated in terms of its ability to satisfy and its effectiveness.

The above-discussed needs and solutions can be deployed in technologies for knowledge management both as CASE (computer-aided software engineering) in the context of ontology creation, where the tool helps the developer in doing the right thing at the right moment, and as knowledge-sharing and -meaning negotiation tools, especially in network systems.

CONCLUSION

The major claim of this article is that an explicit representation of the methodological knowledge employed to provide conceptual analysis and express the model of knowledge by means of formal ontologies is a valuable plus for knowledge management. In the article, the existing major methodologies are described, and it is shown that everyone provides a framework for making tenable decisions upon the correct case to be used in each specific case, depending both upon the knowledge type and the domain. Although a lot of different methodologies for ontology creation are used in different domains, a good methodological approach should not change depending on the domain in which it is applied and on the type of technology that is used (see Figure 2). A metamethodology is needed, which allows the developer to use the same metamethodology even if the domain, the tool for ontology creation, the needs, and so on change during the time.

In particular, both bottom-up and top-down approaches are very important and are both used in different stages of ontology creation. The bidirectional method for developing ontologies gives an explicit answer to the need of merging both approaches, accounting for the need of tenable, if not optimal, trade-offs between the stability of the model of knowledge and the dynamism of the knowledge itself, which is the actual reason for which an explicit methodology is invented.

REFERENCES

Benerecetti, M., Bouquet, P., & Ghidini, C. (2000). Contextual reasoning distilled. *Journal of Theoretical and Experimental Artificial Intelligence, 12*(3), 279-305.

Cocchiarella, N. (1991). Formal ontology. In B. Smith & H. Burkhardt (Eds.), *Handbook of metaphysics and ontology* (pp. 640-647). Munich, Germany: Philosophia Verlag.

Ding, Y., & Foo, S. (2002). Ontology research and development: Part 1. A review of ontology generation. *Journal of Information Science, 3*(28), 123-136.

Dougherty, D. (1992). Interpretative barriers to successful product innovation in large firms. *Organization Science, 3*(2).

Fauconnier, G. (1985). *Mental spaces: Aspects of meaning construction in natural language*. Cambridge, MA: MIT Press.

Fensel, D. (2000). *Ontologies: A silver bullet for knowledge management and electronic commerce*. Berlin: Springer-Verlag.

Fensel, D., van Harmelen, M., Klein, M, & Akkermans, H. (2000). On-to-knowledge: Ontology-based tools for knowledge management. *Proceedings of eBusiness and eWork*, Madrid, Spain.

Fernández, M., Gòmez-Pérez, A., & Juristo, N. (1997). METHONTOLOGY: From ontological art towards ontological engineering. *Working Notes of the AAAI Spring Symposium on Ontological Engineering.*

Fox, M. S., & Gruninger, M. (1994). Ontologies for enterprise integration. *Proceedings of the 2nd Conference on Cooperative Information Systems*, Toronto, Canada.

Fox, M. S., & Gruninger, M. (1998). Enterprise modelling. *AI Magazine*, 109-121.

Gangemi, A., Pisanelli, D. M., & Steve, G. (1998). Ontology integration: Experiences with medical terminologies. In N. Guarino (Ed.), *Formal ontology in information systems* (pp. 163-178). Amsterdam: IOS Press.

Gatius, M., & Rodríguez, H. (1996). A domain-restricted task-guided natural language interface generator. *Proceedings of the 2nd Edition of the Workshop Flexible Query Answering Systems (FQAS'96).*

Ghidini, C., & Giunchiglia, F. (2001). Local models semantics, or contextual reasoning = locality + compatibility. *Artificial Intelligence, 127*(2), 221-259.

Giddens, A. (1984). *The constitution of society.* Berkeley: University of California Press.

Goffman, I. (1974). *Frame analysis.* New York: Harper & Row.

Gruber, T. R. (1998). A translation approach to portable ontology specifications. *Knowledge Acquisition, 5,* 199-220.

Izumi, N., & Yamaguchi, T. (2002). *Semantic coordination of Web services based on multi-layered repository.* PRICAI, 597.

Jasper, R., & Ushold, M. (1999). A framework for understanding and classifying ontology applications. *Proceedings of the 12th Workshop on Knowledge Acquisition, Modelling, and Management,* Canada.

Kuhn, T. (1979). *The structure of scientific revolutions.* Chicago: University of Chicago Press.

Lau, T., & Sure, T. (2002). Introducing ontology-based skills management at a language insurance company. *Modellierung* (pp. 123-134).

Lauser, B., Wildemann, T., Poulos, A., Fisseha, F., Keizer, J., & Katz, S. (2002). A comprehensive framework for building multilingual domain ontologies: Creating a prototype biosecurity ontology. *Proceedings of the International Conference on Dublin Core and Metadata for e-Communities,* 113-123.

Maedche, A., & Staab, S. (2002). Measuring similarity between ontologies. *Proceedings of the European Conference on Knowledge Acquisition and Management: EKAW-2002* (pp. 251-263).

Masolo, C., Borgo, S., Gangemi, A., Guarino, N., & Oltramari, A. (2002). *Wonderweb deliverable d17: Intermediate report 2.0, ISTC-CNR.*

Noy, N. F., & McGuinnes, D. L. (2001). *Ontology development 101: A guide to creating your first ontology.* Stanford, CA: Stanford University.

Orlikowski, W. J. (1992). Learning from notes: Organizational issues in groupware implementation. In J. Turner & R. Kraut (Eds.), *Proceedings of CSCW'92 Conference* (pp. 362-369). New York: The Association for Computing Machinery.

Orlikowski, W. J., & Gash, D. (1994). Technological frames: Making sense of information technology in organizations. *ACM Transactions on Information Systems, 12,* 174-207.

Schwartz, D. G. (2003). From open IS semantics to semantic Web: The road ahead. *IEEE Intelligent Systems, 18*(3), 52-58.

Sowa, J. F. (2000). *Knowledge representation: Logical, philosophical and computational foundations.* Cambridge, MA: Brooks/Cole.

Sure, Y., Erdmann, M., Angele, J., Staab, S., Studer, R., & Wenke, D. (2002). OntoEdit: Collaborative ontology development for semantic Web. *Proceedings of the 1st nternational Semantic Web Conference,* Sardinia, Italy.

Ushold, M. (2000). Creating, integrating and maintaining local and global ontologies. *Proceedings of the 1st Workshop on Ontology Learning (OL-2000) in conjunction with the 14th European Conference on Artificial Intelligence (ECAI 2000).*

Weick, E. K. (1979). *The social psychology of organizing.* Reading, MA: McGraw-Hill.

KEY TERMS

Application-Specific Ontology: An engineering object defining the model of knowledge in a specific application case.

Domain-Specific Ontology: An engineering object defining the model of knowledge in a specific domain. The level of specificity may be very deep, but the name is reserved for those ontologies that are not dependent on specific applications.

Domain Ontology: Either a domain-specific or an application-specific ontology.

Ontological Engineering: The activity of creating models of knowledge and possibly deploying them in actual engineering objects.

Ontology Methodology: A sequence of steps to be deployed in order to achieve one possible goal amongst creating, modifying, re-creating, validating, and evaluating a domain ontology. The very nature of an ontology methodology is more complex in principle, being able to provide the very same goal achievements by means of true work flows. However, these do not actually appear in the current literature.

Top-Level Ontology: An engineering object defining the very general concepts on which a model of knowledge is created. In particular, top-level ontologies give account to the notions of relation, entity, and instance, and model space, time, matter, and the notion of things.

Dynamic Taxonomies

Giovanni M. Sacco
Università di Torino, Italy

INTRODUCTION

End-user interactive access to complex information is one of the key functionalities of knowledge management systems. Traditionally, access paradigms have focused on retrieval of data on the basis of precise specifications: examples of this approach include queries on structured database systems, and information retrieval. However, most search tasks, and notably those typical of a knowledge worker, are exploratory and imprecise in essence: the user needs to explore the information base, find relationships among concepts, and thin alternatives out in a guided way.

Examples of this type of access include the selection of the "right" product to buy, of a candidate for a job, but also finding the likely cause of a malfunction, and so forth. Indeed, exploratory access applies to an extremely wide range of practical situations. Traditional access methods are not helpful in this context, and new access paradigms are needed. Effective end-user access requires a holistic approach, in which modeling, interface, and interaction issues are considered together.

BACKGROUND

Since the vast majority of knowledge is textual and unstructured in nature, information retrieval (IR) techniques (van Rijsbergen, 1979) have been extensively used in the past. IR techniques require almost no editorial work or manual preprocessing of information. However, their limitations have been known for some time: a study on a legal environment reported that only 20% of relevant documents were actually retrieved (Blair & Maron, 1985). Such a significant loss of information is due to the extremely wide semantic gap between the user model (concepts) and the model used by commercial retrieval systems (words). IR systems are also poor from the point of view of user interaction because the user has to formulate his query with no or very little assistance. Finally, results are presented as a flat list with no systematic organization, so that browsing/exploring the knowledge base is impossible.

Hypermedia (see Groenbaek & Trigg, 1994) addresses the problem of browsing/exploration, but it has a number of serious drawbacks: there is no systematic picture of relationships among knowledge base components; exploration is performed one document at a time, which is quite time consuming; and building and maintaining complex hypermedia networks is very expensive.

Traditional taxonomies are used by many systems, such as Yahoo. Here, a hierarchy of concepts can be used to select areas of interest and restrict the portion of the infobase to be retrieved. Taxonomies support abstraction and are easily understood by end-users. However, they are not scalable for large knowledge bases (Sacco, 2002) because they can be used for discrimination just down to terminal concepts, which are no further specialized. As the knowledge base grows, the average number of documents associated to a terminal concept becomes too large for manual inspection.

Solutions based on semantic networks were proposed in the past (e.g., Schmeltz Pedersen, 1993) and are being reconsidered in the current effort on ontologies and Semantic Web. Although more powerful and expressive than plain taxonomies, general semantic schemata are difficult to understand and manipulate by the casual user. They are better suited to programmatic access, and user interaction must be mediated by specialized agents. This increases costs, time to market, and decreases generality and flexibility of user access.

MAIN FOCUS OF THE ARTICLE

Dynamic taxonomies (Sacco, 1987, 2000; also known as faceted classification systems) are a general knowledge management model based on a multidimensional classification of heterogeneous data items and are used to explore/browse complex knowledge bases in a guided yet unconstrained way through a visual interface.

The intension of a dynamic taxonomy is a taxonomy designed by an expert. This taxonomy is a concept hierarchy going from the most general to the most specific concepts. Directed acyclic graph taxonomies modeling multiple inheritance are supported but rarely required. A dynamic taxonomy does not require any other relationships in addition to subsumptions (e.g., IS-A and PART-OF relationships).

In the extension, items can be freely classified under n (n>1) topics at any level of abstraction (i.e., at any level in the conceptual tree). This multidimensional classification is a departure from the monodimensional classification scheme used in conventional taxonomies. Besides being a generalization of a monodimensional classification, a multidimensional classification models common real-life situations. First, items are very often about different concepts: for example a news item on September 11, 2001, can be classified under "terrorism," "airlines," "USA," and so forth. Second, items to be classified usually have different features, "perspectives," or facets (e.g., Time, Location, etc.), each of which can be described by an independent taxonomy.

By taking a "nominalistic" approach—that is, concepts are defined by instances rather than by properties—a concept C is just a label that identifies all the items classified under C. Because of the subsumption relationship between a concept and its descendants, the items classified under C (items (C)) are all those items in the deep extension (Straube & Ozsu, 1990) of C; that is, the set of items identified by C includes the shallow extension of C (i.e., all the items directly classified under C) union the deep extension of C's sons. By construction, the shallow and the deep extension for a terminal concept are the same.

There are two important consequences of this approach. First, since concepts identify sets of items, logical operations on concepts can be performed by the corresponding set operations on their extension. This means that the user is able to restrict the information base (and to create derived concepts) by combining concepts through the normal logical operations (and, or, not).

Second, dynamic taxonomies can find all the concepts related to a given concept C; these concepts represent the conceptual summary of C. Concept relationships other than subsumptions are inferred through the extension only, according to the following extensional inference rule: two concepts A and B are related if there is at least one item d in the knowledge base which is classified at the same time under A or under one of A's descendants and under B or under one of B's descendants. For example, we can infer an unnamed relationship between Michelangelo and Rome, if an item classified under Michelangelo and Rome exists in the knowledge base. At the same time, since Rome is a descendant of Italy, also a relationship between Michelangelo and Italy can be inferred. The extensional inference rule can be seen as a device to infer relationships on the basis of empirical evidence.

The extensional inference rule can be easily extended to cover the relationship between a given concept C and a concept expressed by an arbitrary subset S of the universe: C is related to S if there is at least one item d in S which is also in items (C). Hence, the extensional inference rule can produce conceptual summaries not only for base concepts, but also for any logical combination of concepts. Since it is immaterial how S is produced, dynamic taxonomies can produce summaries for sets of items produced by other retrieval methods such as database queries, shape retrieval, and so forth, and therefore access through dynamic taxonomies can be easily combined with any other retrieval method.

Dynamic taxonomies work on conceptual descriptions of items, so that heterogeneous items of any type and format can be managed in a single, coherent framework. Finally, since concept C is just a label that identifies the set of the items classified under C, concepts are language-invariant, and multilingual access can be easily supported by maintaining different language directories, holding language-specific labels for each concept in the taxonomy. If the metadata descriptors used to describe an item use concepts from the taxonomy, then also the actual description of an item can be translated on the fly to different languages.

Exploration of the Knowledge Base

Dynamic taxonomies can be used to browse and explore the knowledge base in several ways. The preferred implementation follows. The user is initially presented with a tree representation of the initial taxonomy for the entire knowledge base. Each concept label also has a count of all the items classified under it—that is, the cardinality of items(C) for all Cs. The initial user focus F is the universe—all the items in the knowledge base.

In the simplest case, the user can then select a concept C in the taxonomy and zoom on it. The zoom operation changes the current state in two ways. First, concept C is used to refine the current user focus F, which becomes F $\cap$ items(C). Items not in the focus are discarded. Second, the tree representation of the taxonomy is modified in order to summarize the new focus. All and only the concepts related to F are retained, and the count for each retained concept C' is updated to reflect the number of items in the focus F that are classified under C'. The reduced taxonomy is derived from the initial taxonomy by pruning all the concepts not related to F, and it is a conceptual summary of the set of documents identified by F, exactly in the same way as the original taxonomy was a conceptual summary of the universe. In fact, the term *dynamic taxonomy* is used to indicate that the taxonomy can dynamically adapt to the subset of the universe on which the user is focusing, whereas traditional, static taxonomies can only describe the entire universe.

Figure 1. Initial taxonomy: Preparing to zoom on Masaccio

Figure 2. Locations for Masaccio's paintings: Preparing to zoom on USA; candidate items are reduced to 32 from 251

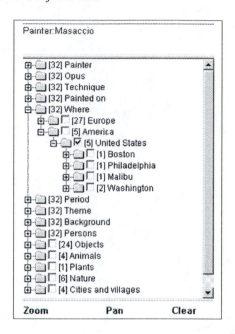

The retrieval process can be seen as an iterative thinning of the information base: the user selects a focus, which restricts the information base by discarding all the items not in the current focus. Only the concepts used to classify the items in the focus and their ancestors are retained. These concepts, which summarize the current focus, are those and only those concepts that can be used for further refinements. From the human computer interaction point of view, the user is effectively guided to reach his goal by a clear and consistent listing of all possible alternatives. This type of interaction is sometimes called guided thinning or guided navigation.

Dynamic taxonomies can be integrated with other retrieval methods in two basic ways. First, focus restrictions on the dynamic taxonomy can provide a context on which other retrieval methods can be applied, thereby increasing the precision of subsequent searches. Second, the user can start from an external retrieval method, and see a conceptual summary of the concepts that describe the result. Concepts in this summary can be used to set additional foci. These two approaches can be intermixed in different iteration steps during a single exploration.

An Example of Interaction

We show a simple systematic exploration on a multimedia knowledge base containing the works of the most important painters of the Italian Renaissance (Piero della Francesca, Masaccio, Antonello da Messina, Paolo Uccello, and Raffaello). Each work was thoroughly classified according to a number of subjects that are shown in Figure 1. The main difference with traditional methods is that no traditional method is able to taxonomically summarize a set of documents: there is no problem in selecting all the works by Masaccio through a database query, but there is no way of knowing where these works or what their themes are without exhaustively inspecting all the items. Conventional taxonomies have the same problem: they give a description of the entire collection, but are unable to summarize subsets of it.

A simple interaction that shows the importance of conceptual summaries follows. In Figure 1, we have the initial taxonomy and we are preparing to zoom on Masaccio. In Figure 2, the taxonomy no longer describes the entire knowledge base, but only the subset of it that consists of Masaccio's paintings. In this reduced taxonomy, we have expanded the location branch (Where) and found out that five paintings are in the USA. A single zoom operation thinned our 251 item knowledge base to only five items. Note that we could have expanded any other branch, according to our interests. Finally, Figure 3 summarizes the Themes for Masaccio's U.S. paintings, after a zoom on USA, and further reduces the number of candidate items to be inspected.

Figure 3. Themes for Masaccio's U.S. paintings: Miracles was clicked; candidate items are reduced from 32 to 5, and then to 1 by selecting the "Miracles" concept

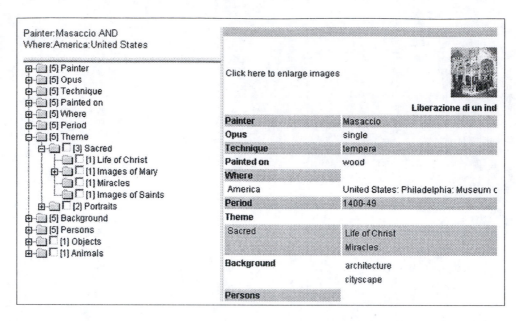

Advantages

The advantages of dynamic taxonomies over traditional methods are dramatic in terms of convergence of exploratory patterns and in terms of human factors. The analysis and experimental data by Sacco (2002) show that three zoom operations on terminal concepts are sufficient to reduce a 1,000,000 item information base described by a compact taxonomy with 1,000 concepts to an average 10 items. Experimental data on a real newspaper corpus of over 110,000 articles, classified through a taxonomy of 1,100 concepts, reports an average 1,246 documents to be inspected by the user of a static taxonomy vs. an average 27 documents after a single zoom on a dynamic taxonomy.

Dynamic taxonomies require a very light theoretical background: namely, the concept of a taxonomic organization and the zoom operation, which seems to be very quickly understood by end-users. Hearst et al. (2002) and Yee et al. (2003) conducted usability tests on a corpus of art images. Despite an inefficient implementation that caused slow response times, their tests show that access through a dynamic taxonomy produced a faster overall interaction and a significantly better recall than access through text retrieval. Perhaps more important are the intangibles: the feeling that one has actually considered all the alternatives in reaching a result. Although few usability studies exist, the recent (2004) widespread adoption of systems based on dynamic taxonomies by e-commerce portals, such as Yahoo, Lycos, BizRate, and so

forth empirically, in late 2003/early 2004 empirically supports this initial evidence.

The derivation of concept relationships through the extensional inference rule has important implications on conceptual modeling. First, it simplifies taxonomy creation and maintenance. In traditional approaches, only the relationships among concepts explicitly described in the conceptual schema are available to the user for browsing and retrieval. The schema designer must therefore anticipate and describe all possible relationships—a very difficult if not helpless task. In dynamic taxonomies, no relationships in addition to subsumptions are required, because concept relationships are automatically derived from the actual classification. For this reason, dynamic taxonomies easily adapt to new relationships and are able to discover new, unexpected ones. Second, since dynamic taxonomies synthesize compound concepts, these need usually not be represented explicitly. This means that the main cause of the combinatorial growth of traditional taxonomies is removed. Sacco (2000) developed a number of guidelines that produce taxonomies that are compact and easily understood by users. Some of these guidelines are similar to the faceted classification scheme by Ranganathan (1965), at least in its basic form: the taxonomy is organized as a set of independent, "orthogonal" subtaxonomies (facets or perspectives) to be used to describe data.

As an example, consider a compound concept such as "15th century Florentine paintings." First, we can break the compound concept into its *facets*: in the case at hand, we will have a Location taxonomy (of which Florence is a descendant), a Time taxonomy (of which the fifteenth century is a descendant), and finally an Art taxonomy (of which painting is a descendant). Second, by taking advantage of the multidimensional classification scheme, the items to be classified under "15th century Florentine paintings" will be classified under Location>Florence, Time>15th century, and Art>Painting instead. The extensional inference rule establishes a relationship between Florence, 15th century, and Painting, and the compound concept can be recovered by zooming on Florence, then on 15th century, and finally on Painting, or any permutation of these concepts since concept composition is commutative. In a conventional classification scheme, such as Dewey (1997) indexing, in which every item is classified under a single concept, we will need to explicitly define a number of different concepts equal to the Cartesian product of the terminals in the three taxonomies. Such a combinatorial growth either results in extremely large conceptual taxonomies or in a gross conceptual granularity (Sacco, 2000). In addition, the dynamic taxonomy approach makes it simple to focus on a concept, such as 15th century, and immediately see all related concepts such as literature, painting, politics, and so forth, which are recovered through the extensional inference rule. In the compound concept approach, these correlations are unavailable because they are hidden inside the concept label.

Additional advantages include the uniform management of heterogeneous items of any type and format, easy multilingual access, and easy integration with other retrieval methods.

Related Areas

Dynamic taxonomies directly derive from the work on the Fact Model (Sacco, 1988), the first semantic data model to include standard inference capabilities based on the conceptual schema itself rather than on external Prolog-like rules. In the Fact Model, relationships among entities (facts) are expressed as irreducible relations (Falkenberg, 1976): one of the standard inference rules in the model (called fact subsumption) states that given a fact F on entities E1, …, En, F is subsumed by all the facts defined on a subset of these entities. This means that, for instance, F(E1, E2) is a generalization of F(E1, …, En), in which E3, …, En are treated as 'don't cares'. In addition, F(E1, E2) exists if there exists at least one fact referencing both entities and at least one tuple in which these entities are not null. If the classification of an item in dynamic taxonomies is seen as a tuple in a fact

which references all the concepts in the taxonomy, the extensional inference rule is derived immediately.

Dynamic taxonomies have obvious connections with Description Logic (Baader, 2003), especially in the interpretation of concepts as sets of instances. Since the model is able to dynamically reconstruct all the combinations of concepts, it can be seen as a device to interactively build and explore hypercubes, in a way applicable to OLAP techniques for databases (see Chaudhuri & Dayal, 1997).

Some of the guidelines for the construction of the taxonomy are similar to basic faceted classification (Ranganathan, 1965; Hearst, 2002). Although some researchers use the term faceted classification instead of dynamic taxonomies, we believe it to be a misnomer because: (a) faceted classification only addresses conceptual modeling and very basic concept composition— conceptual summaries, reduced taxonomies, and guided navigation are totally absent; and (b) faceted classification is a special case of the more general multidimensional classification on which dynamic taxonomies are built.

Finally, agent-based architectures based on user profiles (see Ardissono, 2002, as an example) are a contender for recommender systems and product selection. However, they suffer for a number of important shortcomings with respect to dynamic taxonomies. First, they usually try to acquire knowledge on the user through lengthy dialogs, which are usually perceived as boring and intrusive, and at the same time, often fail to capture a sufficient amount of information. Second, it is often quite difficult to explain to the user why a certain solution was found and which alternatives exist: in short, the properties of selected candidates are not as transparent as they are in dynamic taxonomies.

Applications

Although dynamic taxonomies have an extremely wide application range, the main industrial application is currently e-commerce. Assisted product selection is a critical step in most large-scale e-commerce systems (Sacco, 2003), and the advantages in interaction are so significant as to justify the restructuring of well-established e-commerce portals: current examples include Yahoo, Lycos, BizRate, and so forth.

An interesting application area is multimedia databases, where dynamic taxonomies can be used to integrate access by conceptual metadata and access by primitive multimedia features (color, texture, etc.) into a single, coherent framework (Sacco, 2004). Among other application areas are news archives, encyclopedias, legal databases, multilingual portals, general-purpose search engines, e-auctions, CRM systems, human resources management, medical guidelines (Wollersheim & Rahayu, 2002), and diagnostic systems. Dynamic taxonomies seem especially important as a tool for accessing laws and regulations, and consequently quite relevant for e-government. A number of Web-based commercial systems based on dynamic taxonomies exist. These include Knowledge Processors, Endeca, i411, and Siderean Software.

FUTURE TRENDS

Five broad areas need further investigation:

1. **Extensions to the Model:** Dynamic taxonomies assume a Boolean classification. In some practical cases, a fuzzy (Zadeh, 1965) classification, in which a document can be classified under several concepts with different probabilities, can be more appropriate (Sacco, 2004).
2. **Centralized, Distributed, Federated Architectures:** Effective systems based on dynamic taxonomies must perform the zoom operation and the subsequent reduction of the corpus taxonomy in real time. A slower execution would severely impair the sense of free exploration that the user of dynamic taxonomy systems experiences. Commercial database systems do not achieve a sufficient speed on large to very large information bases, so that special data structures and evaluation strategies must be used (Sacco, 1998). Distributed and federated architectures need also to be investigated since centralized architectures are not always appropriate, because of organization needs and performance and reliability bottlenecks.
3. **Guidelines for Effective Conceptual Schema Design:** The design of effective dynamic taxonomies obviously plays a critical role in practical applications. Sacco (2000) indicates a number of general guidelines for the construction of dynamic taxonomies schemata, which take into account the fact that dynamic taxonomies are able to summarize concepts related to the current focus. Further research is needed to determine more stringent and specific guidelines.
4. **New Application Areas and Environments:** Dynamic taxonomies have an extremely wide application range, and the application areas listed above are but an initial sample. For instance, because of quick convergence, dynamic taxonomies seem the ideal access method for low-resolution wireless devices, especially when a taxonomy design that minimizes breadth is used.
5. **Human Factors Both in General and in Connection with Specific Application Areas:** A critical human factor issue is the presentation and manipulation of the taxonomy, where several alternatives exist (as an example, see Yee et al., 2003, vs. Sacco, 2000, 2004). With respect to specific application areas, dynamic taxonomies may need adaptation or complementary schemes (Sacco, 2003).

CONCLUSION

Exploratory browsing based on dynamic taxonomies applies to most practical situations and search tasks in knowledge management: an extremely wide application range going from multilingual portals, to general-purpose search engines, e-commerce, e-auctions, CRM systems, human resources management, and so forth. In this context, dynamic taxonomies represent a dramatic improvement over other search and browsing methods, both in terms of convergence and in terms of full feedback on alternatives and complete guidance to reach the user goal. For these reasons, we believe them to be a fundamental complement of traditional search techniques, and in fact, systems and Web sites implementing this paradigm are rapidly growing in number.

REFERENCES

Ardissono, L., Goy, A., Petrone, G., & Segnan, M. (2002). Personalization in business-to-customer interaction. *Communications of the ACM, 45*(5), 52-53.

Baader, F., Calvanese, D., McGuinness, D., Nardi, D., & Patel-Schneider, P. (Eds.). (2003). *The description logic handbook.* Cambridge: Cambridge University Press.

Blair, D.C., & Maron, M.E. (1985). An evaluation of retrieval effectiveness for a full-text document-retrieval system. *Communications of the ACM, 28*(3), 289-299.

Chaudhuri, S., & Dayal, U. (1997). An overview of data warehousing and OLAP technology. *ACM SIGMOD Record, 26*(1), 65-74.

Dewey, M., Mitchell, J.S., Beall, J., Matthews, W.E., New G.R., & Matthews, Jr., W.E. (Eds.). (1997). *Dewey decimal classification and relative index* (21st Ed.). OCLC.

Falkenberg, E. (1976). Concepts for modelling information. In G.M. Nijssen (Ed.), *Modelling in database management systems* (pp. 95-109). Amsterdam: North-Holland.

Groenbaek, K., & Trigg, R. (Eds.). (1994). Hypermedia. *Communications of the ACM, 37*(2).

Hearst, M. et al. (2002). Finding the flow in Web site search. *Communications of the ACM, 45*(9), 42-49.

Ranganathan, S.R. (1965). *The colon classification. In S. Artandi (Ed.), Rutgers series on systems for the intellectual organization of information (vol. 4).* Piscataway, NJ: Rutgers University Press.

Sacco, G.M. (1987). Navigating the CD-ROM. *Proceedings of the International Conference on Business of CD-ROM.*

Sacco, G.M. (1988). The fact model: A semantic data model for complex databases. *Information Systems, 13*(1), 1-11.

Sacco, G.M. (1998). *Procedimento a tassonomia dinamica per il reperimento di informazioni su grandi banche dati eterogenee.* Italian Patent 01303603; also U.S. Patent 6,763,349.

Sacco, G.M. (2000). Dynamic taxonomies: A model for large information bases. *IEEE Transactions on Knowledge and Data Engineering, 12*(2), 468-479.

Sacco, G.M. (2002). *Analysis and validation of information access through mono, multidimensional and dynamic taxonomies.* Technical Report, Department of Informatics, University of Torino, Italy.

Sacco, G.M. (2003). The intelligent e-sales clerk: The basic ideas. In H. Krueger & M. Rautenberg (Eds.), *Proceedings of INTERACT'03, the 9th IFIP TC13 International Conference on Human-Computer Interaction* (pp. 876-879).

Sacco, G.M. (2004). Uniform access to multimedia information bases through dynamic taxonomies. *Proceedings of the IEEE 6th International Symposium on Multimedia Software Engineering,* Miami, (pp. 320-328).

Schmeltz Pedersen, G. (1993). A browser for bibliographic information retrieval, based on an application of Lattice Theory. *Proceedings of the 1993 ACM SIGIR Conference* (pp. 270-279).

Straube, D.D., & Ozsu, M.T. (1990). Queries and query processing in object-oriented database systems. *ACM Transactions on Information Systems, 8*(4), 387-430.

van Rijsbergen, C.J. (1979). *Information retrieval.* London: Butterworths.

Wollersheim, D., & Rahayu, W. (2002). Methodology for creating a sample subset of dynamic taxonomy to use in navigating medical text databases. *Proceedings of the IDEAS 2002 Conference,* Edmonton, Canada (pp. 276-284).

Yee, K.-P., Swearingen, K., Li, K., & Hearst, M. (2002). Faceted metadata for image search and browsing. *Proceedings of ACM CHI 2002.*

Zadeh, L. (1965). Fuzzy sets. *Information Control, 8,* 338-353.

KEY TERMS

Extension, Deep: Of a concept C, denotes the shallow extension of C union the deep extension of C's sons.

Extension, Shallow: Of a concept C, denotes the set of documents classified directly under C.

Extensional Inference Rule: Two concepts A and B are related if there is at least one item d in the knowledge base which is classified at the same time under A (or under one of A's descendants) and under B (or under one of B's descendants).

Facet: One of several top-level (most general) concepts in a multidimensional taxonomy. In general, facets are independent and define a set of "orthogonal" conceptual coordinates.

Subsumption: A subsumes B if the set denoted by B is a subset of the set denoted by A ($B \subseteq A$).

Taxonomy: A hierarchical organization of concepts going from the most general (topmost) to the most specific concepts. A taxonomy supports abstraction and models IS-A or PART-OF relations between a concept and its father. Tree taxonomies can be extended to support multiple inheritance (i.e., a concept having several fathers).

Taxonomy, Monodimensional: A taxonomy where an item can be classified under a single concept only.

Taxonomy, Multidimensional: A taxonomy where an item can be classified under several concepts.

Taxonomy, Reduced: In a dynamic taxonomy, a taxonomy, describing the current user focus set F, which is derived from the original taxonomy by pruning from it all the concepts not related to F.

User Focus: The set of documents corresponding to a user-defined composition of concepts; initially, the entire knowledge base.

Zoom: A user interface operation that defines a new user focus by ORing user-selected concepts and ANDing them with the previous focus; a reduced taxonomy is then computed and shown to the user.

E-Learning for Knowledge Dissemination

Shyamala C. Sivakumar
Saint Mary's University, Canada

INTRODUCTION

What is E-Learning?

Today, most organizations need to extend lifelong learning opportunities to their employees in order to be successful in an increasingly competitive global marketplace. Organizations are turning to technological solutions to enable online in-house training and learning for their employees. An integrated approach to e-learning is important because it can be effectively used to analyze employee performance and also to gather information for continuous online and real-time learning of organizational goals to better tailor the educational product and its content. Online learning is made possible by advancements in network infrastructure and the development of voice and multimedia protocols for the seamless transport of information. E-learning involves encouraging the employee to spend time electronically to bring about learning, and to collect information and analyze it with respect to organizational needs, learning processes, and user preferences (Alavi & Leidner, 1999). E-learning ranges from simple computer use in a classroom where instructional materials are stored on a local-area network, to the use of simulation systems used to support teaching activities, or to distance education using broadband-enabled multimedia and shared electronic work spaces. E-learning styles include learner-centric, instructor-centric, and directed environments. E-learning communication modes include synchronous vs. asynchronous modes (time of interaction), and one-to-one, one-to-many, and many-to-many interaction modes. Presentation styles include voice only, voice and video, text only, text and animation, and voice, video, and text. Pedagogical approaches include objectivist, constructivist, and collaborative approaches and situated learning. Also, it is known that learning within organizations is affected by task complexity and the organizational environment (Argyris & Schon, 1996; Bhatt, 2002; Spender, 1996).

This article is organized as follows. We discuss why e-learning is important in creating a knowledge dissemination (KD) system, and why KD systems need a structured e-learning approach. We discuss the role of knowledge officers, practitioners, facilitators and mentors, and employees in enabling knowledge dissemination in such a system. Next we summarize the employee-centric and organizational metrics for evaluating e-learning systems. The main focus of the article is on studying critical factors that affect e-learning not only in the context of organizational requirements, but also in light of technological capability, pedagogical approaches, preferred learning styles, communication modes, and interaction styles across knowledge types. This article proposes an integrated e-learning system-design framework for knowledge dissemination across knowledge types. We discuss future trends in employing e-learning for KD and present conclusions.

BACKGROUND

Why is E-Learning Important in Creating a Knowledge-Dissemination System?

The developer of an e-learning system faces several challenges in designing systems for an online learning environment that ensures strong, effective, and secure learner interaction that best replaces the face-to-face interaction taking place on-site in the workplace and in training sessions (Alavi & Leidner, 1999). In addition to having a clear understanding of the knowledge-type requirements, the challenge is in supporting good pedagogy and learning practices given technical and other constraints. Technical constraints include bandwidth, quality of service (QoS), real-time interactions, support for multiple users, and security requirements. In parallel, instructional design that incorporates appropriate pedagogical techniques into a rich repertoire of learning resources is needed for creating a dynamic e-learning environment. These pedagogical techniques, if tailored to specific knowledge types, can improve productivity by sharing best practices within an organizational community (Agresti, 2003; Castro, Foster, Gunn, & Roberts, 2003; Spender, 1996). An enabling online knowledge-dissemination environment should allow for dynamic networked online interaction to create a non-competitive atmosphere that values both explicit and tacit knowledge dissemination, and the conversion of knowledge between these types to enable learning (Applen, 2002).

Figure 1. Knowledge-dissemination drivers

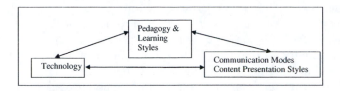

Why do KD Systems Need a Structured E-Learning Approach?

As shown in Figure 1, the rationale for adopting an e-learning technology for knowledge dissemination is influenced by the communication mode, content presentation style, and pedagogy and learning styles employed. However, the influence of organizational requirements and knowledge types on KD drivers (technology, communication modes, and pedagogy and learning styles) has not been studied.

As shown in Figure 2, the three stakeholders typically identified in an organizational e-learning framework are the employees or knowledge users, the knowledge providers in the organization (practitioners, mentors, and experts), and the provider of technology (IMS Global Learning Consortium, n.d). From the organizational perspective, an integrated knowledge-transformation framework for the structured diffusion of knowledge may consist of six processes for evaluating, acquiring, organizing, enabling, transferring, and using knowledge in organizations. In such an e-learning knowledge-management framework, knowledge providers acquire and organize knowledge from diverse sources, which is then suitably formatted and maintained in repositories and databases and is disseminated to users using formal knowledge-transfer mechanisms (Lytras, Pouloudi, & Poulymenakou, 2002).

Figure 2. Stakeholders in an organizational e-learning system

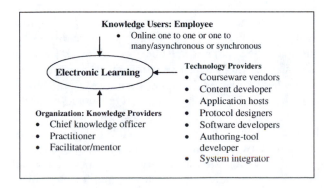

EMPLOYEE-CENTRIC AND ORGANIZATIONAL METRICS FOR EVALUATING AN E-LEARNING SYSTEM

This section discusses employee-centric and organizational metrics for evaluating an e-learning system. We identify metrics first from an employee-centric perspective used to evaluate employee expectations when interacting with a voice- or multimedia-enabled e-learning system. With these e-learning requirements for ensuring successful employee learning in mind, we propose a number of metrics that an organization may use to measure the effectiveness of the system in fostering learning.

The most important measure that an employee will use for repeat interaction with an e-learning system is the ease in using the system. From the employee viewpoint, the convenience of communicating with the system is critical and must be available all the time. The ease of using an e-learning system is a function of system design and is determined by several factors, such as its accessibility, its usability, its reliability, the help available online, having integrated touch points, support for many simultaneous users, the responsiveness of the system, and the appropriateness of system responses to queries (*The E-Learning E-Volution in Colleges and Universities*, 2001). In addition to e-learning objectives, such as tailoring learning modules to address how employees engage in learning (*IMS Learning Design Best Practice and Implementation Guide*, 2002), fostering effective e-learning strategies, and having a rich repertoire of learning resources and aids, instructional design must incorporate the latest techniques in pedagogical research that support learning at a pace that is comfortable to the employee.

The organizational metrics by which e-learning resources may be evaluated include (Janicki & Liegle, 2001; Schocken, 2001) (a) the curriculum content, (b) ease of use, (c) the flexibility of content presentation and management, (d) a continuous employee-assessment facility, (e) the ability to track employee performance through real-time feedback, (f) the ability to employ multimedia simulations, model building, and

153

interaction between users to create a dynamic, engaging environment for learning and to enhance problem-solving techniques on an individual or group basis, and (g) the ability to permit threaded discussions to log participant interactions for further analysis. Also, the organization needs to balance the conflicting metric of finding a cost-effective e-learning solution with employee satisfaction. The availability of off-the-shelf components is a prerequisite to lowering the cost of the system. Employees are also concerned with privacy issues and must be reassured about the nature of the information collected, why it is being collected, and how it may be used. Security measures such as authentication, encryption, authorization, and other measures must be in place to ensure privacy. The communication-channel characteristics, protocols, and technology must be designed for real-time interactions. The technology and protocols used in the e-learning system must be transparent to the employee and support employee touch-point integration. Touch-point integration involves integrating communication across service providers (PSTN, ISP [Internet service provider]), across devices (computer, fax, phone), and across services (e-mail, voice mail, instant messaging). If the employee cannot obtain a satisfactory learning experience from the system, it must be possible for the employee to locate automatically an appropriate mentor or facilitator in a reasonable period of time.

In the next few sections, factors affecting e-learning-system design are assessed with respect to technological capability, pedagogical issues and learning styles, interaction modes, organizational requirements, and knowledge types.

FACTORS AFFECTING E-LEARNING: TECHNOLOGICAL CAPABILITY

In this section we identify a series of requirements (metrics) from a technology perspective that would enable e-learning for knowledge dissemination in an organization, and how each requirement may influence its adoption by the organization. Technology-centric metrics can be broadly classified into courseware, protocol, architecture, infrastructure, engineering, and service metrics (*IEEE 1484.18: Platform and Media Profiles*, 2001).

Courseware consists of multimedia-enabled learning tools, computer software such as simulations, and interactive programs promoting online instruction, laboratories, discussion groups, and chat (*The E-learning E-Volution*, 2001). It is critical that courseware products be developed using pedagogical approaches to create a dynamic, engaging environment that promotes online learning and participation (*IMS Learning Design*, 2002;

Janicki & Liegle, 2001). It is important to design products that take into account the need for self-paced learning.

Protocols deal with the rules for implementing orderly multimedia communication within the e-learning environment. Protocol metrics encompass interoperability, latency, security features, and QoS provisioning (Sivakumar, 2003). The standards bodies such as ITU and the IETF work groups propose their own versions of protocols for achieving similar goals. A critical issue is, then, whether equipment that conforms to one standard can interoperate with equipment conforming to the other standard. In addition, the latency associated with a protocol is implementation dependent and is an important design metric as various implementations by different vendors of the same protocol may have varying latency associated with them. Security is critical to the success of e-learning and includes issues such as whether authentication and nonrepudiation is required, when to use authorization, and what encryption standard is used. Protocol extensibility is an important issue in that a client may propose extensions to the protocol for provisioning custom services.

The architectural viewpoint describes the functions needed of the various logical modules that together implement the e-learning system, the communication channel, and the interactions between them. The architecture must address the critical issue of whether different components can be added in a modular fashion to achieve new functionality. The architecture is typically implemented as a set of logical modules or entities, with a specific functionality associated with each module (*IEEE 1484.18*, 2001). This approach has advantages in that additional functionality can be added by incorporating new logical entities. Critical features such as security and QoS provisioning can now be addressed in a modular framework with an entity assigned the task of ensuring authentication, controlling access, and provisioning QoS before communication is established.

The technology infrastructure deals with the hardware and firmware components with which the e-learning system is designed, including protocol stacks, implementation languages, operating systems, and physical equipment (Sivakumar & Robertson, 2004). Infrastructure metrics that an organization must concern itself with when implementing an e-learning system include the core network technology, the QoS model, and the interoperability of the e-learning infrastructure with legacy systems (*IEEE 1484.18*, 2001). The choice of the core network technology and its architecture impacts bandwidth utilization and, hence, the latency and delay experienced by the employee, and it is an important design constraint. System integration includes the interoperability of various subsystems from different vendors, and the conversion of heterogeneous messages such as video, voice, text, e-mail, and so forth into standard formats to support the creation of a dynamic e-learning environment.

Service requirements deal with the functional requirements expected or offered by the various logical modules in the e-learning system. Critical engineering metrics include the use of codecs (coder or decoder) and echo cancelers for voice conversion before transmission. It may be desirable to include speech-to-text conversion for storing employee interaction data to be used for data mining and possible knowledge-discovery purposes. The issue of backward compatibility, that is, the question of whether devices designed for the current environment can interoperate consistently with legacy systems, is critical and must be addressed. Important service metrics from the service provider's viewpoint include the extensibility of the service model to provide custom (tailored) services to the organization and the community of practice (CoP), and to help support the e-learning system.

The organization may use these metrics to decide whether to adopt a particular courseware, protocol, or technology. Instructors, facilitators, and employees must have an understanding of the various components of the e-learning system, their capabilities, and their deficiencies for a better appreciation of the role of e-learning in the organization and to achieve better employee acceptance of the new technology.

FACTORS AFFECTING E-LEARNING: PEDAGOGICAL ISSUES AND LEARNING STYLES

Four pedagogical techniques that must be part of instructional design in any e-learning environment include the objectivist, constructive, collaborative, and situated learning approaches (Hiltz, Coppola, Rotter, Turoff, & Benbunan-Fich, 2000). The objective approach emphasizes lectures by experts, the constructive approach is skills based with information available only on demand, and the collaborative approach employs group interaction with peers to aid in knowledge construction and problem solving. Information answers *what* questions while knowledge answers the *how* and *why* questions (Rouse, 2002). Classic e-learning systems mimic objectivist learning environments and are structured to impart explicit *what* information. Modern e-learning systems implement constructive pedagogical methods, especially to mimic laboratory environ-

ments that are specifically designed to answer *how* questions. Typically, collaborative learning tools have been used for peer and tutor support (Harris & Figg, 2000).

The objectivist approach is didactic and emphasizes that novices learn by explicitly being informed or taught through the presentation of knowledge in a conventional lecture format. The lectures emphasize the underlying fundamental principles of study and the theoretical foundation of knowledge in a chiefly expert- and knowledge-centric manner (Leidner & Jarvenpaa, 1995). This approach uses a relatively passive method to deliver expert educational content from the expert to practitioner and is most appropriate for imparting factual and procedural knowledge. It is the most extensively used method in higher education environments (Leidner & Jarvenpaa). It is important that the delivery mechanism, course content, and instructional design employed are tailored to deliver factual and procedural information whose content is unambiguous and matches the characteristics of the delivery medium.

The constructivist approach is based on experiential learning where employees construct knowledge through engagement with procedural activities. Typically, this type of learning is supported by laboratories that employ state-of-the-art modeling software, simulators, and other hardware to immerse the employee in a real-world environment. These laboratories are designed to foster practical abilities and skills in employees and correspond to a learner-centric environment (Hiltz et al., 2000; Jonassen, Peck, & Wilson, 1999; Wenger, 1998).

Situated learning has been used in technology-based courses to present academic knowledge in a practical context to teach students problem-solving skills (Wenger, 1998). This is chiefly employed in a laboratory setting to transform novice students into experts in the context of the environments in which they will ultimately work. The application of knowledge in a collaborative laboratory environment is critical to acquiring the problem-solving, reasoning, and management skills needed by potential employees in the workforce (Denning, 1992).

Collaborative learning is a form of constructive learning in which problem solving and the centricity of the learning process is shifted to practitioners as a peer group rather than as individuals. Case studies and project work require employees to analyze the problem and arrive at several alternate solutions based on real-life constraints including financial, technical, and managerial considerations. From a pedagogical point of view, the process of arriving at the solution is deemed to be as important as the final solution.

FACTORS AFFECTING E-LEARNING: COMMUNICATION AND INTERACTION MODES

Communication modes can be broadly classified as synchronous or asynchronous based on the time of interaction. Synchronous systems require the simultaneous participation of employees with experts (i.e., modeling a virtual classroom), and asynchronous systems allow employees to participate at a time and place convenient to them (Kubarek, 1997).

Online interactions can be classified as (a) one-to-many interactions with the system, (b) one-to-one interactions with the equipment, hardware, software, and e-learning learn-ware, (c) many-to-many interactions between peers, or (d) one-to-many interactions between a mentor and employees. Typically, one-to-many interaction in the e-learning system is designed to handle the simultaneous interaction of multiple employees with the system or the expert instructor at the same time. Issues in this type of interaction include how an employee can obtain the attention of the instructor and the number of simultaneous interactions that the system can support without appreciable degradation in the performance of the system. One-to-many interactions are typically synchronous in nature and may involve broadband network connections if employing multimedia communication. Studies have shown that delivering lectures to a remote audience using interactive video (involving two-way audio and videoconferencing) results in no appreciable change in the learning outcomes when compared with traditional on-site, face-to-face instruction (Russell, 1999). These results highlight that the pedagogy embedded in these synchronous mediums of instruction is more important for positive learning outcomes than the instruction medium itself.

In a one-to-one interaction type, the learner interacts with the instructional material embedded in the courseware or laboratory at a time convenient to the learner, typically with no facilitator or instructor present. The one-to-one interaction process is much more complex to implement as the e-learning system is designed to record user input, provide suitable response and access to the learning material, and guide the user through the learning process. The system must also keep track of users' progress and suggest remedial action in case of failure to meet the desired competency level. In general, one-to-many interactions easily lend themselves to synchronous modes, while one-to-one interaction with software, hardware, or courseware is more conducive to asynchronous modes.

FACTORS AFFECTING E-LEARNING: ORGANIZATIONAL REQUIREMENTS AND KNOWLEDGE TYPES

Types of knowledge include tacit knowledge that cannot be explicitly stated; implicit knowledge that can be elicited using questionnaires, interviews, and collaborative discussion groups; and explicit knowledge found in manuals, memos, and training sessions that can be captured as it is created (Nonaka & Takeuchi, 1995). Learning in organizations occurs at several levels including individual, group or collective, corporate, and interorganizational levels (Hwang, 2003). Training approaches that foster reflection during the learning process are especially effective in an organizational setting and can be effected using simulations. Simulations help learners formulate and test different strategies. Mentors and experts can help discuss the results of various strategies and help novice learners learn from interpreting these results. In an organizational context, the learning gained from experience in interorganizational teamwork can be transformed into knowledge and transferred by partnering between these organizations (Wagner, 2003). Such learning is especially appropriate for sharing tacit knowledge about organizational processes and systems. Centralized knowledge repositories such as databases of documents are very effective for disseminating explicit or procedural knowledge while peer-to-peer (p2p) networks are more suited for tacit knowledge dissemination, especially when multimedia video or audio communication is employed in such networks (Kwok & Gao, 2004). In a decentralized p2p network, the members constitute a virtual community of both knowledge providers and knowledge users. From the learner's perspective, learning scenarios are used to organize the learning objects for dissemination. Virtual agencies have been used by U.S. governmental departments to disseminate R & D (research and development) results for better organizational efficiency, the transfer of explicit and tacit technical knowledge, and the alignment of interdepartmental mission goals (Castro et al., 2003).

AN INTEGRATED E-LEARNING SYSTEM-DESIGN FRAMEWORK FOR KNOWLEDGE DISSEMINATION

Figure 3 summarizes how the explicit-tacit, tacit-explicit, tacit-tacit, and explicit-explicit knowledge-con-

Figure 3. Learning styles, pedagogy, communication modes, technology, and organizational requirements across knowledge types

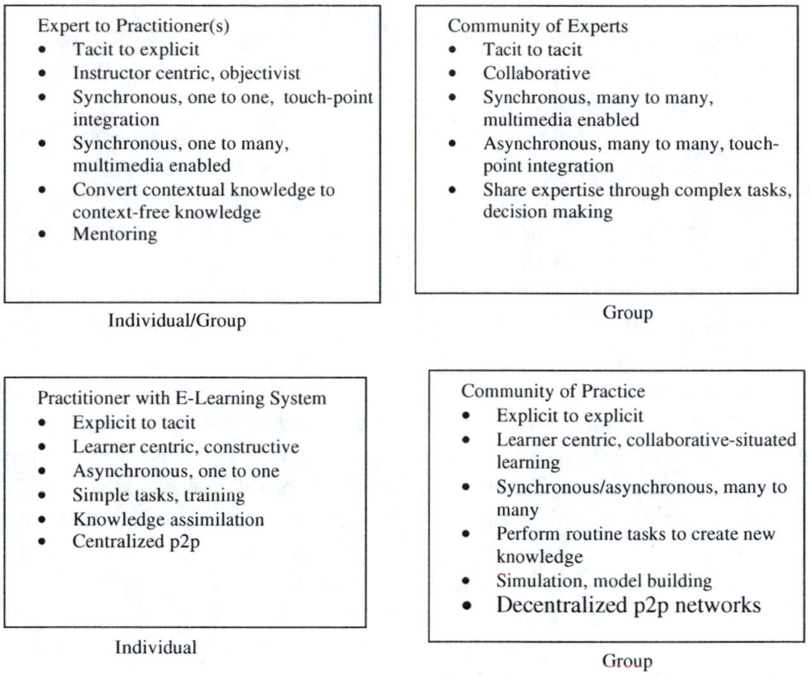

Expert to Practitioner(s)
- Tacit to explicit
- Instructor centric, objectivist
- Synchronous, one to one, touch-point integration
- Synchronous, one to many, multimedia enabled
- Convert contextual knowledge to context-free knowledge
- Mentoring

Individual/Group

Community of Experts
- Tacit to tacit
- Collaborative
- Synchronous, many to many, multimedia enabled
- Asynchronous, many to many, touch-point integration
- Share expertise through complex tasks, decision making

Group

Practitioner with E-Learning System
- Explicit to tacit
- Learner centric, constructive
- Asynchronous, one to one
- Simple tasks, training
- Knowledge assimilation
- Centralized p2p

Individual

Community of Practice
- Explicit to explicit
- Learner centric, collaborative-situated learning
- Synchronous/asynchronous, many to many
- Perform routine tasks to create new knowledge
- Simulation, model building
- Decentralized p2p networks

Group

version models proposed by Nonaka and Takeuchi (1995) influence the choice of pedagogical methods, preferred learning styles, communication modes, interaction styles, organizational requirements, and technology used.

Explicit to implicit knowledge conversion occurs when situated learning occurs in an active environment. Such learning may be achieved with one-to-one asynchronous interaction where the learner interacts with the instructional material embedded in the courseware or laboratory. The one-to-one e-learning system is designed to record user input, provide suitable response and access to learning material, and guide the user through the learning process. This guided practice allows the system to provide corrective feedback (Gagne, 1987). According to Gagne, corrective feedback is one of the most effective teaching strategies that enhances learning and long-term retention of knowledge. At this stage, learning can be thought of as being directed with a distinctly defined sequence of branches (*IMS Learning Design*, 2002). The system also keeps track of the user's progress and suggests remedial action in case of failure to meet the desired competency level. Such embedded learning can be used to present academic knowledge in a practical context to teach employees problem-solving skills (Wenger, 1998), and can be employed in the organization to transform novices into experts in the context of the community in

which they work. This helps the novice gain a broad range of hands-on experience and a large repertoire of knowledge to understand the practical conditions under which to apply specific principles, theories, and techniques.

Explicit to explicit knowledge conversion occurs when members of a community of practice share explicit knowledge to solve a problem in a collaborative style. In a CoP, people who are separated geographically or belong to different work groups share explicit knowledge in a virtual space. Typically, problem solving in a modern enterprise is conducted in a collaborative setting with a good deal of interaction between team members. This makes it imperative that the KD environment model and implement a collaborative online learning environment as it is critical to acquiring the problem-solving, reasoning, and management skills required of novice employees in the workforce (Denning, 1992). Such a CoP can exist within and across organizational boundaries as it is defined by knowledge and consists of users who perform similar work activities (Agresti, 2003). The CoP includes provision for locating experts in the subject area, synchronous and asynchronous collaboration, and sharing resources online in a content-structured format using file or application servers (Agresti; Lewis, 2002). Such content contains explicit knowledge and may include answers to FAQs (frequently asked questions), e-mails, procedures, manuals, and references such as papers and books. However, for a CoP to be successful, it must focus on pressing business needs (Lewis). Also, a facilitator is particularly valuable in monitoring group activities in the CoP and keeping it active and current.

Tacit to explicit knowledge conversion is enabled through the proximity and interpersonal interaction between an expert and practitioner(s) (Hansen, 1999; Nonaka & Takeuchi, 1995; Spender, 1996). Experts have collected tacit knowledge through years of experience in their chosen field, and it would be appropriate to tap into their knowledge by having experts mentor novices or practitioners. Also, mechanisms for the transfer of tacit knowledge (especially complex contextual knowledge) include mentorship and repeated practice over time (Nonaka & Takeuchi; Spender). A practitioner's remote interaction with her or his mentor can be enhanced by integrated communication, that is, when the communication is coordinated across all touch points including e-mail, voice mail, and fax. This may be implemented using an integrated communications system and needs to be in real time to be effective. Automatic call-routing capabilities are an additional asset in routing a call from a practitioner to the mentor within the least possible time. Tacit to explicit knowledge conversion is also enabled through either one-to-one or one-to-many interactions. In synchronous learning environments, proximity and interpersonal interaction between experts and practitioners can be mimicked with two-way videoconferencing that transmits voice and video streams in real time. Many factors contribute to the quality and quantity of information conveyed using multimedia; for example, audio can supplement the information provided by text or video graphics (Schar & Krueger, 2000). Specifically, this approach is advantageous especially when experts with intuitive contextual knowledge explain difficult theoretical concepts or demonstrate advanced techniques to less knowledgeable employees and exploit the prevalence and power of learning by observation (Bandura, 1986). Thus, experts can instruct novices to help reinforce important content-specific organizational knowledge resulting in better retention of knowledge.

Tacit to tacit knowledge conversion occurs when experts within a community of experts (CoE) collaborate synchronously or asynchronously creating documents, tools, and software to share expertise to solve complex problems in their field. Collaborative sessions typically use many-to-many synchronous communication for sharing good practices and training. In addition, collaboration helps in consensus building and decision making. Interaction between experts in a CoE moves knowledge specific to an individual to a CoE or CoP. Asynchronous collaboration is enabled by integrating

communication touch points including e-mail, voice mail, fax, and instant messaging. However, synchronous and asynchronous collaboration tools must be designed to encourage interactions between the CoE and CoP so as to move tacit knowledge from experts to answer questions such as why a particular technique has been employed or why something is done the way it is into the larger CoP.

In this section we posit that an integrated e-learning system-design framework for knowledge dissemination must (a) encourage strong employee interaction by incorporating both synchronous and asynchronous communication modes, (b) add pedagogical and instruction-level knowledge conducive to active, collaborative, self-paced online instruction to enable explicit to tacit (explicit) knowledge conversion, (c) incorporate effective online mentoring and facilitation to mimic the face-to-face interaction taking place on site for enabling tacit to tacit (explicit) knowledge conversion, (d) use employee touch-point integration for practitioner, expert, and mentor communication, (e) integrate authentication and access control into standard e-learning architectures to provide a secure delivery mechanism, and (f) devise high-level metrics to monitor the effectiveness of the e-learning process. Such a system must also be modular, scalable, and reusable across geographically distributed educational applications.

FUTURE TRENDS

Figure 3 provides an exhaustive list of the influence of the pedagogical methods, preferred learning styles, communication modes, interaction styles, organizational requirements, and technology used in knowledge sharing. However, these factors have not been ranked in terms of how important or critical they are to knowledge sharing. Therefore, future work will focus on employing the Delphi method to rank these factors, and further factor analysis could be employed to detect the structure of the relationships between them. Such analysis would help find the critical barriers to knowledge sharing in organizational learning.

CONCLUSION

This article discussed how knowledge types influence the choice of technology, pedagogical method, communication mode, interaction, and learning style employed. In organizational e-learning environments, there are three main design issues that must be considered and addressed. They are technical design, communication- and interaction-process design, and instructional design. In each of these design dimensions, consideration must be given to pedagogical approaches and learning styles from both the organizational-requirement (features and employee capabilities) and knowledge-type perspectives (knowledge conversion). To be effective and in order to meet the needs of a geographically diverse labor force, the designers and deployers of e-learning systems must tailor the courseware content, instructional method, architecture, and delivery mechanism of the system to support the four types of knowledge conversion.

REFERENCES

Agresti, W. (2003). Tailoring IT support to communities of practice. *IT Professional, 5*(6), 24-28.

Alavi, M., & Leidner, D. E. (1999). Knowledge management systems: Issues, challenges and benefits. *Communications of the Association for Information Systems, 1*(7), 1-37.

Applen, J. D. (2002). Tacit knowledge, knowledge management, and active user participation in Website navigation. *IEEE Transactions on Professional Communication, 45*(4), 302-306.

Argyris, C., & Schon, D. A. (1996). *Organizational learning II: Theory, method and practice.* Reading, MA: Addison Wesley.

Bandura, A. (1986). *Social foundations of thought and action.* Englewood Cliffs, NJ: Prentice Hall.

Bhatt, G. D. (2002). Management strategies for individual knowledge and organizational knowledge. *Journal of Knowledge Management, 6*(1), 31-39.

Castro, M., Foster, R. S., Gunn, K., & Roberts, E. B. (2003). Managing R&D alliances within government: The virtual agency concept. *IEEE Transactions on Engineering Management, 50*(3), 297-306.

Denning, P. (1992). Educating a new engineer. *Communications of the ACM, 35*(12), 83-97.

The e-learning e-volution in colleges and universities (pp. 1-142). (2001). The Advisory Committee for Online Learning, Council of Ministers of Education (CMEC), & Industry Canada. Retrieved November 15, 2002, from *http://mlg-gam.ic.gc.ca/sites/acol-ccael/en/report/e-volution_e.pdf*

Gagne, R. M. (1987). *Instructional technology: Foundations.* Hillsdale, NJ: Erlbaum Associates.

Hansen, M. T. (1999). The search-transfer problem: The role of weak ties in sharing knowledge across organization subunits. *Administrative Science Quarterly, 44*(1), 82-111.

Harris, J. B., & Figg, C. (2000). Participating from the sidelines. Online: Facilitating telementoring projects. *ACM Journal of Computer Documentation, 24*(4), 227-236.

Hiltz, S. R., Coppola, N., Rotter, N., Turoff, M., & Benbunan-Fich, R. (2000). Measuring the importance of collaborative learning for the effectiveness of ALN: A multi-measure, multi-method approach. *Journal of Asynchronous Learning Networks, 4*(2), 103-125.

Hwang, A. S. (2003). Training strategies in the management of knowledge. *Journal of Knowledge Management, 7*(3), 92-104.

IEEE 1484.18: Platform and media profiles (pp. 1-188). (2001). IEEE Learning Technology Standards Committee (P1484). Retrieved November 15, 2002, from *http://ltsc.ieee.org/wg18/compilation.pdf*

IMS Global Learning Consortium. (n.d.). Retrieved October 15, 2004, from *http://www.imsproject.org*

IMS learning design best practice and implementation guide. (2002). IMS Global Learning Consortium. Retrieved October 15, 2004, from *http://www.imsproject.org/learningdesign/ldv1p0pd/imsld_bestv1p0pd.html*

Janicki, T., & Liegle, J. O. (2001). Development and evaluation of a framework for creating Web-based learning modules: A pedagogical and systems perspective. *Journal of Asynchronous Learning Networks, 5*(1), 58-84.

Jonassen, D. H., Peck, K. L., & Wilson, B. G. (1999). *Learning with technology: A constructivist perspective.* Upper Saddle River, NJ: Merrill.

Kubarek, D. (1997). *Glossary of distance learning terms.* Retrieved August 14, 2003, from *http://www.cit.cornell.edu/atc/consult/DL/dlglossary.html*

Kwok, S. H., & Gao, S. (2004). Knowledge sharing community in P2P network: A study of motivational perspective. *Journal of Knowledge Management, 8*(1), 94-102.

Leidner, D., & Jarvenpaa, S. (1995). The use of information technology to enhance management school education: A theoretical view. *MIS Quarterly, 19*(3), 265-291.

Lewis, B. (2002). On-demand KM: A two-tier architecture. *IT Professional, 4*(1), 27-33.

Lytras, M. D., Pouloudi, A., & Poulymenakou, A. (2002). Knowledge management convergence: Expanding learning frontiers. *Journal of Knowledge Management, 6*(1), 40-51.

Nonaka, I., & Takeuchi, H. (1995). *The knowledge creating company*. Oxford: Oxford University Press.

Rouse, W. B. (2002). Need to know: Information, knowledge, and decision making. *IEEE Transactions on Systems, Man, and Cybernetics, Part C: Applications and Reviews, 32*(4), 282-292.

Russell, T. L. (1999). *The no significant difference phenomenon*. Raleigh, NC: North Carolina State University & International Distance Education Certification Center.

Schar, S. G., & Krueger, H. (2000). Using new learning technologies with multimedia. *IEEE Multimedia, 7(3),* 40-51.

Schocken, S. (2001). Standardized frameworks for distributed learning. *Journal of Asynchronous Learning Networks, 5*(2), 97-110.

Shale, D. (2002). The hybridization of higher education in Canada. *International Review of Research in Open and Distance Learning, 2*(2), 1-11.

Sivakumar, S. C. (2003). A user interaction framework for e-learning. *Proceedings of the Sixth Annual Conference of Southern Association for Information Systems* (pp. 388-396).

Sivakumar, S. C., & Robertson, W. (2004). Developing an integrated Web engine for online internetworking education: A case study. *Internet Research: Electronic Networking Applications and Policy, 14*(2), 175-192.

Spender, J. C. (1996). Organizational knowledge, learning and memory: Three concepts in search of a theory. *Journal of Organizational Change, 9*(1), 63-78.

Wagner, B. A. (2003). Learning and knowledge transfer in partnering: An empirical case study. *Journal of Knowledge Management, 7*(2), 97-113.

Wenger, E. (1998). *Communities of practice: Learning, meaning and identity*. Cambridge: Cambridge University Press.

KEY TERMS

Asynchronous Systems: They allow students to participate at a time and place convenient to them. In asynchronous systems, interaction between the student and the faculty takes place intermittently through e-mail, HTML (hypertext markup language) content, and/or news or discussion groups. The interaction does not require participation at the same time.

Community of Experts: A collection of people who possess very high knowledge (expertise) in a particular field. They are subject-matter experts and provide intellectual leadership within an organization. A CoE can exist across company divisions and across organizational boundaries.

Community of Practice: An informal community of people bound by a common task or purpose (e.g., similar work activities). A CoP nurtures a critical skill set in an organization. It can exist across company divisions and sometimes across organizational boundaries.

Electronic Learning (E-Learning): Defined as a virtual environment in which the learner's interactions with learning materials, including readings, laboratories, software, assignments, exercises, peers, and instructors, is mediated through the Internet or intranets. E-learning includes the use of simulation systems used to enhance teaching activities and distance education supported by broadband multimedia communication and shared electronic work spaces.

Explicit Knowledge: Defined as context-free knowledge that can be codified using formal and systematic language. Explicit knowledge can be expressed using words (language) or as mathematical formulae, procedures, or principles. Explicit knowledge is easy to codify and communicate.

Synchronous Systems: They require the simultaneous participation of students with faculty in real time. It models a virtual classroom. It involves the use of live chat, white boards, and video and audio conferencing.

Tacit Knowledge: Defined as personal, context-specific knowledge. It is knowledge acquired by experience and practice. It is therefore difficult to formally state, codify, and communicate such knowledge.

Engineering Design Knowledge Management

Z.M. Ma
Northeastern University, China

INTRODUCTION

In recent years, greater global competition is pressuring organizations to produce industrial products with the shortest possible lead times, high quality, and lowest costs. The lifecycle of a product includes many phases such as requirement definition, conceptual design, production, operation, maintenance, and so forth. Each phase in the lifecycle would involve the product information, for example, using some information that comes from other phase(s) and generating some new information during the phase. Engineering design knowledge (EDK) of a product consists of the product information related to the design process of the product.

It should be noticed that modern products are complex, and their developments have increasingly become collaborative tasks among teams that are physically, geographically, and temporally separated (Caldwell et al., 2000; Szykman, *Sriram, Bochenek, Racz, & Senfaute*, 2000). As design becomes increasingly knowledge intensive and collaborative, traditional design databases, which merely provide access to schematics, computer-aided design (CAD) models, and documentation, are inadequate for modern product design (Szykman et al., 2000), and the need for computational design frameworks to support the representation, integration, maintenance, and use of knowledge among distributed designers becomes more critical. The *representation, integration, maintenance,* and *use* of knowledge consist of the knowledge management of engineering knowledge.

BACKGROUND

Nowadays most engineering design is a knowledge-intensive process undertaken by teams dispersed across multiple disciplines. So it needs to be supported with relevant engineering design knowledge. We call *engineering design knowledge* all the standards, laws, and best practices that need to affect the design decision. Engineering design knowledge attempts to integrate three fundamental facts of artifact representation: the physical layout of the artifact (*structure*), an indication of the artifact's overall effect (*function*), and a causal account of the artifact's operation (*behavior*) (Szykman et al., 2000).

The function-behavior-structure (FBS) engineering design model has been developed in Tomiyama, Umeda, and Yoshikawa (1993) and Tomiyama, Mantyla, and Finger (1995). Based on the model, four categories of design knowledge were basically classified (Li & Zhang, 1999): *artifact functions, artifact behaviors, artifact structures,* and the *causalities* among structures, behaviors, and functions. Function knowledge is about the purpose of an artifact; behavior knowledge is about the changes of states of an artifact; structure knowledge is about a set of components and their relationships; causality knowledge is about design constraints, wishes, physical principles, heuristic rules, and so on.

Corresponding to contemporary engineering design, engineering design knowledge is *structured, distributed,* and *evolving.* It is generally already formal or can be easily formalized. It essentially consists of sets of constraints with additional references, justifications, illustrations, examples, and other documentation. This knowledge lends itself to a formal, machine-readable representation. Engineering design knowledge is typically distributed because most engineering artifacts involve a variety of domains of expertise (e.g., electrical, mechanical, styling, and manufacturing) and a variety of stakeholders (e.g., manufacturers, suppliers, servicing agents, legislators). The knowledge is distributed in the sense that each area of expertise and each stakeholder authors, publishes, and maintains their own repository. The SAE (Society of Automotive Engineers) handbook and EPA (Environmental Protection Agency) publications, for example, are published and updated independently of each other. Finally, the knowledge is rapidly evolving because it is meant to be a live reflection of the state of the art and the state of the technology relevant to the engineering domain of interest. The knowledge gets updated asynchronously, and the updated information is made immediately available to the user.

Because engineering design knowledge has a large size, rapid pace of growth and evolution, and distributed ownership, it is better managed as an independent resource rather than hard-coded within the CAD systems or their satellite tools. The management of the engineering knowledge entails its modeling (representation), maintenance, integration, and use.

ENGINEERING DESIGN KNOWLEDGE MANAGEMENT

The management of engineering design knowledge entails its modeling (representation), maintenance, integration, and use. Knowledge modeling consists of representing the knowledge in some selected language or notation. Knowledge maintenance encompasses all activities related to the validation, growth, and evolution of the knowledge. Knowledge integration is the synthesis of knowledge from related sources. The use of the knowledge requires bridging the gap between the objectives expressed by the knowledge and the directives needed to support the designer in creating valid engineering artifacts. The management of engineering design knowledge requires an adequate modeling language and an associate inferencing mechanism. So in this short article, we only focus on the modeling of engineering design knowledge.

Knowledge Modeling

Knowledge modeling and the representation of structural information have been prominent issues in artificial intelligence, knowledge representation, and advanced applications of databases. Although the design knowledge representation itself is not a new subject, there is no commonly agreed approach to the problem, and it still represents an active area of research (Vranes & Stanojevic, 1999). A number of solutions have emerged from these domains, and various researchers have developed models that attempt to capture the facts of structure, function, and behavior (Gorti, Gupta, Kim, Sriram, & Wong, 1998; Vranes & Stanojevic, 1999).

An integrated artifact metamodel was developed in BEST's knowledge representation language, Prolog/Rex (Vranes & Stanojevic, 1999). The Prolog/Rex concepts were used to define generic classes and describe the workpiece, which are instances of generic classes; Prolog/Rex relations were used to describe the relationships between the concepts. Then the knowledge used in the design process was divided into declarative and procedural knowledge. Similarly, in Gorti et al. (1998), an object model was developed which formed the basis of the design knowledge representation. Their model consists of objects, relationships among objects, and classes (object class and relationship class). An object-oriented model has been developed and applied for design knowledge modeling (Mili et al., 2001; Ma & Mili, 2003).

Class with Constraints

Knowledge units were basically constraints (Mili et al., 2001). Constraints are always associated with engineer-

ing artifacts, modeled by classes. Instances of a given class are created and modified through the direct setting and update of their parameters. These parameters, because they are the subjects of direct decisions, are called decision parameters. Most constraints on a class do not constrain directly the decision parameters. They generally refer to more complex and more abstract parameters, called performance parameters. This leads to the modeling of a class using the UML notation in which we represent four compartments: The class name in the top compartment identifies the concept of interest. The bottom compartment contains (a reference to) the constraints that class instances are bound by. These constraints typically refer to parameters of the concept. Some of these parameters are attributes directly set by the designer. They are listed under the second compartment. Most of the parameters referred to in the constraints are measures of "performance" of the class. They are not direct decision parameters, but are functions of some decision parameters. The performance parameters are included in the third compartment along with their expression in terms of decision parameters. The decision parameters used are added to the second compartment.

For example, a door panel may be represented as follows:

Door Panel

Decision parameters
    length: Real
    width: Real
    contour: Curve
Performance parameters
    top to bottom curvature = curvature
        Function (length, contour),
    corner angles = corners
        Function (contour)
Design constraints
    constraint on top to bottom curvature
    constraint on corner angles

Constraints

The most interesting elements in this model are the constraints themselves. In fact, we refer to them as constraints even though they are generally complex documents encompassing source, motivation, rationale, consequences, and a log of the various changes and updates they have undergone. Because of this existing and potential complexity, the constraints are represented within their own class. A number of attributes are used to describe the constraints. These attributes can be very useful when it comes to assessing the authority and criticality of a given constraint. For example, a constraint of type standard authored by a trusted authority from the federal agency EPA is likely to have high criticality. On the other hand, a constraint classified as best practice, whose consequence is a slightly more costly assembly procedure, can conceivably be violated in order to ensure that some other constraint is met.

Constraint

Name:
Source: {EPA, SAE, SME, □ }
Author: (authority)
Classification: {standard, best practice, □ }
Last updated:
Replaces: Constraint
Overrides: (Class, Constraint, Class)
Formula:
Rationale:
Consequences:
Parameters directly referenced: set of parameters
Parameters indirectly referenced: set of Parameters
Replaces older□ not less recent constraints
Overrides weaker□ not stronger constraints

In a word, a class with constraints representing a piece of design knowledge is defined by the quintuplet $<CN, DP, PP, MT, CT>$. Here, CN is the name of the class, and DP, PP, MT, and CT are the sets of decision parameters, performance parameters, methods, and constraints, respectively.

Relationships Among Design Knowledge and Comparison

Since design knowledge is represented by classes with constraints, semantic relationships among design knowledge turn out to be the semantic relationships among classes with constraints. It should be pointed out that, however, the distributed design knowledge may result in syntactic and semantic conflicts among classes with constraints, which affect the identification and determination of the relationships among design knowledge. Here we assume that all possible conflicts are identified and solved.

The following semantic relationships among classes with constraints can be classified in the knowledge model above.

- Subclass relationship
- Part-feature relationship
- Equivalence relationship
- Inclusion relationship
- Approximate equivalence relationship
- Approximate inclusion relationship

Among these relationships, some, like subclass relationship, part-feature relationship, and aggregate relation-

ship, are common in object-oriented model; some, like assembly-component relationship, are crucial for engineering design and manufacturing; and some, like (approximate) equivalence relationship and (approximate) inclusion relationship, are very useful for design knowledge fusion and design knowledge use.

The comparison of design knowledge is a very important topic in the context of design knowledge management. During design of a product, for example, designers would usually think if there has existed a similar product designed before, if there have been some standard parts in CAD systems that could be directly used to design the product, or if some components existed in CAD systems that can be used as references to the designed product. Designers therefore would try to answer these questions by findings from CAD systems or design repositories, when the designed product is very complex or the design repositories are very large and located in heterogeneous systems. In addition, managing design knowledge federations need to integrate knowledge from different sources. In order to cerate the integrated knowledge repositories, it is necessary to identify and capture the semantic relationships among different knowledge models. The purpose of comparing design knowledge is to identify the relationships among design knowledge given above. Since design knowledge is represented by classes with constraints, comparison of design knowledge turns out to be the comparison of classes with constraints. In Ma and Mili (2003), based on the object-oriented knowledge model above, the semantic relationships among design classes with constraints were identified and the methods to determining these relationships were hereby developed. In particular, the comparison of constraints and the semantic relationships on approximate basis were investigated.

Regarding comparison of design knowledge, Tischler, Samuel, and Hunt (1995) focused on the comparison of design knowledge at the artifact structure level, where only the kinematic motion is considered in the domain of machine conceptual design. A conceptual graph (Sowa, 1999) has been used to represent the domain level of an expertise model (Dieng, 1996), and knowledge-intensive design has been represented graphically (Balazs, Brown, Bastien, & Wills, 1997). Therefore, in Li and Zhang (1999), a hybrid graph approach was proposed to represent four kinds of design knowledge: artifact functions, artifact behaviors, artifact structures, and the causalities among structures, behaviors, and functions. Then the comparison of design knowledge turned out to be the comparison of hybrid graphs. Using the Hopfield-Tank neural network algorithm, an algorithm for the graph comparison purpose was developed. Moreover, some research work has also focused on comparison of conceptual graphs (Dieng, 1996; Montes-y-Gómez, Gelbukh, López-López, & Baeza-Yates, 2001).

CONCLUSION

Most of engineering design is a knowledge-intensive process undertaken by teams dispersed across multiple disciplines. So it is essential that engineering design needs to be supported with relevant engineering design knowledge, and engineering design knowledge is better managed as an independent resource rather than hard-coded within the CAD systems or their satellite tools. In this article, we review the issues related to the modeling of engineering design knowledge. In particular, an object-oriented knowledge model to represent design knowledge associated with their categories is presented. Based on the knowledge model, the semantic relationships among design knowledge can be identified and determined. Engineering design knowledge can hereby be compared for design knowledge integration and use.

Engineering design knowledge is represented with the object-oriented model. The management of engineering design knowledge such as maintenance, integration, and use can be achieved in the context of object-oriented database management.

REFERENCES

Balazs, M.E., Brown, D.C., Bastien, P., & Wills, C.E. (1997). Graphical presentation of designs: A knowledge-intensive design approach. In M. Mantyla, S. Finger, & T. Tomiyama (Eds.), *Knowledge intensive CAD,* (Vol. II, pp. 173-188). Chapman & Hall.

Caldwell, N.H.M. et al. (2000). Web-based knowledge management for distributed design. *IEEE Intelligent Systems, 15*(3), 40-47.

Dieng, R. (1996). Comparison of conceptual graphs for modeling knowledge of multiple experts. *Proceedings of the 9th International Symposium on Foundations of Intelligent Systems* (pp. 78-87). Berlin: Springer-Verlag (LNCS 1079).

Gorti, S.R., Gupta, A., Kim, G.J., Sriram, R.D., & Wong, A. (1998). An object-oriented representation for product and design processes. *Computer-Aided Design, 30*(7), 489-501.

Lai, H.C., & Chu, T.H. (2000). Knowledge management: A review of theoretical frameworks and industrial cases. *Proceedings of the 2000 Annual Hawaii International Conference on System Sciences.*

Li, Q., & Zhang, W.J. (1999). Computer comparison of design knowledge. *Proceedings of the Institution of Mechanical Engineers Part B—Journal of Engineering Manufacturing, 212*(8), 635-645.

Ma, Z.M., & Mili, F. (2003). Knowledge comparison in design repositories. *Engineering Applications of Artificial Intelligence, 16*(3), 203-211.

Michael, S.M., & Khemani, D. (2002). Knowledge management in manufacturing technology: An A.I. application in the industry. *Proceedings of the 2002 International Conference on Enterprise Information Systems* (pp. 506-511).

Mili, F., & Ma, Z.M. (2002). Eliciting and formalizing tolerance and leniency in engineering design requirements. *Proceedings of the 2002 International Conference on Fuzzy Systems and Knowledge Discovery, 1* (pp. 96-100).

Mili, F., & Ma, Z.M. (2002). Modeling and maintaining engineering knowledge: Issues and solutions. *Proceedings of the IEEEE 2002 International Conference on Systems, Man, and Cybernetics* (Vol. 3, pp. 567-572).

Mili, F., Shen, W., Martinez, I., Noel, P., Ram, M., & Zouras, E. (2001). Knowledge modeling for design decisions. *Artificial Intelligence in Engineering, 15*, 153-164.

Montes-y-Gómez, M., Gelbukh, A., López-López, A., & Baeza-Yates, R. (2001). Flexible comparison of conceptual graphs. *Proceedings of the 12th International Conference on Database and Expert Systems Applications* (pp. 102-111). Berlin: Springer-Verlag (LNCS 2113).

OMG. (2001). Unified Modeling Language (UML), version 1.4. Retrieved from *http://www.omg.org/technology/documents/formal/uml.htm*

Sowa, J.F. (1999). *Knowledge representation: Logical, philosophical and computational foundations.* Brooks Cole Publishing Co.

Szykman, S., Sriram, R.D., Bochenek, C., Racz, J.W., & Senfaute, J. (2000). Design repositories: Engineering design's new knowledge base. *IEEE Intelligent Systems, 15*(3), 48-55.

Tischler, C.R., Samuel, A.E., & Hunt, K.H. (1995). Kinematic chain for robot hands I: Orderly number-synthesis. *Mechanisms and Machine Theory, 30*(8), 1193-1215.

Tomiyama, T., Mantyla, M., & Finger, S. (1995). *Knowledge intensive CAD,* (volume I). Chapman & Hall.

Tomiyama, T., Umeda, Y., & Yoshikawa, H. (1993). A CAD for functional design. *Annual CIRP, 42*(1), 143-146.

Vranes, S., & Stanojevic, M. (1999). Design knowledge representation in Prolog/Rex. *Engineering Applications of Artificial Intelligence, 12*(2), 221-228.

KEY TERMS

Constraints: As basic knowledge units, the constraints in engineering design are referred to the documents-related engineering design decision, which encompass source, motivation, rationale, consequences, and a log of the various changes and updates they have undergone.

Design Knowledge Comparison: The comparison of engineering design knowledge is to identify and determine the relationships among design knowledge represented in the given knowledge model.

Engineering Design: Encompasses a variety of activities aiming at generating and refining detailed product descriptions prior to their physical realization.

Engineering Design Knowledge: All the standards, laws, and best practices that need to affect design decision are called engineering design knowledge.

Engineering Design Knowledge Management: The management of engineering design knowledge generally entails its modeling (representation), maintenance, integration, and use.

Knowledge Modeling: Consists of representing the knowledge in some selected language or notation.

Object-Oriented Knowledge Model: The knowledge model for knowledge representation, which applies powerful object-oriented modeling technologies such as class, methods, inheritance, envelopment, and so forth.

E

Epistemology and Knowledge Management

Jeremy Aarons
Monash University, Australia

INTRODUCTION

This article surveys and explores the relationship between epistemology and knowledge management (KM). Epistemology is the branch of philosophy concerned with the nature and extent of human knowledge (Klein, 1998b). Knowledge management is clearly deeply indebted to many ideas derived from epistemology. Much of the seminal work in KM discusses epistemology in a fair amount of detail, and explicitly appeals to insights from epistemology in developing a theoretical account of KM. In particular, the groundbreaking works by Sveiby (1994, 1997, 2001), Nonaka (1994), and Nonaka and Takeuchi (1995) make explicit appeal to the philosophical insights in epistemology, which has provided the groundwork for much of their pioneering work in knowledge management. One would thus expect there to be a fairly intimate connection between epistemology and knowledge management. The relationship between these two fields, however, is far from straightforward.

This article argues that traditional philosophical discussions about epistemology are generally quite limited in their application to KM. This is because they focus mainly on the production of individual or personal knowledge, rather than sharing and use of knowledge in a collaborative context. Thus many of the insights from traditional epistemology are largely irrelevant for the enterprise of KM.

There are, however, recent developments in epistemology which seem more promising for KM. This article ends with a brief overview of some of these developments, looking at recent work in both the philosophy of science and social epistemology. These approaches seem extremely promising for developing a sounder philosophical and methodological basis for KM.

BACKGROUND: KNOWLEDGE IN EPISTEMOLOGY

Epistemology—the theory of knowledge—is one of the core branches of philosophy. It is concerned with exploring the nature, sources, and limits of human knowledge (Klein, 1998a). With a history tracing back to Plato and Aristotle, the field of epistemology has attempted to provide an analysis of *what* the concept of knowledge is—a definition of knowledge. Epistemology also attempts to specify what *legitimates* knowledge, so that we can distinguish genuine knowledge from false or spurious knowledge. To a lesser degree epistemologists have also inquired into *how* we acquire knowledge, and whether there are limitations on the scope of our knowledge (Pappas, 1998). Some have even adopted a position of extreme *scepticism*, claiming that genuine human knowledge is impossible (Cohen, 1998).

The focus of contemporary debates in epistemology essentially traces back to the work of Descartes and his method of doubt. In his *Meditations on First Philosophy,* Descartes (1640) undertakes an inquiry into the nature of knowledge. Here Descartes attempts to find the foundational principles upon which our knowledge rests, by trying to identify some sort of fact that we can be entirely certain of. Thus he advocates that we need "to demolish everything completely and start again right from the foundations" (Descartes, 1996, p. 12). For Descartes the real challenge here is scepticism—if there is any possibility of doubt about so-called knowledge being true, then it cannot be genuine knowledge. Descartes' inquiry tries to ascertain just what facts about the external world are beyond scepticism, in order to discover the basis of all our knowledge. Following this methodology Descartes famously arrives at the proposition "cogito ergo sum"—I think, therefore I exist—which he claims puts the proposition "I exist" beyond doubt. Contemporary epistemology has followed strongly in this Cartesian tradition, focusing of the question of the justification of knowledge in the face of scepticism. Because of this, questions about the actual generation of knowledge, and of the uses and contexts of knowledge, have been of peripheral concern for the majority of theorists in epistemology.

In this respect, epistemology has typically defined knowledge as an essentially *personal* item that concerns true facts about the world: knowledge is an individual's *true, justified belief.*[1] Additionally, the majority of research in epistemology has generally been concerned solely with *propositional* knowledge: factual knowledge that can be expressed in a sentence, and can be evaluated for truth or falsehood. Thus traditional approaches to epistemology are concerned primarily with *what* knowledge is and how it can be identified, rather than *how* knowledge is created or used.

KM AND EPISTEMOLOGY

The traditional approach to defining knowledge in epistemology contrasts markedly with the definitions typically proposed in the KM literature. For example, Rumizen defines knowledge as "Information in context to produce actionable understanding" (Rumizen, 2002, pp. 6, 288). Similarly, Davenport and Prusak define knowledge thus:

Knowledge is a fluid mix of framed experience, values, contextual information, and expert insight that provides a framework for evaluating and incorporating new experiences and information. It originates and is applied in the minds of knowers. In organisations, it often becomes embedded not only in the documents or repositories but also in organisational routines, processes, practices, and norms. (1998, p. 5)

These definitions do not view knowledge as essentially personal, true, justified belief, but instead have a notion of knowledge as a practical tool for framing experiences, sharing insights, and assisting with practical tasks. For KM, knowledge is something other than just an individual's understanding of the true facts of the world—it is a *pragmatic* tool for manipulating and controlling the world. It is in this sense that Iivari proposes that knowledge is communal, activity-specific, distributed, and cultural-historical (Iivari, 2000).

Compared to traditional epistemology, KM focuses not so much on the justification knowledge, but instead on understanding the uses of knowledge in order to effectively deal with the practical tasks that involve knowledge-based activity. Thus KM is primarily concerned with knowledge as it is generated, shared, stored, and used within a collaborative environment. KM is also concerned with *all* aspects of knowledge within an organisational framework: the *factual* knowledge of the individuals within the organisation, as well as their *practical* knowledge, *tacit* knowledge, and *technological* knowledge. Thus for KM, knowledge must be far more than just personal certainty about the world—it must involve practical ability as well as conceptual understanding. More importantly, KM is concerned with far more than just the justification of knowledge—it is concerned with the production, storage, and processing of knowledge in a group or shared sense. Thus the relevance of the concept of knowledge for KM is quite different to its relevance for philosophers.

The important point here is that, as far as KM is concerned, there are significant limitations in traditional approaches to epistemology. Traditional epistemology is not concerned with the production and processing of knowledge in a group or shared sense—it is not really concerned with the *pragmatics* of knowledge production

and use. The main issue in epistemology is the status of the final product rather than the process of getting there and what happens after knowledge is acquired. Yet these are precisely the factors that are of interest for KM.

The upshot of this is that, beyond an initial analysis of what knowledge is, the traditional approach to epistemology offers very little in the way of useful insights for KM. Epistemology may offer some assistance when dealing with some forms of explicit knowledge, but beyond that it is of little use. Thus we must look beyond standard epistemology to find useful contributions from philosophy.

On the other hand we also should not stray too far from standard epistemology: KM should not dismiss the importance of the insights of traditional epistemology into the nature of knowledge. Although the different disciplines have fundamentally different interests in the concept of knowledge, the concepts in each discipline are still very closely related. The standard approach in epistemology may be too limited and too narrow for KM, but it also is not totally irrelevant. At its foundation the KM conception of knowledge should at least be *compatible* with the epistemological definition, since even thought the disciplines have different interests in the concept, at its base it is still essentially the same idea. Factual, tacit, practical, technical, and other forms of knowledge must still all meet certain criteria in order to be genuine knowledge: they must correspond to some aspect of the world, accurately reflect a reliable way of manipulating the world, and stand up to the harshest of pragmatic tests. Although precisely what it takes to meet these criteria is the topic of vigorous debate, it is clear that genuine knowledge must have some standards.

FUTURE TRENDS: RELEVANT PHILOSOPHICAL INSIGHTS FOR KM

This article has argued that traditional epistemology can only be of limited use to KM since it focuses on the origins and justification of personal knowledge, rather than the pragmatics of knowledge use, sharing, and dissemination. Since KM is primarily concerned with knowledge as it is generated, shared, stored, and used within a collaborative environment, if we are to look to epistemology to provide a foundation for the tasks of KM, we must look for those areas that can deal with these practical issues, as well as provide insights into these differing forms of knowledge and the relationships between them. The philosophical theory must also help our understanding of the underlying *processes* that are relevant for KM.

The suggestion here is that the most fruitful places to look for relevant philosophical insights for KM is in recent work in both the *philosophy of science* and the emerging field of *social epistemology.* Although there are still limitations associated with these philosophical theories, these areas are engaged with fairly similar questions to those that interest knowledge management, and can thus provide insights into these issues. Thus they should be able to provide some useful theoretical tools that can be applied to building a theoretical account of knowledge work.

Philosophy of Science

There is already a strong tradition within KM of applying insights from the philosophy of science. In particular the works of Kuhn (1970, 1977) and Popper (1959, 1972) have been of great interest to a number of KM theorists. Kuhn's notion of a *paradigm,* a particular world view, has played a pivotal role in understanding how a community of thinkers—or *knowledge workers*—need to share certain base beliefs in order to work together effectively. Kuhn's ideas on incommensurability have also been extremely important for many KM theorists. Popper's insights into the basis of scientific knowledge, and his distinction between Worlds 1, 2, & 3, have also helped enrich the understanding of KM. However KM has paid relatively little attention to more recent developments in the philosophy of science which take a quite different approach in their investigations.

The trend in the philosophy of science over recent years has been to shift from trying to develop a general account of what science is (as evident in the work of Popper and Kuhn), to looking more closely at the fine detail of science. These fine details concern the complex methods by which scientific theories are developed, in terms of how scientists work, reason, *experiment, collaborate,* and so forth. In this way, the emphasis of recent work has been less about the justification of knowledge claims, and more about the *creation* and *use* of knowledge.

There have been two general approaches taken to this type of work. The first falls loosely under the banner of *Social Studies of Science (SSS),* and includes the work of Latour and Woolgar (1979), Latour (1986, 1987, 1998), Charlesworth, Farrall, Stokes, and Turnbull (1989), Knorr Cetina (1981, 1999), and Law and Mol (2001, 2002). This work focuses on sociological investigation into the world of the scientist, looking closely how scientists construct knowledge through their shared understanding of language and observational phenomena, which drives their interpretation of observation and experiment and facilitates their creation of ontological categories. This body of work explores the social details of these processes, uncovering how knowledge plays a pragmatic role in our understanding and manipulation of the world. As such it has provided rich material for application in KM contexts. For example, Latour's (1986) notion of *inscription* plays an

important role in Burstein and Linger's (2003) task-based approach to KM.

The second body of work that looks at the details of scientific knowledge construction is more in the tradition of standard philosophy of science. Unlike *SSS,* this work is not so well known outside the philosophy of science community, and many of its ideas have yet to filter in to other disciplines. This work is closely related to *SSS* in that it similarly looks at the details of how scientists work, and how knowledge claims are constructed and used. However, unlike *SSS,* where ideals such as realism and truth are largely eschewed in favour of more social constructivist modes of thought, this work maintains a connection with realist metaphysical intuitions. Thus Cartwright (1989, 1999) emphasises the importance of *causal capacities* in science, and Dupré (1993) explores the metaphysical implications of the disunity of perspectives that coexist across the ranges of sciences. The detailed work of Galison (1996, 1997) looks at the role of social dynamics and politics in the theoretical life of nuclear physicists. Hacking (1999) also explores these issues in some detail, showing how the social construction of the world does not entail losing contact with traditional epistemological ideals such as accuracy and truth. Finally, Kitcher (1993) develops a complex model of scientific reasoning in a collaborative environment, which factors in the interactions between different researchers in building up a detailed picture of knowledge production in group context.

In science these forms of inquiry can deliver powerful predictions and detailed explanations, by rejecting the central importance of fundamental laws, by being open to the possibility of disunity, and by focussing on solving particular problems in particular contexts rather than developing generally applicable theories. This methodology is particularly applicable in the realms that involve complex physical systems in complex environments, where this approach has significant heuristic power, derived from uncovering and modelling the properties and processes that underlie the complex systems. This approach thus provides powerful insights for guiding our understanding, manipulation, and management of these systems. For these reasons these second set of approaches seem particularly suitable for analysing other types of complex systems, such as those involved in complex organisational environments. They should be directly applicable to these knowledge-based settings, thus providing a methodology for managing and supporting knowledge work. These approaches thus provide a good framework for KM, since they aim to provide a clear account of the underlying processes at work in knowledge production and knowledge-using environments. In doing so they strive to maintain the link between knowledge and truth, and thus provide a good metaphysical foundation for KM research. They also take into account *all* the relevant cognitive factors, including social dynamics and collaborative factors, providing a complete analysis of knowledge production in these contexts. They thus go some way to providing just the sort of pragmatic approaches to knowledge required by KM, over and above the conception of explicit knowledge provided in traditional epistemology.

Social Epistemology

Another promising area of philosophical inquiry is the emerging field of social epistemology (Schmitt, 1998). Work in this area is closely related to the above approaches in philosophy of science, with many of the same people working in this field. Some of the most significant works in this field include Goldman (1999), Longino (2001), Solomon (2001), and Turner (1994, 2002).

Social epistemology is an extension of traditional epistemology, which adds in the relationship between the social and rational factors in its analysis of the knowledge production process. Social epistemology looks at the social context of knowledge, and posits that knowledge may be a collective rather than an individual entity, and may be distributed amongst individuals. Social epistemology focuses on the shared aspect of knowledge, as well as the social situatedness of the knowers. Thus it moves away from the Cartesian paradigm of individual knowledge and the associated challenge of scepticism, and instead views knowledge as being a shared product of groups of individuals.

This reconceptualisation of knowledge as a collaborative entity has obvious advantages for KM. In particular, it is directly appropriate to many of the contexts that concern KM, since these are generally complex collaborative settings, such as in large organisations. Additionally, the closer look at the dynamics of collaborative knowledge in social contexts, as provided by social epistemology, can provide invaluable insights of great relevance to KM. For example, understanding the dynamics involved in the distribution of cognitive labour on a complex task, as discussed by Kitcher (1993), can provide clear guidance for how to provide added support in the form of a KM support system.

The closely related field of social metaphysics (Schmitt, 2003) has delved into very similar issues, including conceptions of joint actions, the autonomy of different social levels, and the relationship between individual and group knowledge. This area of research aims to build an account of the nature of social relations, social entities and institutions, and sociality more generally. As such it can, for example, provide an account of the metaphysical difference between individuals, groups, and the whole of a society. It can also be used to unpack the core theoretical notions of KM and specify the details of its framework. For example, the philosophical tools provided by social metaphysics can give a detailed account of what constitutes *practice* in a collaborative environment (Schatzki, Knorr Cetina, & von Savigny, 2001). Thus it can provide an account of what constitutes a *task* within an organisation, and describe the collaborative nature of the task, and how the task is conceptualised and constituted at different structural levels of an organisation: the individual, group, and enterprise level. In this way the insights from social metaphysics and epistemology can be applied to the particular domain of KM, and can lead to more effective approaches to KM methodology.

CONCLUSION

The conception of knowledge as developed in recent philosophy of science and social epistemology is of great relevance to the pursuits of KM. In particular, it seems that these areas could be very useful for developing a theory of collaborative knowledge work. It also seems clear that these approaches can support this theory within a *realist* and *pluralist* metaphysical framework (as outlined in Cartwright, 1999), and are consistent with the principles of *naturalism* (Quine, 1969). These approaches acknowledge the significant social dimension in knowledge production, while retaining the idea of knowledge being deeply connected to real properties and processes. Thus, applying insights from the social epistemology will make it possible to build a theory of knowledge work that is grounded in reality, but also incorporating the relevant social, practical, and pragmatic concerns that are central to the tasks of knowledge management. The starting point of such an analysis would be to determine precisely what aspects of knowledge are relevant to the enterprise of knowledge management, and to give an account of the factors that underlie these knowledge components. This will involve assessing the relevant cognitive, social, and pragmatic factors involved in KM projects. This will develop into a theoretical foundation for the practical work done in KM that maintains a connection with real-world processes and properties. Such a foundation will avoid the problematic conclusion that knowledge is purely socially constructed, and thus will present a powerful analysis of knowledge work.

However, in terms of the aims of knowledge management, current approaches in the philosophy of science and social epistemology are still somewhat lacking. As they stand they provide a detailed account of knowledge *production*, but little or no account of knowledge *use*. Thus, at present, they have little to say about the pragmatics of knowledge storage, knowledge sharing, and knowledge dispersal, all essential aspects of knowledge management projects.

Part of the problem here is that philosophers typically do not seem to be interested in the sorts of questions that are essential for KM. Epistemology in particular is still largely stuck in the Cartesian paradigm, obsessed with understanding the origins and justification of knowledge rather than the dynamics of knowledge as a process. Here we can actually turn things around and look to KM to provide some inspiration for philosophy. The challenges posed by KM projects can be used to show how these issues are indeed significant ones that need to be investigated in detail. The insights gained from current KM projects can also be fed back into the philosophical theory. This will involve extending the accounts of collaborative knowledge production, as provided by philosophy, to broader accounts of collaborative knowledge use. This is where the practical dimension of KM can actually help to enrich our philosophical understanding of the nature of knowledge, and thereby lead to stronger approaches to KM that are grounded in coherent and sound philosophical theory.

REFERENCES

Baker, A.J. (1998). Anderson, John. In E. Craig (Ed.), *Routledge encyclopaedia of philosophy.* London: Routledge. Retrieved October 6, 2004, from *http://www.rep.routledge.com/article/DD003SECT2*

Burstein, F., & Linger, H. (2003). Supporting post-Fordist work practices: A knowledge management framework for dynamic intelligent decision support. *Journal of Information Technology & People* (Special Issue on KM), *16*(3), 289-305.

Cartwright, N. (1989). *Nature's capacities and their measurement.* Oxford: Clarendon Press.

Cartwright, N. (1999). *The dappled world.* Chicago: University of Chicago Press.

Charlesworth, M., Farrall, L., Stokes, T., & Turnbull, D. (1989). *Life among the scientists: An anthropological study of an Australian scientific community.* Melbourne: Oxford University Press.

Cohen, S. (1998). Scepticism. In E. Craig (Ed.), *Routledge encyclopaedia of philosophy.* London: Routledge. Retrieved June 23, 2004, from *http://www.rep.routledge.com/article/P045*

Davenport, T., & Prusak, L. (1998). *Working knowledge: How organisations manage what they know.* Boston: Harvard Business School Press.

Descartes, R. (1996). *Meditations on first philosophy* (translated by John Cottingham; originally published 1640). Cambridge: Cambridge University Press.

Dupré, J. (1993). *The disorder of things: Metaphysical foundations of the disunity of science.* Cambridge, MA: Harvard University Press.

Galison, P. (1996). Computer simulations and the trading zone. In P, Galison & D. Stump (Eds.), *The disunity of science: Boundaries, contexts, and power* (pp. 118-157). Stanford, CA: Stanford University Press.

Galison, P. (1997). *Image and logic.* Chicago: University of Chicago Press.

Gettier, E.L. (1963). Is justified true belief knowledge? *Analysis,* 23, 121-123. Retrieved June 2004 from *http://www.ditext.com/gettier/gettier.html*

Goldman, A.I. (1999). *Knowledge in a social world.* Oxford: Clarendon Press.

Hacking, I. (1983). *Representing and intervening.* Cambridge: Cambridge University Press.

Hacking, I. (1999). *The social construction of what?* Cambridge, MA: Harvard University Press.

Hume, D. (1888). *A treatise of human nature* (1960 facsimile reprint, edited by L.A. Selby-Bigge). Oxford: Oxford University Press.

Iivari, J. (2000). Reflections on the role of knowledge management in information economy. In F. Burnstein & H. Linger (Eds.), *Knowledge Management for Information Communities. Australian Conference for Knowledge Management and Intelligent Decision Support.* Melbourne, Australia.

Kitcher, P. (1993). *The advancement of science.* Oxford: Oxford University Press.

Klein, P.D. (1998a). Epistemology. In E. Craig (Ed.), *Routledge encyclopaedia of philosophy.* London: Routledge. Retrieved June 15, 2004, from *http://www.rep.routledge.com/article/P059*

Klein, P.D. (1998b). Knowledge, concept of. In E. Craig (Ed.), *Routledge encyclopaedia of philosophy.* London: Routledge. Retrieved June 15, 2004, from *http://www.rep.routledge.com/article/P031*

Knorr Cetina, K.D. (1981). *The manufacture of knowledge: An essay on the constructivist and contextual nature of science.* Oxford: Pergamon Press.

Knorr Cetina, K.D. (1999). *Epistemic cultures: How the sciences make knowledge.* Cambridge, MA: Harvard University Press.

Kornblith, H. (Ed.). (1985). *Naturalizing epistemology.* Cambridge, MA: MIT Press.

Kuhn, T. (1970). *The structure of scientific revolutions.* Chicago: University of Chicago Press.

Kuhn, T. (1977). *The essential tension: Selected studies in scientific tradition and change.* Chicago: University of Chicago Press.

Latour, B. (1986). Visualisation and cognition: Thinking with eyes and hands. In H. Kuklick (Ed.), *Knowledge and society studies in the sociology of culture past and present* (vol. 6, pp. 1-40). Jai Press.

Latour, B., & Woolgar, S. (1979). *Laboratory life: The social construction of scientific facts.* Beverly Hills, CA; London: Sage Publications.

Latour, B. (1987). *Science in action: How to follow scientists and engineers through society.* Milton Keynes: Open University Press.

Latour, B. (1998). *Pandora's hope: Essays on the reality of science studies.* Cambridge, MA: Harvard University Press.

Law, J., & Mol, A. (2001). Situating technoscience: An inquiry into spatialities. *Society and Space, 19,* 609-621.

Law, J., & Mol, A. (Eds.). (2002). *Complexities: Social studies of knowledge.* Duke University Press.

Longino, H. (2001). *The fate of knowledge.* Princeton, NJ: Princeton University Press.

Nonaka. (1994). A dynamical theory of organizational knowledge creation. *Organization Science, 5*(1).

Nonaka & Takeuchi. (1995). *The knowledge creating company.* Oxford: Oxford University Press.

Pappas, G.S. (1998). Epistemology, history of. In E. Craig (Ed.), *Routledge encyclopaedia of philosophy.* London: Routledge. Retrieved June 15, 2004, from *http://www.rep.routledge.com/article/P018*

Polanyi, M. (1966). *The tacit dimension.* Gloucester, MA: Peter Smith (Reprinted 1983).

Popper, K. (1959). *The logic of scientific discovery.* London: Hutchinson.

Popper, K. (1972). *Objective knowledge.* Oxford: Oxford University Press.

Quine, W.V. (1969). Epistemology naturalized. In *Ontological relativity & other essays.* New York: Columbia University Press.

Rumizen, M. (2002). *The complete idiot's guide to knowledge management.* Indianapolis, IN: Alpha.

Schatzki, T.R., Knorr Cetina, K., & von Savigny, E. (Eds.). (2001). *The practice turn in contemporary theory.* London: Routledge.

Schmitt, F. (1998). Social epistemology. In E. Craig (Ed.), *Routledge encyclopaedia of philosophy.* London: Routledge. Retrieved June 15, 2004, from *http://www.rep.routledge.com/article/P046*

Schmitt, F. (Ed.). (2003). *Socializing metaphysics: The nature of social reality.* Rowman & Littlefield.

Solomon, M. (2001). *Social empiricism.* Cambridge, MA: MIT Press.

Sveiby, K.-E. (1994). *Towards a knowledge perspective on organisation.* Doctoral Dissertation, University of Stockholm S-106 91, Sweeden. Retrieved June, 2004, from *http://www.sveiby.com/articles/Towards.htm*

Sveiby, K.E. (1997). *The new organizational wealth—managing & measuring knowledge based assets.* San Francisco: Berrett Koehler.

Sveiby, K.E. (2001). What is knowledge management. Accessed May 2003 from *http://www.sveiby.com/articles/KnowledgeManagement.html*

Turner, S. (1994). *The social theory of practices: Tradition, tacit knowledge and presuppositions.* Chicago: University of Chicago Press.

Turner, S. (2002). *Brains/practices/relativism.* Chicago: University of Chicago Press.

KEY TERMS

Epistemology: The branches of philosophy concerned with exploring the nature, sources, and limits of human knowledge.

Naturalism (Naturalised Epistemology): Philosophical naturalism is the view that the natural sciences provide the best methodology for tackling philosophical problems. Philosophical naturalists view epistemology (and philosophy more generally) as being essentially continuous with science. For our purposes, a naturalised epistemology will be a scientific explanation of how it is that some beliefs come to be knowledge. Naturalism traces back to the work of David Hume (1888) and was first coined by W.V.O. Quine (1969). Also see Kornblith (1985).

Paradigm: A set of practices that define a particular discipline. The now-standard usage for this term traces back to Kuhn (1970), who used it to refer to the set of assumptions, methods, and principles that characterised a particular scientific worldview. The term has now crossed over into much broader usage, and can refer to many different things: a framework, a mindset, a perspective, a way of being. Interestingly, Kuhn himself became frustrated with the philosophical difficulties that surrounded this term, later adopting the concept of a 'disciplinary matrix'.

Pluralism: Pluralism is a broad term that which maintains that there are ultimately many things, or many kinds of thing. Pluralism in the philosophy of science is the claim that there is not necessarily a single true scientific theory—instead, even the best scientific understanding of the world may consist of a number of different, possibly conflicting theories. The Australian philosopher John Anderson summarised this position well when he wrote: "There is not only an unlimited multiplicity of things to which the single logic of events applies but anything whatever is infinitely complex so that we can never cover its characters in a single formula or say that we know 'all about it'" (Baker, 1998).

Pragmatic: Of practical consequence.

Pragmatism: The philosophical tradition associated with the work of William James, John Dewey, and Charles Saunders Peirce, and more recently with Richard Rorty. Pragmatism shares its philosophical roots with *naturalism,* in that it holds the natural world as the final arbiter of truth. However, it also insists on consequences, utility, and practicality as being vital components of truth. Despite this general approach, there are significant differences between the ideas of James, Dewey, and Peirce. Thus in order to distinguish his philosophical approach, C.S. Peirce labelled his doctrine that concepts are to be understood in terms of their practical implications *pragmaticism*.

Realism: The theory that particular things exist independently of our perception. Scientific realism is the view that an object mind-independent reality exists, and that our scientific theories aim to inform us of the nature of this reality.

Scepticism: The view that genuine human knowledge is impossible. *Cartesian* scepticism follows from reasoning presented by Descartes, who showed it is possible to doubt (almost) any particular knowledge claim, and thus those claims cannot be genuine knowledge.

Social Epistemology: "The conceptual and normative study of the relevance to knowledge of social relations, interests and institutions" (Schmitt, 1998). It is an extension of traditional epistemology, which adds in the relationship between the social and rational factors in its analysis of the knowledge production process. Social epistemology looks at the social context of knowledge, and posits that knowledge may be a collective rather than an individual entity, and may be distributed amongst individuals.

Social Metaphysics: This area of research aims to build an account of the nature of social relations, social entities and institutions, and sociality more generally. Much work in this field looks at "how individual human beings figure in social relations and collectives" (Schmitt, 2001).

ENDNOTE

[1] This formal definition of knowledge is quite controversial and is the subject of ongoing vigorous debate (Gettier, 1963). However, most analytic philosophers tend to agree that this definition is *roughly* correct, and the controversy is mainly over the fine details of this approach—especially on the question of what constitutes an adequate justification.

External and Internal Knowledge in Organizations

Rafael Andreu
IESE Business School, University of Nevarra, Spain

Sandra Sieber
IESE Business School, University of Nevarra, Spain

INTRODUCTION: KNOWLEDGE MANAGEMENT AND COMPETITIVE ADVANTAGE

In this article we discuss how knowledge and learning contribute to developing sustainable competitive advantages in firms. We argue that effective knowledge management (KM) initiatives for this purpose should support appropriate learning initiatives (which we define in terms of learning trajectories [LTs] of individuals and groups within the firm) in order to ensure that knowledge needs are adequately covered over time.

Trends in today's environment such as globalization, technological evolution, and deregulation are changing the competitive structure of markets in such a way that the effectiveness of traditional sources of firms' competitive advantage is blurred. More and more, any firm can have access to physical or financial assets, and even to technology, in exactly the same open-market conditions. Consequently, firms need to develop distinctive capabilities, their own "ways of doing things" that are difficult to imitate by competitors. Such capabilities are eventually related to persons in the firm, who at the end of the day develop and apply their abilities and skills, organized in certain ways and based on what these people know. Thus, developing idiosyncratic knowledge that gives meaning to a firm's distinctive ways of doing is increasingly important (Bell, 1973; Drucker, 1993). Idiosyncratic knowledge of this kind is difficult to imitate because it cannot be bought in open markets. That is, it has to be learned, requiring resources, time, effort, and a specific context (organizational, social, etc.) that makes it so path dependent that reproducing it in a firm different from that in which it originated is very difficult (Andreu & Sieber, 2001). In addition, knowledge has three fundamental characteristics that make it especially interesting. First, it is personal in the sense that it originates and resides in persons who assimilate it as the result of their own experiences. They incorporate it into their "base" once convinced of its meaning and implications, articulating it in the context of an organized whole that gives structure and meaning to its different "pieces" (Kolb, 1984). Second, its utilization (through which it does not dissipate) allows persons to understand perceived phenomena (each in his or her own way) and evaluate them, judging how good or convenient those phenomena are for each person at a given time. Third, it serves as a guide for action, helping to decide what to do at a given juncture because action endeavors improve the consequences of perceived phenomena (Andreu & Sieber).

These characteristics make knowledge a solid basis for competitive advantage. As far as it results from the accumulation of persons' experiences, therefore being mainly tacit (Polanyi, 1962), imitating it will be difficult unless precise representations (in the form of explicit knowledge) exist that facilitate its transmission and sharing. The personal experience-accumulation process leading to new knowledge takes place in a social or organizational context (Pentland, 1995; Tyre & von Hippel, 1997), and it unfolds following a different path for each person (dependent, among other things, on his or her previous experience and knowledge). Thus, knowledge is both path and context dependent. To the extent that duplicating contexts and paths in this sense is difficult, knowledge imitation will be costly, and consequently competitive advantages based on it will tend to be sustainable (Grant, 1996; Teece, Pisano, & Shuen, 1997). As a result, knowledge value tends to be higher in the context in which it was developed than it would be in a hypothetical open market. Nevertheless, not all knowledge is the same in terms of potential competitive advantage as we discuss in the next section.

EXTERNAL AND INTERNAL KNOWLEDGE

Competitive forces put pressure on firms not only to streamline their business processes, but also to be able to incorporate relevant knowledge from the environment. In other words, any firm needs access to knowledge that allows it to do something that, although also done by competitors, is demanded and valued by clients. We call this kind of knowledge *external knowledge*. It is brought into a firm from the environment and is useful not only to a particular firm, but also to their competitors in the marketplace. Hence, its market value is approximately equal to its value within the firm. It can be traded in the market and, in general, it tends to be rather technical and explicit, which makes it relatively easy to acquire, be it through training or simply by hiring or buying it (Becker, 1962; Williamson, 1981).

Relying on external knowledge alone, however, does not lead to competitive advantage. Although it may be a competitive necessity, it needs to be complemented by a different kind of knowledge more idiosyncratic and capable of differentiating a firm's offer in the marketplace. It is an organization-specific knowledge that refers to the firm's particular modes of functioning and to its particular organizational context. It acts as an organizational glue when the fast incorporation of external knowledge into a firm may threaten its cohesiveness and sense of unity. It is therefore more valuable inside the organization than in the market, and is less prone to imitation. Developing this kind of knowledge is much less environment driven, and it belongs more to the realm of organizational routines and organizational idiosyncrasy. We call this kind of knowledge *internal knowledge*. Although not valued directly by the labor or factor market, it contributes to achieve competitive advantage as it adds critical value for the customer[1]. Internal knowledge can be understood as the organizational context that (a) plays the role of a skeleton where new knowledge pieces are attached so as to "make global sense" to the firm tradition, culture, and "ways to understand things" (Spender, 1996); and (b) defines the way in which new knowledge will be put to work, hence giving it the idiosyncratic firm's touch that will distinguish its utilization from that of other firms.

The distinction between these two kinds of knowledge is not new. The economics literature has analyzed the differences between general and firm-specific knowledge basically from three perspectives. Becker (1962)

adopted a human-capital approach to study how to price the training of employees, concluding that the firm should cover all firm-specific training while the worker should cover general training as the involved knowledge has a direct market value. Williamson (1981) takes up this argument from a transaction-cost point of view, considering the necessity to protect "skills acquired in a learning-by-doing fashion and imperfectly transferable across employers" (p. 563). From an institutionalist point of view, Doeringer and Piore (1971) consider that the formation of internal labor markets is a consequence of firm-inherited knowledge.

From a more managerial standpoint, there are also contributions that suggest the distinction above. Porter, interviewed by Hodgetts (1999), is very close to the same concept when he distinguishes between "operational improvement" and "positioning." In a similar manner, Edvinsson and Malone's (1997) definition of intellectual capital is close to our concept of internal knowledge. The classic management literature also proposes a similar distinction: Selznick (1957), for example, is very close to the concept of internal knowledge by saying "…we must create a structure *uniquely adapted to the mission and role of the enterprise*..." More recently, Burton-Jones (1999), starting from a conception of the firm as a "knowledge integrator," proposed the so-called Knowledge Supply Model™, where the distinction is made between three internal sources of knowledge and four external sources, the former demanding firm-specific knowledge.

Understood as we propose, a coherent knowledge management initiative has to ensure a proper balance between internal and external knowledge creation and deployment. Our contention is that, thinking in terms of the adequate learning processes leading to the creation and deployment of the appropriate mix of internal and external knowledge in a firm, it is possible to draw conclusions regarding what knowledge management approaches have more or less potential effectiveness for a given firm. Of course, the specificities of each particular firm influence the suitability of a concrete KM approach, but still, a general framework can guide action.

In the context of a generic firm, we propose to think in terms of its knowledge base, understood as a combination of external and internal knowledge components. A schematic representation is shown in Figure 1, where *I* represents a piece of internal knowledge and *E1* to *E4* represent four pieces of external knowledge.

We depict *I* in the center to give the idea of a core, and the different *E*s around it to indicate both the fact that they are closer to the environment and the relative independence there is among each other. Some overlap between *I* and the different *E*s indicates that the part of *I* geared to put the Es into idiosyncratic action needs to be aware of some of the corresponding *E*s' characteristics.

Figure 1. Knowledge base of a firm in terms of internal and external knowledge

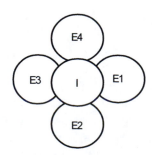

Using this knowledge-base representation of a firm, the next section introduces the concept of learning trajectories and explores the different LTs that can be adopted within a firm. Next, we use these concepts to derive general conditions and goals for effective knowledge management initiatives.

KNOWLEDGE CREATION AND DEPLOYMENT IN THE FIRM: LEARNING TRAJECTORIES

The concept of knowledge-based competitive advantage assumes that a firm has a view of the knowledge base it needs at a given moment. Any firm needs to develop and maintain a mix of internal and external knowledge geared to its particular competitive positioning. One way of configuring this process is through the identification of adequate learning patterns—learning trajectories—that lead to the desired mix of internal and external knowledge. In other words, a firm develops its appropriate mix of knowledge when its members evolve through a right combination of LTs. Thus understood, the LT of an individual is a representation of his or her evolution toward a certain degree of significance to the organization in terms of contributing external or internal knowledge to its relevant knowledge base. Of course, many different individual LTs can be imagined in a firm. Choosing the appropriate ones is a question of matching the knowledge base needed to compete according to the firm's strategy and mission on the one hand, the profiles of the different individuals and groups involved on the other, and the learning procedures judged most effective for each combination of knowledge base and individual or group. Thus, it is impractical to give specific answers for all possible cases. However, the idea of LTs permits us to set up a basic framework useful to design the collection of learning efforts needed and the corresponding KM-based support that might make sense.

One version of such a framework is depicted in Figure 2, where LTs are classified in terms of Internal Knowledge Contents and Degree of Specialization, be it in internal or external knowledge. LTs are represented here as learning paths drawn on the knowledge map of the firm. Depending upon what kind of knowledge the firm needs to develop in order to match its competitive positioning needs, one LT might be more appropriate than another, or a combination of them can be useful across a number of individuals or groups in the firm.

Hence, one can define sorts of stylized LTs that correspond to different career paths of individuals in the organization. In this sense, for example, one LT develops what can be called superspecialists. It corresponds to a career as a specialist in some external knowledge without much idiosyncratic, organization-dependent knowledge. Superspecialists resulting from this kind of LT will probably be highly valued in the market and not as much internally. A firm will not be able to develop competitive advantage with only superspecialists of this kind, however. An extreme example could be that of a movie star who has developed her acting know-how in several movies, but who is not tied to any of them (or their producers) in an organizational sense. The so-called "Hollywood organization" is based in this idea. It consists of a combination of persons, each of whom has excellent knowledge in some specific field, that join efforts toward the achievement of a specific, short-term goal. They stop working together as soon as the goal is achieved as they do not contribute any idiosyncratic knowledge that would give sense to any cooperation over a longer period of time.

On the opposite, an LT targeted only at the development of internal knowledge content is that of the fundamentalist, an organization insider with virtually no external expertise. A firm in which all members have such an LT would not develop competitive advantages, either: It would be like a good movie director without actors. LTs

Figure 2. A classification of LTs

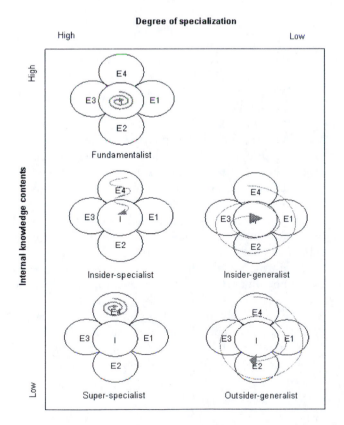

175

of this kind may make sense in extreme cases, but only if they can be complemented with relevant and valued external knowledge holders.

A more balanced LT can be called an insider generalist: A person starts with some external knowledge and proceeds to integrate other *Es* while incorporating more and more *I*. The result, depending on the competitive positioning of the firm, could be an appropriate mix of internal and external knowledge with high competitive-advantage potential. This would correspond to the classical careers of persons who start in one functional department, then pass through other relevant functions, and finally end up at a managing position. During the early stages, these careers incorporate technical skills and add value to the organization through making operating decisions and solving rather structured problems. At later stages, they are valued because they develop integrating capabilities, solving unstructured problems and giving strategic insight to organizational routines.

In contrast, an insider specialist could start from being knowledgeable in an *E* and intensifying in it while incorporating relevant pieces of internal knowledge. This is a typical trajectory of a person who, without ever abandoning a particular function or department, gets more and more involved in firm-specific issues.

Finally, an LT that we call outsider generalist belongs to a person who keeps incorporating different kinds of external knowledge without complementing them with any internal knowledge element. The result is a profile that can be highly valued in the market, but that has difficulties in being well rooted in a specific enterprise.

We could continue with more archetypical LTs. This would miss the point, however. Taken as individual LTs in the context of a desired knowledge map such as that of Figure 1, the idea is that a proper balance of LTs should be designed and managed in order to develop an organization with competitive-advantage potential. Although not a single LT can be considered to be inherently inadequate for the firm's success over time, failure to balance different LTs may give rise to a collection of LTs that might be detrimental to the organization. Although a firm will hardly be able to successfully compete without a good external knowledge base, it will also need to develop a certain critical mass of internal knowledge. This is important for at least two reasons. First, people that follow outsider-generalist or superspecialist LTs may easily leave the firm because they are likely to be highly valued by the market. Second, especially in conditions of soaring environmental change, it is important to have people who are able to give a sense of unity to the organization, which means taking care of internal knowledge development.

LEARNING TRAJECTORIES' GOALS AND CONDITIONS: A BASIS FOR KM SUPPORT

In order to build up, support, and maintain the appropriate external- and internal knowledge bases of a firm, thus contributing to its sustainable competitive advantage, different kinds of LTs need to be fostered in an organization. A variety of initiatives can be designed and deployed for this purpose.

For the development and maintenance of a firm's external knowledge base, two of the LTs above seem particularly adequate: those of the superspecialist and the outsider generalist. Most actual KM initiatives (intra- or extranets, knowledge databases, distance learning arrangements, groupware and communication infrastructures, etc.) are targeted to the development of a good external knowledge base as they typically cover the following areas.

- Infrastructures for experience sharing: Standard best practices and routines, databases, and so forth
- Infrastructures to facilitate coordination among specialists: To the extent that more effective coordination is possible, specialists can concentrate more on their fields of expertise.
- Yellow-pages-type systems to locate who in an organization or the environment has specific experience or knowledge
- Systematized, well-indexed access to market and industry information from standard sources
- Systems that force the utilization of best practices such as ERP, CRM, and so forth
- Training in standard capabilities, available in the open market

Of course, for these supports to be effective they might need to be complemented with others of a more organizational character. For example, adequate control and incentive systems are important when individuals are not willing to share knowledge with others because it is one major source of their value in the marketplace.

Hence, in order to devise adequate organizational supports, questions about market knowledge and its evolution the main technical constraints, possibilities, and innovations and so forth have to be taken into account. Also, the corresponding external knowledge must be codified to the extent possible in order to reduce the impact of workers leaving the organization.

At least three main areas of external knowledge development need to be taken into account. First is the specialization and coordination knowledge for both individuals and teams inside the organization (using ICT-based initiatives to improve coordination efficiency and effectiveness, for example) and between the organization and its environment: structuring relationships with suppliers and clients, formulating strategic alliances for knowledge-sharing purposes, and so forth.

Second is work practices that may enhance external knowledge development and transfer. For example, these include training and education initiatives, the identification of groups of excellence for practice sharing, or the designing and implementing of systems that encapsulate and foster the utilization of general good practices.

Third is the organizational area: incentive and control systems, convenient information-access structures, and so forth.

On the other hand, from the internal knowledge base standpoint, the appropriate LTs differ significantly from those adequate for external knowledge. We argued that internal knowledge has more of a tacit nature, blurred across the organization and "sticky." It cannot be acquired in the market; it has to be developed within the organization. In this context, the insider generalist, insider specialist, and fundamentalist types of LTs in Figure 2 come to mind. They aim at fostering (a) the organization's basic values, (b) routines that facilitate the effective use of these values, (c) the idiosyncratic behavior styles of the organization, both individual and collective, and (d) personal capabilities that fit these styles, facilitating their adoption by organization members.

The sticky nature of internal knowledge implies, as a first consequence, that the usefulness of technology-based traditional KM initiatives will probably be limited as those systems require the encodability of knowledge. In addition, as internal knowledge is context dependent and blurred among organizational members, LTs aimed at its development have to deal with it more as an aggregate than as a set of individual pieces.

According to Szulanski (1996), stickiness is caused mainly by five factors: (a) causal ambiguity and the unprovable nature of the knowledge transferred, (b) the lack of motivation by the knowledge source, which is perceived as unreliable, (c) the characteristics of the knowledge recipient, (d) the lack of absorptive capacity and retentive capacity, and (e) context characteristics such as a barren organizational context and arduous relationships. As a consequence, knowledge-related barriers due to a lack of absorptive capacity, causal ambiguity, and the arduousness of the relationship between the source and the recipient are the main barriers to knowledge transfer within a firm.

Therefore, to enhance internally focused LTs, it is advisable to respond to these three dimensions. The issue about a lack of absorptive capacity, which Cohen and Levinthal (1990) define as the inability to exploit outside sources of knowledge or radical new ways of doing things, suggests exploring ways of broadening the mindsets and searching mechanisms of the organization's members. Fostering an open attitude is a first step in this direction. Systems that "are an integral part of the context" because they are deeply embedded in it can contribute to enhance the understanding and transmission of internal knowledge as they render the organization context "more obvious" to its members.

Regarding causal ambiguity, Tyre and von Hippel (1997) see it as a consequence of imperfectly understood idiosyncratic features of the context. Of course, one way of naturally reducing causal ambiguity is by staying in the organization over long periods of time; this increases the individual's tacit understanding of how the organization functions, its power structure, its culture, and so forth. To the extent possible, the unambiguous recognition of the organization's mental model and value applications to everyday situations contributes to reduce causal ambiguity in this sense. This includes practices such as after-the-fact revisions of why things were done the way they were, be it through mentoring or coaching, or, if possible, concrete mental model representations that contribute to reduce ambiguity.

Finally, implicit in the notion of internal knowledge is its contextual and embedded character. Consequently, in order to develop and deploy it effectively, numerous and multiple individual exchanges are needed so that the appropriate critical mass builds up. In this context, arduous (i.e., distant and laborious) relationships hinder the formation of internal knowledge. Again, this implies that an open and good work atmosphere can enhance internal knowledge formation.

Therefore, internally focused LTs are more likely to be implemented in organizations that have in place initiatives to enhance their absorptive capacity, and that allow for open debates of new ideas or new ways of doing things. Also, the degree of employee retention, especially of those persons who have developed a good understanding of the organization's idiosyncrasies, as well as the encouragement of good relationships between key members and its fostering and nurturing, has a positive impact on the development and maintenance of internal knowledge. For this purpose, mentoring and coaching seem to be especially relevant. Finally, a systematic approach putting adequate organizational structures and systems in place that contribute to making values, styles, and context more obvious and easy to assimilate and understand is a fundamental piece to internal LTs.

As an example, we can refer to the case study of Unión Fenosa and its corporate university (Andreu, Grau, Lara, & Sieber, 2004). The very conception, design, and organization of the corporate university and the courses offered there follow the guidelines that a good combination of external- and internal knowledge development and deployment via LTs would advise. Internal knowledge is subtly interspersed with external knowledge, for example, in the organizational structure of the corporate university itself, which mimics the structure of the company and assigns responsibilities according to it. In fact, learning and teaching from experience as an explicit goal in the company's strategy and mission puts the emphasis on well-balanced LTs in the sense above from the start. Accordingly, managers and employees at all levels are evaluated and promoted by taking explicitly into account, to some extent, the degree to which LTs match the company's needs as they evolve over time in response to environmental and competitive conditions.

CONCLUSION

In this article we have proposed to think in terms of learning trajectories in order to analyze how to achieve the development of a balanced knowledge base in a firm. Such a standpoint puts the emphasis on knowledg development needs and somehow de-emphasizes specific technology-based support, although we recognize the potential of such KM initiatives. Our approach has distinguished between external and internal knowledge in order to characterize a set of archetype LTs with which it is possible to describe the most appropriate knowledge-development course for a specific firm at a given point in time. A particular set of LTs considered appropriate for a specific firm situation gives clear clues about how different kinds of knowledge management systems and supports could help to strike the right internal- and external knowledge balance for that firm. A natural consequence of the proposed analysis is that the KM initiatives that a firm identifies are not all strictly technology based; there is an important complement that in fact defines the critical core of an integrated KM proposition. Thus, we join the view of some notorious recent research efforts that favor a view that enlarges the conception of knowledge management from a system-based view to an organization-wide conception.

REFERENCES

Andreu, R., Grau, A., Lara, E., & Sieber, S. (2004). *Unión Fenosa Corporate University: Teaching and learning from experience* (IESE Business School case).

Andreu, R., & Sieber, S. (2001). Knowledge management and organizational learning: What is the link? In Y. Malhotra (Ed.), *Knowledge management and business model innovation.* Hershey, PA: Idea Group Publishing.

Becker, G. (1962). Investment in human capital: A theoretical analysis. *Journal of Political Economy,* (Suppl. 70), 9-44.

Bell, D. (1973). *The coming of post-industrial society: A venture in forecasting.* New York: Basic Books.

Burton-Jones, A. (1999). *Knowledge capitalism: Business, work, and learning in the new economy.* Oxford University Press.

Cohen, W. M., & Levinthal, D. A. (1990). Absorptive capacity: A new perspective on learning and innovation. *Administrative Science Quarterly, 35*(1), 128-153.

Doeringer, P. B., & Piore, M. J. (1971). *Internal labor markets and manpower analysis.* Lexington, MA: Lexington Books.

Drucker, P. (1993). *Post-capitalist society.* Oxford: Butterworth-Heinemann.

Edvinsson, L., & Malone, M. S. (1997). *Intellectual capital: Realizing your company's true value by finding its hidden brainpower.* New York: Harper Business.

Grant, R. M. (1996). Prospering in dynamically-competitive environments: Organizational capability as knowledge integration. *Organization Science, 7*(4), 375-387.

Hodgetts, R. M. (1999). A conversation with Michael E. Porter: A "significant extension" toward operational improvement and positioning. *Organizational Dynamics, 28*(1).

Kolb, D. A. (1984). *Experiential learning.* Englewood Cliffs, NJ: Prentice Hall.

Pentland, B. T. (1995). Information systems and organizational learning: The social epistemology of organizational knowledge systems. *Accounting, Management and Information Technologies, 5*(1), 1-21.

Polanyi, M. (1962). *Personal knowledge.* New York: Anchor Day Books.

Selznick, P. (1957). *Leadership in administration: A sociological perspective.* Evanston: Row, Peterson and Company.

Spender, J. C. (1996). Making knowledge the basis of a dynamic theory of the firm. *Strategic Management Journal, 17,* 45-62.

Szulanski, G. (1996). Exploring internal stickiness: Impediments to the transfer of best practice within the firm. *Strategic Management Journal, 17,* 27-44.

Teece, D. J., Pisano, G., & Shuen, A. (1997). Dynamic capabilities and strategic management. *Strategic Management Journal, 18*(7), 509-533.

Tyre, M. J., & von Hippel, E. (1997). The situated nature of adaptive learning in organizations. *Organization Science, 8*(1), 71-83.

Williamson, O. (1981). The economics of organization: The transaction cost approach. *American Journal of Sociology, 87*, 548-577.

KEY TERMS

External Knowledge: The kind of knowledge that a firm needs in order to compete but that is standard and available in an open market to any organization on the same conditions of price and functionality. Thus, it can be bought and sold, and therefore it is relatively easily integrated in a firm even if it is implicit and collective.

Internal Knowledge: An organization-specific knowledge that gives idiosyncratic cohesiveness to the integration of external knowledge into a firm. Firm and context dependent, it is an indispensable complement to external knowledge in order to build up knowledge-based competitive advantages when it is appreciated by clients. It is more valuable inside the firm where it originates than in the open market. It is very difficult to be transmitted to a different context.

Learning Trajectory: An individual or collective learning pattern in a firm geared to the development of the adequate mix of internal and external knowledge from which to extract competitive potential. Knowledge management initiatives can be understood, ultimately, as tactical arrangements to support the proper collection of learning trajectories needed at a given juncture for the development of a firm's required knowledge base.

ENDNOTE

[1] Value for the customer is a necessary condition for internal knowledge leading to competitive advantage as otherwise it would complement external knowledge in a meaningless way.

External Knowledge Integration

Jeroen Kraaijenbrink
University of Twente, The Netherlands

Fons Wijnhoven
University of Twente, The Netherlands

INTRODUCTION

As an academic field, knowledge management has concentrated on the creation, storage, retrieval, transfer, and application of knowledge within organizations, while underexposing external knowledge (e.g., Alavi & Leidner, 2001). Although the importance of external knowledge is well recognized (e.g., Cohen & Levinthal, 1990), there remains a need for a better understanding of the organizational processes through which external knowledge is integrated (Grant, 1996; Ranft & Lord, 2002). In particular, we believe that a holistic view on knowledge integration (KI) is both important and lacking. In this article, we address this lacuna in the literature by proposing a process model of KI consisting of three stages—identification, acquisition, and utilization of external knowledge. Our objective is to propose a model consisting of modular subprocesses that parsimoniously reflect the variety of KI concepts in the literature. This model is useful to scholars and practitioners because it provides a better understanding of the various KI subprocesses by putting them together in a coherent way. Such understanding serves as bedrock for solving KI problems and for designing KI solutions (cf. Markus, Majchrzak, & Gasser, 2002).

BACKGROUND

In the current literature, the term KI is used for the integration of knowledge from individuals or departments within an organization (Becerra-Fernandez & Sabherwal, 2001; De Boer, Van den Bosch, & Volberda, 1999; Grant, 1996; Leonard-Barton, 1995; Okhuysen & Eisenhardt, 2002; Szulanski, 1996). Based on the meaning of the word *integration* ("to incorporate into a larger unit," *Merriam Webster Online*) we extend the term KI with three stages that model the incorporation of external knowledge. We call the processes associated with the term KI in the current literature *utilization*. Because external knowledge needs to be acquired before it can be utilized, we include a stage of *acquisition* in the model that precedes the utilization stage.

Correspondingly, to acquire external knowledge it needs to be identified first. Acquisition is therefore preceded in our model by a stage of *identification*.

Although there is excellent research done on each of the KI stages, we found no contribution that covers them all. For their own reasons, scholars concentrate on one or two KI stages and disregard either identification (e.g., Almeida, 1996; Crossan, Lane, & White, 1999; Tsang, 2002), acquisition (e.g., Galunic & Rodan, 1998; Rosenkopf & Nerkar, 2001), or utilization (e.g., Leifer & Huber, 1977; McEvily, Das, & McCabe, 2000; Shenkar & Li, 1999). Other scholars regard KI as a black box or elaborate on explanatory models of successful KI (e.g., De Boer et al., 1999; Hamel, 1991; Hansen, 2002; Lane & Lubatkin, 1998; Mowery, Oxley, & Silverman, 1996; Szulanski, 1996; Zander & Kogut, 1995). As such, they provide an understanding of the outcome of KI but less so of the process. Holistic approaches are found in literature on knowledge transfer (e.g., Appleyard, 1996; Bhagat, 2002; Duncan, 1972; Gupta & Govindarajan, 2000; Kostova, 1999; Newell & Swan, 2000; Szulanski, 1996, 2000). In this article, however, networks and alliances are the objects of research, which limits its contribution to the understanding of the KI process in a single organization.

Though they do not provide a holistic model, these scholars provide us with all the necessary ingredients for a holistic KI model. In this article, we try to put the pieces of the KI puzzle together. We follow a pragmatic approach in which we borrow relevant concepts from literature and position them in the KI model: an approach similar to what Glaser called "transcending"—taking relevant variables from theories while trying to raise their conceptual level (1978, pp. 14-15).

MAIN FOCUS: STAGE MODEL

Although there is no consensus on what constructs form the essential basis of a process model (Curtis, Kellner, & Over, 1992), we define a process as a configuration of connected subprocesses, performed by certain actors.

Figure 1. Stages and subprocesses of knowledge integration

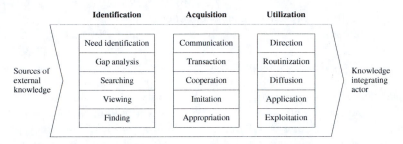

Within this article, we suggest an ordered set of KI subprocesses (see Figure 1) and four views on actors that perform them. An elaboration on the configurations that can be created with these elements is left for future research.

Identification

All subprocesses between initiating a KI process and locating specific external knowledge are considered the identification stage. The apparent relevant theory for this stage is the theory on information seeking. Many information-seeking models follow the process of an information need followed by a successful or unsuccessful search (for an overview, see Case, 2002). These models, however, only partly cover the identification stage, because there are variations in how this stage is initiated. Some seekers start actively from a defined need, while others wait for useful information to appear. Knowledge sources and third parties also can initiate the KI process by pushing an organization to use certain knowledge. Aguilar (1967), Daft and Weick (1984) and Choo (2002) make these distinctions in their work on environmental scanning. At the heart of information-seeking models are information needs. Some authors (e.g., Ellis & Haugan, 1997; Leckie, Pettigrew, & Sylvain, 1996; Wilson, 1999) assume that these needs automatically follow a stimulus or goal. There is, however, substantial evidence that identifying needs is a core problem in information seeking (Choo, Detlor, & Turnbull, 2000; Dervin, 1992; Taylor, 1968). The first subprocess that we propose is therefore *need identification,* which is defined as finding out to a satisfying degree what knowledge an actor needs at a certain moment for a particular purpose. Closely related to need identification is *gap analysis,* which we define as finding out what knowledge an actor is lacking at a certain moment for a particular purpose. It can be beneficial to find out whether knowledge is available internally before looking outside since search costs are likely to be lower within an organization (cf. March, 1991; March &

Simon, 1958) and in personal files (Taylor, 1968). If no additional external knowledge is needed, available knowledge can be exploited (which we consider part of the utilization stage). Once there are indications for what knowledge is needed, companies can search for it. Therefore, a third subprocess that we propose is *searching,* which is defined as intentionally striving to find knowledge or sources of knowledge. This definition suggests that searching is an intentional process regardless of its outcome (cf. Marchionini, 1995). Together, these three subprocesses reflect an information seeking procedure. However, knowledge also can be identified without a focused searching process by broadly scanning the environment. Daft and Weick (1984) call this *viewing.* Daft and Weick do not provide a definition, so we define it as monitoring the existing external knowledge base to detect relevant changes. A final subprocess proposed in the identification stage is *finding,* which we define as coming across knowledge or across sources of knowledge. Finding is an outcome that can occur without searching or viewing, for example, when knowledge is pushed by another organization.

Acquisition

Although there is a conceptual difference between identification and acquisition (Hansen, 1999), searching is often included in the acquisition process (e.g., Gold, Malhotra, & Segars, 2001; Zahra & George, 2002) or defined as the acquisition of information (Johnson, in Case, 2002). However, in our view, searching does not automatically imply acquisition. Since knowledge that crosses organizational borders implies interactions between two or more organizations, social systems theory is highly relevant for this stage. Kuhn and Beam describe three intersystem interactions that we include as subprocesses within the KI model. (Kuhn & Beam, 1982, p. 14)

- **Communication:** An interaction analyzed with respect to its information content

- **Transaction:** An interaction analyzed with respect to its value content
- **Organization:** An interaction analyzed with respect to its joint effectual content

We propose these three interactions as subprocesses in the KI model, but prefer the term "cooperation" above "organization" because of the broader meaning that is given to "organization" in management literature. The subprocesses differ in the way knowledge is transferred. For example, by *communication*, knowledge is acquired by talking to somebody; by *transaction,* it is acquired by buying a document; and by *cooperation,* it is acquired by working together on a project. These three acquisition subprocesses imply the involvement of both the source and the recipient of knowledge. However, knowledge also can be acquired without the involvement of the source. Disregarding illegal activities, such as stealing and spying, this is achieved by imitating a source's behavior or products (Zander & Kogut, 1995). We propose *imitation* as a fourth acquisition subprocess and define it as reproducing knowledge by copying objects or actions from another actor, with or without its assent. Imitation without the source's assent is also called "replication" (Nelson & Winter, 1982). Imitation is, however, also carried out with the assent of the source, for example, when a knowledge source demonstrates how to perform a certain task and the recipient imitates this behavior. Related to knowledge transfer is the transfer of a certain form of property rights, such as patents or copyrights. When one organization buys a document from another organization, this usually automatically involves the acquisition of property rights. In other cases, however, the transfer of property rights is not so natural and might even be problematic, for example, during cooperation (Liebeskind, 1996; Teece, 1998). It is important to include the acquisition of property rights in the KI model because they allow for different ways of utilization (Liebeskind, 1996). Some knowledge may only be used once in an unmodified form, while other knowledge may be fully modified and exploited. We propose *appropriation* as the final subprocess in the acquisition stage and define it as obtaining rights to utilize acquired knowledge in a certain way.

Utilization

As argued in the introduction, knowledge management scholars have extensively researched this KI stage. Researchers on organizational memory (Stein, 1995; Walsh & Ungson, 1991; Wijnhoven, 1999) have distinguished several "mnemonic" processes for utilizing knowledge within an organization. Subprocesses frequently included are acquisition, retention, search, retrieval, and mainte-

nance (Stein, 1995; Walsh & Ungson, 1991). Since acquisition was regarded as a separate stage, we exclude it here.

Grant (1996) observed two primary internal KI "mechanisms"—direction and routinization—which we propose as subprocesses within this stage. *Direction* involves codifying tacit knowledge into explicit rules and instructions so that it can be communicated at low cost throughout the organization (Grant, 1996: 379). *Routinization* is the development of a fixed response to defined stimuli in order to simplify choice (March & Simon, 1958: 142). In dynamic environments, where there are few "defined stimuli," adaptation of the repertoire of these routines is crucial (Argyris & Schön, 1978; Levitt & March, 1988). Organizations can facilitate direction and routinization by a third utilization subprocess: diffusing knowledge throughout the organization. Using the image of a jigsaw puzzle, Galunic and Rodan distinguish two forms of *diffusion*: "A picture on a jigsaw puzzle is distributed when each person receives a photocopy of the picture. The same image would only be dispersed when each of the pieces is given to a different person" (1998: 1198). Like Boisot (1995), by diffusion we not only refer to the active dissemination of knowledge to persons in the organization, but also to the establishment of availability. Therefore, storage of knowledge is included in this subprocess. Unlike routinization, which includes application (Nelson & Winter, 1982), direction and diffusion do not imply that knowledge is applied. A fourth subprocess is therefore distinguished—*application*—which is defined as using knowledge for the purpose(s) for which it was acquired. Knowledge can be applied for other purposes than those for which it was acquired. Organizations might gain maximum advantage from knowledge by reusing it (Markus, 2001) and recombining it (Galunic & Rodan, 1998). Following March (1991) and Schumpeter (1934), we call this fifth and last subprocess in the utilization stage *exploitation*.

Actors

The occurrence and interrelationships of the 15 subprocesses will depend upon the roles that their actors play within the organization. Rather than providing specific roles, we discern four general views on the roles that individuals play within collectives.

The first view stems from the gatekeeper theory (Allen & Cohen, 1969; Tushman, 1977) in which *individuals are representatives* that identify and acquire knowledge for the organization. In the utilization stage, knowledge is elevated to a collective level by direction, routinization, and diffusion into the organizational memory. This view is also central in the information processing perspective (e.g. Daft & Lengel, 1984; Weick, 1979) in which a manager's task is to reduce equivocality within the organization. Although this view might reflect the usual situation in hierarchical organizations, a different situation might well exist in organizations of professionals (cf. Mintzberg, 1979). In such organizations, *individuals are professionals* that identify, acquire, and utilize knowledge themselves. In this second view, each of the subprocesses can be executed individually as well as collectives, such as by collaborative search, group decisions, and group work. Some researchers on collective mind (Weick & Roberts, 1993), organizational decision-making (Simon, 1997), and organizational learning (Argyris & Schön, 1978; Hedberg, 1981; Kim, 1993; March, 1991) emphasize the mutual influence of individuals and collectives. Collectives, like organizations, influence individual knowledge needs and KI processes, while individuals' knowledge and actions, in turn, influence the organization. This third view suggests that *individuals are part of a collective*. People can choose to keep knowledge at the individual level (in their head and personal filing systems) and not make it available to the collective, a central issue in knowledge sharing literature and practice. A fourth view emerges when considering that KI processes can cross business processes and organizational units. Knowledge that is identified, acquired, and applied in one business process or unit also can be used within another business process or unit. This occurs, for example, in new product development, where knowledge acquired and used by a production department also is used in the development of a new product by an R&D department. In this view, *individuals are specialists* that have different areas of expertise.

We believe the proposed stage-model of subprocesses and actors is the most comprehensive of its sort. It extends the most comprehensive existing model that we found (Schwartz, Divitini, & Brasethvik, 2000) with knowledge acquisition and application subprocesses and with an elaboration on the relation between individuals and collectives. The value of these extensions is that the model allows for a more complete analysis of KI than existing models do. This can provide practitioners with a better awareness of the KI process and with an instrument to solve KI problems in their organizations. For example, suppose a company's director notices that his information specialists find and acquire much external knowledge and successfully diffuse it by sending documents to the concerning people in the company. However, he receives many complaints from engineers that this knowledge is not applicable for them. Faced with this problem, the director can use the proposed model to analyze what is going wrong and what can be done to solve this. First, he will observe that *application* is done by different people than the other subprocesses, which suggests that the information specialists act as *representatives* of the engineers. Based on this observation, he might decide that it is better to treat the engineers as *professionals* that can and should identify and acquire the needed knowledge themselves. Second, he can observe that the knowledge is acquired and diffused by means of documents while alternative ways might lead to less loss of relevant details. The KI model makes him aware that *imitation* and *routinization* might be alternatives for respectively *communication* and *diffusion*. Thus, while the model is descriptive, it can facilitate normative decisions by pointing out alternatives for and relationships between KI subprocesses and roles of actors.

FUTURE TRENDS

In this article, we have proposed an ordered set of KI subprocesses and four views on the relation between individual and collective actors. Very important and still lacking are the KI configurations (combinations of subprocesses and roles of individuals) that can be created with them. We suspect that from the numerous theoretically possible configurations, only few appear in practice. It is a challenge to find out which they are and how they relate to organizational effectiveness. Future research should address these open questions, as well as test the completeness and validity of the proposed model. To this end, further decomposition and operationalization of the model into reliable and valid measurement instruments are challenging but necessary steps. Because of its formal approach, we expect the literature on workflow processes to be very useful to find interactions between subprocesses and to check the KI process on completeness (e.g., Van der Aalst, Ter Hofstede, Kiepuszewski, & Barros, 2003).

Considering the growing interconnectivity of organizations over the world, external knowledge becomes more and more important for them. Because of this growing importance for practitioners, we expect a growing attention to KI and KI-related concepts amongst KM researchers in the near and far future. Looking back at the last decade of KM research, we believe there is indeed a growing attention. We find it, however, hard to estimate whether this trend is merely numerical or whether it also reflects cumulativity of knowledge. Huber already remarked in 1991 on the lack of cumulative work and on the lack of synthesis of work from different research groups on organizational learning (Huber, 1991: 107). We have tried to make a step toward synthesis with respect to the integration of external knowledge. This complete volume shows to what extent the KM research community in general has achieved synthesis and also what research challenges there still are.

With the growing attention for interorganizational connectivity, we also expect research attention to shift from large organizations to small organizations and individuals. In networks of companies and individuals, the concept of organization becomes ambiguous. A revealing example is the development of Linux software (Lee & Cole, 2003). The emergence of such networks, where organizational borders and structures are blurred, has significant consequences for KM research and practice. It imposes unanswered questions on, for example, the remaining value of concepts like organizational learning and organizational memory. Because of the diverging meaning of the term *organization,* we have not committed ourselves to a single level of collectiveness in this article. Conversely, we have proposed perspectives on interactions of subprocesses on different levels of collectiveness. We believe these perspectives as well as the KI model remain relevant on the level of organizations, networks, and individuals.

CONCLUSION

We started our analysis with the observation that a comprehensive model of the KI process is both important and lacking. In this article, we have proposed a model that consists of 15 subprocesses ordered in three stages—identification, acquisition, and utilization. This model is comprehensive in its coverage of subprocesses that are involved in KI. However, the current model is like a box of LEGOs®—we have proposed bricks (subprocesses) and types of connections (roles of individuals within collectives), but not the designs (configurations) that can be created with them. Although substantial work still needs to be done, we believe the proposed model is a useful instrument for knowledge management practitioners and researchers because a thorough understanding of the KI process is essential to find and design KI solutions (cf. Keen & Scott Morton, 1978). As a process model, the proposed KI model serves as a kernel theory for design of information systems that are to support the KI process (cf. Markus et al., 2002).

REFERENCES

Aguilar, F.J. (1967). *Scanning the business environment.* New York; London: The MacMillan Company.

Alavi, M., & Leidner, D.E. (2001). Review: Knowledge management and knowledge management systems: Conceptual foundations and research issues. *MIS Quarterly, 25*(1), 107-136.

Allen, T.J., & Cohen, S.I. (1969). Information flow in research and development laboratories. *Administrative Science Quarterly, 14*(1), 12-19.

Almeida, P. (1996). Knowledge sourcing by foreign multinationals: Patent citation analysis in the U.S. semiconductor industry. *Strategic Management Journal, 17*(Winter), 155-165.

Appleyard, M.M. (1996). How does knowledge flow? Interfirm patterns in the semiconductor industry. *Strategic Management Journal, 17*(Winter), 137-154.

Argyris, C., & Schön, D.A. (1978). *Organizational learning: A theory of action perspective.* Reading, MA: Addison-Wesley.

Becerra-Fernandez, I., & Sabherwal, R. (2001). Organizational knowledge management: A contingency perspective. *Journal of Management Information Systems, 18*(1), 23-55.

Bhagat, R. S. e. a. (2002). Cultural variations in the cross-border transfer of organizational knowledge: An integrative framework. *Academy of Management Review, 27*(2), 204-221.

Boisot, M. (1995). *Information space: A framework for learning in organizations, institutions and culture.* London: Routledge.

Case, D.O. (2002). *Looking for information: A survey of research on information seeking, needs, and behavior.* San Diego: Academic Press.

Choo, C.W. (2002). *Information management for the intelligent organization: The art of scanning the environment.* Medford, NJ: Information Today, Inc.

Choo, C.W., Detlor, B., & Turnbull, D. (2000). *Web work: Information seeking and knowledge work on the World Wide Web.* Dordrecht, The Netherlands: Kluwer Academic Publishers.

Cohen, W.M., & Levinthal, D.A. (1990). Absorptive capacity: A new perspective on learning and innovation. *Administrative Science Quarterly, 35*(1), 128-152.

Crossan, M.M., Lane, H.W., & White, R.E. (1999). An organizational learning framework: From intuition to institution. *Academy of Management Review, 24*(3), 522-537.

Curtis, B., Kellner, M.I., & Over, J. (1992). Process modeling. *Communications of the ACM, 35*(9), 75-90.

Daft, R.L., & Lengel, R.H. (1984). Information richness: A new approach to managerial behavior and organizational design. *Research in Organizational Behavior*, 191-233.

Daft, R.L., & Weick, K.E. (1984). Toward a model of organizations as interpretation systems. *Academy of Management Review, 9*(2), 284-295.

De Boer, M., Van den Bosch, F.A.J., & Volberda, H.W. (1999). Managing organizational knowledge integration in the emerging multimedia complex. *Journal of Management Studies, 36*(3), 379-398.

Dervin, B. (1992). From the mind's eye of the 'user': The sense-making qualitative-quantitative methodology. In *Qualitative Research in Information Management* (pp. 61-84). Englewood, CO: Libraries Unlimited.

Duncan, W.J. (1972). The knowledge utilization process in management and organization. *Academy of Management Journal, 15*(3), 273-287.

Ellis, D., & Haugan, M. (1997). Modeling the information seeking patterns of engineers and research scientists in an industrial environment. *Journal of Documentation, 53*(4), 384-403.

Galunic, D.C., & Rodan, S. (1998). Resource combinations in the firm: Knowledge structures and the potential for Schumpeterian innovation. *Strategic Management Journal, 19*, 1193-1201.

Glaser, B.G. (1978). *Theoretical sensitivity: Advances in the methodology of grounded theory.* Mill Valley, CA: The Sociology Press.

Gold, A.H., Malhotra, A., & Segars, A.H. (2001). Knowledge management: An organizational capabilities perspective. *Journal of Management Information Systems, 18*(1), 185-214.

Grant, R.M. (1996). Prospering in dynamically-competitive environments: Organizational capability as knowledge integration. *Organization Science, 7*(4), 375-387.

Gupta, A.K., & Govindarajan, V. (2000). Knowledge flows within multinational corporations. *Strategic Management Journal, 21*, 473-496.

Hamel, G. (1991). Competition for competence and inter-partner learning within international strategic alliances. *Strategic Management Journal, 12*(Summer), 83-103.

Hansen, M.T. (1999). The search-transfer problem: The role of weak ties in sharing knowledge across organization subunits. *Administrative Science Quarterly, 44*, 82-111.

Hansen, M.T. (2002). Knowledge networks: Explaining effective knowledge sharing in multiunit companies. *Organization Science, 13*(3), 232-248.

Hedberg, B. (1981). How organizations learn and unlearn. In P. C. Nystrom & W. H. Starbuck (Eds.), *Handbook of organizational design* (Vol. 1, pp. 8-27). New York: Oxford University Press.

Huber, G.P. (1991). Organizational learning: The contributing processes and the literatures. *Organization Science, 2*(1), 88-115.

Keen, P.G.W., & Scott Morton, M.S. (1978). *Decision support systems: An organizational perspective.* Reading, MA..

Kim, D.H. (1993). The Link between individual and organizational learning. *Sloan Management Review, 35*(1), 37-50.

Kostova, T. (1999). Transnational transfer of strategic organizational practices: A contextual perspective. *Academy of Management Review, 24*(2), 308-324.

Kuhn, A., & Beam, R.D. (1982). *The logic of organization.* San Francisco: Jossey-Bass Inc.

Lane, P.J., & Lubatkin, M. (1998). Relative absorptive capacity and interorganizational learning. *Strategic Management Journal, 19*, 461-477.

Leckie, G.J., Pettigrew, K.E., & Sylvain, C. (1996). Modeling the information seeking of professionals: A general model derived from research on engineers, health care professionals and lawyers. *Library Quarterly, 66*, 161-193.

Lee, G.K., & Cole, R.E. (2003). From a firm-based to a community-based model of knowledge creation: The case of the Linux kernel development. *Organization Science, 14*(6), 633-649.

Leifer, R., & Huber, G.P. (1977). Relations among perceived environmental uncertainty, organization structure, and boundary-spanning behavior. *Administrative Science Quarterly, 22*(2), 235-247.

Leonard-Barton, D. (1995). *Wellsprings of knowledge: Building and sustaining the sources of innovation.* Boston: Harvard Business School Press.

Levitt, B., & March, J.G. (1988). Organizational learning. *Annual Review of Sociology, 14*, 319-340.

Liebeskind, J.P. (1996). Knowledge, strategy, and the theory of the firm. *Strategic Management Journal, 17*(Winter), 93-107.

E

March, J.G. (1991). Exploration and exploitation in organizational learning. *Organization Science, 2*(1), 71-87.

March, J.G., & Simon, H.A. (1958). *Organizations*. New York: John Wiley.

Marchionini, G. (1995). *Information seeking in electronic environments*. Cambridge, MA: Cambridge University Press.

Markus, M.L. (2001). Toward a theory of knowledge reuse: Types of knowledge reuse situations and factors in reuse success. *Journal of Management Information Systems, 18*(1), 57-93.

Markus, M.L., Majchrzak, A., & Gasser, L. (2002). A design theory for systems that support emergent knowledge processes. *MIS Quarterly, 26*(3), 179-212.

McEvily, S.K., Das, S., & McCabe, K. (2000). Avoiding competence substitution through knowledge sharing. *Academy of Management Review, 25*(2), 294-311.

Mintzberg, H. (1979). *The structuring of organizations: A synthesis of the research*. Englewood Cliffs, NJ: Prentice-Hall, Inc.

Mowery, D.C., Oxley, J.E., & Silverman, B.S. (1996). Strategic alliances and interfirm knowledge transfer. *Strategic Management Journal, 17*(Winter), 77-91.

Nelson, R.R., & Winter, S.G. (1982). *An evolutionary theory of economic change*. Cambridge, MA; London: The Belknap Press of Harvard University Press.

Newell, S., & Swan, J. (2000). Trust and inter-organizational networking. *Human Relations, 53*(10), 1287-1328.

Okhuysen, G.A., & Eisenhardt, K.M. (2002). Integrating knowledge in groups: How formal interventions enable flexibility. *Organization Science, 13*(4), 370-386.

Ranft, A.L., & Lord, M.D. (2002). Acquiring new technologies and capabilities: A grounded model of acquisition implementation. *Organization Science, 13*(4), 420-441.

Rosenkopf, L., & Nerkar, A. (2001). Beyond local search: Boundary-spanning, exploration, and impact in the optical disk industry. *Strategic Management Journal, 22*, 287-306.

Schumpeter, J.A. (1934). *The theory of economic development*. Cambridge, MA: Harvard University Press.

Schwartz, D.G., Divitini, M., & Brasethvik, T. (2000). On knowledge management in the Internet age. In D.G. Schwartz, M. Divitini & T. Brasethvik (Eds.), *Internet-based organizational memory and knowledge management*. Hershey, PA: IGP.

Shenkar, O., & Li, J. (1999). Knowledge search in international cooperative ventures. *Organization Science, 10*(2), 134-143.

Simon, H.A. (1997). *Administrative behavior: A study of decision-making processes in administrative organizations* (4th Ed.). New York: The Free Press.

Stein, E.W. (1995). Organizational memory: Review of concepts and recommendations for management. *International Journal of Information Management, 15*(1), 17-32.

Szulanski, G. (1996). Exploring internal stickiness: Impediments to the transfer of best practice within the firm. *Strategic Management Journal, 17*(Winter), 27-43.

Szulanski, G. (2000). The process of knowledge transfer: A diachronic analysis of stickiness. *Organizational Behavior and Human Decision Processes, 82*(1), 9-27.

Taylor, R.S. (1968). Question-negotiation and information seeking in libraries. *College and Research Libraries, 29*, 178-194.

Teece, D.J. (1998). Capturing value from knowledge assets: The new economy, markets for know-how, and intangible assets. *California Management Review, 40*(3), 55-79.

Tsang, E.W. (2002). Acquiring knowledge by foreign partners from international joint ventures in a transition economy: Learning-by-doing and learning myopia. *Strategic Management Journal, 23*, 835-854.

Tushman, M.L. (1977). Special boundary roles in the innovation process. *Administrative Science Quarterly, 22*(4), 587-605.

Van der Aalst, W.M.P., Ter Hofstede, A.H.M., Kiepuszewski, B., & Barros, A.P. (2003). Workflow patterns. *Distributed and Parallel Databases, 14*(1), 5-51.

Walsh, J.P., & Ungson, G.R. (1991). Organizational memory. *Academy of Management Review, 16*(1), 57-91.

Weick, K.E. (1979). *The social psychology of organizing* (2nd ed.). Reading, MA: Addison-Wesley Publishing Company.

Weick, K.E., & Roberts, K.H. (1993). Collective mind in organizations: Heedful interrelating on flight decks. *Administrative Science Quarterly, 38*(3), 357-381.

Wijnhoven, F. (1999). *Managing dynamic organizational memories: Instruments for knowledge management.* Enschede: Twente University Press.

Wilson, T.D. (1999). Models in information behaviour research. *The Journal of Documentation, 55*(3), 249-270.

Zahra, S.A., & George, G. (2002). Absorptive capacity: A review, reconceptualization, and extension. *Academy of Management Review, 27*(2), 185-203.

Zander, U., & Kogut, B. (1995). Knowledge and the speed of the transfer and imitation of organizational capabilities: An empirical test. *Organization Science, 6*(1), 76-92.

KEY TERMS

Knowledge Acquisition: The individual or collective process aimed at obtaining knowledge from another actor, by one or more of the subprocesses of transaction, communication, cooperation, imitation, or appropriation.

Knowledge Appropriation: Individually or collectively obtaining rights to utilize acquired knowledge in a certain way.

Knowledge Finding: Coming across knowledge or sources of knowledge by an individual or a collective, regardless of the engendering process.

Knowledge Identification: The individual or collective process aimed at locating knowledge at a source, by one or more of the subprocesses of need identification, gap analysis, searching, viewing, or finding.

Knowledge Imitation: Individually or collectively reproducing knowledge from another actor by copying its objects or actions, with or without its assent.

Knowledge Integration: The identification, acquisition, and utilization of knowledge that is external to an individual or collective actor.

Knowledge Need Identification: The process of finding out to a satisfying degree what knowledge an individual or collective actor needs at a certain moment for a particular purpose.

Knowledge Search: The intentional individual or collective process of striving to find knowledge or sources of knowledge, regardless of its outcome.

Knowledge Utilization: The individual or collective process aimed at using knowledge by one or more of the subprocesses of direction, routinization, diffusion, application, or exploitation.

Knowledge Viewing: Individually or collectively monitoring the existing external knowledge base to detect relevant changes.

Extracting Knowledge from Neural Networks

Christie M. Fuller
Oklahoma State University, USA

Rick L. Wilson
Oklahoma State University, USA

INTRODUCTION

Neural networks (NN) as classifier systems have shown great promise in many problem domains in empirical studies over the past two decades. Using case classification accuracy as the criteria, neural networks have typically outperformed traditional parametric techniques (e.g., discriminant analysis, logistic regression) as well as other non-parametric approaches (e.g., various inductive learning systems such as ID3, C4.5, CART, etc.).

In spite of this strong evidence of superior performance, the use of neural networks in organizations has been hampered by the lack of an "easy" way of explaining what the neural network has learned about the domain being studied. It is well known that knowledge in a neural network is "mysteriously" encapsulated in its connection weights. It is well accepted that decision-makers prefer techniques that can provide good explanations about the knowledge found in a domain even if they are less effective in terms of classification accuracy.

Over the past decade, neural network researchers have thus begun an active research stream that focuses on developing techniques for extracting usable knowledge from a trained neural network. The literature has become quite vast and, unfortunately, still lacks any form of consensus on the best way to help neural networks be more useful to knowledge discovery practitioners.

This article will then provide a brief review of recent work in one specific area of the neural network/knowledge discovery research stream. This review considers knowledge extraction techniques that create IF-THEN rules from trained feed-forward neural networks used as classifiers.

We chose this narrow view for a couple of important reasons. First, as mentioned, the research in this area is extraordinarily broad and a critical review cannot be done without focusing on a smaller subset within the literature. Second, classification problems are a familiar problem in business. Third, creating basic IF-THEN rules from a trained neural network is viewed as the most useful area in the entire research stream for the knowledge management and data mining practitioner.

With this narrow focus, some aspects of knowledge extraction from neural networks are obviously not mentioned here. With the focus on deterministic IF-THEN rules, outputs that include "fuzziness" (fuzzy logic) are omitted. In addition, research that involves different neural network architectures (e.g., recurrent networks) and/or different knowledge discovery problem areas (e.g., regression/prediction rather than classification) are also excluded from the review.

BACKGROUND

The discussion of the different neural network knowledge extraction techniques are organized around the fundamental premise or process used for rule extraction. Previous researchers (including Tickle, Maire, Bologna, Andrews, & Diederich, 2000) have used the following terms to help segment the different approaches: decompositional, pedagogical, and eclectic.

Decompositional techniques for rule extraction are approaches that perform rule extraction at the individual neuron (or neural component) level. Pedagogical approaches, on the other hand, extract knowledge by treating the entire NN as a "black box," creating rules by correlating inputs to the neural network to the resultant outputs (without considering anything about the structure or weights of the NN). It is reasonable to think of these two terms as extreme points in a continuous spectrum of approaches. Eclectic approaches are techniques that borrow some aspects from each of the two extremes.

Figure 1 helps visualize how these algorithms work. Figure 1 shows a 6-input, 3 hidden neuron, 2 output neural network. Assuming no bias inputs and a fully connected neural network, there would be 24 connection weights (not shown) which represent the knowledge stored in the neural network (after, of course, the NN has been trained on a set of data). The decompositional approaches will examine (at least) the connection weights that lead to each hidden neuron and will "discover rules" such as IF X2 < 7, THEN CONCLUDE Class A. Pedagogical approaches would present systematic random inputs to the neural

Figure 1.

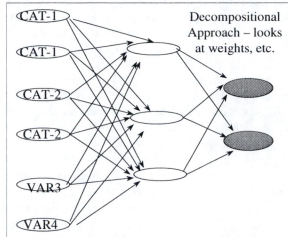

Pedagogical Approach – does not look at internal weights – just inputs and outputs

network, observe the output of the neural networks, and "learn" rules like above through studying the relationship between input and output variations.

The review of pertinent neural network rule extraction algorithms also will include three different measures of technique usefulness (accuracy, fidelity, and comprehensibility) when such measures have been studied. These three different measures of technique usefulness are important in assessing the quality of the different methodologies. Accuracy measures the ability of the derived rule set to classify cases from the problem domain. This is typically reported as percentage correctly classified. Fidelity measures how well classification of cases using rules extracted from the trained NN mimic the classification of just the original NN. Comprehensibility measures the size of the rule set extracted from the neural network, looking at both number of rules and the number of antecedents in the rule. This is a measure of rule complexity.

Additionally, any empirical comparisons to other "competing" rule extraction techniques will also be shared, as well as any empirical comparisons to other comparable well-known knowledge discovery techniques such as inductive learning systems (which might include such well-studied techniques as ID3, C4.5, CART, and See5, among others).

The comparisons to other knowledge discovery techniques that result in decision trees, rules, and so forth are particularly relevant to practice. The techniques discussed in this article use a two-step approach to knowledge elicitation: first, one trains a neural network on a set of cases, and then rules are found through the specific technique. Inductive learning approaches accomplished

this in one step directly from the cases. The ongoing research into the two-step neural network process seeks to explore the contention by Tickle et al. (2000) and others who claim that rule extraction from trained neural networks will (someday) be a better approach than inductive learning systems. This claim stems from the potential for realizing additional correct classifications (which is well documented) possible with neural networks. The quest for this still continues, and results (as shown) show promise. The next section outlines recent progress in this area.

NN RULE EXTRACTION REVIEW

Decompositional Approaches

Su, Hsu, and Tsai (2002) present a decompositional methodology that is similar to many in this category. After a feed-forward NN is trained, important inputs are identified and unnecessary connections are pruned from the network in an iterative fashion. Input data is then transformed into binary form, and then the knowledge (in rules) is extracted by building truth tables for each hidden neuron. The rules are simplified using Karnaugh maps and removing repetitive statements. The classification accuracy of this algorithm showed mixed results when compared to the original neural network model and the inductive learning approach See5. However, their algorithm had increased comprehensibility compared to See5, requiring far fewer attributes to classify the data.

The GLARE approach (GeneraLized Analytic Rule Extraction) is similar, extracting rules from standard feed-forward backpropagation networks requiring binary inputs (Gupta, Park, & Lam, 1999). First, weights between input nodes and hidden nodes are ranked, determining the largest connection weights. Next, another index calculates the importance of the connections between the hidden and output layers using the ranking. This step leads to the extraction of symbolic rules. Using classification accuracy as a benchmark with strictly categorical datasets, GLARE performs as well or better as the inductive learning system C4.5 and the original backpropagation NN. When used with datasets possessing continuous inputs that were converted to Boolean inputs, GLARE's performance suffered significantly.

Vaughn, Cavill, Taylor, Foy, and Fogg (2000) report on a rule extraction method developed for mutli-layer feed-forward neural networks with binary inputs. Their method ranks the activation contributions to each of the hidden neurons, and then repeats the process to determine the significant input neurons. Rules are extracted by combining the significant inputs related to a particular class, in ranked order.

The FERNN (Fast method for Extracting Rules from NN) approach applies a different strategy to the problem. It uses two primary components to generate rules from a neural network (Setiono & Leow, 2000). First, the neural network is trained using an algorithm that seeks to minimize the connection weights of irrelevant inputs. Then, a decision tree is generated from the network's single hidden layer. The algorithm identifies and removes irrelevant inputs while maintaining the network's accuracy. Unlike other algorithms that may apply pruning, FERNN does not require the network to be retrained after connections are removed, which makes rule extraction faster. Rules can be generated from datasets with both continuous and discrete attributes. Empirically, this algorithm was shown to be more accurate than C4.5 for most datasets, while also creating smaller trees. The authors report that FERNN has a high degree of fidelity with the original neural networks.

Fan and Li (2002) present a method for rule extraction in which the hidden neurons are used to partition the input space into subspaces. There are as many partitions as hidden neurons in the network. To extract rules, the data that "fall" in the subspaces are analyzed based on their "classes." The derived rules from this step are then reduced and simplified. The methods were compared to the original NN, genetic algorithms, C4.5, and rough set approaches using the linearly separable IRIS dataset. In this domain, the proposed rule extraction method showed better accuracy and greater comprehensibility than the other methods.

Tsukimoto (2000) presents a decompositional method for extracting rules using Boolean functions. The algorithm is not dependent on any particular network structure or training algorithm and can be applied to NN's with both discrete and continuous values. The only specific requirement is that the NN must have a monotone output function. Experimental results of this algorithm show its accuracy to be slightly better than C4.5 for a binary dataset and slightly worse for discrete and continuous datasets. The comprehensibility of the rules extracted using this method was about the same as C4.5.

Continuous/discrete Rule Extractor via Decision tree Induction (CRED) is another decompositional algorithm that can be used with both discrete and continuous input variables (Sato & Tsukimoto, 2001). In contrast to previous "old" approaches TREPAN (Craven & Shavlik, 1996) and the method of Krishnan et al. (1999) mentioned later in this article, CRED extracts separate trees at the hidden-to-output and input-to-hidden layers instead of a single tree. Rules are formed from these trees, which are then merged and simplified. CRED was tested on several datasets and demonstrated acceptable accuracy levels, but was not compared to other rule extraction or data mining methods.

Schmidt and Chen (2002) use an Aggregate Feed-Forward Neural Network (AFFNN) as a foundation for their rule extraction/neural network approach. The AFFNN is a fully connected network with a single hidden layer, using a combination of pre-and post-processing operations with a modified training routine. The proposed algorithm begins at the output layer, working backward to discover the supporting or related hidden nodes to the specific output neuron, then likewise finds the corresponding supporting input nodes. Fifteen rules were created from the AFFNN in analyzing the well-known MONK-2 dataset with 100% accuracy, compared to inductive learning system ID3 which created a tree with 66 nodes and 110 leaves and had 67.9% accuracy.

Finally, a greedy clustering algorithm (GCA) which fits the decompositional approach was proposed by Setiono and Liu (1998). The GCA creates clusters based on the activation values of the hidden neurons of the neural network. After clusters are formed, they are used to associate output neurons to relevant inputs. For the classic Pima Indian Diabetes dataset, GCA created a more accurate network than C4.5 on testing data and required only one rule to classify the data, compared to 12 rules (with up to ten antecedents) for C4.5. Also, for the aforementioned MONK-2 problem, the GCA created a 100% accurate network requiring one rule to classify the data.

In summary, many different decompositional approaches have been proposed, but few of these studies have directly compared the different approaches. There remain numerous choices for the data mining practitioner, but no clear cut "best" approach. It is interesting to note that much of the early work in this area focused on converting continuous data to binary or discrete data values prior to knowledge extraction. This may be a big drawback of such techniques in real-world settings unless little is lost in accuracy when discretizing the variables.

Pedagogical Approaches

Taha and Ghosh (1999) present a family of approaches for the neural network rule extraction problem starting with BIO-RE, a pedagogical approach. BIO-RE requires a trained network with binary inputs. The authors claim their method is suitable only for a small number of inputs but does not require a particular network structure or training algorithm.

If binary inputs are not suitable or the number of inputs is large, Partial-RE is their alternative approach. Partial-RE identifies dominant node combinations in the network, and extracts rules according to user-specified parameters on completeness. However, performances were problematic if data was not in binary or discretized form.

Finally, the authors also propose Full-RE, a decompositional variant of this rule extraction family that can extract rules from networks with continuous, normal, or binary inputs and is claimed effective for networks of any size. For the IRIS and Wisconsin Breast Cancer data, Full-RE performed favorably to older rule extraction techniques such as NeuroRule (see Setiono & Liu, 1995) and inductive learning approaches such as C4.5, extracting fewer rules with the same or less number of antecedents and had comparable accuracy.

Krishnan, Sivakumar, and Bhattacharya (1999) present a pedagogical method based on genetic algorithms for extracting decision trees from trained neural networks. The method first determines which inputs are relevant to build the decision tree. The tree is then modified systematically to increase comprehensibility or accuracy. This algorithm was less accurate than the original neural network and ID3, but did produce a much smaller tree than ID3. The decision trees resulting from this algorithm were shown to have fidelity over 90%.

Palade, Neagu, and Puscasu (2000) propose a method of rule extraction by interval propagation of an inverted neural network. Their extraction algorithm calculates the required input of the NN for a specified output. The method does not require a particular neural network structure and can utilize continuous inputs and outputs. Unfortunately, this method was not compared to other approaches.

Shigaki and Narazaki (1999) employed a similar approach in the domain of modeling the sintering process used in iron and steel making industry. Their algorithm estimates monotonic regions in the neural network by sampling input vectors. These regions are composed of points with the same class membership and consider various sensitivity patterns. Their approach was not compared to other methods.

Artificial neural-network decision tree algorithm (ANN-DT) is a pedagogical rule extraction technique similar to the inductive learning approach CART (Schmitz, Aldrich, & Gouws, 1999). ANN-DT does not require a particular network structure and input can be discrete or continuous. The algorithm samples the input space of the network, resulting in reduction of the number of rules needed to accurately describe the data. ANN-DT uses a statistical pruning technique similar to that employed by CART. Experimental results showed the ANN-DT algorithm is at least as accurate as CART and has increased fidelity. However, the decision trees created by ANN-DT were more complex for most of the datasets tested.

STAtistics-based Rule Extraction (STARE) is another pedagogical approach. This algorithm limits extracted rules to three antecedents, which increases comprehensibility (Zhou, Chen, & Chen, 2000). The STARE approach also does not require a specific type of network or training method. The rule discretizes continuous attributes while rules are generated. Fidelity also is evaluated as part of the algorithm. Rules not meeting user-specified criteria are not be added to the rule set. Due in part to the limit on the number of antecedents per rule, STARE created more rules than Craven and Shavlik's (1994) approach to rule extraction, but with greater fidelity. Also, STARE had greater classification accuracy when compared to C4.5 for most datasets utilized.

Interestingly, the basic principles of STARE also have been applied to trained neural network ensembles using the Rule Extraction From Neural Network Ensemble (REFNE) approach (Zhou, Jiang, & Chen, 2003). REFNE prioritizes rules and discretizes attributes in a similar manner. Experimental comparisons have been made between REFNE, a trained ensemble, a single neural network, and C4.5. REFNE showed better accuracy than the other three methods. REFNE created more rules per dataset than C4.5, but the rules created by C4.5 had more antecedents per rule.

Again, as with the decompositional approaches, very little comparison has been done between the pedagogical approaches. Many techniques still require discretization of continuous inputs. Systematic analysis of these similar techniques remains lacking in the research literature.

Hybrid/Eclectic Approaches

We end our article by discussing techniques that fit somewhere between the two extreme approaches. Bologna (2000a, 2000b) proposed the Discretized Interpretable Multi Layer Perceptron Model (DIMLP) where neurons of the first hidden layer are connected to only one input neuron. The rest of the network is fully connected. A staircase activation function is used in the first hidden layer (instead of the usual sigmoid function) to transform continuous inputs into discrete values. The extraction technique determines discriminant hyper-plane frontiers, builds a decision tree from this result, and then further prunes and modified the resultant rules. Thus, it uses components of decompositional approaches (pruning, hidden layer analysis) and pedagogical (use of hyper-plane frontiers).

In analyzing the results of DIMLP, it had nearly the same classification accuracy as the original NN on test data and had 100% fidelity on training data. DIMLP also was more accurate than C4.5 on several datasets, but demonstrated less comprehensibility (i.e., more rules and more antecedents per rule).

Interestingly, much like the aforementioned REFNE, DIMLP has recently been extended to generate rules from ensembles of DIMLP networks (Bologna, 2001; Bologna, 2003). Rule extraction from the ensembles showed improved accuracy over rule extraction from single DIMLP

Table 1.

	Category	Data sets used for experiments	Other techniques compared to:	Form of input data:	Specialized Network or Network requirement(s)
Bologna, 2000 a, b	Eclectic	Ionosphere, Monk-1, Monk-2, Monk-3, Pen Based Handwritten digits, Sonar	MLP, C4.5	Neurons of first hidden layer transform continous inputs into discrete values	Each neuron in first hidden layer connected to only one input neuron. Other layers fully connected. Staircase activation function for first hidden layer.
Bologna, 2001, 2003	Eclectic	Arrythmia, Breast-cancer, Wisconsin Breast Cancer(Original and Diagnostic), Dermatology, Echocardiogram, Heart Disease-Cleveland, Heart Disease-Hungarian, Heart Disease-statlog, Hepatitis, Hypothyroid, Iris, Liver-disorders, Lymphography, Pima Indians Di	MLP, CN2, C4.5		Network ensembles. Staircase activation function for neurons in first hidden layer.
Fan & Li, 2002	Decompositional	Iris, *High-pressure air compressor*	NN, Genetic Algorithm, C4.5, Rough Set	Not specified	Hidden-to-output function is linear
Garcez, Broda, & Gabbay, 2001	Eclectic	DNA Sequence Analysis, Monk's, Power Systems Fault Diagnosis	MofN, Subset, Setiono, 1997	Binary	single hidden layer
Gupta, Park, & Lam, 1999	Decompositional	Balloon, BUPA, Glass, Hepatitis, Iris, Postoperative Patient (Post)	NN, C4.5	Inputs converted to boolean	Single hidden layer
Krishnan, Sivakumar, & Bhattacharya, 1999	Pedagogical	Iris, Wine Recognition, Wisconsin Breast Cancer	NN, ID3	No requirement	No special requirements.
Palade, Neagu, & Puscasu, 2000	Pedagogical	*Liquid Tank*	None	Continuous	Nonlinear activation function
Sato & Tsukimoto, 2001	Decompositional	Auto-mpg, Wisconsin University Breast-cancer, BUPA, Credit, IRIS, Machine, Monk 1, Monk 3, University	None	Continuous and Discrete	No special requirements.
Schmidt & Chen, 2002	Decompositional	Iris, Monk-2,	mFOIL, ID3, NN	Binary	Requires pre- and post-processing operations and specialized performance wedge

Table 1 (cont.)

	Category	Data sets used for experiments	Other techniques compared to:	Form of input data:	Specialized Network or Network requirement(s)
Schmitz, Aldrich, and Gouws, 1999	Pedagogical	Abalone, *Sap Flow in Pine Trees, Sine and Cosine Curves*	CART	Discrete or Continuous	No special requirements.
Setiono & Leow, 2000	Decompostional	Monk 1, Monk2, Monk 3, *CNF12a, CNF 12b, DNF 12a, DNF 12b, MAJ12a, MAJ12b, MUX 12*, Australian Credit Approval, Wisconsin Breast Cancer, Heart Disease, Pima Indians, Sonar	N2P2F+C4.5, C4.5	Discrete or Continuous	Minimize augmented cross-entropy error.
Setiono & Liu, 1998	Decompositional	*Contiguity, 5-Bit Parity*, Monks, Pima Indian	ARTMAP, C4.5	Binary, Discrete or Continuous (normalized to [-1,1])	Sigmoid or hyperbolic tangent activation function. Minimize cross entropy error, BFGS training algorithm.
Shigaki & Narazaki, 1999	Pedagogical	*Sintering*	None	Continuous	No special requirements.
Su, Hsu & Tsai, 2002	Decompositional	Pima Indian Liver	NN, See5	Not limited	Output function must be monotone.
Taha & Ghosh, 1999	BIO-RE-Pedagogical; Partial-RE, Full-REDecomposition al	*Artificial Binary Problem*, Iris, Wisconsin Breast Cancer	NeuroRule, C4.5, KT	BIO-Re: Binary, Partial-RE Normalized (0,1), Full-RE: No restriction	Monotonically increasing activation function.
Tsukimoto, 2000	Decompositional	Congressional Voting Records, Iris, Mushroom	C4.5	Discrete or Continuous	Output function must be monotone increasing.Sigmoidal activation function.
Vaughn, Cavill, Taylor, Foy, & Fogg, 2000	Decompositional	*Lower Back Pain*	None	Binary	No special requirements.
Zhou, Chen, & Chen, 2000	Pedagogical	Auto imports, Credit screening, *Fault Diagnosis*, Hepatitis, Iris plant, Lung cancer	Craven & Shavlik,1994, C4.5	Discrete or Continuous	No special requirements.
Zhou, Jiang, & Chen, 2003	Pedagogical	Balance Scale, Congressional Voting Records, Hepatitis, Iris, Statlog Australian Credit approval, Stalog German credit	C4.5	Discrete or Continuous	Network ensemble generated via plurality voting.

Note: For italicized data sets, see cited article for description of data. For all other data sets, source of data is University of California-Irvine Machine Learning Repository (http://www.ics.uci.edu/~mlearn/MLRepository.html).

networks. Therefore, as more and more practitioners use an ensemble approach in their data mining applications, DIMLP offers additional promise.

Finally, Garcez, Broda, and Gabbay (2001) present a method for extracting rules that they claim has high accuracy and fidelity. Their algorithm performs a partial ordering on the set of input vectors of a neural network and then uses a related set of pruning and simplification rules. The method is unique in its use of default negation to capture nonmonotonic rules from the network. This algorithm is slightly less accurate than the classic M of N approach and Setiono's method (Setiono, 1997; Towell & Shavlik, 1993), but the method shows increased fidelity. To achieve this fidelity, the algorithm produces a larger set of rules. The algorithm requires a network with only one hidden layer, but has no specific training requirements.

FUTURE TRENDS

It is clear that no technique or tool has emerged as useful in all (or most) knowledge discovery/data mining circumstances for extracting rules from classification neural networks. Many techniques show promise, but there is a clear lack of systematic study and analysis in the literature. Few comparative studies of rule extraction techniques have been done, and even when such studies have been undertaken, small datasets have been employed. Table 1 provides a comprehensive summary of the techniques previously discussed.

Decision-makers in the knowledge-enabled organizations of today need more than just the high "classification" accuracy that sophisticated techniques like neural networks deliver to their desktop. They also want to gain insight into the problem domain; thus, the explanatory or "lessons learned" knowledge from their analyses is extremely important. Conventional wisdom also would indicate that the simpler the explanation or knowledge extraction results, the higher desirability, larger user acceptance, and bigger payoff to the organization. Thus, the attraction of using NN's (shown to be, for the most part, empirically superior knowledge discovery tools) to provide IF-THEN level explanations (simple yet effective explanations of organizational phenomenon) normally provided by inductive learning systems or by expert knowledge seems worthy of more in-depth study.

We expect future data mining researchers to begin to focus more in this area of knowledge extraction and elicitation, rather than seeking new classification algorithms. Clearly, the potential exists for the organizational usefulness of neural networks to be enhanced by continued progress in this area.

CONCLUSION

The potential of neural network use as data mining tools has not been fully exploited due to the inability to explain the knowledge they learn. In reviewing the literature in this article, it is apparent that there are techniques that may offer this ability, but systematic study of such approaches has been minimal. Our hope is that once this "gap" is filled in the literature, and assuming positive results are found, neural network use by practitioners will be greatly enhanced, which will serve to increase the usefulness and profitability of knowledge management initiatives in many organizations.

REFERENCES

Bologna, G. (2000a). Rule extraction from a multilayer perceptron with staircase activation functions. Paper presented at the *International Joint Conference on Neural Networks*.

Bologna, G. (2000b). Symbolic rule extraction from the DIMLP neural network. In *Hybrid neural systems* (Vol. 1778, pp. 240-254). Berlin: Springer-Verlag Berlin.

Bologna, G. (2001). A study on rule extraction from several combined neural networks. *International Journal of Neural Systems, 11*(3), 247-255.

Bologna, G. (2003). A model for single and multiple knowledge-based networks. *Artificial Intelligence in Medicine, 28*(2), 141-163.

Craven, M.W., & Shavlik, J.W. (1996). Extracting tree-structured representations of trained networks. *Advances In Neural Information Processing Systems, (8)*, 24-30.

Craven, M.W., & Shavlik, J.W. (1994). Using sampling and queries to extract rules from trained neural networks. *Proceedings of the 11th International Conference of Machine Learning*, San Francisco.

Fan, Y., & Li, C.J. (2002). Diagnostic rule extraction from trained feed forward neural networks. *Mechanical Systems and Signal Processing, 16*(6), 1073-1081.

Garcez, A.S.D., Broda, K., & Gabbay, D.M. (2001). Symbolic knowledge extraction from trained neural networks: A sound approach. *Artificial Intelligence, 125*(1-2), 155-207.

Gupta, A., Park, S., & Lam, S.M. (1999). Generalized analytic rule extraction for feed forward neural networks. *IEEE Transactions on Knowledge and Data Engineering, 11*(6), 985-991.

Krishnan, R., Sivakumar, G., et al. (1999). Extracting decision trees from trained neural networks. *Pattern Recognition, 32*(12), 1999-2009.

Palade, V., Neagu, D.-C., & Puscasu, G. (2000). Rule extraction from neural networks by interval propagation. *Proceedings of the 4th International Conference on the Knowledge-Based Intelligent Engineering Systems and Allied Technologies.*

Sato, M., & Tsukimoto, H. (2001). Rule extraction from neural networks via decision tree induction. Paper presented at the *International Joint Conference on Neural Networks.*

Schmidt, V.A., and Chen, C.L.P. (2002). Using the aggregate feedforward neural network for rule extraction. *International Journal of Fuzzy Systems, 4*(3), 795-806.

Schmitz, G.P.J., Aldrich, C., & Gouws, F.S. (1999). ANN-DT: An algorithm for extraction of decision trees from artificial neural networks. *IEEE Transactions on Neural Networks, 10*(6), 1392-1401.

Setiono, R. (1997). Extracting rules from neural networks by pruning and hidden-unit splitting. *Neural Computation, 9*(1), 205-225.

Setiono, R., & Leow, W.K. (2000). FERNN: An algorithm for fast extraction of rules from neural networks. *Applied Intelligence, 12*(1-2), 15-25.

Setiono, R., & Liu, H. (1995). Understanding neural networks via rule extraction. Paper presented at the *Proceedings of International Joint Conference on Artificial Intelligence*, Montreal, Quebec, Canada.

Setiono, R., & Liu, H. (1998). Analysis of hidden representations by greedy clustering. *Connection Science, 10*(1), 21-42.

Shigaki, I., & Narazaki, H. (1999). A machine-learning approach for a sintering process using a neural network. *Production Planning & Control, 10*(8), 727-734.

Su, C.T., Hsu, H.H., & Tsai, C.H. (2002). Knowledge mining from trained neural networks. *Journal of Computer Information Systems, 42*(4), 61-70.

Taha, I.A., & Ghosh, J. (1999). Symbolic interpretation of artificial neural networks. *IEEE Transactions on Knowledge and Data Engineering, 11*(3), 448-463.

Tickle, A.B., Maire, F., Bologna, G., Andrews, R., & Diederich, J. (2000). Lessons from past, current issues, and future research directions in extracting the knowledge embedded in artificial neural networks. In *Hybrid neural systems* (Vol. 1778, pp. 226-239). Berlin: Springer-Verlag Berlin.

Towell, G.G., & Shavlik, J.W. (1993). Extracting refined rules from knowledge-based neural networks. *Machine Learning, 13*(1), 71-101.

Tsukimoto, H. (2000). Extracting rules from trained neural networks. *IEEE Transactions on Neural Networks, 11*(2), 377-389.

Vaughn, M.L., Cavill, S.J., Taylor, S.J., Foy, M.A., & Fogg, A.J.B. (2000). Direct explanations and knowledge extraction from a Multilayer Perceptron network that performs low back pain classification. In *Hybrid neural systems* (Vol. 1778, pp. 270-285). Berlin: Springer-Verlag Berlin.

Zhou, Z.-H., Jiang, Y., & Chen, S.-F. (2003). Extracting symbolic rules from trained neural network ensembles. *AI Communications* (Vol. 16, p. 3). IOS Press.

Zhou, Z.-H., Chen, S.-F., & Chen, Z.-Q. (2000). A statistics based approach for extracting priority rules from trained neural networks. Paper presented at the *Proceedings of IEEE-INNS-ENNS International Joint Conference on Neural Networks*, Como, Italy.

KEY TERMS

Artificial Neural Network: Biologically inspired statistical tools modeled after the structure of the human brain. Neural networks are composed of interconnected units or nodes (a la neurons) with associated weights and activation values. Training or learning rules are incorporated into the network to accomplish forecasting or classification tasks based on the pattern of interconnection throughout the network.

Backpropagation, Feed-Forward NN: A type of neural network popular for use in classification data mining. The neurons in a feed-forward network are organized into an input layer and enable the network to represent the knowledge present in the data.

Data Mining: The discovery of information from a large collection of raw data. This might include processing information to discover relationships and patterns in the data. The data is generally stored in a large database or data warehouse. Neural networks and inductive learning systems are among the collection of techniques used to extract knowledge from these large datasets.

Inductive Learning Systems: Data mining or knowledge discovery tools that learn relationships among a dataset by systematically analyzing cases. Output of these approaches is typically in decision tree (or rule) form. Popular algorithms of this genre include See5, CART, ID3, and C4.5.

Knowledge Discovery: Similar to data mining, this relates to the finding or the process of finding previously unknown patterns or relationships in a set of data. This might be extended to the identification of important or relevant input attributes to be used for classification.

Rules: A typical and useful way for representing knowledge. Can be of many forms, but typically are IF <conditions> THEN <conclusions>. Conditions also are referred to as antecedents, and conclusions as consequents.

Frequent Itemset Mining and Association Rules

Susan Imberman
City University of New York, USA

Abdullah Uz Tansel
Bilkent University, Turkey

INTRODUCTION

With the advent of mass storage devices, databases have become larger and larger. Point-of-sale data, patient medical data, scientific data, and credit card transactions are just a few sources of the ever-increasing amounts of data. These large datasets provide a rich source of useful information. Knowledge Discovery in Databases (KDD) is a paradigm for the analysis of these large datasets. KDD uses various methods from such diverse fields as machine learning, artificial intelligence, pattern recognition, database management and design, statistics, expert systems, and data visualization.

KDD has been defined as "the non-trivial process of identifying valid, novel, potentially useful, and ultimately understandable patterns in data" (Fayyad, Piaetsky-Shapiro, & Smyth, 1996). The KDD process is diagramed in Figure 1.

First, organizational data is collated into a database. This is sometimes kept in a data warehouse, which acts as a centralized source of data. Data is then selected from the data warehouse to form the target data. Selection is dependent on the domain, the end-user's needs, and the data mining task at hand. The preprocessing step cleans the data. This involves removing noise, handling missing data items, and taking care of outliers. Reduction coding takes the data and makes it usable for data analysis, either by reducing the number of records in the dataset or the number of variables. The transformed data is fed into the data mining step for analysis, to discover knowledge in the form of interesting and unexpected patterns that are presented to the user via some method of visualization. One must not assume that this is a linear process. It is highly iterative with feedback from each step into previous steps. Many different analytical methods are used in the data mining step. These include decision trees, clustering, statistical tests, neural networks, nearest neighbor algorithms, and association rules. Association rules indicate the co-occurrence of items in market basket data or in other domains. It is the only technique that is endemic to the field of data mining.

Organizations, large or small, need intelligence to survive in the competitive marketplace. Association rule discovery along with other data mining techniques are tools for obtaining this business intelligence. Therefore, association rule discovery techniques are available in toolkits that are components of knowledge management systems. Since knowledge management is a continuous process, we expect that knowledge management techniques will, alternately, be integrated into the KDD process. The focus for the rest of this article will be on the methods used in the discovery of association rules.

Figure 1. The KDD process

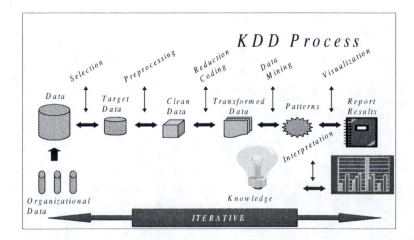

BACKGROUND

Association rule algorithms were developed to analyze market basket data. A single market basket contains store items that a customer purchases at a particular time. Hence, most of the terminology associated with association rules stems from this domain. The act of purchasing items in a particular market basket is called a transaction. Market basket data is visualized as Boolean, with the value 1 indicating the presence of a particular item in the market basket, notwithstanding the number of instances of an item; a value of 0 indicates its absence. A set of items is said to satisfy a transaction if each item's value is equal to 1. Itemsets refer to groupings of these items based on their occurrence in the dataset. More formally, given a set $I = \{ i_1, i_2, i_3, \ldots i_n \}$ of items, any subset of I is called an itemset. A *k-itemset* contains k items. Let X and Y be subsets of I such that $X \cap Y = \phi$. An association rule is a probabilistic implication $X \Rightarrow Y$. This means if X occurs, Y also occurs. For example, suppose a store sells, among other items, shampoo (1), body lotion (2), hair spray (3), and beer (4), where the numbers are item numbers. The association rule *shampoo, hair spray $\Rightarrow$ beer* can be interpreted as, "those who purchase shampoo and hair spray will also tend to purchase beer."

There are two metrics used to find association rules. Given an association rule $X \Rightarrow Y$ as defined above, the support of the rule is the number of transactions that satisfy $X \cup Y$ divided by the total number of transactions. Support is an indication of a rule's statistical significance. Interesting association rules have support above a minimum user-defined threshold called *minsup*. Given the database represented in Figure 2, the support of the association rule *shampoo, hair spray $\Rightarrow$ beer* is equal to the number of transactions where shampoo, hairspray, and beer are equal to 1. This is equal to the shaded region

Figure 2. *Support of shampoo, hair spray $\Rightarrow$ beer 4/12 or 33%*

1. Shampoo	2. Hair Spray	3. Body Lotion	4. Beer
1	0	1	1
1	1	1	0
1	1	1	1
1	0	1	1
0	0	0	1
1	0	1	1
1	1	1	0
1	1	1	1
0	1	0	1
1	1	1	1
1	1	1	1
1	0	0	1

Figure 3. *Support of shampoo and hair spray*

1. Shampoo	2. Hair Spray	3. Body Lotion	4. Beer
1	0	1	1
1	1	1	0
1	1	1	1
1	0	1	1
0	0	0	1
1	0	1	1
1	1	1	0
1	1	1	1
0	1	0	1
1	1	1	1
1	1	1	1
1	0	0	1

and consists of a support of 4 out of 12 transactions, or 33%. Frequently occurring itemsets, called frequent itemsets, indicate groups of items customers tend to purchase in association with each other. These are itemsets that have support above the user-defined threshold, *minsup*.

Given an association rule $X \Rightarrow Y$ as defined above, the confidence of a rule is the number of transactions that satisfy $X \cup Y$ divided by the number of transactions that satisfy X. In Figure 3, the shaded portion indicates the support of Shampoo and Hair Spray. The confidence is then the support of the itemset Shampoo, Hairspray and Beer, divided by the support of Shampoo and Hairspray which equals $4/6 = 66\%$. It is common practice to define a second threshold based on a user-defined minimum confidence called *minconf*. A rule that has support above *minsup* and confidence above *minconf* is an interesting association rule (Agrawal, Imielinski, Swami, 1993; Agrawal & Srikant, 1994; Agrawal, Mannila, Srikant, Toivonen, & Verkamo, 1996).

FINDING ASSOCIATION RULES

Finding association rules above *minconf*, given a frequent itemset, is easily done and linear in complexity. Finding frequent itemsets is exponential in complexity and more difficult, thus necessitating efficient algorithms. A brute force approach would be to list all possible subsets of the set of items *I* and calculate the support of each. Once an itemset is labeled frequent, partitions of the set's items are used to find rules above *minconf*. Continuing our example, assume *minsup* = 65%. Figure 4 lists all the subsets of the set of the items in Figures 2 and 3. The shaded areas indicate the frequent itemsets with support equal to or above 65%. The set of all itemsets forms a lattice, as seen in Figure 5.

Figure 4. Itemsets and their support

Itemset	Support (in percent)	Itemset	Support (in percent)
{1}	83	{2}	58
{3}	75	{4}	83
{1,2}	50	{1,3}	75
{1,4}	66	{2,3}	50
{2,4}	41	{3,4}	58
{1,2,3}	50	{1,2,4}	33
{1,3,4}	58	{2,3,4}	33
{1,2,3,4}	33		

Figure 5. Lattice of itemsets

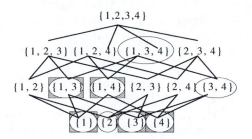

One can see that the brute force method grows exponentially with the number of items in I. In a database containing thousands of items, a brute force approach can become intractable. Algorithms that are exponential relative to the number of variables are said to suffer from "the curse of dimensionality."

If we look at the 1-itemsets in Figure 4, we notice that itemset {2} is below *minsup*. In fact, all supersets of itemset {2} are below *minsup* as well. This is illustrative of the upward closure property of support. If an itemset is not frequent, then the itemset's supersets will not be frequent. Many association rule algorithms use this property to prune the search space for frequent itemsets. Apriori is one such algorithm (Agrawal et al., 1993; Agrawal & Srikant, 1994; Agrawal et al., 1996).

APRIORI ALGORITHM

Apriori uses the upward closure property of support to move level wise through the lattice. To find frequent itemsets, Apriori first scans the data set for the counts of 1-itemsets, since all 1-itemsets are candidates to be frequent. Those frequent 1-itmesets are used to generate the 2-itemsets that are candidates to be frequent. In general, Apriori generates candidate itemsets at a particular level k from the $k-1$ itemsets at level $k-1$. This is done in the algorithm's join step. If two frequent itemsets at level $k-1$ have the same $k-2$ items in common, we form the union of these two sets. The resulting set is a candidate k-*itemset*. Each of these *candidate* itemsets are checked to see if any of their subsets are not frequent. If so, they are pruned from consideration in the prune step, since if you recall, supersets of itemsets that are not frequent, are themselves not frequent. Candidate itemsets that do not have support equal to or above *minsup* are also pruned. The algorithm proceeds level wise through the lattice, until there are no more candidate itemsets generated.

Using the data set from Figure 1, in level 1 of Figure 5, the algorithm starts with all the 1-itemsets as candidate

itemsets. Candidate itemsets in the figure are circled. Counting the support of each itemset, we see that all but {2} are frequent. A box indicates frequent itemsets. Itemsets {1}, {3}, and {4} combine to form candidate 2-itemsets {1,3}, {1,4}, and {3,4}. From the data we see that itemsets {1, 3} and {1, 4} are frequent. Since {1, 3} and {1, 4} have $k-1$ items in common, these itemsets are combined to form the candidate 3-itemset {1, 3, 4}. Itemset {3, 4} is a subset of {1, 3, 4}. Since {3, 4} is not frequent, {1, 3, 4} cannot be frequent. The algorithm stops since we cannot generate any more candidate itemsets.

VARIATIONS ON APRIORI

Researchers have devised improvements to overcome the bottlenecks in the Apriori algorithm. One bottleneck is the time needed to scan the dataset since the dataset is huge, normally terabytes large. Because of this, a lot of the work done by these algorithms is in searching the dataset. The authors of Apriori realized that transactions that do not contain k large itemsets would not contain $k+1$ large itemsets. Thus avoiding further scans of the dataset (Agrawal et al., 1996). Another improvement was to implement the use of transaction identification lists (TID lists). These are the lists of transactions an itemset is contained in. The dataset is scanned only once to create the TID lists for the 1-itemsets. The TID lists for itemsets on any level $k+1$ is created by taking the intersection of the TID lists of the itemsets from level k used in their creation. The problem with TID lists is that initially, the size of the list has the potential to be larger than the dataset. In recognition of this, the authors of Apriori developed Apriori Hybrid, which scans the dataset in the beginning levels of the algorithm, and then switches to TID lists.

Other researchers have taken different approaches to the problem of scanning large datasets. In Dynamic Hashing and Pruning (DHP), it was recognized that in level wise algorithms like Apriori, much of the work is done in generating and counting the 2-itemsets (Park, Chen, & Yu, 1995). The approach here was to hash the candidate 2-itemsets. The number of itemsets in each bin is stored. If the total count of the itemsets in a bin is not larger than or equal to *minsup*, then the itemsets in that bin cannot reach *minsup*. These itemsets are pruned, and the algorithm proceeds as in Apriori.

Another approach was to break the dataset into n partitions such that each partition fits into main memory (Savasere, Oiecninski, & Navathe 1998). The premise is that any global large itemset must also be one of the local frequent itemsets found in a partition. Once frequent itemsets in local partitions are found, the dataset is scanned to determine which of these is global.

Another approach has been to create a random sample from the dataset large enough to fit into memory (Toivonen, 1996). The sample is then used to find frequent itemsets. In order to increase the probability that those itemsets found in the sample would include all frequent itemsets from the dataset, the sample is scanned with a lower support than that used for the dataset. The transactions of the dataset, not in the sample, are then used to check the support counts of the sample frequent itemsets. Thus only one scan of the dataset is required, but there is no guaranty that all frequent itemsets will be found.

Datasets that are increasing in size pose the problem of how to efficiently mine the new data. One could run an algorithm like Apriori on the "new" larger dataset, but this ignores all previous work done in discovering frequent itemsets. In addition it is costly and inefficient since most of the work done in finding frequent itemsets is in scanning the dataset. To avoid redoing one can take an incremental approach whereby you use the information obtained in previous association rule processing to reduce the amount of dataset scans when new transactions are added (Ayan, Tansel, & Arkun, 1999).

Below, we list the notation used in incremental association rule mining.

- DB is the set of old transactions from the original database.
- db is the set of new incoming transactions (the increment).
- $DB+db$ is the set of old and new incoming transactions (the resulting combined dataset).
- $SCDB$ (X) is the support count of itemset X in DB.
- $SCdb$ (X) is the support count of X in db.
- $SCDB+db$ (X) is the support count of X in $DB+db$.

Assume that the size of the increment db is less than the size of the original dataset DB. Define the support count (SC) of an itemset as the number of occurrences of that itemset in the dataset. Figure 6 is an illustration of the incremental approach in terms of the support count of DB (SC_{DB}) plotted against the support count of db (SC_{db}) (Imberman, Tansel, & Pacuit, 2004). For each point (SC_{db}, SC_{DB}) in Figure 6, $SC_{db} + SC_{DB} = SC_{DB+db}$, which is the support count of the new dataset. Let $minSCdb$ be the minimum number of transactions to be frequent in db and $minSCDB$ be the minimum number of transactions to be frequent in DB. Therefore, for all points G on line HC, $SCdb + SCDB = minSCDB+db$. *Line HC partitions the space of itemsets.* All itemsets above and including HC are frequent. All itemsets below HC are not frequent. Triangle HFG represents those itemsets that have become infrequent or have submerged. Triangle GIC represents those itemsets that have become frequent or emerged. The incremental discovery problem can be thought of as efficiently identifying those itemsets in triangles GIC and HFG.

Update With Early Pruning (UWEP; Ayan et al., 1999) has been shown to be an efficient incremental association rule algorithm. Like most incremental algorithms, UWEP uses information found in the increment to prune the search space. First UWEP scans db to find the counts for all the 1-itemsets. In the pruning step, the supersets of the itemsets in DB that are found not frequent in $DB + db$ are pruned from $DB + db$. The frequent itemsets in DB, whose items are absent in db, are checked to see if $SC_{DB} (X) >= SC_{DB + db} (X)$. Frequent itemsets in db are looked at to see if they are frequent in DB. These are frequent by definition. Lastly, for all itemsets that are frequent in DB or db and have not yet been looked at, they are checked to see if they are frequent in $DB + db$.

Besides researching new ways for efficiently finding association rules, researchers have looked at the rules themselves, finding new types of association rules. Association rules are Boolean, looking only at the positive associations between items. Some researchers have looked at the negative dependencies as well, calling these rules

Figure 6. The incremental association rule problem

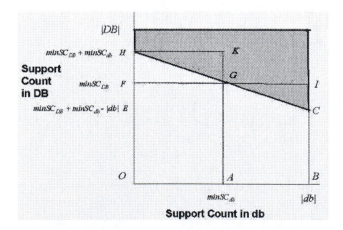

dependency rules (Silverstein, Brin, & Motwani 1998). A dependency rule can express concepts such as *males age 60 or greater = yes* and *smokes = no* ⇒ *buy beer = no*. Imberman et al. (2002) have shown that dependency rules are more expressive for medical data miming than association rules.

Since most data is not Boolean by nature, how can one show associations with numeric and categorical data? Quantitative association rules express associations such as *Age: 30 to 39* and *Owns car = yes* ⇒ *Median Income = 40,000*. One approach was to map each category in a categorical variable, to a Boolean variable and discretize the quantitative variables into intervals (Srikant & Agrawal, 1996). Each interval is mapped onto a Boolean variable. Then any Boolean association rule algorithm can be used to find rules. However, care needs to be exercised in partitioning each variable appropriately. If a quantitative variable is partitioned into too many smaller intervals, minimum support may not be found in any one interval. Therefore some well-supported rules may be missed. Also, confidence can decrease with larger intervals affecting the attainment of minimum confidence. Thus, small intervals might not get minimum support, while large intervals might not get minimum confidence. An approach to solve this problem is to consider all possible continuous ranges (Srikant & Agrawal, 1996). If we were to increase the interval size then we would have no more *minsup* problem. To take care of this we can combine adjacent intervals. But we may still have *minconf* problems. We can solve *minconf* problems by increasing the number of intervals. But doing both leads to two more problems. Given n intervals, there are on average $O(n^2)$ possible ranges. There is therefore a blow up in execution time. Given an interval with support, any range containing that interval also has support. This can lead to a blow up in the number of rules known as the many rules problem. Srikant and Agrawal (1996) posed a solution by setting a user-defined maximum on the size of the interval and using an interestingness measure to filter out uninteresting rules.

The 'many rules problem' has motivated research into the 'interestingness' of rules produced by association rule algorithms. Methods for interestingness involve ordering and grouping association rules in order to facilitate their use and interpretation. Metrics for ordering rules include measures such as confidence, added value, mutual information (Sahar & Mansour, 1999), and conviction measures (Brin, Motwani, Ullman, & Tsur, 1997). Objective interestingness measures seem to cluster into three groups when support and confidence levels are low. Interestingness measures in the same cluster produce similar rule orders. Sahar (1999) along with Mansour (1999) pruned the rule set by discarding 'uninteresting' rules. Sahar worked under the premise that simple rules would already be known by the user and can thus be pruned from the rule set. Sahar (2002) used clustering to group similar rules.

FUTURE TRENDS

Association rule discovery algorithms feed their results into organizational knowledge bases. An important issue is the maintenance and update of discovered association rules as new data becomes available. The incremental algorithms we have summarized above are very useful and cost effective for knowledge management. Research into the combination of sound knowledge management techniques and data mining techniques can make significant contributions to the business environment.

Research into the types of rules that can be generated using the techniques outlined in this article is ongoing. Reduced database scanning by improvements on the basic algorithm is another area of research activity. In addition much current research is being concentrated on finding better data structures for more efficient itemset processing (Gosta & Zhu, 2003). Association rule mining is a very active research field.

CONCLUSION

Association rule algorithms show co-occurrence of variables. One of the major problems inherent in Apriori, and algorithms like Apriori, is that there tends to be a large number of rules generated, some of which are commonly known. In addition, attempts to use the rules generated by association rule algorithms has met with mixed results. On the other hand, Apriori has also been shown to find less obvious patterns in the data (Cox, Eick, Wills, & Brachman, 1997), thereby discovering very valuable knowledge.

ACKNOWLEDGMENTS

This work was supported in part by a grant from The City University of New York PSC-CUNY Research Award Program, awards 65388-00-34 (Imberman) and 65406-00-34 (Tansel).

REFERENCES

Agrawal, R., Imielinski, T., & Swami, A. (1993). Mining association rules between sets of items in large databases. *Proceedings of ACM SIGMOD* (pp. 207-216).

Agrawal, R., Mannila, H., Srikant, R., Toivonen, H., & Verkamo, A.I. (1996). Fast discovery of association rules. In U. Fayyad, G. Piatetsky-Shapiro, P. Smyth, & R. Uthurusamy (Eds.), *Advances in knowledge discovery and data mining* (pp. 307-328). Boston: AAAI/MIT Press.

Agrawal, R., & Srikant, R. (1994). *Fast algorithms for mining association rules.* IBM Res. Rep. RJ9839, IBM Almaden.

Aumann, Y., & Lindell, Y. (1999). A statistical theory for quantitative association rules. *Proceedings of the 5th ACM SIGKDD International Conference on Knowledge Discovery and Data Mining* (pp. 261 -270).

Ayan, N.F., Tansel, A.U., & Arkun, E. (1999). An efficient algorithm to update large itemsets with early pruning. *Proceedings of the 5th ACM SIGKDD International Conference on Knowledge Discovery and Data Mining* (pp. 287-291).

Brin, S., Motwani, R. Ullman, J., & Tsur, S. (1997). Dynamic itemset counting and implication rules for market basket data. *Proceedings of ACM SIGMOD* (pp. 255-264).

Cox, K.C., Eick, S.G., Wills, G.J., & Brachman, R.J. (1997). Visual data mining: Recognizing telephone calling fraud. *Data Mining and Knowledge Discovery, 1*(2), 225-231.

Fayyad, U.M., Piaetsky-Shapiro, G., & Smyth, P. (1996). From data mining to knowledge discovery: An overview. *Advances in knowledge discovery and data mining.* Cambridge, MA: AAAI/MIT Press.

Fukada, T., Yasuhiko, M., Sinichi, M., & Tokuyama, T. (1996). Mining optimized association rules for numeric attributes. *Proceedings of the ACM SIGMOD International Conference on Management of Data* (pp. 13-23).

Gosta, G., & Zhu, J. (2003). Efficiently using prefix-trees in mining frequent itemsets. *Proceedings of the IEEE ICDM Workshop on Frequent Itemset Mining Implementations.* Retrieved from *http://sunsite.informatik.rwth-aachen.de/Publications/CEUR-WS//Vol-90/*

Imberman, S.P., Domanski, B., & Thompson, H.W. (2002). Using dependency/association rules to find indications for computerized tomography in a head trauma dataset. *Artificial Intelligence in Medicine, 26*(1), 55-68.

Imberman, S.P., Tansel, A.U., & Pacuit, E. (2004). An efficient method for finding emerging large itemsets. *Proceedings of the 3rd Workshop on Mining Temporal and Sequential Data, ACM SIGKDD International Conference on Knowledge Discovery and Data Mining.*

Park, J.S., Chen, M.S., & Yu, P.S. (1995). An effective hash based algorithm for mining association rules. *Proceedings of ACM SIGMOD* (pp. 175-186).

Sahar, S. (1999). Interestingness via what is not interesting. *ACM SIGKDD International Conference on Knowledge Discovery and Data Mining* (pp. 332-336).

Sahar, S., & Mansour, Y. (1999). An empirical evaluation of objective interestingness criteria. *Proceedings of the SPIE Conference on Data Mining and Knowledge Discovery* (pp. 63-74).

Sahar, S. (2002). Exploring interestingness through clustering: A framework. *Proceedings of the IEEE International Conference on Data Mining* (ICDM 2002) (pp. 677-681).

Savasere, A., Omiecinski, E., & Navathe, S. (1998). An efficient algorithm for mining association rules in large databases. *Proceedings of the IEEE International Conference of Data Engineering* (ICDE 1998) (pp. 494-502).

Silverstein, C., Brin, S., & Motwani, R. (1998). Beyond market baskets: Generalizing association rules to dependence rules. *Data Mining and Knowledge Discovery, 2*(1), 39-68.

Srikant, R., & Agrawal, R. (1996). Mining quantitative association rules in large relational tables. *Proceedings of the ACM SIGMOD International Conference on Management of Data* (pp. 1-12).

Toivonen, H. (1996). Sampling large databases for association rules. *Proceedings of the 22nd International Conference on Very Large Databases* (VLDB'96) (pp. 135-145).

KEY TERMS

Apriori: A level-wise algorithm for finding association rules. Apriori uses the support of an itemset to prune the search space of all itemsets. It then uses the confidence metric to find association rules.

Association Rule: Given a set $I = \{ i_1, i_2, i_3, \dots i_n\}$ of items, any subset of I is called an itemset. Let X and Y be subsets of I such that $X \cap Y = \phi$. An association rule is a probabilistic implication $X \Rightarrow Y$.

Confidence: Given an association rule $X \Rightarrow Y$, the confidence of a rule is the number of transactions that satisfy $X \cup Y$ divided by the number of transactions that satisfy X.

Data Mining: One step of the KDD process. Can include various data analysis methods such as decision trees, clustering, statistical tests, neural networks, nearest neighbor algorithms, and association rules

Interestingness: Methods used to order and prune the set of rules produced by association rule algorithms.

This facilitates their use and interpretation by the user. Metrics for interestingness include measures such as confidence, added value, mutual information. and conviction measures.

Knowledge Discovery in Databases (KDD): A paradigm for the analysis of large datasets. The process is cyclic and iterative, with several steps including data preparation, analysis, and interpretation. KDD uses various methods from such diverse fields such as machine learning, artificial intelligence, pattern recognition, database management and design, statistics, expert systems, and data visualization.

Quantitative Association Rules: Shows associations with numeric and categorical data. Quantitative rules would express associations such as: *Age: 30 to 39* and *Owns car = yes -> Median Income = 40,000.*

Support: Given an association rule $X \Rightarrow Y$, the support of the rule is the number of transactions that satisfy or match $X \cup Y$, divided by the total number of transactions. Support is an indication of a rule's statistical significance.

UWEP: An incremental association rule algorithm. Incremental association rule algorithms use the information obtained in previous association rule processing to reduce the amount of dataset scans when new transactions are added.

Healthcare Knowledge Management

Kostas Metaxiotis
National Technical University of Athens, Greece

INTRODUCTION

The healthcare environment is changing rapidly, and effective management of the knowledge base in this area is an integral part of delivering high-quality patient care. People all over the world rely on a huge array of organizations for the provision of healthcare, from public-sector monoliths and governmental agencies to privately funded organizations, and consulting and advisory groups. It is a massive industry in which every organization faces a unique combination of operational hurdles. However, what every healthcare system has in common is the high price of failure. Faced with the prospect of failing to prevent suffering and death, the importance of continuously improving efficiency and effectiveness is high on the agenda for the majority of healthcare organizations (Brailer, 1999). Taking also into consideration that the amount of biological and medical information is growing at an exponential rate, it is not consequently surprising that knowledge management (KM) is attracting so much attention from the industry as a whole.

In a competitive environment like the healthcare industry, trying to balance customer expectations and cost requires an ongoing innovation and technological evolution. With the shift of the healthcare industry from a central network to a global network, the challenge is how to effectively manage the sources of information and knowledge in order to innovate and gain competitive advantage. Healthcare enterprises are knowledge-intensive organizations which process massive amounts of data, such as electronic medical records, clinical trial data,

hospitals records, administrative reports, and generate knowledge. However, the detailed content of this knowledge repository is to some extent "hidden" to its users, because it is regularly localized or even personal and difficult to share, while the healthcare data are rarely transformed into a strategic decision-support resource (Heathfield & Louw, 1999). KM concepts and tools can provide great support to exploit the huge knowledge and information resources and assist today's healthcare organizations to strengthen healthcare service effectiveness and improve the society they serve.

The key question which remains is the following: *How can we make knowledge management work in healthcare?* The answer is given in the following sections.

The Healthcare Industry: A Brief Overview

The health care industry is one of the largest single industries all over the world and the largest one in the United States. It has increased by over 65% since 1990 and is expected to double by the year 2007.[1] The IT industry is strategically positioned to become a powerful ally to the healthcare industry as it strives to adopt well-managed cost-efficient strategies. Advanced information technologies can give healthcare providers the opportunity to reduce overall healthcare expenses by lowering the costs of completing administrative and clinical transactions. Nevertheless, in comparison to other industry sectors, the healthcare industry has been slow to embrace e-

Table 1. Percentage of IT implementation in industry (Computer Economics, 1999)

Industry Sector	% in Place
Transportation	57.2
Banking and Finance	52.9
Insurance	48.1
State & Local Government	37.5
Trade Services	36.8
Retail Distribution	35.5
Process Manufacturing	34.9
Discrete Manufacturing	33.3
Wholesale Distribution	33.3
Utilities	26.9
Federal Government	25.0
Healthcare	21.8
Professional Services	21.7

business solutions and other advanced information technologies, as presented in Table 1.

The same study revealed that the healthcare industry spends substantially more on overhead and computer facility maintenance than other industry sectors. In 1997, for instance, the healthcare industry allotted 12% of its budget to maintain existing infrastructure—6% more than the industry norm. The high level of investment in this area by healthcare organizations indicates that many providers operate with the aid of old systems, which require constant repair and maintenance.

At this stage, it is worth emphasizing that the healthcare context differs from other information systems application domains in that it often concerns sensitive and confidential information and leads to critical decisions on people's lives (or quality of life). Thus, stakeholder conflicts have more of an impact than in other areas such as business, trade, and manufacturing. Healthcare is an area with quite intense differences of values, interests, professional backgrounds, and priorities among key stakeholders. Given the complexity of the context, health informatics in general cannot simply focus on technical or information systems aspects alone. It has to take account of their relationship with clinical and managerial processes and practices, as well as deal with multiple stakeholders and organizational cultures and accompanying politics.

Concluding, it should be stressed that healthcare is not only a significant industry in any economy (Folland, Goodman, & Stano, 1997), but also a field that needs effective means to manage data as well as information and knowledge. Managed care has emerged as an attempt to stem the escalating costs of healthcare (Wickramasinghe & Ginzberg, 2001) and improve the quality of services.

THE BACKGROUND OF KM IN HEALTHCARE

An increasing concern with improving the quality of care in various components of the healthcare system has led to the adoption of quality improvement approaches originally developed for industry. These include *Total Quality Management* (Deming, 1986), an approach that employs process control measures to ensure attainment of defined quality standards, and *Continuous Quality Improvement* (Juran, 1988), a strategy to engage all personnel in an organization in continuously improving quality of products and services. Nowadays, the importance of knowledge management is growing in the information society, and medical domains are not an exception. In Yu-N and Abidi (1999), managing knowledge in the healthcare environment is considered to be very important due to the characteristics of healthcare environments and the KM properties. We should always keep in mind that medical

knowledge is complex and doubles in amount every 20 years (Wyatt, 2001).

The healthcare industry is nowadays trying to become a knowledge-based community that is connected to hospitals, clinics, pharmacies, physicians, and customers for sharing knowledge, reducing administrative costs, and improving the quality of care (Antrobus, 1997; Booth, 2001). The success of healthcare depends critically on the collection, analysis, and exchange of clinical, billing, and utilization information or knowledge within and across the organizational boundaries (Bose, 2003).

It is only recently that initiatives to apply KM to the healthcare industry have been undertaken by researchers. Firstly, in the second half of the 1980s, several authors tried to apply artificial intelligence (AI)—with doubtful success—to medicine (Clancey & Shortliffe, 1984; Frenster, 1989; Coiera, Baud, Console, & Cruz, 1994; Coiera, 1996). MYCIN is probably the most widely known of all medical (and not only) expert systems thus far developed (Shortliffe, 1976). And this is despite the fact that it has never been put into actual practice. It was developed at Stanford University solely as a research effort to provide assistance to physicians in the diagnosis and treatment of meningitis and bacteremia infections. PUFF, DXplain, QMR, and Apache III are also some of the most well-known medical expert systems that were developed and put into use (Metaxiotis, Samouilidis, & Psarras, 2000).

De Burca (2000) outlined the conditions necessary to transform a healthcare organization into a learning organization. Fennessy (2001) discussed how knowledge management problems arising in evidence-based practice can be explored using "soft systems methodology" and action research. Pedersen and Larsen (2001) presented a distributed health knowledge management (DKM) model that structures decision support systems (DSSs) based on product state models (PSMs) among a number of interdependent organizational units. The recurrent information for the DSS comes from a network-wide support for PSMs of the participating organizations.

Ryu, Hee Hp, and Han (2003) dealt with the knowledge sharing behavior of physicians in hospitals; their study investigated the factors affecting physicians' knowledge sharing behavior within a hospital department by employing existing theories, such as the Theory of Reasoned Action and the Theory of Planned Behavior. Torralba-Rodriguez and colleagues (2003) presented an ontological framework for representing and exploiting medical knowledge; they described an approach aimed at building a system able to help medical doctors to follow the evolution of their patients, by integrating the knowledge offered by physicians and the knowledge collected from intelligent alarm systems. Also, Chae, Kim, Tark, Park, and Ho (2003) presented an analysis of healthcare quality

Table 2. Important Web sites dedicated to KM in healthcare

Web Site	Description
www.nelh.nhs.uk/knowledge_management.asp	The National Electronic Library for Health has a link dedicated to knowledge management. It describes how to manage explicit knowledge and outlines revolutions in KM in healthcare.
www.who.int	The World Health Organization has launched the Health Academy, which aims to demystify medical and public health practices, and to make the knowledge of health specialists available to all citizens through Web-based technology. The academy will provide the general public with the health information and knowledge required for preventing diseases and following healthier lifestyles.
www.cochrane.org	The Cochrane Collaboration is an international non-profit and independent organization, dedicated to making up-to-date, accurate information about the effects of healthcare readily available worldwide. The major product of the collaboration is the Cochrane Database of Systematic Reviews, which is published quarterly.
www.AfriAfya.org	AfriAfya, African Network for Health Knowledge Management and Communication, is a consortium formed by well-known agencies such as Aga Khan Health Service in Kenya, CARE International, SatelLife HealthNet, PLAN International, and the Ministry of Health in Kenya to harness the power of information and communication technology for community health.
www.hc-sc.gc.ca/iacb-dgiac/km-gs/english/kmhome.htm	The goal of knowledge management at Health Canada is to use the knowledge that resides in the department—in the minds of its staff, in the relationships they have with other organizations, and in their repositories of information—to fulfill their mission: to help the people of Canada maintain and improve their health.
www.ucl.ac.uk/kmc/index.html	The Knowledge Management Centre is part of the School of Public Policy of University College London (UCL). The Knowledge Management Centre's aim is to improve clinical practice, patient outcomes, and health service innovation and efficiency by promoting better health knowledge management by serving as a resource center and making efficient use of its resources internally and across a network of collaborators.

indicators using data mining for developing quality improvement strategies.

Reviewing the literature, it is concluded that a KM-based healthcare management system should have the following objectives (Shortliffe, 2000; Booth & Walton, 2000):

- To improve access to information and knowledge at all levels (physicians, hospital administrators and staff, consumers of health services, pharmacies, and health insurance companies) so that efficiencies and cost reductions are realized.
- To transform the diverse members (care recipients, physicians, nurses, therapists, pharmacists, suppliers, etc.) of the healthcare sector into a knowledge network/community of practice.
- To enable evidence-based decision making to improve quality of healthcare.

Table 2 presents important Web sites dedicated to the promotion and application of KM to healthcare.

THE KNOWLEDGE MANAGEMENT PROCESS IN HEALTHCARE

In order to examine whether knowledge management can really succeed in healthcare, we can analyze this propo-

Figure 1. The knowledge management process cycle

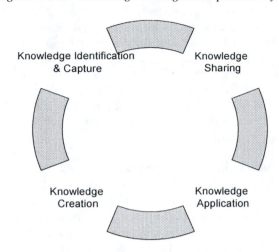

sition in terms of examining the knowledge management process and the likelihood of success for the healthcare organizations in achieving these steps in the process. The KM process consists of four key stages, as shown in Figure 1 (Schwartz, Divitini, & Brasethvik, 2000).

Knowledge identification and capture refer to identifying the critical competencies, types of knowledge, and the right individuals who have the necessary expertise that should be captured. Then, this captured knowledge is shared between individuals, departments, and the like. The knowledge application stage involves applying knowledge—which includes retrieving and using knowledge—in support of decisions, actions, and problem solving, and which ultimately can create new knowledge. As new knowledge is created, it needs to be captured, shared, and applied, and the cycle continues.

Knowledge Identification and Capture in Healthcare

One way to identify the critical knowledge that should be captured and determine the experts in the healthcare organization who have the knowledge on a specific issue (e.g., disease, therapy) is to conduct a knowledge audit. The knowledge audit helps to identify the types of knowledge needed and the appropriate sources (e.g., patient records, medical research literature, medical procedures, drug references) in order to develop a knowledge management strategy for the organization.

On the other hand, the use of intranets is suggested as basic tools for the capture of implicit knowledge. St Helens & Knowsley Health Informatics Service—which covers 320,000 patients—designed and developed an intranet structure with the aim to generate the potential to capture organizational implicit knowledge (Mimnagh, 2002). The real challenge has been to create a health-

community-wide intranet that implements directory services, communities of practice, and lessons learnedt in a way which builds on existing activity and looks for the synergistic effect of adding a KM focus to ongoing work.

Vast amounts of medical knowledge reside within text documents, so that the automatic extraction of such knowledge would certainly be beneficial for clinical activities. Valencia-Garcia and colleagues et al. (2004) presented a user-centered approach for the incremental extraction of knowledge from text, which is based on both knowledge technologies and natural language processing techniques. The system was successfully used to extract clinical knowledge from texts related to oncology and capture it.

Concluding, a key question is whether people would be willing to give up their competitive edge to have their knowledge captured via online repositories, lessons learned, best practices, and the like. This possible dilemma is especially valid in the healthcare sector.

Knowledge Sharing in Healthcare

Productive organizations have the ability to create an environment where specialized knowledge, skills, and abilities of all employees are leveraged to achieve advancements in service industry. However, healthcare organizations cannot be considered as a good example of such organizations. A healthcare organization is a collection of professional specialists who contribute to the delivery of patient care, but also often act competitively inside the organization, without being willing to transfer knowledge because of associated status and power within the organization and the society.

Taking also into account that people in general are not likely to share their knowledge unless they think it is valuable and important, it becomes clear why doctors and physicians are not willing to share and transfer their knowledge. In addition, due to minimal interdisciplinary training, the transfer of tacit knowledge which occurs through apprenticeship style work patterns—for example, internships where junior doctors work alongside a senior clinician in surgery or intensive care—remains problematic (Beveren, 2003).

Effective knowledge management requires a "knowledge sharing" culture to be successful. Especially in healthcare, it is crucial that doctors and physicians understand the benefits of knowledge sharing on a number of levels: benefits to the organization, benefits to patients, and benefits to them personally. The more you can clearly demonstrate these benefits, the more people are likely to be open to change. Doctors and physicians need to be recognized and rewarded in a formal way (e.g., promotions, cash awards) to make knowledge sharing a reality in healthcare.

The Wisecare (Workflow Information Systems for European Nursing Care) project—an EC-funded initiative (1997-1999)—has promoted knowledge sharing using the Internet and online communities. Wisecare provided nurses with a vast amount of information and knowledge about clinical practice through both the Wisecare Web site and data collection tool. This information has been specifically selected to meet their clinical needs and meant nurses had access to relevant knowledge extremely quickly.

Lesson learned systems can also be an effective knowledge sharing approach to be used in healthcare (Yassin & Antia, 2003).

Knowledge Application in Healthcare

Knowledge application refers to taking the shared knowledge and internalizing it within one's perspective and worldviews. For the healthcare organizations the reality is that technology can only fulfill some of their needs. And how well it fulfills them depends critically on managing the knowledge behind them—content management, assigning knowledge roles, and so forth. Tom Davenport (2002), a prominent author on knowledge management, is often quoted as offering the following rule of thumb: your investment in technology in terms of both cost and effort should stay under one-third of the total knowledge management effort—otherwise you are going wrong somewhere.

Knowledge-enabling technologies which can effectively be applied to healthcare organizations are:

- Groupware
- Intranet
- Collaborative tools (e.g., discussion boards, video-conferencing)
- Portals
- Taxonomies

Abidi (2001) presented the Healthcare Enterprise Memory (HEM) with the functionality to acquire, share, and operationalize the various modalities of healthcare knowledge. Davenport (2002) outlined how Partners Health Care System in Boston implemented an enormously successful expert-intervention KM solution. Case studies from the UK's National Health Service (NHS) and the Department of Health illustrated the drive towards modernization and more effective collaborative working among public-sector healthcare systems (Ark Group, 2002).

Knowledge Creation in Healthcare

In general, knowledge creation may take the form of new products or services, increased innovation, and improved customer relationships. In the healthcare setting, knowledge creation can take place in terms of improved organizational processes and systems in hospitals, advances in medical methods and therapies, better patient relationship management practices, and improved ways of working within the healthcare organization. Given the various constraints and barriers occur in the healthcare sector, it takes longer for a new idea to be implemented in the healthcare setting versus that in the business sector.

A few examples of knowledge creation technologies that can be used in healthcare are:

- **Data Mining:** Tools that analyze data in very large databases, and look for trends and patterns that can be used to improve organizational processes.
- **Information Visualization:** Computer-supported interactive visual representations of abstract data to help improve understanding.

CONCLUSION

Knowledge is a critical tool for health, and knowledge management is the capacity to translate research results (knowledge) into policies and practices that can improve the quality of life and lengthen survival. Managing knowledge in a healthcare organization is like trying to knit with thousands of strands of knotted wool; data is held in a number of locations, managed by a variety of people, and stored in every imaginable format. Perhaps in no other sector does knowledge management have such a high promise.

Delivering healthcare to patients is a very complex endeavor that is highly dependent on information. Healthcare organizations rely on information about the science of care, individual patients, care provided, results of care, as well as its performance to provide, coordinate, and integrate services. The traditional single physician-patient relationship is increasingly being replaced by one in which the patient is managed by a team of health care professionals each specializing in one aspect of care. Hence, the ability to access and use the electronic healthcare record (EHCR) of the patient is fundamental. In addition, the transformation of healthcare data into a strategic decision-support resource is fundamental too.

KM can be approached in numerous ways to serve particular needs and conditions. Successful KM practices typically need to be supported by complementary efforts in different domains. IT-related support activities and infrastructures are very important. They serve vital functions, are complex, costly, and often take time to design and implement. In the case of healthcare, building the infrastructure for a KM practice requires extensive effort due to the peculiarities of the health sector (e.g., legal and ethical issues, complex procedures for provision of healthcare, doctors' behavior, etc.).

Coming back to the original question—*How can we make knowledge management work in healthcare?*—and by examining the knowledge management process, we can see that there are positive and negative points as to whether KM will truly work in the healthcare sector. Some people in healthcare think that KM is a passing fad like Total Quality Management, Business Process Reengineering, and other administration-backed initiatives. It is unfortunate to think in this light, as knowledge sharing should be encouraged so that lessons can be learned. KM solutions can facilitate the transfer of patient medical information, access to new treatment protocols as they emerge, knowledge exchange among experts, and so on.

Future research needs to be devoted to measuring the success of KM in healthcare organizations, showing quantitative benefits, and producing a "Return on Investment" index. Measurement is the least-developed aspect of KM because of the inherent difficulty to measure something that cannot be seen, such as knowledge (Bose, 2004). However, this is a very crucial issue since the future usage of KM is heavily dependent on both the quality of the metrics and whether output generated by this metric management would provide tangible value addition to the healthcare organizations. Integration of KM with e-health is also another direction for further research.

REFERENCES

Antrobus, S. (1997). Developing the nurse as a knowledge worker in health—learning the artistry of practice. *Journal of Advanced Nursing, 25*(4), 823-829.

Ark Group. (2002). Inside knowledge. *Knowledge Management, 6*(4).

Beveren, J. (2003). Does health care for knowledge management? *Journal of Knowledge Management, 7*(1), 90-95.

Booth, A. (2001). Managing knowledge for clinical excellence: Ten building blocks. *Journal of Clinical Excellence, 3*(4), 25-32.

Booth, A., & Walton, G. (2000). *Managing knowledge in health services.* Library Association Publishing.

Bose, R. (2003). Knowledge management-enabled healthcare management systems: capabilities, infrastructure and decision support. *Expert Systems with Applications, 24,* 59-71.

Bose, R. (2004). Knowledge management metrics. *Industrial Management & Data Systems, 104*(6), 457-468.

Brailer, D. (1999). Management of knowledge in the modern health care delivery system. *Joint Commission Journal on Quality Improvement, 25*(1), 1-7.

Chae, Y., Kim, H., Tark, K., Park, H., & Ho, S. (2003). Analysis of healthcare quality indicators using data mining and decision support systems. *Expert Systems with Applications, 24,* 167-172.

Clancey, B.C., & Shortliffe, E.H. (1984). *Medical artificial intelligence: The first decade.* Boston: Addison-Wesley.

Coiera, E. (1996). Artificial intelligence in medicine: The challenges ahead. *Journal of the American Medical Association, 6,* 363-366.

Coiera, E., Baud, R., Console, L., & Cruz, J. (1994). *The role of knowledge based systems in clinical practice.* Holland: IOS Press.

Davenport, T. (2002). Making knowledge work productive and effective. *Knowledge Management, 6*(1).

Davenport, T., & Beck, J. (2002). The strategy and structure of firms in the attention economy. *Ivey Business Journal, 66*(4), 48-54.

De Burca, S. (2000). The learning healthcare organization. *International Journal for Quality in Healthcare, 12*(6), 456-458.

Deming, W. (1986). *Out of the crisis.* Cambridge, MA: MIT Press.

Fennessy, G. (2001). Knowledge management in evidence based healthcare: Issues raised when specialist information services searched for the evidence. *Health Informatics Journal, 7*(1), 1-5.

Folland, S., Goodman, A., & Stano, M. (1997). *The economics of health and health care.* Englewood Cliffs, NJ: Prentice-Hall.

Frenster, J. (1989). *Expert systems and open systems in medical artificial intelligence.* Physicians' Educational Series.

Heathfield, H., & Louw, G. (1999). New challenges for clinical informatics: Knowledge management tools. *Health Informatics Journal, 5*(2), 67-73.

Juran, J. (1988). *Juran's quality control handbook* (4th ed.). New York: McGraw-Hill.

Metaxiotis, K., Samouilidis, J.-E., & Psarras, J. (2000). Expert systems in medicine: Academic illusion or real power? *Journal of Informatics in Primary Care*, (February), 3-8.

Mimnagh, C. (2002). Towards capturing implicit knowledge: A practical application of intranet development. *Proceedings of the Conference in Advances in Clinical Knowledge Management 5*, London.

Pedersen, M., & Larsen, M. (2001). Distributed knowledge management based on product state models—the case of decision support in healthcare administration. *Decision Support Systems, 31*, 139-158.

Ryu, S., Hee Hp, S., & Han, I. (2003). Knowledge sharing behavior of physicians in hospitals. *Expert Systems with Applications, 25*, 113-122.

Schwartz, D., Divitini, M., & Brasethvik, T. (2000). Knowledge management in the Internet age. In D. Schwartz, M. Divitini, & T. Brasethvik (Eds.), *Internet-based knowledge management and organizational memory* (pp. 1-23). Hershey, PA: Idea Group Publishing.

Shortliffe, E. (2000). *Medical informatics.* New York: Springer-Verlag.

Shortliffe, E.H. (1976). *Computer-based medical consultations: MYCIN.* Elsevier.

Torralba-Rodriguez, F., Fernandez-Breis, J., Garcia, R., Ruiz-Sanchez, J., Martinez-Bejar, R., & Gomez-Rubi, J. (2003). An ontological framework for representing and exploiting medical knowledge. *Expert Systems with Applications, 25*, 211-230.

Valencia-Garcia, R., Ruiz-Sanchez, J., Vivancos-Vicente, P., Fernandez-Breis, J., & Martinez-Bejar, R. (2004). An incremental approach for discovering medical knowledge from texts. *Expert Systems with Applications, 26*(3), 291-299.

Wickramasinghe, N., & Ginzberg, M. (2001). Integrating knowledge workers and the organization: The role of IT. *International Journal of Healthcare Quality Assurance, 14*(6), 245-253.

Wyatt, J. (2001). *Clinical knowledge and practice in the information age: A handbook for health professionals.* Royal Society of Medicine Press.

Yassin, K., & Antia, B. (2003). Quality assurance of the knowledge exchange process: A factor in the success of child health programs in developing countries. *International Journal of Health Care Quality Assurance, 16*(1), 9-20.

Yu-N, C., & Abidi, S. (1999). Evaluating the efficacy of knowledge management towards healthcare enterprise modeling. *Proceedings of the International Joint Conference on Artificial Intelligence.*

KEY TERMS

Collaborative Tools: Electronic tools that support communication and collaboration—people working together; essentially they take the form of networked computer software.

Distributed Knowledge Management Model: The model which combines the interdependence of one partial product state model to others with the idea of knowledge acquisition rather than just the operational exchange relationship.

Evidence-Based Medicine: Healthcare based on best practice which is encoded in the form of clinical guidelines and protocols.

Groupware: Specific software which allows groups of people to share information and to coordinate their activities over a computer network.

Healthcare Enterprise Memory: A KM info-structure which supports the functionality to acquire, share, and operationalize the various modalities of knowledge existent in a healthcare enterprise.

Information Visualization: Computer-supported interactive visual representations of abstract data which help improve understanding.

Taxonomy: A hierarchical structure for organizing a body of knowledge; it gives a framework for understanding and classifying knowledge.

ENDNOTE

[1] The Health Care Financing Administration, *National Health Expenditures* (1998).

A Hierarchical Model for Knowledge Management

Nicolas Prat
ESSEC Business School, France

INTRODUCTION

Knowledge management (KM) is a multidisciplinary subject, with contributions from such disciplines as information systems (IS) and information technology (IT), strategic management, organizational theory, human-resource management, education science, psychology, cognitive science, and artificial intelligence. In order to take full advantage of these various contributions, the necessity of a multidisciplinary approach to KM is currently widely acknowledged, particularly in the IS and IT, management, and artificial-intelligence communities (Alavi & Leidner, 2001; Dieng-Kuntz et al., 2001; Grover & Davenport, 2001; Nonaka & Konno, 1998; O'Leary & Studer, 2001; Zacklad & Grundstein, 2001).

Several KM models have been proposed in the literature. These models reflect the diversity of disciplines contributing to KM. By describing KM concepts and investigating their relationships, they provide a useful conceptual tool for KM research and practice. However, they suffer from three major limitations.

- They are often incomplete. This may be intentional (in the case of models focusing on a specific aspect of KM) or reflect disproportionate emphasis on one of the disciplines contributing to KM, for example, IS and IT.
- They are inappropriate for navigating between abstraction levels of KM topics ("drill down" or "drill up").
- They do not provide a structure for the quantitative assessment of KM research and/or practice (e.g., for auditing KM practice in a specific company).

This article presents a KM model that aims at providing a solution to these three problems. The model is formalized and structured as a hierarchy, which enables navigation between the abstraction levels of KM topics. Furthermore, by combining this hierarchical structure with the analytic hierarchy process (Saaty, 1980), the KM model may be applied to quantitatively assess KM practice and/or research. The model is organized into three components: knowledge types, KM processes, and *KM context*. It integrates the contribution of previous models and reflects the multidisciplinary aspect of KM.

The article is structured as follows. The next section provides an overview of extant KM models, that is, the background of our work. Then the article presents our hierarchical KM model, develops its three components, and discusses and illustrates how the model may be applied to KM research and practice. Before concluding, we present our view of future trends and research opportunities regarding KM models.

KM MODELS

ISO (2004) defines a model as a "limited representation of something suitable for some purpose." This definition applies to KM models. In broad terms, the purpose of these models is to provide conceptual tools for KM research and/or practice.

Figure 1 proposes a classification of KM models. This classification elaborates on and refines the classification criteria proposed by Holsapple and Joshi (1999) for KM *frameworks*. Figure 1 uses the UML (unified modeling language) formalism (OMG, 2003) for representing classes, generalizations, and generalization constraints. We classify KM models according to four complementary criteria (the first two criteria are those defined in Holsapple and Joshi).

- A KM model is either *descriptive* (i.e., describing the nature of KM phenomena) or *prescriptive* (i.e., proposing methodologies for performing KM).
- KM models are either *broad* or *thematic*. Broad models attempt to cover the whole of KM, while thematic models focus on a specific topic.
- A KM model may be *abstract*, *detailed*, or both (as indicated by the generalization constraint in Figure 1). This classification complements the distinction between broad and thematic models. For example, a broad model may be both abstract (providing a global view of KM concepts or topics) and detailed (enabling navigation into the details of a topic).
- The last classification distinguishes between *semantic* and *analytic* models. Semantic models describe the meaning of KM concepts and their interrelationships. Analytic models adopt a deductive

Figure 1. A classification of KM models

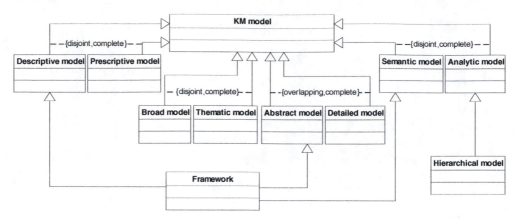

approach, progressively detailing KM topics by decomposing them into subtopics.

In addition to these four classifications, Figure 1 represents two specific types of KM models: frameworks (defined as KM models that are at the same time descriptive, abstract, and semantic) and *hierarchical models* (a special kind of analytic model).

Several KM models have been proposed in the literature (Alavi & Leidner, 2001; Davenport & Prusak, 2000; Despres & Chauvel, 2000; Fowler, 2000; Grover & Davenport, 2001; Handzic, 2001; Holsapple & Joshi, 2004; Newman & Conrad, 2000; Nissen, 2002; Nonaka, 1994). A comparative analysis is presented later in this article. If we consider the above-presented classifications, we notice that existing KM models are often descriptive, abstract, and semantic models, that is, frameworks. All the models are semantic. Consequently, elaborating on the contribution of these models, our objective is to define an integrated, analytic KM model. This broad, analytic model will facilitate navigation into the details of KM topics and enable the quantitative assessment of KM research and/or practice.

A HIERARCHICAL KM MODEL

In this section, we present our KM model and compare it with previous models; we discuss and illustrate how it may be applied to KM research and practice.

Introduction

KM comprises a set of processes. These processes concern knowledge (e.g., knowledge transfer) and are influenced by context (e.g., the organizational culture). Consequently, KM models are often structured around the concepts of KM processes, knowledge, and/or context (Alavi & Leidner, 2001; Despres & Chauvel, 2000; Grover & Davenport, 2001; Handzic, 2001; Holsapple & Joshi, 2004). These concepts form the three basic components of our model.

- The *knowledge types* component characterizes knowledge according to several complementary classifications.
- The *KM processes* component is dedicated to KM activities.
- Finally, the KM context component comprises the factors that influence (positively or negatively) the conduct of KM. Depending or their nature, these factors may (more or less easily) be controlled to improve KM.

The components of our KM model are organized into a hierarchy. The concepts of the model are represented as nodes. The parent-child relationships between nodes are abstraction relationships: A parent node is detailed by its children nodes (or conversely, a child is abstracted into its parent). There are no generally applicable structural criteria indicating when decomposition should stop. This is guided by semantic and practical considerations (e.g., the decomposition of a concept stops when the concept is easy enough to measure in practice or when further decomposition would be meaningless).

We describe the three components of the KM model.

Knowledge Types

The part of the KM model pertaining to knowledge types is represented in Figure 2. Elaborating on previous work, we propose four complementary classifications for characterizing knowledge.

The first classification, which is almost universally adopted in previous KM models, distinguishes between

Figure 2. Knowledge types

tacit and explicit knowledge. Similarly to Nissen (2002), we use the term *explicitness* to name this classification. The distinction between tacit and explicit knowledge was first applied to KM by Nonaka (1994). Tacit knowledge is deeply rooted in the individual's mind and may not be easily codified as opposed to explicit knowledge.

The *reach* classification makes the distinction between individual and collective knowledge. Collective knowledge is further decomposed into group, organizational, and interorganizational knowledge. In general terms, the concept of organizational knowledge may designate knowledge at the organization or at the group level. The reach classification appears in many KM models (e.g., the model of Nissen, 2002, has a reach dimension).

The *abstraction-level* classification distinguishes between specific and general (abstract) knowledge. This distinction appears explicitly in the model of Fowler (2000). The distinction is relevant to KM since knowledge is often more easily transmitted when it is in a specific form (examples). This principle is applied in such methods as case-based reasoning (Kolodner, 1993; Prat, 2001a) and narratives (Soulier, 2000).

The last classification distinguishes between declarative knowledge ("know-what") and procedural knowledge ("know-how"). Since declarative knowledge is made of propositions, this classification is called *propositionality*. Procedural and declarative knowledge are often assimilated to tacit and explicit knowledge respectively. However, the two classifications are not equivalent (For example, the sequence of steps necessary to make a coffee with a coffee machine is procedural knowledge that may easily be made explicit). Procedural knowledge is richer than declarative knowledge. In particular, procedural knowledge comprises the various choice alternatives considered: and the choice criteria (Rolland, Souveyet, & Moreno, 1995). In this respect, the traceability of design processes and decisions is a key research direction for KM (Karsenty, 2001; Prat, 2001b; Zamfiroiu & Prat, 2001).

KM Processes

Figure 3 represents the KM processes component. In contrast with previous KM models, which often focus on the basic processes (knowledge creation, storage, transfer, and utilization) and/or consider all the processes to be at the same level, we distinguish between an operational level comprising the basic processes and a strategic or tactical level (planning, modeling, and control).

Operational processes are the basic processes of KM. Even if the number and names of operational processes may vary, the majority of KM models comprise the same fundamental processes. The typology we use in our model draws heavily from Prat (2001a).

- **Knowledge acquisition** comprises all activities that increase the global stock of knowledge potentially useful to the organization.
- **Knowledge storage** consists in retaining knowledge in individual or collective memory. Knowledge is indexed to facilitate future retrieval.
- **Knowledge transfer** is the sharing of knowledge between individuals, groups, and organizations.
- **Knowledge utilization** is the application of knowledge to business processes.

The *planning*, *modeling*, and *control processes* encompass the following processes.
- The *identification*, *mapping*, and *modeling* of current knowledge or of knowledge necessary to achieve previously defined objectives.
- Evaluation, which may be operated at various levels: the *evaluation* of knowledge, the evaluation of KM projects and/or of KM systems (KMSs) resulting from these projects, and the evaluation of KM.
- Knowledge *update*. This process includes unlearning (forgetting). Although unlearning is often neglected by the IS and IT community, the organiza-

Figure 3. KM processes

tional-theory and strategic-management literature often emphasise this key process, which is often a condition for the acquisition of new knowledge (Huber, 1991; Tarondeau, 2002; Walsh & Ungson, 1991).

- The *protection* of knowledge through various means (patents, firewalls, etc.).

KM Context

This last component of the KM model comprises the factors that may positively or negatively influence KM (Figure 4). Whenever possible, these factors should be used to leverage KM efforts.

Strategy is refined into *mission, vision, objectives, policies* (rules), and *allocated resources*. The latter may be financial, human, or material resources.

The organization comprises the following subtopics:

- *Organizational structure.*
- *Business processes*, into which the KM processes should ideally be incorporated. Following Davenport and Short (1990), we distinguish between operational and managerial processes, the latter being often more knowledge based.
- The *physical work environment.*
- *KM-specific structures*, that is, communities of practice or formal structures.
- *KM-specific functions*: chief knowledge officer (CKO), knowledge manager, technical functions.

The *culture* of an organization is crucial to the success of KM (Grover & Davenport, 2001).

Leadership is mentioned in several KM models, underlying the role of senior management support in the success of KM.

Human-resource management influences *individuals* and their *behaviors*.

Information technologies, techniques, and methods are a key KM enabler and facilitator, although it is generally admitted that technology should not represent more

than one third of a KM project (Davenport & Prusak, 2000; Smith & Farquhar, 2000).

Information technologies, techniques, and methods include *project management methods*, IS development *methods and models, groupware and workflow, document management, databases, data warehouses* and *business intelligence, multimedia*, the *Web*, and *artificial intelligence*. The latter two are discussed in detail below.

The Web comprises architectures (Internet, intranet, extranet, and portals), search engines, and languages (primarily HTML [hypertext markup language] and XML [extensible markup language]).

Artificial intelligence includes the following topics.

- *Expert systems* apply to the representation and utilization of explicit knowledge.
- *Machine learning* permits the generation of new knowledge. Following Michalski (1993), we distinguish three types of learning: inductive learning (from specific to general), analogical learning (specific to specific, or general to general), and deductive learning (general to specific).
- *Intelligent agents* and *multiagent systems* apply to knowledge searching on the Web.
- *Ontologies* also permit the improvement of knowledge searching on the Web in conjunction with XML (semantic Web).
- The *methods and models of knowledge engineering* and *capitalization* include REX (Eichenbaum, Malvache, & Prieur, 1994), MKSM (Ermine, 2001), MEREX (Corbel, 1997), and CommonKADS (Breuker & van de Welde, 1994).

Finally, KM is influenced by the *environment*. Drawing from Holsapple and Joshi (2004) and Reix (2000), we decompose the environment into the *market*; the *competition*; the *technological, cultural,* and *geographical environments; laws and regulations*; and the *governmental, economic, political,* and *social climates*.

Comparison with Previous Models

Table 1 illustrates which topics of our KM model are covered by previous work. For the sake of readability, we only consider the first two detail levels of our model. Table 1 shows that while previous KM models are complementary and thereby contribute to the definition of our model, none of these models covers the whole range of topics covered by ours (this would have been made even more visible if we had considered the more detailed levels of our hierarchy). The most complete model that we have found is the ontology developed by Holsapple and Joshi (2004). However, this ontology, like the other models, is a semantic model, which is inappropriate for navigating

Figure 4. KM context

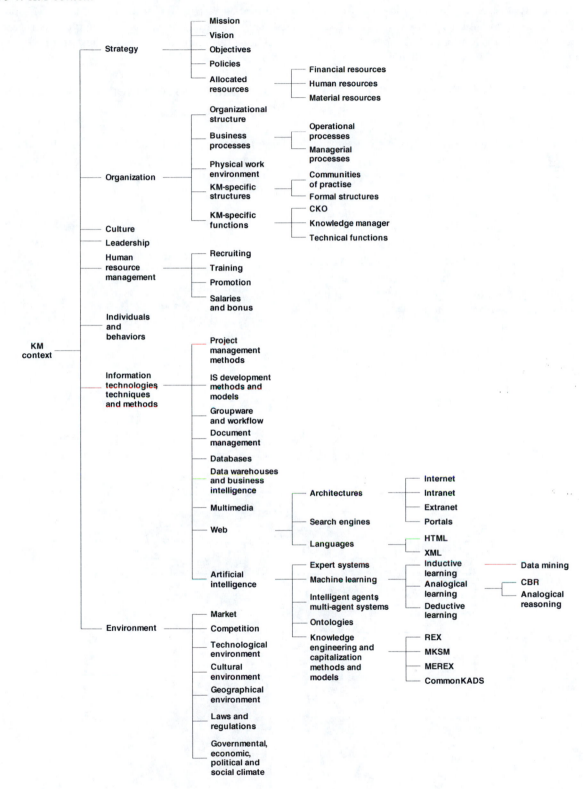

between abstraction levels of KM topics and for quantitatively assessing KM research and practice. On the contrary, navigation and quantitative assessment are facilitated by our hierarchical KM model. This opens the way to different applications both in research and practice.

Application to KM Research and Practice

Navigation Between Abstraction Levels of KM Topics

KM models (more specifically, broad models) should enable researchers and practitioners to examine KM concepts at various levels of detail, and to navigate from abstract levels to detailed levels (drill down) or from detailed levels to abstract levels (drill up). However, even if semantic KM models may comprise concepts of various levels of detail, they do not allow easy navigation between these levels. On the contrary, hierarchies provide a natural mechanism for organizing information of

various detail levels, and for navigating between these levels (Saaty, 1999). Consequently, our KM model, by its very hierarchical structure, enables KM practitioners and researchers to master the complexity of KM phenomena.

Quantitative Assessment of KM Research and Practice

Based on the hierarchical structure of the KM model, the analytic hierarchy process (Saaty, 1980) may be applied to the quantitative assessment of KM by taking the following steps.

1. A subhierarchy of the hierarchical KM model is selected depending on what needs to be assessed and for what purpose.
2. Weights are determined for the nodes of the subhierarchy.
3. The weighed subhierarchy is used for performing evaluations. For each evaluated item, scores are

Table 1. Topics covered by KM models

	Alavi & Leidner (2001)	Davenport & Prusak (2000); Grover & Davenport (2001)	Despres & Chauvel (2000)	Fowler (2000)	Handzic (2001)	Holsapple & Joshi (2004)	Newman & Conrad (2000)	Nissen (2002)	Nonaka (1994)
1. Knowledge types									
1.1. Explicitness									
1.2. Reach									
1.3. Abstraction level									
1.4. Propositionality									
2. KM processes									
2.1. Operational processes									
2.2. Planning, modeling, and control processes									
3. KM context									
3.1. Strategy									
3.2. Organization									
3.3. Culture									
3.4. Leadership									
3.5. Human-resource management									
3.6. Individuals and behaviors									
3.7. Information technologies, techniques, and methods									
3.8. Environment									

Legend:
□ = Not covered   ▨ = Partly or informally covered   ■ = Covered

entered for the end nodes of the subhierarchy. Aggregated scores, including the global score of the item, are calculated based on the previously defined weights.

Assessment of KM Practice

In practice, the KM model can be applied to evaluate (audit) the KM maturity of a given organization. The analytic hierarchy process is perfectly adapted to auditing, as illustrated by the INFAUDITOR system (Akoka, Comyn-Wattiau, & Prat, 1993). The subhierarchy of the KM model chosen for KM auditing typically includes the KM processes and KM context. Weights assigned to the nodes of the subhierarchy reflect the relative priorities of the audited organization with respect to KM (e.g., information technologies, techniques, and methods are more important than leadership, etc.).

We illustrate this application of the KM model with the Cap Gemini and Ernst & Young case (Figure 5). This is simply an illustrating example and by no means a judgment on the way these two companies have handled KM. Information was gathered from secondary sources (Davenport, 1997; Hjertzén & Toll, 1999; Lara, Andreu, & Sieber, 2002). The example was treated using the Descriptor® tool, which supports the analytic hierarchy process (Adexys, 2004).

We consider KM at Ernst & Young and Cap Gemini respectively, before Cap Gemini acquired Ernst & Young in 2000. Our KM model is applied to evaluate and compare KM practices in these two companies. We assume that two levels of detail (not counting the root) are sufficient for getting a first impression of KM practices in the two companies. We exclude the KM types component. Moreover, in the KM context, we exclude the factors environment, and individuals and behaviors (the companies supposedly have limited control on the environment and can control individuals and behaviors only indirectly). We assign weights to the remaining nodes of the subhierarchy. We obtain the weighed subhierarchy represented in the left part of Figure 5 (e.g., information technologies, techniques, and methods count as one third of the KM context). We then use this weighed subhierarchy to assess KM for the two companies, entering scores for the end nodes. The final and intermediary KM scores for the two companies are computed and shown in the table of Figure 5. The final results illustrate the predominant KM

Figure 5. Applying the KM model

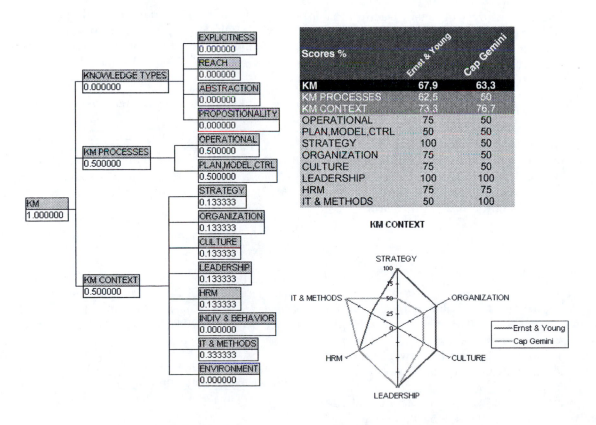

Scores %	Ernst & Young	Cap Gemini
KM	67,9	63,3
KM PROCESSES	62,5	50
KM CONTEXT	73,3	76,7
OPERATIONAL	75	50
PLAN,MODEL,CTRL	50	50
STRATEGY	100	50
ORGANIZATION	75	50
CULTURE	75	50
LEADERSHIP	100	100
HRM	75	75
IT & METHODS	50	100

orientation for the two companies (IT for Cap Gemini and strategy, organization, and culture for Ernst & Young). Based on these results, we may decide to investigate more precisely one aspect of the KM process or context (e.g., the topic of planning, modeling, and control processes). To this end, we would need to change the selection of the subhierarchy and the definition of the weights; however, the approach would remain the same.

Assessment of KM Research

In research, the KM model can be used to compare, contrast, and combine the contributions of different disciplines to KM. Thanks to the hierarchical structure, the commonalities, differences, and profiles of different disciplines can be represented and analyzed at various levels of detail. For example, the score of a given discipline for the tacit-knowledge end node of the KM model can be computed as the frequency in which the word tacit appears in a sample of publications of this discipline relating to KM.

FUTURE TRENDS

By their very structure, hierarchical KM models support navigation between the levels of detail of KM topics. Furthermore, coupled with the analytic hierarchy process, they permit the quantitative evaluation of KM practice and research at various levels of detail. Due to these advantages, we predict a growing interest for such models.

Despite the advantages of hierarchical KM models, they can not replace semantic models for describing and defining KM concepts and explicitly representing the complexity of their relationships. Therefore, since the two types of models do not serve the same purposes, we suggest that they be used complementarily.

Our future research plans concern (a) further applications of our hierarchical KM model to the quantitative assessment of KM research and practice, and (b) ways of combining in practice our KM model with one or several semantic models.

CONCLUSION

In this article, we have presented a hierarchical model for KM research and practice. The model integrates the contributions of previous works. Furthermore, its hierarchical structure eases the navigation between the detail levels of KM topics, and permits quantitative evaluations of KM research and practice.

To the best of our knowledge, no hierarchical KM model had been defined so far. Marchand, Kettinger, and

Rollins (2000) present a model to assess the information orientation of a firm. However, this model has few levels of detail and concerns information rather than knowledge management. Van den Hooff, Vijvers, and de Ridder (2003) present an instrument that companies can use to assess their KM maturity. However, for the most part, this instrument is informal and therefore may not appropriately be called a model.

We do not contend that our KM model is completely stable. However, the hierarchical structure of the model makes it easy to update.

It is our hope that this article will incite more research on hierarchical KM models and on their application to KM-research and practice quantitative assessment.

ACKNOWLEDGMENTS

The author wishes to thank Thomas Lavelle and the anonymous reviewers for their constructive and helpful comments on the present article.

REFERENCES

Adexys. (2004). *Descriptor, version 4.1*. Retrieved June 30, 2004, from *http://www.adexys.com*

Akoka, J., Comyn-Wattiau, I., & Prat, N. (1993). INFAUDITOR: An expert system for information system auditing. *Proceedings of the International Computing Congress (ICC'93)*, Hyderabad, India.

Alavi, M., & Leidner, D. (2001). Knowledge management and knowledge management systems: Conceptual foundations and research issues. *MIS Quarterly, 25*(1), 107-136.

Breuker, J., & van de Welde, W. (Eds.). (1994). *CommonKADS Library for expertise modeling, reusable problem solving components*. Amsterdam: IOS Press.

Corbel, J.-C. (1997). Méthodologie de retour d'expérience: Démarche MEREX de Renault. In J.-M. Fouet (Ed.), *Connaissances et savoir-faire en entreprise*. Paris: Hermès.

Davenport, T. (1997). *Knowledge management case study: Knowledge management at Ernst & Young, 1997*. Retrieved October 15, 2004, from *http://www.bus.utexas.edu/kman/E&Y.htm*

Davenport, T., & Short, J. E. (1990). The new industrial engineering: Information technology and business process redesign. *Sloan Management Review, 31*(4), 11-27.

Davenport, T. H., & Prusak, L. (2000). *Working knowledge: How organizations manage what they know.* Harvard Business School Press.

Despres, C., & Chauvel, D. (2000). How to map knowledge management. In D. Marchand, T. Davenport, & T. Dickson (Eds.), *Mastering information management* (pp. 170-176). London: Prentice Hall.

Dieng-Kuntz, R., Corby, O., Gandon, F., Giboin, A., Golebiowska, J., Matta, N., et al. (2001). *Méthodes et outils pour la gestion des connaissances: Une approche pluridisciplinaire du knowledge management.* Paris: Dunod.

Eichenbaum, C., Malvache, P., & Prieur, P. (1994). La maîtrise du retour d'expérience avec la méthode REX. *Performances Humaines et Techniques, 3-4*(69), 6-20.

Ermine, J.-L. (2001). Capitaliser et partager les connaissances avec la méthode MKSM. In M. Zacklad & M. Grundstein (Eds.), *Ingénierie et capitalisation des connaissances.* Paris: Hermès.

Fowler, A. (2000). The role of AI-based technology in support of the knowledge management value activity cycle. *Journal of Strategic Information Systems, 9*(2-3), 107-128.

Grover, V., & Davenport, T. H. (2001). General perspectives on knowledge management: Fostering a research agenda. *Journal of Management Information Systems, 18*(1), 5-21.

Handzic, M. (2001). Knowledge management: A research framework. *Proceedings of the 2nd European Conference on Knowledge Management (ECKM 2001),* Bled, Slovenia.

Hjertzén, E., & Toll, J. (1999). Knowledge management at Cap Gemini. In *Measuring knowledge management at Cap Gemini AB* (chap. 5, pp. 55-64). Master's thesis, Linköpings Universitet. Retrieved October 15, 2004, from *http://www.tollsoft.com/thesis/paper.html*

Holsapple, C. W., & Joshi, K. D. (1999). Description and analysis of existing knowledge management frameworks. *Proceedings of the 32nd Hawaii International Conference on System Sciences (HICSS 99),* HI.

Holsapple, C. W., & Joshi, K. D. (2004). A formal knowledge management ontology: Conduct, activities, resources, and influences. *Journal of the American Society for Information Science and Technology, 55*(7), 593-612.

Huber, G. P. (1991). Organizational learning: The contributing processes and the literatures. *Organization Science, 2*(1), 88-115.

ISO. (2004). *ISO 18876 integration of industrial data for exchange, access, and sharing: Glossary of terms.* Retrieved October 15, 2004, from *http://www.tc184-sc4.org/ISO18876/glossary.cfm*

Karsenty, L. (2001). Capitaliser le contexte des décisions en conception. In M. Zacklad & M. Grundstein (Eds.), *Management des connaissances: Modèles d'entreprise et applications* (pp. 49-70). Paris: Hermès.

Kolodner, J. (1993). *Case-based reasoning.* San Mateo, CA: Morgan Kaufmann.

Lara, E., Andreu, R., & Sieber, S. (2002). *A case study of knowledge management at Cap Gemini Ernst & Young.* (European Case Clearing House [ECCH] No. 302-164-1)

Marchand, D., Kettinger, W., & Rollins, J. (2000). Information orientation: People, technology and the bottom line. *Sloan Management Review, 41*(4), 69-80.

Michalski, R. S. (1993). Toward a unified theory of learning: Multi-strategy task-adaptive learning. In B. G. Buchanan & D. C. Wilkins (Eds.), *Readings in knowledge acquisition and learning: Automating the construction and improvement of expert systems.* Morgan Kaufmann.

Newman, B., & Conrad, K. (2000). A framework for characterizing knowledge management methods, practices, and technologies. *Proceedings of the 3rd International Conference on Practical Aspects of Knowledge Management (PAKM 2000),* Basel, Switzerland.

Nissen, M. E. (2002). An extended model of knowledge-flow dynamics. *Communications of the Association for Information Systems, 8,* 251-266.

Nonaka, I. (1994). A dynamic theory of organizational knowledge creation. *Organization Science, 5*(1), 14-37.

Nonaka, I., & Konno, N. (1998). The concept of "Ba": Building a foundation for knowledge creation. *California Management Review, 40*(3), 40-54.

O'Leary, D. E., & Studer, R. (2001). Knowledge management: An interdisciplinary approach. *IEEE Intelligent Systems, 16*(1), 24-25.

OMG. (2003). *Unified modeling language (UML) specification, version 1.5.* Retrieved January 15, 2004, from *http://www.omg.org/technnology/documents/formal/uml.htm*

Prat, N. (2001a). Automating knowledge indexing and retrieval in soft domains. *Proceedings of the 2nd European Conference on Knowledge Management (ECKM 2001),* Bled, Slovenia.

Prat, N. (2001b). STEP PC: A generic tool for design knowledge capture and reuse. In R. Roy (Ed.), *Industrial knowledge management: A micro-level approach* (pp. 317-334). London: Springer Verlag.

Reix, R. (2000). *Systèmes d'information et management des organisations.* Paris: Vuibert.

Rolland, C., Souveyet, C., & Moreno, M. (1995). An approach for defining ways of working. *Information Systems Journal, 20*(4), 337-359.

Saaty, T. (1980). *The analytic hierarchy process.* New York: McGraw Hill.

Saaty, T. (1999). *Decision making for leaders.* Pittsburgh, PA: RWS Publications.

Smith, R. G., & Farquhar, A. (2000). The road ahead for knowledge management. *AI Magazine, 21*(4), 17-40.

Soulier, E. (2000). Les récits d'apprentissage et le partage des connaissances dans les organisations: Nouvelles pistes de recherche. *Systèmes d'Information et Management, 5*(2), 59-78.

Tarondeau, J.-C. (2002). *Le management des savoirs.* Paris: PUF. In Collection que sais-je?

van den Hooff, B., Vijvers, J., & de Ridder, J. (2003). Foundations and applications of a knowledge management scan. *European Management Journal, 21*(2), 237-245.

Walsh, J. P., & Ungson, G. R. (1991). Organizational memory. *Academy of Management Review, 16*(1), 57-91.

Zacklad, M., & Grundstein, M. (Eds.). (2001). *Management des connaissances: Modèles d'entreprise et applications.* Paris: Hermès.

Zamfiroiu, M., & Prat, N. (2001). Traçabilité du processus de conception des systèmes d'information. In C. Cauvet & C. Rosenthal-Sabroux (Eds.), *Ingénierie des systèmes d'information.* Paris: Hermès.

KEY TERMS

Knowledge Acquisition: Comprises all activities that increase the global stock of knowledge potentially useful to the organization. An organization may acquire new knowledge through creation or other means (e.g., acquisition of another organization, communication with consultants, etc.).

Knowledge Indexing: Consists in organizing knowledge in individual or collective memory in order to ease its subsequent retrieval.

Knowledge Protection: Ensures that knowledge will be transferred only to authorized individuals, groups, or organizations.

Knowledge Retrieval: Consists in accessing knowledge previously stored in individual or collective memory. Knowledge retrieval makes use of the index defined when that knowledge was stored.

Knowledge Storage: Consists in retaining knowledge in individual or collective memory. When knowledge is stored, it is indexed in memory.

Knowledge Transfer: The sharing of knowledge within or between individuals, groups, and organizations.

Knowledge Utilization: The application of knowledge to business processes. Knowledge has no value per se, but draws its value from concrete application to business processes.

Human Capital in Knowledge Creation, Management and Utilization

Iris Reychav
Bar-Ilan University, Israel

Jacob Weisberg
Bar-Ilan University, Israel

INTRODUCTION

Growing competitiveness, joined with the frequently occurring technological changes in the global age, raise the importance of human capital in the organization, as well as the development and sharing of knowledge resources, which lead to obtaining a competitive advantage.

Perez (2003) presents the human capital as one of the most complex resources for gaining control over organizations. This belief has led managers in the past to base their competitive advantage in the markets and in recruiting resources, on product-related capitals, work processes, or technology.

The human capital of employees has a high financial value and is accumulated via learning processes, which take a central role in the survival and growth of the organization. Since the 1980s, strategic managers and industrialists have identified organizational learning as the basis for obtaining a competitive advantage in the local and international markets (DeGeus, 1988).

The identification and management of the knowledge resource owned by the human capital is quite difficult, since the knowledge is not perceptible and therefore influences the ability to plan activities relating to the use and sharing of knowledge (Davenport, 2001).

A new position has been created in organizations today—that of CKO (Chief Knowledge Officer). This function is required to coordinate processes of knowledge management found within the human capital. However, finance systems are not designed today to reflect the value of the human capital in the company balance sheet (Sveiby, 1997). Gibbert et al. (2000) suggest that organizations should focus on raising the awareness of the importance of the knowledge residing with the human capital in the organization and motivate employees to share their knowledge with the organization and with their colleagues.

The majority of studies dealing with stages of knowledge management and knowledge sharing have focused on technical aspects of systems and communication networks. The present overview focuses on including human capital and its role in the various stages of knowledge management.

BACKGROUND

Human capital in an organization is one of the organization's sources for obtaining a competitive advantage (Ulrich & Lake, 1991), and its importance and contribution for creating knowledge in the organization are great (Collis & Montgomery, 1995).

Perez (2003) identifies four knowledge types characteristic of human capital in the organization, divided according to strategic value and uniqueness to the organization:

1. **Idiosyncratic Human Capital:** A form of human capital unique to the specific organization and having a low strategic value, thus preventing the organization from investing in its development.
2. **Ancillary Human Capital:** A more common form of human capital, having a low strategic value to the organization. It is created during daily activities taking place in the organization.
3. **Core Human Capital:** A unique human capital, essential for the organization to obtain a strategic advantage. Organizations tend to develop the human capital in this category by implementing systems based on skill and on the creation of systems for long-term relationships
4. **Compulsory Human Capital:** A general and essential form of human capital, but one that is not specific to a certain organization; therefore employees are allowed to distribute it between organizations according to alternatives existing in other workplaces.

Most of the recent studies in the field of Knowledge Sharing suggest that the application of a knowledge management program based on the assimilation of databases and technologies does not directly result in the creation and distribution of knowledge (O'Dell & Grayson, 1988, p. 3). Recently, organizations have begun to understand that technology in itself is not a foolproof solution to the problem of knowledge sharing and that more focus should be given to the human capital (Poole, 2000). This shift in perspective has occurred mainly due to the realization that the human capital is the central knowledge carrier in the organization (Quinn, 1992).

Studies in the field of management have shown a recent rise in the popularity of the concept of organizational learning, and its perceived importance for distributing and managing knowledge in an organization, aimed at obtaining a competitive advantage (Collis & Montgomery, 1995; Dierickx & Kool, 1989; Prahalad & Hamel, 1990; Schoemaker, 1992).

A MODEL OF THE HUMAN CAPITAL IN KNOWLEDGE MANAGEMENT

The model suggested in this article (see Figure 1) describes the role of human capital in the knowledge creation processes (A), then moves on to processes of capturing and managing the created knowledge (B) and

mobilizing knowledge-sharing processes between the organization and its individuals, among individuals, and between them and their environment (C). Finally, the model describes the process of incorporating the knowledge at the firm level so as to improve performance and profit, and at the environmental level so as to create databases and prevent loss of knowledge when employees leave the organization (D).

Knowledge Creation

At the individual level, knowledge is created via cognitive processes such as learning, while social systems (i.e., groups) generate knowledge through collaborative interactions (Smith & Lyles, 2003, p. 106).

The factors taking part in the knowledge creation process in an organization may come either from internal or external sources. The knowledge creation process (A_3) consists of the transformation process of raw data (A_1) into information (A_2). In this process, the human capital utilizes technological tools enabling the collection and classification of knowledge. The definition of concepts such as raw data, information, and knowledge is based on the user's perspective, by which the data is considered as raw facts, the information is considered an organized set

Figure 1. Human capital in knowledge management

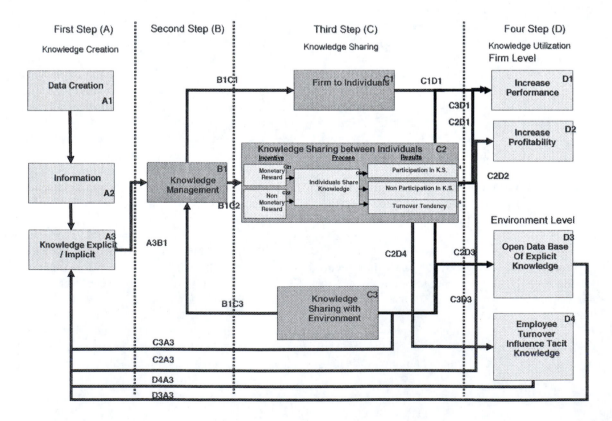

of data, and the knowledge is perceived as meaningful information (Bhatt, 2001).

The idea on which this definition is based is the recursive relationship between the raw data, information, and knowledge managed by the human capital, which is able to determine irrelevant information and return it to its previous status of raw data. Similarly, accumulated knowledge may be considered by the human capital as irrelevant, and returned to a previous status. The raw data, information, and knowledge are relative to each other. The raw data can become critical for a certain individual, resulting in the changing of its status to that of information, which is then combined as a basis for diagnosis and becomes knowledge.

Cohen and Levintal (1990) add that the ability of expanding the knowledge base in an organization depends on the level of learning and on the previous knowledge base of the individuals in the organization, which extend their ability to obtain further knowledge.

Knowledge Management

The literature is based mainly on knowledge management by way of technological tools designed for coping with the explicit knowledge of the human capital.

The explicit knowledge is characterized as structured, having a constant content, and the possibility for documentation and sharing by way of technological systems (Martensson, 2000). The human capital classifies this knowledge and exposes it to the senior management level of the organization (Haldin-Herrgard, 2000).

The main role of the technological systems for knowledge management is to coordinate between the various organizational capitals, while reducing the number of physical and personal limitations.

Knowledge Sharing

Organizations try to locate alternatives for coping with the difficulties of disseminating the knowledge in the organization. One of these alternatives is knowledge sharing, which enables the utilization of organizational knowledge within the existing organizational structure, relationships, and existing compensation structures. The human capital is directly involved in the processes of knowledge sharing, whether consciously or subconsciously. Therefore, a high importance is given to understanding the willingness of individuals in an organization to share knowledge.

Knowledge sharing takes place in two channels—inside the organization and between the organization and its environment.

Knowledge-Sharing Process

Knowledge Sharing Inside the Organization

Two knowledge-sharing processes can be identified in the organization:

- **Knowledge transformation processes (C_1) from the organization to the individuals:** In this process the organizational structure serves as a knowledge-sharing channel (Davenport & Prusak, 1998). The human capital uses the organizational structure to distribute official and explicit knowledge.
- **Knowledge exchange processes (C_2) between individuals:** Individuals in an organization are considered in the literature as the main motivators of the knowledge creation process (Takeachi, 2004). This process is based on the exchange of information, ideas, suggestions, and expertise between individuals (Nahapiet & Ghoshal, 1998; Senge, 1990). In each of the abovementioned processes in which the human capital is involved, various forms of knowledge conversion take place (Nonaka, 2003): socialization (from tacit to tacit), externalization (from tacit to explicit), combination (from explicit to explicit), and internalization (from explicit to tacit).
- **Knowledge sharing with the environment (C_3):** Appleyard (1996) describes the decision to share knowledge as based on two factors: access to knowledge sharing and the usage of knowledge sharing. These factors influence the ability of the individual to share with the environment some of the technical knowledge that has been accumulated in the organization.

The process of exchanging knowledge between individuals and their environment takes place by using IT applications, which electronically distribute information between individuals from different organizations, and between individuals and external databases (Smith & Lyles, 2003, p. 110). One of the methods by which the relationship between the human capital and the environment is represented is the existence of virtual knowledge communities between organizations (Kristot, 1995).

Knowledge and Motivation of Employees

Tampoe (1996) reported that the introduction of a technological system for knowledge sharing would not necessarily influence the level of knowledge sharing in the organization and in its outside environment. Hendriks

(1999) studied the influence of ICTs on the motivation of the knowledge employee and suggested a threefold model, comprising three groups of capitals influencing the sharing of knowledge in the organization:

1. **Factors influencing the current career stage of the individual:** In different career stages, different technological applications will influence the sharing of knowledge in different ways for different individuals.
2. **Factors relating to the content of knowledge sharing, joined with the tendency to share knowledge, or—as described by Davenport and Prusak (1998, p. 96):** a knowledge sharing culture.
3. **Factors relating to the reason for knowledge sharing and the environment in which it is conducted:** A differentiation is noted between situations in which knowledge is distributed in an aim to utilize it, and situations in which individuals create new knowledge from the distributed knowledge, a process referred to as the 'knowledge spiral' (Nonaka & Takeuchi, 1995).

Human Willingness to Participate in Knowledge Sharing

The willingness of the human capital to participate in knowledge-sharing processes can result from an informal commitment to a group inside the organization sharing a common interest in the existence of knowledge, or the existence of skill communities.

One of the most prominent examples for knowledge-sharing activities in organizations is the existence of 'communities of practice', as well as the use of incentives so as to encourage knowledge-sharing processes in the organization.

Communities of Practice

Lave and Wenger (1991) presented the concept of 'communities of practice'. They focused on the fact that most of the learning of the human capital is centered on a specific event. This type of learning combines groups of people having a common interest in a specific issue, and it is conducted informally in a group environment. These communities differ from other groups in the organization in their informal ability to carry a long-term commitment to developing the abilities of all group members, while utilizing processes of exchanging, obtaining, and creating knowledge (Wenger & Snyder, 2000).

The communities of practice have become highly popular in large multi-national organizations due to the high importance of focusing on the search for ways to promote innovation in these organizations (Brown & Duguid, 1991).

Individual Expectations for Compensation

Thibaut and Kelley (1959) and Blau (1964) were some of the first researchers to distinguish between social interactions based on social exchange and those based on economic exchange.

Adams (1965) identified a problem in the organization's ability to provide adequate compensation for knowledge provided by the human capital. Spender (1996) exemplifies the problem found in the field of research and development, in which the value of the knowledge provided may be extremely high for the organization, so high that it surpasses the ability of the organization to adequately compensate the employee for its sharing. In this case there is a risk that the employee will take the knowledge in his possession and share it with competing organizations.

The model suggested in this overview distinguishes between two types of incentives: financial incentive (C_{21}) and non-financial incentive (C_{22}).

Financial Incentives for Knowledge Sharing
Knowledge sharing is conducted via two frameworks—one formal and the other informal.

*   **Compensation for knowledge sharing via a formal framework:** In the formal framework we can identify three levels of compensation for knowledge sharing, and therefore we suggest three levels of compensation: the personal level, the group level, and the inter-group level.
    *   **Compensation at the personal level:** Payment for excellent performance and advancement are some of the most common compensation methods used on this level (Bartol & Srivastava, 2002).
    *   **Compensation at the group level:** Encouraging the human capital to distribute knowledge among group members by way of providing compensation for successful performances of the group. Group measures have been identified as able to promote cooperation, coordination, and motivation of the employees to reach the goals (Dulebohn & Martocchio, 1998). Historically, studies have presented empirical data pointing to a positive correlation between knowledge sharing and group performance (Durham, Knight, & Locke, 1997; Faraj & Sproull, 2000).
    *   **Compensation at the inter-group level:** This method of compensation is essential in multi-national organizations. In this case the human

capital may show an interest in sharing knowledge so as to improve the performance of his organization or business unit, in a similar way to that of the individual's performance in the group level (Gupta & Govindarajan, 1986).

- **Compensation for sharing of knowledge via informal frameworks:** Earl (2001) reported that certain organizations, such as McKinesy and American Express, employ knowledge specialists, whose jobs are to share the knowledge with others in the organization.

Bartol and Srivastava (2002) claim that the compensation for the sharing of tacit knowledge is small due to the difficulty of identifying the transactions taking place during the sharing of that form of knowledge.

Many studies have identified the importance of trust between group members for creating an atmosphere of knowledge sharing (Hedlund & Nonaka, 1993; Nonaka, 1994). The trust factor has also been identified as enabling cooperative behavior between individuals (Mayer, Davis, & Schoorman, 1995; McAllister, 1995).

In a group where the trust capital is central, an informal form of compensation may enhance the trust between group members and create an atmosphere of cooperation, leading to the sharing of knowledge amongst them.

Non-Financial Incentives for Knowledge Sharing

Fishbein and Ajzen's (1975) Theory of Reasoned Action serves as a theoretical framework for explaining the behavior of the individual taking part in knowledge-sharing processes as being affected by the willingness of the individual to take part in these processes.

Human capital has three options in knowledge-sharing processes: one is to participate in these processes (C_{24}), the second is to decide not to participate (C_{25}), and the third is to leave the organization (C_{26}).

The willingness of the individual to participate in knowledge-sharing processes is presented in a multi-faceted two-stage model (Reychav & Weisberg, 2004).

The first stage of the model describes the factors influencing the willingness of the individual to participate in knowledge sharing-processes in the organization, while the second stage describes the results obtained at the individual level.

The willingness of the employees to participate in knowledge-sharing processes is described as affected by the following factors: (1) commitment to the organization, (2) organizational identification, and (3) involvement in one's job.

The results of the employee's behavior in knowledge-sharing processes may lead to an expectation for compensation in return for the employee's investment, while the involvement of employees may reduce their tendency to leave the organization. Organizational identification serves as a method by which the organization affects the behavior of employees by providing compensation for desirable behavior (Cheney, 1983).

Wood (1974) stated that the tendency of employees to concentrate on the activities and characteristics of their job increases their sense of responsibility and willingness to assist other employees and the organization as a whole.

KNOWLEDGE UTILIZATION

The organization strives towards increasing its knowledge-sharing processes and motivating employees to participate in these processes. The model suggested in this article presents the organizational goals, which create the basis for knowledge-sharing processes.

The utilization of knowledge may be divided into two levels. The first is the organizational level, in which the organization strives to apply knowledge-sharing processes so as, for example, to increase organizational performance (D_1) and organizational profitability (D_2) from compensation presented to an external source. The second level is the environmental level, which uses the explicit knowledge disclosed by the organization to its environment (D_3) as part of a marketing strategy or as a survival tool in a competitive market. Otherwise, employees leaving the organization may take along with them both the explicit and tacit knowledge areas, and may share them with competitors (D_4), who may use them as a source for creating further knowledge (D_4A_3, D_3A_3).

The Utilization of Knowledge to Increase Performance

The human factor may use knowledge in order to increase organizational performance (D_1) (Durham, Knight, & Locke, 1997). The main theories mentioned in the literature, presenting the relationship between the existing knowledge and the wish to manage it so as to improve organizational performance, are: (1) the "knowledge-based view of the firm" (Grant, 1996; Conner & Prahalad, 1996; Spender, 1996a), which focuses on the mechanism that enables the organization to reach a competitive advantage; and (2) "the competence-based view of the firm" (Sanchez et al., 1996; Heene & Sanchez, 1997), according to which, organizational capabilities are based on the ability of the human factor to participate in learning processes in the organization and to determine the organizational goals.

The Utilization of Knowledge to Increase Organizational Profitability

Human capital may assist in increasing organizational profitability (D_2) by increasing personal productivity, which in turn contributes to the overall organizational productivity (Darr et al., 1995; Argote & Ingram, 2000).

Tsai (2001) suggested using the profitability measure in order to assess the sharing of knowledge inside the organization, especially when the measured unit is a central one in the organizational network.

Disclosing the Explicit Knowledge to the Environment

The disclosure of knowledge to the environment (D_3) is motivated on two levels—the organizational level and the environmental one. On the *organizational level,* the disclosure of knowledge to the environment may result in an increase to the organization's profitability as a result of selling the knowledge or purchasing further knowledge in return.

On the *environmental level,* the interaction of the human capital with the environment is conducted via technologies supporting the sharing of knowledge. One of the dominant tools for increasing the sharing of knowledge with the environment is the Internet (Marshall, 1997), as well as the use of information communication technologies (ICTs) (McGrath & Hollingshead, 1994).

The Influence of Employee Turnover on Tacit Knowledge

Beyond the influence of employee turnover on the sharing of explicit knowledge of the organization with competitors, the turnover process also has a negative effect on the management and sharing of the tacit knowledge between individuals inside the organization. Baumard (1999) suggested that the main loss of an organization when employees leave it stems from the loss of the tacit knowledge kept by those individuals.

The social structure existing in an organization has a substantial influence on the role of knowledge creation in the organization (Nonaka, 1994). Capelli (2000) states that social systems in the organization influence employees into remaining in the organization by developing a system of trust (Leana & Van Buren, 1999), which increases the sharing of the human capital's tacit knowledge via the existence of personal interactions.

DISCUSSION

The human capital represents one of the most intangible and difficult-to-control assets of the organization (Perez, 2003). A high importance is attributed today to the human capital in the organization and to its influence on the creation of the strategic knowledge, which is unique to the organization.

The accumulation of knowledge by individuals in the organization is based mainly on learning processes, which take a central role in organizational survival and growth.

Until recently, most of the literature studied knowledge management mainly from the technological aspect. The present overview suggests a new direction of thinking, bringing the human capital to the main focus of the knowledge management process. Based on this approach, organizations may be able to define strategies for efficient management of the knowledge held by the human capital of the organization.

This article presented a model that combines the human capital in four main stages, characterizing the process of knowledge management in the organization. In the first stage (A), organizational knowledge is created from internal and external sources. In the second stage (B), the knowledge is managed via technological tools (information systems, databases), which manage mainly the explicit knowledge of the organization.

During the third stage (C), the knowledge is distributed in the organization. Three processes of knowledge sharing can be identified in this stage: the organization provides (transforms) knowledge to individuals (C_1), the individuals exchange knowledge amongst themselves (internal exchange) (C_2), and the organization exchanges knowledge with its environment (external exchange) (C_3). The process describing the internal exchange of knowledge among individuals in the organization (C_2) is a source of knowledge creation inside the organization (C_2A_3), known in the literature as organizational knowledge (Snyder, 1996).

The fourth stage (D) deals with the question: Why is the organization interested in applying the knowledge-sharing processes presented above? In this stage the usability of the knowledge is presented on two levels: on the organizational level the use of knowledge is aimed at increasing the productivity of the individual, and ultimately increasing organizational productivity (D_1) and profitability (D_2). On the environmental level, the organization may on one hand be interested in exposing its explicit knowledge (D_3) by using technological systems (Internet, databases), while on the other hand there is a risk that tacit organizational knowledge will also be distributed outside the organization due to employee turnover (D_4). In each of the last two scenarios, the knowledge shared with the environment may become an external source of knowledge (D_3A_3, D_4A_3) for the organization absorbing it.

FUTURE TRENDS

The issue of knowledge management has been deemed essential in a competitive environment by various sources, including governmental, academic and advisory bodies, as well as industry (Tushman & Nadler, 1986). However, the focus in organizations is on the functionality of knowledge, manifested via the search for tools and technologies that support knowledge management. Therefore, there is substantial potential for studying human capital and its influence on the sharing of knowledge in the overall organizational level (Lang, 2001).

The literature has focused mostly on knowledge management via technological tools aimed at dealing with explicit knowledge in the organization. However, DeLong (1996) reports that these technological systems do not necessarily improve the sharing of knowledge in the organization. We therefore suggest assessing the factors influencing the sharing of knowledge between individuals in the organization, and between organizations and their environment. A study that will deal with the knowledge-sharing processes mentioned in this article, and will suggest ways to manage and apply these processes, may assist organizations in defining a leading strategy towards achieving a competitive advantage.

REFERENCES

Adams, J.S. (1965). Inequity in social exchange. In Berkowitz, L. (Ed.), *Advances in experimental social psychology* (pp. 267-299). New York: Academic Press.

Appleyard, M. (1996). How does knowledge flow? Interfirm patterns in the semiconductor industry. *Strategic Management Journal (1986-1998)*.

Argote, L. & Ingram, P. (2000). Knowledge transfer: A basis for competitive advantage in firms. *Organizational Behavior and Human Decision Processes, 82*(1), 150-169.

Bartol, K.M. & Srivastava, A. (2002). Encouraging knowledge sharing: The role of organizational reward Systems. *Journal of Leadership & Organizational Studies, 9*(1), 64-76.

Baumard, P. (1999). *Tacit knowledge in organizations.* Thousand Oaks, CA: Sage Publications Ltd.

Bhatt, G.D. (2001). Knowledge management in organizations: Examining the interaction between technologies, techniques, and people. *Journal of Knowledge Management, 5*(1), 68-75.

Blau, P. (1964). *Exchange and power in social life.* New York: Wiley.

Brown, J.S. & Duguid, O. (1991). Organizational learning and communities-of-practice: Towards a unified view of working, learning, and innovation. *Organization Science, 2*(1), 198-213.

Capelli, P. (2000). A market-driven approach to retaining talent. *Harvard Business Review, 78*, 103-113.

Cheney, G. (1983). On the various and changing meaning of organizational membership: A field study of organizational identification. *Communication Monographs, 50*, 342-362.

Cohen, W.M. & Levinthal, D.A. (1990). Absorptive capacity: A new perspective on learning and innovation. *Administrative Science Quarterly, 35*, 128-152.

Collis. D.J. & Montgomery, C.A. (1995). Competing on resources: Strategy in the 1990s. *Harvard business Review,* July-August, 118-128.

Conner, K.R. & Prahalad, C.K. (1996). A resource-based theory of the firm: Knowledge versus opportunism. *Organization Science, 7*, 477-501.

Darr, E.D., Argote, L., & Epple, D. (1995). The acquisition, transfer, and depreciation of knowledge in service organizations: Productivity in franchises. *Management Science, 41*(11), 1750-1762.

Davenport, T.H. & Prusak, L. (1998). *Working knowledge.* Boston: Harvard Business School Press.

De Geus, A.P. (1988). Planning as learning. *Harvard Business Review*, March-April, pp. 70-74.

DeLong, D. (1996). *Implementing knowledge management at Javelin Development Corporation: Case study.* Boston: Ernst & Young Center for Business Innovation.

Dierickx, Y. & Cool, K. (1989). Asset stock accumulation and Sustainability of competitive advantage. *Management Science, 35*, 1504-1511.

Dulebohn, J. H. & Martocchio, J.J. (1998). Employee perceptions of the fairness of work group incentive pay plans. *Journal of Management, 24*, 469-488.

Durham, C.C., Knight, D., & Locke, E.A. (1997). Effects of leader role, teamset goal difficulty, efficacy, and tactics on team effectiveness. *Organizational Behavior and Human Decision processes, 72*, 203-231.

H

Earl, M. (2001). Knowledge management strategies: Towards a taxonomy. *Journal of Management Information Systems, 18,* 215-233.

Faraj, S. & Sproull, L. (2000). Coordinating expertise in software development teams. *Management Science, 46,* 1554-1568.

Fishbein, M. & Ajzen, I. (1975). *Beliefs, attitude, intention and behavior: An introduction to theory and research.* Philippines: Addison-Wesley Publishing Company.

Gibbert, M., Jonczyk, C. & Volpel, S. (2000). ShareNet the next generation knowledge management. In I. Davenport & G. Probst (Eds.), *Knowledge management case book, best practices* (pp. 22-39). New York: John Wiley.

Grant, R.M. (1996). Toward a knowledge-based theory of the firm. *Strategic Management Journal, 17*(S), 109-122.

Gupta, A. K. & Govindarajan, V. (1986). Resource sharing among SBUs: Strategic antecedents and administrative implications. *Academy of Management Journal, 29,* 695-714.

Haldin-Herrgard, T. (2000). Difficulties in diffusion of tacit knowledge in organizations. *Journal of Intellectual Capital, 1*(4), 357-365.

Hedlund, G. & Nonaka, I. (1993). Models of knowledge management in the west and Japan. In P. Lorange, et al. (Eds.), *Implementing strategic process: Change, learning and cooperation* (pp. 117-144). Oxford: Basil Blackwell.

Heene, A. & Sanchez, R. (Eds.). (1997). *Competence-based strategic management.* Chichester, UK: John Wiley.

Hendriks, P. (1999). Why share knowledge? The Influence of ICT on the motivation for knowledge sharing. *Knowledge and Process Management, 6*(2), 91-100.

Kristof, A.L., Brown, K.G., Sims, H.P., & Smith, K.A. (1995). The virtual team: A case study and inductive model. In M.M. Beyerlein, M.M., D.A. Johonson, & S.T. Beyerlein (Eds.), *Advances in interdisciplinary studies of work teams 2: Knowledge work in teams* (pp. 229-254). Greenwich, CT: JAI Press.

Lang, J.C. (2001). Managerial concerns in knowledge management. *Journal of Knowledge Management, 5*(1), 43-57.

Lave, J., Wenger, E. (1991). Situated learning. *Legitimate peripheral participation.* Cambridge: University Press.

Leana, C.R. & Van Buren III, H.J. (1999). Organizational social capital and employment practices. *Academy of Management Review, 24,* 538-555.

Marakas, G.M. (1999). *Decision support systems in the twenty-first century.* Englewood Cliffs, NJ: Prentice-Hall..

Marshall, L. (1997). Facilitating knowledge management and knowledge sharing: New opportunities for information professionals. *Online, 21*(5), 92-98.

Martensson, M. (2000). A critical review of knowledge management as a management tool. *Journal of Knowledge Management, 4*(3), 204-216.

Mayer, R. C., Davis, J. H., & Schoorman, F.D. (1995). An integrative model of organizational trust. *Academy of Management Review, 20,* 709-734.

McAllister, D.J. (1995). Affect and cognition based trust as foundations for interpersonal cooperation in organizations. *Academy of Management Journal, 38,* 24-59.

McGrath, J.E. & Hollingshead, A.B. (1994). *Groups interacting with technology, ideas, evidence, issues, and an agenda.* Sage, CA: Thousand Oaks.

Nahapiet, J., & Ghoshal, S. (1998). Social capital, intellectual capital, and the organizational advantage. *Academy of Management Review, 23,* 242-266. Washington, DC: National Academy Press.

Nonaka, I. (1994). A dynamic theory of organizational knowledge creation. *Organization Science, 5,* 14-37.

Nonaka, I. & Takeuchi, H. (1995). *The knowledge-creating company.* Oxford, UK: Oxford University Press.

Perez, J.R. & Pablos, P.O. (2003). Knowledge management and organizational competitiveness: A framework for human capital analysis. *Journal of Knowledge Management, 7*(3), 82-91.

Poole, A. (2000). The view from the floor—What KM looks like through the employee's lens. *Knowledge Management Review, 3,* 8-10.

Prahalad, C.K. & Hamel, G. (1990). The core competence of the corporation. *Harvard Business Review, 68*(3), 79-93.

O'Dell, C. & Grayson, C.J. (1988). *If only we knew what we know: The transfer of internal knowledge and best practice.* New York: The Free Press.

Quinn, JB. (1992). *Intelligent enterprise: A knowledge and service based paradigm for industry.* New York: The Free Press.

Reychav, I. & Weisberg, J. (2004) Antecedents & outcomes of knowledge management: An individual-level model. *ECKM Conference,* Paris.

Sanchez, R., Heene, A. & Thomas, H. (Eds.) (1996). *Dynamic of competence-based competition: Theory and practice in the new strategic management.* Oxford, UK: Elsevier.

Schoemaker, P.J.H. (1992). How to link strategic vision to core capabilities. *Sloan Management Review*, Fall, 67-81.

Senge, P. M. (1990). *The fifth discipline: Five practices of the learning organization.* New York: Doubleday.

Smith, M.E., & Lyles, M.A. (2003). *The Blackwell handbook of organizational learning and knowledge management.* UK: Blackwell

Snyder, W. M. (1996). *Organization learning and performance: An exploration of the linkages between organization learning, knowledge, and performance.* Ph.D. thesis, University of Southern California, USA.

Spender, J. C. (1996). Making knowledge the basis of a dynamic theory of the firm. *Strategic Management Journal, 17*(S2), 45-62.

Spender, J. C. (1996a). Competitive advantage from tacit knowledge? Unpacking the concept and its strategic implications. In B. Moingeon. & A. Edmondson (Eds.), *Organizational learning and competitive advantage* (pp. 56-73). London Sage.

Sveiby, K. (1997). *The new organizational wealth: Managing and Measuring Knowledge-Based Assets.* San Francisco: Berrett-Kochler.

Szulanski, G. (1996). Exploring internal stickiness: Impediments to the transfer of best practice within the firm. *Strategic Management Journal, 17*, 27-43.

Takeuchi, H. & Nonaka, I. (2004). *Hitosubashi on knowledge management.* New York: John Wiley.

Tampoe, M. (1996). Motivating knowledge workers—The challenge for the 1990s. In P.S. Myers (Ed.), *Knowledge management and organizational design* (pp. 179-190). Boston: Butterworth-Heinemann.

Thibaut, J.W. & Kelley, H.H. (1959). *The social psychology of groups.* New York: Wiley.

Tsai, W. (2001). Knowledge transfer in intraorganizational network: Effects of network position and absorptive capacity on business unit innovation and performance. *Academy of Management Journal, 44*(5), 996-1004.

Tushman, M. & Nadler, D. (1986). Organizing for innovation. *California Management Review, 28*(3), 74-88.

Ulrich, D. & Lake, D. (1991). Organizational capability: Creating competitive advantage. *Academy of Management Executive, 5*(1), 77-92.

Wenger, E. & Snyder, WM. (2000). Communities of practice: The organizational frontier. *Harvard Business Review, 78*, 139-146.

Wood, D. (1974) Effect of worker orientation on job attitude correlates. *Journal of Applied Psychology, 59*, 54-60.

H

KEY TERMS

Communities of Practice: Communities of practice is defined as collections of individuals who share the capacity to create and use organizational knowledge through informal learning and mutual engagement (Wenger, 2000, p. 3).

Human Capital: Human Capital is defined as the organizational resource that is most difficult to control- people. Perez (2003), propose a classification of four forms of human capital: idiosyncratic, ancillary, core and compulsory which are distinguished by two dimension: value and uniqueness.

Knowledge: Knowledge is defined as an organized combination of ideas, rules, procedures, and information (Marakas, 1999, p. 264).

Knowledge Management: Knowledge Management is defined as an economic view of the strategic value of organizational knowledge that facilitates the acquisition, sharing and utilization of knowledge (Smith & Lyles, 2003, p. 12).

Knowledge Sharing: Knowledge Sharing is defined as the exchange or transfer process of facts, opinions, ideas, theories, principles and models within and between organizations include trail and error, feedback and mutual adjustment of both the sender and receiver of knowledge (Szulanski, 1996).

Learning Organization: Learning Organization is defined as an entity, an ideal type of organization, which has the capacity to learn effectively (Smith & Lyles, 2003, p. 10)

Organizational Knowledge: Quinn et al. (1996) equate knowledge with professional intellect. According to this view, organizational knowledge is a metaphor, as it is not the organization but the people in the organization who create knowledge.

Organizational Learning: Organizational learning refers to the study of the learning processes of and within organizations (Smith & Lyles, 2003, p. 11).

Tacit Knowledge: Tacit knowledge is defined as knowledge that has not been formalizes or made explicit, as well as to knowledge that cannot be formalized (Nonaka & Takeuchi, 1995). Tacit knowledge is based on the subjective insights, intuitions and is deeply rooted in an individual's actions and experience and ideals, values and emotions (Polanyi, 1966).

ICT and Knowledge Management Systems[1]

Irma Becerra-Fernandez
Florida International University, USA

Rajiv Sabherwal
University of Missouri at St. Louis, USA

INTRODUCTION

Rapid changes in the field of knowledge management (KM) have to a great extent resulted from the dramatic progress we have witnessed in the field of information and communication technology. ICT allows the movement of information at increasing speeds and efficiencies, and thus facilitates sharing as well as accelerated growth of knowledge. For example, computers capture data from measurements of natural phenomena, and then quickly manipulate the data to better understand the phenomena they represent. Increased computer power at lower prices enables the measurement of increasingly complex processes, which we possibly could only imagine before. Thus, ICT has provided a major impetus for enabling the implementation of KM applications. Moreover, as learning has accrued over time in the area of social and structural mechanisms, such as through mentoring and retreats that enable effective knowledge sharing, it has made it possible to develop KM applications that best leverage these improved mechanisms by deploying sophisticated technologies.

In this article we focus on the applications that result from the use of the latest technologies used to support KM mechanisms. Knowledge management mechanisms are organizational or structural means used to promote KM (Becerra-Fernandez, Gonzalez, & Sabherwal, 2004). The use of leading-edge ICT (e.g., Web-based conferencing) to support KM mechanisms in ways not earlier possible (e.g., interactive conversations along with the instantaneous exchange of voluminous documents among individuals located at remote locations) enables dramatic improvement in KM. We call the applications resulting from such synergy between the latest technologies and social or structural mechanisms knowledge management systems. We discuss the topic of KM systems in detail in the next sections.

BACKGROUND

We describe the variety of possible activities involved in KM as broadly intending to (a) discover new knowledge, (b) capture existing knowledge, (c) share knowledge with others, or (d) apply knowledge. Thus, KM relies on four kinds of KM processes as depicted in Figure 1 (Becerra-Fernandez et al., 2004). These include the processes through which knowledge is discovered or captured, and the processes through which this knowledge is shared and applied. These four KM processes are supported by a set of seven KM subprocesses as shown in Figure 1, with one subprocess, socialization, supporting two KM processes (discovery and sharing).

Polyani's (1967) distinction between explicit and tacit is at the heart of most KM papers. These constructs follow in that explicit knowledge is knowledge about things, and tacit knowledge is associated with experience. Nonaka (1994) identified four ways of managing knowledge: combination, socialization, externalization, and internalization. Of the seven KM subprocesses presented in Figure 1, four are based on Nonaka, focusing on the ways in which knowledge is shared through the interaction between tacit and explicit knowledge. New explicit knowledge is discovered through combination, wherein the multiple bodies of explicit knowledge (and/or data and/or information) are synthesized to create new, more complex sets of explicit knowledge. Therefore, by combining, reconfiguring, recategorizing, and recontextualizing existing explicit knowledge, data, and information, new explicit knowledge is produced. In the case of tacit knowledge, the integration of multiple streams for the creation of new knowledge occurs through the mechanism of socialization. Socialization is the synthesis of tacit knowledge across individuals, usually through joint activities rather than written or verbal instructions. Externalization involves converting tacit knowledge into explicit forms such as words, concepts, visuals, or figurative language (e.g., metaphors, analogies, and narratives; Nonaka & Takeuchi, 1995). It helps translate individuals' tacit knowledge into explicit forms that can be more easily understood by the rest of their group. Finally, internalization is the conversion of explicit knowledge into tacit knowledge. It represents the traditional notion of learning.

The other three KM subprocesses—exchange, direction, and routines—are largely based on Grant (1996a,

Figure 1. KM processes

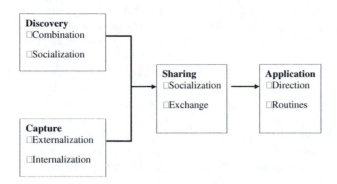

1996b) and Nahapiet and Ghoshal (1998). Exchange focuses on the sharing of explicit knowledge and it is used to communicate or transfer explicit knowledge between individuals, groups, and organizations (Grant, 1996b). Direction refers to the process through which the individual possessing the knowledge directs the action of another individual without transferring to him or her the knowledge underlying the direction. This preserves the advantages of specialization and avoids the difficulties inherent in the transfer of tacit knowledge. Finally, routines involve the utilization of knowledge embedded in procedures, rules, and norms that guide future behavior. Routines economize on communication more than direction as they are embedded in procedures or technologies. However, they take time to develop, relying on constant repetition (Grant, 1996a).

Other KM system characterizations present similar models to describe KM systems. For example, the acquire, organize, and distribute (AOD) model (Schwartz, Divitini, & Brasethvik, 2000) uses a similar characterization to describe organizational memories. Comparing the two models, the acquisition process relates to how we collect knowledge from members of the organization or other resources, and it is related to the processes of knowledge discovery and knowledge capture. The organizing process refers to structuring, indexing, and formatting the acquired knowledge, and it is related to the process of knowledge sharing. Finally, the process of distribution relates to the ability to get the relevant knowledge to the person who needs it at the right time, and it is related to the process of knowledge application.

Knowledge management systems utilize a variety of KM mechanisms and technologies to support the knowledge management processes. Depending on the KM process most directly supported, KM systems can be classified into four types: knowledge-discovery systems, knowledge-capture systems, knowledge-sharing systems, and knowledge-application systems (Becerra-Fernandez et al., 2004). In the next sections, we provide a brief

overview of these four kinds of systems and examine how they benefit from KM mechanisms and technologies.

TYPES OF KNOWLEDGE MANAGEMENT SYSTEMS

Knowledge-discovery systems support the process of developing new tacit or explicit knowledge from data and information or from the synthesis of prior knowledge. These systems support two KM subprocesses associated with knowledge discovery: combination, enabling the discovery of new explicit knowledge, and socialization, enabling the discovery of new tacit knowledge. Thus, mechanisms and technologies can support knowledge-discovery systems by facilitating a combination and/or socialization.

KM mechanisms that facilitate combination include collaborative problem solving, joint decision making, and the collaborative creation of documents. For example, at the senior-management level, new explicit knowledge is created by sharing documents and information related to mid-range concepts (e.g., product concepts) augmented with grand concepts (e.g., corporate vision) to produce new knowledge about both areas. This newly created knowledge could be, for example, a better understanding of the products and corporate vision (Nonaka & Takeuchi, 1995). Mechanisms that facilitate socialization include apprenticeships, employee rotation across areas, conferences, brainstorming retreats, cooperative projects across departments, and initiation processes for new employees. For example, Honda "set up 'brainstorming camps' (*tama dashi kai*)—informal meetings for detailed discussions to solve difficult problems in development projects" (Nonaka & Takeuchi, p. 63).

Technologies facilitating combination include knowledge-discovery or data-mining systems, databases, and Web-based access to data. According to Nonaka and Takeuchi (1995, p. 67), the "reconfiguration of existing information through sorting, adding, combining, and categorizing of explicit knowledge (as conducted in computer databases) can lead to new knowledge." Repositories of information, best practices, and lessons learned also facilitate combination. Technologies can also facilitate socialization, albeit to less extent than they can facilitate combination. Some of the technologies for facilitating socialization include videoconferencing, electronic discussion groups, and e-mail.

Knowledge-capture systems support the process of retrieving either explicit or tacit knowledge that resides within people, artifacts, or organizational entities. These systems can help capture knowledge that resides within or outside organizational boundaries, including within consultants, competitors, customers, suppliers, and prior employers of the organization's new employees. Knowledge-capture systems rely on mechanisms and technologies that support externalization and internalization.

KM mechanisms can enable knowledge capture by facilitating externalization, that is, the conversion of tacit knowledge into explicit form, or internalization, that is, the conversion of explicit knowledge into tacit form. The development of models or prototypes and the articulation of best practices or lessons learned are some examples of mechanisms that enable externalization.

Learning by doing, on-the-job training, learning by observation, and face-to-face meetings are some of the mechanisms that facilitate internalization. For example, at one firm, "the product divisions also frequently send their new-product development people to the Answer Center to chat with the telephone operators or the 12 specialists, thereby 're-experiencing' their experiences" (Nonaka & Takeuchi, 1995, p. 69).

Technologies can also support knowledge-capture systems by facilitating externalization and internalization. Externalization through knowledge engineering is necessary for the implementation of intelligent technologies such as expert systems, case-based reasoning systems, and knowledge-acquisition systems. Technologies that facilitate internalization include computer-based communication. Using such communication facilities, an individual can internalize knowledge from a message or attachment thereof sent by another expert, from an AI- (artificial intelligence) based knowledge-acquisition system, or from computer-based simulations.

Knowledge-sharing systems support the process through which explicit or implicit knowledge is communicated to other individuals. They do so by supporting exchange (i.e., the sharing of explicit knowledge) and socialization (which promotes the sharing of tacit knowledge). Mechanisms and technologies supporting socialization also play an important role in knowledge-sharing systems. Discussion groups or chat groups facilitate knowledge sharing by enabling an individual to explain his or her knowledge to the rest of the group. In addition, knowledge-sharing systems also utilize mechanisms and technologies that facilitate exchange. Some of the mechanisms that facilitate exchange are memos, manuals, progress reports, letters, and presentations. Technologies facilitating exchange include groupware and other team collaboration mechanisms, Web-based access to data, databases, and repositories of information, including best-practice databases, lessons-learned systems, and expertise-locator systems.

Knowledge-application systems support the process through which some individuals utilize knowledge possessed by other individuals without actually acquiring or learning that knowledge. Mechanisms and technologies support knowledge-application systems by facilitating routines and direction.

Mechanisms facilitating direction include traditional hierarchical relationships in organizations, help desks, and support centers. On the other hand, mechanisms supporting routines include organizational policies, work practices, and standards. In the case of both direction and routines, these mechanisms may be either within an organization (e.g., organizational hierarchies) or across organizations (e.g., software-support help desks).

Technologies supporting direction include experts' knowledge embedded in expert systems and decision-support systems, as well as troubleshooting systems based on the use of technologies like case-based reasoning. On the other hand, some of the technologies that facilitate routines are expert systems, enterprise resource-planning systems (ERPs), and traditional management-information systems. As mentioned for KM mechanisms, these technologies can also facilitate directions and routines within or across organizations.

Table 1 summarizes the above discussion of KM processes and KM systems, and also indicates some of the mechanisms and technologies that might facilitate them. As may be seen from this table, the same tool or technology can be used to support more than one KM process.

INFORMATION AND COMMUNICATION TECHNOLOGY INFRASTRUCTURE IN KNOWLEDGE MANAGEMENT SYSTEMS

The knowledge management infrastructure is the foundation on which knowledge management resides. It includes five main components: organization culture, orga-

Table 1. KM systems, subprocesses, mechanisms, and technologies

KM Processes	KM Systems	KM Sub-Processes	Illustrative KM Mechanisms	Illustrative KM Technologies
Knowledge Discovery	Knowledge Discovery Systems	Combination	Meetings, telephone conversations, and documents, collaborative creation of documents	Databases, web-based access to data, data mining, repositories of information, Web portals, best practices and lessons learned
		Socialization	Employee rotation across departments, conferences, brainstorming retreats, cooperative projects, initiation	Video-conferencing, electronic discussion groups, e-mail
Knowledge Capture	Knowledge Capture Systems	Externalization	Models, prototypes, best practices, lessons learned	Expert systems, chat groups, best practices, and lessons learned databases.
		Internalization	Learning by doing, on-the-job training, learning by observation, and face-to-face meetings	Computer-based communication, AI-based knowledge acquisition, computer-based simulations
Knowledge Sharing	Knowledge Sharing Systems	Socialization	See above	See above
		Exchange	Memos, manuals, letters, presentations	Team collaboration tools, web-based access to data, databases, and repositories of information, best practices databases, lessons learned systems, and expertise locator systems
Knowledge Application	Knowledge Application Systems	Direction	Traditional hierarchical relationships in organizations, help desks, and support centers	Capture and transfer of experts' knowledge, troubleshooting systems, and case-based reasoning systems; decision support systems
		Routines	Organizational policies, work practices, and standards	Expert systems, enterprise resource planning systems, management information systems

nization structure, communities of practice, information technology infrastructure, and common knowledge. In this section, we concentrate on the role of ICT infrastructure on KM systems.

Knowledge management is facilitated by the organization's ICT infrastructure. While certain information technologies and systems are directly developed to pursue knowledge management, the organization's overall ICT, developed to support the organization's information-processing needs, also facilitates knowledge management. The ICT infrastructure includes data processing, storage, and communication technologies and systems. It comprises the entire spectrum of the organization's information systems, including transaction-processing systems and management-information systems. It consists of databases and data warehouses, as well as enterprise resource-planning systems. One possible way of systematically viewing the IT infrastructure is to consider the capabilities it provides in four important aspects: reach, depth, richness, and aggregation (Daft & Lengel, 1986; Evans & Wurster, 1999).

Reach pertains to access and connection, and the efficiency of such access. Within the context of a network, reach reflects the number and geographical locations of the nodes that can be efficiently accessed. Keen (1991) also uses the term reach to refer to the locations an ICT platform is capable of linking, with the ideal being able to connect to anyone, anywhere. Much of the power of the Internet is attributed to its reach and the fact that most people can access it quite inexpensively (Evans & Wurster, 1999). Reach is enhanced not just by advances in hardware, but also by progress in software. For instance, the standardization of cross-firm communication standards and languages such as XML (extensible markup language) make it easier for firms to communicate with a wider array of trading partners, including those with whom they do not have long-term relationships.

Depth, in contrast, focuses on the detail and amount of information that can be effectively communicated over a medium. This dimension closely corresponds to the aspects of bandwidth and customization included by Evans and Wurster (1999) in their definition of richness. Communicating deep and detailed information requires high bandwidth. At the same time, it is the availability of deep and detailed information about customers that enables customization. Recent technological progress, for instance, in channel bandwidth, has enabled considerable improvement in depth.

Communication channels can be arranged along a continuum representing their relative richness (Carlson & Zmud, 1999). The richness of a medium is based on its ability to (a) provide multiple cues (e.g., body language, facial expression, tone of voice) simultaneously, (b) provide quick feedback, (c) personalize messages, and (d) use natural language to convey subtleties (Daft & Lengel, 1986). ICT has traditionally been viewed as a lean communication medium. However, given the progress in information technology, we are witnessing a significant increase in its ability to support rich communication.

Finally, rapid advances in ICT have significantly enhanced the ability to store and quickly process information (Evans & Wurster, 1999). This enables the aggregation of large volumes of information drawn from multiple sources. For instance, data mining and data warehousing together enable the synthesis of diverse information from multiple sources, potentially to produce new insights. Enterprise resource-planning systems also present a natural platform for aggregating knowledge across different parts of an organization. A senior IS executive at Price Waterhouse Coopers, for example, remarks, "We're moving quite quickly on to an intranet platform, and that's giving us a greater chance to integrate everything instead of saying to people, 'use this database and that database and another database.' Now it all looks—and is—much more coordinated" (Thomson, 2000, p. 24).

To summarize, the above four ICT capabilities enable knowledge management by enhancing common knowledge or by facilitating the four KM processes. For example, an expertise-locator system (also called knowledge yellow pages or a people-finder system) is a special type of knowledge repository that pinpoints individuals having specific knowledge within the organization (Becerra-Fernandez, 2000, 2001). These systems rely on the reach and depth capabilities of ICT by enabling individuals to contact remotely located experts and seek detailed solutions to complicated problems. Another KM solution attempts to capture as much of the knowledge in an individual's head as possible and archive it in a searchable database (Armbrecht et al., 2001). This is primarily the aim of projects in artificial intelligence, which capture the expert's knowledge in systems based on various technologies, including rule-based systems and case-based reasoning, among others (Wong & Radcliffe, 2000). But the most sophisticated systems for eliciting and cataloging experts' knowledge in models that can easily be understood and applied by others in the organization (see, for example, Ford, Coffey, Cañas, Andrews, & Turner, 1996) require strong knowledge-engineering processes to develop. Such sophisticated KM systems are typically not advocated for use in mainstream business environments primarily because of the high cost involved in the knowledge-engineering effort.

FUTURE TRENDS

The future of knowledge management will be highlighted by three continuing trends: (a) KM will benefit from progress in ICT, (b) KM will continue the shift toward integrating knowledge from a variety of different perspectives, and (c) KM will continue to make trade-offs in numerous important areas.

First, in the future, KM will benefit from continual, and even more dynamic, progress in ICT. Improvements in cost and performance ratios of ICT have caused the cost of digitizing information to approach zero, and the cost of coordinating across individuals, organizational subunits, and organizations to approach zero as well (Grover & Segars, 1996). ICT progress also includes developments in autonomous software-based agents. Thus, the future of KM will be dramatically different due to the inevitable and unpredictable over any long period of time, and quantum changes in ICT and underpinning technologies such as artificial intelligence.

Second, in the future, KM will continue the shift toward bringing together, and effectively integrating, knowledge from a variety of different perspectives. Knowledge management originated at the individual level, focusing on the training and learning of individuals. Over time, the emphasis of knowledge management shifted to groups and entire organizations, and now examples of interorganizational impacts of knowledge management are becoming increasingly common. This trend in the impact of KM is expected to continue with its use across networks of organizations and across governments, enabling collaborations across historical adversaries and integrating knowledge across highly diverse perspectives and disciplines.

Finally, in the future, knowledge management will continue to make trade-offs in numerous important areas. One such trade-off pertains to the use of ICT for sharing. The same communication technologies that support the sharing of knowledge within an organization also enable the knowledge to leak outside the organization to its competing firms. Another trade-off concerns the balance between technology and people. It is essential to maintain a balance between using technology as substitutes for people (e.g., software agents) and using technology to enable collaboration from a wider range of people within and across organizations.

In conclusion, the future of knowledge management is one where people and advanced technologies will continue to work together, enabling knowledge integration across diverse domains with considerably higher payoffs. However, the new opportunities and greater benefits will require the careful management of people and technologies, a synthesis of multiple perspectives, and effectively dealing with a variety of trade-offs. The future of knowledge management will clearly be exciting due to the new opportunities and options, but interesting challenges definitely lay ahead for knowledge managers.

CONCLUSION

We have described the key aspects of knowledge management in this article. We have provided a working definition of knowledge management systems and presented the four types of KM systems: knowledge-discovery systems, knowledge-capture systems, knowledge-sharing systems, and knowledge-application systems. We also discussed how KM systems serve to support KM processes based on the integration of KM mechanisms, technologies, and infrastructure.

REFERENCES

Armbrecht, F. M. R., Chapas, R. B., Chappelow, C. C., Farris, G. F., Friga, P. N., Hartz, C. A., et al. (2001). Knowledge management in research and development. *Research Technology Management, 44*(4), 28-48.

Becerra-Fernandez, I. (2000). The role of artificial intelligence technologies in the implementation of people-finder knowledge management systems. *Knowledge Based Systems, 13*(5), 315-320.

Becerra-Fernandez, I. (2001). Locating expertise at NASA: Developing a tool to leverage human capital. *Knowledge Management Review, 4*(4), 34-37.

Becerra-Fernandez, I., Gonzalez, A., & Sabherwal, R. (2004). *Knowledge management: Challenges, solutions and technologies.* Upper Saddle River, NJ: Prentice Hall.

Becerra-Fernandez, I., & Stevenson, J. M. (2001). Knowledge management systems and solutions for the school principal as chief learning officer. *Education, 121*(3), 508-518.

Carlson, J. R., & Zmud, R. W. (1999). Channel expansion theory and the experiential nature of media richness perceptions. *Academy of Management Journal, 42*(2), 153-170.

Daft, R. L., & Lengel, R. H. (1986). Organization information requirements, media richness, and structural design. *Management Science, 32*(5), 554-571.

Evans, P., & Wurster, T. S. (1999). Getting real about virtual commerce. *Harvard Business Review*, 85-94.

Ford, K. M., Coffey, J. W., Cañas, A. J., Andrews, E. J., & Turner, C. W. (1996). Diagnosis and explanation by a nuclear cardiology expert system. *International Journal of Expert Systems, 9*, 499-506.

Grant, R. M. (1996a). Prospering in dynamically-competitive environments: Organizational capability as knowledge integration. *Organization Science, 7*(4), 375-387.

Grant, R. M. (1996b). Toward a knowledge-based theory of the firm. *Strategic Management Journal, 17*, 109-122.

Grover, V. & Segars, A. H. (1996). IT: The next 1100102 years. *Database, 27*(4), 45-57.

Keen, P. (1991). *Shaping the future: Business design through information technology.* Boston: Harvard Business School Press.

Nahapiet, J., & Ghoshal, S. (1998). Social capital, intellectual capital, and the organizational advantage. *Academy of Management Review, 23*(2), 242-266.

Nonaka, I. (1994). A dynamic theory of organizational knowledge creation. *Organization Science, 5*(1), 14-37.

Nonaka, I., & Takeuchi, H. (1995). *The knowledge creating company: How Japanese companies create the dynamics of innovation.* New York: Oxford University Press.

Polyani, M. (1967). *The tacit dimension.* Garden City, NY: Anchor Books.

Schwartz, D. G., Divitini, M., & Brasethvik, T. (2000). On knowledge management in the Internet age. In D. G. Schwartz, M. Divitini, & T. Brasethvik (Eds.), *Internet-based knowledge management and organizational memory* (pp. 1-23). Hershey, PA: Idea Gruop Publishing.

Thomson, S. (2000). Focus: Keeping pace with knowledge. Information World Review, *155*, 23-24.

Wong, W., & Radcliffe, D. (2000). The tacit nature of design knowledge. *Technology Analysis and Strategic Management, 12*(4), 493-512.

KEY TERMS

Artificial Intelligence: The branch of computer science concerned with making computers behave like humans. Refers to the science that provides computers with the ability to solve problems not easily solved through algorithmic models.

Common Knowledge: An organization's cumulative experiences in comprehending a category of knowledge and activities, and the organizing principles that support communication and coordination.

Knowledge Capture: The process of eliciting knowledge (either explicit or tacit) that resides within people, artifacts, or organizational entities, and representing it in an electronic form such as a knowledge-based system for later reuse or retrieval.

Knowledge Discovery: The development of new tacit or explicit knowledge from data and information or from the synthesis of prior knowledge.

Knowledge Engineering: The process of eliciting an expert's knowledge in order to construct a knowledge-based system or organizational memory.

Knowledge Management: They perform the activities involved in discovering, capturing, sharing, and applying knowledge in terms of resources, documents, and people skills so as to enhance, in a cost-effective fashion, the impact of knowledge on the unit's goal achievement.

Knowledge Management Infrastructure: The long-term foundation on which knowledge management resides. It includes five main components: organization culture, organization structure, communities of practice, information technology infrastructure, and common knowledge.

Knowledge Management Mechanisms: Organizational or structural means used to promote knowledge management. They may (or may not) utilize technology, but they do involve some kind of organizational arrangement or social or structural means of facilitating KM.

Knowledge Management Processes: The broad processes that help in discovering, capturing, sharing, and applying knowledge.

Knowledge Management Systems: They integrate technologies and mechanisms to support KM processes.

Knowledge Sharing: The process through which explicit or tacit knowledge is communicated and appropriated to other individuals.

ENDNOTE

[1] Some sections of this article were adapted from Becerra-Fernandez, Gonzalez, and Sabherwal (2004).

Incentive Structures in Knowledge Management

Hamid R. Ekbia
University of Redlands, USA

Noriko Hara
Indiana University, USA

INTRODUCTION

The role of incentives in organizational behavior has long been recognized and studied (Whyte, 1955; Hertzberg, 1959). This role becomes ever more paramount in knowledge management (KM), where users also become creators and contributors: The voluntary sharing of knowledge by individuals is a key element in the implementation and success of any knowledge-management endeavor. Having gradually recognized this, the KM community has theorized, examined, and implemented various incentive structures to promote knowledge sharing and system use in organizations. This article investigates some of these incentive structures, their underlying assumptions, as well as the issues and questions that they raise for KM theory and practice in general.

The article continues in the next section with a brief history and a general discussion of incentives in organizations. It then discusses the theoretical underpinnings of different approaches to KM as they relate to issues of incentive, and provides examples of practical incentive structures used by organizations. Next, it presents an analysis of the examples in the previous section, discusses possible future trends, and finally draws conclusions in terms of appropriate incentive structures for knowledge sharing.

BACKGROUND: THE CENTRAL DILEMMA OF KNOWLEDGE MANAGEMENT

Organization and management scientists have long studied the role of incentives in organizational behavior. Whyte (1955), for instance, provides a classic study of "the 5 M's of factory life: men, money, machines, morale, and motivation" (p. 1). The dominant scientific management view, which held sway in the incentive systems of the time, was based on an *economic model* of rational human beings who seek to maximize their individual material gains. Whyte challenged this model and replaced it with a *socioeconomic model* that studies human reaction to incentives in the context of their relationships with other human beings (fellow workers, work groups, managers, etc.). He argued that incentives can be symbolic and much broader in character than purely material and monetary, and emphasized that "*we change sentiments and activities through changing interaction*" (p. 227). The lessons of the latter half of the last century, including those of KM, seem to support Whyte's model as a more realistic picture of human organizational behavior.

The situation in knowledge management is obviously different from the factory-floor situation studied by Whyte (1955). Not only are we dealing with a different work environment in terms of organization, management, culture, technology, and so on, we are facing a new type of economic agent, usually referred to as a *knowledge worker* in the literature. Although this term implies a different type of economic activity from earlier ones (e.g., factory work), it does not necessarily mean that knowledge workers have a totally novel psychology in their reaction to incentives. To the contrary, we argue that Whyte's original insights are by and large true of the current work environments as well. To demonstrate this, we introduce what might be called the central dilemma of knowledge management.

A widely studied phenomenon in the social studies of cooperative behavior are the situations known as *social dilemmas:* namely, those where individual rationality (trying to maximize individual gain) leads to collective irrationality (Kollock, 1998; cf Cabrera & Cabrera, 2002). Well-known examples of social dilemmas are the *tragedy of the commons*, where overuse of a shared resource (such as land) by beneficiaries (such as herders) would result in its ultimate depletion (Hardin, 1968), and the phenomenon of *free ride*, where individuals are tempted to enjoy a common resource without contributing to it (Sweeney, 1973). It has been suggested that knowledge sharing can be understood as a special case of a social dilemma (Cabrera & Cabrera; Connolly, Thorn, & Heminger, 1992). That is, if we consider knowledge as a common resource of an organization, individual workers are often faced with the questions of whether or not, to what extent, and under what circumstances should they use, relate to, and contribute to this common property. Although there are clear differences between a natural resource, which is physically constrained in the extent of its use, and knowledge, which is not depleted by use, this conceptualization of knowledge sharing as a social dilemma is rather useful. One way to understand this dilemma is through the fact that contribution to a KM system involves cost (in terms of time, expertise, job security, etc.) that may not be accounted for or paid off by the organizational incentive structures. This is the essence of the central dilemma of KM, which can be articulated as follows:

Why should a knowledge worker contribute to the shared knowledge of the organization if the cost of doing so for the individual is higher than its benefits?

This dilemma gives rise to a tension that is inherent in almost any knowledge-management effort. Incentive structures could therefore be broadly understood as attempts to resolve or reduce this tension. Such attempts should at a minimum address the following questions (Cabrera & Cabrera, 2002, p. 691).

- Why do people share or not share information with coworkers?
- What motivates a person to give up personal knowledge to a third party?
- What are the main barriers that an organization may face when trying to foster knowledge sharing among its employees?
- What can an organization do to overcome those barriers?

The ubiquity of the above dilemma turns these into central questions in the theory and practice of KM. The following discussion demonstrates that various approaches to KM partly diverge on the basis of the answers that they give to the above questions.

INCENTIVES IN KM THEORY

There are different ways to classify KM approaches. For our purposes here, we are going to distinguish among three different views of KM: the techno-centric, human-centric, and socio-technical.

The Techno-Centric View

Roughly speaking, the techno-centric or product-oriented view emphasizes knowledge capture as the main objective of KM. This involves two major dimensions: a cognitive dimension that takes knowledge as something that can be codified, organized, stored, and accessed on the basis of need, and a technical dimension that emphasizes the role of new information and communication technologies in the knowledge-capture process. As such, the techno-centric view tends to formulate and answer the above questions in mainly cognitive and technical terms: People share their knowledge to the extent that they can elicit it and their technologies can capture it. The main barriers to such capturing are therefore either cognitive or technical in character, as are the solutions to overcome the barriers.

As we see, the techno-centric view does not pay much attention to issues of incentive and motivation. Nonaka's (1994) well-known quadrant model might be a rough example of this view: Capture and codify knowledge with expert systems, share knowledge with groupware and intranets, distribute knowledge with databases and desktop publishing, and create knowledge with CAD, virtual reality, and so on. Organizationally, the techno-centric view gives rise to an information-systems model of KM (cf Huysman & de Wit, 2002), concentrating KM efforts within IT departments. It might be fair to say that the techno-centric view, in its purest forms, belongs to the early days of KM and does not have much currency today, although its cognitive component is deep rooted and still holds a strong influence on KM thinking.

The Human-Centric View

The human-centric or process-oriented view, on the other hand, emphasizes the social processes that are needed for the development of trust and reciprocal relationships among individuals. As such, it focuses on person-to-person communication and highlights social constructs such as communities of practice as the main vehicles of KM implementation. According to this view, people are driven toward knowledge sharing by their need for knowledge (Lave & Wenger, 1991). Reciprocity and recognition are, therefore, major motivations for them. Knowledge sharing is often emergent, informal, and hard to create top-down. The barriers to knowledge sharing are often issues of trust, and they can be overcome by building and expanding the right social relationships. Organizationally, the human-centric view is associated with the human-capital view of the firm, and leads to a human-resource-management model of KM (Huysman & de Wit, 2002; see, for example, Desouza & Awazu, 2003). The human-centric view has gained some momentum in recent years, especially around the literature on communities of practice (Lave & Wenger).

The Socio-Technical View

Finally, the socio-technical view thinks of KM as people sharing their knowledge with IT-enabled applications. It considers KM as an integrated socio-technical intervention with coordinated efforts to enroll participants, reward high-quality participation, and resolve issues of trust and commitment. This is the view advocated, among others, by the proponents of social informatics (Kling, 2000). Unlike the techno-centric view, social informatics does not consider IT as a silver bullet that automatically energizes knowledge sharing, and in contrast to the human-centric view, it regards best practices as contextual frames rather than isolated practices. It also puts a large emphasis on power relationships in KM practice (Ekbia & Kling, 2003).

Organizationally, the socio-technical view considers knowledge sharing as an orchestrated process that needs to be supported by both top-down managerial interventions and bottom-up employee and practitioner involvement. Although there seems to be a growing enthusiasm for the socio-technical view, it might take a while before the KM community comes to grips with the full complexity of KM as a socio-technical intervention. As the next discussion illustrates, current practices of KM, even when they involve some kind of incentive structure, are still dominated by either the techno-centric or the human-centric views.

INCENTIVES IN KM PRACTICE

Having recognized the importance of incentives in KM, firms and organizations have devised various schemes to support and motivate knowledge sharing among their employees. The following examples are illustrative of some of the more common schemes. Stevens (2000, p. 54) reports various cases of "innovative strategies that encourage knowledge sharing." Briefly, these included examples range from companies that incorporate this into their hiring process to those that try to develop trust by creating a code of ethics; implementing reward systems on the basis of employee contributions; encouraging knowledge sharing through conferences, classes, and mentoring programs; establishing communities by expanding networks of contacts; or creating role models and KM advocates who keep the ball rolling. It is to be

noticed that many of these incentive schemes are under the strong influence of either the techno-centric or the human-centric views.

Other studies of incentive structures report more or less similar attempted schemes (Angus, 2000; Ward, 2002; Wright, 1998). Generally speaking, current schemes often take the form of extrinsic incentives such as monetary rewards, recognition, and promotion. Popular accounts of incentive systems also tend to focus on similar schemes and, as a result, often portray a rosy picture of the impacts of incentives on employee performance. A rather different picture emerges, however, when employees' opinions are probed. In a survey conducted on a group of knowledge workers, Rupp and Smith (2003) found that 58% of their respondents feel that there is a discrepancy between their merit increase and performance rating. The authors suggest that in order to improve this situation, organizations need to give more responsibilities to employees.

Austin (1996) introduces the phenomenon of "incentive distortion" to demonstrate some of the complications that arise when incentive systems are not built upon employee responsibility. An example comes from a government organization whose task is to help people find jobs. An incentive system, which rewarded employees on the basis of the number of interviews they conducted, actually resulted in a significant rise in the number of interviews, but it also made employees spend little time on finding referrals. Ideally, for the process to be fruitful, the time spent on conducting interviews and finding referrals should be equally divided. To move toward this ideal, management changed the measure of the reward as the ratio of the number of interviews to the number of referrals, only to find out later that employees were deleting the record of interviews in order to distort the ratio.

Barth (2000) introduces some examples of dysfunctional mismatch between incentives and performance measurement. For instance, as part of their performance reviews, IBM employees were asked to contribute their project experience to a company-wide KM system. However, many employees did not submit their contributions until the very last month preceding the reviews. This can be understood in light of the additional burden of the activity, which would take away employees' time and resources from tasks with more direct returns or from what they probably considered more important tasks. Faced with this situation, IBM management introduced a quality-control component that incorporated a kind of expert peer review to evaluate the content and quality of the submissions in terms of their usefulness to other employees. Aside from employee competition, this introduces issues of overhead and cost efficiency for the whole company. The use of selective incentives such as the above incurs a cost for the organization in terms of the monitoring of participation (in addition to the rewards themselves), and this needs to be taken into account in the evaluation of the KM initiative (Cabrera & Cabrera, 2002).

DISCUSSION: FACING THE DILEMMA

"A man always has two reasons for doing anything—a good reason and a real reason." (J. P. Morgan)

The above examples raise a set of questions. How can incentive structures be tailored to improve employee satisfaction? How can managers and KM practitioners prevent incentive distortions from proliferating? At what point are the costs of selective schemes in terms of company overhead, employee time, and employee satisfaction going to tip off the benefits? These (and our earlier) questions should be taken seriously in order for KM efforts to work, and to answer them, the KM community has largely turned to economic theory for a source of ideas.

Davenport and Prusak (1998), for instance, discuss the idea of a "knowledge market" where buyers and sellers of knowledge negotiate a mutually satisfactory price for the exchange. According to this idea, the perceived gain from the exchange in terms of reciprocity, repute, and altruism serve as an incentive for knowledge sharing. As Ba, Stallaert, and Whinston (2001a) have argued, however, it is difficult to quantify these gains into monetary values so that a benefit can be assigned by the organization. Furthermore, knowledge has the characteristics of a public good in that it is nondepletable, and economic theory itself warns us that treating a public good as a private good leads to the underprovision of knowledge and, hence, to organizational loss (ibid; cf Samuelson, 1954). This is related to the free-rider problem and what we called the central dilemma of KM. Ba, Stallaert, and Whinston (2001b) have applied economic theory to discuss an incentive-aligned market mechanism to optimize investment in KM within a firm, but their account focuses almost exclusively on extrinsic motivations such as monetary rewards. To find about intrinsic motivations such as commitment and job satisfaction, however, we need to look elsewhere outside of economic theory.

Social psychologists distinguish intrinsically, vs. extrinsically, motivated activities as ones for which "there is no apparent reward except the activity itself" (Deci, 1976, p. 23). These are behaviors that a person engages in "to feel competent and self-determining" (p. 61). Therefore, they could be either sought as a means of stimulation or as a way of conquering challenges or

reducing incongruities (ibid). Furthermore, industrial psychologists have shown that motivation is a rather fluid and dynamic phenomenon: What motivates one person may not motivate another, what motivates a person may change over time, and people might be always motivated but not necessarily toward organizational goals (Champagne & McAfee, 1989). Similar observations have been made in information-systems research: For example, the report by Constant, Kiesler, and Sproull (1994) reveals that people share knowledge because of their altruistic preferences. These theories and findings might indeed be useful in reducing the tension that arises due to the central dilemma of KM. In her study of a consulting firm with a strong KM initiative, Orlikowski (2000) explains consultants' reluctance to contribute knowledge in terms of the perceived incompatibility between the collaborative nature of the technology, and the individualistic and competitive nature of the organization. Under such circumstances, paying attention to intrinsic motivations might be a key to more effective systems.

What this discussion illustrates is not only that incentive structures are important for KM efforts, but also that they are multifaceted phenomena, the understanding of which requires different levels of analysis from different perspectives: the psychological, social, economical, technical, and so on.

FUTURE TRENDS

Given the multifaceted nature of incentive issues, it would seem that a socio-technical approach, such as proposed by social informatics, holds a stronger promise in addressing them, a trend that is emerging in different quarters of KM theory and practice.

Huysman and de Wit (2002) suggest that, following a first wave where organizations were prone to fall into one of three traps (overemphasis on the role of ICT, individual learning, and managerial needs), KM is moving toward a second wave where the focus is on collective knowledge (social capital) that is routinely shared through personal and electronic networks. Gold, Malhorta, and Segars (2001, p. 187) also introduce an organizational capabilities perspective of knowledge management based on three key infrastructures: the structural (which "refers to the presence of norms and trust"), cultural ("shared contexts"), and technical. Ba et al. (2001a) propose to add an incentive-alignment dimension to the current software-engineering and user-acceptance dimensions of the design and implementation of information systems in organizations.

Cabrera and Cabrera (2002), from the perspective of social dilemmas discussed earlier, suggest a number of interventions with a strong socio-technical character: for example, reducing the cost and increasing the benefits (direct or perceived) of contributing through gain-sharing plans that reward the combined efforts of individuals; increasing the efficacy of contributions through training, feedback mechanisms, and advanced technologies; enhancing group identity and personal responsibility by frequent communication and interaction; and so on.

As these examples indicate, there is a growing trend toward a socio-technical approach that integrates heterogeneous interventions (technical, cultural, structural, etc.) at different levels (micro and macro) of organizational life.

CONCLUSION

The global economy went through a serious transformation in the second half of the 20th century, one aspect of which is the move toward what some analysts call a knowledge economy. Knowledge management is an organizational manifestation of this trend that incorporates novel elements of economic and organizational activity. It would be wrong, however, to conclude from this that everything about the knowledge economy and about knowledge management is novel and unprecedented. There are stable and enduring aspects to all forms of economic activity, and the social psychology of incentive, motivation, and cooperation is one such aspect. Those 21st century factory workers who are unwilling to share their special knowledge (Aeppel, 2002) can probably be explained in similar terms to those that Whyte (1955) used to explain the behavior of their mid 20th century fellow workers, that is, in terms of their material and symbolic relationships to other human beings. By the same token, the reaction of knowledge workers toward incentive structures can also be understood in similar terms.

In this article, we have suggested that KM can be best understood as a socio-technical intervention rather than a purely technological system. A key aspect of this intervention is to motivate individuals to share their knowledge and skills with their fellow workers. This is what turns incentive structures into an indispensable component of any KM effort. The question is how best to implement such structures. To be sure, there is no general answer to this question as particular contexts shape the character of the intervention and structures. But a common lesson that seems to be emerging is that extrinsic motivations alone are not always sufficient and that human beings are often driven by intrinsic motivations such as job satisfaction. It is becoming increasingly clear that even nonmonetary rewards, such

as social recognition, can be effective so long as they are public, infrequent, credible, and culturally meaningful (Lawler, 2000). Similar findings are reported in the literature on communities of practice (Lave & Wenger, 1991; Orr, 1996; Schwen & Hara, 2003). The growing phenomenon of free and open software development, which works through the voluntary contribution of very many individuals, is also a case in point.

In summary, a common recognition of the key role of incentive structures in knowledge management and an associated increase of enthusiasm for socio-technical perspectives seem to be shaping. This does not mean that the path of the future is clear, straightforward, and uncontroversial. There are still many outstanding issues in terms of our understanding of the interplay between various elements and levels: the individual and the social, the cognitive and the technical, the material and the symbolic, the intrinsic and the extrinsic, and so on. A good part of the answer to these questions should inevitably come from outside knowledge management, from the social, organizational, and cognitive sciences as well as technical fields such as computer science. The knowledge-management community can greatly contribute to our better understanding of the above issues by its efforts to integrate those insights in its theory and practice. Organizational incentive structures provide a good starting point for such efforts.

REFERENCES

Aeppel, T. (2002, July 1). Tricks of the trade: On factory floors, top workers hide secrets to success. *The Wall Street Journal*, A1.

Austin, R. D. (1996). *Measuring and managing performance in organizations.* New York: Dorset House Publishing.

Ba, S., Stallaert, J., & Whinston, A. B. (2001a). Introducing a third dimension in information systems design: The case for incentive alignment. *Information Systems Research, 12*(3), 225-239.

Ba, S., Stallaert, J., & Whinston, A. B. (2001b). Optimal investment in knowledge within a firm using a market mechanism. *Management Science, 47*(9), 1203-1219.

Barth, S. (2000). KM horror stories. *Knowledge Management Magazine.* Retrieved February 26, 2004, from *http://www.destinationkm.com/articles/default.asp?ArticleID=923*

Cabrera, A., & Cabrera, E. F. (2002). Knowledge-sharing dilemmas. *Organization Studies, 23*(5), 678-710.

Champagne, M. I., & McAfee, V. W. (1989). *Motivating strategies for performance and opportunity.* New York: Quorum Books.

Connolly, T., Thorn, B. K., & Heminger, A. (1992). Discretionary databases as social dilemmas. In W. B. G. Liebrand, D. M. Messick, & H. A. M. Wilke (Eds.), *Social dilemmas: Theoretical issues and research findings* (pp. 199-208). Tarrytown: Pergamon Press Inc.

Constant, D., Kiesler, S., & Sproull, L. (1994). What's mine is ours, or is it? A study of attitudes about information sharing. *Information Systems Research, 5*(4), 400-421.

Davenport, T., & Prusak, L. (1998). *Working knowledge: How organizations manage what they know.* Boston: Harvard Business School Press.

Deci, E. L. (1976). *Intrinsic motivation.* New York: Plenum Press.

Desouza, K. C., & Awazu, Y. (2003). Knowledge management. *HR Magazine, 48*(11), 107.

Ekbia, H. R., & Kling, R. (2003). Power in knowledge management in late modern times. *Proceedings of the Academy of Management Conference.*

Gold, A. H., Malhorta, A., & Segars, A. H. (2001). Knowledge management: An organizational capabilities perspective. *Journal of Management Information Systems, 18*(1), 185-214.

Hardin, G. (1968). The tragedy of the commons. *Science, 162,* 1243-1248.

Huysman, M., & de Wit, D. (2002). *Knowledge sharing in practice.* Dordrecht: Kluwer Academic Publishers.

Kling, R. (2000). Learning about information technologies and social change: The contribution of social informatics. *The Information Society, 16*(3).

Kollock, P. (1998). Persuasive communication: Measures to overcome real-life social dilemmas. In W. B. G. Liebrand, D. M. Messick, & H. A. M. Wilke (Eds.), *Social dilemmas: Theoretical issues and research findings* (pp. 307-318). New York: Pergammon.

Lave, J., & Wenger, E. (1991). *Situated learning: Legitimate peripheral participation.* Cambridge, MA: Cambridge University Press.

Lawler, E. E., III. (2000). *Rewarding excellence.* San Francisco: Jossey-Bass.

Nonaka, I. (1994). A dynamic theory of organizational knowledge creation. *Organization Science, 5,* 14-37.

Orlikowski, W. (2000). Using technology and constituting structures: A practice lens for studying technology in organizations. *Organization Science, 11*(4), 404-428.

Orr, J. E. (1996). *Talking about machines: An ethnography of a modern job.* Ithaca, NY: Cornel University Press.

Plaskoff, J. (2003). Intersubjectivity and community building: Learning to learn organizationally. In M. Easterby-Smith & M. A. Lyles (Eds.), *The Blackwell handbook of organizational learning and knowledge management.* Blackwell Publishers.

Samuelson, P. (1954). The pure theory of economic expenditure. *Rev. Econom. Statistics, 36*(4), 387-389.

Schwen, T. M., & Hara, N. (2003). Community of practice a metaphor for online design? *The Information Society, 19*(3), 257-270.

Smith, A. D., & Rupp, W. T. (2003). Knowledge workers: Exploring the link among performance rating, pay and motivational aspects. *Journal of Knowledge Management, 7*(1), 107-124.

Stevens, L. (2000). Incentives for sharing. *Knowledge Management,* 54-60.

Ward, S. (2001). Rewarding knowledge sharing at Context Integration, Inc. *KM Review, 5*(1), 3.

Whyte, W. F. (1955). *Money and motivation: An analysis of incentives in industry.* Greenwood Publishing Group.

Write, P. (1998). Do incentive schemes promote knowledge sharing? *Knowledge Management Review, 1*(2), 4-6.

KEY TERMS

Extrinsic Motivations: Those motivations that have a material or symbolic manifestation in the outside world, for example, bonuses, promotions, vacations, reputation, recognition, and so forth.

Free Ride: The tendency of the users of public goods to use them without contributing much or at all to its sharing, usually accompanied with an understatement of the true value of the resource to the free rider.

Incentive Structures: The material or symbolic reward or punishment mechanisms that organizations apply in order to encourage or discourage a certain organizational behavior, in this case, the sharing of knowledge, skills, or insights with other members of the organization.

Intrinsic Motivations: Those motivations that have no external manifestation in terms of rewards, but are psychologically effective in stimulating or driving people to seek self-satisfaction or self-consistency, for example, job satisfaction, commitment, and so forth.

Public Goods: Resources that generally are (or are perceived to be) of some public value or use, and whose consumption by one member of society does not preclude its consumption by others, for example, renewable natural resources such as air, or services such public radio or TV.

Social Dilemma: A situation where individual rationality (in the sense of maximizing personal gain) leads to social irrationality (in the sense of generating a suboptimal outcome for the social group).

Symbolic Incentives: Incentives that do not have material value, but are culturally significant, for example, reputation and recognition.

Inquiring Organizations

Dianne Hall
Auburn University, USA

David Croasdell
University of Nevada, Reno, USA

INTRODUCTION

In order to manage knowledge and operate successfully in today's information-intensive business environments, various organizational forms have emerged (e.g., Mintzberg, 1979; Nonaka, 1994; Nonaka & Takeuchi, 1995). The form that an organization takes has consequences for communication and dissemination of information, and thereby the ability to engage in organizational learning. Some of these forms compress knowledge at the root level of the organization, while others facilitate the search for useful knowledge within the organization. Other forms are capable of supporting organizational members who must synthesize knowledge from diverse sources. If a firm begins to reconfirm that knowledge management and core competencies are at the heart of organizational performance, the demand on organizations to develop core competencies and to create and manage knowledge intensifies. Even after realizing the critical role of knowledge in the present competitive environments, firms are struggling with managing and creating knowledge.

Growing interest in a firm's intellectual capital and collective knowledge have led to ways in which organizations improve knowledge (organizational learning), store knowledge (organizational memory), and share knowledge (knowledge transfer). Although often discussed separately, these three concepts are tightly interwoven, and all must be considered when an organization strives to move toward a knowledge-based competency. These aspects fall under the broad and complex umbrella of knowledge management. In a review of knowledge management literature, Schultze and Leidner (2002, p. 218) suggest a definition of knowledge management as being the "generation, representation, storage, transfer, transformation, application, embedding, and protecting of organizational knowledge." While their definition is not the only one, nor may all researchers or practitioners agree with its appropriateness, it does demonstrate the incredible complexity that knowledge management presents. The authors note that research in knowledge management is a complex interdependency of collaboration (both in knowledge/information sharing and work), organizational memory, and organizational learning.

An organization striving toward knowledge management competency may be best served by incorporating an organizational form that facilitates learning and thus the expansion of organizational memory. However, choosing one form may not be supportive of the multiple types of learning required by such an organization. These organizations should adopt the form of an inquiring organization (Courtney, Croasdell, & Paradice, 1998) and use it to structure flexible subforms that facilitate the learning process.

This article describes inquiring organizations and considers the appropriateness of applying philosophical perspective to organizational form. The next section provides a background to inquiring organizations. The latter part of the article focuses on how inquiring organizations can take on multiple forms. The article concludes with a discussion of areas for future investigation.

BACKGROUND: INQUIRING SYSTEMS, INQUIRING ORGANIZATIONS AND LEARNING

Inquiring systems are characterized by properties described by Churchman (1971), who develops five inquirers based on the writings of five Western philosophers—Leibniz, Locke, Kant, Hegel, and Singer. While an in-depth discussion of the inquirers is not within the scope of this article, each of the inquirers is briefly introduced in the following sections on inquiring organization subforms.

Inquiring systems create and manage knowledge, and provide a component called a guarantor that promotes accuracy and reduces redundancy in organizational memory (Hall, Paradice, & Courtney, 2003). They can provide the basis for a knowledge-oriented organization by facilitating the creation of new organizational knowledge and the adaptation of existing knowledge in wickedly changing situations (Hall et al., 2003). *Inquiring organizations* are based on inquiring systems (Courtney et al., 1998).

Inquiring organizations and learning organizations are terms that are often used interchangeably; however, there is one critical difference between the two. To be an inquiring organization, the organization's philosophical foundation must be laid on the principles of inquiring systems as discussed by Churchman (1971). Both the learning organization and the inquiring organization aspire to learn. Learning organizations primarily engage in double-loop learning (e.g., reacting to a problem by both fixing the problem (single-loop learning) and making changes to underlying norms that may have contributed to the problem) (Argyris & Schön, 1996) and often approach knowledge management in a reactive manner rather than the proactive process of the inquiring organization. However, an inquiring organization *inquires*—that is, it continuously searches and investigates its environment and engages in behavior that examines the learning process itself with an end goal of increasing learning efficiency (triple-loop learning). In this manner, the organization challenges the assumptions on which its behavior is based, effectively examining not the most effective means to an end, but examining the foundation of means themselves (Isaacs, 1993). This provides the capacity to routinely check organizational memory for inaccuracies, redundancies, or information that is no longer relevant (Hall et al., 2003).

Given the complexity of any organization moving toward knowledge competency, one can see that its support needs go beyond managerial style, technology, or process design. A knowledge-based organization must be considered in its entirety; however, providing an adequate foundation that can support such an organization is not easy. Churchman's (1971) inquirers, and the inquiring organization in particular, provide a basis for that foundation.

THE MAIN FOCUS: THE INQUIRING ORGANIZATION

The inquiring organization is a mesh of integrated inquiring systems that operate singly or together depending on the complexity of the environment in which the organizational unit finds itself operating. Each of the inquirers discussed by Churchman (1971) has specific strengths that allow it to operate efficiently in specific contexts, and together the inquirers have the ability to handle the complexity and the chaotic environment in which many modern organizations operate. Each of the inquirers is suited to a particular organizational form and environment. For instance, the Leibnizian inquirer is suited to a hierarchical form where knowledge is pushed throughout the organization. Lockean inquiry is more suited to a network form where information is pulled into the network; knowledge is created specifically for that network's context.

Inquirers in the Churchmanian tradition embody different organizational subforms, but integration of the forms into the inquiring organizational metaform allows homeostasis to survive against the elements, and in doing so, supports the characteristics of an inquiring organization. We therefore define the inquiring organizational metaform as a complex structure of multiple organizational subforms working together for the benefit of the organization. We now discuss the subforms in terms of their architecture and learning characteristics.

The Leibnizian Subform

The Leibnizian inquirer is the most basic of the inquirers and provides the inquiring organization with its initial set of facts (fact nets) and axioms derived from formulas that comprise the foundation of organizational memory. These fact nets are created by identifying and testing a hypothesis using basic axioms stored in the system (Churchman, 1971). This inquirer is considered a closed system; that is, it functions within a limited set of relationships. Learning that is attributed to the Leibnizian inquirer is primarily based in the theory of autopoiesis which is the ability to self-perpetuate and produce through a series of relationships in a closed, stable environment. Organizations or organizational units that exist in an environment of stability and routine do well to adopt the Leibnizian inquirer as their organizational form.

This structured environment requires adherence to rules and regulations; learning within the organization is a push rather than pull process. Learning occurs at the top of the organization and is pushed downward throughout the organization by processes such as demonstration workshops. Because of the explicit nature of the information being passed downward throughout the organization, teaching is not generally a necessary means of information dissemination; the printed rules and handbooks of the organization serve the function well.

The Lockean Subform

The Lockean inquirer is a well-suited system for a relatively stable, but highly social environment. This inquirer is founded on principles of agreement embedded in classification of observations. The Lockean inquirer's members share a common belief and vision, culminating in shared mental models of the organization's environment, tasks, and strategies. Learning is a group effort and does not occur without consensus. Thus, relationships and communication are integral facets of this inquirer (Churchman, 1971).

The learning here is both a push process (e.g., guidelines) and an assimilation process (e.g., the collective observation of senior sales personnel). Rather than demonstrate techniques, formal teaching is likely to involve storytelling by top producers, combined with tried-and-true heuristics generated by those experts to react to specific situations, such as an irate customer. The new salesperson will strive to assimilate actions and processes that are observed to have favorable outcomes for senior sales personnel. This pull process is encouraged through informal indoctrination and by extrinsic motivation factors such as commission percentages.

The Kantian Subform

The Kantian inquirer is designed to incorporate both multiple perspectives and facts to determine models that are appropriate for the situation. Using Leibnizian fact nets to support its data analysis, this inquirer performs modeling techniques to detect causal relationships between perspectives. After a model is chosen as being most appropriate for the particular context through a process known as best-fit analysis, the Kantian inquirer performs an analysis to determine whether that model continues to produce satisfying results; when a model fails to satisfy, it is removed from consideration (Churchman, 1971). This form is most suitable in environments where there is some structure and some ability to formally analyze data, but where a clear solution may not be evident or possible.

Learning in this inquirer is a combination of theoretical and empirical analysis, and is disseminated through the organization via the group members. The nature of the knowledge will affect whether formal or informal teaching applies. Learning may take place in the explicit form (e.g., a change in a process) that would likely be disseminated through a push process as well as being represented in the organization's memory. A new goal, mission, or cultural change may be disseminated less formally through narrative indoctrination.

The Hegelian Subform

The Hegelian inquirer is a more advanced form that seeks to create knowledge through a dialectic process (Churchman, 1971). At its foundation are opposing Leibnizian fact nets that contain the thesis and antithesis perspectives of the question under consideration. Each of these perspectives is examined for their underlying assumptions; these are then paired (one from each side) and examined. As each pair is examined, the assumption with the most applicability to the situation at hand is synthesized into a new perspective that draws on the strength of each of the underlying perspectives (Churchman, 1971). Communica-

tion is critical in this form where learning occurs during the synthesis process and a greater understanding of the context is obtained.

Learning in this form is the outcome of the dialectic. Lessons are disseminated throughout the form itself by communication among the members. Little formal teaching or observing is required because members of these organizations are active in the learning process; however, when this form interacts with other forms, the teaching process would be selected in accordance with the receiving form (e.g., formal workshops for the Leibnizian form).

The Singerian Subform

The Singerian inquirer is the most complex of Churchman's (1971) inquirers. Its primary purpose is to seek out inconsistencies throughout the organization and resolve the inconsistencies through a process of measuring, partitioning, and refining. During this process, the Singerian inquirer "sweeps in" variables and perspectives from as many stakeholders as possible, sometimes using the other inquirers for support. When there are no problems to be solved, the Singerian inquirer challenges the status quo and again enters the measurement process. A subcomponent of the inquirer reruns the models associated with the measurement process to ensure replication throughout the system. This inquirer is appropriate for all environments, but is most appropriate for tumulus environments where fast, efficient action is required and little experience with the problem context is available.

The learning associated with this inquirer is complex in both breadth and depth, and is designed to enlarge the "natural image" with multiple perspectives, partitions, and refinements that allow an organization and its members to engage in a wider variety of innovative and creative tasks. The Singerian organizational form produces knowledge on all levels, and therefore all of the aforementioned learning approaches may be appropriate.

MULTIPLE APPROACHES: THE INQUIRING ORGANIZATIONAL METAFORM

The subforms described above are contained within the inquiring organizational metaform. Rarely does an organization consist of a homogenous set of processes, individuals, cultures, or environments. One common thread that does run throughout the organization, however, is the need for an accurate and dynamic organizational memory. As contributions from any organizational member or unit are stored in organizational memory, other organizational components, such as knowledge discovery components, may develop relationships between the new information and existing information that will be beneficial to another, possibly unrelated, unit, thereby facilitating organizational learning. Growth of organizational memory may be further enhanced in this organizational metaform by the use of a system designed to discover and distribute information, particularly from the external environment. Organizational memory may then be used within the organization to facilitate new or innovative knowledge creation.

Just as the components of an organization may differ vastly, so too may the tasks, environment, and decision-making strategies of different units. These characteristics play an important role in determining an appropriate organizational form to adopt. Because the focus of the inquiring organization is learning and the accompanying growth of organizational memory, care must be taken to structure each organizational unit in a way that provides appropriate structure for the task and environment, but does not limit learning potential. The following examples help clarify how the inquiring organizational metaform may translate into its subforms, all working together to provide proper support to the organization.

Manufacturing firms provide an example that illustrates the existence of varying organizational forms in inquiring organizations. Factory floor workers following standard operating procedures and highly routinized tasks are representative of the Leibnizian form. Team members working together to analyze and reengineer business processes to improve efficiencies and productivity represent the Lockean form. Matching product development and production to market needs and developing strategy to meet consumer needs require model fits typified by the Kantian form of inquiry. Labor talks and negotiated contracts are representative functions of

the Hegelian form. Finally, organizational metrics that are used to inform productivity measures, assign performance bonuses, or modify existing practices would be typical of the Singerian inquirer. New knowledge from these process (e.g., new consumer needs strategy or new productivity measures) are added to organizational memory.

Another organizational form that can be considered is the academic community that exists in higher education. Each form of organizational inquiry exists within the community. Staff members within a given area function at the Leibnizian level using formal mechanisms and routines. The academic work environment is typically stable, and relatively few administrators carry out centralized high-level decision making. Researchers working together through the processes of research and publication are functioning in Lockean communities; committee and service commitments are also Lockean in nature. Kantian forms of inquiry are active when decisions such as budgeting or admissions standards are considered. These tasks are moderately formal, more complicated in nature, and typically include more autonomy in the decision-making process. Hegelian forms of inquiry may exist between students and faculty, and between faculty and the board of trustees. The tenure and promotion process would be typical of Singer inquiry, with the emphasis on measuring output by the number and quality of publications, student evaluation metrics, and quantified contributions to the referent discipline. Individuals go through a process of refining "research" to a specific number of publications, journal quality, contribution matrices, and so forth. These measures may vary by department. The newly created knowledge that arises from this decision scenario may consist of new journal rankings, new productivity measures, and new ratios of service to research. Again, these are added to organizational memory.

Table 1. Organizational structure of Churchman's (1971) inquirers

Form	Characteristics	Primary Learning Style
Leibnizian and Lockean	Formal, routine tasks, stable environment	Top-down dissemination (Leibnizian) Observant assimilation (Lockean)
Kantian	Moderately formal, more complicated tasks, moderately stable environment	Lateral dissemination
Hegelian and Singerian	Informal and often temporary, complicated tasks, turbulent environment	Dialectic (Hegelian) Any of the above (Singerian)

Five organizational subforms have been presented in this article. Discussion has included how each of the subforms may be implemented by or within a given organization, and exemplified how they may work together within an organization under the inquiring organization metaform. Each of the subforms has strengths in particular environments or contexts, but as the metaform, they support the underlying philosophy of the inquiring organization. Managers considering these perspectives can apply the basic principles of each subform as appropriate. Table 1 summarizes the discussion.

FUTURE TRENDS FOR INQUIRING ORGANIZATIONS

Over the last several years, researchers have searched for a unifying theory for knowledge management and the complexities it presents. Clearly, such a theory must support adaptability, flexibility, and the construction of social processes. Two often suggested for the task are Open Systems Theory and Weick's ESR model.

Adaptability is a goal of open systems theory (OST) (Morgan, 1997; von Bertalanffy, 1950, 1968). OST examines an organization for its ability to look beyond its boundaries for information and material, making changes in response to environmental input and learning. These changes are based not only on what it has experienced, but also by combining new information with human experiential knowledge as in an inquiring organization. Weick's (1979, 1995, 2001) Enactment-Selection-Retention (ESR) model of organizing is also concerned with flexibility and information sharing. One of the main premises of ESR is that an adaptive organization is a collective action, and that influence comes not from positional individuals, but from the pattern of communication and relationships inherent in any social organization.

Churchman's (1971) inquirers, OST, and the ESR model each stress the need for communication and information sharing, and propose that an effective organization is a product of its environment, enacts on its environment, and ultimately shapes its environment. Thus, each of these systems is suitable for both stable and unstable environments, and is a potential knowledge management foundation theory. The inquiring organizational metaform described herein goes a step beyond OST and ESR by facilitating knowledge creation within a framework of multiple perspectives.

It is likely that research into a foundational theory for knowledge management will continue. Further development and testing of organizational structures and technologies developed on the foundation of Churchman's (1971) inquiring theory may provide in-

sight into the applicability of this theory as a foundational one. Churchman's (1971) theory has been used as a foundation for organization memory systems and knowledge management systems. Chae, Hall, and Guo (2001) suggest that using Churchman's (1971) inquirers as a foundation for an organizational memory information system can support Huber's (1991) four assumptions about organizational learning: existence, breadth, elaborateness, and thoroughness.

One conceptualized knowledge management system founded on the principles of Churchman's (1971) inquiring systems is proposed to enable organizations to create, manage, and store reliable information that may then be used to support decision making (Hall et al., 2003). This system not only provides technological and social support for an inquiring organization, but places particular emphasis on information acquisition and discovery, a requirement for organizations embroiled in a fast-paced environment. This model was later found to be applicable to Mintzberg, Raisinghani, and Theoret's (1976) seven-stage systems approach to decision making (Hall & Paradice, 2005).

Future research opportunities into inquiring organizations exist in further development and testing of this knowledge management system and its decision-making components. Further, this system was developed using the design theory espoused by Walls, Widmeyer, and El Sawy (1992), which provides yet another research opportunity. For instance, one may ask what advantages and disadvantages exist when a comprehensive theory such as the inquiring systems theory is overlaid on a framework designed to work with focused theories.

To our knowledge, the metaform discussed in this article is unique in the research realm. Thus, many opportunities exist for researchers interested in organizational form. For instance, can heuristics be generally developed to indicate when an organizational unit should invoke a particular subform? Should the lesser subforms be eliminated in favor of the Hegelian and Singerian forms? Is the learning style of a given subform as effective as another? If new and innovative organizational forms are not routinely considered, developed, and tested, will knowledge management fail to reach its full potential?

CONCLUSION

A flexible organizational form such as that underlying an inquiring organization will provide organizations with the ability to withstand tumulus environments and succeed in establishing themselves as knowledge-based systems. The form that supports inquiring organizations allows them to confront different domains, contexts, and environments with an appropriate form, supports knowledge creation and social processes when appropriate, and provides support for quick action. Organizations adopting this flexible and comprehensive form will achieve better advancement toward their knowledge-based goals.

We propose that no one form, process, or system will transform an organization into one with a knowledge orientation. Careful examination of social and technological processes, including the importance of a dynamic organizational memory accessible to all organizational members, is critical. This foundation for viewing the whole organization as a knowledge manager contributes to the future of knowledge management.

REFERENCES

Argyris, C., & Schön, D.A. (1996). *Organizational learning II*. Reading, MA: Addison-Wesley.

Chae, B., Hall, D., & Guo, Y. (2001, August 3-5). A framework for organizational memory and organizational memory information system: Insights from Churchman's five inquirers. *Proceedings of the Americas Conference on Information Systems*, Boston.

Churchman, C.W. (1971). *The design of inquiring systems: Basic concepts of systems and organizations*. New York: Basic Books.

Courtney, J.F., Croasdell, D.T., & Paradice, D.B. (1998). Inquiring organizations. *Australian Journal of Information Systems, 6*(1), 3-15.

Hall, D.J., & Paradice, D.B. (2003). Philosophical foundations for a learning-oriented knowledge management system for decision support. *Decision Support Systems 39*(3), 445-461.

Hall, D.J., Paradice, D.B., & Courtney, J.F. (2003). Building a theoretical foundation for a learning-oriented knowledge management system. *Journal of Information Technology Theory and Application (JITTA), 5*(2), 63-89.

Huber, G.P. (1991). Organizational learning: The contributing processes and the literatures. *Organization Science, 2*(1), 88-115.

Isaacs, W.N. (1993). Taking flight: Dialogue, collective thinking, and organizational learning. *Organizational Dynamics, 22*(2), 24-39.

Mintzberg, H. (1979). *The structuring of organizations: A synthesis of the research*. Englewood Cliffs, NJ: Prentice-Hall.

Mintzberg, H., Raisinghani, D., & Theoret, A. (1976). The structure of 'unstructured' decision processes. *Administrative Science Quarterly, 21*, 246-275.

Morgan, G. (1997). *Images of organizations* (2nd ed.). Thousand Oaks, CA: Sage Publications.

Nonaka, I. (1994). A dynamic theory of organizational knowledge creation. *Organization Science, 5*(1), 14-37.

Nonaka, I., & Takeuchi, H. (1995). *The knowledge-creating company: How the Japanese companies create the dynamics of innovation*. New York: Oxford University Press.

Schultze, U., & Leidner, D. (2002). Studying knowledge management in information systems research: Discourses and theoretical assumptions. *MIS Quarterly, 26*(3), 213-242.

von Bertalanffy, L. (1950). The theory of open systems in physics and biology. *Science, 3*, 23-29.

von Bertalanffy, L. (1968). *General systems theory: Foundations, development, applications*. New York: Braziller.

Walls, J.G., Widmeyer, G.R., & El Sawy, O.A. (1992). Building an information system design theory for vigilant EIS. *Information Systems Research, 3*(1), 36-59.

Weick, K.E. (1979). *The social psychology of organizing* (2nd ed.). New York: Random House.

Weick, K.E. (1995). *Sensemaking in organizations*. Thousand Oaks, CA: Sage Publications.

Weick, K.E. (2001). *Making Sense of the organization*. Oxford: Blackwell Publishers.

KEY TERMS

Homeostasis: The condition of stability that an organization can obtain by being cognizant of and responsive to environmental changes. Homeostasis is one of the most typical properties of highly complex open systems. Such a system reacts to every change in the environment, or to every random disturbance, through a series of modifications of equal size and opposite direction to those that created the disturbance. The goal of these modifications is to maintain the internal balances.

Inquiring Organization: An organization founded on the principles of one or more inquiring systems that seeks to increase its learning potential. Inquiring organizations are learning-oriented organizations that strive to include both creation and management of knowledge in their cache of core competencies. The philosophical foundations of inquiring organizations come from Churchman's (1971) discourse of knowledge creation and inquiring systems from the viewpoints of selected Western philosophers. These perspectives are particularly well suited to knowledge management and serve to differentiate the inquiring organization from other learning organizations.

Inquiring System/Inquirer: Any one of the systems developed by Churchman that supports inquiry and is founded on the philosophies of Leibniz, Locke, Kant, Hegel, or Singer.

Inquiring Theory: The theory espoused by Churchman that systems should be designed to create new knowledge while incorporating ethics and aesthetics, culminating in knowledge that creates the greatest good for the greatest number.

Inquiry: The process of being actively engaged in the pursuit of knowledge.

Leibnizian Fact Net: A knowledge store founded on axioms. Leibnizian inquiry does not begin with inputs that are externally given, but with "innate ideas" where aspects of the symbol stream are under the control of the inquiring system. The truth is the end point of the process of inquiring and is concomitant with internal consistency, completeness, and comprehensiveness. In this inquiring system, all sentences are contingent. A candidate sentence becomes a 'contingent truth' if it can be linked to some sentence in memory. Thus, the memory becomes a *'fact net'* by which the truth of a sentence is verified.

Triple-Loop Learning: When information cannot be processed within the given knowledge system, the system has to be revised. This is what Argyris and Schön call "single- and double-loop learning." Single-loop learning is based on negative feedback and correction of deviation from the norm. Learning is limited to operational actions that are allowed. Single-loop learning works at the level of facts. Learning is focused on the question of how we can reach an existing goal in the best possible way within existing norms. Double-loop learning is directed to correction of "mistakes" based on defined norms. It implies an extra loop reconsidering existing rules and their validity. Triple-loop learning considers not only the facts and the norms, but also the context. Triple-loop learning works on perception and the permanent questioning of inconsistencies in the action theory of the organization.

Integrated Modeling

Thomas Hädrich
Martin-Luther-University Halle-Wittenberg, Germany

Ronald Maier
Martin-Luther-University Halle-Wittenberg, Germany

INTRODUCTION

Modeling is a key task in order to analyze, understand, and improve business processes and organizational structures, and to support the design, implementation, and management of information and communication technologies in general and knowledge management systems (KMSs) in particular. Process-oriented knowledge management (Maier, 2004; Maier & Remus, 2003) is a promising approach to provide the missing link between knowledge management (KM) and business strategy, and to bridge the gap between the human-oriented and technology-oriented views (e.g., Hansen, Nohria, & Tierney, 1999; Zack, 1999). However, existing modeling approaches for business processes, including their extensions for KM, still lack concepts to support knowledge work, which is often unstructured, creative, and learning and communication intensive. Recently, the activity theory has been proposed to provide concepts to analyze knowledge work (e.g., Blackler, 1995), but it has not yet been integrated with business process modeling for designing KM initiatives and KMSs. The following sections analyze the characteristics of knowledge work, distinguish important perspectives for modeling in KM, and discuss extensions of process modeling approaches including activity modeling. Then, the process-oriented and the activity-oriented perspectives on knowledge work are compared and connected by means of the concept of knowledge stance.

BACKGROUND

Knowledge work can be characterized by a high degree of variety and exceptions, strong communication needs, weakly structured processes, an increasing importance on teamwork in the form of project teams, networks, and communities, and it requires a high level of skill and expertise. Inputs and outputs of knowledge work are primarily data, information, or knowledge. Knowledge comprises observations that have been meaningfully organized and embedded in a context through experience, communication, or inference that an actor uses to interpret situations and to accomplish tasks (based on Maier, 2004). Knowledge work consists of a number of specific practices, for example, expressing or extracting experiences, monitoring, translating, and networking (Schulze, 2003).

From an ICT perspective, the main changes in the requirements posed by knowledge work occur due to the considerably higher complexity of data and the focus on organization-wide and interorganizational communication, cooperation, and mobility of knowledge workers. The storage, handling, and sharing of semistructured data require additional ICT systems, such as document , content, and knowledge management systems. Modeling has focused largely on data (entity relationship modeling), objects and classes (object-oriented modeling), and business processes (business process modeling). Knowledge work requires content-, user-, and communication-oriented modeling techniques that show what persons, communities, topics, tools, rules, and other activities and processes are involved, and thus demands concepts and modeling techniques that extend business process modeling to cover these aspects.

PERSPECTIVES FOR MODELING IN KM

Models are representations of a selected portion of the perceived reality of an individual or a group of observers. The design of KM initiatives requires modeling concepts for (a) processes that describe the organizational design, that is, knowledge tasks, flows, roles, and resources, (b) persons by capturing facts about people, that is, their skills, communication, and cooperation in networks and communities, (c) products, that is, the type of knowledge, structures, taxonomies, ontologies, and metadata, and (d) productivity tools, that is, the architecture, functions, and interaction of ICT tools in support of KM (see Figure 1).

A large number of modeling approaches, methods, and techniques have been developed in the literature (e.g., Balzert, 2001). Each of these approaches predominantly focuses on one of the dimensions in Figure 1. For pro-

Figure 1. Perspectives for modeling in knowledge management (based on Maier, 2004)

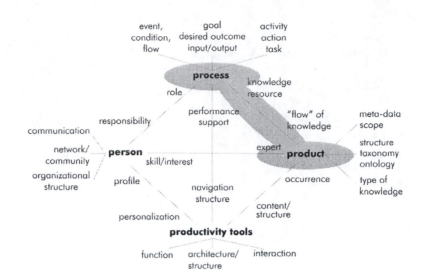

cess-oriented KM, concepts are needed that combine process modeling with the other perspectives, especially with knowledge products and the knowledge-intensive tasks being part of knowledge work.

In recent years, many organizations have applied concepts of business process reengineering (e.g., Davenport, 1993; Hammer & Champy, 1993), and a number of methods and techniques to support business process modeling have been proposed in the literature. Approaches for process modeling distinguish between three levels of granularity that are interconnected: (a) Value chains (Porter, 1985) arrange value-adding activities, (b) business processes connect functions, and (c) work flows orchestrate tasks. As process modeling is a complex task that requires computer support in order to be an economically feasible approach, most methods are applied with the help of a corresponding tool. Examples are ADONIS (Junginger, Kühn, Strobl, & Karagiannis, 2000), ARIS (Scheer, 2001), IEM (Heisig, 2002; Spur, Mertins, & Jochem, 1996), MEMO (Frank, 2002), PROMET (Österle, 1995), SOM (Ferstl & Sinz, 1994), UML-based process modeling (Oestereich, Weiss, Schröder, Weilkiens, & Lenhard, 2003), and the IDEF family of modeling methods (http://www.idef.com). Moreover, there is a number of frameworks and reference models for the definition of work flows that implement business processes (see, e.g., Kumar & Zhao, 1999; WfMC, 2001). The methods differ in formality, semantic richness, and understandability.

Recently, a number of authors have proposed extensions that model (some of) the specifics of KM. Examples are the extensions to ARIS (Allweyer, 1998), PROMET®I-NET (Bach & Österle, 2000; Kaiser & Vogler, 1999), GPO-WM (Heisig, 2002), KMDL

(Gronau, 2003), Knowledge MEMO (Schauer, 2004), and PROMOTE (Hinkelmann, Karagiannis, & Telesko, 2002; Karagiannis & Woitsch, 2003). The main extensions are the introduction of additional object types like knowledge objects, that is, topics of interest, documented knowledge, individual employees, and skills, as well as the introduction of model types like knowledge structure diagrams, communication diagrams, and knowledge maps. More detailed aspects of knowledge-intensive tasks have been implemented in tools for flexible workflow management (Goesmann, 2002). Examples are Bramble (Blumenthal & Nutt, 1995), KnowMore (Abecker, Bernardi, Hinkelmann, Kühn, & Sintek, 1998), MILOS (Maurer & Dellen, 1998, WorkBrain (Wargitsch, Wewers, & Theisinger, 1998), and Workware (Carlsen & Jorgensen, 1998).

The extensions can be classified according to whether they target the abstract level of KM-related organizational design, for example, ARIS and GPO-WM, or whether they target the detailed level of KM-related work flows, for example, PROMOTE and tools for flexible workflow management. None of the extensions provides concepts to model all four perspectives of persons, process, product, and productivity tools, and particularly their relationships. The added concepts describe a portion of the context of knowledge work, but they are not suited to model the often unstructured and creative learning and knowledge practices and their links to business processes.

For example, in the case of ARIS, the added object types "documented knowledge" and "knowledge category," as well as the model types "knowledge structure diagram," "knowledge map," and "communication diagram," give a rough impression of the knowledge needed and produced in each step of a business process, the general knowledge structure, the required skills of the roles, as well as their communication. However, neither of these concepts indicates which knowledge-related actions are possible or required in the process step, with which communities and other processes or activities. Thus, the concepts only describe a fragment of knowledge work, and it remains unclear when and how knowledge is created and applied, and specifically in what occasions and in what context knowledge-oriented actions should be supported, for example, by KMS functions.

The activity theory has been proposed to guide the analysis of knowledge work (see, e.g., Blackler, 1995) and to design information systems, especially group support systems and KMS (see, e.g., Clases & Wehner, 2002; Collins, Shukla, & Redmiles, 2002; Hasan & Gould, 2003; Kuutti, 1997; Sachs, 1995). It places the focus on activities, not to be confused with activities in Porter's (1985) value chain and activities in UML.

The core idea of the activity theory is that human activity is a dialectic relationship between individuals (called agents or subjects) and objects (the purpose of human activity) that is mediated by tools and instruments like cultural signs, language, and technologies in so-called activity systems (see Figure 2, left side). The subject is a part of communities and its connection to them is determined by implicit or explicit social rules. A division of labor (e.g., role system) defines the relation of these communities to the object of the activity system (Engeström, 1987). Intended or unintended results are the outcome of the activities' transformation process.

This is a significant contribution to KM (Hasan & Gould, 2003) since the acquisition of knowledge in modern learning theories is not a simple matter of taking in knowledge, but a complex cultural or social phenomenon (see, e.g., Blackler, 1995).

Activities have a hierarchical structure (see Figure 2, right side). First, the activity is driven by a common motive that reflects a collective need and the reason why the activity exists (Engeström, 1999). Second, an activity is accomplished by actions directed to goals coupled with the motive of the activity. Actions consist of an orientation and an execution phase: The first comprises the planning for action, and the latter is its execution by a chain of operations (Kuutti, 1997). Repeated exercise leads to better planning of the action that then can be conducted more successfully. With enough practice, the separate planning phase becomes obsolete, and actions collapse into operations due to learning and routinization. Third, operations are executed under certain conditions. They are the most structured part that is easiest to automate. An important feature of the activity theory is the dynamic relationship between the three levels. Elements of higher levels collapse to constructs of lower levels if learning takes place. They unfold to higher levels if changes occur and learning is necessary.

An example is the activity of learning to drive a car (Leontiev as cited in Hasan & Gould, 2003). The object is being able to drive. For an unaccomplished driver, the handling of the gearbox happens on the action level. A separate planning and execution phase is necessary for changing gears. For an accomplished driver, driving a car merely is an action with the goal to get somewhere in the context of a broader activity. For him or her, the handling of the gearbox happens nearly unconsciously on the level of operations. If he or she has to drive a different car model with a distinctively designed gearbox, these operations can again unfold into actions.

Activity modeling comprises the identification of activity systems and emphasizes the analysis of the mediating relationships and tensions between its constituting components. Compared to process modeling, the contributions of the activity theory are the consideration of individual or group motives, the notion of communities, a way to conceptualize learning by routinization, and the concept of mediation.

Figure 2. Model and levels of the socially-distributed activity system (Blackler, 1995; Kuutti, 1997)

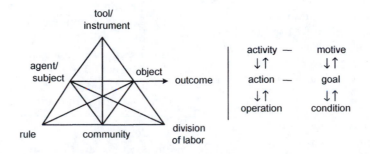

Figure 3. Concept of knowledge stance

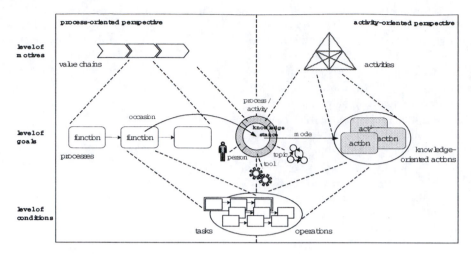

MODELING KNOWLEDGE WORK IN BUSINESS PROCESSES

The concepts provided by the activity theory are well suited to analyze the creative, unstructured, and learning-oriented practices of knowledge work. However, activities primarily aim at the joint creation of knowledge (exploration). Activities lack integration with the value chain and it is not ensured that activities are oriented toward creating customer value (exploitation of knowledge). Therefore, concepts of process and of activity modeling have to be combined in order to get a more comprehensive picture of knowledge work in a business context. This is the aim of the concept of knowledge stance.

A knowledge stance is a class of recurring situations in knowledge work defined by occasion, context, and mode resulting in knowledge-oriented actions (Hädrich & Maier, 2004). It describes a situation in which a knowledge worker can, should, or must switch from a business-oriented function to a knowledge-oriented action (see Figure 3). In a process-oriented perspective, an employee accomplishes functions on the level of goals that belong to a value chain on the level of motives by fulfilling a sequence of tasks on the level of conditions. Simultaneously, he or she can be involved in an activity framing knowledge-oriented actions and corresponding operations. An activity and its corresponding actions and operations can (a) be focused on the business process or (b) pursue a motive not related to the business process (e.g., an effort to build competencies) and thus may make a direct or a more indirect contribution to the process goal.

A business process offers several occasions to learn and to generate knowledge related to the core competencies of the organization. Occasions trigger knowledge stances and are associated with the functions of the business process by offering the opportunity or the need for knowledge-related actions. A knowledge stance is not limited to the generation of knowledge, but may also include the translation and application of knowledge created outside the knowledge stance.

The context comprises all relevant dimensions suitable to describe the actual situation of the worker. It can be structured according to the perspectives for modeling in KM: the process, person, product, and productivity tool. It comprises data about the current process like other subjects involved, desired outcomes, formal rules, or other process steps as well as data about the involved activity like the related community, their objectives, and social rules. Person-related data comprises the level of expertise (e.g., Dreyfus & Dreyfus, 1986), skills, interests, relations to other persons, and position in the organizational structure. The context includes information about what knowledge products and topics are needed, used, or created. Finally, available functions and systems are defined together with privileges to access them.

The mode classifies what actions can be performed and refers to four informing practices (see Schultze, 2000, 2003): (a) Expressing is the practice of the self-reflexive conversion of individual knowledge and subjective insights into informational objects that are independent of the person, (b) monitoring describes continuous, nonfocused scanning of the environment and the gathering of useful just-in-case information, (c) translating involves the creation of information by ferrying it across different contexts until a coherent meaning emerges, and (d) networking is the practice of building and maintaining relationships with people inside and outside the organization.

Context, mode, and occasion are means to specify the set of available, allowed, or required knowledge-

Table 1. Components of knowledge stances

component	description
occasion	is a type of opportunity to learn and to generate knowledge related to the (core) competencies of the organization within the function of a business process
context	describes the actual work situation, i.e., the process/activity context, personal characteristics, as well as topics and tools
mode	classifies knowledge-oriented actions into expressing, monitoring, translating, and networking
action	refers to an unstructured, knowledge-oriented action and is specified by occasion, context, and mode

oriented actions. Examples for actions are (Eppler, 2003) to summarize, prioritize contents, evaluate sources, indicate levels of certitude, compare sources, link content, relate to prior information, add meta-information, notify and alert, ask questions, and offer interaction. In contrast to the clearly defined sequences of functions in the process-oriented perspective, there is no predetermined flow of actions. Table 1 summarizes the components of knowledge stances.

Depending on occasion, context, and mode, it can be decided which KM instruments are suited to support knowledge-oriented actions. When designing KMSs, those knowledge stances are of primary interest that can be supported by ICT. A straightforward approach would be to suggest adequate KMS functions to the user or to automate corresponding operations. This could be accomplished, for example, by offering work flows or user agents known from office applications. The large set of KMS functions available can consequently be tailored to the needs in a stance and thus must obtain information from the context variables as well as the mode and occasion. The context should be derived with as little user effort as possible. The elements and their relation can be represented by a standardized or shared ontology. That

way, inference techniques can be applied and the context can be communicated to and translated for other applications.

The following table shows an example of a knowledge stance for a worker consigned with the maintenance of gas pipes within a specific geographic area (see Table 2). The service is fulfilled by specialized companies under contracts that are renegotiated regularly by the purchasing department of the company.

FUTURE TRENDS

The design of KM instruments and of supporting ICT need structured representations of knowledge work in the context of business processes. It is necessary to integrate both process-oriented and activity-oriented elements for the exploration as well as exploitation of knowledge. The concept of knowledge stance, its integration into a modeling method for KM, and the subsequent design and implementation of ICT-supported KM initiatives promise substantial increases in the productivity of knowledge work.

Table 2. Example of a knowledge stance

element	description
function	regular check of gas pipes, to alert and cooperate with service technicians if necessary (in Process 1)
context	**process/activity:** • Process 1 (maintenance of gas pipes): technical and geographical specifics of the gas pipe, problem type, urgency • Process 2 (negotiation with outsourcing partners): regulations and guidelines to formulate a contract, possible cooperation partners • Activity (cooperation with strategic partners): rules like communication patterns, motives, & objectives of the cooperation partners **person:** experience and internal role of maintenance engineer, other people with relevant technical knowledge **tool:** geographical information system, communication systems, access privileges of the worker **topic:** checklists, documented good/best practices
occasion	Damage on a gas pipe or a related component is identified within Process 1 and can only be repaired by a specialist of a company not yet under contract. Process 1 and Process 2 are connected through actions within the scope of the activity.
mode	The worker builds relationships with persons of another company and thus is in the mode of networking.
actions	search for the right partner, negotiate the specifics of the contract, validate the contract, check the skills of the company's workers

CONCLUSION

This article discussed characteristics of knowledge work and gave an overview of perspectives and approaches for modeling in the context of process-oriented KM. We studied the activity theory as a means to include the dynamic, creative, and often less structured aspects of knowledge work, and proposed the concept of knowledge stance with the following contributions. First, a knowledge stance integrates the process-oriented and the activity-oriented perspectives. The latter is necessary to extend modeling to knowledge-oriented actions. Second, they are a means to design KM instruments and KMSs. The latter could be accomplished, for example, by portals or work spaces that bundle KMS functions and filter contents for knowledge stances, by user agents that guide through an action, and by workflows that routinize parts of actions. To clearly translate into KMS, the concept of knowledge stance needs to be detailed. Overall, the concept seems to be an important step in the quest for adequate extensions of business process modeling to cover aspects of knowledge work.

REFERENCES

Abecker, A., Bernardi, A., Hinkelmann, K., Kühn, O., & Sintek, M. (1998). *Techniques for organizational memory information systems* (DFKI Research Report No. D-98-02). German Research Center for Artificial Intelligence, Karlsruhe, Germany.

Allweyer, T. (1998). Modellbasiertes Wissensmanagement. *Information Management, 13*(1), 37-45.

Bach, V., & Österle, H. (Eds.). (2000). *Customer Relationship Management in der Praxis: Erfolgreiche Wege zu Kundenzentrierten Lösungen.* Berlin, Germany: Springer.

Balzert, H. (2001). *Lehrbuch der Software-Technik* (2nd ed.). Heidelberg, Germany: Spektrum.

Blackler, F. (1995). Knowledge, knowledge work and organizations: An overview and interpretation. *Organization Studies, 16*(6), 1021-1046.

Blumenthal, R., & Nutt, G. J. (1995). Supporting unstructured workflow activities in the Bramble ICN system. *Proceedings of the ACM Conference on Organizational Computing Systems (COOCS'95)* (pp. 130-137).

Carlsen, S., & Jorgensen, H. D. (1998). Emergent workflow: The AIS workware demonstrator. *Proceedings of the Workshop "Towards Adaptive Workflow Systems" of the ACM Conference on Computer Supported Cooperative Work (CSCW'98).*

Clases, C., & Wehner, T. (2002). Steps across the border: Cooperation, knowledge production and systems design. *Computer-Supported Cooperative Work, 11*(1), 39-54.

Collins, P., Shukla, S., & Redmiles, D. (2002). Activity theory and systems design: A view from the trenches. *Computer Supported Cooperative Work, 11*(1), 55-80.

Daconta, M. C., Obrst, L. J., & Smith, K. T. (2003). *The semantic Web: A guide to the future of XML, Web services and knowledge management.* Indianapolis, IN: Wiley.

Davenport, T. (1993). *Business process innovation.* Boston: HBS Press.

Dreyfus, H. L., & Dreyfus, S. E. (1986). *Mind over machine: The power of human intuition and expertise in the era of the computer.* New York: Free Press.

Engeström, Y. (1987). *Learning by expanding: An activity-theoretical approach to developmental research.* Helsinki, Finland: Orienta-Konsultit Oy.

Engeström, Y. (1999). Expansive visibilization of work: An activity-theoretical perspective. *Computer Supported Cooperative Work, 8*(1), 63-93.

Eppler, M. J. (2003). *Managing information quality: Increasing the value of information in knowledge-intensive products and processes.* Berlin, Germany: Springer.

Ferstl, O. K., & Sinz, E. J. (1994). *From business process modeling to the specification of distributed business application systems: An object-oriented approach* [Research Paper]. Department of Business Information Systems, University of Bamberg, Germany.

Frank, U. (2002). Multi-perspective enterprise modeling (MEMO): Conceptual framework and modeling languages. *Proceedings of the 35th Hawaii International Conference on System Sciences (HICSS-35),* Honolulu.

Goesmann, T. (2002). *Ein Ansatz Zur Unterstützung Wissensintensiver Prozesse Durch Workflowmanagementsysteme.* Retrieved October 15, 2004, from *http://edocs.tu-berlin.de/diss/2002/goesmann_thomas.pdf*

Gronau, N. (2003). Modellierung von wissensintensiven Geschäftsprozessen mit der Beschreibungssprache K-Modeler. In N. Gronau (Ed.), Wissensmanagement: Potenziale, Konzepte, Werkzeuge. *Proceedings of the 4th*

Oldenburg Conference on Knowledge Management (pp. 3-29). Berlin, Germany: Gito.

Gruber, T. R. (1993). A translation approach to portable ontology specifications. *Knowledge Acquisition, 5*(2), 199-200.

Hädrich, T., & Maier, R. (2004). Modeling knowledge work. In P. Chamoni, W. Deiters, N. Gronau, R.-D. Kutsche, P. Loos, H. Müller-Merbach, B. Rieger, & K. Sandkuhl (Eds.), *Multikonferenz Wirtschaftsinformatik (MKWI 2004)* (Vol. 2). Berlin, Germany: Akademische Verlagsgesellschaft.

Hammer, M., & Champy, J. (1993). *Reengineering the cooperation.* New York: Harper Business Publishers.

Hansen, M. T., Nohria, N., & Tierney, T. (1999). What's your strategy for managing knowledge? *Harvard Business Review, 77*(3-4), 106-110.

Hasan, H., & Gould, E. (2003). Activity-based knowledge management systems. *Journal of Information & Knowledge Management, 2*(2), 107-115.

Heisig, P. (2002). GPO-WM: Methoden Und Werkzeuge zum Geschäftsprozessorientierten Wissensmanagement. In A. Abecker, K. Hinkelmann, & M. Heiko (Eds.), *Geschäftsprozessorientiertes Wissensmanagement* (pp. 47-64). Berlin, Germany: Springer.

Hinkelmann, K., Karagiannis, D., & Telesko, R. (2002). PROMOTE: Methodologie Und Werkzeug Für Geschäftsprozessorientiertes Wissensmanagement. In A. Abecker, K. Hinkelmann, & M. Heiko (Eds.), *Geschäftsprozessorientiertes Wissensmanagement* (pp. 65-90). Berlin, Germany: Springer.

Junginger, S., Kühn, H., Strobl, R., & Karagiannis, D. (2000). Ein Geschäftsprozessmanagement-Werkzeug fer nächsten Generation. ADONIS: Konzeption und Anwendungen. *Wirtschaftsinformatik, 42*(5), 392-401.

Kaiser, T. M., & Vogler, P. (1999). PROMET®I-NET: Methode für Intranet-basiertes Wissensmanagement. In V. Bach, P. Vogler, & H. Österle (Eds.), *Business Knowledge Management: Praxiserfahrungen Mit Intranet-Basierten Lösungen* (pp. 117-129). Berlin, Germany: Springer.

Karagiannis, D., & Woitsch, R. (2003). The PROMOTE approach: Modelling knowledge management processes to describe knowledge management systems. In N. Gronau (Ed.), *Wissensmanagement: Potenziale, Konzepte, Werkzeuge. Proceedings of the 4th Oldenburg Conference on Knowledge Management* (pp. 35-52). Berlin, Germany: Gito.

Kelloway, E. K., & Barling, J. (2000). Knowledge work as organizational behavior. *International Journal of Management Reviews, 2*(3), 287-304.

Kumar, A., & Zhao, J. L. (1999). Dynamic routing and operational controls in workflow management systems. *Management Science, 45*(2), 253-272.

Kuutti, K. (1997). Activity theory as a potential framework for human-computer interaction research. In B. A. Nardi (Ed.), *Context and consciousness: Activity theory and human-computer interaction* (pp. 17-44). Cambridge, MA: MIT Press.

Leontiev, A. N. (1981). *Problems of the development of the mind.* Moscow: Progress Publishers.

Maier, R. (2004). *Knowledge management systems: Information and communication technologies for knowledge management* (2nd ed.). Berlin, Germany: Springer.

Maier, R., & Remus, U. (2003). Implementing process-oriented knowledge management strategies. *Journal of Knowledge Management, 7*(4), 62-74.

Maurer, F., & Dellen, B. (1998). A concept for an Internet-based process-oriented knowledge management environment. *Proceedings of the Knowledge Acquisition Workshop (KAW98)*, Banff, Canada.

Österle, H. (1995). *Business engineering. Prozeß-und Systementwicklung: Band 1. Entwurfstechniken.* Berlin, Germany: Springer.

Oestereich, B., Weiss, C., Schröder, C., Weilkiens, T., & Lenhard, A. (2003). *Objektorientierte Geschäftsprozessmodellierung mit der UML.* Heidelberg, Germany: dpunkt.

Porter, M. E. (1985). *Competitive advantage: Creating and sustaining superior performance.* New York; London: Free Press.

Sachs, P. (1995). Transforming work: Collaboration, learning, and design. *Communications of the ACM, 38*(9), 36-44.

Schauer, H. (2005). *Knowledge MEMO: Eine Methode zur Planung, Steuerung und Kontrolle ganzheitlichen betrieblichen Wissensmanagements.* Unpublished PhD thesis, University of Koblenz, Koblenz, Germany.

Scheer, A.-W. (2001). *ARIS: Modellierungsmethoden, Metamodelle, Anwendungen.* Berlin, Germany: Springer.

Schmidt, G. (2002). *Prozessmanagement: Modelle und Methoden* (2nd ed.). Berlin, Germany: Springer.

Schultze, U. (2000). A confessional account of an ethnography about knowledge work. *MIS Quarterly, 24*(1), 3-41.

Schultze, U. (2003). On knowledge work. In C. W. Holsapple (Ed.), *Handbook on knowledge management: Vol. 1. Knowledge matters* (pp. 43-58). Berlin, Germany: Springer.

Sinz, E. J. (2001). Modell/Modellierung. In P. Mertins, A. Back, J. Becker, W. König, H. Krallmann, B. Rieger, A.-W. Scheer, D. Seibt, P. Stahlknecht, H. Strunz, R. Thome, & H. Wedekind (Eds.), *Lexikon Der Wirtschaftsinformatik* (pp. 311-313). Berlin, Germany: Springer.

Spur, G., Mertins, K., & Jochem, R. (1996). *Integrated enterprise modelling.* Berlin, Germany: Beuth.

Wargitsch, C., Wewers, T., & Theisinger, F. (1998). An organizational-memory-based approach for an evolutionary workflow management system: Concepts and implementation. *Proceedings of the 31st Hawaii International Conference on System Sciences (HICSS), I* (pp. 174-183).

WfMC. (2001). *The workflow coalition specification: Interface 1. Process definition interchange process model.* Retrieved October 15, 2004, from *http://www.wfmc.org/standards/docs/TC-1016-P_v11_IF1_Process_definition_Interchange.pdf*

Zack, M. H. (1999). Managing codified knowledge. *Sloan Management Review, 40*(4), 45-58.

KEY TERMS

Activity: A socially distributed system composed of individuals, communities, the objects of their activities, and the mediating factors between them. According to the activity theory, the appropriate units of analysis are not the entities and factors in isolation, but the system of relationships between them (Blackler, 1995).

Business Process: A recurring sequence of tasks that transform input goods into output goods and services. It is goal-oriented, starts and ends at the boundaries of an organization, and has to create customer value (Schmidt, 2002).

KM Instrument: A bundle of measures encompassing the organization, human resources, and ICT with the goal of improving KM-related performance indicators. Examples for ICT-related KM instruments are competency-management systems, knowledge maps, or ICT support for communities and knowledge networks.

Knowledge Stance: A recurring situation in knowledge work defined by occasion, context, and a mode resulting in knowledge-oriented actions. It describes a situation in which an employee can, should, or must switch from a business-oriented function to a knowledge-oriented action.

Knowledge Work: Creative work solving unstructured problems that requires the creation, application, packaging, teaching, and acquisition of knowledge (Kelloway & Barling, 2000). It can be categorized with the help of the informing practices of expressing, translating, monitoring, and networking (Schultze, 2003).

Modeling: The goal-oriented representation of a portion of the perceived reality. It is one of the key tasks that help to understand, analyze, and improve knowledge work. A model comprises a source system that is mapped into a target system using defined mapping rules (Sinz, 2001). In the context of organizations, the source system usually is a section of an organizational system, and the target system is a formal or semiformal system.

Ontology: Formal models of an application domain that help to exchange and share knowledge with the help of ICT systems. An ontology is an explicit specification of a shared conceptualization (Gruber, 1993). It represents objects in domains; relationships among those objects; properties, functions, and processes involving the objects; and the constraints on and rules about the objects (Daconta, Obrst, & Smith, 2003).

Integrating Knowledge Management with the Systems Analysis Process

Doron Tauber
Bar-Ilan University, Israel

David G. Schwartz
Bar-Ilan University, Israel

INTRODUCTION

Information systems research has clearly recognized that knowledge management systems (KMSs) have different characteristics and requirements than those of a classic management information system (MIS). Beginning with the relationship drawn between data, information, and knowledge (Alavi & Leidner, 1999, 2001; Bhatt, 2001; Ulrich, 2001; Spiegler, 2000, 2003; Tuomi, 2000), through to the essential nature of unstructured and semi-structured information vs. structured information (Wu, Ling, Lee, & Dobbie, 2001; Lai, Carlsen, Christiansson, & Svidt, 2003; Fensel et al., 2002; Chou & Chow, 2000), there are many elements and areas in which the two diverge.

However although the definition, description, and implementation of a KMS has been recognized as sufficiently distinct from an MIS (Alavi & Leidner, 2001; Hahn & Subramani, 2000; Plass & Salisbury, 2002; Malhotra, 2002), there is no single clear approach to develop a systems analysis and development process that is tailored specifically for a KMS (Alavi & Leidner, 2001; Hahn & Subramani, 2000; Plass & Salisbury, 2002). While the first generation of KMS has been developed as add-on or parallel systems living alongside pre-existing structured management information systems, the next generation of systems development needs to deal with *fusion* systems. A fusion system (Gray et al., 1997) is a system that integrates structured and unstructured knowledge in real time, allowing for full situational assessment based on both information and knowledge resources.

MIS has a long and illustrious history of research and development focusing on creating and refining the systems analysis process. KMS has no such legacy other than what it has inherited directly from MIS. The purpose of this article is to articulate the unique systems analysis and development issues presented by KMS in organizations, explain why tight integration between MIS and KMS development processes is desirable, and illustrate how such integration can be achieved through a modified Knowledge Integrated Systems Analysis (KISA) process for knowledge management.

The KISA process evolved from a series of action research cycles conducted over an information system development project within the Information Systems Development Department and the Chief Information Office of the Israeli Navy. Beginning with a classic IS development approach, each development cycle added new modifications to the process, until a fully integrated process was reached and then applied, without modification, to new integrated KMS-MIS development. The result is a process that is tailored to the needs of fusion systems. The result is an integrated (knowledge and process) system to support the Navy mission lifecycle.

BACKGROUND

According to Demarco (1978):

Analysis is the study of a problem, prior to taking some action. In the specific domain of computer systems development, analysis refers to the study of some business area or application, usually leading to the specification of a new system. (p. 4)

Whitten, Bentley, and Dittman (2001) state that the systems analyst will study "the problems and needs of an organization to determine how people, data, processes, communications, and information technology can best accomplish improvement for the business" (p. 14). No matter what methodology of system analysis is chosen—structured, information modeling or object-oriented methodology—this statement by Demarco made over 25 years ago is still correct. Although methodology changes, still the systems analyst as specified by Yourdon (1989) is the key member of any systems development project and, in fact, this role has not changed. Sircar, Nerur, and Mahapatra (2001) showed that a controversy exists in the literature about the magnitude and nature of the differences between object-oriented (OO) and structured systems development methods. Some authors, as cited by these researchers, believe that the OO approach is merely an evolution from the structured systems development approaches. Others cited by these researchers claim that OO requires an entirely new approach and mindset; still the researchers' emphasize that the primary task of system analysis within the systems development process is to capture the essence of a real-world system through models. This fundamental task has been incorporated into both the structured and the OO development approaches.

Knowledge in an organization can be characterized as unstructured or semi-structured, whereas information and data are fully structured and can be managed by common information management methods. Estimates show that unstructured and semi-structured information account for about 80% of the information volume within organizations (Corp, 2001; Lindvall, Rus, & Sinha, 2003; Ferrucci & Lally, 2004). Therefore, a structured MIS that aids organizational processes will only be addressing 20% of the information management needs. KM flourishes in this gap. Within this gap, most KM projects place an emphasis on knowledge "stock," which tends to dominate an organization's thinking about knowledge (Fahey & Prusak, 1998). According to Schwartz and Te'eni (2000) and Fisher (1999), the problem is "getting the right knowledge to the right person at the right time," or in other words, "delivery of the knowledge to the point of action where it can be applied to the issue at hand" (Schwartz, Divitini, & Brasethvic, 2000).

However, the "right knowledge" is not necessarily the sole property of the knowledge management domain, nor is it to be wholly found in the management information systems domain. The right knowledge is often a fusion of what resides within an MIS with what resides within a KMS. To produce a full knowledge-based situational assessment, *fusion* between the different systems is required. We need to look beyond placing knowledge management systems *alongside* our management information systems and strive to have them tightly integrated or *intertwined*.

The need to utilize new or revised systems analysis methods is founded upon few basic phenomena. First, over time, systems analysis methods have evolved in response to the growing complexity of software systems (Booch, 1994). The two main methods of systems analysis—the Structured (Demarco, 1978; Gane & Sarson, 1979; Yourdon 1989) and Object Oriented (Rumbaugh, Blaha, Premerlani, Eddy, & Lorensen, 1991; Jacobson, Christerson, Jonsson, & Overgaard, 1992; Booch, 1994)—are mainly focused on the structured information as part of the business process. Considering the increase in complexity caused by KM mainly from a technical point of view—the dominant unstructured or semi-structured nature—new or revised methods of system analysis methods are indicated.

Second, as suggested by Jayaratna and Sommerville (1998), current methods and techniques for classic systems analysis lack the ability to close the gap between the ordered world of formality and the complex real world. Adding the lack of structure found in KM to this equation only widens this gap. Since the real world has become more complex, it is the formal methods and techniques that are to be changed.

Third, KM is intended to be viewed as a natural extension of the IS function, and studies show that IS remains responsible for most KM implementation and management (King, Marks, & McCoy, 2002). However, approaching the new field of KMS with the old tools of systems analysis is a recipe for failure. This confusion leads to facts mentioned by researchers, that there is no single clear approach to the development of KMS (Alavi & Leidner, 1999), and that KMSs are developed in ad-hoc and trial-and-error modes (Plass & Salisbury, 2002; Nissen, 2001). The classic system analysis process tends to ignore organizational knowledge and KM process, focusing instead on the organizational processes that involve data and information.

NIMSAD (Normative Information Model-based Systems Analysis and Design) is a systemic framework created by Jayaratna (1994). It is used to understand and evaluate methodologies. Using this framework to examine the structured analysis methodology shows clearly that the classic systems methodology focuses on the flows and structures of formal data and data-related activities, while any aspect beyond this remains outside the area of the practitioner concern (Jayaratna, 1994).

KISA: KNOWLEDGE INTEGRATED SYSTEMS ANALYSIS

One strategy to accomplish this tight coupling between KMS and MIS is to specifically integrate knowledge items (or knowledge artifacts) into the information system. The approach illustrated here is based on the popular UML (Unified Modeling Language) methodology for systems analysis and design. The modified system analysis phases include building the KMS as part of the system analysis process, and adding the knowledge items into the UML charts. The final product of this approach is a unified system that contains two cooperative but independent subsystems, which allow the users to accomplish their processes and use knowledge artifacts at the right time, in the right way. UML is a unification of three methods (Jacobson, Booch, & Rumbaugh, 1999); the unified process is use-case driven, which is a piece of functionality in the system that gives a user (or another system) a result of value. All the use cases together make up the use-case model, which describes the complete functionality of the system. The main reasons for using the use-case model (and the UML as a whole) are the ability of reuse (since use case offers systematic and intuitive means of capturing functionality) and the ability to support the whole development process (most activities such as analysis, design, and testing are performed starting from use cases). According to Fowler and Kendall (2000), the fundamental reason to use the UML involves communication: "I use the UML because it allows me to communicate certain concepts more clearly than the alternatives" (p. 7).

Macro-Level KISA

An Integrated IS + KMS Suit

Information systems cannot be viewed as stand-alone systems, but as interrelated systems that need continuous management rather then one-time planning (Lindgren, Hardless, Pessi, & Nulden, 2002). A system analysis process for a single system that ignores the overall picture is strategically wrong. In other words, planning a system should be part of the information strategy and needs to integrate with the present and future systems. Therefore a KMS should always be part of the overall picture, and a KMS analysis process is part of an overall analysis process. Only the planning of KMS+IS will lead to streamlined, seamless business processes. Today, because most organizations have already established procedural infor-

mation systems, a new KMS analysis process should be part of the strategy and lead to integration with the organizations' legacy systems. Davenport and Glaser (2002) call this approach "just-in-time delivery," stating that the key to success is "to bake specialized knowledge into the jobs of highly skilled workers—to make the knowledge so readily accessible that it can't be avoided."

The integrated suit is illustrated in Figure 1. It should be emphasized that the KMS component or module within the suit allows not only integrated knowledge within the process, but also allows free retrieval of knowledge. For example, knowledge as lessons learned should be available while performing an organizational procedure, like preparing the next week work plan, and also available for a new worker learning the job, by using free retrieval of knowledge.

A Moderated System Analysis Process

Our point of departure is that the IS+KMS suit (as illustrated in Figure 1) is the product of combining IS and KMS methodologies. A classic system analysis process contains the following phases (Whitten et al., 2001; Yourdon, 1989; Demarco, 1978; Gane & Sarson, 1979; Booch, 1994; Pressman, 2000):

1. initial problem/opportunity identification (including feasibility testing)

Figure 1. KMS+IS suite and user roles

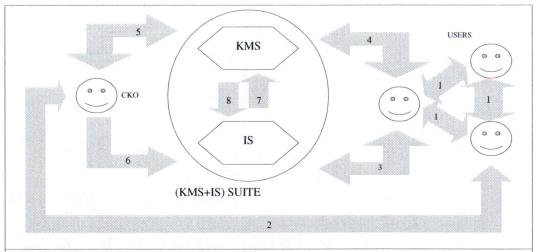

1. Communication and collaboration of the individuals within the organization.
2. Communication of individuals with the CKO with respect to the organizations knowledge needs.
3. A user approaches the suite to fulfill the structured organizational procedural activities (use the IS module).
4. A user approaches the suit to acquire knowledge for unstructured activities (use the KMS module).
5. The CKO organize formalize and store the knowledge to the suite (to the KMS module).
6. The CKO is actively part of changes in the suit (the procedures within the IS), to align with the knowledge used by the process.
7 8. The IS module "calls" the KMS module for knowledge at the moment it is the most valu

Figure 2. Macro view of the moderated system analysis process

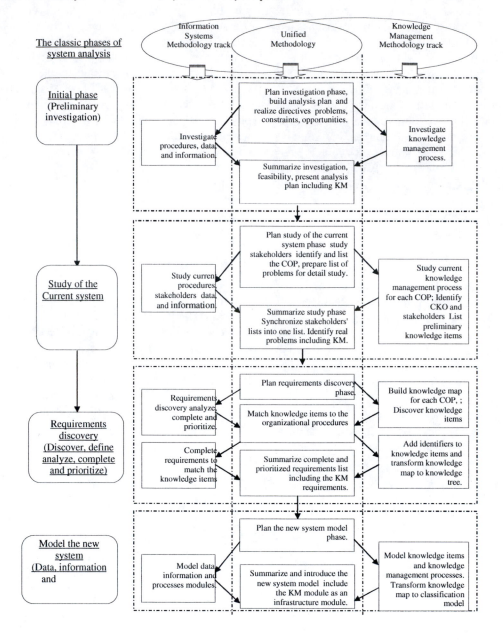

2. study of the current system
3. requirements discovery and analysis
4. data modeling
5. information modeling
6. process modeling

In order to emphasize the main modifications of the integrated system analysis process, we will discuss it from both macro-moderation and micro-moderation points of view.

The main macro-modifications result in the bifurcation of well-known classic system analysis processes into two tracks. As shown in Figure 2, the IS track and the KMS track run in parallel with clearly defined points of intersection. The two tracks must be well planned and synchronized so the work in the two tracks will be able to be done independently (because the tools and the techniques are different) yet synchronously. Each phase begins by planning the KMS and the IS activities to be accomplished

Figure 3. Micro view of the KM-IS interface requirements

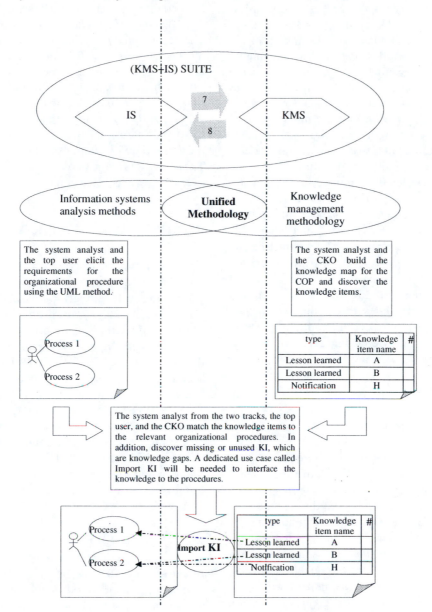

within this phase, then allowing the two tracks to diverge and be done according to their distinct methodologies (meaning IS or KMS methodology). However, as planned, the synchronization demands that the KMS will serve the IS and thus results in a situation in which knowledge serves the organizational procedures by nourishing the organizational procedures with the knowledge items at the appropriate action points.

For example, a well-known tool of KMS methodology is the knowledge map (Vail, 1999). This tool will be still used by the KMS track, but it will also be directed to serve the organizational procedural process as the IS track see and define it. Specifically, the knowledge items to be mapped will have process notification. In other words each item will be able to address the organizational procedures it serves. Another example shows that the modeling of the new organizational procedures as done in the IS track (by UML, DFD, or any other technique) will include the detailed exits points where the user should reach the knowledge items, which had been identified in the KMS track.

The summary of each phase of the KISA process is again the convergence of the two tracks. The synchronization between the two tracks is crucial for the success of the whole process. It demands a clear definition of the activities in each track so full cooperation and no unnecessary overlapping will result. This is actually the *fusion* that is reached by the meeting of the IS group and the KMS group. The process involves not only data and information modeling, but also the knowledge modeling. The system analyst is required to define not only the organizational work procedure, but also the knowledge artifacts that serve each event of these procedures. The new system model also handles the knowledge management process as one of the organizational procedures.

The product of the KISA process is a full systems design, which usually contains the module blueprints. Some of these will be infrastructure modules (which handle the users, workflow mechanism, etc.), while others are operational modules (marketing, finance, etc.). The KM component in the system is the KMS and considered as one of the infrastructure modules; this module will include the KM basic activities such as collect, formalize, store, organize, and share the knowledge that serves on demand (or request) the IS operational modules.

Micro-Level KISA

Micro-moderations are the moderations to the activities within each phase of the system analysis process. Here we describe the interface at requirements elicitation. This activity is the base for the construction of the interface between the operational IS modules that are responsible for the organizational procedures, and the KM module. The process of interface requirements elicitation can be understood as shown in Figure 3. The knowledge items were elicited prior (using the knowledge map in the KMS track), and the requirements for the organizational procedure were discovered in advance (using the UML or the DFD notation). Since not all the knowledge items and not all the organizational procedures were discovered, the meeting point of the two tracks is the place to reveal the missing parts. Now the interface modeling starts by the system analyst in each of the two groups (the IS operational modules group, and the KM module group) working synchronously in the two tracks and matching the knowledge items to their right organizational procedure.

The following example illustrates: Consider that the organizational procedure is Maintenance Planning for a ship type of A. The planner of this process needs the right lessons learned, which were recognized as knowledge items in the KMS. Receiving the right lesson learned at the time of planning is using the right knowledge at the right time for the right person in the right way. In the interface requirements elicitation and modeling stage, the lessons learned that reside in the KMS should be pointed to their right place within the Maintenance Planning procedure. The system analysts from the two groups (accompanied by the top user and the chief knowledge officer) must identify the location in the procedure and the exact identifiers which allow the IS module to request the knowledge items and the KM module to deliver. In this example, the ship type, the location of the maintenance (which shipyard), the time of year, and so forth, will serve as identifiers for these knowledge items of the type of lesson learned. The identifiers of the knowledge items can also be viewed as the knowledge items metadata.

FUTURE DIRECTIONS

The integration of MIS and KMS analysis and design processes will surely lead to the development of new software tools to support increasingly complex interactions between analysts and users. While the development of such tools will probably grow out of the current base of modeling software, there are important techniques from the KM analysis world such as knowledge maps and social network analysis that need to be integrated.

Although the unified methodology presented in this article is robust, as we gain more experience in the analysis and design of fusion systems, we would expect the KISA process to evolve. A finer-grained bifurcation of additional steps in the analysis process will surely lead to tighter integration between KMS and MIS—both in terms of project scope and team composition.

CONCLUSION

Integrating KMS into the system analysis process requires some major modifications, and this integration affects every phase of the systems development process (as shown in Figure 2) and could well be considered a new analysis methodology in its own right. This system analysis approach combines knowledge management and traditional or classic IS system analysis. The approach requires the use of two separate but synchronously integrated tracks, the IS methodology track and the KMS methodology track. Two groups of system analysts conduct the system analysis phases: the KM group is accompanied by the CKO (chief knowledge officer), and the IS group is accompanied by the user representative who operates the organizational procedures. The two groups plan each phase activities together and meet several times along the phase. As the focus of this article was the system analysis process, it was not emphasized that the organizational knowledge management process needs to be modeled and implemented as part of any such integrated project, in order to insure that the KM modules continue to nourish the operational MIS modules.

REFERENCES

Alavi, M., & Leidner, D.E. (1999, January). Knowledge management systems: Emerging views and practices from the field. *Proceedings of the 32nd Annual Hawaii International Conference on System Sciences* (Track 7).

Alavi, M., & Leidner, D.E. (2001). Knowledge management and knowledge management systems: Conceptual foundations and research issues. *MIS Quarterly, 25*(1), 107-136.

Bhatt, G.D. (2001). Knowledge management in organizations: Examining the interaction between technologies, techniques, and people. *Journal of Knowledge Management, 5*(1), 68-75.

Booch, G. (1994). *Object-oriented analysis and design, with applications* (2nd ed.). Addison-Wesley.

Chou, S.T., & Chow, E.T. (2000). Essential factors in knowledge management with COTS product. In. D.G. Schwartz, M. Divitini, & Brasethvic (Eds.), *Internet-based organizational memory and knowledge management.* Hershey, PA: Idea Group Publishing.

Corp, U. (2001). Managing unstructured content in enterprise information portals. *Knowledge Management Journal,* (July).

Davenport, T.H., & Glaser, J. (2002). Just-in-time delivery comes to knowledge management. *Harvard Business Review, 80*(7), 107-111.

Demarco, T. (1978). *Structured analysis and systems specification.* Englewood Cliffs, NJ: Prentice-Hall.

Fahey, L., & Prusak, L. (1998). The eleven deadliest sins of knowledge management. *California Management Review, 40*(3), 265-276.

Fensel, D., Omelayenko, B., Ding, Y., Klein, M., Schulten, E., Botquin, G., Brown, M., Flett, A., & Dabiri, G. (2002). *Intelligent information integration in B2B electronic commerce.* Boston: Kluwer.

Ferrucci, D., & Lally, A. (2004), Building an example application with the unstructured information management architecture. *IBM Systems Journal, 43*(3). Retrieved from *http://www.research.ibm.com/journal/sj/433/ferrucci.html*

Fischer, G. (1999). A group has no head—conceptual frameworks and systems for supporting social interaction. *Information Processing Society of Japan (IPSJ) Magazine, 40*(6), 575-582.

Fowler, M., & Kendall, S. (2000). *UML distilled* (2nd ed.). Addison-Wesley.

Gane, C., & Sarson, T. (1979). *Structured systems analysis—tools and techniques.* Englewood Cliffs, NJ: Prentice-Hall.

Gray, P.M.D., Preece, A., Fiddian, N.J., Gray, W.A., Bench-Capon, T., Shave, M., Azarmi, N., Wiegand, M., Ashwell, M., Beer, M., Cui, Z. et al. (1997). KRAFT: Knowledge fusion from distributed databases and knowledge bases. *Proceedings of the 8th International Workshop on Database and Expert Systems Applications,* Toulouse, France.

Hahn, J., & Subramani, M.R. (2000, December 10-13). A framework of knowledge management systems: Issues and challenges for theory and practice. In W.J. Orlikowski, S. Ang, P. Weill, H.C. Krcmar, & J.I.. DeGrosss (Eds.), *Proceedings of the 21st International Conference on Information Systems (ICIS 2000),* Brisbane, Australia (pp. 302-312).

Jacobson, I., Booch, G., & Rumbaugh, J. (1999). *The unified software development process.* Addison-Wesley.

Jacobson, I., Christerson, M., Jonsson, P., & Overgaard, G. (1992). *Object-oriented software engineering.* Addison-Wesley.

Jayaratna, N. (1994). *Understanding and evaluating methodologies: NIMSAD: A systemic framework.* New York: McGraw-Hill.

Jayaratna, N., & Sommerville, I. (1998). Editorial: The role of information systems methodology in software engineering. *IEEE Proceedings-Software, 145*(4), 93-94.

King, W.R., Marks, P.V., & McCoy, S. (2002). The most important issues in knowledge management. *Communications of the ACM, 45*(9), 93-97.

Lai, Y.-C., Carlsen, M., Christiansson, P., & Svidt, K. (2003, November 15-16), Semantic Web-supported knowledge management system: An approach to enhance collaborative building design. *Proceedings of the ASCE Nashville 4th Joint Symposium on IT in Civil Engineering,* Nashville, TN.

Lindgren, R., Hardless, C., Pessi, K., & Nulden, U. (2002). The evolution of knowledge management systems needs to be managed. *Journal of Knowledge Management*

Practice, 3(March). Retrieved from *http://www.tlainc. com/articl34.htm*

Lindvall, M., Rus, L., & Sinha, S.S. (2003). Software systems support for knowledge management. *Journal of Knowledge Management, 5*(5), 137-150.

Malhotra, Y. (2002). Why knowledge management systems fail? Enablers and constraints of knowledge management in human enterprises. In C.W. Holsapple (Ed.), *Handbook of knowledge management.* Heidelberg: Springer-Verlag.

Nissen, M.E. (2001, July). *Facilitating naval knowledge flow.* Technical Report NPS-GSBPP-01-003, Naval Post Graduate School, Monterey, CA.

Plass, J.L., & Salisbury, L.W. (2002). A living-systems design model for Web-based knowledge management systems. *Educational Technology Research and Development, 50*(1), 35-58.

Pressman, R.S. (2000). *Software engineering: A practitioner's approach* (5th ed.). New York: McGraw-Hill.

Rumbaugh, J., Blaha, M., Premerlani, W., Eddy, F., & Lorensen, W. (1991). *Object-oriented modeling and design.* Englewood Cliffs, NJ: Prentice-Hall.

Schwartz, D.G., & Te'eni, D. (2000). Tying knowledge to action with kMail. *IEEE Intelligent Systems, 15*(3), 33-39.

Schwartz, D.G., Divitini, M., & Brasethvic, T. (2000). On knowledge management in the Internet age. In D.G. Schwartz, M. Divitini, & Brasethvic (Eds.), *Internet-based organizational memory and knowledge management.* Hershey, PA: Idea Group Publishing.

Sircar, S., Nerur, S.P., & Mahapatra, R. (2001). Revolution or evolution? A comparison of object-oriented and structured systems development methods, *MIS Quarterly, 25*(4), 457-471.

Spiegler, I. (2000). Knowledge management: A new idea or a recycled concept? *Communications of the AIS, 3*(June).

Spiegler, I. (2003). Technology and knowledge: Bridging a "generating" gap. *Information & Management, 40,* 533-539.

Tuomi, I. (2000). Data is more than knowledge: Implications of the reversed knowledge hierarchy for knowledge management and organizational memory. *Journal of Management Information Systems, 16*(3), 103-117.

Ulrich, F. (2001). Knowledge management systems: Essential requirements and generic design patterns. In W.W. Smari, N. Melab, & K. Yetongnon (Eds.), *Proceedings of the International Symposium on Information Systems and Engineering (ISE'2001)* (pp. 114-121). Las Vegas: CSREA Press.

Vail, E.F. (1999). Knowledge mapping: Getting started with knowledge management. *Information Systems Management,* (Fall).

Whitten, J.L., Bentley, L.D., & Dittman, K.C. (2001). *System analysis and design methods.* New York: McGraw-Hill.

Wu, X., Ling, T.W., Lee, M.L., & Dobbie, G. (2001). Designing semistructured databases using ORA-SS model. *WISE, 1,* 171-180.

Yourdon, E. (1989). *Modern structured analysis.* Englewood Cliffs, NJ: Prentice-Hall.

KEY TERMS

Data Flow Diagram (DFD): Used to model a system as a network of processes that transform and exchange data as a technique to provide a semantic bridge between users and systems developers. The main components of DFDs are data process, actors, data flow, and data stores.

Fusion System: A system based on an architecture that associates diverse sources of data, information, and knowledge.

NIMSAD (Normative Information Model-based Systems Analysis and Design): A systemic framework created by Jayaratna (1994) for understanding and evaluation of methodologies.

Systems Analysis: Analyze, determine, and model how people, data, information, knowledge, and process can integrate to accomplish improvement of the business.

Unified Modeling Language (UML): A methodology for systems analysis and design. The UML is a unification of three methods (Jacobson, Booch, & Rumbaugh, 1999), the unified process is use-case driven, which is a piece of functionality in the system that gives a user (or another system) a result of value. All the use cases together make up the use-case model, which describes the complete functionality of the system.

Integration of Knowledge Management and E-Learning

Dongming Xu
University of Queensland, Australia

Huaiqing Wang
City University of Hong Kong, Hong Kong

INTRODUCTION

Knowledge management (KM) and e-learning are two concepts that address the requirements of lifelong learning. Over the past several years, there has been an increasing focus on the integration of knowledge management and e-learning systems. By 2003, 70% of organizations implementing knowledge management were linking it with e-learning technically and organizationally (Gartner, 2000). The integration of knowledge management and e-learning enables the creation of great synergies in organizations and business applications. In this article, these two concepts will be presented and their integration will be discussed in detail.

BACKGROUND

E-learning has its historical roots in more than 30 years of development of computer-supported education. The past decade, in particular, has witnessed a dramatic increase in the development of technology-based teaching and learning (Alavi & Leidner, 2001a). E-learning is an instructional process that gives online learners access to a wide range of resources—instructors, learners, and content such as readings and exercises—independently of place and time (Zhang & Nunamaker, 2003). It represents the conscious learning process where objectives and domains are clearly defined, and the focus is set to individual online learner perspectives and demands. Effective and efficient e-learning methods are generally required to ensure that online learners are equipped with the latest knowledge in a timely manner. The previous research has proposed a framework in which e-learning effectiveness is affected by two major components: the human dimension and the design dimension in virtual learning environments (Piccoli, Ahmad, & Ives, 2001). The technology in this framework is geared toward providing effective e-learning. For example, content management is one of the factors in the design dimension, which includes factual knowledge, procedural knowledge, and conceptual knowledge, that has a positive relationship with e-learning effectiveness. The design of interaction enhances the knowledge sharing among learners, and between learners and the instructor.

In contrast to traditional classroom learning, e-learning has several advantages for learners, such as time and location flexibility, relatively cost and time savings, learner-controlled instruction, unlimited access to electronic learning materials, and flexible collaboration between instructors and learners. The previous research has shown that learners benefit from using a variety of e-learning systems. Many e-learning systems present instructional material in a static, passive, and unstructured manner, and give learners little control over the learning content and process. The adaptive e-learning systems integrate knowledge management activities into their e-learning architectures and provide online learners with tailored instruction.

Individuals and groups learn by understanding and then acting, or by acting and then interpreting (Crossan et al., 1999). The process of change in individual and shared thought and action, which is affected by and embedded in the institutions of the organization, is called organization learning (Vera & Crossan, 2003, pp. 122-141). When individual and group learning becomes institutionalized, organizational learning occurs, and knowledge is embedded and created in non-human repositories such as routines, systems, structures, culture, and strategy (Hardaker & Smith, 2002; Crossan et al., 1999).

Knowledge management (KM), on the other hand, has been developed within the business context. The recent interest in organizational knowledge has prompted the use of knowledge management in order to process and manage the knowledge to the organization's benefit (Alavi & Leidner, 2001b). Knowledge management outcomes fall into three main categories: knowledge creation, retention, and transfer (Argote et al., 2003). Knowledge creation occurs when new knowledge is generated in an organization. Knowledge retention involves embedding knowledge in a repository so that it exhibits some persistence over time. Knowledge transfer is evident when experience acquired in one unit affects another. These three categories are closely related.

Table 1. Knowledge management processes and the potential roles of IT (Alavi & Leidner, 2001b)

Knowledge Management Process	Knowledge Creation	Knowledge Storage/Retrieval	Knowledge Transfer	Knowledge Application
Supporting Information Technologies	Data mining Learning tools	Electronic bulletin boards Knowledge repositories Database	Electronic bulletin boards Discussion forums Knowledge directories	Expert systems Workflow management
IT Enablers	Combining new sources of knowledge Just-in-time learning	Support of individual and organizational memory inter-group knowledge access	More extensive internal network More communication channels available Faster access to knowledge sources	Knowledge can be applied in many locations More rapid application of new knowledge through workflow automation
Platform Technology	Groupware and communication technologies			
	INTRANETS			

Lee and Choi (2003) proposed a research framework for studying knowledge management such that the synergy of information technologies, as one of the knowledge management enablers, is positively related to the knowledge management process. Information technology affects knowledge creation in a variety of ways, such as in knowledge sharing, storage, and knowledge flow. Therefore, knowledge management systems are used to rapidly capture, share, organize, and deliver large amounts of corporate knowledge. Knowledge management systems refer to a class of information systems applied to management of organizational knowledge. They are developed to support knowledge management processes in terms of knowledge creation, storage/retrieval, transfer, and application (Alavi & Leidner, 2001b).

Knowledge management processes, also called knowledge management *activities*—form a structured, coordinated system for managing knowledge effectively (Becerra-Fernandez & Sabherwal, 2001). Table 1 illustrates knowledge management processes and the potential roles of information technology (IT). For instance, *knowledge creation* can be achieved through learning tools, such as e-learning systems. Knowledge can be *stored/retrieved* in/from e-learning system repositories and electronic bulletin boards. Discussion forums and electronic bulletin boards provide *knowledge transfer* between learners, and course management and content management can be viewed as *knowledge application* in e-learning environments. Schwartz et al. (2000) stated that knowledge acquisition, distribution, and storage are highly correlated and can fruitfully influence each other. Knowledge acquisition deals with the issues that surround knowledge extraction in its various forms; knowledge distribution tackles the problem of getting the right

knowledge to the right place at the right time (Schwartz & Te'eni, 2000), and knowledge storage undertakes the knowledge repository. Knowledge management is a learning process than requires a continuous re-evaluation of the way knowledge is acquired, organized, and delivered (van der Spek & Spijkervet, 1997).

KNOWLEDGE MANAGEMENT ENABLERS AND KNOWLEDGE MANAGEMENT PROCESSES IN E-LEARNING

The integration of knowledge management and e-learning is an elaboration of knowledge management systems and e-learning systems. Knowledge management could be a cornerstone of e-learning. Effective e-learning leverages traditional e-learning technology such as computing, communication, and multimedia technologies, and knowledge management to create learning environments that can be richer and more flexible, scalable, and cost effective than the standard classroom or lecture hall (Piccoli et al., 2001; Becerra-Fernandez & Sabherwal, 2001). Therefore, e-learning systems integrating with knowledge management are designed to support the rapid capture, delivery, and measurement of knowledge in a Web-based fashion. They are designed to consider online learners' attributes and instructional strategies to provide adaptive, learner control and collaborative e-learning environments, and to thereby maximize e-learning effectiveness.

Recent knowledge management developments enable the education community to provide high-quality multimedia content via the Internet, keep track of online learner activities, or support long-distance communication and

Table 2. Relationship between KM enablers/techniques and KM processes in e-learning

		Knowledge Management Processes in E-Learning				
		Knowledge Creation	Knowledge Storage	Knowledge Retrieval	Knowledge Transfer	E-Learning Application
Knowledge Management Enablers/Techniques in E-Learning	Content Management	+	++	–	–	++
	Course Management	+	+	–	+	++
	Administration and Operation	–	+	++	++	+
	Evaluation Management	+	+	+	+	++
	Interaction/Collaboration	++	+	+	++	+

Note: - less related; + correlated; ++ highly correlated.

cooperation. These developments cover the complete cycle of teaching and learning and its many functional aspects. Based on Lee and Choi's (2003) research framework, an e-learning system is considered to be one knowledge management enabler that provides the infrastructure necessary for the e-learning organization to increase the efficiency of knowledge processes. However, from a broader point of view, the knowledge management enablers and the knowledge management processes in e-learning are correlated at different levels. Knowledge storage and retrieval are classified in one knowledge management process in the previous research (Alavi & Leidner, 2001b). In this article, knowledge storage and knowledge retrieval are divided into two separate processes due to the sequence of the knowledge management process. The knowledge storage process normally occurs at an earlier stage, while the knowledge retrieval process occurs at a later knowledge management stage.

An e-learning environment includes the following five knowledge management enablers: content management, course management, administration/operation, evaluation management, and interaction/collaboration. They are correlated with the knowledge management process in different ways and at different levels, summarized in Table 2. For instance, knowledge creation is highly correlated to interaction/collaboration, but less correlated to the administration and operation functions. This indicates that interaction/collaboration as a knowledge management enabler has a very positive impact on the knowledge creation process, but the administration/operation function has little or no impact on knowledge creation. One may also conclude that these five enablers have positive effects on e-learning applications of different magnitudes.

The classification and definitions of these five knowledge management enablers in e-learning are described below.

- **Content Management:** The American Productivity & Quality Center (APQC, 2001) defines content management as "a system to provide meaningful and timely information to end users by creating processes that identify, collect, categorize, and refresh content using a common taxonomy across the organization." Content management covers pedagogical, psychological, and didactic issues, as well as technical questions. It is a major component of knowledge management. Nearly all relevant e-learning environments offer rich content management functionality. Content management enables the knowledge storage process and the e-learning application process.

- **Course Management:** This includes the ability to share materials and modules across e-learning systems; the ability to edit, comment, and track changes on learners' documents; and the ability to monitor and access learners' e-learning performance. In short, course management offers instructors the ability to electronically maintain and manage class rosters, distribute course materials, administer online exams, and communicate with learners. Course management enables the knowledge creation process.

- **Administration and Operation:** Administration includes user management, administration of access rights, and all aspects of operation. Administration and operation enable the knowledge retrieval and knowledge transfer in e-learning.

- **Evaluation Management:** Self-evaluation can foster effective learning and implement a high degree of learning control. Evaluation management is used to guide learners' e-learning and build their knowledge, and to verify if the information is successfully turned into knowledge. In order for e-learning to be proven effective, learners need to verify that they have succeeded in gaining new knowledge or skills. During this phase, the relationship between information and knowledge becomes visible with respect to e-learning.

- **Interaction/Collaboration:** This supports communicating and collaborating between learner, the systems and organizations, as well as among learners as a pedagogical technique. Interaction and collaboration provide rich functionalities for knowledge sharing, creation, and transfer.

FUTURE TRENDS: INTEGRATING KNOWLEDGE MANAGEMENT AND E-LEARNING

Over the past several years, there has been an increasing focus on the integration of knowledge management and e-learning systems. Both e-learning and knowledge management share a similar focus: how to enhance human knowledge and its use within organizations. Professionals in both fields are increasingly looking for ways to integrate them in order to manage knowledge. The practice of knowledge management has adopted a number of different technologies, from low-tech e-mail to sophisticated, intelligent searches and extended enterprise analytical tools. Whatever the technology, the objective of such adoption is the same: to capture, store, retrieve, and distribute knowledge from internal and external sources, and build upon the intellectual knowledge wealth inherent in the organization. Knowledge management, in general, addresses more of the unintentional, indirect, but continuous learning process. The integrating of e-learning and knowledge management presents exciting opportunities for e-learning systems development and targeted learning based on lifelong learning needs.

Different terminologies have been used for e-learning (Sloman, 2002). Therefore, e-learning environments will be analyzed and classified further. The analysis is based on three main functional dimensions of e-learning systems—collaboration, adaptivity, and learner's control level from low to high—for a particular e-learning system. Combinations of these three dimensions generate eight different scenarios, which show the evolution of e-learning historically, as shown in Figure 1.

In the early days of e-learning, Hypertext Books, Computer-Assisted Instruction (CAI) systems, Communications (CMC), and Group Systems (GSs) were introduced to online learners. These e-learning environments

Figure 1. Evolution of e-learning

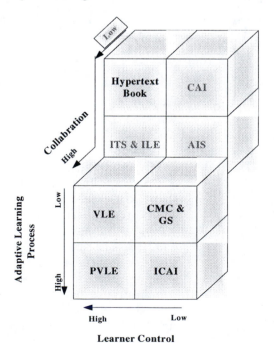

AVLE: Adaptive Virtual Learning Environment

VLE: Virtual Learning Environment

ITS: Intelligent Tutoring System

CMC: Computer-Mediated Communication

CAI: Computer-Assisted Instruction System

ICAI: Intelligent Computer-Assisted Instruction System

AIS: Adaptive Instructional System

ILE: Interactive Learning Environment

GS: Group System

Table 3. The integration relationships between KM processes and e-learning systems

		Hypertext Book	CAI	ITS & IEL	AIS	CMC & GS	ICAI	VLE	AVLE
Knowledge Management Process in E-Learning	Knowledge Creation	–	–	+	+	+	+	+	++
	Knowledge Storage	–	+	+	+	–	+	+	+
	Knowledge Retrieval	–	+	+	+	–	+	+	+
	Knowledge Transfer	–	–	+	+	+	+	+	+
	Application	–	+	+	+	+	+	+	++

Note: - less related; + correlated; ++ highly correlated.

provided online learners with access to up-to-date, relevant learning materials, and the ability to communicate with experts in the field in which they were studying in a very rigid manner. Along with the continuing evolution of information and communication technologies, Virtual Learning Environments (VLEs), Intelligent Tutoring Systems (ITSs), Intelligent Computer-Assistant Instruction (ICAI) systems, Adaptive Instructional Systems (AISs), Interactive Learning Environments (ILEs), and Adaptive Virtual Learning Environments (AVLEs) are developed, Those e-learning environments are making improvements to give online learners more flexibility in their e-learning in terms of collaboration, adaptivity, and learner control to overcome one-size-fits-all instruction, and to provide contextual and adaptive supports for e-learning.

This e-learning evolution framework is proposed based on the analysis of eight scenarios integrating increasing amounts of knowledge management into an e-learning environment (Figure 1). Levels of collaboration, the adaptive learning process, and learner control are measurements used to classify these eight scenarios. As an example, the Hypertext Book-based e-learning systems correspond to a low degree of collaboration, a low degree of adaptivity, and a low degree learner control. On the other hand, the Adaptive Virtual Learning Environments (AVLEs) correspond to a high degree of collaboration, a high degree of adaptivity, and a high degree of learner control. The higher level of collaboration provides better knowledge management processes in terms of knowledge creation, storage, and transfer. Higher levels of the adaptive learning process also have greater impact on the knowledge management process, and higher learner control gives the learner more power to engage in knowledge creation and sharing. Therefore, with the evolution of knowledge management integrated into e-learning environments, AVLE illustrates the future trend of e-learning, which provides adaptive components to personalize learning instruction and match with each learner's individual

cognitive capability in order for knowledge construction to occur.

Table 3 presents the integration relationship among knowledge management processes in e-learning within eight scenarios of e-learning environments. It has been clearly identified that Hypertext Book systems involve very few knowledge management processes. In contrast, the knowledge management processes are well integrated in Adaptive Virtual Learning Environments. Firstly, the knowledge creation process is highly integrated with the AVLEs. Most AVLEs have a "Just-In-Time" e-learning facility, which is an important IT enabler in the knowledge creation process. Some advanced AVLEs have data mining and reasoning capabilities, which are used to help learners analyze their learning performance. Also, the knowledge retrieval process plays an important role in AVLEs, where the contents are retrieved adaptively, based on different individual learners' dynamic situations. Another important knowledge process in AVLEs is knowledge transfer. The communication channels in AVLEs allow learners to publish their opinions and ideas, to access knowledge resources, and to discuss their opinions. For this reason, AVLEs have been attracting more and more attention from educational professionals and development professionals due to their advanced knowledge management facilities and its e-learning effectiveness. In general, the more an e-learning system is integrated with knowledge management processes, the better the learning effectiveness is that can be achieved.

CONCLUSION

E-learning and knowledge management are of increasing importance in this "knowledge economy," and lifelong learning issues will be of continuing significance. Although the integration of e-learning and knowledge management is in its early stage, there are numerous signs of the coming integration that will provide online learners with adaptive e-learning environments. This article has addressed the integration of knowledge management and e-learning to improve the capture, organization, and delivery of corporate knowledge in e-learning. Based on the analysis of knowledge management enablers and knowledge management processes in e-learning, the relationships of these two dimensions are shown in Table 2.

Furthermore, the evolution of e-learning systems has been examined, and eight scenarios have been identified, as shown in Figure 1. Analysis of these eight scenarios helps us to better understand the integration of knowledge management, and to predict the future trends of e-learning systems.

Finally, the integration relationship between knowledge management processes in e-learning and the eight scenarios of e-learning environments is presented in Table 3. The conclusion may be drawn that an e-learning system designed to have a higher level of collaboration, adaptive learning processes, and learner control should better integrate the knowledge management processes. With a higher level of knowledge management integration,, e-learning systems will have more opportunities to achieve e-learning effectiveness.

The proposed relationships in this article between knowledge management enablers and knowledge management processes in e-learning, and between knowledge management processes and e-learning systems, can be viewed as a framework for the integration between knowledge management and e-learning. Such a framework could be very useful for further research, as well as for practitioners in real-world application development.

REFERENCES

Alavi, M., & Leidner, D.E. (2001a). Research commentary: Technology-mediated learning: A call for greater depth and breadth of research. *Information Systems Research, 12*(1), 1-10.

Alavi, M., & Leidner, D.E. (2001b). Review: Knowledge management and knowledge management systems: Conceptual foundations and research issues. *MIS Quarterly, 25*(1), 107-136.

American Productivity & Quality Center. (2001). Is your content out of control? Retrieved from *http://www.apqc.org/portal/apqc/site/generic2?path=/site/km/resources.jhtml*

Argote, L., McEvily, B., & Reagans, R. (2003). Managing knowledge in organizations: An integrative framework and review of emerging themes. *Management Science, 49*(4), 571-582.

Becerra-Fernandez, I., & Sabherwal, R. (2001). Organizational knowledge management: A contingency perspective. *Journal of Management Information Systems, 18*(1), 23-55.

Crossan, M., Lane, H., & White, R. (1999). An organizational learning framework: Dimensions for a theory. *The International Journal of Organizational Analysis, 3*(3), 37-60.

Davenport, T.H., Long, D., & Beers, M.C. (1998). Successful knowledge management projects. *Sloan Management Review, 39*(2), 43-57.

Hardaker, G., & Smith, D. (2002). E-learning communities, virtual markets and knowledge creation. *European Business Review, 14*(5), 342-350.

Lee, H., & Choi, B. (2003). Knowledge management enablers, processes, and organizational performance: An integrative view and empirical examination. *Journal of Management Information Systems, 20*(1), 179-228.

Piccoli, G., Ahmad, R., & Ives, B. (2001). Web-based virtual learning environments: A research framework and a preliminary assessment of effectiveness in basic IT skills training. *MIS Quarterly, 25*(4), 401-425.

Schwartz, D.G., Divitini, M., & Brasethvik, T. (2000). On knowledge management in the Internet age. In D. Schwartz & Brasethvik (Eds.), *Internet-based knowledge management and organizational memory* (pp. 1-23). Hershey, PA: Idea Group Publishing.

Schwartz, D.G., & Te'eni, D. (2000). Tying knowledge to action with k-mail. *IEEE Intelligent Systems, 15*(3), 33-39.

Sloman, M. (2002). *The e-learning revolution: How technology is driving a new training paradigm* (p. 222). New York: AMACOM.

Van der Spek, B.R., & Spijkervetr, A.L. (1997). *Knowledge management: Dealing intelligently with knowledge.* Kenniscertrum CIBIT.

Vera, D., & Crossan, M. (2003). Organizational learning and knowledge management: Toward an integrative framework. In Easterby-Smith and Lyles (Eds.), *The Blackwell handbook of organizational learning and knowledge management* (pp. 122-141). Blackwell Publishing.

Zhang, D., & Nunamaker, J.K. (2003). Powering e-learning in the new millennium: An overview of e-learning and enabling technology. *Information Systems Frontiers, 5*(2), 207-218.

KEY TERMS

Adaptive Virtual Learning Environment (AVLE): An e-learning environment that provides adaptive components to personalize learning instruction, to match with each learner's individual cognitive capability in order for knowledge construction to occur. In AVLEs, individual learners can be uniquely identified, with content that is specifically presented for him or her, and learning progress that can be individually monitored, tailored, and accessed.

Content Management: The American Productivity & Quality Center (APQC, 2001) defines content management as "a system to provide meaningful and timely information to end users by creating processes that identify, collect, categorize, and refresh content using a common taxonomy across the organization." Content management covers pedagogical, psychological, and didactic issues, as well as technical questions. It is a large component of knowledge management.

Course Management: This includes the ability to share materials and modules across course containers, the ability to edit comment and to track changes on learners' documents, and the ability to monitor and access learners' e-learning performance. In short, course management offers instructors the ability to electronically maintain and manage class rosters, distribute course materials, administer online exams, and communicate with learners.

E-Learning: A type of distance learning in which training or educational material is delivered electronically to remote learners via the Internet or an intranet. Broadly speaking, e-learning is known as online learning or Web-based learning. E-learning is an instructional process that gives online learners access to a wide range of resources—teachers, other learners, and content such as readings and exercises—independently of place and time.

Evaluation Management: Used to guide learners' e-learning and build their knowledge, and to verify if the information is successfully turned into knowledge. In order for e-learning to be proven effective, online learners need to verify that they have succeeded in gaining new knowledge or skills. During this phase, the relationship between information and knowledge becomes visible with respect to e-learning.

Knowledge Management Processes: Also called knowledge management activities; may be thought of as the parts of a structured system that manages knowledge effectively. Encompasses four processes: creation, storage, transfer, and application. These processes do not always occur in a linear sequence and are often concurrent.

Organizational Learning: The process of change in individual and shared thought and action, which is affected by and embedded in the institutions of the organization. Organizational learning is descriptive stream, with academics who pursue the question: "How does an organization learn?" When individual and group learning becomes institutionalized, organizational learning occurs.

Intellectual Capital

HY Sonya Hsu
Southern Illinois University, USA

Peter P. Mykytyn Jr.
Southern Illinois University, USA

INTRODUCTION

Today's economy is characterized by a rapid rate of change, globalization, and knowledge-intensive products. This makes knowledge management (KM) vital to organizations. The resource-based view of the firm postulates that a firm's profitability is not only a function of its market and competitive position but also a function of its internal capabilities and know-how in combining its resources to deliver products and services and to enhance organizational performance (Alavi, 2000).

The goal of an effective KM strategy should be to enhance the creation, transfer, and utilization of all types of organizational knowledge (Alavi, 2000). Corporations not only realize that knowledge is the critical resource but also try to manage organizational knowledge more intensely and effectively. For example, Stewart (1997) defined intellectual capital (IC) as the intellectual material—knowledge, information, intellectual property, and experience—that can be put to use for creating wealth.

Several researchers (Bontis, 1996, 2001, 2002a, 2002b; Van Buren, 1999; Mykytyn, Bordoloi, Mckinney, & Bandyopadhyay, 2002; Pike, Rylander, & Roos, 2002) identified the importance of intellectual capital (IC) with Bontis (2002a) indicating that human capital is a major component of IC. Human capital, as well as other components of IC (e.g., innovation capital) is an integral part of knowledge in KM research (Bontis, 2001, 2002a, 2002b; Van Buren, 1999; Pike et al., 2002).

Finally, it does the organization little good if effective KM does not lead to success. This success can be defined as how well an organization engages in KM to innovate and reduce uncertainty. Ultimately, an organization should hope to achieve a competitive advantage.

While there is no clear division between KM and IC, there is an intuitive link between them. Numerous researchers have investigated knowledge components, KM issues, and success achievement in organizations. However, none has included IC components into an integrated research framework. This article presents such a framework.

BACKGROUND

According to Barney (2002), firm resources are "all assets, capabilities, competencies, organizational processes, firm attributes, information, and knowledge that are controlled by a firm" (p. 155). These resources enable the firm to implement strategies that increase its effectiveness and efficiency. Most importantly, the resource-based view of the firm focuses the idiosyncratic, costly to duplicate resources that may give the firm a competitive advantage, such as highly skilled and creative workers, effective managers, and institutional leaders. Barney (2002) further defines these too-costly-to-copy resources as "resource immobility."

Dierickx and Cool (1989) point out that firm resources can be divided into tradable (i.e., unskilled labor, raw materials, and common intellectual property) and nontradable (i.e., firm-specific skills/capabilities, quality reputations, partners royalty, R&D capability, brand loyalty, and customer trust). Whereas tradable resources are mobile and can be acquired easily, the nontradable resources are immobile and must be developed, accumulated, and maintained through time (Hunt, 2000).

"Immobility" in this article differs slightly from Barney's definition. The argument is established by the "how" and "what" to produce those too-costly-to-copy resources. For example, a top management of Toyota can move to Ford but cannot perform at the same scale as in Toyota because of different organizational capabilities, structures, dynamics, processes, and culture. The immobile resources are those that cannot be physically moved from one firm to the others regardless of whether they are copied or stolen. This article attempts to distinguish between mobile and immobile assets, and perhaps establish the argument on increasing the value of mobile assets by the facilitation of immobile assets.

In the spirit of Barney (1991, 1997, 2002), a firm's resources were defined as "capitals." As such, the firm's resources can be divided into financial capital, physical capital, human capital, and organizational capital (Barney, 1991, 1997, 2002). Financial capital includes all money resources. Physical capital is physical technology in a firm. Human capital refers to the training, experience, judgment, intelligence, relationships, and insight of individuals. Organizational capital includes a firm's formal reporting structure; formal and informal planning, controlling, and coordinating systems; its culture and reputation, and its informal relations among groups within firm, between firms and those in its environment (Barney, 2002, p. 156).

Bontis (2002a) defined similar concepts, referring to them as human capital, structure capital, and customer capital. Van Buren (1999), however, replaces Stewart's "structure capital" with two new measures: innovation capital and process capital. Innovation capital is the capability of an organization to innovate and to create new products and services, and process capital represents an organization's processes, techniques, systems, and tools.

Among three definitions of IC, Stewart (1997), Van Buren (1999), and Bontis (2002) all include human capital. Customer capital is the relationship between firms and their customers. Pike et al. (2002) referred to customer capital as relational capital; however, customer capital and relational capital are defined similarly. Structure/process capital by Bontis (2002), innovation/process capital by Van Buren (1999), or organizational capital by Pike et al. (2002) are the most controversial components of IC. Those definitions are titled differently, but they are overlapped in terms of the categories of IC.

Quite controversially, the evaluation of IC also inherits split directions. One direction includes accounting cost base and financial value base. The conventional accounting-based evaluation adjusts its traditional instruments, such as historical transactions, and balanced scorecards (Norton & Kaplan, 1996). These accounting indices were criticized as "lagging measures" (Pike et al., 2002) because they are "cost-based." Acting as a supplemental evaluation to cost-based calculation, the financial value-based approach utilizes net present value to estimate a company's IC with a market value. However, it still demonstrates problems of homogeneity, nonfinancial benefits, and forecasting (Lewis & Lippitt, 1999).

Tobin's q gains its prevalence as an indicator of a firm's intangible value (Hall, 1993; Megna & Klock, 1993). It is a ratio of the capital market value of a firm to its replacement value of its assets. These assets incorporate a market measure of a firm value that is forward-looking, risk-adjusted, and less susceptible to changes in accounting practice (Montgomery & Wernerfelt, 1988). Tobin's q can be as high as 7.00 where intellectual capital is resourceful, such as software industry, whereas q is as low as 1.00 where firms have large capital assets (i.e., steel industry) (Bontis, 2002b).

Other than accounting and financial evaluations, a business-based model is assessed by relative effectiveness of different approaches. Four criteria were established by KnowNet Group (EU/ESPRIT, 2000): (1) it is auditable and reliable; (2) it does not impose a large overhead; (3) it facilitates strategic and tactical management; and (4) it generates the information needed by stakeholders in a firm. Incorporating those criteria of a business-based model into Gold's process capabilities becomes our conceptual model.

Knowledge content can be mobile, which is a characteristic of human capital and innovation capital. KM processes and structures can be immobile, and that is structure capital and KM processes capabilities. This article takes an inward look at an organization's KM processes capabilities that specifically include IC. Of particular interest is a firm's effectiveness captured from mobile and immobile assets, that is, IC, through KM processes capabilities and structure capital.

KM Processes Capabilities

In addition to knowledge capital, integral to KM are processes associated with KM, referred to by Gold, Malhotra, and Segars (2001) as organizational capabilities. Gold et al. (2001) studied KM in an organizational capability perspective, and knowledge processes are perceived as an enabler of the organization to capture, reconcile, and transfer knowledge in an efficient manner. Knowledge processes are acquisition-oriented, conversion-oriented, application-oriented, and security-oriented.

Their descriptions of processes are as follows: (1) The acquisition process includes accumulating knowledge, seeking brand new knowledge, and creating new knowledge out of existing knowledge; (2) the conversion process detects the ability to make knowledge useful; (3) the application process offers effective storage and retrieval mechanisms and enables the organization to quickly access the knowledge depository; (4) the protection process is designed to protect the knowledge within an organization from illegal or inappropriate use or theft.

Intellectual Capital (IC)

- **Human Capital:** Bontis (2001) defined human capital as the combination of knowledge, skill, innovativeness, and ability of a company's individual employees to meet the task. Based on Nonoka (2002), knowledge is created and organized by the very flow of information, anchored on the commitment and beliefs of its holder. Human capital refers to the tacit knowledge embedded in the minds of employees. Ulrich (1998) proposed a measurable definition of human capital which is the product of "competence" and "commitment."

Competence is defined with two aspects: (1) competencies must align with business strategy; (2) competencies need to be generated through more than one mechanism, such as buy, build, borrow, bounce, and bind (Ulrich, 1998). Commitment reflects in how employees relate to each other and feel about a firm (Ulrich, 1998). To foster commitment, Ulrich (1998) indicated three ways: (1) reduce demands, (2) increase resources, and (3) turn demands into resources.

- **Structural Capital:** Bontis (2002a) defined structure capital as the organizational routines and processes that contain the nonhuman storehouses of knowledge. Two components are included in structural capital: a technological component and architectural competencies (Bontis, 2002a). The technological component can be defined as the local abilities and knowledge that are important to day-to-day operation, such as tacit knowledge, proprietary design rules, and unique modes of working together (Bontis, 2002a). The architectural competencies refer to the ability of the firm to integrate its component competencies together in new and flexible ways and to develop new competencies as they are required, for example, communication channels, information filters, and problem-solving strategies that develop between groups, control systems, cultural values, and idiosyncratic search routines (Bontis, 2002a).
- **Innovation Capital:** Innovation capital stands out from all other IC research in that it separates structure/process capital from the companies' capabilities to innovate (Van Buren, 1999). A successful innovation occurs in a cycle, according to Clark (1961). It is developed, profitably utilized, and ultimately loses its value as a source of "rents." An innovation loses its value to produce rents when it is replaced by a latter invention or when it is diffused among rivals. In this article, both objective and subjective measures are accounted for in the intellectual property construct. The objective measure is aligned with Aylen's (2001) audit system of intellectual property, and it includes counts of patents and R&D expenditures (Mykytyn et al., 2002).

The subjective measure includes three dimensions suggested by Teece (1998) for capturing value from intellectual property: (1) appropriability is a function both of the ease of replication and the efficacy of intellectual property rights as a barrier to imitation; (2) markets for know-how are the killer sources to entitle a competitive advantage for intellectual properties, however, they be-

come financial assets when they are traded on the market for monetary rewards; (3) dynamic capabilities are the abilities to sense and to seize new opportunities, and to reconfigure and protect knowledge assets, competencies, and complementary assets and technologies to achieve sustainable competitive advantage.

MAIN FOCUS OF THE ARTICLE

Our article discusses these important KM components in an integrated fashion. The components are addressed below.

Knowledge Process Capabilities and Organizational Effectiveness

Combining or integrating organizational knowledge reduces redundancy, enhances consistency, and improves efficiency by eliminating excess information (Davenport & De Long, 1998). Gold et al. (2001) utilized organizational effectiveness to evaluate the value-added aspect of the organizational resources. Three concepts are used to evaluate organizational effectiveness: improved ability to innovate, improved coordination of efforts, and reduced redundancy of information/knowledge (Gold et al., 2001). Gold et al.'s (2001) results suggested that knowledge infrastructure along with knowledge processes are essential organizational capabilities for effectiveness. Knowledge infrastructure consists of culture, structure, and technology that can be explained by structure capital (Bontis, 2002a, 2002b).

The Mediation of Knowledge Process Capabilities

- **Human Capital and Organizational Effectiveness:** As the service economy grows, the importance of human capital increases (Ulrich, 1998). An experienced, intelligent workforce can marshal the knowledge needed for an information/service economy. Based on research by Davenport and De Long (1998) involving 31 KM projects, it was found that a KM initiative demonstrated some commitment of human capital resources. Ulrich (1998), too, felt that human capital must include an individual's commitment in addition to competence.

An important element of knowledge creation is the focus on the active, subjective nature of knowledge represented by such terms as "belief" and "commitment" that are deeply rooted in the value systems of individuals (Nonaka, 2002). A human capital index created by Ulrich

(1998) may predict other positive outcomes, such as customer loyalty, productivity, and profitability. Bontis (2002b) did not support the relationship between human capital and organizational effectiveness.

The KM processes capabilities are not only embedded in a KM system but also require knowledge workers' inputs and competencies to maneuver around the organizational routines, processes, and functionalities. Human capital is hypothesized to have a positive effect on organizational effectiveness as mediated by KM process capabilities.

- **Innovation Capital and Organizational Effectiveness:** The innovation-oriented approach focuses on explicit knowledge that will eventually facilitate organizational learning. The learned organization will then have better capabilities to innovate and compete. The explicit knowledge can be a database, intellectual property, business designs, business process techniques, or patterns. Technology held proprietary through patents, copyrights, or trade secrets can deter new entrants and achieve a competitive advantage by exploiting economies of scale and scope or through differentiation (Bharadwaj, Varadarajan, & Fahy, 1993). As a major component of innovation capital, intellectual property can be managed as explicit knowledge or act as repositories in a KM system or a database that can be retrieved and reused repeatedly.

The systematic structure of a KM system made intellectual property more accessible and usable. The emphasis on the development and exploitation of knowledge shifts attention from cost minimization to value maximization (Teece, 1998). Aylen (2001) suggested five steps to establish intellectual property capital: conduct an intellectual property audit, incubate new ideas, reduce the ideas to practical form, protect the idea, and exploit the idea. Aylen (2001) also recommended patent databases as a knowledge bank to track the costs and delay associated with the state of a particular product or process.

Besides intellectual property, research and development exspenditure are included in innovation capital that is further defined by appropriateness, markets for know-how, and dynamic capabilities (Teece, 1988). According to Lynn (1998), a significant component of initial management of intellectual assets at Dow Chemical has been its review of patent maintenance within R&D to create objective, major cost savings for the firm.

One famous e-commerce case involving a patent infringement action is Amazon.com vs. Barnesandnoble.com. This case is about Amazon's patented "1-click ordering system." In December 1999, Amazon won a preliminary injunction against Barnesandnoble.com prohibiting any-

one else from employing the "1-click ordering system" (Mykytyn & Mykytyn, 2002). Now Amazon enjoys the increasing rent revenue by leasing the patent "1-click ordering system" to its competitors.

In another patent case involving a deeper understanding of patent application, VisorSoft's newly updated "face-recognition software" was copycatted (Maxwell, 2002) before it went on the market. This software is used in highly secured workplaces, such as airports and banks, that need an accurate identification. It can compare a stored face-print with a person's live image and determine if they were the same. The competitor's software operated exactly like VisorSoft's but was marketed differently. The "continuation patent" known as a "child patent" kept VisorSoft's patent infringement against the competitor, and its argument of being a different process as VisorSoft's was disapproved (Maxwell, 2002). VisorSoft can now recoup its development costs and realize licensing fee from users.

An innovative product goes through creation, conversion, and application processes to present it in the market. It also needs a thorough "protection" process to keep an innovation proprietary. Organizational effectiveness can be defined as a firm's attempts to control and reduce production and marketing costs (Dickson, 1992). Cost-cutting innovations are particularly attractive because their effects are more predictable than other innovations (Dickson, 1992). Innovation capital as evidenced by the accumulation of explicit knowledge is assumed to increase the organizational effectiveness with the facilitation of knowledge process capabilities.

The Mediation of Structure Capital

The essence of structure capital is the knowledge embedded within the routines of an organization (Bontis, 2002a). Also, Bontis' structure capital combined with Van Buren's (1999) process capital echoes knowledge infrastructure in Gold et al. (2001) that involves organizational structure, culture, and technology. Structure capital includes a technological component and architectural competencies (Bontis, 2002a).

Bontis (2002b) found that human capital was not a significant path to a firm's performance, but that structure capital was. On the other hand, when structure capital was analyzed as a mediator, it facilitated human capital in relation to a firm's performance. It showed a valid path from human capital to structure capital, then to a firm's performance.

Bontis' (2002b) study established a relationship between human capital, structure capital, and a firm's performance in a student sample. This article further extends the rationale from structure capital to innovation capital, and attempts to offer some insights. The innovation capital is in response to the rapidly changing environment, and it leads to a constant learning environment for an organization. The constant learning processes are deeply rooted in formalization and routines of an organization, and, in turn, an organization becomes more innovative to compete.

FUTURE TRENDS

Breaking down these streams of ideas, this article tends to utilize four concepts to link to organizational effectiveness. Knowledge process capabilities and structure capital may be direct links to organizational effectiveness, or they may serve a mediating function between human/innovation capital and organizational effectiveness. The conceptual model underlying this article is shown in Figure 1.

From the emergent research agenda, this article attempts to examine if there is a division or a link between IC and KM processes. If there is a division, this study attempts to examine the difference between IC and KM. If there is a link, what effect does one have on the other? This study intends to delineate the "mobile" and "immobile" parts of IC. Human and innovation capitals are content that belong to "mobile" category. On the other hand, KM process capabilities and structural capital are structure and/or process that are "immobile."

Alavi and Leidner (2001) drew some different perspectives on knowledge. They indicated knowledge could be data and information, state of mind, object, process, access to information, and capability. Different views of knowledge lead to different KM, and different knowledge management systems (KMS) are built upon different perceptions of KM. "The view of knowledge as capability suggests a knowledge management perspective centered on building core competencies, understanding the strategic advantage know-how, and creating intellectual capital" (Alavi & Leidner, 2001, p. 110). Most KM research focused on knowledge processes, organization structure, or technology utilization, but not knowledge content per se. On the other hand, IC researchers (Bontis, 1996, 2001,

2002a, 2002b; Van Buren, 1999; Pike et al., 2001) included KM in their studies, however, without a clear distinction from KM or definition of IC.

Finally, structure capital was incorporated to emphasize the importance of how to process knowledge, once it is defined. This study enhances the "understanding of know-how" with an organization's "state of mind" in creating intellectual capital. The organization structure becomes alive when information is actively processed in the minds of individuals through a process of reflection, enlightenment, or learning (Alavi & Leidner, 2001). Beyond organization structure, structure capital refers to the "immobile" organization capability that is also hard to imitate.

Many IC researchers have classified many different categories and/or properties to define IC (Bontis, 1996, 2001, 2002a, 2002b; Van Buren, 1999; Pike et al., 2001; Roos, Roos, Dragonetti, & Edvinsson, 1997; Brooking, 1996). Pike et al. (2002) stated, "There has been a steady convergence" (p. 658) in categorizing an IC model. They concluded a convergent IC model that combined elements created value for an individual company. Those elements include: (1) human capital is represented as attributes of the people (i.e., skill, creativity); (2) organizational capital refers to company-owned items (i.e., systems, intellectual properties); (3) relational capital is external relations with customers, suppliers, and partners.

Focusing on internal resources and a resource-based view with an intention, this article demonstrates an inward examination to a firm. Too, as an extended "immobile" concept, this article attempts to investigate the unique "innovation" capital that may be a valid property ignored by most IC researchers but Van Buren (1999). The focus of IC here is organizational flexibility and immobility that may contribute to organizational process capabilities that comply to any emergent competition a firm may encounter in a marketplace.

Additions to this article are the areas of risk and uncertainty, leading edcoordination, and co-competition among increasing numbers of external members, that is, networks of firms, networks of supply chains, make relational capital unpredictable yet vulnerable.

Figure 1. Conceptual model

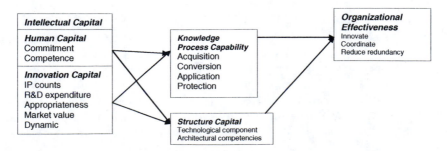

CONCLUSION

This article attempts to delineate KM and IC and more clearly provide definitions that were neglected by either KM researchers or IC researchers. The integration of KM and IC is another goal for this article. Combining the resource-based view and the more recent concept of emergent KM processes, we anticipate introducing innovation capital that consists of intellectual property and other properties. Following Van Buren's (1999) innovation concept, this article focuses more on emergent KM processes rather than static knowledge conversion. Following Ulrich's (1998) human capital index, this article moves forward to more dynamic rather than static working relationships within the firm. Further, we attempt to establish Barney's (1991, 1997, 2002) concepts of "mobile" vs. "immobile" in both KM and IC environment. Finally, this article tries to fill the gaps between the KM and IC research and move forward to an integral explanation to those fields.

REFERENCES

Alavi, M. (2000). Managing organizational knowledge. In R.W. Zmud (Ed.) *Framing the domains of IT management projecting the future...through the past* (pp. 15-28). Cincinnati, OH: Pinnaflex Education Resources, Inc.

Alavi, M., & Leidner, D. (2001). Review: Knowledge management and knowledge management systems: Conceptual foundations and research issues. *MIS Quarterly, 25,* 107-136.

Aylen, D. (2001). Knowledge management: harnessing the power of intellectual property. *Ivey Business Journal, 65.*

Barney, J. (1991). Firm resources and sustained competitive advantage. *Journal of Management, 17,* 99-120.

Barney, J. (1997). *Gaining and sustaining competitive advantage.* Reading, MA: Addison-Wesley.

Barney, J. (2002). *Gaining and sustaining competitive advantage.* Upper Saddle River, NJ: Prentice Hall.

Bharadwaj, S.G., Varadarajan, P.R., & Fahy, J. (1993). Sustainable competitive advantage in service industries: A conceptual model and research propositions. *Journal of Marketing, 57,* 83-99.

Bontis, N. (1996). There's a price on your head: Managing intellectual capital strategically. *Business Quarterly, 43.*

Bontis, N. (2001). Assessing knowledge assets: A review of the models used to measure intellectual capital. *International Journal of Management Reviews, 3,* 41-61.

Bontis, N. (2002a). Intellectual capital: An exploratory study that develops measures and models. In C.W. Choo & N. Bontis (Eds.), *The strategic management of intellectual capital and organizational knowledge.* New York: Oxford University Press.

Bontis, N. (2002b). Managing organizational knowledge by diagnosing intellectual capital: Framing and advancing the state of the field. In C.W. Choo, N. Bontis (Eds.), *The strategic management of intellectual capital and organizational knowledge.* New York: Oxford University Press.

Brooking, A. (1996). *Intellectual capital.* New York: International Thomson Business Press.

Clark, J.M. (1961). *Competition as a dynamic process.* Washington, DC: Brookings Institution.

Davenport, T.H., & De Long, D.W. (1998). Successful knowledge management projects. *Sloan Management Review, 39*(2), 43-57.

Dickson, P.R. (1992). Toward a general theory of competitive rationality. *Journal of Marketing, 56,* 69-83.

Dierickx, I., & Cool, K. (1989). Asset stock accumulation and sustainability of competitive advantage. *Management Science, 35,* 1504-1511.

EU/ESPRIT (2000). Knownet: Knowledge management with Intranet technologies. *Project EP28928.* Retrieved from *www.know-net.org/*

Gold, A.H., Malhotra, A., & Segars, A.H. (2001). Knowledge management: An organizational capabilities perspective. *Journal of Management Information Systems, 18,* 185-215.

Hall, B.H. (1993). The stock market's valuation of R&D investment during the 1980s. *AEA Papers and Proceedings, 70,* 259-264.

Hunt, S. (2000). *A general theory of competition: Resources, competences, productivity, economic growth.* UK: Sage.

Lewis, E., & Lippitt, J. (1999). Valuing intellectual assets. *Journal of Legal Economics, 9,* 31-48.

Lynn, L.E. (1998). The management of intellectual capital: the issues and the practice. Management accounting issues paper 16, *Management Accounting Practices Handbook.* Hamilton, Ontario: Society of Management Accountants of Canada.

Maxwell, R. (2002). Smart patents; Is your intellectual capital at risk? *Forthought,* April, 2-3.

Megna, P., & Klock, K. (1993). The impact of intangible capital on Tobin's q in the semiconductor industry. *AEA Proceedings Paper, 83*, 265-269.

Montgomery, C., & Wernerfelt, B. (1988). Diversification, Ricardian rents and Tobin's q. *Rand J. of Economic, 19*, 623-632.

Mykytyn, K., Bordoloi, B., Mckinney, V., & Bandyopadhyay, K. (2002). The role of software patents in sustaining IT-enabled competitive advantage: A call for research. *Journal of Strategic Information Systems, 11*, 59-82.

Mykytyn, P.P. Jr., Mykytyn, K. (2002). Computer software patents: A dilemma in competitive advantage IT research. *Communications of the Association for Information Systems, 8*, 109-130.

Nonaka, I. (2002). A dynamic theory of organizational knowledge creation. In C.W. Choo & N. Bontis (Eds.), *The strategic management of intellectual capital and organizational knowledge*. New York: Oxford University Press.

Norton, D., & Kaplan, R. (1996). *The balanced scorecard: Translating strategy into action*. Boston: Harvard Business School.

Pike, S., Rylander, A., & Roos, G. (2002). Intellectual capital: Management and disclosure. In C.W. Choo & N. Bontis (Eds.), *The strategic management of intellectual capital and organizational knowledge*. New York: Oxford University Press.

Roos, J., Roos, G., Dragonetti, N., & Edvinsson, L. (1997). *Intellectual capital: Navigating the new business landscape*. New York: Macmillan.

Stewart, T.A. (1997). *Intellectual capital: The new wealth of organizations*. New York: Double-Day/Currency.

Teece, D.J. (1988). Capturing value from technological innovation: Integration, strategic partnering, and licensing decisions. *Interface, 18*, 46-61.

Teece, D.J. (1998). Capturing value from knowledge assets: The new economy, markets for know-how, and intangible assets. *California Management Review, 40*, 55-79.

Ulrich, D. (1998). Intellectual capital = competence x commitment. *Sloan Management Review, 39*, 15-26.

Van Buren, M.E. (1999). *A yardstick for knowledge management*. *Training & Development, 53*, 71-8.

KEY TERMS

Human Capital: Human capital is the combination of knowledge, skill, innovativeness, and ability of a company's individual employees to meet the task. It refers to the tacit knowledge embedded in the minds of employees.

Human Capital Index: A measurable definition of human capital is defined by the product of "competence" and "commitment." While they align with business strategy, competencies need to be generated through more than one mechanism, such as buy, build, borrow, bounce, and bind. Commitment is concerned with how employees relate to each other and feel about a firm.

Innovation Capital: The innovation-oriented approach focuses on explicit knowledge that will eventually facilitate organizational learning. The learned organization will then have better capabilities to innovate and compete.

Intellectual Capital: It refers to intellectual material—knowledge, information, intellectual property, and experience—that can be put to use for creating wealth.

Intellectual Property: Intellectual property includes business designs, business process techniques, or patterns. Technology held proprietary through patents, copyrights, or trade secrets can deter new entrants and achieve a competitive advantage by exploiting economies of scale and scope or through differentiation. Five steps are suggested to establish intellectual property capital: conduct an intellectual property audit, incubate new ideas, reduce the ideas to practical form, protect the idea, and exploit the idea.

Knowledge Management Process Capabilities: Knowledge processes are perceived as an enabler of the organization to capture, reconcile, and transfer knowledge in an efficient manner. Knowledge processes are acquisition-oriented, conversion-oriented, application-oriented, and security-oriented.

Organizational Effectiveness: It is used to evaluate the value-added aspect of the organizational resources. Three concepts are included: improved ability to innovate, improved coordination of efforts, and reduced redundancy of information/knowledge.

Structure Capital: The knowledge embedded within the routines of an organization involves organizational structure, culture, and technology. Structure capital includes a technological component and architectural competencies.

Intellectual Capital and Knowledge Management

Gil Ariely
University of Westminster, UK and Interdisciplinary Center Herzliya, Israel

INTRODUCTION

Knowledge management (KM) and intellectual capital (IC) are not one and the same, and although some overlap is apparent, the relationship is far from trivial and requires exploration. Some intellectual capital such as brand is not knowledge, and some knowledge that cannot be transformed into value is not intellectual capital.

This article illustrates the paradigm of IC and its measurement, focusing then on tensions in the relationship of KM and IC and their origins.

Sullivan (2000) moves us toward the understanding of KM as *value creation* in all its aspects, vs. IC, or ICM (IC management), as *value extraction* (thus, measurement, accountability, explicability, etc.). He defines intellectual capital very briefly as "knowledge that can be converted into profit" (p. 192), implying that some quantification of the value of knowledge is required.

BACKGROUND

The history and development of intellectual capital and intellectual-capital management somewhat correlate to that of knowledge management, and it seems superfluous to elaborate on the practicality of intellectual capital, where practice was preliminary to theory. The IC movement is a paradigm derived from a practical need: to bridge the apparent gap between the firm's books and the classic accounting vehicle, and the actual market value. According to Petty and Guthrie (2000):

[t]he intellectual capital movement is undeniably grounded in practice (Roos et al., 1997; Larsen et al., 1999; Mouritsen, 1998). The development of intellectual capital reports, for instance, can be traced back to the desire for individuals working with or within businesses to improve their understanding of what comprised the value of the business so as to manage better those things that generate value. (Sveiby, 1997; Edvinsson & Malone, 1997; Johanson et al., 1999)

They also say (p. 158; see also the definition of IC in "Key Terms"), "Often, the term 'intellectual capital' is treated as being synonymous with 'intangible assets.'"

The paradigm of IC is established rather commonly in the literature as divided into three subdomains: human capital, organizational capital, and customer capital (or human capital, structural capital, and relational capital; Bontis, 2002; Edvinsson & Malone, 1997; Stewart, 1997; Sullivan, 1998). This division is meaningful toward measurement, a focal point of the IC movement.

IC Measurement and Models

Valery Kanevsky and Tom Housel write, "Understanding how to accelerate the conversion of knowledge into money is the real challenge in the information age" (as cited in Von Krogh, Roos, & Kleine, 1998, p. 269). Tracking that process of conversion into value leads to measurement. Roos, Roos, Edvinsson, and Dragonetti (1998) emphasize that the definition of intellectual capital must be clear and measurable: In order to manage intellectual capital, it must be measured.

However, the measurement of knowledge assets triggers both great interest and great skepticism. Indeed, the measurement of IC is still being experimented with various models.

One of the ultimate goals of measuring intellectual capital is its proper acknowledgement and reporting, similar to the more familiar accounting and reporting system of tangible assets in firms. The perspective of the stocks and flows forms of knowledge (following the resource-based view of the firm) inspired a comparison to familiar forms of accounting reporting. According to Bontis, Dragonetti, Jacobsen, and Roos (1999):

In a way, the identification of stocks creates a series of still photos of the company's intangible resources, whereas the flows provide the animation. Adding a flow perspective to the stock perspective is akin to adding a profit and loss statement to a balance sheet in accounting. The two perspectives combined (or the two reporting tools, in the case of accounting) provide much more information than any single one alone.

Indeed, Lev (2000a, 2000b) says, "Accounting's 500 year exceptional durability is being severely tested...a major contributor to such asymmetries are the archaic accounting rules which treat most investments in knowledge as regular expenses."

As to the principle behind actually calculating intellectual capital, Mouritsen, Bukh, Larsen, and Johansen (2002, p. 11) say, "Authors such as Edvinsson and Malone, and Stewart suggest that intellectual capital is a combination of human, structural and customer capital, whose worth can be identified by subtracting the firm's book value from its market value."

Although measuring IC is recognized to be crucial, frameworks have not yet reached statutory recognition as paradigms, thus allowing us but a sample and flavour of some available models and tools implemented toward the metrics of "intangibles" within the scope of this article. This is not due to the lack of models, but to the lack of standards. Further literature reviews of the tools elaborate beyond the scope this theatre allows (Bontis et al., 1999).

According to Petty and Guthrie (2000), "it is the limitations of the existing financial reporting system for capital markets and other stakeholders [that] have motivated an evolving dialogue on finding new ways to measure and report on a company's intellectual capital." The product of this dialogue is a plethora of new measurement approaches that all have the aim, to a greater or lesser extent, of synthesising the financial and non-financial value-generating aspects of the company into one external report. Principal among the new reporting models are the intangible asset monitor (Sveiby, 1988; 1997; Celemi, 1998); the balanced scorecard (Kaplan and Norton, 1992; 1996); the Skandia value scheme (Edvinsson and Malone, 1997; Edvinsson, 1997); and the intellectual capital accounts (DATI, 1998).

It is interesting to compare the frameworks of several of the main classification schemas for reporting intellectual capital. These three principal ones, which emerge prominent in IC literature, show progress toward alignment within the IC paradigm (Table 1).

A conclusion from this comparison is that by now there are the first signs of an aligning idea in the perception of intellectual capital, hence, its measurement. There is clear identification in classification between capital relating to human assets, and capital relating to structure—be it internal or inclusive of the external values.

Moreover, entwined in all frameworks is the profound realization of the value and qualitative characteristics of the attempts to quantify the qualitative via various proxy indicators, as the nature of knowledge, and in particular the nature of its value, is qualitative.

But we must remember that there is no widely accepted standard, and firms may measure their intangible assets rather than be obliged to do so. What measure, metric, tool, or approach is preferable is purely dependent on the circumstances of the organization as there is no binding authoritative view or legislation in the matter (although the need for it is reoccurring in the literature; Bassi & Van Buren, 1999; Van Buren, 1999).

Tools that resemble the familiar accounting tools for reporting are being developed, such as intellectual-capital statements (Mouritsen et al., 2002; Mouritsen, Larsen, Bukh, & Johansen, 2001), and attempts through practice raise a lantern for future recognition and regularity (Wyatt, 2002).

THE RELATIONSHIP BETWEEN KM AND IC

To sum up intellectual capital, and in particular its possible measurement and reporting, it is possible to consider intellectual capital as the knowledge phase in accounting using the principle analysis of knowledge; that is, the accounting reports and balance sheets familiar to us consist merely of the information of the firm, whilst the intellectual-capital reports are in fact the actual accounting knowledge of the firm and its values.

We have so far taken "raw financial data" (Edvinsson & Malone, 1997, p. 77), the signals, and put them in formation in order to inform (hence it becomes information) in the accounting reports. The knowledge of the firm, mostly tacit, was created in the mind of the reader, be it an accountant, investor, or so on, using other various tacit and explicit sources to inform. The intellectual-capital movement is trying to make explicit as much of this

Table 1. IC paradigm

Developed by	Framework	Classification
Sveiby (1997, 1998)	The intangible-asset monitor	Internal structure External structure Competence of personnel
Kaplan and Norton (1992)	The balanced scorecard	Internal-processes perspective Customer perspective Learning and growth perspective Financial perspective
Edvinsson and Malone (1997)	Skandia value scheme	Human capital Structural capital

knowledge as possible; much of it arrives as qualitative data and qualitative information.

Continuing the "IC equals firm's tree roots" metaphor (Edvinsson & Malone, 1997, p. 10), although such an effort is not futile, the full (tacit) underground nature of the roots as well as the effect of the soil (context) can never be exposed in full. Evermore, trying to examine the roots in depth by taking out the tree in full cannot be done without harming the roots, as is taking them out of their soil. Thus, we are left with data collected through secondary methods attempting to x-ray the roots from above ground, or inductively taking a sample of the roots. These inseparable connections are discussed further when we recall the dualities incorporated in the concept of value.

The empiric foundation of this article was research implementing grounded theory in a multiple-case study in three organizations (the National Health Service, National Transportation Authority, and the military), from which the illustrated theory emerged. The organizational creation of the paradigms of KM and IC and their relationship was examined by researching KM as a methodology toward IC (Ariely, 2003): an array of methods transformed into perceived value and intellectual capital.

Knowledge is first and foremost inherent in people and in interactions. Viewing knowledge as part of human capital leads to the idea that managing knowledge is part of the structural capital (although not limited to structure). So, successful KM is in itself part of the organization's intellectual capital in addition to the knowledge incorporated in it as a process and in its people. But in order to fully understand the relationship between KM and IC, which surrounds the transformation of knowledge and managing it into value, we must stop to consider the meaning of value within the dual contexts of KM and IC.

What Does Value Mean?

The duality in the definition of value (see "Key Terms") is crucial since the meanings of the word reflect on the quantitative—vs.—qualitative tensions incorporated in the concept of value. Patrick Sullivan (2000) writes,

Economists view value *as the sum of a stream of benefits (or income) stretching into the future, summed and discounted to a net present value in dollars. Yet value has meaning for many others besides economists [p. 247]...The economics of information applies to any idea, expression of an idea, or fact that is known by one person and is potentially of value to another.* (p. 271)

Any capital or currency is dependent upon its market: so is intellectual capital. Its value, as any currency, is in the eyes of the beholder. Diamonds may be worthless on a deserted, isolated island, or they may bring their worth as a tool to start a fire, multiplying perhaps their true value to our Robinson Crusoe beyond any market value.

The value of knowledge implemented toward action in one context (or having the potential to be) may be absolutely worthless in another. Sullivan (2000) further explores the concept of value, differentiating between defensive and offensive value types for the organization, and creating the organization's value chain.

The relative value placed on innovative ideas is largely dependent upon the firm's view of itself, and upon the reality of the marketplace. Put another way, each firm exists within a context that shapes the firm's view of what is or is not of value. (p. 247; see also Sullivan, 1998; Sveiby, 2001; Von Krogh, Nonaka, & Nishiguchi, 2000).

The perception of the value of the organization's intellectual capital is what becomes its intellectual property and intellectual assets. Assessing it is essential as is assessing the investment in intellectual capital (Bassi & Van Buren, 1999) similarly to any other capital. Furthermore, there is a different value to knowledge, and different behaviours of intellectual capital and intellectual property in different organizational contexts (Sullivan, 2000), for example, intellectual-capital development at a spin-off company (Manfroy & Gwinnell, 1998) in mergers and acquisitions (Sullivan, 2000). According to Joyce and Stivers (1999), "[r]esults indicate that firms...tend to differ in organizational structure and technology orientation, as well as in the perception of the value of various non-financial performance factors and intangible assets."

The operative meaning is that things that are valuable do not necessarily have intrinsic value. They are *value-able*, with the potential for value, perception making their value ability come true within the organization and in its environment.

Tension Between Production Factors

The tensions that lie beneath the surface between knowledge management and intellectual capital are derived from their basically different nature in relation to the conservative production factors (land, capital, labour). Intellectual capital relates to capital, whilst knowledge management relates to labour. Yet the behaviour of IC is not the same as capital. Mouritsen et al. (2002, p. 10) note that "[i]ntellectual capital is, even if it refers to 'capital,' not a conventional accounting or economic term." The rules for its depreciation, creation, and so forth are complex and irrelevant to "hard capital" (e.g., depreciation of knowledge occurs when it is not used, contrary to tangible assets).

The management of people as human resources has been dealt with within the division of labour. However, when arguing that knowledge is not just people, but their "cognitive contact with reality" (Zagzebski, 1999), their knowledge might be acknowledged, but not managed directly in the classic definition of management in the same way we manage resources within the division of labour. Streatfield and Wilson (1999, p. 70) say, "We cannot manage knowledge directly—we can only manage information about the knowledge possessed by people in organizations." Indeed, we can always manage the yellow pages, which are pointers to knowledge. These pointers accrue in themselves information about the formations of the knowledge.

As to the tensions between the division of knowledge and the division of labour, Klein and Scarbrough (2002) emphasize that:

[t]he very identification of knowledge as a factor of production as distinct from labour, and the irreducibility of the one to the other invites conflict between the two. While much of the literature on knowledge management seeks to legitimise and exploit knowledge as a quasi-autonomous resource of the organization, we see knowledge as simultaneously different from, but not wholly independent from labour.

Indeed, the management of resources such as knowledge in the postindustrial age suggests a much more permissive and updated approach to management.

Boisot and Griffiths (1999) note that "[i]n a 'post Marxist' world, knowledge workers are once more becoming the owners of the means of production," owning the most important production factors: knowledge and intellectual capital.

Epistemological Tensions

As our ground is knowledge, it is worth going into geological depth about the theoretical layers beneath it. There lies one more real foundation for the tension between these two domains of knowledge—knowledge management vs. intellectual capital—perhaps to a degree, between their correlating communities of practice (with the overlap that exists between the fields existing between the communities, too). Some tensions date, as geological issues tend to, as far in the past as the origins of that ground.

There is an epistemological diversity, as in many fields, amongst thinkers in the most intrinsic approaches to the world, knowledge, truth, and validity. However, it reflects on not only the derived methodological researching ideology, but rather on the core itself.

For instance, many approach the field of intellectual capital from the need to measure and quantify the organization's value (Petty & Guthrie, 2000), the very need that arouses interest in IC at first being the apparent gap between the firm's actual value and its "book value," by using conservative accounting measures. Accountants, as well as many managers, tend to derive from the epistemological foundations of positivism since positivism seems to have been management's mainstream (Johnson & Duberley, 2000) and the most appropriate for Taylor's scientific approach of the industrial age.

It is the same behaviour of knowledge as a differentiated production factor from the conservative ones in the industrial age (land, labour, capital) that justifies a different epistemological, philosophical approach.

Many approach the field of knowledge management from very different epistemological foundations and approaches, such as social constructivism. Wenger (1998, p. 141) says:

Knowing is defined only in the context of specific practices, where it arises out of the combination of a regime of competence and an experience of meaning. Our knowing—even of the most unexceptional kind—is always too big, too rich, too ancient and too connected for us to be the source of it individually.

Hence, "[k]nowledge *is* socially constructed" (Despres, 2002), which tends to form a real challenge for positivists' measurement.

It is that tension, derived from epistemological differences, that highlights the need for an attempt to approach the field of intellectual capital from a social constructivist's orientation. Also, the derived approach and methodology, in order not to neglect the real essence of value, which is interwoven with perceptions, is constructed socially.

Einstein reminded us that not all that can be counted counts, and not all that counts can be counted. Value and perception become components (or methods in the array) of the modeled methodology. It is perception that brings realization to the potential for value of value-ables.

The emotive theory of values, as one of the principles of logical positivism, acknowledges that "[s]tatements of value are neither true or false, but are simply expressions of attitude" (Cruise, 1997; Gross, 1970; Wedberg, 1984). We can extend that principle within the definitions of value. Thus, one type of value is dependent on the other—on values, perception, and attitude.

Indeed it follows that some tension is also derived from the very essence of the term measurement, which implicitly tries to quantify the very qualitative.

Figure 1.

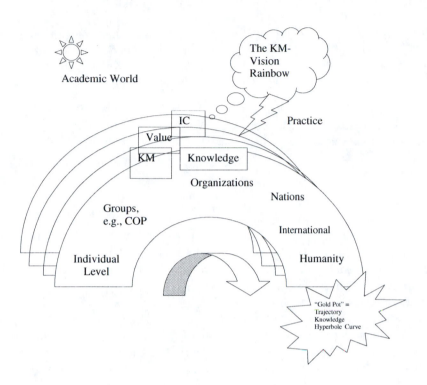

FUTURE

Viewing knowledge management as a catalyst for the creation of human knowledge moves us up the trajectory curve in the hyperbola of human-knowledge creation by allowing us to build better on past generations and current knowledge.

The importance of the connection to intellectual capital is a catalyst for the industry to invest in research and the implementation of KM and IC. This brings the short- and medium-term benefits that organizations and management so often seek, but brings us all the long-term benefits from the blossoming of KM, knowledge, and knowledge on knowledge. According to McElroy (2002, p. 30):

Not surprisingly, managers interested in getting their arms around intellectual capital are searching for ways to describe, measure, and manage their intangible assets with a particular emphasis on capturing their favorable effects on the bottom line and on shareholder values.

Indeed, through a different visualization from the hyperbola of knowledge creation, we can imagine a rainbow model on which the different dimensions are aligned (e.g., value) from an individual level to humanity.

While the academic world should shed light on the whole spectrum, practitioners tend to focus on organizational levels due to economic reasons. The benefits for humanity go beyond organizations, supporting a trajectory knowledge-creation hyperbola. Carrillo (1999) says:

In Post Capitalist Society, Peter Drucker wonders whether anyone will dare to undertake the intellectual manifesto of the Knowledge Economy, something like The K-Capital. One of the most distinctive challenges to the KM movement is the extent to which it is capable of gaining self-awareness and self-management capabilities. To the extent that this happens, it will be able to facilitate the process for achieving the best human account on the principles of knowledge economics.

It seems clear that the intellectual-capital movement picked up the glove dropped in 1993 by Peter Drucker.

CONCLUSION

Exploring the relationships between knowledge management and intellectual capital by incorporating epistemological tensions reveals one such relationship that can be modeled into an empirically grounded methodology.

Knowledge, and managing all of its elements (knowledge creation, sharing, and transfer, etc.), becomes part of the organization's intellectual capital. The intellectual capital is then transformed through its value to the organization (a matter of perception, as discussed, dependant on the eye of the beholder) into the organization's owned intellectual property so that it can be protected.

Explicitly exploring knowledge management as a mechanism that moves us toward intellectual capital and property allows the KM process to become part of the intellectual capital in itself.

According to Fahy (2000):

The management literature highlights that executives play a role in the process of converting resources into something of value to customers (Williams, 1992). This involves resource identification, development, protection and deployment (Amit & Schoemaker, 1993) and managerial skill in these activities is in itself a source of sustainable competitive advantage (Castanias & Helfat, 1991). It is important that future research finds suitable ways of operationalising this management role.

Knowledge management is indeed a suitable way, and managerial skill in KM and IC activities, and the activities themselves, are indeed yet another resource that is valueable, hence potentially another source of sustainable competitive advantage.

The proxy indicators used in different organizations to express the value of qualitative knowledge and of managing it are unique to each and even amorphous. The problem with their acceptance by the society in which they exist is the epistemological tension that results from past industrial-age managerial education and accounting systems that were dominated by positivism. Organizationally, these indicators are derived from the organization's perception of value in light of core competencies and the organizational mission and vision. Such an evolution of thought and of paradigms within the organizations occurred in a spiral manner, collecting and recollecting on previous evolution, and leading to an aligning idea that allows the perception of unification amongst paradigms.

Thus, an epistemological, evolutionary adaptation is required in managerial education complementing that of the postindustrial age rather than suffice for the positivistic approach.

Furthermore, the empiric results and the emerging theory support and accord the evolution of the KM and IC paradigms by and large and their relationship, aiming at an aligning idea, or perception of unification, between them as experienced in many domains in the history of science (Kuhn, 1962).

REFERENCES

Ariely, G. (2003). *Knowledge management as a methodology towards intellectual capital: A roadmap.* Paper presented at the KMAC2003 OR Society International Conference, Aston.

Bassi, L. J., & Van Buren, M. E. (1999). Valuing investments in intellectual capital. *International Journal of Technology Management, 18*(5-8), 414-432.

Boisot, M., & Griffiths, D. (1999). Possession is nine tenths of the law: Managing a firm's knowledge base in a regime of weak appropriability. *International Journal of Technology Management, 17*(6), 662-676.

Bontis, N. (2001). Assessing knowledge assets: A review of the models used to measure intellectual capital. *International Journal of Management Reviews, 3*(1), 41-60.

Bontis, N. (2002). *All aboard! Take a knowledge journey.* IICR.

Bontis, N., Dragonetti, N. C., Jacobsen, K., & Roos, G. (1999). The knowledge toolbox: A review of the tools available to measure and manage intangible resources. *European Management Journal, 17*(4), 391-402.

Brennan, N., & Connell, B. (2000). *Intellectual capital: Current issues and policy implications.* Paper presented at the 23rd Annual Congress of the European Accounting Association, Munich, Germany.

Carrillo, F. J. (1999). *The knowledge management movement: Current drives and future scenarios.*

Committee on Intellectual Property Rights in the Emerging Information Infrastructure, N. R. C. (2000). *The digital dilemma: Intellectual property in the information age.* Retrieved from *http://www.nap.edu/openbook/0309064996/html/1.html*

Cruise, P. L. (1997). Are proverbs really so bad? Herbert Simon and the logical positivist perspective in American public administration. *Journal of Management History, 3*(4), 342-359.

Drucker, P. F. (1993). *Post-capitalist society* (1st ed.). New York: HarperBusiness.

Edvinsson, L., & Malone, M. S. (1997). *Intellectual capital* (1st ed.). New York: HarperBusiness.

Fahy, J. (2000). The resource-based view of the firm: Some stumbling-blocks on the road to understanding sustainable competitive advantage. *Journal of European Industrial Training, 24*(2), 94-104.

Gross, B. (1970). *Analytical philosophy: An historical introduction.* New York: Pegasus Press.

Johnson, P., & Duberley, J. (2000). *Understanding management research.* Sage.

Joyce, T., & Stivers, B. P. (1999). Knowledge and innovation focus. *International Journal of Technology Management, 18*(5-8), 500-509.

Kaplan, R.S., & Norton, D.P. (1992). The Balanced Scorecard. Measures that drive performance. *Harvard Business Review,* Jan-Feb.

Kaps, G., & Nohr, H. (2001). Measurement of success in knowledge management using balanced scorecards (Part 1). *Nfd Information-Wissenschaft Und Praxis, 52*(2), 89-97.

Klein, J., & Scarbrough, H. (2002). *Knowledge management and institutional failure.*

Kuhn, T. S. (1962). *The structure of scientific revolutions.* Chicago: University of Chicago Press.

Lev, B. (2000a). *Knowledge and shareholder value.*

Lev, B. (2000b). *New accounting for the new economy.*

Manfroy, W., & Gwinnel, H. (1998). Intellectual capital development at a spin-off company. In P.H. Sullivan (Ed.), *Profiting from intellectual capital: Extracting value from innovation.* New York: Wiley.

McElroy, M. W. (2002). Social innovation capital. *Journal of Intellectual Capital, 3*(1), 30-39.

Morey, D., Maybury, M. T., & Thuraisingham, B. M. (2000). *Knowledge management: Classic and contemporary works.* Cambridge, MA: MIT Press.

Mouritsen, J., Bukh, P. N., Larsen, H. T., & Johansen, M. R. (2002). Developing and managing knowledge through intellectual capital statements. *Journal of Intellectual Capital, 3*(1), 10-29.

Mouritsen, J., Larsen, H. T., Bukh, P. N., & Johansen, M. R. (2001). Reading an intellectual capital statement: Describing and prescribing knowledge management strategies. *Journal of Intellectual Capital, 2*(4), 359-383.

OECD. (1999). Programme notes and background to technical meeting and policy and strategy forum. Paper presented at *Measuring and Reporting Intellectual Capital, An International Symposium.*

Petty, R., & Guthrie, J. (2000). Intellectual capital literature review: Measurement, reporting and management. *Journal of Intellectual Capital, 1*(2), 155-176.

Roos, J., Roos, G., Edvinsson, L., & Dragonetti, N. C. (1998). *Intellectual capital: Navigating in the new business landscape.* New York: New York University Press.

Stewart, T. A. (1997). *Intellectual capital: The new wealth of organizations* (1st ed.). New York: Doubleday/Currency.

Streatfield, D., & Wilson, T. (1999). Deconstructing "knowledge management." *Aslib Proceedings, 51*(3), 67-71.

Sullivan, P. H. (1998). *Profiting from intellectual capital: Extracting value from innovation.* New York: Wiley.

Sullivan, P. H. (2000). *Value-driven intellectual capital: How to convert intangible corporate assets into market value.* New York: Wiley.

Sveiby, K.-E. (1997). *The new organizational wealth: Managing & measuring knowledge-based assets* (1st ed.). SanFrancisco: Berrett-Koehler Publishers.

Sveiby, K.-E. (1998). Intellectual capital: Thinking ahead. *Australian CPA* , June, pp. 18-22.

Sveiby, K.-E. (2001). A knowledge-based theory of the firm to guide in strategy formulation. *Journal of Intellectual Capital, 2*(4), 344-358.

Taylor, F.W. (1911). *Principles of scientific management.* New York: Harper Row.

Van Buren, M. E. (1999). A yardstick for knowledge management. *Training & Development, 53*(5), 71-.

Von Krogh, G., Nonaka, I. O., & Nishiguchi, T. (2000). *Knowledge creation: A source of value.* New York: St. Martin's Press.

Von Krogh, G., Roos, J., & Kleine, D. (1998). *Knowing in firms: Understanding, managing, and measuring knowledge.* London: Sage.

Wedberg, A. (1984). *A history of philosophy.* Clarendon Press.

Wenger, E. (1998). *Communities of practice: Learning, meaning, and identity.* New York: Cambridge University Press.

Wyatt, A. (2002). Towards a financial reporting framework for intangibles: Insights from the Australian experience. *Journal of Intellectual Capital, 3*(1), 71-86.

Zagzebski, L. (1999). What is knowledge? In *The Blackwell guide to epistemology* (pp. 92-116).

KEY TERMS

Dynamic Model of a Relationship Between Paradigms: Following Kuhn's (1962) concepts of scientific paradigms, the model of the relationship between KM and IC is dynamic and entwined in other dominant paradigms in the correlating and overlapping scientific and practitioners' communities.

Epistemological Tension: A tension between paradigms or domains of knowledge that is in fact derived from a deeper difference in the epistemological foundations on which they were built.

Evolutionary Aligning Idea: A framing idea created over time in an evolutionary manner aimed to align a paradox or tension between paradigms toward a perception of unification.

Human Capital: Includes "[a]ll individual capabilities, the knowledge, skill, and experience of the company's employees and managers" (Edvinsson & Malone, 1997, p. 34), as well as culture and values in the organization, creativity, and innovativeness.

Intellectual Capital (IC): Defined by the OECD as "[t]he economic value of two categories of intangible assets of a company:

1. organizational ('structural') capital; and
2. human capital.

More precisely, structural capital refers to things like proprietary software systems, distribution networks, and supply chains. Human Capital includes human resources within the organization (i.e., staff resources) and resources external to the organization, namely customers and suppliers." This is sometimes differentiated from relational capital.

Intellectual Property (IP): It is "the time limited monopoly (a copyright or patent) given to one who has made a contribution to that progress." The tensions between the freedom of speech and ownership are beyond the scope of this article. It is sufficient to define IP as the protection measure for IC once identified and defined.

Relationship Capital: It is the relationships with the firm's customers, but also with suppliers and the environment in whole (also referred to as customer capital).

Structural Capital: It is the "embodiment, empowerment, and supportive infrastructure of human capital" (p. 35) and includes IT systems, databases, organizational concepts, documentation and trademarks, patents, and copyrights, that is, all that is left behind when the staff is going home (also referred to as organizational capital).

Value: According to Webster Dictionary, it is the following:

1. fair return or equivalent in goods, ervices, or money for something exchanged
2. the monetary worth of something: marketable price
3. relative worth, utility, or importance <a good *value* at the price> <the *value* of base stealing in baseball> <had nothing of *value* to say>
7. something (as a principle or quality) intrinsically valuable or desirable <sought material values inste4ad of human *values* —W.H. Jones>

The duality in the above definition of value is crucial, since the meanings of the word reflect on the quantitative vs. qualitative tensions incorporated in the concept of value in economy.

Intelligence and Counterterrorism Tasks

Antonio Badia
University of Louisville, USA

INTRODUCTION

At the end of the Cold War, the intelligence situation (characterized in the past by a confrontation among equals and information scarcity) changed radically to the current situation of today, characterized as an asymmetric threat: On one side, there is still a nation, but on the other, there is a relatively small group of individuals brought together by a common ideology, usually with ethnic and religious elements. These individuals can only confront their opponent by using subterfuge, deception, and terrorist acts. They try to disguise their activities by infiltrating society at large and seeking refuge in anonymity. This kind of conflict has long been analyzed in the military literature under names like *low-intensity conflict* (LIC) or *operation other than war* (OOTW; for more on this perspective, the reader is referred to the classic work by Kitson, 1971). The task of the nations under terrorist threat is to detect the group's individuals and their intentions before they can carry out destructive actions. For this, their intelligence services count with large amounts of raw data obtained from many different sources: signal intelligence, open sources, tips from informants, friendly governments, and so forth. However, this data is not always reliable and almost never complete, and the truly interesting events are usually to be found hidden among large amounts of similar looking facts. To deal with this situation, intelligence officers use sophisticated information technology tools. Several authors have pointed out that this task is not at all dissimilar from the task that strategists in business intelligence (BI) and knowledge management (KM) face: As in KM, in intelligence the challenge is that "the right knowledge must get to the right people at the right time" (Pappas & Simon, 2002). Therefore, intelligence experts may learn something from studying BI and KM, and their history and milestones, while business strategists may also be enlightened by the history and lessons of military intelligence (after all, military intelligence is an ancient discipline; in contrast, KM can be considered a newcomer). In this article, we describe the intelligence analysis cycle and compare it with the KM cycle (we assume the reader is familiar with KM, but not with intelligence tasks). We point out the similarities (and the differences) between the two, and highlight several ways in which military intelligence may benefit from the hindsights and techniques developed by KM practitioners. We also briefly describe tools and methods from military intelligence that KM practitioners may find illuminating. We close with a discussion of future trends and some conclusions.

BACKGROUND: INTELLIGENCE ANALYSIS

The ultimate goal of intelligence analysis is to provide a customer, military or civilian, with the best possible information to help in making policy, strategic, and tactical decisions that affect national security[1]. In this task, intelligence is used to refer to knowledge and information, the basic end product of the analysis. Such analysis is carried out by highly trained analysts who work in a continuous process involving the following steps[2].

- **Need Analysis:** Customers (policy makers and others) make requests that the analyst must translate to specific requirements and tasks in order to make sure that the final product answers the needs of the customer. Customer demands often need interpretation or analysis before they can be expressed as an intelligence requirement (Krizan, 1996). The customer may have additional constraints on the intelligence product; the request may have time constraints (short term vs. long term) or scope constraints (broad or strategic vs. narrow or tactical).
- **Collection:** This refers to the gathering of raw (uninterpreted) data. Nowadays, there is an abundance of data due to the variety and richness of sources:
  - Signal intelligence (SIGINT) includes information from radar, telemetry, and intercepted communications.
  - Imagery intelligence (IMINT) refers to images delivered by electronic means, mostly satellites.
  - Measurement and signature intelligence (MASINT) is data produced from sensors (chemical, acoustic, etc.) other than SIGINT and IMINT.

- Human-source intelligence (HUMINT) refers to data provided by informants, either through clandestine means, official contacts with allied nations, or diplomatic missions.

- Open-source intelligence (OSINT) refers to publicly available information (radio, television, newspapers, commercial databases, etc.); this is in contract with all previous sources, which are usually classified and not open.

- **Processing and Exploitation:** In this stage, the raw data is converted to a form suitable for further analysis. This includes the translation of documents in foreign languages, analysis of sensor data, decoding of messages, and so forth. These tasks consume a large amount of resources from intelligence agencies since many of them are labor intensive, and specialized personnel are needed to carry them out. Moreover, in this phase, the evaluation of the accuracy, reliability, and meaning of the raw data (which continues in the next step) gets started.

- **Analysis and Production:** In this stage, the processed data are integrated, interpreted, and evaluated. In this crucial phase, the analyst must assess how reliable and complete the data pieces are, how distinct pieces of data can be interpreted, and how they fit in an overall picture. The first task is needed since many times the sources of information are not trustworthy, and an adversary may leave indications that actually mislead an intelligence agency in order to disguise real intentions. The second task is needed since raw data is rarely unambiguous; the same act (for instance, buying fertilizer) may signal completely different intentions depending on the context (to work on a farm or to prepare explosives). The last task is needed since data is rarely complete; after all collection is done, analysts usually have only fragmented and sometimes unrelated evidence. Finally, even after some conclusion is reached, there are two tasks left. First, analysts try to verify their work by correlating finished intelligence with data from other sources, looking for supporting evidence and/or inconsistencies. Because the process is far from exact, and is based on partial, tentative evidence, all conclusions reached are by necessity also tentative, best estimate interpretations. Note that in this step we go from facts to interpretation and judgment; hence, it is in this step that the danger is greater for presumptions, biases, and other problems to arise. Second, the created intelligence must be tailored to the customer, and an effort must be made to make sure that the product answers the customer's needs. In particular, the information produced must be relevant to the original answer, as accurate as possible (and, if uncertain, accompanied by some measure of its certainty), objective, usable (i.e., actionable), and timely.

- **Dissemination:** This is simply the process of delivering the finished product to the consumer. Sometimes, this is followed by the consumers providing feedback to the intelligence analyst so that the process can be improved.

While some intelligence is produced in response to a specific demand from a consumer, other intelligence is produced simply in order to keep track of ongoing events, to detect trends and patterns, or to be aware of events that may develop. As a result, finished intelligence can be of one of several categories, depending on its origin, subject, type of analysis, and/or intended use. With regard to origin, intelligence may be analyst driven, event driven, or scheduled (periodical). With regard to subject, intelligence may be economic, geographic, political, scientific, and so forth. With regard to the type of analysis, intelligence can be descriptive or inferential; in the latter case, it can be about the past, the present (warnings), or the future (forecasts; Waltz, 2003).

In the United States alone, there are several intelligence agencies that are collectors of data and/or producers of finished intelligence based on several departments. Collaborations among these agencies have been notably absent in the past.

KM IN INTELLIGENCE ANALYSIS

The idea that KM has a role to play in intelligence analysis is not new. In a seminar paper, Brooks (2000) already stated our main thesis, namely, because of similarities in goals, issues, and tasks, KM could lend significant insight when analyzing intelligence work and vice versa. The book by Waltz (2003) has this very same thesis at its core. Moreover, the 9/11 Commission has stated that some of the most serious failures in intelligence that had been observed (the lack of communication between the FBI and CIA, and the obsolete information technology deployed at the FBI) stem from not having an adequate knowledge management strategy in place: "In essence, the agency didn't know what it knew." Also, the book by Krizan (1996) starts with a prologue under the subtitle "National Intelligence meets Business Intelligence." But the most revealing proof of the influence of KM in intelligence work may be the creation, by the Central Intelligence Agency, of a nonprofit enterprise (In-Q-Tel) devoted to identifying promising technologies and funding companies developing them. In this article, we focus on the influence of KM on intelligence work, concretely on techniques and tools of KM that could have an impact on intelligence tasks. We will also briefly mention aspects in which intelligence work is influencing KM, although this is not our main topic.

In order to achieve our goal, we start by listing similarities and differences between KM and intelligence as this will help us understand which methods may transfer.

- **Relationship with a Customer:** Both BI and intelligence have the need to satisfy a customer (the policy maker or military command in the intelligence case, the company executive in the BI case). Furthermore, in both cases, customers may not articulate the exact needs in terms conducive to the intelligence task, but in terms that make sense to themselves. Also, in both cases, the customer requires actionable intelligence, that is, information that supports decision making and planning. It is up to the analyst to ensure that the final product of analysis has, at least to some degree, several characteristics that will make it useful to the customer: It is to be accurate, objective, usable, relevant, and timely. Finally, because we live in an era where access to information is easy, both BI and intelligence analysts need to add value, going beyond what the customer already knows (which may be quite a lot) by offering analytical skills.

- **Data Analysis:** Both in the BI and intelligence cases, analysts have at their disposal large amounts of raw data (usually from open sources); however, the information sought is usually hidden within this massive set of uninterpreted, unconnected set of facts. Both BI and intelligence rely on IT to deal with this large amount of data (Waltz, 2003). However, there is no procedure that will yield the needed results on each case. Several techniques must be used in the analysis, and many times the analysis relies also on the intuition and experience of the analyst. Another similarity is the fact that scenarios under analysis have widened considerably. In BI, it is routine now to watch data on many different fields, from technology to politics to the weather. Also in intelligence, routine political analysis is being complemented by historical, economical, and other analyses.

- **Transformation of Tacit Knowledge:** Both companies and intelligence organizations have a large deal of tacit (implicit) knowledge in the heads of senior personnel and in the informal networks developed over time as a byproduct of work processes. Analysts, either in business or intelligence,

absorb and internalize information; this manifests itself externally in social interaction (meetings, memos, etc.; Waltz, 2003). In both cases, it is very important to leverage (by making explicit, recording, and cataloguing) as much as possible this internal knowledge. This is a difficult task but it offers the possibility of a large payoff in the form of expertise that is kept in house when people leave the organization (Von Krogh, Ichijo, & Nonaka, 2000).

An important difference is the adversarial nature of the intelligence scenario. Each party tries to protect information about itself by hiding it and by deception. While in industry there is also a need and a practice for a certain amount of secrecy, there is usually no need for deception (at least not on a large, organized scale). Hence, intelligence must deal with information that may not be trustworthy; the sources must be carefully considered and the information has to be cross-checked with other available information. BI does not have to bother itself with these issues. As a consequence, the amount of what we called processing and exploitation is much smaller in BI than it is in Intelligence. The analysis phase also takes on a different character. Because of the need to evaluate the reliability of sources in intelligence work, evaluating and selecting evidence is an important part of the analysis; this step is rarely needed in BI.

Another important difference is the reserved nature of sources in intelligence work. This has consequences throughout the intelligence cycle: Sometimes it is not possible to go back to the source for additional information, and sometimes results cannot be disseminated as this would compromise the source of some data. This is why sometimes the intelligence process has been described as "the process of the discovery of secrets by secret means" (Waltz, 2003, p. 2).

Finally, a crucial difference is the extreme need for security in intelligence work. While companies are more and more aware of the need for security (due to industrial espionage, market competition, and malicious attacks to their networks), in the intelligence world there are a series of long standing procedures to restrict access, usually based on credentials (clearance levels) and on policies like need-to-know.

KM TECHNIQUES IN INTELLIGENCE

Based on our previous analysis, we can sketch a list of KM techniques that are bound to be beneficial for intelligence analysis.

- **Creation of an Organizational Memory, including a Best-Practices Repository:** Since much work by the analyst relies on his or her experience and intuition, such experience and intuition are great resources that must be kept and shared. Best-practices repositories do just that. Such repositories help not only to improve ongoing analysis, but they aid in the purpose of training (Clift, 2003; Pappas, & Simon, 2002). The intelligence community has recognized the importance of this approach and has tried to incorporate it into its practice, for instance, by collecting best practices (called *tradecraft* in the intelligence world); however, this has been done mainly in print (Product Evaluation Staff, Directorate of Intelligence, Central Intelligence Agency, 1996) without the support of IT tools that would facilitate searching and dissemination (Watson, 2002).

- **Creation of Communities of Interest and Communities of Expertise:** Many times, intelligence analysis requires considerable expertise in more than one area: Economical, political, military, and historical knowledge may be needed for a single task. No person is likely to possess all the knowledge so the analyst must frequently consult experts. Connecting analysts to the right person to consult for a given task would increase the quality of the analysis. Note that, in creating such communities, the intelligence agencies face the same problems that companies do, for instance, the common good problem (the cost of the effort to providers outweigh the benefit to consumers since the provider does not benefit). Several solutions applied in business may be useful here, too: Reduce the cost to providers (make it as easy as possible to give advice, etc.) and/or reward them. Ultimately, one should strive to achieve equilibrium (mutual reciprocity) as providers also become consumers; at this point, the problem goes away. However, starting may be difficult since communities need critical mass: They are only good if enough people use them. In fact, bootstrapping the community may be the hardest part (Clawson & Conner, 2004).

- **Information Management Tools:** KM has special information management needs that databases do not fulfill, so certain tools and techniques are of special interest in KM. The same tools could be very useful to the intelligence analyst. Among them, we point out the following:

- **Document Management Tools:** A considerable amount of information accessed by the analyst is disseminated in documents of several types: memos, reports, and so forth. Clearly, one of the challenges in the intelligence process is to find the relevant facts from among all the data available from different sources. Databases can easily index, sort, and access with efficiency-structured data, that is, data that has been entered in a certain format, usually specified in advance by a database designer. However, data in documents tend to be semistructured (i.e., they have irregular, dynamic structures) or unstructured (i.e., any structure is implicit and not known beforehand), and databases tend not to deal well with this sort of data. On the other hand, information retrieval (IR) systems deal well with such data, but usually offer only limited search capabilities (keyword-based processing). A new generation of tools, however, is emerging around information extraction (IE) technology to specifically address the challenges of managing document-based information. Such tools can be a valuable aid for the analyst, especially since often the information in documents (e-mails, memos, etc.) may lead to tacit knowledge (Asprey & Middleton, 2003). As an example, what people write in e-mails, memos, and so forth gives strong clues as to what their expertise is. In the context of intelligence work, though, such tools must include sophisticated access control (separate privileges for viewing, versioning, annotating, and printing, for instance) in order to deal with security issues (Mena, 2004).

- **Collaborative Tools:** Due to the complexity of today's intelligence analysis, most analysts are experts in a well-defined domain. This specialization means that complex problems that are best attacked from several angles must be tackled by groups, not individuals. However, successful teams require good organization, effective communication, cooperation, and a shared mental model or at least vocabulary. Therefore, collaborative tools (groupware, communication tools, etc.) could be used in this regard. Intelligence agencies are well aware of this situation: Collaborative tools using commercial web technologies are being developed through the Joint Intelligence Virtual Architecture program to assist today's analyst in locating and accessing valuable data, assessing such data, producing an informed analytic product, and moving that product to where it will be of value. (Clift, 2003) Common in KM, such tools are only recently being adopted by the intelligence community, probably because of concerns about security and access. However, the potential payoff of such systems is high, especially if the dissemination of information (based on predefined profiles or dynamic requests) is added to the process being modeled.

- **Work Flow Management (WM) Tools:** Because each step in the intelligence process (see above) is likely to be given to a different expert, the final product is the result of a collaborative process, a true team effort. The members of this team must communicate easily and effectively; the better the communication, the more likely the final product will be of high quality. WM tools help control collaborative processes and therefore are very relevant in this area. Thus, just like collaborative tools address collaboration at the process level, work flow management tools support collaboration at the analysis level.

- **Intelligent Indexing and Search Tools for Multimedia Data:** Due to the variety of sources, intelligence analysts work with data in several formats. The need to link all available data, unearthing unknown connections, means that all data should be indexed and tagged to facilitate further analysis. These tools are especially important nowadays because they help combat information overload and because with abilities like push-pull (subscribe query) dissemination and intelligent text processing (sometimes in multilingual environments), the tools support the knowledge exchange cycle, facilitating the transformation between tacit and explicit knowledge (Waltz, 2003).

- **Cognitive or Analytical Tools:** Used especially in the analysis and production phase, these tools focus on the reasoning process itself: keeping track of hypotheses, goals, and their interrelationships, choosing among alternatives, and performing what-if analysis. The importance of these tools is that they help counteract natural biases and shortcomings of the analyst's mental model. Because these are part of internalized knowledge, such biases are difficult to identify and deal with, and they constitute a serious problem in intelligence work (Heuer, 1999) where dealing with deception and hard-to-interpret information is part of everyday work (Waltz, 2003).

Note that the above list relies heavily on IT tools and techniques. Clearly, there is more to KM than IT. In fact, it is well known that managerial and organizational changes are needed in order to support KM (Davenport & Prusak, 1998; O'Leary, & Studer, 2001). Therefore, strategies to make the tools work within the organization are an integral part of KM. Some authors state that real KM is not achieved until there is a culture change in the organization (Brooking, 1999; Davenport and Prusak). To support organizational learning, collaboration, and team problem solving, businesses have adopted a variety of strategies (Choo & Bontis, 2002). Such experiences are another source of knowledge from which intelligence agencies may greatly benefit since historically they have worked on a very different mindset-one that encouraged secrecy.

INTELLIGENCE IN KM

As it is often the case, the adoption of KM techniques in intelligence (and in the military at large) has resulted in the adaptation of old techniques to new circumstances, or even the development of new ones. As a result, intelligence officers have also contributed some concepts that are useful to KM at large. It is notable, in this context, that military strategy has recently become trendy in business circles, with books like the classic *Art of War* by Sun-Tzu being recommended literature for executives. Another notable trend is the adoption of KM techniques in the military at large; in fact, the Army has declared "information superiority" as one of the key concepts of the Army of the future in the "Joint Vision 2020," a report from the U.S. Joint Chiefs of Staff issued in 2000[3]. One area where intelligence leads the way is the emphasis on security. As stated above, in a business environment, the situation is not openly adversarial but is competitive nonetheless. Malicious network attacks by hackers, disruptive tactics used by competitors in other countries (industrial espionage, etc.), and the fact that a country's economy is also a target in terror warfare have made businesses more and more aware of the need for strict security policies and methods. Data mining techniques, common in business to better understand clients and the market, are also being used to protect from internal and external threats: "To protect from insider threat, an organization could mine employee's information to learn about travel patterns, emails, phone conversations, work habits, computer usage, [and] Web usage" to determine if an individual is likely to betray the organization (Thuraisingham, 2003, p. 359). Measures like compartmentalization, access based on clearance levels, and need-to-know policies will help in this regard, although they must be carefully implemented so that they do not restrict the flow of information or collaborative efforts.

Another area in which intelligence agencies are well versed is the need for appropriate training. Because analysts must have a thorough formation phase to be useful to their agency, several practices (including mentoring from senior analysts) have been adopted that should be considered in a business setting.

Finally, some concrete techniques seem to have great potential for transfer. For instance, the institution of postmortem analysis, especially of failures, facilitates the creation of an institutional memory and is a great resource for further analysis, like "meta-analysis of the causes and consequences of analytical success and failure" (Heuer, 1999). Such practices, therefore, should be readily adopted in the business world, although resistance to them should be expected and will have to be dealt with through managerial measures. Another particular technique developed in the intelligence community is *link analysis*: the search for relationships among seemingly unrelated pieces of information in order to uncover previously unknown connections. This technique forms the basis for social network analysis (Sageman, 2004) and could prove very useful in BI. Finally, there are tools like modeling and simulation tools (especially in the modeling and simulation of the analysis process) and data visualization tools, which are already in use in the intelligence community but are still not as common in BI. It is very likely that such tools will become more and more important in the latter.

FUTURE TRENDS

There is no doubt that the future will see still further interaction between the KM and intelligence communities. Their similarities mean that they will continue learning from each other and influencing each other. On the intelligence side, as the commoditization of sensors and other data acquisition technologies means that all parties will have access to most of the same data, the emphasis will shift to analysis and synthesis (Waltz, 2003). Also, a fast changing environment means that the ability to cope with change will be needed by the intelligence community. The business world, having recognized this need some time ago, has already addressed the problem (although not all techniques from the business world will be readily applicable, like sharing information with business partners and suppliers, due to security concerns; Bennet & Bennet, 2003). Overall, KM processes and methods will become more and more relevant. Thus, it is likely that, in the near future, each area surveyed in this article will continue to be developed and lead to further interaction.

Some areas that will require further attention in the near future include how to share data securely; it will be necessary to track how information is being accessed and used in order to make sure that security is not compromised. Thus, collaboration tools will have to add this ability. Also, the stress on information access and dissemination means that new techniques for personalization, profiling, and distribution (like push-pull systems; Glance, Arregui, & Dardenne, 1998) will become more and more appealing to intelligence organizations.

Finally, the introduction of collaboration and other tools will foster the development of informal communities in intelligence organizations. Efforts in the business world to nurture and sustain such communities will provide guidance to the intelligence community (Clawson & Conner, 2004).

CONCLUSION

There is a strong connection between knowledge management and intelligence work that only now has begun to be explored with the depth it deserves. Several authors have already pointed out that intelligence organizations need KM due to the size and complexity of the data being processed, the level of expertise needed to process the data, and the sophistication of the final product, which must have the qualities of actionable knowledge. Here we have provided only a short introduction to this line of work. Some preliminary conclusions can be drawn already: The parallelisms this analysis unearths are resulting in a cross-pollination of techniques and tools that can only be beneficial to professionals on both sides, and there are still many parallelisms to be uncovered. Thus, it is important to continue work in this direction, especially in times of need like the present one.

REFERENCES

Asprey, L., & Middleton, M. (2003). *Integrative document and content management: Strategies for exploiting enterprise knowledge.* Hershey, PA: IGP.

Bennet, A., & Bennet, D. (2003). *Organizational survival in the new world: The intelligent complex adaptive system.* Amsterdam: Elsevier. (Kmci Press Series).

Berkowitz, B., & Goodman, A. (2000). *Best truth: Intelligence in the information age.* New Haven, CT: Yale University Press.

Borghoff, U., & Pareschi, R. (Eds.). (1998). *Information technology for knowledge management.* Berlin: Springer-Verlag.

Brooking, A. (1999). *Corporate memory: Strategies for knowledge management.* London: International Thomson Business Press.

Brooks, C. C. (2000). Knowledge management and the intelligence community. *Defense Intelligence Journal, 9*(1), 15-24.

Choo, C. W., & Bontis, N. (2002). *The strategic management of intellectual capital and organizational knowledge.* New York: Oxford University Press.

Clawson, J., & Conner, M. (Eds.). (2004). *Creating a learning culture: Strategy, technology, and practice.* Cambridge University Press.

Clift, A. D. (2003). Intelligence in the Internet era. *Studies in Intelligence, 47*(3). Retrieved from *http://www.cia.gov/csi/studies/vol47no3/article06.html*

A consumer's guide to intelligence. (1998). Arlington, VA: Office of Public Affairs, Central Intelligence Agency.

Davenport, T., & Prusak, L. (1998). *Working knowledge.* Cambridge, MA: Harvard Business School Press.

Donnely, H. (2003). Portal open army doors. *Military Information Technology, 7*(5). Retrieved September 28, 2004, from *http://www.mit-kmi.com/*

Glance, N., Arregui, D., & Dardenne, M. (1998). Knowledge pump: Supporting the flow and use of information. In U. Borghoff & R. Pareschi (Eds.), *Information technology for knowledge management* (chap. 3, pp. 35-53). Springer-Verlag.

Heijst, G. V., van der Spek, R., & Kruizinga, E. (1998). The lessons learned cycle. In U. Borghoff & R. Pareschi (Eds.), *Information technology for knowledge management* (chap. 2, pp. 17-34). Springer-Verlag.

Heuer, R. J. (1999). *Psychology of intelligence analysis.* Center for the Study of Intelligence, Central Intelligence Agency. Retrieved from *http://www.cia.gov/csi/books/19104/index.html/*

Kitson, F. (1991). *Low intensity operations: Subversion, insurgency and peacekeeping.* London: Faber and Faber.

Krizan, L. (1996). *Intelligence essentials for everyone.* Washington, DC: Joint Military Intelligence College.

Mena, J. (2004). *Homeland security techniques and technologies.* Charles River Media.

O'Leary, D., & Stude, R. (2001). Guest editors' introduction: knowledge management—An interdisciplinary approach. *IEEE Intelligent Systems, 16*(1), 24-25, January 2001.

Pappas, A., & Simon, J. M. (2002). The intelligence community: 2001-2015. *Studies in Intelligence, 46*(1). Retrieved from *http://www.cia.gov/csi/studies/vol46no1/article05.html*

Popp, R., Armour, T., Senator, T., & Numrych, K. (2004). Countering terrorism through information technology. *Communications of the ACM.*

Product Evaluation Staff, Directorate of Intelligence. (1996). *A compendium of analytic tradecraft notes* (Vol. 1), Langley, VA: Central Intelligence Agency.

Sageman, M. (2004). *Understanding terror networks.* Philadelphia: University of Pennsylvania Press.

Schreiber, G., Akkermans, H., Anjewierden, A., de Hoog, R., Shadbolt, N., Van de Velde, W., et al. (2000). *Knowledge engineering and management: The Common KADS methodology.* Cambridge, MA: MIT Press.

Thuraisingham, B. (2003). *Web data mining and applications in business intelligence and counter-terrorism.* Boca Raton, FL: CRC Press.

Von Krogh, G., Ichijo, K., & Nonaka, I. (2000). *Enabling knowledge creation: How to unlock the mystery of tacit knowledge and release the power of innovation.* New York: Oxford University Press.

Waltz, E. (2003). *Knowledge management in the intelligence enterprise.* Norwood, MA: Artech House Information Warfare Library.

Watson, I. (2002). *Applying knowledge management: Techniques for building corporate memories.* San Francisco: Morgan Kaufmann.

KEY TERMS

Asymmetric Threat: An adversarial situation characterized by the inequality in resources between the contenders, which usually results in one of them resorting to covert and terrorist activities to continue the conflict.

Business Intelligence: The process of gathering information in the field of business. The goal is to gain competitive advantage. The information gathered usually refers to customers (their needs, their decision-making processes), the market (competitors, conditions in the industry), and general factors that may affect the market (the economy at large, technology, culture).

Community: A group of people that share common characteristics. In a community of interest, there is a common role on a common task; in a community of expertise, there is a common area of knowledge and professional experience.

Intelligence Cycle: A complete process of intelligence data, divided into data collection, data processing and exploitation, data analysis, and production and dissemination.

Intelligence Data Sources: The origins of data captured in the data-collection phase; the term covers both people (HUMINT) and mechanical or technical means (SIGINT, IMINT, MASINT).

Military Intelligence: A discipline that focuses on gathering, analyzing, and disseminating information about adversaries, present and future, and conflict conditions (like the area of operations), both for tactical and strategical purposes.

ENDNOTES

[1] In this article, we will not distinguish between national and military intelligence (Waltz, 2003) as we are interested in a high-level analysis for which this distinction is not very productive.

[2] Our description of the intelligence cycle is, out of necessity, highly summarized; the interested reader is referred to *A Consumer's Guide to Intelligence* (1998), Krizan (1996), and Waltz (2003).

[3] As an example of KM tools already in use in the U.S. Army, the Program Executive Office Command, Control and Communications Tactical (PEO C3T) has developed a knowledge-center Web portal that has served as a precursor and model for the service-wide Army Knowledge Online (AKO) Internet site. The portal has a variety of technology products and capabilities, such as project-management tools, repositories, work-flow applications, and similar tools, and it serves as the daily operations center of the workforce for PEO C3T and other Army agencies. This tool has put recent emphasis on externalizing tacit knowledge. Efforts to capture knowledge and create communities of practice among subject-matter experts have also been extended (Donnelly, 2003). Outside the Army, the FBI has recently developed the Secure Collaborative Operational Prototype Environment for Counterterrorism (SCOPE), a data mart with more than 34 million documents related to counterterrorism, in which several knowledge-management tools (like collaboration tools) are being used.

Interesting Knowledge Patterns in Databases

Rajesh Natarajan
Indian Institute of Management Lucknow (IIML), India

B. Shekar
Indian Institute of Management Bangalore (IIMB), India

INTRODUCTION

Knowledge management (KM) transforms a firm's knowledge-based resources into a source of competitive advantage. Knowledge creation, a KM process, deals with the conversion of tacit knowledge to explicit knowledge and moving knowledge from the individual level to the group, organizational, and interorganizational levels (Alavi & Leidner, 2001). Four modes—namely, socialization, externalization, combination, and internalization—create knowledge through the interaction and interplay between tacit and explicit knowledge. The "combination" mode consists of combining or reconfiguring disparate bodies of existing explicit knowledge (like documents) that lead to the production of new explicit knowledge (Choo, 1998). Transactional databases are a source of rich information about a firm's processes and its business environment. Knowledge Discovery in Databases (KDD), or data mining, aims at uncovering trends and patterns that would otherwise remain buried in a firm's operational databases. KDD is "the non-trivial process of identifying valid, novel, potentially useful, and ultimately understandable patterns in data." (Fayyad, Piatetsky-Shapiro, & Smyth, 1996). KDD is a typical example of IT-enabled combination mode of knowledge creation (Alavi & Leidner, 2001).

An important issue in KDD concerns the glut of patterns generated by any knowledge discovery system. The sheer number of these patterns makes manual inspection infeasible. In addition, one cannot obtain a good overview of the domain. Most of the discovered patterns are uninteresting since they represent well-known domain facts. The two problems—namely, rule quality and rule quantity—are interdependent. Knowledge of a rule's quality can help in reducing the number of rules. End-users of data mining outputs are typically managers, hard pressed for time. Hence, the need for automated methods to identify interesting, relevant, and significant patterns. This article discusses the interestingness of KDD patterns. We use the association rule (AR) (Agrawal, Imielinski, & Swami, 1993) in a market-basket context as an example of a typical KDD pattern.

However, the discussions are also applicable to patterns like classification rules.

BACKGROUND

The Rule Quantity Problem: Solution Perspectives

The rule quantity problem may be a result of the automated nature of many KDD methods, such as AR mining methods. In one study, Brin, Motwani, Ullman, and Tsur (1997) discovered 23,712 rules on mining a census database. Approaches to alleviate this problem aim at reducing the number of rules required for examination while preserving relevant information present in the original set. Redundancy reduction, rule templates, incorporation of additional constraints, ranking, grouping, and visualization are some of the techniques that address the rule quantity problem.

In AR mining, additional constraints in conjunction with support and confidence thresholds can reveal specific relationships between items. These constraints reduce the search space and bring out fewer, relevant, and focused rules. Rule templates (Klemettinen, Mannila, Ronkainen, Toivonen, & Verkamo, 1994) help in selecting interesting rules by allowing a user to pre-specify the structure of interesting and uninteresting class of rules in inclusive and restrictive templates, respectively. Rules matching an inclusive template are interesting. Such templates are typical post-processing filters. Constraint-based mining (Bayardo, Agrawal, & Gunopulos, 2000) embeds user-specified rule constraints in the mining process. These constraints eliminate any rule that can be simplified to yield a rule of equal or higher predictive ability. Association patterns like negative ARs (Savasere, Omiecinski, & Navathe, 1998; Subramanian, Ananthanarayana, & Narasimha Murty, 2003), cyclic ARs (Ozden, Sridhar, & Silberschatz, 1998), inter-transactional ARs (Lu, Feng, & Han, 2000), ratio rules (Korn, Labrinidis, Kotidis, &

Faloutos, 1998), and substitution rules (Teng, Hsieh, & Chen, 2002) bring out particular relationships between items. In the market-basket context, negative ARs reveal the set of items a customer is unlikely to purchase with another set. Cyclic association rules reveal purchases that display periodicity over time. Thus, imposition of additional constraints offers insight into the domain by discovering focused and tighter relationships. However, each method discovers a specific kind of behaviour. A large number of mined patterns might necessitate the use of other pruning methods. Except for rule templates, methods that enforce constraints are characterized by low user-involvement.

Redundancy reduction methods remove rules that do not convey new information. If many rules refer to the same feature of the data, then the most general rule may be retained. "Rule covers" (Toivonen, Klemettinen, Ronkainen, Hatonen, & Mannila, 1995) is a method that retains a subset of the original set of rules. This subset refers to all rows (in a relational database) that the original ruleset covered. Another strategy in AR mining (Zaki, 2000) is to determine a subset of frequently occurring closed item sets from their supersets. The magnitude of cardinality of the subset is several orders less than that of the superset. This implies fewer rules. This is done without any loss of information. Sometimes, one rule can be generated from another using a certain inference system. Retaining the basic rules may reduce the cardinality of the original rule set (Cristofor & Simovici, 2002). This process being reversible can generate the original ruleset if required. Care is taken to retain the information content of the basic unpruned set. Redundancy reduction methods may not provide a holistic picture if the size of the pruned ruleset is large. Further, the important issue of identification of interesting patterns is left unaddressed. For example, a method preserving generalizations might remove interesting exceptions.

Visualization techniques take advantage of the intuitive appeal of visual depiction that aids in easy understanding (Hilderman, Li, & Hamilton, 2002). Various features like use of graphs, colour, and charts help in improved visualization. Rules depicted in a visual form can be easily navigated to various levels of detail by iteratively and interactively changing the thresholds of rule parameters. The main drawback in visualization approaches is the difficulty of depicting a large rule/attribute space. In addition, understandability of visual depiction decreases drastically with increase in dimensions. Hence, a user might fail to detect an interesting phenomenon if it is inlaid in a crowd of mundane facts. However, for browsing a limited rule space, visualization techniques provide an intuitive overview of the domain.

A user might be able to get a good overview of the domain with a few general rules that describe its essentials. Mining generalized association rules using product/attribute taxonomies is one such approach (Srikant & Agrawal, 1995). If all items at lower levels of a product taxonomy exhibit the same relationship, then rules describing them may be replaced by a general rule that directly relates product categories. General Rules, Summaries, and Exceptions (GSE) patterns introduced by Liu, Hu, and Hsu (2000) is an approach to summarization. The general rules, along with summaries, convey an overview while exceptions point to cases differing from the general case. Another approach is to group rules on the basis of exogenous criteria such as economic assessment, profit margin, period of purchase, and so forth (Baesens, Viaene, & Vanthienen, 2000). Clustering techniques group "similar" rules (Gupta, Strehl, & Ghosh, 1999) by imposing a structure on them. Rules within each group can then be studied and evaluated based on this structure. Most of the techniques stated help in consolidating existing knowledge rather than identifying new/latent knowledge.

The Rule Quality Problem: Solution Perspectives

The "rule-quality" problem is a consequence of most of the discovered patterns referring to obvious and commonplace domain features. For example, Major and Mangano (1995) mined 529 rules from a hurricane database of which only 19 were found to be actually novel, useful, and relevant. The most common and obvious domain facts are easily discovered since they have strong presence in databases. In addition, such facts form a core component of the user's domain knowledge due to repeated observation and application. Examination of these patterns is a waste of time since they do not further a user's knowledge. Ranking rules based on their interestingness is one approach that may address the rule-quality problem.

INTERESTINGNESS MEASURES

Interestingness measures try to capture and quantify the amount of "interest" that any pattern is expected to evoke in a user. Interesting patterns are expected to arouse strong attention from users. "Interestingness," an elusive concept, has many facets that may be difficult to capture and operationalize. Some of them may be domain and user-dependent. In other cases, depending on the context, the same features may be domain and user-independent. Capturing all features of interestingness in one single measure simultaneously is an arduous task. Therefore, researchers typically concentrate on those features that are important and relevant for a particular application. Thus, operationalization of interestingness may be context-dependent. Information retrieval and KM literature allude to "relevance ranking" schemes that bring out the relevance of a particular piece of knowledge such as document and Web site. Interestingness in KDD is a much more complex concept with many facets in addition to relevance. Although relevance contributes to interestingness, a relevant pattern may not be interesting if it is commonplace knowledge. Thus, the interplay of various facets like relevance, novelty, unexpectedness, surprisingness, user knowledge, and others together determine the interestingness of a KDD pattern. A broad classification of interestingness measures may be based on user-involvement.

Objective Measures of Interestingness

Objective measures quantify a pattern's interestingness in terms of its structure and the underlying data used in the discovery process. Researchers have used measures developed in diverse fields such as statistics, social sciences, machine learning, information theory, and others to measure specific data characteristics. These include statistical measures like confidence, support (Agrawal, Imielinski, & Swami, 1993), lift (Piatetsky-Shapiro & Steingold, 2000), conviction (Brin, Motwani, Ullman, & Tsur, 1997), rule interest (Brin et al., 1997), and others. Information theoretic measures such as entropy, information content, the Kullback and the Hellinger measures have also been used in other data mining studies (Hilderman & Hamilton, 1999). Occurrence of odd events/phenomena such as Simpson's paradox is also deemed interesting (Freitas, 1998). Freitas (1999) has adopted a multi-criteria approach for evaluation of objective interestingness. Incorporation of rule-quality factors such as disjunct size, imbalance of class distributions, misclassification costs, and asymmetry help in the objective evaluation of a rule's "surprisingness." With A→B denoting an AR, P(A) and P(B) denoting the probabilities of occurrence of sets A and B, respectively, we have the following key properties (Piatetsky-Shapiro & Steingold, 2000) that should satisfy a good objective measure of interestingness (RI)

1. RI=0, if A and B are statistically independent, that is, P(A,B)=P(A).P(B)
2. RI monotonically increases with P(A,B), other parameters such as P(A) and P(B) being fixed.
3. RI monotonically decreases with P(A) (or P(B)), other parameters (i.e., P(A,B) and P(B) or P(A)) being constant.

It may be observed that these properties are tied to the co-occurrence of A and B. The interestingness of A→B increases with increase in the co-occurrence of A and B relative to individual occurrences of A or B.

Objective measures are strongly domain- and user-independent. They reveal data characteristics that are not tied to domain/user-related definitions. However, this property may limit their power of discrimination. Since any objective measure has to hold across domains, it takes care of a limited aspect of data that is common across domains. Hence, objective measures cannot capture all complexities of the discovery process (Silberschatz & Tuzhilin, 1996). Many objective measures are based on strength of the dependence relationship between items (Shekar & Natarajan, 2004b). Conventionally, interestingness is regarded as being directly proportional to strength of the dependence relationship. However, this view may lead to erroneous results (Brin et al., 1997). For example, while "Support" is useful in measuring the statistical significance of a rule, rules that are most obvious to the user have high support values. Similarly, other objective measures have their own limitations and biases.

It is also common for different objective measures to convey contradictory evaluation or conceal certain facts about a domain. Therefore, it is not only important to select the appropriate measure(s) for each domain, but also specify the correct order of application (Tan, Kumar, & Srivastava, 2004). Only then, the truly interesting rules would get revealed. An important application of objective measures is their use as initial filters to remove definitely uninteresting or unprofitable rules. Rules that reflect insignificant presence of transactions do not warrant further attention and hence may be removed by objective measures.

Subjective Measures of Interestingness

Users play an important role in the interpretation and application of KDD results. Therefore, interestingness measures need to incorporate user-views in addition to data-related aspects. Users differ in their beliefs and interests since they may have varied experience, knowledge, and psychological makeup. In addition, they also may have varying goals and difference of opinions about the applicability and usefulness of KDD results. This variation in interest enhances the importance of injecting subjectivity into interestingness evaluation (Silberschatz & Tuzhilin, 1996). "Actionability" and "Unexpectedness" are two facets that determine subjective interestingness (Silberschatz & Tuzhilin, 1996). Interesting rules may be unexpected (i.e., surprising to the user) or actionable (translating results into actions).

Actionability is an important criterion in KM because organizational performance often depends more on the ability to turn knowledge into effective action, rather than on knowledge itself (Alavi & Leidner, 2001). Actionable patterns are interesting since they offer opportunity for direct action. However, operationalization of "actionability" has proved to be an extremely difficult task due to the inherent difficulty in associating patterns with actions. Also, it may not be possible to pre-specify all possible actions. Studies centered on actionability tend to be domain-specific (Silberschatz & Tuzhilin, 1996). The demand that patterns be related to actions is one difficult task in all but the narrowest of domains where actions are clearly defined. The KEFIR system (Matheus, Piatetsky-Shapiro, & McNeill, 1996) is a typical example. Adomavicius and Tuzhilin (1997) propose an approach to defining actionability, using "action hierarchy." An action hierarchy is a tree (Deo, 1989) of actions with patterns and pattern templates (KDD queries) assigned to its nodes. This approach provides a framework for operationalizing actionability with some domain independence.

Roddick and Rice (2001) bring out the temporal and dynamic nature of interestingness. Using events in the sporting arena as a running example, they show how "anticipation" has a critical effect on both: selection of interesting events and variation of interestingness threshold as events unfold. However, the concept of anticipation needs to be further explored. Information about a subject is interesting if the user has some prior knowledge about it and also if this knowledge is relevant to user-goals (Ram, 1990). Accordingly, interestingness may be defined as a heuristic that measures relevance of the input to a person's knowledge goals. "Knowledge goals" (Ram, 1990) is related to acquiring some piece of information required for a reasoning task. If a piece of information is relevant to "knowledge goals," interest toward it increases.

Silberschatz and Tuzhilin (1996, p. 971) argue that "the majority of actionable patterns are unexpected and that the majority of unexpected patterns are actionable."

Hence, they hypothesize that unexpectedness is a good approximation for actionability and vice-versa. Since unexpectedness is easier to operationalize than actionability, most studies concerning subjective interestingness employ "unexpectedness" as the main subjective criterion. Approaches to determination of subjective interestingness using "unexpectedness" tend to follow the general approach given below:

- Eliciting user-views
- Representing user-views in a form suitable for computation
- Mining the database to extract rules about the domain
- Comparing mined rules with user-views to determine the degree of conflict
- Presenting and labeling, rules that conflict user-views (on attributes such as relationship, strength, and direction), as interesting

However, methods using unexpectedness may differ in implementation details such as representation schema, method of comparison, and interestingness measures (Padmanabhan & Tuzhilin, 1999; Liu, Hsu, Mun, & Lee, 1999, Shekar & Natarajan, 2004a). One limitation of this methodology is the knowledge acquisition issue. Eliciting views from users is difficult, and acquired knowledge could be incomplete. Users may not be able to completely specify all their views about a domain. This may result in a large number of rules having high interestingness scores. Many of these rules might concern attributes, relationships, and beliefs, the user has failed to specify. Other limitations are more approach-specific, such as specifying a priori probabilities in the Bayesian approach (Silberschatz & Tuzhilin, 1996) and fuzzy membership functions (Liu et al., 1999). Figure 1 displays a partial classification of the approaches toward interestingness in KDD. Pruning and ranking of patterns on the basis of interestingness measures is an intuitive approach to rule quality and rule quantity problems.

Figure 1. Partial classification of interestingness measures (based on Silberschatz and Tuzhilin, 1996)

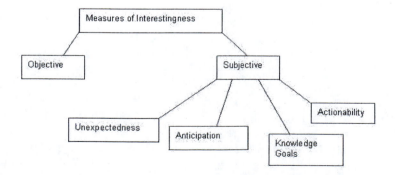

FUTURE TRENDS

Interestingness, an elusive concept, may have many facets intrinsic to a particular domain. A combination of objective and subjective measures may be necessary to reveal interesting patterns. Some issues concerning application of interestingness measures may be generic while others may be domain-specific. One important issue is the genesis of interestingness and its constituent features. Unexpectedness and actionability do not characterize interestingness in its totality. There might be other domain-dependent features worthy of consideration and incorporation. A detailed study of interestingness in specific domains and across domains can help in capturing and operationalizing subtle features. These features could then form the basis for more comprehensive interestingness evaluation.

Another issue concerns the joint application of objective and subjective measures. Objective measures could be used as a first filter to remove rules that are definitely uninteresting. This should be based on certain requirements, such as significance and predictive ability. Subjective measures can then bring in user-biases and beliefs into interestingness evaluations. Interaction between objective and subjective measures has not been sufficiently explored. In addition, few studies have considered the appropriateness of applying a specific interestingness measure across domains. The effect of changing the order of application of interestingness measures and the interaction between them are issues worthy of future study. Some relationships are a logical consequence of a firm's operational business rules. Such knowledge, being intuitive and tacit due to daily application, may not be specified during the knowledge elicitation phase. Incorporating such logical inferences in subjective measures is another issue for future research.

An important consideration with storing knowledge in KM systems is context inclusion (Alavi & Leidner, 2001). Without contextual information, knowledge may not be efficiently and effectively operationalized. Interestingness may be strongly domain and user-dependent and hence highly subjective. On the other hand, if objective measures can be made context-dependent by infusing them with domain-related data definitions, then the user-dependence may be reduced. This might allow sharing of KDD results across an organization.

Application of interestingness measures during the various phases of knowledge discovery has its own advantages and disadvantages. If the dataset is large, then it may be advantageous to mine rules and then apply interestingness measures. On the other hand, for a small one, application of interestingness measures during the mining phase may be preferable. Ideally, a data mining system should contain a repository of interestingness measures, both objective and subjective. Choice of measures could be based on the patterns mined, application, and purpose of the user. Here, the importance of integrating mining methods with interestingness evaluation cannot be over-emphasized.

Another problem with rule ranking concerns the possible lack of relationship among interesting rules. Thus, two consecutive interesting rules could pertain to different domains/sub-domains. Hence, it may be difficult for a user to connect them and obtain an overview of the domain. Combining methods that address the rule quantity problem with interestingness might partially address this problem. Clustering of similar rules could possibly be studied as a pre-processing step followed by a ranking scheme based on interestingness. Thus, a user might be able to obtain an overview of the domain and also discover implicit hidden knowledge brought out by interesting rules. Visualization techniques that display interestingness evaluations in an intuitive and understandable manner may be helpful.

CONCLUSION

Initial focus in the KDD community was with respect to algorithm development—toward newer and faster methods operating on large datasets. This resulted in a large number of patterns—sheer numbers of which contributed to incomprehensibility. The importance of understandability of discovered patterns, especially with respect to practical applications has been acknowledged. Recent literature in KDD has focused on various approaches to alleviate the rule quality and rule quantity problem. Ranking patterns according to interestingness is an important approach to addressing the rule quality problem. Interestingness is both data-driven and user-view driven. Correspondingly, patterns may be evaluated on the basis of objective and subjective measures. However, interestingness is an elusive concept, whose many facets are both difficult to capture and difficult to operationalize. Many of these facets are yet to be identified. Future research pertaining to interestingness is expected to yield results with respect to more complete characterizations. KM deals with the creation, storage/retrieval, transfer, and application of relevant knowledge in any organization. Interestingness measures and other methods, which address the problem of immensity of mined patterns are vital contributors to knowledge creation processes in KM. It is not uncommon to find organizations struggle to make sense of data captured through automated processes. Frameworks and methodologies for selecting relevant and significant patterns that add to organizational knowledge are expected to feature as important issues in KM.

REFERENCES

Adomavicius, G., & Tuzhilin, A. (1997). Discovery of actionable patterns in databases: The action hierarchy approach. *Proceedings of the 3rd International Conference on Data Mining and Knowledge Discovery (KDD 1997),* Newport Beach, California (pp. 111-114). AAAI Press.

Agrawal, R., Imielinski, T., & Swami, A. (1993). Mining association rules between sets of items in large databases. *Proceedings of the 1993 ACM SIGMOD International Conference on Management of Data,* Washington, DC. (pp. 207-216). ACM Press.

Alavi, M., & Leidner, D.E. (2001). Knowledge management and knowledge management systems: Conceptual foundations and research issues. *MIS Quarterly, 25*(1), 107-136.

Baesens, B., Viaene, S., & Vanthienen, J. (2000). Post-processing of association rules. *Proceedings of the Workshop on Post-Processing in Machine Learning and Data Mining: Interpretation, Visualization, Integration, and Related Topics Within The 6th ACM SIGKDD International Conference on Knowledge Discovery and Data Mining (KDD 2000),* Boston (pp. 20-23). Retrieved from *www.cas.mcmaster.ca/~bruha/kdd2000/kddrep.html*

Bayardo Jr., R.J., Agrawal, R., & Gunopulos, D. (2000). Constraint-based rule mining in large, dense databases. *Data Mining and Knowledge Discovery, 4*(2/3), 217-240.

Brin, S., Motwani, R., Ullman, J.D., & Tsur, S. (1997). Dynamic itemset counting and implication rules for market basket data. *Proceedings of the ACM SIGMOD International Conference on Management of Data,* Tucson, AZ (pp. 255-264). ACM Press.

Choo, C.W. (1998). *The knowing organization.* New York: Oxford University Press.

Cristofer L., & Simovici D. (2002). Generating an informative cover for association rules. *Proceedings of the 2002 IEEE International Conference on Data Mining (ICDM 2002),* Maebashi City, Japan (pp. 597-600). IEEE Computer Society Press.

Deo, N. (1989). *Graph theory with wpplications to engineering and computer science.* India: Prentice Hall of India Private Limited.

Fayyad, U.M., Piatetsky-Shapiro, G., & Smyth, P. (1996). From data mining to knowledge discovery: An overview. In U. M. Fayyad, G. Piatetsky-Shapiro, P. Smyth, & R. Uthurusamy (Eds.), *Advances in knowledge discovery and data mining* (pp. 1-34). AAAI/MIT Press.

Freitas, A.A. (1998). On objective measures of rule surprisingness. *Proceedings of the Second European Symposium on Principles of Data Mining and Knowledge Discovery, (PKDD-98), Lecture Notes in Artificial Intelligence.* (LNAI 1510), Nantes, France (pp. 1-9). Springer-Verlag.

Freitas, A.A. (1999). On rule interestingness measures. *Knowledge-Based Systems, 12,* 309-315.

Gupta, G.K., Strehl, A., & Ghosh, J. (1999). Distance based clustering of association rules. *Proceedings of Intelligent Engineering Systems through Artificial Neural Networks, (ANNIE 1999)* (Vol. 9, pp. 759-764). ASME Press.

Hilderman, R.J., Li, L., & Hamilton, H.J. (2002). Visualizing data mining results with domain generalization graphs. In U. M. Fayyad, G. G. Grinstein, & A. Wierse Andreas (Eds.), *Information visualization in data mining and knowledge discovery* (pp. 251-270). Academic Press.

Hilderman, R.J., & Hamilton, H.J. (1999). *Knowledge discovery and interestingness measures: A survey.* Technical Report, Department of Computer Science, University of Regina, Canada.

Klemettinen, M., Mannila, H., Ronkainen, P., Toivonen, H., & Verkamo, I.A. (1994). Finding interesting rules from large sets of discovered association rules. *Proceedings of the 3rd International Conference on Information and Knowledge Management (CIKM 1994)* (pp. 401-407). ACM Press.

Korn, F., Labrinidis, A., Kotidis, Y., & Faloutos, C. (1998). Ratio rules: A new paradigm for fast, quantifiable data mining. *Proceedings of the 24th International Conference on Very Large Databases (VLDB 1998),* New York (pp. 582-593). Morgan Kaufmann Publishers.

Liu, B., Hsu, W., Mun, L., & Lee, H. (1999). Finding interesting patterns using user expectations. *IEEE Transactions on Knowledge and Data Engineering, 11*(6), 817-832.

Liu, B., Hu, M., & Hsu, W. (2000). Multi-level organization and summarization of the discovered rules. *Proceedings of the ACM SIGKDD International Conference on Knowledge Discovery & Data Mining (KDD 2000),* Boston (pp. 208-217). ACM Press.

Lu, H., Feng, L., & Han, J. (2000). Beyond intra-transaction association analysis: Mining multi-dimensional inter-transaction association rules. *ACM Transactions on Information Systems, 18*(4), 423-454.

Major, J.A., and Mangano, J.J. (1995). Selecting among rules induced from a hurricane database. *Journal of Intelligent Information Systems, 4,* 39-52.

Matheus, C., Piatetsky-Shapiro, G., & McNeill, D. (1996). Selecting and reporting what is interesting: The KEFIR application to healthcare data. In U. M. Fayyad, G. Piatetsky-Shapiro, P. Smyth, & R. Uthurusamy (Eds.), *Advances in knowledge discovery and data mining* (pp. 495-516). AAAI/MIT Press.

Ozden, B., Sridhar, R., & Silberschatz, A. (1998). Cyclic association rules. *Proceedings of the 14th International Conference on Data Engineering (ICDE 1998)* (pp. 412-421). IEEE Computer Society Press.

Padmanabhan, B., & Tuzhilin, A. (1999). Unexpectedness as a measure of interestingness in knowledge discovery. *Decision Support Systems, 27*(3), 303-318.

Piatetsky-Shapiro, G., & Steingold, S. (2000). Measuring lift quality in database marketing. *ACM SIGKDD Explorations Newsletter, 2*(2), 76-80.

Ram, A. (1990). Knowledge goals: A theory of interestingness. *Proceedings of the 12th Annual Conference of the Cognitive Science Society,* Cambridge, MA.

Roddick, J.F., & Rice S. (2001). What's interesting about Cricket?: On thresholds and anticipation in discovered rules. *ACM SIGKDD Explorations Newsletter, 3*(1), 1-5, ACM Press.

Savasere, A., Omiecinski, E., & Navathe, S. (1998). Mining for strong negative associations in a large database of customer transactions. *Proceedings of the 14th International Conference on Data Engineering (ICDE 1998)* (pp. 494-502). IEEE Computer Society Press.

Shekar, B., & Natarajan, R. (2004a). A framework for evaluating knowledge-based interestingness of association rules. *Fuzzy Optimization and Decision Making, 3*(2), 157-185.

Shekar, B., & Natarajan, R. (2004b). A transaction-based neighbourhood-driven approach to quantifying interestingness of association rules. *Proceedings of the 4th IEEE International Conference on Data Mining (ICDM 2004),* Brighton, UK (pp. 194-201). IEEE Computer Society Press.

Silberschatz, A., & Tuzhilin, A. (1996). What makes patterns interesting in knowledge discovery systems. *IEEE Transactions on Knowledge and Data Engineering, 8*(6), 970-974.

Srikant, R., & Agrawal, R. (1995). Mining generalized association rules. *Proceedings of the 21st International conference on Very Large Databases (VLDB 1995),* Zurich, Switzerland (pp. 407-419). Morgan Kaufmann Publishers.

Subramanian, D.K., Ananthanarayana, V.S., & Narasimha Murty, M. (2003). Knowledge-based association rule mining using AND-OR taxonomies. *Knowledge-Based Systems, 16,* 37-45.

Tan, P., Kumar, V., & Srivastava, J. (2004). Selecting the right interestingness measure for association patterns. *Information Systems, 29*(4), 293-331.

Teng, W., Hsieh, M., & Chen, M. (2002). On the mining of substitution rules for statistically dependent items. *Proceedings of IEEE International Conference on Data Mining (ICDM 2002)* (pp. 442-449). IEEE Computer Society Press.

Toivonen, H., Klemettinen, M., Ronkainen, P., Hatonen, K., & Mannila, H. (1995). Pruning and grouping discovered association rules. *Proceedings of the Mlnet Workshop on Statistics, Machine Learning and Knowledge Discovery in Databases,* Herakhion, Crete, Greece.

Zaki, M.J. (2000). Generating non-redundant association rules. *Proceedings of the 6th ACM SIGKDD International Conference on Knowledge Discovery and Data Mining (KDD 2000)* (pp. 34-43). ACM Press.

KEY TERMS

Actionability: Actionability of a pattern indicates its usefulness. Essentially, a pattern is actionable if a user can act on it to his or her advantage. Though it has a great practical orientation, actionability is difficult to operationalize due to the inherent difficulty in mapping patterns to useful actions.

Association Rules: Association rules are implication rules that bring out hidden relationships among attributes, on the basis of co-occurrence of attributes. In the market-basket context, they inform about items that are likely to be purchased together, thereby providing an insight into customer purchasing behaviour. Formally, an Association rule is an implication of the form $A \Rightarrow B$, where A and B can be single items or sets of items, with no commonality between sets A and B, e.g. *{Bread}⇒{Butter}, {Bread, Jam}⇒{Butter},* and so forth. An AR is characterized by two measures, support (a statement of generality) and confidence (a statement of predictive ability). These rules are very general, having a simple interpretation with minimal restrictions on their structure. *{Bread}⇒{Butter}* with support =20% and confidence = 60% means that 60% of the transactions that contain Bread also contain Butter and they are purchased together in 20% of the transactions.

Interestingness: Interestingness is an elusive concept that is very difficult to characterize and operationalize. A pattern is interesting if it arouses attention in the minds of the examiner. Interestingness has many facets like unexpectedness, actionability, prior knowledge, and knowledge goals, in addition to many unidentified domain-dependent features. Features of interestingness may be user-dependent, domain-dependent, or/and there might be a temporal aspect associated with it.

Interestingness Measures: Interestingness measures try to capture and quantify the amount of "interest" that a pattern is expected to evoke in a user. They can be further classified into objective and subjective measures of interestingness.

Objective Measures of Interestingness: Objective measures of interestingness are data-driven and have some element of domain-independence. They measure interestingness of a pattern in terms of its structure and the underlying data used in the discovery process. Typical examples of such objective measures of interestingness are support and confidence. Many objective measures of interestingness trace their origin to traditional statistical, AI, machine learning, and allied literature. Objective measures do not capture all the complexities of the pattern discovery process and might sometimes bring out contradictory results.

Patterns: Knowledge extracted by data mining tools and techniques is usually expressed in the form of patterns. Fayyad, Piatetsky-Shapiro, and Smyth (1996) have defined a pattern in the context of data mining as: "A pattern is an expression E in a language L describing facts in a subset F_E of F (where F is the database). E is called a pattern if it is simpler (in some sense) than the enumeration of facts in F_E." Patterns describe essential characteristics of a domain, in a simple, concise and intelligible form. For example, rule "If Age is less than 18 then not allowed to vote," is a pattern that describes the essential characteristics of individuals who are not eligible to vote. Patterns might have varied representation schemas, structure, interpretation, and so forth.

Subjective Measures of Interestingness: Subjective measures not only depend on the structure of a rule and the data used in the discovery process, but also on the user who examines the pattern. These measures recognize the diversity in users due to varied tastes, beliefs, experience, and knowledge. Consequently, a pattern that might be of interest to one user might not interest another. From a subjective point of view, unexpectedness, and actionability are two reasons for a pattern to be interesting to the user.

Unexpectedness: A pattern is interesting to the user if it is "surprising" to the user. This unexpectedness might be due to the pattern contradicting the belief system of the user: The greater the contradiction, the higher the unexpectedness. Most of the data mining studies use unexpectedness as the primary criterion for operationalizing subjective interestingness.

User-Beliefs: User-beliefs are viewpoints and opinions that users hold about a domain due to their knowledge and experience. From the interestingness perspective, a pattern that contradicts user-beliefs is interesting. Intensity of interestingness increases with an increase in this conflict.

Intranet and Organizational Learning

Kees Boersma
Vrije Universiteit Amsterdam, The Netherlands

Sytze Kingma
Vrije Universiteit Amsterdam, The Netherlands

INTRODUCTION

In this article, we will analyze the cultural dimension of intranets as knowledge management tools within organizations. An intranet is an information communication technology (ICT) based upon Internet technology (http://www, TCP/IP). The intranet phenomenon was introduced in the early 1990s following the idea that it can integrate all the computers, software, and databases within a particular organization into a single system that enables employees to find and share all the information they need for their work (Bernard, 1997; Cortese, 1996). Intranets function as a computer-mediated communication (CMC) tool and are used as computing networks used for sharing organizational information. While Internet technology is leading, access is restricted exclusively to organizational members (by means of electronic firewalls). In a study to the role of intranets in strategic management decisions, Curry and Stancich (2000) define Intranets as "…private computing networks, internal to an organization, allowing access only to authorized users" (p. 250). The term *private* indicates that an intranet is a network that can be accessed only by members of a particular organization. The term *network* emphasizes the connection between computers that enables corporate communication. Intranets run on open but controlled networks that enable organization members to employ the same WWW servers and browsers, which are distributed over the local area network (LAN).

In recent debates on strategic management and learning, an organizational learning *culture* has been introduced as one of the main 'critical success factors' underlying the effective use of intranets (Carayannis, 1998). The aim of this article is to analyze the cultural aspects of intranets as tools in organizational learning processes. It is not so much a presentation of the instrumental effects of intranets for the learning organization culture—the way an intranet influences organizational learning processes is not taken for granted, but studied by the way it is used in different settings. We will present a framework for analyzing the cultural dimension of intranets within specific organizational contexts.

Many studies of intranets dealing with the effectiveness and efficiency of knowledge sharing and knowledge management take a static and deterministic point of view. That means that the focus is on structural constrains, without paying attention to the actual use of intranets. In contrast with this, we plea for an approach focusing upon communicative actions, and stress the communication between people on the intranet on the basis of normative agreement and feelings of mutual understanding and belonging. We furthermore highlight three dimensions from which this cultural context of an intranet can be defined, studied, and analyzed. These dimensions, which indeed apply to any enterprise system (ES) and which in a way also represent historical phases in the development of technology (Silverstone & Haddon, 1996), will in our contextual analysis be specified as the 'constitution' of an intranet, the intranet as a 'condition' of the learning organization, and the (unintended) 'consequences' of intranet use. An analysis on these levels is crucial for those scholars who want to grasp the cultural dimension in the actual use of intranets as a knowledge management tool.

Intranet and Organizational Culture

Often, the objective for the implementation of an intranet is that it will facilitate knowledge sharing among members within a single organization. There is a growing body of publications that see an intranet as a tool for organizational learning (e.g., Carayannis, 1998; Curry & Stancich, 2000; Scott, 1998; Sridhar, 1998; Ottosson, 2003). With regard to knowledge management, it has been analyzed in terms of knowledge banks, e-learning platforms, expert networks, online information sharing tools, and the like. Recently, intranets were identified as an infrastructure supporting knowledge management (Harvey, Palmer, & Speier, 1998; Damsgaard & Scheepers, 2001). In this body of literature, intranets are presented as promising knowledge management ICT tools in the sense that intranets will be complementary to or even replace existing information and communication carriers within and among organizations. In addition, intranets are seen as promising instruments for information sharing and collaboration across departments, functions, and information systems (Damsgaard & Scheepers, 1999). Internet-based ICTs like an intranet are even introduced as radical and disruptive innovations, since the implementation is intended strongly to influence the knowledge base of the organization (Lyytinen & Rose, 2003; Mustonen-Ollila & Lyytinen, 2003).

Together with the stories on the promising aspect of intranets, however, came the stories about organizational restrictions, misalignments, and user resistance. Discussions can be found about organizational constraints, such as the lack of standards, immature interfaces, weak linkages to other information systems, bandwidth availability and information overload, and the lack of an internal organization to authorize, support, and organize the quality of the information. On many occasions, it is the organizational culture that has been introduced as an explanation for misalignments or as a condition for a successful implementation and use of intranets (Damsgaard & Scheepers, 2001, p. 5). Curry and Stancich (2000) state: "To obtain maximum value from an intranet, both the 'soft' cultural issues of information sharing and change in work processes must be addressed alongside the 'hard' systems issues of managing the intranet as an information system and a business resource" (p. 255). Moreover, it has been argued that a cultural shift to information sharing is necessary to solve problems of information sharing by means of intranets (Harvey et al., 1998). A positive culture, in this respect, is the motivation to create, share, and use information and knowledge to solve problems with each other within the organization.

It is, however, difficult and often misleading to establish direct causal links between organizational culture and the performance of intranets, since we must realize that culture is part and parcel of the entire organization and affects all kinds of actions and relations (Alvesson, 2002). The definition of 'organizational culture' is itself problematic. It has been described in the literature as a pattern of shared assumptions often produced by top management (Schein, 1992). Such a description of culture as a set of shared assumptions is rather oversimplified (Martin, 1992). Empirical research provides us with a far more complex picture, and shows that tensions can grow and remain between the individuals' interests and organization aims. Because of cognitive and normative diversity within an organization, the attribution of meaning (which is an important part of the cultural process) is complicated and leads to integration as well as fragmentation, and unity as well as diversity.

In line with this, organizational culture has been defined as a sensemaking process (Weick, 1995). That means that we have to study how individual workers give meaning to their actions. In using intranets, like texts such as reports, statistics, protocols, and minutes, the organizational members give meaning to their activities. In this way "...we can understand such interpretations as stemming from the very use of intranet itself" (Edenius & Borgerson, 2003, p. 131). The use of an intranet can generate a kind of consensual knowledge and, as long as different workers get into mutual trust, this can lead to a feeling of belonging. To use an intranet is making sense of experiences, routines, and insights. On a more abstract level, Wenger introduced the term 'communities of practice' to describe the process of people who share common goals or interests and how the people interact with each other to learn how to do better. These communities are formed by people who engage in a process of collective learning in a shared domain of human endeavor (Wenger, 1998; Wenger, McDermott, & Snyder, 2002). Communities of practice enable practitioners to share knowledge, to create a link between learning and performance, and to make connections among others across structural organizational boarders. Because of this, we will discuss intranet and organizational culture in terms of 'shared' meaningful work practices, while at the same time recognizing the existence of multiple working cultures dealing with intranets.

Intranet and Organizational Learning

As argued above, an intranet can facilitate knowledge sharing among organization members. The idea is that the knowledge put on the intranet is explicit knowledge (in the terms of Polanyi) that can easily be shared by members of the user group. However, the term 'knowledge sharing' is problematic, because the people's tacit knowing—that is, how to do things—is never fully shared (Walsham, 2002). Only if the data (the explicit knowledge) on the intranet is connected to the tacit knowing, then can the intranet offer something interesting to that user—it can generate a kind of consensual knowledge. That implies that the user must have the skills and competence in selecting the appropriate explicit knowledge. In other words, the knowledge is not in the computer system, but within the human being. It is the end-users that give sense to the data and messages on the intranet by means of their tacit knowing.

Like other ICTs, intranets are the outcome of choices made by individual actors or groups and of organizational constraints that together influence the character of this particular technology. This is known in the literature as the process of mutual shaping (Williams & Edge, 1996; Orlikowski, 2000). While using intranets, actors produce and reproduce communication and information patterns within organizations. Organizational learning on intranets thus can be analyzed as a social process of structuration (in line with Berends, Boersma, & Weggeman,

2003). From this structurationist framework it has been stressed, in particular by Orlikowski (2000), that individual actors are always situated actors. In using ICT tools actors reproduce at the same time important normative and power relations. Thus linkages can be specified between on the one hand the meanings attributed to technologies and on the other hand the normative prescriptions and power relations of organizations.

It has been argued before that an intranet is as good as its content (Curry & Stancich, 2000; White, 2004). Intranets facilitate communication and information sharing among organization members only if the employees can find the data they need, can judge the information to be valid and current, and can trust the persons—gatekeepers—who are responsible for the content of the intranet. However, Edenius and Borgerson (2003) argue that this idea of the intranet as being a container-like tool, where knowledge is seen as a stable stock of fixed information, takes a conventional rational discussion about knowledge management as a starting point. According to them, this view underestimates that an intranet works as a dynamic configuration that also produces knowledge. In other words, the use of an intranet is part of the living act of knowing.

The use of intranet as a tool for knowledge management needs actors who creatively realize learning practices and communication patterns as part of organizational cultures. That means that organizational learning consists of changing organizational practices via the development of knowledge, realized in social practices (Gherardi & Nicolini, 2001). The benefit of knowledge sharing (i.e., learning processes) throughout the organization via an intranet cannot be reduced to individual learning, or individual learning plus something extra such as the sharing of knowledge. Individuals will benefit from intranets in terms of information sharing only if the technology 'fits' into their daily routines embedded within organizational cultures. In this perspective, the organizational knowledge is part of and lives in a constellation of communities of practice (Wenger, 1998). The intranet can be a challenge for these communities, because it offers a platform for sharing knowledge and mutual understanding.

In defining an intranet from this point of view, three different but mutually related dimensions should be taken into account. These dimensions include the constitution of the intranet (stressing the redefinition of learning practices), the intranet as a condition of organizations (stressing the virtualization of organizations), and the intended as well as unintended consequences of the intranet (stressing the globalization of organizations and power relations). In the interaction between these three dimensions of intranet, we find how organizational cultural aspects shape this technology and how this technology in its turn influences organizational cultures.

Three Dimensions of an Intranet

The first dimension in our approach is the study of the constitution of an intranet. This dimension refers to the material, time-spatial, appearance of intranets. It concerns the artifacts and persons intranets are made of, including PCs, cables, mainframes, software packages, interfaces, reports, and intranet programmers and operators. Similar to the argument Downey (2001) makes for the Internet, intranet workers can only be revealed if we consider the artifacts, labor, and space simultaneously. Therefore a cultural study of the intranet should pay serious attention to the material and geographical aspects of these systems. Conceptions of organizational culture usually not only refer to values and rules, but also to material artifacts (Schein, 1992), which increasingly consist of ICT systems. In line with the discussion above, the evolution of intranets can only be interpreted by studying the interests and perceptions of the various actors that use this ES. An intranet is not a given technology, although it has some scripts (i.e., standard procedures for users), but is a malleable tool shaped by social forces within the organization.

The second dimension, the intranet as a condition for organizations, refers to the functional integration of knowledge (sub)systems by the use of an intranet. An intranet may contribute to the development of 'network enterprises', defined by Castells (1996). This type of organization is rather flexible because it can both reallocate its means of production and change its goals. The intranet, as a knowledge-sharing tool, can function within network organizations as an enabling tool to reconfigure themselves. Like the Internet, intranets create new patterns of social behavior and communication (DiMaggio, Hargittai, Neuman, & Robinson, 2001). Knowledge sharing within network organizations is facilitated but not determined by ICT systems like intranets. In this respect, the borders within and between organizations are constantly reinterpreted, because the structure of the intranet makes it possible to bind people working at different locations together—it is the virtual space of the intranet that is the new condition for a learning environment. In a way, intranets link employees, divisions, and companies, and provide information anytime and anyplace, and enable and reinforce network structures. The aspect of an intranet as a virtual dimension of an organization where partners are located over a wide area linked seamlessly together, however, is yet to be reached due to the relative recency of the system (Kim, 1998).

The third dimension highlights the consequences of the use of an intranet for organizational culture and the wider environment. This dimension refers to the actual effects of an intranet, and concerns the intended as well as unintended consequences. Effects concerning the scaling-up and globalization and the managerial control over knowledge flows seem particularly relevant for the cultural analysis of an intranet. Organizations are embedded in extended networks and operate often in global markets. In some way they have to control these global operations and manage knowledge flows in this context in a coordinated manner. The intended and unintended use enhances the capacity of panoptic control and disciplinary power—an architecture of power closely associated with ICT systems (Zuboff, 1988). Management can use the stored information on the intranet to monitor and interfere with the performance of individuals and groups. At the same time individuals can be empowered by the system and carry out their tasks with more responsibility based on their own insights, preferences, and information from the intranet. However, there are unintended consequences due to these virtual aspects. While the use of an intranet can lead to a sense of belonging, a possible decrease in face-to-face communication is the other side of the coin (Hine, 2000). This can easily lead to a loss of shared identity and weaken social relationships with colleagues within the same organization. Participation on the intranet in this respect is rather anonymous, without much engagement, and therefore maybe less effective as a tool for knowledge management.

FUTURE RESEARCH

Intranets are likely to be further developed in many organizations in the near future as a new communication infrastructure. It is presented both within popular management literature as in international journals as another promising bandwagon for organizations (Lynch, 1997). There is a growing number of managers that implement intranets as a solution for knowledge sharing within the organization. Future research should study the consequences of intranets as a tool for knowledge management to understand the organizational cultural aspects in the way it is presented in this article. It is the people who work with the system that give meaning to the data on an intranet. To understand how people give meaning to the (data on) an intranet, we have to follow the evolution of intranets (within specific contexts) over a longer period of time. This means that "attempts to create unified, universally applicable models or 'best practice' guidelines for designing and implementing intranets are futile. Instead we have to recognize organizational diversity and that the technology is embedded in, and shaped by, its social context" (Bansler, Damsgaard, Scheepers, Havn & Thommesen, 2000, p. 18). We want to argue that it is necessary to integrate both the individual contributions (i.e., the use of technology), group dynamics, and the organizational cultural aspects in a well-balanced manner during the implementation and use of intranets in the process of organizational learning.

Important questions to raise in this respect are inspired by the way Hine (2000) questions the 'virtual life' on the Internet:

- How do the users of an intranet understand its capacity, and how do they interpret it as a medium of communication?
- How does the intranet affect the organization of social relationships within the organization, and is this different to the way in which 'real life' is organized?
- What are the implications of an intranet for the authority and power relations within the organization?
- How do people define the boundary between the real data and the virtual data on the intranet?

CONCLUSION

Because users give meaning to the intranet, "…organizations need to carefully consider how their intranet should be deployed so as to reap the maximum benefit in terms of knowledge creation" (Damsgaard & Scheepers, 2001, p. 11). Intranets are not a pre-given and unproblematic tool for knowledge management. Instead, the implementation and use of an intranet as a tool for knowledge sharing needs a careful understanding of its social-cultural impact and at the same time has to be seen as a cultural phenomenon in itself. This means that an intranet should not be treated as the explanans (the thing or solution that explains the communication problem); in other words, with the help of the intranet, we can solve our communication problems—but rather as the explanandum (the thing or solution that has to be explained): What are the cultural features that shaped the intranet, and in what way does the use of intranets shape and reshape communication patterns within the organization?

In order to understand the cultural aspects of intranets, we have to incorporate the sensemaking processes both during the managerial implementation process as well as in a socio-cultural analysis. In our approach this means a careful analysis of the condition of intranets (what socio-technical choices are made to build the technology), intranet as a constitution (what kind of organization is made possible by the intranet), and the consequences of intranets (how the intranet affects the communication patterns within the organization). This perspective offers the possibility to integrate the 'virtual' communication on the intranet with the patterns of social behavior in the 'real' world.

REFERENCES

Alvesson, M. (2002). *Understanding organizational culture*. London: Sage Publications.

Bansler, J.P., Damsgaard, J., Scheepers, R., Havn, E., & Thommesen, J. (2000). Corporate intranet implementation: Managing emergent technologies and organizational practices. *Journal of the Association for Information Systems, 1*, 1-25.

Berends, H., Boersma, K., & Weggeman, M. (2003). The structuration of organizational learning. *Human Relations, 56*(9), 1035-1056.

Bernard, R. (1997). *The corporate intranet* (2nd Ed.). New York: John Wiley & Sons.

Carayannis, E.G. (1998). The strategic management of technological learning in project/program management: The role of extranets, intranets and intelligent agents in knowledge generation, diffusion, and leveraging. *Technovation, 18*(11), 697-703.

Castells, M. (1996). *The rise of the network society. (Vol. 1)* Oxford: Malden, Blackwell.

Cortese, A. (1996). Here comes the intranet. And it could be the simple solution to companywide information-on-demand. *Business Week,* (February).

Curry, A., & Stancich, L. (2000). The intranet: An intrinsic component of strategic information management? *International Journal of Information Management, 20,* 249-268.

Damsgaard, J., & Scheepers, R. (1999). Power, influence and intranet implementation. A safari of South African organizations. *Information Technology & People, 12*(4), 333-358.

Damsgaard, J., & Scheepers, R. (2001). Harnessing intranet technology for organisational knowledge creation. *Australian Journal of Information Systems,* (December), 4-15.

DiMaggio, P., Hargittai, E., Neuman, W.R, & Robinson, J.P. (2001). Social implications of the Internet. *Annual Review of Sociology, 27,* 307-336.

Downey, G. (2001). Virtual webs, physical technologies, and hidden workers. The spaces of labor in information Internetworks. *Technology and Culture, 42*(2), 209-235.

Edenius, M., & Borgerson, J. (2003). To manage knowledge by intranet. *Journal of Knowledge Management, 7*(5), 124-136.

Gherardi, S., & Nicolini, D. (2001). The sociological foundations of organizational learning. In M. Dierkes, A.B. Antal, J. Child, & I. Nonaka (Eds.), *Handbook of organizational learning and knowledge* (pp. 35-60). Oxford: Oxford University Press.

Harvey, M., Palmer, J., & Speier, C. (1998). Implementing intra-organizational learning: A phased-model approach supported by intranet technology. *European Management Journal, 16*(3), 341-354.

Hine, C. (2000). *Virtual ethnography*. London: Sage Publications.

Kim, J. (1998). Hierarchical structure of intranet functions and their relative importance: Using the analytic hierarchy process for virtual organizations. *Decision Support Systems, 23,* 59-74.

Lynch, G. (1997). Intranets: Just another bandwagon? *Industrial Management & Data Systems, 97*(4), 150-152.

Lyytinen, K., & Rose, G.M. (2003). Disruptive information system innovation: The case of Internet computing. *Information Systems Journal, 13,* 301-330.

Martin, J. (1992). *Cultures in organizations. Three perspectives*. Oxford: Oxford University Press.

Mustonen-Ollila, E., & Lyytinen, K. (2003). Why organizations adopt information system process innovations: A longitudinal study using Diffusion of Innovation theory. *Information Systems Journal, 13,* 275-297.

Orlikowski, W.J. (2000). Using technology and constituting structures: A practice lens for studying technology in organizations. *Organization Science, 11*(4), 404-428.

Ottosson, S. (2003). Dynamic product development of a new intranet platform. *Technovation, 23,* 669-678.

Schein, E.H. (1992). *Organizational culture and leadership*. San Francisco: Jossey-Bass.

Scott, J.E. (1998). Organizational knowledge and the intranet. *Decision Support Systems, 23,* 3-17.

Silverstone, R., & Haddon, L. (1996). Design and the domestication of information and communication technologies: Technical change and everyday life. In R. Mansell & R. Silverstone (Eds.), *Communication by design* (pp. 44-74). Oxford: Oxford University Press.

Sridhar, S. (1998). Decision support using the intranet. *Decision Support Systems, 23,* 19-28.

Walsham, G. (2002). What can knowledge management systems deliver? *Management Communications Quarterly, 16*(2), 267-273.

Wenger, E. (1998). *Communities of practice: Learning, meaning and identity.* Cambridge: Cambridge University Press.

Wenger, E., McDermott, R., & Snyder, W. (2002). *Cultivating communities of practice: A guide to managing knowledge.* Boston: Harvard Business School Press.

Weick, K. (1995). *Sensemaking in organizations.* London: Sage Publications.

White, M. (2004). Does your intranet have a win-win strategy? *EContent, 27*(3), 41.

Williams, R., & Edge, D. (1996). The social shaping of technology. *Research Policy, 25*(6), 865-899.

Zuboff, S. (1988). *In the age of the smart machine.* New York: Basic Books.

KEY TERMS

(Partly derived from Hine, 2000, pp. 157-162; Wenger, 1998.)

Bandwidth: Term used to denote the capacity of a communication channel for information: a narrow bandwidth implies slow or limited communication. It describes the carrying capacity of the user's connection or the server connection. It is commonly measured in bits or bytes per second instead.

CMC (Computer-Mediated Communication): A general term referring to a range of different ways in which people can communicate with one another via a computer network. Includes both synchronous and asynchronous communication, one-to-one and many-to-many interactions, and text-based or video and audio communication.

Communities of Practice: Communities formed by people who engage in a process of collective learning in a shared domain of human endeavor. For a community of practice to function, it needs to generate and appropriate a shared repertoire of ideas, commitments, and memories. It also needs to develop various resources such as tools, documents, routines, vocabulary, and symbols that in some way carry the accumulated knowledge of the community.

Intranet: A restricted-access or internal network that works like the Internet (http://www). It enables employees, or those with access, to browse or share resources. Intranets are private computing networks, internal to an organization, used for sharing organizational information.

LAN (Local Area Network): A group of computers and associated devices that share a common communications line or wireless link, and typically share the resources of a single processor or server within a small geographic area.

Organizational Culture: Refers to the way people give meaning to their actions in an organizational setting. Because of cognitive and normative diversity within an organization, the attribution of meaning is complicated and leads to organizational cultural integration as well as fragmentation, and unity as well as diversity.

Knowledge Calibration

K

Ronald E. Goldsmith
Florida State University, USA

Kishore Gopalakrishna Pillai
Florida State University, USA

INTRODUCTION

The purpose of this article is to describe the concept of *knowledge calibration* within the context of knowledge management. Knowledge calibration is a concept borrowed from the psychology of decision making. It refers to the correspondence between knowledge accuracy and the confidence with which knowledge is held. Calibration is a potentially important concept for knowledge management because it describes one of the subtle errors that can lead to poor decisions. Where the correspondence between the accuracy of one's knowledge and the confidence in that knowledge is high, decisions are described as well calibrated; but poor correspondence implies miscalibrated decisions. Since one concern of the field of knowledge management is the best use of knowledge for decision-making purposes, this topic is relevant.

BACKGROUND

A variety of scientists, including meteorologists, statisticians, and psychologists, have been interested in measuring and in explaining judgments of confidence and their relation to accuracy (e.g., Harvey, 1997; Yates, 1990). Most of these studies report that people are systematically overconfident about the accuracy of their knowledge and judgment. In fact, scholars have even considered overconfidence as a stylized fact of human cognition.

The construct "calibration of knowledge" refers to the correspondence between accuracy of knowledge and confidence in knowledge (see Figure 1). High accuracy and high confidence in knowledge promote high calibration; confidence in these decisions is justified. Low accuracy and low confidence also promote high calibration. In this case, decision makers are aware of their ignorance and are unlikely to overreach. A lack of correspondence between accuracy and confidence means *miscalibration*. Miscalibrated individuals are either overconfident or underconfident—situations that can result in costly mistakes in decision making.

For example, a description of the difficulties Xerox had in successfully bringing their new inventions to market (Carayannis, Gonzalez, & Wetter, 2003) reveals that, among other problems, managers placed great faith in their knowledge of the market, technology, and future trends that was subsequently proved to be misplaced. One could argue that the Bush Administration's decision to go to war with Iraq in order to destroy weapons of mass destruction that did not exist, but were claimed to exist on the basis of high confidence in flimsy evidence, is also an example of miscalibration and its influence on decision making.

Although several approaches to improving knowledge calibration have been suggested, little effort has been made to integrate them into the field of knowledge management. A new dimension of the discourse on knowledge management can be added by examining the implications of the construct of knowledge calibration to knowledge management. In the subsequent paragraphs, we elaborate on how this can be achieved and why it is important.

MAIN FOCUS

Literature on knowledge management has focused on: (a) defining the constructs of knowledge and knowledge management; (b) describing processes associated with knowledge creation, storage and retrieval, transfer, and application; and (c) developing and implementing systems to facilitate these processes. Implicit in these tasks is the idea that knowledge is embedded in individu-

Figure 1. Accuracy-confidence matrix

	Confidence	
Accuracy	High	Low
High	Good calibration	Miscalibration
Low	Miscalibration	Good calibration

als, groups, as well as in physical structures (Alavi & Leidner, 2001; Brown & Duguid, 2000). These discussions implicitly assume that knowledge available in the organization will be used in decision making and that such use will enable users to make better decisions. As research has noted, however, knowledge, which as commonly used refers to accurate or correct knowledge, is not the sole factor affecting decision quality. Users have to access and wisely use the knowledge in decision making before KM systems can be said to improve management activity. One instance of this can be found in the "knowledge/use-reuse" situation where knowledge is developed and stored for reuse by its creators later on or by other subsequent users (Markus, 2001). If the knowledge is not well recorded, stored, or made easily retrievable, users will be few and their effectiveness compromised. A further problem is described by the impact of new technologies on marketing management, where Tapp and Hughes (2004, p. 293) argue that "...KM systems have increased the *supply* of knowledge 'objects' (explicit, recorded, packets of knowledge), but that *usage* of these 'objects' by other workers (the crucial added value) remains elusive." The skill with which users and re-users take advantage of knowledge depends on many factors, including capturing, packaging, and distribution of the knowledge (Markus, 2001). Moreover, the confidence with which the decision maker accepts that knowledge also affects the way he/she uses the knowledge to make decisions. In other words, knowledge calibration affects the quality of *decision making*.

Ideally, organizations are better served if all individuals have high calibration, arising from high accuracy and high confidence in the knowledge. This is not to deny that there could be cases where *overconfidence* can be justified as a functional adaptation to motivate the implementation of decisions (Russo & Schoemaker, 1992). Investigation of subtleties in the context of knowledge management can be the focus of later research. At this stage, the critical issues pertaining to knowledge calibration in the context of knowledge management are: (a) What factors contribute to miscalibration? (b) How can they be reduced or eliminated? and (c) What organizational practices can help promote calibration through knowledge management systems?

Factors Contributing to Miscalibration

Where does miscalibration come from? Although miscalibration is likely due to multiple causes and their interactions, two principal sources can be identified for our purposes: internal (personal) and external (structural). That is, miscalibration can arise from cognitive causes as well as from the quantity of information provided and how it is presented to the user.

Alba and Hutchinson (2000, pp. 139-142) summarize the main cognitive causes. These first include *failures of memory* due to distortion or incompleteness. *Memory* is often biased in the direction of a prior judgment, thus increasing overconfidence. Memory might be incomplete when decision-consistent facts are more easily recalled, better decision options fail to be considered, or where other aspects of the knowledge interfere with recall and consideration. Underconfidence can also arise when the consequences of decisions fail to be considered. The difficulty and frequency with which outcomes can be imagined reduces the perceived likelihood of an outcome. A second cognitive source of miscalibration comes from *misweighting evidence*, thereby not optimally incorporating decision inputs into the decision process. For example, decision makers often fail to use base rates in solving problems. They rely on available cues instead of valid ones. They overemphasize extreme instances, irrelevant data, and easy-to-understand information. Overconfidence can come from poor appraisal of the diagnosticity of information where diagnosticity varies with its ease of use. *Motivational* factors may induce decision makers to fail to consider hypothesis-disconfirming evidence, accept confirmation uncritically, or limit their search to supportive evidence only. Having some familiarity or expertise with the decision task might induce overconfidence where the decision tasks are inordinately difficult, as in turbulent environments where it is difficult for everybody to see the future. Finally, overconfidence arises where expertise is not helpful to the decision.

Alba and Hutchinson (2000, pp. 142-144) and others describe some of the ways in which information is presented (inappropriate decision inputs) that can also induce sub-optimal levels of confidence. Too much information, where the assumption is made that greater amounts of information yield better decisions, or nondiagnostic information can cause overconfidence. *Misattribution* of information, as when fragments of retrieved information are interpreted as having been recalled from prior knowledge so that inference is interpreted as recall, can induce miscalibration. The number of operations needed to get an answer, familiarity with judgments, and the ease with which information can be retrieved may play a role. Another example of misattribution can be found in the "sleeper effect," where the source of information is forgotten over time, but the information itself is remembered; confidence in even poor information may increase if its provenance is lost.

Empirical evidence from the literature on information systems suggests that the design of both the information dimensions (quantity, form, format, etc.) and the inquiring system play key roles in user calibration. Oskamp (1965) used clinical psychology case studies to discover that increasing the quantity of information provided to decision makers produced miscalibration because it increased their decision confidence, but did not improve their decision quality. More information caused the confidence to soar out of proportion to the actual correctness of their decisions. Chervany and Dickson (1974) studied the effects of information overload on decision confidence, quality, and time. They found that decision makers using statistically summarized data outperformed those using raw data, but took longer and were less confident in their decisions. Familiarity with the decision task can promote overconfidence, as can the illusion of control, where decision makers come to believe that they have more influence on decision outcomes than they really do.

Ways to Improve Calibration

In general, it can be stated that calibration can be improved by promoting (1) accuracy of knowledge and (2) optimal levels of confidence in the knowledge. While accuracy can be viewed in monotonic terms, in as much as more of it is better, the knowledge management system should strive to promote optimal levels of confidence. Overconfidence and underconfidence mean miscalibration, and research has recorded the widespread prevalence of the former (Einhorn & Hogarth, 1981; Tversky & Kahneman, 1974). Hence, there is a need to build checks into the knowledge management system to promote optimal levels of confidence.

Bell (1984) compared different forms of presenting information and found a convergence between decision confidence and *decision quality*. Decision confidence based on information presented as text was greater than that for information presented in numeric form, but subjects found it easier to identify inconsistencies when the information was presented in numeric form rather than in textual form.

Literature also suggests that that using decision support systems—and by extension, knowledge management systems—also affects calibration. McIntyre (1982) found that the calibration of subjects using a DSS was worse than that of their unaided counterparts. He speculated that the DSS might have contributed to miscalibration (in the form of underconfidence) because it led subjects to believe that much better decisions existed than those from which they had selected.

Design features of a knowledge management system can also influence user calibration. Studies have examined the effects of design features on user calibration in the context of decision support systems. Davis,

Kottemann, and Remus (1991) and Davis and Kottemann (1994) hypothesized that the use of a "what-if" inquiry design creates an illusion of control, causing users to overestimate the effectiveness of the what-if DSS design. Their results supported this hypothesis. Despite performance effects to the contrary, and the availability of tools whose recommendations would have led to much better decisions, subjects continued their use of the what-if design feature. That is, subjects maintained their overconfidence in the efficacy of the what-if inquiry design feature despite negative feedback and the availability of better tools. Davis and his coauthors concluded that an illusion of control was created by using the what-if feature of the DSS and that this illusion overwhelmed any negative feedback, including poor performance, in formulating the subject's attitude about the efficacy of the what-if DSS design feature.

Aldag and Powers (1986) also have suggested the illusory benefits of using a DSS. In their study, subjects analyzed strategic management cases and, assuming the role of a consultant, made written recommendations. Although the recommendations of those who used the DSS were judged no better than their unaided counterparts, the DSS-aided subjects reported more confidence in their recommendations than did those that were unaided, again resulting in miscalibration (Kasper, 1996). These illusory benefits were also found when the aid is an expert system. Faust (1986) provides a series of rules or necessary conditions for improving calibration. In summary form, his rules are: (1) decrease information overload and misleading illusory data; (2) present evidence that disconfirms and refutes one's position; (3) distinguish between knowledge and speculation, between knowledge and metaknowledge; and (4) generate competing alternative hypotheses. Kasper (1996) reviews relevant literature on decision support systems and opines that the design of both the information (overload, misleading, disconfirming, speculative) and the inquiring system (generate competing alternative hypotheses) plays key roles in user calibration. Thus, basic research into reducing miscalibration suggests ways in which knowledge management systems can incorporate features to improve calibration.

Knowledge Management and Knowledge Calibration

How then can knowledge management systems be applied to improving knowledge calibration to enhance decision making? Knowledge is described as consisting in two forms. *Tacit* knowledge can be summarized as personal or subjective knowledge (mental models, know-how, skills), and *explicit* knowledge is "articulated, codified, and communicated in symbolic form and/or natural language" (Alavi & Leidner, 2001, p. 110). Miscalibration can arise from overconfidence in both tacit and explicit knowledge. Accounts of the sources of overconfidence that stress the role of expertise and familiarity (Alba & Hutchinson, 2000) imply that the *interaction* of tacit and explicit knowledge can result in overconfidence as well. While explicit knowledge can be identified more easily, and systems and procedures can be developed to deal with it, for example through feedback and training, dealing with tacit knowledge poses a greater challenge.

When managers access the (explicit) knowledge base prior to decision making, a feature could be added to the retrieval mechanism that explicitly asks them to rate their confidence in the information retrieved. However, for information surrounded by uncertainty, such as strategic decisions for future action, managers could be trained to use such a KM rating system to make them more cautious in their use of this information. *Simulations*, games, and case studies, where the use of a feedback mechanism can be incorporated to reduce overconfidence, can be developed. By requiring decision makers to explicitly state their level of confidence, this aspect of the decision can be analyzed and critiqued by others involved in the decision process, and the decision maker can gain insight into his/her style of information use. Information sources can also be evaluated by these rating systems, leading to their modification and to improvement.

Calibration of explicit knowledge involves an implicit calibration of *tacit knowledge* as well, but dealing with miscalibration arising from tacit knowledge requires additions to the existing systems. The system should be capable of tapping into the tacit knowledge base of the user, and in an interactive manner, gauge the level of miscalibration. Obviously, this presupposes a tacit knowledge base within the system, which might go against the very notion of tacit knowledge itself (as something that cannot be made explicit). Still, we feel that at least some dimensions of such knowledge will lend itself to assessment of calibration. For example, evaluating the outcomes of using tacit knowledge by comparing them with the performance people expect of themselves could improve some aspects of decision making (cf. Alba & Hutchinson, 2000, p. 133). Decision making simulations could be designed to deliberately confound experts so as to make them more cautious in their conclusions, training them to pay attention to their assumptions and consider alternative hypotheses.

In this regard, we bring to attention the concepts of transactive and mechanistic memory that have been discussed (Lynn & Reilly, 2002; Wegner, 1987). *Transactive memory* refers to the set of individual memory systems in combination with their intercommunications; transactive memory exists as a property of a group as group members share their memories through their interactions with each other and with external memory storage devices. *Mechanistic memory* refers to information accessed from mechanical systems. A part of transactive memory can be conceptualized as overlapping with tacit knowledge. Codifying such transactive memory and systematizing it will enable the creation of interactive procedures that could assess the level of miscalibration of users (cf. Markus, 2001). While this is an idea at an incipient stage, research can look into its possible developments.

With modern IT advances, an intelligent agent could be developed to serve as a sounding board to evaluate decisions under different confidence conditions. Such systems would have to be developed to realistically challenge managers while not promoting underconfidence as found by McIntyre (1982). Miscalibration is more likely in turbulent rather than stable environments and in emergent knowledge processes (new product development, strategy making) because there is high uncertainty, less time for feedback, and little direct experience (cf. Markus, Majchrzak, & Gasser, 2002). Such scenarios encourage the formation of more tacit and less explicit knowledge. IT could be used to present such scenarios to managers in training sessions to accustom them to their environment and alert them to the dangers of overconfidence as well as ways to reduce its harmful impact.

Some researchers have examined issues that address these questions. Kasper (1996) proposes a theory of decision support systems for user calibration. Kasper's theory utilizes the theory of symbolic representation in problem solving (Kaufmann, 1985) according to which the quality of mental acts (including calibration) depends upon matching the appropriate symbolic representation and reasoning to problem novelty. Hence, the DSS design theory for user calibration is based on the notion that user calibration depends upon designing a DSS so that it effectively supports the users' symbolic representation in problem solving, and it contends that DSS designs for user calibration depend upon problem novelty.

Following the guidelines suggested by Faust (1986) and building on Kasper (1996), it can be suggested that future research and development should be devoted to devising ways to adjust KM systems so that:

- They reduce information overload, perhaps screening information so that irrelevant and illusory data can be removed, and only the most crucial and relevant information delivered.
- They incorporate negative or disconfirming information in the retrieval system so that decision makers are exposed to counter-arguments.

- They rate information to distinguish degrees of speculation.
- They require/suggest competing hypotheses that can be analyzed and rejected or accepted side by side with the favored course of action.

FUTURE TRENDS

Possible avenues for research into knowledge calibration in knowledge management include learning more about how decision makers interact with IT systems if the latter include explicit mechanisms to reduce overconfidence. More should be learned about the best ways to integrate knowledge calibration into training in the use of DSS. Which methods work best in reducing overconfidence? Increasing attention is being devoted to novel IS contexts, such as emergent knowledge processes, organizational activity patterns that exhibit "an emergent process of deliberations with no best structure or sequence; requirements for knowledge that are complex (both general and situational), distributed across people, and evolving dynamically; and an actor set that is unpredictable in terms of job roles or prior knowledge" (Marcus et al., 2002, p. 179). A variety of causes seem to induce miscalibration. Future research could focus on delineating more precisely the relationships among these prospective influences. Do multiple causes lead to the same phenomenon, or are there different types of miscalibration, perhaps with different causes? Recent theories of information foraging (Pirolli & Card, 1999) offer new insights into how humans acquire information; integrating these theories with KC and KM is an exiting prospect.

The challenge is to integrate these ideas into the ongoing dialogue on knowledge management, and formulate a dynamic theory of knowledge management systems for user calibration. Given the rapid increase in the research efforts and output on knowledge management, such a theory is likely to evolve over the course of the next few years.

CONCLUSION

Miscalibration seems to be pervasive feature of decision-making environments. We argue that more study should be devoted to it in KM. "The processes of knowledge creation, storage/retrieval, and transfer do not necessarily lead to enhanced organizational performance; effective knowledge application does" (Alavi & Leidner, 2001, p. 129). This brief outline makes a case for the incorporation of knowledge calibration into knowledge management research and practice as one aspect of improving knowledge application. The stream of research on knowledge management can be enriched by integrating relevant thought streams that have the potential of adding a new dimension to our understanding of knowledge management. For instance, Meso, Troutt, and Rudnicka (2002) recently highlighted how naturalistic decision-making research can enhance knowledge management. In the same fashion we hope that the idea outlined above catalyzes the synthesis of thoughts on knowledge calibration into the body of knowledge management research.

REFERENCES

Alba, J.W., & Hutchinson, J.W. (2000). Knowledge calibration: What consumers know and what they think they know. *Journal of Consumer Research, 27*(2), 123-156.

Alavi, M., & Leidner, D.E. (2001). Knowledge management and knowledge management systems: Conceptual foundations and research issues. *MIS Quarterly, 25*(January), 107-136.

Aldag, R.J., & Powers, D.J. (1986). An empirical assessment of computer-assisted decision analysis. *Decision Sciences, 17*(April), 572-588.

Bell, J. (1984). The effect of presentation form on judgment confidence in performance evaluation. *Journal of Business Finance and Accounting, 11*(March), 327-346.

Brown, J.S., & Duguid, P. (2000). *The social life of information.* Boston: Harvard Business School Press.

Carayannis, E., Gonzalez, E., & Wetter, J. (2003). The nature and dynamics of discontinuous and disruptive innovations from a learning and knowledge management perspective. In L.V. Shavinina (Ed.), *The international handbook on innovation* (pp. 115-138). Amsterdam: Elsevier Science.

Chervany, N.L., & Dickson, G.W. (1974). An experimental evaluation of information overload in a production environment. *Management Science, 20*(October), 1335-1344.

Davis, F.D., Kottemann, J.E., & Remus, W.E. (1991). What-if analysis and the illusion of control. *Proceedings of the 24th Annual Hawaii International Conference on System Sciences, 3,* (pp. 452-460).

Davis, F.D., & Kottemann, J.E. (1994). User perceptions of decision support effectiveness: Two production planning experiments. *Decision Sciences, 25*(January), 57-78.

Einhorn, H.J., & Hogarth, R.M. (1981). Confidence in judgment persistence of the illusion of validity. *Psychological Review, 85*(May), 395-416.

Faust, D. (1986). Learning and maintaining rules for decreasing judgment accuracy. *Journal of Personality Assessment, 50*(April), 585-600.

Goldman, A.I. (1999). *Knowledge in a social world.* Oxford: Clarendon Press.

Harvey, N. (1997). Confidence in judgment. *Trends in Cognitive Science, 1,* 78-82.

Kasper, G.M. (1996). A theory of decision support system design for user calibration. *Information Systems Research, 7*(February), 215-232.

Kaufmann, G. (1985). A theory of symbolic representation in problem solving. *Journal of Mental Imagery, 9*(February), 51-70.

Lynn, G.S., & Reilly, R.R. (2002). *Blockbusters.* New York: Harper Business.

Markus, M.L. (2001). Toward a theory of knowledge reuse: Types of knowledge reuse situations and factors in reuse success. *Journal of Management Information Systems, 18*(1), 57-93.

Markus, M.L., Majchrzak, A., & Gasser, L. (2002). A design theory for systems that support emergent knowledge processes. *MIS Quarterly, 26*(3), 179-212.

McIntyre, S. (1982). Experimental study of the impact of judgment-based marketing models. *Management Science, 28*(January), 17-33.

Meso, P., Troutt, M.D., & Rudnicka, J. (2002). A review of naturalistic decision making research with some implications for knowledge management. *Journal of Knowledge Management, 6*(January), 63-73.

Oskamp, S. (1965). Confidence in case-study judgments. *Journal of Consulting Psychology, 29*(March), 261-265.

Pirolli, P., & Card, S. (1999). Information foraging. *Psychological Review, 106*(4), 643-675.

Russo, J.E., & Schoemaker, P.J.H. (1992). Managing overconfidence. *Sloan Management Review,* (Winter), 7-17.

Tapp, A., & Hughes, T. (2004). New technology and the changing role of marketing. *Marketing Intelligence & Planning, 22*(3), 284-296.

Tversky, A., & Kahneman, D. (1974). Judgment under uncertainty: Heuristics and biases. *Science, 185*(September), 1124-1131.

Wegner, D.M. (1987). Transactive memory. In B. Mullen & G.R. Goethals (Eds.), *Theories of group behavior* (pp. 185-208). New York: Springer-Verlag.

Yates, J.F. (1990). *Judgment and decision making.* Englewood Cliffs, NJ: Prentice-Hall.

KEY TERMS

Calibration: Correspondence between accuracy and confidence. Calibration exists when there is correspondence.

Decision Making: The process and the act of making decisions.

Knowledge Calibration: Correspondence between knowledge accuracy and confidence with which knowledge is held.

Mechanistic Memory: Refers to information accessed from mechanical systems.

Miscalibration: Implies a lack of correspondence between accuracy and confidence.

Overconfidence: Exists when a person holds confidence more than what is warranted by the accuracy of his/her knowledge; overconfidence implies miscalibration.

Tacit Knowledge: Personal or subjective knowledge, which includes mental models, know-how, skills, and so forth.

Transactive Memory: Refers to the set of individual memory systems in combination with their intercommunications; transactive memory exists as a property of a group as group members share their memories through their interactions with each other and with external memory storage devices.

Knowledge Communication

Martin J. Eppler
University of Lugano, Switzerland

INTRODUCTION: THE IMPORTANCE OF KNOWLEDGE COMMUNICATION IN MANAGEMENT

Communicating professional knowledge is a key activity for today's specialized workforce. The efficient and effective transfer of experiences, insights, and know-how among different experts and decision makers is a prerequisite for high-quality decision making and coordinated, organizational action (Straub & Karahanna, 1998). Situations of such deliberate (interfunctional) knowledge transfer through interpersonal communication or group conversations (Gratton & Goshal, 2002) can be found in many business constellations, as the following typical examples illustrate:

Technology experts present their evaluation of a new technology to management in order to jointly devise a new production strategy (McDermott, 1999). Engineers who have discovered how to master a difficult manufacturing process need to convey their methods to engineers in other business units (Szulanski, 1996, 1999). Legal experts brief a management team on the implications of new regulations on their business model (Wilmotte & Morgan, 1984). Experts from various domains need to share their views and insights regarding a common goal in order to agree on a common rating of risks, requirements (Browne & Ramesh, 2002), industries, or clients. Project leaders need to present their results to the upper management and share their experiences of past projects in order to assess the potential of new project candidates (Schindler & Eppler, 2003). Scientists who work as drug developers present new avenues for future products that business unit managers must assess. Market researchers present their statistical analyses of recent consumer surveys to the head of marketing (Boland et al., 2001). Strategy consultants present the findings of their strategic company assessment to the board of directors in order to devise adequate measures (Creplet, Duouet, Kern, Mehmanzapir, & Munier, 2001).

What these diverse situations all have in common is the problem of *knowledge asymmetry* (Sharma, 1997) that has to be resolved through interpersonal communication. While the manager typically has the authority to make strategic or tactical decisions, he or she often lacks the specialized expertise required to make an informed decision on a complex issue (Watson, 2004). Because of the wide scope of decisions that need to be made, a manager frequently has to delegate the decision preparation to experts who—based on their professional training and previous experience—can analyze complex situations or technological options in a more reliable manner. The results of such analyses then need to be communicated back to the manager, often under considerable time constraints. The knowledge communication challenge, however, begins long before that, at the time when the manager has to convey his or her knowledge needs and decision constraints to the experts in order to delegate the analysis task effectively.

BACKGROUND: THE CONCEPT OF KNOWLEDGE COMMUNICATION

Based on the reasoning described in the previous section, we define *knowledge communication* as the (deliberate) activity of interactively conveying and co-constructing insights, assessments, experiences, or skills through verbal and non-verbal means. Knowledge communication has taken place when an insight, experience, or skill has been successfully reconstructed by an individual because of the communicative actions of another. Knowledge communication thus designates the successful transfer of know-how (e.g., how to accomplish a task), know-why (e.g., the cause-effect relationships of a complex phenomenon), know-what (e.g., the results of a test), and know-who (e.g., the experiences with others) through face-to-face (co-located) or media-based (virtual) interactions. This type of knowledge communication can take place synchronously or asynchronously.[1] The first mode of communication refers to (often face-to-face) real-time interactions, while the latter designates delayed (usually media-based) interactions.

We use the term *knowledge dialogues* for the first type of (synchronous) knowledge communication, stressing the interactive and collaborative style of knowledge exchange in this communication mode (see Isaacs, 1997; Nonaka, Toyama, & Konno, 2000). Depending on the knowledge-focused goal of such dialogues, we distinguish among *Crealogues* (that focus on in the creation of new insights), *Sharealogues* (facilitating knowledge transfer), *Assessalogues* (focusing on the evaluation of new insights), and *Doalogues* (e.g., turning understanding into committed action, i.e., 'talk the walk'). Each type of knowledge dialogue requires different behavior and interaction patterns and support measures (e.g., whereas Assessalogues require critical, convergent evaluation tools, Crealogues require an open atmosphere for divergent thinking and rapid idea generation without judgment).

With regard to asynchronous knowledge communication, we refer to the concept of *knowledge media* (see Eppler, Röpnack, & Seifried, 1999) as enabling knowledge transfer through technology-based communication, collaboration, e-learning, aggregation, retrieval, and archiving services. Knowledge media can be differentiated in terms of their target community, such as scientific knowledge media, public knowledge media, professional knowledge media, and so forth. The concept of knowledge media in general stresses the importance of a community that collaborates regularly using a common platform that consists not only of IT functionalities, but also of common communication norms and (usage) rules.

In this understanding, knowledge communication is *more* than communicating information (e.g., facts, figures, events, situations, developments, etc.) or emotions (e.g., fears, hopes, reservations, commitment) because it requires conveying context, background, and basic assumptions. It requires the communication of personal insights and experiences. Communicating insights requires the elicitation of one's rationale and reasoning (i.e., one's argumentation structure); of one's perspective, ratings, and priorities; and of one's hunches and intuition. At times it may even be necessary to present an overview of the expert's relevant skills along with his/her previous professional experiences and credentials (Lunce, Iyer, Courtney, & Schkade, 1993) in order to build trust and enable an adequate atmosphere for effective knowledge transfer. Thus, in addition to pure information (and at times emotion), a myriad of other indicators need to be provided in order to transfer knowledge. These indicators help the person who requires insights from another to understand the other's perspective, to reconstruct the other's insights correctly, and to connect them to one's own prior knowledge.

Still, knowledge communication does not only differ in terms of *what* is communicated (knowledge in context rather than isolated data or information[2]), but also *how* one communicates. The transfer of information can often be successful without additional effort beyond an ordinary, everyday communication style. Communicating expertise-based, complex insights, by contrast, calls for didactic tricks and at times sophisticated indirect speech acts and visualization means that help the other side to become actively involved in the communication and engage in a collaborative, goal-directed sense-making process—a prerequisite for the construction of new knowl-

edge (see Weick, 1995). The process of knowledge communication hence requires more reciprocal interaction between decision makers and experts because both sides only have a fragmented understanding of an issue and consequently can only gain a complete comprehension by iteratively aligning their mental models. All of this means that when we communicate knowledge, we are still communicating information and emotions, but we also create a specific type of context so that this information can be used to re-construct insights, create new perspectives, or acquire new skills.

This (interpersonal) communication perspective on knowledge transfer has already been emphasized by other researchers—who explicitly label this view as 'knowledge communication' (Scarbrough, 1995, p. 997; Antonelli, 2000; Harada, 2003; Reiserer, Ertl, & Mandl, 2002)—and by several practitioners (e.g., Watson, 2004). Nevertheless, these authors have often treated knowledge communication as a kind of black box that is described only in broad terms and general traits, such as the major communication goals or steps. By examining the communication problems that often impede knowledge transfer in detail, we can look into this black box and propose pragmatic ways of improving knowledge communication, especially among experts and managers where the chasm between in-depth knowledge and decision authority is particularly apparent.

PROBLEMS IN COMMUNICATING KNOWLEDGE AMONG EXPERTS AND DECISION MAKERS

In order to better understand the problems that can impede the effective transfer of decision-relevant knowledge from experts to managers and from managers to experts, we will review relevant constructs and prior findings from social and engineering sciences, as there are in fact numerous concepts that describe issues related to sub-optimal knowledge transfer. These concepts regard topics such as interdepartmental knowledge transfer, professional communication, decision making, communication technology, or the nature of expert knowledge. By screening these disciplines and topic areas, we can establish a first overview of possible knowledge communication problems and we can create a systematic terminology to speak more explicitly (and consistently) about knowledge communication barriers.

Previously identified barriers of knowledge communication are summarized in Table 1. There are three main criteria for including concepts in this table: First, the concept has to be closely related to problems of interpersonal, professional knowledge transfer.[3] Second, the

Table 1. Key research concepts that illustrate knowledge communication barriers

Key Concept/Knowledge Communication Barrier	Description	References
Cognitive biases (confirmation, availability, recency, dichotomized reasoning, framing, anchoring, representativeness, etc.)	Knowledge may not be correctly interpreted or used due to biases in one's reasoning, such as listening only to those insights that confirm one's prior opinion.	Tversky & Kahnemann, 1974
Decision problems (plunging in, shooting from the hip, poor feedback, taking shortcuts, frame blindness, etc.)	The decision maker may for example believe that he/she can make a complex decision right away without looking further at the provided analysis.	Russo & Shoemaker, 1989
Communication biases (audience tuning, misattribution bias, saying-is-believing, shared reality)	The knowledge is inadvertently manipulated through communication itself: • *Audience Tuning*: Communicators spontaneously tune their messages to: –the personal characteristics of the audience, or –the situational factors. • *Misattribution Bias:* Communicators tend to consider their audience-tuned messages to be about the topic of the message rather than about the audience. • *Saying-Is-Believing Effect:* Autopersuasion has stronger effects because one does not activate regular mechanisms of critical reflection. • *Shared Reality*: You consider your audience-tuned message to provide objective, accurate information on the message topic because it was shared with others.	Higgins, 1999
Argumentation fallacies (begging the question, overgeneralizing, personal attacks, defective testimony, problematic premise, slippery slope, red herring, etc.)	In demonstrating one's ideas and insights, people fall into argumentative traps, such as begging the question (circular reasoning), over-generalizing, appealing to false majorities or false expertise, reasoning ad consequentiam (what should not be true, cannot be true) or reacting with direct attacks at a person (at hominem) rather than at a knowledge claim.	van Eemeren et al., 1992
Defensive routines (skilled incompetence, learned helplessness, easing-in, etc.)	New knowledge is sometimes not accepted (or provided) due to mechanisms or habits that prevent the identification and acceptance of one's own ignorance. This may lead to a reduced effort to understand complex issues (learned helplessness).	Argyris, 1986, 1990
Knowledge disavowal	A number of factors have been found which limit information use in organizations, such as not spending enough time collecting advice, refusal to share, fear of exposure, and so forth. Knowledge disavowal occurs when reliable and relevant information is not shared among decision makers.	Zaltman, 1983; Deshpande & Kohli, 1989
Knowledge sharing hostility	Knowledge communication fails because the 'knowledge givers' are reluctant to share their insights due to micropolitics, strenuous relationships, or fear.	Husted & Michailova, 2002
Micropolitics of knowledge	The 'knowledge claims' of an expert are discredited by the decision makers due to their differing (hidden) agenda, because of a coalition of people with an alternative view, or due to the expert's lack of formal authority.	Lazega, 1992

Table 1. Key research concepts that illustrate knowledge communication barriers, cont.

Key Concept/Knowledge Communication Barrier	Description	References
Internal knowledge stickiness	Knowledge can sometimes not be transferred because of arduous relationships or casual ambiguities regarding the knowledge, or because of the lack of absorptive capacity of the knowledge receivers.	Szulanski, 1996, 1999
Groupthink	A (management) team may not truly listen to the input of an expert because of the team's group coherence, and group dynamics sometimes block outside advice and feel omniscient.	Janis, 1982
Information overload	An individual is sometimes not able to integrate new information into the decision-making process because too much complex information has to be interpreted too quickly.	O'Reilly, 1980; Eppler & Mengis, 2004
Self/other effect	Individuals tend to discount advice and favor their own opinion.	Yaniv & Kleinberger, 2000
Knowing-doing gap/smart talk trap	Sometimes organizations know where a problem resides and how to tackle it, but do not move from knowledge to action (due to unhealthy internal competition or lacking follow-up).	Pfeffer & Sutton, 2000
Absorptive capacity	Limited ability of decision makers to grasp the knowledge of the expert based on lack of prior knowledge.	Bower and Hilgard, 1981; Cohen & Levinthal, 1990
Paradox of expertise	Experts sometimes find it difficult to articulate their knowledge or rephrase their insights in a way that a non-expert can understand. Sometimes experts indicate other rules than they actually apply.	Johnson, 1983
Ingroup outgroup behavior	We tend to interact more with likewise groups than with others, thus reducing our chances to acquire radically new knowledge.	Blau, 1977
Task closure	In our communication, we may choose to use a one-way communication medium because it permits us to close an open task without having to have a conversation. Thus leaner communication channels are used that may be necessary. In other words: We tend to want to close a communication process in order to complete an open task.	Straub & Karahanna, 1998; Meyer, 1962
Set-up-to-fail syndrome	Managers are projecting their initial expectation of an expert's likely performance unto him/her, leading to the self-fulfilling prophecy of (at times) lower performance. This is aggravated by de-motivating feedback to the expert.	Manzoni & Barsoux, 2002
ASK problem	Anomalous State of Knowledge: When a decision maker does not have the knowledge base to really know what to ask for. People need to know quite a bit about a topic to be able to ask or search for relevant information.	Belkin, 1980; Chen et al., 1992
Not-invented-here (NIH) syndrome	Knowledge from others is sometimes rejected because it originated elsewhere.	Katz & Allen, 1982
Preference for outsiders	This is the opposite of the NIH syndrome and describes the tendency of managers to value outside knowledge higher than internal knowledge because it has a higher status, it is scarcer (because of difficult access), and it is less scrutinized for errors than internal knowledge.	Menon & Pfeffer, 2003
False consensus effect	We assume others see situations as we do, and fail to revise our framing.	Manzoni & Barsoux, 2002

Table 1. Key research concepts that illustrate knowledge communication barriers, cont.

Key Concept/Knowledge Communication Barrier	Description	References
Inert knowledge	The knowledge that the decision maker has acquired from the expert does not come to mind when it is needed or useful for decision making or actions. The transferred knowledge is stuck in the situation where it has been acquired.	Whitehead, 1929
Hidden profile problem	One often does not know other people's background (profile)—that is, what they know and could contribute to a problem's solution. The knowledge that is thus frequently shared in a discussion is what is expected by everyone.	Stasser 1992; Stasser & Stewart, 1992
Common knowledge effect	The tendency of a group to focus merely on commonly shared (rather than unique) pieces of information.	Gigone & Hastie, 1993
Lack of common ground	Common ground refers to the manager's and expert's assumptions about their shared background beliefs about the world. If those assumptions are wrong or inconsistent, communication becomes more difficult.	Clark & Schaefer, 1989; Olson & Olson, 2000
Cassandra syndrome	The decision makers do not give sufficient weight or attention to an expert's warning because they face many other important problems. Only when the situation has deteriorated dramatically do they start taking the expert's advice.	Mikalachki, 1983

concept has to describe a problem of major impact on the quality of knowledge transfer (rare or very specific issues are not included). Third, the concept has to be influential—that is, it has to be cited with the same construct label by several authors (other than the creator of the concept). The resulting list in Table 1 first includes 'umbrella' concepts that designate a group of closely related problems, such as cognitive biases, decision-making problems, argumentation fallacies, communication biases, or defensive routines, and then concepts that label individual problems, such as the not-invented-here syndrome or the ASK problem.

The problems listed in Table 1 are neither mutually exclusive nor collectively exhaustive. Nevertheless, Table 1 summarizes many of the key pitfalls in communicating knowledge. It is in the nature of the phenomenon that these problems are not isolated, but that they rather interact in many, sometimes unpredictable ways.

Based on the concepts from Table 1, and based on 10 focus groups[4] and 10 personal interviews with engineers who frequently collaborate with managers in their companies, as well as interviews with 20 IT managers[5] who regularly interact with experts for their decision making, we distinguish among five types of knowledge communication problems. These are briefly summarized below, followed by examples of each type of problem, cited from both experts and managers.

The first type of knowledge communication problems is *expert-caused* difficulties. These mistakes make it cumbersome for the decision maker to grasp the insights of a specialist. This type of problem also includes issues that

make it difficult for the manager to explain his or her own constraints and priorities. Examples of this kind of problem are the use of overly technical jargon, not relating the insights to the manager's situation, starting with details before an overview is given, or lacking interest of the expert in related (but relevant) issues. From the list provided in Table 1, knowledge-sharing hostility and the paradox of expertise clearly belong to this category.

The second type of knowledge communication challenges is *manager-caused* problems that leave it unclear to the expert what the manager actually expects from him or her (briefing). This makes it difficult for the expert to convey what he or she knows. Management mistakes make it harder for the manager to fully profit from the offered expertise. For example, a manager's reluctance to discuss detailed problems may have major effects on an issue, such as lack of concentration and attention or lack of technical know-how. From the list in Table 1, the decision problems, the ASK problem, the Cassandra syndrome, or the inert knowledge problem are typical examples of this group.

The third type of knowledge communication problems are caused by the *mutual behavior* of experts and managers, including their experiences or attitudes (e.g., reciprocal stereotypes). Examples from the list of concepts that belong to this group are lacking feedback on both sides, the set-up to fail syndrome, groupthink, and ingroup outgroup behavior.

Fourth, we see problems caused by the *interaction situation* of the expert-manager interaction, such as time constraints, communication infrastructure, distractions, interventions from others, and so forth. The problem of information overload in Table 1 can arise due to the time constraints in a communication situation. But the hidden profile problem can also be due to the communicative situation, where the background of the participants is not fully revealed or discussed at the beginning of a manager-expert interaction.

The fifth and final type of knowledge communication problems includes issues that are caused indirectly by the *overall organizational context* of managers and experts, such as their organizational constraints and their differing tasks, priorities, and interests. The 'micropolitics of knowledge' concept listed in Table 1 would be an example of the (negative) impact of the organizational context on the transfer of knowledge.

CONCLUSION AND FUTURE TRENDS

Many studies in knowledge management examine the structural, macro aspects of knowledge transfer on an organizational level (Szulanski, 1999). There are also studies that examine the general motivational barriers to such transfers (Husted & Michailova, 2002). The field of knowledge communication, by contrast, examines the micro perspectives of knowledge transfer, thus highlighting the role of adequate or inadequate communication behavior patterns for knowledge transfer. These examined patterns go beyond the question of motivation and encompass issues such as the use of adequate language, timing, group interventions, or media use for knowledge transfer. This article has defined this approach as knowledge communication. It has outlined the various problems that exist when individuals (particularly experts) communicate their knowledge to others (e.g., managers).

Future knowledge management research should examine ways of facilitating and thus improving knowledge communication. This can be achieved through such tools as knowledge visualization suites, dialogue techniques, or knowledge elicitation methods. In doing so, future research should pay particular attention to the influence of (expert and manager) behavior, and to situational and organizational factors that affect the quality of knowledge communication.

REFERENCES

Alavi, M., & Leidner, D. (2001). Knowledge management and knowledge management systems: Conceptual foundations and research issues. *MIS Quarterly, 25*(1), 107-136.

Alvesson, M. (1993). Organizations as rhetoric: Knowledge-intensive firms and the struggle of ambiguity. *Journal of Management Studies, 30*(6), 997-1020.

Antonelli, C. (2000). Collective knowledge communication and innovation: The evidence of technological districts. *Regional Studies, 34*(6), 535-547.

Argyris, C. (1986). Skilled incompetence. *Harvard Business Review, 64*(5), 74-79.

Argyris, C. (1990). *Overcoming organizational defenses.* New York: Prentice-Hall.

Belkin, N.J. (1980). Anomalous states of knowledge as a basis for information retrieval. *Canadian Journal of Information Science, 5,* 133-143.

Blackler, F. (1995). Knowledge, knowledge work and organizations. *Organization Studies, 16*(6), 1021-1046.

Blau, P.M. (1977). *Inequality and heterogeneity: A primitive theory of social structure.* New York: The Free Press.

Boland, R.J., Singh, J., Salipante, R., Aram, J.D., Fay, S.Y., & Kanawattanachai, P. (2001). Knowledge representations and knowledge transfer. *Academy of Management Journal, 44*(2), 393-417.

Bower, G.H., & Hilgard, E.R. (1981). *Theories of learning.* Englewood Cliffs, NJ: Prentice-Hall.

Bouty, I. (2000). Interpersonal and interaction influences on informal resource exchanges between R&D researchers across organizational boundaries. *Academy of Management Journal, 43*(1), 50-65.

Bradley, S. & Braude, M. (1995). The "magic quadrant" process. *Gartner Research Note*, (February 22). Retrieved October 8, 2001, from *www.gartnerweb.com*

Bromme, R., Rambow, R., & Nückles, M. (2001). Expertise and estimating what other people know: The influence of professional experience and type of knowledge. *Journal of Experimental Psychology, 7*(4), 317-330.

Browne & Ramesh (2002). Improving information requirements determination: A cognitive perspective. *Information & Management, 39,* 625-645.

Chen, H. (1994). Collaborative systems: Solving the vocabulary problem. *IEEE Computer*, (May), 58-69.

Clark, H.H., & Schaefer, F.S. (1989). Contributing to discourse. *Cognitive Science, 13,* 259-294.

Creplet, F., Duouet, O., Kern, F., Mehmanzapir, B., & Munier, F. (2001). Consultants and experts in management consulting firms. *Research Policy, 30,* 1517-1535.

Davenport, T., & Prusak, L. (1998). *Working knowledge: How organizations manage what they know.* Boston: Harvard Business School Press.

Deshpande, R., & Kohli, A.K. (1989). Knowledge disavowal: Structural determinants of information processing breakdown in organizations. *Knowledge, 11*(2), 155-169.

Eppler, M., Röpnack, A., & Seifried P. (1999). Improving knowledge intensive processes through an enterprise knowledge medium. In J. Prasad (Ed.), *Proceedings of the 1999 ACM SIGCPR Conference 'Managing Organizational Knowledge for Strategic Advantage: The Key Role of Information Technology and Personnel'* (pp. 222-230).

Eppler, M., & Mengis, J. (2004). The concept of information overload. *The Information Society—An International Journal, 20*(5), 1-20.

Gigone, D., & Hastie, R. (1993). The common knowledge effect: Information sharing and group judgment. *Journal of Personality and Social Psychology, 65,* 959-974.

Goldhaber, G.M., Yates, M.P., Porter, D.T., & Lesniak, R. (1978). Organizational communication. *Human Communication Research, 5,* 76-96.

Gratton, L., & Ghoshal, S. (2002). Improving the quality of conversations. *Organizational Dynamics, 31,* 209-223.

Gülich, E. (2003). Conversational techniques used in transferring knowledge between medical experts and non-experts. *Discourse Studies, 5*(2), 235-263.

Harada, T. (2003). Three steps in knowledge communication: The emergence of knowledge transformers. *Research Policy, 32,* 1737-1751.

Higgins, T. (1999). Saying is believing effects: When sharing reality about something biases knowledge and evaluations. In L. Thompson, J. Levine, & D. Messick (Eds.), *Shared cognition in organization: The management of knowledge.* Mahwah, NJ: Lawrence Erlbaum.

Husted, K., & Michailova, S. (2002). Diagnosing and fighting knowledge-sharing hostility. *Organizational Dynamics, 31*(1), 60-73.

Isaacs, W. (1997). *Dialogue and the art of thinking together: A pioneering approach to communicating in business and in life.* New York: Doubleday.

Janis, I. (1982). *Groupthink: Psychological studies of policy decisions and fiascoes.* Boston: Houghton Mifflin.

Johnson, P.E. (1983). What kind of expert should a system be? *Journal of Medicine and Philosophy, 8,* 77-97.

Katz, R., & Allen, T.J. (1982). Investigating the Not Invented Here (NIH) syndrome: A look at the performance, tenure, and communication patterns of 50 R&D project groups. *R&D Management, 12*(1), 7-19.

Kirmeyer, S.L., & Lin, T. (1987). Social support: Its relationship to observed communication with peers and superiors. *Academy of Management Journal, 30*(1), 151-162.

Lazega, E. (1992). *Micropolitics of knowledge. Communication and indirect control in workgroups.* New York: deGruyter.

Lunce, S.E., Iyer, R.K., Courtney, L.M., & Schkade, L.L. (1993). Experts and expertise: An identification paradox. *Industrial Management and Data Systems, 93*(9), 3-9.

Manzoni, J.-F., & Barsoux, J.-L. (2002). *The set-up-to-fail syndrome, how good managers cause great people to fail.* Cambridge. Harvard Business School Press.

McDermott, R. (1999). Learning across teams. *Knowledge Management Review, 8,* 32-36.

McLeod, J.M., & Chaffee, S.H. (1973). Interpersonal approaches to communication research. *American Behavioral Scientist, 16*(4), 469-499.

Menon, T., & Pfeffer, J. (2003). Valuing internal vs. external knowledge: Explaining the preference for outsiders. *Management Science, 49*(4), 497-513.

Meyer, R.L. (1962). *A communications theory of urban growth.* Boston: MIT Press.

Mikalachki, A. (1983). Does anyone listen to the boss? *Business Horizons,* (January-February), 18-24.

Newman, J., & Newman, R. (1985). Information work: The new divorce? *British Journal of Sociology, 24,* 497-515.

Nonaka, I., Toyama, R., & Konno, N. (2000). SECI, ba and leadership: A unified model of dynamic knowledge creation. *Long Range Planning, 33,* 5-34.

O'Reilly, C.A. (1980). Individuals and information overload in organizations: Is more necessarily better? *Academy of Management Journal, 23,* 684-696.

Olson, G., & Olson, J. (2000). Distance matters. *Human-Computer Interaction, 15*(2-3), 107-137.

Pfeffer, J., & Sutton, R.I. (2000). *The knowing-doing gap: How smart companies turn knowledge into action.* Boston: Harvard Business School Press.

Probst, G., Romhardt, K., & Raub, S. (1999). *Managing knowledge: Building blocks for success.* London: John Wiley & Sons.

Reiserer, M., Ertl, B., & Mandl, H. (2002). Fostering collaborative knowledge construction in desktop videoconferencing. Effects of content schemes and cooperation scripts in peer teaching settings. *Proceedings of the International Workshop on Barriers and Biases in Computer-Mediated Knowledge Communication—and How They May Be Overcome,* Münster, Germany.

Russo, J.E., & Shoemaker, P.J.H. (1989). *Decision traps.* New York: Simon and Schuster.

Scarbrough, H. (1995). Blackboxes, hostages and prisoners. *Organization Studies, 16*(6), 991-1019.

Schindler, M., & Eppler, M. (2003). Harvesting project knowledge: A review of project learning methods and success factors. *International Journal of Project Management, 21,* 219-228.

Sharma, A. (1997). Professional as agent: Knowledge asymmetry in agency exchange. *Academy of Management Review, 22*(3), 758-798.

Starbuck, W.H. (1992). Learning by knowledge-intensive firms. *Journal of Management Studies, 29,* 147-175.

Stasser, G., Stewart, D.D., & Wittenbaum, G.M. (1995). Expert roles and information exchange during discussion: The importance of knowing who knows what. *Journal of Experimental Social Psychology, 31,* 244-265.

Stasser, G., & Stewart, D. (1992). Discovery of hidden profiles by decision-making groups: Solving a problem versus making a judgment. *Journal of Personality and Social Psychology, 63,* 426-434.

Straub, D., & Karahanna, E. (1998). Knowledge worker communications and recipient availability: Toward a task closure explanation of media choice. *Organization Science, 9*(2), 160-175.

Szulanski, G. (1996). Exploring internal stickiness: Impediments to the transfer of best practices within the firm. *Strategic Management Journal, 17*(Winter), 27-43.

Szulanski, G. (1999). The process of knowledge transfer: A diachronic analysis of stickiness. *Organizational Behavior and Human Decision Processes, 82*(1), 9-27.

Tsoukas, H. (1996). The firm as a distributed knowledge system: A constructionist approach. *Strategic Management Journal, 17,* 11-25.

Tversky, A., & Kahnemann, D. (1974). Judgment under uncertainty: Heuristics and biases, *Science, 1.185,* 1124-1131.

van Eemeren, H., & Grootendorst, R. (1992). *Argumentation, communication, and fallacies: A pragma-dialectical perspective.* Mahwah, NJ: Lawrence Erlbaum.

Vaughan, D. (1997). *The Challenger launch decision.* Chicago; London: The University of Chicago Press.

von Krogh, G., & Roos, J. (1995). *Organizational epistemology.* New York: St. Martin's Press.

Watson, C.M. (2004). Don't blame the engineer. *Sloan Management Review,* (Winter), 26-29.

Weick, K.E. (1995) *Sensemaking in organizations.* Thousand Oaks, CA: Sage Publications.

Whitehead, A.N. (1929). *The aims of education and other essays.* New York: McMillan.

Wilmotte, R.M., & Morgan, P.I. (1984). The discipline gap in decision making. *Management Review,* (September), 21-24.

Yaniv, I., & Kleinberger, E. (2000). Advice taking in decision making: Egocentric discounting and reputation formation. *Organizational Behavior and Human Decision Processes, 83,* 260-281.

Zaltman, G. (1983). Knowledge disavowal in organizations. In R.H. Kilmann, K.W. Thomas, D.P. Slevin, R. Nath, & S.L. Jesell (Eds.), *Producing useful knowledge for organizations* (pp. 173-187). New York: Praeger.

KEY TERMS

Knowledge Asymmetry: Designates the gap in the level of understanding regarding a particular topic among two or more people, for example among decision makers and experts regarding decision-relevant insights. Knowledge asymmetry cannot be resolved in the same manner as information asymmetry, as the mere transfer of information is insufficient for a mutual level of understanding. Hence, collaborative sense making processes need to take place in order to overcome knowledge asymmetry.

Knowledge Communication: The (deliberate) activity of interactively conveying and co-constructing insights, assessments, experiences, or skills through verbal and non-verbal means. It designates the successful transfer of know-how (e.g., how to accomplish a task), know-why (e.g., the cause-effect relationships of a complex phenomenon), know-what (e.g., the results of a test), and know-who (e.g., the experiences with others) through face-to-face (co-located) or media-based (virtual) interactions.

Knowledge Dialogue: Designates conversations that have as their prime objective the manipulation of knowledge, that is to say to create new knowledge (Crealogues), share knowledge (Sharealogues), evaluate knowledge (Assessalogues), or apply and utilize knowledge (Doalogues). Participants in knowledge dialogues pay special attention to the role of language in creating new insights, conveying what one knows to others, or critically examining arguments. In the case of Doalogues that convert knowledge into action, as in the other three types of knowledge-focused talk, conversations are not just held, but actively managed.

Knowledge Media: Information technology-based infrastructures that enable knowledge codification and transfer. They are platforms for the exchange of insights, experiences, and methods among scientific communities and communities of practice. Knowledge media offer various electronic knowledge services, such as expert directories (who knows what), knowledge maps (how are areas of knowledge related), notification services (what is new), or communication and learning services (such as application sharing or visualized chat sessions).

Specialist: A person with considerable experience in a domain who has engaged in a deliberate practice in that domain for an extended period of time (i.e., more than 10 years); somebody who is recognized by a domain-related community as a person with proven problem-solving skills in a particular area.

ENDNOTES

[1]	Both modes can be used in one-to-one or one-to-many contexts. Both modes can rely on speech, text, graphics, and other means of communication (i.e., verbal and non-verbal).

[2]	Our distinction between data, information, and knowledge follows the mainstream conception found in current literature (e.g., Davenport & Prusak, 1998). We view data as isolated recordings that are often generated automatically and cannot be directly used to answer questions. Information is connected, condensed, or generally processed data that allows an individual to answer questions. Knowledge is what enables an individual to ask relevant questions (Newman & Newman, 1985, p. 499). It refers to the capability of an individual to solve problems (Probst, Romhardt, & Raub, 1999). Information only becomes knowledge if a person interprets that information correctly, connects that piece of information with his or her prior knowledge, and can apply it to problems or decisions (see also Alavi & Leidner, 2001).

[3]	The concept does not have to originate in the context of interpersonal communication research, but its application to it must be obvious and fruitful, as in the example of the ASK problem. The ASK problem was first discussed in the information retrieval community, but it has ramifications for interpersonal knowledge communication as well.

[4]	Each focus group lasted for approximately one hour and consisted of 12-20 participants. The focus groups were conducted in 2002 and 2003 in Switzerland and Germany, with engineers and IT specialists from eight companies (each employing more than 1,000 people). Focus group facilitation and documentation was provided by the research team. The topic of the focus group discussion was "communication problems among engineers/specialists and managers."

[5]	Each interview lasted between 30 minutes and two hours. Interviewees were mostly senior IT managers or chief information officers of medium-sized and large Swiss companies, as well as select line managers with considerable experience. The main topic of the interviews was "problems in the knowledge communication with specialists."

Knowledge Creation

Nilmini Wickramasinghe
Illinois Institute of Technology, USA

INTRODUCTION

Knowledge management (KM) is a newly emerging approach aimed at addressing today's business challenges to increase efficiency and efficacy of core business processes, while simultaneously incorporating continuous innovation. The need for knowledge management is based on a paradigm shift in the business environment where knowledge is now considered to be central to organizational performance and integral to the attainment of a sustainable competitive advantage (Davenport & Grover, 2001; Drucker, 1993). Knowledge creation is not only a key first step in most knowledge management initiatives, but also has far reaching implications on consequent steps in the KM process, thus making knowledge creation an important focus area within knowledge management. Currently, different theories exist for explaining knowledge creation. These tend to approach the area of knowledge creation from either a people perspective—including Nonaka's Knowledge Spiral, as well as Spender's and Blackler's respective frameworks—or from a technology perspective—namely, the KDD process and data mining.

The following discusses each of these major theories on knowledge creation and suggests the benefits of taking a holistic approach to knowledge creation—namely, incorporating both the people and technology perspectives in all knowledge creation endeavors, and thereby facilitating the realization of a broader knowledge base, better knowledge inputs to impact on the consequent KM steps, and hence an increased likelihood in more successful knowledge management initiatives.

Figure 1. The KM Triad

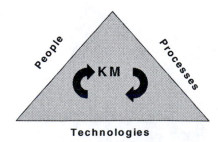

BACKGROUND

Knowledge Management

Knowledge management offers organizations many strategies, techniques, and tools to apply to their existing business processes so that they are able to grow and effectively utilize their knowledge assets. In essence then, knowledge management not only involves the production of information, but also the capture of data at the source, the transmission and analysis of this data, as well as the communication of information based on or derived from the data to those who can act on it (Swan et al., 1999). Integral to knowledge management is incorporating the socio-technical perspective of people, processes, and technologies (Wickramasinghe & Mills, 2001). We can visualize this in terms of the KM Triad as shown in Figure 1. The significance of the KM Triad is to emphasize that knowledge can be created by people and/or technologies, and can also be embedded in processes.

Broadly speaking, knowledge management involves four key steps of creating/generating knowledge, representing/storing knowledge, accessing/using/re-using knowledge, and disseminating/transferring knowledge (Davenport & Prusak, 1998; Alavi & Leidner, 2001; Markus, 2001). By combining the KM Triad with these four key steps, it is possible to form the KM Diamond as shown in Figure 2. The KM Diamond highlights the importance of the impact of the three elements of KM—namely, people, process, and technology—on the four steps of knowledge management. In other words, successful KM initiatives require consideration and interactions among all of these components.

Knowledge creation, generally accepted as the first step for any knowledge management endeavor (as depicted in Figure 2), requires an understanding of the knowledge construct as well as its people and technology dimensions. Given that knowledge creation is the first step in any knowledge management initiative, it naturally has a significant impact on the other consequent KM steps (depicted in Figure 2), thus making knowledge creation a key focal point of many theories currently in the literature. In order to fully appreciate the need for taking a holistic approach to knowledge creation, it is important to first discuss the subtleties of the knowledge construct itself.

Figure 2. The KM Diamond

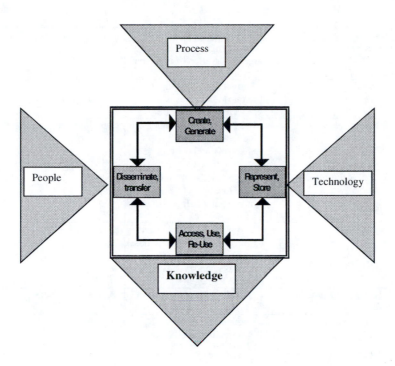

Historical Understanding of Knowledge

We owe much of our current understanding of knowledge today to the discussions and debates of ancient Greek philosophers such as Socrates, Plato, and Aristotle. The knowledge construct and trying to pin it down, as well as define the process of knowing itself, dominated their thinking. For these ancient Greek philosophers, knowledge was a homogenous construct that ultimately was representative of the truth. Thus knowledge was truth. Other important challenges to what knowledge is then came in the 17th and 18th centuries when philosophers such as Decartes, Leibnitz, and Locke challenged the ideas of knowledge as faith and developed ideas of knowledge as accurate, provable facts, while other philosophers such as Hegel and Kant defined knowledge as divergent meaning or justified true beliefs. Since the 19th century, many different philosophical schools of thought have emerged, and they have all tried to once again pin down this elusive, yet important knowledge construct. Table 1 summarizes the major perspectives.

The Multifaceted Knowledge Construct

As with many concepts in organizational theory, the existence of duality as discussed by Orlikowski (1992) applies when we examine the knowledge construct. Traditionally researchers have turned to Burrell and Morgan's

(Malhotra, 2000) well-established framework of objective and subjective characterizations, or a more recent approach elaborated on by Schultze and Leidner (2002) is Deetz's four discourses of organizational inquiry to highlight these dualities. In trying to manage knowledge, it is necessary first to understand the binary nature of knowledge—namely, its objective and subjective components (Malhotra, 2000) or consensus/dissensus dimensions (Schultze & Leidner, 2002). Knowledge can exist as an object, in essentially two forms: explicit or documented and formal knowledge—that is, "know-what"—and tacit or experiential—that is, "know-how" (Polyani, 1958, 1966; Nonaka & Takeuchi, 1995; Beckman, 1999). It is well established that while both types of knowledge are important, tacit knowledge is more difficult to identify and thus manage (Malhotra, 2000; Newell, Robertson, Scarbrough, & Swan, 2002). Of equal importance, though perhaps less well defined, knowledge also has a subjective component and can be viewed as an ongoing phenomenon, being shaped by social practices of communities (Boland & Tenkasi, 1995). The objective elements of knowledge can be thought of as primarily having an impact on process, while the subjective elements typically impact innovation. Both effective and efficient processes as well as the functions of supporting and fostering creativity and innovation are key concerns of knowledge management. Thus, we have an interesting duality in knowledge management (Wickramasinghe, 2001) that some have called a

Table 1. Multiple perspective on knowledge (Wickramasinghe & Sharma, 2005)

School of Thought	Basic Ideas on Knowledge	Some Proponents
Positivism	Knowledge is gained from the observation of objective reality.	Comte
Constructivism	Knowledge is constructed in our minds, thus is not objective.	Erlangen School
Critical Theory	Uses knowledge to integrate the tension between reality of society and the real societal function of science.	Habermas, Horkheimer
Critical Rationalism	All knowledge must be open to empirical falsification before it can be accepted.	Popper
Empiricism	Knowledge can be created from experiments, and thus only mathematics and natural sciences can provide secure knowledge.	Locke, Russel
Sociology of Knowledge	Knowledge is a socially constructed reality.	Mannheim, Scheler
Pragmatism	Knowledge represents a local reality based on our experiences.	Dewey

contradiction (Schultze, 1998) and others describe as the *loose-tight* nature of knowledge management (Malhotra, 2000).

The *loose-tight* nature of knowledge management comes to being because of the need to recognize and draw upon several distinct philosophical perspectives, including the Lockean/Leibnitzian stream and the Hegelian/Kantian stream. Models of convergence and compliance representing the *tight* side are grounded in a Lockean/Leibnitzian tradition. Such a perspective views the pursuit of knowledge and its management as necessary to provide the correct solution to a problem or decision, and thus enables organizational effectiveness and efficiencies to ensue (Wickramasinghe, 2005). This in turn leads to the development of models that are essential to support the information processing aspects of knowledge management, most notably by enabling efficiencies of scale and scope and thus supporting the objective view of knowledge management (Malhotra, 2000; Wickramasinghe, 2005). In contrast, the *loose* side provides agility and flexibility in the tradition of a Hegelian/Kantian perspective. Such models recognize the importance of divergence of meaning and the need to support discourse within communities of practice (Boland & Tenkasi, 1995), which is essential to support the "sense-making," subjective view of knowledge management. In terms of knowledge creation then, in order to ensure the creation of a rich, germane, and useful knowledge base, it is prudent to be mindful of these philosophical perspectives that highlight the key dynamics relating to different types of knowledge creation.

MAIN FOCUS: THEORIES ON KNOWLEDGE CREATION

The processes of creating and capturing knowledge, irrespective of the specific philosophical orientation (i.e., Lockean/Leibnitzian versus Hegelian/Kantian), is the central focus then of both the psycho-social and algorithmic theories of knowledge creation. However, to date knowledge creation has tended to be approached from one or the other perspective, rather than a holistic, combined perspective (Wickramasinghe, 2005).

The Psycho-Social Driven Perspective to Knowledge Creation

In this section three well-known psycho-social knowledge creation theories—Nonaka's Knowledge Spiral, and Spender's and Blackler's respective frameworks—are presented. Organizational knowledge is not static;

rather it changes and evolves during the lifetime of an organization (Davenport & Prusak, 1998; Malhotra, 2000). Furthermore, it is possible to change the form of knowledge, that is, to transform existing tacit knowledge into new explicit knowledge and existing explicit knowledge into new tacit knowledge, or to transform the subjective form of knowledge into the objective form of knowledge (Nonaka & Nishiguchi, 2001; Nonaka, 1994).

This process of transforming the form of knowledge, and thus increasing the extant knowledge base as well as the amount and utilization of the knowledge within the organization, is known as the knowledge spiral (Nonaka, 1994). In each of these instances, the overall extant knowledge base of the organization grows to a new, superior knowledge base. According to Nonaka (1994):

1. Tacit-to-tacit knowledge transformation usually occurs through apprenticeship type relations where the teacher or master passes on the skill to the apprentice.
2. Explicit-to-explicit knowledge transformation usually occurs via formal learning of facts.
3. Tacit-to-explicit knowledge transformation usually occurs when there is an articulation of nuances; for example, as in healthcare if a renowned surgeon is questioned as to why he does a particular procedure in a certain manner, by his articulation of the steps the tacit knowledge becomes explicit.
4. Explicit-to-tacit knowledge transformation usually occurs as new explicit knowledge is internalized; it can then be used to broaden, reframe, and extend one's tacit knowledge.

These transformations are often referred to as the modes of socialization, combination, externalization, and internalization, respectively (Nonaka & Nishiguchi, 2001).

The following scenario serves to depict these knowledge transformations in the context of healthcare (Wickramasinghe et al., 2004). Specifically, the scenario outlines the application of the knowledge spiral in the domain of reconstructive orthopedic surgery. Advancing age often leads to the degeneration of a patient's knee and hip joints such that reconstruction of the joint with metal and plastic components is often required. Given the explosion of the population over the age of 65 over the next 40 years, these devices are being implanted in increasingly larger numbers during major surgical procedures in which the degenerative joint surfaces are removed and replaced with the artificial components. There are a multitude of variables in these reconstructions, ranging from the patient characteristics and healthcare status to the implant design and implantation methodologies. The surgeon's tacit knowledge determines the 'best' implant design and combinations and implantation methodologies that are used for each particular patient. The examination of the clinical results leads to the explicit knowledge that determines if those choices are appropriate for each patient population.

However, the examination of the results of these interventions has been limited at the very least to just a few of the thousands of clinical data points and rarely to more than one surgeon or one clinical site. Moreover, at each clinical site, the data of interest is often housed in divergent databases from administrative, clinical, financial, imaging, and laboratory sources. The complete and accurate examination of the clinical results of joint replacement requires an examination of each of these data sets for the relationships that may exist within and across databases. Post-operative and regular radiographs of these implanted devices are used by clinicians to determine if the implant methodologies, such as device alignment and bone-implant interface, are appropriate. Migration of the implant within the host bone or wearing of the plastic component can be visualized on the radiographs and is indicative of impending failure of the component. Combinations of the various data sources—that is, *combinations of explicit knowledge*—will assist with the handling of failures and complications, and offer the clinicians the opportunity to develop solutions to problems as or even before the problems develop into patient symptoms—that is, *increase the existing knowledge base*. The knowledge transformations of the knowledge spiral from *extant explicit and tacit knowledge* to the creation of new explicit and tacit will assist in the search of clinical perfection and ultimately lead to improved clinical outcomes and increased healthcare value. Thus, in this one simple scenario from healthcare, all four of Nonaka's knowledge transformations are being effected.

Integral to this changing of knowledge through the knowledge spiral is that new knowledge is created (Nonaka, 1994); this can bring many benefits to organizations, as seen in the above scenario of the orthopedic reconstruction of knee and hip joints. Specifically, in today's knowledge-centric economy, processes that effect a positive change to the existing knowledge base of the organization and facilitate better use of the organization's intellectual capital, as the knowledge spiral does, are of paramount importance. It is noteworthy that while the knowledge spiral is well discussed in the literature as a cornerstone in knowledge creation, few frameworks, if any, exist on how to actualize the transformations of the knowledge spiral as evidenced by extensive literature review studies (Schultze & Leidner, 2002; Alavi & Leidner, 2001).

Two other primarily people-driven theories that focus on knowledge creation as a central theme are Spender's and Blackler's respective frameworks (Newell et al., 2002). Spender draws a distinction between individual knowledge and social knowledge, each of which he claims can be implicit or explicit (Newell et al., 2002; Spender, 1998). From this framework we can see that Spender's definition of implicit knowledge corresponds to Nonaka's tacit knowledge. However, unlike Spender, Nonaka does not differentiate between individual and social dimensions of knowledge; rather he just focuses on the nature and types of the knowledge itself. In contrast, Blackler (Newell et al., 2002; Blackler, 1995) views knowledge creation from an organizational perspective, noting that knowledge can exist as encoded, embedded, embodied, encultured, and/or embrained. In addition, Blackler emphasized that for different organizational types, different types of knowledge predominate and highlighted the connection between knowledge and organizational processes (Newell et al., 2002; Blackler, 1995).

Blackler's types of knowledge can be thought of in terms of spanning a continuum of tacit (implicit) through to explicit, with embrained being predominantly tacit (implicit) and encoded being predominantly explicit, while embedded, embodied, and encultured types of knowledge exhibit varying degrees of a tacit (implicit)/explicit combination. In other words, Blackler takes a more integral calculus perspective to the types of knowledge. An integrated view of all the three frameworks is depicted in Figure 3. What is important to note here is that this integrated view is not in conflict with any of the philosophical perspectives discussed earlier. This means that the existence of tacit and explicit knowledge, and more importantly the knowledge spiral itself, the most general of the three psycho-social frameworks, is relevant to both the Lokean/Leibnitzian and Hegelian/Kantian perspectives, as well as the other philosophical perspectives identified in Table 1. One key benefit of such an integrated view (as in Figure 3) is that it shows the interrelationships among these three frameworks and how their respective views of knowledge map to each other.

Specifically, from Figure 3 we can see that Spender's and Blackler's perspectives complement Nonaka's conceptualization of knowledge creation and more importantly do not contradict his thesis of the knowledge spiral wherein the extant knowledge base is continually being expanded to a new knowledge base, be it tacit/explicit (in Nonaka's terminology), implicit/explicit (in Spender's terminology), or embrained/encultured/embodied/embedded/encoded (in Blackler's terminology). What is important to underscore here is that these three frameworks take a primarily people-oriented perspective of knowledge creation.

Figure 3. People-driven knowledge creation grid/map

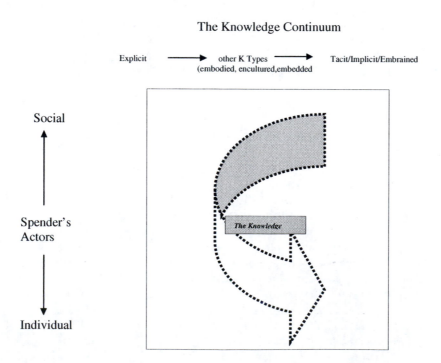

The Algorithmic Perspective to Knowledge Creation

In contrast to the above, primarily people-oriented frameworks pertaining to knowledge creation, knowledge discovery in databases (KDD), and more specifically data mining, approaches knowledge creation from a primarily technology-driven perspective. In particular, the KDD process focuses on how data is transformed into knowledge by identifying valid, novel, potentially useful, and ultimately understandable patterns in data (Fayyad, Piatetsky-Shapiro, & Smyth, 1996; Adriaans & Zantinge, 1996; Becerra-Fernandez, 2001; Chung & Gray, 1999). KDD is primarily used on data sets for creating knowledge through model building, or by finding patterns and relationships in data using various techniques drawn from computer science, statistics, and mathematics as illustrated in Figure 4 (Cabena, Hadjinian, Stadler, Verhees, & Zanasi, 1998).

From an application perspective, data mining and KDD are often used interchangeably. Figure 5 presents a generic representation of a typical knowledge discovery process. Knowledge creation in a KDD project usually starts with data collection or data selection, covering almost all steps (described above and illustrated in Figure 5) in the KDD process. As depicted in Figure 5, the first three steps of the KDD process (i.e., selection, preprocessing, and transformation) are considered exploratory data mining, whereas the last two steps (i.e., data mining and interpretation/evaluation) in the KDD process are considered predictive data mining.

The primary tasks of data mining in practice tend to be description and prediction. Description focuses on find-

Figure 4. Key techniques involved in data mining (adapted from Wickramasinghe et al., 2004)

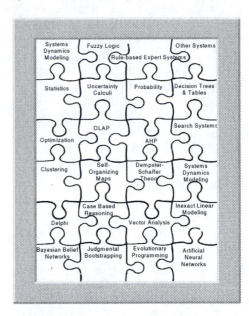

ing human-interpretable patterns describing the data, while prediction involves using some observations or attributes to predict unknown or future values of other attributes of interest. The relative importance of description and prediction for particular data mining applications can vary considerably. The descriptive and predictive tasks are carried out by applying different machine learning, artificial intelligence, and statistical algorithms. Irre-

Figure 5. Integrated view of the knowledge discovery process (adapted from Wickramasinghe et al., 2004)

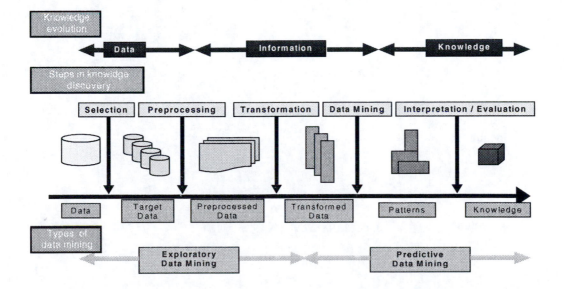

spective of the type of data mining, knowledge creation is the ultimate goal.

Figure 5 captures all the major aspects connected with data mining and the KDD process, and emphasizes the integral role of the KDD process to knowledge creation showing how data is transformed into knowledge via information. However, unlike the frameworks discussed earlier, where knowledge is subdivided into various constituent parts, it is important to note that typically in the KDD process, the knowledge component itself is treated as a homogeneous block.

FUTURE TRENDS

"Land, labor, and capital now pale in comparison to knowledge as the critical asset to be managed in today's knowledge economy." Peter F. Drucker

The nations that lead the world into the next century will be those who can shift from being industrial economies, based upon the production of manufactured goods, to those that possess the capacity to produce and utilize knowledge successfully. The focus of the many nations' economy has shifted first to information-intensive industries such as financial services and logistics, and now toward innovation-driven industries, such as computer software and biotechnology, where competitive advantage lies mostly in the innovative use of human resources. This represents a move from an era of standardization to customization, to an era of innovation where knowledge, its creation and management hold the key to success (Bukowitz, & Williams, 1997; Drucker, 1993, 1999).

In today's knowledge economy, it is indeed vital to begin to take a holistic approach to knowledge creation, and thus combine the people-driven and technology-driven theories of knowledge creation into an integrative, all-encompassing meta framework in order to truly capture the subtle nuances and complexities of knowledge creation (refer to Figure 6). The two significant ways to create knowledge are: (1) synthesis of new knowledge through socialization with experts—a primarily people-dominated perspective, and (2) discovery by finding interesting patterns through observation and a combination of explicit data—a primarily technology-driven perspective (Becerra-Fernandez et al., 2004). By incorporating a people perspective into data mining, it becomes truly possible to support both these knowledge creation scenarios and thereby realize the synergistic effect of the respective strengths of these approaches in enabling superior knowledge creation to ensue.

Figure 6. Holistic view of knowledge creation

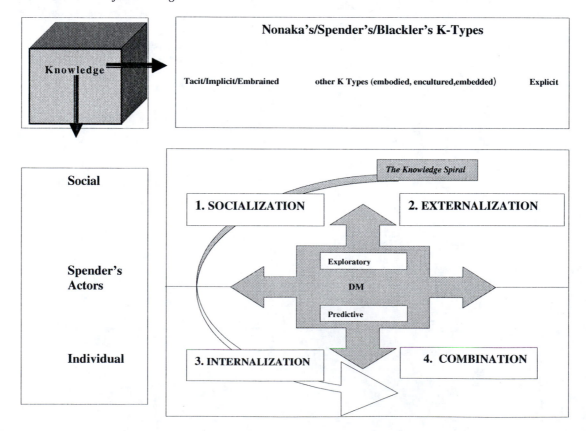

DISCUSSION AND CONCLUSION

The preceding discussions have highlighted the key knowledge creation theories that focus on either a people-driven perspective or a technology-driven perspective. Irrespective of which knowledge creation perspective is adopted, it is important for effective knowledge creation to firstly realize that knowledge is a multifaceted construct and knowledge management is a multidimensional approach (consequently the individual steps of knowledge management also should exhibit this multidimensionality).

Given the importance of knowledge management in today's knowledge economy, it is indeed useful to combine the people-driven and technology-driven perspectives into an integrative, all-encompassing meta framework in order to truly capture the subtle nuances and complexities of knowledge creation, and hence realize the synergistic effect of the respective strengths of these frameworks. For example, from the KDD process perspective, we can see how knowledge is created from data, while from the people-driven perspective, we can see the various types of knowledge. Furthermore, such an integrative meta framework or holistic perspective to knowledge creation provides a broader scope and thus better accommodates the different possible knowledge creation scenarios. This is particularly important in today's competitive business environment, as KM is becoming more prevalent in organizations irrespective of the organizational structures or industry. For example, more structured organizations would be more likely to use explicit knowledge more than tacit knowledge, while dynamic and informal organizations are likely to use more tacit/implicit knowledge (Spiegler, 2003; Wickramasinghe & Mills, 2001). Similarly, technologically savvy organizations would be more likely to create knowledge (and consequently achieve a strategic advantage) by using the KDD process.

Thus, knowledge creation involves a people dimension, technology dimension, and the processes that link the people and technology. In addition, knowledge creation plays a catalytic role in effecting knowledge management. Hence, the need for an integrative meta framework and holistic perspective that serves to bring these two key dimensions together—that is, an amalgamation of data mining with the knowledge spiral.

ACKNOWLEDGMENT

The author wishes to acknowledge Adam Fadlalla for his suggestions and contribution in earlier versions and the development of these ideas.

REFERENCES

Adriaans, P., & Zantinge, D. (1996). *Data mining.* Addison-Wesley.

Alavi, M., & Leidner, D. (2001). Review: Knowledge management and knowledge management systems: Conceptual foundations and research issues. *MIS Quarterly, 25*(1), 107-136.

Becerra-Fernandez, I. et al. (2004). *Knowledge management.* Upper Saddle River, NJ: Prentice-Hall.

Becerra-Fernandez, I., & Sabherwal, R. (2001). Organizational knowledge management: A contingency perspective. *Journal of Management Information Systems, 18*(1), 23-55.

Beckman, T. (1999). The current state of knowledge. In Liebowitz (Ed.), *Knowledge management handbook.* London: CRC Press.

Blackler, F. (1995). Knowledge, knowledge work and organizations—an overview and interpretation. *Organization Studies, 16*(6), 1021-1046.

Boland, R., & Tenkasi, R. (1995). Perspective making, perspective taking. *Organizational Science, 6,* 350-372.

Bukowitz, W.R., & Williams, R.L. (1997). New metrics for hidden assets. *Journal of Strategic Performance Measurement, 1*(1), 12-18.

Cabena, P., Hadjinian, P., Stadler, R., Verhees, J., & Zanasi, A. (1998). *Discovering data mining from concept to implementation.* Englewood Cliffs, NJ: Prentice-Hall.

Chung, M., & Gray, P. (1999). Special section: Data mining. *Journal of Management Information Systems, 16*(1), 11-16.

Davenport, T., & Grover, V. (2001). Knowledge management. *Journal of Management Information Systems, 18*(1), 3-4.

Davenport, T., & Prusak, L. (1998). *Working knowledge.* Boston: Harvard Business School Press.

Drucker, P. (1999). Beyond the information revolution. *The Atlantic Monthly,* (October), 47-57.

Drucker, P. (1993). *Post-capitalist society.* New York: Harper Collins.

Fayyad, Piatetsky-Shapiro, Smyth. (1996). From data mining to knowledge discovery: An overview. In Fayyad, Piatetsky-Shapiro, Smyth, & Uthurusamy (Eds.), *Advances in knowledge discovery and data mining.* Menlo Park, CA: AAAI Press/MIT Press.

Malhotra, Y. (2000). Knowledge management and new organizational form. In Y. Malhotra (Ed.), *Knowledge management and virtual organizations*. Hershey, PA: Idea Group Publishing.

Markus, L. (2001). Toward a theory of knowledge reuse: Types of knowledge reuse situations and factors in reuse success. *Journal of Management Information Systems, 18*(1), 57-93.

Newell, S., Robertson, M., Scarbrough, H., & Swan, J. (2002). *Managing knowledge work*. New York: Palgrave.

Nonaka, I. (1994). A dynamic theory of organizational knowledge creation. *Organizational Science, 5,* 14-37.

Nonaka, I., & Nishiguchi, T. (2001). *Knowledge emergence*. Oxford: Oxford University Press.

Nonaka, I., & Takeuchi, H. (1995). *The knowledge-creating company: How Japanese companies create the dynamics of innovation*. Oxford: Oxford University Press.

Orlkowski, W. (1992). The duality of technology: Rethinking the concept of technology in organizations. *Organization Science, 3*(3), 398-427.

Parent, M., Gallupe, R., Salisbury, W., & Handelman, J. (2000). Knowledge creation in focus groups: Can group technology help? *Information & Management, 38,* 47-58.

Polyani, M. (1958). *Personal knowledge: Towards a post-critical philosophy*. Chicago: University Press Chicago.

Polyani, M. (1966). *The tacit dimension*. London: Routledge & Kegan Paul.

Schultze, U. (1998, December). Investigating the contradictions in knowledge management. *Proceedings of IFIP*.

Schultze, U., & Leidner, D. (2002). Studying knowledge management in information systems research: Discourses and theoretical assumptions. *MIS Quarterly, 26*(3), 212-242.

Spender, J. (1998). Pluralist epistemology and the knowledge-based theory of the firm. *Organization, 5*(2), 233-256.

Spiegler, I. (2003). Technology and knowledge: Bridging a "generating gap." *Information and Management, 40,* 533-539.

Swan, J., Scarbrough, H., & Preston, J. (1999). Knowledge management—the next fad to forget people? *Proceedings of the 7th European Conference on Information Systems*.

Wickramasinghe, N., & Mills, G. (2001). MARS: The electronic medical record system. The core of the Kaiser galaxy. *International Journal of Healthcare Technology Management, 3*(5/6), 406-423.

Wickramasinghe, N. et al. (2004). Realizing the value proposition for healthcare by incorporating KM strategies and data mining techniques with use of information communication technologies. *International Journal of Healthcare Technology and Management,* forthcoming.

Wickramasinghe, N. (2005). The phenomenon of duality: A key to facilitate the transition from knowledge management to wisdom for inquiring organizations. In J. Courtney, J. Haynes, & D. Paradice (Eds.), *Inquiring organizations: Moving from knowledge management to wisdom*. Hershey, PA: Idea Group Publishing.

Wickramaisnghe, N., & Sharma, S. (2005). *The fundamentals of knowledge management*. Upper Saddle River, NJ: Prentice-Hall.

KEY TERMS

Data Mining and KDD Process: Knowledge discovery in databases (KDD) (and more specifically data mining) approaches knowledge creation from a primarily technology-driven perspective. In particular, the KDD process focuses on how data is transformed into knowledge by identifying valid, novel, potentially useful, and ultimately understandable patterns in data (Fayyad et al., 1996). From an application perspective, data mining and KDD are often used interchangeably.

Explicit Knowledge: Formal knowledge—that is, "know-what" represents knowledge that is well established and documented.

Hegelian/Kantian Perspective of Knowledge Management: Refers to the subjective component of knowledge management; can be viewed as an ongoing phenomenon, being shaped by social practices of communities and encouraging discourse and divergence of meaning, and the recognition of the existence of multiple approaches.

Knowledge Creation: The first step in the KM process (the other steps include represent/store, access/use/reuse, disseminate/transfer); impacts the other consequent steps.

Knowledge Spiral: Developed by Nonaka, refers to the process of transforming the form of knowledge, and thus increasing the extant knowledge base as well as the amount and utilization of the knowledge within the organization. The key transformations effected by the knowledge spiral include socialization (tacit-tacit knowledge transfer), combination (explicit-explicit knowledge transfer), internalization (explicit-tacit knowledge transfer), and externalization (tacit-explicit knowledge transfer).

Lockean/Leibnitzian Perspective of Knowledge Management: Refers to the objective aspects of knowledge management, where the need for knowledge is to improve effectiveness and efficiencies and the search for the correct approach.

Tacit Knowledge: Experiential knowledge—that is, "know-how" represents knowledge that is gained through experience and through doing.

Knowledge Flow

Vincent M. Ribière
New York Institute of Technology, USA

Juan A. Román
National Aeronautics and Space Administration (NASA), USA

INTRODUCTION

Various models and frameworks have been used to represent the flows of knowledge in an organization. The first and most popular of these remains the spiraling SECI (socialization, externalization, combination, internalization) model presented by Nonaka and Konno (1998), Nonaka and Takeuchi (1995), and Nonaka and Toyama (2003), which presents the various knowledge interactions and creations between tacit and explicit knowledge. Knowledge flows can also be represented and assessed through the knowledge life cycle.

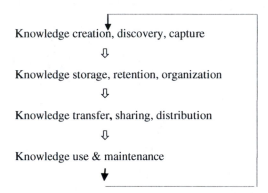

Knowledge creation, discovery, capture

⇩

Knowledge storage, retention, organization

⇩

Knowledge transfer, sharing, distribution

⇩

Knowledge use & maintenance

In this article, we describe knowledge flows through a third lens that is based on how people obtain and/or share the knowledge that they need to perform their work. We found a certain agreement on a typology defining two main strategies for knowledge flows: *codification* vs. *personalization*.

BACKGROUND

The Codification Strategy

The codification strategy is intended to collect, codify, and disseminate information. It relies heavily on information technology. One of the benefits of the codification approach is the reuse of knowledge. According to Davenport and Prusak (1998, p. 68):

The aim of codification is to put organizational knowledge into a form that makes it accessible to those who need it. It literally turns knowledge into a code (though not necessarily a computer code) to make it as organized, explicit, portable, and easy to understand as possible.

The codification strategy has been named and described in different ways by various authors. In 1999, Hansen, Nohria, and Tierney published an article in the *Harvard Business Review* titled "What's your strategy for managing knowledge?" In this article, they describe how different companies focus on different practices and strategies in order to manage their knowledge. The first approach is called codification, where the strategy centers on the computer:

Knowledge is codified and stored in databases, where it can be accessed and used easily by anyone in the company. Knowledge is codified using a *people-to-documents approach*: it is extracted from the person who developed it, made independent of that person, and reused for various purposes. (Hansen et al., p. 108)

Hansen et al. illustrate this strategy with the case of two consulting companies, Anderson Consulting and Ernst & Young, which adopted this strategy due to the fact that their activity mainly focused on implementation projects rather than on purely innovative projects. Stephen Denning (1998), former CKO of the World Bank, describes two different ways of sharing knowledge: the *collecting dimension* and the *connecting dimension*. The collecting dimension is described as the "capturing and disseminating of know-how through information and communication technologies aimed at codifying, storing and retrieving content, which in principle is continuously updated through computer networks" (Denning, p. 10).

Know-Net (2000), a "Leading Edge Total Knowledge Management [KM] Solution" developed by an European consortium, incorporates such an approach. Know-Net calls it the *product view* and the *process view*. The product-view approach is described as focusing on products and artifacts containing and representing knowledge. This implies the management of documents, and their creation, storage, and reuse in computer-based corporate memories. The competitive strategy is to exploit organized, standardized, and reusable knowledge.

Natarajan and Shekhar (2000) present two models, the *transformation model* and the *independent model*, that clearly comply with the previous descriptions. The transformation model deals with explicit knowledge, relying mainly on document capture, structured databases, knowledge-extraction tools, text mining, and search and retrieval applications.

A Lotus white paper, describing KM and collaborative technologies, categorizes KM applications as *distributive* or *collaborative*: "*Distributive applications* maintain a repository of explicitly encoded knowledge created and managed for subsequent distribution to knowledge consumers within or outside the organization" (Zack & Michael, 1996).

As we can observe, all these descriptions and definitions are very closely related in depicting a codification strategy. For the remainder of this article, we will adopt the codification naming in order to refer to the type of approaches previously described.

The Personalization Strategy

The personalization strategy focuses on developing networks for linking people so that tacit knowledge can be shared. It invests moderately in IT. This approach corresponds to the Nonaka and Takeuchi (1995), and Nonaka and Toyama (2003) personalization phase of the SECI model where knowledge flow and creation happen during an exchange of tacit knowledge. The authors, who previously defined the codification strategy, also provide their own definition of the personalization strategy. Hansen et al. (1999) named it personalization. It focuses on dialogue between individuals as opposed to knowledge in a database: "Knowledge that has not been codified—and probably couldn't be—is transferred in brainstorming sessions and one-on-one conversations" (Hansen et al.). An investment is made in building networks of people, where knowledge is shared not only face-to-face, but also over the telephone, by e-mail, and via videoconference. Hansen et al. illustrate this strategy with the case of three consulting companies, McKinsey, BCG, and Bain, which adopted this strategy since they mainly focus on customized and

Figure 1. The codification strategy

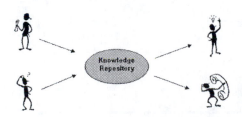

innovative projects. Stephen Denning (1998) defines this strategy as the connecting dimension:

It involves linking people who need to know with those who do know, and so developing new capabilities for nurturing knowledge and acting knowledgeably. For example, help desks and advisory services (small teams of experts whom one can call to obtain specific know-how or help in solving a problem) can be very effective in the short term in connecting people and getting quick answers to questions, thus accelerating cycle time, and adding value for clients.

Know-Net (2000) defines this as the process-centered approach, which focuses on knowledge management as a social communication process. It facilitates conversations to exchange knowledge and can be improved by various aspects and tools of collaboration and cooperation support.

Natarajan and Shekhar (2000) use the independent-model designation to describe the tools that attempt to find solutions for the sharing of tacit knowledge. They list a number of technologies that could be used to facilitate the sharing of knowledge. Among them are technologies such as Web-based training used for skill-enhancement programs. Yellow pages, Web crawlers, broadcast applications, communities of practice (using expert locators, collaboration, virtual work-space applications), and the sharing of best practices (using knowledge repositories and discussion-group-based applications) are also examples of knowledge sharing.

Zack and Michael (1996) talk about the collaborative approach that focuses primarily on supporting interaction and collaboration among people holding tacit knowledge. They highlight that:

in contrast to distributive applications, the repository associated with collaborative applications is a by-product of the interaction, rather than the primary focus of the application. This repository of messages is dynamic and its content emergent. The ability to capture and structure emergent communication within a repository provides a more valuable, enduring, and leverageable knowledge by-product than the personal notes or memories of a traditional conversation or meeting. Collaboration technologies, therefore, can support a well-structured repository of explicit knowledge while enabling the management of tacit knowledge. The knowledge repository represents a valuable means to manage the explication, sharing, combination, application, and renewal of organizational knowledge. (Zack & Michael).

Figure 2. The personalization strategy

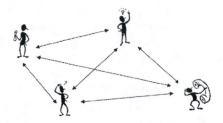

Once again, we can observe that all of these descriptions and definitions are very similar and depict the same type of processes and tools. Personalization approaches facilitate the person-to-person knowledge transfer. For the rest of this article, we will adopt the personalization designation in order to refer to the type of approaches previously described.

Codification vs. Personalization

What is the best strategy for managing knowledge? Hansen et al. (1999) noted that effective organizations excel by primarily emphasizing one of the strategies and using the other in a supporting role. They postulate that companies trying to excel at both strategies risk failing at both. They refer to a 20-80 split between codification and personalization. This proposal raised much discussion in the literature (Koenig, 2004) and in the HBR forum referring to this article (HBR Forum, 1999). Denning (1998) mentioned that organizations that focus entirely on a personalization approach, with little or no attempt at codification, can be very inefficient.

In order to select an adoption strategy, Tiwana (2002) designed a checklist based on the recommendations of Hansen et al. They recommended examining the company's competitive strategy (What value do customers expect from the company? How does the knowledge that resides in the company add value to customers' goals?). Once the competitive strategy is clear, three additional questions might be investigated.

• Does your company offer standardized or customized products?

• Does your company have a mature or innovative product?

• Do people rely on explicit or tacit knowledge to solve problems?

Companies having standardized products and/or mature products might want to focus on a codification approach. In contrast, companies having customized and/or innovative products might want to focus on a personalization approach. People relying on explicit knowledge will

also be more disposed to adopt a codification approach. Furthermore, recent research highlights the critical role that organizational culture and interpersonal trust have in the selection of these two KM strategies (Ribière, 2001; Ribière & Tuggle, 2005; Román-Velázquez, 2004; Román, Ribière, & Stankosky, 2004). They demonstrated that the success of a KM strategy might be directly impacted by the type of organizational culture present in the organization.

The next section of this article presents the findings of an empirical study of U.S. organizations, covering the government, for-profit, and nonprofit sectors. The study was conducted to characterize the strategic approach for knowledge flow within the different sectors.

Empirical Study

The data analyzed in this article were collected during two independent research studies performed by Ribière (2001) and Román-Velázquez (2004), which evaluated the KM strategy (codification and personalization) that employees predominantly use to facilitate the flow of knowledge throughout the organization. Ribière's research developed a list of 23 items that were theoretically divided into two groups: one for codification and one for personalization. However, Román-Velázquez modified and reduced the list to 20 items based on an extensive literature review (Hoyt, 2001; Kemp, Pudlatz, Perez, & Munoz Ortega, 2001; Marwick, 2001; McKellar & Haimila, 2002; Shand, 1998) and after detailed conversations with expert practitioners in the field of KM, human resources, experiment design, and information technology (Boswell, 2002; Naus, 2002; Reed, 2002; Rhoads, 2002). In addition, the model was validated during previous research and found to be accurate and reliable (Román-Velázquez; Román-Velázquez et al., 2004).

For this study, the data were concatenated, creating a new data set with 431 respondents (N = 431) as described in Table 1. A total of 13 indicator variables were retained for analysis. The variables were evaluated using a seven-point scale where 1 is *Very Minimum Extent*, 7 is *Very Great Extent*, and 0 is assigned to responses for *Don't Know* and *Don't Exist*. This study employed inferential statistical analysis, using the data collected

Table 1. Responses by category

	Frequency	Percent	Cumulative Percent
For-profit	66	15.3	15.3
Government	313	72.6	87.9
Non-profit	52	12.1	100.0
Total	431	100.0	

Table 2. Descriptive statistics for the technologies, support tools, and processes utilized throughout the organization

Technologies, Support Tools & Processes[1]	C / P	Mean	Standard Deviation
Intranet/Extranet	C	5.74	1.55
Phone calls/Teleconferencing	P	5.40	1.81
Search Engines/Information Retrieval System	C	4.77	1.98
Working Groups/Communities of Practice	P	4.26	2.02
Document Management/Content Management	C	4.05	2.05
Web-based Training/e-Learning	C	3.97	1.92
Mentoring/Tutoring	P	3.87	2.04
Videoconferencing	P	3.77	2.04
Benchmarking/Best Practices	C	3.69	2.00
Multimedia Repositories	C	3.45	2.09
Data Mining/Knowledge Discovery Tools	C	3.30	2.11
Expertise Locator/Directory of Expertise	P	3.19	2.23
Story Telling	P	3.14	2.13

N = 431   C: codification -   P: personalization

from respondents to make estimates about a much larger population. The confidence levels and confidence intervals are two key components of the sampling error estimates and refer to the probability that our estimations are correct (Babbie, 1998; Sekaran, 1992). Using N = 431 as the responses collected and a 95% confidence level, the confidence interval is calculated to be ± 4.72.

The data analysis revealed mean score values for the 13 indicator variables ranging from 5.47 to 3.14 as shown in Table 2. Their mean score provides an indication of their usage and popularity. The table can be analyzed using two perspectives: by the absolute mean score compared to all items, and by considering the KM strategy that each item represents independently.

A closer inspection of the results showed that a total of five items had high scores: mean scores above 4.0 (midpoint). They were intranets and extranets, phone calls and teleconferencing, search engines and information-retrieval systems, working groups and communities of practice, and document management and content management. The frequent use of these technologies and tools by employees increases the flow of knowledge within the organization, therefore having a greater impact than all the others.

Intranet/extranet scores at the top of the tools usage for a codification strategy. It is not surprising since intranets and extranets are often the first technology that organizations deploy in order to facilitate intra- and extraorganizational collaboration and knowledge ex-change. It is the core component necessary to deploy a portal. Intranet/extranet is followed by search engines and information-retrieval systems, and document management and content management. The easy retrieval and archival of documents and content remain core functionalities of the codification approach that increase the velocity of codified knowledge flow. These technologies within the codification strategy can be categorized as enabling the sharing of knowledge from one to many or many to many, and were utilized by the majority of the respondents within the government, for-profit, and non-profit sectors.

Regarding the personalization strategy, phone calls and teleconferencing were found to be the most utilized ways to share tacit knowledge between people within all the sectors included in the study. This finding can be explained by the fact that this technology has been available for decades and knowledge workers are familiar with them. Their use is often the employees' first and instinctive reaction when looking for help or advice. In second position are working groups and communities of practice. During the past years, a strong emphasis on communities and their benefits has emerged in the KM literature. This success is due to the fact that their implementation is simple, and knowledge workers perceived them as a good way to learn and connect with other knowledge workers. Furthermore, organizations that have silos utilized them as a good way to breach boundaries across silos and to foster collaboration and knowledge

Figure 3. Codification and personalization factors as dominant strategic approaches for the flow of knowledge within the organization

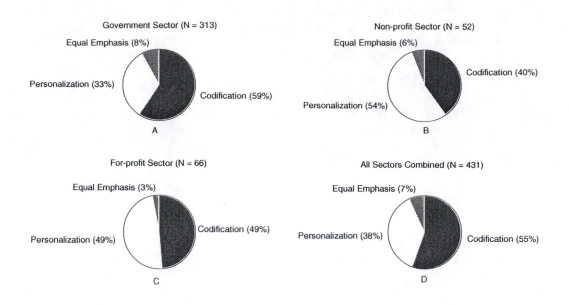

exchanges. Mentoring and tutoring tools take the third position of the personalization strategy. One way to pass on or share the tacit knowledge that older employees have acquired throughout their career is to mentor and/or tutor new or younger colleagues. Once again, this practice is not new, but it remains one of the most popular and the most efficient way to transfer tacit knowledge. Both communities and mentoring and tutoring are support tools and processes that are being widely used within the government sector to address the potential human-capital crisis that is looming with the exodus of baby boomers from the workforce. As of fiscal year 2002, approximately 71% of the government's permanent employees will be eligible for either regular or early retirement by 2010. Of those eligible, 40% are expected to do so (The President's Management Agenda Fiscal Year 2002).

A more in-depth analysis of the data was performed using the validated knowledge-flow model in order to identify the dominant KM strategy within the different sectors under consideration. The analysis reveals that codification is the dominant strategy employed by 59.4% (N = 186) of respondents in the government sector, with 32.6% (N = 102) utilizing a dominant personalization strategy. Only 8% (N = 25) utilized both in a balanced manner (equal emphasis) as shown in Figure 3A. This outcome could be an indication that the large numbers of rules and statutory regulations that guide and define the nature of government business is a major factor driving the dominant KM strategy of codification. However,

Figure 3B shows the nonprofit sector having a nearly opposite strategic approach, with 53.8% (N = 28) of respondents utilizing a dominant personalization strategy and 40.4% (N = 21) a dominant codification strategy. It also shows a reduction to 6% in the number of respondents that are utilizing a balance codification and personalization strategies. The results provide evidence that the nonprofit sector leverages more on the flow of knowledge between people than on documents. This characteristic could be due to the business nature of most nonprofit organizations. On the other hand, the data analyzed in the for-profit sector show the respondents are equally divided in their selection of a dominant KM strategy. Figure 3C shows that a total of 49% of respondents utilize a dominant codification strategy with the same number utilizing a dominant personalization strategy. In addition, only 3% of respondents employ a completely balanced approach utilizing both dominant strategies. This balanced approach is the lowest of all the three sectors. Lastly, Figure 3D illustrates all sectors combined.

Based on the above results, if we were to describe the KM strategic approach for knowledge flow as a continuum, we would have the government sector at one end and the nonprofit sector at the other end. The for-profit sector would fall approximately in the middle of the continuum. Moreover, it demonstrates that the sectors are considerably different from each other. This highlights the fact that many organizations have found that both codification and personalization approaches are needed for an effective knowledge-management effort. The emphasis of one approach over the other or its balance depends heavily on the organization's overall strategy. The correct emphasis depends on the manner in which the organization serves its clients and stakeholders, the economics of its business (e.g., for-profit, nonprofit, government), the human capital it possesses, and the culture of the organization. The above results demonstrate that the types of technologies, tools, and processes that CKOs, KM architects, KM managers, and other decision makers should select for implementation need to be carefully evaluated based on the many influencing factors identified above in order to achieve their expected benefits.

FUTURE TRENDS

KM practices and technologies are constantly evolving. The Gartner (2003) research group published a knowledge-management "hype cycle" that describes the evolution and maturity of KM technologies. During the past years, an emergence of synchronous collaborative technologies has emerged, and some have been rapidly adopted to facilitate knowledge flows. As an example, instant messaging is increasingly used for business purposes in order to facilitate presence awareness and knowledge exchange. Portal solutions like Microsoft Sharepoint 2003 already embed this capability. When employees access information on the portal (document, electronic discussion posting, expertise profile, etc.), they can see if the author is currently logged in and can eventually contact him or her by instant messaging or by e-mail. New wireless devices will also provide new ways to facilitate knowledge exchange. New tools, practices, and technologies will provide new knowledge-flow channels, but the underlying knowledge-flow strategies (codification and personalization) will remain the same. We believe that companies will attach more and more importance to personalization strategies since it can be viewed by some companies and authors (Wick, 2000) as a logical evolution from the codification approach.

CONCLUSION

It is important to remember that the codification and personalization KM strategies are not incompatible. Companies must use both strategies simultaneously, but might need to put more emphasis on one of these strategies than on the other. Hansen et al. (1999) suggested a 20-80 split between these two strategies, but our empirical study demonstrated that in practice, there is not such a clear distinction between the emphasis associated to each.

Companies interested in launching a KM initiative or companies working on taking their KM initiative to the next level need to asses what strategy will best fit their needs and which will be the most likely to succeed based on their organizational culture. Focusing on the right knowledge-flow strategy is one of the keys to a successful KM journey.

REFERENCES

Babbie, E. (1998). *The practice of social research* (8th ed.). Belmont, CA: Wadsworth Publishing Company.

Boswell, H. W. (2002). KM survey suggestions. In J. Roman (Ed.). Greenbelt, MD: COMPANY.

Davenport, T., & Prusak, L. (1998). *Working knowledge: How organizations manage what they know.* Boston: Harvard Business School Press.

Denning, S. (1998). *What is knowledge management?* Retrieved from *http://www.worldbank.org/ks/index.html*

Encyclopedia Britannica Ready Reference (10th ed.) [CD]. (2001). Encyclopaedia Britannica, Inc.

Gartner. (2003). *Hype cycle for knowledge management* (No. R-20-0010).

Hansen, M. T., Nohria, N., & Tierney, T. (1999). What's your strategy for managing knowledge? *Harvard Business Review*, 106-116.

HBR Forum. (1999). Retrieved January 2001 from *http://www.hbr.org*

Hoyt, B. J. (2001). *KM technology & tools listing.* Retrieved October 15, 2004, from *http://www.kmnews.com*

Kemp, J., Pudlatz, M., Perez, P., & Munoz Ortega, A. (2001). *KM technologies and tools.* European KM Forum.

Know-Net. (2000). *The approach.* Retrieved from *http://www.know-net.org*

Koenig, M. E. D. (2004). Knowledge management strategy: Codification versus personalization (A false dichotomy). In M. E. D. Koenig & K. T. Srikantaiah (Eds.), *Knowledge management lessons learned: What works and what doesn't?* Medford, NJ: Information Today.

Marwick, A. D. (2001). Knowledge management technology. *IBM Systems Journal, 40*(4), 814-830.

McKellar, H., & Haimila, S. (Eds.). (2002). *KMWorld buyers' guide* (Fall 2002 ed.). Medford, NJ: KM World & Information Today.

Merriam-Webster Dictionary & Thesaurus. (Version 2.6) [CD]. (2002). Merriam-Webster's, Inc.

Natarajan, G., & Shekhar, S. (2000). *Knowledge management: Enabling business growth.* New Delhi, India: Tata McGraw-Hill.

Naus, S. A. (2002). *KM server suggestions.* Greenbelt, MD.

Nonaka, I., & Konno, N. (1998). The concept of Ba: Building a foundation for knowledge creation. *California Management Review, 40*(3), 40-54.

Nonaka, I., & Takeuchi, H. (1995). *The knowledge creating company.* Oxford: Oxford University Press.

Nonaka, I., & Toyama, R. (2003). The knowledge-creation theory revisited: Knowledge creation as a synthesizing process. *Knowledge Management Research and Practice, 1*(1), 2-10.

Pollock, N. (2002). *Knowledge management and information technology encyclopedia* (1st ed.). Fort Belvoir, VA: Defense Acquisition University Press.

Reed, D. E. (2002). KM survey suggestions. In J. Roman (Ed.), Greenbelt, MD.

Rhoads, E. (2002). *KM survey suggestions.* Washington, DC.

Ribière, V. (2001). *Assessing knowledge management initiative successes as a function of organizational culture.* DSc dissertation, George Washington University, Washington, DC.

Ribière, V., & Tuggle, F. D. (2005). The role of organizational trust in knowledge management tools and technology use and success. *International Journal of Knowledge Management, 1*(1).

Román-Velázquez, J. A. (2004). *An empirical study of knowledge management in the government and nonprofit sectors: Organizational culture composition and its relationship with knowledge management success and the approach for knowledge flow.* DSc dissertation, George Washington University, Washington, DC.

Román-Velázquez, J. A., Ribière, V., & Stankosky, M. A. (2004). Organizational culture types and their relationship with knowledge flow and knowledge management success: An empirical study in the US government and nonprofit sectors. *Journal of Information & Knowledge Management (JIKM), 3*(2).

Sekaran, U. (1992). *Research methods for business* (2nd ed.). New York: John Wiley & Sons.

Shand, D. (1998). Harnessing knowledge management technologies in R&D. *Knowledge Management Review, 3*, 20-26.

Tiwana, A. (2002). *The knowledge management toolkit: Orchestrating IT, strategy, and knowledge platforms* (2nd ed.). Upper Saddle River, NJ: Prentice Hall.

Wick, C. (2000). Knowledge management and leadership opportunities for technical communicators. *Technical Communications.*

Zack, M. H., & Michael, S. (1996). *Knowledge management and collaboration technologies* (White paper). The Lotus Institute, Lotus Development Corporation.

KEY TERMS

Benchmarking/Best Practices: The continuous process of measuring products, services, and practices against others. It is mostly used to identify processes, services, and so forth generally considered to be superior in approach, and results in other methods internal or external to the enterprise.

Codification Strategy: The codification strategy (vs. personalization strategy) is intended to collect, codify, and disseminate information. Knowledge is codified using a people-to-documents approach. This strategy relies heavily on IT. One of the benefits of the codification approach is the reuse of knowledge (Hansen et al., 1999).

Data Mining/Knowledge-Discovery Tools: Extraction of meaningful information from masses of data (e.g., data warehouse) usually employing algorithms to correlate among many variables faster than humanly possible.

Directory of Expertise/Expert Locator: A directory with listings of individuals, their expertise, and contact information used to locate knowledgeable personnel within the enterprise.

Document-/Content-Management Systems: Information management tools that provide the storage, retrieval, tracking, and administration of documents within an organization.

Internet/Intranet/Extranet: A worldwide system of computer servers from which users at any computer can extract information or knowledge. Intranets and extranets are Internet-like networks whose scope is to restrict access to internal personnel or external partners within an enterprise, with the goal of fostering information and knowledge sharing.

Mentoring/Tutoring: The task of providing formal or informal advice, support, and knowledge to another person by someone of substantial experience who nurtures the career of a protégé.

Multimedia Repositories: Specialized databases that make different types of media, such as text, sound, video, computer graphics, and animation, available to users across an enterprise to promote reuse and reduce redundancy.

Personalization Strategy: The personalization strategy (vs. codification strategy) focuses on developing networks for linking people so that tacit knowledge can be shared. Hansen et al. (1999) say, "Knowledge that has not been codified—and probably couldn't be—is transferred in brainstorming sessions and one-on-one conversations. It invests moderately in IT. One of the benefits of the personalization approach is to leverage knowledge.

Phone Call/Teleconferencing: An interactive communications session using the telephone between two or more users who are geographically separated.

Search Engine/Information Retrieval System: A program that searches documents for specified keywords or phrases and returns a list of the documents where the keywords were found.

Storytelling: A method to illustrate a point, convince listeners, and effectively transfer knowledge by narrating management actions, employee interactions, or other relevant events within an organization.

Videoconferencing: Information technology tool that transfers video (closed-circuit television) as well as audio, and is used by two or more people working together at different physical locations for collaboration in real time.

Web-Based Training/E-Learning: Training or organized learning without the physical presence of a teacher, that is, CD-ROMs, webcasts, video, and so forth.

Working Groups/Communities of Practice: A group of individuals with a common working practice who do not constitute a formal work team. The group cuts across traditional organizational boundaries and enables individuals to acquire new knowledge—otherwise unavailable—at a faster rate.

Some of these definitions were extracted and/or adapted from the Knowledge Management and Information Technology Encyclopedia (Pollock, 2002), Encyclopedia Britannica Ready Reference (2001), and the Merriam-Webster Dictionary & Thesaurus (2002).

ENDNOTE

[1]   All these technologies are defined in the "Key Terms" section of this article.

Knowledge in Innovation Processes

Marco Paukert
Fraunhofer Institut für Integrierte Publikations–und Informationssysteme, Germany

Claudia Niederée
Fraunhofer Institut für Integrierte Publikations–und Informationssysteme, Germany

Matthias Hemmje
FernUniversität Hagen, Germany

INTRODUCTION

The success of industrial and scientific research has always been dependent on new discoveries and innovations, but tighter budgets and increasing global competition push the pace with which innovation must happen nowadays. Bringing new products to the market before competitors do constitutes a crucial competitive advantage for many companies and organizations. Accelerating discovery and innovation is increasingly dependent on the use of advanced information and knowledge technology for building environments that support the innovation process systematically and efficiently (cf. Specht, Beckmann, & Amelingmeyer, 2002; Amidon, 2002). Such environments depend on a number of advanced knowledge management technologies and have to adapt to the wide variety of innovative practices, innovation cultures, organizational context, and application areas where innovation takes place. It is essential that the functionalities of such are aligned with the needs of innovators and their context.

Innovation starts with an adequate identification of goals including an appropriate problem description and ends with the successful exploitation of the problem solution. Therefore, innovation is understood as dealing with complex problem-solving processes in whose activities knowledge of different types is applied and created. Systematic support of innovation processes requires efficient management of knowledge with respect to activities like acquisition, creation, enrichment, retrieval, reuse, and combination of such knowledge.

When taking a closer look at innovation activities in different areas, a common core innovation process can be identified that consists of six overlapping but distinguishable phases. The specific characteristics of the innovation process imply an innovation-specific, multi-stage knowledge lifecycle and knowledge management support that reflects the dependency on the innovation environment and the characteristics of the innovation process.

BACKGROUND

Innovation is the successful exploitation of new ideas which can be products or processes. It happens in the scientific domain (development of new scientific approaches, theories, methodologies, etc.) and organizations (new products, processes, marketing campaigns, etc.). Innovation is used by many scientific disciplines in many different shades. Nevertheless the core understanding of innovation can be identified as mentioned above (cf. Specht et al., 2002; Rogers, 1998; OECD, 1997).

Independent of the domain, innovation is a knowledge-intensive process. This means that proper knowledge management is necessary to support the innovation process successfully. To achieve a basis for this, a knowledge lifecycle model can be applied as a means of supporting externalization and application of innovation process and resource knowledge while following the general baseline of all approaches of knowledge management that knowledge is more useful if it does not reside in the minds of individuals, but is applied and made available to others (c.f. Alavi & Leidner, 1999), and that this is even crucial for the creation of new knowledge (Borghoff & Pareschi, 1998; Spiegler, 2000). Revisiting KM theory, several models for knowledge flow and knowledge lifecycles have been proposed that capture the dynamics of knowledge, its transformation and relationship to the respective application context (e.g., Nonaka & Takeuchi, 1995; Borghoff & Pareschi, 1998; Fischer & Ostwald, 2001). In the case of this article, the specific application context in the focus of our work is innovation processes. Therefore, the knowledge lifecycle model discussed here focuses on the specific needs of innovators with regards to managing their innovation resources in an appropriate way. The research work in which this model was developed was almost entirely performed in the context of the European project INNOVANET (IST-2001-38422).

Innovations lead to problem solutions which can differ in the degree of novelty of the solution and the amount of change implied. The terminology of TRIZ

(Theory of Inventive Problem Solving, an algorithmic approach for solving difficult technical and technological problems) suggests five levels of innovation (Shulyak, 1977). This ranges from small evolutionary changes implementing improvements of existing systems or products on the lowest level to revolutionary changes on the highest level that offer solutions outside the confines of contemporary scientific knowledge. As discussed later, the partition into an evolutionary and a revolutionary type of innovation has an important impact on the activities in the knowledge lifecycle and on adequate process support.

In the remainder of this article, the innovation knowledge lifecycle model is introduced and framed as a representation medium supporting a conceptual basis for externalization, management, and optimization of application of knowledge and knowledge resources in the context of innovation processes. The model is based on a thorough study of the state of the art in both innovation management and knowledge management theory. Within this article, an innovation-focused approach to represent and apply a knowledge management methodology is implemented. However, readers can also benefit from the general discussion around the proposed view of knowledge management activities and practices, while considering innovation as one contextual condition within which knowledge is applied. Finally, the IKLC model as introduced can also be considered as a valuable instrument that enables better understanding and better documentation of innovation processes during their preparation as well as during their execution. In turn, the model is the formal basis for achieving greater transparency, control, and efficiency within knowledge-intensive innovation processes.

MAIN FOCUS OF THE ARTICLE

The Innovation Knowledge Lifecycle (IKLC) is a domain-independent metamodel. It describes the phases of the innovation process in the Innovation Process Model, validated by Paukert, Niederée, Muscogiuri, Bouquet, and Hemmje (2003), and the knowledge flow in each of the innovation phases on an abstract level (Knowledge Lifecycle Model, mentioned above). The Knowledge Lifecycle itself includes a problem cycle and a knowledge cycle (see Figure 1).

The problem cycle (left side of Figure 1) is connected with the innovation process as a whole:

- **Become aware:** In a specific domain, there is a pool of actual and potential problems. By certain dynamics—changes in the environment, personal interests, and so forth—specific problems gain awareness and they receive the status of known problems.
- **Select problem:** The set of known problems is the starting point for innovation. Selecting a problem is a crucial step that is driven by various factors like market needs, innovation strategies, available resources, and so forth. The choice of the "right" problem is an essential precondition for successful innovation.
- **Contribute:** If the innovation process is successful, it provides a solution for the problem it was triggered by. The innovation process provides a contribution to the set of solved problems. When exploited, innovation also changes its environment, which in turn may lead to new challenges and problems, triggering further innovation (thus closing the

Figure 1. Innovation Knowledge Lifecycle (IKLC)

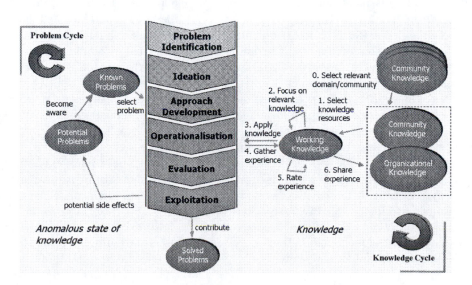

345

cycle). The problem cycle complements the knowledge cycle and can be compared to the anomalous state of knowledge (a user's inability to describe and articulate a problem), as discussed by Belkin, Oddy, and Brooks (1982) for the area of information retrieval.

The knowledge cycle (right side of Figure 1) models the knowledge flow in the innovation process, with a special focus on knowledge application. Especially, it follows the argument of Fischer and Ostwald (2001) that knowledge creation should be integrated into the work process and is not a separate activity. The knowledge cycle distinguishes three basic knowledge types: community knowledge; organizational knowledge, shared by a specific community or within an organization; and working knowledge, the knowledge at hand in a concrete working or task context. In the case of an individual activity, this is the personal knowledge of an individual, whereas in the case of a team effort, the working knowledge is the relevant joint knowledge of the members. The knowledge cycle indicates a linear process of seven steps—nevertheless, feedback loops in-between are possible:

- **Step 0: Select Relevant Domain/Community:** An innovation process is embedded into an application domain with an associated community, whose knowledge is applied. While this knowledge is sufficient for minor scale innovations, facing problems of a totally new kind requires radically new solutions and knowledge. For these revolutionary developments exploring knowledge of different domains/communities is needed. The identification of one or more relevant knowledge domains is an iterative process that requires the exploration of different knowledge domains, the development of an understanding of this knowledge, and assessment of the relevance for the current task.

- **Step 1: Select Knowledge Resources:** After identifying relevant domains/communities, adequate knowledge resources for the innovation task are selected. This can be a knowledge object, a collection of knowledge objects or an expert; selected and acquired knowledge becomes working knowledge. Identifying knowledge objects also includes internalization of the knowledge (Nonaka & Takeuchi, 1995).

Selecting domains and focusing on knowledge resources is only necessary if the existing working knowledge is not sufficient. Typically, revolutionary innovations require more new knowledge and also knowledge from different domains. Thus, more effort will be put into these first two steps.

- **Step 2: Focus on Relevant Knowledge:** Only a small part of the knowledge is relevant for solving the problems in a specific situation. The process of focusing on relevant knowledge objects may be a mental process if an individual has enough background knowledge to judge the knowledge resources. In case one individual does not have enough knowledge to focus on the relevant knowledge, negotiation and cooperation with others become necessary.

- **Step 3: Apply Knowledge:** The selected knowledge has to be applied in a specific task in the innovation process, for example, deciding on a certain evaluation method or choosing a specific representation language. Before the knowledge can be applied, it may require adaptation to the context of use. The effort to be spent depends on the match of the current task context and the context the knowledge was learned from.

- **Step 4: Gather Experience:** By applying knowledge to a task, experiences are made to what kind of result this application leads by observing the performance and the emerging results. For sharing the insights from this knowledge application, at least a minimum of externalization is necessary.

- **Step 5: Rate Experience:** The gathered experience is set into relationship with the goals of the innovation process or the current activity, and it is rated in this context. This rating provides the basis for the decision about further actions. The rating provides the basis for further applications of the same knowledge. Depending on the rating it may be considered more often or it may be neglected because it was not helpful. Cooperative activities require rating negotiation between team members.

- **Step 6: Share Experience:** Gathering and rating of experiences producing new knowledge. Ideally, the rated experience and the resulting knowledge are made explicit as knowledge objects, so they can be shared with others, thus closing the knowledge cycle. This requires extra effort, which has to be well motivated (Fischer & Ostwald, 2001). Even negative experiences represent knowledge that might become valuable at a later point in time (Ruggles & Little, 1997).

The model described above takes into account another fundamental dimension related to the IKLC, called the contextual dimension. Many studies from philosophy (e.g., Kuhn, 1962), organization science (e.g., Boland & Tenkasi, 1995), cognitive science (e.g., Fauconnier, 1985; Johnson-Laird, 1992), and knowledge representation (cf. Giunchiglia, 1993; McCarthy, 1993) stress the fact that knowledge cannot be viewed simply as a collection of "objective facts" about reality, as any "fact" presupposes a context which contributes to give it a definite meaning. Assuming that each community has its own shared context, which facilitates communication and knowledge sharing, it must be taken into account that communication and knowledge sharing across different communities presupposes a process of "perspective taking" (Boland & Tenkasi, 1993), which is qualitatively different from the process of "perspective making," which means building and using the shared perspective within a single community (Bouquet, Serafini, & Zanobini, 2003). This has an important impact on many of the described phases. For example, the way a community acquires another community's knowledge is not a simple step of incorporation, but may require a "translation" from one language to another, from a conceptual schema to another, and so forth. Analogously, the perception of how relevant a problem is depends also on a community's context, as many examples show that relevance is relative to what is implicitly assumed (cf. Paukert et al., 2003).

Model of the Innovation Process

As outlined earlier, the following model is based on a study of theories in the innovation domain as well as in the KM domain. It has been validated within an intensive evaluation procedure (Paukert et al., 2003). In the following, the model is presented without introducing its derivation to give priority to explaining the innovation domain as a KM application context. Understanding the properties of the introduced exemplar application domain is crucial for fully taking advantage of the IKLC model, even for transferring its generic properties into other KM application domains. Considering the wide variety of possible innovation forms and innovation application

Figure 2. Innovation Process Model (IPM)

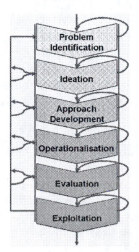

domains, generalizations are difficult. However, on an abstract level it is possible to identify six basic phases of an innovation process. They are described in the following innovation process model whose phases are common to most innovation processes (Paukert et al., 2003). The phases are depicted in Figure 2.

There is basically a sequential order between these phases. But there are also overlaps and loops between the phases, where, due to (intermediate) results or external events, revisiting earlier phases becomes necessary. This need for feedback is also stressed by Pérez-Bustamente (1999). In the following, the six phases are described in detail.

Problem Identification Phase

Each innovation is started by a problem that the innovative process is expected to solve. Systematically, two forms can be distinguished (Pérez-Bustamente, 1999):

- **proactive** forms, which include trend setting, recognition of market opportunity, need creation, and identification of research opportunity; and
- **reactive** forms, which include open problems in production or processes, changed requirements, and reaction to changed environments.

Regardless of how the innovation is started, the problem needs a proper description. The more people are involved, the more detailed and explicit the problem representation has to be. A first validation of the problem checks the adequacy of the description with respect to the targeted problem as well as the novelty of the problem. Further, a first estimation about the feasibility and the relevance of the problem has to be conducted to reduce the risk of investing resources into further steps. Clearly, these considerations are influenced by the innovation strategy of the involved organization.

Ideation Phase

In the Ideation phase, ideas are generated and collected which are thought to contribute to a possible solution to the described problem. These activities form the core of the innovation process since the subsequent phases are directly dependent on the decisions made at this point. There are several (systematic) ways to discover ideas for solving the problem such as analogy, data mining, paradigm shift, and luck. These all involve the exploration and selection of the current state of the art. The amount of needed knowledge in this phase increases, the more revolutionary the innovation is supposed to be since new domains may be required to find an appropriate solution to the problem.

For negotiating factors like adequacy for the problem, novelty, and feasibility, the ideas have to be formalized and described.

Approach Development Phase

Approach Development is the first step towards solidifying the idea towards an implemented solution. In this phase a conceptual model for the implementation is developed which describes its planned solution on a conceptual level. This phase takes the description, the problem, and the idea as input.

The first set of activities in this phase involves the identification of a useful approach for conceptually describing the implementation of the idea. This involves exploration, selection, application, and creation of related knowledge in terms of technologies, methodologies, and formalisms. The approach and the conceptual model have to be validated for adequacy, novelty, and feasibility of operationalization before they can be considered a valid input for the operationalization phase.

Operationalization Phase

In the Operationalization phase, the developed approach is actually implemented according to the developed model. The goal during operationalization is to achieve results which show that the selected approach adequately resolves the initial problem. This may require a number of iterative steps that are conducted to increase the quality of the solutions to achieve a maximum outcome. Operationalization can become quite resource consuming, making the validation in the preceding phase a crucial activity.

Validating the activities in this phase checks the adequacy of the operationalization with respect to the chosen approach. Also, it checks if it is possible to scale up the developed approach from, for example, a prototype production to a mass production process and with respect to exploitation.

Evaluation Phase

In addition to the validation activities which conclude each developmental cycle during operationalization, there is a separate Evaluation phase which tests the results produced during the innovation process. Negative evaluation results can lead to revision of individual decisions, or they can even lead to cancellation of the entire innovation process. The evaluation requires careful planning of the experimental design and analysis to ensure representative and valid results. The evaluation criteria and methods depend on the domain and intended application area.

For revolutionary innovation activities, the evaluation phase is much more challenging than for evolutionary innovation, since revolutionary innovation often also invalidates the traditional best-practice methods of evaluation applied so far.

Exploitation Phase

In this integral part of innovation, the results of the prior phases are distributed in order to gain benefit from them and to meet the goals of the innovation request it was triggered by: a company takes the newly developed product and will try to market it as profitable as possible, or a new process is implemented and integrated into the operational workflow for its improvement and to obtain more cost-effective performance. In the scientific domain, innovations—new insights, methodologies, theories—are disseminated via publication into scientific communities of interest.

Depending on the type of innovation—evolutionary or revolutionary—the demands towards the knowledge lifecycle vary. In an evolutionary innovation scenario—like selling soft drinks in green bottles instead of brown plastic bottles—less knowledge is required than in a revolutionary innovation scenario—like opening new power resources.

An evolutionary innovation requires no knowledge from external domains; the domain knowledge is well known and so are the knowledge resources. Only small shifts of focus have to be made. Applying, gathering, rating, and sharing the knowledge are well-understood operations, although the motivation of systematic knowledge sharing is a challenge in many organizations.

A revolutionary innovation demands knowledge which is out of the main domain of the innovator. Domains will have to be identified which are thought to hold the necessary knowledge. Being unacquainted within these domains, innovators are missing the prerequisite knowledge to decide about the important knowledge resources at first. Also, the process of focusing on the relevant knowledge may take longer since the criteria for these activities are not familiar yet. Applying, gathering, and rating knowledge may require new methods and strategies, whereas sharing the acquired knowledge is less of a problem since this activity is domain-independent.

FUTURE TRENDS

Future steps will concentrate on developing a framework for systematic innovation support. Such innovation support and the knowledge management tools applied in innovation have to be flexible and adaptable in order to take into account that:

- the different phases of the innovation process have specific requirements;
- innovating organizations and teams have their own specific innovation practices, and innovation culture and requirements; and
- requirements and cultural characteristics of innovation culture can change over time (Paukert, Niederée, & Hemmje, in press).

For an Innovation Engineering Environment (IEE) for systematic innovation support by knowledge technology, the following four core technology areas were identified:

- **Innovation Process Management:** This component is necessary to support the general management of innovation processes. Even though innovation processes present peculiar aspects, an innovation process is first of all a process, and as such it must be managed. This component contains tools that allow innovation managers to plan, log, and monitor the phases and the related activities and resources.
- **Generic Innovation Support Components:** This core component's sub-components provide classes of functionalities which are intrinsic to knowledge management functionality of any innovation process, independently from domain and application. Examples include: adequate representation, intelligent matchmaking, discovery, and interaction support.
- **Application-Specific Support Components:** Effective innovation support also requires tools that are domain-specific. This is especially true for approach development and operationalization. Examples of such tools are design and simulation tools. In the design of the IEE, it is important to enable the flexible integration of existing and newly developing application-specific tools.
- **Innovation Environment Configuration Support:** This functionality has to be specialized for the different phases. This may include method and tool selection, tool configuration, and user interface design. IEE specialization results in a system architecture that provides specific support based on the generic tools and functionalities suggested by the IKLC.

These four core technology areas have been identified and validated within the resulting research roadmap work (see www.innovanet.eu.com). Implementing solutions to these technology challenges within ongoing knowledge technology R&D will promote and support a more systematic approach to managing innovation. Following a meta design approach (Fisher, 2000), tools for the customization step can finally be part of the overall knowledge-based innovation management framework itself, increasing the flexibility of the approach and enabling involvement of the innovators themselves into the customization process. This allows the adaptation of the system to the requirements of individual organization sand teams, as well as the evolution of the system when the innovation factors change or the environment changes.

CONCLUSION

Although it is generally understood that innovation is a knowledge-intensive process with specific requirements, the work on systematic support of the innovation process by an Innovation Engineering Environment is still in an early state. This article lays a conceptual foundation for the further work in building tools and systems for more systematically supporting the innovation process by information and knowledge technology, with the final aim of contributing to the acceleration of innovation.

In designing and building IEEs that are applicable in different domains, the wide spectrum of existing innovation processes (mostly deviations from the presented innovation process model) is a large challenge and requires flexible and adaptable solutions. However, aiming for a common core of innovation support functionality reduces the overall effort, keeps the R&D activities in this area focused, and eases the adoption of successful innovation cultures and practices across the borders of individual organizations and domains.

Some of the current trends in information and knowledge technology promise to be supportive of the successful development of information technologies:

- the success of service-oriented architectures implemented by Web services can be exploited for building adaptive IEEs, where (Web) services in support of specific innovation activities can be easily and dynamically integrated;
- the Semantic Web activities resulted in widely accepted approaches and exchangeable formats for describing innovation resources and the process itself; and
- the currently increased activities in the area of ontology development and exploitation, which is triggered by the Semantic Web activities, will result in pragmatic and scalable approaches for intelligent decision making and for the interoperable mediation of innovation resources, especially also across the borders of domains as it is required for revolutionary innovation activities.

In spite of the large challenges of this task, it is expected that there will be considerable progress in more systematic and efficient innovation support in the near future.

REFERENCES

Alavi, M., & Leidner, D. (1999). Knowledge management systems: Issues, challenges, and benefits. *Communication of the AIS, 1*(February). Retrieved June 24, 2004, from *http://cais.isworld.org/articles/1-7/article.htm*

Amidon, D.M. (2002). The innovation superhighway. *Frontiers of entrepreneurship and innovation: Readings in Science Park policies and practices.* International Association of Science Parks.

Belkin, N.J., Oddy, R.N., & Brooks, H.M. (1982). ASK for information retrieval: Part II. Results of a design study. *Journal of Documentation, 38,* 145-164.

Boland, J.R., & Tenkasi, R.V. (1995). Perspective making and perspective taking in communities of knowing. *Organizational Science, 6,* 350-372.

Borghoff, U., & Pareschi, R. (1998). *Information technology for knowledge management.* Berlin, Heidelberg: Springer-Verlag.

Bouquet, P., Serafini, L., & Zanobini, S. (2003, October 23-25). Semantic coordination: A new approach and an application. *Proceedings of the 2nd International Semantic Web Conference (ISWC-03),* Sanibel Island, FL.

Fisher, G. (2000). Social creativity, symmetry of ignorance and meta-design. *Knowledge-Based Systems Journal, 13,* 527-537.

Fischer, G., & Ostwald, J. (2001). Knowledge management: Problems, promises, realities, and challenges. *IEEE Intelligent Systems, 16,* 60-72.

Fauconnier, G. (1985). *Mental space: Aspects of meaning construction in nature language.* Cambridge, MA: Bradford Books.

Giunchiglia, F. (1993). Contextual reasoning. *Epistemologia,* (Special Issue on I Linguaggi e le Macchine XVI), 345-364.

Johnson-Laird, P. (1992). *Mental models.* Cambridge: Cambridge University Press.

Kuhn, T.S. (1962). *The structure of scientific revolutions.* Chicago: The University of Chicago Press.

McCarthy, J. (1993). Notes on formalizing context. *Proceedings of the 13th International Joint Conference on Artificial Intelligence (IJCAI'93),* Chambery, France (pp. 555-560).

Nonaka, I., & Takeuchi, H. (1995). *The knowledge creating company.* Oxford: Oxford University Press.

OECD (Organization for Economic Cooperation and Development). (1997). The Oslo manual: Proposed guidelines for collecting and interpreting technological innovation data. Retrieved from *http:// www.oecd.org/ findDocument/0,2350,en_2649_34409_1 _119669_1_1_1, 00 .html*

Paukert, M., Niederée, C., Muscogiuri, C., Bouquet, P., & Hemmje, M. (2003). Knowledge in the innovation process: An empirical study for validating the innovation knowledge lifecycle. *Proceedings of the 4th European Conference on Knowledge Management* (pp. 725-738). Oxford, UK.

Paukert, M., Niederée, C., & Hemmje, M. (in press). Adapting organizational knowledge management cultures to the knowledge lifecycle in innovation processes. In M. Rao (Ed.), *KM chronicles: Cultures of knowledge.*

Pérez-Bustamente, G. (1999). Knowledge management in agile innovative organizations. *Journal of Knowledge Management, 3,* 6-17.

Rogers, M. (1998). *The definition and measurement of innovation.* Melbourne Institute Working Paper Series No. 10/98.

Ruggles, R., & Little, R. (1997). *Knowledge management and innovation—an initial exploration.* White Paper, Ernst&Young LLP.

Shulyak, L. (1977). Introduction to TRIZ. In G. Altshuller (Ed.), *40 principles.* Worchester, MA: Technical Innovation Center.

Specht, G., Beckmann, C., & Amelingmeyer, J. (2002). *F&E management.* Stuttgart: Schäffer-Poeschel-Verlag.

Spiegler, I. (2000). Knowledge management: A new idea or a recycled concept. *Communication of the AIS, 3*(March). Retrieved April 22, 2004, from *http://cais.isworld.org/ articles/1-7/article.htm*

KEY TERMS

Evolutionary Innovation: A type of innovation which contains narrow extensions or improvements of an existing product or process which is not substantially changed. The applied changes are rather small and incremental; the knowledge needed is inside the innovator's domain.

Innovation: The successful exploitation of a new idea. This may be in the industrial domain (products, processes, campaigns) or the scientific domain (theories, insights, methodologies).

Innovation Engineering Environment (IEE): A flexible and adaptable framework based on information and knowledge technology for systematic innovation support. It includes four core components: Innovation Process Management, Generic Innovation Support Components, Application-Specific Configuration Support, and Innovation Environment Configuration Support.

Innovation Knowledge Lifecycle: Model of the knowledge-related activities in which the innovation process is embedded; this includes a problem cycle that feeds the innovation process and that can also be triggered by innovation, as well as a knowledge cycle that describe activities around knowledge objects within the innovation process on an abstract level.

Revolutionary Innovation: A type of innovation that provides solutions outside the confines of contemporary scientific knowledge and best practice in an area, and represents pioneering work.

K

Knowledge Integration

Hans Berends
Eindhoven University of Technology, The Netherlands

Hans van der Bij
Eindhoven University of Technology, The Netherlands

Mathieu Weggeman
Eindhoven University of Technology, The Netherlands

INTRODUCTION

In most organizations, specialized knowledge is dispersed over organization members (Tsoukas, 1996). Organization members have different educational backgrounds and working experiences and develop different perspectives. Yet, the development and production of complex goods and services normally requires the application of multiple disciplines and perspectives. Therefore, the integration of knowledge is an important task for managers and other organization members (Carlile, 2002; De Boer, Van den Bosch, & Volberda, 1999; Galunic & Rodan, 1998; Grant, 1996a, 1996b; Kogut & Zander, 1992; Okhuysen & Eisenhardt, 2002; Ravasi & Verona, 2000).

Knowledge integration has to be realized through the actions of the specialists involved, but knowledge management professionals can facilitate this task. Several mechanisms can be deployed to realize knowledge integration. An important question is what instrument is suited for what circumstances, for example, which knowledge integration mechanisms fit an exploration strategy and which mechanisms fit an exploitation strategy (March, 1991). If organizations do not explore, they can get stuck in a suboptimal or deteriorating situation. In contrast, if organizations do not exploit, they will have high costs and low incomes. Yet, exploitation and exploration require contrasting approaches to knowledge integration.

The next section presents the theoretical background on the topic of knowledge integration. Subsequently, we describe the knowledge integration mechanisms that can be found in the literature and basic conditions for the successful utilization of these mechanisms. We introduce a framework that distinguishes knowledge integration mechanisms, which can be used to assess the value of particular mechanisms for different situations. This framework is applied in a discussion of the knowledge integration approaches that are required for explo-

ration and exploitation. The concluding section suggests directions for future research.

BACKGROUND

Several disciplines have contributed to the study of knowledge integration. Economists and strategy theorists formulated the outlines of a knowledge-based view of the firm (Demsetz, 1991; Grant, 1996b; Galunic & Rodan, 1998; Kogut & Zander, 1992; Nelson & Winter, 1982; Teece, Pisano, & Shuen, 1997). They have built upon work in organization science, including the information processing perspective (Galbraith, 1973; Tushman & Nadler, 1978) and earlier work on the differentiation and integration of tasks (Lawrence & Lorsch, 1967; Thompson, 1967). Disconnected from those studies, social psychologists studied the effectiveness of knowledge integration under different conditions in experimental studies (e.g., Hollingshead, 1998; Stasser, Stewart, & Wittenbaum, 1995; Wegner, 1987). Combining insights from these disciplines, the problem of knowledge integration can be sketched as follows.

The development and production of complex goods and services requires a wide and expanding range of technological, marketing, and organizational knowledge (Demsetz, 1991; Grant, 1996a, 1996b; Tsoukas, 1996). For example, Ford not only needs a competency in road vehicles and engines, but in 15 other major technological fields as well, including chemical processing, metallurgy, semiconductors, and instruments and controls (Granstrand, Patel, & Pavitt, 1997). In addition to the breadth of knowledge involved, the depth of technologies—their analytical sophistication—also is increasing (Wang & Von Tunzelmann, 2000).

A single individual cannot have the breadth and depth of knowledge required for the development and production of most goods and services. Individuals have restricted learning capacities (Simon, 1991). Furthermore, due to the situatedness of learning processes (Lave & Wenger, 1991), individuals are only able to become experts in fields in which they are actively involved. Finally, learning processes are characterized by an increasing rate of return (Levinthal & March, 1993). That is, the more knowledge one has in a particular field, the easier it is to learn something new within that field. For these reasons, individuals have to specialize in a certain field in order to develop the level of expertise required. It is through the specialization of individuals in different fields, and hence the differentiation of knowledge, that an organization is able to acquire both the required breadth and depth of knowledge (Carlile, 2002; Marengo, 1993; Wegner, 1987).

When the knowledge required for innovation or production lies dispersed across individuals, departments, and organizations, a fundamental task for organization members and management is to integrate that knowledge. The differentiation of knowledge creates a need for knowledge integration. We define knowledge integration as "the process in which different pockets of knowledge, which are valuable for a particular organizational process and held by different organization members, are applied to that organizational process." As we will discuss next, this process can be realized through several mechanisms.

KNOWLEDGE INTEGRATION MECHANISMS

Six different knowledge integration mechanisms can be found in the current literature: (1) sequencing, (2) decision support systems, (3) direction, (4) thinking along, (5) group problem-solving, and (6) knowledge transfer. These mechanisms can be used separately and in combination with each other. This section describes each of them and discusses two basic conditions for the successful utilization of these mechanisms.

Sequencing

The first mechanism for knowledge integration is the sequencing of tasks (Demsetz, 1991; Grant, 1996b; Nelson & Winter, 1982). This mechanism exploits the specialization of organization members. As a knowledge integration mechanism, sequencing refers to the assignment of tasks to those organization members who have the relevant knowledge for it. When routines of sequenced tasks are created, individuals only need to know their part of the routine in order to realize that specialized knowledge is applied in a coordinated way (Nelson & Winter, 1982, p. 101).

Decision Support Systems

Decision support systems are a second way to integrate knowledge. When specialists codify their knowledge and embed it in a decision support system, their original specialist knowledge can be integrated in the practices of a wide range of other organization members (e.g., Davenport & Glaser, 2002). Advances in information technology and knowledge engineering have greatly enhanced the feasibility of this approach to knowledge integration, though there are also clear limits to its applicability (e.g., Dreyfus, 1992).

Direction

Specialists in one area of knowledge can issue rules, directives, and operating procedures to guide the behavior of non-specialists, less mature specialists, and specialists in other fields (Grant, 1997, p. 451). Demsetz (1991) called this mechanism "direction." Rules and directives can be interpreted as translations of a wider body of explicit and tacit knowledge into a limited instruction. The organization members applying these rules and directives do not need to fully understand the wider body of knowledge underlying them.

Thinking Along

Berends, Debackere, Garud, and Weggeman (2004) introduced thinking along as another knowledge integration mechanism. Thinking along takes place in interactions between organization members, but it differs from knowledge transfer. Thinking along consists in the temporary application of one's knowledge to somebody else's problem. The application of this knowledge—including tacit knowledge—may yield ideas, hypotheses, suggestions, comments, and questions that contribute to the process of knowledge creation. These contributions are much easier to communicate than the background knowledge used to produce them. Yet, through thinking along, that background knowledge gets applied to the organizational process involved. In the study of Berends et al. (2004) this mechanism was frequently found in the interactions between industrial researchers.

Group Problem-Solving

Okhuysen and Eisenhardt (2002) limit the concept of knowledge integration to group problem-solving. This mechanism consists of the direct combination of knowledge previously dispersed over individuals in order to solve a problem or make a decision. Okhuysen and

Eisenhardt emphasize that this is not just a passive process of combining pieces of knowledge in a way comparable to building with LEGO blocks or making a jigsaw puzzle. The integration of knowledge involves the active use of knowledge and the generation of new ideas, aided by the combination of knowledge. In contrast with thinking along, group problem-solving concerns a shared problem and symmetrical contributions from those involved. Group problem-solving is widely researched in field studies, such as multi-disciplinary innovation projects (e.g., Carlile, 2002; Huang & Newell, 2003), and in experimental studies (e.g., Okhuysen & Eisenhardt, 2002; Stasser et al., 1995).

Knowledge Transfer

Knowledge transfer is presumably the most widely studied mechanism for knowledge integration (e.g., Hansen, 1999; Szulanski, 1996). Though knowledge integration can be realized through knowledge transfer, knowledge transfer alone does not constitute knowledge integration. Knowledge integration requires that the receivers of knowledge are able to absorb it, combine it with their existing knowledge, and apply it to an organizational process. Past research has discovered a wide range of factors that enable or constrain knowledge transfer (e.g., Cummings & Teng, 2003; Szulanski, 1996; Van der Bij, Song, & Weggeman, 2003). Among these factors are characteristics of knowledge such as its tacitness, characteristics of senders such as their motivation, characteristics of receivers such as their absorptive capacity, characteristics of relationships such as the level of trust, and characteristics of the organizational context such as the communication infrastructure. Furthermore, the literature distinguishes several types of knowledge transfer. For example, Dixon (2000) discerns five types of knowledge transfer: serial transfer, near transfer, far transfer, strategic transfer, and expert transfer. Dixon argues that these types of knowledge transfer are suited for different situations and conditions.

Past research has identified several conditions for successful knowledge integration. Two conditions are fundamental. First, organization members need to recognize opportunities for knowledge integration (Galunic & Rodan, 1998). Social psychologists have stressed the importance of a well-developed transactive memory system (Wegner, 1987). Transactive memory refers to the metaknowledge people have about the knowledge and skills of others (Wegner, 1987). Research has shown that such knowledge about others enhances sequencing (Moreland, 1999), thinking along (Berends et al., 2004), group problem-solving (Stasser et al., 1995; Okhuysen & Eisenhardt, 2002), and knowledge transfer (Hollingshead, 1998).

Second, many authors have mentioned the importance of shared understanding (e.g., Galunic & Rodan, 1998; Grant, 1996a; Tushman, 1978). The specialization of organization members not only enables an organization to acquire the range of required expertise, it also creates diverging thought worlds and frames of reference (Carlile, 2002; Dougherty, 1992). Boundaries between groups and practices may create serious barriers to knowledge integration. A basic level of common knowledge and a shared conceptual framework may help to overcome these barriers. Ethnographic field studies have emphasized the role of boundary objects for the success of knowledge integration. A boundary object is an object that is shared and shareable across different contexts and enables collaboration across boundaries (Carlile, 2002; Star & Griesemer, 1989). An example of such a boundary object is the drawing of a new machine, which can be used by different disciplines contributing to the machine.

CHARACTERIZING KNOWLEDGE INTEGRATION MECHANISMS

The existing literature describes a range of knowledge integration mechanisms. However, it does not offer a conceptual framework to distinguish and order these mechanisms. Grant (1996b), for example, does not offer an integrated perspective on the mechanisms he introduces. This deficiency in the literature limits our ability to assess the suitability of mechanisms for different organizational processes and conditions. As a first step toward filling this gap, we introduce a dimension that characterizes and distinguishes knowledge integration mechanisms.

Knowledge integration mechanisms differ in the degree to which the application of a piece of knowledge, which is valuable for realizing an organizational process, involves somebody else other than the person having that piece of knowledge. The knowledge of an organization member can be integrated into an organizational process by directly applying it, by incorporating it in a decision support system, by translating it into a rule, by using it when thinking along with someone, by using it in group problem-solving, and by transferring it to someone else. These options differ in the amount of effort required from other persons to realize that the knowledge is applied to a specific organizational process. Two extremes are knowledge transfer and sequencing. Knowledge transfer demands high involvement from the organization members receiving knowledge, since they should absorb the knowledge and apply it in their part of the organizational process. In contrast,

Figure 1. Characterization of knowledge integration mechanisms with regard to the required involvement of other organization members

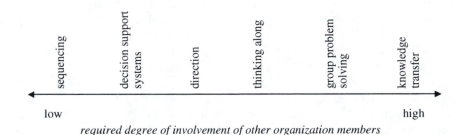

required degree of involvement of other organization members

sequencing only requires that everyone applies his or her knowledge to his or her own task: "While each organization member must know his job, there is no need for anyone to know anyone else's job" (Nelson & Winter, 1982, p. 105).

Figure 1 locates each of the knowledge integration mechanisms discussed in the previous section on a continuum from a low to a high degree of involvement of other organization members. Integrating knowledge via rules and directives, for example, lies between the extreme cases of sequencing and knowledge transfer. To some degree it is like knowledge transfer. Organization members other than the ones issuing a rule are needed to apply rules in an organizational process. Yet, to the degree that rules and directives are translations of larger bodies of knowledge, direction does not require as much involvement of other organization members as the transfer of those complete bodies of knowledge would have taken. Similarly, decision support systems, thinking along, and group problem-solving occupy intermediate positions.

EXPLOITATION AND EXPLORATION

Knowledge integration mechanisms characterized by a high or a low degree of involvement have different advantages and disadvantages. This has implications for their suitability for different organizational processes and conditions. In this section, we will focus on the distinction between exploitation and exploration (March, 1991). Whereas exploration is related to the creation of new knowledge and value, exploitation involves the extraction of value from existing intellectual capital (Sullivan, 1999). Several authors have argued that exploration and exploitation are facilitated by sharply different organizational characteristics (Benner & Tushman, 2003; Hill & Rothaermel, 2003; Levinthal & March, 1993; McNamara & Baden-Fuller, 1999). We

will argue that exploration and exploitation also require different approaches to knowledge integration.

Exploitation is served by mechanisms that require a low degree of involvement of other organization members—except when those other organization members are able to reuse knowledge. Exploitation refers to "the use and development of things already known" (Levinthal & March, 1993, p. 105). Exploitation requires that available knowledge is applied where effectively possible, to low costs. In general, low degrees of involvement are less costly. Being deeper involved in the application of knowledge to a particular part of an organizational process takes more time and effort. Particularly, if knowledge has to be transferred to someone else to be applied, this requires time and effort of both sender and receiver. Efficient knowledge integration is realized when the division of tasks is in accordance with the division of knowledge. That is, it is most efficient when a task is assigned to the person who has the relevant knowledge for it. This minimizes the costs associated with knowledge transfer. Thus, Grant (1996b, p. 114) states: "If production requires the integration of many people's specialist knowledge, the key to efficiency is to achieve effective integration while minimizing knowledge transfer through cross-learning by organizational members."

Matching the division of tasks to the division of knowledge—and thus avoiding mutual involvement—can be done primarily by sequencing, but direction and decision support systems also exploit specialization. As Grant (1996b, p. 115) writes: "Thus it is highly inefficient for a quality engineer to teach every production worker all that he knows about quality control. A more efficient means of integrating his knowledge into the production process is for him to establish a set of procedures and rules for quality control." To a lesser degree, the matching of tasks to knowledge can be realized by thinking along. In thinking along, the person having relevant knowledge is not assigned a separate task, but applies his or her knowledge to a problem of somebody else and communicates resulting ideas for solving that problem.

Matching the division of tasks to the division of knowledge is more important when the knowledge involved is tacit and when boundaries exist between bodies of knowledge (Carlile, 2002). Those conditions make knowledge transfer more difficult, and therefore make it more important to avoid (Berends et al., 2004).

This reasoning points at limits to the usefulness of knowledge transfer. However, as stated, when other organization members are able to reuse knowledge in later activities, knowledge transfer may be valuable. When knowledge is in line with someone's specialization, economies of scale and scope make its transfer to that person more valuable (Grant & Baden-Fuller, 2004). For example, this is the case when best practices are transferred from one production facility to another one that uses the same kind of process (Szulanski, 1996).

Exploration requires a different approach to knowledge integration than exploitation. Exploration is "the pursuit of new knowledge, of things that might come to be known" (Levinthal & March, 1993, p. 105). Schumpeter and many later authors have argued that innovation stems from the recombination of existing pieces of knowledge (e.g., Galunic & Rodan, 1998; Nelson & Winter, 1982). Accordingly, scholars working within the resource-based view argue that the innovative potential of a firm lies in its capability to recombine knowledge and other resources (Kogut & Zander, 1992; Teece et al., 1997). Furthermore, several authors have emphasized that exploration requires the generation of variety (Benner & Tushman, 2003; March, 1991). Given that "most new ideas are bad ones" (Levinthal & March, 1993), many ideas have to be suggested and tried before a successful innovation is created. Combining the ideas that innovation is realized through the recombination of knowledge and that exploration requires a variety of alternatives, we claim that exploration requires knowledge integration mechanisms that create variety in opportunities for knowledge recombination. We will argue that a higher degree of involvement facilitates such variation and that, therefore, group problem-solving, thinking along, and knowledge transfer are particularly suited for exploration.

That a higher degree of involvement enables variation in knowledge integration can be attributed to three factors. First, a higher degree of involvement gives more freedom to apply knowledge in diverse ways. For example, in an ethnographic study within a research organization, we observed the following interaction. In a biweekly cluster meeting, one researcher, Patrick, told about a lubricant he used to enhance the coating of optical discs. Jason, one of his colleagues, who worked

on the coating of television screens, responded: "That's a nice solution. It might also work for the coating of screens. I will try that." When knowledge is transferred to others, those persons can decide in what ways to use that knowledge and, thus, how to integrate it with their existing knowledge.

Second, a higher degree of involvement enables one to detect more opportunities for the combination of knowledge. Galunic and Rodan (1998) introduced the notion of detection capability to refer to the capability to detect opportunities for fruitful recombinations of knowledge. In the previous example, Jason used his capability to detect a possible new application of the idea presented by Patrick. In group problem-solving or thinking along, each person involved can use his or her capability to detect ways to combine knowledge. Thus, especially when several people are jointly involved, the chances are higher that new combinations of knowledge are detected.

Third, the value of joint involvement for exploration also originates from the unexpected associations and reactions that interactions can trigger (Berends et al., 2004). For example, Okada and Simon (1997) found that specifically the questioning of each other's ideas is one of the strengths of group problem-solving. A question may trigger a new problem representation, which may trigger new ideas, which in turn may raise evaluative comments, and so on. Such a process prompts the knowledge bases of each of the persons involved in heterogeneous and unexpected ways.

CONCLUSION

Knowledge integration is of crucial importance when production or innovation requires knowledge from several organization members. The literature suggests several mechanisms for knowledge integration (though these mechanisms are not always interpreted in this particular way). In this article, we contributed to the study of knowledge integration by introducing a dimension that captures important differences between knowledge integration mechanisms. This dimension is the degree of involvement of other organization members that is required by a knowledge integration mechanism. Furthermore, we used this dimension in a discussion of the value of different mechanisms for exploitation and exploration.

Future research is required for the further development of theoretical and practical insight in knowledge integration. First, a number of conceptual issues require additional attention. What other dimensions can be used to differentiate knowledge integration processes and mechanisms? What is the relationship between task integration mechanisms and knowledge integration mechanisms? Second, theory building should extend beyond what has been presented in this article and include other characteristics of knowledge integration, contextual factors, and organizational outcomes. Furthermore, the arguments on the suitability of knowledge integration strategies for exploration and exploitation presented in this article should be rigorously tested. Third, we need more insight in the way in which each of the knowledge integration mechanisms can be realized and facilitated. Special attention is required for strategies to overcome boundaries between disciplines and strategies to deal with uncertainty and ambiguity within disciplines. We believe that the advancement of insight will be served by continuing the utilization of a multitude of methodological approaches, including qualitative field studies (e.g., Ravasi & Verona, 2000), quantitative survey research (e.g., Hansen, 1999), experimental studies (e.g., Stasser et al., 1995), and simulation studies (e.g., Marengo, 1993).

REFERENCES

Benner, M.J., & Tushman, M.L. (2003). Exploitation, exploration, and process management: The productivity dilemma revisited. *Academy of Management Review, 28*(2), 238-256.

Berends, H., Debackere, K., Garud, R., & Weggeman, M. (2004). *Knowledge integration by thinking along.* ECIS Working Paper 04.05, Eindhoven: Eindhoven University of Technology, Eindhoven Centre for Innovation Studies.

Carlile, P.R. (2002). A pragmatic view of knowledge and boundaries: Boundary objects in new product development. *Organization Science, 13*(4), 442-455.

Cummings, J.L., & Teng, B.S. (2003). Transferring R&D knowledge: The key factors affecting knowledge transfer success. *Journal of Engineering and Technology Management, 20*(1-2), 39-68.

Davenport, T.H., & Glaser, J. (2002). Just-in-time delivery comes to knowledge management. *Harvard Business Review, 80*(7), 107-112.

De Boer, M., Van den Bosch, F.A.J., & Volberda, H.W. (1999). Managing organizational knowledge integration in the emerging multimedia complex. *Journal of Management Studies, 36*(3), 379-398.

Demsetz, H. (1991). The theory of the firm revisited. In O.E. Williamson, S.G. Winter, & R.H. Coase (Eds.), *The nature of the firm.* New York: Oxford University Press.

Dixon, N.M. (2000). *Common knowledge.* Boston: Harvard Business School Press.

Dougherty, D. (1992). Interpretative barriers to successful product innovation in large firms. *Organization Science, 3*(2), 179-202.

Dreyfus, H.L. (1992). *What computers still can't do.* Cambridge, MA: MIT Press.

Galbraith, J.R. (1973). *Designing complex organizations.* Reading, MA: Addison-Wesley.

Galunic, D.C., & Rodan, S. (1998). Resource combinations in the firm: Knowledge structures and the potential for Schumpeterian innovation. *Strategic Management Journal, 19*(12), 1193-1201.

Granstrand, O., Patel, P., & Pavitt, K. (1997). Multi-technology corporations: Why they have "distributed" rather than "distinctive core" competences. *California Management Review, 39*(4), 8-25.

Grant, R.M. (1996a). Prospering in dynamically-competitive environments: Organizational capability as knowledge integration. *Organization Science, 7*(4), 375-387.

Grant, R.M. (1996b). Toward a knowledge-based theory of the firm. *Strategic Management Journal, 17*(Winter Special Issue), 109-122.

Grant, R.M. (1997). The knowledge-based view of the firm: Implications for management practice. *Long Range Planning, 30*(3), 450-454.

Grant, R.M., & Baden-Fuller, C. (2004). A knowledge accessing theory of strategic alliances. *Journal of Management Studies, 41*(1), 61-84.

Hansen, M.T. (1999). The search-transfer problem. *Administrative Science Quarterly, 44*(1), 82-111.

Hill, C.W., & Rothaermel, F.T. (2003). The performance of incumbent firms in the face of radical technological innovation. *Academy of Management Review, 28*(2), 257-284.

Hollingshead, A.B. (1998). Retrieval processes in transactive memory systems. *Journal of Personality and Social Psychology, 74*(3), 659-671.

Huang, J.C., & Newell, S. (2003). Knowledge integration processes and dynamics within the context of cross-functional projects. *International Journal of Project Management, 21*(3), 167-176.

Kogut, B., & Zander, U. (1992). Knowledge of the firm, combinative capabilities, and the replication of technology. *Organization Science, 3*(3), 383-397.

Lave, J., & Wenger, E. (1991). *Situated learning*. Cambridge: Cambridge University Press.

Lawrence, P.R., & Lorsch, J.W. (1967). *Organization and environment: Managing differentiation and integration*. Boston: Harvard Business School Press.

Levinthal, D., & March, J. (1993). The myopia of learning. *Strategic Management Journal, 14*(Winter Special Issue), 95-112.

March, J.G. (1991). Exploration and exploitation in organizational learning. *Organization Science, 2*(1), 71-87.

Marengo, L. (1993). Knowledge distribution and coordination in organizations. *Revue Internationale de Systémique, 7*(5), 553-571.

McNamara, P., & Baden-Fuller, C. (1999). Lessons from the CellTech case: Balancing knowledge exploration and exploitation in organizational renewal. *British Journal of Management, 10*(4), 291-308.

Moreland, R.L. (1999). Transactive memory: Learning who knows what in work groups and organizations. In L.L. Thompson, J.M. Levine, & D.M. Messick (Eds.), *Shared cognition in organizations*. Mahwah, NJ: Lawrence Erlbaum.

Nelson, R.R., & Winter, S.G. (1982). *An evolutionary theory of economic change*. Cambridge, MA: Harvard University Press.

Okada, T., & Simon, H.A. (1997). Collaborative discovery in a scientific domain. *Cognitive Science, 21*(2), 109-146.

Okhuysen, G.A., & Eisenhardt, K.M. (2002). Integrating knowledge in groups: How formal interventions enable flexibility. *Organization Science, 13*(4), 370-386.

Ravasi, D., & Verona, G. (2001). Organising the process of knowledge integration: The benefits of structural ambiguity. *Scandinavian Journal of Management, 17*(1), 41-66.

Simon, H.A. (1991). Bounded rationality and organizational learning. *Organization Science, 2*(1), 125-134.

Star, S.L., & Griesemer, J.R. (1989). Institutional ecology, "translations" and boundary objects. *Social Studies of Science, 19*(3), 387-420.

Stasser, G., Stewart, D.D., & Wittenbaum, G.M. (1995). Expert roles and information exchange during discussion. *Journal of Experimental Social Psychology, 31*(3), 244-265.

Sullivan, P.H. (1999). Profiting from intellectual capital. *Journal of Knowledge Management, 3*(2), 132-142.

Szulanski, G. (1996). Exploring internal stickiness: Impediments to the transfer of best practice within a firm. *Strategic Management Journal, 17*(Winter Special Issue), 27-44.

Teece, D.J., Pisano, G., & Shuen, A. (1997). Dynamic capabilities and strategic management. *Strategic Management Journal, 18*(7), 509-533.

Thompson, J.D. (1967). *Organizations in action*. New York: McGraw-Hill.

Tsoukas, H. (1996). The firm as a distributed knowledge system. *Strategic Management Journal, 17*(Winter Special Issue), 11-25.

Tushman, M.L. (1978). Technical communication in R&D laboratories: The impact of project work characteristics. *Academy of Management Journal, 21*(4), 624-645.

Tushman, M.L., & Nadler, D.A. (1978). Information processing as an integrating concept in organizational design. *Academy of Management Review, 3*(3), 613-624.

Van der Bij, H., Song, X.M., & Weggeman, M. (2003). An empirical investigation into the antecedents of knowledge dissemination at the strategic business unit level. *Journal of Product Innovation Management, 20*(2), 163-179.

Wang, Q., & Von Tunzelmann, G.N. (2000). Complexities and the functions of the firm: Breadth and depth. *Research Policy, 29*(7/8), 805-818.

Wegner, D.M. (1987). Transactive memory. In B. Mullen & G.R. Goethals (Eds.), *Theories of group behavior* (pp. 185-208). New York: Springer Verlag.

KEY TERMS

Direction: Direction refers to specialists issuing rules, directives, and operating procedures to guide the behavior of non-specialists, less mature specialists, and specialists in other fields. Rules and directives can be interpreted as translations into a limited instruction of a wider body of explicit and tacit knowledge on a subject.

Division of Knowledge: The division of knowledge refers to the way in which knowledge is dispersed over organization members, groups, and departments. The division of knowledge varies from a low degree of differentiation (a high degree of redundancy) to a high degree of differentiation (a low degree of redundancy).

Exploitation: Exploitation refers to the use and development of things already known. It consists of making the most of current knowledge and learning how to execute current activities better. Exploitation is the opposite of exploration. If organizations do not exploit, they will have high costs and low incomes.

Exploration: Exploration refers to the pursuit of new knowledge, of things that might come to be known. It consists of learning completely new things and is associated with radical innovation. Exploration is the opposite of exploitation. If organizations do not explore, they can get stuck in a suboptimal or deteriorating situation.

Knowledge Integration: In most organizations, the knowledge required for innovation and production lies dispersed over individual organization members, groups, and departments. The performance of organizations depends on the integration of that specialized knowledge. Knowledge integration is the process in which different pockets of knowledge, which are valuable for a particular organizational process and held by different organization members, are applied to that organizational process.

Knowledge Integration Mechanism: Knowledge integration mechanisms are mechanisms through which the process of knowledge integration can be realized. The existing literature describes sequencing, decision support systems, direction, thinking along, group problem-solving, and knowledge transfer as knowledge integration mechanisms.

Sequencing: As a knowledge integration mechanism, sequencing refers to the assignment of tasks to those organization members who have the relevant knowledge for it. When creating routines of sequenced tasks, individuals only need to know their part of the routine in order to realize a coordinated application of knowledge.

Thinking Along: Thinking along consists in the temporary application of one's knowledge to somebody else's problem. This includes the application of tacit knowledge, intuitions, associations, and hunches. The application of this knowledge may yield ideas, hypotheses, suggestions, comments, questions, and so on.

K

Knowledge Intermediation

Enrico Scarso
University of Padova, Italy

Ettore Bolisani
University of Padova, Italy

Matteo Di Biagi
University of Padova, Italy

INTRODUCTION

Since knowledge is increasingly regarded as the central source of competitive advantage, a "cognitive" interpretation of business activities becomes vital. With regard to this, the flourishing field of knowledge management (KM) provides useful insights into approaches to a systematic and explicit management of knowledge. Furthermore, the development of Internet technologies raises expectations of new opportunities to acquire, process, and distribute knowledge. Little research has, however, been done on the *new businesses* that may originate from a combination of KM practices and the use of new technologies. In particular, since the activities of knowledge creation and sharing are not bound to the single organisation, there is room for the development of innovative services that enable a "knowledge-based use" of network technologies such as the Internet. In fact, an increasing number of examples of innovative "knowledge-intensive" firms based on the Web can be found, but there is the need for better understanding of the contents and issues associated with such emerging ventures.

This article focuses on the business of "knowledge intermediation" via the Web, that is, the provision of technology-based services designed to support knowledge flows between organisations. In detail, the aims are: (1) to explore the development of a new business model that combines the use of information and communication technologies with a KM capability; (2) to suggest preliminary classifications; and (3) to highlight possible economic opportunities and problems as well.

BACKGROUND

As the day-by-day practice shows, it is very unlikely that the single firm can own or internally generate all the knowledge assets required for the business (Quintas, Lefrere, & Jones, 1997; Bolisani & Scarso, 2000). As a consequence, companies are increasingly realising that their knowledge resources derive in significant part from the system of interorganisational relationships established with customers, vendors, business partners, institutions, and even competitors. Such *knowledge networks* (i.e., formal or informal agreements to share knowledge, explore innovations, and exploit new ideas, Millar, Demaid, & Quintas, 1997; Pyka, 1997, 2002; Warkentin, Sugumaran, & Bapna, 2001; Peña, 2002) constitute a basic and distinctive feature of the current knowledge-based economy.

Until now, most of the literature on KM has focused on knowledge generated, transferred, and used within a single organisation, while little work has been done to understand how to manage knowledge across organisations (Parise & Henderson, 2002; Spring, 2003). Hence, it is necessary to analyse whether and how the principles and approaches elaborated in "traditional" KM have to be reframed to perform *knowledge network management* (Seufert, von Krogh, & Bach, 1999). This sort of "extended KM" clearly raises more problematic issues than managing knowledge within the single firm. For instance, attempts to communicate meanings may be difficult due to the lack of common goals, languages, values, and mental schemes. As a matter of fact, a *cognitive distance* or *gap* may separate knowledge sources and users, which makes the sharing of useful knowledge difficult. Furthermore, reciprocal trust is needed, since a knowledge exchange may be easily exposed to the risk of opportunistic behaviours. Also, the effective "functioning" of a knowledge network involves the subdivision of "cognitive tasks" and KM competencies among the participants. Finally, an adequate technological infrastructure may be required to handle the large amounts of contents scattered in a wide context.

For this reason, new kinds of "mediating services" can be of great use: to fill the cognitive gap between players; to facilitate the flowing of knowledge inside the network (Spring, 2003); to act as "organizational translators" (Teece, 1998) between different interests, values, and culture of interconnecting partners; to implement and manage Internet-based interorganisational KM systems; to build network trust, and so forth. There is already evidence of companies providing such innovative services (see Bolisani, Di Biagi, & Scarso, 2003). The purpose here is to verify whether a "KM viewpoint" can be of help to describe more formally the new businesses of knowledge intermediation that we will name "knowledgemediary" (KMY). In particular, their distinctive features, key competences, and critical managerial issues are illustrated and discussed.

CONCEPT DEFINITION

To better specify the notion of *knowledgemediary*, it is useful to briefly recall its antecedents.

Knowledge-Intensive Business Services (KIBS)

The term KIBS was introduced to define business service firms providing knowledge-intensive, technology-based services with a high level of supplier-user interaction, generally produced by employing a highly qualified labour force (Nählinder, 2002). KIBS play the crucial role of both creating knowledge for (or together with) their customers, and assisting the circulation of knowledge from one firm to another. This knowledge brokering function is generally a byproduct of their work, that mainly consists in "solving problems for the clients." A growing number of studies about KIBS highlights the relevant contribution given by such services in the present economic systems (OECD, 1997; Roberts, Andersen, & Hull, 2000; Nählinder, 2002), as well as their special features, that is, they are innovative, act as vehicles of innovation, and connect firms, thus performing the function of "cognitive interface" between different business partners. Miles (1996) proposes a useful distinction between "traditional" KIBS (e.g., classical consulting services) and T-KIBS (i.e., services that concern or are based on the use of information and communication technologies, including Internet-based applications). Our notion of KMY has its roots inside the T-KIBS category.

Intermediation and Internet Applications

As mentioned, KMY services imply a mediating capability by their very nature, since they act in the middle of an interorganisational context. It is, however, necessary to specify the particular kind of intermediation that can be of interest here.

First, it is important to note that even the activity of intermediaries in traditional trade (e.g., identification of demand needs; information on products and suppliers; comparisons; market intelligence; distribution of information on products; customer targeting; demand orientation, etc.) involves *cognitive contents* (Sarkar, Butler, & Steinfield, 1995). In substance, a significant part of the value added by an intermediary consists of "bridging" over the *cognitive gap* between buyers and sellers, thereby facilitating the exchange of knowledge for settling transactions. Such cognitive implications of the intermediation activity also are underlined by the economic theories. For instance, according to the *transaction costs* theory, the choice between in-house direct sale and use of external intermediaries is based on the complexity, specificity, and uncertainty of economic exchanges (Rangan, Menezes, & Maier, 1992), that is on the *cognitive aspects* of a transaction. Also, in the *principal-agent* theory, agents are delegated to assist principals with their economic counterparts, in order to reduce the decisional complexity produced by *knowledge shortages* (Pratt & Zeckhauser, 1985). Another important problem concerns the *quality of information* exchanged by trading partners, and the *signalling (transferring) mechanisms* employed for this (Choi, Stahl, & Whinston, 1997).

The cognitive connotation of intermediation raises peculiar issues for Internet-based businesses. In fact, although the huge amount of information available on the Web extends the cognitive capabilities of the surfers, the growing size and complexity of the cyberspace and the resulting "information overload" effect makes its exploitation very difficult. In such context there may be the need for "knowledge mediators," capable of assisting the users in the management of online sources. Indeed, theoretical arguments and empirical observations show that the diffusion of Internet applications generally implies the development of new forms of intermediaries (Sarkar, Butler, & Steinfield, 1995), such as *infomediaries* (online firms specialising in online customer profiling and analysis of navigation traces), *cybermediaries* (online companies that specialise in electronic transactions such as Web malls, comparison sites, credit card clearing services, etc.), and so on.

Knowledge Mediators in KM Processes

The notion of "knowledge mediator" is also relevant to the literature of KM. For instance, the resort to "domain experts" is recommended for a corporate Web portal, in order to facilitate the extraction of knowledge from internal sources and its delivery to end users (Mack,

Ravin, & Byrd, 2001). The presence of a "knowledge broker" is often suggested for the good functioning of knowledge exchanges (e.g., the concept of "knowledge markets," Davenport & Prusak, 1998; Markus, 2001; Matson, Patiath, & Shavers, 2003; Kafentzis, Mentzas, Apostolou, & Georgolios, 2004). The task here consists of assisting sources and recipients to match their different interpretative contexts, translating meanings and values, and supporting the whole knowledge transfer process.

Knowledge Transfer Process

To better understand the role played by a knowledge mediator, we can refer to a representation of the *knowledge transfer* process (Hendriks & Vriens, 1999; Tuomi, 2000; Garavelli, Gorgoglione, & Scozzi, 2002). Figure 1 depicts the particular case of knowledge transferred through electronic communication. A piece of knowledge content must be first *externalised* (i.e., converted in the appropriate format, language, and data), transmitted, and then *internalised* (i.e., understood and assimilated by the receiver¾cf. Sharratt & Usoro, 2003). The success of this process requires: an "interpretative context" (or background) shared by the interconnecting partners; a mutual interest in transferring knowledge; and established "trust" (i.e., the parties should not doubt the quality of the knowledge transferred and its use). Such conditions can be

better satisfied thanks to the action of a knowledge mediator, who can assist or perform the externalisation/internalisation processes and help generate trust. In addition, the mediator might deal with the development and management of the technical infrastructure that underpins the transfer process.

Conceptual Roots of KMY Services

The following points represent the conceptual roots of the kind of firms that we named KMY (Figure 2). To summarise, the recognition of knowledge as a core resource for business and the increasing resort to external competencies explains the growing importance ascribed to "extended" KM processes. However, since a single firm may encounter several problems in accessing external sources and managing knowledge relations, this may open opportunities for innovative intermediating services that combine different services and capabilities:

- solving knowledge-intensive problems and applying extended KM ("KM capability")
- acting as an interface between knowledge sources and users, thus favouring knowledge exchanges ("mediating capability")
- designing and/or using information and communication technologies as a fundamental support of its activities ("technological capability")

Figure 1. The knowledge transfer process (adapted from Hendriks & Vriens, 1999)

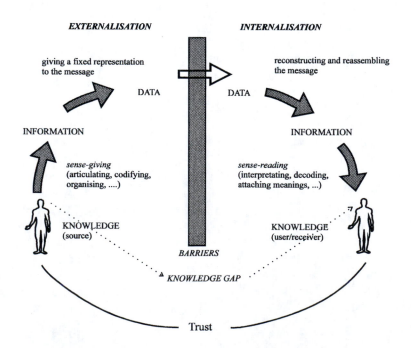

Figure 2. Conceptual roots of KMY services

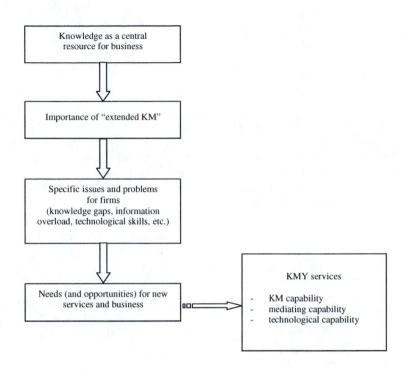

The practical foundations of the services provided by a KMY can be associated to the following aspects:

- a basic competence in managing knowledge transfer between firms/organisations, for example, to identify knowledge needs of the users, to research and select sources and knowledge contents, to perform processes of codification/de-codification, and so forth

- the capability of selecting the most adequate solution for settling a knowledge transaction in accordance to the specific circumstances of application (namely, nature of players involved, kind of knowledge exchanged, property rights, legal implications, payments, etc.)

- and, finally, the capability of using and integrating the technology into the KM processes

It is worth noting that such services can be provided by completely new startups but also by existing companies that can create departments specialising in KMY activities. Indeed, the focus of some existing companies (as in the case of consulting firms, or even media groups) is information or knowledge transfer. However, even in this case, the novelty is that KMY services represent the evolution and enrichment of traditional activities, thanks to the organic integration of KM com-

petencies, mediating capabilities, and the advanced use of new technologies.

To specify in more detail the possible features of a KMY service, we outline a framework and propose a reference taxonomy, by considering a typical situation denoted by the presence of: the *user* (typically a business user: firm, professional, etc.); a *source*, that provides or sells knowledge (other firms, university departments, research centres, etc.); and a *KMY*. For this purpose, we also refer to a scheme of a *knowledge transaction* (Figure 3), that is, a situation where economic players exchange knowledge contents with one another, by means of KMY services. The notion of transaction is essential to analyse the economic value of knowledge exchanges used in business processes.

Similarly to other economic exchanges, a knowledge transaction implies the transfer of a kind of goods (i.e., knowledge) from a source to a receiver, and a flow of payments. Clearly, there are peculiar aspects that should be considered when knowledge is the object of economic exchange. While in a traditional transaction, it is the buyer that makes a payment in favour of the seller (and, in addition, the intermediation service is paid by one or both parts); in the case of a knowledge transaction, it may be less clear who pays for what. For instance, in some cases knowledge sources can be "free," and the user can be asked to pay for the intermediation

Figure 3. Knowledge transaction by means of KMY services

service (e.g., the research activity performed by the KMY). Another important issue regards *pricing*. Since knowledge is typically an *experience good* (i.e., its value can be estimated after acquisition and use), it is very difficult to establish a *market price*, and consequently the pricing of KMY services also is harder. Other special questions concern the *property rights protection*, namely the attempts to avoid opportunistic behaviour associated with the exchange of knowledge.

All things considered, our analytical framework consists of six dimensions.

a. **Knowledge flows:**
   - knowledge asked or researched by the users
   - knowledge delivered by the source (not necessarily on demand)
   - knowledge that represents an additional (and original) contribution of the KMY

b. **Knowledge forms and contents:**
   - tacit vs. explicit knowledge components: referring to the knowledge transfer process, the explicit component can be more easily "decontextualised" and transferred in formal modes, while the tacit component is tightly connected to the interpretative framework shared by the parties involved in the transfer process
   - range and scope of knowledge, for example, multidisciplinary vs. specialised knowledge
   - object of knowledge, for example, know-about, know-how, know-why, know-who, know-with

c. **KM process implied in delivering KMY services:**
   - acquisition (identifying and cataloguing sources, analysing nature and formats of knowledge, etc.)
   - selection (choice of the specific knowledge contents to be transferred in relation to the specific uses)
   - internalisation (assistance to users in the assimilation of knowledge)
   - externalisation and distribution (assistance to sources in the delivery of knowledge)

d. **Service structure and competencies needed:**
   - organisational-managerial component: KM competencies (see point c), knowledge of the

sector/market where the KMY operates, capability of managing interorganisational network relations, and intermediation skills
   - technical components: tools used to support interorganisational KM processes in an Internet environment, as well as the skills to select, configure, and use them

e. **Management of knowledge transactions:**
   When knowledge is the object of an economic exchange, the transaction raises specific questions in relation to the transfer, protection, and replication of the property rights. It also should be analysed what service of knowledge transfer is paid for. More generally, the issues involved are:
   - mechanisms used for the economic exchange (formats, times, contracts, etc.)
   - mechanisms used for payments
   - duration of the transactional relations (e.g., spot, repetitive, or project-based relation)

f. **Model and structure of relations established by the KMY:**
   - bilateral relations with a single user or source (i.e., KMY as a sort of "private consultant")
   - relations with multiple and indistinct sources and users, with players belonging to a specific sector, value chain, or business community

EMPIRICAL INVESTIGATIONS

Despite their novelty, various examples of KMYs can be found in the business arena. Here, the features of some emergent categories or *models* are described, just as they were identified on the basis of an empirical exploration of the current experience in the field (see Bolisani, Di Biagi, & Scarso, 2003).

- **Mediator:** Its main role is to activate knowledge flows from sources to users. Examples include KMY services for professional consulting. The clients submit queries that are interpreted by the KMY, that also selects the appropriate professional, and takes care of the correct transmission of the answer as well as payment execution, and so forth. Other examples are human-based search engines, that is, services that provide assistance in information retrieval through the Net. In this case, users formulate complex queries interpreted by the KMY operators that also search on the Net and provide possible answers. Thus, the mediator model focuses on the management of "know-who" knowledge (i.e., knowledge of the possible sources and of their "quality" or reliability). Accordingly, the "reputation" that the KMY builds is crucial. Another key issue is the KM process of interpretation/de-contextualization of queries, which is vital especially considering that the entire relation occurs on the Internet with no face-to-face interactions.

- **Facilitator:** Its key function is to build appropriate environments for knowledge transfer, by identifying the optimal mechanisms or technology (i.e., a database, a document exchange, an online form, etc.), by processing codification/de-codification, and so on. A typical example is that of "job seeking" online services: The KMY performs a collection, selection, and presentation of job ads that are classified in a common format to facilitate retrieval. It is crucial for facilitators to have a "standard" process of collection, de-contextualization, and presentation of knowledge contents from heterogeneous sources to undifferentiated users. All this raises peculiar issues, such as the selection, explication, and standardisation of knowledge contents to be presented through a common interface (e.g., a Web portal). While knowledge coming from sources can be the "know-about" type, the added contribution of the KMY service is essentially a "know-with" component (i.e., how to connect different contents).

- **Aggregator:** This KMY service performs preliminary recognition and mapping of knowledge sources for a specific business community or market; knowledge contents are then made available to the users on demand. Examples are "vortal" (vertical portal) services, supplying market and technical information for specific business communities. The "aggregator" model refers to a common situation: a multiplicity of heterogeneous sources, and several potential users belonging to the same business community. The highly specific knowledge contents, which also can have heterogeneous formats, must be aggregated and collected for the community. The added service of the aggregator rests on the capability of selecting and reformulating contents that "may be" of interest for the users, which requires high competence of the business sector. In addition, the contents collected have to be converted and proposed in the appropriate form.

- **Manager:** This is the most complex model of KMY, since it combines many of the services described. Examples can be the online services for virtual business communities, or for communities of practice. In this case, an Internet-based platform for "knowledge sharing" is provided to all the firms and professionals serviced. This sort of Web portal, reserved to registered users, is based on a "flexible" system for sharing all the documents and contents needed. Since the mediating role of the KMY and the business relations between the users are closely intertwined, the kind of knowledge that the KMY has to manage is highly specific, but at the same time requires extreme flexibility to manage exceptions and innovations.

CONCLUSION AND FUTURE TRENDS

The main point here is that the practical transition toward the knowledge economy implies the implementation of new businesses that combine the explicit management of knowledge with an advanced use of Internet-based technologies. To investigate such issue, we attempted to introduce new approaches to the analysis of online business models by integrating "classical" themes of e-commerce (i.e., the characteristics of online transactions and the role of intermediation) with the emerging discipline of KM. The definition of KMY is strictly functional to this purpose, and is used to analyse new businesses of online intermediation by considering their role in KM processes in an explicit and direct way. Clearly, one limitation is that the empirical evidence is still insufficient to draw a conclusion. Actually, any new study of emerging business models necessarily suffers from scarce empirical confirmations. In any case, our early findings (see Bolisani, Di Biagi, & Scarso, 2003) apparently show that the perspective adopted could be promising.

Although the approach proposed here has descriptive aims, the findings also can provide useful insights into practical managerial aspects of new business implementation. In particular, the classifications of business models previously discussed, and the evaluation of the specific opportunities and problems associated with each specific KMY feature, can be of use for the implementation of new services based explicitly on KM practices and Internet technologies.

Having said that, there is still work to do to transform the analysis into a more complete subject of research. In particular, the *transactional nature* of KMY services should be investigated more thoroughly, with direct reference of knowledge as the object of economic exchange. As regards managerial guidelines, an important issue concerns the *practical implementation* of an online strategy for a KMY service. There is especially the need to integrate a descriptive or analytical approach (that can be useful to make classifications or illustrate problems) to more normative prescriptions.

REFERENCES

Bolisani, E., Di Biagi, M., & Scarso, E. (2003). Knowledge intermediation: New business models in the digital economy. *Proceedings of the 16th Bled eCommerce Conference* (pp. 987-999).

Bolisani, E., & Scarso, E. (1999). Information technology management: A knowledge-based perspective. *Technovation, 19,* 209-217.

Choi, S., Stahl, D.O., & Whinston, A.B. (1997). *The economics of electronic commerce.* Indianapolis: MacMillan.

Davenport, T.H., & Prusak, L. (1998). *Working knowledge: How organizations manage what they know.* Boston: Harvard Business School Press.

Garavelli, A.C., Gorgoglione, M., & Scozzi, B. (2002). Managing knowledge transfer by knowledge technologies. *Technovation, 22,* 269-279.

Hendriks, P.H.J., & Vriens, D.J. (1999). Knowledge-based systems and knowledge management: Friends or foes? *Information & Management, 35,* 113-125.

Kafentzis, K., Mentzas, G., Apostolou, D., & Georgolios, P. (2004). Knowledge marketplaces: Strategic issues and business models. *Journal of Knowledge Management, 8*(1), 130-146.

Mack, R., Ravin, Y., & Byrd, R.J. (2001). Knowledge portals and the emerging digital knowledge workplace. *IBM Systems Journal, 40*(4), 925-954.

Markus, M.L. (2001). Toward a theory of knowledge reuse: Types of knowledge reuse situations and factors in reuse success. *Journal of Management Information Systems, 18*(1), 27-93.

Matson, E., Patiath, P., & Shavers, T. (2003). Stimulating knowledge sharing: Strengthening your organization's internal knowledge market. *Organizational Dynamics, 32*(3), 275-287.

Miles, I. (1996). *Innovation in services: Services in innovation.* Manchester, UK: Manchester Statistical Society.

Millar, J., Demaid, A., & Quintas, P. (1997). Trans-organizational innovation: A framework for research. *Technology Analysis & Strategic Management, 9*(4), 399-418.

Nählinder J. (2002). Innovation in knowledge intensive business services. State of the art and conceptualisations. *ISRN Liu–Tema-T-WP-244-SE,* June.

OECD (1997). *Statistics on value added and employment, services.* Paris, OECD.

Parise, S., & Henderson, J.C. (2001). Knowledge resource exchange in strategic alliance. *IBM Systems Journal, 40*(4), 908-924.

Peña, I. (2002). Knowledge networks as part of an integrated knowledge management approach. *Journal of Knowledge Management, 6*(5), 469-478.

Pratt, J.W., & Zeckhauser, R.J. (Eds.). (1985). *Principals and agents. The structure of business.* Boston: Harvard Business School Press.

Pyka, A. (1997). Informal networking. *Technovation, 17,* 207-220.

Pyka, A. (2002). Innovation networks: From the incentive-based to the knowledge-based approaches. *European Journal of Innovation Management, 5*(3), 152-163.

Quintas, P., Lefrere, P., & Jones, G. (1997). Knowledge management: A strategic agenda. *Long Range Planning, 30*(3), 385-391.

Rangan, K.V., Menezes, M.A.J., & Maier, E.P. (1992). Channel selection for new industrial products: A framework, method, and application. *Journal of Marketing, 56,* 69-82.

Roberts, J., Andersen, B., & Hull, R. (2000). In B. Andersen, J. Howell, R. Hull, I. Miles, & J. Roberts (Eds.) *Knowledge and innovation in the new service economy* (pp. 10-35). Cheltenham, UK: Edward Elgar.

Sarkar, M.B., Butler, B., & Steinfield, C. (1995). Intermediaries and cybermediaries: A continuing role for mediating players in the electronic marketplace. *Journal of Computer Mediated Communication, 1*(3).

Seufert, A., von Krogh, G., & Bach, A. (1999). Towards knowledge networking. *Journal of Knowledge Management, 3*(3), 180-190.

Sharratt, M., & Usoro, A. (2003) Understanding knowledge-sharing in online communities of practice. *Electronic Journal on Knowledge Management, 1*(1), 187-196.

Spring, M. (2003). Knowledge management in extended

operations networks. *Journal of Knowledge Management, 7*(4), 29-37.

Teece, D.J. (1998). Capturing value from knowledge assets: The new economy, markets for know-how, and intangible assets. *California Management Review, 40*(3), 55-79.

Tuomi, I. (2000). Data is more than knowledge: Implications of the reversed knowledge hierarchy for knowledge management and organizational memory. *Journal of Management Information Systems, 16*(3), 103-117.

Warkentin, M., Sugumaran, V., & Bapna R. (2001). E-knowledge networks for inter-organizational collaborative e-business. *Logistics Information Management, 14*(1/2), 149-162.

KEY TERMS

Cybermediary: An online company specialising in electronic transactions and digital intermediation. The term was introduced by Sarkar, Butler, and Steinfield (1995).

Experience Goods: Goods whose value can be estimated after acquisition and use. This raises the problem of pricing and other marketing issues. Generally speaking, digital goods (e.g., books, music, software, news, and, of course, information) are all experience goods.

Extended Knowledge Management: KM methods and practices applied to inter-firm knowledge management. The adjective "extended" means activities that span the organisational boundaries, involving suppliers, customers, vendors, business partners, and institutions.

Knowledge Networks: Inter-firm formal or informal agreements whose main goal is to share knowledge and exploit new ideas. Knowledge networks provide the member firms with access to complementary knowledge resources, and extend their core capabilities. In a knowledge network each node represents a unique repository of knowledge whereas the links represent economic and strategic ties that enable knowledge flows among nodes.

Knowledge-Intensive Business Services (KIBS): Business service firms which provide knowledge-intensive, technology-based services with a high level of supplier-user interaction, generally produced by employing a highly educated labour-force.

Knowledge Transaction: An economic exchange whose object is knowledge.

Knowledgemediary: An online company providing services to support knowledge transactions. Such companies are able to solve knowledge-intensive problems; to act as broker between knowledge sources and users; and to design and use information and communication technologies for knowledge management aims.

Knowledge Management Agents

Leon Sterling
University of Melbourne, Australia

APPLYING AGENTS WITHIN KNOWLEDGE MANAGEMENT

The agent has existed as a concept for thousands of years. In the human context, an agent is a person that performs some task on your behalf, for example, a travel agent planning flights and accommodation for your holiday, or a real-estate agent helping you buy or sell a house, or someone arranging marriages. Some Biblical laws specifically refer to agents.

In the much more recent software context, an agent is loosely a program that performs a task on your behalf. Agents have grown in popularity since the introduction of the PC (personal computer) as the target environment for application software has increased in complexity. Software systems must now operate robustly in a networked, global environment comprised of diverse, distributed technologies. Furthermore, the environment is dynamic, and frequent change is inevitable. Having automated help is almost a necessity.

Despite many attempts, there is no universally agreed technical definition of agents. An oft-cited reference by Franklin and Graeser (1996) gives almost a dozen different definitions. Let us consider a textbook definition given by Wooldridge (2002, p. 15). An agent is "an encapsulated computer system, situated in some environment, and capable of flexible autonomous action in that environment in order to meet its design objectives."

Essential characteristics of the agent paradigm that can be elicited from this definition are:

*   The autonomy of individual agents, or their ability to act for themselves and to achieve goals
*   The reactivity of individual agents in response to changes in the environment
*   The modularity of individual agents and classes to allow the easy development of complex systems
*   The ability of agents to communicate effectively and interact with legacy systems

Optional characteristics of the agent paradigm, which emerge from broader considerations of agents than the above definition, include mobility in moving around a network and the ability to reason.

This article rests on the metaphoric view of agents as entities performing tasks on one's behalf. Agents are presumed useful for building software to interact with complex environments such as the Internet or within complex organizations such as universities and multinational corporations. Expected of a program being viewed as an agent is an ability to sense and be aware of the environment in which it is situated, an ability to communicate with other agents, and an ability to take action in its situated environment. According to these three expectations, sophisticated e-mail programs such as Microsoft's Outlook and Qualcomm's Eudora can be viewed as agents. They are situated on the Internet and sense various aspects of the Internet, including when Internet connections are live and when new mail arrives. They communicate with other e-mail clients by sending and receiving messages. They take actions such as raising alerts when mail has arrived, sending mail that has been queued once an Internet connection is restored, or filtering messages according to rules.

We now connect with knowledge. Organizations operating in today's software environment need to represent, interact with, and above all, maintain a large collection of knowledge, including, for example, business practices, trade secrets, intellectual property, organizational hierarchies, promotional organizational descriptions, and knowledge of both its own policies and policies of relevant, external regulatory bodies. There is out of necessity great diversity in the form, content, and context of the knowledge. Most of this knowledge is in unstructured or semistructured form. The problem of the representation and maintenance of such knowledge within an organization can be loosely called the knowledge management problem.

For the purposes of this article, there is no need to define the knowledge management problem or knowledge management, for that matter, more precisely. However, we note that the term knowledge management subsumes the term content management. Referring to knowledge rather than content suggests some concern with formalizing knowledge explicitly.

How might agents be applicable to the knowledge management problem? As a running, concrete example, consider knowledge management issues related to the responsibilities of a university lecturer in charge of a subject[1]. She or he must prepare, deliver, and maintain content in a variety of forms, possibly including lecture notes, papers, and media presentations. Let us particularly focus on one component of the task, namely, maintaining a Web site for the subject.

Several possibilities exist for enlisting the help of agents. An obvious first task for agents is to help with the acquisition of knowledge, which is obtaining content and placing it on the Web site.

What type of software agent might be useful for the acquisition of knowledge? It is natural to envisage a custom Web crawler (http://en.wikipedia.org/wiki/Web_crawler), Programs that trawled specified Web sites looking for content were early applications built to exploit the World Wide Web. Building a Web-crawling agent immediately raises important considerations. The agent should be aware of important regulatory issues such as the fact that downloading mp3 files is illegal in some countries without the authorised permission of the copyright holder. The agent should also be aware of conventions such as the robots.txt protocol (http://en.wikipedia.org/wiki/Robots.txt_protocol) in which guidelines are given about parts of a file hierarchy that should be ignored by well-behaved agents. There are many similar policies of which a knowledge-acquiring agent would need to be aware. These policies demonstrate some of the complexities that need to be taken into account in building agents.

Search engines are based on exhaustive trawls and efficient indexing of files using techniques from information retrieval. Agents can also be constructed using techniques derived from experience in building knowledge-based expert systems. Consider the task of tracking down a particular paper by a particular author. One may have been referred to the paper by word of mouth or by the need to cite a final version of the paper for which you only had a preliminary version. A prototype citation-finding agent, CiFi (Loke, Davison, & Sterling, 1996), was built for this task. CiFi used the following three strategies for finding papers. First, CiFi tried to find a link from the author's home page[2] using heuristics about possible keywords such as research and publications. Then CiFi looked for a link from a page of publications or technical reports linked from the author's department. Finally, CiFi sent an e-mail to the author asking for the file or citation.

A challenge in building CiFi was making it work on a variety of Web sites. Ideally, a single agent is desirable that can operate successfully over a range of Web sites. CiFi was not particularly intelligent or effective. It clearly reflected a bias to papers written by researchers within universities. It failed, for example, to find white papers written by companies. It would have had difficulty adapting to current spam filters if its e-mail message was blocked. Having agents adapt to changing circumstances is a desirable property. However, CiFi is

indicative of an agent that might be applied to a knowledge management task.

Another task that might be assigned to an agent is to look for new articles by particular authors. Suppose you respect the work of a particular researcher and want to be notified of any of his or her new publications. It is possible for an agent to look for changes on a Web site and alert you that a new publication may be present[3]. In general, reporting changes or the presence or absence of documents is a task that the reader should have no difficulty in identifying as being potentially useful within his or her own organization. Providing new information or reminding participants that the next step in a work flow needs to happen can be helpful. Such an agent can be viewed as being a facilitator. Facilitation was espoused by Winograd and Flores (1987) as an alternative model for agents rather than artificial intelligence.

Let us return to specific tasks within Web-site management. Content on a Web page may be made available through links to other resources. However, it is frustrating when browsing to find outdated links on Web pages. An agent could check periodically whether links are still live. It would need to sense the result of its search and update the links on the page.

Here is another task for an agent. Some of the knowledge on a Web site can be usefully cross-linked. For example, an online quiz would be enhanced for self-study by having links from questions to material where the correct answer can be found. These links may be provided once the student has attempted the quiz. An agent could construct these links automatically. Of course, any changes to content would mean that the cross-links would need to be checked. A prototype agent called QuizHelper that can perform this task has been described in Chan and Sterling (2003).

Several of the above suggestions for agents address the performance of maintenance activities. Maintenance is key for knowledge management. The reader can doubtless imagine maintenance activities in his or her own environment that might be performed by an agent. Some maintenance activities are already happening automatically, for example, through alerts about software updates or the downloading of security patches.

A different type of task that an agent can perform is monitoring the use of a program.

For a program developed to help students learn material, an educator may want an agent to assess if the program is being used properly by the students. The assessment may be used to give feedback to the software developers or to try to ascertain whether the student is meeting learning objectives. The conceiving of agents to monitor student interaction with a program suggests good design questions. How is the agent going to sense what the student is doing? How are student actions going to be interpreted? How can student activities be matched to learning objectives?

Now imagine a system consisting of several of these agents working together performing tasks in a domain. A system consisting of multiple cooperating agents is known as a multiagent system. The conceiving of separate tasks being performed by separate agents simplifies the conceptualisation of how the system may be built. We discuss the building of multiagent systems later.

Agents need to be aware of the environmental context, and there is growing work on the representation of the context and the environment. Explicit models of the environment and context are examples of models of knowledge, our next topic. It is a challenge to handle the knowledge of different agents in a multiagent system, and this leads us to the important but difficult and conceptually rich area of agent ontology.

While ontology is discussed in other articles in this volume, we address it briefly as ontology is an important topic for agents and one that is underestimated by agent researchers. The most common definition of an ontology is "an explicit specification of a conceptualisation."[4] In practice, an ontology is an explicit, formal knowledge-representation scheme.

As stated previously, an ability to communicate is intrinsic to an agent. In order for meaningful communication to occur between agents, they must understand what each other's terms mean. Clearly, knowledge management tasks are easier if all agents involved, including humans and software agents, agree on the vocabulary they are using.

Agent developers until now have assumed that each application would have a suitable ontology. Explicit languages have been developed for agent communication, notably KQML as discussed by Finin, Labrou, and Mayfield (1997), and the more recent standard, ACL, being developed by FIPA (Foundation for Intelligent Physical Agent; http://www.fipa.org). Both KQML and ACL are based on the speech-act theory originally espoused by Searle (1969). Communication by an agent using KQML has a field for an ontology. It is presumed that by knowing what ontology an agent uses, correct meaning will be applied. ACL is more sophisticated and even provides a specification for an ontology agent "for registering and serving ontologies to agents" (http://www.fipa.org/specs/fipa00086/).

There are several dimensions to consider with respect to an ontology. Is it general purpose or domain specific? Is it maintained centrally, or distributed among several agents? Do all agents use the same ontology or is meaning negotiated between different ontologies? Does each task have its own ontology? Where should the ontology come from? One possibility is that an organi-

zation maintains its own ontology that constitutes its single organizational view of the world. An alternative possibility has been that someone develops a single ontology to which developers refer. The prototypical example of a single ontology is Cyc, which has been under development for 20 years. An open-source version of Cyc is available at http://www.opencyc.org. A recent development with regard to Cyc is the use of contexts to represent local knowledge.

Knowledge depends on context. Different cultures do things differently, and the behaviour of an agent needs to be culturally appropriate. An increasingly common view is that agents should be allowed to have diverse views. Cultural issues should not be underestimated. Even within organizations, there is a need to interact with outside organizations, be they commercial, regulatory, or cooperative. Outside organizations will have a different view of the world and hence a different ontology. When agents communicate or cooperate in tasks, their knowledge may need to be matched, a process we call knowledge mediation.

An approach to achieving knowledge mediation is by viewing tasks as context, as advocated in Lister and Sterling (2003). Agents only need to be able to match up sufficient knowledge to perform a task rather than to match a complete ontology. While partial matching may lead to difficult maintenance issues should a task be repeated, it seems more realistic and akin to how people interact despite clearly different views of the world. This raises the issue of modeling tasks for agents. The knowledge of a domain is usually separate from the knowledge of performing tasks in the domain. In building an agent application, this needs to be taken into consideration.

The next topic to be considered is the practice of building multiagent systems. How should multiagent systems be built for knowledge management applications? Today's dynamic, distributed, heterogeneous environment presents a problem for software developers. Traditional software engineering has demanded the complete specification of a software application before issuing assurances that the application will work correctly. Producing a complete specification of requirements is not realistic and almost certainly impossible given the inevitable changes. It is questionable whether current software-development techniques are adequate[5]. The relatively new paradigm of agent-oriented programming (Wooldridge, 2002) has emerged as a potential successor to object-oriented programming, and in principle is better able to address the new demands on software.

While substantial experience has been accumulated in building individual agents, building a multiagent system remains a challenge. The first complete methodology proposed to guide the process of developing a multiagent system was Gaia (Wooldridge, Jennings, & Kinny, 2000). According to Gaia, a multiagent system is conceived as a computational organization of agents, with each agent playing a specific role, or several roles, within the organization and cooperating with other agents toward the achievement of a common application (i.e., organizational) goal. The field of agent-oriented software engineering has blossomed since 2001 to address the question of how to develop agents systematically. No single methodology has emerged as the best choice for developers.

A good overview of the range of methodologies for building multiagent systems can be found in Bergenti et al. (2004). Almost all methodologies highlight roles, goals, and agents as important new concepts for building multiagent systems rather than object-oriented systems. However, just as there is no agreed-on definition for agents, there is no agreed-on definition for roles and goals. Let us consider them briefly.

Roles are abstractions of agents, and they specify high-level aspects of an agent such as responsibilities, constraints, and permissions. It is useful to clarify in what role an action to be undertaken by an agent is to be performed. Goals are high-level representations of the purpose of a system. They specify what is to be achieved, the aspect of system analysis, rather than how something is to be achieved, which is system design and implementation. Eliciting system requirements in terms of roles and goals can be intuitive and different than the established object-oriented practice of using cases.

For many applications, we will want to consider a system as consisting of both humans and software agents. Knowledge management certainly involves people. A distinct advantage of the agent paradigm is that it facilitates thinking in terms of systems consisting of both humans and software agents. Thinking of a system in terms of roles and goals blurs the difference between human agents and software agents, which from experience is useful during elicitation.

Design proceeds once roles and goals have been elicited. Agents are chosen to fulfill one or many roles. The agents will perform tasks and activities to achieve goals and follow protocols. There is a growing body of literature on appropriate protocols for multiagent systems. The use of agents can help to abstract interface issues. Agents can serve as a wrapper around legacy systems. The interacting agents are designed to communicate correctly. How an agent communicates with the legacy program becomes an internal matter that does not need to be addressed by the system as a whole. Agents can also be designed to consume services, a view consistent with the current vision of Web services.

This article has been concerned with relating two topics: knowledge management and multiagent systems. We have considered how agents might be applied to knowledge management by identifying some knowledge management tasks that might usefully be performed by agents. We discussed how agents might be developed to perform the tasks, highlighting the extra concepts of goals and roles that are useful for the development of agents. In conclusion, knowledge management can be viewed as a system where humans and software agents cooperate. Research has been performed that indicates that building agents to perform knowledge management tasks is promising.

REFERENCES

Bergenti, F., Gleizes, M. P., & Zambonelli, F. (2004). *Methodologies and software engineering for agent systems: The agent-oriented software engineering handbook*. Norwell, MA: Kluwer.

Chan, K., & Sterling, L. (2003). Light-weight agents for e-learning environments. *Foundations of Intelligent Systems: Proceedings of the 14th International Symposium, ISMIS 2003* (pp. 197-205).

Finin, T., Labrou, Y., & Mayfield, J. (1997). KQML as an agent communication language. In J. Bradshaw (Ed.), *Software agents*. Cambridge, MA: MIT Press.

Franklin, S. P., & Graeser, A. G. (1996). Is it an agent, or just a program? A taxonomy for autonomous agents. In J. P. Muller, M. J. Wooldridge, & N. R. Jennings (Eds.), *Intelligent agents III*. Berlin: Springer-Verlag.

Gómez-Pérez, A., Fernández-López, M., & Corcho, O. (2004). *Ontological engineering*. London: Springer-Verlag.

Lister, K., & Sterling, L. (2003). Tasks as context for intelligent agents. In J. Liu, B. Faltings, N. Zhong, R. Lu, & T. Nishida (Eds.), *Proceedings of the 2003 IEEE/WIC International Conference on Intelligent Agent Technology* (pp. 154-160). IEEE Computer Society.

Loke, S. W., Davison, A., & Sterling, L. S. (1996). CiFi: An intelligent agent for citation finding on the World-Wide Web. In Springer lecture notes in artificial intelligence: Vol. 1114. *Proceedings of the 4th Pacific Rim International Conference on Artificial Intelligence (PRICAI-96)* (pp. 580-592).

Searle, J. R. (1969). *Speech acts: An essay in the philosophy of language*. Cambridge, MA: Cambridge University Press.

Shakes, J., Langheinrich, M., & Etzioni, O. (1997). Dynamic reference sifting: A case study in the homepage domain. *Proceedings of the 6th International World Wide Web Conference* (pp. 189-200).

Winograd, T., & Flores, F. (1987). *Understanding computers and cognition: A new foundation for design.* Reading, MA: Addison Wesley Publishing Inc.

Wooldridge, M. J. (2002). *An introduction to multiagent systems.* Chinchester, UK: John Wiley.

Wooldridge, M. J., Jennings, N. R., & Kinny, D. (2000). The Gaia methodology for agent-oriented analysis and design. *International Journal of Autonomous Agents and Multi Agent Systems, 3*(3), 285-312.

KEY TERMS

Agent: An encapsulated computer system situated in some environment that is capable of flexible, autonomous action in that environment in order to meet its design objectives.

Goal: A high-level representation of the purpose of a multiagent system.

Knowledge Management Problem: The problem of the representation and maintenance of diverse, dynamic knowledge within an organization.

Knowledge Mediation: The process of matching the knowledge of agents when they communicate or cooperate in tasks.

Multiagent System: A system consisting of multiple cooperating agents.

Ontology: An explicit specification of a conceptualisation.

Role: An abstraction of an agent used to elicit requirements for a multiagent system.

Web Crawler: A program that browses the World Wide Web in a methodical, automated manner.

ENDNOTES

[1] In the United States, a subject is called a course, a fact that illustrates the ontology problem discussed later in the article.

[2] Finding an author's home page is an interesting task in and of itself, and agents have been developed to accomplish the task. The best known is Ahoy!, which was retired in 2000. More information can be found in Shakes, Langheinrich, and Etzioni (1997). Note that the need for such an agent has been essentially obviated by Google.

[3] A free Web service was developed to notify users of Web-site changes several years ago. It is worth commenting that some people view the task an agent performs as a service, and the metaphor of intelligent services is used to describe similar concepts being discussed in this article. This is not the place to debate the relative merits of the agent metaphor vs. the services metaphor.

[4] This definition of ontology is given by Gruber, and it is discussed at length in Gómez-Pérez, Fernández-López, and Corcho (2004).

[5] It is a belief underlying the article that current software-development methods are inadequate, but the argument is beyond the scope of this article.

Knowledge Management Governance

Suzanne Zyngier
Monash University, Australia

K

INTRODUCTION

There are many barriers to the implementation of knowledge management (KM) strategies. These include the lack of time and financial resources allocated to sharing knowledge, a lack of organizational understanding of the philosophy and the benefits of KM, and a lack of skills in KM. However, survey data show that the greatest acknowledged obstacle to the implementation of a KM strategy is the management culture of the organization (Chase, 1997; Zyngier, 2001). These obstacles reveal a problem in the implementation of an organizational KM strategy. The problem lies not in the implementation of a given strategy per se, but in the lack of governance of that strategy.

The governance process is a framework of authority that ensures the delivery of anticipated or predicted benefits of a service or process (Farrar, 2001). The operationalization of that strategy is therefore executed in an authorized and regulated manner. Governance mechanisms must be invoked to guide both the initial implementation and the ongoing control and authority over KM strategies. A governance framework will provide the management of risk, review mechanisms and fiscal accountability in leveraging tacit knowledge, and the sharing of explicit knowledge within an organization. Knowledge is not simply a series of artefacts to be managed. This article identifies the processes in KM that are subject to governance. KM governance centres the decision-making authority as an executive framework to deliver the expected benefits of the strategy and for these benefits to be delivered in a controlled manner. This is achieved by the establishment of checks and balances in the implementation of the strategy. It ensures that evaluation measures feedback that enables deliberate adjustment of the delivery of the strategy, and that needs and expectations are being met. If the needs and expectations of the organization cannot be met, then the governance process should then be able to establish and manage the cause.

The first part of this article discusses KM strategy development and shows the origins of KM governance in the concept of the use of governance principles and practices. The second part will discuss the central issues in KM governance, being authority, evaluation, measurement, and risk management. The third part will suggest a structure or model for KM governance explaining how this operates in an organizational context, and suggests future trends for this research.

BACKGROUND

The Role of Leadership

Executive management leads and establishes the culture and consequent ability of an organization to capture, share, and manage its knowledge. In the past, leaders in organizations were empowered to order changes, and then all that was required of the organization was to implement the plan (Bridges & Mitchell, 2000). The culture of an organization is developed by the structure, attitude, and example of management. Krogh, Ichijo, and Nonaka (2000) describe how effective management and the support of knowledge creation depends on the physical, virtual, and emotional context in which they are manifested. Where there is a strong commitment at the level of executive management to change organizational culture, an organization is able to begin to create the values that lead to knowledge sharing across boundaries (Hackett, 2000; O'Dell, Grayson, & Essaides, 1998). Currently, interpretations of knowledge management leadership (Rumizen, 2002; Tiwana, 2002) endow the leader with the responsibility to direct, conduct, or guide functions in the implementation of such a strategy.

The terms knowledge champion, leader, and sponsor are used interchangeably in the knowledge management literature. The terms variously indicate a person who initiates a KM strategy, or one who supports and promotes the initiation of such a strategy. Therefore, the person or persons responsible for the implementation of a KM strategy may have the sole responsibility for the development and implementation of a KM strategy. This cannot ensure buy in from the organization as a whole. These risks are revealed as found in Australian and international surveys that have disclosed some of the obstacles to KM strategies (Chase, 1997; Davis, McAdams, Dixon, Orlikowski, & Leonard, 1998; DeLong & Fahey, 2000; Ewyk, 1998; Fang, Lin, Hsiao, Huang, &

Fang, 2002; Hackett, 2000; IC² Institute at the University of Texas at Austin, 2001; McAdam & Reid, 2001; Zyngier, 2001).

KM Strategy Development

KM literature describes many approaches to the development of a strategy or plan to be implemented as a means of achieving the organizational objectives of sharing tacit and explicit knowledge within the organization. Strategies are usually grounded in a theoretical methodology that will provide the greatest leverage in implementation (Zack, 1999), with each meeting perceived needs in the organization. There are two categories of strategies: deliberate and emergent strategies. Deliberate strategies must be articulated in a plan that must then be implemented. Emergent strategies are those that emerge in the organization as part of the process of learning what works well and what does not. Mintzberg (1994) suggests that strategic planning processes fail when they are not constructed to understand, internalise, and synthesise, that is, to learn from the successes or failures of the strategic process as it is implemented. In this sense, strategic planning would be a static and inviolate process. This is where the concepts of strategic approaches to KM are vulnerable unless the strategy is conceived of as a learning or evolutionary process. This being so, a KM strategy or plan is not rigid, but is an operational process that will enable learning and can evolve to take into account new and emerging environments within and outside the organization. KM obstacles lie not in the plan, but in the processes of control or regulation that surround the planning, implementation, feedback, and ongoing development of the plan. These processes are governance processes.

Governance Principles and Practice

There are a number of current contending uses of the term governance. In this article, governance refers to the governance processes of control or regulation within companies, interpreted as the implementation of authority through a framework that ensures the delivery of anticipated or predicted benefits of a service or process in an authorized and regulated manner (Weill & Woodham, 2003). This approach forms a context for analysis, management, risk management, and the ongoing development of strategies to manage organizational knowledge. It is also a means of developing measures of the effectiveness of those strategies. Governance will be affected by the composition of the membership of the governing body, the personal characteristics and history of the individuals involved, and the visions and principles enshrined in organizational structures and processes.

There are two main theories in the governance literature that relate to the purpose of the corporation and whose interests it should serve (Farrar, 2001; Van den Berghe & De Ridder, 1999). These are:

1. the shareholder model where the primacy focus of serving shareholder interest and value is the underlying philosophy or driver of governance, and cost minimisation and profit maximisation are paramount, and

2. the stakeholders model where the primary interest is on all stakeholders including the organization's owners or shareholders, creditors, employees, and the local communities in which the firm exists.

The stakeholders or consultative model may be considered a less managerially neat option due to the need to consult and reconcile conflicting interests; however, where decisions are made and endorsed by the majority of stakeholders, there is greater acceptance of decisions and activity around those decisions (Vinten, 2000).

In the stakeholder model, a greater contribution of decision making is expected at all levels. Internal stakeholder governance processes are not merely good management processes, but can also be viewed in terms of ensuring that a wide range of organizational needs are represented and being met. While to-date governance principles have rarely been applied to other managerial strategies, this approach is seen in the work of the IT Governance Institute (2001), the IT Governance Institute and COBIT Steering Committee (2000), and the British Standards Institution and Technical Committee (2002). The notion of IS and IT governance activity is already apparent as a subset of governance. This framework similarly facilitates the provision of feedback mechanisms within other managerial strategies to serve as a model of continuous improvement in organizational structures. Responsiveness to stakeholder interests enhances the capacity of the organization to identify and analyse a greater range of risks and to better deliver services or products.

Governance is at the centre of the decision-making authority. It is a framework to deliver the expected benefits of investments in a controlled manner through the establishment of checks and balances in the mode of service delivery. It ensures that evaluation feeds back into the service delivery strategy, and that stakeholder needs and expectations are being met. This approach is echoed by Galliers' (1999) sociotechnical approach to business and IS strategy formations, and the management of organizational transformation that takes into account the organizational environment, business strategies and processes, and required infrastructure. He sees that implementation requires the allocation of responsibilities with clearly defined objectives, timescales, and performance measures. This is paralleled by ongoing evaluation and review, including long-term planning and perspective, and the recognition and accounting for consequential or emergent strategies.

Weill and Woodham (2002) propose that the design of governance mechanisms is constructed in the context of the competing operational, structural, and infrastructural forces that operate within a business in harmony with organizational objectives. A governance framework must understand how decisions are made in key domains. These domains are principles, infrastructure strategies, architecture and investment, and prioritisation. Thus, governance will concentrate on the relationships and processes that develop and maintain control over the infrastructure, and human resources utilized in order to deliver the service to the organization. It provides check and balance mechanisms that enable the decision-making processes and results in IT contributing as a value-adding function in service of the enterprise.

An emphasis on strategy, risk management, the delivering of financial value, and performance measurement indicates the ongoing management of best practice. Applied to organizational IT, it is suggested that "at the heart of the governance responsibilities of setting strategy, managing risks, delivering value and measuring performance, are the stakeholders values, which drive the enterprise and IT strategy" (IT Governance Institute, 2001, p. 10). This is not a linear mechanism, but it is intended to feed back both the positive and negative aspects of performance. These response mechanisms will in turn moderate and improve practice in addition to responding to the internal and external effects in the organizational environment.

FOCUS ON KM GOVERNANCE

The delivery of a KM strategy in an organization exists and provides services to meet the needs for the creation, dissemination, and utilization of tacit and explicit knowledge to fulfill organizational objectives. How this function is fulfilled is reflected in the timeliness of service delivery and the satisfaction levels of internal and also, potentially, external clients. The processes and principles that act as a framework for the examination, regulation, supervision, and revision of KM strategies are termed KM governance. Wiig (1997) described governance functions as those of the monitoring and facilitation of knowledge-related activities within the implementation process. There is little in the literature that

separates descriptions of strategy implementation from the authority framework that governance provides. Knowledge management governance processes determine organizational knowledge-access conditions, quality maintenance, decision-making processes, and means for resolving KM obstacles.

Authority

KM governance can meet process objectives through the development of an effective understanding of the potential of KM within the organization, an effective understanding of the role of KM within the organization, and the alignment of KM with the value proposition and strategy of the organization. Finally, it also meets process objects through the regular review, approval, and monitoring of KM investments in infrastructure and in human resources. KM governance centres on the decision-making authority, an executive framework to deliver the expected benefits of the strategy. This can then be delivered in a controlled manner through the establishment of evaluation, measurement, and risk management in service delivery. It ensures that these processes feed back into the service delivery strategy, and that all stakeholder needs and expectations are being met. If they cannot be met, then the governance process will be able to establish the reason and resolution.

Risk Management

Governance processes manage the risks of KM to acknowledge and challenge the cultural issues, structural obstacles, and other relevant issues as they arise during the implementation and ongoing operation of the strategy. The management of these risks assists in their resolution and strengthens strategies to manage knowledge within the organization. The need for risk management in KM was formally indicated in 2001 (Standards Australia) with the need to identify the assets, risks, and controls associated with the implementation of strategy. Obstacles to the effective management of organizational knowledge include a management culture in the organisation that hinders KM with concomitant change-management issues. Additionally, the philosophy of knowledge management is often inadequately understood in the organisation, and conflicts of organizational priorities are problematic for the development and initiation of a KM strategy. For many organizations, the development of criteria for knowledge collection is difficult (Chase, 1997; Zyngier, 2001).

Risk management is a proactive strategy of analysis and aids in the anticipation of risks to the KM strategy before they arise (Standards Australia, 2003). By engaging with the risks, it becomes possible to develop a means of risk resolution. The resolution may require organizational change management, the provision of additional financial or infrastructural support, or a realignment of the original strategy in light of unforeseen or emergent activity within the organization. Risk management requires regular evaluation of the strategy and the organization that it serves.

Evaluation and Measurement

Governance in KM implies and demands deliberate consideration of the strategies in place in the long and medium term. KM governance processes incorporate evaluation and measurement in order to prove the value of practices, and to progress and develop existing practices. Governance mechanisms must maintain a collective knowledge of trends in industry, technology, and the corporate structural and social environment.

Evaluation looks at both successes of and obstacles to the implementation of a KM strategy. The evaluation of successes must take into account the contribution made to the aims and objectives of the organization. When the successes make a contribution, they should be continued. When they do not make a contribution, consideration should be given to their continuance. The evaluation of obstacles to the KM strategy implies the capacity to question why the risk may not have been foreseen and therefore managed. The evaluation of obstacles must take into account the barriers they create for the aims and objectives of the organization. When this is the case, can these ends be achieved utilizing an alternative solution or method?

There are a number of criteria currently used to establish the return on investment (ROI) for KM strategies: Liebowitz and Wright (1999) look at human capital growth, Sveiby (1997) uses intangible assets, and some use the balanced scorecard (Kaplan & Norton, 1996) with a number of measures including financial, growth, customer, and internal business processes. Probst, Raub, and Romhardt (2000) look at the normative, operational, and strategic goals of the strategy to see if they are being met. Other common techniques include simple measures of staff retention or an improvement in the product-to-market delivery time, both in quantity, and in quality. If these are evident and are the only variance from usual practice, then the strategy is seen as successful.

A KM Governance Framework

KM literature deals with the need for the alignment of strategy with organizational aims and objectives, and for leadership of that strategy. This process is supported by information and communications technology and operates in the organizational context of the corporate governance principles. There is an explicit link between the market and the organization in its aims and objectives that lead to governance processes.

The governance framework presents the functions of KM as supporting the aims, objectives, and governance processes of the organization in the context of the broader environment of its external stakeholders, which includes its customers and consultants and the regulatory environment. The KM strategy is developed by KM leaders in the planning of a process of the identification, acquisition, development, sharing and distribution, utilization, and finally retention of knowledge (Probst et al., 2000; Tiwana, 2002). The practice of KM implementation follows with the execution of a course of action that is intended to fulfill the aims and objectives of the plan in order to support the aims and objectives of the organization as a whole. The relationship between the KM strategy and the KM implementation is in theory a unidirectional one where implementation is merely the following through of the strategic plan. In practice, this relationship may be more interactive as those responsible for the implementation may also have a level of responsibility for the development of the strategic plan. KM governance is the layer exercising the authority processes and principles that act as a framework for the examination, regulation, supervision, and revision of KM strategies.

The KM strategy is developed by KM practitioners. The interaction between the development of strategy and governance is twofold. The governance process develops the principles and rationale for the impetus and momentum of the strategy, the management of risks, the financial control, and the accountability for stakeholder response. The governance process also evaluates KM activity according to previously defined and articulated performance measures.

The KM strategy is implemented or operationalized by KM staff, and supported and promoted by champions in the organization. The implementation of the strategy is evaluated according to the criteria established by the governance body. Evaluation will also take into account changes in product and customers, changes in the regulatory environment, and inputs from consultants or industry partners. It reflects the aims and objectives of the organization that it serves. The KM strategy is planned and may be revised as the need arises. The evaluation data flows from the KM implementation to the governance body, which then feeds its decision(s) back to the redevelopment of the strategy.

Companies that rely on or utilize KM for the transfer of strategic knowledge should work to establish KM

Figure 1. Framework for KM governance

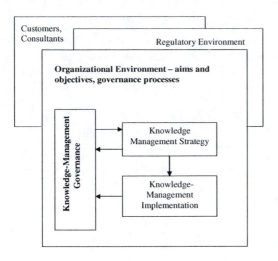

governance committees including one for stakeholder representation. There are two fundamental objectives in this governance process. These are as follow:

- to ensure that KM delivers value to the identified stakeholders. This value is derived from the value proposition of the organization and the organizational strategies put in place to achieve those ends.
- to control and to minimise the risk to the KM strategy. The strategy must be capable of adjustments required in response to perceived flaws in its capacity to effectively transfer knowledge. A KM strategy is not a single prescribed formula that can fit all organizations or even fit organizations within a particular industry segment.

KM governance can meet the previous objectives through:

- the sponsorship of an effective understanding of the role and potential of KM within the organization,
- the alignment of KM with the value proposition and strategy of the organization,
- the regular evaluation review, approval, and monitoring of KM investments in infrastructure and in human resources, and
- the management of the risks of KM.

In acknowledging knowledge as the organization's strategic asset and differentiator, it can be seen that the ultimate responsibility of the KM governance process is to ensure the governance of KM as a means of pursuing success in the implementation of a KM strategy in the organization.

FUTURE TRENDS

KM governance is currently a subject of extensive research that has built the model described. Future research possibilities may lie in looking in depth at the interrelationships between governance and stakeholders, in evaluation and measurement, in risk-management techniques, and in authority over infrastructure and investments.

The governance model described was developed from research undertaken with Australian and global organizations (Zyngier, Burstein, & McKay, 2005). Future research possibilities may lie in testing this model and developing others in other operating environments.

CONCLUSION

Governance processes operate to manage the risks of KM to acknowledge and contend with the cultural issues, structural obstacles, and other relevant issues as they arise during the implementation and ongoing operation of a strategy. The management of these risks will assist in the resolution of such issues and in turn strengthen the strategies to manage knowledge that are employed within the organization. Acknowledging knowledge as the organization's strategic asset and competitive differentiator is not the ultimate responsibility of the governance process. The effective governance of KM may be a means of pursuing success. However, the governance of KM implies more than this. It implies and demands strategic thinking about the strategies in place for long-term and medium-term planning. Such strategies should not be regarded as linear in direction, but they should incorporate feedback both in the positive and negative aspects of the KM strategy that will in turn modify, progress, and develop existing plans and practices.

This article has outlined the theoretical framework of internal organizational governance and its application in strategies to manage organizational knowledge for the implementation of those strategies. Governance functions operate to ensure that KM delivers value to the identified stakeholders and provides a control mechanism to minimise risks to the successful implementation of a KM strategy. The governance framework given for these processes and practices may better enable an effective and coordinated outcome for KM strategies that ensures the delivery of anticipated benefits in an authorized and regulated manner.

REFERENCES

Bridges, W., & Mitchell, S. (2000). Leading transition: A new model for change. *Leader to Leader, 16.*

British Standards Institution & Technical Committee BDD/3. (2002). *BS 15000-1:2002 IT service management, Part 1: Specification for service management.* London: British Standards Institution.

Chase, R. L. (1997). The knowledge-based organisation: An international survey. *Journal of Knowledge Management, 1*(1), 38-49.

Davis, S., McAdams, A., Dixon, N., Orlikowski, W., & Leonard, D. (1998). *Twenty questions on knowledge in the organisation.* Business Intelligence and Ernst & Young Center for Business Innovation. Retrieved from *http://webarchive.org/web/20001212102500/www.businessinnovation.ey.com/research/researchf.htm*

DeLong, D. W., & Fahey, L. (2000). Diagnosing cultural barriers to knowledge management. *The Academy of Management Executive: Ada, 14*(4), 113-127.

Denning, S. (2001). *The springboard: How storytelling ignites action in knowledge-era organisations.* Woburn, MA: Butterworth-Heinemann.

Earl, M. J., & Scott, I. A. (1999). What is a chief knowledge officer? *Sloan Management Review, 40*(2), 29.

Ewyk, O. v. (1998). *MIS98 Mindshare conference knowledge management survey results.* Retrieved September 22, 2000, from *www.hci.com.au/hcisite/articles/mis98srvy.htm*

Fang, S.-C., Lin, J.L., Hsiao, L. Y. C., Huang, C.-M., & Fang, S.-R. (2002). The relationship of foreign R&D units in Taiwan and the Taiwanese knowledge-flow system. *Technovation, 22,* 371-383.

Farrar, J. (2001). *Corporate governance in Australia and New Zealand.* South Melbourne, Australia: Oxford University Press.

Galliers, B. (1999). Editorial: Towards the integration of e-business, knowledge management and policy considerations within an information systems strategy framework. *Journal of Strategic Information Systems, 8,* 229-234.

Hackett, B. (2000). *Beyond knowledge management: New ways to work and learn* (Research Rep. No. 1261-00-RR). New York: The Conference Board.

IC² Institute at the University of Texas at Austin. (2001). *The information and knowledge management audit.* Retrieved January 10, 2001, from *www.glis.utexas.edu/~coast/audit/*

IT Governance Institute. (2001). *Board briefing on IT governance.* Rolling Meadows, IL: Information Systems Audit and Control Foundation.

IT Governance Institute & COBIT Steering Committee. (2000). *COBIT framework* (3rd ed.). Rolling Meadows, IL: IT Governance Institute.

Kaplan, R., & Norton, D. (1996). *The balanced scorecard.* Boston: Harvard Business School Press.

Krogh, G. V., Ichijo, K., & Nonaka, I. (2000). *Enabling knowledge creation: How to unlock the mystery of tacit knowledge and release the power of innovation.* Oxford: Oxford University Press.

Liebowitz, J., & Wright, K. (1999). A look toward valuating human capital. In J. Liebowitz (Ed.), *Knowledge management handbook* (pp. 5.1-5.13). Boca Raton, FL: CRC Press.

McAdam, R., & Reid, R. (2001). SME and large organisation perceptions of knowledge management: Comparison and contrasts. *Journal of Knowledge Management, 5*(3), 231-241.

Mintzberg, H. (1994). The fall and rise of strategic planning. *Harvard Business Review,* 107-114.

O'Dell, C., Hasanali, F., Hubert, C., Lopez, K., Odem, P., & Raybourn, C. (2000). Successful KM implementation: A study of best-practice organizations. In C. Holsapple (Ed.), *Handbook on knowledge management: Vol. 2. Knowledge directions* (pp. 411-443). Berlin, Germany: Springer-Verlag.

Probst, G., Raub, S., & Romhardt, K. (2000). *Managing knowledge: Building blocks for success.* Chichester, UK: John Wiley & Sons.

Rumizen, M. C. (2002). *The complete idiot's guide to knowledge management.* Indianapolis, IN: Alpha A Pearson Education Company.

Standards Australia. (2001). *HB 275-2001 knowledge management: A framework for succeeding in the knowledge era.* Sydney, Australia: Standards Australia International Limited.

Standards Australia. (2003). *AS 5037-(Int)2003 knowledge management interim Australian standard.* Sydney, Australia: Author.

Sveiby, K. E. (1997). *The new organizational wealth: Managing and measuring knowledge-based assets.* San Francisco: Berrett-Koehler Publishers, Inc.

Tiwana, A. (2002). *The knowledge management toolkit: Orchestrating IT, strategy, and knowledge platforms* (2nd ed.). Upper Saddle River, NJ: Prentice Hall PTR.

Van den Berghe, L., & De Ridder, L. (1999). *International standardisation of good corporate governance: Best practices for the board of directors.* Boston: Kluwer Academic Publishers.

Vinten, G. (2000). The stakeholder manager. *Management Decision.*

Weill, P., & Woodham, R. (2002). *Don't just lead, govern: Implementing effective IT governance* (White Paper No. 326). Boston: CISR.

Wiig, K. M. (1997). Knowledge management: An introduction and perspective. *The Journal of Knowledge Management, 1*(1), 6-14.

Zack, M. H. (1999). Managing codified knowledge. *MIT Sloan Management Review, 40*(4), 45.

Zyngier, S. (2001). *Knowledge management strategies in Australia: Preliminary results of the survey of the knowledge management uptake in Australian companies* (Research Rep. No. 1/2001). Caulfield East, Australia: Monash University.

Zyngier, S., Burstein, F., & McKay, J. (2005). Governance of strategies to manage organizational knowledge—A mechanism to oversee knowledge needs. In M. Jennex (Ed.), *Knowledge management case book.* Hershey, PA.: Idea Group Publishing.

KEY TERMS

Authority: An established power to enforce moral or legal decisions. Organizational authority is accountable for its actions. Authority is a right to demand and instruct subordinates. Authority may also be delegated or be derived from delegated control. The organization may mandate power to a role, position a group or individual in authority, or power may be assigned or sanctioned by consensus.

Evaluation: The assessment of the effectiveness of service delivery and the identification of obstacles or barriers to service delivery. Some means of evaluation include understanding the perceptions of improvement in the organization in the manner in which it formalizes knowledge processes, knowledge structures, and underlying systems. These in turn will affect the operations, products, or services delivered. Another means of evaluation of the effectiveness of a KM strategy is through establishing increased awareness and participation in that strategy. The balanced scorecard (Kaplan & Norton, 1996) is a technique that considers these human issues.

Governance: A process that is a framework of authority to ensure the delivery of anticipated or predicted benefits of a service or process. The operationalization of the particular organizational strategy is therefore executed in an authorized and regulated manner. Governance acts to manage risk, evaluate and review strategic goals and objectives, and exercise fiscal accountability to ensure the return on investment of those strategies.

Measurement: Substantially a quantitative tool. It may rely on a direct comparison of performance before and subsequent to the initiation and establishment of a KM strategy. The organization may choose to measure its performance in market competitiveness and acceptance, or it may look at the contribution of the KM strategy to financial benefits and viability. It can also measure contributions to and the growth in the volume of explicit knowledge content stored and used by staff. Some knowledge managers may regard the increase in the resources attached to the project as a measure of the acceptance and, hence, the understanding of the value of KM to their organization.

Organizational Environment: Refers to the aims and objectives of the organization in the context of the way in which it structures itself and its activities. The structure of the organization is the way in which the organization is arranged for the implementation of authority. Generally, this structure is either a hierarchical structure, a flat structure, or a management matrix. A hierarchical structure is typically shaped like a pyramid with power or control centralized in a CEO (chief executive officer) who has managers reporting back. These managers have subordinates who also exercise delegated authority over their subordinates. There may be several layers of authority and delegation depending on the size and complexity of the organization. Ultimately, power and control lies in the CEO. A management matrix has a series of control mechanisms where the workforce may report to their direct superior, and additionally to one of a series of team leaders. This requires a sequence of devolved authorities and responsibilities. A flat organizational structure has devolved power and responsibilities without a cascading series of reporting structures.

Return on Investment: Commonly used as an accounting term to indicate how well an organization has used its investment in resources. In a knowledge-management context, ROI describes the return on both the human and financial capital invested in that strategy. Some measures may include sustainable growth, calculable efficiencies in product development cycles, improved decision making, better ability to initiate and integrate new employees, lower rates of staff turnover reflecting improved employee morale, and better ability to retain customers reflecting trust in employees' expertise.

Risk Management: A tactic to minimise the susceptibility of the KM strategy to risk and subsequent failure or ineffectiveness. Risk must be analysed to assess the potential exposure to the chance of human or infrastructural barriers. Examples of these risks may include:

- a management culture in the organisation that hinders KM,

- the fact that the philosophy of KM is not understood in the organisation,
- conflicts of organizational priorities, and
- the fact that the development of criteria for knowledge collection is clouded.

Risk may also threaten operational or financial elements of the strategy. Examples of risks to processes may include:

- a lack of understanding of the knowledge types and artefacts associated with specific business functions,
- current informal, organic knowledge-transfer strategies and systems,
- risks associated with system development, and
- risks associated with managing changes and their implementation, and additionally managing expectations of the staff and executive management.

Knowledge Management in Professional Service Firms

K

Dieter Fink
Edith Cowan University, Australia

Georg Disterer
Hannover University of Applied Sciences and Arts, Germany

INTRODUCTION

For professional service firms, such as consultants, accountants, lawyers, architects, and engineers, knowledge is a capacity to act. Knowledge can be used to take action and to serve the client. As market pressures increase, so does the demand for securing and exploiting knowledge for the firm. In addition, a shortage of high-potential professional service providers has increased the 'war for talent' in which firms compete in employing the most talented professionals. These situations are exacerbated by the decrease in lifelong loyalty, a traditional value within professional groups, and the departure and retirement of professionals, often the most experienced ones.

For professional service firms, the main assets are intellectual, not physical, and they have to seek new ways to leverage their professional intellect. It is therefore not surprising that the emergence of technology-enabled knowledge management (KM) has attracted much attention from those firms. The special relevancy of KM to professional service firms is clear: "…in professional services, we are selling the expertise of our people" (Townley, 2002, p. 4; see also Chait, 1999; Foy, 1999). If knowledge is the 'product' or the dominant ingredient, it is worth it to manage that asset, and to establish and manage systematically the acquisition, synthesis, and sharing of insights and experiences. Indeed consultants are seen as the earliest and most successful adopters of KM (Simmons, 2004; Terrett, 1998; Skyrme, 1999).

The core business of these firms is to provide highly developed knowledge-based services grounded on the existence of intellectual assets. "Thus, it makes sense that managing those assets effectively is now looked at as a vital aspect of maintaining competitiveness" (Davis, 1998, p. 11). Intellectual assets exist in various forms, and their exploitation is only restricted by the capacity and readiness of humans to do so. Quinn, Anderson, and Finkelstein (1996) observed:

The capacity to manage human intellect—and to convert it into useful products and services—is fast becoming the critical executive skill of the age. As a result, there has been a flurry of interest in intellectual capital, creativity, innovation, and the learning organization, but surprisingly little attention has been given to managing professional intellect. (p. 71)

BACKGROUND: PROFESSIONAL KNOWLEDGE

Much debate has taken place in recent years on what constitutes knowledge and knowledge management. In this respect comprehensive analyses is provided of this topic by researchers such as Drucker (1988), Swan, Scarborough et al. (1999), Tidd and Driver (2001), and Schultze and Leidner (2002). However, far less has been written about the nature of professional knowledge. Some understanding can be gained by examining the levels at which it operates. According to Quinn et al. (1996), professional knowledge operates at four levels as follows:

- **Cognitive knowledge (know-what):** This is the basic mastery of a discipline that professionals achieve through education and training.
- **Advanced skills (know-how):** This is the ability to apply cognitive knowledge into effective execution in a complex real world.
- **Systems understanding (know-why):** The deep knowledge of cause-and-effect relationships underlying a discipline, expressed as highly trained intuition.
- **Self-motivated creativity (care-why):** This is the will, motivation, and adaptability for success, enabling renewal of knowledge in the face of today's rapid changes.

To perform their knowledge work, professionals in the first instance acquire cognitive knowledge (know-what) by undergoing education. To advance their knowledge, to reach the know-why stage, they enter into a period of training in a professional firm, usually in the form of articles of clerkship, under the supervision of an experienced professional. As further knowledge is gained, they

Figure 1. Professional knowledge and value

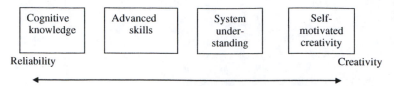

are able to demonstrate systems understanding (know-why) and self-motivated creativity (care-why). For professionals, the value of knowledge increases markedly as they move up the knowledge scale from cognitive knowledge to self-motivated creativity. Figure 1 shows the various forms of professional knowledge on a scale.

Evans and Volery (2000) defined the nature of services being able to be offered by professional service providers as intelligence, consulting, counseling, relationship networking, education, and training.

- **Intelligence:** The provision of quality information to sharpen, improve, or support the 'cleverness' of clients in situations such as decision making. Professional knowledge is required to structure and present the information so that is has optimum utility for clients.
- **Consulting:** The customization of information to satisfy the particular circumstances of a client. Consulting requires the ability to apply and transfer a high level of professional knowledge to the client.
- **Counseling:** Acting as mentor to the client, the service provider works with the client to structure, identify, and recommend appropriate approaches to the client's problems. High levels of professional experience, knowledge, and motivation are required and provide a good example of a 'care-why' knowledge type.
- **Relationship networking:** The ability of the service provider to bring clients into contact with other clients or parties that may have the potential to provide them with business benefits. At these meetings, exchanges take place in the form of information, ideas, experiences, and so forth.

- **Education and training:** Similar to counseling but in a more formal and structured setting, the service provider imparts knowledge, information, and skills to clients.

To understand the nature of professional services, they should be compared with the nature of products. This was done by Alexander and Hordes (2003) as reflected in Table 1.

It can be deduced that professional knowledge services are intangible in nature in that they do not have the physical dimensions and components of products. It is therefore not usually possible for a client to see, touch, or feel the professional service he or she is about to receive. Furthermore, the production and consumption of services occurs simultaneously. Usually this requires the service provider and client to be present during the conveying of the service. A further characteristic makes professional knowledge services heterogeneous—that is, neither homogenous nor of a standardized quality. The context in which services are demanded and delivered constantly change.

KNOWLEDGE MANAGEMENT

According to a well-recognized paper by Hansen, Nohria, and Tierney (1999), professional service firms employ two very different KM strategies. The authors used the consulting business as an example, but pointed out that the approach can be generalized across all professional service firms. According to them, some professional service firms concentrate on the codifiable knowledge of their employees and try to capture, store, and reuse it. In the

Table 1. Distinction between products and services

Dimension	Product	Service
Production	Built	Performed
Production Costs	Uniformity	Uniqueness
Involvement	Rarely	Usually
Quality Control	Compare output to specification	Compare expectation to experience
Poor Quality Procedure	Recall	Apologize and atone
Moral and Skill Level	Important	Vital

codification approach, also called "people-to-documents" approach, knowledge is made independent of the individual who developed it and is reused for various purposes, for example within other consulting projects, for other industries, or in other countries.

The application of this strategy results in a repository of systematically encoded knowledge for subsequent distribution and usage. Because the approach exhibits a flow of knowledge into and out of a central repository, the approach could be named "integrative" (Zack, 1998, p. 92). This school of thought aims to codify and reuse knowledge to improve efficiency. As knowledge is transferred into documents and/or files and can be handled as knowledge products, the approach is akin to a "product-centered" KM approach (Mentzas, Apostolou, Young, & Abecker, 2001).

In other professional service firms, the most valuable knowledge is believed to be closely tied to the person who developed it. This knowledge is mainly transferred by direct person-to-person contact; the approach is therefore called a "personalization" approach (Hansen et al., 1999). As supporting communication processes among people is its main focus, it could be named an "interactive" approach (Zack, 1998) or "process-centered" approach (Mentzas et al., 2001). The approach is anchored in organizational learning theory and aims to build up organizational memory by facilitating learning processes. Strictly speaking the personalization strategy is not 'really' about the management of knowledge, but more about management of communication and conversation between people.

The main characteristics of codification and personalization strategies are summarized in Table 2.

The two approaches, codification and personalization, are not mutually exclusive (Hansen et al., 1999; Earl, 2001; Zack, 1998) but must be combined appropriately. However, the approaches give distinct hints about the use of information and communications technology (ICT) to support KM.

Codification focuses on identifying and explicating knowledge into knowledge objects in order to give access to knowledge to all employees of the professional service firm. Extraction processes are implemented to identify

specific knowledge and experiences, and make them more generic. Sometimes special roles like "knowledge harvesters" (DeVoss, 2000) or "catalysts" (Fitter, 2000) are defined to establish responsibilities for identifying, systemizing, editing, and documenting valuable knowledge in the form of checklists, precedents, or forms. The knowledge objects are then stored in databases that allow flexible and fast access and retrieval. Various ICT-enabled functions support the access, such as:

- classification systems to retrieve objects by keywords;
- full-text search features;
- topic maps to visualize content and relations between items; and
- push features, which alert a user when certain knowledge items are changed or when they are added to a specific topic.

Personalization fosters communication and conversation between employees of a professional service firm—across time, space, and hierarchy. Conservative habits within firms sometimes hinder free conversation across hierarchies or lines of business. Especially in large and globally distributed firms, employees can lose opportunities to exchange ideas and suggestions. ICT is therefore used to connect people and to mediate communication using features such as:

- expert finder systems containing profiles of employees so that their special expertise can be retrieved or they can be contacted for advice;
- communities of practice are built with the use of ICT, where employees with similar professional interests (e.g., consulting services for retail industry, auditing of banks) can meet and have discussions in an electronic environment;
- use of electronic blackboards, group calendars, or mailing lists to establish and support groups of employees working together;
- conference systems fostering personal contact and face-to-face communication.

Table 2. The two main KM approaches

Approach 1	Approach 2	References
codification	personalization	Hansen et al., 1999
people-to-documents	people-to-people	Hansen et al., 1999
integrative	interactive	Zack, 1998
product-centered	process-centered	Mentzas et al., 2001
knowledge as object	knowledge embedded in people	Wasko & Faraj, 2000
knowledge as object	knowledge as process	Garavelli, Gorgolione, & Scozii, 2002

The literature reflects several comprehensive descriptions of how ICT can be used in innovative ways to support KM in professional consultancy service firms. They include Alavi (1997), Bartlett (1996), Christensen and Baird (1997), Ezingeard, Leigh, and Chandler-Wilde (2000), Heisig, Spellerberg, and Spallek (2003), Hirsh, Youman, and Hanley (2001), Manville (1999), Martiny (1998), Tallman, Horwitch, and Armacost (2002), Vorbeck and Habbel (2001), and Vorbeck, Heisig, Martin, and Schütt (2003). The large extent of publications may partly be driven by the desire of consultancies to promote their services to other firms doing KM projects by demonstrating their KM competencies through the media of publications.

In addition to describing KM systems, empirical data is available on how KM systems are used by professionals. An analysis of the KM system in one consultancy provides insight into the knowledge usage patterns of consulting professionals (Kautz & Mahnke, 2003). The case organization is a large global consulting firm with more than 100,000 employees located in more than 100 countries. The KM initiative of the firm started in 1995, with the case analysis being conducted in 2000. Figure 2 gives the knowledge sources professionals used when they need knowledge or information about a specific topic.

Kautz and Mahnke (2003) also identified serious problems and factors causing non-adoption of KM systems:

- The KM system is not used as the primary store of knowledge.
- Mostly general information is searched within the KM databases.

Figure 2. Information sources used by consultants

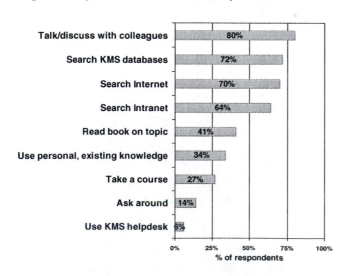

- Only half of the users are participating in knowledge networks.
- Usage is limited by professionals' lack of time.
- Participation in development of KM systems is low.
- Various functions of KM systems are not used heavily.

Other empirical findings from broader samples indicate more clearly that "lack of time," "lack of sharing culture," and "lack of general understanding of knowledge management" are the major barriers to KM initiatives (e.g., Ruggles, 1998; KPMG, 2003). It can therefore be concluded that technological issues may not be the dominant ones when supporting KM in professional service firms. Moreover, various cultural barriers need to be overcome to foster knowledge sharing (Disterer, 2003). For example it has been found that sharing knowledge is an "unnatural" behavior for many (Quinn et al., 1996; Barua & Ravindran, 1996; Holloway, 2000; Colier et al., 1996). People issues are seen to be critical for successful knowledge sharing: "In fact, if the people issues do not arise, the effort underway is probably not knowledge management. If technology solves the problem, yours was not a knowledge problem" (Ruggles, 1998, p. 88).

Linked to knowledge sharing is the question of what role incentives and rewards play in encouraging professionals to share their tacit knowledge. Laupase and Fink (2002) found from a series of case studies of management consulting firms that reward systems did motivate consultants to share knowledge with each other. The most effective scheme was found to be sharing knowledge in informal meetings and offering non-financial, intrinsic rewards. Consultants were found to be most comfortable in an informal environment, as they felt it was easier to engage and to ask further follow-up questions. They were also more in favor of intrinsic rewards, such as being recognized, encouraged to participate in decision making, and feeling a sense of belonging.

However, an opposing view to the preparedness of knowledge sharing exists. In professional service firms, employees compete directly with each other through their special knowledge, gifts, and talents. It might be part of the individual culture of the high-performing employees that they compete for the best positions in their career paths because they like to compete and to excel on principle (Quinn et al., 1996). Thus, with internal competition knowledge workers would be very cautious to openly share their knowledge with colleagues, because they would possibly give up individual advantages. Furthermore, they are often rewarded to build a unique expertise in a certain area and to provide that expertise to clients, rather than to share it with colleagues. Additionally, many professional service firms bill services to the clients based on chargeable hours. This approach tends to devalue an activity that is not 'billable', like helping colleagues with their professional problems.

As seen above, various individual and social barriers must be taken into account when initiating and establishing KM in professional service firms. Disterer (2003) categorized those barriers and gives a list of possible actions to foster knowledge sharing. These range from cultural actions like building trust and mutual understanding and support for give-and-take attitudes within the firm (to build up a knowledge-friendly culture), organizational actions to form groups of people working on similar issues, and human resource (HR) management to provide incentives and rewards to the professionals in order to enhance knowledge sharing.

A recent survey by the American Productivity and Quality Center (APQC) gives some insights about how top consulting firms organize their KM activities (Simmons, 2004). The survey shows that the most efficient firms do have a core KM team that centrally develops strategies, directs and coordinates activities, facilitates projects, and builds central systems like search engines and portals. Beside these central functions, the actual knowledge work is carried out in the decentralized business lines. The cost for all KM operations was found to be a median 0.5% of the revenue.

FUTURE TRENDS

It is expected that one major trend will be providing clients direct access to the knowledge base of professional service firms. Databases with 'lessons learned' and 'best practices' are shared with clients in order to raise customer loyalty. Ongoing information services to clients generated by software agents and pushed to clients will improve the client relationship. In the legal area, some examples are known where law firms are providing document assembly generators to enable clients to build up contracts on their own (Parnham, 2002).

Technology-enabled client services, mainly delivered through e-mail or on the Web, will consolidate existing client relationships, for example through more frequent interactions, and also invigorate them by the addition of new forms of client value. Fink (2001) investigated the evolution of professional accounting firms and found that "KM provides the opportunity to develop entrepreneurial versus the administrative capabilities of the firms" (p. 494). Opportunities identified included knowledge support and knowledge brokering. However, risks such as the reduction of context and a shift of power to the client were also acknowledged.

Integrating internal content of a knowledge base with external content will be a further challenge. Software agents will search through external databases and build references to internal knowledge objects. For better access to the knowledgebases, mobile access for those professionals working at the clients' premises will have to be implemented.

CONCLUSION

The management of knowledge in professional service firms deserves much attention since knowledge is the key resource of these firms. Effective KM systems therefore need to be developed and utilized. This article has shown that the value of professional knowledge increases over time, which in turn increases the urgency to have it captured and made available to those with lesser knowledge and/or experience. However, the nature of professional knowledge (intangible, perishable, heterogeneous) poses particular challenges to implementing KM systems.

It is clear that ICT has opened up many opportunities to supporting the KM activities of professional service firms. However, a number of strategic choices have to be made and importantly the use of ICT has to be supported by effective HR management. Essentially there are two approaches to KM, the codification or product approach and the personalization or process approach. Whatever approach is used, there are many obstacles that need to be overcome before KM systems are operational and become fully utilized. Success is largely dependent on the human element within the firms. Issues such as incentives and rewards for knowledge sharing need to be identified and resolved within the firms.

Many case studies have been published on leading professional firms and their experiences with KM. Valuable lessons can be learned from them. Furthermore, more developments are on the horizon which will ensure that the topic of KM in professional service firms will remain topical for years to come.

REFERENCES

Alavi, M. (1997). *KPMG Peat Marwick U.S.: One great brain.* Harvard Business School Case 9-397-108.

Alexander, J.A., & Hordes, M.W. (2003). The service marketing challenge: How to defy obstacles and better promote your offerings. *Professional Service Journal, 3*(17). Retrieved October 5, 2004, from *www.internetviz-newsletter.com/PSJ/e_article000198268.cfm?x=b11,0*

Bartlett, C.A. (1966). *McKinsey & Company: Managing knowledge and learning.* Harvard Business School Case 9-396-357.

385

Barua, A., & Ravindran, S. (1996). Reengineering information sharing behavior in organizations. *Journal of Information Technology, 11*(3), 261-272.

Chait, L.P. (1999). Creating a successful knowledge management system. *Journal of Business Strategy, 20*(March), 23-26.

Christensen, C.M., & Baird, B. (1997). *Cultivating capabilities to innovate: Booz Allen & Hamilton.* Harvard Business School Case 9-698-027.

Collier, B., DeMarco, T., & Fearey, P. (1996). A defined process for project postmortem review. *IEEE Software, 3*(4), 65-72.

Davis, M.C. (1998). Knowledge management. *Information Strategy, 15*(1), 11-22.

DeVoss, D. (2000). Knowledge harvesters dig deep. *Knowledge Management Magazine, 8.* Retrieved September 29, 2004, from *www.destinationkm.com/articles/default.asp?ArticleID=877*

Disterer, G. (2002). Social and cultural barriers for knowledge databases in professional service firms. In D. White (Ed.), *Knowledge mapping and management.* Hershey, PA: Idea Group Publishing.

Disterer, G. (2003). Fostering knowledge sharing: Why and how? In A.P.D. Reis & P. Isaias (Eds.), *Proceedings of the IADIS International Conference E-Society,* Lisbon.

Drucker, P. (1988). The coming of the new organization. *Harvard Business Review, 66*(1), 45-53.

Earl, M. (2001). Knowledge management strategies: Toward a taxonomy. *Journal of Management Information Systems, 8*(1), 215-233.

Evans, D., & Folery, T. (2000). Online business development services for entrepreneurs: An exploratory study. *Proceedings of the ICSB World Conference,* Brisbane.

Ezingeard, J.N., Leigh, S., & Chandler-Wilde, R. (2000). Knowledge management at Ernst & Young UK: Getting value through knowledge flows. *Proceedings of the 21st International Conference on Information Systems,* Brisbane.

Fink, D. (2001). Knowledge management in small and medium sized professional accounting firms: Progress and challenges. *Wirtshaftsinformatik, 43*(5), 487-496.

Fitter, F. (2000). Catalysts for knowledge. *Knowledge Management Magazine, 7.* Retrieved September 29, 2004, from *www.destinationkm.com/articles/default.asp?ArticleID=882*

Foy, P.S. (1999). Knowledge management in industry. In J. Liebowitz (Ed.), *The knowledge management handbook.* Boca Raton.

Garavelli, A.C., Gorgolione, M., & Scozii, B. (2002). Managing knowledge transfer by knowledge technologies. *Technovation, 22*(5), 269-279.

Hansen, M.T., Nohria, N., & Tierney, T. (1999). What's your strategy for managing knowledge. *Harvard Business Review, 77*(2), 106-116.

Heisig, P., Spellerberg, F., & Spallek, P. (2003). Knowledge management: The holistic approach of Arthur D. Little Inc. In K. Mertins, P. Heisig, & J. Vorbeck (Eds.), *Knowledge management—concepts and best practices* (2nd ed.). Berlin: Springer-Verlag.

Hirsh, C., Youman, M., & Hanley, S. (2001). Creating knowledge-based communities of practice—lessons learned from KM initiatives at AMS. In R.C. Barquin, A, Bennet, & S.G. Remez (Eds.), *Knowledge management: The catalyst for e-government, management concepts.* Vienna.

Holloway, P. (2000). Sharing knowledge—and other unnatural acts. *Knowledge Management Magazine, 1,* 17-18.

Kautz, K., & Mahnke, V. (2003). Value creation through IT-supported knowledge management? The utilization of a knowledge management system in a global consulting company. *Informing Science, 6,* 75-88.

Knowles, C. (2002). Intelligent agents without the hype: Why they work best with well structured content. *Business Information Review, 19*(4), 22-28.

KPMG. (2003). *Insights from KPMG's European knowledge management survey 2002/2003.* KPMG Consulting, NL.

Laupase R., & Fink, D. (2002). Do reward systems encourage tacit knowledge sharing in management consulting firms? *Proceedings of Information Resources Management Association International Conference,* Seattle.

Manville, B. (1999). A complex adaptive approach to KM: Reflections on the case of McKinsey & Company. *Knowledge Management Review, 8*(May), 26-31.

Martiny, M. (1998). Knowledge management at HP Consulting. *Organizational Dynamics, 27*(2), 71-77.

Mentzas, G., Apostolou, D., Young, R., & Abecker, A. (2001). Knowledge networking: A holistic solution for leveraging corporate knowledge. *Journal of Knowledge Management, 5*(1), 94-106.

Parnham, R. (2002). Lawyers in the know. *The European Lawyer,* (October), 20-22.

Quinn, J.B., Anderson, P., & Finkelstein, S. (1996). Managing professional intellect: Making the most of the best. *Harvard Business Review,* (March-April), 71-80.

Ruggles, R. (1998). The state of the notion: Knowledge management in practice. *California Management Review, 40*(3), 80-89.

Schultze, U., & Leidner, D. (2002). Studying knowledge management in information systems research: Discourses and theoretical assumptions. *MIS Quarterly, 26*(3), 213-242.

Simmons, L. (2004). Benchmarking with the best consultancies. *Knowledge Management Review, 6*(6), 28-31.

Skyrme, D.J. (1999). Knowledge management: Making it work. *The Law Librarian, 31*(2), 84-90.

Swan, J., Scarborough, H. et al. (1999). Knowledge management—the next fad to forget people? *Proceedings of European Conference on Information Systems,* Copenhagen.

Tallman, S., Horwitch, M., & Armacost, R. (2002). Bain & Company—CP/KM experts. Retrieved September 29, 2004, from *www.bain.com/bainweb/PDFs/cms/Marketing/10709.pdf*

Terrett, A. (1998). Knowledge management and the law firm. *Journal of Knowledge Management, 2*(1), 67-76.

Tidd, J., & Driver, C. (2001). *Technological and market competencies and financial performance. From knowledge management to strategic competence* (pp. 94-125). London: Imperial College Press.

Townley, C. (2002). Let's treat knowledge like the people they are. *Professional Review, 2*(4), 4.

Vorbeck, J., Heisig, P., Martin, A., & Schütt, P. (2003). Knowledge management in a global company—IBM global services. In K. Mertins, P. Heisig, & J. Vorbeck (Eds.), *Knowledge management—concepts and best practices* (2nd ed.). Berlin: Springer-Verlag.

Vorbeck, J., & Habbel, R. (2001). Sophisticated information technology to promote knowledge sharing and communication—Booz Allen & Hamilton. In K. Mertins, P. Heisig, & J. Vorbeck (Eds.), *Knowledge management.* Berlin: Springer-Verlag.

Wasko, M.M., & Faraj, S. (2000). IT is what one does: Why people participate and help others in electronic communities of practice. *Journal of Strategic Information Systems, 9*(2), 155-173.

Zack, M.H. (1998). Managing codified knowledge. Retrieved September 29, 2004, from *www.cba.neu.edu/~mzack/articles/kmarch/kmarch.htm*

KEY TERMS

ICT-Enabled Knowledge Management: ICT facilitates both knowledge personalization and codification. Examples of the former are expert finder systems containing profiles of employees with special expertise, communities of practice where employees with similar professional interests can meet, and electronic blackboards. Examples of the latter are classification systems to retrieve objects by keywords, full-text search features, and topic maps.

Incentives and Rewards: To encourage knowledge sharing, incentives and rewards are offered. Research has established that intrinsic rewards, such as being recognized and being encouraged to participate in decision making, are powerful motivators. On the other hand, it is argued that with internal competition, knowledge workers would be very cautious about openly sharing their knowledge with colleagues so not to give up individual advantages.

Knowledge Codification: The documentation of knowledge—that is, the conversion of tacit knowledge into an explicit form. ICT is often a strong facilitator to support this strategy of knowledge management. For example, knowledge objects are stored in databases that allow flexible and fast access and retrieval. It is a product-centric view of knowledge management.

Knowledge Personalization: The application of specific knowledge to the context of the client's circumstances. An understanding of the client's needs is essential, and strong relationships between the knowledge provider and the knowledge receiver need to be developed so that knowledge is accepted and utilized. It is a process-centric view of knowledge management.

Knowledge Sharing: The sharing of knowledge possessed by experienced professionals with those less experienced. This is not an easy task since much knowledge is of a tacit nature, which needs to be made explicit and communicated. Reward systems are often used to encourage knowledge sharing, and knowledge possessed is regarded as a competitive advantage not to be given up readily.

Professional Knowledge: Knowledge or intellect applied by people employed in professional services firms in their endeavor to meet the demands of their clients. Professional knowledge develops through states—know-what, know-how, know-why, and care-why. Value of the application of such knowledge to the professional firm and client increases in later knowledge states.

Professional Service Firm: Firms formed to meet the demands of clients, such as lawyers, public accountants, financial advisers, and so forth. They can be of different sizes ranging from sole professional to multi-national firms. They can be run by a sole professional or in partnership with other professionals.

Knowledge Management in Safety–Critical Systems Analysis

K

Guy Boy
EURISCO International, France

Yvonne Barnard
EURISCO International, France

INTRODUCTION

Knowledge management in the design of safety-critical systems addresses the question of how designers can share, capitalize, and reuse knowledge in an effective and reliable way. Knowledge management is situated in groups, organizations, and communities, playing different roles in the design process. Design of safety-critical systems has specific properties, such as dealing with complexity, traceability, maturity of knowledge, interaction between experts, awareness of the status of information, and trust in knowledge. Documentation is of crucial importance in design processes, ensuring that these properties are taken care of in a proper and reliable way. However, writing is not an easy task for engineers, and support is needed. Several knowledge management solutions, both tools and organizational setups, are available to support design work, such as active notification of changes, personal and team workspaces, active design documents and knowledge portal solutions.

SITUATING KNOWLEDGE MANAGEMENT

Knowledge management (KM) has become an important research topic, as well as a crucial issue in industry today. People have always tried to organize themselves in order to capitalize, reuse, and transfer knowledge and skills among each other within groups. Poltrock and Grudin (2001) propose the triple distinction team-organization-community for groups. KM tools and organizational set-ups usually emerge from the requirements of one of these kinds of groups. Note that we do not dissociate a KM tool from the group that is likely to use it.

A team is a small group of persons that work closely with each other, but not necessarily in the same location. A leader often coordinates its work. Team participants typically fulfill different roles. They strongly need to communicate. The following groups are examples of teams: software development teams, proposal writing teams, conference program committees, and small operational groups such as customer support or research project teams. Support technologies include: buddy lists, instant messaging, chat, Groove (a peer-to-peer team collaboration environment), Quickplace (provides an instant virtual team room where information is managed), BSCW (both a product and a free service for managing information for self-organizing groups, Bentley, Horstmann, & Trevor, 1997), video conferencing, data conferencing, and eRoom (team workspaces with shared workspaces, calendars, and discussions through a Web browser).

The structure of an organization is typically hierarchical. Modern organizations are usually geographically distributed. They strongly need to be coordinated. The following groups are examples of organizations: companies, governments or government agencies, and non-profit organizations. Support technologies include: e-mail, calendars, workflow, Lotus Notes (an integrated collaboration environment), intranet applications and webs, document management systems, and broadcast video.

Communities share a common interest but no structure. They are usually geographically distributed and provide services to people (e.g., the European KM Forum, Amazon.com). The following groups are examples of communities: citizens of a city or neighborhood, special-purpose chat groups, virtual world citizens, auction participants, stamp collectors, and retired people. Support technologies include: Web sites, chat rooms, and virtual worlds.

In the field of safety-critical systems, teams, organizations, and communities inter-relate in order to insure quality on both products and processes. They are highly constrained. Usually teams are made to carry out projects and programs; they may be multi-national for example. Organizations are made to manage people within a consistent space, such as a national company that is more appropriate to handle social laws and customs of the country where it is chartered. Communities are made to help people who share the same kind of work practice to refer among each other, such as a community of electrical engineers. We summarize these distinctions in Figure 1.

Figure 1. An individual may belong to a project team, a company, and a professional association at the same time.

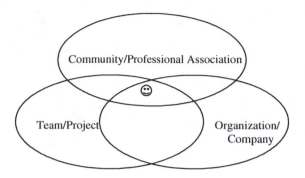

A project team exists only during the time of the related project. A company may have several projects or programs that themselves may involve people from others companies. A company may become obsolete when the type of products it produces is no longer appropriate with the current market. Professional communities survive the obsolescence of both projects and companies. They actually may also become obsolete when either technology and/or the social world change.

In this article, we will present specific issues brought by the design of safety-critical systems, and human factors related to documentation generated and used in design processes. We will also focus on related current design issues. The specificity of safety-critical design knowledge will be presented. Several KM management solutions will be discussed. The article concludes with a discussion on the difficulties and challenges of KM in engineering.

The article is coming from several knowledge management projects performed in cooperation with groups of engineers in large aerospace and telecommunication companies. In particular, most recent findings come from the European Research and Development project WISE (IST-2000-29280; www.ist-wise.org). In WISE (Web-Enabled Information Services for Engineering), we study work-practices of engineers in large manufacturing companies, and we design practical methods to easily share and access essential knowledge and information for their tasks. These methods are supported by the development of an engineering knowledge portal application. The industrial partners involved in this project are Nokia and Airbus. Other partners are Cyberstream Interface SI, PACE, EURISCO International, Norwegian Computing Centre Helsinki University of Technology, and Technical University of Berlin.

Designing Safety-Critical Systems

Safety-critical systems have specific properties that directly affect the way knowledge management is carried out. Examples of safety-critical systems are aircraft, power plants, medical equipment, and telecommunication systems. They are basically complex, as complete as possible, and described by mature knowledge. Safety is not only a matter of end-user emotion, attention, and cognition; it is also a matter of organization and people involved in the whole lifecycle of related products. They involve experts that need to cooperate. For that matter, traceability of decisions is crucial.

Safety-Critical Systems Communities as Families

People working on safety-critical systems, in domains such as aerospace, nuclear power plants, and medicine, form strongly connected communities of practice that could be seen as families. They have their own meetings, workshops and conferences, even journals, where they can exchange experience, foster research, and improve knowledge on safety-critical systems in general. These communities work across organizations and teams. They tend to become references and initiate standards in the related field. They are recognized bodies for knowledge validation, providing principles for assessing knowledge maturity.

Dealing with Complexity

Even if the designers of safety-critical systems should always have in mind to design for simplicity, what they have to do is inherently complex. Systems are complex, and processes to design and develop these systems are complex. In the design process, designers rely on knowledge that is available in the form of handbooks, lessons learned, and best practices. Designers have to take into account the experiences with older systems, on which the new system is usually building, making sure that incidents and accidents that have happened are no longer possible in the new design. Designs are verified and validated in extensive, well-defined processes. In the end of the design process, certification by different authorities and certification bodies can also play a large role. In order to get a system certified, one has to be able to justify the choices that were made, to prove, as far as possible, that all knowledge about problems with similar systems has been taken care of, and that the system will function safely in all kinds of difficult and even disastrous scenarios.

Targeting Completeness in an Open World

Safety-critical systems require complete definition of their (cognitive) functions that they involve in terms of role, context of validity and use, and appropriate resources that they need to accomplish their functions (Boy, 1998). A cognitive function analysis is usually mandatory when we need to demonstrate that the system being designed satisfies a set of safety requirements. Completeness does not apply only to the mandatory kinds of functions, but also to the situations that end-users may encounter when they are using the systems. Completeness is difficult and often impossible to reach. This is why groups that design safety-critical systems use simulators in order to multiply the number of situations and cover a broader spectrum. They incrementally accumulate and articulate related knowledge by categorizing relevant situations.

Maturity of Knowledge and Maturity in Design

We claim that knowledge is constructed—let us say designed. The design of knowledge is incremental. Safety-critical systems are designed over time. They are tested, modified several times, and certified. Their use is carefully observed and documented. The resulting observation product, usually called experience feedback, is provided to designers who use it to modify their current understanding of the artifacts they have designed. Knowledge about these artifacts becomes progressively mature through this incremental process. There are short-loop design-knowledge validation processes that lead to official documents guiding the design process. There are also long-loop design-knowledge validation processes that involve experience feedback on already mature artifacts. In particular, engineers involved in safety analysis have an everyday need in using internal official documents. For example for a system safety analyst, requirements, courses, applicable documents, lessons learned (in-service experience), FAQs, lists of experts, previous similar deliverables, review results, validation and verification checklists/action lists, and system review action lists are crucial information that needs to be easily accessed.

Dealing with Drafts

Not all documents are finalized and approved at any time. Designers have to deal with draft documents, addressing questions such as how one can recognize that a document is ongoing, how versioning is taken into account, how revisions are managed. The validation of a document is related to the appropriate list of signatures. When a document is validated, it becomes "official." Each design rationale description should be appropriately contextualized. including its status (i.e., mainly the revision and approval dates) and background information (where it is coming from and who did it). In order to follow appropriate guidelines to edit and publish such a document, training may be necessary and guidelines should be easily available. From a broader standpoint, our investigations led to the distinction between private and public spaces of a document—that is, each technical document has a private space where it is invisible outside of a specific community, and a public space where it is visible by a wider community.

Awareness and Communication Between Experts

Situation awareness is a key issue in safety-critical systems. It is much studied at use time. However, it requires more attention at design and development times. People may make errors because they are not aware of the current situation or state of the art. Is Team 1 aware of current actions and productions of Team 2 at the right time? Is Team 1 aware of what Team 3 did a few years ago on the same topic or a similar one? How can we increase awareness? In some cases, it would be nice to have the appropriate information pushed to the front so potential users are aware of its existence. In addition, efficient search mechanisms should provide the necessary means to pull appropriate information when needed. In both cases, context-sensitive algorithms, which may take the form of software agents, are necessary.

When designers know about a type of incident or accident that involved a piece of equipment that they are designing, they (at least try to) design artifacts in order to provide users with the necessary means to handle related situations in the best possible way. They are expert in their field (i.e., design). People who are likely to provide this "incident/accident" knowledge are human factors specialists, end-users themselves or experiences laid down in appropriate databases and knowledge bases. In any case, experts need to communicate either in a live way, such as using computer-supported cooperative work environments, or in a remote way, such as using knowledge bases. Space-time constraints usually impose choices in the way such communication would happen.

Traceability in Space and Time

One of us carried out an exhaustive study on traceability within a large aircraft manufacturing company (Boy, 2001). Traceability is not only information retrieval, it also deals with awareness that potential knowledge exists somewhere, and finally when this knowledge is found, it must be understood correctly. Whether they are project teams, corporate organizations, or professional communities, groups have difficulty providing clear explanations of why things were done in a certain way. This is due to the geographical spread-out of people composing these groups, speed of technology evolution, high turnover of personnel, and lack of documentation of the design process. We will see below that writing is a key issue that cannot be removed from the design activity. People need to know salient reasons that pushed other people to design artifacts they are currently responsible for. This remains true during the whole lifecycle of an artifact.

Trust in Knowledge

Whenever someone gets knowledge from someone else, a crucial issue is to figure out if it is reliable. Do I trust this knowledge without experiencing it? What are the processes that I would need to implement to believe that this knowledge is reliable? The use of Web technology opens our horizons to a wider spectrum of knowledge providers, but we are less sure that acquired knowledge might be trusted. The level of maturity needs to be clearly understood. Consequently, knowledge should come with contextual information that reinforces our understanding of its maturity and context if used.

In the study of Bonini, Jackson, and McDonald (2001), three dimensions of trust were found of importance: belief, dependence, and experience. If you have to trust the information coming from others, you have to be confident in the other and the information provided, you are dependent because you need the information, and you rely on the experience you have with this person and the information. In design processes, the designer is regularly in a dependent position, because preliminary versions are shared between group members and designs of other, related systems are often also in a not yet stable version (participatory design).

Especially in the design of safety-critical systems, one has to make sure that the knowledge that is shared is correct and can be trusted. For this reason extensive validation and document version management is in place in industries. One should avoid the risk of basing one's design on information that has not been verified, and designers should be aware what the latest version of a document is in order to use it.

DESIGN IS WRITING, AND WRITING IS DESIGN

Knowledge management for safety-critical systems mostly deals with documentation since everything should be traceable and formally validated. Consequently, the way things are written is crucial. However, writing is not always perceived as a key issue in engineering and design. Engineers are not scientists who base their careers on the number and quality of the papers they produce. A technical document may be generated the day before delivery just because it was planned to do so. Engineering culture is based on creativity and efficiency, based on very specific languages, often in the form of drawings and schematics that cannot be understood by an outsider. Engineers do not perceive the writing-for-all philosophy as relevant.

Two Separate Worlds: Engineering and Literature

The distinct worlds of engineering and literature barely met during the last century. The human-computer interaction (HCI) community has nicely introduced *design* "into the picture" since user interfaces require a subtle combination amount of technique and graphical art. There, science and arts met. In knowledge management, a deeper step is required. Designers need to step into literature. They need to write technical documents describing requirements, specifications, job orders, evaluation rationale, training and performance support, experience feedback, and a large variety of official documents. It has been observed that people who are already in senior positions in an organization know the benefit of good documentation, and tend to write more than younger employees who do not have as much experience. Document content should satisfy the objectives, thus answering the question: Why and for whom are we writing this document?

In addition, in international environments such as contemporary European multi-national companies, writing in English may be a difficult task for non-native English-speaking personnel. The result is that produced English-written documents may be difficult to understand

The Time-for-Writing Issue

Project deadlines are always very short and do not allow enough time for decent writing. In an engineering organization, the real job is design, not writing. People are usually awarded on design performance issues, not on documentation issues. Writing time should be clearly planned in a project schedule and given the same priority as other activities, so that when there is an extension in the duration of the project, writing is not the last item on the agenda when there is little time left to perform it, as is often the case.

What is Obvious for Someone (Expert) is Not Necessarily for Someone Else

There is no consensus whether writing has improved over the years, for example, in the aeronautics domain. However, some people think that most aerospace technical documents generated during the 1960s are remarkably precise. They were not ambiguous. Work was very well done. People had time and resources to write properly. Other people think that current engineers do not capitalized the necessary technical background to produce appropriate and sufficiently detailed technical documents. It is very important that a selected group of readers reviews all documents. If someone does not understand a technical document, then it should be modified and improved towards a better comprehension. We should apply to documents the same kind of usability testing and user-centered design procedures as for systems. Human factors principles are very similar. Sometimes we say "writing is design, and design is writing."

Redefining Prose Rules Using Multimedia

This statement claims that the quality of technical documentation contributes to the quality of design. We usually write for potential readers. In the same way, we design for potential users. Researchers know that several persons must review papers before being delivered outside. We also know that several persons must test artifacts before being delivered outside. The reader of a multimedia document has become a user of a software application. From this viewpoint, reading a physical note, report, or book has evolved towards interacting with a computer. Writing has also evolved towards design of interactive software. Writing words, phrases, paragraphs, and chapters has become designing objects and software agents. Static paper documents have become (inter)active documents.

The active part of a book (system) is the reader (user). In addition, the organization of the book (system), the way phrases (objects) are written (designed), style, and lexicon used suggest reader (user) activity. Sometimes, the reader (user) hardly understands what the author (designer) wanted to express. Instead of mobilizing the cognition of the reader (user) on interaction problems, the most important part of the cognitive activity of the reader (user) should be centered on the understanding and interpretation of (active) document content.

Toward Simplicity

Design documents are not only outputs of design processes, but also inputs—that is, formulating design ratio-
nale contributes to improving the design itself. There are two issues of simplicity: documenting to improve the simplicity of use of a system being developed, and reducing the difficulty of generating technical documents—that is, making it simpler. Simplest systems are best used. In most cases, when systems are too complicated, they are not used at all. This is true both for the system being developed and for its documentation.

Writing from Bottom-Up (Annotations) vs. Top-Down (Requirements)

People tend to write little notes either by using Post-Its, personal notebooks, page marks, and so on. They annotate what they do and use these notes in order to improve the capacities of their own short-term and long-term memories. If this kind of practice is very useful to people themselves, for a short term, interoperability becomes a problem when such knowledge needs to be exchanged with others or reused by the same person after a longer period of time. Annotations can be considered as pragmatic knowledge that needs to be structured if it is to be used by others. People cannot structure such knowledge in the first place because it is intrinsically situated—that is, it is captured in context to keep its full sense. This is why a mechanism that would support annotation generation and why structuring can be a powerful tool.

APPROPRIATE TOOLS AND ORGANIZATIONAL SETUPS

In industries that develop safety-critical systems, a variety of knowledge management tools are available. Also in R&D projects (including projects in the European Frameworks), many KM tools have been developed. It is clear that tools cannot be designed and used without appropriate organizational setups. People adapt to technology and groups, whether they are teams, organizations, or communities. However, adaptation can be limited by the constraints imposed by tools and socio-cultural habits of the people involved.

Active Notifications of Changes in Design

Designers of safety-critical systems are expected to be proactive people who manage information using available tools in their organizational setups. However, information technology is capable of augmenting their initial skills. Software agents may provide assistance in a variety of tasks that require routine, and usually boring, actions. Safety-critical technology always incrementally changes due to accidents and incidents, customer requirements and needs that continuously evolve, and refinement of the technology itself. There is always a discrepancy between these effective changes of technology and its related operational documentation. People need to be notified about changes in order to operate such technology in a safe way. When such notification is timely, it is usually passive and left to the expertise or intuition of the user; it may not be noticed. This is why a system that would provide proactive notification of changes would be tremendously useful. In the WISE environment, people can subscribe to documentation, indicating about which changes (updates, deletion, status changes, etc.) they want to be notified, by e-mail or in the active work environment.

Supporting the Writing Process

Above we have emphasized the importance of writing for the design process. Tools are available that can support engineers in documenting their work, and capture annotations during the design work, not just after the design is finished. An example of such a tool is the Computer Integrated Documentation (CID) system developed at NASA (Boy, 1991). Another example can be found in the IMAT (Integrating Manuals and Training) system developed for designing learning material (de Hoog et al., 2002). Also in the WISE workspace, the engineer is enabled to make annotations to all different kinds of knowledge objects and to choose whether to share them with team members or others.

Crisp and clearly understood design rationale is a good indicator of maturity in design. Formalisms have been developed to describe design rationale such as gIBIS (*graphical Issue-Based Information System*) (Conklin & Begeman, 1989) or QOC (*Questions Options Criteria*) (MacLean, Young, Bellotti, & Moran, 1991). They support the elicitation of design rationale and enable the documentation of design decisions, development plans, and systems that are effectively developed.

Organization of Personal and Team Workspaces

In current communication and cooperation software, very efficient search engines are available; bottlenecks are elsewhere. They are in the way people categorize incoming information with respect to what is already available on their desktop. This categorization is a strong condition for further retrieval and traceability. People organize their workspace in order to perform their tasks efficiently and manage time and content accordingly. They use Post-Its, bookmarks, document piles, proximity for urgent or fre-

quent access, and so on. In any case, people do not stop to fine-tune their initial categorization to better fit their everyday needs. In the WISE project we have developed a environment in which users have a personal workspace in which they can organize the knowledge they need for their task, as well as a workspace for groups in which knowledge can be pre-structured and shared. The environment consists of a portal that gives access to the companies' documentations, databases, and tools, including search facilities on all knowledge objects thus available, of whatever format or location.

Active Design Documents

The concept of active design document (ADD) (Boy, 1997) was developed to support designers of safety-critical systems in knowledge management. Active documentation may take various forms and involve different kinds of content. An ADD is defined by four categories that organize a designer's workspace: interface objects, interaction descriptions, contextual links, and design rationale.

Interface objects (IOs) provide appropriate, useful, and natural illusions of designed artifacts. IOs have their own behavior reflecting the behavior of related artifacts. They enable users to test usefulness and usability of related artifacts. They provide concrete feeling and grasp of the use of an artifact, its learning requirements, its purpose hands-on, and so forth. Their progressive integration leads to a series of prototypes and, in the end, the final product.

Interaction descriptions (IDs) provide the specification of user-artifact dialogue. IDs may be expressed in either natural language, or a domain-specific technical language ranging from textual descriptions in simplified English (operational procedures for example) to a knowledge representation like the interaction blocks (Boy, 1998). A main advantage of using interaction blocks is to enable formal testing of interaction complexity, and expressing contexts and abnormal conditions of use explicitly.

A test user either follows IDs and produces an activity by using appropriate related IOs, or interacts directly with IOs and verifies the validity of related IDs. In both cases, he or she tests the links between IOs and IDs in context (i.e., in the context of the task being performed). The corresponding category is called *contextual links* (CLs). This is where usefulness and usability evaluations (sometimes annotations) are stored in the form of either free text or specific preformatted forms.

Design rationale (DR) provides the reasons why the IOs and IDs of an artifact have been designed the way they are, and design alternatives that were not chosen. DR is commonly implemented by using semi-formal languages such as gIBIS or QOC already mentioned.

ADDs are tools that support not only communication and mediation, but also prototyping and evaluation. They enable their users to store design knowledge according to a concrete and systematic formalism. Creation and maintenance of such ADDs enable an entire organization to maintain awareness of their design processes and products.

Interoperable Documents and the Portal Concept

Documents should be interoperable. This requirement induces two kinds of issues: standards and integrated environments. When people exchange documents across teams, organizations, and communities, they expect the others to be able to process what they provide. This is commonly a matter of standards. In a closed world where an organization can cope with an integrated environment in the form of intranet for example, people do not have to worry about standards. Nevertheless, standards progressively emerge from the extensive use of specific types of documents.

Designers require KM environments that are user-centered (easy to use and avoid overload) and integrated within their current tasks. They should have easy access to KM services at each design step. For example, in a safety assessment process, there should be information provided for performing safety analysis and related documents. In other words, the designer workspace should be (re)designed in such a way that he or she has easy access to experience feedback (e.g., not only a list of what is necessary to do and forbidden (checklists), but providing deep knowledge to foster preventive design actions and avoid later corrective actions) at any time. Having this knowledge available at the designer's desktop at all times can be realized by a KM portal. A portal means that it provides access to knowledge, wherever it is located, but does not contain this knowledge itself. In the KM portal developed in WISE, designers have access to knowledge available in, for example, databases with experience feedback, lessons learned, and best practices, to all kinds of relevant documents, and to people who can bring interesting knowledge and experience. Access to all these sources is provided in the same manner and with a single search facility.

CONCLUSION

The way knowledge is exchanged during the design and the further lifecycle of a safety-critical system induces several factors related to systems (complexity, completeness, maturity, traceability) and people (expertise, writing, simplicity, drafts, information credibility, uncertainty, and awareness).

Several actual developments influence the design processes of safety-critical systems: more people from different organizations (within the company or (sub)contractors) get involved, more procedures are in place (such as certification procedures, involving human factors in particular), and product development needs to be faster than before. These evolutions have a direct impact on the increase of both the number and content of documents. Information technology provides new means to generate, maintain, and use such documents. A main issue is to improve the use of such means.

Important questions remain to be answered: Does this technology change the job of engineers? Does it free up engineers from boring tasks? Or does it create new ones? Answers to these questions are complex. However, this article contributes by providing categories of KM solutions such as the organization of personal and team workspaces, active design documents, and knowledge portals. Usefulness and usability of such solutions need to be tested carefully in a real-world environment with a critical mass of people involved. This is very difficult to do since experts and specialists (e.g., designers of safety-critical systems) are always occupied, busy, and constrained into an already existing KM system, often very far from the solutions proposed. Transformations should be incremental, accepted by the people involved. Implementing a new KM system is also redefining a new philosophy of work, a new culture. This is hard to do and hard to implement! This is the main reason why the design of new KM systems must be human-centered—that is, team-centered, organization-centered, and community-centered. Each of these types of group has its own motivations, requirements, and constraints.

REFERENCES

Bentley, R., Horstmann, T., & Trevor, J. (1997). The World Wide Web as enabling technology for CSCW: The case of BSCW. *Computer-Supported Cooperative Work: Special Issue on CSCW and the Web, 6.*

Bonini, D., Jackson, A., & McDonald, N. (2001). Do I trust thee? An approach to understanding trust in the domain of air traffic control. *Proceedings of IEE People in Control,* UMIST, Manchester, UK.

Boy, G.A. (1991, December). Indexing hypertext documents in context. *Proceedings of the Hypertext'91 Conference,* San Antonio, TX.

Boy, G.A. (1997). Active design documents. *Proceedings of the ACM DIS'97 Conference.* New York: ACM Press.

Boy, G.A. (1998). *Cognitive function analysis.* Stamford, CT: Ablex.

Boy, G.A. (1999). *Traceability.* EURISCO-Airbus Report T-99-060-V3.

Conklin, E.J., & Begeman, M.L. (1989). gIBIS: A tool for all reasons. *Journal of the American Society for Information Science, 40,* 200-213. (This article describes a graphical support tool for IBIS.)

de Hoog, R., Kabel, S., Barnard, Y., Boy, G., DeLuca, P., Desmoulins, C., Riemersma, J., & Verstegen, D. (2002). Reusing technical manuals for instruction: Creating instructional material with the tools of the IMAT project. In Y. Barnard, M. Grnadbastien, R. de Hoog, & C. Desmoulins (Eds.), *Ingrating Technical and Training Documentation, Proceedings of the ITS2002 Workshop, 6th International Conference on Intelligent Tutoring Systems,* San Sebastian, Spain/Biarritz, France.

MacLean, A., Young, R.M., Bellotti, V.M.E., & Moran, T.P. (1991). Questions, options and criteria: Elements of design space analysis. *Human-Computer Interaction, 6,* 201-250. (This article describes the background for designing space analysis and the QOC notation. It explains how it can be used in the design process and to study reasoning in design. Other articles of interest on this topic also appear in this issue of the journal.)

Poltrock, S.E., & Grudin, J. (2001, July 9-13). Collaboration technology in teams, organizations, and communities. Tutorial. *Proceedings of the 8th IFIP TC13 IFIP INTERACT Conference on Human-Computer Interaction,* Tokyo, Japan.

Knowledge Management Ontology

Clyde W. Holsapple
University of Kentucky, USA

K.D. Joshi
Washington State University, USA

INTRODUCTION

Many definitions of ontology are posited in the literature (see Guarino, 2004). Here, we adopt Gruber's (1995) view which defines ontologies as simplified and explicit specification of a phenomenon. In this article, we posit an ontology that explicates the components of knowledge management (KM) phenomena. This explicit characterization of knowledge management can help in systematically understanding or modeling KM phenomenon.

In the past decade, KM has received significant attention within the information systems community, however, the community has not provided a well-integrated framework to help unify this sub-discipline. Therefore, in an effort to provide a comprehensive and unified view of KM, we introduce a formal characterization of a KM ontology collaboratively developed with an international panel of KM practitioners and researchers. Prior articles have either detailed various portions of this ontology and described panelists' piecewise evaluations of them (Holsapple & Joshi, 2000, 2001, 2002c) or outlined a more definitional and axiomatic version of this ontology (Holsapple & Joshi, 2004). Here, however, we provide a concise integrated view of the whole ontology.

Several methodologies for designing and developing ontologies have been proposed in the literature for many domains and for various objectives. For instance, Noy and McGuinness (2001) have posited seven steps for developing a basic ontology, whereas others, such as Guarino (retrieved 2004), have discussed the application of ontological principles in various context. Our ontolology development process, although unique in certain aspects, incorporates many of the principles recommended in the literature.

BACKGROUND

The ontology was developed through a process of four phases including the preparatory, anchoring, collaborative, and application phases (Holsapple & Joshi, 2002a).

In the preparatory phase, standards and criteria for ontology development and evaluation were created. In the anchoring phase, an initial ontology by consolidating, synthesizing, organizing, and integrating concepts from the past literature was developed. During the third phase, a panel of 31 KM practitioners and researchers collaborated in two Delphi rounds to further refine, modify, and evaluate the initial ontology. The last phase involved illustrating the application and utility of the developed ontology.

KNOWLEDGE MANAGEMENT ONTOLOGY

This ontology defines knowledge management as an entity's (such as an individual, group, organization, community, nation) deliberate and organized efforts to expand, cultivate, and apply available knowledge in ways that add value to the entity, in the sense of positive results in accomplishing its objectives or fulfilling its purpose (Holsapple & Joshi, 2004).

Many definitions of knowledge can be found in the literature (see Nonaka, 1994; Alavi & Leidner, 2001; Marshall & Brady 2001; Randall, Hughes, O'Brien, Rouncefield, & Tolmie, 2001; Sutton, 2001). The objective of the Delphi process was to characterize knowledge management behaviors that can accommodate various perspectives on the nature of knowledge. Therefore, no single definition of knowledge was developed or adopted. Knowledge can be represented in mental, behavioral, symbolic, digital, visual, audio, and other sensory patterns that may occur in various object and process formats. Knowledge has a variety of attributes including mode (tacit vs. explicit), type (descriptive vs. procedural vs. reasoning), orientation (domain vs. relational vs. self), applicability (local vs. global), accessibility (public vs. private), immediacy (latent vs. currently actionable), perishability (shelf-life), and so forth. More complete and detailed listings of attribute dimensions for characterizing knowledge have been advanced but are beyond the scope of this article (Holsapple & Joshi, 2001; Holsapple, 2003a) In the interest of being

Figure 1. Architecture of a KM episode (adapted from Holsapple & Joshi, 2004)

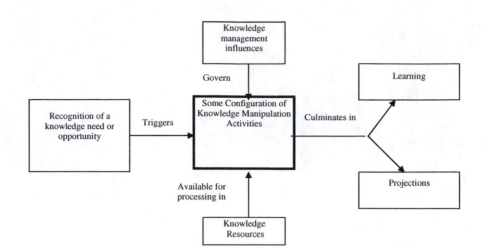

generic, the ontology is neutral on these differential views.

This ontology adopts an episodic view to knowledge work. In other words, an entity's knowledge management work is viewed as a collection of episodes. These episodes, which vary in structure, function, and purpose, unfold in various settings to accomplish a range of different tasks. This ontology characterizes a *knowledge management episode* (KME) (see Figure 1) as a configuration of *knowledge manipulation activities*, by a collection of *knowledge processors*, operating on available knowledge *resources*, subject to knowledge management *influences*, and yielding *learning* and/or *projections* (Holsapple & Joshi, 2004). Knowledge management episodes are triggered to satisfy a knowledge need or opportunity; it concludes when that need/opportunity is satisfied or terminated. Some examples of KME include decision-making, problem-solving, and brainstorming episodes.

KME is considered to have a learning outcome when the state of an entity's knowledge resources is altered. On the other hand, projection outcomes are expressions or manifestations—in the form of knowledge, material, capital, or behavior—of an entity's KME that are released into its environment. The resulting alteration in the state of the entity's knowledge base or environment due to learning or projection can be functional or dysfunctional in nature. The three primary components that drive the execution of a KME are the *knowledge manipulation activities, knowledge resources,* and *knowledge management influences.*

Knowledge Manipulation Activities Component

Knowledge manipulation refers to the processing of usable knowledge representations embedded within an entity's knowledge resources. Knowledge processors that possess skills for performing knowledge manipulations activities can be human participants or computer-based parts in an entity. Numerous classifications of knowledge manipulation activities have been forwarded by KM researchers (see Alavi & Leidner, 2001; Holsapple & Joshi, 2002c). However, they often fail to provide a unifying view due to the use of differing terminology and varying levels of manipulation activities. This ontology provides a relatively comprehensive, unifying, elemental characterization of the major knowledge manipulation activities that occur during knowledge work.

As illustrated in Table 1, the Delphi process uncovered elemental knowledge manipulation activities, their sub-activities, and their interrelationships. The five types of basic knowledge manipulation activities that can occur during knowledge work include *knowledge acquisition, knowledge selection, knowledge generation, knowledge assimilation,* and *knowledge emission.*

The knowledge resulting from the execution of a knowledge manipulation activity by a processor can be transferred for further processing to other instances of knowledge manipulation activities. In other words, knowledge flows into and out of knowledge manipula-

Table 1. The Ontology's Knowledge Manipulation Activity Component (Adapted from Holsapple and Joshi, 2004)

Knowledge Manipulation Activity	Sub-Activities within This Activity	Knowledge Flows into This Activity from	Knowledge Flows Released from This Activity to
Acquisition	Identification, Capturing, Organizing, Transferring	Entity's Environment	Assimilation, Generation, Emission
Selection	Identification, Capturing, Organizing, Transferring	Entity's Knowledge Resources	Acquisition, Assimilation, Generation, Emission
Generation	Monitoring, Evaluating, Producing, Transferring	Acquisition, Selection	Assimilation, Emission
Assimilation	Assessing/valuing, Targeting, Structuring, Transferring	Acquisition, Selection, Generation	Entity's Knowledge Resources
Emission	Targeting, Producing, Transferring	Acquisition, Selection, Generation	Entity's Environment

tion activities. A knowledge flow can be initiated through a pull or a push mechanism. So, a processor performing an instance of an activity could push that resulting knowledge to another instance of an activity or it could transfer that knowledge to satisfy the knowledge request from some other activity instance. In order to establish, coordinate, and control the knowledge flows among activity instances, processors also transfer ancillary messages to the interacting instances. These ancillary messages provide feedback, clarification, and evaluation of actual knowledge flow.

The ontology's five elemental knowledge manipulation activities that resulted from the Delphi process are characterized as follows (see Holsapple & Joshi, 2004 for a more formal discussion of these activities).

A knowledge *acquisition* activity involves identification of knowledge from the entity's environment and making it available in a suitable representation to an appropriate activity. The knowledge *selection* activity is similar to knowledge acquisition with one difference: Knowledge selection identifies knowledge from within an entity's knowledge resources as opposed to from the entity's environment. A knowledge *generation* activity derives or discovers knowledge in the context of existing knowledge. A knowledge *assimilation* activity culminates in learning by altering an entity's knowledge resources. A knowledge *emission* activity applies the existing knowledge to produce projections for release into the environment. The knowledge assimilation and emission activity involves usage and application of entity's existing knowledge to create knowledge.

Each of the five knowledge manipulation activities are comprised of sub-activities. Next, we will describe the sub-activities as well as the incoming and outgoing knowledge flows for each of the knowledge manipulation activities.

Knowledge acquisition (knowledge selection) is accomplished through a set of sub-activities which include identification of appropriate knowledge from the external sources (within the entity's existing resources), capturing the identified knowledge, organizing captured knowledge, and transferring the organized knowledge to an appropriate activity. A knowledge acquisition activity receives knowledge flows from an entity's environment and delivers the acquired knowledge to an activity that immediately uses the knowledge and/or to one that assimilates it within the entity for subsequent use. A knowledge selection activity receives knowledge flows from an entity's knowledge resources and delivers the selected knowledge to the acquisition, use, and/or assimilation activities.

The generation of knowledge entails monitoring the entity's knowledge resources and the external environment and attaining required knowledge (via selection or acquisition), evaluating the obtained knowledge in terms of its utility and validity for the production of knowledge, producing knowledge by creating, synthesizing, analyzing, and constructing knowledge from a base of existing knowledge, and transferring the produced knowledge to an appropriate activity. A knowledge generation activity receives knowledge flows from knowledge selection or acquisition activities and delivers the generated knowledge to assimilation and/or emission activities.

Knowledge assimilation involves assessing and valuing knowledge to be assimilated, targeting knowledge resources where knowledge would be situated, structuring knowledge into forms appropriate for the targets, and transferring the knowledge representations as targeted. A knowledge assimilation activity receives knowledge flows from knowledge acquisition, selection, or generation activities and produces knowledge flows that are transferred/embedded into the entity's knowledge resources.

The emission activity involves targeting elements of the environment to determine what projections need to be produced, producing projections for the target, and transferring the projections to targets which involves packaging and delivery. A knowledge emission activity receives knowledge flows from knowledge selection, acquisition, and/or generation activities and delivers the packaged knowledge (i.e., projections) to targets in the environment.

Knowledge assimilation and emitting activities, which result in learning and projection respectively, are very critical to effective knowledge work. These activities, if executed effectively, can add value to an entity in terms of enhanced knowledge, profits, and performance. The knowledge processed by the knowledge manipulation activities are embedded within different types of knowledge resources that are characterized below.

Knowledge Resource Component

An organizational resource is a source of value, revenue, wealth, or rent to an organization (Holsapple & Joshi, 2004). Traditionally, organizations have recognized and effectively managed three types of resources: financial, human, and material. However, knowledge assets are recognized as crucial organizational resources (Drucker, 1993) for creating and maintaining a competitive advantage (Holsapple & Singh, 2001). More organizations are attempting to manage knowledge resources with a degree of systematic, deliberate, or explicit effort devoted to managing the other three resources. Knowledge resources are entities where organizational knowledge is embedded and can be manipulated by an organization in ways that yield value. A taxonomy characterizing knowledge resources, a component of our knowledge management ontology, which was developed through the Delphi process is described next.

Some classes of knowledge resources exist independent of an entity's existence whereas the others depend on the existence of an entity. The resources that exist independent of an entity are called *content* knowledge resources. The resources that are dependent on the existence of an entity are called *schematic* resources. Schematic knowledge is embedded within the behaviors that manifests in an organization. The four kinds of schematic resources include *culture, infrastructure, strategy,* and *purpose.* An organization's cultural knowledge resource holds organizational values, principles, norms, traditions, unwritten rules, and informal procedures. An organization's infrastructure structures an organization's participants in terms of the roles that have been defined for participants to fill, the relationships among those roles, and regulations that govern the use of roles and relationships (Holsapple & Luo, 1996). An organization's strategy consists of planning knowledge for utilizing organization's infrastructure, culture, knowledge artifacts, and participants' knowledge (as well as other organizational resources). An organization's purpose consists of

directional knowledge used to align entity's strategy, infrastructure, and culture.

The two types of content knowledge resources include *participants' knowledge* and knowledge embedded within *artifacts*. These resources can exist without an entity that host, own or create these resources. Knowledge artifacts are objects without any processing skills, but have knowledge embedded within them that can be processed by human or computer processors. Participants' knowledge is the knowledge possessed by knowledge processors that participate in an organization.

The last class of knowledge resources that is accessible to an entity are the resources in its environment. The environment's knowledge resources are a crucial source for replenishing and augmenting an organization's knowledge resources.

Knowledge Management Influences Component

Knowledge influences are factors that shape and govern the execution of knowledge manipulation activities during a KM episode. The Delphi methods revealed three classes of KM influences, including *managerial influences, resources influences,* and *environmental influences.* Managerial influences incorporate administrative activities established and executed by an entity that affect its knowledge work. Resource influences are comprised of organizational resources that are employed to carry out entity's knowledge work. Environmental influences are factors external to an entity (i.e., in its environment) that affect its conduct of knowledge management.

The managerial influences include knowledge *leadership*, knowledge *coordination*, knowledge *control*, and knowledge *measurement*. Leadership facilitates fruitful knowledge work. Knowledge coordination involves management of dependencies among knowledge manipulation activities, knowledge resources, knowledge processors, and knowledge management episodes. Knowledge control involves ensuring that needed knowledge resources and processors are available in sufficient quality and quantity, subject to required security. Knowledge measurement involves assessing and valuing knowledge resources, knowledge processors, knowledge manipulation activities, managerial influences, knowledge management episodes, and overall conduct of knowledge management.

The ontology recognizes an entity's resources as influences on how a KM episode unfolds. This includes not just its knowledge resources, but also the other more traditional resources such as financial, material, and human. The third class of influence includes an entity's environment. Unlike managerial influences (and, to a considerable extent, resource influences), environmental influences are factors over which an entity typically has limited (or no) control. These factors may operate as constraints, impediments, or facilitators of the entity's knowledge management efforts. The Delphi process yielded six major classes of environmental influences: competition, fashion, markets, technology, time, and the GEPSE (governmental, economic, political, social, and educational) climate.

FUTURE TRENDS

This article provides a general purpose ontology that is very generic in nature and applicable to various knowledge contexts. Although, on one hand the ontology's general nature broadens its applicability, it also limits it from capturing the nuances of a specific knowledge context. Therefore, by adopting this ontology as its foundation, future research needs to develop context-specific ontologies that focus on characterizing a specific KM episode in a more detailed fashion. For instance, in order to better understand how the knowledge management conduct unfolds during an information system development (ISD) process, it is crucial to explicate and characterize the KM conduct in the context of an ISD process. Such an effort could entail enumeration of knowledge manipulation activities and its relationships specific to this task, identification of knowledge resources involved in this type of knowledge work, and uncovering influences that facilitate or constrain knowledge processing in an ISD process.

This ontology provides concepts and components associated with KM episodes. However, it does not offer measures for these constructs. Future research needs to create measurement scales that operationalize the ontology's constructs for measuring and testing the execution of KM episodes within organizations.

Future research and practice needs to continually test and examine this ontology's utility and applicability and develop it further through improvements, refinements, and modifications.

CONCLUSION

The posited ontology identifies and characterizes major elements of KM in a unified and relatively comprehensive manner. It provides a characterization of KM episodes that consists of three components: knowledge manipulation activities, knowledge resources, and knowledge influences. Moreover, it provides a taxonomy for an entity's knowledge resources where knowledge

may be stored, embedded, and/or represented. It identifies and relates knowledge manipulation activities that operate on those resources. It recognizes factors that influence the conduct of KM in an organization.

The ontology in its current form provides a foundation for systematic KM research, study, and practice. It provides researchers with a unified and comprehensive view of KM that is crucial for studying KM (e.g., Holsapple & Singh, 2000; Holsapple & Singh, 2001; Massey, Montoya-Weiss, & O'Driscoll, 2002; Holsapple & Jones, 2003). It gives practitioners a frame of reference for evaluating KM practices and identifying KM opportunities. It forwards a structure and content for developing a formal KM curriculum (e.g., Holsapple, 2003b, 2003c; Weidner, 2003).

This ontology is an initial step toward initiating conceptual development in the KM field. This ontology can be developed further through added breath and depth. It can be extended in a normative direction by adding elements that prescribe methods and technologies for the conduct of KM.

REFERENCES

Alavi, M., & Leidner, D. (2001). Knowledge management and knowledge management systems: Conceptual foundations and research issues. *MIS Quarterly, 25*(1), 107-136.

Drucker, P. (1993). *Post-capitalist society*. New York: Harper Collins.

Gruber, T.R. (1995). Toward principles for the design of ontologies used for knowledge sharing. *International Journal of Human and Computer Studies, 43*(5/6), 907-928.

Guarino, N. (2004). Understanding, building, and using ontologies. Retrieved 2004, from *http://ksi.cpsc.ucalgary.ca/KAW/KAW96/guarino/guarino.html*

Holsapple, C., & Luo, W. (1996). A framework for studying computer support of organizational infrastructure. *Information and Management, 31*(1), 13-24.

Holsapple, C., & Singh, M. (2000, March 31-April 2). The knowledge chain. *Proceedings of the Annual Conference of the Southern Association on Information Systems.*

Holsapple, C., & Singh, M. (2001). The knowledge chain model: Activities for competitiveness. *Expert Systems with Applications, 20*(1), 77-98.

Holsapple, C.W., & Joshi, K.D. (2000). An investigation of factors that influence the management of knowledge in organizations. *Journal of Strategic Information System,* *9*(2-3), 235-261.

Holsapple, C.W., & Joshi, K.D. (2001). Organizational knowledge resources. *Decision Support Systems, 31*(4), 39-54.

Holsapple, C.W., & Joshi, K.D. (2002a). A collaborative approach to ontology design. *Communications of the ACM, 44*(2), 42-47.

Holsapple, C.W., & Joshi, K.D. (2002c). Knowledge manipulation activities: Results of a Delphi study. *Information and Management, 39*(6), 477-490.

Holsapple C. (2003a). Knowledge and its attributes. In C. Holsapple (Ed.), *Handbook on knowledge management: Knowledge matters* (pp. 165-188). Berlin: Springer-Verlag.

Holsapple, C. (Ed.) (2003b). *Handbook on knowledge management: Knowledge matters.* Berlin: Springer-Verlag.

Holsapple, C.W., & Jones, K. (2003, August 4-5). Toward an elaboration of the knowledge chain model. *Proceedings of the Americas Conference on Information Systems,* Tampa, FL.

Holsapple, C.W., & Joshi, K.D. (2004). A collaboratively designed ontology of knowledge management. *Journal of the American Society for Information Science and Technology, 55*(7), 593-612.

Marshall N., & Brady, T. (2001). Knowledge management and the politics of knowledge: Illustrations from complex products and systems. *European Journal of Information Systems, 10*(2), 99-112.

Massey, A.P., Montoya-Weiss, M.M., & O'Driscoll, T.M. (2002). Knowledge management in pursuit of performance: Insights from Nortel Networks. *MIS Quarterly, 26*(3), 269-289.

Nonaka, I. (1994). A dynamic theory of organizational knowledge creation. *Organization Science, 5*(1), 14-37.

Noy, N.F., & McGuinness, D.L. (2001). Ontology development 101: A guide to creating your first ontology. *SMI technical report SMI-2001-0880.*

Randall, D., Hughes, J., O'Brien, J., Rouncefield, M., & Tolmie P. (2001). Memories are made of this: Explicating organisational knowledge and memory. *European Journal of Information Systems, 10*(2), 113-121.

Sutton D.C. (2001). What is knowledge and can it be managed? *European Journal of Information Systems, 10*(2), 80-88.

Weidner, D. (2003) Book review. *In thought and practice, 2*(1). Retrieved from *www.kmpro.org/journal/Book_Review/Handbook_on_Knowledge_Management.cfm*

KEY TERMS

Content Knowledge Resource: A knowledge resource that exists independently of an organization to which it belongs.

Environmental Influences: Factors external to an entity (i.e., in its environment) that affect its conduct of knowledge management.

Knowledge Management: An entity's systematic and deliberate efforts to expand, cultivate, and apply available knowledge in ways that add value to the entity, in the sense of positive results in accomplishing its objectives or fulfilling its purpose.

Knowledge Management Episode: Is aA configuration of knowledge manipulation activities, by a collection of knowledge processors, operating on available knowledge resources, subject to knowledge management influences, and yielding learning and/or projections

Knowledge Manipulation Activities: Knowledge manipulation activities process usable knowledge representations embedded within an entity's knowledge resources.

Managerial Influences: Administrative efforts undertaken by an entity that affect its conduct of knowledge management.

Resource Influences: An entity's resources that are deployed to execute and affect its conduct of knowledge management.

Schematic Knowledge Resource: A knowledge resource whose existence depends on the existence of the organization.

Knowledge Management Processes

Frank Land
London School of Economics and Political Science, UK

Urooj Amjad
London School of Economics and Political Science, UK

Sevasti-Melissa Nolas
London School of Economics and Political Science, UK

INTRODUCTION

Knowledge management (KM), as a topic for academic research and practical implementation, has had a short history dating back only to the early 1990s. Due to knowledge management's recent debut as we know it, it is not surprising that much of the writing and research on the subject is controversial. In this article we note the need of a critical awareness of desirable and undesirable shades of knowledge management processes (Land, Nolas, & Amjad, 2005).

BACKGROUND AND FOCUS

Knowledge is both disseminated and acquired. As observers we cannot know what intentions lay behind the act of dissemination, or what motivates the acquirer to acquire. We cannot blindly assume information—a major component of knowledge—as interpreted, facilitated, conceptualised, or experienced, is automatically for everyone's benefit. The process of knowledge management may have a desired or detrimental outcome for society, an organisation, a team, or the individual. Indeed, the outcome of a KM activity, say knowledge sharing, is largely unpredictable. The reality is the outcome may benefit one group at the expense of another. Benefiting one group at the expense of the other is addressed by the following conceptual fusions.

KM is a continuum of desirable and undesirable political processes. This article suggests that the combined concepts of *knowledge management*, organisational politics (OP), and coevolution (CE) make a contribution to the understanding of KM, whether in its benign or its darker manifestation. Because knowledge management is a purposeful activity, it can never be neutral. Hence the article sets out to forewarn practitioners and thinkers in the area of KM that care must be taken since knowledge (K) can be manipulated for both altruistic and selfish purposes.

If the study of KM is to have an enduring future, it must take a more holistic stance. We suggest the concept of "coevolution" (McKelvey, 2002; Lewin & Volberda, 1999; Lewin et al., 1999) provides a way of understanding the implications of knowledge management on the organisation and its employees. Coevolution describes the mutual influences among actors in a collective, as well as their environment. Mutual influences can have desirable and undesirable, constructive and destructive effects. In the case of an organisation, coevolution can be envisaged as being effected in a set of multi-dimensional networks, themselves part of a larger set of networks to which they are linked.

Any event or activity will have some (possibly unknown) impact on other succeeding or collateral activities. Their responses will in turn trigger impacts and responses in further activities, including possibly in the activity that acted as the initial trigger. Each activity evolves on a trajectory which may have been planned, but the outcome and direction is often unexpected. The pattern of responses in diverse activities leads to their *coevolution*. The coevolution of *power* and knowledge contribute to the discussion of the darker sides of knowledge management by offering an understanding of *shades of desirable and undesirable forms of knowledge management*. The concept of coevolution permits us to replace the simple ethical/non-ethical dichotomy and attempts to explain the dynamics in a continuum of knowledge management processes, actuated by motives, mediated by sources, and realised via the dissemination and acquisition of knowledge. Nevertheless, the complex pattern woven by coevolution remains uncertain, and permits the *emergence* of the unexpected.

KM occurs at all levels in the organisation. It may be a planned formal process supported by KM software designed to increase the effectiveness of a team of knowledge workers. Equally it may be a hidden process of *knowledge manipulation* by a group attempting to direct the organisation on a path away from its formal objectives. It may be an informal process, the reaction of a group of people responding to an initiative they believe will damage them. But whatever the intention behind the process, both the study of *organisational politics* and coevolution suggest that the outcome will be uncertain. Outcomes, sometimes unexpected, emerge from the responses of organisational actors. In order to deal with the problem of uncertainty and emergence, at both an analytical and practical level, the article introduces the concepts of *desirable* and *undesirable coevolution* for looking at was *is* and not what *ought* to be.

CORE IDEAS OF THE ARTICLE

Knowledge, Power, and Their Dynamic Interactions

This article links together:

* Knowledge Management (KM)
* Organisational Politics (OP) and
* The concept of Coevolution (CE)

All three share a common concept: *power.* Knowledge management, despite much of the rhetoric surrounding the concept, is not a power-neutral process. If, as has been suggested (Land et al., 2005), knowledge is managed in order to achieve goals, be they benign or corrupt, political processes are invoked in the management process.

KM, OP, and CE all involve power, and each is profoundly affected by the way power is distributed. Knowledge management in its idealised form is independent of power. In reality the existence of an asymmetric power balance enables those with the power, often those who have formal authority, to present knowledge in directions of their choosing. Those with lesser power may respond by using knowledge to achieve their ends in more subtle and primarily informal ways, of which the spreading of rumours is one typical way. A central idea of KM is that knowledge, if considered a commodity, is manoeuvred toward shades of desirable and undesirable directions by multiple stakeholders.

OP, summarised as a wide range of descriptions of formal and informal power relationships in organisations, has been studied and documented at least since the 1970s (e.g., Pettigrew, 1973; Mintzberg, 1983; Pfeffer, 1997). OP provides a theoretical lens with which to conceptualise and observe both constructive and destructive aspects of KM.

Most academic literature agrees KM is an essential activity for a modern enterprise to flourish in a global competitive economy, and many practicing managers share this view. Despite the slippery meaning of KM, a positive relationship between knowledge and truth—and

hence KM—is implicitly assumed. An interpretist view of KM is that people are capable of being aware of their own actions, further assuming knowledge and understanding are 'good' or at least neutral (Schultze, 1999). In other words, interpretivists take for granted people are self-aware, but optimistically believe knowledge management to be an inherently constructive and positive process. However, Schultze also notes that the open sharing of knowledge may not occur in competitive business environments associated with competitive advantage.

The inspiration for thinking about the interrelationship of knowledge management and power is found in the following concepts of coevolution and organisational politics.

Organisational Politics

The study of organisational politics suggests the driving force enabling organisational politics to occur is power, and in particular the asymmetrical distribution of power. Organisations are overlapping sets of political networks, rule, and role systems, engaging in coalition building as part of manipulative, selfish, under-the-table dealings, as well as for constructive purposes aimed at furthering the aims of that organisation.

The informal and formal organisation becomes part of the discussion, since it is the informal organisation where much of the political activity occurs—behind the scenes. Pfeffer (1997, p. 136), in support of this position, notes: "...these less formal methods rely more on power and influence, leverage individuals' positions in social networks, and entail ongoing negotiations among organisational participants." However, identifying political behavioural patterns for the sake of efficiency is not enough. "The skill is to try and prevent individual and organisational pathological circumstances from arising by recognising the appropriate and inappropriate behaviours that individuals and groups will and will not be able to accept" (Kakabadse & Parker, 1984, p. 101).

Three aspects of KM as a political process within an organisation are dependency, strategies for enacting power, and decision making.

Taking Pettigrew's (1973, p. 26) position that "Power is...a property of social relationships, not an attribute of the actor...Dependency is...a product of an imbalance of exchange between individuals and the ability of one actor to control others through his [/her] possession of resources," knowledge can be a critical resource. Hence the desirable or undesirable directions of K manipulation can trigger that dependency to be constructive or destructive. For example, a senior manager may become dependent on the knowledge (experience) of a junior manager, therefore strengthening the expertise and performance of the team. The senior manager is dependent on the knowledge of the junior manager. Her/his own performance is governed by the presence or absence of the subordinate.

A specific arena in an organisational politics context is a decision-making process, which determines specific actions to be taken. Influencing a decision in the making is more effective than attempting to do so after action on the decision has been taken (Mintzberg, 1983, p. 206). In practice, manipulation of information and knowledge, designed to influence the decision maker, takes place at all levels in the organisation and for many reasons.

Organisational politics provide the geo-political landscape for describing KM processes, alerting us to the manipulative nature of KM. Viewing KM as political is not an end in itself. Kakabadse and Parker (1984, pp. 104-105) summarise organisational politics and offer a remedy:

Problems arise when an individual group rejects, misunderstands, or responds with inappropriate behaviours [for example, providing false information] to the actions of other individuals or groups. In the literature, it is their negative interactions that have, to date, been labelled 'political.' We suggest that one way of reducing negative interactions is to strive for multi-rationality. Multi-rationality is a process whereby actors begin to understand their own values, beliefs, and norms; are able to assert their individuality but are equally able to accept that others hold a different rationale.

Coevolution

Tasaka (1999) describes coevolution as "a process in which each part interacts with and influences the other parts, thereby stimulating their mutual development." The coevolution of power and knowledge contribute to the discussion of knowledge management by emphasising the intricacy of the interactions, the uncertainty of what the outcomes of the interactions will be, and the opportunities the interactions provide for the manipulation of information and knowledge.

Interactions cannot be clearly classified as desirable or undesirable. Every process creates interactions. As knowledge management creates interactions, we cannot predict that the outcome of coevolution will yield what was intended. As a consequence of the multi-rationalities operating in the real world, some individuals or groups may see the outcomes as desirable, where others judge them detrimental to the organisation or to themselves. Ignoring the 'power' dimensions of the situation being studied gives the impression that organisational space is neutral, and that the action of entering the space is also neutral (Land et al., 2005). Constant change and mutual influencing among actors, processes, and scenarios add to the awareness of the non-neutrality of KM.

Coevolution explains how first-order effects trigger other second-order effects, which in turn trigger further effects. Further effects produce a cascade of non-deterministic effects where the impacts will be emergent and cannot be second-guessed. An example of this is the desire for clarity of organisational strategy, leading perhaps, in the interest of clarity, to rigidly defined organisational roles. But the imposition of stricter controls to enforce the predefined organisational architecture may have the undesired consequence of inhibiting innovation and stifling initiative.

The following two examples illustrate power dynamics and KM processes. CE is used to highlight the intricate interaction in these instances of post-merger integration (PMI) and water management. PMI is an example of what happens inside an organisation, and the case of water management here is an example of inter-organisational relationships.

Example 1: Post-Merger Integration

Organisation, a national leader in its sector, experienced a merger in 2000. The results of the merger were *Organisation's* unclear strategic goals, as voiced through semi-structured interviews in 2002. This lack of clarity trickled down to a particular department (henceforth *Department*) and other teams that interacted with the *Department*. Unclear strategic goals and how to operationalise them on an individual, team, and department level emerged in the following ways. Hierarchical relationships and prioritisation of work tasks are very much interrelated. The essence of this is that senior-level management commented on being out of touch with what is happening at middle-management levels. Being out of touch with middle-management levels—clearly a failure of KM—translates into prioritisation problems, where the operational levels know what the daily capabilities are and the senior management may have an overall understanding of what needs to be done to achieve organisational goals, but not the knowledge of realistic capabilities on everyday tasks. For example, a new deadline must be met sooner than previously understood by the operational and middle-management levels. Pressure is then put on the subsequent levels to produce for this deadline. The operational levels become frustrated because a particular piece of equipment is down for the moment, making the task even more difficult, and further delaying other needed, regular tasks. Being out of touch with what is happening in daily routines then becomes a vicious cycle of no space for initiative and heavy-handedness from senior management, toward operational management.

The primary problem identified here is ambiguity of roles and strategy. One common solution to alleviate such ambiguity is increasing the amount of information to the same people and to more people. In other words, change the KM processes with higher volume of information and more interaction. However, increasing the quantity of knowledge to alleviate the management levels' ambiguity of roles and strategy is not the straightforward solution. Becker (2001, pp. 1046-1048) argues for acknowledging a difference between the meanings of uncertainty and ambiguity. He states "ambiguity" is *structural* uncertainty, whereas "uncertainty" is *stochastic*, in other words random or probabilistic uncertainty. The point being that, faced with a decision problem that is due to structural rather than random uncertainty, increasing the knowledge and information at hand may further increase the structural uncertainty (ambiguity) instead of alleviating it. "What is required is to make people communicate, assimilate cognitive frameworks, and develop understanding…to support processes that lead to understanding, not just access to information"(Becker, 2001, p. 1048).

The implementation of organisational strategy is shaped by the individual priorities of the relevant organisational actors. And the implementation process is itself driven by KM processes employed by stakeholders operating in various hierarchical levels in the organisation. Ambiguity in priorities and ambiguity in roles can facilitate perverse knowledge management outcomes.

Past research identifies inherent ambiguity and issue politicisation as impediments to effective post-merger integration (Vaara, 2002, p. 887).[1] Merger failure has been linked to lack of clearly defined roles, responsibilities, and incentives (Deloitte & Touche, 2002). "Increased ambiguity—due to unclear goals, roles, and procedures—allows greater opportunity for political behaviour to be employed in reaching objectives" (Parker, Dipboye, & Jackson, 1995). Political behaviour can be a problem if the power dynamics of KM processes are not realised for their constructive and destructive implications. What this means for KM processes is that multiple interpretations imply conflicting discourses which can be both constructive and destructive. People in the organisation may have a different idea of where the organisation should be headed, how it should get there, and who is responsible for getting it there. How each person at each organisational level is shaping the motivation, transfer, interpretation, and implementation of KM processes brings into question the desirable or undesirable dimensions of KM.

Returning to the case study's ambiguity of roles and strategy during their post-merger integration, KM processes are seemingly part of the problem, and instinctively part of the solution—in terms of simply increasing information flows. Cyclical misinterpretation of expectations and responsibilities among organisational levels demonstrates miscommunicated and misunderstood knowledge management processes. However, the desired perception of clarity does not necessarily mean a desirable set of KM processes exists. Where 'better KM' may be considered part of an eventual solution, we might actually ask: How are the KM processes occurring within an arena of organisational politics or power relationships?

Example 2: Water Management

Knowledge management power relationships also exist among organisations. The following illustrates how inter-organisational relationships relate to each other in the case of water regulation in England and Wales. Every five years a review of water prices occurs. The changes in water pricing for all consumers stem from EU and UK regulatory requirements ranging from water quality, to the cost of infrastructure improvement. Maloney (2001) describes the multi-stakeholders' interactions as processes of negotiation and sanctions. The regulatory review of water price limits in England and Wales illustrate a form of knowledge management as multi-stakeholders coping with ever-changing rules (regulations) and the blurred boundaries of organisations' roles (expectations and responsibilities as public, private, and civil society).

The purpose of the periodic review, according to the Office of Water Services (OFWAT), the independent economic regulator for water for all of England and Wales, is "…to make sure that the companies are able to carry out and finance their functions under the Water Industry Act 1991" (OFWAT, 1998). OFWAT also claims they aim to set price limits that allow each company to carry out their functions while protecting the interests of customers in two ways: (1) enabling well-managed companies to finance the delivery of services in line with relevant standards and requirements, and (2) providing incentives for companies to improve efficiency and service delivery. Notice how these two main objectives already imply the non-neutrality of the ensuing knowledge management processes. First, each organisation will interpret and implement "relevant standards and requirements" to the advantage of each organisation, perhaps even unintended conflicting interpretations. Second, "providing incentives for companies to improve efficiency" is a form of KM manipulation. The water companies must provide draft business plans early in the regulatory review process to the independent economic regulatory agency (OFWAT), along with more public sector organisations such as the Environment Agency and Department for Rural Affairs and Agriculture. The negotiations that take place between the regulators and the regulated—how the business plans fit with regulatory requirements, while simultaneously sustaining the companies—illustrates how a KM process can move in many directions. The way a draft business plan is presented can persuade how the regulators decide to advise on reshaping the business plan to adjust with newer EU regulations, for example.

Governance according to the Global Water Partnership includes power and different levels of authority, and regulation is housed under the broad roof of governance—governance that in itself lends to KM manipulation.

The Global Water Partnership argues:

Governance looks at the balance of power and the balance of actions at different levels of authority. It translates into different systems, laws, regulations, institutions, financial mechanisms, and civil society development and human rights, essentially the rules of the game. Usually improving governance means reform. (GWP, 2003)

To organise how we approach thinking and acting on these observations may be to identify the changes of multi-level (EU-UK) organisations and types (public-private-civil society), recognising power asymmetries and their interconnections. For example if the European Union's Water Framework Directive is raising the standards in London, by driving the 2004 regulatory review process toward more stringent policies, we may want to ask how London's customers and the water company Thames Water is adjusting to these new standards, and doing to affect the new standards?

FUTURE TRENDS

As KM becomes a more comfortable topic for researchers, and numerous governments and private sector organisations buy into the language and concepts of KM, a responsibility resides with the advocates of KM of the potential abuse of KM processes. The maturing of the eventual field of KM is on the horizon. KM is slowly moving away from defining it, debating its use, gathering, storing, sharing it, toward questions of what does it essentially mean for communication and productivity. KM for better or worse—as some would say "repackaging old ideas with glossy new ones"—is here to stay. How are we going to welcome this emerging discipline that seemingly unites information systems, organisations, and politics, to name a few? One of those ways may include obvious answers such as further empirical work and sharpening of definitions. Behind any method researchers and other applied practitioners of KM choose, they should note that control is not the solution and where attempted, frequently backfires.

CONCLUSION

This article proposes the significance of conceptualising KM as a political process, with notions from OP and CE. OP provides a familiar and documented contextual boundary where power-ridden processes of KM interact. CE further energises the explanation of power-ridden KM processes by giving vocabulary and meaning to changing patterns of interaction. The PMI and water management examples illustrate KM as a political process in the real world. In this specific case of PMI, information travels among hierarchical levels of an organisation, producing conflicting expectations that worsen the politics within that organisation. As for the water management case, local, national, and international levels of organisation interact with different types of organisations—public, private, and to some extent civil society. The inter-organisational dynamics lend to multi-layer knowledge management processes among them: infrastructure improvement needs based on changing water quantity/quality, what can be reasonably charged to customers, and the question of the regulations imposing desirable behaviour.

KM processes are manipulated for constructive and destructive purposes. A context of organisational politics and a paradigm of coevolution are not the only ways of highlighting an agenda for KM. OP and CE provide ways of highlighting and connecting what we already understand as relationships of power and knowledge. KM as a growing area of research and practice has and will open new ways of thinking, while revisiting old. Wielding KM's full capabilities also includes responsibly using and interpreting the hidden and obvious agendas.

ACKNOWLEDGMENT

We would like to acknowledge the LSE Complexity Group for providing the space in which the present collaboration could develop. The LSE Complexity Group's work has been enabled by the support of our academic advisors, business partners, and EPSRC (Engineering and Physical Science Research Council) awards, including a three-year collaborative action research project, Integrating Complex Social Systems (ICoSS) under the Systems Integration Initiative entitled *Enabling the Integration of Diverse Socio-Cultural and Technical Systems within a Turbulent Social Ecosystem* (GR/R37753). Details of the LSE Complexity Research Programme and the ICoSS Project can be found at http://www.lse.ac.uk/complexity.

REFERENCES

Becker, M.C. (2001). Managing dispersed knowledge: Organizational problems, managerial strategies, and their effectiveness. *Journal of Management Studies, 38*(7), 0022-2380.

Deloitte & Touche. (2001). *Solving the merger mystery, maximizing the payoffs of mergers and acquisitions.*

GWP (Global Water Partnership). (2003). *Effective water governance: Learning from the dialogues.*

Kakabadse, A., & Parker, C. (1984). *Power, politics, and organizations: A behavioural science view.* New York: John Wiley & Sons.

Land, F., Nolas, S.M., & Amjad, U. (2006). Theoretical and practical aspects of knowledge management. In D.G. Schwarz (Ed.), *Encyclopaedia of knowledge management* (pp.855-861). Hershey, PA: Idea Group Reference.

Lewin, A., Long, C., & Carroll, T. (1999). The coevolution of new organizational forms. *Organization Science, 10*(5), 535-550.

Lewin, A., & Volberda, H. (1999). Prolegomena on coevolution: A framework for research on strategy and new organizational forms. *Organization Science, 10*(5), 519-534.

Maloney, W.A. (2001). Regulation in an episodic policy-making environment: The water industry in England and Wales. *Public Administration, 79*(3), 625-642.

McKelvey, B. (2002). Managing coevolutionary dynamics. *Proceedings of the European Group for Organizational Studies* (EGOS 2002).

Mintzberg, H. (1983). *Power in and around organizations.* Englewood Cliffs, NJ: Prentice-Hall.

OFWAT (Office of Water Services). (2004). *Introduction to the Water Framework Directive.*

Parker, C.P., Dipboye, R.L., & Jackson, S.L. (1995). Perceptions of organizational politics: An investigation of antecedents and consequences. *Journal of Management, 21*(5), 891-912.

Pettigrew, A. (1973). *The politics of organizational decision-making.* Harper and Row, Barnes and Noble Import Division, USA.

Pfeffer, J. (1997). *New directions for organization theory: Problems and prospects.* Oxford: Oxford University Press.

Schultze, U. (1999). Investigating the contradictions in knowledge management. In T.J. Larsen, L. Levine, & J.I. De Gross (Eds.), *Information systems: Current issues and future changes* (pp. 155-174). Laxenberg, Austria: IFIP.

Tasaka, H. (1999). Twenty-first century management and the complexity paradigm. *Emergence, 1*(4), 115-123.

Vaara, E. (2002). On the discursive construction of success/failure in narratives of post-merger integration. *Organization Studies, 23*(2), 211-248.

KEY TERMS

Coevolution: Describes the mutual influences among actors in a collective, as well as their environment; mutual influences can be desirable and undesirable, constructive or destructive. In the case of an organisation, it can be envisaged as a set of multi-dimensional networks, themselves part of a larger set of networks to which they are linked. Nodes in the networks represent entities such as offices, factories, teams, and individuals. They are linked formally or informally to other nodes. Activities at any node send messages—and by implication, knowledge—to other nodes in the form of feedback, or feed-forward, thereby triggering activities in those nodes. The messages may use the formal or the informal links in the network. They may be sent intentionally, or accidentally.

Desirable/Undesirable Coevolution: A heuristic with which to talk about knowledge management as a process along a continuum.

Emergence: The process by which often unexpected outcomes result from the interaction of different activities and occurrences within an organisation.

Goal Setting: Defining goals, be they benign or corrupt; political processes are invoked. The goals themselves can be constructive or destructive, formally or informally arrived at, at the level of the organisation or the individual, public or private.

Knowledge Manipulation: The abuse of knowledge management; when information is hidden, distorted, withheld for a particular purpose.

Power: The capability and possibility to influence and/or direct the course of some action.

Organisational Politics: Wide range of descriptions of formal and informal power relationships in organisations.

ENDNOTE

[1] Vaara (2003) identified four in total. The issues not mentioned here are cultural confusion and organizational hypocrisy, because they are not central to this article's purpose.

Knowledge Management Software

Rodrigo Baroni de Carvalho
FUMEC University, Brazil

Marta Araújo Tavares Ferreira
Federal University of Minas Gerais (UFMG), Brazil

INTRODUCTION

Due to the vagueness of the concept of knowledge, the software market for knowledge management (KM) seems to be quite confusing. Technology vendors are developing different implementations of the KM concepts in their software products. Because of the variety and quantity of KM tools available on the market, a typology may be a valuable aid to organizations that are searching and evaluating KM software suitable to their needs.

The objective of this article is to present a typology that links software features to knowledge processes described in the SECI (socialization, externalization, combination, internalization) model developed by Nonaka and Takeuchi (1995). KM solutions such as intranet systems, content-management systems (CMSs), groupware, work flow, artificial intelligence- (AI) based systems, business intelligence (BI), knowledge-map systems, innovation support, competitive intelligence (CI) tools, and knowledge portals are discussed in terms of their potential contributions to the processes of socialization, externalization, internalization, and combination.

BACKGROUND

KM intends to be an area of research and practice that deepens the understanding of knowledge processes in organizations and develops procedures and instruments to support the transformation of knowledge into economic and social progress. In fact, different aspects of these issues have been studied for decades in many different disciplines as R&D (research and development) and innovation management, information systems management, information science, computer science, library studies, innovation economics, science and technology social studies, epistemology, and many others. Maybe one of the most important contributions of the KM concept is the creation of a space (in academy and in the business world) where these many groups and points of view may discuss and work together.

KM studies analyze people, organizations, processes, and technology. Although technology is not the main component of KM, it would be naive to implement KM without considering any technological support. According to Stewart (1998), the intellectual capital of an organization has three dimensions: human capital, structural capital, and client capital. Structural capital is defined as the organizational systems and structures that store and transfer knowledge, and it includes the quality and extent of information systems, databases, patents, written procedures, and business documents. From this perspective, KM software should be considered as an important component of the structural capital of organizations.

This article assumes that IT has a supporting role, not the main role, in a KM program. According to Terra (2000), KM has seven dimensions: strategy, culture and organizational values, organizational structure, human resource skills, IT, measuring, and environmental learning. Therefore, IT is only one of the dimensions of KM, and technology alone does not transform information into knowledge. The KM ultimate challenge is to increase the chances of innovation through knowledge creation. The role of IT in this context is to extend the human capacity of knowledge creation through the speed, memory extension, and communication facilities of technology.

Nonaka and Takeuchi (1995) have analyzed the knowledge-creation process of Japanese organizations and developed a framework (SECI model). This model relates the knowledge creation of firms to four knowledge conversion processes.

- **Socialization (S):** the process of sharing tacit knowledge through shared experiences. As apprentices learn the craft of their masses through observation, imitation, and practice, so do employees of a firm learn new skills through on-the-job training.
- **Externalization (E):** where tacit knowledge is articulated into explicit knowledge with the help of metaphors and analogies. Externalization is triggered by dialog and collective reflection.
- **Combination (C):** the process of converting explicit knowledge into more systematic sets of explicit knowledge.

- **Internalization (I):** where explicit knowledge is converted into tacit knowledge. This usually occurs when explicit knowledge is put into practice. It is also related to shared mental models and work practices.

These interactions build a continuous spiral from the individual to organizational level. Ponzi (2004) used bibliometric techniques to analyze 2,240 source records obtained from scientific citation indexes. His research revealed that Nonaka and Takeuchi (1995) is the top most cited reference in the KM area and the most influential work. Due to this popularity, we have decided to use the SECI model to help individuals who already know this framework but need a better understanding of the KM software market.

There are some related works concerning KM software categorization: Barnes (2001), Bellaver and Lusa (2002), Davenport and Prusak (1998), Fernandez, Gonzalez, and Sabherwal (2004), Maier (2004), Malhotra (2000), Rollet (2003), Ruggles (1997), and Tiwana (2002). None of these academic works establish a direct relationship between the KM systems and the SECI model. The authors usually prefer to use their own KM framework to analyze the link between knowledge processes and KM systems. There is also another type of proposal for categorization, that is, Microsoft (2000), which has been developed by vendors and is very IT based. It is not the objective of this article to discuss the differences and the similarities among these proposals, but they have been considered in the development of the typology presented here.

MAIN FOCUS OF THE ARTICLE

The main objective of this article is to present a typology of KM solutions present on the market that comprehends 10 categories, each of which emphasizes specific KM aspects. It also intends to identify which of the knowledge-conversion processes (Nonaka & Takeuchi, 1995) is supported by each software category. This article concludes by presenting some trends in KM software development and suggesting some guidelines for the launching of KM programs supported by IT.

To accomplish our objective, it was necessary to explore the software market in order to classify KM tools. The major difficulty in accomplishing this task was the establishment of limits on a growing market. A sample of KM software was constructed through information collected on KM-related sites selected in Nascimento and Neves (1999), on advertisements in KM magazines (*KM World*, *KM Magazine*, and *DM Review*), and in digital libraries (http://brint.com). The exploratory research resulted in a list of 26 software vendors that were contacted, from which 21 sent folders, technical briefings, and demo versions of their software. The analysis of each KM system basically consisted of an installation and feature checkup. It was tested if the features advertised by the vendor were really supported by the KM system. After the analysis of these tools, it was possible to identify some common features among them, which originated the typology's first version. This version (Carvalho, 2000) was composed of eight categories.

After this period, Collins (2003), Detlor (2004), Firestone (2003), Kim, Chaudhury, and Rao (2002), and Raol, Koong, Liu, and Yu (2002) published research related to the evaluation of KM software and the emergence of knowledge portals. Due to the development of the KM software market and influenced by the previously mentioned works, this typology was reviewed and updated in 2004. As a result, two new categories have been incorporated: competitive intelligence tools and knowledge portals. The KM systems are then discussed in terms of their contributions to the four knowledge conversion modes developed by Nonaka and Takeuchi (1995).

As a result of this research, 10 KM software categories are presented as follows:

- Intranet-based systems
- Content management systems
- Groupware
- Work flow
- Artificial intelligence-based systems
- Business intelligence
- Knowledge map systems
- Innovation support tools
- Competitive intelligence tools
- Knowledge portals

Intranet-Based Systems

An intranet is an appropriate tool to systematize and add the explicit knowledge that is dispersed through departments. Intranets are organizational assets and an important part of the structural dimension of intellectual capital, as described by Stewart (1998). The communication in intranets is usually passive because the user has to pull the information. Nevertheless, the efficient usage of intranets is closely related to a wider comprehension of information management contribution to organizational performance. An intranet, like other systems described in this article, should be understood as a part of the organizational information context, and its usefulness is influenced by culture, values, and principles concerning strategic information management.

This explains why, despite the wide and varied set of features made possible by intranets, they have been used in most organizations primarily for basic information access, that is, the retrieval of corporate documents (Choo, Detlor, & Turnbull, 2000).

According to Choo et al. (2000), intranets are quite helpful in promoting the externalization, combination, and internalization processes. The combination process is supported by unified access to multiple content sources, and internalization occurs when there is a dissemination of success stories and best practices on the intranet. Part of the intranet content is generated by employees who have decided to document their experiences and externalize their knowledge. Web server software, such as Apache HTTP (hypertext transfer protocol) Server, offers the basic features for intranet deployment.

Content Management Systems

CMSs manage repositories of important corporate documents and contribute to the organization of the vast amount of documents generated by office activities. Paperwork is still a reality, and each document is a source of nonstructured information that could be lost if not well organized. According to Rollet (2003), existing paper documents are brought into the CMS through scanning, and optical character recognition (OCR) software analyzes the resulting image files and translates them into computer-readable text. Bennet (1997) states that CMSs provide more efficient retrieval, and better security and version control of documents. File Net and Excalibur Retrieval Ware are examples of CMSs. These systems have many features-cataloging, metadata, searching, versioning, and indexing-that were inherited from the traditional information retrieval (IR) systems, which are studied in the field of library science.

CMSs deal only with the explicit dimension of knowledge, supporting then the combination process. The focus of CMS is primarily on providing access to existing documents in any available media: fax, e-mails, HTML (hypertext markup language) forms, computer reports, paper, video, audio, or spreadsheets.

Groupware

Organizations are searching for flexible structures that can easily adapt to a changing environment. The need of cooperation between geographically dispersed work groups is a critical issue to global organizations. Groupware systems have a push style where information is sent to the user. Groupware is a blend of synchronous (like chat), asynchronous (like e-mail), and community-focused tools (like e-groups). Informal communication predominates in a groupware environment. Groupware

systems are well suited to support communities of practice, where specialists of a given domain of knowledge, who may be dispersed all over the world, exchange their expertise in order to find solutions to specific problems.

According to Nonaka and Takeuchi (1995), the externalization of tacit knowledge is induced by dialog and collective reflection. Groupware helps this process by permitting collaboration and the exchange of nonstructured messages. Discussion groups and chats are common groupware features that make possible the gradual articulation of tacit knowledge. The development of technologies, such as videoconferencing and instant messaging, has contributed to a better quality of interaction among groupware users. These enriched virtual environments provide a suitable context for the socialization and internalization processes. Choo et al. (2000) present online apprenticeship as an example of socialization supported by groupware. The Microsoft groupware suite (MS Exchange, MS Outlook, MS Messenger) and the Lotus family (Notes, Sametime, Lotus Workplace) are examples of groupware packages.

Work Flow

Work flow systems support standardized business processes. These systems regulate the information flow from person to person, place to place, and task to task in processes that require ordered and structured information. The objective of work flow systems is to establish and accelerate the process flow, following its steps and tracking each activity that composes the process. They make explicit the knowledge that is embedded in standard processes, mainly supporting the formal codification of existing knowledge (externalization).

Cruz (1998) defines the three basic elements of work flow, also called the three *R*s model.

- **Roles:** set of skills to execute a specific task
- **Rules:** features that define how the data should be processed
- **Routes:** logical paths for the knowledge flow through the process

Work flow systems, like ARIS Toolset, present features that support the graphical representation of existing processes. These systems are also used for business process reengineering (BPR) because they make explicit who does what in what order, and what products or services are produced. Another interesting feature of work flow systems is simulation, which permits the dynamic analysis of business processes. The simulation supplies information about the execution of processes, process weak points, and resource bottlenecks. Work flow systems are usually integrated with groupware and CMSs in order to provide an organized document flow across knowledge workers, supporting then the execution of a business process.

Artificial Intelligence-Based Systems

AI is the computer-science field that has produced the first studies relating information to knowledge. Expert systems, CBR (case-based reasoning) systems, and neural networks are some types of systems that use AI techniques. An expert system is built on the observation of a specialist at work and on the mapping of part of his or her knowledge into derivation rules.

As Davenport and Prusak (1998) explain, CBR systems support learning from a set of narratives or cases related to a problem. When a user has a problem, he or she can check in the case database in order to find if it is related to a problem that has already been solved. CBR systems use pattern matching algorithms to retrieve cases that are more similar to the problem stated before. The user can interact with the system by analyzing the solutions of existing cases and refining the search. CBR systems have been successfully used in help desk and call-center applications. They help contributors to externalize what has been learned from experience through the narrative of cases.

On the other hand, frequent users of the CBR system can internalize the knowledge that is represented into the system. This knowledge can also be restructured and represented in another manner. According to Rollet (2003), fundamental prerequisites for AI methods are suitable ways of representing knowledge, and automated reasoning typically uses highly formalized knowledge bases consisting of explicit rules, using, for instance, predicate logic. AI is also important for the development of software components, like intelligent agents, that can be used in a wide range of information systems, helping search and retrieval features.

Neural networks, like CA-Neugents, are more sophisticated systems that use statistical instruments to process cause-effect examples and to learn the relationships involved in the solution of problems. Neural networks are very flexible and intelligent systems because each new input results in an automatic reprogramming and consequent addition of new relationships.

Business Intelligence

Business intelligence is a set of tools used to manipulate a mass of operational data and to extract essential business information from them. BI systems comprehend the following:

- **Front-end systems:** They consist of a comprehensive set of data analysis tools like OLAP (online analytical processing), data mining, query, and reporting.
- **Back-end systems:** DBMSs (database management systems), data warehouses, and data marts.

DBMSs are the basis of a BI solution. First, the operational data generated by business transactions are extracted from the DBMS, filtered by some criteria, and then moved to the data warehouse. After this BI back-end loading step, the front-end tools are able to identify hidden patterns inside the data, and the user is free to build his or her own queries and strategic reports. BI systems, like Business Objects and Oracle 10g BI, provide end users with self-service access to information stored in data marts, data warehouses, and online transaction processing (OLTP) systems. As Choo (1998) explains, organizations are using analysis tools to reveal patterns that would otherwise remain buried in their huge operational databases; software for OLAP, a front-end BI tool, allow users to create multidimensional views of large amounts of data as they "slice and dice" the data in various ways to discover patterns and trends.

The focus of BI is decision making. BI systems excel in the job of sorting, categorizing, and structuring information, and facilitating the reconfiguration of existing information (combination) as well as creating new information.

Knowledge Map Systems

Also known as expertise locators, knowledge maps work like yellow pages that contain a "who-knows-what" list. A knowledge map does not store knowledge. The map just points to people who own it, creating opportunities for knowledge exchange.

A standard knowledge map is fed with profiles of competencies of the members of an organization. The knowledge map provides an expert locator feature that helps users to find the expert's best suited to work on a specific problem or project. A knowledge map categorizes an organization's expertise into searchable catalogs. By using a knowledge map, it is easier to identify people in terms of whom they know, what they know, and how proficient they are at a given task.

Human resource specialists use knowledge maps to match existing competencies with strategic targets and to identify what kinds of know-how, essential for growth, are currently available. According to Terra (2000), knowledge maps facilitate tacit knowledge exchange because they provide faster expert search and increase the chance of personal meetings. This approximation can probably result in face-to-face contacts that promote shared experiences and learning by observation, imitation, and praxis (socialization).

Innovation Support Tools

Amidon (2000) defines innovation as the application of new ideas to products or services. The result of innovation can be observed by the number of new patents, the design modifications of existing products, and the development of new products. Innovation support tools are systems that contribute to knowledge generation along the product design process. These tools intend to create a virtual environment that stimulates the multiplication of insights and are especially used in industrial R & D. An innovation support tool may include different features.

- A technical database where patents, articles, and research projects are recorded
- Graphic simulation features, which can facilitate internalization
- Combinatory tools, which help to consider unusual possibilities in the design of innovations

Innovation support tools, like Goldfire Innovator from Invention Machines, are generally based on a scientific content or patent database that allows users to conceive new products, correct product defects, design feature modifications to existing products, identify technology trends and future product road maps, or improve production processes. The combination process is also supported because an engineer can combine existing explicit knowledge to generate new patents or product specifications.

Competitive Intelligence Tools

FULD & Company Inc. (2000) describes the CI cycle in five steps.

- **Planning and direction:** the identification of questions that will drive the information gathering phase
- Published information collection
- **Primary source collection:** information gathering from people rather than from published sources
- **Analysis and production:** the transformation of the collected data into meaningful assessment
- **Report and inform:** the delivery of critical intelligence in a coherent manner to corporate decision makers

FULD and Company Inc. (2000) has evaluated the CI software offered on the market and has concluded that

they offer better support to the second and fifth steps of the CI cycle. The other steps are very human based and are only slightly benefited by technology. In the second step, software agents perform the automatic collection of timely information from news feeds and search the Internet and corporate intranets. In the fifth step, CI tools accelerate the dissemination of reports by sending e-mail reports according to users' preferences. CI tools concentrate on the combination process of the knowledge conversion spiral. They act like a probe on information sources: The information that is obtained is filtered and classified before dissemination so it is disseminated in an adequate format to facilitate combination. On the other hand, CI tools contribute to sense making, which is related to the internalization process. According to Choo (1998), organizations first have to make sense of what is happening in their environments in order to develop a shared interpretation that can serve as a guide to action.

Knowledge Portals

In an attempt to consolidate various departmental intranets, organizations are constructing corporate intranets or portals (Choo et al., 2000). A great contribution of portals is the integration of heterogeneous information sources, providing a standard interface to the users. According to the authors, a portal's primary function is to provide a transparent directory of information already available elsewhere, not to act as a separate source of information itself. Common elements contained in corporate portal design include an enterprise taxonomy or classification of information categories that helps to ease retrieval, a search engine, and links to internal and external Web sites and information sources.

The personalization feature of portals enables end users to organize their work by community, interest, task, or job focus. Besides providing personal access to knowledge, portals help users in the job of building community places. Online awareness and real-chat capabilities are available throughout the portal. Therefore, the user can see who is online, connect with them instantly, and get immediate answers.

But portals are evolving into more complex and interactive gateways so that they may integrate in a single solution many KM tools' features presented before. They are becoming single points of entry through which end users and communities can perform their business tasks, and evolving into virtual places where people can get in touch with other people who share common interests. Knowledge portals are the next generation of EIPs (enterprise information portals). Knowledge portals support all knowledge processes described

Table 1. Categories of knowledge management software: Summary table

Category	Dominating Knowledge Conversion Processes	Origin of Concepts	Examples
Intranet-Based Systems	Externalization, Combination, Internalization	Computer Networks (Web Technology)	Apache HTTP Server
Content Management Systems	Combination	Information Science	Excalibur Retrieval Ware and File Net
Groupware	Socialization, Externalization, Internalization	CSCW (Computer-Supported Cooperative Work)	Lotus Family (Notes, Sametime) and MS Suite (Exchange, Outlook, Messenger)
Work Flow	Externalization	Organization and Methods	ARIS Toolset (IDS Scheer)
Artificial Intelligence-Based Systems	Externalization, Combination, Internalization	Artificial Intelligence	Neugents (Computer Associates)
Business Intelligence	Combination	Database Management	Business Objects and Oracle 10g BI
Knowledge Maps	Socialization	Information Science and Human Resource Management	Gingo (Trivium) and Lotus Discovery Server
Innovation Support Tools	Combination, Internalization	Innovation and Technology Management	Goldfire Innovator (Invention Machines)
Competitive Intelligence Tools	Combination	Strategic Management and Information Science	Knowledge Works (Cipher Systems) and Vigipro (CRIQ/CGI)
Knowledge Portals	Socialization, Externalization, Combination, Internalization	Computer Networks and Information Science	Hummingbird and Plumtree

in the SECI model because portals are in fact the amalgamation of many KM systems presented before.

Table 1 presents the 10 classes of KM software discussed in this article, their main contribution to knowledge conversion processes, the disciplinary origin of their main concepts, and some examples. The examples are merely illustrative and do not represent a recommendation or preference for any technology vendor.

It is interesting to notice how KM software covers a large spectrum of features, information resources, and users. For instance, CMSs are made to retrieve documents while knowledge map systems exist to find people. Like CMSs, BI supports the combination process. However, CMSs deal basically with documents that are usually nonstructured and appear in a great variety of formats, while the basic BI structure is a database record with specific attributes and a standardized format. Finally, the users of innovation support tools are usually technicians, engineers, or scientists who are involved in some creative design process inside an R & D department, while managers are BI's typical users.

FUTURE TRENDS

There seems to be a trend of functional convergence in KM systems. Preserving initial features, vendors are incorporating extra features from others categories described in the typology presented in this article, transforming their products into KM-integrated suites. For instance, a BI system may start to offer a knowledge map feature in a new version. So, it seems that increasingly, KM software will be classified in more than one of the presented categories, which can be alternatively considered as an array of features for KM systems.

The portal technology is the materialization of this convergence trend. Scientific research about portal features and types of KM systems seems to merge, following the movement of the KM software market. Collins (2003) and Detlor (2004) are examples of this recent approach. According to Collins, the knowledge portal's basic features are BI, collaboration, and content management. As a result, a basic portal will require the integration of at least four KM systems presented in this article: the intranet, CMS, groupware, and BI.

Integration can be a cumbersome task and may not be seen as a short-term project, especially in the case where there are heterogeneous systems scattered all over the organization. Firestone (2003) emphasizes the role of XML (extensible markup language) in portal architecture and presents relations between portal-integration efforts and the current research concerning EAI (enterprise application integration). The better choice is to consider a knowledge portal as a gradual project, allowing organizations to expand later the capabilities and functionalities delivered through the portal.

CONCLUSION

The wise selection of KM software requires a previous analysis of an organization's knowledge needs. Among the considerations to be addressed in some organizations is the fact, for instance, that a low level of socialization may be the critical point; in other ones, externalization may need to be improved.

As to the adoption process, it is interesting to notice the differences between KM software and ERP (enterprise resource planning) systems. ERPs are usually implemented in a top-down style, and the organization generally has to adjust its processes to the system in a short period of time. It is impossible to do the same with a KM system. The commitment and motivation of members are crucial to any KM program, much more than better KM software. KM requires a long term strategy to involve people and break paradigms. Also, policies referring to participation, flexibility, autonomy, and career evolution must surely be adapted.

KM software can be considered an interdisciplinary business because their development requires not only technical skills, but also a deep understanding of social and managerial aspects. In this sense, Choo et al. (2000) suggest that intranet designers look for the lessons learned from the field of CSCW. Recommendations include the need to ensure that everyone benefits from groupware, the need to understand the current work practice, and the involvement of users in design.

As a result of the research presented in this article, we conclude that KM software is evolving in order to offer an integrated platform for organizational knowledge conversion processes. But this does not mean that the resources of KM software are already well exploited by the organizations that have adopted them. As reported in literature and as we have ourselves learned from the study of two Brazilian organization systems (Carvalho, 2000), their potential is most frequently underevaluated and unexplored. In fact, their actual utilization stresses mainly their support of information access and retrieval, while their communication and collaboration dimensions are yet to be discovered.

The implementation of KM systems is a complex process. The KM software needs not only to be integrated to the existing IT infrastructure, but to the organizational culture, procedures, and human resource policy as well. The correct balance between managerial and technical aspects constitutes one of KM-tool adoption's greatest challenges. According to Detlor (2004), culture and user behaviors are the key drivers and inhibitors of internal sharing, and organizations should develop ways of stimulating people to use and contribute to KM systems.

Many organizations that are implementing KM programs focus exclusively on the conversion of human capital into structural capital. They think of KM as an opportunity to extract part of the knowledge of their employees and store it in knowledge bases. This approach misunderstands the dynamic and complex characteristics of knowledge, its tacit-prevailing nature, and the fact that, more than existing knowledge, the incessant creation of knowledge is the distinctive feature.

The KM concept has recently been severely criticized (Berkman, 2001), and one of the reasons for this may be the excessive emphasis on software and methodologies per se. This argument emphasizes the importance of considering technology in its context, that is, of relating it to the complexity of knowledge processes in order not to over (or under) estimate technology, or to miss the opportunity of bringing knowledge to where it belongs: the center of organizational attention.

REFERENCES

Amidon, D. (2000). *Knowledge innovation.* Retrieved from *http://www.entovation.com*

Barnes, S. (2001). *Knowledge management systems: Theory and practice.* London: Thomson Learning Europe.

Bellaver, R., & Lusa, J. (2002). *Knowledge management strategy and technology.* Norwood, MA: Artech House.

Bennet, G. (1997). *Intranets: Como implantar com sucesso na sua empresa.* Rio de Janeiro, Brazil: Campus.

Berkman, E. (2001). When bad things happen to good ideas. *Darwin Magazine.* Retrieved from *http://www.darwinmag.com*

Carvalho, R. B. (2000). *Aplicações de softwares de gestão do conhecimento: Tipologia e usos.* MSc dissertation, Programa de Pós-Graduação em Ciência da Informação da UFMG, Belo Horizonte, Brazil.

Choo, C. W. (1998). *The knowing organization.* Oxford, UK: Oxford University Press.

Choo, C. W., Detlor, B., & Turnbull, D. (2000). *Web work: Information seeking and knowledge work on the World Wide Web.* Dordrecht, Germany: Kluwer Academic Publishers.

Collins, H. (2003). *Enterprise knowledge portals.* New York: Amacon.

Cruz, T. (1998). *Workflow: A tecnologia que vai revolucionar processos.* São Paulo, Brazil: Atlas.

Davenport, T., & Prusak, L. (1998). *Working knowledge: How organizations manage what they know.* Boston: HBS Press.

Detlor, B. (2004). *Towards knowledge portals.* Boston: Kluwer Academic Publishers.

Fernandez, I., Gonzalez, A., & Sabherwal, R. (2004). *Knowledge management and KM software package.* Harlow, UK: Pearson.

Firestone, J. (2003). *Enterprise information portals and knowledge management.* Burlington, UK: Butterworth-Heinemann.

FULD & Company Inc. (2000). *Intelligence software report.* Retrieved from *http://www.fuld.com*

Kim, Y., Chaudhury, A., & Rao, H. (2002). A knowledge management perspective to evaluation of enterprise information portals. In *knowledge and process management* (Version 9, pp. 57-71). Indianapolis, IN: John Wiley & Sons.

Maier, R. (2004). *Knowledge management systems: Information and communication technologies for knowledge management.* Heidelberg, Germany: Springer-Verlag.

Malhotra, Y. (2000). *Knowledge management and virtual organizations.* Hershey, PA: IGP.

Microsoft. (2000). Knowledge management: Produtividade organizacional. *ComputerWorld, 319,* 11-12.

Nascimento, N., & Neves, J. T. R. (1999). A gestão do donhecimento na World Wide Web: Reflexões sobre a pesquisa de informações na rede. *Perspectivas em Ciência da Informação, 4,* 29-48.

Nonaka, I., & Takeuchi, H. (1995). *The knowledge creating company.* New York: Oxford Press.

Ponzi, L. (2004). Knowledge management: Birth of a discipline. In *Knowledge management lessons learned.* Medford, NJ: Information Today.

Raol, J., Koong, K., Liu, L., & Yu, C. (2002). An identification and classification of enterprise portal functions and features. *Industrial Management Data Systems, 102.* Retrieved from *http://www.emerald insight.com/0263-55777.htm*

Rollet, H. (2003). *Knowledge management: Processes and technologies.* Boston: Kluwer Academic Publishers.

Ruggles, R. (1997). *Knowledge management tools.* Burlington, UK: Butterworth-Heinemann.

Stewart, T. (1998). *Capital intelectual.* Rio de Janeiro, Brazil: Campus.

Terra, J. C. C. (2000). *Gestão do conhecimento: O grande desafio empresarial.* São Paulo, Brazil: Negócio Editora.

Tiwana, A. (2002). *The knowledge management toolkit: Practical techniques for building a knowledge management system.* New York: Prentice Hall.

KEY TERMS

Competitive Intelligence: Set of interrelated measures that aim at systematically feeding the organizational decision process with information about the organizational environment in order to make it possible for people to learn about it, to anticipate its evolution, and to make better decisions in consequence.

CSCW (Computer-Supported Cooperative Work): Branch of computer science dedicated to the study of groupware technologies.

Enterprise Information Portal (EIP): Single Web interface to corporate information.

Expert System: A special type of artificial intelligence system that contains a limited domain knowledge base, an inference mechanism to manipulate this base, and an interface to permit the input of new data and user dialog.

Groupware: Type of software that is designed to help teams that are geographically dispersed who need to work together.

Intelligent Agent: Software component capable of acting autonomously by perceiving the environment, evaluating choices, and deciding on actions without checking the user.

Knowledge Portal: A personalized interface to online resources for knowledge workers to integrate applications and data. It is an evolution of EIP.

Neural Networks: A system composed of a large number of software nodes connected by weighted links. The system learns by adjusting those weights through repetitive learning cycles.

OLAP (Online Analytical Processing): Front-end tool that allows the analysis of multidimensional data. It is commonly used in business intelligence systems.

Knowledge Management Strategy Formation

K

Clyde W. Holsapple
University of Kentucky, USA

Kiku Jones
University of Tulsa, USA

INTRODUCTION

Knowledge-based organizations (Holsapple & Whinston, 1987; Paradice & Courtney, 1989; Bennet & Bennet, 2003) are intentionally concerned with making the best use of their knowledge resources and knowledge-processing skills in the interest of enhancing their productivity, agility, reputation, and innovation (Holsapple & Singh, 2001). A key question that confronts every knowledge-based organization is concerned with how to approach the task of forming a KM strategy. Beyond aligning KM strategy with an organization's vision and overall strategy for achieving its mission, how does the creator of a KM strategy proceed? How is the created (or adopted) KM strategy communicated and evaluated? What can be done to avoid blind spots, gaps, and flaws in the strategy?

One way to begin to answer such questions is to study successful cases of organizational knowledge management (e.g., see Smith & McKeen, 2003; O'Dell et al., 2003; van der Spek, Hofer-Alfeis, & Kingma, 2003; Bennet & Porter, 2003; Oriel, 2003; Wolford & Kwiecien, 2003; Kelly & Bauer, 2003; DeTore & Balliet-Milholland, 2003). Such cases can give specific KM strategies to consider emulating or adapting. They can lead to an understanding of various issues to consider in the act of forming a KM strategy. Other cases can even identify dysfunctional elements to avoid during KM strategy formation and use (Malhotra, 2003).

A complementary approach to answering such questions is to employ a general-purpose model as a guide for KM strategy formation. This can be used regardless of the nature of the organization or its particular circumstances. It guides the strategy formation process in the sense of providing a structure for identifying the KM activities that a strategy can or should address in its efforts to maximize performance. A KM director uses the model to assess where the organization presently stands with respect to each of the identified activities, to consider new initiatives for each of the activities (customized to the organization's particular circumstances), and to furnish dimensions for evaluating competitive standing.

Here, we examine the Knowledge Chain Model for guiding KM strategy formation. It is important to understand that this is *not* a process model that specifies some sequence of steps to be followed in devising KM strategies. Rather, it is a model that identifies key factors that need to be considered in the development of KM strategies. These factors are "key" in the sense that they are potential sources of greater competitiveness. They are areas of activity that, if performed better than competitors, will yield superior organizational performance through better productivity, agility, innovation, and/or reputation. Creators of KM strategies need to pay close attention to the techniques and technologies selected and deployed in each of the key activity areas in both their own organizations and in other (e.g., competing) organizations.

BACKGROUND

The notion of a strategy has varied meanings (Mintzberg & Quinn, 1996). Here, we regard strategy as being a systematic plan of action for deliberately using an organization's resources in ways that fulfill its purpose (e.g., mission, duty, vision). A knowledge management strategy, then, is a plan for marshaling and applying knowledge-oriented resources in the interest of supporting the organization's purpose. These knowledge-oriented resources include the organization's *knowledge processing capabilities* and its *knowledge assets* (Holsapple & Joshi, 2004). The classes of knowledge assets include knowledge held by an organization's participants, various artifacts belonging to the organization (e.g., documents, manuals, videos), the organization's culture, and its particular infrastructure of roles, relationships, and regulations. The knowledge processing capabilities include the skills of both individual participants (both human and computer-based processors) and collective participants (e.g., groups, teams, communities) in the organization.

Knowledge Processing Capabilities

An organization's knowledge processing capabilities can be categorized into those that are technologically based and those that are practice based. Capabilities can depend on a combination of these two. In any case, knowledge processing capabilities manifest in the actual activities that an organization performs as it operates on its knowledge assets. KM strategy determines what technologies and practices will be adopted in any given instance of a KM activity.

Information technology (IT) is being subsumed by *knowledge technology*. IT systems for automated transaction handling, record storage, and reporting remain important. However, the emphasis going forward is on technological systems that support knowledge amplification within and across organizations. This knowledge technology involves the use of computer and communication technologies to automatically acquire, derive, or discover knowledge needed by decision makers and researchers on a just-in-time basis. Knowledge technology fosters knowledge sharing and unleashes the creative potential inherent in knowledge-worker collaboration. It includes technology that measures and coordinates the activities of knowledge workers. Knowledge technology provides a basis for organizational memory and learning. It also involves technology to personalize timing and presentation of knowledge delivery according to knowledge-worker profiles.

Human cognitive and communicative acts are the other part of the KM equation. This part comprises *knowledge practices* and their alignment with an organization's vision and plans. These practices are based on knowledge ontologies, methods, techniques, metrics, incentives, and processes. They are concerned with issues of organizational infrastructure (roles, relationships, regulations), culture, ethics, training, skills, and core competencies.

Knowledge Assets

One way for an organization to begin developing a KM strategy is to ascertain the competitiveness of its present knowledge position. Zack (1999) suggests that competitive knowledge position can be categorized in terms of the degree of innovation relative to its competitors within an industry:

- **Core Knowledge:** The basic body of knowledge required of all players in an industry in order to remain competitive.
- **Advanced Knowledge:** Knowledge that distinguishes an organization from other players in its industry in a degree sufficient for achieving a competitive edge.
- **Innovative Knowledge:** Knowledge held/applied by an organization that is so distinctive that it is the basis for being a market leader in the industry.

By evaluating its knowledge assets relative to these three categories, an organization's competitive knowledge position becomes evident. Zack goes on to advocate using a strength-weakness-opportunity-threat (SWOT) analysis to recognize deficiencies in an organization's knowledge position, as well as knowledge strengths that can be leveraged. Of course, organizations will differ in both their knowledge positions and in the strategies that they devise for working from these positions within their environments.

Zack (1999) advises that to find its own unique connection between strategy and knowledge assets, an organization should be alert for the need to increase knowledge assets in a particular area (e.g., ensuring sufficient core knowledge, fending off threats), opportunities to more fully exploit existing knowledge assets, the potential to generate new knowledge internally (especially advanced or innovative knowledge), and the potential of acquiring knowledge from external sources.

Developing KM Strategy

An organization should recognize that its KM strategy can be connected not only to its knowledge assets, but also to its knowledge processing capabilities (see Figure 1). Thus, in addition to guiding KM strategy formation through an analysis of an organization's actual and potential knowledge assets, there needs to be an analysis of possible practices and technologies that may be adopted for operating on those assets. This analysis of knowledge processing capabilities may follow the format used for knowledge assets. The capabilities can be classified into core, advanced, and innovative categories to understand the organization's knowledge processing capabilities relative to those of competitors. Further, via a SWOT approach, an organization needs to ascertain whether to increase knowledge processing capabilities in a particular area such as assimilating knowledge, whether opportunities to more fully exploit existing knowledge processing capabilities exist, whether new practices/technologies can be developed in-house, or whether the practices/technologies can be implemented via outsourcing, alliances, and/or purchase.

What is missing from this consideration of KM strategy development is an appreciation of the fundamental kinds of KM activities that are candidates for strategic focus. More broadly, fundamental kinds of

Figure 1. Aspects of knowledge management strategy

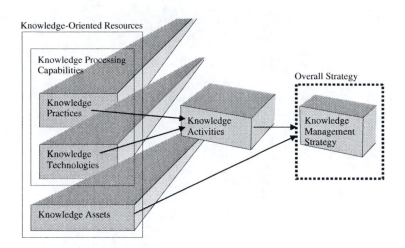

business activities for strategic focus are known. In management theory, the Value Chain Model identifies the basic kinds of business activities that can be focal points for competitiveness (Porter, 1985). The value chain is composed of distinct activities (called "value activities") that an organization performs in the course of doing business. These value activities fall into nine generic categories: five primary and four secondary, and translate an organization's broad competitive strategy into specific action steps required to achieve competitiveness.

By formulating a strategy to perform one or more of the value activities better than competitors, the organization can attain a competitive advantage. Analogously, it would be helpful for KM strategists to have a model that identifies basic kinds of KM activities that can be focal points for competitiveness. By formulating a plan involving practices and/or technologies to perform one or more of these KM activities better than competitors, the organization can attain a competitive advantage. The Knowledge Chain Model identifies these activities, thereby offering guidance to those who formulate KM strategy.

THE KNOWLEDGE CHAIN MODEL

Although it is analogous to the Value Chain Model, the Knowledge Chain Model (KCM) is *not* derived from the Value Chain Model (Holsapple & Singh, 2000, 2001). Rather, it is derived from a collaboratively engineered ontology of knowledge management. Moreover, the KCM is supported by empirical studies that show a connection between each of its KM activities and organizational competitiveness. It is important to understand that (like

Porter's Value Chain Model), the KCM is *not* a process model. Rather, it identifies activities of particular interest to persons formulating strategy. Instances of the activities occur simultaneously, serially, in parallel, and in loops combining to form various patterns in the course of organizational operations.

Several researchers have proposed models derived from the Value Chain Model to help understand various aspects of IT (e.g., Rockart & Short, 1991). One of these, called the Information/Knowledge Value Chain, adapts the value chain to propose a linear process model that describes stages in an organization's processing of information and knowledge (King & Ko, 2001). The authors use this model as a basis for developing a framework that can be used to evaluate KM efforts in terms of cognitive, post-cognitive, behavioral, learning, and organizational impact assessments (King & Ko, 2001). They briefly suggest another use of the model: namely, that planners sequentially consider each stage in the Information/Knowledge Value Chain to design strategic systems. This consideration can involve brainstorming or other approaches to stimulating ideas about the stage, with the aim of uncovering better ways to implement it. Brainstorming and similar approaches can also be applied to any of the Knowledge Chain Model's activities.

Here, we first present highlights of the original KCM. Because the original model has been further developed, we then describe this more detailed version of the KCM.

The Original Knowledge Chain Model

The Knowledge Chain Model identifies nine crucial activities that knowledge-driven enterprises can per-

Figure 2. The original Knowledge Chain Model

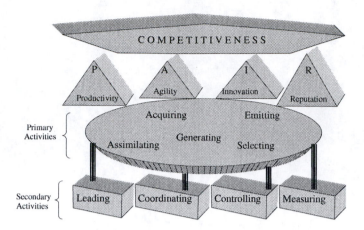

form in ways that yield competitive advantage (Holsapple & Singh, 2000, 2001). These activities are derived from an ontology of knowledge management phenomena that was collaboratively engineered with an international array of KM practitioners and researchers (Joshi, 1998; Holsapple & Joshi, 2002, 2003, 2004). Like Porter's Value Chain Model, it is a basic tool for diagnosing competitive advantage and finding ways to enhance it.

The Knowledge Chain Model includes five primary activities that an organization's knowledge processors perform in manipulating knowledge assets. These five activities are identified in the KM ontology as the five generic KM activities involved within knowledge management episodes: acquiring, selecting, generating, assimilating, and emitting knowledge. In addition, the KCM includes four secondary activities that support and guide performance of the primary activities. These four KM activities are identified in the KM ontology as managerial influences on the conduct of knowledge management: leading, coordinating, controlling, and measuring knowledge management initiatives. The KMC recognizes four ways in which improvements in the design and execution of KM activities can aid competitiveness: better productivity, greater agility, greater innovation, and enhanced reputation (i.e., the PAIR approaches to competitiveness).

Figure 2 shows how the elements of the Knowledge Chain Model are related. Observe that no process is specified in the model. As with the Value Chain Model, the impetus is on identification of key activities on which to concentrate in formulating strategies for adding value and improving competitiveness. The fact that the Value Chain Model and the KCM each have nine activities appears to be coincidental, as the KCM is not derived from the Value Chain Model and there is no particular correspondence between any KCM activity

and any value chain activity. Indeed, all of the KCM activities can be applied to the study or implementation of knowledge processing within any one of the value chain activities.

The KCM disaggregates a knowledge-based firm's knowledge processing and systematically examines all the discrete but interrelated primary and secondary KM activities that the firm performs. The result is a means for analyzing the sources of competitive advantage. The economics of how each KM activity is performed will affect whether a firm's cost structure is high or low relative to competitors. How each KM activity is performed will also affect its contribution to meeting customer needs and hence its degree of differentiation from other firms. Comparing the knowledge chains of competitors can reveal differences that determine competitive advantage.

Table 1 summarizes the KM activities that comprise an organization's knowledge chain. Anecdotal evidence indicates that this set of interrelated knowledge activities appears to be common across diverse organizations, appears to be capable of being performed with various practices and technologies so as to promote competitiveness, and appears to do so in the four PAIR directions (Holsapple & Singh, 2001). Moreover, a survey of KM practitioners indicates that each of the knowledge chain activities can be performed in ways that contribute to competitiveness along the PAIR directions (Singh, 2000).

KM skills of an organization's participants need to be cultivated and applied in the performance of these activities. When a specific instance of a KM activity occurs in an organization, it is performed by one or more knowledge processors, some human and others computer based. Multiple processors may be able to perform a given type of KM activity. Conversely, mul-

Table 1. KM activity classes in the Knowledge Chain Model (adapted from Holsapple & Singh, 2001)

Category	Activity Class	Description
Primary	Knowledge Acquisition	Acquiring knowledge from external sources and making it suitable for subsequent use
Primary	Knowledge Selection	Selecting needed knowledge from internal sources and making it suitable for subsequent use
Primary	Knowledge Generation	Producing knowledge by either discovery or derivation from existing knowledge
Primary	Knowledge Assimilation	Altering the state of an organization's knowledge resources by distributing and storing acquired, selected, or generated knowledge
Primary	Knowledge Emission	Embedding knowledge into organizational outputs for release into the environment
Secondary	Knowledge Measurement	Assessing values of knowledge resources, knowledge processors, and their deployment
Secondary	Knowledge Control	Ensuring that needed knowledge processors and resources are available in sufficient quality and quantity, subject to security requirements
Secondary	Knowledge Coordination	Managing dependencies among KM activities to ensure that proper processes and resources are brought to bear adequately at appropriate times
Secondary	Knowledge Leadership	Establishing conditions that enable and facilitate fruitful conduct of KM

tiple types of KM activity may be performed by a given processor.

Knowledge acquisition refers to the activity of identifying knowledge in the organization's external environment and transforming it into a representation that can be *assimilated*, and/or used for knowledge *generation* or *emission*. Selecting knowledge refers to the activity of identifying needed knowledge within an organization's existing knowledge resources and providing it in an appropriate representation to an activity that needs it (i.e., to an *acquiring*, *assimilating*, *generating*, and *emitting* activity). Generation is an activity that produces knowledge by discovering it or deriving it from existing knowledge, where the latter has resulted from *acquisition*, *selection*, and/or prior *generation*. Derivation involves the use of process knowledge (e.g., procedures, rules) and descriptive knowledge (e.g., data, information) to generate new process and/or descriptive knowledge employing KM skills that are of an analytical, logical, and constructive nature. Although the result is "new" to the processor that derives it, it may have previously existed but not have been assimilated, or it may already exist elsewhere in the organization but not be subject to facile selection. Discovery generates knowledge in less structured ways, via skills involving creativity, imagination, and synthesis.

Assimilating is an activity that alters an organization's knowledge resources based on *acquired*, *selected*, or

generated knowledge. It receives knowledge flows from these activities and produces knowledge flows that impact the organization's state of knowledge. Emitting knowledge is an activity that uses existing knowledge to produce organizational outputs for release into the environment. It yields projections (i.e., embodiments of knowledge in outward forms) for external consumption, in contrast to *assimilation* which may also yield projections, but which are retained as knowledge assets. Emission is only partially a KM activity because it also can involve physical activities such as production through raw material transformation.

In characterizing the KCM's primary activities, we have strictly adopted the activity definitions existing in the underlying KM ontology. Some KM authors use some of the same terms but with different meanings. For instance, Davenport and Prusak (1998) use the term "knowledge generation" to mean not only generation as it is defined in Table 1, but to also include knowledge acquisition activity. However, just as there is a fundamental distinction between making something and buying something, the distinction between generating knowledge oneself and obtaining knowledge from external sources deserves to be made. As another example, some authors use the term "knowledge acquisition" to include not only acquisition as recognized in the ontology, but to include knowledge selection as well. However, this suggests that it is possible to acquire what we already possess, as well as what we do not possess. Like the ontology on which it is based, the KCM holds that the distinction between acquiring knowledge that is not possessed and selecting from knowledge that is possessed is an important one. Thus, in using the Knowledge Chain Model, it is important to be true to the definitions of its activities rather than confusing them with alternative definitions that are not as sharp in making distinctions.

Secondary activities support and guide the performance of primary KM activities. Measurement involves the valuation of knowledge resources and knowledge processors, including quantitative methods, qualitative assessment, performance review, and benchmarking. It is a basis for evaluation of control, coordination, and leadership; for identifying and recognizing value-adding processors and resources; for assessing and comparing the execution of KM activities; and for evaluating the impacts of an organization's conduct of KM on bottom-line performance. Control is concerned with ensuring that needed knowledge resources and processors are available in sufficient quantity and quality subject to required security and constraints on integrity and privacy. Quality is controlled with respect to two dimensions: knowledge validity (accuracy and consistency) and knowledge utility (relevance and importance). Controlling the quality of knowledge is a significant issue for KM, because the value of knowledge and returns achieved from knowledge resources depend on its quality. Protection involves protection from loss, obsolescence, unauthorized exposure, unauthorized modification, and erroneous assimilation.

Coordination refers to guiding the conduct of KM in an organization. It involves managing dependencies among knowledge resources, among knowledge manipulation activities, between knowledge resources and other resources (i.e., financial, human, and material), and between knowledge resources and KM activities. It involves marshaling sufficient skills for executing various activities, arranging those activities in time, and integrating knowledge processing with an organization's operations. An organization's approach to problem solving, decision making, experimentation, and organizational learning, all of which are knowledge-intensive endeavors, can depend on how it coordinates its KM activities. Of the four secondary KM activities, leadership is central. It sets the tone (i.e., shapes the culture) for coordination, control, and measurement that manifest. It qualifies the expression of each primary activity. In short, leadership establishes enabling conditions for achieving fruitful KM through the other eight activities. The distinguishing characteristic of leadership is that of being a catalyst through such traits as inspiring, mentoring, setting examples, engendering trust and re-

spect, instilling a cohesive and creative culture, establishing a vision, listening, learning, teaching, and knowledge sharing.

The Extended Knowledge Chain Model

The Knowledge Chain Model can be developed in further detail by identifying specific KM activity types that belong to each of the nine classes shown in Table 1 (Holsapple & Jones, 2003, 2004, 2005). In all, over 60 specific KM activities, organized into the nine classes, have been determined to yield this extended version of the KCM. These more detailed activities have been developed from an interpretive analysis of the knowledge management literature and have been judged in a survey of practitioners who lead KM initiatives as capable of being performed in ways that contribute to organizational competitiveness (Jones, 2004). The distinct KM activity types for each class are illustrated in Figure 3. For full descriptions and examples of each of the detailed KM activities, refer to Jones (2004) and Holsapple and Jones (2004, 2005). These elaborations also include taxonomies for organizing the specific KM activity types within each of the nine KCM classes.

Using the Knowledge Chain Model to Guide KM Strategy Formation

Clearly, formulating a KM strategy is not a trivial task. Moreover, it needs to be developed in concert with other aspects of an organization's overall strategy (e.g., marketing strategy, financial strategy). This development could be after the fact, devised to be aligned with and supportive of pre-existing business strategy. Alternatively, KM strategy formulation may be an integral part of an organization's overall strategy development. In either event, KM strategy is concerned with design and deployment of a suitable mix of practices and technologies for performing the knowledge management activities that can contribute to organizational performance and competitiveness. But exactly what are these crucial KM activities? The extended version of the Knowledge Chain Model answers this question in considerable detail. As such, it can help guide KM strategy formation.

Knowledge technologies, knowledge practices, and knowledge assets are the building blocks of a KM strategy (recall Figure 1). As discussed previously, Zack (1999) has provided a way of analyzing knowledge assets that can guide KM strategy formation. The KCM provides a structure for dealing with the practice and technology aspects of KM strategy. An appropriate combination of the possibilities for these two factors

Figure 3. The extended Knowledge Chain Model

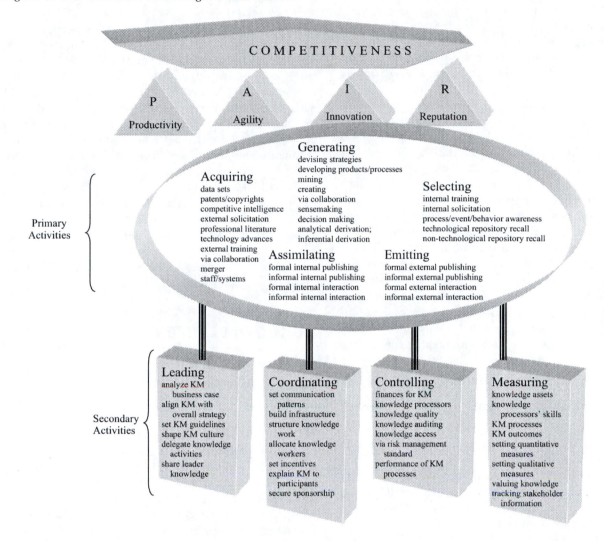

needs to be determined in formulating a plan for implementing each of the KM activities identified by the Knowledge Chain Model. For a given organization, the determination of what specific technology/practice mix is appropriate for each of the KM activities depends on two classes of situational factors: the organization's available assets (i.e., human, financial, knowledge, material) and the nature of the environment (e.g., social, political, regulatory, market, industry) in which the organization finds itself.

As a starting point, the KM strategist needs to understand where the organization presently is with respect to each of the KCM activities. A SWOT analysis for each activity can be helpful. For a particular KCM activity,

what are the current practices and technologies (if any) that are being used, to what extent does this approach to implementing the activity contribute to PAIR, what practices/technologies do competitors use to implement the activity? Next, the KM strategist needs to brainstorm and develop insights about possibilities for performing the KCM activity in ways that enhance organizational performance (e.g., in one or more of the PAIR directions). What alternative practices/technologies are feasible candidates for implementing the activity in light of the organization's asset situation and environment situation? Do available knowledge assets (e.g., patents, culture, infrastructure, data warehouses), human assets (e.g., knowledge processing skills), or material assets (e.g., automated knowledge processing skills) allow the strategist to plan on value-adding practices/technologies for implementing the activity? Do present or anticipated environmental factors suggest competitive threats or opportunities in the performance of the activity? These should be factored into KM strategy development relative to the KCM activity.

Another way to look at KM strategy formation is more of a top-down approach. Here, the strategist settles on one (or more) of the PAIR directions as being most consistent with or important to the overall business plan. Suppose that it is agility that the organization most wants to compete on. Each of the KCM activities is then examined from the standpoint of how the present way of performing it contributes to agility. The KM strategist asks whether there are practices/technologies that can be economically adopted as part of the plan to make the organization better able to respond to rapid, perhaps unexpected, changes in its environment or assets. The KM strategy then becomes tied to the overall strategy of excellent response-ability. Empirical study of the original KCM gives clues as to which of the nine activity classes are likely to have greatest potential for impacts on agility (Singh, 2000).

FUTURE DIRECTIONS

While the KMC offers guidance to KM strategists in structuring both the planning and the plan for driving KM initiatives, it does not offer prescriptions about what practices/technologies to adopt in specific asset/environment situations or for achieving results in a specific PAIR dimension.

The KM activities identified by the KMC are not the only determining factors that can lead to competitiveness. There are other forces that influence how the conduct of KM ultimately unfolds in an organization: resource influences (e.g., knowledge assets) and environmental influences (Joshi, 1998). This suggests that the KCM could be extended to include resource and environmental factors, which both constrain and enable the execution of KM activities. One future research direction is to investigate this extension.

The KMC is descriptive in nature. Its intent is to identify KM activities that researchers and practitioners need to consider in managing knowledge to enhance organizational performance. An obvious next step is prescriptive, further developing the KMC to lay out candidate practices and technologies for each of the KM activities.

CONCLUSION

In the interest of being competitive, a knowledge-based organization must adopt, design, and implement knowledge management activities better than other organizations. The Knowledge Chain Model identifies nine classes of KM activities and over 60 specific KM activities that appear to be common across diverse organizations. The KMC holds that individually, and in combination, these KM activities can be contributors to competitiveness. Evidence from the literature provides support for this assertion, as do results of surveys of leaders of KM initiatives. Thus, rather than simply saying that KM can yield a competitive advantage, the Knowledge Chain Model provides structure to designers of KM strategy, ensuring full consideration of the varied KM activities that can be sources of competitiveness in the directions of better productivity, agility, innovation, and/or reputation.

ACKNOWLEDGMENT

This work is supported in part by a grant from the Kentucky Science and Engineering Foundation.

REFERENCES

Bennet, A., & Porter, D. (2003). The force of knowledge: A case study of KM implementation in the Department of Navy. In C.W. Holsapple (Ed.), *Handbook on knowledge management: Knowledge directions*. Berlin/Heidelberg: Springer-Verlag.

Bennet, D., & Bennet, A. (2003). The rise of the knowledge organization. In C.W. Holsapple (Ed.), *Handbook on knowledge management: Knowledge matters*. Berlin/Heidelberg: Springer-Verlag.

Davenport, T., & Prusak, L. (1998). *Working knowledge: How organizations manage what they know*. Boston: Harvard Business School Press.

DeTore, A., & Balliet-Milholland, J. (2003). Transforming theory into fact: Hands-on knowledge management initiatives built on a reinsurer's pile of junk. In C.W. Holsapple (Ed.), *Handbook on knowledge management: Knowledge directions*. Berlin/Heidelberg: Springer-Verlag.

Holsapple, C.W., & Jones, K.G. (2003, August). Toward an elaboration of the Knowledge Chain Model. *Proceedings of the Americas Conference on Information Systems*, Tampa, FL.

Holsapple, C.W., & Jones, K.G. (2004). Exploring primary activities of the knowledge chain. *Knowledge and Process Management, 11*(3).

Holsapple, C.W., & Jones, K.G. (2005). Exploring secondary activities of the knowledge chain. *Knowledge and Process Management, 12*(1).

Holsapple, C.W., & Joshi, K.D. (2002). A collaborative approach to ontology design. *Communications of the ACM, 45*(2).

Holsapple, C.W., & Joshi, K.D. (2003). A knowledge management ontology. In C.W. Holsapple (Ed.), *Handbook on knowledge management: Knowledge matters.* Berlin/Heidelberg: Springer-Verlag.

Holsapple, C.W., & Joshi, K.D. (2004). A formal knowledge management ontology conduct, activities, resources, and influences. *Journal of the American Society for Information Science and Technology, 55*(7).

Holsapple, C.W., & Singh, M. (2000, March 31-April 2). The Knowledge Chain Model. *Proceedings of the 3rd Annual Conference of the Southern Association for Information Systems,* Atlanta, GA.

Holsapple, C.W., & Singh, M. (2001). The Knowledge Chain Model: Activities for competitiveness. *Expert Systems with Applications, 20*(1).

Holsapple, C.W., & Whinston, A.B. (1987). Knowledge-based organizations. *The Information Society, 5*(2).

Jones, K.G. (2004). *An investigation of activities related to knowledge management and their impacts on competitiveness.* PhD Dissertation, Carol M. Gatton College of Business and Economics, University of Kentucky, USA.

Joshi, K.D. (1998). *An investigation of knowledge management characteristics: Synthesis, Delphi study, analysis.* PhD Dissertation, Carol M. Gatton College of Business and Economics, University of Kentucky, USA.

Kelly, T., & Bauer, D. (2003). Managing intellectual capital, via e-learning, at Cisco. In C.W. Holsapple (Ed.), *Handbook on knowledge management: Knowledge directions.* Berlin/Heidelberg: Springer-Verlag.

King, W.R., & Ko, D. (2001). Evaluating knowledge management and the learning organization: An information/knowledge value chain approach. *Communications of the AIS, 5*(14).

Malhotra, Y. (2003). Why knowledge management systems fail: Enablers and constraints of knowledge management in human enterprises. In C.W. Holsapple (Ed.), *Handbook on knowledge management: Knowledge matters.* Berlin/Heidelberg: Springer-Verlag.

Mintzberg, H., & Quinn, J. (1996). *The strategy process: Concepts, contexts, cases.* Englewood Cliffs, NJ: Prentice-Hall.

O'Dell, C., Hasanali, F., Hubert, C., Lopez, K., Odem, P., & Raybourne, C. (2003). Successful KM implementations: A study of best practice organizations. In C.W. Holsapple (Ed.), *Handbook on knowledge management: Knowledge directions.* Berlin/Heidelberg: Springer-Verlag.

Oriel, S.L. (2001). *From* inventions management to intellectual capital management at the Dow Chemical Company: A 100+ year journey. In C.W. Holsapple (Ed.), *Handbook on knowledge management: Knowledge directions.* Berlin/Heidelberg: Springer-Verlag.

Paradice, D.B., & Courtney, J.F. Jr. (1989). Organizational knowledge management. *Information Resources Management Journal, 2*(3).

Porter, M. (1985). *Competitive advantage: Creating and sustaining superior performance.* New York: The Free Press.

Rockart, J., & Short, J. (1991). The networked organization and the management of interdependence. In M. Scott Morton (Ed.), *The corporation of the 1990s: Information technology and organizational transformation.* Oxford: Oxford University Press.

Singh, M. (2000). *Toward a knowledge management view of electronic business: Introduction and investigation of the Knowledge Chain Model for competitiveness.* PhD Dissertation, Carol M. Gatton College of Business and Economics, University of Kentucky, USA.

Smith, H.A., & McKeen, J.D. (2003a). Knowledge management in organizations: The state of current practice. In C.W. Holsapple (Ed.), *Handbook on knowledge management: Knowledge directions.* Berlin/Heidelberg: Springer-Verlag.

van der Spek, R., Hofer-Alfeis, J., & Kingma, J. (2003). The knowledge strategy process. In C.W. Holsapple (Ed.), *Handbook on knowledge management: Knowledge directions.* Berlin/Heidelberg: Springer-Verlag.

Wolford, D., & Kwiecien, S. (2003). Driving knowledge management at Ford Motor Company. In C.W. Holsapple (Ed.), *Handbook on knowledge management: Knowledge directions.* Berlin/Heidelberg: Springer-Verlag.

Zack M.H. (1999). Developing a knowledge strategy. *California Management Review, 41*(3).

KEY TERMS

Knowledge Assets: An organization's schematic and content knowledge resources, including knowledge held by the organization's participants, various artifacts belonging to the organization (e.g., documents, manuals, videos), the organization's culture, and its particular infrastructure of roles, relationships, and regulations.

Knowledge Chain Model: A model that identifies generic knowledge management activities, which are keys to achieving competitive advantage and therefore can guide the formation of KM strategies.

Knowledge Management Strategy: A plan for marshaling and applying knowledge-oriented resources (knowledge assets and knowledge processing capabilities) in the interest of supporting the organization's purpose.

Knowledge Processing Capabilities: The practices and technologies of an organization that can be used operating on knowledge assets.

Primary Activities in the Knowledge Chain: Activities that an organization's knowledge processors perform via various practices and technologies in manipulating knowledge assets within knowledge management episodes: acquiring, selecting, generating, assimilating, and emitting knowledge.

Secondary Activities in the Knowledge Chain: Activities that support and guide performance of the primary activities via various practices and technologies: leading, coordinating, controlling, and measuring knowledge management initiatives.

Strategy: A systematic plan of action for deliberately using an organization's resources in ways that fulfill that organization's purpose.

Value Chain Model: Identifies nine generic, distinct categories of activity that an organization performs in the course of doing business, which¾if performed better than competitors, can yield a competitive advantage for the organization.

Knowledge Management Success Models

Murray E. Jennex
San Diego State University, USA

INTRODUCTION

Alavi and Leidner (2001, p. 114) defined knowledge management systems (KMSs) as "IT-based systems developed to support and enhance the organizational processes of knowledge creation, storage/retrieval, transfer, and application." They observed that not all KM initiatives will implement an IT solution, but they support IT as an enabler of KM. Maier (2002) expanded on the IT concept for the KMS by calling it an ICT system that supported the functions of knowledge creation, construction, identification, capturing, acquisition, selection, valuation, organization, linking, structuring, formalization, visualization, distribution, retention, maintenance, refinement, evolution, access, search, and application. Stein and Zwass (1995) define an organizational memory information system (OMIS) as the processes and IT components necessary to capture, store, and bring to bear knowledge created in the past on decisions currently being made. Jennex and Olfman (2004) expanded this definition by incorporating the OMS into the KMS and adding strategy and service components to the KMS.

Additionally, we have different ways of classifying the KMS and/or KMS technologies, where KMS technologies are the specific IT and ICT tools being implemented in the KMS. Alavi and Leidner (2001) classify the KMS and KMS tools based on the knowledge lifecycle stage being predominantly supported. This model has four stages: knowledge creation, knowledge storage and retrieval, knowledge transfer, and knowledge application. It is expected that the KMS will use technologies specific to supporting the stage for which the KMS was created to support. Marwick (2001) classifies the KMS and KMS tools by the mode of Nonaka's (1994) SECI model (socialization, externalization, combination, and internalization) being implemented. Borghoff and Pareschi (1998) classify the KMS and KMS tools using their knowledge management architecture. This architecture has four classes of components—repositories and libraries, knowledge-worker communities, knowledge cartography or mapping, and knowledge flows—with classification being based on the predominant architecture component being supported. Hahn and Subramani (2001) classify KMS and KMS tools by the source of the knowledge being supported: a structured

artifact, structured individual, unstructured artifact, or unstructured individual. Binney (2001) classifies the KMS and KMS tools using the knowledge spectrum. The knowledge spectrum represents the ranges of purposes a KMS can have and include transactional KM, analytical KM, asset management KM, process-based KM, developmental KM, and innovation and creation KM. Binney does not limit a KMS or KMS tool to a single portion of the knowledge spectrum and allows for multipurpose KMS and KMS tools. Zack (1999) classifies KMS and KMS tools as either integrative or interactive. Integrative KMS or KMS tools support the transfer of explicit knowledge using some form of repository and support. Interactive KMS or KMS tools support the transfer of tacit knowledge by facilitating communication between the knowledge source and the knowledge user. Jennex and Olfman (2004) classify the KMS and KMS tools by the type of users being supported. Users are grouped into two groups based on the amount of the common context of understanding they have with each other, resulting in the classifications of process- or task-based KMS and KMS tools, or generic or infrastructure KMS and KMS tools.

Regardless of the classification of the KMS, once a KMS is implemented, its success needs to be determined. Turban and Aronson (2001) list three reasons for measuring the success of a knowledge management system.

- To provide a basis for company valuation
- To stimulate management to focus on what is important
- To justify investments in KM activities

All are good reasons from an organizational perspective. Additionally, from the perspective of KM academics and practitioners, the measurement of KMS success is crucial to understanding how these systems should be built and implemented.

To meet this need, several KM and/or KMS success models are found in the literature. Models of KM success are included as a Churchman (1979) view of a KMS can be defined to include the KM initiative driving the implementation of a KMS (also, the counterview is valid as looking at KM can also include looking at the KMS).

What is KM or KMS success? This is an important question that has not been fully answered as researchers are finding it difficult to quantify results of KM and KMS efforts. This article presents several KM and KMS success models. Two basic approaches are used to determine success. The first looks at the effective implementation of KM processes as the indicator of a successful implementation, with the expectation that effective processes will lead to successful knowledge use. These models identify KM processes by looking at KM and KMS success factors. The second approach looks at identifying impacts from the KM or KMS implementation, with the expectation that if there are impacts from using knowledge, then the KM or KMS implementation is successful. These models consider success a dependent variable and seek to identify the factors that lead to generating impacts from using knowledge. The following models, found through a review of the literature, use one or both of these approaches to determine KM or KMS success.

KNOWLEDGE MANAGEMENT SUCCESS MODELS

Bots and de Bruijn: Knowledge Value Chain

Bots and de Bruijn (2002) assessed KM and determined that the best way to judge good KM was through a knowledge value chain. Good KM is defined as using KM to improve organizational competitiveness. However, measuring the KM impact on competitiveness is considered difficult, so ultimately it was concluded that good KM is when the KM initiative matches the model provided in Figure 1 and the KM processes are implemented well. KM is assessed for effectiveness at each step of the knowledge process and is good if each of the indicated activities is performed well with the ultimate factor being that the KM enhances competitiveness. Figure 1 illustrates the KM value chain. The model was developed by viewing and contrasting KM through an analytical (technical) perspective and an actor (user)

perspective. These perspectives are conflicting, and KM assessment occurs by determining how well the KMS meets each perspective at each step.

Massey, Montoya-Weiss, and O'Driscoll KM Success Model

Massey, Montoya-Weiss, and O'Driscoll (2002) present a KM success model based on their Nortel case study. The model is based on the framework proposed by Holsapple and Joshi (2001) and reflects that KM success is based on understanding the organization, its knowledge users, and how they use knowledge. It recognizes that KM is an organizational change process and KM success cannot separate itself from organizational change success, with the result being that KM success is essentially defined as improving organizational or process performance. The model is presented in Figure 2. Key components of the model are the following.

- **KM Strategy:** The processes using knowledge and what that knowledge is; the sources, users, and form of the knowledge; and the technology infrastructure for storing the knowledge
- **Key Managerial Influences:** Management support through leadership, the allocation and management of project resources, and the oversight of the KMS through the coordination and control of resources and the application of metrics for assessing KMS success
- **Key Resource Influences:** The financial resources and knowledge sources needed to build the KMS
- **Key Environmental Influences:** The external forces that drive the organization to exploit its knowledge to maintain its competitive position

Lindsey KM Success Model

Lindsey (2002) considered KM success as being defined by Kaplan and Norton's (1992) balanced-scorecard

Figure 1. Bots and de Bruijn (2002) KM value chain

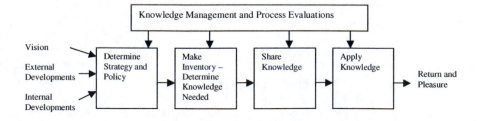

Figure 2. Massey et al. (2002) KM success model

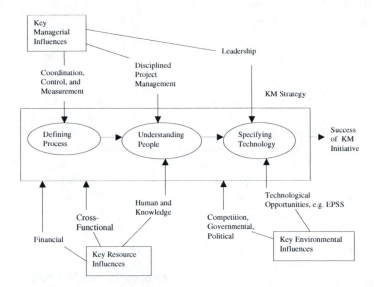

approach and proposed a KM effectiveness model based on combining the organizational capability perspective theory (Gold, Malhotra, & Segars, 2001) and the contingency-perspective theory (Becerra-Fernandez & Sabherwal, 2001). The model defines KM effectiveness in terms of two main constructs: knowledge infrastructure capability and knowledge process capability, with the knowledge process capability construct being influenced by a knowledge task. The knowledge infrastructure capability represents social capital and the relationships between knowledge sources and users, and it is operationalized by the technology (the network itself), structure (the relationship), and culture (the context in which the knowledge is created and used). The knowledge process capability represents the integration of KM processes into the organization, and it is operationalized by acquisition (the capturing of knowledge), conversion (making captured knowledge available), application (degree to which knowledge is useful), and protection (security of the knowledge). Tasks are activities performed by organizational units and indicate the type and domain of the knowledge being used. Tasks ensure the right knowledge is being captured and used. KM success is measured as a combination of the satisfaction with the KMS and the effectiveness of KM processes. Figure 3 illustrates the Lindsey model.

Jennex-Olfman KMS Success Model

Jennex and Olfman (2004) present a KMS success model that is based on the DeLone and McLean (1992,

Figure 3. Lindsey (2002) KM effectiveness model

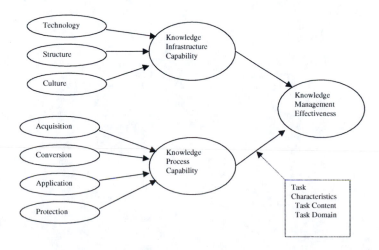

2003) IS success model. Figure 4 shows the KMS success model. This model evaluates success as an improvement in organizational effectiveness based on the use of and impacts from the KMS. Descriptions of the dimensions of the model follow.

- **System Quality:** how well the KMS performs the functions of knowledge creation, storage and retrieval, transfer, and application; how much of the OM is codified and included in the computerized portion of the OM; and how the KMS is supported by the IS staff and infrastructure.

- **Knowledge and Information Quality:** ensures that the right knowledge and OM with sufficient context is captured and available for the right users at the right time.

- **Use and User Satisfaction:** indicates the actual levels of KMS use as well as the satisfaction of the KMS users. Actual use is most applicable as a success measure when the use of a system is required. User satisfaction is a construct that measures satisfaction with the KMS by users. It is considered a good complementary measure of KMS use when use of the KMS is required, and the effectiveness of use depends on users being satisfied with the KMS.

- **Perceived Benefit:** measures perceptions of the benefits and impacts of the KMS by users and is based on Thompson, Higgins, and Howell's (1991) perceived-benefit model. It is good for predicting continued KMS use when use of the KMS is volun-

tary, and the amount and/or effectiveness of KMS use depends on meeting current and future user needs.

- **Net Impact:** An individual's use of a KMS will produce an impact on that person's performance in the workplace. Each individual impact will in turn have an effect on the performance of the whole organization. Organizational impacts are typically not the summation of individual impacts, so the association between individual and organizational impacts is often difficult to draw; that is why this construct combines all impacts into a single construct. This model recognizes that the use of knowledge and OM may have good or bad benefits, and allows for feedback from these benefits to drive the organization to either use more knowledge and OM or to forget specific knowledge and OM.

Maier KMS Success Model

Maier (2002) also proposes a KMS success model based on the DeLone and McLean IS success model (1992). This model is similar to the Jennex-Olfman model. A breakdown of the dimensions into constructs is not provided, but specific measures for each dimension are identified. This model is illustrated in Figure 5 and uses the following dimensions.

- **System Quality:** taken directly from DeLone and McLean (1992) and refers to the overall quality of the hardware and software

Figure 4. KMS success model of Jennex and Olfman (2004)

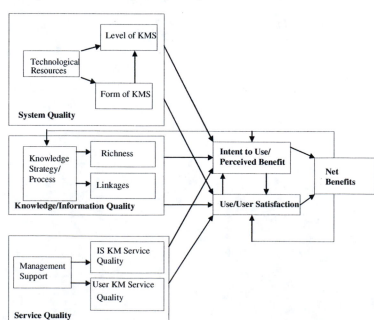

Figure 5. Maier (2002) KMS success model

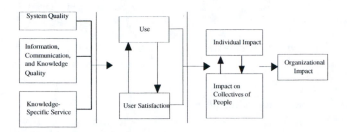

- **Information, Communication, and Knowledge Quality:** the quality of the stored data, information, and knowledge, and the quality of knowledge-flow methods

- **Knowledge-Specific Service:** how well subject-matter experts and KMS managers support the KMS

- **System Use and User Satisfaction:** taken directly from DeLone and McLean (1992) and refers to actual KMS use and the satisfaction users have with that use

- **Individual Impact:** taken directly from DeLone and McLean (1992) and refers to the impacts KMS use has on an individual's effectiveness

- **Impact on Collectives of People:** the improved effectiveness within teams, work groups, and/or communities that comes from using the KMS

- **Organizational Impacts:** taken directly from DeLone and McLean (1992) and refers to improved overall organizational effectiveness as a result of KMS use

FUTURE TRENDS

There are two areas needing research. The first is in defining KM and KMS success and quantifying the factors that define or reflect this success. Two promising approaches are in identifying success measurements with respect to DeLone and McLean's (2002) IS success model, or to Kaplan and Norton's (1992) balanced-scorecard approach.

The second area is to improve the generalizability of the models by establishing quantitative support across a broad range of organizations and users. This is necessary for showing that the models are not just reflective of the conditions observed in the case study leading to their generation.

CONCLUSION

Many KM and KMS success and effectiveness models have been proposed. Most are based on case study research that looked in depth at KM or a KMS in an organizational setting. This type of research yields good insight into organizational and user processes and mechanics, giving researchers an excellent perspective from which to build models that explain their observations. Additionally, all of these models have some level of theoretical foundation. The use of established theory coupled with observation yields useful models. The models presented in this article are all useful to researchers exploring KM and KMS success and effectiveness. Also, these models are useful to practitioners and KMS designers as they provide guidance into what to look at when determining KM and KMS success, and what to include in a KMS.

REFERENCES

Alavi, M., & Leidner, D. E. (2001). Review: Knowledge management and knowledge management systems: Conceptual foundations and research issues. *MIS Quarterly, 25*(1), 107-136.

Becerra-Fernandez, I., & Sabherwal, R. (2001). Organizational knowledge management: A contingency perspective. *Journal of Management Information Systems, 18*(1), 23-55.

Binney, D. (2001). The knowledge management spectrum: Understanding the KM landscape. *The Journal of Knowledge Management, 5*(1), 33-42.

Borghoff, U. M., & Pareschi, R. (1998). *Information technology for knowledge management.* Berlin, Germany: Springer-Verlag.

Bots, P. W. G., & de Bruiin, H. (2002). Effective knowledge management in professional organizations: Going by the rules. *Proceedings of the 35th Hawaii International Conference on System Sciences.*

Churchman, C. W. (1979). *The systems approach* (Rev. Ed.). New York: Dell Publishing.

DeLone, W. H., & McLean, E. R. (1992). Information systems success: The quest for the dependent variable. *Information Systems Research, 3,* 60-95.

DeLone, W. H., & McLean, E. R. (2003). The DeLone and McLean model of information systems success: A ten year update. *Journal of Management Information Systems, 19*(4), 9-30.

Gold, A. H., Malhotra, A., & Segars, A. H. (2001). Knowledge management: An organizational capabilities perspective. *Journal of Management Information Systems, 18*(1), 185-214.

Hahn, J., & Subramani, M. R. (2000). A framework of knowledge management systems: Issues and challenges for theory and practice. *Proceedings of the 21st International Conference on Information Systems* (pp. 302-312).

Holsapple, C. W., & Joshi, K. D. (2001). Knowledge management: A three-fold framework. *The Information Society, 18*(1), 47-64.

Jennex, M. E., & Olfman, L. (2002). Organizational memory/knowledge effects on productivity: A longitudinal study. *Proceedings of the 35th Hawaii International Conference on System Sciences, HICSS35.*

Jennex, M. E., & Olfman, L. (2004). Modeling knowledge management success. *Proceedings of the Conference on Information Science and Technology Management, CISTM.*

Kaplan, R. S., & Norton, D. P. (1992). The balanced scorecard: The measures that drive performance. *Harvard Business Review.*

Lindsey, K. (2002). Measuring knowledge management effectiveness: A task-contingent organizational capabilities perspective. *Proceedings of the 8th Americas Conference on Information Systems* (pp. 2085-2090).

Maier, R. (2002). *Knowledge management systems: Information and communication technologies for knowledge management.* Berlin, Germany: Springer-Verlag.

Marwick, A. D. (2001). Knowledge management technology. *IBM Systems Journal, 40*(4), 814-830.

Massey, A. P., Montoya-Weiss, M. M., & O'Driscoll, T. M. (2002). Knowledge management in pursuit of performance: Insights from Nortel networks. *MIS Quarterly, 26*(3), 269-289.

Nonaka, I. (1994). A dynamic theory of organizational knowledge creation. *Organization Science, 5*(1), 14-37.

Stein, E. W., & Zwass, V. (1995). Actualizing organizational memory with information systems. *Information Systems Research, 6*(2), 85-117.

Thompson, R. L., Higgins, C. A., & Howell, J. M. (1991). Personal computing: Toward a conceptual model of utilization. *MIS Quarterly, 15*(1), 125-143.

Turban, E., & Aronson, J. E. (2001). *Decision support systems and intelligent systems* (6th ed.). Prentice Hall.

Zack, M. H. (1999). Managing codified knowledge. *Sloan Management Review, 40*(4), 45-58.

KEY TERMS

Knowledge Management Effectiveness: The measure of how well KM processes are implemented.

Knowledge Management Success: The improvement in organizational performance that comes from using knowledge as a result of a knowledge management initiative. Success can be expressed as the result of the impacts caused by the use of knowledge and/or the effective implementation of KM processes.

Knowledge Management System: KMSs are the "IT-based systems developed to support and enhance the organizational processes of knowledge creation, storage/retrieval, transfer, and application" (Alavi & Leidner, 2001, p. 114).

Knowledge Management System Effectiveness: The measure of how well the components of a KMS are implemented or perform their intended functions.

Knowledge Management System Success: The improvement in organizational performance that comes from using knowledge as a result of a knowledge management system. Success can be expressed as the result of the impacts caused by the use of the KMS or the effective implementation of KMS processes. A Churchman (1979) perspective of systems supports the use of KMS success as a surrogate for or complementary measure of KM success.

Knowledge Processes: The organizational processes for managing knowledge; specifically, the formal processes for knowledge capture and reuse, how the knowledge will be stored, and the metrics for measuring the effectiveness of knowledge use.

Knowledge Management System Success Factors

Murray E. Jennex
San Diego State University, USA

INTRODUCTION

What does it take to build a successful knowledge management system (KMS)? Knowing the essential success factors is useful as it provides researchers and practitioners with the basic requirements for building a successful KMS. Also, if we take a Churchman (1979) view of systems, it can be argued that determining KMS success factors will also help us determine KM initiative success factors as Churchman found it difficult to separate the system from the process requiring the system. However, what is KM or KMS success? The literature does not provide a consensus on this, although two concepts of success can be identified. The first considers KM or KMS a success if knowledge use through the initiative or system improves the organization's ability to compete. The second considers KM or KMS a success if the KM processes implemented through the KMS (discussed later) are implemented effectively. Both success concepts imply that the KMS has to be used. Therefore, KM and KMS success factors are those factors that encourage or help users to use the KMS to effectively perform KM functions.

What is a KMS? Alavi and Leidner (2001, p. 114) define KMSs as "IT-based systems developed to support and enhance the organizational processes of knowledge creation, storage/retrieval, transfer, and application." They observed that not all KM initiatives will implement an IT solution, but they support IT as an enabler of KM. Maier (2002) expanded on the IT concept for the KMS by calling it an ICT system that supports the functions of knowledge creation, construction, identification, capturing, acquisition, selection, valuation, organization, linking, structuring, formalization, visualization, distribution, retention, maintenance, refinement, evolution, access, search, and application. Stein and Zwass (1995) define an organizational memory information system (OMIS) as the processes and IT components necessary to capture, store, and bring to bear knowledge created in the past on decisions currently being made. Jennex and Olfman (2004) expanded this definition by incorporating the OMIS into the KMS and adding strategy and service components to the KMS.

This article uses a literature review to identify these success factors. Studies looking at KM, KMS, OM, and OMS or OMIS were reviewed and the success factors extracted. KM studies were included as a Churchman (1979) view of a KMS can be defined to include the KM initiative driving the implementation of a KMS (also, the same logic can be applied for including OM with OMS studies). OM and OMS studies are included with KM and KMS as Jennex and Olfman (2002) found that KM and OM are essentially the same with the difference being the players. End users tend to use KM where KM is concerned with the identification and capture of key knowledge. Information systems personnel tend to be concerned with OM where OM is the storage, search, retrieval, manipulation, and presentation of knowledge. KMS and OMS are the systems built to support KM and OM, and are essentially systems designed to manage organizational knowledge.

The literature review identified many KMS success factors that are summarized below. To make sense of these factors, they were analyzed for key words and concepts and combined into generic success factors. Definitions for the generic success factors were generated by combining and simplifying the concepts included in the base success factors. The generic success factors are also presented and discussed. The generic success factors were ranked based on the number of articles the base success factors appeared in. The article concludes with a ranked list of KMS success factors.

KMS SUCCESS FACTORS

A successful KMS should perform well the functions of knowledge creation, storage and retrieval, transfer, and application. However, other factors can influence KMS success. Mandviwalla, Eulgem, Mould, and Rao (1998) summarized the state of the research and described several strategy issues affecting the design of a KMS. These include the focus of the KMS (who are the users), the quantity of knowledge to be captured and in what formats, who filters what is captured, and what reliance and/or limitations are placed on the use of individual memories.

Additional technical issues affecting KMS design include knowledge storage and repository considerations, how information and knowledge is organized so that it can be searched and linked to appropriate events and use, and processes for integrating the various repositories and for reintegrating information and knowledge extracted from specific events. Some management issues include how long the knowledge is useful, access locations as users rarely access the KMS from a single location (leads to network needs and security concerns), and the work activities and processes that utilize the KMS.

Ackerman (1994) studied six organizations that had implemented his Answer Garden system. Answer Garden is a system designed to grow organizational memory in the context of help-desk situations. Only one organization had a successful implementation because expectations of the capabilities of the system exceeded the actual capabilities. Ackerman and Mandel (1996) found that a smaller task-based system was more effective on the suborganization level because of its narrower expectations. They refer to this narrower system as "memory in the small."

Jennex and Olfman (2000) studied three KM projects to identify design recommendations for building a successful KMS. These recommendations include the following:

- Develop a good technical infrastructure by using a common network structure, adding KM skills to the technology support skill set, using high-end PCs (personal computers), integrating databases, and standardizing hardware and software across the organization.

- Incorporate the KMS into everyday processes and IS by automating knowledge capture.

- Have an enterprise-wide knowledge structure.

- Have senior management support.

- Allocate maintenance resources for the OMS.

- Train users on the use and content of the OMS.

- Create and implement a KM strategy or process for identifying and maintaining the knowledge base.

- Expand system models and life cycles to include the KMS, and assess system and process changes for impact on the KMS.

- Design security into the KMS.

- Build motivation and commitment by incorporating KMS usage into personnel evaluation processes, implementing KMS use and satisfaction metrics, and identifying organizational culture concerns that could inhibit KMS usage.

Additionally, Jennex and Olfman (2002) performed a longitudinal study of KM on one of these organizations and found that new members of an organization do not use the computerized KMS due to a lack of context for understanding the knowledge and the KMS. They found that these users needed pointers to knowledge more than codified knowledge.

Jennex, Olfman, and Addo (2003) investigated the need for having an organizational KM strategy to ensure that knowledge benefits gained from projects are captured for use in the organization by surveying year 2000 (Y2K) project leaders. They found that benefits from Y2K projects were not being captured because the parent organizations did not have a KM strategy or process. Their conclusion was that KM in projects can exist and can assist projects in utilizing knowledge during the project.

Davenport, DeLong, and Beers (1998) studied 31 projects in 24 companies. Eighteen projects were determined to be successful, five were considered failures, and eight were too new to be rated. Eight factors were identified that were common in successful KM projects. These factors are as follow:

- Senior management support.
- Clearly communicated KMS purposes and goals.
- Linkages to economic performance.
- Multiple channels for knowledge transfer.
- Motivational incentives for KM users.
- A knowledge-friendly culture.
- A solid technical and organizational infrastructure.
- A standard, flexible knowledge structure.

Malhotra and Galletta (2003) identified the critical importance of user commitment and motivation through a survey study of users of a KMS being implemented in a healthcare organization. They found that using incentives did not guarantee a successful KMS. They created an instrument for measuring user commitment and motivation that is similar to Thompson, Higgins, and Howell's (1991) perceived-benefit model, but is based on the self-determination theory that uses the perceived locus of causality.

Ginsberg and Kambil (1999) explored issues in the design and implementation of an effective KMS by building a KMS based on issues identified in the literature and then experimentally implementing the KMS in a field setting. They found knowledge representation, storage, search, retrieval, visualization, and quality control to be key technical issues, and incentives to share and use knowledge to be the key organizational issues.

Alavi and Leidner (1999) surveyed executive participants in an executive development program with respect to what was needed for a successful KMS. They found organizational and cultural issues associated with user motivation to share and use knowledge to be the most significant. They also found it important to measure the benefits of the KMS and to have an integrated and integrative technology architecture that supports database, communication, and search and retrieval functions.

Holsapple and Joshi (2000) investigated factors that influenced the management of knowledge in organizations through the use of a Delphi panel consisting of 31 recognized KM researchers and practitioners. They found leadership and top management commitment and support to be crucial. Resource influences such as having sufficient financial support, a high skill level of employees, and identified knowledge sources are also important.

Koskinen (2001) investigated tacit knowledge as a promoter of success in technology firms by studying 10 small technology firms. Key to the success of a KMS was the ability to identify, capture, and transfer critical tacit knowledge. A significant finding was that new members take a long time to learn critical tacit knowledge, and a good KMS facilitates the transference of this tacit knowledge to new members.

Barna (2003) studied six KM projects with various levels of success (three were successful, two failed, and one was an initial failure turned into a success) and identified two groups of factors important to a successful KMS. The main managerial success factor is creating and promoting a culture of knowledge sharing within the organization by articulating a corporate KM vision, rewarding employees for knowledge sharing, creating communities of practice, and creating a best-practices repository. Other managerial success factors include obtaining senior management support, creating a learning organization, providing KMS training, and precisely defining KMS project objectives.

Design and construction success factors include approaching the problem as an organizational problem and not a technical one; creating a standard knowledge submission process; having methodologies and processes for the codification, documentation, and storage of knowledge; and having processes for capturing and converting individual tacit knowledge into organizational knowledge. Also, organizations should create relevant and easily accessible knowledge-sharing databases and knowledge maps.

Cross and Baird (2000) propose that KM would not improve business performance simply by using technology to capture and share the lessons of experience. It was postulated that for KM to improve business performance, it had to increase organizational learning through the creation of organizational memory. To investigate this, 22

projects were examined. The conclusion was that improving organizational learning improved the likelihood of KM success. Factors that improved organizational learning include the following:

- Supporting personal relationships between experts and knowledge users.
- Providing incentives to motivate users to learn from experience and to use the KMS.
- Providing distributed databases to store knowledge and pointers to knowledge.
- Providing work processes for users to convert personal experience into organizational learning.
- Providing direction to what knowledge the organization needs to capture and learn from.

Sage and Rouse (1999) reflected on the history of innovation and technology and identified the following issues:

- Modeling processes to identify knowledge needs and sources.
- A KMS strategy for the identification of knowledge to capture and use, and of who will use it.
- Incentives and motivation to use the KMS.
- An infrastructure for capturing, searching, retrieving, and displaying knowledge.
- An understood enterprise knowledge structure
- Clear goals for the KMS.
- The measurement and evaluation of the effectiveness of the KMS.

Yu, Kim, and Kim (2004) explored the linkage of organizational culture to knowledge management success. They found that KM drivers such as a learning culture, knowledge-sharing intention, KMS quality, rewards, and KM team activities significantly affected KM performance. These conclusions were reached through a survey of 66 Korean firms.

DISCUSSION

These studies provide several success factors. To summarize them, they have been reviewed and paraphrased into a set of ranked success factors where the ranking is based on the number of sources citing them. Table 1 lists the final set of success factors in their rank order. Additionally, success factors SF1 through SF4 are considered the key success factors as they were mentioned by at least half of the success factor studies.

Table 1. KMS success factor summary

ID	Success Factor	Source
SF1	An integrated technical infrastructure including networks, databases/repositories, computers, software, KMS experts	Alavi and Leidner (1999), Barna (2002), Cross and Baird (2000), Davenport et al. (1998), Ginsberg and Kambil (1999), Jennex and Olfman (2000), Mandviwalla et al. (1998), Sage and Rouse (1999), Yu et al. (2004)
SF2	A knowledge strategy that identifies users, user experience-level needs, sources, processes, storage strategies, knowledge, and links to knowledge for the KMS	Barna (2002), Ginsberg and Kambil (1999), Holsapple and Joshi (2000), Jennex et al. (2003), Koskinen (2001), Mandviwalla et al. (1998), Sage and Rouse (1999), Yu et al. (2004)
SF3	A common enterprise-wide knowledge structure that is clearly articulated and easily understood	Barna (2002), Cross and Baird (2000), Davenport et al. (1998), Ginsberg and Kambil (1999), Jennex and Olfman (2000), Mandviwalla et al. (1998), Sage and Rouse (1999)
SF4	Motivation and commitment of users including incentives and training	Alavi and Leidner (1999), Barna (2002), Cross and Baird (2000), Davenport et al. (1998), Ginsberg and Kambil (1999), Jennex and Olfman (2000), Malhotra and Galletta (2003), Yu et al. (2004)
SF5	An organizational culture that supports learning and the sharing and use of knowledge	Alavi and Leidner (1999), Barna (2002), Davenport et al. (1998), Jennex and Olfman (2000), Sage and Rouse (1999), Yu et al. (2004)
SF6	Senior management support including the allocation of resources, leadership, and providing training	Barna (2002), Davenport et al. (1998), Holsapple and Joshi (2000), Jennex and Olfman (2000), Yu et al. (2004)
SF7	Measures established to assess the impacts of the KMS and the use of knowledge, as well as to verify that the right knowledge is being captured	Alavi and Leidner (1999), Davenport et al. (1998), Jennex and Olfman (2000), Sage and Rouse (1999)
SF8	A clear goal and purpose for the KMS	Ackerman (1994), Barna (2002), Cross and Baird (2000), Davenport et al. (1998)
SF9	A learning organization	Barna (2002), Cross and Baird (2000), Sage and Rouse (1999), Yu et al. (2004)
SF10	Easy knowledge use supported by the search, retrieval, and visualization functions of the KMS	Alavi and Leidner (1999), Ginsberg and Kambil (1999), Mandviwalla et al. (1998)
SF11	Work processes designed to incorporate knowledge capture and use	Barna (2002), Cross and Baird (2000), Jennex and Olfman (2000)
SF12	The security/protection of knowledge	Jennex and Olfman (2000), Sage and Rouse (1999)

FUTURE RESEARCH TRENDS

Many of the above KMS success factors were identified through qualitative research with their importance established through bibliographical analysis. Future research needs to consolidate these factors into a single KMS success-factor model. To be useful, the generated KMS success model needs to be quantitatively validated against a variety of organizations. This will improve the validity and general application of the model.

CONCLUSION

Many studies have been performed that have identified KM success factors. The summary of Table 1 is a useful summary of success factors and their importance, and is useful for researchers and practitioners. However, more research into KM and KMS success is needed. The success factors presented in this article were generated from a literature survey. The studies used for this litera-ture survey utilized a variety of methods including sur-veys, case studies, Delphi studies, and experimentation. A total of 78 projects or organizations were investigated using case studies, and approximately 100 organizations were surveyed. Overall, in addition to the case studies mentioned, four surveys were administered and one Delphi study and experiment were performed. However, this is not sufficient research to definitively state that all KM success factors have been identified and their importance determined. Only a few of the sources were able to con-duct any kind of statistical analysis or hypothesis testing, leaving a qualitative analysis basis for most of these success factors. This leaves an opportunity for research-ers.

REFERENCES

Ackerman, M. (1994). Definitional and contextual issues in organizational and group memories. *Proceedings of the 27th Annual Hawaii International Conference on System Sciences* (pp. 191-200).

Ackerman, M., & Mandel, E. (1996). Memory in the small: An application to provide task-based organizational memory for a scientific community. *Proceedings of the 29th Annual Hawaii International Conference on System Sciences* (pp. 323-332).

Alavi, M., & Leidner, D. E. (1999). Knowledge management systems: Emerging views and practices from the field. *Proceedings of the 32nd Hawaii International Conference on System Sciences*.

Alavi, M., & Leidner, D. E. (2001). Review: Knowledge management and knowledge management systems: Conceptual foundations and research issues. *MIS Quarterly, 25*(1), 107-136.

Barna, Z. (2003). *Knowledge management: A critical e-business strategic factor.* Unpublished master's thesis, San Diego State University, San Diego.

Churchman, C. W. (1979). *The systems approach* (Rev. ed.). New York: Dell Publishing.

Cross, R., & Baird, L. (2000). Technology is not enough: Improving performance by building organizational memory. *Sloan Management Review, 41*(3), 41-54.

Davenport, T. H., DeLong, D. W., & Beers, M. C. (1998). Successful knowledge management projects. *Sloan Management Review, 39*(2), 43-57.

Ginsberg, M., & Kambil, A. (1999). Annotate: A Web-based knowledge management support system for document collections. *Proceedings of the 32nd Hawaii International Conference on System Sciences*.

Holsapple, C. W., & Joshi, K. D. (2000). An investigation of factors that influence the management of knowledge in organizations. *Journal of Strategic Information Systems, 9*, 235-261.

Jennex, M. E., & Olfman, L. (2000). Development recommendations for knowledge management/organizational memory systems. *Proceedings of the Information Systems Development Conference 2000*.

Jennex, M. E., Olfman, L., & Addo, T. B. A. (2003). The need for an organizational knowledge management strategy. *Proceedings of the 36th Hawaii International Conference on System Sciences, HICSS36*.

Jennex, M. E., & Olfman, L. (2002). Organizational memory/knowledge effects on productivity: A longitudinal study. *Proceedings of the 35th Hawaii International Conference on System Sciences, HICSS35*.

Koskinen, K. U. (2001). Tacit knowledge as a promoter of success in technology firms. *Proceedings of the 34th Hawaii International Conference on System Sciences*.

Malhotra, Y., & Galletta, D. (2003). Role of commitment and motivation as antecedents of knowledge management systems implementation. *Proceedings of the 36th Hawaii International Conference on System Sciences*.

Mandviwalla, M., Eulgem, S., Mould, C., & Rao, S. V. (1998). Organizational memory systems design. Unpublished working paper for the Task Force on Organizational Memory presented at the *31st Annual Hawaii International Conference on System Sciences*.

Sage, A. P., & Rouse, W. B. (1999). Information systems frontiers in knowledge management. *Information Systems Frontiers, 1*(3), 205-219.

Thompson, R. L., Higgins, C. A., & Howell, J. M. (1991). Personal computing: Toward a conceptual model of utilization. *MIS Quarterly, 15*(1), 125-143.

Yu, S.-H., Kim, Y.-G., & Kim, M.-Y. (2004). Linking organizational knowledge management drivers to knowledge management performance: An exploratory study. *Proceedings of the 37th Hawaii International Conference on System Sciences, HICSS36*.

KEY TERMS

Knowledge Management Success: The improvement in organizational performance that comes from using knowledge as a result of a knowledge management initiative. Success can be expressed as the result of the impacts caused by the use of knowledge and/or the effective implementation of KM processes.

Knowledge Management System Success: The improvement in organizational performance that comes from using knowledge as a result of a knowledge management system. Success can be expressed as the result of the impacts caused by the use of the KMS or the effective implementation of KMS processes.

Knowledge Management System Success Factor: Anything necessary to encourage or increase the effective use of a KMS.

Knowledge Processes: The organizational processes for managing knowledge; specifically, they are the formal processes for knowledge capture and reuse, determining how the knowledge will be stored, and metrics for measuring the effectiveness of knowledge use.

Organizational Memory: The means by which knowledge from the past is brought to bear on present activities, resulting in higher or lower levels of organizational effectiveness (Stein & Zwass, 1995; Walsh & Ungson, 1991).

Organizational Memory System: The system created to capture, store, search, and retrieve knowledge from a repository.

Knowledge Management Systems

Ronald Maier
Martin-Luther-University Halle-Wittenberg, Germany

Thomas Hädrich
Martin-Luther-University Halle-Wittenberg, Germany

INTRODUCTION

Knowledge management systems (KMSs) are seen as enabling technologies for an effective and efficient knowledge management (KM). However, up to date the term knowledge management system has often been used ambiguously. Examples are its use for specific KM tools, for KM platforms, or for (a combination of) tools that are applied with KM in mind. So far, investigations about the notion of KMS remain on the abstract level of what a KMS is used for, for example, "a class of information systems applied to managing organizational knowledge" (Alavi & Leidner, 2001, p. 114). The following two sections define the term KMS and obtain a set of characteristics that differentiates KMS from traditional information systems, such as intranet infrastructures, document- and content-management systems, groupware, or e-learning systems. Then, two ideal architectures for KMS are contrasted. It is discussed which KMS architecture fits what type of KM initiatives, and some empirical findings on the state of practice of KMS are summarized. The last sections give an outlook on future trends and conclude the article.

BACKGROUND

A review of the literature on information and communication technologies to support KM reveals a number of different terms in use, such as knowledge warehouse, KM software, KM suite, KM (support) system, and KM technology as well as learning-management platform, learning-management portal, learning-management suite, learning-management system, or organizational-memory (information) system (e.g., Alavi & Leidner, 2001; Maier, 2004; McDermott, 1999; Mentzas, Apostolou, Young, & Abecker, 2001; Nedeß & Jacob, 2000; Schwartz, Divitini, & Brasethvik, 2000; Seifried & Eppler, 2000; Stein & Zwass, 1995). In addition to these terms meaning a comprehensive platform in support of KM, many authors provide more or less extensive lists of individual tools or technologies that can be used to support KM initiatives as a whole or for certain processes, life-cycle phases, or tasks thereof (e.g., Allee, 1997; Binney, 2001; Borghoff & Pareschi, 1998; Hoffmann, 2001; Jackson, 2003; Meso & Smith, 2000; Ruggles, 1998).

TOWARD A DEFINITION OF KNOWLEDGE MANAGEMENT SYSTEMS

Recently, the terms KM tools and KMS have gained wide acceptance both in the literature and on the market. Consequently, we use the term KMS being well aware that there are a number of similar conceptualizations that complement the functionality and architectures of KMS. In the following, we will summarize the most important characteristics of KMS as found in the literature.

Goals

The primary goal of KMS is to bring knowledge from the past to bear on present activities, thus resulting in increased levels of organizational effectiveness (Lewin & Minton, 1998; Stein & Zwass, 1995). Thus, a KMS is the technological part of a KM initiative that also comprises person-oriented and organizational instruments targeted at improving the productivity of knowledge work (Maier, 2004). KM initiatives can be classified according to the strategy in human-oriented personalization initiatives and technology-oriented codification initiatives (Hansen, Nohria, & Tierney, 1999). They can further be distinguished according to the scope into enterprise-specific initiatives and initiatives that cross organizational boundaries. According to organizational design, initiatives can establish a central organizational unit responsible for KM, or they can be run by a number of projects and/or communities. The initiatives can focus on a certain type of content along the knowledge life cycle, for example, ideas, experiences, lessons learned, approved knowledge products, procedures, best practices, or patents. Finally, the organizational culture can be characterized as open, trustful, or collective where willingness to share knowledge is high; or as confidential, distrustful, or individual where there are high barriers to knowledge sharing (see Maier, 2004, for a definition of and empirical results about this typology of KM initiatives). The type of initiative determines the type of KMS for its support.

Processes

KMSs are developed to support and enhance knowledge-intensive tasks, processes, or projects (Detlor, 2002; Jennex & Olfmann, 2003) of, for example, knowledge creation, organization, storage, retrieval, transfer, refinement and packaging, (re)use, revision, and feedback, also called the knowledge life cycle, ultimately to support knowledge work (Davenport, Jarvenpaa, & Beers, 1996). In this view, a KMS provides a seamless pipeline for the flow of explicit knowledge through a refinement process (Zack, 1999).

Comprehensive Platform

Whereas the focus on processes can be seen as a user-centric approach, an IT-centric approach provides a base system to capture and distribute knowledge (Jennex & Olfmann, 2003). This platform is then used throughout the organization. In this case, a KMS is not an application system targeted at a single KM initiative, but a platform that can be used either as is to support knowledge processes or as the integrating base system and repository on which KM application systems are built. Comprehensive in this case means that the platform offers functionality for user administration, messaging, conferencing, and the sharing of (documented) knowledge, that is, publishing, searching, retrieving, and presenting.

Advanced Knowledge Services

KMSs are ICT platforms on which a number of integrated services are built. The processes that have to be supported give a first indication of the types of services that are needed. Examples are rather basic services, for example, collaboration, work-flow management, document and content management, visualization, search, and retrieval (e.g., Seifried & Eppler, 2000); or more advanced services, for example, personalization, text analysis, clustering and categorization to increase the relevance of retrieved and pushed information, advanced graphical techniques for navigation, awareness services, shared work spaces, and (distributed) learning services as well as the integration of and reasoning about various (document) sources on the basis of a shared ontology (e.g., Bair, 1998; Borghoff & Pareschi, 1998; Maier, 2004).

KM Instruments

KMSs are applied in a large number of application areas (Tsui, 2003) and specifically support KM instruments, such as (a) the capture, creation, and sharing of good or best practices, (b) the implementation of experience-management systems, (c) the creation of corporate knowledge directories, taxonomies, or ontologies, (d) competency management, (e) collaborative filtering and handling of interests used to connect people, (f) the creation and fostering of communities or knowledge networks, or (g) the facilitation of intelligent problem solving (e.g., Alavi & Leidner, 2001; McDermott, 1999; Tsui, 2003). Thus, KMSs offer a targeted combination and integration of knowledge services that together foster one or more KM instruments.

Specifics of Knowledge

KMSs are applied to managing knowledge that is described as "personalized information…related to facts, procedures, concepts, interpretations, ideas, observations, and judgements" (Alavi & Leidner, 2001). From the perspective of KMS, knowledge is information that is meaningfully organized, accumulated, and embedded in a context of creation and application. KMSs primarily leverage codified knowledge, but also aid communication or inference used to interpret situations and to generate activities, behaviour, and solutions. KMSs help to assimilate contextualized information, provide access to sources of knowledge, and, with the help of shared context, increase the breadth of knowledge sharing between persons rather than storing knowledge itself (Alavi & Leidner, 2001).

Participants

The internal context of knowledge describes the circumstances of its creation. The external context relates to the retrieval and application of knowledge (Barry & Schamber, 1998; Eppler, 2003). Contextualization is one of the key characteristics of KMS (Apitz, Lattner, & Schäffer, 2002) that provides a semantic link between explicit, codified knowledge and the persons that hold or seek knowledge in certain subject areas. Thus, it creates a network of artifacts and people, of memory and of processing (Ackerman & Halverson, 1998). Decontextualization and recontextualization turn static knowledge objects into knowledge processes (Ackerman & Halverson, 1998). Meta-knowledge in a KMS is sometimes as important as the original knowledge itself (Alavi & Leidner, 2001). Therefore, users play the roles of active, involved participants in the knowledge network fostered by KMS.

Figure 1. Characteristics of KMS

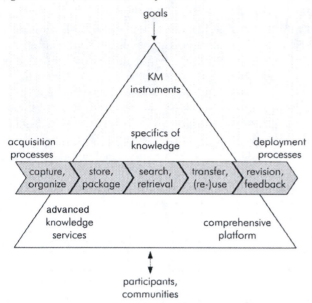

In addition to the previous characteristics, a KMS has to be aligned with the specifics of its application environment, the goals, and the types of KM initiatives as well as the acquisition and deployment processes required for managing knowledge (see Figure 1).

Consequently, a KMS is defined as a comprehensive ICT platform for collaboration and knowledge sharing with advanced knowledge services built on top that are contextualized and integrated on the basis of a shared ontology, and personalized for participants networked in communities. KMSs foster the implementation of KM instruments in support of knowledge processes targeted at increasing organizational effectiveness.

Actual implementations of ICT systems certainly fulfill the characteristics of an ideal KMS only to a certain degree. Thus, a continuum between traditional IS and advanced KMS might be imagined with minimal requirements providing some orientation (see Maier & Hädrich, 2004).

ARCHITECTURES FOR KNOWLEDGE MANAGEMENT SYSTEMS

There are basically two ideal types of architectures of KMS: centralistic KMS and peer-to-peer (p2p) KMS.

Many KMS solutions implemented in organizations and offered on the market are centralistic client-server solutions (Maier, 2004). Figure 2 shows an ideal layered architecture for KMS that represents an amalgamation of theory-driven (e.g., Apitz et al., 2002; Zack, 1999),

market-oriented (e.g., Applehans, Globe, & Laugero, 1999; Bach, Vogler, & Österle, 1999), and vendor-specific architectures (e.g., Hyperwave, Open Text Livelink). A thorough analysis of these architectures and the process of amalgamation can be found in Maier, 2004. The ideal architecture is oriented toward the metaphor of a central KM server that integrates all knowledge shared in an organization and offers a variety of services to the participant or to upward layers (see Figure 2).

Data and knowledge sources include organization-internal as well as organization-external sources, and sources of structured as well as semi-structured information and knowledge.

Infrastructure services provide basic functionality for synchronous and asynchronous communication, sharing of data and documents as well as the management of electronic assets. Extraction, transformation, and loading tools provide access to data and knowledge sources. Inspection services (viewers) are required for heterogeneous data and document formats.

Integration services help to meaningfully organize and link knowledge elements from a variety of sources by means of an ontology. They are used to analyze the semantics of the organizational knowledge base and to manage metadata about knowledge elements and users. Synchronization services export and (re)integrate a portion of the knowledge work space for work off-line.

Figure 2. Architecture of a centralized KMS

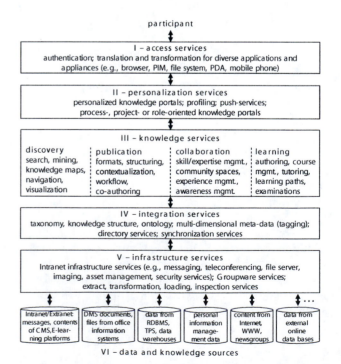

Knowledge services provide intelligent functions for discovery, that is, the search, retrieval, and presentation of knowledge elements and experts; publication, that is, the structuring, contextualization, and release of knowledge elements; collaboration, the joint creation, sharing, and application of knowledge; and learning, the authoring that is supported by tools and tools for managing courses, tutoring, learning paths, and examinations as well as the reflection on learning and knowledge processes established in the organization (commonly referred to as double-loop learning; see Argyris & Schön, 1978).

Personalization services provide more effective access to the large amounts of knowledge elements. Subject-matter specialists or managers of knowledge processes can organize a portion of the KMS contents and services for specific roles or develop role-oriented push services. The services can be personalized with the help of, for example, (automated) interest profiles, personal category nets, and personalized portals.

Access services transform contents and communication to and from the KMS to fit heterogeneous applications and appliances. The KMS has to be protected against eavesdropping and unauthorized use by tools for authentication and authorization.

Recently, the peer-to-peer (p2p) metaphor has gained increasing attention from both academics and practitioners (e.g., Barkai, 1998; Schoder, Fischbach, & Teichmann, 2002). There have been several attempts to

design information-sharing systems or even KMSs to profit from the benefits of this metaphor (Benger, 2003; Maier & Sametinger, 2004; Parameswaran, Susarla, & Whinston, 2001; Susarla, Liu, & Whinston, 2003). This promises to resolve some of the shortcomings of centralized KMS, for example:

- to reduce the costs of the design, implementation, and maintenance of a centralized knowledge server,
- to overcome the limitations of a KMS that focuses on organization-internal knowledge whereas many knowledge processes cross organizational boundaries,
- to reduce the barriers to actively participate and share in the benefits of a KMS, and
- to seamlessly integrate the shared knowledge work space with personal knowledge work spaces and messaging objects.

However, there is no common architecture or an agreed list of functions yet for this type of KMS. Generally, the p2p label is used for different architectures, for example, pure p2p architectures or hybrid architectures such as assisted and super p2p architectures (e.g., Dustdar, Gall, & Hauswirth, 2003). The more functionality for central coordination that is required in a p2p system, as is the case in a KMS, the more likely it is

Figure 3. Architecture of server and peer

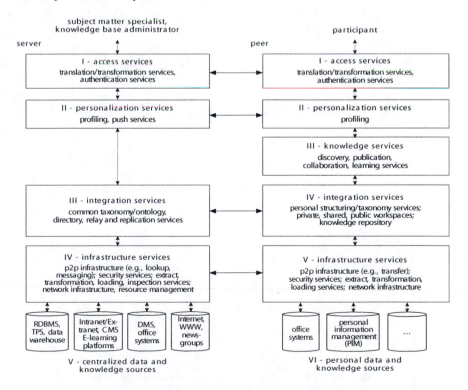

that some kind of assistance by a server is needed to coordinate the system (hybrid architecture). Still, the difference to the centralized architecture is that p2p systems allow users to develop personal knowledge bases locally and to directly share knowledge with other peers without the need to design a shared space on a server. Figure 3 depicts the architecture of a peer and a server to assist the network. Both architectures basically consist of the same layers as the architecture of the centralized KMS.

The differences between a single peer's architecture and the centralistic architecture are the following:

- Infrastructure services handle personal data and knowledge sources and provide the p2p infrastructure for locating peers, exchanging data with other peers, and assuring the security of the personal knowledge base.

- Integration services handle the meta-data of the knowledge objects in the personal knowledge base and establish a personal ontology. Private work spaces contain information that is only accessible by its owner. Public work spaces hold knowledge objects that are published via the Internet. Protected work spaces contain knowledge objects that are accessible by a single peer or a group of peers that the owner explicitly grants access to.

- Knowledge services build upon the knowledge base, just as in the centralized case. The knowledge repository is now spread across a number of collaborating peers.

- Personalization services build on individual user profiles and on centralized personalization services provided by the server.

- Access services are similar to those in the centralized KMS architecture.

The differences between a server's architecture and the centralistic architecture are the following:

- Infrastructure services enable a server to access a number of additional shared data and knowledge sources. He provides services for lookup and message handling that improve the efficiency of the p2p infrastructure.

- Integration services offer a shared ontology for the domain handled by, for example, a network of subject-matter specialists. This addresses the challenge in a distributed KMS that the personal knowledge bases cannot be integrated without a mapping of ontologies. The server might offer replication services to peers that sometimes work off line.

- There are no central knowledge services in addition to the peers' services.

- Personalization services include profiles and push services that ease in accessing the organized collection of (quality-approved or even-improved) knowledge that the subject-matter specialists administer.

- Access services are restricted to the administration of the server, the central knowledge structure, and the profiles for personalization.

DISCUSSION

Centralized KMSs offered on the market differ with respect to the extent and intensity with which they cover the services included in the centralized architecture. Some focus on learning management (e.g., Hyperwave), integration (e.g., Lotus Notes/Workspace), discovery (e.g., Verity K2 Enterprise), publication (e.g., Open Text Livelink), collaboration (e.g., Quovix CommunityBuilder), or on access and personalization (portal solutions, e.g., Plumtree Corporate Portal, SAP Enterprise Portal). In addition to several research prototypes (e.g., Benger, 2003; Maier & Sametinger, 2004), Groove Networks Groove is an example for a p2p collaboration tool that is readily available on the market and at least offers some of the functions that are needed in KM (Maier & Hädrich, 2004).

Table 1 shows for what type of KM initiative centralized and p2p KMSs are suited. Consequently, a centralized KMS seems to be more adequate for a KM initiative

Table 1. Type of KMS and type of KM initiative

characteristics	centralized KMS	p2p-KMS
strategy	codification	personalization
organizational design	central	decentralized
content	primarily lessons learned, (approved) knowledge products, and secured knowledge, but also ideas, experiences, and individual contents	individual contents, ideas, and results of group sessions and experiences
organizational culture	both types of culture (restrictive or loose user privileges)	open, trustful culture

that can be described as a codification initiative restricted to the organization's boundaries and managed by a central organizational unit that fosters the handling of all types of knowledge. A p2p information-sharing system targets a KM initiative that can be described as a personalization initiative involving members from a number of institutions. Thus, the initiative is managed decentrally, requiring an open, trustful, collective organizational culture and a focus on the exchange of individual knowledge, ideas, and experiences.

However, there are still serious technical challenges that have to be overcome in p2p computing in general. These challenges concern connectivity, security, and privacy, especially the risk of spreading viruses, unauthorized access to confidential and private information, the installation of unwanted applications, fault tolerance, availability, and scalability (Barkai, 1998). There are also organizational issues that have to be resolved before a p2p KMS can be fully deployed in an organization, for example, the coordination issue, meaning that structuring and quality management of the knowledge contained in a p2p network have to be supported.

In the following, the state of practice of KMS is summarized in the form of theses that describe activities concerning KMS in German-speaking countries as investigated in an empirical study conducted by one of the authors (Maier, 2004).

1. Almost all large organizations have an intranet and/or groupware platform in place that offers a solid foundation for KMS. These platforms, together with a multitude of extensions and add-on tools, provide good basic KM functionality, for example, the easy sharing of documents and access to company information.

2. Large organizations have also already implemented KM-specific functions. Most rely on the centralized KMS architecture, but many experiment with p2p solutions. Many of the implemented functions are not used intensively, in some cases due to technical problems, but mostly because they require substantial organizational changes and significant administrative effort.

3. The majority of organizations relies on organization-specific developments and combinations of tools and systems rather than on standard KMS solutions. The market for KMS solutions is a confusing and dynamic one, and integration with existing systems is often difficult. Organizations might also fear the loss of strategic advantages if they exchange their homegrown KMS solutions for standard software.

4. There has been a strong emphasis on explicit, documented knowledge. This is not surprising as in many cases large amounts of documents have already existed in electronic form, and improved handling of documents and the redesign of corresponding business processes can quickly improve organizational effectiveness. Recently, there has been a trend toward collaboration and learning functions because technical requirements for media-rich electronic communication can now be met at reasonable costs.

5. Comprehensive KMSs are highly complex ICT systems because of (a) the technical complexity of advanced knowledge services and of large volumes of data, documents, messages, and links as well as contextualization and personalization data, (b) the organizational complexity of a solution that affects business and knowledge processes throughout the organization, and (c) human complexity due to the substantial change in habits, roles, and responsibilities that is required as KMSs have to be integrated into daily practices of knowledge work.

6. In many organizations, a multitude of partial systems is developed without a common framework that could integrate them. Some organizations also build enterprise knowledge portals that at least integrate access to ICT systems relevant for the KM initiative. Only recently have comprehensive and integrated KMSs offered functionality integrated within one system and realized the vision of an enterprise knowledge infrastructure (Maier, Hädrich & Peinl, 2005).

FUTURE TRENDS

Generally, there has been a shift in the perspective of KMS vendors as well as organizations applying those systems from a focus on documents containing knowledge, and thus from a pure codification strategy, to a combination and integration of functions for handling internal and external contexts, locating experts, managing competency, and so forth that bridges the gap to a personalization strategy (Maier, 2004). Advanced functions supporting collaboration in teams and communities, tools linking knowledge providers and seekers, and e-learning functionality have been integrated into many centralized KMSs. This trend will continue as many organizations strive to profit from the promised benefits of comprehensive ICT platforms for the increase of productivity of knowledge work and, consequently, of organizational effectiveness.

CONCLUSION

This article has studied the notion of the term KMS. Ideal architectures for centralized and peer-to-peer KMSs were contrasted. Each of these architectures targets a different type of KM initiative. Summing up, it seems that centralized KMSs offered on the market more and more live up to the expectations of organizations ready to apply ICT to support a KM initiative. Peer-to-peer KMSs promise to resolve some of the shortcomings of centralized KMS, especially concerning the time-consuming effort to build and maintain a central knowledge repository. However, major challenges still lie ahead until peer-to-peer systems can truly be called KMSs and can be used to support the still-growing share of users involved in knowledge work.

There seem to be four main approaches to deploying KMSs in organizations: (a) A KMS can be seen as a general infrastructure that supports knowledge work throughout the organization, (b) business processes, projects, and/or theme-oriented activities are the nexus of knowledge and thus are specifically targeted by KMSs, (c) communities and knowledge networks can be fostered by ICT, which aids knowledge sharing throughout the life cycle of these organizational entities, and (d) certain types of knowledge, for example, lessons learned and best practices, can be at the core of the design of a KMS.

REFERENCES

Ackerman, M. S., & Halverson, C. (1998). Considering an organization's memory. *Proceedings of ACM 1998 Conference on Computer Supported Cooperative Work* (pp. 39-48).

Alavi, M., & Leidner, D. E. (2001). Review: Knowledge management and knowledge management systems: Conceptual foundations and research issues. *MIS Quarterly, 25*(1), 107-136.

Allee, V. (1997). *The knowledge evolution: Expanding organizational intelligence.* Boston: Butterworth-Heinemann.

Apitz, R., Lattner, A., & Schäffer, C. (2002). Kontextbasiertes Wissensmanagement in der Produktentwicklung als Grundlage für anpassungsfähige Unternehmen. *Industrie Management, 18*(3), 32-35.

Applehans, W., Globe, A., & Laugero, G. (1999). *Managing knowledge: A practical Web-based approach.* Reading, MA: Addison-Wesley.

Argyris, C., & Schön, D. (1978). *Organizational learning: A theory of action perspective.* Reading, MA: Addison-Wesley.

Bach, V., Vogler, P., & Österle, H. (Eds.). (1999). *Business Knowledge Management: Praxiserfahrungen mit Intranet-basierten Lösungen.* Berlin, Germany: Springer.

Bair, J. (1998). *Dimensions of KM technology selection* (Rep. No. T-05-0592). Stamford, CT: Gartner Group.

Barkai, D. (1998). *Peer-to-peer computing: Technologies for sharing and collaborating on the Net.* Hillsboro, OR: Intel Press.

Barry, C. L., & Schamber, L. (1998). Users' criteria for relevance evaluation: A cross-situational comparison. *Information Processing & Management, 34*(2-3), 219-236.

Benger, A. (2003). Dezentrales, selbstorganisierendes Wissensmanagement. In N. Gronau (Ed.), Wissensmanagement: Potenziale, Konzepte, Werkzeuge. *Proceedings of the 4th Oldenburg Conference on Knowledge Management* (pp. 155-170). Berlin, Germany: Gito.

Binney, D. (2001). The knowledge management spectrum: Understanding the KM landscape. *Journal of Knowledge Management, 5*(1), 33-42.

Borghoff, U. M., & Pareschi, R. (Eds.). (1998). *Information technology for knowledge management.* Berlin, Germany: Springer.

Davenport, T. H., Jarvenpaa, S. L., & Beers, M. C. (1996). Improving knowledge work processes. *Sloan Management Review, 37*(4), 53-65.

Detlor, B. (2002). An informational perspective towards knowledge work: Implications for knowledge management systems. In D. White (Ed.), *Knowledge mapping and management* (pp. 195-205). Hershey, PA: IRM Press.

Dustdar, S., Gall, H., & Hauswirth, M. (2003). Peer-to-Peer-Architekturen. In S. Dustdar, H. Gall, & M. Hauswirth (Eds.), *Software-Architekturen für verteilte Systeme* (pp. 161-198). Berlin, Germany: Springer.

Eppler, M. J. (2003). *Managing information quality: Increasing the value of information in knowledge-intensive products and processes.* Berlin, Germany: Springer.

Hansen, M. T., Nohria, N., & Tierney, T. (1999). What's your strategy for managing knowledge? *Harvard Business Review, 77*(3-4), 106-116.

Hoffmann, I. (2001). Knowledge management tools. In K. Mertins, P. Heisig, & J. Vorbeck (Eds.), *Knowledge man-*

agement: Best practices in Europe (pp. 74-94). Berlin, Germany: Springer.

Jackson, C. (2003). *Process to product: Creating tools for knowledge management.* Retrieved October 15, 2004, from *http://www.brint.com/members/online/120205/jackson/*

Jennex, M., & Olfmann, L. (2003). Organizational memory. In C. W. Holsapple (Ed.), *Handbook on knowledge management: Vol. 2. Knowledge directions* (pp. 207-234). Berlin, Germany: Springer.

Lewin, A. Y., & Minton, J. W. (1998). Determining organizational effectiveness: Another look, and an agenda for research. *Management Science, 32*(5), 514-553.

Maier, R. (2004). *Knowledge management systems: Information and communication technologies for knowledge management* (2nd ed.). Berlin, Germany: Springer.

Maier, R., & Hädrich, T. (2004). Centralized versus peer-to-peer knowledge management systems. Paper presented at the *5th European Conference on Organizational Knowledge, Learning and Capabilities (OKLC)*, Innsbruck.

Maier, R., Hädrich, T., Peinl, R. (2005). *Enterprise Knowledge Infrastructures*. Berlin, Germany: Springer.

Maier, R., & Sametinger, J. (2004). Peer-to-peer information workspaces in Infotop. *International Journal of Software Engineering and Knowledge Engineering, 14*(1), 79-102.

McDermott, R. (1999). Why information technology inspired but cannot deliver knowledge management. *California Management Review, 41*(4), 103-117.

Mentzas, G., Apostolou, D., Young, R., & Abecker, A. (2001). Knowledge networking: A holistic solution for leveraging corporate knowledge. *Journal of Knowledge Management, 5*(1), 94-106.

Meso, P., & Smith, R. (2000). A resource-based view of organizational knowledge management systems. *Journal of Knowledge Management, 4*(3), 224-234.

Nedeß, C., & Jacob, U. (2000). Das Knowledge Warehouse vor der Gefahr der Komplexitätsfalle. In H. Krallmann (Ed.), *Wettbewerbsvorteile durch Wissensmanagement: Methodik und Anwendungen des Knowledge Management* (pp. 91-116). Stuttgart, Germany: Schäffer-Poeschel.

Parameswaran, M., Susarla, A., & Whinston, A. B. (2001). P2P networking: An information sharing alternative. *IEEE Computer, 34*(7), 1-8.

Ruggles, R. L. (1998). The state of the notion: Knowledge management in practice. *California Management Review, 40*(3), 80-89.

Schoder, D., Fischbach, K., & Teichmann, R. (Eds.). (2002). *Peer-to-peer.* Berlin, Germany: Springer.

Schwartz, D. G., Divitini, M., & Brasethvik, T. (2000). On knowledge management in the Internet age. In D. G. Schwartz, M. Divitini, & T. Brasethvik (Eds.), *Internet-based organizational memory and knowledge management* (pp. 1-23). Hershey, PA: IGP.

Seifried, P., & Eppler, M. J. (2000). *Evaluation führender Knowledge Management Suites: Wissensplattformen im Vergleich.* St. Gallen, Switzerland: Net Academy Press.

Stein, E., & Zwass, V. (1995). Actualizing organizational memory with information systems. *Information Systems Research, 6*(2), 85-117.

Susarla, A., Liu, D., & Whinston, A. B. (2003). Peer-to-peer enterprise knowledge management. In C. W. Holsapple (Ed.), *Handbook on knowledge management: Vol. 2. Knowledge directions* (pp. 129-139). Berlin, Germany: Springer.

Tsui, E. (2003). Tracking the role and evolution of commercial knowledge management software. In C. W. Holsapple (Ed.), *Handbook on knowledge management: Vol. 2. Knowledge directions* (pp. 5-27). Berlin, Germany: Springer.

Zack, M. H. (1999). Managing codified knowledge. *Sloan Management Review, 40*(4), 45-58.

KEY TERMS

Architecture: Used to describe the basic building blocks, functions, interfaces, and relationships of complex systems on an abstract level of detail. It is also used as a blueprint or reference model for implementing information systems, for example, enterprise architectures, information-system architectures, or software architectures.

Knowledge Management Initiative: A systematic effort in the form of a project, for example, that aims at generally fostering KM and specifically implementing a KM instrument in an organization.

Knowledge Management Instrument: A bundle of measures encompassing organization, human resources, and ICT with the goal of improving organizational effectiveness. The support of KM instruments distinguishes KMS from more traditional ICT.

Knowledge Management System: A comprehensive ICT platform for collaboration and knowledge sharing with advanced knowledge services built on top that are contextualized and integrated on the basis of a shared ontology, and personalized for participants networked in communities. KMSs foster the implementation of KM instruments in support of knowledge processes targeted at increasing organizational effectiveness.

Knowledge Process: A service process supporting the flow of knowledge within and between knowledge-intensive business processes. Knowledge processes comprise a number of functions on knowledge, for example, capture, organization, storage, packaging, search, retrieval, transportation, (re)use, revision, and feedback, and they can be supported by KMS.

Knowledge Work: Creative work solving unstructured problems that can be characterized by a high degree of variety and exceptions, strong communication needs, weakly structured processes, teamwork in the form of project teams, networks and communities, and a high level of skill and expertise that require advanced ICT support.

Peer-to-Peer: Denotes the idea of a network of equals (peers) that provide resources such as CPU time, storage area, bandwidth, or information to each other so that collaborative processes are enabled avoiding a central coordinating instance.

Knowledge Organizations

Daniel L. Davenport
University of Kentucky Chandler Medical Center, USA

Clyde W. Holsapple
University of Kentucky, USA

INTRODUCTION

An important endeavor within the field of knowledge management (KM) is to better understand the nature of knowledge organizations. These are variously called knowledge-based organizations, knowledge-centric organizations, knowledge-intensive organizations, knowledge-oriented organizations, and so forth. One approach to doing so is to study the characteristics of specific organizations of this type such as Chaparral Steel (Leonard-Barton, 1995), Buckman Labs, World Bank, or HP Consulting (O'Dell, 2003). A complementary approach is to study various frameworks that have been advanced for systematically characterizing the elements, processes, and relationships that are found in knowledge organizations. Here, we examine three such frameworks that are representative of the variety in perspectives that have been advocated for understanding the nature of knowledge organizations. These frameworks share a view that sees knowledge as a key organizational asset that enables action. However, they differ in emphases (e.g., asset vs. action) and constructs.

This article is organized as a systematic review of the three frameworks. The content relies heavily on the original presentations found in the referenced publications. Space limitations do not permit a comparative analysis or synthesis of the frameworks. Nevertheless, taken together, the reviews do offer valuable vantage points for studying knowledge organizations and useful departure points for more detailed consideration of these as well as other frameworks concerned with knowledge organizations.

The Intangible Assets Framework of Knowledge Organizations, as developed by Karl Sveiby (1997), is considered first. It relies on the concept of intangible assets and characterizes companies for whom these assets are important. Second, the Knowledge Management Cycle Framework introduced by Wiig, de Hoog, and van der Spek (1997) emphasizes the cyclical nature and means of managing an organization's knowledge assets. Third, the Knowledge Flow Framework advanced by Newman (2003) emphasizes flows of knowledge

assets in the sense of agents performing transformations on knowledge-bearing artifacts.

Each framework description starts with a brief overview of the framework from the perspective of its creator(s). It continues by describing and defining the elements, processes, and relationships of the framework in encyclopedic format. Additional references to related works by other authors also are provided for readers who wish to further explore the framework's perspective. Where pictorial renditions of a framework are available, they are reproduced to visually tie together the concepts.

BACKGROUND

Frameworks are cognitive structures used to organize our thinking about a particular domain of interest. They give us concepts pertaining to the domain and guidance about relationships among those concepts, thereby forming a basic understanding of what is observed in a domain, for formulating new ideas about a domain, and for operating or managing in a domain. As such, KM frameworks are useful to academicians in framing research and building theory, to practitioners in learning about and executing KM, and to educators for organizing and presenting KM. Here, the KM domain of interest involves knowledge organizations.

The notion of organizations that explicitly recognize and cultivate knowledge as a key resource began to gain prominence in the 1980s (Holsapple & Whinston, 1987; Paradice & Courtney, 1989). It was seen as being on a par with the traditional organizational resources of people, materials, and finances. Knowledge was seen as pervading all functional areas of organizational management from strategy to operations, from human resources to technological systems, from economics and accounting to finance and marketing. The processing of an organization's knowledge resources was seen as an important (or even indispensable) aspect of nearly all organizational work. A confluence of forces led to the widespread rise of knowledge organizations in the 1990s, and the accompanying interest in more fully understanding these organizations and their possibilities (Bennet & Bennet, 2003).

Growing out of this interest, various frameworks of the knowledge organization have been advanced by researchers and practitioners. Although we do not exhaustively survey them here, we do review three that represent a diversity of views about an organization's knowledge assets and its use of those assets. Thus, the article serves as an introduction to the realm of knowledge organization frameworks and a foundation for review, comparison, and contrast of perspectives on organizational knowledge assets and their utilization.

AN INTANGIBLE ASSETS FRAMEWORK OF KNOWLEDGE ORGANIZATIONS

Within the intangible assets (IA) framework, people are the only true agents in business. All assets and structures, whether tangible or intangible, are seen as being the result of human actions. The intangible assets of an organization are those embedded in the competences of its human resources and in its internal and external structures of interactions among these people. Knowledge organizations are those for which the greatest value lies in intangible assets (Sveiby, 1997).

Knowledge and Intangible Assets

The IA framework regards knowledge as being the capacity to take action. It is seen as tacit, action-oriented, supported by rules, and constantly changing (Sveiby, 1997). These assets are invisible in the sense that there is typically no accounting for them. They are intangible in that they are neither brick, nor mortar, nor money. They are comprised of two components: the competences of the organization's personnel and the organizational structures (internal and external) that allow them to interact (Sveiby, 1997). The IA framework does not regard structures as objects, but rather as being constructed in a constant process by people interacting with each other (Weick, 1995). They are not statically visible, but are events that link together. Knowledge management, based on the IA view, is "the art of creating value from intangible assets" (Sveiby, 1997, p. 1).

Knowledge Organizations

The IA framework conceives of knowledge organizations as having relatively few tangible assets, and having intangible assets that exceed tangible assets in value. In Figure 1, the dark line separates the visible and tangible from the invisible and intangible. The professional services or business services sector is a close equivalent of knowledge organizations (e.g., DeTore & Balliet-Milholland, 2003). Most employees of these companies are highly qualified and highly educated professionals, that is, they are knowledge workers. Their work consists largely of using their own competencies to produce or transfer knowledge, sometimes with the assistance of suppliers of information or specialized knowledge (Sveiby, 1997).

As indicated in Figure 2, the IA focus in a knowledge organization is on the key concepts of employee competence, internal structure, and external structure. They are defined as follows:

- **Individual competence:** Employee competence involves the capacity to act in a wide variety of situations to create both tangible and intangible assets. Individual competence is comprised of five interdependent elements: (1) explicit knowledge, (2) skill, (3) experience, (4) value judgments, and (5) social network (Sveiby, 1997).
- **Internal structure:** Internal structure includes patents, concepts, models, and computer and administrative systems. These are created by the employees and are generally owned by the organization. However, they may be acquired elsewhere. In addition, organizational culture is part of the internal structure, as are management, legal structure, manual systems, attitudes, and R&D software (Sveiby, 1997).
- **External structure:** External structure includes relationships with customers and suppliers. It also encompasses brand names, trademarks, and the company's reputation or image. In the IA framework, to manage the external structure is to manage the flows of knowledge in customer and supplier relationships (Sveiby, 1997).

Value is created through knowledge transfers and conversions between and within these three elements. A knowledge organization would not exist if not for their

Figure 1. The balance sheet of a knowledge (Sveiby, 1997)

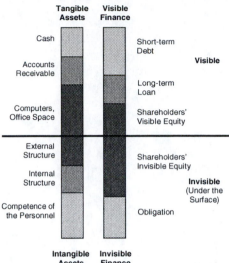

Figure 2. The organization from a knowledge-based organization perspective (Sveiby, 2001)

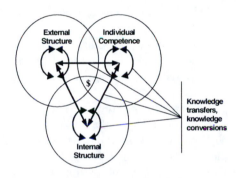

personnel with competences in handling knowledge assets, internal structure that allows them to collaborate, and external structure that allow customers and suppliers to support and enhance their knowledge bases. For a knowledge organization, external structures are based not so much on financial flows as on knowledge flows involving intangible assets.

Personnel Categories in Knowledge Organizations

The IA framework categorizes personnel within a knowledge organization along two dimensions according to levels of professional and organizational competence. This yields the four categories shown in Figure 3, which are defined as follows (Sveiby, 1997, pp. 57-60):

- **Support staff:** "The support staff assists both the professionals and the managers. They have no spe-

cial qualifications of their own to give them status in a knowledge organization."

- **Professionals:** "The most highly skilled professionals—the experts—are the genuine income generators. Experts are characterized by a dedication to their jobs and their professions, a love of solving problems, and a dislike of routine."
- **Managers:** "Managers are in many ways the opposite of professionals. They are capable of managing and organizing, have learned to work through other people, and enjoy doing so."
- **Leaders:** Leaders are the people whom others want to follow. They are informally "appointed" by their followers. "Leadership involves two tasks: deciding where the organization should go and persuading others to follow. The most successful leaders of knowledge organizations are usually former experts, but they are rarely the most outstanding experts."

Ensuring suitable quantities, degrees of competence, and interaction structures for these four personnel categories, as well as the appropriateness of the mix among the categories, strongly influence a knowledge organization's performance and viability over time.

Further Reading

More information on this Intangible Assets Framework of Knowledge Organizations can be found at www.sveiby.com and Sveiby (2001). Related perspectives on the knowledge organization that emphasize intangible assets are found in Stewart (1997), Davenport and Prusak (1998), and Teece (2003).

A KNOWLEDGE MANAGEMENT CYCLE FRAMEWORK

Whereas the IA framework focuses on intangible knowledge assets in people and structures, the Knowledge Management Cycle Framework emphasizes the use of

Figure 3. Four personnel categories in knowledge organizations (Sveiby, 1997)

Figure 4. The knowledge management cycle (Wiig, de Hoog, & van der Spek, 1997)

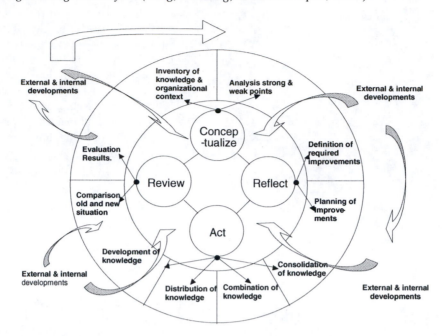

knowledge assets. A knowledge organization is viewed as manifesting a cyclic process of four activities: review, conceptualize, reflect, and act. During the cycle, analysis, plans, and actions are formulated in terms of four basic operations on knowledge that can be executed in organizations: development, distribution, consolidation, and combination.

Basic Concepts

The Knowledge Management Cycle Framework, illustrated in Figure 4, provides a model for how a knowledge organization's knowledge assets are used. Observe that the cycle proceeds in a clockwise fashion and that it can be impacted by both external and internal influences. The frameworks' specific definitions of terms are given in Figure 4 (Wiig, de Hoog, & van der Spek, 1997).

- **Review:** In this phase, a knowledge organization monitors and evaluates its performance. Review involves comparing old situations with the new, and evaluating the results of improvement plans relative to original goals and objectives.
- **Conceptualize:** This part of the cycle involves selecting a knowledge resource in the organization, and analyzing its strong and weak points. This analysis includes developing an understanding of the ways in which knowledge assets are bound to organizational roles participating in business processes.

- **Reflect:** Reflection is concerned with defining and deciding on knowledge management improvement plans. It includes developing the "optimal" plans for correcting knowledge bottlenecks and analyzing them for risks that accompany their implementation.
- **Act:** The final phase of the cycle implements plans chosen in the reflect phase. According to the framework, actions entail four basic operations on knowledge assets: development, distribution, consolidation, and combination (Wiig, de Hoog, & van der Spek, 1997).
- **Development:** Development of knowledge assets is said to occur through purchase, learning programs, and machine-based learning from databases.
- **Distribution:** Distribution is delivering knowledge assets to the points of action through knowledge-based systems, manuals, and network connections.
- **Consolidation:** This operation is described as taking steps to prevent an organization's knowledge assets from disappearing. It includes the knowledge-based systems, tutoring programs, and knowledge transfer programs.
- **Combination:** In this framework, combination refers to finding synergies among and reusing existing knowledge assets.

Within any iteration of the knowledge cycle, the organization takes action based on its knowledge assets.

It is through knowledge cycle iterations that an organization's knowledge asset base is enhanced, thereby improving performance and viability of the knowledge organization.

Further Reading

More information about this Knowledge Management Cycle Framework can be found in van der Spek and de Hoog (1995), de Hoog et al. (1999), and van der Spek and Spijkervet (1995). In a related vein, a seven-phase knowledge life cycle has been advanced by APQC and Arthur Anderson: share, create, identify, collect, adapt, organize, apply (O'Dell & Grayson, 1997). Moreover, one portion of the KM ontology deals with specific kinds of manipulations that a knowledge organization can perform on knowledge resources in the context of KM episodes rather than KM cycles (Holsapple & Joshi, 2004).

A KNOWLEDGE FLOW FRAMEWORK

The Knowledge Flow Framework advanced by Newman presents "the foundations for a basic understanding of knowledge flows, agents, artifacts, and transformations critical to any examination of knowledge processing. In doing so, it attempts to bridge the gap between a conceptual understanding of how knowledge contributes to corporate objectives, and the practical issues of knowledge management and knowledge engineering" (Newman, 2003, p. 301). As such, it furnishes a unifying vision for some of the concepts provided by the other two frameworks. This framework focuses on enablers for organizational process tasks, rather than concentrating on knowledge assets or on sequences of knowledge utilization phases. It serves as a basis for analyzing knowledge flows that permeate a knowledge organization.

Knowledge Flows

Knowledge flows are "sequences of transformations performed by agents on knowledge artifacts in support of specific actions or decisions" (Newman, 2003, p. 304). As depicted in Figure 5, these include knowledge creation, retention, transfer, and utilization flows.

Agents

Agents are specialized objects or roles played by people, organizations, societies, automata, and so forth. They are the knowledge processors within a knowledge organization and are the active components in knowledge flows (Newman, 2003):

- **Individual agents:** The framework defines these as being human processors. They sit at the center of every knowledge flow and can deal with tacit artifacts that automated agents cannot.
- **Automated agents:** Automated agents are non-human processors. They are "any human construct that is capable of retaining, transferring, or transforming knowledge artifacts. They are not exclusively computers, e.g. a camera....They can perform many types of transformations on explicit artifacts much faster and with a greater degree of repeatability than can individual agents" (Newman, 2003, pp. 308-309).
- **Collective agents:** Newman (2003) defines these as specific collection of individual and automated agents. They are not necessarily homogeneous and may exhibit characteristics unexhibitable by any single agent. They may possess "group"-level tacit knowledge and may retain knowledge beyond the life of any individual or automated agent.

Figure 5. Knowledge flows

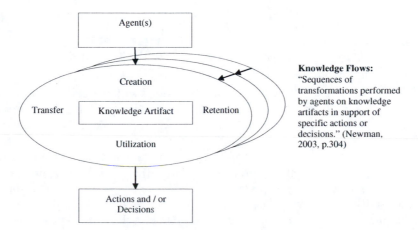

Knowledge Flows: "Sequences of transformations performed by agents on knowledge artifacts in support of specific actions or decisions." (Newman, 2003, p.304)

Knowledge Artifacts

In this framework, knowledge artifacts are "documents, memories, norms, values, and other things that represent the inputs to, and outputs of, the knowledge-enabled activities of agents" (Newman, 2003, p. 303). Essentially, this framework uses the term "artifact" to refer to a representation that is usable for one or more agents in their knowledge work. This notion is consistent with Newell's (1982) conception of knowledge as that which is conveyed by representations that are usable to some processor (i.e., that give that processor the ability to take action).

The phrase "knowledge artifact" refers simultaneously to two kinds of representation: cognitive knowledge artifacts and physical knowledge artifacts. The former deal with mental and behavioral representations. The latter are more concerned with symbolic, audio, video, and digital representations.

- **Cognitive knowledge artifact:** This refers to awareness and understanding of a particular aspect of our real or metaphysical world. It is commonly referred to simply as knowledge (Newman, 2003).
- **Physical knowledge artifact:** This is a "representation of the associated cognitive knowledge artifact" (Newman, 2003, p. 305).

Along another dimension, the Knowledge Flow Framework partitions knowledge artifacts into three classes, depending on the extent to which the representation is capable of codification and transfer among agents:

- **Explicit knowledge artifacts:** These have been codified in a way that makes it possible to touch, see, hear, feel, and/or manipulate them. They can be readily transferred from one person to another (Newman, 2003).
- **Implicit knowledge artifacts:** These are artifacts whose meanings are not explicitly captured, but can be inferred (Newman, 2003).
- **Tacit knowledge artifacts:** These defy expression and codification. They may be more prevalent and influential than either explicit or implicit artifacts (Newman, 2003).

Transformations

Transformations are the behaviors that agents perform on artifacts. The Knowledge Flow Framework organizes transformations into four general categories: knowledge creation, knowledge retention, knowledge transfer, and knowledge utilitzation. Newman (2003) defines them as follows:

- **Knowledge creation:** In this framework, "creation" refers to all behaviors through which new knowledge enters a knowledge-based system. It can occur internally through knowledge generation or from external sources via acquisition. It includes such activities as knowledge development, discovery, capture, and elicitation.
- **Knowledge retention:** This refers to an organization's storage, maintenance, and retrieval of previously created knowledge.
- **Knowledge transfer:** This kind of transformation refers to all behaviors through which agents share knowledge and knowledge artifacts. Knowledge transfer includes, but is not limited to, communication, translation, conversion, filtering, and rendering.
- **Knowledge utilization:** Finally, there are transformations in which agents use knowledge to further the goals and aims of the organization. All such behaviors are directly concerned with applying knowledge to enable decisions and actions. A "knowledge utilization event" is a specific decision or action enabled by the knowledge flow.

FURTHER READING

More information about the Knowledge Flow Framework can be found in Newman (1996, 2000). This framework's constructs are largely consistent with the KM ontology (Holsapple & Joshi, 2004). For instance, a knowledge utilization event is what the KM ontology recognizes as a particular kind of KM episode, knowledge artifacts are knowledge representations in KM ontology parlance, agents are what the KM ontology calls knowledge processors, and transformations map into the KM ontology's knowledge manipulations.

FUTURE TRENDS

Future efforts at better understanding knowledge organizations will proceed at both micro and macro levels. At the micro level, researchers will study the nature of knowledge work done by an organization's agents (Schultze, 2003). At the macro level, efforts will continue in the direction of devising increasingly complete and unified frameworks for characterizing knowledge organizations. It is likely that some of these efforts will integrate notions of knowledge assets, knowledge processing cycles, and knowledge flows with concepts

K

from business process management (Smith & Fingar, 2002) and social networking (Brass, 1992).

In a prescriptive vein, frameworks of the knowledge organization will be applied to devise specific strategies or prescriptions for how knowledge organizations can enhance performance (Sveiby, 2001). Normative frameworks of knowledge organizations will be devised suggesting what the nature of these organizations should be, rather than describing what is or has been. For instance, knowledge organizations will be seen as intelligent complex adaptive systems (Bennet & Bennet, 2004) and as value networks (Allee, 2003)

CONCLUSION

The frameworks presented here are sampling of efforts made to describe elements and relationships that exist in knowledge organizations. The coverage is more suggestive than exhaustive. Frameworks of knowledge organizations will continue to appear and evolve, symptomatic of the rich and varied nature of these organizations. At some point the diverse frameworks may converge. However, for the present, creative tension still exists in the differing perspectives and, as Sveiby says so eloquently, (Lelic, 2002, p. 1):

The conceptual framework of knowledge management is unusual in its ambiguity, extraordinary in its depth, unfathomable in its rapid expansion, and—best of all—has no single trademark or copyright owner.

The frameworks represent a spectrum of current points of view about the nature knowledge organizations and are useful to those pursuing the study and execution of knowledge management. The diversity presented gives even the experienced knowledge manager or academician reason to pause and consider varying perspectives on this topic. For the novice, it presents an approachable and important introduction to the domain of knowledge organizations.

REFERENCES

Allee, V. (2003). *The future of knowledge: Increasing prosperity through value networks*. Amsterdam: Butterworth-Heinemann.

Bennet, A., & Bennet, D. (2004). *Organizational survival in the new world*. Amsterdam: Butterworth-Heinemann.

Bennet, A., & Bennet D. (2003). The rise of the knowledge organization. In Clyde W. Holsapple (Ed.), *Handbook on knowledge management 1: Knowledge matters* (pp. 5-20). Berlin: Springer-Verlag.

Brass, D.J. (1992). Power in organizations: A social network perspective. In G. Moore & J.A. Whitt (Eds.), *Research in politics and society* (pp. 295-323). Greenwich, CT: JAI Press.

Davenport, T.H., & Prusak, L. (1998). *Working knowledge : How organizations manage what they know*. Boston: Harvard Business School Press.

de Hoog, R., et al. (1999). Investigating a theoretical framework for knowledge management. In J. Leibowitz (Ed.), *Knowledge management handbook* (pp. 1-18). Boca Raton, FL: CRC Press.

DeTore, A., & Balliet-Milholland, J. (2003). Transforming theory into fact: Hands-on knowledge management initiatives built on a reinsurer's pile of junk. In Clyde W. Holsapple (Ed.), *Handbook on knowledge management 2: Knowledge directions* (pp. 533-548). Berlin: Springer-Verlag.

Holsapple, C.W., & Joshi, K. (2004). A formal knowledge management ontology: Conduct, activities, resources, and influences. *Journal of the American Society for Information Science and Technology, 55*(7), 593-612.

Holsapple, C.W., & Whinston, A.B. (1986). Knowledge-based organizations. *The Information Society, 5*(2), 77-90.

Lelic, S. (2002). The knowledge: Karl-Erik Sveiby. *Knowledge Management Magazine, 6*(1), 1.

Leonard-Barton, D. (1995). *Wellsprings of knowledge*. Boston: Harvard Business School Press.

Newell, A. (1982). The knowledge level. *Artificial Intelligence, 18*(1), 87-127.

Newman, B.D. (1996). Knowledge management vs. knowledge engineering: The knowledge management theory papers. Retrieved from *www.km-forum.org#http://www.km-forum.org#*

Newman, B.D. (2003). Agents, artifacts, and transformations: The foundations of knowledge flows. In Clyde W. Holsapple (Ed.), *Handbook on knowledge management 1: Knowledge matters* (pp. 301-316). Berlin: Springer-Verlag.

Newman, B.D., & Conrad, K. (2000). A framework for characterizing knowledge management methods, practices, and technologies. *Data Administration Newsletter* (TDAN.COM). (12)

O'Dell, C. & Grayson, C.J. (1997). *Identifying and transferring internal best practices*. Houston, TX: APQC.

Stewart, T.A. (1997). *Intellectual capital: The new wealth of organizations*. New York: Doubleday/Currency.

O'Dell, C., et al. (2003). Successful KM implementations: A study of best practice organizations. In Clyde W. Holsapple (Ed.), *Handbook on knowledge management 2: Knowledge directions* (pp. 411-442). Berlin: Springer-Verlag.

Paradice, D. & Courtney, J. (1989). Organizational knowledge management. *Information Resource Management Journal, 2*(3), 1-13.

Schultze, U. (2003). On knowledge work. In Clyde W. Holsapple (Ed.), *Handbook on knowledge management 1: Knowledge matters* (pp. 43-58). Berlin: Springer-Verlag.

Smith, H., & Fingar, P. (2002). *Business process management*. Tampa, FL: Megan-Kiffer Press.

Sveiby, K.E. (1996, 2001). What is knowledge management? Retrieved July 16, 2003, from *www.sveiby.com/articles/KnowledgeManagement.html*

Sveiby, K.E. (1997). *The new organizational wealth: Managing & measuring knowledge-based assets*. San Francisco: Berrett-Koehler Publishers, Inc.

Sveiby, K.E. (2001). A knowledge-based theory of the firm to guide strategy formulation. *Journal of Intellectual Capital, 2*(4), 1-16.

Teece, D. (2003). Knowledge and competence as strategic assets. In Clyde W. Holsapple (Ed.), *Handbook on knowledge management 1: Knowledge matters* (pp. 129-152). Berlin: Springer-Verlag.

van der Spek, R., & de Hoog, R. (1995). A framework for knowledge management methodology. In Karl M. Wiig (Ed.), *Knowledge management methods: Practical approaches to managing knowledge* (pp. 379-393). Arlington, TX: Schema Press.

van der Spek, R., & Spijkervet, A. (1995). *Knowledge management: Dealing intelligently with knowledge*. Utrecht, The Netherlands: Kenniscentrum CIBIT.

Weick, K.E. (1995). *Sensemaking in organizations*. Thousand Oaks, CA: Sage Publication.

Wiig, K.M., de Hoog, R., & van der Spek, R. (1997). Supporting knowledge management: A selection of methods and techniques. *Expert Systems with Applications, 13*(1), 15-27.

KEY TERMS

Agents: "Specialized objects or roles played by people, organizations, societies, automata, and so forth within knowledge-based systems. They are the active components of knowledge flows" (Newman, 2003, p. 308).

Competence: The capacity to act in a wide variety of situations to create both tangible and intangible assets (Sveiby, 1997).

Intangible Assets: Assets normally unaccounted for on a balance sheet but reflected in the market value of a firm; composed of employee competence, and the internal and external structures of the firm (Sveiby, 1997).

Knowledge Artifacts: "The documents, memories, norms, values, and other things that represent the inputs to, and outputs of, the knowledge-enabled activities of agents" (Newman, 2003, p. 303).

Knowledge Flows: "Sequences of transformations performed by agents on knowledge artifacts in support of specific actions or decisions" (Newman, 2003, p. 304).

Knowledge Management Cycle: A cyclical process of reviewing, conceptualizing, reflecting, and acting to manage knowledge in the organization (Wiig, de Hoog, & van der Spek, 1997).

Knowledge Organization: An organization where intangible assets make up a large part of the market value of the firm; business service firms are close equivalents to knowledge organizations (Sveiby, 1997).

Knowledge Worker: Highly qualified and highly educated professionals whose work consists largely of using their own competencies to convert information into knowledge, sometimes with the assistance of suppliers of information or specialized knowledge (Sveiby, 1997).

Knowledge Producers and Consumers

Atreyi Kankanhalli
National University of Singapore, Singapore

Bernard C.Y. Tan
National University of Singapore, Singapore

Kwok-Kee Wei
City University of Hong Kong, Hong Kong

INTRODUCTION

In a knowledge-based economy, organizations find it difficult to compete based upon the individual knowledge of a few organizational members. This provides the rationale for *knowledge management* wherein organizational knowledge must be shared, combined, and reused in order to enable organizations to compete more effectively. Hence, *knowledge sharing* is considered an essential process in knowledge management. Unfortunately, sharing is often unnatural for the parties involved in it, that is, knowledge contributors or producers and knowledge seekers or consumers. Hoarding knowledge and not accepting knowledge from others are natural tendencies that are difficult to change (Davenport & Prusak, 1998). *Knowledge contributors* may be inhibited from sharing their knowledge due to perceptions of loss of power, lack of time or incentives, and other barriers. *Knowledge seekers* may find it laborious to seek advice from others and desire to discover solutions for themselves. Therefore, it is vital to understand and foster the *motivations* of knowledge contributors and seekers toward participating in knowledge sharing.

With the attention to knowledge management and the knowledge-based view of the firm, research in knowledge sharing and its motivations has gained interest over the last decade and a half. The initial focus of research was on investigating what motivates knowledge contribution (e.g., Orlikowski 1993; Constant, Kiesler, & Sproull, 1994) as this appeared to be a more intractable problem than motivating knowledge seeking. Subsequently, knowledge seeking behavior also has been researched (e.g., Goodman & Darr, 1998; Jarvenpaa & Staples, 2000; Kankanhalli, Tan, & Wei, 2001), although there is still considerably more attention devoted to studying knowledge contribution behavior.

Concurrently, the role of technology (known as *knowledge management system* or KMS) in enabling knowledge sharing has received research interest. However, in spite of the advent of new technology enabled forms of knowledge sharing such as knowledge logging (the enterprise flavor of blogging), the challenges of promoting knowledge sharing persist. This is because culture and management issues appear to dominate over technological issues in ensuring knowledge sharing success. For example, Ruppel and Harrington (2001) found that employee acceptance of or resistance to Intranets as a knowledge-sharing environment was more of a management and culture problem rather than a technology hurdle. Calls have been made to address both social and technical issues together (Zack, 1999) in order to be able to reap the benefits of knowledge management that have been experienced by some organizations (Davenport & Prusak, 1998).

BACKGROUND

Knowledge sharing is typically defined in two ways depending on the perspective toward knowledge. Researchers who view knowledge as an object tend to use the term "knowledge transfer" while others who see knowledge as a process use the term "knowledge sharing" (Allee, 1997). The notions of knowledge sharing and knowledge transfer can be combined by defining knowledge sharing as voluntary activities (process) of transferring or disseminating knowledge from one person to another person or group in an organization (Hansen, Nohria, & Tierney, 1999). A number of theoretical perspectives have been used to investigate the motivation of knowledge contributors and seekers.

Public Goods Theory

One of the initial lenses employed in studying motivations in knowledge sharing has been public goods theory (e.g., Thorn & Connolly, 1987; Fulk, Flanagin, Kalman, Monge, & Ryan, 1996). Knowledge shared in an organization through means such as a knowledge repository (referred to as a discretionary database in some previous literature) can be considered as a public good, that is, non-excludable, non-rival, and exhibiting jointness of supply. Knowledge shared is considered non-excludable because other repository users who did not contribute to its production are not prevented from access to the knowledge. The knowledge is non-rival because even if one consumer uses the knowledge, it still remains available to others, who also may apply the knowledge in their own situations. The knowledge contributed exhibits jointness of supply because it costs as much to produce for use by one person as for use by many.

Research along this perspective tends to focus on the motivational dilemma faced by knowledge contributors to such repositories. The dilemma for knowledge contributors is that collective interests bid them to share knowledge whereas self-interest may discourage them from contributing. Collective interest suggests that knowledge contributed will allow it to be combined or reused for greater benefit to the organization (Fulk et al., 1996). However, self-interest seems to dictate that contributing knowledge would reduce the unique knowledge possessed by the individual and thereby make him or her more replaceable in the organization (Kollock, 1999). In a broader sense, the dilemma for the community is that all members of the community stand to gain if everyone contributes. However, individually members are better off free-riding on the contributions of others. Therefore, research along this stream tries to understand how to promote collective action of knowledge contribution when it does not appear individually rational (Wasko & Faraj, 2000).

Expectancy Theory

Another perspective on studying motivation for knowledge contribution and seeking has attempted to apply more rational theories of motivation such as expectancy theory (Vroom, 1964) to understand the phenomenon. These studies (e.g., Kalman, 1999) suggest that individuals contribute knowledge based on their expectancy of certain benefits. Kalman's research found that organizational commitment, organizational instrumentality (the belief that sharing knowledge will produce organizational gain), and connective efficacy (the belief that the repository can be used to reach other people) positively influence individual's motivation to contribute to a repository.

Studies on knowledge seeking also have made use of expectancy theory (e.g., Nebus, 2004). Nebus' study proposed that the relationship between perceived value from knowledge seeking and knowledge seeking behavior is moderated by the perceived expectation of obtaining value. The perceived value from knowledge seeking depends on contributor's expertise and credibility while the perceived expectation of value depends on trust, obligation, and contributor's willingness to help. The perceived cost of seeking depends on monetary and time costs as well as the seeking risk in terms of the distance between the contributor and seeker.

Technology Adoption Theories

Theories of technology adoption have been applied to study motivation to use technologies for knowledge sharing. Particularly, the theory of planned behavior (Ajzen, 1991), which has been applied to technology adoption, has been used for this purpose. The theory proposes that the intention to use a technology depends on the attitude toward the technology, subjective norms, and perceived behavioral controls. Studies of knowledge contribution (e.g., Bock & Kim, 2002) have sought to find the antecedents of attitude, subjective norms, and perceived behavioral controls for knowledge contributors. Bock and Kim (2002) found that anticipated reciprocal relationships affected the attitude toward knowledge contribution while autonomy, innovativeness, and fairness of the organization impacted the subjective norm to contribute knowledge. As expected, attitude and subjective norm were positively related to knowledge contribution intention and to actual knowledge contribution behavior. Anticipated extrinsic rewards were found to play a facilitating role in individual's knowledge contribution.

The theory of planned behavior in conjunction with the task-technology fit model (Goodhue & Thompson, 1995) has been used to explain knowledge seeking behavior (Kankanhalli et al., 2001). Kankanhalli and colleagues' study found that technology-related factors (perceived output quality) and organization-related factors (availability of resources) directly impact seeking behavior, while task factors (task interdependence and task tacitness) play a moderating role on the effect of incentives on knowledge seeking from repositories.

Gaps in Literature

Prior empirical studies tend to focus on the benefits (acting as motivators) rather than the costs (acting as inhibitors) of knowledge contribution. This is in spite of the fact that practitioner literature (e.g., O'Dell & Grayson, 1998) and conceptual academic literature (e.g., Ba, Stallaert, & Whinston, 2001) suggest that costs are important in determining knowledge contribution behavior. Another feature of the prior research is that most studies consider knowledge sharing for all electronic media without focusing on a particular form of KMS. Even when studies are situated in the context of a particular technology, they may not refer specifically to the technology features and the consequences thereof. However, it is likely that differences in antecedent factors of contributing and seeking and the relative importance of antecedent factors can be expected for different forms of KMS. Further, since most empirical studies have been single case studies or surveys within one organization, there is a lack of theoretically grounded, empirically generalizable results regarding the phenomenon of interest.

Considering these gaps, newer research in knowledge sharing attempts to develop socio-technical frameworks for knowledge contribution and knowledge seeking via KMS considering both cost and benefit factors as antecedents. Organizational community factors that provide the context in which sharing takes place also are included in the frameworks. Particular forms of KMS for knowledge sharing are being studied (e.g., Goodman & Darr, 1998; Wasko & Faraj, 2000) and more generalizable research is being undertaken (e.g., Kankanhalli et al., 2001; Bock & Kim, 2002) as knowledge about the phenomena evolves.

FOCUS

This section describes a sample of the newer approaches toward explaining knowledge contribution and knowledge seeking behaviors that can obtain better explanatory power as compared to previous studies. They make use of social exchange theory, which accounts for both costs and benefits of knowledge sharing using collective technologies such as knowledge repositories.

Social Exchange Theory

Social exchange theory explains human behavior in social exchanges (Blau, 1964), which differ from economic exchanges in that obligations are not clearly specified. In such exchanges, people do others a favor with a general expectation of some future return but no clear expectation of exact future return. Therefore, social exchange assumes the existence of relatively longer-term relationships of interest as opposed to one-off exchanges (Molm, 1997). Knowledge sharing through knowledge repositories can be seen as a form of generalized social exchange (Fulk et al., 1996) where more than two people participate and reciprocal dependence is indirect, with the repository serving as intermediary between knowledge contributors and seekers. Knowledge contributors share their knowledge with no exact expectation of future return. Knowledge seekers con-

sume knowledge without certainty of when they will reciprocate in the future. The quantity and value of knowledge contributed or consumed is difficult to specify.

Resources (tangible and intangible) are the currency of social exchange. Resources given away during social exchange or negative outcomes of exchange can be seen as costs. Resources received as a result of social exchange or positive outcomes of exchange can be seen as benefits. Social exchange theory posits that people behave in ways that maximize their benefits and minimize their costs (Molm, 1997). This is in agreement with knowledge management research, which suggests that increasing the benefits and reducing the costs for contributing or seeking knowledge can encourage knowledge sharing using KMS (Goodman & Darr, 1998; Wasko & Faraj, 2000; Markus, 2001).

During social exchange, costs can be incurred in the form of opportunity costs and actual loss of resources (Molm, 1997). Opportunity costs are the rewards foregone from an alternative behavior not chosen. During social exchange, benefits can be extrinsic or intrinsic in nature (Vallerand, 1997). Extrinsic benefits are sought as means to ends. Intrinsic benefits are sought after as ends by themselves. Research has established extrinsic and intrinsic benefits as drivers of human behavior in several domains including knowledge sharing (Osterloh & Frey, 2000). Although cost and benefit factors can impact knowledge contribution and seeking, this impact is likely to be contingent upon contextual factors (Orlikowski, 1993; Goodman & Darr, 1998). *Social capital theory* accounts for several important contextual factors.

Social Capital Theory

Social capital theory emphasizes the resources (social capital) embedded within networks of human relationships (Nahapiet & Ghoshal, 1998). The theory posits that social capital provides the conditions necessary for knowledge transfer to occur. Three key aspects of social capital that can define the context for knowledge transfer are trust, norms, and identification (Nahapiet & Ghoshal, 1998). Prior research has hinted on the moderating role of aspects of social capital in knowledge sharing (Constant et al., 1994; Jarvenpaa & Staples, 2000).

Trust is the belief that the intended action of others would be appropriate from our point of view. It indicates a willingness of people to be vulnerable to others due to beliefs in their good intent and concern, competence and capability, and reliability (Mishra, 1996). Generalized trust (trust within a community) has been viewed as a key contextual factor affecting cooperation and the effectiveness of knowledge transfer (Adler, 2001).

Figure 1. Framework for knowledge contribution/seeking

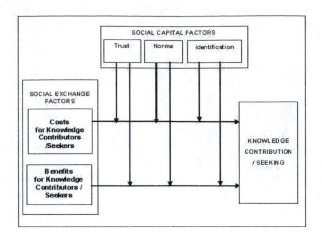

A norm represents a degree of consensus in the social system (Coleman, 1990). Pro-sharing norms that have been reported to enhance knowledge transfer are norms of teamwork (Starbuck, 1992), collaboration and sharing (Orlikowski, 1993; Goodman & Darr, 1998; Jarvenpaa & Staples, 2000), willingness to value and respond to diversity, openness to conflicting views, and tolerance for failure (Leonard-Barton, 1995). The first two norms can create an atmosphere where people are motivated to share knowledge as an accepted common practice. The last three norms can be crucial to promote knowledge sharing by reducing the risks of sharing.

Identification is a condition where the interests of the individual merge with the interests of the organization, resulting in the creation of an identity based on those interests (Johnson, Johnson, & Heimberg, 1999). Three key components of identification have been identified: similarity of values, membership, and loyalty toward the organization (Patchen, 1970). Similarity is the extent to which members of an organization possess joint goals and interests. Membership is the degree to which self-concept of members is linked to the organization. Loyalty refers to the extent to which members support and defend their organization. Identification can enhance communication and knowledge transfer among organizational members (Nahapiet & Ghoshal, 1998).

A framework for explaining knowledge contribution and knowledge seeking incorporating constructs from social exchange theory and social capital theory is shown in Figure 1.

Knowledge Contributor Motivation

In the contributor framework, opportunity costs (e.g., contribution effort) and other costs (e.g., loss of knowledge power) are proposed to negatively impact knowl-edge contribution. Both extrinsic (e.g., economic rewards) and intrinsic (e.g., enjoyment in helping others, and image) benefits are proposed to positively affect knowledge contribution. Contextual factors (i.e., trust, norms, and identification) may moderate the relationships between cost and benefit factors and knowledge contribution. For example, trust can moderate the relationship between contribution effort and knowledge contribution, and identification may moderate the relationship between economic rewards and knowledge contribution.

Knowledge Seeker Motivation

In the seeker framework, both opportunity costs (e.g., seeker effort) and other cost factors (e.g., future obligation) are proposed to negatively impact knowledge seeking. Extrinsic (e.g., economic reward) and intrinsic (e.g., knowledge growth) benefits are proposed to positively affect knowledge seeking. Contextual factors (i.e., trust, norms, and identification) can moderate the relationships between cost and benefit factors and knowledge seeking. For example, identification may moderate the relationship between future obligation and knowledge seeking while pro-sharing norms can moderate the relationship between knowledge growth and knowledge seeking.

FUTURE TRENDS

Based on practice and previous research, several avenues for future research are suggested. The directions are discussed in terms of studying additional motivational influences and relationships, application of theories across other settings (e.g., different KMS, users, organizations, and other nations or cultures), and extension to allied socio-technical problems.

Additional Influences and Relationships

Additional motivational influences in terms of individual costs (e.g., system learning cost, review cost, and follow-up cost), benefits (e.g., network benefit), organizational context (e.g., size of KMS user community), and task factors (e.g., task interdependence and tacitness) can be included in the frameworks to possibly enhance explanatory power. Interactions and links among cost, benefit, and social capital factors and between factors from different theoretical perspectives can be explored. This will allow us to understand why certain costs or benefits dominate others and why certain factors moderate the effect of others on knowledge contribution or seeking.

Investigation of Different Knowledge Sharing Contexts

Studies examining usage of different types of KMS for knowledge sharing could be conducted based on previous frameworks. The effect of different user demographics on perceived costs and benefits and consequent usage of KMS could be assessed. This will allow specific usage enhancement measures to be catered for different demographic groups. Similar studies could be conducted across different industry sectors. For example, knowledge sharing models could be compared across sectors where different cost, benefit, and contextual influences are expected. Further, the models could be extended to other national and cultural settings. Since knowledge sharing behavior may be culture-dependent and knowledge sharing in global organizations is likely to extend across cultural boundaries, studies of cross-country or cross-cultural nature can better inform the applicability of knowledge sharing theories under different national and cultural conditions.

Allied Socio-Technical Problems

Knowledge contributor and seeker perspectives can be combined to formulate an overall model for knowledge sharing. Other aspects of social capital such as structural and cognitive aspects could be investigated to observe their effect on the motivation, access, and shared understanding for knowledge transfer. Frequency of knowledge transfer transactions as well as contribution and seeking cost per transaction could be studied. These parameters may vary for different forms of KMS and direct knowledge transfer. This may allow for explanation of user decision to choose a particular KMS or form of knowledge transfer. Organizational controls for monitoring knowledge contribution and seeking behavior could be investigated. Finding better ways of monitoring such behavior could help to design appropriate incentive systems for promoting knowledge sharing. Mandates for KMS usage could be explored to understand whether they produce full compliance, and whether the quality of knowledge contributions and reuse would be different for mandated vs. voluntary use. Mechanisms for seekers to evaluate contribution quality could be studied with the purpose of facilitating knowledge seeking.

CONCLUSION

Conceptual frameworks based on social exchange theory and social capital theory can be applied to explain and predict knowledge contribution and knowledge seeking behavior in different contexts. The research has practical implications for organizational management and technology architects. Implications are suggested to promote knowledge sharing by enhancing significant benefits and alleviating significant costs for knowledge contributors and seekers.

Encouraging Knowledge Contribution

Contributor benefits such as enjoyment in helping others and knowledge self-efficacy need to be increased in order to encourage knowledge contribution. Enjoyment in helping others could be increased by connecting knowledge seekers with contributors and allowing them to express their appreciation of how useful the knowledge contributed has been in their work. Perceptions of knowledge self-efficacy could be enhanced by highlighting knowledge contribution success stories and their positive impact on organizational performance. Economic rewards for knowledge contribution could be targeted toward individuals who have greater identification with the organization. High identification individuals may be more readily motivated by incentives to contribute knowledge. Negative effects of contribution effort on knowledge contribution could be alleviated through increasing trust. Higher trust could be promoted by ensuring that credit is given for knowledge contributions, that is, all knowledge contributions are duly acknowledged. Alternatively when trust is low, contribution effort could be reduced by allocating time for their employees to share knowledge and integrating knowledge sharing into work processes.

Encouraging Knowledge Seeking

Seeker benefits such as perceived utility of results and knowledge growth need to be increased to encourage knowledge seeking. Perceived utility of results could be increased by ensuring that knowledge repositories are populated with relevant, accurate, and timely knowledge pertaining to the needs of seekers. This requires that contributors be encouraged to share their knowledge using various recommendations suggested in the preceding section and the quality of knowledge be vetted by implementing appropriate content review processes. Perceptions of knowledge growth can be increased by highlighting the learning benefits of seeking knowledge. If seekers are convinced of personal knowledge growth, they may be motivated to seek knowledge even when knowledge found is not directly relevant to their immediate work. Promoting employees' personal growth and development would also lead to higher employee satisfaction and morale in the long-term. Such measures would be necessary particularly under conditions of low pro-sharing norms. High pro-sharing norms could override the need for such benefits.

Technology Considerations

KMS technology designers could promote usage of their products for knowledge sharing by reducing knowledge contribution effort and increasing utility of results for knowledge seekers. KMS should be designed so that entry of knowledge is as minimally onerous to contributors as possible. Mechanisms to facilitate knowledge entry include intelligent acquisition and improved content taxonomy. An interactive system that prompts for knowledge and organizes the knowledge can reduce contribution effort. A comprehensive domain categorization that captures inter-category relationships can ease contribution effort. Knowledge contribution effort also can be reduced by allowing more natural forms of knowledge acquisition (e.g., audio or video contribution) as opposed to purely text contribution. This may be particularly appropriate for more tacit forms of knowledge.

Utility of results for knowledge seekers can be increased by designing filtering, indexing, and retrieval technologies that ensure appropriate content goes into KMS and can be readily found. Indexing and retrieval technologies need to be designed that can efficiently customize and refine searches and provide relevance feedback. Knowledge seekers need to be provided information about the quality of knowledge retrieved to enable them to make reasonable judgments about reuse. Examples of such information include quality ratings and reviews.

Although large amounts of investments are being made in knowledge management initiatives, a significant number of organizations have difficulties with implementing these initiatives due to the challenges of motivating employees to contribute and reuse knowledge. The above discussion attempts to explain the motivations of knowledge contributors and knowledge seekers and thereby throw light on this problem. Organizational knowledge leveraging would be possible only if both contributors and seekers are motivated.

REFERENCES

Adler, P.S. (2001). Market, hierarchy, and trust: The knowledge economy and the future of capitalism. *Organization Science, 12*(2), 215-234.

Ajzen, I. (1991). The theory of planned behavior. *Organizational Behavior and Human Decision Processes, 50*, 179-211.

Allee, V. (1997). *The knowledge evolution: Expanding organizational intelligence.* Boston: Butterworth-Heinemann.

Ba, S., Stallaert, J., & Whinston, A.B. (2001). Research commentary: Introducing a third dimension in information systems design: The case for incentive alignment. *Information Systems Research, 12*(3), 225-239.

Blau, P.M. (1964). *Exchange and power in social life.* New York: J. Wiley.

Bock, G.W., & Kim, Y.G. (2002). Breaking the myths of rewards: An exploratory study of attitudes about knowledge sharing. *Information Resource Management Journal, 15*(2), 14-21.

Coleman, J. (1990). *Foundations of social theory.* Cambridge, MA: Harvard University Press.

Constant, D., Kiesler, S., & Sproull, L. (1994). What's mine is ours, or is it? A study of attitudes about information sharing. *Information Systems Research, 5*(4), 400-421.

Davenport, T.H., & Prusak, L. (1998). *Working knowledge: How organizations manage what they know.* Boston: Harvard Business School Press.

Fulk, J., Flanagin, A.J., Kalman, M.E., Monge, P.R., & Ryan, T. (1996). Connective and communal public goods in interactive communication systems. *Communication Theory, 6*(1), 60-87.

Goodhue, D.L., & Thompson, R.L. (1995). Task-technology fit and individual performance. *MIS Quarterly, 19*(2), 213-236.

Goodman, P.S., & Darr, E.D. (1998). Computer-aided systems and communities: Mechanisms for organizational learning in distributed environments. *MIS Quarterly 22*(4), 417-440.

Hansen, M.T., Nohria, N., & Tierney, T. (1999). What's your strategy for managing knowledge? *Harvard Business Review 77*(2), 106-116.

Jarvenpaa, S.L., & Staples, D.S. (2000). The use of collaborative electronic media for information sharing: An exploratory study of determinants. *Journal of Strategic Information Systems, 9*(2-3), 129-154.

Johnson, W.L., Johnson, A.M., & Heimberg, F. (1999). A primary and second order component analysis of the organizational identification questionnaire. *Educational and Psychological Measurement, 59*(1), 159-170.

Kalman, M.E. (1999). *The effects of organizational commitment and expected outcomes on the motivation to share discretionary information in a collaborative database: Communication dilemmas and other serious games.* Doctoral dissertation, University of Southern California.

Kankanhalli, A., Tan, B.C.Y., & Wei, K.K. (2001). Seeking knowledge in electronic knowledge repositories: An exploratory study. *Proceedings of the International Conference on Information Systems,* New Orleans (pp. 123-133).

Kollock, P. (1999). The economies of online cooperation: Gifts and public goods in cyberspace. In M. Smith & P. Kollock (Eds.), *Communities in cyberspace* (pp. 220-239). New York: Routledge.

Leonard-Barton, D. (1995). *Wellsprings of knowledge: Building and sustaining the source of innovation.* Boston: Harvard Business School Press.

Markus, M.L. (2001). Towards a theory of knowledge reuse: Types of knowledge reuse situations and factors in reuse success. *Journal of Management Information Systems, 18*(1), 57-94.

Mishra, A.K. (1996). Organizational responses to crisis: The centrality of trust. In R.M. Kramer & T.R. Tyler (Eds.), *Trust in organizations: Frontiers of theory and research* (pp. 261-287). Thousand Oaks, CA: Sage.

Molm, L.D. (1997). *Coercive power in social exchange.* New York: Cambridge University Press.

Nahapiet, J., & Ghoshal, S. (1998). Social capital, intellectual capital, and organizational advantage. *Academy of Management Review, 23*(2), 242-266.

Nebus, J. (2004). Learning by networking: Knowledge search and sharing in multinational organizations. *Academy of International Business Annual Meeting.*

O'Dell, C., & Grayson, C.J. (1998). If only we knew what we know: Identification and transfer of internal best practices. *California Management Review, 40*(3), 154-174.

Orlikowski, W.J. (1993). Learning from notes: Organizational issues in groupware implementation. *Information Society, 9*(3), 237-251.

Osterloh, M., & Frey, B.S. (2000). Motivation, knowledge transfer, and organizational forms. *Organization Science, 11*(5), 538-550.

Patchen, M. (1970). *Participation, achievement, and involvement on the job.* Englewood Cliffs, NJ: Prentice Hall.

Ruppel, C.P., & Harrington, S.J. (2001). Spreading knowledge through Intranets: An analysis of the organizational culture leading to Intranet adoption and use. *IEEE Transactions on Professional Communications, 44*(1), 37-52.

Starbuck, W.H. (1992). Learning by knowledge-intensive firms. *Journal of Management Studies, 29*(6), 713-740.

Thorn, B.K., & Connolly, T. (1987). Discretionary databases: A theory and some experimental findings. *Communication Research, 14*(5), 512-528.

Vallerand, R.J. (1997). Toward a hierarchical model of intrinsic and extrinsic motivation. *Advances in Experimental Social Psychology, 29,* 271-360.

Vroom, V.H. (1964). *Work and motivation.* New York: Wiley.

Wasko, M.M., & Faraj, S. (2000). It is what one does: Why people participate and help others in electronic communities of practice. *Journal of Strategic Information Systems, 9*(2-3), 155-173.

Zack, M.H. (1999). Managing codified knowledge. *Sloan Management Review, 40*(4), 45-5.

KEY TERMS

Expectancy Theory: An individual will act in a certain way based on the expectation that the act will be followed by a given outcome and on the attractiveness of that outcome to the individual.

Identification: Identification is a condition where the interests of the individual merge with the interests of the organization, resulting in the creation of an identity based on those interests.

Knowledge Contributor: A person who provides knowledge that may be shared with other organizational members (used interchangeably with knowledge producer).

Knowledge Seeker: A person who searches for and acquires knowledge from other organizational members (used interchangeably with knowledge consumer).

Knowledge Sharing: Voluntary activities (process) of transferring or disseminating knowledge from one person to another person or group in an organization.

Norms: A norm represents acceptable attitudes and behaviors by consensus among members of a community.

Public Goods Theory: A good or service is said to have "public" characteristics if private producers cannot capture all of the benefits associated with its consumption. Once such a good is produced, people can enjoy the benefits that it provides without having to pay for them. Consequently, it is argued that public goods will either be "underproduced" in the free market or not produced at all.

Social Capital Theory: Social capital theory emphasizes the resources (social capital) embedded within networks of human relationships. The theory posits that social capital provides the conditions necessary for knowledge transfer to occur.

Social Exchange Theory: According to social exchange theory, people engage in social exchange when the benefits outweigh the costs of exchange. The costs and benefits can be tangible or intangible, physical or psychological.

Theory of Planned Behavior: According to the theory, human behavior is guided by three kinds of beliefs: beliefs about the likely outcomes of the behavior and the evaluations of these outcomes (attitude); beliefs about the normative expectations of others and motivation to comply with these expectations (subjective norms); and beliefs about the presence of factors that may facilitate or impede performance of the behavior and the perceived power of these factors (perceived behavioral controls). As a general rule, the more favorable the attitude and subjective norm, and the greater the perceived control, the stronger should be the person's intention to perform the behavior in question. Intention is assumed to be the immediate antecedent of actual behavior.

Trust: Trust is the belief that the intended action of others would be appropriate from our point of view. It indicates a willingness of people to be vulnerable to others due to beliefs in their good intent and concern, competence and capability, and reliability.

Knowledge Representation

Gian Piero Zarri
University of Paris IV/Sorbonne, France

INTRODUCTION

In 1982, Allen Newell introduced the "knowledge level" principle (Newell, 1982) and revolutionized the traditional way of conceiving the relationships between knowledge management and computer science. According to this principle, the knowledge level represents the highest level in the description of any structured system: Situated above and independent from the "symbol level," it describes the observed behaviour of the system as a function of the knowledge employed, and independently of the way this knowledge is eventually represented/implemented at the symbol level. "The knowledge level permits predicting and understanding behaviour without having an operational model of the processing that is actually being done by the agent" (Newell, 1982, p. 108). An arbitrary system is then interpreted as a *rational agent* that interacts with its environment in order to attain, according to the knowledge it owns, a given goal in the best way; from a strict knowledge level point of view, this system is then considered as a sort of "black box" to be modeled on the basis of its input/output behaviour, without making any hypothesis on its internal structure. To sum up, the knowledge level principle emphasises the *why* (i.e., the goals), and the *what* (i.e., the different tasks to be accomplished and the domain knowledge) more than the *how* (i.e., the way of implementing these tasks and of putting this domain knowledge to use).

BACKGROUND

The emergence of the knowledge principle produced a shift of emphasis, in the (computerized) knowledge management domain, from a pure "representational" attitude to a "modeling" one, that is, a shift from the production of tools for implementing the knowledge a system will use to that of tools for building up models of the behaviour of the system in terms of that knowledge. An example of this is the Knowledge Acquisition and Design Structuring (KADS) methodology (Schreiber, Wielinga, & Breuker, 1993; Schreiber, Akkermans, Anjewierden, de Hoog, Shadbolt, Van de Velde, & Wielinga, 1999). A fundamental step in the KADS approach is, in fact, the set up of a general "conceptual model" of the system, which an observer (a knowledge engineer) creates by abstracting from the problem-solving behaviour of some experts. According to the knowledge principle, the conceptual model does not include any detailed constraint about the implementation level. This last function is assigned to the "design model," which corresponds to the (high level) specifications of the final knowledge-based system (KBS), and which represents the transformations to be executed on the conceptual model when we take into account the external requirements (e.g., specialised interfaces, explanation modules, etc.). The conceptual model is built up according to a four-layer structured approach: Each successive layer interprets the description given at the lower layer. A first layer concerns the "static domain knowledge," that is, the domain concepts and their attributes, the domain facts, the structures representing complex relations, and so forth. The static knowledge can be viewed as a declarative theory of the domain. A second type of knowledge concerns the "knowledge sources" and the "metaclasses." A knowledge source is defined as an elementary step in the reasoning process (an inference) that derives new information from the existing one; KADS presupposes the existence of a set of canonical inferences such as "abstraction, association, refinement, transformation, selection, computation." Metaclasses describe the role that a group of concepts plays in the reasoning process (e.g., observable, hypothesis, solution, etc.). The third layer contains knowledge describing how inferences can be combined to fulfill a certain goal, that is, how to achieve operations on metaclasses. The most important type of knowledge in this category is the "task": A task is a description of a problem-solving goal or subgoal, as "diagnose a patient with these particular symptoms." The fourth category of knowledge is the "strategic knowledge," which settles the general goals that are relevant to solve a particular problem; how each goal can be achieved is determined by the task knowledge.

One of the main attractions of this structured, analytical approach to the automation of knowledge management resides in the fact that all the methodologies based implicitly or explicitly on the knowledge level principle embrace the idea that the set up of KBSs can be facilitated by the development of libraries of reusable components. These pertain mainly to two different classes, (1) reusable "ontologies" (see also Zarri, "RDF and OWL" in this Volume) and (2) reusable problem-solving methods, which define classes of operations for problem-solving. Chandrasekaran (1990) is one of the first to suggest the development of reusable components under the form of "generic tasks," where a generic task defines both a class of application tasks with common features, and a method for performing these tasks.

An additional manifestation of this general tendency toward generalisation, abstraction, and reuse in the knowledge management domain are the activities aimed at the construction of general and reusable "corporate memories," (see van Heijst, van der Spek, & Kruizinga, 1996; Brooking, 1998; Beckett, 2000). Knowledge has been recognised as one of the most important assets of an enterprise and a possible success factor for any industrial organization, on the condition that it can be controlled, shared, and reused in an effective way. Accordingly, the core of the organization can then be conceived under the form of a general and shared organizational memory, that is, of an online, computer-based storehouse of expertise, experience, and documentation about all the strategic aspects of the organization. The construction and practical use of corporate memories becomes then the main activity in the knowledge management of a company, a focal point where several computer science and artificial intelligence disciplines converge: knowledge acquisition (and learning), data warehouses, database management, information retrieval, data mining, case-based reasoning, decision support systems, querying (and natural language querying) techniques, and so forth.

A clear discrimination between "knowledge" and "symbol" level is often not so easy to attain. For example, some methodologies that make reference to the knowledge level principle go in reality against Newell's approach because the structure they impose on the knowledge is a function of *how* a specific class of applications is implemented and dealt with, and the models they produce are then valid only in a very specific context. On a more pragmatic level, reuse can be very difficult to obtain, because there is often a significant semantic gap between some abstract, general method, and a particular application task. Moreover, discovering and formalising a set of elementary tasks independently from any specific application domain is a particularly hard endeavour which meets all sort of embarrassing problems, ranging from the difficulties in defining the building blocks in a sufficiently general way to the ambiguities concerning which aspects (the model or the code) of the blocks can really be reused. This explains why a (not trivial) number of "pure" knowledge-level proposals are still theoretical proposals, characterised by a limited implementation effort.

Indiscriminate use of the "modeling" approach risks forgetting that the basic technological support for implementing effective knowledge management is nevertheless provided by the knowledge representation (and processing) techniques. The building blocks, the generic tasks, the reusable modules, the shareable ontologies, and so forth must be formalised using one or more of the ordinary knowledge representation techniques developed in the last 50 years such as rules, logic, or frames. In this article, knowledge management will then be seen essentially as an application of the usual knowledge representation (and processing) techniques: creating and using, for example, large corporate memories requires that, first off all, the knowledge be represented, store,d and computer-managed in a realistic and efficient way.

TYPES OF KNOWLEDGE REPRESENTATION SYSTEMS

"Knowledge is power!" according to the well-known slogan spread abroad by Edward Feigenbaum—more precisely, Feigenbaum stated that: "...the power...does not reside in the inference method; almost any inference method will do. The power resides in the knowledge" (Feigenbaum, 1984, p. 101). Reviewing the different solutions for representing knowledge proposed in these last 50 years, we can isolate two main groups:

- The "symbolic" approach. This is characterised by (1) the existence of a well-defined, one-to-one (bijective) correspondence between *all the entities* of the domain to be modeled (and their relationships) and the *symbols* used in the knowledge representation language, and (2) by the fact that the knowledge manipulation algorithms (inferences) take explicitly into account this correspondence.
- The "soft programming" approach. Here, only the input and output values have an explicit, bijective correspondence with the entities of a given problem to be modeled. For the other elements and factors of the problem, (1) it is often impossible to establish a *local correspondence* between the symbols of the knowledge representation system and such elements and factors; (2) the resolution processes are not grounded on any explicit correspondence notion; (3) statistical and probabilistic methods play an important part in these resolution processes.

Given the present popularity of "ontologies" (a sort of symbolic approach) in all the domains requiring the concrete application of knowledge representation tools—

including the knowledge management context, (e.g., Staab, Studer, Schnurr, & Sure, 2001)—it is very likely that knowledge management specialists will have to make use of symbolic (ontological) tools in the practice of their discipline. On the other hand, (1) information about soft systems is, apparently, less omnipresent than its symbolic counterpart in the knowledge management literature, and (2) bio-inspired intelligent information systems are broadly seen as one of the next frontiers of computer science. We will then supply here some (very limited) information about soft systems and an essential bibliography. For an in-depth discussion of the symbolic approach (see Bertino, Catania, & Zarri, 2001, p. 105-170; Zarri, "RDF and OWL" in this Volume).

THE SOFT PROGRAMMING PARADIGM

Neural Networks

Neural networks represent probably the most well-known example of soft programming paradigm. As genetic algorithms, their inner model can be considered as (loosely) "biologically inspired." More than on a loose analogy with the organisation of the brain—in this contest, only the (very simplified) concepts of "neuron" and "synapse" have been preserved—the biological foundations of neural networks reside in the self-organising principles that are characteristic of living systems. When a threshold number of interconnections (synapses) have been established between a set of neurons—and if the network has been carefully "programmed"—a form of self-organising activity appears that allows an external observer to affirm that the network "learns": it learns, for example, to associate a pattern with another, to synthesise a common pattern from the set of examples, to differentiate among input patterns and so forth where "pattern" must be understood here according to its more general meaning.

A neural network is made up of several "layers," where any number of neurons (processing units) can be present in each of the layers. Each neuron maps the inputs received from all the other neurons situated in a lower layer (or some external stimuli) to a one-dimensional output. This last is a function, among other things, of the "weights" associated with the connections (synapses) between the neurons in layer n and neurons in layer n-1, that is, of the "strength" of these connections. "Learning" is normally implemented by modifying the weights of the connections: For example, the "backpropagation method" consists in adjusting the weights making use of the difference, for a given distribution of input values, between the desired output values of

the network and the values really obtained. Using then a training set made up of couples of input-output patterns, the weights are cyclically modified so that the differences are eventually minimised according, for example, to a least-squares sense. See Wasserman (1989) and Anderson (1995) for a detailed account of neural networks' theory.

Neural networks are particularly useful for *capturing associations* or *discovering regularities* within a set of patterns, especially when (1) the number of variables or the diversity of data is very great, and (2) the relationships between the variables are not well understood and, therefore, are difficult to describe using traditional (symbolic) methods. Accordingly, "classical" applications of neural networks concern banking (credit scoring, recovery scoring, forecasting the behaviour of new costumers, identifying "good risks"), financing (predicting share prices and volatilities, portfolio and asset management), industry (predicting demand for a product or a service, servo-control for machines or chemical reactors), marketing (marketing and mailing targeting, turnover prediction, data mining), public administration (analysis and prediction of crime, tax fraud detection, economic forecasting), and so forth. In these domains, neural network present, with respect to the corresponding "symbolic solutions," the fundamental advantage of freeing the knowledge engineer from the necessity of constructing a faithful "model" of the situation at hand, and of formatting correspondingly the data: *with neural networks, the model is already there, even if it must be appropriately tuned (learning)*. Moreover, at the difference of many symbolic solutions, neural networks are relatively insensible to missing or erroneous values. On the other hand, neural networks—because of the lack of a one-to-one correspondence between entities to be modeled and symbols—are "black boxes" that do not explain their decisions. Moreover, their possible domains of applications are surely limited in number with respect to those where a symbolic approach can be appropriate.

Genetic Algorithms

Darwinian evolution—based on the principle of the "only the strongest survive strategy"—characterises the biological metaphor that is behind the creation of the genetic algorithms (GAs). According to this strategy, individuals compete in nature for food, water, and refuge, and for attracting a partner: The most successful individuals survive and have a relatively large number of offsprings. Their (outstanding) genetic material will then be transmitted to an increasing number of individuals in each successive generation; the combination of such outstanding characteristics ("chromosomes" or "genotypes") will be able to produce *individuals whose suitability ("fitness") to the environment will sometimes transcend that of their parents*. In this way, species can evolve—John Holland (Holland, 1975) and his colleagues of the University of Michigan are unanimously recognized as the first researchers to have envisaged the utilization of this strategy to solve the usual computer science problems.

The first step in the utilisation of the GAs approach consists then in the creation of a "population" of individuals (from a few tens to a few hundreds) that are represented by "chromosomes" (sometimes called "genotypes"). From the point of view of the problem to be solved, each chromosome represents a set (list) of parameters that constitutes a potential solution for the problem: for example, in a problem requiring a numerical solution, a chromosome may represent a string of digits; in a scheduling problem, it may represent a list of tasks; in a cryptographic problem, a string of letters, and so forth. Each item of the list is called a "gene." Traditionally, the parameters (genes) are coded using some sort of binary alphabet (i.e., a chromosome takes the form of a string of n binary digits).

The initial population is then modified and "improved" making use of two genetic operators, "crossover" and "mutation." Crossover takes two selected individuals, the "parents," and cuts their gene strings at some randomly (at least in principle) chosen position, producing two "head" and two "tail" substrings. The tail substrings are then switched, giving rise to two new individuals called "offsprings," which inherit some genes from each of the parents: The offsprings are then created through the exchange of genetic material. Mutation is applied to the offsprings after crossover, and consists into a random modification of the genes with a certain probability (normally a small one, e.g., 0.0001) called the "mutation rate." Note that mutation—that can be conceived, in biological terms, as an error in the reproduction process—is the only way to create truly new individuals (crossover makes use of already existent genetic material).

Genetic algorithms are part of *a wider family of biologically inspired methods called in general "evolutionary algorithms," which are search and optimisation procedures all based on the Darwinian evolution paradigm evoked here*, and consisting then in the simulation of the evolution of particular individuals through the application of processes of selection, reproduction, and mutation. Apart from GAs, other evolutionary methodologies are known under the name of "Evolution Strategies," "Evolutionary Programming," "Classifier Systems," and "Genetic Programming." Ge-

netic Programming domain has emerged in these last years as particularly important. Genetic Programming can be seen as a variation of GAs where the evolving individuals are computer programs instead of chromosomes formed of fixed-length bit strings; when executed, the programs supply then a solution of the given problem (see Koza, 1992). In Genetic Programming, programs are not represented as lines of ordinary code, but rather as "parse trees" corresponding to a coding syntax in prefix form, analogous to that of LISP. The nodes of the parse trees correspond then to predefined functions ("function set") that are supposed to be appropriate for solving problems in general in a given domain of interest, and the leaves (i.e., the terminal symbols) correspond to the variables and constants ("terminal set") that are proper to the problem under consideration. Crossover is then implemented by swapping randomly selected sub-trees among programs; mutation, normally, is not implemented.

The classical reference in the GAs field is still Goldberg (1989); a good introductory book is Mitchell (1998).

Fuzzy Knowledge Representation Techniques

The fuzzy logic paradigm also is based on some sort of biologically inspired approach, even if the analogy looks less evident. It is related to the fact that *fuzzy logic intends to simulate the way humans operate in ordinary life*, that is, on a continuum, and not according a crisp "nothing-or-all" Aristotelian logic. Humans use some forms of gradually evolving linguistic expressions to indicate that, with respect to a given thermal environment, they are "comfortable," "cold," or "freezing." Fuzzy logic allows to quantify such "fuzzy" concepts, and to represent then our sensations about temperature making use of numeric values in the range of 0 (e.g., "comfortable") to 1 (e.g., "freezing," with 0.7 representing then "cold").

More precisely, according to the "fuzzy sets" theory—this theory, introduced by Zadeh (1965) makes up the core of the fuzzy logic paradigm (see also, in this context, Zimmerman, 1991; Kosko, 1992)—every linguistic term expressing degrees of qualitative judgements, like "tall, warm, fast, sharp, close to," and so forth corresponds to a specific fuzzy set. The elements of the set represent then different "degrees of membership," able to supply a numeric measure of the congruence of a given variable (e.g., temperature) with the fuzzy concept represented by the linguistic term.

Knowledge representation according to the fuzzy logic approach consists then in the computation, for a collection of input values, of their degree of membership with respect to a group of fuzzy sets. For a fuzzy application dealing with a temperature regulation system, the fuzzy sets to be considered for the variable "temperature" will be "cold," "cool," "comfortable," "warm," and "hot." The process allowing us to determine, for each of the inputs, the corresponding degree of membership with respect to each one of the defined sets is called "fuzzification"; the degrees are calculated making use of appropriate "membership functions" that characterise each one of the sets. In this way, an input value of 83° F will be translated into two fuzzy values, 0.2 which represents the degree of membership with respect to the fuzzy set "hot," and 0.8 representing the degree of membership with respect to the fuzzy set "warm," (see Viot, 1993 for the technical details). Imprecise, approximate concepts like "warm" and "hot" are then translated into computationally effective, smooth, and continuous terms.

The fuzzy logic paradigm is *widely used in industrial applications, especially for systems without a precise mathematical model and characterised by a high level of uncertainty.* These applications range from household appliances such as dishwashers and washing machines that make use of fuzzy logic to find out the optimal amount of soap and the correct water pressure, to self-focusing cameras and embedded micro-controllers. Fuzzy logic also is used in special kinds of expert systems like decision support systems and meteorological forecast systems.

The Symbolic Paradigm

Knowledge representation systems that follow the symbolic approach range between two possible basic forms (as usual, mixed forms are possible):

- Pure *rule-based representations* supporting inference techniques that can be assimilated to first order logic procedures (*inference by resolution*). Within this first pole, is at least pragmatically useful to distinguish between the systems developed in a logic programming context and the simplest Expert Systems based on the standard production rules paradigm.
- Pure *frame- or object-based representations* supporting *inference by inheritance*, and also admitting defaults and procedural attachment. A particular class of inheritance-based systems that are today particularly fashionable are the ontology-based systems and their formal counterpart, the description logics (terminological logics) systems.

The Rule-Based Approach

Expression (a) below represents a so-called "Horn clause" (named after Alfred Horn, who first investigated their properties), that is, a kind of well-formed formula (*wff*) of the first-order predicate calculus characterised by the fact of having *at most* one positive "literal," 'A.' Horn clauses are particularly important in artificial intelligence because they represent the basis of the logic programming paradigm and constitute the formal framework of programming languages like PROLOG and DATALOG.

$$A \vee \neg B_1 \vee \neg B_2 \ldots \vee \neg B_n \qquad n \geq 0 \qquad \text{(a)}$$

Applying to (a) a series of logical transformations based, *inter alia*, on the well-known de Morgan's laws, formula (a) can be transformed into (b)—(see Bertino, Catania, & Zarri, 2001, pp. 112-113)—where '$\wedge$' represents now the "conjunction" or "logical and" symbol, and '$\supset$' is the "implication" symbol.

$$(B_1 \wedge B_2 \ldots \wedge B_n) \supset A \qquad n \geq 0 \qquad \text{(b)}$$

Making use of the standard notation for representing implication, we can write (b) as (c), where the arrow '$\rightarrow$' is the connective "if" representing the implication and a "comma" still represents a "logical and":

$$B_1, B_2, \ldots B_n \rightarrow A \qquad n \geq 0 \qquad \text{(c)}$$

In (c), $B_1 \ldots B_n$ is now the "antecedent," or the "conditions," of the implication, and A is the "consequent" or the "conclusion." Therefore, formula (c) states that, if the different conditions B_1, B_2, ..., B_n are *all verified* (TRUE), they imply the conclusion A; we can write (c) succinctly as:

$$\textit{If } B \textit{ Then } A. \qquad \text{(d)}$$

Formula (d) corresponds to the well-known notation used for the "*production rules*" that still constitute one of the basic operational tools used in all sort of artificial intelligence, cognitive science, knowledge management and Semantic Web applications. Their derivation from "classical" first order logic sketchily outlined is very important, given that the theory of production rule can then be easily brought back to the well-known formal context proper to theorem proving (resolution principle) and logic programming, (see Bertino, Catania, & Zarri, 2001, p. 107-122). Note, however, that production rule systems can only implement a reduced subset of the *full* first order logic.

The functioning of a typical "*expert system*" (ES) that makes use of *production rules* can be described as follows:

- The system includes a "*rule base*," that is, an unordered collection of production rules having the format of (c). We give now to the B$_i$ the meaning of "*conditions*" (facts) that must be satisfied, and to A the meaning of the "*action/actions*" that must be performed if the conditions are satisfied. The B$_i$ represent the "*left-hand side*" (LHS) of the rule *r*, A the "*right-hand side*" (RHS).

- The system also includes a "*working memory*" (WM) where the facts submitted are stored as input to the system or automatically inferred during its functioning.

- During its functioning, the system repeatedly performs a "*recognise-act*" cycle, which can be characterised as follows in the case of "*condition-driven*" or "*forward-chaining*" ESs:

  - In the "*selection phase*," for each rule *r* of the rule base, the system: (1) determines whether LHS(*r*) is satisfied by the current WM contents, that is, if LHS(*r*) matches the facts stored in the WM ("*match subphase*") and, if so, (2) it adds the rule *r* to a particular rule subset called the "*conflict set*" (CS) ("*addition subphase*"). When all the LHS are false, the system halts.

  - In the "*conflict resolution phase*," a rule of the CS is selected for execution. If it is impossible to select a rule, the system halts.

  - In the "*act phase*," the actions included in RHS(*r*) are executed by the interpreter—this is often called "*firing a rule*." Firing a rule will normally change the content of WM and, possibly, the CS. To avoid cycling, the set of facts ("*instantiation*") that has instantiated the LHS variables of the fired rule becomes ineligible to provoke again the firing of the same rule, which, of course, can fire again if instantiated with different facts.

A way of schematising the recognise-act cycle is represented in Figure 1. The name of "*conflict set*" is due to the fact that, amongst all the competing selected rules that are in agreement with the current state of WM, it is necessary to choose the only rule to be executed by the interpreter in the current cycle—choosing and executing multiple rules is possible, but more complex. The specific procedures to be implemented for performing the resolution of the conflicts depend on the application, and can be very complicated, given that the execution of a rule may lead other rules to "*fire*," or on the contrary, prevent their firing and so forth. It is then possible to make use of user-defined priorities: The user is allowed to choose a particular strategy, such as giving preference to rules that operate on the most recent information added to WM, or that match the highest number of items, or the most specific rule, the

Figure 1. The "recognise-act" cycle

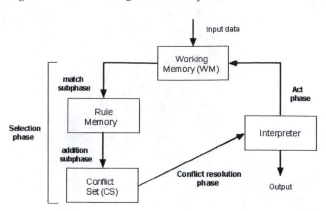

one with the most detailed LHS that matches the current state of WM. It is also possible to make use of pre-defined criteria for ordering the rules, which may be static (i.e., a priority ordering is assigned to the rules when they are first created) or dynamic.

Production systems can be classified into two different categories according to the way rules are compared with data of WM. When the comparison is between LHS(*r*) and WM as illustrated in Figure 1, we have the "*condition-driven*" or "*forward-chaining*" systems). But it is also possible to compare RHS(*r*) with WM ("*action-driven*," or "*backward-chaining*" systems). An example of a backward-chaining system is given by MYCIN, a software designed to perform medical diagnosis (prescribe antibiotic therapy) in the field of bacterial infections that represents one of the best known and historically important expert system (see Shortliffe, 1976). More details can be found in Bertino, Catania, & Zarri (2001, p. 125-131).

The Inheritance-Based Approach

Inheritance is one of the most popular and powerful concepts used in the artificial intelligence and knowledge representation domains. It represents, at the same time:

- **Static:** A *static* structuring principle that allows to group together similar notions in classes, and to economise in the description of some attributes of the entities of the low-level classes because these descriptions can be inherited from the entities of the high-level classes;

- **Dynamic:** A *dynamic* inferencing principle that allows to make deductions about the properties (attributes) of the low-level entities that are *a priori* unknown because these properties can be deduced from those that characterise the high-level entities—with the well-known problems linked with the fact that, for example, "penguins" and "ostriches" pertain to the class "birds," but they cannot inherit from the description of this general class the property "can_fly";

- **Generative principle:** A *generative principle* that allows to define new classes as variants of the existing ones: The new class inherits, in fact, the general properties and behaviours of the parent class, and the system builder must only specify how the new class is different.

The inheritance principle is normally used to set up *hierarchies of "concepts"—"ontologies" or "taxonomies,"* where the first are differentiated from the second because they add to the plain description of the hierarchical links among the concepts also an explicit definition/description of these concepts. Ontologies/taxonomies are then structured as *inheritance hierarchies* making use of the well-known IsA link—also called AKindOf (Ako), SuperC, and so forth (see Figure 2). A relatively unchallenged—see however, Brachman, (1983)—semantic interpretation of IsA states of this relationship among concepts, when noted as (IsA *B A*), means that concept *B* is a *specialisation* of the more general concept *A*. In other terms, *A* subsumes *B*. This assertion can be expressed in logical form as:

$$\forall x \ (B(x) \rightarrow A(x)) \ ; \tag{e}$$

(e) says that, if any *elephant_* (*B*) IsA *mammal_* (*A*), and if clyde_ is an *elephant_*, then clyde_ is also a *mammal_*—as usual, the *concepts_* are written down in italics, and their instances_ (e.g., clyde_, an "individual") in roman characters. When (e) is interpreted strictly, it also implies that a given concept *B* and all its instances *must* inherit *all* the features (properties) and their values of *all* the concepts C_i in the hierarchy that have *B* as a specialization; we speak in this case of "strict inheritance." Note that, under the strict inheritance hypothesis, totally new properties can be added to *B* to differentiate it (specialize it) with respect to its parents.

Relation IsA is transitive: This means that, for example, having both $\forall x \ (C(x) \rightarrow B(x))$ and $\forall x \ (B(x) \rightarrow A(x))$, we can deduce from this that $\forall x \ (C(x) \rightarrow A(x))$. This property is particularly important because it allows, in an inheritance hierarchy like that of Figure 2, to represent explicitly only the IsA relationships that associate directly two nodes (i.e., without the presence of intermediary nodes). All the residual IsA relationships are then explicitly derived only when needed: For example, from Figure 2 and from the transitive property of IsA, we can explicitly assert that (IsA *chow_ mammal_*).

The necessary complement of IsA for the construction of well-formed hierarchies concerns some form of

Figure 2. A simple inheritance hierarchy

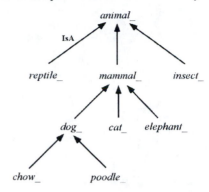

InstanceOf link, used to introduce the "instances" (concrete examples) of the general notions represented by the concepts. The difference between (IsA *B A*) and (InstanceOf *C B*) is normally explained in terms of the difference between the two options of (1) considering *B* as a subclass of *A* in the first case, operator '$\subset$', and (2) considering C as a member of the class *B* in the second, operator '$\in$'. Unfortunately, this is not sufficient to eliminate any ambiguity about the notion of instance, which is much more controversial than that of concept. Problems about the definition of instances concern: (1) the possibility of accepting that concepts (to the exclusion of the root) could also be considered as "instances" of their generic concepts; (2) the possibility of admitting several levels of instances, that is, instances of an instance. For a discussion about these problems and the possible solutions, see Bertino, Catania, and Zarri (2001, p. 138).

We can now associate to any concept a "structure" (a "*frame*") to reflect the knowledge human beings have about (1) the intrinsic properties of these concepts and (2) the network of relationships, other than the hierarchical one, the concepts have each other. As already stated, we are now totally in the "ontological" domain, and this sort of frame-based ontologies can be equated to the well-known "semantic networks" (see Lehmann, 1992).

Basically, a "frame" is a set of properties, with associated classes of admitted values, that is linked to the nodes representing the concepts. Introducing a frame corresponds then to establishing a new sort of relationship between the concept C_i to be defined and *some* of the other concepts of the ontology. The relationship concerns the fact that the concepts $C_1, C_2 \ldots C_n$ used in the frame defining C_i indicate now the "class of fillers" (specific concepts or instances) that can be associated with the "slots" of this frame, the slots denoting the main properties (attributes, qualities, etc.) of C_i. There is normally no fixed number of slots, nor a particular order imposed on them; slots can be accessed by their names.

Figure 3. A simple example explaining the "inheritance of properties/attributes"

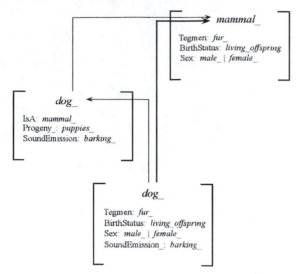

Figure 3 (an "ontology") reproduces a fragment of Figure 2 (a "taxonomy") where the concepts are now associated with their (highly schematized) defining frames—note that the two fillers *male_* | *female_* also could have been replaced by their subsuming concept *sex_*. This figure makes explicit what "inheritance of properties/attributes" means: Supposing that the frame for *mammal_* is already defined, and supposing now to tell the system that the concept *dog_* is characterised by the two specific properties Progeny and SoundEmission, what the frame *dog_* really includes is represented in the lower part of Figure 3.

Even if, under the influence of the Semantic Web work (see Zarri, "RDF and OWL" in this Volume), the "classic" frame paradigm sketched here is moving toward more formalized, logic-based (and XML/RDF-based) types of representation, nevertheless this paradigm still constitutes the foundation for the setup of a large majority of knowledge repositories all over the world; often, a knowledge base is nothing more than a "big" ontology formed of concepts/individuals represented under the form of frames. The most well-known tool for the setup of large knowledge bases making use of the frame model is Protégé-2000, developed for many years at the Medical Informatics Laboratory of the Stanford University (California, USA) (e.g., Noy, Fergerson, & Musen, 2000; Noy, Sintek, Decker, Crubezy, Fergerson, & Musen, 2001). Protégé-2000 represents today a sort of standard in the frame-based ontological domain.

FUTURE TRENDS

Knowledge representation systems that follow the "soft programming" paradigm are expected to evolve into the new "bio-inspired intelligent information systems." These are systems capable of extracting meaning associated to complex patterns of sensor stimuli and of generating well coordinated sequences of elementary actions complying with a set of higher level goals. The systems should show autonomous growth in perceptual, motor, and cognitive abilities. Examples can concern the construction (1) of hardware/software "artifacts that live and grow" (ALGs), that is, artifacts that self-adapt and evolve beyond pure programming, and (2) of perception-response systems (PRSs) inspired by the sophistication of solutions adopted by living systems, where "perception" refers to the sensorial, cognitive, and control aspects (covering vision, hearing, or any other modalities) used by the biological organisms to interact with the environment.

With respect now to the "symbolic approach," the most up-to-date rule-based systems are those used in a Semantic Web context (see Zarri, "RDF and OWL" in this Volume). In the inheritance- and frame-based domain, Protégé-2000 is still the *de facto* standard; on a more theoretical level—and thanks at least partly, once again, to the success of the Semantic Web research—description logics (DLs) have gained particular importance in these last years. DLs (Baader, Calvanese, McGuinness, Nardi, & Patel-Schneider, 2002) are an axiomatized, inheritance-based system characterised by the presence of a mechanism for the automatic classification of concepts as its main reasoning component. One of the main reasons for the introduction of DLs has been the wish to offer a formal and logically-sound foundation for frame-based systems (see Minker & Grant in this Volume).

CONCLUSION

In this article, we started with the fundamental revolution in the relationships between knowledge management and computer science that followed the introduction of the "knowledge level" principle, and of the new emphasis on the "modeling" principles that resulted from that. Notwithstanding the corresponding, indisputable progresses at the theoretical and methodological level, we have then shown that the adoption of the knowledge level principle does not eliminate the need—when creating and using, for example, large organizational memories—for making certain that the required "knowledge" be represented, stored, and computer-managed in a realistic and efficient way. Knowledge representation represents then one of the key, enabling factors for knowledge management.

Confronted with the choice of selecting specific knowledge representation tools, we must choose between two conflicting paradigms, the "symbolic" approach—where there is a precise, one-to-one correspondence between the entities of the domain to be dealt with and the symbol intended to represent them – and the "soft programming" approach, where this correspondence is totally blurred. In a knowledge management context, the symbolic paradigm ("ontologies") seems to be, presently, the predominant one; given, however, the importance that the new "bio-inspired intelligent information systems"—an evolution of the "soft programming" approach—should have in the future, the soft programming techniques (neural networks, genetic algorithms, and fuzzy logic) are of growing importance.

REFERENCES

Anderson, J.A. (1995). *An introduction to neural networks*. Cambridge, MA: MIT Press.

Baader, F., Calvanese, D., McGuinness, D., Nardi, D., & Patel-Schneider, P.F. (Eds.) (2002). *The description logic handbook: Theory, implementation and applications*. Cambridge: University Press.

Beckett, R.C. (2000). A characterization of corporate memory as a knowledge system. *Journal of Knowledge Management, 4*(4), 311-319.

Bertino, E., Catania, B., & Zarri, G.P. (2001). *Intelligent database systems*. London: Addison-Wesley and ACM Press.

Brachman, R.J. (1983). What IS-A is and isn't: An analysis of taxonomic links in semantic network. *IEEE Computer, 16*(10), 30-36.

Brooking, A. (1998). *Corporate memory: Strategies for knowledge management*. London: Thomson Business Press.

Chandrasekaran, B. (1990). Design problem solving: A task analysis. *AI Magazine, 11*(4), 59-71.

Fegenbaum, E.A. (1984). Knowledge engineering: The applied side of artificial intelligence. In *Annals of the New York Academy of Sciences, 246*, 91-107.

Goldberg, D.E. (1989). *Genetic algorithms in search, optimization, and machine learning*. Reading, MA: Addison-Wesley.

Holland, J.H. (1975). *Adaptation in natural and artificial systems*. Ann Arbor, MI: University of Michigan Press.

Kosko, B. (1992). *Neural networks and fuzzy systems: A dynamical systems approach to machine intelligence*. Englewood Cliffs, NJ: Prentice Hall.

Koza, J. (1992). *Genetic programming*. Cambridge, MA: The MIT Press.

Lehmann, F. (Ed.). (1992). *Semantic networks in artificial intelligence*. Oxford: Pergamon Press.

Mitchell, M. (1998). *An introduction to genetic algorithms*. Cambridge, MA: The MIT Press.

Newell, A. (1982). The Knowledge Level. *Artificial Intelligence, 18*, 87-127.

Noy, F.N., Fergerson, R.W., & Musen, M.A. (2000). The knowledge model of Protégé-2000: Combining interoperability and flexibility. In Knowledge Acquisition, Modeling, and Management. *Proceedings of the European Knowledge Acquisition Conference, EKAW'2000*. Berlin: Springer-Verlag.

Noy, N.F., Sintek, M., Decker, S., Crubezy, M., Fergerson, R.W., & Musen, M.A. (2001). Creating Semantic Web contents with Protégé-2000. *IEEE Intelligent Systems, 16*(2), 60-71.

Schreiber, G., Akkermans, H., Anjewierden, A., de Hoog, R., Shadbolt, N., Van de Velde, W., & Wielinga, B. (1999). *Knowledge engineering and management: The CommonKADS Methodology*. Cambridge, MA: The MIT Press.

Schreiber, G., Wielinga, B., & Breuker, J. (1993). *KADS: A principled approach in knowledge-based system developments*. London: Academic Press.

Shortliffe, E.H. (1976). *Computer-based medical consultations: MYCIN*. New York: American-Elsevier Publications.

Staab, S., Studer, R., Schnurr, H.-P., & Sure, Y. (2001). Knowledge processes and ontologies. *IEEE Intelligent Systems, 16*(1), 26-34.

van Heijst, G., van der Spek, R., & Kruizinga, E. (1996). Organizing corporate memories. In B.R. Gaines & M. Musen (Eds.), *Proceedings of the 10th Banff Knowledge Acquisition for Knowledge-Based Systems Workshop*, Calgary: Department of Computer Science of the University.

Viot, G. (1993). Fuzzy logic: Concepts to constructs. *AI Expert 8*(11), 26-33.

Wasserman, P.D. (1989). *Neural computing: Theory and practice*. New York: Van Nostrand Reinhold.

Zadeh, L.A. (1965). Fuzzy sets. *Information and Control, 8*, 338-353.

Zimmermann, H.J. (1991). *Fuzzy set theory and its applications* (2nd Ed.). Norwell, MA: Kluwer.

KEY TERMS

Frame-Based Representation: A way of defining the "meaning" of a concept by using a set of properties ("frame") with associated classes of admitted values—this "frame" is linked with the node representing the concept. Associating a frame with the concept c_i to be defined corresponds to establishing a *relationship* between c_i and *some* of the other concepts of the ontology; this relationship indicates that the concepts $c_1, c_2 \dots c_n$ used in the frame defining c_i denote the "class of fillers" (specific concepts or instances) that can be associated with the "slots" (properties, attributes, qualities, etc.) of the frame for c_i.

Genetic Operators, Crossover and Mutation: "Crossover" takes two selected chromosomes, the "parents," and cuts their gene (bit) strings at some randomly chosen position, producing two "head" and two "tail" substrings. The tail substrings are then switched, giving rise to two new individuals called "offsprings," which inherit each some genes from each of the parents: The offsprings are then created through *the exchange of genetic material*. "Mutation" consists into a random modification of the genes with a certain probability (normally a small one, e.g., 0.0001) called the "mutation rate."

Inheritance-Based Knowledge Representation: Ontologies/taxonomies are structured as hierarchies of concepts ("inheritance hierarchies") by means of "IsA" links. A semantic interpretation of this relationship among concepts, when noted as (IsA *B A*), means that concept *B* is a *specialisation* of the more general concept *A*. In other terms, *A* subsumes *B*. This assertion can be expressed in logical form as:

$$\forall x\,(B(x) \rightarrow A(x)) \qquad (1)$$

(1) says that, for example, if any *elephant_* (*B*, a concept) IsA *mammal_* (*A*, a more general concept), and if clyde_ (an instance or individual) is an *elephant_*, then clyde_ is also a *mammal_* – in more concise terms, *A* subsumes *B*. When (1) is interpreted strictly, it also implies that the instances of a given concept *B must* inherit *all* the features (properties) of *all* the concepts in the hierarchy that have

B as a specialization; we speak in this case of "strict inheritance."

IsA and Instance of links: The necessary complement of IsA for the construction of well-formed hierarchies is the InstanceOf link, used to introduce the "instances" (concrete examples) of the general notions represented by the concepts. The difference between (IsA *B A*) and (InstanceOf C *B*) can be explained by considering *B* as a *subclass* of A in the IsA case, operator 'Î' and by considering C as a *member of the class B* in the InstanceOf case, operator 'Î' The notion of instance is, however, much more controversial than that of concept. Problems about the definition of instances concern, for example, (1) the possibility of accepting that concepts (to the exclusion of the root) also could be considered as "instances" of their generic concepts; (2) the possibility of admitting several levels of instances (i.e., instances of an instance).

Knowledge Representation, Soft Programming Approach: In this case (neural networks, genetic algorithms, etc.), only the input and output values have an explicit correspondence with the entities of the domain. For the other elements and factors, it is normally impossible to establish a *local correspondence* between them and the symbols of the knowledge representation system, and the resolution processes (where statistical and probabilistic methods play an important role) are not grounded on any explicit notion of correspondence.

Knowledge Representation, Symbolic Approach: The "classical" way of representing knowledge. According to the symbolic approach, there is a well-defined, one-to-one (bijective) correspondence between *all the entities* of the domain to be modeled (and their relationships), and the *symbols* used in the knowledge representation language. Moreover, the knowledge manipulation algorithms (inferences) take explicitly into account this correspondence.

"Learning Rules" for Neural Networks: They concern the modification of the weights w of the connections among neurons according to a specific input pattern. The learning method based on backpropagation consists in adjusting the weights making use of the difference, for a given pattern of input values to the network, between the *desired activation levels for the neurons of the output layer* and the *levels really obtained*. Using then a training set made up of couples of input-output patterns, the weights are cyclically modified so that the differences are eventually minimised according to a least-squares sense.

Ontologies vs. Taxonomies: In a taxonomy (and in the most simple types of ontologies), the *implicit* definition of a concept derives simply by the fact of being inserted in a network of *specific/generic relationships* (IsA) with the other concepts of the taxonomy/hierarchy. In a "real" ontology, we also must supply some *explicit* definitions for the concepts—or at least for a majority among them. This can be obtained, for example, by associating a "frame" (a set of properties/attributes with associated classes of admitted values, see Protégé-2000) with these concepts.

Rule-Based Knowledge Representation: A (symbolic) way of representing knowledge under the form of "rules" of the type: "*If* B *Then* A", where B, the "antecedent" or "condition," *is* a *conjunction* of literals $B_1 \wedge B_2 \wedge \ldots B_n$, and A, the "consequent" or the "conclusion," *can* be a *disjunction* of literals, $A_1 \vee A_2 \ldots A_n$. The meaning of the rule is then: if the different conditions B_i are *all verified* (TRUE), they imply the conclusion A, or a set of alternative conclusions which are expressed by the different A_i. This type of representation can be reduced to first order logic (resolution principle).

K

Knowledge Representation in Pattern Management

Pankaj Kamthan
Concordia University, Canada

Hsueh-Ieng Pai
Concordia University, Canada

INTRODUCTION

The reliance on past experience and expertise is critical to any development. Patterns are a reusable form of knowledge gained by experts in solving problems that occur repeatedly in a domain. The concept of a pattern was introduced by Christopher Alexander in the 1970s (Alexander, 1979).

Patterns have found widespread use since their inception. Applications of patterns originated in the civil engineering and urban planning domains as an approach to design buildings, roadways, and towns (Alexander, 1979). Since then, patterns have been applied to various areas including use cases (Adolph, Bramble, Cockburn, & Pols, 2002), software design (Gamma, Helm, Johnson, & Vlissides, 1995), human-computer interaction (Borchers, 2001), electronic business (Adams, Koushik, Vasudeva, & Galambos, 2001), and configuration management (Berczuk & Appleton, 2003), to name a few in computing.

As the number of patterns grows and its user community broadens, the need for an effective management of patterns arises. If not addressed, patterns may, for example, fail to communicate their purpose to the user community, could be misused, or be virtually inaccessible when called upon. This can adversely affect further acceptance and evolution of patterns as means for solving frequently occurring problems.

This article discusses issues in pattern management as they relate to knowledge representation (KR). Although deemed important (Vlissides, 1998), there has been little attention in this area and one of the goals of this work is to fill that void. The article is organized as follows. We first provide a brief background on patterns within the context of pattern management. Next, requirements for representing patterns are given and different ways of representing patterns, along with an analysis of each approach, are discussed in detail. This is followed by an outline of some future directions and trends that representation of pattern knowledge is likely to take. Finally, we present concluding remarks.

BACKGROUND

Patterns are important, as they are time- and technology-independent abstractions that suggest proven, reusable solutions to common problems in a domain. In a software context, patterns represent knowledge and experience that underlies many redesigns and reengineering efforts of engineers that have struggled to achieve greater reuse and flexibility in their software (Devedzic, 2002).

Patterns are related to, but different from other forms of knowledge such as principles, guidelines, and frameworks: Patterns are at a lower level of abstraction with respect to principles, and in fact, patterns often rely on principles for the quality and acceptance of their solutions; patterns are more concrete compared to guidelines, which often tend to be prescriptive, vague, and targeted more toward an expert rather than a novice; patterns are at a higher level of abstraction with respect to frameworks, although frameworks often make use of patterns to provide reusable code components.

An abstract model of patterns can be given as follows: A pattern P consists of a finite set of *elements*, that is, $P = \{E_1, E_2, ..., E_i\}$, where each element is part of pattern description as given. These elements form an anatomy of a pattern where they act as placeholders for pattern content and enable the pattern to be described completely for practical use. Typical elements are:

- **Name:** The unique, often metaphoric, name of the pattern by which it is known in the community.
- **Context:** The environment, situation, or interrelated conditions within the scope of which the PROBLEM recurs, and for which the SOLUTION is desirable.
- **Problem:** An issue that needs to be investigated and resolved, and is typically constrained by the CONTEXT in which it occurs.
- **Forces:** These describe relevant assumptions and constraints of the PROBLEM and how they interact/conflict with one another. These help determining the kinds of tradeoffs that must be considered to arrive at a SOLUTION.

- **Solution:** The response to the PROBLEM in a CONTEXT that helps resolve the issue(s).
- **Rationale:** The reasoning behind and suitability of the pattern as a justified choice toward solving the PROBLEM.
- **Resulting Context:** The state of the entity (such as a software process or a software product) after applying the pattern, including both the positive and negative consequences.
- **Related Patterns:** The patterns that may be applicable as a result of the new context in which the entity finds itself.
- **Example:** The instance(s) of "real-world" situation(s) where the specified pattern has been applied.

This list could be extended to include other elements, for example, ANTI-PATTERNS (non-examples of the use of the pattern) or include elements of metadata (author information, version control, and so forth). The choice of both elements and element names varies in the community. Also, some of these elements (such as EXAMPLE) can be repeated while some of the elements (such as RATIONALE) are considered as optional.

A collection of patterns along with their (often implicit) context-driven relationships gives rise to a *pattern language*. A pattern language PL consists of a finite set of patterns $P_1, P_2, ..., P_j$ and a finite set of non-reflexive relationship types $R_1, R_2, ..., R_k$, that is, PL = $\{P_1, P_2, ..., P_j; R_1, R_2, ..., R_k$ such that $P_u R_t P_v$ for some u, $v \in \{1, 2, ..., j\}, u \neq v$, and $t \in \{1, 2, ..., k\}\}$. From a graph drawing perspective, a pattern language could be viewed as a directed acyclic graph (DAG) where $P_1, P_2, ..., P_j$ are the nodes and $R_1, R_2, ..., R_k$ are the vertices. Pattern languages differ from each other with respect to the domain that they correspond to, but need not be mutually exclusive (unrelated). For example, a pattern language for high-level user interface design of software is considered to be different from that for low-level source code design. However, the choices of patterns at the higher level could influence (restrict) the possibilities for selecting patterns at the lower level.

Pattern management involves various, not necessarily mutually exclusive, activities (Figure 1) that include pattern integration (combining patterns from a pattern language), pattern dissemination (making patterns available on a medium such as on an electronic network), pattern mining (pattern elicitation/discovery), pattern validation (designating potential candidate patterns and tracking them to qualification), pattern authoring (documenting and editing), pattern representation (explicitly specifying the syntactical and semantical knowledge inherent in a pattern), pattern selection and use (from a given set of options, choosing a pattern suitable for a

Figure 1. Activities in pattern management

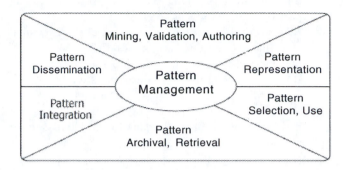

problem and applying it), pattern archival (storing patterns expressed in a representation for future use), and pattern retrieval (searching and finding a pattern from a given archive). Tasks involved in these activities have been shown (May & Taylor, 2003) to fit in the Nonaka SECI model of knowledge (Nonaka & Takeuchi, 1995).

The issue of adequate representation of patterns is central to pattern management as it directly or indirectly impacts other activities, including authoring, selection, integration, dissemination, archival, and retrieval. According to the COCOMO II cost estimation model (Boehm et al., 2001), reuse comes with a cost of adaptation to new contexts and a proper representation is crucial in this respect. Therefore, we next focus primarily on pattern representation from the perspective of knowledge management.

REPRESENTATION OF PATTERNS

There is a need for pattern representation at three levels: representing knowledge inherent in an individual pattern, representing relationships of patterns within a pattern language, and representing relationships across pattern languages. In this regard, technical requirements that we consider necessary for a language to be suitable for pattern representation, in no particular order of priority, are:

- **R1:** A representation must be able to accurately reflect the elements that constitute a pattern and their properties. To do that, a representation must have both a [R1.1] syntactical and [R1.2] semantical basis. This is necessary to be able to clearly express the syntax and semantics of relations among patterns and between pattern languages. It also makes it possible to check the validity of a pattern description with respect to its representation language.
- **R2:** A representation must allow means for unique identification of the pattern and its elements. This

is important for traceability, cross-reference, and transclusion (the inclusion of one resource, or a part thereof, within another resource).

- **R3:** A representation must enable reuse. It is desirable that it provides support for [R3.1] hypertext that facilitates reuse via transclusion.
- **R4:** The community of pattern users may be geographically dispersed. Therefore, a representation should enable sharing by providing support for internationalization and means for global dissemination.
- **R5:** The elements of a pattern may need to be represented in a variety of different forms such as text, graphic, mathematical symbols, and so forth. Therefore, a representation must accommodate the possible heterogeneous nature of a pattern.
- **R6:** A representation must strive for high quality. For practical purposes, quality is viewed as a collective of attributes (ISO, 1994) that are quantifiable (Fenton & Pfleeger, 1997). The desirable quality attributes include [R6.1] interoperability (for cross-tool interpretability), [R6.2] maintainability (for longevity of pattern descriptions), [R6.3] efficiency (for archival and transmission purposes), [R6.4] non-proprietary/standardized (for unrestricted, stable use), and [R6.5] usability (for broad use and outreach).
- **R7:** A representation should be amenable to automated processing (such as for manipulation or transformation). The processing tools should be reasonably [R7.1] easy to create and use, [R7.2] robust, [R7.3] fast, [R7.4] cost-feasible, and [R7.5] widely available.
- **R8:** The representation should have a low learning curve. In particular, it should be easy to express a pattern in the representation language.

Not all requirements may be applicable to all representations. We use [+R*] to denote strong conformance and [-R*] to denote weak conformance with these requirements, respectively. In the remainder of this section, we discuss informal (natural), semi-formal, and formal language representations and their adequacy to express patterns with respect to these requirements.

TRADITIONAL APPROACHES FOR REPRESENTATION OF PATTERNS

The natural language representation of patterns that was originally introduced in (Alexander, 1979) and used widely since then (Gamma et al., 1995) is a largely narrative form of structured text. It was targeted for dissemination via print medium and seems to have served well for many years. Although easy to learn and use ([+R8]), it suffers from various limitations that prevent it from taking advantage of potential benefits offered by the electronic medium of communication, in general, and today's management systems, in particular. For instance, there is no standard way to verify whether a pattern is compliant with the notation ([-R1]), it is not possible to reuse pattern elements without actually copying them or to reference pattern elements for, say, indexing purposes ([-R3]), and its structure cannot be readily exploited for machine-use and for automated processing (Gomes et al., 2002) ([-R7]). Efforts to resolve the issues inherent to a natural language representation have led to movement toward the formalization of pattern representations.

The Unified Modeling Language (UML) (Booch, Jacobson, & Rumbaugh, 2005) is a standard [+R6.4], semi-formal language for visually modeling the structure and behavior of object-oriented software systems. The Object Constraint Language (OCL) (Warmer & Kleppe, 2003) is the formal expression language for UML that allows users to write constraints and queries over object models. Visual rendering has the ability to present structures with complex relationships that could enhance comprehensibility (Schauer & Keller, 1998). Learning and using UML and OCL require little training ([+R8]) for use and there are various modelers in the market today to generate UML models ([+R7]). As an example, solution instances of the software design patterns of (Gamma et al., 1995) have been illustrated using UML in (Braude, 2004). However, UML and OCL together are limited to expressing only partial solution instances of patterns ([-R1]). It is not readily possible to indicate universally unique identifiers in UML ([-R2]). In addition, lack of sufficient constructs for expressing pattern solutions have led to non-standard extensions of UML (Dong & Yang, 2003).

LePUS (Eden, Hirshfeld, & Yehudai, 1999) and BPSL (Taibi & Ngo, 2003) are formal specification languages based on first-order logic and/or temporal logic for software design patterns such as those of Gamma et al. (1995). They also are limited to representing only the solution instance of patterns ([-R1]).

SEMANTICAL REPRESENTATION OF PATTERNS

In order to represent the knowledge inherent in a domain, we need to classify the domain into concepts and the relations between them. The declarative knowledge of a domain is often modeled using *ontology*. Formally, ontology is defined as an explicit formal specification of a conceptualization that consists of a set of terms in a domain and relations among them (Gruber, 1993).

There is a natural affinity between patterns and ontologies (Devedzic, 2002). Like patterns, ontologies are forms for knowledge sharing and reuse. By means of documentation, patterns help make implicit expert knowledge explicit; ontologies, on the other hand, help make implicit domain knowledge explicit. Therefore, an ontological representation is suitable in providing a semantical (logical) basis for the domain of patterns.

There are a number of languages available for specification of ontologies (Gómez-Pérez, Fernández-López, & Corcho, 2004) that differ in various ways: variations in power of syntactical constructs, semantical origin, expressiveness, reasoning support, and availability of processing tools. Selecting the one suitable amongst them depends on several factors, including scope of the ontology being built, availability of tools (stable and robust editors, capable and fast reasoners), and whether the resulting ontology fits in well with other organizational knowledge management products.

Ontologies vary in their complexity, which in turn depends upon various factors: complexity of the domain whose knowledge is represented; conclusions that can be drawn from it; and goals and underlying semantical basis of the representation language. The result is that we have a spectrum of ontologies where only those with a logical foundation yield themselves to automated reasoning.

Description Logics as a Basis for Ontology Specification Languages

Description Logics (DL) (Baader, McGuinness, Nardi, & Schneider, 2003) is a family of KR formalisms that form a decidable subset of the first-order predicate logic. DL is tailored for expressing knowledge about concepts and concept hierarchies. The basic building blocks are concepts, roles, and individuals. Concepts describe the common properties of a collection of individuals and can be considered as unary predicates that are interpreted as sets of objects, whereas roles are interpreted as binary relations between objects. Each DL also defines a number of language constructs (such as intersection, union, role quantification, and so forth) that can be used to define new concepts and roles. The main reasoning tasks are classification, satisfiability, subsumption, and instance checking.

The main advantage of DL languages compared to other KR languages such as those based on semantic networks (Sowa, 1991) and frames (Brachman & Levesque, 1985) is a well understood declarative semantics ([+R1.2]), where the meaning of a construct is given by the description and its models. There are well-investigated algorithms (Baader & Sattler, 2001) with publicly available mature implementations ([+R7]) of DL languages to verify a number of properties of an ontology (such as correctness, completeness, decidability, and complexity).

Ontological Inferences

A pattern language that is represented as a simple taxonomy cannot be reasoned with and only trivial inferences can be deduced from it. Therefore, the interest is in pattern ontology with logical constraints that can be reasoned with, and from which complex and "interesting" inferences can be derived.

The quality of retrieval related to patterns is largely concerned with two attributes: accuracy and efficiency. In traditional pattern management systems (PMS), the retrieval process is based upon a keyword match in the archive for patterns and has various limitations toward accuracy. In general, a traditional PMS has no specific mechanism to differentiate between synonyms or homonyms, and is not able to extract implicit knowledge. As a consequence, there may exist some patterns that are important for a pattern user but are not retrieved.

One of the motivations for using DL-based ontologies in the study of patterns is the interesting inferences that can be drawn based on *concept* match that would otherwise not have been possible with a traditional PMS. The following examples illustrate the possibilities:

- **Example 1:** Let P_1 be a pattern in pattern language PL_1, where the element FORCES is used to represent a set of constraints of the pattern, and let P_2 be a pattern in pattern language PL_2, where the element CONSTRAINTS is used to represent a set of constraints of the pattern. In order to understand the meaning of the corresponding pattern elements of PL_1 and PL_2, an ontology can be used that declares/specifies that the term FORCES has an equivalent meaning as the term CONSTRAINTS. As the result, when the pattern user is looking for patterns with certain FORCES, not only the contents of FORCES element of pattern P_1 will be searched, but contents of the CONSTRAINTS element of pattern P_2 also will be searched.
- **Example 2:** Consider a pattern that contains the following statement in its FORCES: "This pattern is not intended for GUI applications." Now, since the keyword "GUI" appears in the pattern description, this pattern would typically be included in the results returned in a traditional PMS when the user searches for patterns that can be applied to GUI applications. This is because the meaning of the

(logical) word "not" is not understood by a traditional PMS and, in general, the meaning of the pattern description is not relevant. Therefore, the fact that a keyword appears in a pattern description does not necessarily mean that a pattern returned in the search result is relevant. This problem is circumvented in the use of a DL-based ontology for patterns.

The ontological approach to patterns does present certain obstacles. Although a principled and systematic approach to ontological development is highly desirable (Gómez-Pérez et al., 2004), creation of high quality ontology is a nontrivial and arduous endeavor ([-R8]). Also, although there are robust, well-supported tools for authoring and reasoning with ontologies ([+R7]), there is a steep learning curve involved ([-R8]). The efficiency of deriving an inference from a given ontology depends on the complexity of the ontology, algorithms implemented in the reasoner, and underlying user goals. Although a simple fetch and return could take just a few seconds, a complex query formulation that has to traverse recursively through several classes could take hours under the same computing environment ([-R6, -R7]).

SYNTACTICAL REPRESENTATION OF PATTERNS

The content of pattern elements needs to be adequately represented for any further action. Descriptive markup (Coombs, Renear, & DeRose, 1987) provides a rich and mature model for text, with well-defined syntax and semantics (Sperberg-McQueen, Huitfeldt, & Renear, 2000) that allows focusing on the content rather than processing or presentation. Extensible Markup Language (XML) (Bray, Paoli, Sperberg-McQueen, Maler, & Yergeau, 2004) is a vendor-neutral [+R6.4] meta-language that provides directions for expressing the syntax of descriptive markup languages. Instances of these markup languages are hierarchically structured documents that typically consist of content encapsulated within elements and attributes, and grammatical instructions on how to process them. A markup language for representing Mobile Application patterns that satisfies many of the requirements [R1-R8] is introduced in Pai (2002).

There are a number of technologies that strengthen the XML framework. XML Schema (Fallside, 2001) provides a grammar for structural and datatype constraints on the syntax and content of the elements and attributes in XML documents ([+R1]). XML Linking

Figure 2. A pattern represented in XML transformed to multiple computing environments

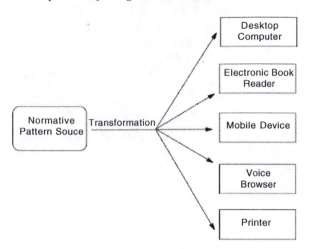

Language (XLink) (DeRose, Maler, & Orchard, 2001) provides powerful bidirectional linking capabilities necessary for hypertext ([+R3.1]). Namespaces in XML (Bray, Hollander, & Layman, 1999) is mechanism for uniquely identifying elements and attributes of XML documents specific to a markup language, thus making it possible to create heterogeneous documents that unambiguously mix elements and attributes from multiple different XML documents ([+R5]). XSL Transformations (XSLT) (Clark, 1999) is a style sheet language for transforming XML documents into other formats. There is a mature base of publicly available tools for authoring and processing XML and its ancillary technologies ([+R7]).

Representing the anatomy of a pattern in an XML document provides various advantages toward archival, retrieval, and processing. Each pattern element can be uniquely identified and can be referred to from both inside and outside the document it is contained in ([+R2]). It is possible to separate the structure of a pattern from its presentation, thereby enabling a pattern to be rendered on multiple devices via a transformation, without making substantial modifications to the original document source (Figure 2). For example, a pattern represented in XML could be transformed using a XSLT style sheet into HTML for presentation on a desktop computer.

Since XML is based on Unicode for its character set, pattern documents have a strong support for internationalization ([+R4]): elements of a pattern or their content could be represented simultaneously in different natural languages or make use of special symbols; as a byproduct, it also fosters collaborative authoring and encourages global dissemination of patterns.

- **Example:** The following illustrates a simple XML document instance representing a generic pattern:

```
<xml version="1.0" encoding="UTF-8">
<PATTERN ID="...">
<HEAD>
 <!--Metadata Elements -->
<AUTHOR>...</AUTHOR>
<VERSION>...</VERSION>
</HEAD>
<BODY>
 <!-- Core Elements -->
<NAME>...</NAME>
<PROBLEM>...</PROBLEM>
<CONTEXT>...</CONTEXT>
<SOLUTION>...</SOLUTION>
<EXAMPLE MEDIA-TYPE="...">...</EXAMPLE>
</BODY>
</PATTERN>
```

The presence of ellipsis reflects some legally allowable content. The precise semantics of desirable XML elements (PATTERN, NAME, PROBLEM, CONTEXT, SOLUTION, EXAMPLE) and attributes (ID, MEDIA-TYPE) can be given by an ontology. An XML Schema can provide the structural (order and cardinality) and datatype constraints for all the XML elements and attributes.

There are certain obstacles in the use of XML for representing patterns. Unless compressed, XML grammars and documents can be prohibitively large for network transmission and machine interpretation. They also can appear to be verbose [-R6.3] and can be error-prone for direct authoring. The tools for authoring and processing patterns tend to be different than the tools for XML, which adds an extra layer of effort ([-R8]).

INTERDEPENDENCY OF PATTERN REPRESENTATION LANGUAGES

Some of the pattern representation languages discussed are not necessarily exclusive and can in fact complement each other. XML is not meant to be a mechanism for conceptual modeling of a domain and has limited capabilities toward relationship management. XML grammar languages such as XML Schema provide only syntactical but, for our purpose, insufficient semantical constraints on the elements and attributes included in XML documents. For example, it would not in general be possible to conclude from an XML Schema that if the pattern SOLUTION element suggests a shopping system, then the RELATED PATTERN element must point to a payment system pattern. Such issues can be compensated by using pattern ontology. On the other hand,

among the possible choices, XML is a suitable candidate for underlying syntax of pattern ontology languages. As pattern ontologies grow in size, there is a need for visualization during authoring. To a certain extent, this capability can be provided by the use of UML (by using Class Diagrams for concepts and properties, using Associations for roles, and including constraints using OCL where needed).

FUTURE TRENDS

As the number of patterns/pattern languages evolve and are shared among people with diverse backgrounds around the world, appropriate representation of patterns will become crucial. The Semantic Web (Hendler, Lassila, & Berners-Lee, 2001) has recently emerged as an extension of the current Web that adds technological means for better knowledge representation, interpretation, and reasoning. With its origins (Schwartz, 2003) in classical Artificial Intelligence (AI), Semantic Web has been labeled as the future of distributed knowledge management (Daconta, Obrst, & Smith, 2003).

Ontology specification languages based on XML syntax and DL semantics designed specifically for Semantic Web applications are beginning to appear. The Web Ontology Language (OWL) (Dean & Schreiber, 2004) is an XML-based ontology specification language initiative of the World Wide Web Consortium (W3C) to standardize and streamline past similar efforts under one banner. There are three sub-languages of OWL that are designed to be increasingly expressive (OWL Lite, OWL DL, and OWL Full). In our experience, only OWL DL provides the right balance for ontological representation of patterns due to its semantical foundations in DL and available reasoning support. Equipped with ontologies, powerful querying schemas, and other related technologies in the Semantic Web framework, pattern users will be able to access desirable patterns for the problem at hand with precision under distributed computing environments. For that to succeed, it is also imperative that ontological bases for patterns are openly accessible and are efficient. Initiatives toward ontological representation of patterns, particularly in modern ontology specification languages, are in their infancy (Henninger, 2002) and we hope that recent stabilization of OWL will encourage the pattern community to work in that direction.

Automation of activities in pattern management will continue to be an important area of research. In this regard, placing patterns within the framework of case-based reasoning (CBR) (Kolodner, 1993), an AI approach to learning and problem-solving based on past experience, can be quite useful. For example, pattern selection and use that traditionally has been a human activity could (at least partially) be automated using CBR, where a case is a situation in which a design pattern was applied in the past to a specific software design (Gomes et al., 2002). The issues due to interrelationships (Althoff, 2001) and heterogeneity that this gives rise to could be ameliorated by ontological (Wu, Lou, & Chen, 2003) and XML representations (Coyle, Hayes, & Cunningham, 2002) of cases. The computing challenges that remain here will be adaptation when the case-based representations of patterns are feature-rich and when they are large in number.

CONCLUSION

The raison d'être for patterns as reusable knowledge is to transcend wisdom from experts to novices. To be successful in that regard, the continually evolving ecosystem of patterns needs to be readily available and systematically managed. This requires a transition from a natural language representation to formal representation of knowledge inherent in patterns.

UML, along with OCL to a certain extent, and XML-based markup languages working choreographically with DL-based ontology languages to a large extent are equipped to do that. To successfully represent a pattern, we also need to achieve a delicate balance between graphical depictions and descriptive text where the two act synergistically (Vlissides, 1998).

To realize the true potential of patterns, we must foster an environment where the user community can freely and effectively communicate. The Semantic Web provides a vehicle to advance this social aspect of patterns.

ACKNOWLEDGMENTS

We would like to thank Dr. Volker Haarslev (Concordia University, Montreal, Canada) for his insights on Description Logics, and the reviewers for their helpful comments and suggestions for improvement.

REFERENCES

Adams, J., Koushik, S., Vasudeva, G., & Galambos, G. (2001). *Patterns for e-business: A strategy for reuse.* IBM Press.

Adolph, S., Bramble, P., Cockburn, A., & Pols, A. (2002). *Patterns for effective use cases.* Addison-Wesley.

Alexander, C. (1979). *The timeless way of building.* Oxford University Press.

Althoff, K.-D. (2001). Case-based reasoning. In S.K. Chang (Ed.), *Handbook of software engineering and knowledge engineering* (Vol. 1). World Scientific.

Baader, F., McGuinness, D., Nardi, D., & Schneider, P.P. (2003). *The description logic handbook: theory, implementation and applications.* Cambridge University Press.

Baader, F., & Sattler, U. (2001). An overview of tableau algorithms for description logics. *Studia Logica, 69,* 5-40.

Berczuk, S., & Appleton, B. (2003). *Software configuration management patterns: Effective teamwork, practical integration.* Addison Wesley.

Boehm, B.W., Abts, C., Brown, A.W., Chulani, S, Clark, B.K, Horowitz, E., Madachy, R., Reifer, D., & Steece, B. (2001). *Software cost estimation with COCOMO II.* Prentice Hall.

Booch, G., Jacobson, I., & Rumbaugh, J. (2005). *The unified modeling language reference manual* (2nd Ed.). Addison-Wesley.

Borchers, J. (2001). *A pattern approach to interaction design.* John Wiley & Sons.

Brachman, R.J., & Levesque, H.J. (1985). *Readings in knowledge representation.* Morgan Kaufmann.

Braude, E.J. (2004). *Software design: From programming to architecture.* John Wiley & Sons.

Bray, T., Hollander, D., & Layman, A. (1999). *Namespaces in XML.* W3C Recommendation. World Wide Web Consortium (W3C).

Bray, T., Paoli, J., Sperberg-McQueen, C.M., Maler, E., & Yergeau, F. (2004). *Extensible Markup Language (XML) 1.0* (3rd Ed.). W3C Recommendation. World Wide Web Consortium (W3C).

Clark, J. (1999). *XSL Transformations (XSLT) Version 1.0.* W3C Recommendation. World Wide Web Consortium (W3C).

Coombs, J.H, Renear, A.H., & DeRose, S.J. (1987). Markup systems and the future of scholarly text processing. *Communications of the ACM, 30*(11), 933-947.

Coyle, L., Hayes, C., & Cunningham, P. (2002, December 10). Representing cases for CBR in XML. *Proceedings of the 7th UKCBR Workshop*, Cambridge, UK.

Daconta, M.C., Obrst, L.J., & Smith, K.T. (2003). *The Semantic Web: A guide to the future of XML, Web services, and knowledge management.* John Wiley & Sons.

Dean, M., & Schreiber, G. (2004). *OWL Web Ontology Language Reference.* W3C Recommendation. World Wide Web Consortium (W3C).

DeRose, S., Maler, E., & Orchard, E. (2001). *XML Linking Language (XLink) Version 1.0.* W3C Recommendation. World Wide Web Consortium (W3C).

Devedzic, V. (2002). Understanding ontological engineering. *Communications of the ACM, 45*(4), 136-144.

Dong, J., & Yang, S. (2003). Extending UML to visualize design patterns in class diagrams. *15th International Conference on Software Engineering and Knowledge Engineering (SEKE 2003)*, San Francisco.

Eden, A.H., Hirshfeld, Y., & Yehudai A. (1999). *Towards a mathematical foundation for design patterns.* Technical Report 1999-004, Department of Information Technology, Uppsala University, Uppsala, Sweden.

Fallside, D.C. (2001). *XML Schema Part 0: Primer.* W3C Recommendation. World Wide Web Consortium (W3C).

Fenton, N.E., & Pfleeger, S.L. (1997). *Software metrics: A rigorous & practical approach.* International Thomson Computer Press.

Gamma, E., Helm, R., Johnson, R., & Vlissides, J. (1995). *Design patterns: Elements of reusable object-oriented software.* Addison-Wesley.

Gomes, P., Pereira, F., Paiva, P., Seco, N., Ferreira, J., & Bento, C. (2002, September 4-7). Using CBR for automation of software design patterns. *Proceedings of the 6th European Conference on Case Based Reasoning (ECCBR 2002)*, Aberdeen, Scotland.

Gómez-Pérez, A., Fernández-López, M., & Corcho, O. (2004). *Ontological engineering.* Springer Verlag.

Gruber, T.R. (1993). Toward principles for the design of ontologies used for knowledge sharing. In *Formal ontology in conceptual analysis and knowledge representation.* Kluwer Academic Publishers.

Hendler, J., Lassila, O., & Berners-Lee, T. (2001). The Semantic Web. *Scientific American, 5*(1).

Henninger, S. (2002). Using the Semantic Web to construct an ontology-based repository for software patterns. *Proceedings of the 2002 Workshop on the State of the Art in Automated Software Engineering*, Irvine, CA (pp. 18-22).

ISO. (1994). ISO 8402:1994. *Quality management and quality assurance—Vocabulary.* International Organization for Standardization (ISO).

Kolodner, J. (1993). *Case-based reasoning.* Morgan Kaufmann.

May, D., & Taylor, P. (2003). Knowledge management with patterns. *Communications of the ACM, 46*(7), 94-99.

Nonaka, I., & Takeuchi, H. (1995). *The knowledge-creating company: How Japanese companies create the dynamics of innovation.* Oxford University Press.

Pai, H. (2002). *Applications of extensible markup language to mobile application patterns.* Master's thesis, McGill University, Canada.

Schauer, R., & Keller, R.K. (1998). Pattern visualization for software comprehension. *Proceedings of the 6th International Workshop on Program Comprehension (IWPC'99)*, Ischia, Italy (pp. 4-12).

Schwartz, D.G. (2003). Open IS semantics and the Semantic Web: The road ahead. *IEEE Intelligent Systems, 18*(3), 52-58.

Sowa, J.F. (1991). *Principles of semantic networks: Explorations in the representation of knowledge.* Morgan Kaufmann.

Sperberg-McQueen, C.M., Huitfeldt, C., & Renear, A. (2000). Meaning and interpretation of markup. *Markup Languages: Theory & Practice, 2*(3), 215-234.

Taibi, T., & Ngo, D.C.L. (2003). Formal specification of design patterns: A balanced approach. *Journal of Object Technology, 2*(4), 127-140.

Vlissides, J. (1998). Notation, notation, notation. *C++ Report*, April.

Warmer, J., & Kleppe, A. (2003). *The object constraint language: Precise modeling with UML* (2nd ed.). Addison-Wesley.

Wu, Z., Lou, G., & Chen, H. (2003, June 24). CaseML: A RDF-based case markup language for case-based reasoning in Semantic Web. *Proceedings of the ICCBR 2003 Workshop on "From Structured Cases to Unstructured Problem Solving Episodes for Experience-Based Assistance,"* Trondheim, Norway.

K

KEY TERMS

Description Logics: A highly expressive formalism that allows users to specify concepts, properties of concepts, and relationships among concepts, by writing independent logical propositions.

Inference: A logical conclusion derived by making implicit knowledge explicit.

Markup: Syntactically delimited characters added to the data of a document to represent its structure.

Pattern: A proven solution to a recurring problem in a given context.

Pattern Language: A set of interrelated patterns expressed in some notation that, as a whole, provides a vocabulary for solving problems arising in some domain.

Pattern Representation: An expression in some natural or formal language to make the knowledge inherent in a pattern processable for human and machine interpretation.

Ontology: An explicit formal specification of a conceptualization that consists of a set of terms in a domain and relations among them.

Knowledge Reuse

Ilan Oshri
Erasmus University Rotterdam, The Netherlands

K

INTRODUCTION

Knowledge reuse is the process through which knowledge is captured, validated, stored, and retrieved. Through the reuse of knowledge, organizations may exploit internal capabilities and improve the effectiveness of their exploration activities (March, 1999). Knowledge reuse processes emphasize the centrality of knowledge within an organization by aligning information systems and communication technologies with human activity and organizational mechanisms, such as learning processes and organizational structures. The process of knowledge reuse can be systematic and planned; however, it can also be carried out in an informal manner through social networks and interpersonal ties (Newell, 2004). While knowledge reuse is explored from an entitative perspective, in which knowledge is generic, accessible, and codifiable, other views, such as social construction (Lave & Wenger, 1991), are also considered in this article. Furthermore, various contexts are considered in this article; however, the emphasis in this article is on knowledge reuse activities in product development and project management contexts.

In this article, the concept of knowledge reuse will be explored. First, a review of recent discussions in the academic and practical literature will be presented. Following this, a discussion about the processes, contexts, mechanisms, and challenges involved in reusing knowledge will be developed. Lastly, future research in this area and conclusions will be offered.

BACKGROUND

The study of knowledge reuse has evolved from the field of software development through object-oriented software development practices (Banker & Kauffman, 1991) to more strategic management concepts such as modularization and product design (Sanchez & Mahoney, 1996). Several authors (e.g., Markus, 2001) introduced knowledge reuse as an important concept in knowledge management. The practical relevance of knowledge reuse was considered from software and hardware engineering perspectives (Sanderson & Uzumeri, 1994), the management of multi-project environments (Cusumano & Nobeoka, 1998), and as a phase in the evolution of a firm (Victor & Boynton, 1998). More recently, research has explored additional scenarios for knowledge reuse providing further insight about the reuse of project-specific knowledge (Newell, 2004), templates, information about bids, components, and platforms (Nightingale, 2000).

Various mechanisms and processes have been associated with knowledge reuse. First and foremost, knowledge reuse has been perceived as a process that is based on documenting, verifying, indexing, and retrieving information from repositories (Markus, 2001). Indeed, the information systems approach to knowledge reuse is vital. Nonetheless, knowledge reuse is also an outcome of an informal, people-based activity (Newell, 2004), which can also be complementary to the information system approach. In this respect, the challenges organizations face when attempting to reuse knowledge involve aspects associated with both information systems and human behavior. On the one hand, knowledge re-users face challenges in properly storing, indexing, filtering, verifying, and retrieving information from repositories. On the other hand, these challenges intimately relate to motivational factors to share knowledge, which are human-related factors. The above topics will be discussed in detail in the following sections.

MAIN FOCUS OF THE ARTICLE

The Concept of Knowledge Reuse: Some Examples

Knowledge reuse is defined as the process through which knowledge is captured, verified, filtered, stored, and retrieved (Markus, 2001). There are at least three actors involved in this activity: the knowledge creator who creates the knowledge, the knowledge broker or intermediary who prepares the knowledge for reuse by synthesizing and documenting the knowledge, and the knowledge re-user who retrieves the knowledge and re-applies it in different contexts (Markus, 2001). Knowledge reuse activities are arguably related to organizational effectiveness through the exploitation of existing knowledge and resources (Dixon, 2000).

There are several knowledge processes related to the reuse of knowledge. In particular, knowledge sharing and transfer are two knowledge processes that were often associated with knowledge reuse. Unlike knowledge sharing and transfer, reusing knowledge is an activity in which specific knowledge or design is transferred from a knowledge holder to a knowledge seeker in order to make use and re-apply the knowledge or the design in different contexts. Some car models made by Toyota, for example, share the same components. This was achieved through the transfer of these components between different project teams. In such an activity, a knowledge base will be populated with information about designs and components; and through a knowledge search mechanism, a re-user will be able to verify, retrieve, and reapply a particular component. In this reuse activity, a modification of the reused design may take place in order to adjust the reused design to the requirements and specifications of the new product.

Advantages and Disadvantages in Reusing Knowledge

The advantages associated with the reuse of knowledge are many. By reusing knowledge, organizations may also avoid "reinventing the wheel" in terms of products, components, templates, and processes, thus freeing up resources to other core activities, be these customer responsiveness or innovation. In the context of product development, some more specific contributions were associated with the reuse of knowledge such as lower risk in new product development and a robust design (Nightingale, 2000), shorter time to market, reduced R&D costs, and higher responsiveness to customer needs (Datar, Clark, Sunder, Surendra, & Kannan, 1997; Nayak, Chen, & Simpson, 2000).

However, reusing knowledge may also bring stress to organizations. Excessive exploitation, in particular, may lead to a trap in which organizations that operate in "suboptimal stable equilibriums" and enjoy the cost effectiveness associated with the reuse of knowledge may suffer from a lack of explorative activities that are crucial for the future development of organizations (March, 1999). Furthermore, information distortion, in the form of missing information or false information, could possibly negatively affect the reuse process and outcome (Carley & Lin, 1997). Therefore, to avoid these pitfalls, organizations require an understanding of the various aspects involved in knowledge reuse, and may design their internal processes and systems to respond to such challenges.

The Process of Knowledge Reuse

Several processes are involved in the reuse of knowledge. From an information systems perspective (Markus, 2001), the reuse of knowledge is based on the use of repositories

and may involve four processes: First, knowledge is captured through documentation, something that can be a by-product of the work process or as an intentional activity using information systems. Capturing knowledge can also include filtering knowledge and preparing the knowledge for future reuse. Second, knowledge is classified and formatted by relating the content to existing and new classification schemes, and through the contextualization and de-contextualization of the content. Third is distributing the knowledge by either pull or push mechanisms. Populating a repository is an example of a pull mechanism, while an automatic e-mail that informs knowledge workers about project management templates available to reuse is a push mechanism. The reuse activity is the last stage in which the re-user is (re)applying the knowledge and updates the knowledge source with contextual context that may serve future re-users.

From a learning perspective (Prencipe & Tell, 2001), the reuse of knowledge can take place at three levels of the organization—individual, group or team, and organizational—through mechanisms that relate to experience accumulation, knowledge articulation, and knowledge codification. Knowledge reuse is more systematic and exploitative in nature when the learning is based on knowledge codification at the three levels of the organization, and tends to be more explorative in nature when the learning is based on accumulative experience at the individual level.

From a strategic management perspective (Victor & Boynton, 1998), knowledge reuse is a step towards building sustainable and dynamic capabilities. A full renewal lifecycle of a product from a knowledge-based perspective may consist of the creation of knowledge, the transformation of new knowledge into modular products and components, and the reuse of these modules, according to market needs, by reconfiguring and re-applying knowledge.

Achieving successful knowledge reuse requires the involvement of each of the aspects mentioned above. Information systems aspects are important for the storage and retrieval of the knowledge, while the learning aspects are key for the improvement of reuse activities. The following section will address the contexts within which knowledge reuse may occur.

The Context of Knowledge Reuse

Knowledge reuse may take place in different contexts, such as between organizations (inter-firm knowledge reuse) or within an organization (intra-firm knowledge reuse). Sharing knowledge and designs between firms is not free of challenges. Issues pertaining to trust between suppliers of a supply chain may impede the sharing of knowledge. Furthermore, proprietary issues may restrict the reuse of designs across firms. Nonetheless, in recent years, research and development have seen an improvement in the level of knowledge sharing between firms. In particular, examples from the automobile industry provide an insight into the systems and processes that support product delivery through information sharing within a supply chain (Childerhouse, Hermiz, Mason-Jones, Popp, & Towill, 2003).

In the context of intra-firm knowledge reuse, firms put the emphasis on making generic and specific knowledge available for reuse through repositories, social networks, and interpersonal connections. Recent years have seen a growing interest in reusing project-specific knowledge (Newell, 2004). Projects have become a central vehicle through which companies learn—hence, requiring a systematic method to capture the learning and experiences and reusing them over time. The reuse of project-specific knowledge and the broad firm context will be discussed below.

Mechanisms Involved in Knowledge Reuse

Various mechanisms are mentioned in the context of knowledge reuse. These can be divided into three areas: information systems, managerial practices, and social networks mechanisms.

Information systems support knowledge reuse through the use of repositories (Markus, 2001). These repositories store and make available various types of information such as internal and external knowledge, data or documents, specific or generic information, or as a pointer to experts.

Managerial practices may include several mechanisms through which knowledge reuse is supported. Sharing work procedures is one important mechanism for knowledge reuse. In this respect, commonality across tools and technical procedures is important and may include, for example, the use of identical development tools (e.g., C++ or Microsoft Office) across several software development projects. Furthermore, shared work procedures may also include the involvement of different stakeholders in a decision-making process to ensure that past learning, from various perspectives, will be included in the process. Sharing past experiences, for example, is achieved when a multi-functional product development team meets every week to assess progress and suggest solutions, based on their individual and shared learning.

Furthermore, the organization of experts and expertise within the firm may have an impact on the possibilities of reusing knowledge. In this respect, two modes of organizing were considered. First is the functional structure in which experts and expertise are centered within the functional department and contribute to the project objectives from their departments. Second is the project-centered structure in which experts and expertise from different departments work as a project team towards common project goals. While the functional structure offers more possibilities to reuse knowledge within the department, mainly with regard to technologies and product concepts, the project-centered structure presents opportunities to reuse lessons learned between multi-functional teams with regard to product development process. The matrix structure, which combines functional with project-centered structures, includes the possibilities to reuse expert technical knowledge within the functional structure with the learning from past projects about the process of product development within project teams.

Another managerial practice that gained attention in recent years is project management practices (Cusumano & Nobeoka, 1998). Through a careful coordination of projects, the reuse of knowledge between projects can be improved. In this context, the emphasis has been on the reuse of components and platforms from a source project to other projects that are carried out concurrently.

Reward schemes were also considered as a driver to encourage knowledge reuse. Reward systems were designed to remunerate knowledge workers who documented and indexed valuable knowledge, as well as knowledge workers who made a useful (re)use of existing knowledge by reapplying concepts and solutions to new product and process introductions.

While technology and managerial practices dominated the discussion about knowledge reuse, social networks and interpersonal connections contributing to knowledge reuse are no less important to the exploitation of internal capabilities (Newell, 2004). Person-to-person communications, informal encounters, and social rituals within communities of practice are among the various activities that drive knowledge reuse through social interactions (Prencipe & Tell, 2001; Wenger, 1998).

There are several scenarios in which the mechanisms involved in knowledge reuse may play a role. Managerial practices, in particular project management practices, will enhance the reuse of knowledge between projects in a project environment. In this scenario, the use of information systems may further assist in documenting, screening, and retrieving knowledge to be re-configured and re-applied by another project team. Social interaction as a vehicle for knowledge reuse is more an explorative activity which drives knowledge exchanges between knowledge creators and re-users; however, it may enjoy the planning and discipline introduced by project management practices.

Challenges in Knowledge Reuse

The reuse of knowledge may face a number of challenges. From an information system perspective, there are several challenges at the individual, group, and organizational levels. Knowledge can be either tacit or explicit (Polanyi, 1966). Articulating tacit knowledge is a difficult task, let alone capturing, storing, and retrieving it. This is perhaps the most challenging task that a knowledge re-user is facing.

Secondly, properly creating and indexing knowledge may generate mistakes or confusion about the "true" meaning of the information stored or retrieved (Markus, 2001). A common problem, for example, is to search for specific information. The common system of indexing generates problems for knowledge seekers because of a misplacement of the information within the indexing system.

Thirdly, the costs involved in creating repositories by carefully documenting and indexing knowledge for future reuse are very high. Furthermore, data entries are long and can hardly be justified as a central activity within product development.

Lastly, the "stickiness" of knowledge presents additional barriers to transfer and reuse knowledge. The recipient's lacks of absorptive capacity is one example of the recipient's inability to value, assimilate, and apply new knowledge (Szulanski, 1996, p. 31).

From a managerial perspective, the process of knowledge reuse may face challenges in the area of the organizational structure, project management coordination, and planning and reward systems. In terms of the organizational structure, while adopting either a functional or project-centered structure would present advantages for knowledge reuse within and across projects respectively, each structure still cannot support the reuse of knowledge across the organization. The matrix organization combines functional departments and cross-functional teams in the form of projects. Under this structure, projects usually succeed in integrating knowledge across functional areas, therefore increasing the possibilities to reuse knowledge and designs (Cusumano & Nobeoka, 1998).

Rewarding knowledge re-users has also posed challenges in terms of the criteria that define what a valuable knowledge reuse process is. Some of the criteria suggested in this context are at the project level. Criteria assessing the exploitation of resources, for example, included: man/month software development saved following the reuse process, total reduction in project costs, and a shorter product lead-time. Both the number of hits per index in a repository and the number of times an existing solution was reapplied in different contexts were considered as criteria for the value and quality of a reuse process. Because a reuse process can also be based on social interactions, a process that is often unplanned and undocumented, rewarding those involved can be a difficult task.

Lastly, planning a reuse process through project management practices may not always be possible (Cusumano & Nobeoka, 1998). Indeed, in companies that can plan product introductions in advance, the possibilities to design and monitor the reuse of knowledge between projects are feasible. This is mainly the case in mass-producing companies such as Toyota and Sony. On the other hand, many organizations cannot rely on the project planning approach. Suppliers of complex systems and products (CoPS), for example, may not be able to plan in advance the reuse of knowledge by solely relying on project management practices. This is because of contractual arrangements between the supplier and the client that define the production time interval, the design, and the number of units to be produced (Hobday, 2000). For this reason, suppliers of CoPS are more likely to rely on information systems and social interactions as the drivers for knowledge reuse (Prencipe & Tell, 2001). In summary, the challenges involved in achieving a successful reuse process are many, bringing together aspects from the social, information system, and human behavior perspectives.

FUTURE TRENDS

Two main future trends can be considered: practical and research themes.

From a practical viewpoint, potential developments are in three areas: defining the role of knowledge facilitator in knowledge reuse activities, motivating individuals and teams to engage in knowledge reuse activities, and balancing between exploitation (reuse) and exploration (innovation) activities.

Firms face major challenges in building and successfully maintaining knowledge systems. Several studies confirmed that it takes more than information systems to reuse knowledge (Markus, 2001; Newell, 2004). It has been suggested that knowledge facilitators (also known as knowledge brokers and knowledge managers) can improve the capture and filtering of knowledge for reuse (Markus, 2001). Instead of relying on project teams to carry out the storage of knowledge in a repository, firms should follow some recent successful examples, such as Booz-Allen, in which knowledge managers accompanied the project team making sure that knowledge generated during the project is captured, indexed, and prepared for reuse (Markus, 2001). In addition to the need to continuously improve technology-based indexing and searching mechanisms, the development of transactive memory, a concept which emphasizes the idea of "who knows what," can be enhanced through the involvement of knowledge facilitators, acting as knowledge brokers.

While the rationale for reusing knowledge is well grounded in the economies of efficiencies, in practice empirical evidence suggests that many organizations do not pursue this activity. In many cases the reason for this behavior is a lack of awareness and incentives that would encourage individuals and teams to seek solutions in-house prior to launching an explorative activity which may well be a "reinvention of the wheel." Managers should consider developing educational programs relating to the many aspects involved in reusing knowledge, including methodologies that fit their organization and incentive schemes that link reuse activities to individual, team, and organizational performance.

Lastly, while this article represents a call to undertake knowledge reuse activities, organizations should still consider achieving a balance between exploitative and explorative activities. When launching a new product, for example, an assessment of the costs involved in reconfiguring an existing design for reuse versus developing a design from scratch should be undertaken.

From a theoretical viewpoint, future research trends may consider understanding the process and context of reuse activities in the following scenarios: (i) reuse of intangible products such as financial products, (ii) reuse of processes, and (iii) reuse between firms also coined here as inter-firm reuse process.

The study of processes and innovation of intangible products, in particular in the financial services, is very limited. More specifically, little is known about the reuse of knowledge of intangible products as opposed to tangible products (e.g., the broad research on reuse in the context of the automobile industry or the aircraft industry).

The study of knowledge reuse has traditionally focused on the potential to reuse products or sub-systems within products. More research is needed into the potential to reuse processes and templates of operations in the broad context of the firm, and more specifically within and between projects.

Lastly, knowledge reuse is perceived as an intra-firm activity. Little is known about the process through which inter-firm knowledge reuse can be achieved, the mechanisms involved in the reuse that may support it, and the challenges involved in the process.

CONCLUSION

This article explored the concept of knowledge reuse. Aspects associated with knowledge reuse were reviewed from information system, social, and strategic management perspectives. While research and practice has traditionally focused on information systems to support the reuse of knowledge, other tools and practices, such as managerial practices and social networks, were reviewed as complementary vehicles. While research and practice has made significant progress in understanding knowledge reuse contexts and processes, far more investment in methodologies, tools, and processes is still needed in order to exploit the potential offered by this practice.

REFERENCES

Banker, R.D., & Kauffman, R.J. (1991). Reuse and productivity in integrated computer-aided software engineering: An empirical study. *MIS Quarterly, 12*(2), 375-401.

Carley, K.M., & Lin, Z. (1997). A theoretical study of organizational performance under information distortion. *Management Science, 43*(7), 976-998.

Childerhouse, P., Hermiz, R., Mason-Jones, R., Popp, A., & Towill, D.R. (2003). Information flow in automotive supply chains—present industrial practice. *Industrial Management and Data Systems, 103*(3/4), 137-150.

Cusumano, M.A., & Nobeoka, K. (1998). *Thinking beyond lean: How multi-project environment is transforming product development at Toyota and other companies.* New York: The Free Press.

Datar, S., Clark, J., Sunder, K., Surendra, R., & Kannan, S. (1997). New product development structures and time-to-market. *Management Science, 43*(4), 452-464.

Dixon, N.M. (2000). *Common knowledge: How companies thrive by sharing what they know.* Boston: Harvard Business School Press.

Drucker, P. (1969). *The age of discontinuity.* NJ: Transaction Publisher.

Hobday, M. (2000). The project-based organization: An ideal form for managing complex products and systems? *Research Policy, 29*(Special Issue), 872-893.

Lave, J., & Wenger, E. (1991). *Situated learning legitimate peripheral participation.* Cambridge: Cambridge University Press.

March, J.G. (1999). *The pursuit of organizational intelligence.* Malden, MA: Blackwell.

Markus, M.J. (2001). Toward a theory of knowledge reuse: Types of knowledge reuse situations and factors in reuse success. *Journal of Management Information Systems, 18*(1), 57-93.

Nayak, R., Chen, W., & Simpson, T. (2000, September 10-13). A variation-based methodology for product family design. *Proceedings of the ASME Design Automation Conference* (Paper No. DAC14264), Baltimore.

Newell, S. (2004). Enhancing cross-project learning. *Engineering Management Journal, 16*(1), 12-21.

Nightingale, P. (2000). The product-process-organization relationship in complex development projects. *Research Policy, 29*(Special Issue), 913-930.

Polanyi, M. (1962). *Personal knowledge: Toward a post critical philosophy.* New York: Harper Torchbooks.

Prencipe, A., & Tell, F. (2001). Inter-project learning: Processes and outcomes of knowledge codification in project-based firms. *Research Policy, 30*(9), 1373-1394.

Sanchez, R., & Mahoney, J.T. (1996). Modularity, flexibility and knowledge management in product and organization design. *Strategic Management Journal, 17*(Special Issue), 63-76.

Sanderson, S., & Uzumeri, M. (1994). Managing product families: The case of the Sony Walkman. *Research Policy, 24*, 761-782.

Szulanski, G. (1996). Exploring internal stickiness: Impediments to the transfer of best practice within the firm. *Strategic Management Journal, 17*(Special Issue), 27-43.

Turner, J.R. (1993). *The handbook of project-based management.* Maidenhead: McGraw-Hill.

Victor, B., & Boyton, A.C. (1998). *Invented here.* Boston: Harvard Business School Press.

Wenger, E. (1998). *Communities of practice; learning, meaning and identity.* Cambridge: Cambridge University Press.

Winter, S. (1987). Knowledge and competence as strategic assets. In D.J. Teece (Ed.), *The competitive challenge: Strategies for industrial innovation and renewal* (pp. 159-184). Cambridge, MA: Ballinger Publishing Company.

KEY TERMS

Inter-Project Learning: A learning activity in which project-specific knowledge, templates, or designs are transferred from a source project to other projects.

Knowledge Facilitator: A knowledge worker who ensures that knowledge is captured, indexed, and was made available for reuse.

Knowledge Worker: Participants in an economy where information and its manipulation are the commodity and the activity (Drucker, 1969). Some examples of knowledge workers include, but are not limited to, researchers, product developers, engineers, and resource planners.

Project and Project Environments: A project is a temporary endeavor in which human, material, and financial resources are organized in a novel way, to undertake a unique scope of work, for a given specification, within constraints of cost and time, so as to achieve beneficial changes defined by quantitative and qualitative objectives. A project environment is a cluster of projects within a firm, in which a set of products is developed.

Project Management Practices for Reuse: Project coordination mechanisms that ensure an overlap in development time between two projects to ensure that designs developed in one project will be reused by other projects.

Repository: In information technology, a central place in which an aggregation of data is kept and maintained in an organized way, usually in computer storage.

Social Networks for Reuse: Organizational mechanisms that emphasize interpersonal interactions as a source for knowledge reuse between individual and teams.

Knowledge Sharing

William R. King
University of Pittsburgh, USA

INTRODUCTION

Knowledge sharing (KS) is critical to organizations that wish to use their knowledge as an asset to achieve competitive advantage. Knowledge management systems (KMSs) can be primary enablers of knowledge sharing in an organization.

A major focus of knowledge sharing is on the individual who can explicate, encode, and communicate knowledge to other individuals, groups, and organizations. In particular, the employment of some KMSs requires individuals to contribute their knowledge to a system rather than keeping it to themselves or sharing it only through personal exchanges.

Another major focus of knowledge sharing is on knowledge sharing in teams since teams have become so prominent in management thought and practice, and because some of the long-presumed benefits of teams such as "higher labor productivity, a flatter management structure and reduced employee turnover" have been validated (Glassop, 2002, p. 227).

A major distinction between knowledge sharing and knowledge transfer (terms that may sometimes be used interchangeably) is that transfer implies focus, a clear objective, and unidirectionality, while knowledge may be shared in unintended ways multiple directionally without a specific objective (see article titled "Knowledge Transfer").

Of course, knowledge may also be shared in intended ways, such as when a team attempts to develop mutual knowledge, a common ground, or knowledge that the parties know they share in common (Cramton, 2001).

BACKGROUND

Some people presumably have a tendency to share knowledge just as some people have a tendency to be talkative. Others follow the "knowledge is power" dictum, probably learned in organizational settings; these people may hoard knowledge and be reluctant to share it.

Knowledge sharing may occur between and among individuals, within and among teams, among organizational units, and among organizations. Sharing among individuals within teams is a particularly important focus whether the teams are temporary sets of interdependent individuals bound by a collective aim, problem-solving groups (also usually temporary in nature), self-managing teams, or cross-functional teams (Glassop, 2002). Virtual teams, those in which individuals primarily communicate using electronic means, are becoming a more important focus of KS.

Sharing behavior may be differentiated in terms of the sharing of explicit knowledge (that which is written down or encoded in some fashion) vs. the sharing of tacit knowledge (that which exists in the mind of an individual; Nonaka, 1994), or some combination of the two varieties. Individuals may have different propensities to share explicit and tacit knowledge. They may consider explicit knowledge, such as reports and memos that are in their possession, to be owned by the organization that paid them to produce the documents, whereas they may consider that knowledge that is in their heads belongs to them (Constant, Kiesler, & Sproull, 1994).

Knowledge-management systems of two general varieties are both driven primarily by knowledge sharing. The two types are referred to as repositories and networks, or as the codification and personalization types of KMS strategies (Kankanhalli, Tanudidjaja, Sutanto, & Tan, 2003). Repositories are databases of knowledge usually contributed by individuals, teams, or organizations for potential use by others. The best example is a best-practices repository. Networks facilitate communications among team members or among groups of individuals who are not necessarily identified a priori.

Information technology can enable both types: in the former case, enabling sharing across widely dispersed elements of an organization, and in the latter case, enabling communities of practice involving people who discover that they have common practices or interests to form and share knowledge either within an organization or among various organizations. Probably the best known interorganization community is that which develops and maintains the open-source Linux system (Lee & Cole, 2003).

ISSUES IN KNOWLEDGE SHARING

Organizations have taken different views on knowledge sharing. Some, believing that there is a danger in giving away secrets or viewing sharing as a diversion from individuals' primary work, have not encouraged sharing. Others, believing that there is great potential benefit in disseminating knowledge within an organization and perhaps beyond its boundaries, support it. Of course, the tenets of knowledge management presume that sharing is generally both beneficial and necessary if an organization is to realize its potential.

Many researchers and those organizations and managers that wish to encourage knowledge sharing have focused on how they might best motivate individuals to share their most valuable personally held knowledge. The concept of knowledge as a public good can serve to illustrate this issue.

Knowledge as a Public Good

A fundamental issue of KMS is demonstrated by the notion of knowledge as a public good. A public good is something that is available to all members of a community or organization regardless of whether they contributed to the constitution of the good. A fundamental problem with public goods is that they are subject to the free-rider problem whereby an individual enjoys the benefits without contributing to the institution or maintenance of the common asset, which may result in an undersupply of the good.

Thorn and Connolly (1987) conducted research that conceptualized information in a database as a public good. They identified cost as a factor for individuals considering sharing their valuable personally held information in terms of sharing cost: the time and/or effort that is required from the individual to share knowledge through a computer-based system. They concluded that this cost is something that is considered by the potential sharer when making the decision of whether to contribute.

Constant et al. (1994) identified positive motivators for individuals to contribute, even when the personal costs may be high. These include the enhancement of self-esteem, the reinforcement of an individual's understanding of their own knowledge, and the shared values of organizational citizenship (Bolino & Turnley, 2003).

Goodman and Darr (1999) identified the contextual conditions in the organization affecting an individual's decision to share his or her knowledge through a KMS. They determined that a sharing culture is necessary prior to the implementation of such a system. They also identified shared rewards as an important element in producing such a culture. Such intangible and cultural variables may well constitute the accepted wisdom among KMS practitioners.

Motivating Knowledge Sharing

Organizations generally rely on either formal supervisory controls or more general organizational support to motivate knowledge sharing. Examples of the former are guidelines that specify what is appropriate sharing behavior and the monitoring of the knowledge that individuals provide to a KMS. Illustrative of the latter is the development of cultural norms that promote sharing.

These quite-different views of how knowledge sharing can be motivated are illustrated in studies conducted by Perlow (1998) and Alvesson (1993).

Perlow (1998) studied knowledge workers in a software-development group where the management of the organization instituted a stringent means of controlling the employees. The company imposed strict demands by monitoring employees, standing over them, and routinely checking up on them. Management instituted mandatory meetings, deadlines, and extra work to ensure that the employees were working in the best interest of the firm. This approach is referred to as supervisory control.

Alvesson (1993) performed a case study of a computer consulting company. The study found that management felt that the company operated efficiently because management strove to have a strong interpersonal culture in the organization. This culture was based on focusing on the organization as a community instead of viewing it as merely a collection of individuals. This approach reflects a general approach referred to as social exchange.

Supervisory Control

Organizations can operate in formal ways that encourage knowledge sharing, for example, by using employment contracts that specify that knowledge and information that is collected or generated in the course of work belongs to the organization. However, such legalistic approaches are difficult to enforce.

However, other forms of supervisory control may have an impact on an individual's willingness to share his or her knowledge through a KMS (Loebecke, Van Fenema, & Powell, 1999). Supervisory control is defined as efforts by management to increase the likelihood that individuals will act in ways that will result in the achievement of organizational objectives (Stajkovic & Luthans, 2001).

Supervisory control is important because an assumption in agency theory, and in some other management literature, is that the goals of the employer and the employee are, to some degree, divergent, necessitating a need for control in order to align the goals of the two actors (Flamholtz, 1996). The exact nature of the supervisory-control mechanisms needed to produce goal congruence is unresolved because of the widely varied types of control mechanisms that have been utilized and studied. For example, supervisory-control mechanisms may consist of the use of power, leadership, building clans, or information processing.

Social Exchange

Social-exchange theory posits that people contribute to others commensurate with the contributions that they perceive are being made by others to them. This theory views the contributions that individuals make to an organization as reciprocal arrangements. Reciprocal arrangements occur when an individual performs some type of action for another individual, group, or organization. The action is performed without a specific economic contract that ensures that the action will be repaid. Rather, the individual who performs the action does so because he or she believes that the action will be reciprocated at some future time, though the exact time and nature of the reciprocal act is unknown and unimportant (Turnley, Bolino, Lester, & Bloodgood, 2003).

This exchange relationship develops from a series of mutual exchanges between two actors until such time as a relationship exists whereby mutual exchanges become a normative behavior. Unlike an economic-exchange relationship, in the social-exchange relationship, the potential result of any behavior is based on a trust that the relationship will proceed as in past exchanges (Meyer, Stanley, Herscovitch, & Topolnytsky, 2002).

This relationship of mutual exchange may exist between individuals or between an individual and an organization. Over a period of time, an individual may develop opinions about the exchange relationship between himself or herself and the organization by observing the relationship, the organization, other employees and their relationship with the organization, and individuals who are external to the organization. In this way, employees personify the organization through the actions of their supervisors and coworkers.

Research has demonstrated the relationship between social exchange and positive outcomes in organizations (Allen, Shore, & Griffeth, 2003). Social exchange has been found to be important in exploring why individuals have high feelings of loyalty to their organization. It has also been found to be important in explaining why individuals exhibit positive behaviors in their organizations when these positive behaviors are not formally required (Liao & Chuang, 2004).

Perceived Organizational Support

The emphasis on social exchange from an individual to an organization and vice versa was used by Eisenberger, Huntington, Hutchison, and Sowa (1986) in developing the concept of perceived organizational support (POS) to explain how individuals in organizations can become committed to their organizations. They proposed that "employees develop global beliefs concerning the extent to which the organization values their contributions and cares about their well-being" (p. 501). They developed a reciprocal view of the relationship between employee and employer in which the employee shares a strong level of commitment to his or her organization if he or she perceives that the organization has a strong commitment in return. They surmised that high levels of POS will create a feeling of obligation in the employee, whereby the employee will feel obligated to support organizational goals.

Other research supports this conclusion. Eisenberger, Fasolo, and Davis-LaMastro (1990) showed that POS demonstrated a positive relationship to conscientiousness in the performance of job-related responsibilities and a commitment to making the organization a better place through fostering innovation. Lynch, Eisenberger, and Armeli (1999) found a positive relationship between a high level of POS and a high level of extra-role behaviors, and that the reverse was also true; that is, if there is a low level of POS, there is a low level of extra-role behaviors from individuals in an organization. POS has become a much-used construct in various areas of social science and business (Fuller, Barnett, Hester, & Relyea, 2003).

The Effects of Supervisory Control and Organizational Support

Numerous studies have identified the differences between theories of economics (e.g., supervisory control) and theories of sociology (e.g., organizational support), and their impacts on the achievement of organizational goals. Often, these studies propose that the theories of economics and sociology rely on differing assumptions and therefore cannot be considered to be similar (Adaman & Madra, 2002). In fact, some even contend that the cross-pollination of the disparate theories is inappropriate and should be avoided (e.g., Oleson, 2003).

Modern consideration of rational man as a utility maximizer and social man as a conglomeration of complex motivational forces in an organization trace back to Barnard (1938), who recognized the importance of the "willingness of persons to contribute efforts to the cooperative system" (p. 83). This willingness was considered to be different than the tangible and more easily measurable elements of motivation derived from a supervisory-control system. He emphasized that if individuals in organizations were only concerned with a direct relationship with the structured control system as a means of dictating the exact amount of work that they would accomplish, then the organization would be unable to function. He posited that the helpful behaviors exhibited by employees that are difficult to measure acted as the glue that allowed operations in organizations to run relatively seamlessly.

Katz and Kahn (1966) further developed this idea by distinguishing between in-role behaviors and "innovative and spontaneous behaviors," positing that innovative and spontaneous behaviors make an organization "intrinsically cooperative and interrelated" (p. 339). They proposed that these behaviors are so ingrained in the fabric of the organization that they are seemingly transparent to management and thus are often taken for granted. However, these behaviors ought not to be so taken since much of the work that is accomplished in organizations is difficult for management to specify.

March and Simon (1958) approached organizations from the perspective of social psychology. They acknowledged that individuals make their decisions on much more than purely economic bases and presented propositions that allude to the vast array of influences in an organization that impact the decision-making processes of individuals. Specifically, they focused on the effects that group norms and expectations have on individuals. These norms and expectations are not easily measurable in an economic framework; however, they are important in an organization that is attempting to accomplish specific objectives.

Davis, Schoorman, and Donaldson (1997) contributed to this economics-vs.-sociology discussion by recognizing that viewing individuals as utility maximizers may not account for the complex set of factors that can motivate individuals to accomplish things that do not always seem to directly maximize their utility. They stressed that other motivational elements that are not based on economic assumptions of utility maximization are necessary to account for the motivational elements in individuals and organizations.

FUTURE TRENDS

The issue of how best to motivate individuals to share their most valuable personal knowledge is not completely resolved. The conventional wisdom is that the creation of a knowledge-sharing culture is the best way,

although that is not empirically well validated (Goodman & Darr, 1999).

Among the other research findings related to knowledge sharing that appear to have value are the following:

a. Knowledge sharing involves both costs and benefits (not necessarily economic; Constant et al., 1994; Thorn & Connolly, 1987).

b. Contrary to some popular wisdom, supervisory control appears to be more important than perceived organizational support in terms of both the frequency of submissions and the perceived effort expended in contributing to a KMS (King & Marks, in press; since this study was done in a military organization, the results may be limited to similar contexts).

c. Concern with self-interest has a negative effect on sharing-related attitudes (Constant et al., 1994). This might suggest that an organization that creates a highly competitive culture, such as by having the policy of attempting to counsel 10% of the lowest performers out of the organization each year, might have difficulties in motivating knowledge sharing.

d. Dispersed (not colocated) computer-mediated teams have difficulties in knowledge sharing that are greater than those experienced in colocated teams in part because of the difficulties in establishing social presence—the degree to which the medium facilitates the awareness of other people and the development of interpersonal relationships (Cramton, 2001).

e. Systems variables, such as use and usefulness, appear to have important moderating effects on individuals' sharing behavior through a KMS (King & Marks, in press).

CONCLUSION

Economic, behavioral, and social factors must be considered when assessing the issue of how to motivate individuals to contribute their most valuable personally held knowledge to others who they may not even know, as in contributing to a KMS.

Most interest and research in knowledge sharing has focused on this supply-side issue: that is, how to motivate people to share. However, some researchers have focused on the demand side: individuals' knowledge-seeking and knowledge-acquisition behavior. This perspective addresses potential users of knowledge and how they search for it when they have a question or problem. Expert networks have been established in organizations such as Microsoft to enable such search, and of course, communities of practice also facilitate this demand-side viewpoint of sharing.

REFERENCES

Adaman, F., & Madra, Y. M. (2002). Theorizing the "Third sphere: A critique of the persistence of the economic fallacy". *Journal of Economic Issues, 36*(4), 1045-1078.

Alavi, M., & Leidner, D. (2001). Knowledge management systems: Issues, challenges, and benefits. *CAIS, 1*(7), 2-36.

Allen, D. G., Shore, L. M., & Griffeth, R. W. (2003). The role of perceived organizational support and supportive human resource practices in the turnover process. *Journal of Management, 29*(1), 99-118.

Alvesson, M. (1993). Cultural-ideological modes of management control: A theory and a case study of a professional service company. In S. Deetz (Ed.), *Communication yearbook 16* (pp. 3-42). London: Sage.

Barnard, C. (1938). *The functions of the executive.* Cambridge, MA: Harvard University Press.

Bolino, M. C., & Turnley, W. H. (2003). Going the extra mile: Cultivating and managing employee citizenship behavior. *Academy of Management Executive, 17*(3), 60-71.

Constant, D., Kiesler, S., & Sproull, L. (1994). What's mine is ours, or is it? A study of attitudes about information sharing. *Information Systems Research, 5*(4), 400-421.

Cramton, C. D. (2001). The mutual knowledge problem and its consequences for dispersed collaboration. *Organization Science: A Journal of the Institute of Management Sciences, 12*(3), 346.

Davis, J., Schoorman, F., & Donaldson, L. (1997). Toward a stewardship theory of management. *Academy of Management Review, 22*(1), 20-47.

Eisenberger, R., Fasolo, P., & Davis-LaMastro, V. (1990). Perceived organizational support and employee diligence, commitment, and innovation. *Journal of Applied Psychology, 75,* 51-59.

Eisenberger, R., Huntington, R., Hutchison, S., & Sowa, D. (1986). Perceived organizational support. *Journal of Applied Psychology, 71*(3), 500-507.

Flamholtz, E. (1996). *Effective management control: Theory and practice.* Boston: Kluwer Academic Publishers.

Fuller, J. B., Barnett, T., Hester, K., & Relyea, C. (2003). A social identity perspective on the relationship between perceived organizational support and organizational commitment. *Journal of Social Psychology, 143*(6), 789-791.

Glassop, L. I. (2002). The organizational benefits of teams. *Human Relations, 55*(2), 225-250.

Goodman, P., & Darr, E. (1999). Computer-aided systems and communities: Mechanisms for organizational learning in distributed environments. *MIS Quarterly, 22*(4), 417-440.

Kankanhalli, A., Tanudidjaja, F., Sutanto, J., & Tan, B. (2003). The role of IT in successful knowledge management initiatives. *Communications of the ACM, 46*(9), 69-74.

Katz, D., & Kahn, R. (1966). *The social psychology of organizations.* New York: Wiley.

King, W. R., & Marks, P. V. (in press). *Motivating knowledge sharing through a knowledge management system.*

Lee, G. K., & Cole, R. E. (2003). From a firm-based to a community-based model of knowledge creation: The case of the Linux Kernel development. *Organization Science: A Journal of the Institute of Management Sciences, 14*(6), 633.

Liao, H., & Chuang, A. (2004). A multilevel investigation of factors influencing employee service performance and customer outcomes. *Academy of Management Journal, 47,* 41-58.

Loebecke, C., Van Fenema, P., & Powell, P. (1999). Coopetition and knowledge transfer. *Database for Advances in Information Systems, 30*(2), 14-25.

Lynch, P., Eisenberger, R., & Armeli, S. (1999). Perceived organizational support: Inferior versus superior performance by wary employees. *Journal of Applied Psychology, 84*(4), 476-483.

March, J., & Simon, H. (1958). *Organizations.* New York: John Wiley & Sons.

Meyer, J. P., Stanley, D. J., Herscovitch, L., & Topolnytsky, L. (2002). Affective, continuance, and normative commitment to the organization: A meta-analysis of antecedents, correlates, and consequences. *Journal of Vocational Behavior, 61*(1), 20-52.

Nonaka, I. (1994). A dynamic theory of organizational knowledge creation. *Organization Science, 5*(1), 14-37.

Oleson, T. (2003). Debunking economics: The naked emperor of the social sciences. *Journal of Economic Issues, 37*(1), 228-231.

Perlow, L. (1998). Boundary control: The social ordering of work and family time in a high-tech corporation. *Administrative Science Quarterly, 43*(2), 328-357.

Stajkovic, A. D., & Luthans, F. (2001). Differential effects of incentive motivators on work performance. *Academy of Management Journal, 44*(3), 580-590.

Thorn, B., & Connolly, T. (1987). Discretionary data bases: A theory and some experimental findings. *Communication Research, 14*(5), 512-528.

Turnley, W. H., Bolino, M. C., Lester, S. W., & Bloodgood, J. M. (2003). The impact of psychological contract fulfillment on the performance of in-role and organizational citizenship behaviors. *Journal of Management, 29*(2), 187-207.

KEY TERMS

Knowledge Sharing: The exchange of knowledge between and among individuals, and within and among teams, organizational units, and organizations. This exchange may be focused or unfocused, but it usually does not have a clear a priori objective.

Knowledge Transfer: The focused, objective-seeking communication of knowledge between individuals, groups, or organizations such that the recipient of knowledge (a) has a cognitive understanding, (b) has the ability to apply the knowledge, or (c) applies the knowledge.

Mutual Knowledge: The common ground, or knowledge that a team possesses and knows that it possesses.

Perceived Organizational Support: A construct or measure of the degree to which individuals perceive that their organization has a strong commitment to them, in which case they are likely to have a strong commitment to it.

Public Good: Something that is shared by all members of a community whether or not they have contributed to the constitution or maintenance of the good.

Social-Exchange Theory: The theory that people contribute to the welfare of others, either individuals, groups, or organizations, to a degree that is commensurate with their perceptions of the contributions that are made by others to them (over the long run).

Social Presence: The degree to which a knowledge-sharing medium, such as a network, facilitates an awareness of other people and the development of interpersonal relationships.

Supervisory Control: Formal actions by management to enhance the likelihood that employees will act in ways that management wishes them to act or in ways that are beneficial to the organization.

Knowledge Sharing Barriers

Keith L. Lindsey
Trinity University, USA

INTRODUCTION

To ensure continued existence, an organization must develop ways to share the knowledge that is possessed within that organization with the people who need, or who will need, that knowledge. This critical organizational task transcends departmental boundaries and is a necessary element for the maintenance of every organizational function. Improving the efficiency of knowledge sharing is a highly desirable goal because it offers a promise of compounded returns as the organization works harder and smarter. As business practices have developed over the last few decades, knowledge workers have developed a variety of mechanisms and routines to share knowledge, but these have not yet been well studied. Specifically, the barriers to knowledge sharing remain somewhat elusive.

A better understanding of the knowledge-sharing process may provide managers with a set of tools that could be used to identify and combat barriers to knowledge sharing, which could lead to much more efficient organizational routines. In this article, the process of knowledge sharing will be examined by framing the knowledge-sharing transaction as a form of communication in order to identify and isolate the barriers to that type of communication. Once the barriers are isolated, they can be overcome.

BACKGROUND

In order to manage knowledge, researchers must first develop an understanding of the way that knowledge flows through an organization. The flow of knowledge is reflected in the most basic construct of this article: knowledge sharing. Opposing that flow of knowledge, barriers to knowledge sharing present a challenge to every organization. However, when the managers of an organization embark on a journey to improve knowledge sharing within that organization, they are met by a host of confusing issues. If they review the literature, they find a wide variety of issues that are thought to prevent knowledge sharing, each of which is typically deemed the most critical by the researcher who is promoting it. If they hire outside consultants, they may be offered solutions to problems that they do not even have. Until the managers are able to objectively measure how the specific barriers to knowledge sharing are perceived to exist within their organization, they will be unsure of the optimum method of overcoming those barriers. The first step to objectively measuring knowledge workers' perceptions of barriers to knowledge sharing in an organizational environment is the identification of the many barriers to knowledge sharing that exist within the organization.

It is proposed that barriers to knowledge sharing should actually be measured in terms of knowledge workers' perceptions of barriers to knowledge sharing. Though the difference is subtle, it acknowledges the fact that many decisions are made on a subconscious level, and that there is no surety that knowledge workers are cognizant of the particular barriers that they face, or even if they are, they will not always act rationally to promote the organizational good. In addition, even when knowledge workers understand why they act, they may not be able to explain their actions to researchers, and thus their perceptions must be used as a proxy to measure the effect of a barrier to knowledge sharing.

The concept of knowledge sharing is best illustrated by Foy (1999, p. 15.2): "facilitating learning, through sharing, into usable ideas, products and processes." This definition implies that the focus should be on sharing knowledge within an organization for a specific purpose. Thus, this concept diverges somewhat from the field of learning (because learning may or may not have an organizational imperative or objective) but may still draw from that field because learning is an artifact from the knowledge-sharing process.

UNMASKING BARRIERS TO KNOWLEDGE SHARING

The Knowledge-Sharing Process

A common tendency in knowledge management (KM) research has been to build on the work to understand knowledge that was begun in the 1960s. Polanyi (1962, 1967), who introduced the concepts of tacit and explicit knowledge, is widely cited. Nonaka's (1994) and Nonaka and Takeuchi's (1995) further research into the way that knowledge is created in organizations has also been of significant influence. Perhaps because of these three great contributors, most of the constructs that have been researched as possible barriers to knowledge sharing are cognitive or behavioral based. From the factors-for-success literature (Bennett & Gabriel, 1999; Broadbent, Weill, & St. Clair, 1999; Davenport & Prusak, 1998; Purvis, Sambamurthy, & Zmud, 2001), an emphasis has been placed on determining the factors that enable KM systems. The globalization research (Chow, Deng, & Ho, 2000; Gupta & Govindarajan, 2000; Hofstede, 1980; Hofstede, Neijen, Ohayv, & Sanders, 1990; Okunoye, 2002) emphasizes culture, including both the national and the organizational culture. McDermott and O'Dell (2001) found that organizational culture was more important to knowledge sharing than the approach or commitment to KM.

Barriers to Knowledge Sharing

The KM literature yields several articles that describe knowledge sharing as it occurs in sample organizations. KM researchers have identified a host of barriers to knowledge sharing, but generally focus on a single knowledge-sharing context. The issues that could potentially constitute barriers to knowledge sharing that have been identified in the KM literature are summarized in Table 1.

Note that there are some conflicting factors, such as expected rewards. Barson et al. (2000) and Weiss (1999) determined that rewards were important factors for encouraging knowledge sharing, while Bock and Kim (2002) found rewards were not significant. This conflict is disturbing, however, these researchers examined differing sets of barriers and used different knowledge-sharing contexts, and these differences could account for the differing results.

Communications

In just over 50 years, a great deal of communications research has been conducted, and this research has the potential to contribute some rigor to the field of KM. Though communications research initially ignored context, some recent results have noted the potential importance of context when the message to be communicated

Table 1. Summary of potential barriers to knowledge sharing

Study	Issues
APQC (1996)	culture, technology, measurement
Buckman Model (1998)	simplicity, access, usability, motivation to participate
Okunoye (2002)	operating environmental factors, national culture and beliefs, local orientation
Bock & Kim (2002)	associations, contribution, (but not reward)
Fraser, Marcella & Middleton (2000)	lack of a *knowledge-sharing facility*
Weiss (1999)	time limitations, lack of rewards, common practices in professional services, lack of recognition, lack of reciprocity
Ellis (2001)	contribution, accuracy, recognition
Dixon (2002)	absorptive capacity, understanding of the context, perception that gaining knowledge will be of worth, confidence in the knowledge, feeling that the knowledge fits into current context
Hall (2001)	user friendliness
Levina (2001)	low trust, lack of contextual clues, memory loss, discontinuity in progress toward goals, inability to voice relevant knowledge, unwillingness to listen, and differences in unit: subculture, unit goals, local problem constraints, professional cultures, professional goals, specialized languages and methodologies, national cultures, languages
Dyer & Nobeoka (2000)	network that motivates participation, prevention of free riders, and reduction of the costs of knowledge search
McDermott & Odell (2001)	obvious link between knowledge sharing and business problems, tools and structures for knowledge sharing consistent with the overall style of the organization, reward and recognition systems that support knowledge sharing, availability of time
Barson, et al. (2000)	Personal - internal resistance, self-interest, trust, risk, fear of exploitation, fear of contamination, proprietary thinking, skepticism toward sharing, lack of common ground, and fear – of exploitation, contamination, penalty, becoming redundant, losing power, losing resources, losing confidentiality Organizational - targeting, costs, proprietary knowledge, distance, and technological - available technology, legacy systems, efficiency and effectiveness of system, compatibility of system Multidimensional - culture, rewards, and existing resources
Cabrera & Cabrera (2002)	payoffs for contributing, enhanced efficacy perceptions, strengthened group identity and personal responsibility

is complex. The work of Tucker, Meyer, and Westerman (1996) indicated that communication processes that enhance shared experiences (context) could result in improved organizational performance. The issue of context and the way that context emerges was further addressed by Augier, Shariq, and Vendelo (2001). They investigated the ways that context might emerge and be transformed, and the relationship between context and knowledge sharing. Consistent with Tucker et al., they found that context emerges as a result of the experiences that an individual brings to a situation. They also determined that context may subsequently transform over time as an individual's experiences change. Their final finding constitutes an important rationale to pursue the current research. They found that, for complex, unstructured problems, knowledge sharing will not occur unless there is a shared context. This research supports the conclusions drawn from the KM research that context is a variable that should be explicitly manipulated.

The Communication Process

This section will develop the communication model that will form the communication framework for evaluating knowledge sharing. The communication model employed in this research is presented in Figure 1. This model will be used to facilitate the identification of a complete set of barriers to knowledge sharing by providing a framework that suggests that barriers could be encountered in each area of the model.

This model is based upon the Shannon and Weaver (1949) transmission model of communication, a model suggested by Szulanski (2003) to be fundamental to most research on knowledge transfer. The Shannon and Weaver model has been adapted by Schramm (1965) to model human communication. Schramm made the model somewhat more generic by substituting encoding and decoding for Shannon and Weaver's transmitter and receiver. In addition, since Shannon and Weaver's original model was intended to apply to electronic transmission, noise was only conceptualized to affect the message while it was within the channel. In recognition that human communication is subject to a far wider range of interferences, the

model presented in Figure 1 accounts for noise within each step of the communication process. Finally, to acknowledge the importance of meaning and context, a feedback loop is included. The feedback loop is based on the Osgood-Schramm circular model of communication (McQuail & Windahl, 1981), however, while the Osgood-Schramm model conceptualizes communication as an unending circular pattern of messages, this model (with a single feedback loop) acknowledges the directionality of knowledge sharing.

As defined by Jablin (1979), communication is the process used to transfer information and influence from one entity to another. The combination of information and influence could certainly be viewed as knowledge, and thus, the transfer of knowledge from one entity to another could be viewed either as knowledge sharing or communication.

Barriers to Communication

This section reports the result of a literature review to identify potential barriers to knowledge sharing that have been studied from a communications perspective. Table 2 summarizes the barriers to communication that have been addressed in the communications literature. In order to validate the assertion that these barriers are representative of a complete set of barriers to communication, they have been subjectively categorized using the elements of the communication model, and it can be seen that each element is represented. Some barriers are applicable to more than one category, for example, cultural differences apply to both sender and receiver. These barriers are listed only once in the table since only a single entry is necessary for barrier identification.

The communications literature presents a more broad perspective concerning these barriers to communication, and these barriers can clearly be deemed barriers to knowledge sharing. While there is a high degree of duplication, this is only indicative of the close relationship between communication and knowledge sharing.

Summary of Barriers to Communication and Knowledge Sharing

The list of barriers from the KM literature can be supplemented by the list of barriers to communication in order to create a more complete list of barriers to knowledge sharing. It is through this action that the importance of the communication framework is highlighted. After combining both lists, 124 barriers to knowledge sharing are identified. Table 3 presents these barriers, organized in alphabetical order.

Figure 1. The communications model

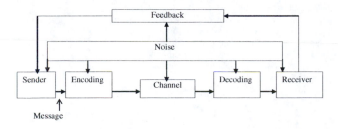

Table 2. Summary of potential barriers to communication

Category	Study	Issues
Sender		
	Blagdon (1973)	power and status relationships, information ownership
	Golen & Boissoneau (1987)	status or position, poor organization of ideas
	Gupta & Govindarajan (2000)	motivational disposition of source (willingness to share), perceived value of source unit's knowledge
	Johlke, Duhan, Lewis (2000)	ambiguity regarding ethical situations, peers, or rewards communicating goal achievements
Encoding		
	Blagdon (1973)	specialization of jobs
	Bennett & Olney (1986)	poor communication skills (lack of clarity and conciseness)
	Golen & Boissoneau (1987)	know-it-all attitude
	Hulbert (1994)	cultural differences play a significant role in encoding/decoding messages
	Buckman (1998)	global constraints including culture
Channel		
	Westmeyer, DiCioccio, & Rubin (1998)	appropriateness of a channel, effectiveness of a channel
	Weiss (1999)	use of static channels, use of dynamic channels
	Gupta & Govindarajan (2000)	existence and richness of transmission channels
	Johlke et al. (2000)	communication mode
Feedback		
	Golen & Boissoneau (1987), Messmer (1998)	improper feedback
	Lewis (2000)	sense making and feedback
Message		
	Johlke et al. (2000)	communication content, communication direction, communication frequency
Decoding		
	Golen (1980)	tendency not to listen
	Golen, Burns, & Gentry (1984)	information overload
	Rogers & Roethlisberger (1991)	tendency of the receiver to evaluate
	Golen & Boissoneau (1987)	defensiveness, differences in perceptions, emotional reactions, inability to understand nonverbal communication, prematurely jumping to conclusions, information overload, tendency not to listen
	Messmer (1998)	state of mind, preoccupation with an ongoing task, passive listening
Receiver		
	Golen (1980)	communicator's lack of credibility, hostile attitude
	Golen et al. (1984)	personality conflicts
	Golen & Boissoneau (1987)	lack of credibility, lack of interest in the subject matter, lack of subject-matter knowledge, lack of trust, lack of understanding of technical language, personality conflicts, prejudice or bias, resistance to change, hostile attitude, overly competitive attitude, either-or thinking
	Golen, Catanach, & Moeckel (1997)	credibility/background, conflict
	Gupta & Govindarajan (2000)	absorptive capacity of receiving unit, motivational disposition of receiving unit
	Lewis (2000)	establishing legitimacy
Noise		
	Blagdon (1973)	physical distance between members of an organization
	Golen & Boissoneau (1987)	inappropriate physical appearance, speaking too loudly, fear of distortion or omission of information, informal social groups or cliques, too many gatekeepers, physical distance between members of an organization, poor spatial arrangements, physical noise and distractions, use of profanity
	Buckman (1998)	structural barriers associated with hierarchical organizations
	Messmer (1998)	ambiguity regarding the knowledge-sharing task or procedures
	Johlke et al. (2000)	ambiguity regarding customers, ambiguity regarding supervisor support
	Lewis (2000)	creating and communicating vision
	McPhee, Corman, & Dooley (2002)	employees know what the knowledge is
	Lehr & Rice (2002)	use of measures

Table 3. Combined list of barriers to knowledge sharing

absorptive capacity of receiving unit
access to the knowledge
ambiguity regarding:
ethical situations
knowledge seekers
peers
reward
supervisor support
the knowledge-sharing task
professional goals
appropriate communication mode
appropriateness of the sharing channel
availability of:
dynamic channels to share knowledge
knowledge-sharing technology
static channels to share knowledge
time to dedicate to knowledge sharing
communication direction
communication frequency
communication of organizational vision
communicator's lack of credibility
compatibility of legacy systems
sharing systems
confidence in the knowledge
cultural differences
defensiveness for gaining knowledge
desire to retain information ownership
differences in perceptions of workers
discontinuity in progress toward goals
effectiveness of sharing channel
effectiveness of the sharing system
efficiency of the sharing system
either-or thinking
emotional reactions to sharing
employees can identify the knowledge
richness of transmission channels
existing resources sufficient to share
expected:
associations with other sharers
contribution to the organization
recognition for sharing knowledge
rewards for sharing knowledge
obvious link between sharing and
the business' problems
operating environmental factors
org. communicates goal achievements
overly competitive attitude
passive listening
perceived value of source's knowledge
perception that knowledge will be of worth
personality conflicts
physical distance between workers
physical noise and distractions
poor communication skills (lack of)
poor organization of ideas
poor spatial arrangements
power and status relationships
prejudice or bias
prematurely jumping to conclusions
preoccupation with an ongoing task
prevention of free riders
professional cultures
proprietary knowledge
proprietary thinking
questionable accuracy of information
receiver perceives enhanced efficacy

feeling that the knowledge fits current context
fear of:
becoming redundant
distortion or omission of information
exploitation once knowledge is shared
losing confidentiality
losing power once knowledge is shared
losing resources once knowledge is shared
penalty if knowledge is shared
risk
global constraints including culture
high costs of knowledge search
hostile attitude toward knowledge sharing
improper feedback
inability to understand nonverbal cues
inability to voice relevant knowledge
inappropriate physical appearance
informal social groups or cliques
information overload
internal resistance to knowledge sharing
know-it-all attitude
knowledge-sharing structures match compatibility of
the organization's style
knowledge-sharing system simplicity
knowledge workers have a local orientation
lack of:
a knowledge-sharing facility
clarity and conciseness
common ground
contextual clues
interest in the subject matter
motivation to participate
reciprocity
subject-matter knowledge
trust
understanding of technical language
willingness to share
local problem constraints
measurement of knowledge transfer
memory loss
motivational disposition of source
multiple languages used by knowledge workers
resistance to change
satisfactory content of the sharing transaction
self-interest
sender must establish legitimacy
sense making
skepticism toward sharing
specialization of jobs
specialized languages and methodologies
state of mind
status or position
strengthened group identity
strengthened personal responsibility
structural barriers in hierarchical organizations
tendency of the receiver to evaluate
time limitations
too many gatekeepers
understanding of the context
unit goals
unit subculture
unwillingness to listen
usability of the knowledge
use of a network that motivates participation
user friendliness of knowledge-sharing system

Note that there is a significant level of duplication, which was expected since knowledge sharing and communication are similar events. The important issue is that by framing the knowledge-sharing transaction as a communication event, the communication model yielded significantly a larger and richer set of potential barriers to knowledge sharing derived from the communications literature.

FUTURE TRENDS

The most pressing issue is the resolution of conflicting reports, such as the importance of expected rewards. Recall that Barson et al. (2000) and Weiss (1999) determined that rewards were important factors for encouraging knowledge sharing, while Bock and Kim (2002) found rewards were not significant. As these researchers examined differing sets of barriers and used different knowledge-sharing contexts, this conflict is not an indication that some of the research may have been faulty. By analyzing a single, comprehensive set of barriers to knowledge sharing, future researchers may be able to resolve conflicts such as this.

Another important need is to analyze these barriers to knowledge sharing for context dependency. Recent research by Augier et al. (2001) noted that knowledge sharing requires a shared context, so it is possible that when the knowledge-sharing context changes, the barriers to knowledge sharing may change as well. Now that a single broad set of potential barriers to knowledge sharing has been identified, the set may be analyzed over several different knowledge-sharing contexts to determine whether knowledge workers' perceptions of these barriers change with the conditions.

An important prerequisite for measuring context dependency is the development of an instrument to measure knowledge workers' perceptions of which barriers pertain to their specific knowledge-sharing task. Once a valid, reliable tool for identifying which barriers are important within an organization is made available, future researchers may then study a large number of organizations in order to draw general conclusions about knowledge workers.

After common barriers to knowledge sharing are identified, researchers can then work to develop ways to manage and improve the knowledge-sharing process in order to lessen (or even eliminate) the greatest barriers. This action could unlock vast organizational potential by improving the efficiency of knowledge sharing within an organization.

CONCLUSION

The exhaustive list of barriers to knowledge sharing presented in Table 3 begs reduction through further analysis. The Delphi method could be used to do this and to rank the factors accordingly; alternatively, factor analysis could be employed to reduce the data and detect structure in the relationships between them. A third alternative, which may be more difficult to accomplish but is of greater value to the development of management practices, would be to devise a field experiment to observe how knowledge workers perceive each of these barriers. By adopting a communications framework, this comprehensive set of potential barriers to knowledge workers was derived, and now this set can provide a structure for the objective analysis of all barriers simultaneously. Researchers can analyze these barriers in an organizational environment to determine which, if any, are most important, or at least which are perceived to be most important to knowledge workers. By sampling a large number of individuals, a pattern may be seen to emerge indicating areas that are worthy of management attention.

Knowledge sharing is a field that, as of yet, has not received a great deal of researcher attention. Rigorous research, based in theory, concerning knowledge sharing and the barriers to knowledge sharing can help frame this field as a legitimate academic pursuit and provide a basis for the discovery of fundamental truths that may be of real use to managers as the need for knowledge sharing becomes more important.

REFERENCES

Alavi, M. & Leidner, D. E. (2001). Review: Knowledge management and knowledge management systems: Conceptual foundations and research issues. *MIS Quarterly, 25*(1), 107-136.

American Productivity and Quality Center (APQC). (1996). *Knowledge management: Consortium benchmarking study final report.* Retrieved November 14, 2002, from *http://www.store.apqc.org/reports/Summary/knowmng.pdf*

Augier, M., Shariq, S., & Vendelo, M. (2001). Understanding context: Its emergence, transformation and role in tacit knowledge sharing. *Journal of Knowledge Management, 5*(2), 125-136.

Barson, R. J., Foster, G., Struck, T., Ratchev, S., Pawar, K., Weber, F., et al. (2000). *Inter- and intra-organisational barriers to sharing knowledge in the extended supply chain.* Retrieved December 2, 2002, from e2000 conference proceedings Web site: *http://www.corma.net/download/e2000.doc*

Bennett, J. C., & Olney, R. J. (1986). Executive priorities for effective communication in an information society. *The Journal of Business Communication, 23*(2), 13-22.

Bennett, R., & Gabriel, H. (1999). Organisational factors and knowledge management within large marketing departments: An empirical study. *Journal of Knowledge Management, 3*(3), 212-225.

Blagdon, C. (1973). Barriers to communication. *Business Communication Quarterly, 36*(3), 12.

Bock, G. W., & Kim, Y. G. (2002). Breaking the myths of rewards: An exploratory study of attitudes about knowledge sharing. *Information Resources Management Journal, 15*(2), 14-21.

Broadbent, M., Weill, P., & St. Clair, D. (1999). The implications of information technology infrastructure for business process redesign. *MIS Quarterly, 23*(2), 159-182.

Buckman, R. H. (1998). Knowledge sharing at Buckman Labs. *The Journal of Business Strategy, 19*(1), 11-15.

Cabrera, A., & Cabrera, E. F. (2002). Knowledge-sharing dilemmas. *Organization Studies, 23*(5), 687-710.

Chow, C. W., Deng, F. J., & Ho, J. L. (2000). The openness of knowledge sharing within organizations: A comparative study in the United States and the People's Republic of China. *Journal of Management Accounting Research, 12*, 65-95.

Davenport, T. H., & Prusak, L. (1998). *Working knowledge: How organizations manage what they know.* Boston: Harvard Business School Press.

Dixon, N. (2002). The neglected receiver of knowledge sharing. *Ivey Business Journal, 66*(4), 35-40.

Dyer, J. H., & Nobeoka, K. (2000). Creating and managing a high-performance knowledge-sharing network: The Toyota case. *Strategic Management Journal, 21*(3), 345-367.

Ellis, K. (2001). Dare to share. *Training, 38*(2), 74-77.

Foy, P. S. (1999). Knowledge management in industry. In J. Liebowitz (Ed.), *Knowledge management handbook* (pp. 15.1-15.10). New York: CRC Press.

Fraser, V., Marcella, R., & Middleton, I. (2000). Employee perceptions of knowledge sharing: Employment threat of synergy for the greater good? A case study. *Competitive Intelligence Review, 11*(2), 39-52.

Golen, S., Burns, A. C., & Gentry, J. W. (1984). An analysis of communication barriers in five methods of teaching business subjects. *The Journal of Business Communication, 21*(3), 45-52.

Golen, S. P. (1980). An analysis of communication barriers in public accounting firms. *The Journal of Business Communication, 17*(5), 39-51.

Golen, S. P., & Boissoneau, R. (1987). Health care supervisors identify communication barriers in their supervisor-subordinate relationships. *Health Care Supervisor, 6*(1), 26-38.

Golen, S. P., Catanach, A. H., Jr., & Moeckel, C. (1997). The frequency and seriousness of communication barriers in the auditor-client relationship. *Business Communication Quarterly, 69*(3), 23-37.

Gupta, A., & Govindarajan, V. (2000). Knowledge flows in multinational corporations. *Strategic Management Journal, 21*, 473-496.

Hall, H. (2001). Input-friendliness: Motivating knowledge sharing across intranets. *Journal of Information Science, 27*(3), 139-146.

Hofstede, G. (1980). *Culture's consequences.* Beverly Hills, CA: Sage.

Hofstede, G., Neijen, B., Ohayv, D. D., & Sanders, G. (1990). Measuring organizational cultures: A qualitative and quantitative study across twenty cases. *Administrative Science Quarterly, 35*(2), 286-316.

Hulbert, J. E. (1994). Overcoming intercultural communication barriers. *The Bulletin of the Association for Business Communication, 57*(1), 41-44.

Jablin, F. M. (1979). Superior-subordinate communication: The state of the art. *Psychological Bulletin, 86*, 1201-1222.

Johlke, M. C., Duhan, D. F., Howell, R. D., & Wilkes, R. W. (2000). An integrated model of sales managers' communication practices. *Journal of the Academy of Marketing Sciences, 28*(2), 263-277.

Lehr, J. K., & Rice, R. E. (2002). Organizational measures as a form of knowledge management: A multitheoretic, communication-based exploration. *Journal of the American Society for Information Science and Technology, 53*(12), 1060-1073.

Levina, N. (2001). Sharing knowledge in heterogeneous environments [Electronic version]. *Reflections: The SoL Journal, 2*(2), 32-42.

Lewis, L. K. (2000). Communicating change: Four cases of quality programs. *The Journal of Business Communication, 37*(2), 128-155.

McDermott, R., & O'Dell, C. (2001). Overcoming cultural barriers to sharing knowledge. *Journal of Knowledge Management, 5*(1), 76-85.

McPhee, R. D., Corman, S. R., & Dooley, K. (2002). Organizational knowledge expression and management. *Management Communication Quarterly: McQ, 16*(2), 274-281.

McQuail, D., & Windahl, S. (1981). *Communication models for the study of mass communications.* London: Longman.

Messmer, M. (1998). Improving your listening skills. *Strategic Finance, 79*(9), 14.

Nonaka, I. (1994). A dynamic theory of organizational knowledge creation. *Organizational Science, 5*(1), 14-37.

Nonaka, I., & Takeuchi, H. (1995). *The knowledge-creating company: How Japanese companies create the dynamics of innovation.* Oxford: Oxford University Press.

Okunoye, A. (2002). Where the global needs the local: Variation in enablers in the knowledge management process. *Journal of Global Information Technology Management, 5*(3), 12-31.

Polanyi, M. (1962). *Personal knowledge: Toward a post-critical philosophy.* New York: Harper Torchbooks.

Polanyi, M. (1967). *The tacit dimension.* London: Routledge & Keoan Paul.

Purvis, R. L., Sambamurthy, V., & Zmud, R. W. (2001). The assimilation of knowledge platforms in organizations: An empirical investigation. *Organization Science, 12*(2), 117-135.

Rogers, C. R., & Roethlisberger, F. J. (1991). Barriers and gateways to communication. *Harvard Business Review, 69*(6), 105-111.

Schramm, W. (1965). How communication works. In W. Schramm (Ed.), *The process and effects of mass communication* (pp. 3-26). Urbana, IL: University of Illinois Press.

Shannon, C. E., & Weaver, W. (1949). *The mathematical theory of communication.* Urbana, IL: University of Illinois Press.

Szulanski, G. (2003). *Sticky knowledge: Barriers to knowing in the firm.* Thousand Oaks, CA: Sage.

Tucker, M. L., Meyer, G. D., & Westerman, J. W. (1996). Organizational communication: Development of internal strategic competitive advantage. *The Journal of Business Communication, 33*(1), 51-69.

Weiss, L. (1999). Collection and connection: The anatomy of knowledge sharing in professional service firms. *Organization Development Journal, 17*(4), 61-77.

Westmeyer, S. A., DiCioccio, R. L., & Rubin, R. B. (1998). Appropriateness and effectiveness of communication channels in competent interpersonal communication. *Journal of Communications, 48*(3), 27-36.

KEY TERMS

Application: Knowledge integration to create organizational capability through directives, organizational routines, and self-contained task teams.

Barriers to Knowledge Sharing: Characteristics of the knowledge-sharing environment that may limit or preclude the knowledge-sharing transaction. The evaluation of barriers to knowledge sharing should actually be measured in terms of knowledge workers' perceptions of barriers to knowledge sharing since knowledge workers may not be able to elucidate the actual barriers.

Creation: An interaction between individuals that includes the exchange of tacit and explicit knowledge.

Knowledge Sharing: A transaction that results in a transfer of knowledge to or from a knowledge worker. The definition provided by Foy (1999, p. 15-2) is "facilitating learning, through sharing, into usable ideas, products and processes."

Knowledge-Sharing Context: The impetus for the knowledge-sharing transaction. This refers to the way that the knowledge is to be transferred. A framework that could be used for knowledge-sharing contexts could be drawn from Alavi and Leidner's (2001) description of four major knowledge-management processes, briefly described below:

Knowledge Worker: Anyone whose work involves tasks that require the processing of information. These tasks include collecting, analyzing, synthesizing, structuring, storing, retrieving, and using information.

Storage/Retrieval: Focuses on issues relating to organizational memory, both tacit and explicit.

Transfer: Includes a variety of interactions between individuals and groups; within, between, and across groups; and from groups to the organization.

Knowledge Sharing Between Individuals

Carolyn McKinnell Jacobson
Marymount University, USA

INTRODUCTION

As Peter Drucker (2000) has pointed out, the foundation of the 21st century organization is no longer money or capital or even technology; it is knowledge. In order for that knowledge to create value, it must be shared. Some discussions of knowledge sharing in organizations and, indeed, some knowledge management initiatives seem to assume that given the right technology and/or the proper culture, knowledge will flow readily throughout the firm. Technologies that facilitate knowledge sharing (e.g., databases, intranets, and groupware) currently exist and are constantly improving. But technologies are only part of the knowledge management equation.

In 1997, the Ernst and Young Center for Business Innovation conducted a study of 431 U.S. and European organizations (Ruggles, 1998). Of those responding, only 13% rated their organizations as good or excellent at sharing knowledge internally. Even when knowledge was accessible, only 30% reported that their organizations were good or excellent at using that knowledge in making decisions. When asked what was the biggest obstacle to knowledge sharing within their organizations, 54% cited culture. To understand knowledge sharing within an organization, we must look beyond culture and start with the individual.

BACKGROUND

There has been much written about defining, creating, assessing, and changing organizational culture. In most of these writings, the focus has been the organization as a whole (e.g., Deal & Kennedy, 1982; Kotter & Heskett, 1992; Schein, 1999) or its subdivisions (e.g., Sackmann, 1992). The focus has not been on the individual or on knowledge sharing.

What exactly do we mean by knowledge sharing? There are numerous definitions of knowledge ranging from the pragmatic to the philosophical. We shall adopt a definition based on Turban (1992) that knowledge is information that has been organized and analyzed to convey understanding, experience, learning, and expertise so that it is understandable and applicable to problem solving or decision making. Although knowledge sharing and knowledge transfer are often used interchangeably, we shall make a distinction between them. Knowledge sharing as used here refers to an exchange of knowledge between two individuals: one who communicates knowledge and one who assimilates it. Knowledge sharing focuses on human capital and the interaction of individuals. Knowledge transfer focuses on structural capital and the transformation of individual knowledge to group or organizational knowledge, which becomes built into processes, products, and services. Strictly speaking, knowledge can never be shared. Because knowledge exists in a context, the receiver interprets it in light of his or her own background.

Several authors have looked at the organizational factors that inhibit the sharing of knowledge. Believing that most people "have a natural desire…to share what they know," O'Dell and Grayson (1998, p. 16) attribute the lack of internal knowledge sharing in organizations to "a set of organizational structures, management practices, and measurement systems that *discourage*-rather than encourage-sharing" (p. 17). Szulanski (1996, 2003) identifies four sets of factors that determine how readily knowledge will be shared within the firm: the characteristics of knowledge, the characteristics of the source, the characteristics of the recipient, and the organizational context. Hubert Saint-Onge, chief executive officer (CEO) of Konverge Digital Solutions Corp, offers a different explanation for the lack of knowledge sharing: "Sharing knowledge is an unnatural act. You can't just stand up and say 'Thou shalt share knowledge'-it won't work" (as cited in Paul, 2003).

E. von Hippel (1994) coined the phrase "sticky information" to describe "the incremental expenditure required to transfer that unit of information to a specified locus in a form usable by a given information seeker" (p. 430). The higher the incremental expenditure, the stickier the information is. Stickiness may be an attribute of the information itself, or it may refer to attributes and choices made by someone seeking information or by someone providing it.

If we are to understand knowledge sharing, we must examine what happens at the level of the individuals who are at the core of the knowledge sharing process. Maslow's (1987) hierarchy of needs provides one widely accepted explanation of the behavior and attitudes of individuals in organizations. Maslow identified five levels of human needs: physiological (e.g., food, water), safety (e.g., security, protection), social (e.g., love, affection, sense of belonging), esteem (e.g., respect and recognition from others, personal sense of competence), and self-actualization (e.g., fulfillment of one's potential). According to Maslow, an unsatisfied need motivates behavior. Because these five needs exist in a hierarchy, a lower level need must be satisfied before the next higher level need is activated until the highest level, self-actualization, is reached. The more the self-actualization need is satisfied, the stronger it grows. Although there may be a variety of ways to satisfy a need, individuals can be expected to engage in knowledge sharing behaviors to the extent that they perceive that knowledge sharing leads to the satisfaction of a need.

Shannon and Weaver (1949) provide us with a transmission model of communication. Their model consists of six basic elements: the source, encoder, message, channel, decoder, and receiver. Although this model is often referred to in explaining human communication, it was actually designed for information theory and cybernetics, and is therefore technologically oriented. As a result, it does not address factors that can affect human communication, such as the context of the communication or the content of the message itself. Nevertheless, it provides insight into the communication process by dividing that process into discrete units.

Berlo's (1960) model of communication also refers to the source, message, channel, and receiver, but his focus is on interpersonal dyadic communication. The source and receiver are defined in terms of communication skills, knowledge, social systems, culture, and attitudes. Communication skills include speaking, writing, listening, reading, and thinking or reasoning. Knowledge

refers to the source's knowledge of his or her own attitudes, options for producing a message, choices of communication channels, and subject matter. Social systems are produced through communication and refer to the collective behaviors and structures associated with a group of individuals who have interdependent goals. Culture, which consists of our shared beliefs, values, and behaviors, will influence our communication patterns as well. Finally, attitudes toward self, the subject matter, and the receiver also affect communication.

Models of the communication process, such as Berlo's (1960) model, apply to communication in general and not specifically to knowledge sharing, although knowledge sharing requires communication in some form (verbal or nonverbal, written or spoken, etc.). From an organizational semiotics perspective, knowledge sharing can therefore be analyzed in terms of communication functions.

Previous work on knowledge sharing has often focused on teams or groups and has overlooked important factors that affect the exchange of knowledge between two individuals. As Nonaka and Takeuchi (1995, p. 59) have pointed out, "An organization cannot create knowledge without individuals." The purpose of this article is to describe a model of knowledge sharing between individuals in organizations.

A MODEL OF KNOWLEDGE SHARING

Borrowing from the work of Shannon and Weaver (1949) and from Berlo (1960), we focus on six factors involved

Figure 1. A model of knowledge sharing between individuals in an organizational context (based on Shannon & Weaver, 1949)

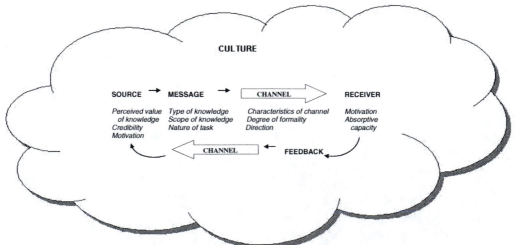

in knowledge sharing: the knowledge source, the message, the knowledge receiver, the communication channel, feedback, and the environment or culture in which the knowledge sharing occurs (see Figure 1).

Knowledge Source

The knowledge source is an individual who possesses knowledge and transmits it. The transmission of knowledge may or may not be intentional (Hendriks, 1999). An example of unintentional transmission would be someone acquiring knowledge by watching you perform a task. Three characteristics relate to the knowledge source. The first characteristic suggests that, because the flow of knowledge between individuals has a cost associated with it, knowledge that is perceived by the source as being more valuable is more likely to be shared than knowledge that is perceived to be of lesser value or duplicative (Gupta & Govindarajan, 2000). Of course, it is always possible that the possessor of the knowledge does not realize the value of that knowledge. The second characteristic is the credibility of the source. Knowledge is more likely to be shared if the source is seen as credible. Factors associated with credibility include trustworthiness, status, education, and position (Szulanski, 2003).

The third characteristic relates to the motivation of the source to share knowledge. Individuals or groups who perceive that their unique, valuable knowledge provides them with power or status in the organization will be less likely to share that knowledge (Gupta & Govindarajan, 2000; Szulanski, 2003). Conversely, those individuals who are motivated to share their knowledge will have a positive effect on knowledge sharing (Gupta & Govindarajan). This motivation may arise from altruism (a desire to help others or to help the organization), from a passion for the subject, or from a desire to be recognized as an expert, what Maslow (1987) referred to as the esteem need). It may also arise from the expectation that, at some point in the future, the receiver will be willing to return the favor, either as knowledge shared or in some other form (Davenport & Prusak, 1998).

What kinds of rewards should an organization provide to motivate employees to share knowledge? In three large scale studies on knowledge management, the American Productivity and Quality Center concluded, "…if the process of sharing and transfer is not inherently rewarding, celebrated and supported by the culture, then artificial rewards won't have much effect" (O'Dell & Grayson, 1998, p. 82). If knowledge sharing helps people do their work better or more efficiently, or if it provides them with recognition as experts, they will be motivated to do it (Maslow, 1987). This is not to say that explicit rewards

should never be used. In 1993, the most active participants in Buckman Laboratories' online knowledge sharing network received a surprise trip to a conference in Arizona, a $150 leather bag, and an IBM Thinkpad 720. The bag and computer quickly became status symbols around the company (O'Dell & Grayson).

The Message

The second factor in the knowledge sharing process involves the message itself. What is the type of knowledge that is being shared, and what is the scope of that knowledge (Dixon, 2000)? Although there are various typologies of knowledge (e.g., Blackler, 1995; Collins, 1993; Machlup, 1980; Quinn, Anderson, & Finkelstein, 1996; Wiig, 1994), we shall adopt Nonaka and Takeuchi's (1995) widely accepted framework because it focuses on the individual as central to the knowledge-creation process: "An organization cannot create knowledge without individuals" (p. 59). Based on the distinction first made by Michael Polanyi (1967), Nonaka and Takeuchi describe knowledge as existing on a continuum ranging from explicit to tacit. Explicit knowledge, sometimes referred to as codified knowledge, is objective knowledge that can be transmitted in formal, systematic language. It deals with past events or objects and can be transmitted electronically in documents and databases. Tacit knowledge is personal and context specific. It is more difficult to capture and express, existing primarily in people's heads (Nonaka & Takeuchi). Most knowledge found in organizations is a combination of the two, falling somewhere between the two ends of the continuum. Although explicit knowledge is generally considered easier to share than tacit knowledge, it may be that tacit knowledge simply requires different channels or different transmission processes. In a study of attitudes about information sharing in a technical context (Constant, Kiesler, & Sproull, 1994), it was found that participants were willing to share explicit knowledge in the form of documents that belonged to the organization. Although the participants were also willing to share personal expertise (tacit knowledge) such as providing assistance with a software package, when sharing tacit knowledge they expected something in return (e.g., acknowledgement of their expertise).

The scope of the knowledge, the second characteristic of the message, refers to the number of functional areas in the organization that will be affected by the knowledge being shared. Knowledge that is narrower in scope is generally less complex and more explicit, making it easier to share. Knowledge that involves multiple functional areas tends to be more complex and therefore more difficult to share (Dixon, 2000).

A third characteristic of the message concerns the nature of the task. Tasks may be routine or nonroutine, and may occur regularly or infrequently. Routine tasks that occur regularly involve knowledge that can be readily shared. Nonroutine tasks that occur less frequently or only under unusual circumstances make knowledge sharing more challenging. If the knowledge source and the intended receiver are doing similar tasks in similar contexts, knowledge can be shared more easily (Dixon, 2000).

Knowledge Receiver

The knowledge receiver, the target of the communication, is the third factor in the knowledge sharing process. The effectiveness of the knowledge sharing process will depend on the receiver's motivation and absorptive capacity. Motivation may be influenced by the "not-invented-here" syndrome, which suggests that we tend to regard knowledge from another source as less valuable than what we already know. This may derive from our reluctance to admit that someone else is more competent than we are. It might also derive from power struggles in the organization, which cause us to denigrate or disregard any knowledge contributions from an individual or a unit that we perceive to be a competitor. Or we may simply not see the value or relevance of that knowledge (Gupta & Govindarajan, 2000).

Several companies have created awards to encourage employees to use knowledge from other sources. Understanding the reluctance to use knowledge from another source and the motivation associated with recognition, Texas Instruments created the NIHBIDIA Award (Not Invented Here But I Did It Anyway) for ideas borrowed either from inside or outside of the company. British Petroleum bestows a Thief of the Year award to the person who has "stolen" the best idea (Davenport & Prusak, 1998).

The second characteristic related to the receiver is his or her capacity to absorb new knowledge, which is influenced by the ability to recognize the value of new knowledge that is encountered, to assimilate that knowledge, and to apply it (Cohen & Levinthal, 1990). Prior related knowledge will increase our ability to absorb new knowledge. Similarly, if the source of that knowledge is an individual like ourselves in terms of education, background, and so forth, we are more likely to absorb new knowledge or change our attitudes and behavior (Dixon, 2000; Gupta & Govindarajan, 2000; Szulanski, 2003).

Davenport and Prusak (1998) recount the story of a group of 23 surgeons who specialize in coronary artery bypass surgery. They wanted to find out if skill sharing and observing one another in surgery would improve their success rate. They started by sharing their success rates and comparing them with statistics of other surgeons in the medical center and in the region. They also received training in continuous improvement techniques. The overall result was that these surgeons achieved a 24% drop in the mortality rate associated with the surgery. A major factor in the success of this project was that these surgeons all worked in the same area of specialization and all shared almost identical training and experience. The similarity in background and experience allowed them to easily understand and absorb each other's words and actions.

Communication Channel

The fourth factor in the knowledge sharing process is the communication channel, or the means by which a message is communicated. A communication channel may involve seeing, hearing, touching, smelling, or tasting (Berlo, 1960). Telephone, the Internet, braille, airwaves, and roadside billboards are all examples of communication channels. Knowledge sharing will be enhanced by the richness, bandwidth, and reliability of the communication channel. For example, knowledge sharing may be facilitated by face-to-face meetings that involve seeing and hearing as opposed to electronic communication (e.g., e-mail, databases, or direct mail) that only involves seeing. Channels can be either formal or informal. Formal mechanisms for linking organizational units might include task forces, permanent committees, or formally appointed liaison personnel. Informal mechanisms would involve ad hoc, interpersonal interactions among employees. The better your relationships with your coworkers and the more opportunities you have to interact, the greater the possibility of knowledge sharing. These interactions are typically horizontal (peer to peer) or vertical (e.g., corporate mentoring programs or internships; Gupta & Govindarajan, 2000; Szulanski, 2003).

Some organizations have created open office spaces to encourage face-to-face interaction among employees. Newspaper offices have used this model for some time because editors understand that it facilitates rapid knowledge sharing so that deadlines can be met. Sun Microsystems' offices in Menlo Park, California, use architectural design to encourage interaction and knowledge sharing. Only about one third of their floor space is devoted to offices; the rest is designed to encourage informal project discussions with lots of light, comfortable couches, and white boards (Fisher & Fisher, 1999). Hewlett-Packard has also made open space offices compulsory for its subsidiaries (Sveiby, 1997).

Feedback

It can be argued that knowledge sharing has not occurred unless the knowledge receiver has assimilated what has been communicated. This can be determined by the response (either verbal or nonverbal) of the receiver. Feedback may consist of a verbal reply, a nod, or the successful completion of a task, indicating that the receiver understood the message. Conversely, a puzzled look may signal a lack of understanding. The receiver's response may thus influence future messages from the knowledge source. If the receiver has assimilated the knowledge, it should lead to increased value for the organization, either through a change in behavior or through the development of a new idea that leads to a change of behavior.

Culture

Finally, the knowledge sharing process takes place within an organizational culture, which Schein (1985) has defined as a "shared view." Culture is reflected in an organization's values, norms, and practices such that values are manifested in norms, which determine specific practices (De Long & Fahey, 2000). Excellent companies have shared values that are clear to all employees throughout the organization (Peters & Waterman, 1982) and that determine how employees think and act. De Long and Fahey describe four aspects of organizational culture that influence knowledge-related behaviors: culture shapes assumptions about which knowledge is important; it mediates the relationships among individual, group, and organizational knowledge; it creates the organizational context for social interactions; and it impacts the creation and adoption of new knowledge.

One of the values that must be part of a knowledge sharing culture is trust, which is defined in terms of respecting the ownership of ideas (Andrews & Delahaye, 2000; Zand, 1972). Knowledge sharers must know that they will get credit and that others will reciprocate. Trust must be visible, it must be ubiquitous, and it must start at the top (Davenport & Prusak, 1998). Top management in particular must emulate trustworthiness because their actions define the values of the organization.

When asked to name the three critical factors in knowledge management, Robert Buckman, president, chairman, and CEO of Bulab Holding, Inc., replied, "Culture, culture, culture" (as cited in O'Dell & Grayson, 1998, p. 71). If top management believes that power comes from accumulating and hoarding knowledge, then knowledge sharing will not occur. In Buckman's view, "The most powerful individuals will be those who do the best job of transferring knowledge to others" (p. 77).

FUTURE TRENDS

Knowledge has arguably become the most important resource for organizations today. Because organizations cannot create knowledge without people, the knowledge worker has become an organization's single greatest asset. If knowledge is to create a competitive advantage for the organization, it must be shared. Any effort to effect knowledge sharing must begin with an understanding of the factors that influence knowledge sharing between individuals.

As the examples above clearly illustrate, organizations are beginning to address some of the issues involved in knowledge sharing. What is needed now is a model that brings all the relevant factors together in an organized fashion, and that model is provided here. Wiig and Jooste (2003) point out that the first generation of knowledge management in the 1990s focused on "visible aspects of work…The new second generation approaches seek greater impacts and better business results and therefore require more effective methods" (pp. 300-301). This model of knowledge sharing between individuals provides a shift from the isolated projects of the first generation to integrated practices, and from the more narrow applications of the 1990s to a broader approach and deeper understanding of knowledge sharing.

Understanding the factors involved in knowledge sharing is a first step in understanding how to manage the knowledge sharing process. Although a detailed framework for managing knowledge sharing is beyond the scope of this article, three general suggestions are offered.

First, an organization that values knowledge sharing must ensure that its culture (e.g., norms, values, and practices) consistently supports it. Individuals must receive appropriate rewards for knowledge sharing, and they must receive credit for their ideas. Knowledge sharing is facilitated when people share the same work culture (Davenport & Prusak, 1998), but it must be recognized that cultures are not always homogeneous throughout an organization (McDermott & O'Dell, 2001). An essential element of culture is trust, which must be ubiquitous, must be visible, and must be modeled from the top of the organization on down (Davenport & Prusak).

Second, motivation is a key factor for both the source and the receiver. With reference to Maslow's (1987) hierarchy of needs, knowledge workers are motivated by esteem and self-actualization needs. Individuals can be expected to engage in knowledge sharing behaviors to the extent that doing so satisfies these needs. Managers who want to promote knowledge sharing should therefore provide employees with opportunities for satisfying these needs through creative and challenging work, recognition, and promotion. Managers should also try to minimize or remove any obstacles that block need satisfaction and therefore inhibit knowledge sharing.

Herzberg's (1968) two factor theory provides us with another perspective on motivation. According to Herzberg, factors that produce job satisfaction (motivators) are separate and distinct from those that lead to job dissatisfaction (hygiene factors). Motivators relate to job content and include achievement, recognition for achievement, advancement, growth, and responsibility. These factors can increase job satisfaction, but they will not prevent job dissatisfaction. Hygiene factors relate to job context and include company policy, supervision, working conditions, salary, and security. These factors do not motivate behavior, but they may lead to dissatisfaction and therefore decreased motivation if they are absent. A manager's goal should be to keep job dissatisfaction low and job satisfaction high. High satisfaction can be expected to result in increased effort (i.e., increased motivation of the knowledge source and receiver) and receptivity to ideas and suggestions (i.e., the absorptive capacity of the receiver; Locke, 1970).

Third, managers need to provide and promote opportunities for knowledge sharing. While such opportunities are necessary for knowledge sharing, they are not sufficient and must be in conjunction with the proper culture and motivation. These opportunities may range from informal face-to-face meetings to formal electronic communication systems (e.g., e-mail, discussion boards). Mentoring programs may be used to encourage more seasoned employees to share knowledge with new hires. A physical environment that includes open office space and areas for informal interaction may also encourage knowledge sharing.

This model of knowledge sharing between individuals in an organizational context provides a framework for future research to explore these factors in greater depth. For example, how do the characteristics of the communication channel interact with the characteristics of the source or the receiver? Are some communication channels more appropriate for some kinds of messages? Is this model valid for all kinds of knowledge? How can trust be built in a colocated community? Are the same methods for building trust in a colocated community also effective in a virtual community? How can trust be built in a cross-cultural community? What is the relationship between this model and various organizational, or even national, cultures?

CONCLUSION

There have been several systematic research studies of knowledge sharing in organizations (e.g., Constant et al., 1994; O'Dell & Grayson, 1998; Ruggles, 1998), but much of what we think we know is based on anecdotal evidence. This model offers us a starting point for a more systematic and scientific approach. A better understanding of organizational knowledge sharing at the dyadic level will provide a foundation for understanding knowledge sharing within and among groups, and ultimately, within and among organizations.

REFERENCES

Andrews, K. M., & Delahaye, B. L. (2000). Influences on knowledge processes in organizational learning: The psychosocial filter. *The Journal of Management Studies, 37*(6), 797-810.

Berlo, D. K. (1960). *The process of communication: An introduction to theory and practice.* New York: Holt, Rinehart & Winston, Inc.

Blackler, F. (1995). Knowledge, knowledge work and organizations: An overview and interpretation. *Organizational Studies, 16*(6), 1021-1046.

Cohen, W. M., & Levinthal, D. A. (1990). Absorptive capacity: A new perspective on learning and innovation. *Administrative Science Quarterly, 35*, 128-152.

Collins, H. (1993). The structure of knowledge. *Social Research, 60*, 95-116.

Constant, D., Kiesler, S., & Sproull, L. (1994). What's mine is ours, or is it? A study of attitudes about information sharing. *Information Systems Research, 5*(4), 400-422.

Davenport, T. H., & Prusak, L. (1998). *Working knowledge: How organizations manage what they know.* Boston: Harvard Business School Press.

De Long, D. W., & Fahey, L. (2000). Diagnosing cultural barriers to knowledge management. *The Academy of Management Executive, 14*(4), 113-127.

Deal, T. E., & Kennedy, A. A. (1982). *Corporate cultures: The rites and rituals of corporate life.* Reading, MA: Addison-Wesley Publishing Co.

Dixon, N. M. (2000). *Common knowledge: How companies thrive by sharing what they know*. Boston: Harvard Business School Press.

Drucker, P. F. (2000). Knowledge work. *Executive Excellence, 17*(4), 11-12.

Fisher, K., & Fisher, M. D. (1999). Shedding light on knowledge work. In J. W. Cortada & J. A. Woods (Eds.), *The knowledge management yearbook, 1999-2000* (pp. 157-167). Boston: Butterworth-Heinemann.

Gupta, A., & Govindarajan, V. (2000). Knowledge flows within multinational corporations. *Strategic Management Journal, 21*, 473-496.

Hendriks, P. (1999). Why share knowledge? The influence of ICT on the motivation for knowledge sharing. *Knowledge and Process Management, 6*(2), 91-100.

Herzberg, F. (1968). One more time: How do you motivate employees? *Harvard Business Review, 46*(1), 53-62.

Kotter, J. P., & Heskett, J. L. (1992). *Corporate culture and performance*. New York: Free Press.

Locke, E. A. (1970). Job satisfaction and job performance: A theoretical analysis. *Organizational Behavior and Human Performance, 5*, 484-500.

Machlup, F. (1980). *Knowledge: Its creation, distribution, and economic significance: Vol. 1. Knowledge and knowledge production*. Princeton, NJ: Princeton University Press.

Maslow, A. (1987). *Motivation and personality* (3rd ed.). New York: Harper and Row.

McDermott, R., & O'Dell, C. (2001). Overcoming cultural barriers to sharing knowledge. *Journal of Knowledge Management, 5*(1), 76-85.

Nonaka, I., & Takeuchi, H. (1995). *The knowledge creating company: How Japanese companies create the dynamics of innovation*. New York: Oxford University Press.

O'Dell, C., & Grayson, C. J., Jr. (1998). *If only we knew what we know*. New York: Free Press.

Paul, L. G. (2003). Why three heads are better than one: How to create a know-it-all company. *CIO*. Retrieved from *http://www.cio.com/archive/120103/km.html*

Peters, T. J., & Waterman, R. H., Jr. (1982). *In search of excellence: Lessons from America's best-run companies*. New York: Harper & Row.

Polanyi, M. (1967). *The tacit dimension*. Garden City, NY: Anchor Books.

Quinn, J. B., Anderson, P., & Finkelstein, S. (1996). Managing professional intellect: Making the most of the best. *Harvard Business Review, 74*(2), 71-80.

Ruggles, R. (1998). The state of the notion: Knowledge management in practice. *California Management Review, 40*(3), 80-89.

Sackmann, S. A. (1992). Culture and subcultures: An analysis of organizational knowledge. *Administrative Science Quarterly, 37*(1), 140-161.

Schein, E. H. (1985). *Organizational culture and leadership*. San Francisco: Jossey-Bass.

Schein, E. H. (1999). *The corporate culture survival guide: Sense and nonsense about culture change*. San Francisco: Jossey-Bass.

Shannon, C. E., & Weaver, W. (1949). *The mathematical theory of communication*. Chicago, IL: University of Illinois Press.

Sveiby, K. E. (1997). *The new organizational wealth*. San Francisco: Berrett-Koehler Publishers, Inc.

Szulanski, G. (1996). Exploring internal stickiness: Impediments to the transfer of best practice within the firm. *Strategic Management Journal, 17*, 27-43.

Szulanski, G. (2003). *Sticky knowledge: Barriers to knowing in the firm*. London: SAGE Publications.

Turban, E. (1992). *Expert systems and applied artificial intelligence*. New York: Macmillan.

von Hippel, E. (1994). "Sticky information" and the locus of problem solving: Implications for innovation. *Management Science, 40*(4), 429-439.

Wiig, K.M. (1994). *Knowledge management: The central management focus for intelligent-acting organizations*. Arlington, TX: Schema Press.

Wiig, K. M., & Jooste, A. (2003). Exploiting knowledge for productivity gains. In C. W. Holsapple (Ed.), *Handbook on knowledge management* (pp. 289-308). Berlin, Germany: Springer.

Zand, D. (1972). Trust and managerial problem solving. *Administrative Science Quarterly, 17*, 229-239.

KEY TERMS

Communication Channel: The medium used to convey the message. The channel could involve seeing, hearing, smelling, feeling, or tasting. Various media (e.g., e-mail, Web sites, telephone) may be more or less appropriate for various messages.

Dyadic Communication: Communication between two people: the source and the receiver. A dyadic approach to communication stresses the role of the relationship between the source and the receiver.

Knowledge Sharing: An exchange of knowledge between two individuals: one who communicates knowledge and one who assimilates it. In knowledge sharing, the focus is on human capital and the interaction of individuals. Strictly speaking, knowledge can never be shared. Because it exists in a context; the receiver interprets it in light of his or her own background.

Knowledge Transfer: An exchange of knowledge in which the focus is on structural capital (knowledge that has been built into processes, products, or services) and on the transformation of individual knowledge to group knowledge or organizational knowledge.

Message: What the source produces (e.g., the spoken word, a written memo, a physical motion). It is assumed that meaning is encoded in the message and that the receiver is able to decode that meaning.

Organizational Culture: A set of widely shared beliefs, values, norms, and practices that describe how to think, feel, and act within an organizational setting.

Receiver: The destination of the message or the person who decodes the message. This requires skills, for example, in listening or reading.

Source: An originator of a message or the person who encodes the message. This requires skills, for example, in speaking or writing. This person may have a variety of purposes in mind (e.g., to persuade someone, to be friendly, to provide information). In this model, we focus on the purpose of sharing knowledge.

Knowledge Sharing in Legal Practice

K

Chad Saunders
University of Calgary, Canada

INTRODUCTION

Given the reliance on knowledge-based resources over traditional assets, the professional context serves as a heightened environment in which to investigate knowledge sharing. Within legal practice, the success of a law firm is connected to the firm's ability to leverage knowledge (Sherer, 1995), and this has led to a call for knowledge management to be a business imperative within legal practice (Parsons, 2004; Rusanow, 2003).

An underlying assumption within much of the knowledge management literature is that knowledge sharing is universally beneficial and to be encouraged both within and across organizations. However, in legal practice, sharing is often difficult to achieve or counter to current professional practice. This issue is most salient when considered in the context of the often-contradictory results observed by larger law firms implementing information technologies to increase knowledge sharing throughout their organization. In the remainder of this article, four perspectives that employ a *logic of opposition* (Robey & Boudreau, 1999) are used to explore the often contradictory outcomes observed when using information technology to increase knowledge sharing by considering factors both impeding and enhancing sharing within legal practice.

BACKGROUND

Despite the recognition of the importance of knowledge in the various professions, a deliberate effort to manage knowledge within the legal profession is a more recent development (Parsons, 2004; Rusanow, 2003).

Knowledge management initiatives are often implemented with the intent of improving aspects of the knowledge management problematic, and this is invariably associated with the implementation of information technology to assist or enable such initiatives (Grover & Davenport, 2001). Knowledge sharing has been identified as a key process in leveraging knowledge assets (Jarvenpaa & Staples, 2000; Nahapiet & Ghoshal, 1998), and within professional practice knowledge management, initiatives are often directed towards improving knowledge sharing throughout the organization (Weiss, 1999). Knowledge sharing in a legal context is typically motivated by a desire

to share legal knowledge, but there is a growing interest in extending such efforts to knowledge of the client, industry, staff skills, key stakeholders, and the firm's market and financial position.

Within legal practice, inconsistent findings have been observed with respect to technology-based initiatives aimed at increasing knowledge sharing throughout the firm (Cabrera & Cabrera, 2002; Gottschalk, 1999; Hunter, Beaumont, & Lee, 2002; Terrett, 1998). For many firms the implementation of information technology represents the arrival of 'knowledge management' within the organization. This view positions information technology as a determinant or enabler of radical organizational change that once implemented transforms the organization to one where key processes such as knowledge sharing are not only possible but also inevitable. This deterministic logic of the organizational impacts of information technology has been critiqued and an alternate, more complex relationship purported between information technology and organizations that is emergent and reciprocal in nature (DeSanctis & Poole, 1994; Hirschheim, 1985; Kling, 1980; Markus & Robey, 1988; Orlikowski, 2000; Orlikowski & Robey, 1991; Schultze & Leidner, 2002; Walsham, 1993). These authors point to the possibility for different conceptualizations to the logic of determination for the relationship between organizations and technology. The logic of determination explains change as the result of variation in a set of predictor variables that account for the orderly relationships among the variables in a theoretical model; in contrast the logic of opposition is more suitable for accounting for contradictory outcomes by considering forces both promoting and impeding change (Robey & Boudreau, 1999).

Knowledge Sharing in Legal Practice

Institutional theory, organizational politics, organizational culture, and organizational learning draw upon a logic of opposition and are employed in the remainder of this article to account for the contradictory outcomes of information technology by considering the forces both enhancing and impeding knowledge sharing within legal practice. For the following discussion, these theoretical lenses are directed towards medium (300-750 lawyers) and large (greater than 750 lawyers) law firms in order to highlight the competing forces both enhancing and impeding knowledge sharing. These forces are anticipated to manifest in smaller firms, but to a lesser degree since many of these competing forces are influenced by the size of the practice, the level of geographic dispersion, the nature of the growth strategy (internal expansion or acquisition), and the nature of the competitive environment. Within the legal profession, larger firms are quickly becoming the norm as firms expand through rapid growth fueled by acquisition. Accompanying this growth is an increasing reliance on professional management beyond the traditional collegial shared management from which many of these firms originated. This tension has provided a heightened environment in which to consider the contradictory consequences of efforts to use information technology to improve knowledge sharing and a unique opportunity to highlight how alternate conceptualizations can be used to embrace these contradictions in practice.

Institutional Theory

Institutional theory points to the importance of historical and professional traditions and enduring values that are supported by the organization (Robey & Boudreau, 1999). Institutional theories have historically explained why organizational structures and values endure, despite strong reasons and efforts aimed at changing them (Robey & Boudreau, 1999).

Institutions consist of cognitive, normative, regulative structures and activities that provide stability and meaning to social behavior. Institutions are transposed by various carriers—cultures, structures, and routines—and they operate at multiple levels of jurisdiction. (Scott, 1995, p. 33)

Contemporary institutional theory exhibits a logic of opposition, recognizing that while the institutional environment presents normative forces that pressure conformity to maintain legitimacy, a wide variety of organizational responses may be manifest, and change in this context must be considered in terms of the structural factors both enhancing and impeding change (Robey & Boudreau, 1999).

Shifts in the discourses surrounding the wider institutional context of the legal profession have given rise to new conceptualizations of professionalism and partnerships. A new archetype has been proposed that characterizes professional practice through an amalgamation of components of professionalism and partnership—referred to as the P2 form to highlight the differences between the familiar M-form (Greenwood, Hinings, & Brown, 1990) and the recently proposed

managerial professional business (Cooper, Hinings, Greenwood, & Brown, 1996). The P2 form emphasizes a fusion of ownership and control, where managerial tasks revolve among the owners with minimal hierarchy and strong links with clients and the local office. Managerial professional business (MPB) in contrast emphasizes effectiveness and efficiency, with client service and competition serving as the guiding force for a formalized central management team. Within the MPB form, there is increased specialization among lawyers, and integration is accomplished using hierarchy, cross-functional teams, and rules and procedures.

The increased focus on client needs while reducing forces within the firm for sharing increases the outside pressure to share. That is, clients are driving many of the knowledge management initiatives within law firms as they demand increased accountability, and are not willing to pay for 'reinventing the wheel' and are therefore demanding that firms ensure that their lawyers are sharing knowledge. From management's point of view, having the client receive mixed advice because internally the lawyers are not sharing is viewed very negatively. At the same time these clients are realizing that the firm has considerable additional knowledge that is relevant to their business so they are further demanding that the firm share that information with them. Management is eager to satisfy such requests since they wish the client to treat the firm as a 'trusted advisor' on a host of matters in a long-term relationship with the firm (Hunter et al., 2002). This produces competing demands on individual lawyers to hoard their knowledge on the one hand since they see this as guaranteeing their position within the firm by providing their specialized service to the client, while on the other hand knowing that their position also depends on how well they perform with others who also work for the same client.

The need for increased sharing usually begins with the development of a knowledge repository that is centrally administered. This is consistent with the MPB form since it assists in the goal increasing managerial influence throughout the firm. This is particularly important as firms typically consist of multiple offices of national and international affiliates. Centralized technologies based upon knowledge repositories might offer the ability to share knowledge, while at the same time affect institutional norms and cross-organizational boundaries that impede the very sharing that these technologies are intended to support. The very arrival of a specialized knowledge management group or a chief knowledge officer while demonstrating management support for such initiatives as increased knowledge sharing may also effectively separate the practicing lawyers from involvement with knowledge management initiatives within the organization.

The MPB form places significant emphasis on economic performance and efficiency, and this often conflicts with professional and personal expectations of work such as the connection to the public good or the desire for more personal time. The impinging on professional autonomy and representative democracy of the traditional P2 form conflicts with notions of hierarchical control and bureaucracy. Since the MPB form is essentially layered on top of the existing P2 form, there are inherent contradictions that arise, as these forms co-exist within the same organization.

Accounting for contradictory outcomes of information technology employing an institutional theory perspective highlights the dual consideration of the normative pressures on these organizations to not change in order to maintain legitimacy (e.g., highlighted by the factors constituting the P2 form) and forces enhancing change as in the case of the factors implicated in addressing increased pressure from clients (e.g., the MPB form).

Organizational Politics

Organizational politics draws our attention to opposing forces in the form of political resistance to change that must be balanced by negotiation and compromise; change emerges from groups with incompatible opposing interests politically jockeying for position, using information technology as a resource to such political ends along the way (Robey & Boudreau, 1999). Interestingly, it is not assumed that political conflicts can be resolved and that power struggles may be enduring aspects of the political climate. Organizations are regarded as arenas where the contributions and rewards of various parties are sometimes aligned, often misaligned, and occasionally realigned (Bacharach, Bamberger, & Sonnenstuhl, 1996). Professional management establishes an interesting power dynamic within the law firm. Traditionally, management was a shared responsibility and almost an afterthought, or at least something in addition to individual legal practices that had to be performed. The partners were essentially all at the same level, and all the other lawyers wished to be partners someday. However, formal management, while providing a central authority to facilitate sharing throughout the firm, also impedes that process by introducing a power dynamic that was not present when management responsibilities were shared. Before there was no 'us' and 'them', while now there is a clear distinction. Ironically, knowledge management in legal practice may drive a wedge between those demanding that sharing occur and those whom they wish to share (Hunter et al., 2002).

One of the underlying tenets of legal practice has been that 'knowledge is power', since progression within the firm is perceived to be based upon competitive advantage arising from withholding certain knowledge from others (Terrett, 1998). This power to essentially refuse to share was legitimated since there was a professional expectation of autonomy so one could not be forced to share. This autonomy was extends to the relationship with clients whereby individual lawyers essentially 'owned' particular clients, so there was no pressure to share with others since the individual lawyer could directly serve the needs of the client. The key metric for performance under this 'one-on-one' relationship with clients was the billable hour, and this was not negatively affected by knowledge hoarding as the client's needs were met and any inefficiencies resulting from 'reinventing the wheel' were rewarded since the lawyer was paid on a hourly basis. It is detrimental for lawyers to share under this regime since they potentially lose power and income. Incentives and metrics that focus exclusively on individual performance tend to impede knowledge sharing in this context, since they do not account for the positive externalities or recognize the additional value at the group or firm level that can result from such sharing. Consideration for metrics that encourage knowledge sharing focus on factors surrounding mentorship (e.g., student recruitment), industry-level measures that depend on the overall performance of the firm (e.g., market share), or group-level measures (e.g., customer satisfaction with legal team or peer recognition). Varied incentive structures attempt to encourage individual performance while aligning individual goals with those of the group or firm. That is, incentives make explicit the value associated with sharing among the group or firm.

The shifting power from individual lawyers to a central authority has eroded individual autonomy that has further contributed to changing power dynamics, so lawyers are now more mobile, with alternate career paths emerging apart from remaining with the firm for life by progressing to becoming a partner. In conjunction with this is the emerging practice of parachuting individual lawyers into the firm in a lateral move rather than the traditional vertical progression. These individuals are intended to bring a valuable knowledge base and a following of key clients. This climate may at first seem to not be conducive to knowledge sharing (e.g., reduced loyalty), but there may be other political forces at work. For example, attaching oneself to such 'stars' may prove extremely beneficial, and the infusion of new talent may enhance sharing as new practices are adopted.

The push from clients for increased cost accounting has shifted the legal practice of lawyers towards more attention being paid to financial cost considerations for the client and not exclusively on their legal requirements. Information technology in the form of extranets that permit secure access by clients to their ongoing legal files has tended to solidify this practice and shifted the power from the lawyers to the client, as they demand increased transparency and real-time updates on the progress of their file. A parallel power dynamic is evidenced in a reliance on information systems aimed at increasing sharing *between* law firms (Gottschalk, 2001; Khandelwal & Gottschalk, 2003).

The political considerations within a law firm highlight the competing forces for sharing that accompany an increased reliance on formal management. This view also points to the role of incentives in adequately addressing the positive externalities that can accompany group- and firm-level sharing while countering the individual pressures to hoard knowledge. Finally, the political perspective directs our attention to the increased pressure from clients for increased sharing to facilitate improved transparency and real-time updates, and the need for management to counter existing practices that discourage such sharing.

Organizational Culture

Organizational culture demonstrates the importance of recognizing that technology alone will not overcome resistance stemming from cultural persistence and that further steps will need to be taken to address these concerns in the long term (Robey & Boudreau, 1999). Information technologies are considered cultural artifacts that come to symbolize various beliefs, values, and assumptions (Robey & Boudreau, 1999). Three views of organizational culture have been identified: (1) integration—where culture is unified and consistent, and thus opposing organizational change; (2) differentiation—where conflicts occur at the boundaries between subcultures; and (3) fragmentation—where opposing and irreconcilable interpretations may be entertained simultaneously within and across subcultures, and thus culture is viewed as inherently ambiguous and contradictory (Martin, 1992).

The integration perspective points to areas of strong consensus where values, assumptions, and behaviors are shared, and highlights difficulties in implementing change due to cultural drag, thus producing friction between existing patterns and emerging ones (Robey & Boudreau, 1999). Lawyers are not generally viewed as great information sharers, owing to a career progression based upon acquiring a unique knowledge base and thus facilitating a culture of knowledge hoarding rather than sharing (Rusanow, 2003). Time-based billing further encouraged a reluctance to share since sharing required additional time for which the lawyers could not justify billing to clients, and lawyers were reluctant to dedicate 'non-billable' hours to sharing when they could be working for clients. Information technology in the

integration perspective is therefore used to essentially force knowledge-sharing practice by 'culturing' lawyers in knowledge management (Rusanow, 2001). These efforts are then aligned with incentives that contribute to producing an essentially homogenous sharing culture for the firm over time.

The differentiation perspective suggests that even though a homogenous culture may exist within a group, there may be significant differences between groups, even within the same organization or area of specialization. Subcultures shape assumptions about what knowledge is worth managing, expectations of who must share and who can hoard or control specific knowledge, and contributes to the context for social interaction which influences how knowledge will be shared (De Long & Fahey, 2000). Subcultures have significant implications for knowledge sharing since common subcultures are essential for knowledge sharing, without which the tacit knowledge that provides the background understanding for explicit knowledge is not available (Heaton & Taylor, 2002). This implies that where practices are common, sharing can occur (Brown & Duguid, 1991). Using this perspective it is clear that even within the same firm, lawyers may not be able to share their knowledge because their areas of practice are so different. This would explain why it might be easier for lawyers to share with lawyers in another firm than with lawyers in their own firm. Sub-cultural differences are not always a threat, as such differences can also serve as the impetus for a more constructive dialogue, highlighting the complexities that arise in sharing across and even within subcultures.

The fragmentation perspective provides that any cultural symbol can be interpreted in different ways and irreconcilable interpretations can exist simultaneously (Robey & Boudreau, 1999). Even the technological artifact may embody certain cultural features that may affect the use of that technology in practice, and this can be expected to vary between individuals using the same technological artifact. Using technologies to increase sharing under the fragmentation perspective would imply that depending on how the cultural symbol of the technology is interpreted, it may increase or decrease levels of sharing. For example, if the information technology is seen as representing a centralized management culture that is divorced from the more collegial environment in which lawyers are accustomed, then this is likely to reduce sharing significantly. However, if the technology is seen to promote a customer-focused legal practice that is aligned with a preferred collegial culture, then sharing is likely to increase.

Since many of these firms have pursued an aggressive growth strategy fueled by acquisitions, the result is a firm that does not grow its own culture so much as it inherits numerous cultures from the acquired firms. Part of that acquisition is a legacy information technology situation that likely is inextricably linked with the culture of the acquired organization. Attempts to change the existing system or to introduce new systems are likely going to be viewed as a direct assault on the very culture of the firm. Such changes are also counter to the professional culture of lawyers. A collegial environment that provides the lawyer with considerable autonomy in their practice that is essentially self-regulated and underpinned with a connection to the public good and mentorship characterizes this professional culture. Any changes that adversely affect this professional culture are likely to be met with resistance. Within this professional culture are entwined legitimate legal reasons for not sharing such as protection of client confidentiality and intellectual property rights. The ability to segregate knowledge in this context can outweigh the benefits gained by sharing such knowledge with others within the firm.

Organizational culture offers considerable insight into the forces both impeding and enhancing knowledge sharing within legal practice. Multiple acquisitions and the considerable autonomy afforded to individual lawyers and offices on how they operate have left these larger firms severely fragmented. Efforts to increase knowledge sharing in this context must address the multiple cultural differences represented. By appealing to the professional cultures of these lawyers, considerable inroads can be made. The collegial context in which they were trained and the reliance on mentorship all provide unifying connections that can facilitate sharing both within one office and across the offices of these large organizations.

Organizational Learning

Organizational learning considers how organizations learn new responses and why they often fail to learn, while learning organizations achieve higher performance through their ability to learn from past experiences (Senge, 1990). Information technology through the organizational learning lens can have a role to play in both enabling and disabling organizational learning (Robey & Boudreau, 1999).

Learning relies upon an organizational memory, which can be defined as understandings shared by members of an organization about its identity, mental maps, and routines for thought and action (Fiol & Lyles, 1985). While such benefits can accrue for learning, organizational memory may be a poor guide for future action if things change, and therefore organizations must spend considerable time updating their memory (Fiol & Lyles, 1985). The prevailing technology-focused view of knowledge management in legal practice is aimed at capturing the organizational memory in a knowledge repository that can then be shared throughout the firm. However, looking at the constituent aspects of organizational memory, it is unlikely that such aspects could be captured so conveniently.

Legal practice has a strong tradition of mentorship that serves as the basis for learning and firm profits. This mentorship model is built upon the firm's ability to leverage the professional skills of the senior partners with the efforts of the juniors. The underlying motivation for many of the knowledge management initiatives within legal practice is that by improving knowledge management processes such as sharing, the firm will be able to better leverage junior lawyers while simultaneously increasing the effectiveness of the senior partners. While information technology can contribute significantly to knowledge sharing efforts by providing alternate communication channels or the availability of information that was not previously easily accessible, these changes do not necessarily provide the improved learning envisioned to originate from increased sharing. For example, even though e-mail may provide a new channel between senior partners and juniors, juniors may be reluctant to avail of that channel and thus maintain institutional norms, whereby juniors do not have direct access to senior partners.

The mentorship model is the preferred mode of learning with respect to the formalized relationship between junior lawyers and their more senior mentors. This relationship facilitates considerable sharing between the junior and the senior mentor, but the sharing is predominately unidirectional, with the junior lawyer being on the receiving end. This is likely an excellent learning model for the juniors, but may also impede sharing in other aspects. The mentorship model relies on the junior lawyer performing work for the mentor who then bills the client at their senior rate; in return the junior lawyer receives the case experience and guidance needed to progress in the firm. However, it is easy to envision with the forces already discussed in play that such a learning relationship can be shifted so that the junior is essentially performing the work without the benefits of the mentorship. Similarly, this model pairs mentor to junior, often to the exclusion of other lawyers, thus potentially reducing sharing opportunities that would be available if the junior worked with a range of lawyers. Mentorship at the more senior level is not generally as formalized; and when viewed through the increased pressures for individual performance and a reliance on a more centralized management, it is not hard to envision how such mentoring opportunities quickly are moved to the background in favor of short-term gains.

Firm-wide information systems that provide the lawyers with access to best practices, legal precedents, lists of experts, and a searchable knowledge base may in fact be contributing to the erosion of mentorship opportunities. By relying on the information systems as the source of such insights, the lawyers may be robbing themselves of the opportunity to both mentor and be mentored, and the associated benefits of such relationships.

Despite these challenges, the mentorship model appears to be one of the strengths of professional practice, albeit at risk of erosion within certain professional management- and technology-focused environments. The ability to formalize the mentorship model beyond the junior lawyers appears to offer considerable potential for addressing the competing forces both impeding and enhancing knowledge sharing within legal practice.

FUTURE TRENDS

The theoretical perspectives presented draw upon a logic of opposition that sheds new light on the contradictory findings of the effects of technology on knowledge sharing within law firms. Structuration theory (Giddens, 1984) may be a useful theoretical position to take in this regard since the concept of *duality of structure* points to a reciprocal connection between action and structure. A structuration view of information technology directs our attention to organizational consequences of these technologies as being produced and reproduced through human action (Orlikowski, 2000; Orlikowski & Robey, 1991; Schultze & Orlikowski, 2004).

Legal practice provides a heightened environment in which to investigate the forces both enabling and constraining knowledge sharing. Many of the implications are unique to the legal context of larger firms, but given the growing prominence of geographically dispersed service organizations that rely almost exclusively on their knowledge for their survival and the increased use of information technology to support these practices, the experience in these larger law firms may very well represent things to come for many organizations.

Future studies drawing upon a conceptualization of technology that simultaneously enables and constrains knowledge sharing over time would appear to be particularly beneficial to the field of knowledge management.

CONCLUSION

This article highlights the difficulty in offering prescriptive advice on how to use information technology to increase knowledge sharing within law firms, since any action aimed at increasing knowledge sharing can over time simultaneously produce the opposite effect. There are often good reasons why key aspects of legal practice are counter to knowledge sharing, so expecting lawyers to fundamentally change their practice in order to improve knowledge sharing is problematic if not considered in the context of the range of forces both enabling and constraining such sharing.

Institutional theory highlights the dual consideration of the normative pressures on these organizations to remain the same in order to maintain legitimacy and forces enhancing change in order to remain competitive. The professional institution of a law firm provides certain expectations for conduct, appearance, and practice which if not met severely affect the credibility of the firm. However, competitive pressures fueled by rapid expansion through acquisition have placed strong opposing forces that are shifting these firms to rely on centralized professional management approaches. The customer-centric view this shift entails has produced a push for increased sharing within the firm to produce a consistent and more transparent story for the client, while simultaneously reducing the sharing as individual lawyers see their value to the client as being guaranteed by hoarding their knowledge.

Organizational politics draws our attention to political resistance that impedes knowledge sharing that must be balanced with negotiation and compromise. Legal practice with its reliance on collegial shared management has traditionally relied on power originating from seniority in the firm, but this power is shifting towards professional managers for decisions on how the firm should operate. Firm-wide information systems are seen to both improve professional practice by increasing sharing, while at the same time serving to push a wedge between the lawyers and management that in turn impedes sharing.

Organizational culture points to the role that multiple acquisitions and professional autonomy have played in producing fragmented cultures for these larger firms. Professional cultures might serve as a link between these diverse organizational cultures by appealing to their collegial background and reliance on mentorship. Information technology in this context can be seen as a cultural artifact, and as such any attempt at changing or replacing the technology can be seen as a challenge to the organizational or professional culture that the technology espouses.

Organizational learning highlights the role played by the mentorship model in legal practice. The emerging professional management and a reliance on information systems for improved sharing may in fact be eroding this mode of learning within these large law firms. The mentorship model still appears to offer the most promise for improved knowledge sharing within legal practice, if combined with new approaches to mentorship that draw upon the available technologies and match professional expectations for practice.

The contradictory results observed by law firms when using information technology to improve knowledge sharing throughout their organizations provides an opportunity to employ alternate theoretical positions that instead of treating these findings as a problem embraces them and offers an explanation as to why they were observed. There are other theoretical positions that draw upon a logic of opposition (and other logics) that may prove useful in considering additional aspects of knowledge management in legal practice. This article provides insight into many of the opposing forces that arise within legal practice, and while not an exhaustive list, it is hoped that this will serve as the basis for further work.

REFERENCES

Bacharach, S.B., Bamberger, P., & Sonnenstuhl, W.J. (1996). The organizational transformation process: The micropolitics of dissonance reduction and the alignment logics of action. *Administrative Science Quarterly, 41,* 477-506.

Brown, J.S., & Duguid, P. (1991). Organizational learning and communities of practice: Toward a unified view of working, learning, and innovation. *Organization Science, 2*(1), 40-57.

Cabrera, A., & Cabrera, E.F. (2002). Knowledge-sharing dilemmas. *Organization Studies, 23*(5), 687-710.

Cooper, D.J., Hinings, B., Greenwood, R., & Brown, J.L. (1996). Sedimentation and transformation in organizational change: The case of Canadian law firms. *Organization Studies, 17*(4), 623-648.

De Long, D.W., & Fahey, L. (2000). Diagnosing cultural barriers to knowledge management. *Academy of Management Executive, 14*(4), 113-127.

DeSanctis, G., & Poole, M.S. (1994). Capturing the complexity in advanced technology use: Adaptive structuration theory. *Organization Science, 5*(2), 121-147.

Fiol, C.M., & Lyles, M.A. (1985). Organizational learning. *Academy of Management Review, 10,* 803-813.

Giddens, A. (1984). *The constitution of society: Outline of a theory of structuration.* Berkeley: University of California Press.

Gottschalk, P. (1999). Knowledge management in the professions: Lessons learned from Norwegian law firms. *Journal of Knowledge Management, 3*(3), 203-211.

Gottschalk, P. (2001). Predictors of inter-organizational knowledge management: Lessons learned from law firms in Norway. *Knowledge and Process Management, 8*(3), 186-194.

Greenwood, R., Hinings, C.R., & Brown, J. (1990). "P2-form" strategic management: Corporate practice in professional partnerships. *Academy of Management Journal, 33*(4), 725-755.

Grover, V., & Davenport, T.H. (2001). General perspectives on knowledge management: Fostering a research agenda. *Journal of Management Information Systems, 18*(1), 5-21.

Heaton, L., & Taylor, J.R. (2002). Knowledge management and professional work. *Management Communication Quarterly, 16*(2), 210-236.

Hirschheim, R.A. (1985). *Office automation: A social and organizational perspective.* Chichester, UK: John Wiley & Sons.

Hunter, L., Beaumont, P., & Lee, M. (2002). Knowledge management practice in Scottish law firms. *Human Resource Management Journal, 12*(2), 4-21.

Jarvenpaa, S.L., & Staples, D.S. (2000). The use of collaborative electronic media for information sharing: An exploratory study of determinants. *Journal of Strategic Information Systems, 9*(2-3), 129-154.

Khandelwal, V.K., & Gottschalk, P. (2003). Information technology support for interorganizational knowledge transfer: An empirical study of law firms in Norway and Australia. *Information Resources Management Journal, 16*(1), 14-23.

Kling, R. (1980). Social analyses of computing: Theoretical perspectives in recent empirical research. *Computing Surveys, 12,* 61-110.

Markus, M.L., & Robey, D. (1988). Information technology and organizational change: Causal structure in theory and research. *Management Science, 34*(5), 583-598.

Martin, J. (1992). *Cultures in organization: Three perspectives.* Oxford, UK: Oxford University Press.

Nahapiet, J., & Ghoshal, S. (1998). Social capital, intellectual capital, and organizational advantage. *Academy of Management Review, 23*(2), 242-266.

Orlikowski, W. (2000). Using technology and constituting structures: A practice lens for studying technology in organizations. *Organization Science, 11*(4), 404-428.

Orlikowski, W., & Robey, D. (1991). Information technology and the structuring of organizations. *Information Systems Research, 2*(2), 143-169.

Parsons, M. (2004). *Effective knowledge management for law firms.* Oxford, UK: Oxford University Press.

Robey, D., & Boudreau, M.-C. (1999). Accounting for the contradictory organizational consequences of information technology: Theoretical directions and methodological implications. *Information Systems Research, 10*(2), 167-185.

Rusanow, G. (2001). Culturing lawyers in knowledge management. *Knowledge Management Asia-Pacific, 1*(1), 1-11.

Rusanow, G. (2003). *Knowledge management and the smarter lawyer.* New York: ALM Publishing.

Schultze, U., & Leidner, D.E. (2002). Studying knowledge management in information systems research: Discourses and theoretical assumptions. *MIS Quarterly, 26*(3), 213-242.

Schultze, U., & Orlikowski, W. (2004). A practice perspective on technology-mediated network relations: The use of Internet-based self-serve technologies. *Information Systems Research, 15*(1), 87-106.

Scott, W.R. (1995). *Institutions and organizations.* Thousand Oaks, CA: Sage Publications.

Senge, P.M. (1990). *The fifth discipline.* New York: Currency Doubleday.

Sherer, P.D. (1995). Leveraging human assets in law firms: Human capital structures and organizational capabilities. *Industrial and Labor Relations Review, 48*(4), 671-691.

Terrett, A. (1998). Knowledge management and the law firm. *Journal of Knowledge Management, 2*(1), 67-76.

Walsham, G. (1993). *Interpreting information systems in organizations.* Chichester, UK: John Wiley & Sons.

Weiss, L. (1999). Collection and connection: The anatomy of knowledge sharing in professional service firms. *Organizational Development Journal, 17*(4), 61-77.

KEY TERMS

Billable Hours: The practice whereby lawyers track the work they perform for various clients on an hourly basis. This time is billed on an hourly rate to the client. Lawyers also track their activities that are not billable to a particular client and usually attempt to minimize the amount of these non-billable hours.

Billing Model: Under time-based billing, a client's fee is based upon the number of hours spent on the client's case, while under value-based billing, the fee is a mutually agreed value of the law firm's work for the client.

Duality of Structure: The concept in structuration theory that structure is the medium and the outcome of the conduct it recursively organizes.

Logic of Determination: Explains organizational change in terms of the variation of a set of predictor variables.

Logic of Opposition: Explains organizational change by identifying forces both promoting change and impeding change.

Organizational Memory: Understandings shared by members of an organization about its identity, mental maps, and routines for thought and action.

Senior Partner: Partners in the firm who share in the profits of the law firm and generally play a key role in recruiting new business through their networks and reputation.

Knowledge Structure and Data Mining Techniques

Rick L. Wilson
Oklahoma State University, USA

Peter A. Rosen
University of Evansville, USA

Mohammad Saad Al-Ahmadi
Oklahoma State University, USA

INTRODUCTION

Considerable research has been done in the recent past that compares the performance of different data mining techniques on various data sets (e.g., Lim, Low, & Shih, 2000). The goal of these studies is to try to determine which data mining technique performs best under what circumstances. Results are often conflicting—for instance, some articles find that neural networks (NN) outperform both traditional statistical techniques and inductive learning techniques, but then the opposite is found with other datasets (Sen & Gibbs, 1994; Sung, Chang, & Lee, 1999: Spangler, May, & Vargas, 1999). Most of these studies use publicly available datasets in their analysis, and because they are not artificially created, it is difficult to control for possible data characteristics in the analysis. Another drawback of these datasets is that they are usually very small.

With conflicting empirical results in the knowledge discovery/data mining literature, there have been numerous calls for a more systematic study of different techniques using synthetic, well-understood data. The rationale for synthetic data is that various factors can be manipulated while others are controlled, which may lead to a better understanding of why technique X outperforms technique Y in some, but not all, circumstances (Scott & Wilkins, 1999).

This call for research dates back to Quinlan's seminal work in inductive learning algorithms. In his 1994 study that analyzed the difference between neural networks and inductive decision trees, Quinlan conjectures the existence of what he called S-problems and P-problems. In his definition, S-problems are those that are unsuited for NN's, while P-problems are those unsuited for decision tree induction. More recently, the review work on neural networks by Tickle, Maine, Bologna, Andrews, and Diederich (2000) propose that determining whether a classification task belongs to the P-problem or S-problem set is a very important research question.

Recently, other researchers have proposed that the composition of the underlying knowledge in a dataset, or knowledge structure (KS), may be pertinent in understanding why knowledge discovery techniques perform well on one dataset and poorly on others. This term has been used by Hand, Mannila, and Smyth (2001), and Padmanabhan and Tuzhilin (2003) to refer to this phenomenon, while Scott and Wilkins (1999) used a similar term, structural regularities, to describe the same concept.

The goal of this article is to explore in more detail how the existence of a database's underlying *knowledge structure* might help explain past inconsistent results in the knowledge discovery literature. Management scholars will recognize the term knowledge structure, as Walsh (1995) refers to it as a "mental template...imposed on an information environment to give it form and meaning." Therefore, for the knowledge discovery context, we propose that knowledge structure is analogous to the form and meaning of the knowledge to be discovered in a database. Though we will not explore the concept too deeply, one also can define knowledge structure through the use of a parameter set P as proposed by Hand et al. (2001). The parameter set would be attribute-value pairs that detail the existence of a specific knowledge structure for a given knowledge concept/database pair.

This knowledge structure concept is an abstract concept, which may make it hard to visualize. Typically, when a knowledge worker is using a technique to extract knowledge from a database, they will not have any idea about the underlying knowledge structure of the concept of interest. But, researchers have hypothesized that knowledge discovery in a database is optimized when the formalism of the tool matches this underlying structure of the knowledge (Hand et al., 2001). Based on this, we conjecture that if a knowledge worker did know the knowledge structure parameter values prior to exploring the data, he or she could find the optimal tool for the knowledge discovery process.

From a historical perspective, past knowledge discovery and data mining research results could be explained by whether a particular knowledge discovery tool was or was not a good "match" with the underlying knowledge structure. The idea of matching the tool to the structure is somewhat analogous to the concept of task-technology fit, studied in the MIS literature during the mid 1990s (Goodhue, 1995).

Recent research in other related areas has found that contradictory or difficult to explain results could be related to the concept of knowledge structure (Wilson & Rosen, 2003). In this study, the well-known IRIS and BUPA Liver datasets were used to examine the efficacy of knowledge discovery tools in protected (by data perturbation) confidential databases. The IRIS dataset is known to possess linearly separable classes, while the BUPA Liver dataset cases has been historically difficult to correctly classify for all knowledge discovery tools. An outcome of this research was the proposal that knowledge discovery tool effectiveness in a protected (perturbed) database could be impacted by both the database's underlying knowledge structure and the *noise* present in the database. The concept of *noise* is simply the degree to which the different classes can be separated or differentiated by the optimal tool, or, alternatively, a surrogate measure of how difficult cases are to classify (e.g., Li & Wang, 2004).

Through a simple example, the article will attempt to provide some evidence that the underlying knowledge structure present in a database could have significant impacts on the performance of knowledge discovery tools. Building on past postulation, the example also will explore whether the so-called "match" between the knowledge structure and the knowledge discovery tools' own formalism is important to the classification accuracy of the knowledge discovery task.

BACKGROUND

To investigate the possible impact of what has previously been defined as knowledge structure, a hypothetical database/classification task will be formulated. Thus, the investigation of knowledge structure in this article will be limited to a classification domain. The concepts of knowledge structure can be extended to all kinds of knowledge discovery tasks: prediction/regression, clustering, and so forth. We choose classification as our focus because it is a well-studied area and is easily illustrated in this experiment.

To this end, a 50,000 record fictitious bank database, previously used in another work (see Muralidhar, Parsa, & Sarathy, 1999), will serve as the database for the study. The data, in its original form, has five attributes (Home Equity, Stock/Bonds, Liabilities, Savings/Checking, and CD's) with known means, standard deviations, and so forth.

To simulate the existence of an important knowledge concept, a sixth binary categorical (class) variable was systematically added to the database, representing some important knowledge to a data analyst (perhaps differentiating between profitable customers and not-so-profitable customers). How the class variable was systematically created is addressed and is related to the knowledge structure parameters.

We chose a very simplistic definition of knowledge structure types in our continuing example. Two different knowledge structures were employed, decision tree and linear. The *decision tree* (DT) structure means that the researchers created a decision tree using all five variables, and then the data was applied to the tree to determine class membership (either '0' or '1') in the sixth variable, for each individual case. The specific tree used was chosen such that all variables were found in the tree and that there were an equal number of the two distinct classes created (25,000 cases each of 'class 0' and 'class 1'). The tree itself was obviously somewhat arbitrary, but does represent a scenario where the underlying structure of the knowledge concept was in a decision tree form.

The second structure used was a linear format (LINEAR). A strictly linear relationship was created using all five variables, to determine class membership (either '0' or '1') in the sixth variable for each individual case. Again, the resulting values for the sixth variable included 25,000 cases for each 'class 0' and 'class 1.' This again represents the situation where the underlying knowledge concept of interest is in a linear form.

While these two structures may be overly simplistic, their choice allows us to explore the possible impact of the concept of knowledge structure with minimal moderating factors. Ultimately, the notation of Padmanabhan and Tuzhilin (2003) may be a more formal and more accurate approach to describe this phenomenon, and we will return to this later in the article.

For each of the two exemplar knowledge structures (DT and LINEAR), we created another database that involved adding "noise" to the class variable. The purpose of adding noise is to have the synthesized datasets replicate knowledge discovery situations where a perfect discrimination between classes is not possible, as is true in the case of the previously mentioned BUPA Liver dataset. One could argue that real-world databases are more likely than not to have a high degree of noise.

To introduce noise into each of the noise-free datasets (referred to as the 0% noise case), the class variable of 25% of the cases in each class were randomly switched. Thus, the balance of the two different classes was preserved (25,000 of each), and 25% of the cases were now put into the wrong class.

Thus, four different datasets were synthesized—a dataset where the underlying knowledge structure was a decision tree with 0% noise, a dataset where the underlying knowledge structure was a linear relationship with 0% noise, and the complimentary datasets where inaccuracy, in the form of 25% noise, was added into the class variable. These four different datasets represent a diverse spectrum of knowledge discovery scenarios.

In our quest to investigate how knowledge discovery tools may be impacted by the structure of knowledge, there are many possible tools that could be utilized. To try to get a wide view of possible impacts, we present the results from four "standard" approaches: discriminant analysis, the decision tree procedure CART (Classification and Regression Tree Analysis), logistic regression, and a standard feed-forward back-propagation neural network.

Discriminant analysis was selected because it uses (for the two class case) a linear regression-based approach for classifying cases. Thus, from Hand et al.'s (2001) contention that classification/knowledge discovery is optimized when the formalism of the tool matches the underlying structure of the knowledge, one would expect discriminant analysis to perform the best when the underlying knowledge structure was linear.

However, there are many citations in the statistics literature that state when dealing with binary (or categorical) dependent variables, logistic regression is superior in performance to discriminant analysis. Thus, we study both approaches, since they represent tools whose underlying formalism is linear. Both were implemented using standard statistical routines in SPSS.

Using the same rationale, the CART algorithm was selected, as it is a well-known and well-documented inductive decision tree algorithm (see Weiss & Kulikowski, 1991). Given the contention of matching structure to tool formalism, one would expect CART to perform better for those datasets with a decision tree knowledge structure. Again, this tool was implemented using standard defaults in the SPSS package Answer Tree.

Finally, feed-forward, back-propagation neural networks were implemented and used in this study. As another non-parametric technique (like CART), neural networks are often times compared to traditional statistical tools in classification problems. Many claim that they are universally the best classifiers, though results do not necessarily support this claim. Neural network researchers might postulate that they may be immune to knowledge structure impacts since they are alleged to be able to find all types of classification knowledge patterns. The neural network software used in this study was SPSS's Neural Connection, again using standard default values for training, network structure, and the like.

The dependent measure of interest in this study was the classification accuracy of the knowledge discovery tool. Since we had datasets of equal class membership, individual class accuracy was not of particular interest. Ten-fold cross-validation (with stratified samples) was used to ensure a robust measure of tool classification accuracy (see Weiss & Kulikowski, 1991, for more details). An instance was labeled as correctly classified when the tool classification matched the actual class value of the database instance. The correct number of classifications was assessed both for the training (development) and testing partitions. Due to the large size of our simulated dataset and the use of cross-validation, the accuracy of the tools for the training and testing set were nearly identical. Therefore, for simplicity, we report only the results of the testing sets.

RESULTS

Table 1 shows the average classification accuracy over the 10 trials for the experiment. The rows represent the four different knowledge discovery techniques used: logistic regression (LR), multiple discriminant analysis (MDA), the decision tree inductive learning algorithm of CART, and back propagation neural networks (NN). The columns represent the two different levels of Noise (0% and 25%). The top half of Table 1 shows the results when the *decision tree* knowledge structure was used to create the synthetic database, the bottom half, the results when a *linear* structure was used. Figures 1 and 2, respectively, show the results in graphical format.

Table 1. Average classification accuracy

	Noise	Level
KS=Tree	Zero	Twenty Five
LR	72.9	61.2
MDA	72.6	61.2
CART	100	75
NN	98.7	72.5

KS=Linear	Zero	Twenty Five
LR	100	74.3
MDA	98.7	74.2
CART	87.1	68.5
NN	99.9	74.7

Figure 1. Tree KS

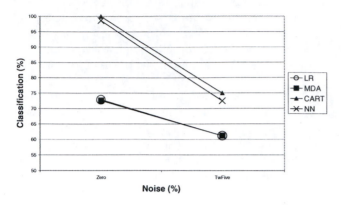

Figure 2. Linear KS

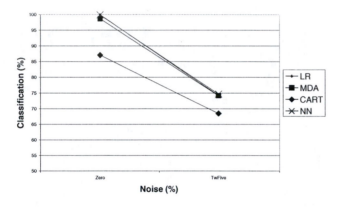

Knowledge Structure: Decision Tree

For the datasets whose knowledge was generated via decision trees, the CART decision tree approach had 100% classification accuracy for the 0% noise case, and 75% accuracy for the 25% noise case. As the formalism of the knowledge discovery approach exactly matches the knowledge structure, these results are not surprising.

The poor performance of the linear-based methods, multiple discriminant analysis and logistic regression may be surprising. They do a very poor job of classification when applied to the decision tree knowledge structure (approximately 73% correct in the 0% noise case). Thus, the unmatched approaches were approximately 27% worse than the matched approaches. This is fairly strong evidence of the potential impact of matching the knowledge discovery approach to the true underlying knowledge structure. Similar results are also true for the 25% noise rate; however, the impact is dampened in

magnitude due to the already poor performance of MDA and LR.

The results of the neural network for both noise levels are very good but are statistically significant different (worse) than CART. Even considering this, the neural network seems less susceptible to performance impact than the linear knowledge discovery techniques. Summarizing from a statistically statistical standpoint, CART performs statistically better than all three other techniques, neural networks performs better than discriminant analysis and logistic regression, and the two linear approaches are equivalent performers.

Knowledge Structure: Linear

Interestingly, for the linear knowledge structure and 0% noise, logistic regression performs perfectly (100% average correctly classifications). Discriminant analysis has just a small average "miss" rate (1.3%). Neural networks also perform very close to perfect (an average of 99.9% correct), while CART performs significantly worse (practically and statistically) at an 87.1% average correct classifications. Of importance is the finding that CART's performance when applied to a database with an unmatched knowledge structure is not nearly as poor as the performance of the linear tools when applied to databases with an unmatched knowledge structure.

With the noise level at 25%, it is surprising to see that neural networks perform better than all other techniques (though their classification accuracy is not statistically different from the two linear approaches). These results provide some credence to the robustness of neural networks when considering potential impacts of knowledge structure. Of course, this may be true only for this study.

Overall, for the linear knowledge structure databases, the two linear approaches and neural networks show no statistical differences, while all three perform statistically significantly better than the performance of CART. This is true for both with and without noise.

FUTURE TRENDS AND DISCUSSION

The results provide some evidence that knowledge structure and its relationship to the tools used could impact the results of knowledge analysis. Certainly, the small study undertaken could not claim to be comprehensive, but the evidence found would suggest consideration should be given to this concept of knowledge structure by practitioners and researchers alike.

Of course, the knowledge possessed by a database will likely never perfectly fit one specific knowledge structure (or at least as generically as they have been defined here). Similarly, the inclusion of noise into the synthetic database is at best a surrogate measure of the inherent difficulty to find hidden knowledge in a set of database cases. This difficulty could stem from relevant attributes not appearing in the database (missing information) or just because the knowledge/relationships resist easy quantification.

How might this knowledge structure concept be implemented or further quantified? Using the notation used in Padmanabhan and Tuzhilin (2003), perhaps the knowledge structure of a database can be identified as an n-tuple of the knowledge concept itself plus some measure (say on a continuous 0 to 1 scale) of how similar the knowledge structure is to a set of exemplars. This 0 to 1 scale also could be a measure of noise as it relates to the exemplar structures.

As a continuing example, consider the database already analyzed here, with five continuous attributes, one class variable indicating good/bad customer (noted by abbreviation GB), and suppose we also have another class variable indicating whether the customer is considered a likely target (0/1 value) for a new marketing campaign for a new product (noted by NP). Let us also assume (unrealistically) that there are four specific exemplar knowledge structures in the universe of knowledge discovery: decision trees (DT), linear (L), type 3 (T3), and type 4 (T4).

The four versions of the synthetic database used in the article might then be defined by a parameterized function KS = f(database, DT, L, T3, T4), such that the database with KS=DT and no noise would be KS=(GB,1,0,0,0), and with 25% noise KS=(GB, .75, 0,0,0). Likewise, the two datasets with underlying knowledge being linear would have parameterized KS values of (GB,0,1,0,0) and (GB, 0,.75,0,0), respectively.

Continuing with the example, if the knowledge structure of the concept new product target (NP) had mixed components of decision tree, linear and Type 4 structure, it might have a parameterized value of (NP, .3, .4, 0, .1). In summary, assuming that knowledge structure does continue to show promise as an explanatory factor in knowledge discovery results, future studies working to formalize and further operationalize this knowledge structure concept seem very important.

Some might view this problem of trying to quantify a database knowledge structure as not useful. We would argue that better understanding the dynamics of data mining and knowledge discovery is exactly the kind of problem that should be studied in academic research. The field needs better ways of ensuring the correct or best tool is used in knowledge discovery rather than depending upon pure chance. The use of multiple tools (and multiple variations of individual tools, such as ensembles of neural networks) is certainly a good strategy, but researchers should continue to look for new and innovative ways to help guide the data mining practitioner. Researchers should help practitioners better understand when and where these tools are most useful, and not just simply continue to deploy new tools.

The results of this article are another example of the potential of neural networks to seemingly approximate many types of functions (or knowledge structures), unlike the other three tools employed. Unfortunately, we cannot yet consider using only neural networks as a knowledge discovery tool given their present inability to explain the knowledge the tool has discovered (Li & Wang, 2004). There is an ongoing stream of research (e.g, Tickle et al., 2000) focusing on developing techniques whereby neural network knowledge is made more understandable for the decision-maker, but it is still at primitive stages of development. Should this research lead to further enhancement of neural networks to better explain their results, then perhaps the search for the "holy grail" of knowledge discovery tools has been found. Unfortunately, the maturity of this research indicates this is not reasonable over the next few years.

However, neural networks may play an expanded role in knowledge structure determination through this same "natural" ability to learn any function. Perhaps they can somehow be trained to recognize exemplar and combined knowledge structures in various synthetic databases, and then the results of this trained network can be applied to real datasets under analysis. In this way, the decision-maker would have an improved idea on which knowledge discovery tool will likely optimize their results.

CONCLUSION

Many researchers have long been seeking the penultimate knowledge discovery technique. This article has provided evidence that the underlying knowledge structure that exists in a specific database could impact knowledge discovery results. It seems reasonable to further expand and clarify our definition of knowledge structure, work at further understanding how to operationalize this concept, and then merge this with ongoing streams of research that seek to enhance knowledge discovery tools, all resulting in providing better tools for the practitioner. Through this multifaceted approach we can continue to add deeper understanding to the operation of the many powerful analytic tools on the desktops of today's knowledge workers.

REFERENCES

Goodhue, D. (1995). Understanding user evaluations of information systems. *Management Science, 41*(12), 1827-1844.

Hand, D., Mannila, H., & Smyth, P. (2001). *Principles of data mining*. Cambridge, MA: MIT Press.

Li, R., & Wang, Z. (2004). Mining classification rules using rough sets and neural networks. *European Journal of Operations Research*, forthcoming.

Lim, T.S., Low, W.Y., & Shih, Y.S. (2000). A comparison of prediction accuracy, complexity, and training time of thirty-three old and new classification algorithms. *Machine Learning, 40*(3), 203-229.

Muralidhar, K., Parsa, R., & Sarathy, R. (1999). A general additive data perturbation method for database security. *Management Science, 45*(10), 1399-1415.

Padmanabhan, B., & Tuzhilin, A. (2003). On the use of optimization for data mining: Theoretical interactions and eCRM opportunities. *Management Science, 49*(10), 1327-1343.

Quinlan, J.R. (1994). Comparing connectionist and symbolic learning methods. In R. Rivest, (Ed.), *Computational learning theory and natural learning systems: Constraints and prospects* (pp. 445-456). Cambridge, MA: MIT Press.

Scott, P.D., & Wilkins, E. (1999). Evaluating data mining procedures: Techniques for generating artificial data sets. *Information and Software Technology, 41*(9), 579-587.

Sen, T.K., & Gibbs, A. M. (1994). An evaluation of the corporate takeover model using neural networks. *Intelligent Systems in Accounting, Finance and Management, 3*(4), 279-292.

Spangler, W., May, J.H., & Vargas, L.G. (1999). Choosing data-mining methods for multiple classification: Representation and performance measure implication for decision support. *Journal of Management Information Systems, 16*(1), 37-62.

Sung, T.K., Chang, N., & Lee, G. (1999). Dynamics of modeling in datamining: Interpetive approach to bankruptcy prediction. *Journal of Management Information Systems, 16*(1), 63-85.

Tickle, A., Maine, F., Bologna, G., Andrews, R., & Diederich, J. (2000). Lessons from past, current issues, and future research directions in extracting the knowledge embedded in artificial neural networks. In S. Wernster & R. Sun (Eds.), *Hybrid neural systems* (pp. 226-239). Heidelberg: Springer-Verlag Telos.

Walsh, J. (1995). Managerial and organizational cognition: Notes from a trip down memory lane. *Organizational Science, 6*(3), 280-321.

Weiss, S., & Kulikowski, C. (1991). *Computer systems that learn*. San Mateo: Morgan Kauffman.

Wilson, R.L., & Rosen, P.A. (2003). The impact of data perturbation techniques on data mining accuracy. *Journal of Database Management, 14*(2), 14-26.

KEY TERMS

Classification and Regression Trees (CART): A tool for data mining that uses decision trees. CART provides a set of rules that can be applied to a new dataset for predicting outcomes. CART segments data records by creating binary splits.

Knowledge Structure: A parameterized concept that could help explain why a specific knowledge discovery technique performs best for a particular knowledge discovery task. The concept is analogous to the form and meaning (i.e., underlying structure) of the knowledge to be discovered in a database, and defined by a set of parameters P.

Logistic Regression: Special form of regression in which the dependent variable is a nonmetric, dichotomous (binary) variable. Although some differences exist, the general manner of interpretation is quite similar to linear regression.

Multiple Discriminant Analysis: A multivariate technique that can be used if the single dependent variable is dichotomous or multichotomous, and therefore nonmetric. The goal of this technique is to understand the difference between groups and to predict the likelihood that an entity will belong to a particular group based on several metric independent variables.

Neural Network: A system of processing elements, called neurons, connected together to form a network. The fundamental and essential characteristic of an artificial neural network is the ability to learn; they are not programmed but learn from examples through repeated adjustments of their weights.

Noise: In this article, it can be viewed in two similar ways. Noise is a statistical concept that represents some form of variation in a database. In the context of using a perturbation approach to protect confidential data, noise is added to mask the confidential data item. From the perspective of using a knowledge discovery tool, noise represents the ease or difficulty in classifying individual records correctly (i.e., relative ease in defining or finding the knowledge). The noisier a database is, the more difficult it is to gain insight into knowledge present.

P-Problems: Where all of the input variables are always relevant to the classification. Decision tree methods are unsuitable for P-Problems.

S-Problems: Where the relevance of a particular input variable depends on the values of other input variables. Back-propagation neural networks will require inordinate amounts of learning time for these types of problems, so they are unsuitable for S-Problems.

Knowledge Synthesis Framework

Kam Hou Vat
University of Macau, Macau

INTRODUCTION

The last decade of the 20th century saw explosive growth in discussions about knowledge—knowledge work, knowledge management, knowledge-based organizations, and the knowledge economy (Cortada & Woods, 2000). At the center of such discussions are the two notions of process and knowledge. The former represents not only the organization's operations characterized by clearly defined inputs, outputs, and flows, but also management practices which give the organization its depth and means for handling change and turbulence. The latter is represented by a range of complexity and intellectual richness, from Plato's "justified true belief" (Nonaka & Takeuchi, 1995) to a more mundane "the capacity to act" (Sveiby, 1997). How knowledge is characterized, used, and even created within an organization is a very complicated process. Nevertheless, we believe that each member of an organization has his or her own knowledge space, which is subject to some level of description, and thus may be architected, integrated, and designed into an organization (Davenport & Prusak, 1998; Levine, 2001). As the source of wealth shifts from capital to knowledge (Drucker, 1992), it is clear that organizations that actively seek to create their own communal knowledge space from that, which exists among its members, will have a decided advantage over those who do not. One working definition of knowledge is hereby interpreted in terms of its potential for action and its ability to change context and goals—the rules of relevance and adaptation. Yet, what is the means by which a communal knowledge space may be built? And how would an organization use it for advantage? To answer these questions, this article is divided into five sections: The Background of Knowledge Synthesis; Pursuing the Ideal of a Learning Organization; Scaffolding the Knowledge Framework; Future Trends of IS Design for Knowledge Sharing; and Conclusion.

The first provides the foundations on understanding the knowledge phenomenon as it is happening in many an organization today. The second serves as a digest in capturing some basic ideas of the learning organization. The third brings forth our conception of an actionable framework of knowledge synthesis, applicable to the Internet-based development of present-day organizations. The fourth discusses some of the challenges in information systems (IS) design for knowledge work. The fifth concludes the article by reiterating the challenges in doing organizational knowledge synthesis.

The theme of this article is to investigate strategies to enhance knowledge sharing through the idea of a learning organization. Its aim is to conceive appropriate design of IS support so as to expand an organization's capacity to adapt to future challenges.

THE BACKGROUND OF KNOWLEDGE SYNTHESIS

To situate our discussions about knowledge work in an organization, we first resort to the classification scheme of knowledge tasks from Charles Perrow (1970) on the basis of their analyzability (the degree to which search activity is needed to solve a problem) and variability (the number of exceptions—new or unexpected—encountered while performing a task). There are four task subtypes: craft, routine, engineering, and non-routine. *Routine* tasks are characterized by the combination of low variability and high analyzability. Namely, few exceptions are encountered in the work process, and when an exception does occur, little search behavior is required to handle it. *Craft* tasks are characterized by the combination of low variability and low analyzability. This means only a narrow range of exceptions being encountered, but a high level of search activity is needed to find a solution to problems. *Engineering* tasks are characterized by the combination of high variability and high analyzability. Namely, the number or variety of exceptions that workers may encounter in the task is high, but finding a solution is relatively easy because well-understood standard procedures should have been established to handle the exceptions. Finally, *non-routine* tasks are characterized by the combination of high variability and low analyzability. It is the most complex and least routine of the four tasks in Perrow's classification. These tasks are complex because not only is the number of unexpected situations large, but search activity is high: Each new situation creates a need to expend resources to deal with it. A key goal of management is to analyze and refine what have been craft and non-routine tasks, and transform them into routine and engineering tasks. They constantly seek to reduce the ambiguity and uncertainty by routinizing work and the business rules governing that work.

Nonetheless, organizational tasks are increasingly being craft and non-routine. Such knowledge work is not easily subject to process explicitness (clearly defined specifications). As tasks become more unanalyzable (i.e., craft, non-routine), the level of ambiguity increases and requires people with relatively more experience and tacit knowledge, and a certain level of rich information. Similarly, as tasks become more variable (i.e., engineering and non-routine), the level of uncertainty increases thereby requiring people with more training, formal education, explicit knowledge, and high quantities of information. Obviously, such is the backdrop behind which many an enterprise today has been developing their contexts for organizational knowledge synthesis.

In order to develop a communal knowledge space— one that develops new forms of knowledge from that which exists among its members—we must describe how and with what an organization performs its work, say, in terms of its core capabilities (i.e., strategic processes) and core competencies (i.e., knowledge areas applied to capabilities) (Stalk, Evans, & Shulman, 1992). Oftentimes the alignment context is expressed in terms of the dynamics of the people-process-system issue. Namely, we need to design suitable information systems to help people with knowledge to perform the processes involved to produce results of value to the organization. In fact, Zuboff (1988) has written extensively on the interaction of people and information technology (IT), and the all-important shift in management thinking from automating to informating. In practice, *automating* typically refers to the use of IT during process change to substitute the deployment of humans. Automating serves to lower uncertainty and increase management control. *Informating*, in contrast, refers to the effect IT may have on the understanding and transparency of a process. Informating makes people more productive through their use of and process integration with IT. It serves to increase the capacity of people to understand the entire value-adding business process. Thus, informating concerns itself with the connection people have with their specific tasks as well as the whole flow of work. Certainly, the notion of knowledge must be incorporated. While informating concerns IT and task integration, the idea of *knowledging* (Savage, 1996) refers to individual and organizational learning, and is characterized by the process of knowledge creation and the active involvement of the individual with his or her work. Knowledging includes a dynamic interaction between the known (explicit) and the vision (tacit) forms of knowledge. In fact, each context from automating to informating to knowledging may be thought of as a stage, a progression requiring additional alignment threads and trade-off. In particular, the trade-off between individualism and community may impact the movement from informating to knowledging. Individualism drives individual knowledge and rewards, and thus encourages informating, while a community emphasizes sharing and is more closely associated with knowledging, including the interaction of computers, people, lateral relations, business processes, and organizational learning (including knowledge creation). Thereby, in order to create a communal knowledge space for the organization, each successive organizational transformation, from automating to informating to knowledging, requires higher levels of process abstraction and a broad range of process integration and alignment threads.

PURSUING THE IDEAL OF A LEARNING ORGANIZATION

Nowadays, enterprises including educational institutes are challenged to do things faster, better, and more cost effectively in order to remain competitive in an increasingly global economy. There is a strong need to share knowledge in a way that makes it easier for individuals, teams, and enterprises to work together to effectively contribute to an organization's success. This idea of knowledge sharing has well been exemplified in the notion of a learning organization (LO) (Garvin, 1993; King, 1996; Levine, 2001; Senge, 1990; Vat, 2001). Basically, a learning organization could be considered as an organization that focuses on developing and using its information and knowledge capabilities in order to create higher-value information and knowledge, to modify behaviors to reflect new knowledge and insights, and to improve bottom-line results. Based on this characterization of LO, there are many possible IS instances that could be incorporated into a learning organization. The acronym "LOIS" (Learning Organization Information System) (Vat, 2003; Williamson & Lliopoulos, 2001) as applied to an organization is often used as a collective term representing the conglomeration of various information systems, each of which, being a functionally defined subsystem of the enterprise LOIS, is distinguished through the services it renders. For example, if a LOIS could support structured and unstructured dialogue and negotiation among the organizational members, then the LOIS subsystems might need to support reflection and creative synthesis of information and knowledge, and thus integrate working and learning. They should also help document information and knowledge as it builds up, say, by electronic journals. Or, they have to make recorded information and knowledge retrievable, and individuals with information and knowledge accessible. Collectively, a LOIS can be considered as a scheme to improve the organization's chances for success and survival by continuously adapting to the external environment. Consequently, we stand a better chance of increasing social participation and shared understanding within the enterprise, and thus foster better learning. Although we believe that this positioning of LOIS represents a significant vision of a future generation of information systems, there are serious questions to be addressed in connection with knowledge capture and transformation, as well as intellectual asset management within the enterprise. All these have consequences for organization transformation in such areas as strategies, structures, processes, systems, and people. More importantly, the philosophy underlying the LOIS design should recognize that our knowledge is the amassed thought and experience of innumerable minds, and the LOIS helps capture and reuse those experiences and insights in the enterprise. The notion that emerges strongly resembles the classical history paradigm of learning from past events, necessitating the collection of data and repeated re-interpretation of its meaning, significance, and impact for next generations. That is also the idea of organizational learning (Senge et al., 1994), supported by an organizational memory (Conklin, 1996)—the means by which knowledge from the past is continuously brought to bear on present activities. It should possibly result in higher or lower levels of organizational effectiveness (Stein, 1992) in terms of the decision making, organizing, leading, designing, controlling, communicating, planning, and motivating functions of the management process. The cultivation of a communal knowledge space based on the organizational memory is fundamental to enterprises that intend to establish, grow, and nurture a digital learning organization (Hackbarth & Groven, 1999), where individuals grow intellectually and expand their knowledge by unlearning inaccurate information and relearning new information. Oftentimes, there is the essential difference between doing it the way we always did it (single-loop learning) and arriving at an innovative solution that establishes new patterns and relationships (double-loop learning) (Argyris, 1992; Senge et al., 1994).

SCAFFOLDING THE KNOWLEDGE FRAMEWORK

In order to create the communal knowledge space for the entire organization, an organization needs a vision that orients the entire organization to the kind of knowledge it must acquire, and wins spontaneous commitment by the individuals and groups involved in knowledge creation (Dierkes, Marz, & Teele, 2001; Stopford, 2001). It is top management's role to articulate this knowledge vision and communicate it throughout the organization. A knowledge vision should define what kind of knowledge the organization should create in what domains. It helps determine

how an organization and its knowledge base will evolve in the long run (Leonard-Barton, 1995; Nonaka & Takeuchi, 1995). On the other hand, the central requirement for organizational knowledge synthesis is to provide the organization with a strategic ability to acquire, create, exploit, and accumulate new knowledge continuously and repeatedly in a circular process. To meet this requirement, we need an actionable framework, which could facilitate the installation of this strategic ability. It is believed that there are at least three major elements constituting the knowledge framework of a learning organization, including the knowledge architecture, the knowledge synthesis process, and the technical knowledge infrastructure. The first, being a component of the overall organizational architecture, is responsible for generating an ever-growing body of organizational knowledge. The second provides the formal methodology for collecting, integrating, and disseminating knowledge. The third, increasingly being virtualized over the Internet in every organization, should allow every individual to gain access to knowledge wherever and whenever it is needed.

The Knowledge Architecture

Following the idea of a learning organization, we suggest the creation of a number of architectural components in the knowledge architecture (Vat, 2001, 2003), which are intended to facilitate learning, and the creation, acquisition, plus distribution of knowledge among organizational members.

- **The IL-component:** The individual learning (IL) (Kim, 1993) component serves to provide training and education for individuals through the institution of workshops, apprenticeship programs, and the establishment of informal mentoring programs. Typically, an IL component provides free use of the organization's IS infrastructure to access unstructured material in order to pursue an explicit educational path, and to access structured learning material purposely designed for online self-learning. The organization that adopts the IL component in pursuit of a learning organization is betting on its people; namely, enhanced individual learning will translate into improved organizational behaviors and performance.
- **The OL-component:** The organizational learning (OL) (Grant, 1996; Probst & Buchel, 1997) component focuses on the use of a communities of practice approach, leading to the formation of collaborative groups composed of professionals who share experience, knowledge, and best practices for the

purposes of collective growth. The conceptual basis is that group-based organizational competencies and capacities can be developed, refined, and enhanced to enable the organization to adapt to changing circumstances and demands, through such ideas as teamwork, empowerment, case management, or development-centered career paths.

- **The IPM-component:** This component deals with the issue of intellectual property management (IPM) (Stewart, 1997; Sveiby, 1997; Wiig, 1997) underlying the activities that are involved in leveraging existing codified knowledge assets in the form of patents, brands, copyrights, research reports, and other explicit intellectual properties of the organization. The organization that pursues the IPM component in support of a learning organization may devise a financial incentive that allows individuals and groups to be rewarded for the creation and leveraging of intellectual properties.

- **The KM-component:** The knowledge management (KM) (O'Leary, 1998) component focuses on the acquisition, explication, and communication of mission-specific professional expertise that is largely tacit in nature to organizational participants in a manner that is focused, relevant, and timely (Grant, 1996; King 1999; van der Spek & De Hoog, 1995; Wiig, 1993). The conceptual basis is that an organization's tacit knowledge can, in part, be made explicit, and leveraged through the operation of KM-related processes and systems developed for knowledge sharing.

The Knowledge Synthesis Process

Knowledge synthesis is a social as well as an individual process. Sharing tacit knowledge requires individuals to share their personal beliefs about a situation with others. At that point of sharing, justification becomes public. Each individual is faced with the tremendous challenge of justifying his or her beliefs in front of others—and it is this need for justification, explanation, persuasion, and human connection that makes knowledge synthesis a highly fragile process. To bring personal knowledge into a social context, within which it can be amplified or further synthesized, it is necessary to have a field that provides a place in which individual perspectives are articulated and conflicts are resolved in the formation of higher-level concepts. In a typical organization, the field for interaction is often provided in the form of an autonomous, self-directed work team, made up of members from different functional units. It is a critical matter for an organization to decide when and how to establish such a team of interaction in which individuals can meet and interact. This team triggers organization knowledge synthesis

through several steps. First, it facilitates the building of mutual trust among members, and accelerates creation of an implicit perspective shared by members as tacit knowledge. Second, the shared implicit perspective is conceptualized through continuous dialogue among members. Tacit field-specific perspectives are converted into explicit concepts that can be shared beyond the boundary of the team. It is a process in which one builds concepts in cooperation with others. It provides the opportunity for one's hypothesis or assumption to be tested. As Markova and Foppa (1990) argue, social intercourse is one of the most powerful media for verifying one's own ideas.

Next comes the step of justification, which determines the extent to which the knowledge created within the team is truly worthwhile for the organization. Typically, an individual justifies the truthfulness of his or her beliefs based on observations of the situation; these observations, in turn, depend on a unique viewpoint, personal sensibility, and individual experience. Accordingly, when someone creates knowledge, he or she makes sense out of a new situation by holding justified beliefs and committing to them. Indeed, the creation of knowledge is not simply a compilation of facts, but a uniquely human process that cannot be reduced or easily replicated. It can involve feelings and belief systems of which we may not even be conscious. Nevertheless, justification must involve the evaluation standards for judging truthfulness. There might also be value premises that transcend factual or pragmatic considerations. Finally, we arrive at the stage of cross-leveling knowledge (Nonaka, Toyama, & Konno, 2002). During this stage, the concept that has been created and justified is integrated into the knowledge base of the organization, which comprises a whole network of organizational knowledge.

The Knowledge Infrastructure

The knowledge infrastructure supporting the idea of a learning organization is based on a simple philosophy; namely, various knowledge services, in support of a specific LOIS context (say, the creation of a communal knowledge space), must be interpreted as the essential means to realize the particular synthesis processes for organizational knowledge transfer. And such services could be made available to their users in the form of different distributed Web-based applications, which are each designed and tested incrementally and iteratively according to the purposeful activities of the organizational scenarios. The challenge is how to design the infrastructure to enable spontaneous knowledge capture and transfer so as to turn the scattered, diverse knowledge of individual knowledge workers into well-structured knowledge assets ready for reuse in the organization (De Hoog, Benus, Vogler, & Metselaar, 1996). Accordingly, adoption of a three-tiered configuration—composed of respectively the front-end KM services (KMS), the middle-layer KM architecture (KMA), and the back-end organizational memory (OM)—is suggested (Vat, 2000, 2002).

- **The knowledge management services (KMSs):** The design of front-end KM services is an attempt to recognize the human assets within the minds of individuals, and to leverage them as organizational assets that can be accessed and used by a broader set of individuals on whose decisions the organization depends. According to Nonaka and Takeuchi (1995), organizational knowledge can be created through the interactions between tacit and explicit knowledge based on the SECI (socialization, externalization, combination, and internalization) process. Consequently, our KM services can be devised based on these four modes of interactions. The 'knowledge socialization' process usually occurs in the form of informal communication when someone raises a question for discussion or an issue that requires a response. The 'knowledge internalization' process occurs when we are actively searching for methods or lessons learned to solve problems at hand. We internalize knowledge by doing, and also by observing what other people have done in a similar context and by example. The 'knowledge externalization' process is aimed at structuring knowledge and making it available to other users. It involves concept mapping, tacit knowledge categorization, and representation. The 'knowledge combination' process involves various knowledge sharing and decision coordination.
- **The knowledge management architecture (KMA):** The KMA acts as the middle layer supporting the front-end KMS through the back-end OM. Its logical requirements are to satisfy the KM concerns to create, retain, share, and leverage knowledge from the personal level to the team level, the organizational level, and even the inter-organizational level. Its development is conceived from two architectural perspectives: the business architecture and the technology architecture. The former involves the development of management solutions that are related to modeling the business functionality of the organization—namely, business strategies, processes, and structures that enhance and facilitate organization-wide knowledge leveraging. The latter involves the development of information and communications technology (ICT) components within an intranet-based knowledge medium to translate the organization's business vision into effective electronic applications that support the intra- and inter-organizational KM services.

- **The organizational memory (OM):** The KM processes involved in organizational learning often require iterations of references and modification of the components developed in the business and the technology architectures of the KMA. This requirement implies the importance of a reusable asset repository for storing various business-specific and technology-related components in the form of tacit and explicit knowledge items. The OM could be designed to fulfill this specific requirement. For example, it could be structured into the business repository and the technology repository. Typically the business repository stores knowledge items we can use to standardize definitions of organizational and process models. And we can archive existing process components, which can then be recalled later by coworkers in other departments to be reused or modified for new process models. Similarly, the technology repository stores technology resources such as 'business objects', pre-built and purchased components, developer documentation, and numerous other technology standards.

FUTURE TRENDS OF IS DESIGN FOR KNOWLEDGE SHARING

According to Checkland and Holwell (1995), the main role of an information system is that of a support function. The IS function is to support people taking purposeful action by indicating that the purposeful action can itself be expressed via some activity models, which are called the "human activity systems" (HAS) models from the perspective of soft systems methodology—SSM (Checkland & Scholes, 1990). The job of providing IS support can then be thought about as entailing a pair of systems, one a system which is served (the people taking the action), and the other a system which does the serving. Thereby, whenever a system serves or supports another, it is a very basic principle of SSM (Checkland, 1983) that the necessary features of the serving system can be worked out only on the basis of a prior account of the system served. This is because the nature of the system served—the way it is thought about—will dictate what counts as service, and hence what functions the system which provides that service must contain (Checkland, 1981, p. 237). Thus, an IS strategy concerning support to an organization, such as a LOIS, can be coherently designed and set up only on the basis of a clear concept of the knowledge sharing context. This is true not only for the IS strategy of the learning organization as a whole, but also for the thinking concerning each detailed system created within that strategy. Consequently, the process of IS development needs to start not with attention quickly focused on data and technology, but with a focus on the actions served by the intended organizational system. Once the actions to be supported have been determined and described (using various HAS-based activity models), we can proceed to decide what kind of support should be provided, say: automating action which is currently being carried out by people; or *informating* people (providing information support to people) (Zuboff, 1988); or *knowledging* teams of people (facilitating their social and mental exchange) (Savage, 1996) as they carry out their tasks. In each case, we need to determine what will help people take the desired action, and what will help to monitor the action and make adjustments if desired outcomes are not emerging. Often the monitoring and control needs to be thought about carefully in terms of some declared measures of performance, which should derive from how the purposeful activity is conceptualized. The key point is that in order to create the necessary IS support that serves the intended organizational scenario, it is first necessary to conceptualize the organizational system that is to be served, since this order of thinking should inform what relevant services would indeed be needed in the IS support.

CONCLUSION

This article describes an initiative to develop an actionable framework for knowledge synthesis, paying particular attention to the design issues in support of participatory knowledge construction, in the context of organization transformation in today's prevailing knowledge economy. Our discussion intends to clarify the ideal of a learning organization (LO) which is designed to help transfer learning from individuals to a group, provide for organizational renewal, keep an open attitude to the outside world, and support a commitment to knowledge. In particular, we have elaborated the design issues of the LOIS support that help structure and facilitate knowledge interconnectivity, in terms of a three-tiered technical knowledge infrastructure comprising the front-end knowledge management services, the mid-layer of knowledge management architecture, and the back-end organizational memory. To realize the LOIS support, it is also necessary to examine the underlying processes in which, in a specific organizational context, a particular group of people can conceptualize their world and hence the purposeful action they wish to undertake. We need to understand why, among these people, certain data are selected and treated as relevant items in order to get the best

possible definitions of accepted purposes and the intentional action that follows from pursuing them. The examination of meanings and purposes, in support of designing the necessary IS functions, should be broadly based, and its richness will be greater the larger the number of people who take part in it. Nevertheless, the examination should try to home in on the question: If we want to pursue this purpose, which seems meaningful to us, what would we have to do and how could we do it? Remembering the many possible relationships that have to be managed, we have to acknowledge the rarity of complete consensus among different people. What are sought are often the accommodations, which enable some meaningful work to be sustained in undertaking actions relevant to plausible purposes. This consequently provides the basis for ascertaining the organization's communal knowledge space: namely, what IS support is truly needed by those undertaking their actions, and how modern IT can help to provide that support.

REFERENCES

Argyris, C. (1992). *On organizational learning.* Cambridge, MA: Blackwell Business.

Checkland, P. (1981). *Systems thinking, systems practice.* Chichester: John Wiley & Sons.

Checkland, P. (1983). Information systems and systems thinking: Time to unite? *International Journal of Information Management, 8,* 230-248.

Checkland, P., & Holwell, S. (1995). Information systems: What's the big idea? *Systemist, 17*(1), 7-13.

Checkland, P., & Scholes, J. (1990). *Soft systems methodology in action.* Chichester, UK: John Wiley & Sons.

Conklin, E.J. (1996). Designing organizational memory: Preserving and utilizing intellectual assets of an organization's members to compete in a knowledge-based economy. Retrieved September 30, 2004, from *www.touchstone.com/tr/whitepapers.html*

Cortada, J.W., & Woods, J.A. (Eds.). (2000). *The knowledge management yearbook 2000-2001.* Boston: Butterworth-Heinemann.

Davenport, T.H., & Prusak, L. (1998). *Working knowledge: How organizations manage what they know.* Boston: Harvard Business School Press.

De Hoog, R., Benus, B., Vogler, M., & Metselaar, C. (1996). The CommonKADS organization model: Content, usage, and computer support. *Expert Systems with Applications, 11*(1), 247-260.

Dierkes, M., Marz, L., & Teele, C. (2001). Technological visions, technological development, and organizational learning. In M. Dierkes, A.B. Antal et al. (Eds.), *Handbook of organizational learning and knowledge* (pp. 282-304). Oxford: Oxford University Press.

Drucker, P.F. (1992). The new society of organizations. *Harvard Business Review,* (September-October).

Garvin, D.A. (1993). Building a learning organization. *Harvard Business Review, 71*(4), 78-91.

Grant, R.M. (1996). Toward a knowledge-based theory of the firm. *Strategic Management Journal, 17*(Winter Special Issue), 109-122.

Hackbarth, G., & Grover, V. (1999). The knowledge repository: Organization memory information systems. *Information Systems Management, 16*(3), 21-30.

Kim, D. (1993). The link between individual and organizational learning. *Sloan Management Review,* (Fall), 37-50.

King, W.R. (1996). IS and the learning organization. *Information Systems Management, 13*(3), 78-80.

King, W.R. (1999). Integrating knowledge management into IS strategy. *Information Systems Management, 16*(4), 70-72.

Leonard-Barton, D. (1995). *Wellsprings of knowledge: Building and sustaining the sources of innovation.* Boston: Harvard Business School Press.

Levine, L. (2001). Integrating knowledge and processes in a learning organization. *Information Systems Management,* (Winter), 21-32.

Markova, I., & Foppa, K. (Eds.). (1990). *The dynamics of dialogue.* New York: Harvester Wheatsheaf.

Nonaka, I., Toyama, R., & Konno, N. (2002). SECI, Ba and leaderships: A unified model of dynamic knowledge creation. In S. Little, P. Quintas, & T. Ray (Eds.), *Managing knowledge: An essential reader* (pp. 41-67). London: Sage Publications.

Nonaka, I., & Takeuchi, H. (1995). *The knowledge creating company: How Japanese companies create the dynamics of innovation.* Oxford: Oxford University Press.

O'Leary, D.E. (1998). Enterprise knowledge management. *IEEE Computer, 31*(3), 54-61.

Perrow, C. (1970). *Organizational analysis: A sociological view.* Belmont, CA: Wadsworth.

Probst, G., & Buchel, B. (1997). *Organizational learning: The competitive advantage of the future.* Herdsfordshire, UK: Prentice-Hall (Europe).

Savage, C.M. (1996). *Fifth generation management (revised edition): Co-creating through virtual enterprising, dynamic teaming and knowledge networking.* Boston: Butterworth-Heineman.

Senge, P. (1990). *The fifth discipline: The art and practice of the learning organization.* London: Currency Doubleday.

Senge, P., Kleiner, A., Roberts, C., Ross, R.B., & Smith, B.J. (1994). *The fifth diciplin fieldbook: Strategies and tools for building a learning organization.* New York: Currency Doubleday.

Stalk Jr., G., Evans, E., & Shulman, L.E. (1992). Competing on capabilities: The new rules of corporate strategy. *Harvard Business Review,* (March-April).

Stein, E.W. (1992). A method to identify candidates for knowledge acquisition. *Journal of Information Systems, 9*(2), 161-178.

Stewart, T.A. (1997). *Intellectual capital: The new wealth of organizations.* New York: Doubleday.

Stopford, J.M. (2001). Organizational learning as guided responses to market signals. In M. Dierkes, A.B. Antal et al. (Eds.), *Handbook of organizational learning and knowledge* (pp. 264-281). Oxford: Oxford University Press.

Sveiby, K.E (1997). *The new organizational wealth.* Berrett-Koehler.

Van der Spek, R., & De Hoog, R. (1995). A framework for a knowledge management methodology. In K.M. Wiig (Ed.), *Knowledge management methods* (pp. 379-393). Arlington, TX: Schema Press.

Vat, K.H. (2000, November 1-2). Designing knowledge infrastructure for virtual enterprises in organizational learning. *Proceedings of the 10th Annual Business Information Technology Conference* (BIT2000), Manchester, England (CD-ROM Paper No. 45).

Vat, K.H. (2001, November 1-4). Towards a learning organizational model for knowledge synthesis: An IS perspective. *CD-Proceedings of the 2001 Information Systems Education Conference* (ISECON2001), Cincinnati, OH.

Vat, K.H. (2002). Designing organizational memory for knowledge management support in collaborative learning. In D. White (Ed.), *Knowledge mapping and management* (pp. 233-243). Hershey, PA: IRM Press.

Vat, K.H. (2003, March 1-2). An IS-based architectural modeling for learning organization: A conceptual walkthrough. *Proceedings of the 6th Annual Conference of the Southern Association for Information Systems* (SAIS2003) (pp. 55-62), Savannah, GA.

Wiig, K.M. (1993). *Knowledge management: The central management focus for intelligent-acting organizations.* Arlington, TX: Schema Press.

Wiig, K.M. (1997). Integrating intellectual capital and knowledge management. *Long Range Planning, 30*(3), 399-405.

Williamson, A., & Lliopoulos, C. (2001). The learning organization information system (LOIS): Looking for the next generation. *Information Systems Journal, 11*(1), 23-41.

Zuboff, S. (1988). *In the age of the smart machine: The future of work and power.* New York: Basic Books.

KEY TERMS

Double-Loop Learning: Together with single-loop learning, they describe the way in which organizations may learn to respond appropriately to change. Single-loop learning requires adjustments to procedures and operations within the framework of customary, accepted assumptions, but fails to recognize or deal effectively with problems that may challenge fundamental aspects of organizational culture, norms, or objectives. Double-loop learning questions those assumptions from the vantage point of higher order, shared views, in order to solve problems.

IS Support: An information system (IS) function supporting people taking purposeful action. This is often done by indicating that the purposeful action can itself be expressed via activity models, through a fundamental re-thinking of what is entailed in providing informational support to purposeful action. The idea is that in order to create IS support which serves, it is first necessary to conceptualize the organizational system that is served, since this order of thinking should inform what relevant services would indeed be needed in the IS support.

Knowledge Infrastructure: A technical infrastructure supporting the development of organizational knowledge, whose design philosophy is often organization-specific. An example is to consider the infrastructure as a three-tiered system comprising the front-end knowledge management services, the middle knowledge management architecture, and the back-end organizational memory.

Knowledge Sharing: A process of leveraging the collective individual learning of an organization, such as a group of people, to produce a higher-level organization-wide intellectual asset. It is supposed to be a continuous process of creating, acquiring, and transferring knowledge accompanied by a possible modification of behavior to reflect new knowledge and insight, and produce a higher-level intellectual content.

Knowledge Synthesis: The broad process of creating, locating, organizing, transferring, and using the information and expertise within the organization, typically by using advanced information technologies.

Learning Organization: An organization that helps transfer learning from individuals to a group, provide for organizational renewal, keep an open attitude to the outside world, and support a commitment to knowledge. It is also considered as the organization that focuses on developing and using its information and knowledge capabilities in order to create higher-value information and knowledge, to modify behaviors to reflect new knowledge and insights, and to improve bottom-line results.

Organizational Memory: A learning history that tells an organization its own story, which should help generate reflective conversations among organizational members. Operationally, an organizational memory has come to be a close partner of knowledge management, denoting the actual content that a knowledge management system purports to manage.

Soft Systems Methodology: A methodology that aims to bring about improvement in areas of social concern by activating in the people involved in the situation a learning cycle that is ideally never-ending. The learning takes place through the iterative process of using systems concepts to reflect upon and debate perceptions of the real world, taking action in the real world, and again reflecting on the happenings using systems concepts. The reflection and debate is structured by a number of systemic models of purposeful activities. These are conceived as holistic ideal types of certain aspects of the problem situation rather than as accounts of it. It is also taken as given that no objective and complete account of a problem situation can be provided.

Knowledge Transfer

William R. King
University of Pittsburgh, USA

INTRODUCTION

The term *knowledge transfer* (KT) is often used in a generic sense to include any exchange of knowledge between or among individuals, teams, groups, or organizations, whether intended or unintended.

However, knowledge transfer, as it has been formally studied, reflects intended unidirectional exchange, as when an enterprise resource planning (ERP) systems consultant transfers implementation knowledge to a potential user of a system, or when a franchiser's training team transfers knowledge about how to operate a franchise to a franchisee's team. Such knowledge transfers are between a clearly defined source and a recipient, have a focus, and have a clearly identified objective.

Although this unidirectional, focused, objective-oriented view is widely held among those who have a professional or academic interest in the KT process, there are different schools of thought concerning exactly when transfer can be said to have taken place between a source and a recipient. Some adopt the view that knowledge must both be communicated and applied before it has been transferred; others take the view that if the recipient of knowledge has the capacity to apply it, transfer has occurred. Still, others assume that if it has been cognitively transferred (e.g., understood), it has been transferred. Each of these viewpoints appears to be useful in certain circumstances, so there is no universal agreement on which is best.

However, there is agreement that knowledge transfer is different from knowledge sharing, which may be an unfocused exchange among individuals or groups who have little intention to send or receive knowledge (see article titled "Knowledge Sharing" in this encyclopedia). Of course, knowledge sharing may also have a focus as when persons engage in a brainstorming group session in order to generate new ideas or enhance creativity.

Perhaps the best way to conceptualize knowledge transfer and knowledge sharing is that they are at two ends of a spectrum. The knowledge transfer end is formalized, with a clearly defined purpose, and is unidirectional. The knowledge-sharing end is multidirectional, informal, and has no clear objective and few rules. Between these extremes lies a wide range of possible combinations involving individuals, teams, groups, organizational units, and organizations. Different people may use different terminology to describe these possible situations, but the end points are well grounded in theory and in practice.

BACKGROUND

Knowledge that is transferred may be either tacit, explicit, or a combination of both (Nonaka, 1994). When a master craftsman works to develop the skill and knowledge of an apprentice, he is transferring tacit knowledge. When a physician highlights a finding in a medical research paper and sends it to an associate, she is transferring explicit knowledge. When an ERP consultant shows a potential system user how to use tools and tables to implement a system, he or she is transferring a combination of tacit and explicit knowledge.

Knowledge transfer is very important because without it, every problem-solving approach or operating skill would have to be reinvented each time that the knowledge is needed. Indeed, it may not be overstating the case to say that knowledge transfer is a fundamental process of civilization. Certainly, it is a focus of learning, which is critical to all advancement.

As treated here, knowledge transfer is the communication of knowledge from a source so that it is learned and applied by a recipient (Argote, 1999; Darr & Kurtzberg, 2000). The source and recipient may be individuals, groups, teams, organizational units, or entire organizations in any combination.

Knowledge is usually defined as a justified belief that increases an individual's capacity to take effective action (Alavi & Leidner, 2001). Explicit knowledge is transmittable in formal, systematic language. Tacit knowledge "dwells in a comprehensive cognizance of the human mind and body" (Nonaka, 1994).

One of the central tenets of KT relates to the ease of transfer across individuals, groups, and organizations. Codified knowledge may be transferred in the form of documents and manuals. When the codified knowledge is of the know-what (concerning the state of the world) variety, the passage of the materials may complete the transfer. However, when the codified knowledge is of the know-how (competence) variety, complementary discussion or practice involving both the source's and recipient's tacit knowledge is often necessary to complete the transfer (Edmondson, Pisano, Bohmer, & Winslow, 2003).

When the knowledge to be transferred is tacit, the proximity of the source and recipient and their interpersonal interactions influence the likelihood of successful KT. Some tacit knowledge may be verbalized, explicated, codified, and communicated to others. This is an important mechanism of knowledge transfer, although many other processes are valid and useful as well. Some tacit knowledge may not be transferable, or at least will require demonstrations by the source and practice by the receiver.

Commercial knowledge, which may be either explicit or tacit, "... is not truth, but effective performance; not right, but 'what works' or even 'what works better'" (Demarest, 1997). Commercial knowledge is an important focus of practical knowledge transfer in organizations. It is exemplified by the implementation knowledge—sets of rules, tools, guidelines, and ways to effectively employ them—that is conveyed by a consultant who is aiding a client in implementing or customizing a complex information system in the client's organization. For instance, in this context, consultants may transfer knowledge about testing procedures to clients who learn and apply this knowledge as evidenced by the clients developing test scripts, conducting tests of individual modules, and running integration tests to ascertain whether data are correctly passed between modules.

ISSUES IN KNOWLEDGE TRANSFER

The best way to measure KT has not been uniquely determined. First, there are the conceptual issues, noted earlier, concerning when transfer shall be deemed to have taken place. Whichever definition is adopted, transfer is usually measured through surrogates. For instance, Szulanski (1996) measures "stickiness": the difficulty in transferring knowledge in an organization. A few studies (e.g., Ko, Kirsch, & King, 2005) have used direct measures for specific contexts, for instance, by observing a recipient's ability to perform tasks that are related to the objectives of the transfer. However, most studies have not used behavioral measures of successful KT.

A major issue in knowledge transfer has to do with the antecedents, or determinants, of effective KT. In other words, what factors most importantly influence successful knowledge transfer?

Argote (1999) depicts four categories of antecedents for knowledge transfer between organizations: characteristics of the relationships among organizations, characteristics of the knowledge transferred, character-istics of the organizations, and characteristics of the transfer process. After examining a number of such factors, Szulanski (1996) identified two categories of antecedent factors: knowledge barriers and motivational barriers to the transfer of best practices between sets of individuals in an organization. Ko et al. (2005) added communications factors because such factors have been found to be important in KT in information systems implementation processes (Hartwick & Barki, 2001).

Knowledge-Related Factors

An arduous relationship, causal ambiguity, shared understanding, knowledge observability, and absorptive capacity are widely believed to be important knowledge-related antecedent factors for successful KT. These factors are related to the source's and/or recipient's knowledge base or ability to acquire knowledge when it is needed, as well as to their knowledge relationship. An arduous relationship refers to the quality of the relationship between the source and recipient. Successful transfer usually requires many interactions for the knowledge to be successfully transferred. An arduous relationship, one that is emotionally laborious and distant, is likely to adversely influence knowledge transfer (Faraj & Sproull, 2000).

Causal ambiguity refers to "ambiguity about what the factors of production are and how they interact during production" (Szulanski, 1996, p. 30). Taken literally, this refers to the production of goods, but it may also apply to the production of knowledge. Although this interpretation is untested, it is not unreasonable to posit that if the source and recipient understand how knowledge has been produced and to what it relates, this relative absence of ambiguity might facilitate transfer.

Shared understanding represents the extent to which a source's and recipient's work values, norms, philosophies, problem-solving approaches, and prior work experience are similar. Studies suggest that having similar heuristics and similar shared experiences are important to knowledge transfer (Hansen, Nohria, & Tierney, 1999). Without shared understanding, there is a tendency for the source and recipient to disagree, which leads to poor outcomes. Shared understanding probably removes barriers to understanding and acceptance between the two parties and enhances their ability to work toward a common goal.

Knowledge observability leads to more effective transfer. Knowledge observability is "how easy it is to understand the activity by looking at and examining different aspects of the process or final product" (Zander, 1991, p. 47). The basic premise underlying this concept is that knowledge may be a sticky asset, making it difficult to transfer (Szulanski, 1996). Knowledge observability makes knowledge less sticky, which should enable better transfer (Birkinshaw, Frost, & Ensign, 2002).

Absorptive capacity is the ability of a recipient to recognize the value of the source's knowledge, assimilate it, and apply it. This capacity is largely a function of the recipient's existing stock of knowledge prior to the transfer, which enables a recipient to value, assimilate, and apply new knowledge successfully (Galbraith, 1990).

Motivational Factors

Factors such as a lack of incentives, a lack of confidence, "turf protection," and the "not-invented-here" syndrome are considered to be motivational factors that may influence knowledge transfer. Not all of these have been extensively studied, but motivation in general has been shown to be a positive factor in transfer. For instance, in a technological transfer context, knowledge-acquiring firms were found to accelerate the speed of KT when other companies were perceived to be developing similar products (Zander & Kogut, 1995).

For practical purposes, it is useful to distinguish between intrinsic and extrinsic motivation. Intrinsic motivation exists when the activity "... is valued for its own sake and appears to be self-sustained" (Calder & Shaw, 1975, p. 599). In contrast, extrinsic motivation comes from external sources. Intrinsic motivation in an organizational setting can be influenced by appropriate personnel selection. Extrinsic motivation can, on the other hand, be influenced by specific rewards for transferring knowledge, the inclusion of knowledge transfer as an element of personnel evaluations, and other explicit forms of reward or recognition.

A best-practices repository is a good illustration. Technically, this involves knowledge sharing since one person or unit contributes a practice to be shared by initially unidentified others. However, once a best practice has been identified by a potential user, the source is typically contacted with questions and requests for complementary tacit knowledge. At that point, it becomes a KT process. In such instances, it has been found that careful screening of the ideas that are submitted provide the best results. Many firms have a committee that carefully evaluates each best-practice submission. Only those that are the best of the best actually get put into the repository. The submitter's name is prominently displayed on the best practice, thereby conferring status on those whose ideas have passed this rigorous test. Similar recognition is given to those who make significant contributions to the well-known open-source Linux software (Lee & Cole, 2003).

Communications Factors

The information systems literature has identified various communications factors as impediments to successful system implementation (e.g., Hartwick & Barki, 2001). Among the most important are source credibility and communications competence.

Source credibility is a communications factor that reflects the extent to which a recipient perceives a source to be trustworthy and an expert (Grewal, Gotlieb, & Brown, 1994). When source credibility is high, the knowledge presented is perceived to be useful, thereby facilitating transfer. When source credibility is low, recipients tend to be less-readily persuaded and may heavily discount the value of the knowledge that is the focus of the intended transfer. The transfer of knowledge between departments in a firm has been found to be importantly influenced by the credibility of the source (Slaughter & Kirsch, 2000).

Communications competence is the ability to demonstrate the appropriate communications behavior in an organizational setting. Communications within a dyad requires both the encoding and decoding of messages. Encoding competence is the ability to clearly put ideas into words or symbols, have a good command of language, and be easily understood. A study of communications encoding competence suggests that subordinates form either positive or negative perceptions about their supervisor based on this ability (Berman & Hellweg, 1989).

Decoding competence refers to a recipient's ability to listen, be attentive, and respond quickly. This capability has also been shown to affect working relationships and to create opportunities to improve relationships.

Many studies have shown that communications competence is important for resolving conflicts, having effective teams, and providing opportunities to improve the quality of relationships; all of these outcomes are correlated with successful knowledge transfer.

FUTURE TRENDS

The KT source and recipient model appears to be a powerful analytic tool for many situations in which knowledge must be communicated and learned by someone who is less experienced and is less qualified than the source.

A major need that is beginning to be filled is for measures of successful knowledge transfer that incorporate the impact aspect of transfer whether it is cognitive or behavioral.

Some research results that are either widely accepted or recently developed are the following:

1. An arduous relationship between the source and recipient negatively affects KT (e.g., Szulanski, 1996).
2. Shared understanding between the source and recipients is particularly important to successful KT (Ko et al., 2005).
3. Absorptive capacity has long been believed to be important in influencing effective KT (e.g., Galbraith, 1990).
4. Knowledge observability is important to successful KT (e.g., Birkinshaw et al., 2002).
5. Intrinsic motivation may be more important than extrinsic motivation in KT.
6. Source credibility is important in KT, while the source's encoding competence may not be so important (e.g., Ko et al., 2005).

CONCLUSION

Knowledge transfer is done more efficiently when the knowledge to be transferred is relatively more explicit and relatively less tacit. Most organizations use structures and processes such as routines and standard procedures to codify as much of the knowledge that is to be transferred as is possible (Cohen & Bacdayan, 1994; March & Simon, 1958).

This is important because in the general situation of transferring knowledge, there is the assumption that meaning is universal and that the contexts of the sender and receiver are relatively homogeneous. In fact, the meaning that is given to knowledge is situational, cultural, and contextual. Thus, knowledge transfer should be more successful when these factors are similar for the sender and receiver. This is why the transfer of knowledge in complex systems implementation and in franchisee training is based on so many standard procedures, routines, and documented knowledge, and why individuals are chosen to offer and receive such training that come from the same backgrounds. For example, the trainers have invariably served in the operating capacities for which they are instructing the trainee.

Of course, some tacit knowledge cannot be explicated, so it can only be transferred through demonstrations, as in apprentice training. This is a very expensive and time-consuming process, so the goal in most organizational settings is to put knowledge that needs to be transferred into as explicit a form as is feasible.

Other practical guidelines involving successful knowledge transfer are the following: (largely derived from Ko et al., 2005).

1. It is important to create situations where the source and recipient can interact frequently, thereby nurturing their relationship and enhancing the flow of knowledge.
2. Individuals who have the least need for new knowledge should be selected to be the initial recipients of knowledge (because the recipient's absorptive capacity is so important for effective KT). This means that KT in a professional setting should not initially be viewed as training.
3. When widespread training is necessary, a two-stage strategy may be useful. First, have those with the least need (those that are already best qualified) take part in the KT process; then have them transfer knowledge to those that are more in need of the new knowledge.
4. Personnel with the highest level of intrinsic motivation should be assigned to KT; extrinsic rewards are not effective, except perhaps in the earliest stages of KT.
5. Consulting firms and others who are being evaluated as potential sources of knowledge should be required to commit to the use of specific individuals in the KT process since the abilities of the individuals' sources are critical.

REFERENCES

Alavi, M., & Leidner, D. (2001). Knowledge management systems: Issues, challenges, and benefits. *CAIS, 1*(7), 2-36.

Argote, L. (1999). *Organizational learning: Creating, retaining and transferring knowledge.* Boston: Kluwer Academic Publishers.

Berman, S. J., & Hellweg, S. A. (1989). Perceived supervisor communication competence and supervisor satisfaction as a function of quality circle participation. *Journal of Business Communication, 26*(2), 103-122.

Birkinshaw, J. M., Frost, T. S., & Ensign, P. C. (2002). Centers of excellence in multinational corporations. *Strategic Management Journal, 23*(11), 997-1019.

Calder, B. J., & Shaw, B. M. (1975). Self-perception of intrinsic and extrinsic motivation. *Journal of Personality and Social Psychology, 31*, 599-605.

Cohen, M. D., & Bacdayan, P. (1994). Organizational routines are stored as procedural memory: Evidence from a laboratory study. *Organization Science: A Journal of the Institute of Management Sciences, 5*(4), 554-569.

Darr, E. D., & Kurtzberg, T. R. (2000). An investigation of partner similarity dimensions on knowledge transfer. *Organizational Behavior & Human Decision Processes, 82*(1), 28-45.

Demarest, M. (1997). Understanding knowledge management. *Long Range Planning, 30*(3), 374-385.

Edmondson, A., Pisano, G. P., Bohmer, R., & Winslow, A. (2003). Learning how and learning what: Effects of tacit and codified knowledge on performance improvement following technology adoption. *Decision Sciences, 34*(2), 197-223.

Faraj, S., & Sproull, L. (2000). Coordinating expertise in software development teams. *Management Science, 46*(12), 1554-1568.

Galbraith, C. S. (1990). Transferring core manufacturing technologies in high technology firms. *California Management Review, 32*(4), 56-70.

Grewal, D., Gotlieb, J. B., & Brown, S. W. (1994). Consumer satisfaction and perceived quality: Complementary or divergent constructs? *Journal of Applied Psychology, 79*(6), 875-886.

Hansen, M. T., Nohria, N., & Tierney, T. (1999). What's your strategy for managing knowledge? *Harvard Business Review, 77*(2), 106-116.

Hartwick, J., & Barki, H. (2001). Interpersonal conflict and its management in information system development. *MIS Quarterly, 25*(2), 195-228.

Ko, D. G., Kirsch, L. J., & King, W. R. (2005). Antecedents of knowledge transfer from consultants to clients in enterprise system implementations. *Management Information Systems Quarterly, 29*(1), 59-85.

Lee, G. K., & Cole, R. E. (2003). From a firm-based to a community-based model of knowledge creation: The case of the Linux kernel development. *Organization Science: A Journal of the Institute of Management Sciences, 14*(6), 633.

March, J. G., & Simon, H. A. (1958). *Organizations.* New York: John Wiley & Sons.

Nonaka, I. (1994). A dynamic theory of organizational knowledge creation. *Organization Science, 5*(1), 14-37.

Slaughter, S., & Kirsch, L. J. (2000). *Transferring evaluative knowledge: The case of software metrics* (GSIA Working Paper No. 2000-08). Pittsburgh, PA: Carnegie Mellon University.

Szulanski, G. (1996). Exploring internal stickiness: Impediments to the transfer of best practice within the firm. *Strategic Management Journal, 17*, 27-43.

Zander, U. (1991). *Exploiting a technological edge: Voluntary and involuntary dissemination of technology.* Doctoral dissertation, Institute of International Business, Stockholm School of Economics, Stockholm, Sweden.

Zander, U., & Kogut, B. (1995). Knowledge and the speed of the transfer and imitation of organizational capabilities: An empirical test. *Organization Science: A Journal of the Institute of Management Sciences, 6*(1), 76-93.

KEY TERMS

Commercial Knowledge: An important focus of practical knowledge transfer in business. It is "...not truth, but effective performance; not right, but 'what works' or even what works better'" (Demarest, 1997). It is exemplified by the implementation knowledge—sets of rules, tools, guidelines, and ways to effectively employ them—that is conveyed by a consultant who is aiding a client in implementing or customizing a complex information system.

Communications-Related Antecedent Factors: Source credibility and communications competence (in terms of both encoding and decoding capabilities) are communications-related antecedent factors for effective knowledge transfer.

Explicit Knowledge: Knowledge that exists in and is transmittable in formal, systematic language.

Knowledge-Related Antecedent Factors: An arduous relationship, causal ambiguity, shared understanding, knowledge observability, and absorptive capacity are important knowledge-related antecedent factors for effective knowledge transfer.

Knowledge Sharing: The exchange of knowledge among individuals within and among teams, organizational units, and organizations. This exchange may be focused or unfocused, but it usually does not have a clear objective.

Knowledge Transfer: The focused, unidirectional communication of knowledge between individuals, groups, or organizations such that the recipient of knowledge (a) has a cognitive understanding, (b) has the ability to apply the knowledge, or (c) applies the knowledge.

Motivation-Related Antecedent Factors: Intrinsic and extrinsic motivational factors have been studied as antecedent factors for effective knowledge transfer. Other factors such as a lack of incentives, a lack of confidence, and the not-invented-here syndrome have been widely discussed, but not widely studied.

Tacit Knowledge: Knowledge that is known in the mind of an individual. Some of it may be verbalized, made explicit, and encoded to become explicit knowledge; some of it may not be explicable so that it must be demonstrated if it is to be transferred, as in a master craftsman showing an apprentice how to do something and the apprentice subsequently practicing what has been demonstrated.

Knowledge Transfer Between Academia and Industry

Franz Hofer
Graz University of Technology, Austria

INTRODUCTION

Many policy makers and researchers consider knowledge transfer between academia and industry as one of the most promising measures to strengthen economic development. The idea of linking academia and industry is not new. Back in 1910 *research universities* were established, which strongly emphasized industry-related research as part of their activities and were funded by enterprises in order to tap this knowledge (see Matkin, 1990, for the history of technology transfer at four U.S. research universities—MIT, U.C. Berkeley, Penn State, and Stanford). Knowledge transfer has increased considerably during the last few decades. Many universities have established offices aimed at improving relations with industry. The performance of these offices varies considerably. One example for a quantitative performance indicator is license revenues of U.S. universities (Artley, Dobrauz, Plasonig, & Strasser, 2003). Only a handful of examined universities actually draw profit from it. The majority pay more for legal advice and fees than they earn from license income. It is obvious that the performance variances depend on many factors like staff resources at the transfer offices, type of university research (basic vs. applied, technical vs. non-technical domains), the *brand* of the university as well as prior industrial relationships, to name just a few. Not all of these factors can be changed in the short run, but knowing them and streamlining actions towards their improvement can lead to sustainable changes, in the end positively influencing economic performance. Despite the long history and recent efforts to improve university-industry collaborations, the full potential does not yet seem to be exploited (Starbuck, 2001). Jankowski (1999) and Clough (2003) confirm the decrease of federal funding for universities and point to increasing collaborations between academia and industry, which in their view comprises the danger of leaving *fundamental frontier research*, vital for breakthrough innovations, behind. At the same time, industry increasingly relies on external knowledge sources to keep up with the pace of their competitors (Business-Higher Education Forum, 2001; Tornatzky, 2000). In many cases, these external sources are customers and suppliers (Adametz & Ploder, 2003; Dachs, Ebersberger, & Pyka, 2004). This may be due to similar rationales, profit, and already-existing customer-client relationships. However, industry more and more turns to universities when looking for support. According to Godin and Gingras (2000), universities are still one of the major producers of knowledge, despite an increase of other R&D institutions. Collaborations between academia and industry bring partners with different competencies together and cover the whole range of the R&D chain, from basic research to application. By fulfilling the needs of both partners, universities as well as enterprises, and building up trust, knowledge transfer leads to knowledge flows and production of new knowledge, and thus creates a fertile environment for innovation. The article at hand examines motives as well as barriers related to knowledge transfer out of a systemic as well as a process-related view and provides some general suggestions for further improvements.

BACKGROUND

The earlier focus of knowledge transfer between academia and industry was on technology, in the sense of technological processes and artifacts inhibiting technological knowledge without paying much attention to the soft facts important for the success or failure of the transfer. Nowadays, technology transfer often comprises more than technological knowledge, including data as well as technology-related organizational knowledge (Abramson, Encarnacao, Reid, & Schmolch, 1997). As Schumpeter (1912) explained, technology is not exclusively the base of innovations. Using the term knowledge transfer instead of technology transfer reinforces Schumpeter's view of innovation, which additionally includes, for example, social innovations like new organizational structures or incentive systems (see Hofer, Adametz, & Holzer, 2004, for an example of a knowledge transfer program implemented by a university of technology in collaboration with a *classical* university). Knowledge transfer schemes range from regional programs and initiatives to national and international ones. Besides the different geographical focus, also the target group, at which knowledge transfer measures are aimed, can differ (broad approach vs. focus on specific industrial sectors). All these characteristics influence knowledge transfer at the operative level and require diverse additional partners and processes. Knowledge transfer between academia and industry as understood herein refers to activities, aimed at enabling and facilitating industry to tap knowledge produced at universities. The article examines knowledge transfer in general without limiting it to certain geographic borders. Knowledge transfer does not only comprise large collaborative R&D projects, but also measures like informal consulting as well as diploma theses commissioned by enterprises. The primary objective of knowledge transfer is to strengthen the competitiveness of both partners, leading in succession to improved economic development.

MAIN FOCUS OF THE ARTICLE

The article addresses regional as well as national governments trying to provide the right framework for parties involved in knowledge transfer—universities' managers, who would like to establish closer links with industry, as well as representatives of industry, who plan to or already use external knowledge sources like universities. The first part of this article deals with motives at different organizational levels of the parties directly involved; the second part discusses barriers negatively influencing knowledge transfer. The article concludes with some suggestions for future actions in order to amplify motives and overcome barriers, thus increasing the performance of knowledge transfer initiatives and programs.

What are the Driving Forces in Knowledge Transfer?

In order to improve knowledge transfer between academia and industry, it is not sufficient to examine solely existing barriers; one must also examine possible motives, as the driving power must be identified and intensified. This is not only important at the agency but also the individual level, where knowledge transfer ultimately takes place (Lipscomb & McEwan, 2001). The following comments are based on the results of a literature study performed for a paper presented at the 2004 *Exploiting Change in the 21st Century* international conference (Hofer, 2004). Motives for universities to get involved in knowledge transfer are mainly financial as well as legal ones. At many universities, the share of industrial funding already makes up a substantial part of the total budget. Without the financial commitment of industry, these universities would have to cut their expenses dramatically. The trend of increasing industrial funding of universities is likely to grow even more in the future, with governments stabilizing or even cutting resources and increasingly interdisciplinary R&D projects demanding researchers from various professional areas. But universities are involved not only for financial

reasons, but also because they are legally bound to perform knowledge transfer with industry. For example, the Austrian *Universitaetsgesetz 2002* [University Law 2002] lists "support to practically use and apply universities' R&D results" as one of the primary tasks of Austrian universities. Etzkowitz (2003) calls this additional task the *third mission* of universities besides doing research and educating students. Despite all perils like stronger emphasis on applied research, universities at the agency level are committed to perform knowledge transfer with industry and thus offering their knowledge. The commitment at the individual level does not always reflect this opinion. This is comprehensible if one considers that legal claims at this level do not exist as part of contracts between universities and their employees. Usually, there are no financial benefits, which recompense researchers for efforts to perform knowledge transfer with industry, except for researchers, whose jobs directly depend on external funds. Knowledge transfer does not seem to be perceived as important as other tasks (Kremic, 2003). If the researcher's employment does not depend directly on industrial funding, that person is free to decide whether or not and to which degree to get involved in knowledge transfer. Therefore the issue of what motivates researchers at universities to invest some of their time budget in projects with industrial partners is of particular interest. The majority of literature referred to in the following regards individuals in public laboratories. It is assumed that governmental scientists and their universities' counterparts are motivated by similar factors because of the similar framework such as public funding and similar kinds of R&D. Differently from their colleagues, university researchers must also teach their students, thus having even more time constraints. Studies performed by Large, Belinko, and Kalligatsi (2000), Schartinger, Schibany, and Gassler (2001), and Spivey, Munson, and Flannery (1994) identified personal interest and satisfaction as the primary motives of researchers to deal with industry. They do not seem to be motivated by extrinsic factors like additional income. Frey and Osterloh (2000) describe researchers as people typically motivated by intrinsic motives, which additionally confirms the results of the various studies. The main objective of private industries is to make profits, to be profitable for their owners, and to be a better investment than other corporations (Kremic, 2003). Industry collaborates with universities because it promises to be profitable. However, large-scale enterprises (e.g., in the life science industry) in some cases are funding blue-sky research at universities; they do not do it for the sake of basic research, but because this gives them the right to be first to exploit possible inventions and to recruit high potentials before others get a hold of them. Challenges like fast and highly specialized knowledge production, shorter product lifecycle due to increasing share of data as part of products, and increased marketing of universities, which present themselves as R&D partners of industry, push enterprises to get involved in knowledge transfer activities.

Large et al. (2000) identified various motives of individuals at enterprises for collaborating with public laboratories. The first three motives for enterprises' individuals are: (1) expected technical benefits for the end user, (2) expected proprietary knowledge for the manufacturer, and (3) expected financial benefits for the manufacturer. The comparison with the motives identified for scientists reveals a stronger profit-orientation on the part of the manufacturers. Kremic (2003), who points to the strong link between enterprises' performance and employment, also supports this view.

What are the Forces Hindering Involvement in Knowledge Transfer?

Motives are one side of the coin, but knowing what hinders industry and academia to transfer knowledge mutually is equally important in order to design holistic approaches. The following section will systematically examine barriers and suggest efforts to overcome them by providing suitable measures. The first part focuses on barriers deduced with the aid of system theory. The second part examines process-based barriers. The two directly involved parties here are universities and industry. As socio-technological systems, they consist of various elements: individuals as

carriers of knowledge; data in the form of, for example, publications or entries in databases; and technical devices supporting information and documentation processes as well as data exchange. Links connect the elements of both systems, whereby these relations are not necessarily physical ones.

The knowledge transfer system displayed in Figure 1 shows the two primary parties: academia and industry. This form of knowledge transfer takes place directly between universities and industry. Reinhard (2001) lists four types of barriers, which apply to the systemic view and can equally apply to both parties: (1) not knowing each other, (2) not being allowed to work with each other, (3) not wanting to work with each other, and (4) not being able to work with each other. High search costs limit the possibilities on both sides to look for suitable partners (Beise & Spielkamp, 1996). The use of the Internet can actually help to limit such costs (Czarnitzki & Rammer, 2003), but especially for risky projects with insecure outcomes, it cannot replace prior hands-on experience. Additional barriers, which are part of the prior classification, are different organizational structures and objectives, prior or current projects of the university with enterprises' competitors, lack of motivation, or low qualification, which negatively influences the absorption capability (Reinhard, 2001). The fifth barrier identified from the systemic view stems from the characteristics of knowledge. Unlike products, which can be rather easily priced and tested, knowledge is characterized as an

Figure 1. Knowledge transfer system—the system consists of two sub-systems, academia and industry, with various elements, which are linked with each other. Knowledge transfer takes place on an inter-organizational level between the two sub-systems.

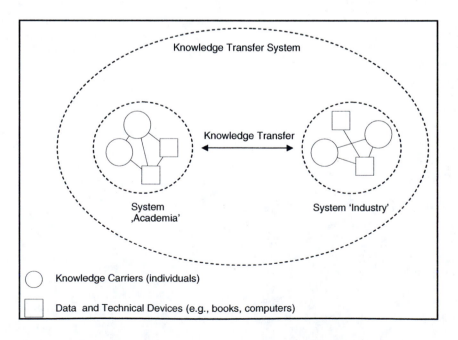

experience good (Watanabe, Yoneyama, Senoo, Fukushima, & Senoh, 2004). This makes it difficult for industry in an early stage to identify suitable knowledge sources. To some extent the identified barriers differ, taking into account various geographic extensions. For example, the characteristics of knowledge will always remain the same, but enabling extensive face-to-face communication facilitates the decision on both sides whether collaboration could be fruitful or not. The following process-related view complements the systemic view and reveals additional barriers hindering the full exploitation of knowledge transfer. Although the whole range of knowledge transfer measures requires different processes (Pries & Guild, 2004), the following examination focuses on a general process definition, which should make it possible to apply the results to specific knowledge transfer processes. Processes are defined as a sum of various activities with a defined beginning and end which transform and/or transport objects (physical ones or data) following defined rules. They are logical, spatial, and chronological chains of activities (Remus & Schub, 2003; Schwickert & Fischer, 1996). The main reason to introduce process management is to overcome intra- and/or inter-organizational functional barriers, thus reducing 'frictional losses' and improving the quality of outcome.

Knowledge transfer processes can be divided into two major types: (1) looking for external knowledge, and (2) offering internal knowledge. If in need of external knowledge, sub-processes look like this: (a1) identifying missing knowledge, which at the same time demands the identification of the internal knowledge stock; (b1) identifying possible knowledge providers; and (c1) balancing

knowledge needs and offers. Sub-processes for knowledge providers are: (a2) identifying the internal knowledge stock; (b2) identifying possible knowledge customers, which look for this kind of knowledge; and (c2) balancing knowledge needs and offers. The sub-processes at this level are the same, only the order is different. Hence, knowledge transfer processes have an intra- as well as inter-organizational dimension. Therefore, it is not sufficient to optimize processes solely at the interface of universities and industry. Additionally, internal processes like brokering of external enquiries and responsibilities for processes have to be taken into account. Some of the properties—like subjects, inputs, outputs, and internal and external factors influencing the process—are closely connected with the barriers identified above. Additional barriers identified with the help of the process-related view are associated to the trigger and process owner. Knowledge transfer processes between academia and industry can be triggered either by enquiries from industry or by universities (e.g., promoting proactive support services). Besides these *physical* triggers, other processes can also act as starting point; for example, successful R&D projects can automatically lead to defined knowledge transfer processes. In the past, industry often acted as a trigger and knocked at the *ivory tower* for support, but due to environmental changes like decreasing public funding, universities are more actively looking for contacts with industry. It is necessary for a holistic knowledge transfer approach to consider different forms of triggers and design the processes accordingly. Another important action to remove barriers is the unmistakable assignment of process owners. They are responsible

Figure 2. Processes' properties—the process-related view enables the identification of further barriers using the properties that characterize processes.

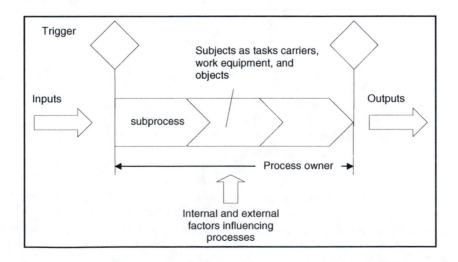

for their processes, ranging from initial enquiries to the delivery of the outcome to the customer. This is especially important in the beginning of potential collaborations, in the idea or pre-project phase, where industry usually evaluates different collaboration partners. Due to the involvement of intermediaries, who are usually not the professionals (the ones actually performing the collaborative research project), handing over responsibility to the professionals at the right moment is critically important for further collaborations. If this happens too early, it could lead to unnecessary delays and misunderstandings. If it happens too late, both partners, academia and industry, perceive intermediaries as unnecessary bureaucratic entities slowing down the project advancement.

DIRECTIONS FOR FURTHER IMPROVEMENTS OF KNOWLEDGE TRANSFER ACTIVITIES

Simultaneously increasing motives and lowering barriers should help to further improve the accessibility of research institutions like universities to industry and thus promote economic development. The benefits for universities at the agency level are quite clear, but knowledge transfer ultimately depends on individuals. Especially, intrinsic motives like satisfaction and personal interest seem to play a major role for researchers (Frey & Osterloh, 2000; Large et al., 2000; Schartinger et al., 2001; Spivey et al., 1994). The motives for industry to use academic knowledge at the agency level are mainly *profit driven*, because of the close link between fulfilling the requirements of the employers and employment; this motive is likely to be valid also for individual employees in industry. Specifically, relations between universities' researchers and small and medium-sized enterprises seem to have potential for further improvements. Small and medium-sized enterprises typically lack strategic tools. Therefore, they usually concentrate on short-term projects and as a result on short-term profit. This limits the possibility to exploit knowledge transfer with academia, and in succession leads to a perceived low value of universities' research. The main barriers identified relate to: (1) not knowing each other, (2) not being allowed to work with each other, (3) not wanting to work with each other, (4) not being able to work with each other, (5) characteristics of knowledge, (6) not considering different forms of triggers, and (7) unclear assignment of process owners. Some of the barriers can be lowered or even eliminated by universities and industry on their own; others require additional support by, for example, intermediaries, governments, or funding agencies. The barriers given in the systemic view make it clear that a mix of different partners can greatly enhance knowledge transfer. The support by funding agencies as well as governments can play a vital role. The task of intermediaries is to bridge the gap between universities and industry. They can offer support services that are out of reach for research departments at universities because of time restraints. Funding agencies as well as funding programs introduced by governments can support the upgrading of industry's absorption capabilities, an important requirement for successful collaborations with external partners like universities. Setting up suitable processes, which consider barriers related to the different possible forms of triggers and clear assignments of process owners, are tasks of the involved institutions. The more partners, the more complex are such tasks. However, as already mentioned earlier, only collaboration between complementary partners can provide the necessary *critical mass* to lower some of the barriers. Thus it is important to consider which institutions should be involved in knowledge transfer programs in order to facilitate such activities. Above all, changing external factors is a task that ultimately requires the support of local, regional, and national governments. The main results show the necessity of: (1) deciding at whom the knowledge transfer activities should be aimed, (2) the integration of additional partners besides universities and industry, and (3) arranging effective processes to eliminate barriers and increase motivation.

FUTURE TRENDS

Trends like growing global competition and rapidly changing environment put pressure on industry as well as academia. They have to establish and deepen their contacts with each other in order to keep up front. Therefore, knowledge transfer between academia and industry will increase in importance, and the winners will be the ones who fully understand how to utilize such activities. Traditional boundaries between institutions like universities, industry, and governments will be blurred further, thus following the idea of Etzkowitz and Leydesdorff (1995) which promotes close collaborations between universities, industry, and governments—the so-called *triple-helix model*.

CONCLUSION

Building on the framework provided here, the key for successful knowledge transfer activities lies in the following three key measures: (1) knowing the target group, (2) integrating all necessary parties, and (3) setting up the right processes. This requires the commitment and efforts of all involved parties. Despite global markets, regions still play important roles with respect to knowledge transfer, which includes amongst others tacit knowledge, learning, and innovation (Morgan, 2001). Therefore, establishing and enhancing regional initiatives and programs aimed at bringing academia and industry together could form the central part of regional economic development efforts and act as a springboard for national and international knowledge transfer measures. Through increasing intra-regional knowledge transfer, the collaboration capabilities of all involved parties will increase and thus make regions ready for other advanced measures.

REFERENCES

Abramson, H.N., Encarnacao, J., Reid, P.P., & Schmolch, U. (1997). *Technology transfer systems in the United States and Germany: Lessons and perspectives*. Washington, DC: National Academy Press.

Adametz, C., & Ploder, M. (2003). *Innovationsbericht Steiermark 2003* [Innovation survey styria 2003]. Graz: Forschungsgesellschaft JOANNEUM RESEARCH mbH.

Artley, R.J., Dobrauz, G., Plasonig, G.E., & Strasser, R.R. (2003). *Making money out of technology: Best practice in technology exploitation from academic sources*. Solothurn: ETeCH AG.

Beise, M., & Spielkamp, A. (1996). *Technologietransfer von Hochschulen: Ein Insider-outsider-effekt [Technology transfer from higher education institutes: The insider-outsider effect]*. Discussion Papers, 96-10.

Business-Higher Education Forum. (2001). *Working together, creating knowledge: The university-industry collaboration initiative*. Washington, DC: Business-Higher Education Forum.

Clough, G.W. (2003). National priorities for science and technology: A view from the academic sector. In A.H. Teich, S.D. Nelson, S.J. Lita, & A.E. Hunt (Eds.), *AAAS science and technology policy yearbook 2003* (pp. 23-31). Washington, DC: American Association for the Advancement of Science.

Czarnitzki, D., & Rammer, C. (2003). Technology transfer via the Internet: A way to link public science and enterprises. *Journal of Technology Transfer, 28*, 131-147.

Dachs, B., Ebersberger, B., & Pyka, A. (2004). Why do firms co-operate for innovation? A comparison of Austrian and Finish CIS 3 results. *Volkswirtschaftliche Diskussionsreihe des Instituts für Volkswirtschaftslehre der Universitaet Augsburg* [Discussion series of the Institute for Economics at the University of Augsburg], *255*.

Etzkowitz, H. (2003). The European entrepreneurial university: An alternative to the U.S. model. *Industry & Higher Education, 17*, 325-335.

Etzkowitz, H., & Leydesdorff, L. (1995). The Triple Helix of university-industry-government relations: A laboratory for knowledge based economic development. *EASST Review, 14*, 11-19.

Frey, B.S., & Osterloh, M. (2000). *Managing motivation: Wie sie die Neue Motivationsforschung für ihr Unternehmen Nutzen Können* [Managing motivation: How you can use current motivation research for your enterprise]. Wiesbaden: Dr. Th. Gabler GmbH.

Godin, B., & Gingras, Y. (2000). The place of universities in the system of knowledge production. *Research Policy, 29*, 273-278.

Hofer, F. (2004, June). Understanding the motives to further improve knowledge transfer activities: A case of the Graz Region (Austria). *Proceedings of the TTI2004 Conference of Technology Transfer and Innovation Ltd.*, Edinburgh.

Hofer, F., Adametz, C., & Holzer, F. (2004). Technology and knowledge transfer scheme in the Graz region—10 years of experience. *Industry & Higher Education, 18*, 177-186.

Jankowski, J.E. (1999). Trends in academic research spending, alliances, and commercialization. *Journal of Technology Transfer, 24*, 55-68.

Kremic, T. (2003). Knowledge transfer: A contextual approach. *Journal of Technology Transfer, 28*, 149-158.

Large, D., Belinko, K., & Kalligatsi, K. (2000). Building successful knowledge commercialization teams: Pilot empirical support for the theory of cascading commitment. *Journal of Technology Transfer, 25*, 169-180.

Lipscomb, M., & McEwan, A.M. (2001). Technology transfer in SMEs: The TCS model at Kingston University. In H.H. Hvolby (Ed.), *Proceedings of the 4th SMESME International Conference: Stimulating Manufacturing Excellence in Small & Medium Enterprises* (pp. 406-413). Aalborg: Department of Production at Aalborg University.

Matkin, G.W. (1990). *Technology transfer and the university*. New York: Macmillan.

Morgan, K. (2001, September). The exaggerated death of geography: Localized learning, innovation, and uneven development. *Proceedings of the Conference of the Eindhoven Centre for Innovation Studies,* Eindhoven University of Technology.

Pries, F., & Guild, P. (2004). Analyzing the commercialization of university research: A proposed categorization scheme. In Y. Hosni, R. Smith, & T. Kahlil (Eds.), *Proceedings of IAMOT 2004—the 13th International Conference on Management of Technology* (Paper Identification Number: 652). Washington, DC: International Association for Management of Technology.

Reinhard, M. (2001). Absorptionskapazitaet und nutzung externen technologischen wissens in unternehmen [Absorption capability and the use of external technological knowledge in enterprises]. *ifo Schnelldienst, 54,* 28-39.

Remus, U., & Schub, S. (2003). A blueprint for the implementation of process-oriented knowledge management. *Knowledge and Process Management, 10,* 237-253.

Schartinger, D., Schibany, A., & Gassler, H. (2001). Interactive relations between universities and firms: Empirical evidence for Austria. *Journal of Technology Transfer, 26,* 255-268.

Schumpeter, J.A. (1912). *Theorie der Wirtschaftlichen Entwicklung* [Theory of economic development]. Leipzig: Duncker & Humblot.

Schwickert, A.C., & Fischer, K. (1996). Der Geschaeftsprozess als Formaler Prozess—Definition, Eigenschaften, Arten [The business process as formal process—definition, characteristics, and types]. *Arbeitspapiere WI des Lehrstuhls für Allgemeine Betriebswirtschaftslehre und Wirtschaftsinformatik der Universität Mainz* [working papers WI of the Institute for Business Economics at the University of Mainz], *4.*

Spivey, W.A., Munson, J.M., & Flannery, W.T. (1994). Understanding the environs that impact knowledge transfer and knowledge transition. *Journal of Technology Transfer, 19,* 63-73.

Starbuck, E. (2001). Optimizing university research collaborations. *Research Technology Management,* (January-February), 40-44.

Tornatzky, L.G. (2000). *Building state economies by promoting university-industry technology transfer.* Washington, DC: National Governor's Association.

Watanabe, T., Yoneyama, S., Senoo, D., Fukushima, M., & Senoh, K. (2004). Visualizing the invisible: A marketing approach of the technology licensing process. In Y. Hosni, R. Smith, & T. Kahlil (Eds.), *Proceedings of IAMOT 2004—the 13th International Conference on Management of Technology* (Paper Identification Number: 565). Washington, DC: International Association for Management of Technology.

KEY TERMS

Collaboration: A project between at least two partners. The partners show consideration for each other and do not try to selfishly fulfill their own needs. Each partner enters collaborations voluntarily. Because of the impossibility to clearly specify all activities and control collaborations exactly, trust plays a major role.

Data: The generic term for signs, symbols, and pictures. Data can be saved, processed, printed, and so on. They are not bound to individuals.

Foresight: The Foresight Methodology provides tools and systematic approaches to integrate various partners and views in order to provide the necessary framework for, for example, measures to improve economic development. It is closely connected with the Triple-Helix Model.

Information/Documentation: Information is a process with data as input and knowledge as output. An individual is the subject who transforms the data into knowledge. Relations between two technical devices are data exchange processes. Relations between two or more individuals are communication processes. The reverse information process is called documentation process (e.g., writing an article).

Knowledge: Knowledge is exclusively bound to individuals or group of individuals. They can generate knowledge, for example, by the information process. Knowledge does not exist in databases, books, or articles. Only by interaction with individuals does data become knowledge of the respective individual.

Process Management: Strong functional orientation does not nowadays meet customer needs. The aim of process management is to overcome functional barriers and to deliver the results customers desire.

System Theory: System Theory facilitates the illustration of complex and complicated relations between different elements. Thus, it enables specific views, suited for the respective purpose of the system.

Triple Helix: Introduced by Etzkowitz and Leydesdorff in 1995. The idea of the Triple-Helix Model is the close collaboration between industry, universities, and governments in order to provide suited infrastructure necessary for innovations and economic development.

Knowledge Visualization

K

Martin J. Eppler
University of Lugano, Switzerland

Remo A. Burkhard
University of St. Gallen, Switzerland

INTRODUCTION

Making knowledge visible so that it can be better accessed, discussed, valued, or generally managed is a longstanding objective in knowledge management (see Sparrow, 1998). Knowledge maps, knowledge cartographies, or knowledge landscapes are often heard terms that are nevertheless rarely defined, described, or demonstrated. In this article, we review the state of the art in the area of knowledge visualization, and describe its background and perspectives. We define the concept and differentiate it from other approaches, such as information visualization or visual communication. Core knowledge visualization types, such as conceptual diagrams or visual metaphors, are distinguished, and examples of their application in business are shown and discussed. Implications for research and practice are summarized, and future trends in this domain are outlined.

The Concept of Knowledge Visualization

Generally speaking, the field of knowledge visualization examines the use of visual representations to improve the *creation* and *transfer* of knowledge between at least two people. Knowledge visualization thus designates all graphic means that can be used to construct and convey complex insights. Beyond the mere transport of facts, people who employ knowledge visualization strive to transfer insights, experiences, attitudes, values, expectations, perspectives, opinions, and predictions, and this in a way that enables someone else to re-construct, remember, and apply these insights correctly. Examples of knowledge visualization formats are heuristic sketches (e.g., ad-hoc drawings of complex ideas), conceptual diagrams (such as Porter's Five Forces diagram), visual metaphors (such as Plato's cave metaphor of reality), knowledge animations (such as a rotating double helix), knowledge maps (such as a landscape of in-house experts), or domain structures (e.g., a co-citation network of knowledge management literature). All these formats capture not just (descriptive) facts or numbers, but prescriptive and prognostic insights, principles, and relations. They are used as indirect (and at times ambiguous) communication in order to trigger sense-making activities and to motivate viewers to re-construct meaning. Thus, the 'what' (object), the 'why' (goal), and the 'how' (methods) of knowledge visualization differ from information visualization. These differences are further described in the following section.

The Differences Between Knowledge and Information Visualization

A related field and precursor to knowledge visualization is information visualization. Information visualization is an advancing field of study both in terms of academic research and practical applications (Card, Mackinlay, & Shneiderman, 1999; Chen, 1999a; Spence, 2000; Ware, 2000). Information visualization offers novel visual applications for the interactive browsing and analysis of data with the aim to derive new insights by seeing trends, outliers, or clusters. Card et al. (1999) define information visualization, as "the use of computer-supported, interactive, visual representations of abstract data to amplify cognition." This definition is well established among computer scientists active in this field. The information visualization fields neglects, however, the potential of visualizations as a medium for the transfer of complex knowledge. Another neglected aspect relates to the integration of non-computer based visualization methods (e.g., posters, physical objects, etc.) as architects, artists, and designers use them. This is the objective of knowledge visualization and at the same time the main difference to information visualization: information visualization and knowledge visualization are both exploiting our innate abilities to effectively process visual representations, but the way of using these abilities differs in both domains. Information visualization aims to explore large amounts of abstract (often numeric) data to derive new insights or simply make the stored data more accessible. Knowledge visualization, in contrast, facilitates the transfer and creation of knowledge among people by giving them *richer means of expressing what they know*. While information visualization typically helps to improve information retrieval and access, and generally optimizes the presentation of large data sets—particularly in the interaction of humans and computers—knowledge visualization primarily is used to *augment knowledge-intensive communication among individuals*. Such visual communication of knowledge is relevant for several areas within knowledge management, as described in the next section.

Application Areas within Knowledge Management

Knowledge visualization can help to solve several predominant, knowledge-related problems in organizations. First, there is the omnipresent problem of knowledge *transfer* (or knowledge asymmetry). Knowledge visualization offers a systematic approach to transfer knowledge at various levels: among individuals, from individuals to groups, between groups, and from individuals and groups to the entire organization. To do so, knowledge must be recreated in the mind of the receiver (El Sawy, Eriksson, Carlsson, & Raven, 1997). This depends on the recipient's cognitive capacity to process the incoming stimuli (Vance & Eynon, 1998). Thus, the person responsible for the transfer of knowledge not only needs to convey the relevant knowledge at the right time to the right person, he or she also needs to convey it in the right *context* and in a way so that it can ultimately be used and remembered. Graphics such as rich but easily understandable visual metaphors can serve exactly this purpose, as the brain can process images often more easily than text. In this context, visualization can also facilitate the problem of *inter-functional knowledge communication*—that is, the communication among different stakeholders and experts with different professional backgrounds. Visual methods for the transfer of complex knowledge are thus one emergent sub-discipline within knowledge visualization.

Another application area of visualization within knowledge management is knowledge creation. Knowledge visualization offers great potential for the *creation* of new knowledge in groups, thus enabling innovation. Knowledge visualization offers methods to use the creative power of imagery and the possibility of fluid re-arrangements and changes. It inspires and enables groups to create new knowledge, for instance by use of heuristic sketches or visual metaphors. Unlike text, these graphic formats can be quickly and collectively changed, and thus propagate the rapid and joint improvement of ideas.

A further, more general, application goal of knowledge visualization is its use as an effective strategy against *information overload*. Information overload (see Eppler, Mengis, 2004) is a major problem in knowledge-intensive organizations. Knowledge visualizations help to compress large amounts of reasoned information with the help of analytical frameworks, theories, and models that ab-

sorb complexity and render it accessible. This can be a vital prerequisite for the three application domains mentioned previously (transfer, creation, and communication).

Although these application fields have existed for several years, the potential of visual representations is often lost because there is little assistance for non-professional visualizers to make use of the power of complex visualization. Thus, a conceptual framework should be developed that enables practitioners to better use and apply visual representations of knowledge. In the next section, we briefly outline relevant background areas that have paved the way for knowledge visualization as a new discipline. Then, we will present a first general framework to guide the application of knowledge visualization.

BACKGROUND

The field of knowledge visualization is an emerging one, merging approaches from information visualization, didactic techniques, visual cognition, and visual communication research, as well as more practical approaches, such as business diagramming or visual programming languages. Below, we briefly review two of these central disciplines.

Visual Cognition and Perception

A majority of our brain's activity deals with processing and analyzing visual images. Several empirical studies show that visual representations are superior to verbal-sequential representations in different tasks (Larkin & Simon, 1987; Glenberg & Langston, 1992; Bauer & Johnson-Laird, 1993; Novick, 2001). Similarly, Miller (1956) reports that a human's input channel capacity is greater when visual abilities are used. The reason for this has been researched by Gestalt psychologists. Their findings indicate that our brain has a strong ability to identify patterns in graphics (Koffka, 1935). In addition, research on visual imagery (Kosslyn, 1980; Shepard & Cooper, 1982) suggests that visual recall seems to be better than verbal recall. It is still not entirely clear how images are stored and recalled, but it is clear that humans have a natural ability to remember and use images. Three related fields of research—instructional psychology, MIS, and media didactics—investigate the learning or performance outcomes of text-alone versus text-picture. Again, visualization seems to outperform text alone. Mandl and Levin (1989), Weidenmann (1989), and Swaab, Postmes, Neijens, Kiers, and Dumai (2002) present clearly different results in knowledge acquisition or task performance from text and pictures. All of these studies lead to one unambiguous conclusion: If visualization is applied correctly, it dramatically increases our ability to think and communicate.

Visual Communication Studies

Different isolated research fields contribute valuable results for the visual communication of knowledge. These are contributions in the field of visualizing information in print (Bertin, 1974; Tufte, 1990, 1997), cognitive art and hypermedia design (Horn, 1998), information architecture (Wurman, 1996), and contributions in the fields of graphics design, interface design, interaction design, and human-computer interaction. From a theoretical perspective, there are different contributions that help to improve the transfer of knowledge, particularly communication science (Fiske, 1982), visual communication sciences (Newton, 1998; Stonehill, 1995), and cognitive psychology (Farah, 2000). These contributions show how visual representations affect our social cognition processes both positively (improving understanding) and negatively (manipulating perception and interpretation). Many systematic approaches that examine visualization in communication, however, have so far been rooted in the mass media sector. They have primarily described how newspapers and television use graphic representations to convey meaning. How to use such formats actively for knowledge transfer is rarely discussed in these contributions. We use insights from these and other domains to categorize the main application parameters of knowledge visualization in the next section.

A Framework for Knowledge Visualization

For an effective creation and transfer of knowledge through visualization, at least three perspectives (Table 1) should be considered. These perspectives answer three key questions with regard to visualizing knowledge, namely:

1. What type of knowledge is visualized (object)?
2. Why should that knowledge be visualized (purpose)?
3. How can the knowledge be represented (method)?

The answers to these three questions are obviously highly interconnected. Listing possible answers to these key questions leads to a first conceptual framework that can provide an overview of the knowledge visualization field (see Table 1).

The *knowledge type perspective* can be used to identify the type of knowledge that needs to be transferred. For our framework we distinguish among five types of knowledge: declarative knowledge (know-what), procedural knowledge (know-how), experiential knowledge or experience (know-why), orientation knowledge (know-where), and people-related knowledge (know-who) (for this distinction, see for example Alavi & Leidner, 2001). Today, there is no validated prescriptive framework that links visualization formats to knowledge types and that offers specific representation formats for particular knowledge types.

With the help of the *visualization goal perspective*, we distinguish among several reasons why a visual knowledge representation is used. Goals for knowledge visualization use that can be anticipated are knowledge sharing through visual means, knowledge crafting or creation, learning from visual representations, codifying past experiences visually for future users, or mapping knowledge (Vail, 1999) so that experts, for example within a large organization, can be more easily identified.

The *visualization format perspective* structures the visualization methods to six main groups: heuristic sketches, conceptual diagrams, visual metaphors, knowledge animations, knowledge maps, and domain structures.

Having given an overview of the main formats of knowledge visualization, we will discuss each of the six types, and how they can be matched with adequate

Table 1. The three different perspectives of the knowledge visualization framework

Knowledge Type (what?)	Visualization Goal (why?)	Visualization Format (how?)
Know-what	Transferring (clarification, elicitation, socialization)	Heuristic Sketches
Know-how	Creating (discovery, combination)	Conceptual Diagrams
Know-why	Learning (acquisition, internalization)	Visual Metaphors
Know-where	Codifying (documentation, externalization)	Knowledge Animations
Know-who	Finding (e.g., experts, documents, groups)	Knowledge Maps
	Assessing (evaluation, rating)	Domain Structures

Figure 1. Freud's heuristic sketch for theory development[2]

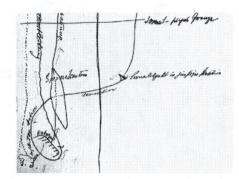

Figure 2. Various sketches helped to assist and inspire the group reflection processes in an urban planning workshop[3]

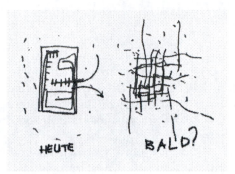

knowledge types and applied for specific application contexts.

Heuristic Sketches: Creating New Insights Individually or in Groups

Heuristic sketches are drawings that are used to assist the group reflection and communication process by making knowledge-in-progress explicit and debatable. Generally a sketch is defined as "a rough drawing or painting in which an artist notes down his preliminary ideas for a work that will eventually be realized with greater precision and detail."[1] In the context of knowledge management, we call these sketches heuristic sketches to highlight their problem-solving potential. The main benefits of heuristic sketches are: (1) they represent the main idea and key features of a preliminary study; (2) they are versatile and accessible; (3) they are fast and help to quickly visualize emergent notions; (4) the use of a pen on a flipchart attracts the attention towards the communicator; and (5) heuristic sketches allow room for one's own interpretations and foster the creativity in groups. Examples of heuristic sketches are shown in Figures 1 and 2.

Conceptual Diagrams: Structuring Information and Illustrating Relationships

Conceptual diagrams as seen in Figure 3 are schematic depictions of abstract ideas with the help of standardized shapes (such as arrows, circles, pyramids, or matrices). They are used to structure information and illustrate relationships. For the transfer and creation of knowledge, conceptual diagrams help to make abstract concepts accessible, to reduce the complexity to the key issues, to amplify cognition, and to discuss relationships (Eppler, 2003).

An example of a particularly knowledge-intensive conceptual diagram is the Toulmin chart, based on the argumentation theory of Steven Toulmin (1964). Such a chart helps to breakdown an argument into different parts (such as claim, reasons, and evidence); this is useful when evaluating the validity of a claim.

Visual Metaphors: Relating Domains to Improve Understanding

A metaphor provides the path from the understanding of something familiar to something new by carrying ele-

Figure 3. An overview of frequently used conceptual diagrams

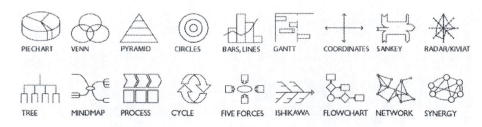

Figure 4. The negotiation bridge: A visual metaphor that outlines a negotiation method[4]

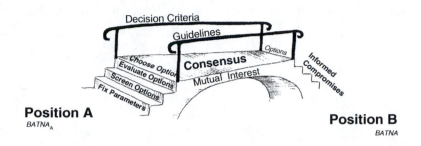

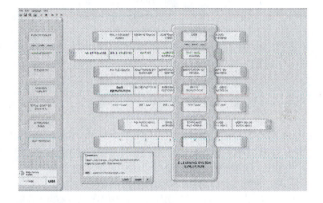

Figure 5. The Infoticle application allows exploring large-time varying datasets[5]

Figure 6. The interactive parameter ruler enables teams to explore alternatives in real time[6]

ments of understanding from the mastered subject to a new domain. This is why Aristotle calls the metaphor a *tool of cognition*. A metaphor provides rapid information, is highly instructive, and facilitates the process of learning. As Worren, Moore, and Elliott (2002, p. 1230) have pointed out, metaphors can also improve memorability and coordination in groups. Visual metaphors used for knowledge transfer or creation can either be natural objects or phenomena (e.g., mountains, icebergs, tornado), or artificial, man-made objects (e.g., a bridge, a ladder, a temple), activities (e.g., climbing, etc.), or concepts (e.g., war, family). Their main feature is that they organize information meaningfully. In doing so, they fulfill a dual function. First, they position information graphically to organize and structure it. Second, they convey an implicit insight about the represented information through the key characteristics (or associations) of the metaphor that is employed.

In Figure 4 the metaphor of a bridge was used to convey how to lead successful negotiations.

Knowledge Animations: Dynamic and Interactive Visualizations

Knowledge animations are computer-supported interactive visualizations that allow users to control, interact, and manipulate different types of information in a way that fosters the transfer and creation of knowledge. By interacting with the information, new insights are created or shared. Knowledge animations help to fascinate and focus people, to enable interactive collaboration and persistent conversations, and to illustrate, explore, and discuss complex issues in various contexts. In the *Infoticle* application (Vande Moere, Mieusset, & Gross, 2004), the animation of data-driven particles (Infoticles) helps to explore large time-varying datasets and allows seeing the behavior of individual data entries in the global context of the whole dataset.

In similar ways, the interactive parameter ruler (Figure 6; Eppler, 2004) enables teams and individuals to explore alternatives in real time through sliders in the ruler appli-

Figure 7. The tube map visualization (1.2×2.4 meter) presents an overview and details on a project. Each line represents one target group, each station a project milestone. Each line (target group) stops at the stations (milestones) where the target groups are involved. The stations are tagged with descriptions, dates, or instructions.

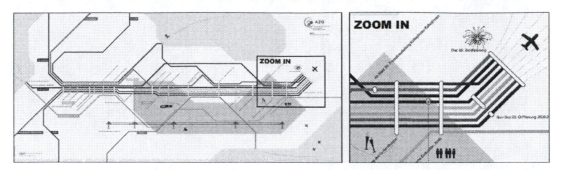

cation. As they enter evaluation criteria or decision options and move them into various positions, participants develop a common understanding regarding a complex issue. The joint visual interaction is thus a catalyst for collective knowledge development and transfer in groups.

Knowledge Maps: Navigating and Structuring Expertise

Knowledge maps (Eppler, 2002) are graphic formats that follow cartographic conventions to reference relevant knowledge. A knowledge map generally consists of two parts: a ground layer which represents the context for the mapping (such as an island), and the individual elements that are mapped within this context (e.g., towns). The ground layer typically consists of the mutual context that all employees can understand and relate to, such as a business model, a product, the competency areas, or a geographic map. The elements that are mapped onto such a shared context range from experts and communities of practice to more explicit and codified forms of knowledge such as articles, patents, lessons learned bases, or expert systems. Knowledge maps are thus graphic directories of knowledge-sources, -assets, -structures, -applications, or -development stages.

In Figure 7 the customized *Tube Map Visualization*[7] illustrates a five-year quality development project. The subway-lines represent individual target groups and the stations milestones. The knowledge map was printed on a poster (2.4×1.2 meters) and located in front of an elevator to foster creativity and initiate discussion. An evaluation can be found in Burkhard and Meier (2004).

Domain Structures: Visualizing Intellectual Structures

Knowledge domain visualization focuses on identifying and visually representing the dynamics of scientific fron-

tiers in a multidisciplinary context and allows new ways of accessing knowledge sources (authors, institutions, papers, journals, etc.) by visualizing linkages, relationships, and structures of scientific domains (Chen, 1998, 1999b, 2000, 2003). New algorithms can be integrated in novel interfaces for the exploration of digital libraries where new search paradigms become decisive (Kleiboemer, Lazear, & Pederson, 1996; Chen, Houston, Sewell, & Schatz, 1998; Sebrechts, Vasilakis, Miller, Cugini, & Laskowski, 1999; Sutcliffe, Ennis, & Hu, 2000). Examples for such systems are *Envision* (Fox et al., 1993, 2002) or *Gridvis* (Weiss-Lijn, McDonnell, & James, 2001). An overview of such systems is presented by Nowell, France, Hix, Heath, and Fox (1996) and Börner and Chen (2002). While this knowledge visualization format is currently only used for knowledge management in scientific communities, future application in corporate settings can be envisioned (for communities of practice).

CONCLUSION

Knowledge visualization offers solutions for the transfer and creation of knowledge, and stresses an important and often neglected potential that knowledge management researchers and practitioners can exploit: our innate ability to effectively process visual representations. Knowledge visualization also offers new development roads for the discipline of information visualization, as it extends the field with regard to other knowledge types and knowledge processes other than information exploration (namely knowledge transfer and knowledge creation in groups), because: (1) it uses computer-based and non-computer based visualization methods; (2) it points to psychological, social, and cognitive factors of different recipients; and (3) it integrates findings from other research fields such as knowledge management, communication science, architecture, or psychology. This article presented both a theoretical framework and application examples to highlight the great potential of visualization for knowledge management. Specifically, this potential relates to cognitive (c), social (s), and emotional (e) benefits of visualization. These factors can be summarized in the CARMEN acronym:

- **Coordination:** Visual representations help to coordinate knowledge workers, and to structure communication and group processes (e.g., knowledge maps, visual tools for collaboration, heuristic sketches). (s)
- **Attention:** Visual representations allow users to gain attention by addressing emotions (e.g., advertising) and to keep attention (e.g., sketching on a flipchart) by identifying patterns, outliers, and trends (e.g., information visualization). (c)
- **Recall:** Visual representations improve memorability, remembrance, and recall, because we think in images (e.g., visual metaphor, stories, and conceptual diagrams). (c)
- **Motivation:** Visual representations inspire, motivate, energize, and activate viewers (e.g., knowledge maps, mutual stories, instructive diagrams). (e)
- **Elaboration:** Visual representations lead to further understanding and appreciation of concepts and ideas as one interacts with them (e.g., discussing scenarios of a new product by the use of heuristic sketches or a physical model). (c)
- **New Insights:** Knowledge visualizations can reveal previously hidden connections and lead to sudden insights—'a-ha' experiences. By visualizing experiences in a group, for example, root causes of certain errors can surface. Visual representations support the creation of new insights by embedding details in context and showing relationships between objects (e.g., information visualization, visual metaphors). (c)

As far as the limitations are concerned, there is evidence that visualization can have drawbacks with regard to specific contexts. One should thus not neglect the risks inherent in using such forms of visualization, namely the difficult maintenance of the diagrams and maps, the reification of (at times) invalid views, and hence the possible manipulation of users, or the possible distortion of reality through misinterpretations. Future research will have to investigate these potential negative effects empirically in authentic application contexts (e.g., Blackwell & Green, 1999). As a reminder, we summarize the potential drawbacks of knowledge visualization with the COMMA acronym:

- **Confusion:** If knowledge visualizations do not respect certain rules and conventions, or if the used metaphors or analogies are difficult to understand, they can be confusing and obstruct knowledge transfer.
- **Overload or oversimplification:** Knowledge visualization that does not respect the cognitive constraints of visual perception quickly becomes overloaded and de-motivating. On the other side of this spectrum, visualizations may also simplify ideas or concepts by leaving out too many vital elements.
- **Misuse or misrepresentation:** Visualizations may also be used where they are not really necessary and where a text may convey an insight (e.g., because of its sequential structure) more adequately than a text. They may misrepresent a given domain, for example, by employing an unfit metaphor or diagrammatic template. Misuse may also result from a haphazard look at a picture.
- **Manipulation:** As stated above, visualization is a powerful instrument that can be used to cover up logical flaws, incomplete reasoning, or distorted evidence. Consequently, visualizations must always be viewed critically.
- **Ambiguity:** As graphic symbols are typically open to various interpretations, compilations of such symbolic forms in knowledge visualizations may at times be ambiguous. Because of this, it is crucial to provide written or verbal explanations to accompany complex graphics.

In terms of future trends, knowledge visualization will evolve with regard to new *formats* and new *application areas*. The potential to combine various formats (such as diagrams, maps, and metaphors) in a complementary way (as architects use them) seems obvious. It also seems clear that knowledge visualization will be used in other settings than just the traditional computer desktop environment. Examples of new application areas for knowledge visualization can be found in the visual communication of corporate missions, strategies, value propositions, and business scenarios. New applications can also be envisioned by combining knowledge visualization with other innovative approaches in knowledge management, such as storytelling. Storytelling is in fact a closely related knowledge management tool, as it strives for rich, mental imagery (Loebbert, 2003). We believe that stories can be combined with knowledge visualization formats (as in visualized story trails) to trigger and accelerate the creation and dissemination of knowledge in organizations.

In conclusion, we believe that additional time and budget for knowledge visualization should be allocated in future corporate KM initiatives and in future research initiatives on knowledge management. Knowledge visualization clearly is an idea whose time has come. To put this idea into practice, however, requires not only imagination, but also dedication to continuous assessments and improvements.

REFERENCES

Alavi, M., & Leidner, D. (2001). Knowledge management and knowledge management systems: Conceptual foundations and research issues. *MIS Quarterly, 25*(1), 107-136.

Bauer, M., & Johnson-Laird, P. (1993). How diagrams can improve reasoning. *Psychological Science, 4*(6), 372-378.

Bertin, J. (1974). *Graphische Semiologie. Diagramme, Netze, Karten.* Berlin: Walter de Gruyter.

Blackwell, A.F., & Green, T.R.G. (1999). Does metaphor increase visual language usability? *Proceedings of the 1999 IEEE Symposium on Visual Languages (VL'99)* (pp. 246-253).

Börner, K., & Chen, C. (2002). *Visual interfaces to digital libraries.* Heidelberg: Springer-Verlag (LNCS).

Burkhard, R., & Meier, M. (2004, June 30-July 2). Tube map: Evaluation of a visual metaphor for interfunctional communication of complex projects. *Proceedings of I-KNOW '04,* Graz, Austria (pp. 449-456).

Card, S.K., Mackinlay, J.D., & Shneiderman, B. (1999). *Readings in information visualization; Using vision to think.* Los Altos, CA: Morgan Kaufmann.

Chen, C. (1998). Bridging the gap: The use of pathfinder networks in visual navigation. *Journal of Visual Languages and Computing, 9*(3), 267-286.

Chen, C. (1999a). *Information visualisation and virtual environments.* London: Springer.

Chen, C. (1999b). Visualizing semantic spaces and author co-citation networks in digital libraries. *Information Processing and Management, 35*(3), 401-420.

Chen, C. (2000, July 19-21). Domain visualization for digital libraries. *Proceedings of the International Conference on Information Visualisation (IV2000)* (pp. 261-267). London.

Chen, C. (2003). *Mapping scientific frontiers: The quest for knowledge visualization.* London: Springer.

Chen, H., Houston, A., Sewell, R.R., & Schatz, B.R. (1998). Internet browsing and searching: User evaluations of category map and concept space techniques. *Journal of the American Society for Information Science, 49*(7), 582-603.

El Sawy, O.A., Eriksson, I., Carlsson, S.A., & Raven, A. (1997, November 6-8). Understanding the nature of shared knowledge creation spaces around business processes: An international investigation. *Proceedings of the Carnegie Bosch Institute Conference on Knowledge in International Corporations,* Rome.

Eppler, M. (2002). Making knowledge visible through knowledge maps. In C.W. Holsapple (Ed.), *Handbook on knowledge management* (pp. 189-206). Berlin: Springer-Verlag.

Eppler, M. (2003). *Managing information quality. Increasing the value of information in knowledge-intensive products and processes.* Berlin: Springer-Verlag.

Eppler, M. (2004). Facilitating knowledge communication through joint interactive visualization. *Journal of Universal Computer Science, 10*(6), 683-690.

Farah, M.J. (2000). *The cognitive neuroscience of vision.* Malden, MA: Blackwell.

Fiske, J. (1982). Communication theory. In J. Fiske (Ed.), *Introduction to communication studies* (pp. 6-24). London; New York: Methuen.

Fox, E., North, C., Wang, J., Abhishek, A., Anil, B., & Supriya, A. (2002). Enhancing the ENVISION interface for digital libraries. *Proceedings of the 2nd ACM/IEEE-CS Joint Conference on Digital Libraries* (pp. 275-276). Portland, OR: ACM Press.

Fox, E.A., Hix, D., Nowell, L.T., Brueni, D.J., Wake, W.C., Heath, L.S., & Rao, D. (1993). Users, user interfaces, and objects: ENVISION, a digital library. *Journal of the American Society for Information Science, 44*(8), 480-491.

Glenberg, A., & Langston, M. (1992). Comprehension of illustrated text: Pictures help to build mental models. *Journal of Memory and Language, 31*(2), 129-151.

Horn, R. (1998). *Visual language: Global communication for the 21st century.* Brainbridge Island, WA: MacroVU.

Kleiboemer, A.J., Lazear, M.B., & Pederson, J.O. (1996). Tailoring a retrieval system for naive users. *Proceedings of the 5th Symposium on Document Analysis and Information Retrieval (SDAIR96),* Las Vegas (pp. 209-216).

Koffka, K. (1935). *The principles of Gestalt psychology.* New York: Harcourt Brace.

Kosslyn, S.M. (1980). *Images and mind.* Cambridge, MA: Harvard University Press.

Larkin, J., & Simon, H. (1987). Why a diagram is (sometimes) worth ten thousand words. *Cognitive Science, 11,* 65-99.

Lin, X., White, H.D., & Buzydlowski, J. (2001, August 6-12). Associative searching and visualization. *Proceedings of the International Conference on Advances in Infrastructure for Electronic Business, Science, and Education on the Internet (SSGRR01),* L'Aquila, Italy.

Lin, X., White, H.D., & Buzydlowski, J. (2003). Real-time author co-citation mapping for online searching. *Information Processing and Management: An International Journal, 39*(5), 689-706.

Loebbert, M. (2003). *Storymanagement—der Narrative Ansatz für Management und Beratung.* Stuttgart: Klett-Cotta.

Mandl, H., & Levin, J.R. (1989). *Knowledge acquisition from text and pictures.* Amsterdam: North-Holland.

Miller, G.A. (1956). The magical number seven, plus or minus two: Some limits on our capacity for processing information. *Psychological Review, 63,* 81-97.

Novick, L.R. (2001). Spatial diagrams: Key instruments in the toolbox for thought. In D.L. Medin (Ed.), *The psychology of learning and motivation* (pp. 279-325). San Francisco: Academic Press.

Nowell, L.T., France, R.K., Hix, D., Heath, L., & Fox, E. (1996). Visualizing search results: Some alternatives to query-document similarity. *Proceedings of the ACM SIGIR Conference on Research and Development in Information Retrieval (SIGIR96),* Zurich, Switzerland (pp. 67-75).

Sebrechts, M.M., Vasilakis, J., Miller, M.S., Cugini, J.V., & Laskowski, S.J. (1999). Visualization of search results: A comparative evaluation of text, 2D, and 3D interfaces. *Proceedings of the 22nd Annual International ACM SIGIR Conference on Research and Development in Information Retrieval* (pp. 3-10). Berkeley, CA: ACM Press.

Shepard, R.N., & Cooper, L.A. (1982). *Mental images and their transformations.* Cambridge, MA: MIT Press.

Sparrow, J. (1998). *Knowledge in organizations.* Thousand Oaks, CA: Sage Publications.

Spence, B. (2000). *Information visualization.* San Francisco: ACM Press.

Sutcliffe, A.G., Ennis, M., & Hu, J. (2000). Evaluating the effectiveness of visual user interfaces for information retrieval. *International Journal of Human-Computer Studies,* (53).

Swaab, R.I., Postmes, T., Neijens, P., Kiers, M.H., & Dumai, A.C.M. (2002). Multiparty negotiation support: The role of visualization's influence on the development of shared mental models. *Journal of Management Information Systems, 19*(1), 129-150.

Toulmin, S. (1964). *The uses of argument.* Cambridge, UK: Cambridge University Press.

Tufte, E. (1990). *Envisioning information.* Cheshire: Graphics Press.

Tufte, E. (1997). *Visual explanations.* Cheshire: Graphics Press.

Vance, D., & Eynon, J. (1998). On the requirements of knowledge-transfer using information systems: A schema whereby such transfer is enhanced. *Proceedings of the 4th Americas Conference on Information Systems,* Baltimore (pp. 632-634).

Vande Moere, A., Mieusset, K.H., & Gross, M. (2004). Visualizing abstract information using motion properties of data-driven particles. *Proceedings of the Conference on Visualization and Data Analysis 2004, IS&T/SPIE Symposium on Electronic Imaging 2004,* San Jose, CA.

Ware, C. (2000). *Information visualization: Perception for design.* San Francisco: Morgan Kaufmann.

Weidenmann, B. (1989). When good pictures fail: An information-processing approach to the effect of illustrations. In H. Mandl & J.R. Levin (Eds.), *Knowledge acquisition from text and pictures.* Amsterdam: Elsevier, North.

Weiss-Lijn, M., McDonnell, J.T., & James, L. (2001). Visualizing document content with metadata to facilitate goal-directed search. *Proceedings of the 5th International Conference on Information Visualization (IV01)* (pp. 71-76).

White, H.D., Buzydlowski, J., & Lin, X. (2000). Co-cited author maps as interfaces to digital libraries: Designing pathfinder networks in the humanities. *Proceedings of the IEEE International Conference on Information Visualization (IV00),* London (pp. 25-30).

Worren, N., Moore, K., & Elliott, R. (2002). When theories become tools: Toward a framework for pragmatic validity. *Human Relations, 55*(10), 1227-1250.

Wurman, R.S. (1996). *Information architects.* Zurich: Graphis Press Corp.

KEY TERMS

Conceptual Diagrams: Schematic depictions of abstract ideas with the help of standardized shapes such as arrows, circles, pyramids, matrices, and so forth.

Heuristic Sketches: Ad-hoc drawings that are used to assist the group reflection and communication process by making unstable knowledge explicit and debatable.

Information Visualization: The use of computer-supported methods to interactively explore and derive new insights through the visualization of large sets of information.

Knowledge Animations: Interactive applications that consist of interactive mechanisms that foster the reconstruction of knowledge or the generation of new insights.

Knowledge Domain Visualization: Focuses on identifying and visually presenting the dynamics of scientific frontiers in a multidisciplinary context, and allows new ways of accessing knowledge sources by visualizing linkage, relationships, and the structures of scientific domains.

Knowledge Maps: Cartographic depictions of knowledge sources, structures, assets, and development or applications steps. Knowledge maps do not directly represent knowledge, but reference it for easier identification and assessment.

Knowledge Visualization: Designates all graphic means that can be used to develop or convey insights, experiences, methods, or skills.

Visual Metaphors: Graphic depictions of seemingly unrelated graphic shapes that are used to convey an abstract idea by relating it to a concrete phenomenon.

ENDNOTES

[1] Sketch. *Encyclopedia Britannica.* Retrieved August 4, 2003, from *http://www.britannica.com/eb/article?eu=69864*

[2] Reproduced by permission of A.W. Freud et al./ Paterson Marsh Ltd., London.

[3] With permission from the Swiss Federal Institute of Technology (ETH): *http://www.sciencecity.ethz.ch*

[4] BATNA in this context is an abbreviation for Best Alternative to a Negotiated Agreement. See Lewicki, R.J., Saunders, D.M., & Minton, J.W. (1997). *Essentials of negotiation.* Boston: Irwin McGraw-Hill.

[5] With permission from the Swiss Federal Institute of Technology (ETH): *http://blue-c.ethz.ch/*

[6] Image by www.lets-focus.com/Martin J. Eppler

[7] Copyright by vasp datatecture GmbH, *www.vasp.ch.* Image with permission from vasp datatecture GmbH.

Learning in Organizations

Irena Ali
Department of Defence, Australia

Leoni Warne
Department of Defence, Australia

Celina Pascoe
University of Canberra, Australia

INTRODUCTION

In work life, socially based learning occurs all the time. We learn from interactions between peers, genders, functional groups, and across hierarchies, and it happens in ways not normally recognized as learning (Jordan, 1993). Therefore, use of the term "social" learning reflects that organizations, organizational units, and work groups are social clusters, as are study groups and task groups, and thus learning occurs in a social context.

In this situation, social learning is defined as learning occurring within or by a group, an organization, or any cultural cluster and it includes:

- The procedures by which knowledge and practice are transmitted across posting cycles, across different work situations and across time;
- The procedures that facilitate generative learning—learning that enhances the enterprise's ability to adjust to dynamic and unexpected situations and to react creatively to them.

Social learning represents important processes that contribute to individuals' abilities to understand information, create knowledge from that information, and share what they know. Social learning is therefore intrinsic to knowledge management.

This article is based on research conducted by the Enterprise Social Learning Architectures (ESLA) team. The ESLA team was created in 1998 to carry out a research study into "social learning" and the organizational culture that supports such learning. The study, spanning a period of four years, took place in a number of different settings within the Australian Defence Organisation (ADO).

The findings of this research are of importance because the ADO, like other organizations, faces the problem that much of the organization's memory and knowledge is "walking out the door" in terms of the skills, experience, and the corporate knowledge of its ex-employees. In the current climate, the competitive edge lies in gaining the *knowledge edge*, and to do so requires an understanding of how new knowledge is generated within groups, what motivates people to share what they know, how it is shared between and managed amongst members of an organization, and to what extent organizational culture influences social learning. In this article, we explore some of the organizational factors that enhance social learning and as such, are instrinsically related to knowledge management, as there is a symbiotic relationship between the two concepts.

BACKGROUND

A key assumption underlying the study was that research aimed at explicating social learning requires a socio-technical approach. Many organizations invest heavily in implementing information technology in the hope of providing a seamless solution to managing information resources and organizational knowledge. Unfortunately, these initiatives are often implemented without much regard to how people in organizations go about creating, acquiring, sharing, and making use of information (Bednar, 2000; Davenport, 1994; Vandeville, 2000). The greatest knowledge base in the company does not reside in a computer database somewhere but in the heads of the individuals associated with that organization. These individual knowledge bases are continually changing and adapting to the real world in front of them. Therefore, these individual knowledge bases need to be connected together so that they can do whatever they do best in the shortest possible time. New communication technology will certainly support information sharing where physical proximity is not a possibility. However, the technology alone will not create the trust and interpersonal context necessary to achieve a true network. It is, therefore, necessary to prepare the cultural ground. Values cannot be shared electronically or via bits of paper. Organizations are not based on electronic networks, rather, relationships must be initially constructed through face-to-face interactions (Davenport, 1994). Thus, knowledge sharing will depend on the quality of conversations, formal or informal, that people have (Davenport & Prusak, 1998).

Research on the cultural aspects of those organizations that foster new knowledge and generative learning suggests that employee trust and open communication play an integral role. Higher levels of trust between managers and employees are correlated with more open communication (Ruppel & Harrington, 2000). Schein (1993) and Phillips (1997) suggest that information sharing promotes common identity, mutual trust, and organizational learning and is directly related to organizational cultures that foster generative learning. Schein (1993) also claims that opening up and sharing encourages integration between organizational subcultures and, in turn, organizational adaptation to change. Organizations have a responsibility to create a culture in which learning occurs and that culture will determine the quality of learning that takes place. Such a culture provides the opportunity for personal contact so that tacit knowledge, which cannot effectively be captured in procedures or represented in documents and databases, can be transferred (Davenport & Prusack, 1998; Webber, 1993). For this to occur, the focus has to be on increasing the ability of the individual, as it would be the collective result of many individual actions that would produce a result for the whole of the organization. In a culture that values knowledge, managers recognize not just that knowledge generation is important for business success but also that it should be nurtured.

The methodology of the study evolved over time and included qualitative and quantitative aspects. The research team used ethnographic techniques in the form of fieldwork, which entailed observing the work taking place in different settings, and using directed questioning to clarify issues. In addition to ethnographic observations, the ESLA team undertook extensive, semi-structured interviews with a stratified sample of staff to ensure that an adequate representation was achieved. More than 60 interviews were conducted, and all interviews and field notes were transcribed, coded, and analyzed using the qualitative software package N'Vivo.

The quantitative method involved a questionnaire consisting of Likert scale questions, some open-ended questions, as well as questions ranking listed attributes. In addition, the questionnaires were designed to collect some demographic data about study participants. The response rate for the questionnaires was more than 90%.

The combination of methods offered complementary perspectives of each of the settings. The observations and interviews provided data that offered the insiders' points of view and also shed light on unique aspects of the various social settings that were studied, adding richness to the data. On the other hand, the quantitative surveys enabled generalizations across the settings and answered "what if" types of questions.

SOCIAL LEARNING ENABLERS

A set of overarching organizational values will determine what type of learning culture and organizational communication climate prevails within any company. The ESLA research findings indicate that in organizational cultures characterized by trust, transparency of decision-making, empowerment and forgiveness of mistakes, sharing of information is widespread. It is difficult to determine whether the organizational cultural values are an organizational "property" adopted by its staff or whether these values are influenced by individuals and their belief system. However, within the same organization, different units were operating according to a different "cultural code". This seems to indicate that each individual staff member can mold their organizational culture within the spheres of their responsibility or influence and, as stated earlier, it is the collective sum of individual actions that results in learning at the organizational level.

In addition to the overarching values, the research identified an additional set of factors that supports and enables effective social learning. These factors fall into two categories. The first, *Learning Capability Development*, refers to *characteristics in the environment* and provides a context in which the second category operates, such as organizational infrastructure. This second category is referred to as *Enablers* and represents *processes and strategies* that, if present and effectively applied in an enterprise, can facilitate social learning, such as Common Identity, Team Building, Access to Information, Development of Individual Expertise, and Induction and Enculturation.

As depicted in Figure 1, all of these social learning factors can, from time to time, be either inhibited or challenged by issues such as political and economic vagaries, budget uncertainty, organizational restructures, retrenchments, and so forth.

A graphical representation of the structured social learning architecture is shown in Figure 2.

A common finding through all the settings studied was the impact of trust and open communication on the enablers of generative and social learning. This is because of trust's impact on willingness to share knowledge and to voice ideas. Higher levels of risk-taking behavior have been found to result from increased trust in co-worker relationships (Mayer, Davis, & Schoorman, 1995) and from supervisors showing concern for employees' ideas and feelings (Oldham & Cummings, 1996). Addition-

Figure 1. Factors impacting on social learning in organizations

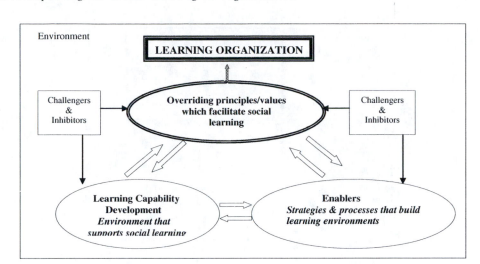

ally, greater risk-taking can result from increased trust for supervisors, in that co-workers' preparedness to act in innovative ways is a form of risk-taking, and it can be encouraged by supervisors' acceptance of mistakes as learning tools, which is a form of trust (Costigan, Itler, & Breman, 1998). Moreover, employees see themselves as more motivated and more likely to take initiative in professional development activities when they have higher levels of trust for their supervisors (Costigan et al., 1998).

The ESLA research findings point to a recursive relationship between trust and employees' sense of empowerment and self-esteem. Employees who are feeling good about themselves and their value to the organization are likely to be motivated, reliable, and have loyalty to the organization. This loyalty will precipitate higher productivity, higher staff retention rates, and the willingness to share knowledge and ideas with others, thus contributing to the knowledge base of the organization. These relationships are depicted in Figure 3.

The literature supports the findings that trust is pivotal in climates of organizational change and when environments are uncertain (Kramer & Tyler, 1995). The results of the ESLA quantitative surveys indicate that trust in leaders and their decision-making played an important part, with just over half (53%) of respondents saying that they trust decisions made by their leaders. It is interesting to note that the higher up the hierarchical chain, the greater the level of agreement with this statement. Nevertheless, the need for more transparency of organizational decision-making was often repeated. One of the interviewees put it very succinctly:

We need a far more open information network that actually allows us to see how the organization works.

The ESLA research data clearly points out that the qualities of certain leaders and the team cultures these leaders create are associated with high levels of trust within those teams, and a generally positive attitude toward collaboration and teamwork. For instance, in teams characterized by cohesiveness and strong team spirit, leaders took on the role of a facilitator, rather than a traditional command-control role, thus allowing people to shape their work themselves. These leaders empowered people to go and seek out their own solutions rather than mandating actions, and they positioned people in ways so as to leverage their unique strengths, to make their own decisions, and have their own responsibilities. They encouraged a wide span of communication so that the individuals in need of information were able and free to consult not only their immediate work group but also the entire organization and beyond and any network that they needed to go to for information. This way these individuals were able to solve their problems quickly and to provide a rapid response to the customer. Moreover, these leaders used frequent two-way feedback to convey their expectations, as well as asking the staff to provide feedback on their own performance. The ESLA team was told that this type of leadership also gave the staff a tremendous opportunity to explore, improvise, and learn.

The ESLA researchers also were given examples of team leaders who motivated people and built trust by providing every opportunity for their personal and professional development. These leaders were able to motivate people in order to bring the best out of team members and to achieve results. Additional methods of team motivation that were observed included celebrating individual and team achievements, and always looking for something positive to say about each team member.

Figure 2. Structured social learning architecture

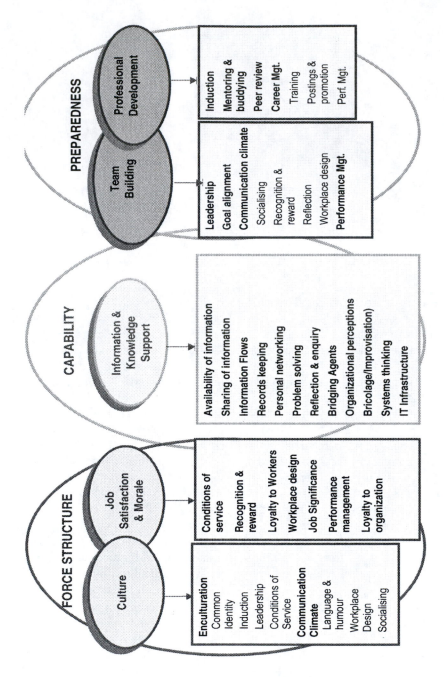

Figure 3. The role of trust in organizations

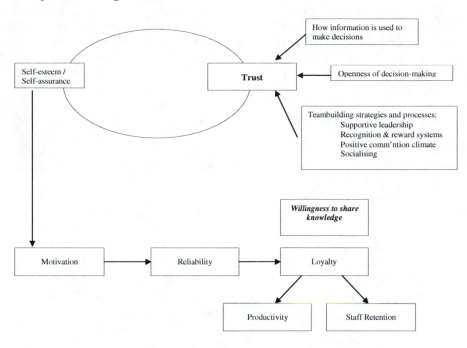

Leaders of successful teams were able to set realistic expectations of their team. Numerous staff interviewed said that knowing what their leaders are expecting of them is one of the most important factors for successful teamwork because it allowed the team to have achievable goals. Furthermore, staff were constantly kept informed and in the loop by e-mails, drop-ins, and meetings. In many cases, at the onset of a new posting, leaders were forthcoming with their vision and expectations of the team, as is indicated by the following:

...the first day he started, he sat us all down in a big meeting for about two and a half hours and he said this is what I expect of you and he had the white-board out and then we could let him know what we expected of him and it was a good way to start.

However, this practice was not prevalent throughout all the settings under study. The survey data points out that 58% of respondents in one of the settings felt that their supervisors did not communicate their expectations of day-to-day work requirements well. This breakdown in communications, along with a lack of transparency in decision-making processes, became a fertile breeding ground for organizational politics and low morale and subsequently diminished opportunities for social learning.

The interview data and the survey data clearly indicated that good communication skills were considered to be one of the most valued factors of effective leadership, as stated by one of the informants:

...if I pick on three things, I'd say communication skills, observation skills, you know your ability to observe and to take in data, and then also a bit of a brain on your head so you can make sensible decisions, on the basis of that.

In most instances, staff spoke very highly about their leaders, and 83% felt that in their team good leadership enhanced teamwork; however, the ESLA team was made aware that:

...some of the people we have in positions of authority don't have a schmick about manpower management, they really don't. Some are good, I mean it's not a manual skill, it's an emotional skill.

The power of positive feedback, recognition, and reward cannot be overemphasized, not only for building a team's performance but also for the building of trust. This recognition must apply not only to big tough jobs but equally to quiet, unassuming day-to-day tasks. Mitchell (2000) points out that making employees feel appreciated, focusing attention on their good ideas, inviting them to extend themselves, and saying "thank you, we know that you are a good employee, we value you and your work," is a big factor in motivation. A positive self-image and self-confidence is one of the early steps toward effective motivation. A person who feels motivated and feels good about himself or herself acts with confidence. Individuals empower themselves by receiving positive feedback and add to the empowerment of others when recognition is given freely (Katzenback & Smith, 1993).

A lack of day-to-day recognition of one's work came through very strongly as an issue. The research data indicated that recognition of one's achievements and good work was well established in some teams; however, this practice was not widespread throughout all the settings studied. In some units, the managers used recognition and praise as an empowering tool within their teams; however, the same managers were often not recognized themselves, by their own superiors.

[Recognition] it's something that your boss says to you each day, saying, 'Jeez, that piece of writing was really good, mate. You did a great job there.' It's that sort of mentality that we have to get through to our senior managers...

Most of the respondents (86%) indicated that recognition comes foremost from their immediate team members and 62% said that their supervisors always acknowledge their positive contributions at work. The researchers were told that in some teams there are special celebrations once an important piece of work is satisfactorily completed or milestones are reached. Such celebrations reinforce for workers that their efforts are valuable to the team's functions and products. It is clear that the benefits of recognition and reward flow in two directions, on one side there is a benefit for the individual and their willingness to share knowledge, and on the other, the supervisors are gaining respect and trust from their staff. The following quote depicts this:

...the flow on effect of that [recognition] is that the rest of the group say, 'Hey gees, you know, yeah she has done a good job. Yes and she's been recognized for it. Yeah. It's not such a bad group that we were working for.' And the flow on to me is they see that I care, as a supervisor, and I'm prepared to recognize good work. But culturally—culturally we don't put the importance on this, I think, that we should...

The research data strongly indicates that socializing plays an important role in trust building and social learning. The aspect of "feeling good" about work colleagues is an important motivating factor and a factor contributing to building trust amongst employees and, again, their willingness to share knowledge. Maslow's theory of motivation identifies a sense of belonging to a group and getting to know each other as a vital step in the life of a team and in achieving set goals. As they get to know each other, the team members derive satisfaction from belonging to a cohesive team, but more importantly, they become aware of each other's strengths and weaknesses, what they can or cannot do, their expertise and experience. This knowledge facilitates utilizing each team member to their full potential.

The respondents indicated that work-related social activities led to a greater sense of team spirit (85%). These social activities were not just frivolous functions; they were core activities that were ultimately task oriented. As one of the respondents put it:

...it is important and we do, we have time out where we go for coffee and to chat, it's team building and getting to know each other, and I think that's really important because you need to get to know the personalities on your team....We talk about work things when we're having coffee, but it's joking and fun.

Scholars use the term *social capital* to refer to human relationships that make organizations work effectively. Healthy social relationships in organizations build trust, make people learn faster and be more productive and creative (Prusak & Cohen, 2001). However, building successful social relationships in organizations during times of constant change, staff shortages, and pressure to deliver with fewer resources is extremely difficult.

...People in the headquarters need to let off steam, so if everybody was just working constantly five days a week with no let-up, you know, you'd start to get cracks in the organization. So people do appreciate it, [socializing] you know, when it happens...

The ESLA research data indicates that social activities lead to greater team cohesion and enhanced team morale. Informal social gatherings allow people to get to know each other, build trust and stronger relationships, and (more importantly) share knowledge. Many interviewees stated that during such informal social gatherings they learn more about what is happening in other units in the organization than through formal channels.

CONCLUSION

Social learning requires individuals to be willing to share their knowledge and to be willing to voice their ideas. In this way, shared knowledge empowers not only the individual, but also the team and the organization as a whole.

The ELSA research findings indicate that the requisite cohesion and commitment arises from effective leadership, transparency in decision-making and communication, appropriate reward and recognition, socializing, and commitment to a common goal. However, trust appears to be an overriding requirement, one that provides the glue that binds these processes and strategies for effective social learning and building of corporate knowledge. Knowledge sharing cannot be mandated, it must occur willingly. It is for this reason that trust must underpin the team building behaviors and attitudes that result in the confidence and cohesion needed to openly share knowledge, construct new knowledge, and build stronger organizations.

The implications of the research are that organizations seeking to improve information sharing and knowledge generation need to develop a greater awareness of the processes and strategies of organizational learning. Organizational knowledge is distributed across functional groups and its generation and continual existence is dependent on the overall organizational culture. This study indicates that information sharing and subsequent knowledge generation would be successful when interactive environments are cultivated before other solutions are implemented, particularly those based on technology alone.

REFERENCES

Ali, I., Pascoe, C., & Warne, L. (2002). Interactions of organizational culture and collaboration in working and learning. *Educational Technology and Society, 5*(2), 60-69.

Ali, I., Warne, L., Agostino, K., & Pascoe, C. (2001, June 19-22). Working and learning together: Social learning in the Australian Defence Organization. *Informing Science Conference IS2001—Bridging Diverse Disciplines Proceedings (CD-ROM)*, Krakow, Krakow University of Economics, Poland.

Bednar, P. (2000). A contextual integration of individual and organizational learning perspectives as part of IS analysis. *Informing Science, 3*(3), 145-156.

Costigan, R.D., Itler, S.S., & Breman, J.J. (1998). A multi-dimensional study of trust in organizations. *Journal of Management Issue, 10*(3), 303-317.

Davenport, T.H. (1994). Saving IT's soul: Human-centered information management. *Harvard Business Review,* March-April.

Davenport, T.H., & Prusack, L. (1998). *Working knowledge: How organizations manage what they know.* MA: Harvard Business School Press.

Jordan, B. (1993). *Ethnographic workplace studies and computer supported co-operative work.* Interdisciplinary Workshop on Informatics and Psychology. Scharding, Austria.

Kazenback, J.R., & Smith, D.K. (1993). The discipline of teams. *Harvard Business Review,* March-April, 111-120.

Kramer, R.M., & Tyler, T.R. (1995). *Trust in organizations, frontiers of theory and research.* Sage Publications.

Mayer, R.C., Davis, J.H., & Schoorman E.D. (1995). An integrative model of organizational trust. *Academy of Management Journal, 20*(3), 709-734.

Mitchell, S. (2000). *Be bold and discover the power of praise.* East Roseville: Simon & Schuster.

Oldham, G.R., & Cummings, A. (1996). Employee creativity: Personal and contextual factors at work. *Academy of Management Journal, 39*(3), 607-635.

Phillips, R.A. (1997). A stakeholder theory and principle of fairness. *Business Ethics Journal, 7*(1), 51-66.

Prusak, L., & Cohen, D. (2001). How to invest in social capital. *Harvard Business Review,* June, 86-93.

Ruppel, P.C., & Harrington, S.J. (2000). The relationship of communication, ethical work climate, and trust to commitment and innovation. *Journal of Business Ethics, 25,* 313-328.

Schein, E.H. (1993). Organizational culture and leadership. *Organizational Dynamics, 22*(2), 40-51.

Vandeville, J. (2000). Organizational learning through the collection of 'Lessons Learned.' *Informing Science, 3*(3), 127-133.

Warne, L. Ali, I., & Pascoe, C. (2002). Sharing knowledge through effective team building: Trust vs. the information power dynamic. *Proceedings of the Australian Conference for Knowledge Management and Intelligent Decision Support,* In F. Burstein & H. Linger (Eds.), Melbourne, (pp. 73-85).

Warne, L., Ali, I., & Pascoe, C. (2003). *Social learning and knowledge management: A journey through the Australian Defence Organization: The final report of the enterprise social learning architectures task,* DSTO-RR-0257, AR 012-854, Defence Systems Analysis Division, DSTO Information Sciences Laboratories, South Australia.

Webber, A.M. (1993). What's so new about the new economy? *Harvard Business Review*, January/February, 24-42.

KEY TERMS

Communication Climate: Extent to which there is an open and free exchange of information, transparency of decision-making, and conflict is constructively managed.

Knowledge: An understanding gained through experience or learning—the sum, or a subset, of what has been perceived and discovered by an individual. Knowledge exists in the minds of individuals and is generated and shaped through interaction with others.

Knowledge Management: In an organizational setting, it must, *at the very least*, be about how knowledge is acquired, constructed, transferred, and otherwise shared with other members of the organization, in a way that seeks to achieve the organization's objectives.

Social Capital: Human relationships that make organizations work effectively.

Social Learning: Learning occurring in or by a cultural cluster and including procedures for transmitting knowledge and practices across different work situations/settings and time.

Social Learning Enablers: Organizational processes and strategies that, if present and effectively applied in an enterprise, can facilitate social learning.

Systemic Understanding: A holistic view of an organization and its inter-relationships, an understanding of the fabric of relationships and the likely effect of interrelated actions.

Learning Networks and Service-Oriented Architectures

George Tsekouras
University of Brighton, UK

George Roussos
University of London, UK

INTRODUCTION

The value of knowledge assets in creating competitive advantage and subsequently wealth through innovation has never been greater (Teece, 1998). It is increasingly being acknowledged that the resources and the competencies developed within the organisation as well as the mechanisms for building up and reconfiguring these competencies is the only defence against a fierce competition (Penrose, 1959; Prahalad & Hamel, 1990; Teece, Pisano & Shuen, 1997). However, the nature of knowledge production has changed dramatically over the last years. According to Gibbons et al. (1994), the knowledge production has moved from mode 1 to mode 2. The new mode:

- requires transdisciplinary approaches
- is characterised by heterogeneity of skills
- is context-sensitive involving an intense interaction between producers and users of knowledge

The highly complex and rapidly changing character of contemporary knowledge production makes it almost impossible for single organisations to acquire the full set of required skills. Even large corporations with abundant resources need to turn to other organisations in order to cope with new knowledge requirements. Learning through networking with other firms gives the opportunity not only to share expenses and resources, but more significantly, to listen to new ideas, challenge one's own inherent assumptions, and embrace new perspectives.

The challenge associated with this is to set up an infrastructure to support shared learning and reflection on a regular and sustainable basis. To answer this problem, the mechanism of the so-called learning networks (LN) has been introduced. Learning networks do not refer to networks of organisations where learning simply happens—as is the case with every network—but to interorganisational networks where structures have been established with the primary purpose of increasing the participants' knowledge. These networks:

- involve representatives of different organisations, mainly but not exclusively, private firms
- are formally established with clear and defined boundaries for participation
- have an explicit structure for operation with regular processes that can be mapped to the learning cycle
- have a primary learning target—some specific learning/knowledge which the network is going to enable
- can assess the learning outcomes which feed back to the operation of the network.

The formal character of the network provides an institutionalised organisational platform which represents a permanent structure for identifying knowledge gaps and satisfying knowledge needs, allows evaluation, and accumulates experience regarding the support required by learners. More significantly, the lasting character of membership in learning networks facilitates the development of trust relationships among learners.

Information technology can play a critical role in supporting LNs. Yet, the majority of current KM systems have been designed under the assumption that they will be used within a single organisation or that a single organisation will be responsible for their operation. KM systems appropriate for interorganisational use dictates that several challenges are met. For example, interorganisational information systems must not only provide reliable infrastructures for the organisation itself but also must be capable of sharing resources seamlessly within their network of learning partnerships. These operating conditions demand that such systems are both flexible and operate transparently. Over the past few years, service-oriented architectures have emerged as a framework that addresses this requirement both effectively and efficiently. In this article, we discuss the current use of Web-based service architectures to support LNs and then outline future trends.

BACKGROUND

The new rules of competition (Teece, 1998) have demanded from organisations to build a concrete strategy for learning and continuous change (Argyris & Schon, 1996). Initially, loads of competent tutors and specialised trainers stormed the companies and apparently their resources, delivering high-quality training courses and material. It was only when Orr (1990a, 1990b) observed technicians in Xerox that it was realized that real value learning is intrinsically blended with communities which:

- make their own decisions
- practice the acquired knowledge
- improvise their approaches

In a similar vein, Lave and Wenger (1991) have talked of situated learning—learning that is intrinsically linked to the environment where it is situated—while Cook and Brown (1999) regard organisational learning governed by *epistemology of practice* rather than *epistemology of possession* (i.e., knowledge is fundamentally associated with practice and cannot be transferred as a commodity). These contributions have made Stamps (2000) wonder whether "learning is social [and] training is irrelevant" and Wenger (1998, 2000) suggest that real value learning can only happen in "communities of practice." Behind all these approaches, there is the notion that knowledge management cannot be separated from the tacit knowledge (Polanyi, 1966), that is, the knowledge we possess but we cannot tell. Nonaka and Takeuchi (1995) observed the process of knowledge creation within an organisation to conclude that knowledge is generated by regular exchanges between tacit and explicit knowledge. Tsoukas (2002) argues that tacit knowledge cannot be translated or converted into explicit knowledge:

We cannot operationalise tacit knowledge but we can find new ways of talking, fresh forms of interacting and novel ways of distinguishing and connecting...New knowledge comes about...when our skilled performance is punctuated in new ways through social interaction.

Meanwhile, a variety of scholars and policymakers have noticed the phenomenal success of *clusters of different companies*. Becattini (1989, 1990) described the Italian experience where networks of small firms and other institutions have helped certain regions to achieve one of the highest rates of economic development and one of the lowest rates of unemployment in Europe. Several case studies point to the same conclusion: Southern Germany, South-West Belgium, Northern Denmark, M4 corridor in UK, Silicon Valley in California (Sengenberger & Pyke, 1990; Saxenian, 1991). Even in less developed economies like Brazil and Pakistan, the collective efficiency developed within clusters has phenomenal results (Bessant & Tsekouras, 2001). It is becoming clear that simple factors such as proximity do not, of themselves, explain the success of clustering. Humphrey and Schmitz identify the importance of developing trust relations, whilst Sengenberger and Pyke (1992) point out the readiness amongst firms for cooperation which help the firms to build shared learning mechanisms.

Building on the understanding developed in the two areas, a new approach has been developed to combine the virtues of both. More specifically, it was realised that significant knowledge benefits can be captured *when communities of practice develop across firms boundaries*, sharing experiences from their organisations. Using the mechanism of learning networks, practitioners groups are set up to reflect collectively and learn from each other, following a number of principles:

- Firms[1], represented by managers, are allocated in small groups with up to 20 members
- All necessary decisions for learning are made by the learners themselves rather than experts and tutors
- Learning is practical and derives from the discussion of the concrete experience of the group members rather than the introduction of abstract concepts
- Part of the participants duties is to go to their own organisations, try out the learned approaches, come back to the group, and report their experience
- The group becomes a forum for sharing concerns, get psychological support, but also receive feedback on their own ideas from other practitioners
- Experts and tutors may be invited occasionally, only when needed
- Knowledge resources are used but only in conjunction with their practical learning

Of course, knowledge interactions between different firms is not a new phenomenon (Nonaka & Takeuchi, 1995; Von Hippel, 1988). The challenge presented to learning networks was to develop the managerial capabilities required for sustaining and improvising these activities on a long-term basis[2]. In other words, the challenge for learning networks is to develop the organisational processes and the managerial capabilities which allow the systematic emergence and development of communities of practice between different firms. A critical enabler of this strategy is the appointment of a specially dedicated *facilitator* to assist the group's practitioners in their structured reflection. The facilitators have gone through special training (e.g., how to enhance group dynamics, how to tackle disagreement between members) and accumulate relevant experience over time. The learning groups receive further support by the network, that is, a wider organisation which includes all group members as well as those which are not in any group at a certain time. The network has its Managing Director, usually called *the Network Moderator,* who is responsible for providing a common ground for all different groups operating at a time, ensuring the interface between them and the cross-fertilisation of their experience.

The so-called learning networks range from networks focusing on:

- single issues (e.g., the British Quality Foundation)
- particular sectors (e.g., Industry Forum by the Society of Motor Manufacturers and Traders, CIRIA for the construction industry in UK)
- specific regions and particular sectors (e.g., AC Styria for the automotive sector in the Austrian region of Styria)
- specific regions without any sector or topic focus (e.g., Plato network in Ireland)

The benefits of the learning network approach is obvious for SMEs because it gives them a permanent forum for obtaining knowledge in an inexpensive way. Convinced by the advantages of the approach, multinational enterprises have also adopted the concept in three forms:

- internal learning networks between different units or departments of the enterprise, sometimes located in different parts of the world (e.g., Black & Decker)
- joint learning networks among themselves and their suppliers (e.g., the suppliers clubs in TOYOTA / Bessant et al., 2003)
- inter-corporations learning networks among the main players of a sector to share ideas, reflect jointly, and exchange good practices (e.g., SCRIA in the aerospace industry and CRINE in the energy sector in UK)

The potential of KM systems can contribute significantly to the improvement of the learning network processes. On one hand, the innovative scheme of learning networks represents a unique opportunity for KM systems to offer added value to businesses and their managers. Time after time, systems developers discover that successful and cost-effective design of information systems require a combination of theory and practical experience as well as dynamic and proven organisational designs which the information architectures can match.[3] A good match between the information systems and the organisational layout can speed up the development process, reduce costs, increase productivity, improve the quality of software, and more significantly increase the relevance of KM systems to users. The next section reviews the value added that KM systems can offer to learning networks and their members.

PORTAL SERVICE ARCHITECTURES FOR LEARNING NETWORKS

Learning networks face the challenge of increasing the level and the knowledge-intensity of interaction among their members while at the same time they want to shorten the cycle of formation, trust development and knowledge sharing within groups. In order to do so, they have to improve their organisational processes that support directly or indirectly the knowledge interactions between the members. These processes include the decision-making, collaborative learning, and dissemination of and harvesting knowledge. Traditionally, all learning network processes were carried out primarily through physical meetings. This imposed significant limitations to the network activities due to severe time and travelling restrictions. For instance, if a manager-member of a group missed a session, he or she could not make up for it while the communication with other group fellows, the group facilitator, or even the network moderator was limited to the times of actual meetings.

The development of Web-based information systems gave the opportunity to learning networks to:

- facilitate planning and management of learning activities, including the decision-making for a number of issues such as the focus of learning, the strategic direction of the network, and so forth
- enhance communication and informal knowledge sharing among the network members
- support organisation of and access to network resources including learning material and "members details and photos" of other network fellows[4]
- facilitate the knowledge dissemination to the organisations of the firms represented in a group, namely the managers not participating to a group

Most often such activities are supported via a portal operated by the network broker. The network moderator and the group facilitators are ultimately responsible for the content, although virtual interactions such as net meetings and asynchronous communications are encouraged among the network and group members. Needless to say, implementation of a Web-based system does not automatically solve all the problems and the cautious reader should keep in mind the multitude of problems related to the architecture and deployment of IT in any organisational context.

The economics of rolling-out, populating with content, and maintaining such portals are more complex. Three distinguishing strategies have been identified (Tsekouras et al., 2004). Firstly, *the liberal approach*, where a general support effort is assumed by the broker to "have the ball rolling" in different areas. The broker's effort is rather limited and hopes to see the main initiative—and therefore its cost—undertaken by the network members.

Second is the catalytic intervention strategy, similar to what is called *the "Clinton approach"* (Greenstein, 2000). This strategy consists of very focused intervention by the broker, who therefore undertakes limited effort to roll out the system. The broker uses its intelligence to identify the critical, for its network, portal areas, and concentrates all its efforts to these areas. This strategy is definitely more intelligent than the liberal approach, but it also carries a significant higher risk since it puts "all its eggs in one basket."

Finally, *the heavyweight strategy* is where the network moderator is very active in uploading resources, updating the portal with the forthcoming events and learning sessions, filling in the personal details of the network members, and so forth. This incurred the broker a heavy cost in terms of days of work which is undertaken with the hope of high return on investment. This strategy is the most resource-intensive but also the less risky one. However, it requires the broker to be absolutely convinced for the potential benefits.

On the demand side, three generic patterns of usage have been identified regarding the practitioners-members of the network. The first pattern is reading in connection with *the networks conventional activities namely physical learning sessions and events*. The primary objective of this behaviour is to get prepared for or remembered of the organised sessions of the network, most of which are—at least currently—physical meetings.

The second pattern aims to *improve the communication with the network broker in order to exploit his cognitive capability and accumulated experience to direct their own learning*. In this pattern, the network members rely on the brokers' capability to direct them to useful news, new learning developments, and new sources of knowledge in order to update their knowledge and their own skills.

The third pattern is the one with the objective of bringing *the learners-network members directly in touch with other fellow members or experts* in order to learn from them. This virtual and direct transfer of knowledge can happen either in association with an actual meeting or on its own merit—as is the case with the virtual sessions at predefined times.

Despite the significant enhancement of the learning network processes by the LN portal, careful study reveals a broad set of challenges still unresolved by these systems. Although current Web technologies have provided the means for extensive electronic interaction between the network members, the sharing of information and knowledge resources must always go through the central network portal, creating a number of economic or cognitive bottlenecks. Indeed, before a network member can access network information or resources, a person must identify the relevant information or resource, seek the licence from the owner of the relevant information to share it in the network, upload the content in the network portal, and dispatch a notification to network members to alert them to the relevant update.

Carrying out these activities in full requires that considerable resources be consumed. Hence, the most effective strategy for increasing the knowledge-intensive interactions between the members is not necessarily the most efficient one from the resources point of view—what is called the heavyweight approach. Moreover, although individual organisations willingly participate in network exchanges, they remain independent and they want to keep control of their own resources. In other words, organisation's members may accept to share access to part of their own resources with other organisations' members but it is unlikely to consent to pass ownership of these resources to the network broker or other network members.

Third, in distributed computing systems the only trusted party to carry out the required steps is the network brokers, namely the network moderator or the group facilitators. However, the network brokers face significant cognitive limitations. For instance, it is almost impossible for the brokers to be aware of the full set of available knowledge resources existing in different members; even if he or she was, he or she would not be able to review, select, and disseminate all these resources on his or her own.

Finally, as the network grows, the brokers find it increasingly difficult to cope with the escalating responsibilities and demands of their tasks. As a result, the network should move from a "solar configuration" where the broker is the central node of interaction to a "spider web configuration." This configuration presupposes intelligent brokers, concentrating on the most critical aspects of learning networks such as building trust, resolving conflicts, and removing barriers, with the network members turning into active nodes of interaction and learning.

In short, while Web technologies have provided the means for extensive electronic interactions between network members, such interactions are significantly limited by financial and cognitive factors. In consequence, such interactions rarely go beyond the simple exchange of information. In the following section, we discuss how the emerging next generation service architectures can potentially help overcome these restrictions flexibly and transparently.

FUTURE TRENDS

Service-oriented architecture (SOA) (Stojanovic & Dahanayake, 2003) shifts the emphasis of information systems design from particular applications and application development frameworks toward well-defined and self-contained elements of functionality that do not depend on external context or state. Thus, systems are constructed by linking together services as needed so as to achieve specific goals. The value of SOA lies in the fact that it can effectively abstract enterprise architectures using the concept of the so-called Service Bus, that is, a shared communications medium on which services may connect to and use in a plug-and-play manner.

In particular, in the case of highly decentralized, heterogeneous, and geographically distributed systems, SOA offers distinct advantages. In this context, SOA can help develop systems: that are scalable and can cater to large numbers of ever-changing users; that are trustworthy so as to protect confidential information; and last but not least, that are not constrained in terms of the particular technical choices. In particular, heterogeneity and distribution imply that there are frequent non-trivial issues regarding synchronization and concurrency as well as compatibility. To address these issues, numerous frameworks have been developed over the past decades, which employ middleware services and may rely heavily on reusable code and design patterns. Such frameworks need to address multiple issues including efficient and effective handling of remote processes, data, and input/output; naming; brokering, trading, and leasing resources; multiple levels of software abstractions; multiple attributes; security and trust management; threading and synchronization; and, finally, distributed transaction processing. In this context, SOA provides a novel solution which offers a significant advantage over all other solutions, namely its conceptual simplicity.

In the context of learning networks, SOA fulfils well a number of core requirements:

- Individual organisations can participate in a SOA by offering their resources to other network members without sacrificing control. In fact, they can define their own security policies and trust relationships and enforce them at the service level.
- Brokering and mediation bottlenecks can be readily bypassed, thus removing the information management limitations of the portal approach. In fact, relationships can be developed bilaterally in a peer-to-peer manner.
- Networks become scalable with additional members joining without unbalancing the existing relationships and systems. Moreover, network configurations can evolve in time and change with the topology of partner relationships without disturbing the established relationships of knowledge sharing.
- Different types of resources can be made available under the same service-based interface. For example, structured and unstructured information as well as computational resources can be made readily available under the common interaction paradigm of a service interface.
- Finally, it becomes possible to integrate the resources and process of the learning network to the internal workings of the network members as appropriate. Use of the services is automated and thus less manual effort is required in updating and maintaining resources.

Different technologies can be used to develop SOA. Currently, two candidates seem to attract most interest, namely Web services and the Grid. A Web service is a software system identified by its location on the World Wide Web and whose interface and supported modes of interaction are described using XML. The use of XML-based technologies, including the Universal Description, Discovery and Integration Protocol, and the Web Services Description Language, allow other systems to discover and use the service transparently as well as adapt their operation to meet its requirements. Interaction between systems using the Web service is also carried out using XML messages transferred over the Internet. Web services allow for the loose integration of service components and have the distinct advantage of employing widely available and standardised Web technologies.

Using Web Services, we can develop learning network infrastructures for controlled but open resource sharing especially where we have to deal with well-defined and possibly structured knowledge sources. For example, the case of the spider model architecture can be directly translated into a Web-based distributed and decentralised infrastructure, where network partners are in control of their own resources and are given discretionary access to resources of other members.

Often, the functionality offered by Web services does not fulfil all the requirements of a specific situation. In this case, a set of technologies that have become known as the Grid can be used to provide tighter coupling.

The Grid (Foster & Kesselman, 2003) is an umbrella term used to refer to a selection of technologies, protocols, services, application programming interfaces, software development kits, and turnkey systems to support coordinated resource sharing and problem-solving in dynamic, multi-institutional, virtual organisations. Although the Grid was initially focused primarily on advanced distributed supercomputing applications with emphasis on extreme computational power and data storage, today it commonly includes major technology trends, such as Internet, enterprise, distributed, and peer-to-peer computing to address much more mainstream situations. Indeed, resource sharing supported by the Grid can cater for process building through direct access to computers, software, data, and other resources, as is required by a range of collaborative problem-solving and resource brokering strategies. This type of sharing and collaborative learning is highly controlled, with resource providers and consumers defining clearly and carefully just what is shared, who is allowed to share, and the conditions under which sharing occurs. A set of individuals and/or institutions defined by such sharing rules form what is referred to in Grid parlance as a virtual organisation.

An early example of the use of SOA to support LNs can be observed in the Bloomsbury Bioinformatics Consortium (Orengo, Jones, & Thornton, 2003). This LN brings together researchers and practitioners in institutes located in the Bloomsbury of London with the common aim of developing innovative bioinformatics solutions for the medical industry. Interorganisational learning is assisted by the operation of a network infrastructure developed on the peer-to-peer Grid model, which allows for sophisticated levels of control over shared resources. Moreover, sharing of resources can be carried out in a cost-sensitive manner while embracing issues of quality of service, scheduling, co-allocation, and accounting. Finally, learning resources are annotated following a scheme which is uniform and representative of the particular learning network structure. To this end, the Consortium employs Semantic Web technologies, namely the Resource Description Framework, to describe themes and relationships between the different elements. Development of domain-specific ontologies is seen as a key element for collaborative relationships.

CONCLUSION

The blending of action learning with the network approach has produced a very powerful mechanism for sharing knowledge between different organisations, what has become known more widely as learning networks. This has generated unique results of learning and upgrading not only in terms of the skills of the involved individuals but also in terms of the processes of the relevant organisations. However, physical and practical constraints have limited the amount and the quality of the knowledge interactions among the members of the network. The first generation of Web technologies have enabled virtual and thus more convenient and longer lasting communication with other network partners as well as the network moderator and facilitators. The Web-based information systems also have given network members the opportunity to share resources through a centralised portal. However, these systems request major resource investment from the network brokers, generating a new set of constrains mainly related to the cognitive and practical limitations of the broker. In addition, these systems could not resolve the critical issues of efficient accumulation and ownership of the network resources.

The service-oriented architecture offers the opportunity to tackle these issues in an efficient and transparent way. Sharing of resources is feasible without losing the ownership rights, while the network brokers have to define the rules of sharing rather than collecting and disseminating the resources. The biggest advantage of these solutions is that they enable the transformation of learning networks from a solar broker-critical configuration to a spider web open resource configuration, allowing the flexible development of bipolar knowledge interactions without disturbing the overall balance of the system. Yet, the issues associated with the implementation of these new technologies need to be thoughtfully deliberated and carefully resolved.

REFERENCES

Argyris, C., & Schon, D. (1996). *Organisational learning II* Addison-Wesley.

Beamish, N.G., & Armistead, C.G. (2001). Selected debate from the arena of knowledge management: New endorsements for established organizational practices. *International Journal of Management Reviews, 3*(2), 101-111.

Becattini, G. (1989). Sectors and/or districts: Some remarks on the conceptual foundations of industrial economics. In E. Goodman & J. Bamford (Eds.), *Small firms and industrial districts in Italy.* London: Routledge.

Becattini, G. (1990). The Marshallian industrial district as a socio-economic notion. In F. Pyke, G. Becattini & W. Sengenberger (Eds.), *Industrial districts and inter-firm cooperation in Italy.* International Institute for Labour Studies, Geneva.

Bessant, J., Kaplinsky, R., & Lamming, K. (2003). Putting supply chain learning into practice. *International Journal of Operations & Production Management, 23*(2), 167-184.

Bessant, J., & Rush, H. (1995). Building bridges for innovation: The role of consultants in technology transfer. *Research Policy, 24,* 97-114.

Bessant, J., & Tsekouras G. (2001). Developing learning networks. *A.I. & Society, Special Issue on Networking, 15,* 82-98.

Best, M. (1990). *The new competition.* Oxford, UK: Polity Press.

Buchel, B., & Raub S., (2002). Building knowledge-creating value networks. *European Management Journal, 20* (6), 587-596.

Burner, M. (2003). The deliberate revolution: Transforming integration with XML Web services. *ACM Queue, 1*(1), 12-20.

Cook, S.D., & Brown, J.S (1999). Bridging epistemologies: The generative dance between organizational knowledge and organizational knowing. *Organization Science, 10*(4), July-August, 381-400.

Foster, I., & Kesselman, C. (2003). *The grid: Blueprint for a new computing infrastructure.* Morgan Kaufmann.

Gibbons, M., Limoges, C., Nowotny, H., Schwartzman, S., Scott, P., & Trow, M. (1994) *The new production of knowledge: Science and research in contemporary societies.* London: Sage.

Greenstein, F. (2000). *The presidential difference: Leadership style from Roosevelt to Clinton.* Martin Kessier books, Free Press.

Humphrey, J., & Schmitz, H. (1996). The triple C approach to local industrial policy. *World Develoment, 24*(12), 1859-1872.

Lave J., & Wenger, E. (1991). *Situated learning: Legitimate peripheral participation.* Cambridge: Cambridge University Press.

Leonard-Barton, D. (1995). *Wellsprings of knowledge.* Boston: Harvard Business School Press.

McDermott, R. (1999). Why information technology inspired but cannot deliver knowledge management. *California Management Review, 41*(4), 103-117.

Monday, P.B. (2003). *Web services patterns: Java Edition.* New York: Academic Press.

Nonaka, I., & Takeuchi, H. (1995). *The knowledge creating company.* New York: Oxford University Press.

Orengo, C.A., Jones, D.T., & Thornton, J.M. (2003). *Genes, proteins and computers.* BIOS Scientific Publishers.

Orr, J. (1990a). *Talking about machines: An ethnography of a modern job.* Doctoral thesis, Cornell University.

Orr, J. (1990b). Sharing knowledge, celebrating identity: War stories and community memory in a service culture. In D.S. Middleton & D. Edwards (Eds.), *Collective remembering: Memory in society.* Beverly Hills, CA: Sage Publications.

Penrose, E. (1959). *Theory of the growth of the firm.* New York: John Wiley & Sons.

Polanyi, M. (1966). *The tacit dimension.* London: Routledge & Keegan Paul.

Prahalad, C., & Hamel, G. (1990). The core competence of the corporation. *Harvard Business Review*, May-June, 79-91.

Saxenian, A. (1991). The origins and dynamics of production networks in Silicon Valley. *Research Policy, 20.*

Schmitz, H., (1995). Collective efficiency: Growth path for small-scale industry. *Journal of Development Studies, 31*(4), 529-566.

Sengenberger, W., & Pyke, F. (1992). Industrial districts and local economic regeneration: research and policy issues. In F. Pyke & W. Sengenberger (Eds.), *Industrial districts and local economic regeneration* (pp. 1-30). International Institute for Labour Studies, Geneva.

Stamps, D. (2000). Communities of practice: Learning is social. Training is irrelevant. In E. Lesser, M. Fontaine, J. Slusher, (Eds.), *Knowledge and communities* (pp. 53-64). Butterworth-Heinemann.

Stojanovic, Z., & Dahanayake, A. (2004). *Service-oriented software system engineering: Challenges and practices.* Hershey, PA: Idea Group Publishing.

Teece, D. (1998). Capturing value for knowledge assets: The new economy, markets for know-how, and intagible know-how and intangible assets. *California Management Review, 40*(3), Spring, 55-79.

Teece, D., Pisano, G., & Shuen, A. (1997). Dynamic capabilities and strategic management. *Strategic Management Journal, 18,* 509-33.

Tsekouras, G., Swift, G., Coughlan, C., Berry, M., Steiner, G., & Sochos, A. (2004). *Final evaluation report.* Knowlaboration Project, IST-2001-32505, EU, Luxembourg.

Tsoukas, H. (2002). Do we really understand tacit knowledge? In M. Easterby-Smith & M.A. Lyles (Eds.), *Handbook of organizational learning and knowledge.* Blackwell.

Von Hippel, E. (1988). *The sources of innovation.* Oxford: Oxford University Press.

Wenger, E. (1998). Communities of practice: The key to knowledge strategy. In E. Lesser, M. Fontaine, & J. Slusher (Eds.), *Knowledge and communities* (pp. 3-20). Butterworth-Heinemann.

Wenger E., & Snyder W. (2000). Communities of practice: The organisational frontier. *Harvard Business Review,* Jan-Feb, 139-145.

KEY TERMS

The Learning Network Facilitators: The network managers who are responsible for running the network processes on the ground such as network sessions, workshops, visits, and so forth etc. Their role is far from being tutors or experts to teach network members new knowledge. More specifically, the facilitators organise the practical aspects of networking (e.g., venue, dates), ease the learning process of the managers who participate in the network sessions, and unblock the change management process in their organisations. Their job requires strong inter-personal skills and a competence in tackling the human aspects of learning and change.

The Learning Network Members: The primary *clients* of learning networks; the term refers to all managers and practitioners who are in the network in order to acquire new knowledge. They are supposed to act as company representatives rather than as individuals, although during the course of shared learning they have to make decisions on their own. In some cases, especially when their organisation is a large company, they also assume the role of the liaison officers in the sense of connecting various individuals and departments within the organisation with discussions and learning within the network.

The Learning Network Moderator: (Also called *Network co-ordinator, or Network broker,* this) is the Managing Director of the network . The Network Moderator deals with the strategic decisions of the network (e.g., learning focus, selection criteria for accepting members, etc.) and plays a bridging role between the network members and the Network Board. The Network Moderator is the person who monitors the activities of the network facilitators, engages in nurturing, and disciplinary behaviour. He/she is also responsible for maintaining a database of speakers and facilitators for the network, promoting and publishing the activities of the network.

Learning Network Referral Procedure: Refers to the procedure by which new organisations-members are recruited for Learning Networks. The central feature of this procedure is that it uses existing members and their industrial and social relationships in order to recruit new members. Learning networks use the social networks of existing members, to spread the word about the network, attract interest to its activities, or even recruit new members. Existing network members also can also refer to the network when they face problems with other collaborating or supplying companies.

Learning Networks: Inter-organisational networks where structures have been established with the primary purpose of increasing the participants' knowledge. These networks involve representatives of different organisations, mainly, private firms. They are formally established with clear and defined boundaries for participation, and have a explicit structure for operation with regular processes. The outcomes of the network can be fully assessed and evaluated; these results feed back to the network, giving it the opportunity to improvise. A typical structure for a learning network include the Network Moderator, the Network Facilitators, and the Network Members.

The Service-Oriented Architecture: A design pattern for the construction of information systems. Its value lies in the fact that it can abstract enterprise architectures using the concept of the so-called Service Bus, that is, a shared communications medium on which services may connect to and use in a plug-and-play manner. This is the equivalent of a bus in a computer architecture, which provides the foundation for core and peripheral components to connect and communicate transparently with each other. Different internal and external systems may connect to the bus transparently.

Web Services:. A Web service is a software system identified by its location on the World Wide Web, whose interface and supported modes of interaction are described using XML. Interaction between systems using the web Web service also is carried out using XML messages transferred over the Internet. Web services allow for the loose integration of service components and have the distinct advantage of employing widely available and standardised Web technologies.

ENDNOTES

[1] These firms can be even in the same sector, but they should not be direct competitors in the sense of targeting the same market niche.

[2] The effectiveness of communities-based learning has been a concern for managers in intraorganisational context (Buchel & Raub, 2002).

[3] The failure of developers to take sufficiently into account these issues have led to a significant amount of criticism against KM systems (McDermott, 1999; Beamish & Armistead, 2001).

[4] The access to contact information of other network fellows has been acknowledged as a very important contribution by the network members "as we only meet monthly [and] it's handy to refresh memory (face to name)" (Tsekouras et al., 2004).

Legal Knowledge Management

John Zeleznikow
Victoria University, Australia

INTRODUCTION

Legal practice is primarily concerned with the transfer of legal knowledge from practitioners or clients. Whilst lawyers may draft contracts and make representations on behalf of their clients, their primary task is to advise their clients on appropriate remedies and courses of action. Rodríguez Morcón, Pérez García, and Sigüenza Pizarro Rodriguez (2002) claim that a lawyer sells what he knows, often in the form of a document (a contract, an opinion, a report) and much more often in a trial before a court or in a negotiation with a counterpart. Khandelwal and Gottschalk (2003) claim that lawyers can be defined as knowledge workers. They are professionals who have gained knowledge through formal education (explicit) and through learning on the job (tacit).

To carry out their daily work, lawyers also have to manage a great many sources of information. It is important for them to be aware of current changes in legislation and jurisprudence, and to consult books and articles. But it is also necessary to manage the information that is generated from within the practice in the course of lawyers' relationships with their clients. In a law firm's day-to-day work, a mass of information and knowledge is generated which has to be managed efficiently, so that it is easily, quickly. and intuitively accessible whenever it is needed by any of the firm's offices. Rusanow (2003) defines legal knowledge management as the leveraging of the firm's collective wisdom by using systems and processes to support and facilitate the identification, capture, dissemination, and use of the firm's knowledge to meet its business objectives.

We commence by emphasising the difficulty of developing generic legal knowledge management approaches given the multiplicity of different legal systems. We next focus on maintaining legal knowledge using an argumentation-based approach and building legal knowledge-based systems for World Wide Web. Since the goal of the legal process is to avoid litigation, we conclude by discussing how knowledge can be managed to provide Online Dispute Resolution.

BACKGROUND

One of the major difficulties in providing generic legal knowledge management tools is the fact that legal practice is very context dependent. Whilst the laws of gravity are fairly uniform throughout our earth, this is definitely not the case with legal norms. Even within Western Europe, Canada, and the United States, there are distinct legal traditions—namely Common Law and Civil Law.

David and Brierly (1985) note that common law and civil law legal traditions share similar social objectives (individualism, liberalism, and personal rights), and they have in fact been joined in one single family, the *Western law* family, because of this functional similarity. Other countries may have a code of law based upon tribal practice or religious principles.

Even within one country, there may be various modes of legal practice or major regional differences in the way law is practised. For example, in the United States, a state court determines Family Law. Because of the varying legislation between states, lawyers often engage in *forum shopping* to obtain an advantage for their client.

As well as regional differences, the different courts in the same region may rely upon distinct *burdens of proof*—the necessity or duty of affirmatively proving a fact or facts in dispute on an issue raised between the parties in a cause (Black, 1990). Except as otherwise provided by the common law, the burden of proof requires proof by a preponderance of the evidence (or the balance of probabilities). In a criminal case, the government must prove all the elements of the crime beyond a reasonable doubt. Except in cases of tax fraud, the burden of proof in a tax case is generally on the taxpayer.

Hence law is very domain specific. An ontology is an explicit conceptualization of a domain (Gruber, 1995). Legal ontologies represent legal norms and are very significant for developing legal knowledge-based systems on the World Wide Web.

Building generic legal ontologies is not possible. Breuker, Elhag, Petkov, and Winkels (2002) claim that unlike engineering, medicine, or psychology, law is not ontologically founded. They claim law is concerned with constraining and controlling social activities using documented norms. Zeleznikow (2004) conducts an overview of legal ontologies.

CLIME, e-COURT, and FFPOIROT are all legal ontology projects funded by the European Union. Because of the plethora of legal systems in Europe, there is a great need to develop legal ontologies that are applicable across the European Union.

Given the domain specific nature of legal knowledge, and the fact that law firms exploit their legal knowledge for commercial gain, legal knowledge management has often been conducted in-house. Perhaps the one exception to this rule has been legal aid organisations, which provide advice to a large number of indigent clients.

LEGAL KNOWLEDGE MANAGEMENT, DECISION SUPPORT, AND THE WORLD WIDE WEB

Gottschalk (1999) states that the use of advanced technologies enables the law firm to take advantage of the most appropriate tools to improve efficiency, increase effectiveness, streamline communication, and reduce costs for their clients. A law firm is a collection of fiefdoms—each lawyer has his or her own clients and keeps the information about them private. One of the greatest objectives of knowledge management in law firms seems to be consistency of work output in an increasingly global market. Knowledge management support systems in law firms are concerned with capturing and codifying knowledge, creating knowledge, distributing knowledge, and sharing knowledge (Edwards & Mahling, 1997).

Russanow (2003) claims that information technology creates an expectation of faster and alternative legal services. In the age of instantaneous communication, lawyers have been forced to find quicker ways to deliver traditional legal services. Knowledge management systems and processes enable lawyers to work more efficiently and provide legal services quicker than ever before.

The Internet has also opened a whole new market for lawyers to sell their services. Lawyers must examine how they will use technology to deliver services to their clients. Online advisory and drafting tools, developed and managed by law firms, are becoming commonplace. Knowledge management systems and processes provide the foundation of online services.

Ross (1980) states that the principal institution of the law in action is not trial: it is settlement out of court. Alternative dispute resolution involves alternatives to the traditional legal methods of solving disputes. It is difficult to construct a concise definition of alternative dispute resolution (to litigation) for resolving disputes. Online dispute resolution, the application of information communication technology in alternative dispute resolution, has become a new and enhanced technique for dispute resolution.

Russanow (2003) further claims that a large firm may find that there is little sharing of knowledge across practice groups and offices. There are a number of cultural reasons for this. Where the partner compensation model rewards the individual rather than the firm, practice groups tend to operate as separate business units, focused only on growing their own practices. There is no incentive to share work with others, since there may be no reward for referring work to colleagues. Indeed, there may be overlap in areas of practice between lawyers in different practice groups. These groups may be competing with each other in the market. Lawyers may also believe that their knowledge base is their power base, and that sharing that knowledge would dilute their value.

This lack of knowledge sharing between individuals and practice groups means that the firm is not leveraging its multi-practice, multi-office infrastructure. Practice groups are not looking at cross-selling opportunities with other practice groups. These inefficiencies and lost business opportunities may directly impact the firm's revenue. In some instances, the lack of cross-referrals to other, more appropriate practice groups may even affect the firm's risk exposure.

Carine (2003) claims key elements of knowledge management are collaboration, content management, and information sharing. These elements can occur concurrently.

Collaboration refers to colleagues exchanging ideas and generating new knowledge. Common terms used to describe collaboration include knowledge creation, generation, production, development, use, and organisational learning

Content management refers to the management of an organisation's internal and external knowledge using information management skills and information technology tools. Terms associated with content management include information classification, codification, storage and access, organisation, and coordination.

Information sharing refers to ways and means to distribute information and encourage colleagues to share and reuse knowledge in the firm. These activities may be described as knowledge distribution, transfer, or sharing.

Effective information technology (IT) support for knowledge management can serve as a competitive advantage and as a professional aid to law firms. To examine IT support for knowledge management in Norwegian law firms, Gottschalk (1999) conducted a study that involved two phases of data collection and analysis. The first phase was an initial field study of the largest law firm in Norway to identify issues and attitudes towards IT and knowledge management in a law firm as a basis for the survey approach in the second phase. The semi-structured interviews conducted in the initial field study documented a strong belief in the potential benefits from knowledge management. The second phase was a survey of Norwegian law firms. Firm culture, firm knowledge, and use of information technology were identified as potential predictors of information technology support for knowledge management in law firms in Norway. The extent to which law firms in Norway use information technology to support knowledge management is significantly influenced by the extent firms generally use information technology.

FUTURE TRENDS: LEGAL DECISION SUPPORT ON THE WORLD WIDE WEB

Susskind (2000) indicates that until recently, there was only limited use of IT by legal professionals. While the use of word processing, office automation, case management tools, client and case databases, electronic data/document interchange tools, and fax machines is now standard, for example, only recently have law firms commenced using IT for knowledge management purposes. He claims that the use of knowledge-based legal knowledge management tools will become common in large firms by 2007 and in all legal firms by 2012.

But how will such systems be constructed?

Argumentation has been used in knowledge engineering in two distinct ways: to structure knowledge and to model discourse (Stranieri & Zeleznikow, 2004). Stranieri, Zeleznikow, and Yearwood (2001) have used Toulmin's theory of argumentation to manage legal knowledge. Toulmin (1958) concluded that all arguments, regardless of the domain, have a structure that consists of six basic invariants: claim, data, modality, rebuttal, warrant, and backing. Every argument makes an assertion based on some data. The assertion of an argument stands as the

claim of the argument. Knowing the data and the claim does not necessarily convince us that the claim follows from the data. A mechanism is required to act as a justification for the claim. This justification is known as the warrant. The backing supports the warrant and in a legal argument is typically a reference to a statute or a precedent case. The rebuttal component specifies an exception or condition that obviates the claim.

A system they constructed called Split-Up (Stranieri, Zeleznikow, Gawler, & Lewis, 1999) provides advice upon how Australian Family Court judges distribute marital property following divorce. Figure 1 illustrates one argument from the Split-Up system. We can see from that figure that there are three data items. Each of these is the claim item of other arguments, leading to a tree of arguments where the ultimate claim of the system is the root of the tree. In the argument in Figure 1, the inference mechanism is a neural network. The network, once trained with appropriate past cases, will output a claim value (percentage split of assets) given values of the three data items.

Figure 1 illustrates one argument from the Split-Up system. In 20 of the 35 arguments in Split-Up, claim values were inferred from data items with the use of neural networks, whereas heuristics were used to infer claim values in the remaining arguments. The Split-Up system produces an inference by the invocation of inference mechanisms stored in each argument. However, an explanation for an inference is generated after the event, in legal realist traditions by first invoking the data items that led to the claim. Additional explanatory text is supplied by reasons for relevance and backings. If the user questions either data item value, she is taken to the argument that generated that value as its claim.

Figure 1. Argument for percentage split of assets to the husband

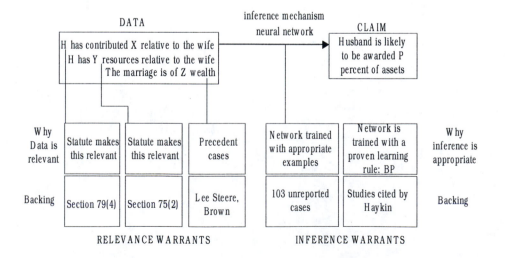

The Split-Up system performed favourably on evaluation. Currently, the tree of arguments is being modified in conjunction with domain experts from Victoria Legal Aid (VLA) to accommodate recent changes in legislation. The argument-based representation facilitates the localization of changes and makes maintenance feasible. The use of the argument-based representation of knowledge enables machine-learning techniques to be applied to model a field of law widely regarded as discretionary. JUSTREASON, developed by JUSTSYS (www.justsys.com.au) is a knowledge management shell that integrates a rule-based reasoning approach with argumentation structures similar to those used in the Split-Up system. To date the argument structure has been trialed in systems in family law (35 arguments), refugee law (200 arguments), sentencing (23 arguments), copyright law (50 arguments), evaluation of eyewitness evidence (23 arguments), and eligibility for legal aid (8 arguments).

The argument structure is also being used to support *online dispute resolution*. Lodder and Zeleznikow (2005) argue that an online dispute resolution environment can be appropriately designed through the use of *dialogue tools* and *negotiation systems* in a *three-step model*. Their proposal involves the use of collaboration and information sharing. The model involves: (a) determining the BATNA (according to Fisher and Ury, a BATNA—Best Alternative to a Negotiated Agreement—is what would occur if the issue were not resolved), which is a form of information sharing; (b) attempting to resolve the existing issues in conflict using argumentation techniques—a collaborative approach to resolving the dispute; (c) for those issues not resolved in (b), we use compensation/trade-off strategies to advise on a possible sequencing and resolution of a dispute—a further attempt at sharing information given the disputants' preferences. If the advice suggested in (c) is not acceptable to the parties, return to (b) and repeat the process recursively until either the dispute is resolved or a stalemate occurs.

We are currently using the JustReason Shell as a tool for building our online dispute resolution environment. It allows for the development of decision support systems to advise upon BATNAs, provides support for the disputants to conduct discussions and negotiations (argumentation), and allows for the use of game theory techniques to advise upon trade-offs. Our online dispute environment has been tested in the domain of property distribution in Australian Family Law.

CONCLUSION

In this article, we have noted that generic legal knowledge management is difficult, since legal knowledge is very domain and region dependent. Recently, there has been an increased focus on providing legal knowledge through the World Wide Web. We argue that future legal knowledge management systems that provide support for dispute resolution will become available on the World Wide Web. We introduce one approach for building such systems.

REFERENCES

Black, H.C. (1990). *Black's law dictionary*. St. Paul, MN: West Publishing Company.

Breuker, J., Elhag, A., Petkov, E., & Winkels, R. (2002). Ontologies for legal information serving and knowledge management. *Proceedings of Jurix 2002, the 15th Annual Conference on Legal Knowledge and Information Systems* (pp. 73-82). Amsterdam: IOS Press.

Carine, H. (2003, August 24-27). Applying knowledge management in law firm alliances. *Proceedings of the 10th Asia Pacific Special Health and Law Librarians Conference,* Adelaide, Australia.

David, R., & Brierley, J.E.C. (1985). *Major legal systems in the world today*. London: Stevens & Sons.

Edwards, D.L., & Mahling, D.E. (1997). Towards knowledge management systems in the legal domain. *Proceedings of Group 97, ACM,* (pp. 158-166), Phoenix, AZ.

Gottschalk, P. (1999). Use of IT for knowledge management in law firms. *The Journal of Information, Law and Technology, 3.* Retrieved from *http://www.law.warwick.ac.uk/jilt/99-3/gottschalk.html*

Gruber, T.R. (1995). Towards principles for the design of ontologies used for knowledge sharing. *International Journal of Human-Computer Studies, 43,* 907-928.

Khandelwal, V.K., & Gottschalk, P. (2003). Information technology support for interorganizational knowledge transfer: An empirical study of law firms in Norway and Australia. *Information Resource Management Journal, 16*(1), 14-23.

Lodder, A.R., & Zeleznikow, J. (2005). Developing an online dispute resolution environment: Dialogue tools and negotiation systems in a three-step model. *Harvard Negotiation Law Review, 10,* 287-338.

Rodríguez Morcón, C., Pérez García, J., & Sigüenza Pizarro, J.A. (2002). Knowledge management in a law firm. *UPGRADE, 3*(1), 51-55. Retrieved from *http://www.upgrade-cepis.org*

Ross, H.L. (1980). *Settled out of court*. UK: Aldine Publishing.

Rusanow, G. (2003). *Knowledge management and the smarter lawyer*. New York: ALM Publishing.

Stranieri, A., Zeleznikow, J., Gawler, M., & Lewis, B. (1999). A hybrid–neural approach to the automation of legal reasoning in the discretionary domain of family law in Australia. *Artificial Intelligence and Law, 7*(2-3), 153-183.

Stranieri, A., Zeleznikow, J., & Yearwood, J. (2001). Argumentation structures that integrate dialectical and monoletical reasoning. *Knowledge Engineering Review, 16*(4), 331-348.

Stranieri, A., & Zeleznikow, J. (2001). WebShell: The development of Web-based expert systems. *Research and Development in Expert Systems XVIII. Proceedings of ES2001—The 21ˢᵗ SGES International Conference on Knowledge Based Systems and Applied Artificial Intelligence* (pp. 245-258). London: Springer-Verlag.

Stranieri, A., & Zeleznikow, J. (2004). Knowledge discovery from legal databases. *Springer Law and Philosophy Library, 69*.

Susskind, R. (2000). *Transforming the law: Essays on technology, justice and the legal marketplace*. Oxford: Oxford University Press.

Toulmin, S. (1958). *The uses of arguments*. MA: Cambridge University Press.

Zeleznikow, J. (2004). Building intelligent legal decision support systems: Past practice and future challenges. In J.A. Fulcher & L.C. Jain (Eds.), *Applied intelligent systems: New directions* (pp. 201-254). Berlin: Springer-Verlag.

KEY TERMS

Argumentation: Involves a family of concepts that can be broadly grouped into three categories: a) concepts related to the process of engaging in an argument, b) procedures or rules adopted to regulate the argument process, and c) argument as a product or artefact of an argument process.

BATNA (Best Alternative to a Negotiated Agreement): What would occur if an issue in dispute is not resolved.

Burden of Proof: The necessity or duty of affirmatively proving a fact or facts in dispute on an issue raised between the parties in a cause.

Civil Law: May be defined as that legal tradition which has its origin in Roman law and was subsequently developed in Continental Europe. It is highly systematised and structured, and relies on declarations of broad, general principles, often ignoring the details.

Common Law: The legal tradition that evolved in England from the 11th century onwards. Its principles appear for the most part in reported judgments, usually of the higher courts, in relation to specific fact situations arising in disputes that courts have adjudicated.

Explicit Knowledge: Can be expressed in words and numbers and shared in the form of data, scientific formulae, specifications, manuals, and the like. This kind of knowledge can be readily transmitted between individuals formally and systematically.

Online Dispute Resolution: The application of information communication technology to support alternative dispute resolution.

Ontology: An explicit conceptualization of a domain. Legal ontologies represent legal norms and are very significant for developing legal knowledge-based systems on the World Wide Web.

Tacit Knowledge: Highly personal and hard to formalize, making it difficult to communicate or share with others. Subjective insights, intuitions, and hunches fall into this category of knowledge. Tacit knowledge is deeply rooted in an individual's actions and experience, as well as in the ideals, values, or emotions he or she embraces.

Toulmin Argument Structure: Toulmin stated that all arguments, regardless of the domain, have a structure that consists of four basic invariants: claim, data, warrant, and backing. Every argument makes an assertion. The assertion of an argument stands as the claim of the argument. A mechanism is required to act as a justification for the claim, given the data. This justification is known as the warrant. The backing supports the warrant and in a legal argument is typically a reference to a statute or precedent case.

Logic and Knowledge Bases

J. Grant
Towson University, USA

J. Minker
University of Maryland at College Park, USA

INTRODUCTION

Knowledge bases (KBs) must be able to capture a wide range of situations. One must be able to represent and answer questions regarding indefinite information where it is not clear that there is a unique answer to a question. One must also represent and answer questions about negative information. We discuss a powerful way to represent such information, namely through reasoning about knowledge bases using logic.

In the real world, information known at one time may change. However, in first-order logic, information once known cannot change. This phenomenon is known as *monotonicity*. Since KBs deal with incomplete information, they are not monotonic. We shall discuss a form of *logic programming*, below, which is able to handle nonmonotonic information and situations required by KBs such as definite and indefinite data, and logical and default negation.

The question of how to adapt first-order logic to handle complex situations started in the 1950s. Early systems handled problems in an ad hoc way. Several primitive deductive databases (DDBs), function-free logic programs, were developed in the 1960s. Robinson (1965) developed a general method for automated theorem proving to perform deduction. This method is known as the *Robinson Resolution Principle*; it is a generalization of *modus ponens* to first-order predicate logic. Green and Raphael (1968) were the first to recognize the importance and applicability of the work performed by Robinson and developed a system using this principle.

November 1977 is generally considered to be the start of the modern era of DDBs. A workshop, "Logic and Data Bases," was organized in Toulouse, France, by Gallaire and Nicolas in collaboration with Minker. The workshop included researchers who had performed work in deduction from 1969 to 1977 using the Robinson Resolution Principle. The book *Logic and Data Bases*, edited by Gallaire and Minker (1978), contained these papers. Many significant contributions were described in the book. Nicolas and Gallaire discussed the difference between model theory and proof theory. They demonstrated that the approach taken by the database community was model theoretic—that is, the database represents the truths of the theory, and queries are answered by a bottom-up search. However, in logic programming, answers to a query use a proof theoretic approach, starting from the query, in a top-down search. Reiter discussed the *closed world assumption* (*CWA*), whereby in a theory, if one cannot prove that an *atomic formula* is *true*, then the negation of the atomic formula is assumed to be true. The *CWA* is a *default rule* that permits one to make a decision on negation even if the decision may not be correct.

Reiter's paper elucidated three major issues: the definition of a query, an answer to a query, and how one deals with negation. Clark presented an alternative theory of negation, the concept of if-and-only-if conditions that underlie the meaning of negation, called negation-as-finite-failure. The Reiter and Clark papers are the first to formally define default negation in logic programs and deductive databases. Several implementations of deductive databases were reported. Nicolas and Yazdanian described the importance of integrity constraints in deductive databases. The book provided, for the first time, a comprehensive description of the interaction between logic and databases, and knowledge bases.

References to work on the history of the development of the field of deductive databases and to a description of early systems may be found in Minker (1996).

BACKGROUND

Much of the world's data is stored in relational databases. A relational database consists of tables, each with a fixed number of rows. Each row of a table contains information about a single object. For example, an employee table may contain columns for an employee number, name, address, age, salary, and department name. Each row contains data about one employee. In the same database a department table may contain department name, department number, phone number, and manager's employee number. The connection between the two tables is provided by the common column on department name. Relational databases also allow for integrity constraints that prevent some types of incorrect updates. For example, the specification of employee number as the key of the employee table means that only one row is allowed for any employee number.

Writing a relational database in logic formalism, we associate a predicate with each table, using the same name for convenience. Then an atomic formula (atom), such as,

Department(sales, 5, 1234567, 11223),

means that there is a row in the Department table with the values listed there. In general, an atom consists of a predicate and a set of arguments which may be constants, variables, or function symbols with arguments. We shall deal only with function-free atoms. Deductive databases extend the concept of relational databases by allowing tables to be defined implicitly by using a formula. In this example, we may define an intensional predicate,

Supervisor(emp1,emp2)←Employee(emp1,_,_,_,_,dept1),
                       Department(dept1,_, _, emp2)

to stand for the fact that emp2 is the manager of emp1's department. We use underscores to indicate irrelevant attributes.

This type of definition is allowed for relational databases, where it is called a *view*.

However, the following definition:

Superior(emp1, emp2) ← Supervisor(emp1, emp2)

Superior(emp1, emp2) ← Supervisor(emp1, emp3),
                       Superior(emp3, emp2)

where superior stands for the supervisor, the supervisor's supervisor, and so on, uses recursion and was not allowed in the original relational database framework.

More formally, a deductive database, DDB, is a triple, *<EDB, IDB, IC>*. *EDB*, the extensional database, is a set of facts, namely the rows in tables. *IDB*, the *intensional database*, is a set of rules that implicitly define new tables. *IC* is a set of *integrity constraints*. All three parts of a *DDB* are written as logic formulas. Queries are also written as logic formulas. For example, the query:

← Employee(_, name, address, _, _, deptname),
            Department(deptname, 5, _,_)

asks for the names and addresses of employees in department 5, including the name of the department, while the query:

← Supervisor(11223, emp)

asks for the supervisors of employee *11223*.

The *IDB*, in the general case, contains a set of rules of the form:

$$A1, \ldots, An \leftarrow B1, \ldots, Bm, \text{not } Bm{+}1, \ldots, \text{not } Bm{+}k \quad (1)$$

where all the Ai, $1 \le i \le n$, and Bj, $1 \le j \le m + k$, are literals (atoms or logically negated atoms, e.g., $\neg p$, where p is an atom), and *not* stands for default negation. Whereas logical negation specifies that an atom is definitely not *true*, default negation *not* is an implicit form of negation that permits one to conclude that a defaulted atom is not *true*, even if it is not explicitly known to be not *true*. The left-hand side of the reverse implication is called the *head* and the right hand side is the *body*. The meaning of such a rule is:

A1 or . . . , or An is true if B1 and . . . , and Bm
and not Bm+1 and , . . . , not Bm+k are true.

A *logic program* is a collection of rules of the form (1). Since we deal only with function-free rules, we call such a set of rules a *deductive database*. There are different kinds of deductive databases depending upon the rules used.

The first generalization of relational databases permitted function-free recursive Horn rules in a database—that is, rules in which n = 1 and k = 0. These deductive databases are called *Datalog* databases. Formulas where the head is empty are also allowed: they stand for queries and some types of integrity constraints. When the formula is considered to be a query, $Q(X1, \ldots, Xn)$, and hence the head is empty and the free variables are $X1, \ldots, Xn$, an answer to the query has the form $< a1, \ldots, an >$ so that $Q(a1, \ldots, an)$ follows from the database.

MAIN FOCUS OF THE ARTICLE

Datalog Semantics

Van Emden and Kowalski (1976) formalized the semantics of logic programs that consist of Horn rules, where the rules are not necessarily function-free. They recognized that these programs can be characterized in three distinct ways: by model, fixpoint, or proof theory, leading to the same semantics. When the logic program is function-free, their work provides the semantics for *Datalog* databases. Horn rules may be recursive, that is, a predicate on the left-hand side of a rule may have the same predicate on the right-hand side of the rule. Hence,

Datalog allows for more general knowledge bases than the relational model.

Model theory deals with the collection of models (a set of atoms that are *true* in the theory) that captures the intended meaning of the database. Fixpoint theory deals with a fixpoint operator that constructs the collection of all atoms that can be inferred to be true from the database. Proof theory provides a procedure that finds answers to queries with respect to the database. Van Emden and Kowalski (1976) showed that there is a unique minimal model, which is the same as all of the atoms in the fixpoint, and are exactly the atoms provable from the theory.

To deal with negation, one can subtract from the set of all atoms formed from the predicates and constants in the database, the minimal set of answers to the DDB. If an atom is contained in this set, then it is assumed *false*.

Initial approaches to answering queries in DDBs did not handle recursion and were primarily top-down (or backward reasoning). However, answering queries in relational database systems was bottom-up (or forward reasoning) to find all answers. Several approaches were developed to handle recursion to improve search time. Two of them are called the *Alexander* and *magic set methods*. They take advantage of constants in the query, and effectively compute answers using a combined top-down and bottom-up approach.

Integrity constraints are important to KBs. They are used primarily to assure that a KB update is consistent. Reiter (1978) showed that Datalog databases can be queried with or without ICs and the answer to the query is identical. However, ICs provide *semantic* information about the data in the KB and can be used to optimize search for answers to queries. The use of ICs to constrain search is called *semantic query optimization (SQO)*. Semantic query optimization has been incorporated into some relational databases. A topic related to SQO is that of *cooperative answering systems*. The objective is to give a user the reason why a particular query succeeded or failed (see Minker, 1996, for references).

The first article on magic sets may be found in Bancilhon, Mayer, Sagiv, and Ullman (1986). A description of the magic set method to handle recursion in DDBs may be found in Ullman (1988a, 1988b). For work on the fixpoint theory of Datalog, and the work of Van Emden and Kowalski, see Lloyd (1987). A comprehensive survey and references to work in cooperative answering systems is in Gaasterland, Godfrey, and Minker (1992). References to alternative definitions of ICs, semantic query optimization, and cooperative answering may be found in Minker (1996).

Stratified Deductive Databases

Datalog databases provide additional capabilities for KBs. However, they are still not able to handle more complex situations. There may be a need to handle both logical and default negation in some applications. The logic programming formalism handles these situations by permitting more complex rules which have a literal (i.e., an atomic formula or the negation of an atomic formula) in the head and literals with possibly negated-by-default literals in the body of a rule. Such rules are called *extended*, where in Formula (1) n = 1, m $\geq$ 0, k $\geq$ 0, and the *As* and *Bs* are literals. Such databases combine *classical negation* ($\neg$) and *default negation (not)*, and are called *extended DDBs*.

Logic programs that use default negation in the body of a clause were first defined in 1986 by Apt, Blair, and Walker (1988) and Van Gelder (1988) as stratified logic programs in which A1 and the Bj, $1 \leq j \leq m+k$, in Formula (1) are atomic formulas, and there is no recursion through negation. They show that there is a unique preferred minimal model, computed from strata to strata, termed the *perfect model* by Przymusinski (1988). In a stratified theory, rules are placed in different strata, where the definition of a predicate in the head of a rule is in a higher stratum than the definitions of predicates negated in the body of the rule. The definition of a predicate is the collection of rules containing the predicate in their head. One computes positive predicates in a lower stratum, and a negated predicate's complement is true in the body of the clause if the positive atom has not been computed in the lower stratum. The identical semantics is obtained, independent of how the database KB is stratified. This DDB is termed *Datalog$^\neg$*. If a KB can be stratified, then there is no recursion through negation, and the database is called *Datalog$^\neg_{strat}$*.

If the rule:

Happyemp(emp1) ← Employee(emp1), not
   Supervisor(emp1, 11223)

is added to the predicates given earlier, a stratified program is obtained with two strata. The lowest stratum contains *Employee, Department*, and *Supervisor*, since *Happyemp* depends negatively on *Supervisor*, it must be in a higher stratum.

Non-Stratified Deductive Databases

In some KBs it is useful to allow recursion through negation. Once this happens, the KB is no longer stratified. Consider the following simple example:

```
r1: rich(X) ← not poor(X)
r2: poor(X) ← not rich(X)
r3: satisfied(joe) ← poor(joe)
r4: satisfied(joe) ← rich(joe).
```

Non-stratified *KBs* may not have unique answers to queries. Additionally, there may be more than one semantics that define answers to queries in such KBs, and hence alternative ways to answer queries. One such semantics is the *answer set semantics (ANS)* developed by Gelfond and Lifschitz (1988), and another semantics is the *well-founded semantics (WFS)* developed by Van Gelder, Ross, and Schlipf (1991). The different semantics for *ANS* and *WFS* are illustrated on the above example.

The first two rules, namely that an individual is rich if not poor and poor if not rich, are recursive through negation. Thus this KB is not stratified. But note that by the last two rules, *joe* is satisfied if he is *poor* and also if he is *rich*. By using the answer-set semantics (ANS), there are two answer sets, namely $S1 = \{poor(joe),$ $satisfied(joe)\}$ and $S2 = \{rich(joe), satisfied(joe)\}$. A query is answered *"yes"* if it is *true* in all answer sets and *"false"* if it is *false* in all answer sets. In this case we can conclude $\{rich(joe)$ *or* $poor(joe),$ $satisfied(joe)\}$, that is, *joe* is *rich* or *poor*, and *joe* is satisfied.

The semantics for ANS is defined first for programs without default negation as the smallest set of literals *S*, with the property that if all the literals of a rule in the program are in *S*, then the head is also in *S*. Consider now a program *P* with default negation and candidate answer set *C*. Obtain a new program P^1 without default negation as follows: for any rule that has a default negation *not L* in the body with $L \in C$, the rule is eliminated (the rule cannot apply); for the remaining rules all the default negations are eliminated (the default negation must be true). Since P^1 does not have negation, its semantics may be computed by the first method. If the semantics to P^1 is the set *C*, then *C* is accepted as the semantics for the original program *P*. If *C* is the answer set of P^1, it is called an answer set of *P*.

The *well-founded semantics (WFS)* coincides with the *ANS* on *stratified programs*. In the case of non-stratified programs, WFS uses three truth values: *true*, *false*, and *unknown*. In the example above, all three atoms: *satisfied(joe)*, *poor(joe)*, and *rich(joe)*, would be considered as *unknown*.

Disjunctive Databases

So far we have considered only definite databases (i.e., where in Formula (1) $n = 1$). Disjunctive databases are useful for KBs when information, either in the EDB or IDB, is indefinite (i.e., in some formulas $n > 1$). Hence, disjunctive databases permit the representation of indefinite knowledge such as $p \lor q$, where it is not known if *p* is *true*, or *q* is *true*, but it is known that $p \lor q$ is true. Such KBs are called *extended disjunctive deductive databases (EDDDBs)* or $Datalog^{\neg}_{disj.ext}$. An important special case, *disjunctive deductive databases (DDDBs)*, or $Datalog^{\neg}_{disj,}$ allows only atoms in Formula (1). Minker (1982) started the study of DDDBs and showed how to answer both positive and negated queries.

For positive queries over DDDBs, it suffices to show that the query is satisfied in every minimal model. For negated queries, Minker developed the *Generalized Closed World Assumption (GCWA)*, which assigns the value *true* to a negated atom if the atom does not appear in any minimal model. Minker and others then developed various techniques for answering queries in DDDBs.

Various semantics have been given for EDDDBs. The most prominent of these is the *Answer Set Semantics (ANS)* modified appropriately from the definite case.

TOOLS FOR IMPLEMENTING KBS

The development of KB systems using logic has been facilitated by enhancements made to relational databases through techniques within DDDBs added to the language SQL, through deductive database implementations, and through implementations of the well-founded and answer set semantics for non-stratified and disjunctive databases. In addition, we discuss the use of logic in a large knowledge base system, *Cyc*.

SQL

The *SQL:1999* standard includes queries involving recursion and hence recursive views. The recursion must be linear with at most one invocation of the same recursive item. Default negation is stratified and applies only to predicates defined without recursion. *SQL:1999* allows a general class of ICs, called *Asserts*, that allow for arbitrary relationships between tables and views that express types of ICs generally associated with DDDBs.

Linear recursion is implemented as a part of the client server of *IBM's DB2* system using *magic sets*.

Techniques from semantic query optimization also have been incorporated into *DB2*.

Datalog

Several prototype implementations of *Datalog¬* have been developed; however, only two systems are active: *Aditi*, developed at the University of Melbourne under the direction of Dr. K. Ramamohanarao (1993), and *LDL++*, developed at UCLA under the direction of Dr. Carlo Zaniolo (see Arni, Ong, Tsur, Wang, & Zaniolo, 2003).

Well-Founded Semantics and Answer Set Semantics

The most important implementations for extended DDBs are the Well-Founded Semantics and the Answer Set Semantics. See Minker (1996) for a discussion of alternate proposals and alternative systems. Rao, Sagonas, Swift, Warren, and Friere (1997) developed a system, *XSB*, that computes the well-founded semantics. The system extends the full functionality of *Prolog*, an important logic programming language, to the WFS. The use of XSB for medical diagnosis is described in Swift (1999). XSB also permits the user to employ *Smodels*, discussed below, and is available on the Internet as open source.

Niemelä and Simons (1996) developed *Smodels* to compute the answer sets of programs in *Datalog with negation*. *Smodels* is presently considered the most efficient implementation of Answer Set Semantics. The system can be licensed from a company in Finland called Neotide.

Implementation of Disjunctive Deductive Databases

Eiter, Leone, Mateis, Pfeifer, and Scarcello (1997) developed *DLV (DataLog with Or)* to compute answer sets for disjunctive deductive databases. The work is a joint effort between the Technical University of Austria and the University of Calabria, Italy.

Cyc

Cyc, developed by Lenat (1995), is both a knowledge base and a system that contains a set of tools to manipulate the database. The *Cyc KB* consists of a large quantity of basic human knowledge: facts, rules of thumb, and heuristics for reasoning about objects and events that arise in normal life situations. There are approximately 200,000 terms and several dozen assertions about and involving each term. The database is being continually updated by human knowledge experts.

The Cyc system contains an inference engine that performs logical deduction (including *modus ponens*, and universal and existential quantification). It also contains special inferencing mechanisms, such as inheritance and automatic classification, as special cases. It also includes special purpose inferencing modules for handling a few specific classes of inference such as handling equality, temporal reasoning, and mathematical reasoning. It contains a variety of interface tools that permit the user to browse, edit, and extend the Cyc KB, to pose queries to the inference engine, and to interact with the database integration module and other features in the system.

Knowledge Base Management

A *knowledge base* consists of a large set of data, the description of the data (metadata), and a potentially large set of rules. A *Knowledge Base Management System (KBMS)* provides the capabilities to manage, manipulate, and handle the KB. Many capabilities may be required of a KBMS. We discuss some of the more important ones.

The KBMS must provide a language to represent the facts, the description of the facts, the integrity constraints associated with the database, and the rules in the KB. Facts may be temporal in nature. Users may specify preferences in what they would like for answers to queries, and may also specify priorities. The language must provide a capability to enter, delete, or modify data and rules in the KB. It must provide an ability to query all parts of the KB: the data, the description of the data (metadata), and the rules.

In addition to the language, the underlying system should permit many of the following capabilities:

1. **An inference capability to use the rules, the data description, and the facts to derive new information:** The inference capability must have a nonmonotonic reasoning capability. This is needed since it is not possible to include all the negative data that might be known in any realistic problem, and one must make conclusions in the absence of information. The inference mechanism should also permit the mixing of the metadata (that is, the description of the data), together with the rules and facts.

2. **A mechanism to update (i.e., enter, delete, or modify) the KB:** Depending upon the inference mechanism used, this might require careful attention (e.g., Fernandez, Grant, & Minker, 1996).

3. **A capability to optimize a query:** Unless there is a query optimizer, queries may take excessive amounts of time. This is true even in relational database systems that do not have an inference capability.

4. **The ability to integrate multiple KBs:** This is required in many KBSs such as in organizations that are distributed. Inconsistencies may arise when integrating such systems, and there is the need for handling the integration to provide correct answers to users (see Grant & Minker, 2002; Levy, 2000).

5. **The ability to provide cooperative answers to users:** For example, there is a need to know when a query can never be answered because of the nature of the database, or because there may be no data about the query currently in the database (see Gaasterland et al., 1992). The user might require that a route for a trip not go through a particular city, or a plane have at most one intermediate stop.

6. **The ability to provide data mining, or the discovery of knowledge in a database:** There are several distinguished forms of human reasoning identified by the philosopher Pierce (1883). *Deduction* is an analytic process based on the application of general rules to particular cases, with the inference as a result. The focus of this article is on providing explicit knowledge that exists in a database through deduction. Data mining or discovery are forms of analytic reasoning called *induction*, which infer the rule from the case and the result. That is, it discovers a general rule (see Plotkin, 1969; Shapiro, 1981; Hand, Manilla, & Smythe, 2001). Another form of reasoning, *abduction*, uses synthetic inference, which generates hypotheses H such that $(KB\ U\ H)$, where KB is the knowledge base, implying a consequence, C' (see Kakas, Kowalski, & Toni, 1993).

Logic-based languages provide a powerful method for constructing KBMSs. All work developed for DDBs and extended DDBs concerning semantics and complexity apply directly to KBMS. Baral and Gelfond (1994) describe how extended DDBs may be used to represent KBs. The features of KBMSs as described in this section can be used to implement all of the capabilities discussed above. Many of the systems already have these capabilities. Hence, they can allow the KB experts to focus on the database, the description of the data, the specification of the rules, and integrity constraints of the KB. They can then employ an appropriate DDB system that has the required semantics.

Applications

Many applications of KBs exist in a wide variety of fields. We mention only a few here. *Abduction* is a method of reasoning used to find explanations of observations. This concept has been used in areas such as medical diagnosis and legal reasoning. Information agents, able to handle data on the World Wide Web, have been proposed for solving information retrieval problems. Data integration deals with the integration of data in different databases. The planning problem in artificial intelligence is closely related to the ANS. The handling of preferences and inconsistencies are other areas where KBs are useful.

We illustrate the use of a DDB formalism for KBs with two examples. Consider a *family KBs* with the following rules and data:

parent(pat, mike) ←
father(X, Y), mother(X, Y) ← parent(X, Y).

The first statement is a fact, the second is a disjunctive rule. From this KB we conclude that pat is mike's father or mike's mother.

A second example deals with eligibility for a scholarship in a university KB. Basically, students with a high grade point average (GPA) or who are athletes and have a good GPA are eligible. Some students are not eligible. Students who are neither eligible nor not eligible are interviewed.

eligible(X) ← gpa(X, high)
eligible(X) ← athlete(X), gpa(X, good)
¬eligible(X) ← ¬gpa(X, good), ¬gpa(X, high)
interview(X) ← eligible(X), not ¬eligible(X)
gpa(sam, good) ←
athlete(sam) ←
gpa(mary, good) ←
¬athlete(mary) ←.

From this KB, eligible(sam) and interview(mary) can be deduced using the answer set semantics.

FUTURE TRENDS AND CONCLUSION

The field of KBs has been enhanced by developments in DDBs. Future developments, discussed briefly below, will make it easier for users to develop KBs.

Relational databases have already incorporated techniques from DDBs. Other tools such as the incorporation of *join elimination,* and *SQO* techniques such as equalities and arithmetic constraints can be added to the

SQL language. Additional tools that provide cooperative responses to users can also be incorporated in future versions of SQL. It is unclear if additional features of DDBs can be added without major revisions to the relational systems.

DDBs have not yet been made available as commercial systems. The future of commercial systems in this area is not promising except for the XSB system that provides the well-founded semantics; Smodels that provides the answer set semantics; and DVL that provides a disjunctive semantics. These systems already are in use, primarily in university communities. KB systems have been implemented using these systems. Should such systems become commercial, they will make it easier to develop KBs.

REFERENCES

Apt, K.R., Blair, H.A., & Walker, A. (1988). Towards a theory of declarative knowledge. In J. Minker (Ed.), *Foundations of deductive databases and logic programming* (pp. 89-148). San Francisco: Morgan-Kaufmann.

Arni, F., Ong, K., Tsur, S., Wang, H., & Zaniolo, C. (2003). The deductive database system ldl++. *Theory and Practice of Logic Programming, 3,* 61-94.

Bancilhon, F., Maier, D., Sagiv, Y., & Ullman, J. (1986) Magic sets and other strange ways to implement logic programs. *Proceedings of the ACM Symposium on Principles of Database Systems.*

Baral, C., & Gelfond, M. (1994). Logic programming and knowledge representation. *Journal of Logic Programming, 19/20,* 73-148.

Eiter, T., Leone, N., Mateis, C., Pfeifer, G., & Scarcello, F. (1997). In J. Dix, U. Furbach, & A. Nerode (Eds.), *Proceedings of the 4th International Conference on Logic Programming and Nonmonotonic Reasoning (LPNMR'97)* (pp. 363-374), Berlin: Springer-Verlag (LNAI 1265).

Fernandez, J.A., Grant, J., & Minker, J. (1996). Model theoretic approach to view updates in deductive databases. *Journal of Automated Reasoning, 17*(2), 171-197.

Gaasterland, T., Godfrey, P., & Minker, J. (1992). An overview of cooperative answering. *Journal of Intelligent Information Systems, 1*(2), 162-207.

Gallaire, H., & Minker, J. (1978). *Logic and data bases.* New York: Plenum Press.

Gelfond, M., & Lifschitz, V. (1988). The stable model semantics for logic programming. In R.A. Kowalski & K.A. Bowen (Eds.), *Proceedings of the 5th International Conference and Symposium on Logic Programming* (pp. 1070-1080).

Grant, J., & Minker, J. (2002). A logic-based approach to data integration. *Theory and Practice of Logic Programming, 2*(3), 293-321.

Green, C.C., & Raphael, B. (1968). The use of theorem-proving techniques in question-answering systems. *Proceedings of the 23rd National ACM Conference.*

Hand, D., Mannila, H., & Smyth, P. (2001). *Principles of data mining.* Boston: The MIT Press.

Kakas, A.C., Kowalski, R.A., & Toni, F. (1993). Abductive logic programming. *Journal of Logic and Computation, 6*(2), 719-770.

Lenat, D.B. (1995). Cyc: A large-scale investment in knowledge infrastructure. *Communications of the ACM, 38*(11), 32-38.

Levy, A.Y. (2000). Logic-based techniques in data integration. In J. Minker (Ed.), *Logic-based artificial intelligence* (pp. 575-595). Norwell, MA: Kluwer.

Lloyd, J.W. (1987). *Foundations of logic programming* (2nd Ed.). Berlin: Springer-Verlag.

Minker, J. (1982). On indefinite databases and the closed world assumption. *Lecture Notes in Computer Science, 138,* 292-308.

Minker, J. (1996). Logic and databases: A 20-year retrospective. In D. Pedreschi & C. Zaniolo (Eds.), Logic in databases. *Proceedings of the International Workshop (LID'96)* (pp. 3-57), San Miniato, Italy. Berlin: Springer-Verlag.

Niemela, I., & Simons, P. (1996). Efficient implementation of the well-founded and stable model semantics. In I. Niemela & T. Schaub (Eds.), *Proceedings of JICSLP-96.* Boston: The MIT Press.

Pierce, C.S. (1883). A theory of probable inference. Note B. The logic of relatives. *Studies of logic by members of the Johns Hopkins University* (pp. 187-203). Baltimore: Johns Hopkins University.

Plotkin, G.D. (1969). A note on inductive generalisation. In B. Meltzer & D. Michie (Eds.), *Machine Intelligence 5* (pp. 153-163). Edinburgh: Edinburgh University Press.

Przymusinski, T.C. (1988). On the declarative semantics of deductive databases and logic programming. In J. Minker (Ed.), *Foundations of deductive databases and logic programming* (pp. 193-216). San Francisco: Morgan-Kaufmann.

Ramamohanarao, K. (1993). An implementation overview of the Aditi deductive database system. *Proceedings of the 3rd International DOOD Conference* (DOOD'93) (pp. 184-203), Phoenix, AZ. Berlin: Springer-Verlag (LNCS 760).

Rao, P., Sagonas, K., Swift, T., Warren, D.S., & Friere, J. (1997). XSB: A system for efficiently computing well-founded semantics. In J. Dix, U. Ferbach, & A. Nerode (Eds.), *Proceedings of Logic and Nonmonotonic Reasoning: 4th International Conference* (LPNMR'97) (pp. 430-440).

Reiter, R. (1978). Deductive question-answering on relational data bases. In H. Gallaire & J. Minker (Eds.), *Logic and data bases* (pp. 149-177). New York: Plenum Press.

Robinson, J.A. (1965). A machine-oriented logic based on the resolution principle. *Journal of the ACM, 12*(1), 23-41.

Shapiro, E.Y. (1981). An algorithm that infers theories from facts. *Proceedings of the 7th International Joint Conference on Artificial Intelligence* (IJCAI'81). San Francisco: Morgan-Kaufmann.

Swift, T. (1999). *Tabling for non-monotonic programming.* Technical report, SUNY Stony Brook, USA.

Ullman, J.D. (1988a). *Principles of database and knowledge-base systems I.* Rockville, MD: Computer Science Press.

Ullman, J.D. (1988b). *Principles of database and knowledge-base systems II.* Rockville, MD: Computer Science Press.

Van Emden, M.H., & Kowalski, R.A. (1976). The semantics of predicate logic as a programming language. *Journal of the ACM, 23*(4), 733-742.

Van Gelder, A. (1988). Negation as failure using tight derivations for general logic programs. In J. Minker (Ed.), *Foundations of deductive databases and logic programming* (pp. 149-176). San Francisco: Morgan-Kaufmann.

Van Gelder, A., Ross, K.A., & Schlipf, J. (1991). Unfounded sets and well-founded semantics for general logic programs. *Journal of the ACM, 38*(3).

KEY TERMS

Datalog: A class of deductive databases that may contain various types of negation and disjunction.

Deductive Database: An extension of relational database that allows relations to be implicitly defined by rules.

Disjunctive Database: A database that allows indefinite information.

Implicit Knowledge: Knowledge not explicitly given in the knowledge base but derivable from it using various assumptions.

Inference: Derivation using rules and assumptions.

Integrity Constraint: A rule that must be satisfied by the database or knowledge base if it is consistent.

Knowledge Base: An entity comprising facts, rules, and integrity constraints used for collecting and querying diverse types of information.

Negation: Logical negation specifies that an atom is definitely false; default negation permits the conclusion, based on some default rule, that an atom is false.

Nonmonotonic: A type of system where the addition of new information may change old information.

Semantic Query Optimization: The use of integrity constraints to constrain search in answering queries.

Mapping Group Knowledge

Duncan Shaw
Aston University, UK

INTRODUCTION

During group meetings it is often difficult for participants to effectively: *share* their knowledge to inform the outcome; *acquire* new knowledge from others to broaden and/or deepen their understanding; *utilise* all available knowledge to design an outcome; and record (to *retain*) the rationale behind the outcome to inform future activities. These are difficult because, for example: only one person can share knowledge at once which challenges effective sharing; information overload makes acquisition problematic and can marginalize important knowledge; and intense dialog of conflicting views makes recording more complex.

This article reports on the social process of mapping group knowledge which aims to better support the processes of sharing, acquiring, utilising and retaining, knowledge during group meetings. Mind mapping, causal mapping (Eden, forthcoming), concept maps (Gaines & Shaw, 1995a), and various mapping techniques reported in Huff and Jenkins (2002) have been used to structure and represent individual thinking and knowledge about an issue. Software now exist to support these mind-mappers (e.g., MindMap®, KMap, Decision Explorer). However, often individuals cannot solve problems themselves and instead need insight from a range of people who can collectively address the problem. For example, groups are often used where issues are so complex that they require the involvement of a number of diverse knowledge holders. Also groups are often used where political considerations suggest that the involvement of various key people would facilitate the implementation of actions.

Thus, the principles of mapping individual knowledge have been applied to small groups of people to support their collective structuring and thinking about an issue. Approaches such as Dialog Mapping (Conklin, 2003), concept mapping (Gaines & Shaw, 1995a), and Journey Making (Eden & Ackermann, 1998a) can all support the process of mapping group knowledge during meetings. While it is possible to deploy these approaches using flipchart paper and pens, software have been developed to support these particular approaches (i.e., Compendium, KMap, and Group Explorer, respectively). These software aim to capture, represent, and model the participants' knowledge in a more versatile manner than is possible on paper, enabling more effective navigation and consideration of the breadth and depth of issues.

This article begins with an introduction to the research on mapping knowledge. Then it reviews the benefits for knowledge management of engaging groups in mapping their collective knowledge. An example of a computer-based mapping methodology is briefly introduced—the Journey Making approach. Future research directions and implications for knowledge management conclude the article.

BACKGROUND TO RESEARCH ON MAPPING

Much work has been performed on the applications of cognitive and causal mapping, for example mapping for: negotiation (Bonham, 1993), strategic management (Carlsson & Walden, 1996), strategy (Fletcher & Huff, 1994; Bougon & Komocar, 1994), communication (Te'eni, Schwartz, & Boland, 1997), litigation (Ackermann, Eden, & Williams, 1997), IS requirements planning (McKay, 1998), consumer branding (Henderson, Iacobucci, & Calder, 1998), and knowledge management (Shaw, Edwards, Baker, & Collier, 2003b).

Also work has been conducted on other types of mapping, for example: knowledge networks, which represent the knowledge around a process (Gordon, 2000); mapping knowledge contained on an intranet (Eppler, 2001); and integrating concept maps with other applications to build the knowledge base (Gaines & Shaw, 1995b). With the exception of knowledge networks, that work differs to cognitive/causal mapping which concentrates more on the social process of generating knowledge through personal reflection and/or collaboration.

This article focuses on maps built by groups of knowledge holders during facilitated workshops. This body of literature is smaller, but includes: exploring how to facilitate the process of capturing knowledge from groups using mapping (Johnson & Johnson, 2002), group mapping using computers (Eden & Ackermann, 1998a; Shaw, 2003), using group mapping in a research study (Casu, Thanassoulis, & Shaw, 2002; Edwards, Collier, & Shaw, 2004), and using group mapping for knowledge management (Gaines, 2002). These studies tend to focus on improving the process of conducting a group mapping session and building group maps.

In terms of analysing the content of maps, research has focused on analysing the nature of individual cognitive maps, for example, analysing the themes in the maps (Jenkins & Johnson, 1997), and the number of concepts in the maps and the number of in/out arrows linking concepts (Eden, forthcoming). Some exploration of the properties of group maps (albeit sometimes group maps which have been generated by merging the cognitive maps of individuals) has also been performed (e.g., McKay, 1998; Eden & Ackermann, 1998b; Shaw, 2003). Shaw, Ackermann, and Eden (2003a) offer a typology for how managers access and share knowledge during group mapping activities.

The research on mapping concentrates on the deployment, evaluation, and improvement of the methods often leading to practical and theoretical advances of mapping techniques.

We now review the general benefits of mapping group knowledge.

MAPPING KNOWLEDGE FOR KNOWLEDGE MANAGEMENT

To structure the following discussion, we return to the sharing, acquisition, utilisation, and retention of knowledge to explore how mapping supports each of these. Below we assume that there are 5-12 people (participants) in a group who are mapping their knowledge. The knowledge is being captured in a map, and the process of mapping is being supported by a facilitator. This map is publicly displayed for all participants to see. This arrangement is characteristic of Dialog Mapping, concept mapping, and Journey Making (see Figure 1).

Sharing Knowledge

Sharing knowledge in a group meeting is not a straightforward activity. The group decision support systems experimental literature (see Fjermestad & Hiltz, 1998, for a review) has identified a range of factors which inhibit the sharing of knowledge, for example: "production blocking" when people cannot generate new ideas because they are trying to remember the ideas they want to share, and "evaluation apprehension" that your contributions will be negatively evaluated by the group.

When group mapping, one way of partially avoiding these inhibitors is through participants sharing knowledge by either writing it onto cards or typing it into a networked computer which is running a brainstorming software. These bring the advantage that many participants can share their knowledge simultaneously as they are not constrained to waiting for others to finish speaking before they can share their own opinion. Consequently lots of knowledge can be shared very quickly to the map, enabling the group to focus on discussing the knowledge that has been shared rather then trying to access the knowledge that each member holds. Furthermore, anonymity of who contributed the knowledge gives participants the freedom to share knowledge which they are not too sure of (or which is controversial)—allowing the group to evaluate its legitimacy.

Mapping also encourages creativity by providing stimuli (on the public display of knowledge) in the form of other peoples' ideas from which to gain inspiration. Also, facilitators can offer participants different types of sessions in which to share their knowledge, whether they share their knowledge whilst knowing/without knowing/

Figure 1. Participants in a Journey Making mapping workshop

partially knowing what other participants have shared (see Shaw, 2003, for more details). Finally, sharing knowledge directly into the map enables the participants to select/craft their own wording of contributions, without their knowledge being interpreted and reworded by a facilitator. For more details on these points, see Gaines and Shaw (1995c), Eden and Ackermann (1998a), and Shaw (2003).

Acquiring New Knowledge

Acquiring knowledge in group meetings can be problematic, as often the knowledge is poorly shared and poorly managed when shared, making identification of the key issues difficult. Information overload can also hinder the acquisition of new knowledge (Grise & Gallupe, 1999).

Through mapping, the facilitator will aim to capture the knowledge in a format where individuals can engage in a structured discussion of, what emerges through discussion to be, the key points. By communicating perspectives in only a few words, the public screen can display the breadth of issues. Through discussion, detail can be added to those issues, ensuring the requisite depth of knowledge is acquired and integrated into the group's consideration of the issues. Participating in this discussion is a key source of new information (acquiring knowledge) where people come to appreciate the legitimacy of competing perspectives—but not necessarily agree with that perspective.

Through mapping the participants share and discuss knowledge about the relationships between the issues. This enables them to enrich their appreciation of the issues with new knowledge about their causes and consequences. This is in contrast to a brainstorm where the issues are discussed, but not necessarily the relationship between the issues in a systematic, structured fashion.

In mapping, the acquisition of knowledge is a catalyst for synthesising knowledge across participants. The aim is often for the participants to build a shared understanding of what are the critical pieces of knowledge that must be incorporated into any decision or action plan. This shared understanding often does not extend to consensus on what should be done. Instead, the action plan should contain enough of what the different participants are interested in that they are willing to accept actions which they are less interested in.

Utilising Knowledge

Due to the problems of sharing and acquiring knowledge in group workshops, it is often difficult to gather appropriate knowledge to utilise. Furthermore, bounded rationality, decision-making heuristics, group thinking, and information overload can make the effective usage of shared and acquired knowledge problematic. However, in map-

ping workshops process support aims to take the group through the issues in a structured and transparent way, to overcome these problems and effectively utilise the knowledge in the group.

Mapping aims to support the utilisation of knowledge, primarily through helping participants to cope with the complexity of multiple perspectives that have been shared. By modelling the knowledge on a public screen, the participants do not need to retain the knowledge in their head or try themselves to integrate different pieces of knowledge from different people. The facilitator, using the model/map, will display the knowledge on the public screen and provide structure to reduce the cognitive demands on the recipients (i.e., manage its complexity). Thus the effects of information overload might be reduced, allowing participants to concentrate on utilising the knowledge for the purposes of the workshop.

For example, in strategy development workshops, the knowledge is utilised to identify and agree on a portfolio of actions which will progress the organisation/group in the required direction. Knowledge will be used to design appropriate actions by understanding drivers and prerequisites for action, exploring consequences of action, identifying incompatibilities across actions, and appreciating issues of action implementation.

Retaining Knowledge

Knowledge retention can be problematic over the short and long term. At one extreme, people can forget what they heard less than 10 minutes ago as they are overwhelmed with a spiralling conversation that is continuous, offering them new knowledge. At the other extreme, organisations want to retain knowledge for future use, perhaps over years.

Mapping in group workshops assists in the short-term 'retention' of knowledge by publicly displaying the knowledge either on a flip-chart or via a projector. The display is used as a shared device through which the group communicates—that is, participants make reference to the publicly displayed model as they illustrate their reasoning for holding particular opinions. This prevents group members from having to retain the argument in their heads.

The maps can also act as a long-term record of what was agreed and the rationale behind this agreement. These can be circulated around the organisation, but might be difficult to interpret for those not in the workshop. Progress against actions can be logged with reference to the maps (Shaw et al., 2003b).

We now review one particular workshop approach that maps group knowledge—the Journey Making approach.

THE JOURNEY MAKING APPROACH

Journey Making has been selected for further description because it is supported by a mapping software that, like KMap, offers a group the functionality to share their knowledge through a networked computer directly into an electronic map.

Journey Making stands for the *JO*int *U*nderstanding, *R*eflection, and *NE*gotiation of strateg*Y* (Eden & Ackermann, 1998a). This facilitator-led approach arose from a need to support groups in their strategy making endeavours. Through jointly understanding the range of pertinent issues in a problem, it is believed that a group is in a better position to tackle that problem. Reflection on the range of potential causes of the problem, and consequences of taking action to address the problem, engage the whole group (individually and collectively) in critical thinking and discussion. The range of potential actions to address the problem are rigorously considered with the aim of participants accepting the legitimacy of competing actions (or rejecting actions) through social negotiation. The outcome is typically an action plan that contains a portfolio of strategic actions that when implemented, the group believes, will tackle the problem.

Underpinning Journey Making is an aim of providing participants with a process through which they:

- *Surface* their own views in a group as other people do the same, and then…
- Collectively *explore* (not just get told about) the commonality/differentiation between those views, in order to…
- Learn about the *connections* across these multiple views (i.e., identify how the issues affect/are affected by each other), enabling them to…
- *Build* their knowledge through developing a richer appreciation of these connections (i.e., thinking through the causes and consequences of issues), to…
- *Expand* their individual and collective knowledge of the topic beyond that which they held prior to the workshop, enabling them to…
- *Select* an appropriate combination of actions which are thought to have the desired impact when implemented.

Mapping is central to this process as the following discussion will show.

MAPPING KNOWLEDGE IN JOURNEY MAKING WORKSHOPS

In a computer-supported Journey Making workshop, computer technology assists in the sharing, capturing, and displaying of views, and the voting on options. Walking into a typical Journey Making room (Figure 1), the participant would often see: 8-10 laptop computers sitting in a horseshoe running a group decision support software (Group Explorer); a projector displaying causal mapping software (Decision Explorer) on a very large projection screen; and a facilitator facing the group with computers in front of him/her.

In a Journey Making workshop, normally between 5-16 participants share their knowledge to the causal map through computers. During the brainstorm (or 'gathering' in Journey Making terminology, as the process is designed to gather occupational views, not purely lateral thoughts), the participants type their knowledge, views, and opinions (in the form of 'contributions' of 4-10 words in length) into their own networked computer which is running Group Explorer software. All contributions are made anonymously, in that issues are not identified to the individuals who made them. For example, in response to a question about how to encourage learning and sharing of knowledge in the workplace, one manager might type: "utilise the existing expertise of existing people"; another might suggest that the company should address the issue that "individuals experience outside of the business is not capitalised." These would then be displayed on the map (see Figure 2).

The facilitator, on his/her own computer screen, will move all the participants' contributions into content-related clusters and display those clusters on a public screen (using a projector) for all the participants to read and be stimulated by. Participants can then type in more contributions in response to either the stimulus 'question' or after reading what others have contributed on the public screen.

Also, participants can share knowledge of the relationship between different contributions. When building group maps, these relationships (represented in the map as an arrow) are usually causal as the group is exploring the causes of problems and drivers that will cause/bring change. For example, the participants building the map in Figure 2 thought that "individuals' experience outside of the business is not capitalised," but if addressed, could be one way of "utilis[ing] the existing expertise of existing people."

Following the gathering, the facilitator will encourage a group discussion around the issues represented on the map. This discussion will aim to surface more contributions to be added to the map, as well as further structure

Figure 2. An extract from a group map

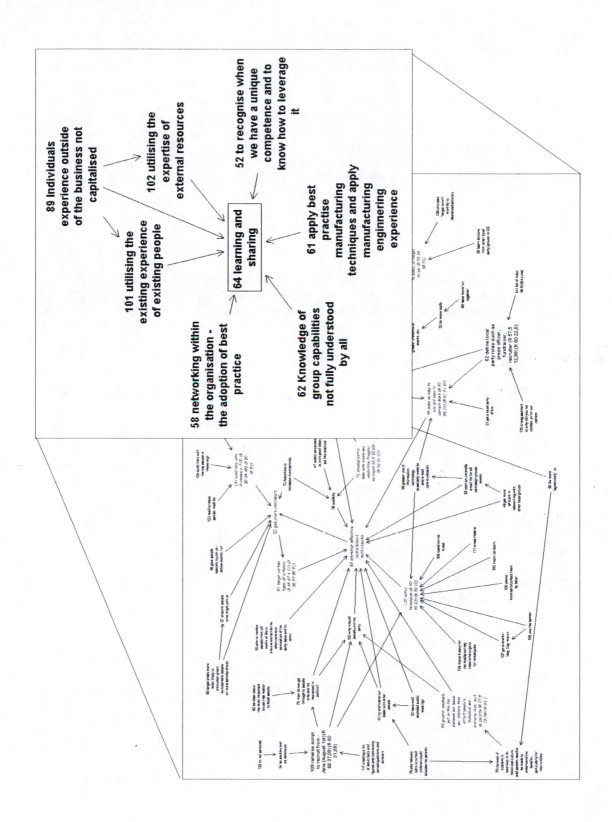

the contributions by identifying more causal relationships/links.

The product of this work will be a structured causal map which reflects the participants' knowledge of the situation and on which the participants can begin to consider which actions should be implemented in the organisation, and exploring the effects these actions might have if implemented. Through exerting effort in building and negotiating a feasible action plan (and understanding the benefits from implementing it), the facilitator will aim for group members to build commitment to implementing the actions. This commitment will help ensure that the implementation of actions is followed through to completion.

FUTURE TRENDS

As evident from earlier discussions, researchers are using the principles of mapping to gather and structure knowledge in a range of ways. For mapping in group workshops, much of this attention aims to evaluate the existing methods as a catalyst for their improvement. In terms of improving the mapping aspect of these workshops, researchers are continually reflecting on practice of mapping in groups (Johnson & Johnson, 2002), offering new ways of conducting workshops to collect knowledge with more breadth and/or depth (Shaw, 2003), offering methods for interrogating maps during workshops (Eden, forthcoming), and developing new software to support different types of group mapping.

In the Operational Research community, researchers are examining how the results from mapping activities can feed into other methods of analysis, for example, multi-criteria decision models (Belton, Ackermann, & Shepherd, 1997) and data envelopment analysis models (Casu et al., 2002). In this way mapping can be effective for multi-methodology applications (as shown in Mingers & Gill, 1998) where a combination of different methods are combined to better address the issues.

The use of computer technology gives new access to the way in which participants contribute knowledge to group maps during workshops. Being able to log the knowledge shared by participants in a computer database enables post-workshop analyses of what each person shared when, and how that was used by the group to inform the final outcome. Complementing this data with video recordings of group discussion and social negotiation would enable the entire workshop to be amenable to post-workshop analyses. A fruitful direction for research would be to use these data to better understand the way in which knowledge is shared and used during these meetings.

Another direction for research would be to explore the impact of a workshop on the organisation—taking a longitudinal perspective through to the implementation of actions and the role of mapping in this.

CONCLUSION

During meetings, the structured collection and representation of knowledge can support the participants' acquisition, utilisation, and retention of available knowledge. We suggest that mapping is able to support the participants when they share, reflect upon, synthesise, expand, record, and creatively employ knowledge to better achieve the aims of the meeting. Through formal mapping methodologies such as Dialog Mapping, concept mapping, and Journey Making, facilitators can better support groups in these endeavours. However, more research to evaluate mapping approaches is needed to inform the continuous development of the techniques and of the software that supports them.

REFERENCES

Ackermann, F., Eden, C., & Williams, T. (1997). Modelling for litigation: Mixing qualitative and quantitative approaches. *INTERFACES, 27,* 48-65.

Belton, V., Ackermann, F., & Shepherd, I. (1997). Integrated support from problem structuring through to alternative evaluation using COPE and VISA. *Journal of Multi-Criteria Decision Analysis, 6,* 115-130.

Bonham, G.M. (1993). Cognitive mapping as a technique for supporting international negotiation. *Theory and Decision, 34,* 255-273.

Bougon, M.G., & Komocar, J.M. (1994). Directing strategic change: A dynamic holistic approach. In A.S. Huff (Ed.), *Mapping strategic thought* (pp. 135-163). Chichester: John Wiley & Sons.

Carlsson, C., & Walden, P. (1996). Cognitive maps and a hyperknowledge support system in strategic management. *Group Decision and Negotiation, 6,* 7-36.

Casu, B., Thanassoulis, E., & Shaw, D. (2002). Using a group decision support system to aid input-output identification in data envelopment analysis. In A. Emrouznejad, R. Green, & V. Krivonozhko (Eds.), *Proceedings of the International Data Envelopment Analysis Symposium* (pp. 159-164). Moscow, Russia.

Conklin, J. (2003). *Wicked problems and social complexity.* Working paper of the CogNexus Institute. Retrieved from *http://www.cognexus.org*

Eden, C., & Ackermann, F. (1998a). *Making strategy: The journey of strategic management.* London: Sage Publications.

Eden, C., & Ackermann, F. (1998b). Analysing and comparing causal maps. In C. Eden & J.C. Spender (Eds.), *Managerial and organisational cognition* (pp. 192-209). London: Sage Publications.

Eden, C. (forthcoming). Analyzing cognitive maps to help structure issues or problems. *European Journal of Operational Research.*

Edwards, J.S., Collier, P.M., & Shaw, D. (2004). *Management accounting and knowledge management.* London: Chartered Institute of Management Accountants.

Eppler, M.J. (2001). Making knowledge visible through intranet knowledge maps: Concepts, elements, cases. *Proceedings of the 34th Annual Hawaii International Conference on Systems Sciences,* Los Alamitos, CA.

Fjermestad, J., & Hiltz, S.R. (1998). An assessment of group support systems experiment research: Methodology and results. *Journal of Management Information Systems, 15*(3), 7-149.

Fletcher, K.E., & Huff, A.S. (1994). Strategic argument mapping: A study of strategy reformulation at AT&T. In A.S. Huff (Ed.), *Mapping strategic thought* (pp. 135-194). Chichester: John Wiley & Sons.

Gaines, B.R. (2002). Organizational knowledge acquisition. In C.W. Holsapple (Ed.), *Handbook on knowledge management: Volume 1* (pp. 317-347). Berlin, Heidelberg: Springer-Verlag.

Gaines, B.R., & Shaw M.L.G. (1995a). Concept maps as hypermedia components. *International Journal of Human-Computer Studies, 43*(3), 323-361.

Gaines, B.R., & Shaw, M.L.G. (1995b). WebMap: Concept mapping on the Web. *World Wide Web Journal, 1*(1), 171-183.

Gaines, B.R., & Shaw, M.L.G. (1995c). Collaboration through concept maps. In J.L. Schnase & E.L. Cunnius (Eds.), *Proceedings of Computer Support for Collaborative Learning'94* (pp. 135-138). Mahwah, NJ.

Gordon, J.L. (2000). Creating knowledge maps by exploiting dependent relationships. *Knowledge-Based Systems, 13*(2-3), 71-79.

Grise, M.L., & Gallupe, R.B. (1999). Information overload in face-to-face electronic meetings: An integrative complexity approach. *Journal of Management Information Systems, 16,* 157-185.

Henderson, G.R., Iacobucci, D., & Calder, B.J. (1998). Brand diagnostics: Mapping brand effects using consumer associative networks. *European Journal of Operational Research, 11,* 306-327.

Huff, A.S., & Jenkins, M. (2002). *Mapping strategic knowledge.* London: Sage Publications.

Jenkins, M., & Johnson, G. (1997). Linking managerial cognition and organisational performance: A preliminary investigation using causal maps. *British Journal of Management, 8,* S77-S90.

Johnson, P., & Johnson, G. (2002). Facilitating group cognitive mapping of core competencies. In A.S. Huff & M. Jenkins (Eds.), *Mapping strategic knowledge* (pp. 220-236). London: Sage Publications.

McKay, J. (1998). Using cognitive mapping to achieve shared understanding in information requirements determination. *The Australian Computer Journal, 30,* 139-145.

Mingers, J., & Gill, A. (1998). *Multimethodology: Theory and practice of combining management science methodologies.* Chichester: John Wiley & Sons.

Shaw, D. (2003). Evaluating electronic workshops through analysing the 'brainstormed' ideas. *Journal of the Operational Research Society, 54*(7), 692-705.

Shaw, D., Ackermann, F., & Eden, C. (2003a). Sharing knowledge in group problem structuring. *Journal of the Operational Research Society, 54*(9), 936-948.

Shaw, D., Edwards, J.S., Baker, B., & Collier, P.M. (2003b). Achieving closure through knowledge management strategy. *Electronic Journal of Knowledge Management, 1*(2), 197-205.

Te'eni, D., Schwartz, D.G., & Boland, R.J., (1997). Cognitive maps for communication: Specifying functionality and usability. In J. Carey (Ed.), *Human factors in management information systems: The Relationship between user interface design and human performance* (pp. 83-100). Greenwhich, CT: Ablex.

KEY TERMS

Causal Link: An arrow on a group map which represents a causal relationship between the two issues represented by the contributions it links.

Causal Relationship: The causality that exists between ideas/opinions; often can be thought of as drivers or consequences of action. For example, "implement KM system" needs "support from top management" and "make resources available" (both drivers), and the organisational impact might be "better utilisation of information" and/or "improved operational capabilities" (both consequences).

Cognitive Map: A structured representation of contributions, structured with links, to represent one person's knowledge of the topic. Often a map is built by oneself or by an interviewer during an interview.

Contribution: A piece of knowledge about an issue. Represents a participant's view, idea, perspective, thought, or opinion. A contribution should be about 4-10 words in length, to ensure it is understandable when read, but not too wordy.

Decision Explorer: A software often used in Journey Making events that supports the representation and analysis of maps. The Decision Explorer maps are projected onto a public screen for all participants to read, and illustrate their opinion using, during the workshop.

Gathering: An event where participants share their knowledge with the group on a particular topic. A gathering focuses exclusively on occupational knowledge and encourages an evaluation of the legitimacy of other peoples' contributions. A gathering is unlike a brainstorm in that it encourages evaluation, and discourages 'wild and wacky' ideas instead encouraging ideas that are potentially feasible for implementation. Following a gathering, facilitated group discussion is conducted on the contributions shared.

Group Explorer: A software used in a group which (in part) enables each participant to directly insert his/her knowledge (in the form of contributions and causal links) into a group map. Group Explorer works with Decision Explorer, which displays the group map on the public screen.

Group Map: A structured representation of the contributions of a range of people. The contributions are structured with links that are agreed by the group members during intensive, facilitated discussion of the issues that follow a gathering.

Journey Making: Group mapping activities are often a central part of a group's *JO*int *U*nderstanding, *R*eflection, and *NE*gotiation of strateg*Y*. The methodology aims to support groups in their development of a feasible strategy that they are individually and collectively committed to implementing.

Mathematical Knowledge Management

William M. Farmer
McMaster University, Canada

M

INTRODUCTION

Mathematical knowledge is significantly different from other kinds of knowledge. It is abstract, universal, highly structured, extraordinarily interconnected, and of immense size. Managing it is difficult and requires special techniques and tools.

Mathematicians have developed (over the last two or three millennia) many techniques for managing mathematical knowledge. For example, there is a large collection of techniques based on the use of special symbols and notations. Although these techniques are quite effective and have greatly advanced mathematical practice, they are primitive in the sense that the only tools they require are pencil and paper, typesetting machines, and printing presses.

Today mathematics is in a state of transition. Mathematicians are using the Internet in new ways to find information and to share results. Engineers and scientists are producing new kinds of mathematical knowledge that is oriented much more to practical concerns than to theoretical interests. This is particularly true in the field of software development where software specifications and code are forms of mathematical knowledge. Computers are being pushed to perform more sophisticated computations and to mechanize mathematical reasoning. Mathematical knowledge, as a result, is being produced and applied at an unprecedented rate.

It is becoming increasingly difficult to effectively disseminate mathematical knowledge, and to ascertain what mathematical results are known and how they are related to each other. Traditional ways of managing mathematical knowledge are no longer adequate, and current computer and communication technology do not offer an immediate solution. Since mathematical knowledge is vital to science and technology, and science and technology is vital to our society, new ways of managing mathematical knowledge based on new technology and new theory are needed.

This article introduces the main issues of managing mathematical knowledge. It is organized as follows. The Background section describes mathematics as a process of creating, exploring, and connecting mathematical models. The special characteristics of mathematical knowledge and the four main activities that constitute the management of mathematical knowledge are discussed in the Main Focus of the Article. The Future Trends section introduces *Mathematical Knowledge Management* (MKM), a new field of research, and discusses some of the challenges it faces. The article ends with a conclusion, references, and a list of key terms.

The management of mathematical knowledge is an emerging field of research. Researchers are just starting to build a foundation for it. This article focuses on the core concerns of the field. Except for a few remarks, it does not discuss the parallels between mathematical knowledge management and mainstream knowledge management. Nor does it discuss how techniques for managing mathematical knowledge can be applied to the management of other kinds of knowledge. These are important topics for future research.

BACKGROUND

People often associate mathematics with a body of knowledge about such things as numbers, spatial relationships, and abstract structures. However, this view of mathematics is misleading. It suggests that mathematics is something static and dead, but mathematics is actually the opposite—dynamic and alive. It is more productive and accurate to view mathematics as a process for comprehending the world that consists of three intertwined activities (Farmer & von Mohrenschildt, 2003).

The first activity is the *creation of mathematical models* that represent mathematical aspects of the world. Mathematical models come in many forms. A well-known and important example is the model of real number arithmetic composed of the set of real numbers, and operations and relations involving the real numbers such as +, ×, and <. Real number arithmetic includes various *submodels* such as arithmetic of the natural numbers 0,1,2,... and arithmetic of the rational numbers like 2/3, 31/17, and so forth. Real number arithmetic and its submodels capture the essential elements of counting, measurement, motion, and much more. Real number arithmetic itself is a submodel of complex number arithmetic and many other mathematical models.

The second activity is the *exploration of mathematical models* to learn what they say about the mathematical aspects of the world they model. There are several means of exploration. The explorer can state a conjecture about a model and then attempt to *prove* that the conjecture is true by virtue of being a logical consequence of the defining properties of the model. The explorer can also formulate a problem concerning the model and then *compute* a solution to it by mechanically manipulating a representation of the problem using rules determined by the model. A third approach, which is sometimes very effective, is to *visualize* some facet of the model with a diagram, picture, or animation.

The last activity is the *connection of mathematical models* by identifying and recording relationships between models. Models can be related to one another in various ways. Examples includes two models being equivalent in a certain sense, one model containing another as a submodel, and one model generalizing another model. A collection of interconnected models facilitates the creation and exploration of new models. New models can be built from old models, and then the results about the old models can be applied to these new models according to how they are connected. Thus, models rarely need to be developed from scratch.

MAIN FOCUS OF THE ARTICLE

Mathematical knowledge is knowledge about mathematical models. Each piece of mathematical knowledge is understood relative to a *context* of a mathematical model or group of mathematical models. For example, the statement "there is no square root of -1" is true in the model of real number arithmetic, but actually false in complex number arithmetic (the square root of -1 is the complex number i). Although a piece of mathematical knowledge is not meaningful without its context, the context of mathematical knowledge is often not explicitly stated. For example, one might say that as a mathematical fact, "every nonzero number has a multiplicative inverse" without mentioning the context of the statement. Of course, this statement is true for rational number arithmetic and real number arithmetic, but false for natural number arithmetic.

The context for understanding mathematical knowledge is analogous to the context for understanding other kinds of knowledge. Knowledge, mathematical or otherwise, that is applied out of its proper context is not reliable. The context of a piece of knowledge, mathematical or otherwise, is often imprecise or not fully articulated. However, a context for mathematical knowledge, unlike a context for many other kinds of knowledge, can be made as precise as is desired.

Mathematical knowledge is *direct* knowledge about mathematical models, but it is also *indirect* knowledge about the mathematical aspects of the world which are being modeled. As indirect knowledge, mathematical knowledge is useful, often even vital, to engineers and scientists. It is routinely used to help solve real-world problems.

Mathematical knowledge has several characteristics that sharply distinguish it from other kinds of knowledge. These characteristics make managing mathematical knowledge significantly different from managing other kinds of knowledge.

Abstractness

A mathematical model is an abstraction of the world; it ignores everything about the world except some part of the world's underlying mathematical structure. Other kinds of knowledge can be abstract, but mathematical knowledge is inherently abstract. Moreover, mathematics is, to a large degree, the study of abstractions.

Universality

Direct knowledge about a mathematical model is indirect knowledge about any situation in the world that exhibits the mathematical structure captured by the model. For example, it is true in the model of rational number arithmetic that, for any two integers m,n, if m/n is an integer, then $m = m/n + ... + m/n$ (n times) is sum of equal integers. As a result, *any* set of m objects can be divided into n subsets of equal size if m is divisible by n. Mathematical knowledge is thus universal in the sense that it can be applied to every domain of interest that exhibits the right kind of mathematical structure.

Language

Mathematical knowledge is usually expressed in a language with a carefully controlled syntax and a precise, unambiguous semantics. The language allows one to express statements about a certain collection of objects. The language may be an *informal* language based on a natural language such as English in which ordinary words such as "implies" and "function" have special meanings. The language may also be a *formal* language that can be read, analyzed, and presented by software.

Semantics

Unlike other kinds of knowledge, mathematical knowledge can be given a precise semantics. This is usually done by representing the context of the mathematical knowledge as a "mathematical theory." For example, an *axiomatic theory* is a pair $T = (L,A)$ where L is a language and A is a set of statements of L called *axioms*. The axioms express properties that the objects of L are assumed to possess. A mathematical model is a *model* of T if it has the same objects as *L* and it satisfies each axiom in *A*. *T* thus represents "axiomatically" the context composed of the models of *T*. A piece of mathematical knowledge about the context represented by *T* can then be expressed as a statement of *L* that is true in each model of *T*.

Representation

A body of mathematical knowledge can be represented in different ways. It can be represented *declaratively* as an explicit set of statements or as the set of logical consequences of a mathematical theory. It can be represented *procedurally* as the knowledge that is embodied in a computation system such as a calculator. It can be represented *visually* by diagrams and animations. A body of mathematical knowledge can also be represented by a combination of declarative, procedural, and visual means.

Proof

Most knowledge is obtained by empirical observation and experimentation. Mathematical knowledge is usually not obtained empirically. One way that it is obtained is by proving a conjecture within a context. A *proof* is an argument that shows that a statement *S* of a language *L* is a logical consequence of the axioms of an axiomatic theory $T = (L,A)$, and therefore, that *S* is true in each model of *T*. In other words, a proof verifies a conjecture by logical reasoning alone.

Computation

Another way that mathematical knowledge is obtained is by computing a solution to a problem. A *computation* from an expression *A* of a language *L* to an expression *B* of *L* is a sequence of meaning-preserving, mechanical manipulations that transform *A* into *B*. *A* expresses a problem to be solved and *B* expresses a solution to the problem. For example, *A* could be the equation

$$x^2 - 3x + 2 = 0,$$

B could be the statement

$$x = 1 \text{ or } x = 2,$$

and a computation of *A* from *B* could be the sequence of manipulations that are used to algebraically solve a quadratic equation like *A*.

Interconnectedness

The body of mathematical knowledge is extraordinarily interconnected. The same piece of knowledge may appear in many different places and in many different forms. For example, the models of real number arithmetic and rational number arithmetic—which are quite different in certain ways—both satisfy a common set of properties about +, ×, and <.

Size

The body of mathematical knowledge is unimaginably immense. It can even be argued that it is inherently infinite and thus possibly even bigger than the physical world. For instance, the model of natural number arithmetic, which is relatively simple, includes facts about each of the infinitely many natural numbers.

Mathematical Knowledge

Mathematical knowledge is produced by exploring mathematical models by means of proof, computation, and visualization. Mathematicians and other mathematics practitioners have traditionally been more concerned about its production than its management. As a result, the management of mathematical knowledge has historically been a collection of loosely related activities and for the most part not a highly disciplined process. In our opinion, there are four major activities—articulation, organization, dissemination, and access—that would be crucial components of any disciplined approach to the management of mathematical knowledge.

Articulation

Mathematical knowledge cannot be communicated unless it is *articulated*. An articulated body of mathematical knowledge has three components. The first is the *language* in which it is expressed. The second is the *context* of mathematical models within which it is understand. And the third is the *representation* by which it is conveyed.

Most mathematical knowledge is not articulated at all or only partially articulated. Many mathematical details have never been articulated; they reside only in the minds of mathematicians.

Mathematicians rediscover the details using hints provided by the original discoverer. Since fully articulating mathematical knowledge is burdensome, in most cases the language, context, and representation are only partially presented. The user of the knowledge is expected to be able to fill in what is missing as needed. This works well with human users who have strong mathematical skills. It does not work as well with students and average human users, and it does not work at all when the user is a computer program.

Organization

The prodigious size and interconnectedness of mathematical knowledge is a huge obstacle to effective management. Articulated mathematical knowledge needs to be carefully organized to avoid redundancy, to capture connections, and to express results in a compact form. This requires identifying and abstracting common structure and then formalizing it as a mathematical theory.

Mathematicians have always been very interested in organizing mathematical knowledge. However, their interest in the organization of mathematical knowledge is usually motivated by research or education and not by the practical management of mathematical knowledge. To be effectively managed, mathematical knowledge must be organized in a more practical way.

Dissemination

After mathematical knowledge is articulated and organized, it needs to be disseminated. The traditional modes of dissemination are as natural language text in journals and textbooks, and as computation procedures in calculators and mathematical software. Emerging modes of dissemination are as digital information that is accessible on the World Wide Web, and as formally represented declarative and procedural knowledge that is incorporated in mechanized mathematics systems such as computer algebra systems and computer theorem proving systems.

Historically, only the most general and widely applicable mathematical knowledge has been disseminated to the public. Mathematical knowledge generated by engineering and scientific endeavors, such as software development, is usually not widely disseminated even though it would be of value to many mathematics practitioners. New approaches and technology are needed to disseminate this latter, more practical kind of mathematical knowledge.

Access

People need software tools for finding the mathematical knowledge they require in a body of knowledge that has been disseminated. Tools are needed for doing searches and making queries, for performing deductions and computations with mathematical software systems, and for understanding how the knowledge has been articulated and organized. These software tools need to be much more sophisticated and easier to use than current tools. For example, search engines must understand the semantics of mathematical languages and, for example, when syntactically distinct expressions such as x^2+1 and $1+x.x$ are semantically equivalent.

How effectively mathematical knowledge can be accessed strongly depends on how the mathematical knowledge is previously formed. Mathematical knowledge needs to be articulated, organized, and disseminated so that access is facilitated.

FUTURE TRENDS

Mathematical Knowledge Management (MKM) is a new interdisciplinary field of research in the intersection of mathematics, computer science, library science, and scientific publishing. The objective of MKM is to develop new and better ways of managing mathematical knowledge using sophisticated software tools. MKM is expected to serve mathematicians, scientists, and engineers who produce and use mathematical knowledge; educators and students who teach and learn mathematics; publishers who offer mathematical textbooks and disseminate new mathematical results; and librarians and mathematicians who catalog and organize mathematical knowledge.

The challenges facing MKM researchers are daunting. The following are some of the major issues (expressed as questions) that are challenging researchers in MKM:

1. What kind of tools are need to put mathematical knowledge on the World Wide Web? (see, e.g., the MathML (*www.w3.org/Math*), MoWGLI (*www.mowgli.cs.unibo.it*), and Open-Math (Dalmas, Gaëtano, & Watt, 1997) programs)
2. What kind of software support is needed to convert an informal articulation of mathematical knowledge into a formal articulation? (see, e.g., Davenport, 2003)
3. How should the context of mathematical knowledge be expressed?
4. How should mathematical knowledge be organized? (see, e.g., Brownie & Stanway, 2003)
5. How can libraries of mathematical knowledge be searched? (see, e.g., Bancerek & Redneck, 2003)
6. How can mathematical knowledge be shared between mathematical systems? (see, e.g., Carette, Farmer, & Wajs, 2003)

7. How can declarative representations of mathematical knowledge be integrated with procedural representations? (see, e.g., Farmer & von Mohrenschildt, 2003)

8. What role should universities, governments, professional societies, and publishers play in disseminating mathematical knowledge?

9. Who should own and administer mathematical knowledge?

10. How should the role of mathematicians differ from the role of librarians in the task of organizing mathematical knowledge?

11. How should disseminated mathematical knowledge be certified?

12. What mechanism should be used to standardize and integrate MKM software tools?

The grand challenge of MKM is to develop a *universal digital mathematics library* (UDML). Composed of many heterogeneous, intercommunicating systems, it would be easily accessible via the World Wide Web. It would be constructed in an open, cooperative fashion in the same way that the Internet was constructed. Never finished, it would continuously grow and in time would contain essentially all mathematical knowledge (intended for the public). It would also be continuously reorganized and consolidated as new connections and discoveries were made.

A UDML would contain a highly structured and interconnected mixture of axiomatic, algorithmic, diagrammatic, and other kinds of mathematical knowledge. Each piece of mathematical knowledge in it would carry a certification of its correctness (relative to a specified set of assumptions). It would also include an integrated collection of tools for exploring its contents. It is important to note that a UDML would be a library and not an archive. That is, its primarily purpose would be to make mathematical knowledge widely accessible, not just to store and catalog mathematical knowledge.

Creating a UDML will be a Herculean project requiring the development of many new kinds of technology. Some of this technology is being developed now on current formal mathematics library projects including the NIST Digital Library of Mathematical Functions (*dlmf.nist.gov*), the Formal Digital Library (*www.nuprl.org/FDLproject*), Hypatheon (DiVito, 2004), Logosphere (*www.logosphere.org*), Mizar (*mizar.org*), and the Wolfram Functions site (*functions.wolfram.com*).

As a new field of research, MKM was launched by the First International Workshop on MKM (*www.risc.uni-linz.ac.at/institute/conferences/MKM2001*) in September 2001 in Hagenberg, Austria. Organized by Bruno Buchberger and Olga Caprotti, MKM 2001 led to the founding of the MKM Consortium in December 2001

under the leadership of Michiel Hazewinkel and to a special issue (Buchberger, Gonnet, & Hazewinkel, 2003) of the *Annals of Mathematics and Artificial Intelligence* dedicated to MKM.

The MKM Consortium is an international group of researchers dedicated to the promotion of research and interest in MKM. It has organized two subsequent international MKM conferences: the Second International Conference on MKM (*www.cs.unibo.it/MKM03*) was held in February 2003 in Bertinoro, Italy, and the Third International Conference on MKM (*mizar.org/MKM2004*) was held September 19-21, 2004, in Bialowieza, Poland. The MKM Consortium currently consists of a European Chapter (*monet.nag.co.uk/mkm/index.html*) and a North American Chapter (*imps.mcmaster.ca/na-mkm*).

CONCLUSION

Mathematical knowledge has special characteristics that require management techniques and technology different than the techniques and technology needed for other kinds of knowledge.

Researchers in the new field of MKM are beginning to develop new and better software for managing mathematical knowledge. Since mathematical knowledge is universal knowledge about mathematical aspects of the world, this software, and certainly the ideas on which it is based, may be applicable to the abstract and mathematical parts of other kinds of knowledge.

REFERENCES

Bancerek, G., & Redneck, P. (2003). Information retrieval in MML. In A. Asperti, B. Buchberger, & J.H. Davenport (Eds.), *Mathematical knowledge management. Proceedings of MKM 2003,* (pp. 119-132). Berlin: Springer-Verlag (LNCS 2594).

Brownie, J., & Stanway, T. (2003). Managing digital mathematical discourse. In A. Asperti, B. Buchberger, & J.H. Davenport (Eds.), *Mathematical knowledge management. Proceedings of MKM 2003,* (pp. 45-55). Berlin: Springer-Verlag (LNCS 2594).

Buchberger, B., Gonnet, G., & Hazewinkel, M. (Eds.). (2003). Mathematical knowledge management. *Annals of Mathematics and Artificial Intelligence, 38*(Special Issue), 1-232.

Carette, J., Farmer, W.M., & Wajs, J. (2003). Trustable communication between mathematics systems. In T. Hardin & R. Rioboo (Eds.), *Calculemus 2003* (pp. 58-68). Rome: Arcane.

Dalmas, S., Gaëtano, M., & Watt, S.M. (1997). An Open-Math 1.0 implementation. *Proceedings of the International Symposium on Symbolic and Algebraic Computation (ISSAC-97)* (pp. 241-248). ACM Press.

Davenport, J.H. (2003). MKM from book to computer: A case study. In A. Asperti, B. Buchberger, & J.H. Davenport (Eds.), *Mathematical knowledge management. Proceedings of MKM 2003* (pp. 45-55). Berlin: Springer-Verlag (LNCS 2594).

DiVito, B.L. (2004). Hypatheon: A mathematical database for PVS users. Retrieved from *http://imps.mcmaster.ca/na-mkm-2004/proceedings/pdfs/divito.pdf*

Farmer, W.M., & von Mohrenschildt, M. (2003). An overview of a formal framework for managing mathematics. *Annals of Mathematics and Artificial Intelligence, 38,* 165-191.

KEY TERMS

Axiomatic Theory: Consists of a language and a set of statements of the language called *axioms*. The language allows one to express statements about a certain collection of objects, and the axioms express properties that the objects of the language are assumed to possess. An axiomatic theory represents a collection of mathematical models—namely, those models that have the same objects as the language of the theory and that satisfy the axioms of the theory.

Computer Algebra System: A software system that performs symbolic computations.

Computer Theorem Proving System: A software system that is used to discover, develop, or verify formal deductions.

Context: In mathematics, a mathematical model or group of mathematical models within which a piece of mathematical knowledge is understood.

Mathematical Knowledge Management (MKM): A new interdisciplinary field of research in the intersection of mathematics, computer science, library science, and scientific publishing. The objective of MKM is to develop new and better ways of managing mathematical knowledge using sophisticated software tools.

Mathematical Model: A model of certain mathematical aspects of the world. Mathematical models come in many forms. A common form is a collection of objects together with a collection of operations on and relationships between the objects.

Proof: A mathematical *proof* of a statement S in an axiomatic theory T is an argument that shows that S is a logical consequence of the axioms of T. Proofs are used to discover, certify, and communicate mathematical knowledge.

Measuring Knowledge Management Capabilities

M

Uday Kulkarni
Arizona State University, USA

Ronald Freeze
Arizona State University, USA

INTRODUCTION

As business professionals know, creating awareness of a problem and its impact is a critical first step toward the resolution of the problem. That which does not get measured, does not get managed (Redman, 1998). In fact, measurement is a precursor to improvement. This is true for knowledge management (KM) capabilities of an organization. "In today's knowledge-based economy," Alan Greenspan recently said, "70% of organizational assets are knowledge assets." Knowledge assets are intangible capabilities, and there is a recognized need to "make a greater effort to quantify the value of such intangible assets" (Teece, 1998b). How does one measure the worth of an organization's knowledge assets? What does one mean by knowledge assets anyway?

In this article, we afford some formal structure to the idea of measuring knowledge management capabilities of an organization, with the ultimate goal of improving business performance through better management of knowledge assets. We describe a large-scale effort at Intel to assess such capabilities with a view to enhance them. This project started in May of 2002. We describe the different types of knowledge assets identified, the potential capabilities associated with managing knowledge assets, the metrics devised for their measurement, and the assessment methodology that is being standardized across the corporation. We also provide results of the initial validation of the instrument and its ability to ascertain KM capabilities correctly. Hundreds of knowledge workers (Davenport, 2003) have so far participated in this study to benchmark KM capabilities of their units. Some units are already planning the next steps for improving their KM capabilities.

BACKGROUND: WHAT IS KNOWLEDGE?

The direction required to quantify the value of knowledge assets begins to come into focus when one realizes their diversity in an organizational setting. Some knowledge assets are "grounded in the experience and expertise of individuals," that is, tacit knowledge, while others can be stored as knowledge objects that exist on their own, that is, explicit knowledge (Fahey & Prusak, 1998; Teece, 1998a). Therefore, to describe knowledge assets that exist across organizations, domains that encompass knowledge work and can be studied for improving on-the-job productivity must be identified. For this reason, we start with classifying the whole gamut of knowledge residing in an organization into a knowledge-asset framework.

We categorize institutional knowledge assets into four areas: expertise, lessons learned, knowledge documents, and data. This categorization resulted from the realization that knowledge in each area has a unique (a) mix of tacit and explicit content, (b) method of transfer and contextual value, and (c) life cycle (creation to application), including its shelf life. To contrast the unique nature of each knowledge area, its characterization along these three dimensions needs to be understood.

Expertise

Expertise is high in tacit knowledge. Individuals in an organization are often considered experts within a particular domain. The transfer of expertise occurs via consultation, collaboration, mentoring, and observation, that is, through personal interaction. The shelf life of this type of knowledge depends on the currency of the knowledge in the context of its application, and it can be extended by renewal and learning. The availability of experts and the ability of an organization to locate required expertise for a given situation quickly can result in performance improvement (Dooley, Corman, & McPhee, 2002).

Lessons Learned

Lessons learned are the essence of learning from past successes and failures. They represent highly specific knowledge gained while completing a project or task. They lie toward the tacit end of the tacit-explicit continuum. Undocumented lessons are in the heads of people who learned them. To the extent lessons are documented, their transferability is improved (in a networked organization), but their applicability remains highly contextual. Recognizing the similarities between the characteristics of the current task with those of an earlier one from which the lesson was learned is an important step in their application. This type of knowledge is created when one recognizes that something substantial of recurring value has been learned. The shelf life of a lesson depends on its generalizability and the persistence of the context. The more generalized a lesson, the broader is its applicability and the longer its life. Organizations that exploit this type of knowledge have reported substantial cost savings (O'Dell & Grayson, 1998).

Knowledge Documents

Knowledge documents represent explicit knowledge such as project reports, technical reports, policies and procedures, research reports, publications, pictures, drawings, diagrams, audio and video clips, and so forth. Knowledge documents encompass internally generated as well as external information (Zack, 1999). Market research reports and operating manuals of complex machinery are good examples. Knowledge documents contain the background knowledge that can be referred to by a knowledge worker to educate themselves—to increase their awareness and understanding—about an area that they work in. Well understood taxonomies and archives, as well as the ease of access of relevant documents, is important to maximize the transferability and reuse of this knowledge. In contrast to lessons learned, the knowledge contained in knowledge documents is more permanent.

Data

The most explicit form of knowledge is contained in data used for strategic and tactical decision making (Fahey & Prusak, 1998). Here we do not refer to operational data generated by the day-to-day transactions of a business, but aggregated and historical data such as that stored in a data warehouse. Such data can be a constant source of useful knowledge when used for analytical processing, detecting patterns, modeling business situations, and so forth. The quality of metadata (design of the structure and descriptions of data) determines the availability and usability of this type of knowledge. The shelf life of data as a knowledge source can be very long; many retail corporations have spent millions of dollars on creating large data warehouses that store years of summary data for discovering trends and patterns (knowledge) that can have a direct impact on strategic decisions.

One may argue that there is a substantial overlap among the knowledge assets described above. While we recognize that the lines separating these knowledge assets are gray, the core characteristics of the knowledge areas differ substantially, and therefore the knowledge needs of an organization can be more clearly understood if they are broken up among the different types of knowledge assets. Hansen, Nohria, and Tierney (1999) describe the differing views of knowledge in different organizations and show how an organization's business strategy drives its knowledge needs. We found that, particularly in large organizations, the functional nature of a business unit emphasizes the unit's knowledge needs.

While each business unit within Intel utilized all types of knowledge, we found that the importance, and therefore the strategic focus of a business unit, varied based on its core functional responsibility. TMG, an organizational unit focused on the rapid ramp-up of production operations, required a high level of capability within the lessons-learned category. Identifying shortcomings within this unique capability area therefore became critical. In contrast, SSG, a unit responsible for the development of system software solutions, required emphasis on different capability areas, namely, in expertise and knowledge documents. Being able to assess the existing capability levels in these differing knowledge areas is not only essential for benchmarking, but also for directing efforts to improve them and to monitor progress over time. The importance of KM capability assessment is validated by the actions of the business units subsequent to the assessment; most of the business units have already started investing in planned KM initiatives in those knowledge areas that are deemed important but low in capability level.

WHAT DOES MANAGING KNOWLEDGE MEAN?

Like any other intangible asset, knowledge needs to be managed in order to maximize its value by fully exploiting its utility. Each type of knowledge asset has its own unique characteristics as described above, however, a common framework can be applied to understand how it can be managed. One such framework stems from the concept of the knowledge life cycle (Alavi & Leidner, 2001). The four distinct stages of the knowledge life cycle are creation and capture, storage and archival, retrieval and transfer, and application and reuse. We found that, although these stages seem to apply only to explicit knowledge, they do apply to tacit knowledge as well. For example, in the context of highly tacit knowledge such as expertise, the capture stage corresponds to the process of identifying domain experts and registering their expertise. This information about specific fields of expertise is then stored in an expertise database. The retrieval stage occurs when a potential user of knowledge searches for and locates the appropriate expert, and the application stage is the culmination of the life cycle resulting in a consultation with the expert. The knowledge life-cycle framework can thus be applied to manage both explicit and tacit knowledge.

In assessing KM capabilities of an organization, ascertaining how well each stage of the knowledge life cycle is managed becomes important. Stages of the life cycle may be assisted by the necessary technology support and the integration of KM-related activities into normal business processes. While technology automates parts of the knowledge life cycle, process integration ensures participation in KM-related activities. In addition, the cultural underpinnings of an organization determine the extent to which organizational knowledge may be shared.

Technology Support

Although technology is not the solution to managing knowledge, it provides the means to participate in certain stages of the knowledge life cycle. KM systems are a class of information systems built around this need. Examples of KM systems that offer support for sharing knowledge in various capability areas are a form-based registration system for capturing the areas of expertise of experts, a storage and retrieval system for categorizing and searching knowledge documents, a data warehouse with decision-support and modeling tools, and so forth.

Process Integration

If knowledge-sharing activities are made part of normal business processes, it is more likely to result in higher KM capabilities. Purely voluntary participation in KM-related activities is hard to come by because its direct and immediate benefits are difficult to measure. Nevertheless, large and small organizations have started embedding knowledge capture and access activities into work flows. Examples of such practices are routine engagement in reflective activities after reaching major milestones of projects to capture lessons learned, or looking for relevant knowledge documents at the beginning of a new task or project.

The Role of Culture

Organizational culture plays a significant role in defining the extent to which knowledge may be shared. The environments in which employees work can affect both the supply and demand aspects of every type of knowledge. On the supply side, it is the willingness to share expertise, taking the time to catalog important knowledge documents, and investing time in postmortems and debriefings to capture lessons learned from completed projects and tasks. On the demand side, culture can promote looking for and reusing available knowledge.

The existence of a positive knowledge-sharing culture is a precondition for an organization to have any capability in KM (Adams & Lamont, 2003). No amount of sophisticated KM systems and process changes can enhance KM capabilities if the culture discourages sharing and promotes hoarding. Organizations that have this problem and recognize it need to work on creating the appropriate environment for their knowledge workers. As a first step, immediate supervisors may encourage the regular sharing of work-related problem solutions and be role models by demonstrating knowledge-sharing behavior. The next higher level in this direction may be reached by recognizing and rewarding knowledge-sharing behavior, and instituting training and education on systems and processes used for knowledge sharing. At the highest level, the top management of the company may demonstrate its commitment by having a well articulated KM strategy and setting goals for KM-related undertakings.

HOW CAN ONE MEASURE KNOWLEDGE MANAGEMENT CAPABILITY?

Since KM assessment is an opportune topic, a few assessment tools and frameworks have been developed and presented at practitioner conferences and Web sites of such companies. Noteworthy among these are two methods, both based on the five level capability maturity model of the Software Engineering Institute (Humphrey, 1995). One is from Siemens that divides KM-related issues into eight key areas and a progressive maturity-level scale (Ehms & Langen, 2002; Langen, 2002), and another is from InfoSys Technologies focusing on three key result areas and a maturity model (Kochikar, 2002). However, apart from the terminology and some semantic transformations from software engineering to KM, there is no detailed description of the model, no operational classification of different types of knowledge, and no definitions of levels in terms of goals. For example, the general and specific goals of each level and the activities needed to attain the various levels of maturity are not available. Moreover, there is no scientific study reporting attempts made to test for content and construct validity of either the measurement instrument or the process adopted.

Our case-study team consisted of experts from Intel Corporation from process management, value measurement, change management, and information technology, in addition to the external academic researchers (authors). We undertook a structured conceptual develop-

ment process to design a knowledge management capability assessment (KMCA) instrument. With the identification of knowledge-asset areas, a consistent nomological measure across all knowledge areas was needed to identify the capability level achieved within each area of knowledge.

Development of the KMCA Instrument

The KMCA model also adapts the framework of the five level capability maturity model to the KM context. The conceptual structure of the KMCA emphasizes the top-down design of the measurement instrument. The five

Table 1. Capability levels

Capability Level	General Goals	Examples of Specific Goals
Level 1: Possible	Knowledge sharing is not discouraged. There is a general willingness to share. People who understand the value of sharing do it. The meaning of knowledge assets is understood.	Previous lessons learned can be found with perseverance.
		Some experts are willing to share expertise when consulted.
Level 2: Encouraged	The culture encourages the sharing of knowledge assets. The value of knowledge assets is recognized. Knowledge assets are stored/tracked in some fashion.	Supervisors encourage regular meetings to share knowledge/solutions.
		Experts and their expertise are identifiable.
		The importance of prior lessons learned is recognized.
Level 3: Enabled/ Practiced	The sharing of knowledge assets is practiced. Systems/tools to enable KM activities exist. Rewards/incentives promote knowledge sharing.	Organizational leadership understands how KM is applied to business.
		Lessons learned are captured.
		Taxonomies and centralized repositories for knowledge documents exist.
		Experts are able to register their expertise.
		Historical data is available for decision making.
Level 4: Managed	Employees expect to locate knowledge. Training is available. KM-related activities are part of work flow. Systems/tools for supporting KM activities are easy to use. KM capabilities and benefits are assessed. Leadership exhibits commitment to KM. Leadership provides a KM strategy.	Senior management sets policy, guidelines, and goals with respect to KM.
		Tools to locate experts are easy to use.
		Capturing, storing, and using lessons learned are part of normal work process.
		Knowledge-document retrieval is fast and easy.
		Historical data utilized for decision making is easy to access and manipulate.
Level 5: Continuous Improvement	KM processes are reviewed/improved. KM systems/tools are widely accepted, monitored, and updated. The KM assessment generates realistic improvement.	Senior management periodically reviews the effectiveness of KM investments to the whole organization.
		Recent improvements in document access have been implemented.
		Expert and expertise identification has expanded and been refined.
		New tools for data manipulation are tested and implemented.
		The impact of lessons learned on operations is communicated.

capability levels of the KMCA are described in terms of their general goals in Table 1. The general goals indicate the milestones to be achieved in order for an organization (or an organizational unit) to reach the corresponding capability level. These goals are general enough to apply to each of the four knowledge capability areas. One can see that lower level goals are easier to achieve than higher level goals. This progression gives the questionnaire the ability to discern between capability levels accurately, an important design aspect of the KMCA.

The KMCA team mapped each general goal to one or more specific goals for each knowledge area: expertise, lessons learned, knowledge documents, and data. For example, consider one of the general goals of Capability Level 3 (see Table 1): "Systems/tools to enable KM activities exist." Emanating from this general goal, one of the corresponding specific goals for the expertise area is "Experts are able to register their expertise in an expertise profiling system." Such mapping was completed for each general goal of each capability level (for every capability area). Specific goals of each capability level of each knowledge area were then mapped to one or more specific practices, which are work practices that employees could identify with in their day-to-day work life. Specific practices were, in turn, converted into questions for the first version of the questionnaire. By strictly adhering to this procedure, the team was not only able to include questions representing all levels (Level 1 through Level 5), but also able to maintain the relative progression of levels of questions within each area.

The prototype and subsequent versions of the instrument were developed and validated in four distinct phases over a 24 month period. These phased activities and accomplishments are described in Table 2, which details the deliberate, step-by-step process. The questionnaire consists of sections for each knowledge area and one for the cultural aspects of an organization. Within each section, questions are grouped by the components of that knowledge area. For example, the components under the knowledge documents section are taxonomy, the categorization process, the repository, the search and retrieval process, and the application and use process. Each question is mapped to a capability level according to the specific goals of that level. The final questionnaire consists of about 120 questions that can be completed in about 20 minutes.

Instrument Validation

Translation validity, which includes both the face and content validity of items included in the instrument, attempts to assess the degree to which the accurate translation of the constructs occurs while

Table 2. Instrument construction in validation

	Activities	Accomplishments
Phase 1 May 2002– Aug. 2002	Background research and identification of knowledge capability areas. Conceptual design of the instrument, capability levels, goals, and initial survey construction. Focus group of 12 knowledge workers.	Confirmation of knowledge areas. Initial questionnaire with about 145 questions and a 45-minute completion time. Applicability of the survey to the work environment (face and content validity).
Phase 2 Aug. 2002– Nov. 2002	Survey administration to 38 volunteers from one business unit.	Ability of the instrument to measure KM capabilities of the unit (criterion-related validity). Survey modification based on open-ended feedback (face and content validity).
Phase 3 Nov. 2002– Aug. 2003	Full-scale pilot study administration to a large business unit. Elimination of redundant questions after data analysis, formatting, and readability improvements. Interrater reliability test utilizing six domain experts on KM.	Final questionnaire with about 120 questions and a 20-minute completion time. Improvement in the instrument's ability to recommend specific KM practices. Ability of the instrument to discern between capability levels.
Phase 4 Aug. 2003– May 2004	Final version administered to three large business units (population 650 to 1,000 employees). Confirmatory factor analysis and other testing of capability areas, their components, and measurement accuracy.	Ascertaining the ability of the instrument to measure capability levels in each knowledge area. Response bias test indicated no bias. Ability to make comparisons of KM capabilities within and between business units.

operationalizing the instrument (Trochim, 2001). This was a major focus in the early phases of the project, which provided substantial input as to the applicability of the concepts to Intel.

The criterion-related validity assesses the measurement accuracy of the instrument. It checks the predictive capability of the instrument based on the theory of the construct. In our case, this is the ability of our instrument to accurately measure the capability level of an organization in each knowledge area. Because of the strict design considerations, we expected to observe that for each capability area, all the requirements of a lower level of capability would be fully met before requirements of any of the higher levels are met. Results from the three business units at Intel confirmed this expectation, and we conclude that the capability levels are a progression. We also expected the KMCA to be able to compare relative capabilities across knowledge areas within a single organization and across multiple organizations for a given knowledge area. Our results also confirmed this expectation. The overall results thus confirm that the mapping from general goals to specific goals and practices, and then to actual questions was accurately accomplished, and that KMCA is able to measure and compare the separate KM capabilities of organizations.

Up to this point, we have focused on item construction and its translation to knowledge areas and levels. The overall goal is one of establishing the four capability areas as measurable constructs. For this final step,

we used confirmatory factor analysis and represented each capability area as a latent factor whose measurement consistency was established using two measurement model forms: (a) the general-specific model and (b) the second-order model (Chen, West, & Sousa, in press). The results of both structural equation models provided fit indices for all capability areas, indicating models of good fit. The significance of the general factor and the second-order factor representing the overall capability area provides strong evidence supporting these knowledge assets as measurable capabilities. Using both measurement models within each business unit provided experimental rigor and external validity.

Measurement Results

The results of the KMCA are in the form of capability-level scores in each knowledge area accompanied by a report describing the highlights and detailed information concerning the status of KM capability in each area. Figure 1 shows a sample page from the results of the lessons-learned knowledge area pertaining to one of the business units at Intel. "Usage" summarizes the usage and importance of the knowledge area to the unit. The observations are factual statements that convey to the business unit the highlights of the unit's capability in a particular area. The recommendations are prescriptions for action. The specificity of the recommendations allows a unit to start planning for KM initiatives. Addi-

Figure 1. Sample KMCA results page

Unit Name:	_____
Capability Area:	*Lessons Learned*
Capability Level Achieved:	*3 (on a scale of 1 to 5, with 5 being the highest)*

Highlights:

Usage

o   Ninety percent of the respondents use lessons learned.

o   Among the four knowledge areas, lessons learned were considered the least important to the job.

o   Individuals use lessons learned three to four times a week and spend a total of 30 to 60 minutes a week looking for lessons learned.

Observations

–   Looking for lessons learned is part of work practices; lessons learned do provide insights that promote successful practices and avoiding mistakes.

–   Although the electronic storage system for lessons learned seems to be adequate, it is deficient in terms of ease of use, documentation, accessibility, and search categories.

Recommendations

✓   Electronic storage and search systems for lessons learned need improvement.

✓   A systematic process for the capture and periodic review of existing lessons learned needs to be instituted.

Detailed Information:

Component Analysis: Detailed analysis of each component of the lessons-learned area: capture, taxonomy, repository, and application and use

Descriptive Statistics: Detailed statistics regarding the response rate, mean, variance, maximum, minimum, and so forth for every question

Summary of open-ended qualitative comments made by respondents

tionally, "Detailed Information" contains the capability analysis of each component of the knowledge area (which, in the case of lessons learned, are capture, taxonomy, repository, and application and use), descriptive statistics, and a summary of respondents' qualitative comments.

As a consequence of the KMCA, one of the business units, SSG, has already started major efforts in most of the suggested directions. SSG has constituted five overlapping teams of knowledge workers to plan and design KM initiatives: one in each of the knowledge areas and one specifically to address organizational culture in the context of knowledge sharing. The long-term effect of these efforts needs to be seen.

FUTURE TRENDS: IMPACT ON BUSINESS PERFORMANCE

Ultimately, the proof of the pudding is in eating. Assessing KM capabilities is an interim step toward the ultimate goal of making a positive impact on business performance. The direct impact of KM initiatives on bottom-line performance metrics, such as profit, revenue, and market share, is difficult to establish. Nonetheless, efforts need to be made in choosing the appropriate metrics. In the case of semiautonomous business units, bottom-line metrics are not pertinent. In such cases, indicators more relevant to the business of the unit, such as productivity, quality (of the product or service), and responsiveness, may be chosen. Complicating the relationship between KM initiatives and business performance is the fact that the gestation period for reaping benefits is longer, unlike installations of new equipment or implementations of business process changes. Thus, investments in KM initiatives must be viewed longitudinally.

Of the three large business units that have participated in the KM capability assessment at Intel, one is a manufacturing unit (TMG), another is responsible for providing systems software embedded in chips (SSG), and the third is the corporate quality-assurance unit (CQN). The population surveyed within the manufacturing unit was the engineers and technicians responsible for maximizing the yield and quality of semiconductor wafers using the most sophisticated and expensive equipment in its category. By far, the most important goal of this group is keeping the machines up and running at the optimum levels. Given the nature of their responsibility, as a relatively short-term measure of performance, we devised a metric to measure the delay experienced in getting the right knowledge (expertise, lessons learned, knowledge documents, and data) to the right person whenever needed. A longer term metric of performance

is the average down times and ultimately the yield of the particular factory.

In the case of the other two units, although there are no direct measures of white-collar productivity, the effects of knowledge sharing and reuse can be observed by way of time saved in isolating a problem, finding solutions, and completing projects. The effects of knowledge sharing may also result in better decisions in choosing vendors, arriving at more accurate lab test results, and so forth. Hence, in addition to the quantitative measures of time spent to get the knowledge, we used qualitative measures such as the adequacy of various knowledge sources in satisfactorily fulfilling the requirements of individual managers.

As one moves away from the direct impact of KM initiatives to improvements over the long term, confounding factors obfuscate the relationship between KM and business performance. The benefits of KM become harder to assert, and investments in KM initiatives become harder to justify.

CONCLUSION

Knowledge management is increasingly viewed as a way to improve firm performance and potentially to provide a competitive advantage. Successes have been documented in corporate initiatives (sometimes referred to as KM initiatives) by utilizing knowledge in the form of best practices that resides within the firm. The descriptions of success have been predominantly anecdotal. To allay the complexity of the concept of knowledge assets, we identified four distinct types of knowledge assets, each with its own mix of tacit-explicit content, method of transfer, and life cycle. Through our case study, we demonstrated that it is not only possible to obtain a realistic assessment of KM capabilities of an organization in each knowledge area, but that the assessment offers specific directions for improving such capabilities. We found that the business units that we analyzed had differing knowledge-area emphases and capabilities based on the business unit's function and objectives. These results have several implications going forward for both business practice and research.

From a business perspective, our study demonstrates that the assessment of KM capabilities can be prescribed as a key component of an organization's KM program. Since organizations possess and require varied capabilities in different areas of knowledge, a capability assessment (such as the KMCA) should occur as one of the first steps toward improvement. Additionally, an organization should conduct a macrolevel review of its business goals and the knowledge needs of its processes to most effectively achieve those goals. Once a review of these goals and knowledge needs is completed, an assessment of the capability areas will provide an alignment analysis of the fit with the stated business objectives. Initiatives can then be designed to target those knowledge capabilities that are deemed important but deficient within the organization. Such goal-directed targeting of specific capabilities via well-designed initiatives, coupled with the tracking of business performance metrics, would greatly enhance the effectiveness of a KM program. The ability to correctly measure knowledge capabilities and prescribe improvements thus provides an initial step to capitalize fully on the management of knowledge.

For successfully contributing to research in the area of KM capability assessment, two items need to be kept in focus: the choice of success metrics and the longitudinal nature of this research. The business performance metrics chosen must be measurable and should be an acceptable measure of success of KM initiatives; they are critical in establishing relationships between KM capabilities and business performance. Since the return on investments in KM initiatives of any kind—systems, processes, or cultural aspects—usually occurs over an extended period, an organization participating in such a scientific study has to recognize the long-term nature of its commitment. A standardized instrument that can measure various KM capabilities consistently over long periods becomes an essential component of the undertaking.

REFERENCES

Adams, G. L., & Lamont, B. T. (2003). Knowledge management systems and developing sustainable competitive advantage. *Journal of Knowledge Management, 7*(2), 142-154.

Alavi, M., & Leidner, D. (2001). Review: Knowledge management and knowledge management systems: Conceptual foundations and research issues. *MIS Quarterly, 25*(1), 1-7-136.

Chen, F. F., West, S. G., & Sousa, K. H. (in press). A comparison of general-specific and second-order models of quality of life. *Structural Equation Modeling*.

Davenport, T. H. (2003). A measurable proposal. *CIO Magazine*.

Dooley, K. J., Corman, S. R., & McPhee, R. D. (2002). A knowledge directory for identifying experts and areas of expertise. *Human Systems Management, 21*, 217-228.

Ehms, K., & Langen, M. (2002). Holistic development of knowledge management with KMMM. *Siemens AG*.

Fahey, L., & Prusak, L. (1998). The eleven deadliest sins of knowledge management. *California Management Review, 40*(3), 265

Hansen, M. T., Nohria, N., & Tierney, T. (1999). What's your strategy for managing knowledge? *Harvard Business Review, 77*(2), 106.

Humphrey, W. S. (1995). *A discipline for software engineering*. Reading, MA: Addison-Wesley.

Kochikar, V. P. (2002). *The knowledge management maturity model: A staged framework for leveraging knowledge*. Unpublished manuscript.

Langen, M. (2002). *Knowledge management maturity model: KMMM methodology for assessing and developing maturity in knowledge management*.

O'Dell, C., & Grayson, C. J. (1998). If only we knew what we know: Identification and transfer of internal best practices. *California Management Review, 40*(3), 154.

Redman, T. C. (1998). The impact of poor data quality on the typical enterprise. *Communications of the ACM, 41*(2), 79-82.

Teece, D. J. (1998a). Capturing value from knowledge assets: The new economy, markets for know-how, and intangible assets. *California Management Review, 40*(3), 55.

Teece, D. J. (1998b). Research directions for knowledge management. *California Management Review, 40*(3), 289.

Trochim, W. M. (2001). *The research methods knowledge base* (2nd ed.). Retrieved from *http://atomicdogpublishing.com*

Zack, M. H. (1999). Developing a knowledge strategy. *California Management Review, 41*(3), 125.

KEY TERMS

Data: Highly explicit knowledge derived from the data in databases and data warehouses used for strategic decision making after summarizing, analyzing, mining, and so forth.

Expertise: Highly tacit, domain-specific knowledge gained through experience, formal education, and collaboration.

Knowledge Assets: Intangible assets that encompass knowledge as well as the ability of an organization to leverage that knowledge.

Knowledge Capability Area (also referred to as Knowledge Area or Capability Area): A subset of knowledge assets identified as either expertise, lessons learned, knowledge documents, or data.

Knowledge Documents: Documented knowledge with an established, extended shelf life that resides in an explicit form and may originate internally or externally.

Knowledge Life Cycle: The activities encompassing the treatment of knowledge as it moves through the stages of creation and capture, storage, retrieval and transfer, and application and reuse.

Lessons Learned: Task- or situation-specific knowledge gained while completing tasks or projects, also referred to as best known methods, best practices, and internal benchmarking.

M

Measuring Organizational Learning as a Multidimensional Construct

Juan C. Real
Pablo de Olavide University, Spain

Antonio Leal
University of Seville, Spain

Jose L. Roldan
University of Seville, Spain

INTRODUCTION

The traditional way of measuring learning as a result has been through the so-called learning and experience curves. The learning curves, developed within the production framework (Levitt & March, 1988), relate the manufacturing cost of a product to the accumulated experience in its production. This establishes that its cost decreases as the number of units made increases. At first, although this relationship was limited to the direct labour cost, it later extends to the total production cost.

In the 70s, the Boston Consulting Group applied this idea to the manufacturing sectors with experience curves. These curves expand the learning effect to activities other than those typical of production (Albernathy & Wayne, 1974). They describe the influence that experience acquired through the repetition of a specific activity has on the variable cost and/or price.

Another form of learning evaluation is the half-life curves that measure the time taken in obtaining an improvement of 50% in a determined measurement performance: The greater slope curves indicate a faster learning (Garvin, 1993).

These systems of evaluation are, nevertheless, incomplete for a learning organization. The cognitive level, changes in conduct, and its influence on performance improvement must be taken into account in assessing a company's learning. Surveys, questionnaires, and interviews are, in this case, more useful (Garvin, 1993).

The research has, however, advanced with great slowness due to two matters: first, as a result of the complexity and multidimensional nature of the object of study; second, the absence of a solid common starting-point, caused by the theoretical disagreement that exists concerning the very definition of the concept and its dimensions. In this line, organization learning (OL), as multidimensional construct, has been analyzed through the dimensions related to the OL capability, according to a series of phases that define a sequential time process, or by means of a knowledge-creation process.

BACKGROUND

In spite of the extensive existing literature on OL, there are very few attempts to operate this construct (Chaston, Badger, & Sadler-Smith, 1999), especially case studies that try to induce theory from practice (Easterby-Smith & Araujo, 1999).

OL, as a result, has been treated as a uni-dimensional construct (Levitt & March, 1988), whereas its analysis as a lasting process connected with knowledge acquisition and performance improvement has allowed us to go further into its complex and multidimensional character.

Easterby-Smith, Crossan, and Nicolini (2000, p. 789) consider the question of the OL measurement to be lacking in methodological and epistemological debate. In most cases, a contingent vision prevails in which the methods used are appropriate for different kinds of research problems. In general, the studies in this field reveal three perspectives:

a.   A macro/positivist perspective that uses quantitative methods—its unit of analysis being the organization or its significant subunits.

b.   A micro/interpretative perspective, where the researchers are interested in the phenomenon known as "communities of practice." They collect qualitative data via formal interviews or informal conversations and they use the individual as their unit of analysis.

c.   Intermediate perspective typically focusing on case studies. This assumes a combination of the previous methodologies. The studies follow the interpretative tradition to the extent that the researchers gather data mainly from interviews and observation. They differ in the sense that the focus is in on the complete case, or on comparisons between similar cases.

As Easterby-Smith et al. (2000) indicate, the different methods are appropriate for different kinds of research problems. Although the European works mainly use the interpretative methods, North American works place more emphasis on the quantitative empirical investigation. We will take this latter approach in this work to analyze the OL measurement, since this will allow its complex and multidimensional nature to be

perceived via a quantitative analysis of its dimensions (Slater & Narver, 1995).

ORGANIZATIONAL LEARNING AS A MULTIDIMENSIONAL CONSTRUCT

The academic field has, in the last decade, shown an increasing interest in the development of a measurement scale that allows the valuing of the OL as a multidimensional construct, made up of a set of attributes or related dimensions. Thus, following a prescriptive approach (Vera & Crossan, 2003), there is a first workgroup referring to how organizations should really learn. In this

Table 1. The measurement of the organizational learning capability

Author(s)	OL dimensions (items)	Unit of analysis	Research objective
Goh (2003)	• Clarity of mission and vision (4) • Leadership commitment and empowerment (5) • Experimentation and rewards (5) • Effective transfer of knowledge (4) • Teamwork and group problem-solving (3)	Individual: A longitudinal study with two samples formed by individuals of two companies	To describe a tool to measure an organization's learning capability
Goh & Richards (1997)	• Clarity of purpose and mission (4) • Leadership commitment and empowerment (5) • Experimentation and rewards (5) • Transfer of knowledge (4) • Teamwork and group problem-solving (3)	Individual: 632 people from four organizations, two from the public sector and two from the private sector	To measure the managerial practices that facilitate organizational learning or the conditions and enablers that can help an organization become a learning organization
Hult (1998)	• Team orientation (5) • Systems orientation (4) • Learning orientation (4) • Memory orientation (4)	International strategic business unit (SBU): A sample of 179 domestic and 167 international SBUs	To examine the role of organizational learning in the strategic sourcing process of a multinational service corporation
Hult & Ferrell (1997)	• Team orientation (5) • Systems orientation (4) • Learning orientation (4) • Memory orientation (4)	International strategic business unit (SBU): A sample of 179 domestic and 167 international SBUs	To develop and test a measurement of learning capability (OLC) using the purchaising process of a multinational corporation
Jerez-Gómez et al. (2004)	• Management commitment (5) • System perspective (3) • Openness and experimentation (4) • Knowledge transfer and integration (4)	Organization: 111 firms from the chemical industry	To develop a measurement scale for organizational learning capability
Yeung et al. (1999)	• Generate and generalize ideas with impact (24) • Incompetencies for learning (34)	Strategic business unit (SBU): 268 SBUs from large size and a wide variety of industries	To establish how variables of context (industry, business strategy and organizational culture) can influence how and why an organization learns, and how the organizational learning capability will affect business performance

Table 2. Basic aspects of learning organization and their relationship with the learning capability dimensions

Learning capability dimensions	Related factors according to authors revised
Personal mastery	• Team orientation (Hult, 1998; Hult & Ferrell, 1997) • Experimentation (Goh, 2003; Goh & Richards, 1997) • Generate and generalize ideas with impact (Yeung et al., 1999) • Openness and experimentation (Jerez-Gómez et al., 2004)
Mental models	• Learning orientation, systems orientation (Hult, 1998; Hult & Ferrell, 1997) • Incompetencies for learning (Yeung et al., 1999) • System perspective (Jerez-Gómez et al., 2004)
Shared vision	• Leadership commitment and empowerment (Goh & Richards, 1997) • Learning orientation, systems orientation (Hult, 1998; Hult & Ferrell, 1997) • Clarity of mission and vision (Goh, 2003; Goh & Richards, 1997) • System perspective (Jerez-Gómez et al., 2004)
Team learning	• Learning orientation, team orientation (Hult, 1998; Hult & Ferrell, 1997) • Transfer of knowledge (Goh, 2003; Goh & Richards, 1997) • Teamwork and group problem-solving (Goh, 2003; Goh & Richards, 1997) • Knowledge transfer and integration (Jerez-Gómez et al., 2004)
Systems thinking	• System perspective (Jerez-Gómez et al., 2004)

way, an organization should show a high degree of learning in each and every one of the dimensions defined for its learning capability to be considered as high. In the line of the same prescriptive approach, a second workgroup is centred on how the organizations should manage their knowledge following a series of stages or phases. A third workgroup gathers a set of proposals considering OL to be a process of knowledge creation (Vera & Crossan, 2003).

Within the first workgroup, we find authors, such as Goh (2003), Goh, and Richards (1997), Hult (1998), Hult and Ferrell (1997), Jerez-Gómez, Céspedes-Lorente and Valle-Cabrera (2004), and Yeung, Ulrich, Nason, and von Glinow (1999). They identify as OL dimensions the critical components for the learning organization or intelligent organization, so described initially by Senge (1990). These are shown in Table 1.

OL is defined as the "to learn to learn" capability or "meta-learning": the organization follows a continuous change model, permanently challenging its basic assumptions and theories in use (Swiering & Wiersma, 1992). This idea of learning capability presents a clear link to the learning orientation concept or propensity of the company toward learning in connection with different elements that have to be present for OL to occur (Day, 1994; Galer & van der Heijden, 1992; Sinkula, Baker, & Noordewier, 1997). In order to build an organization with learning capacity, Senge (1990) considers as fundamental the implementation of a series of principles or management practices, that he calls "learning disciplines." Table 2 shows the relationship between these disciplines and the key dimensions of the works that use a learning capability measurement.

Personal mastery discipline means individuals clarify and rethink their personal vision, thus guiding future creation. This proposal implies experimentation and the search of innovative and flexible solutions to current and future problems allowing for the creation of ideas.

Mental models refer to assumptions or thinking schemes that conform the acts of the organization's members. For the organization, it is vitally important to be able to modify behavior lines set out in its organizational memory, offering a space for new knowledge creation. This is especially useful when such behavior lines do not correspond to the facts and continue to prevail and guide organizational activity.

Building a shared vision is the shared ideal that agglutinates individual energies of organizational members and guides them in a common direction, generating a tension that leads to learning. This thought is supported by the managerial commitment, which implies that the management acknowledges the relevance of learning in the organization and supports it, promoting the development of a culture that fosters a learning atmosphere as a key value.

With reference to team learning, such learning can only be carried out via experience interchanges among individuals. This means generalizing ideas, that is, sharing ideas in the organization. Following this principle, there is the organizational ability to transfer knowledge both externally and internally. Teamwork allows an organization's members to be able to share knowledge and increase their understanding about needs and the ways in which other colleagues, in other parts of the organization, work.

Table 3. The measurement of OL as a process

Author(s)	OL dimensions (items)	Unit of analysis	Research objective
Pérez et al. (2004)	• Knowledge external acquisition (10) • Knowledge internal acquisition (7) • Knowledge distribution (7) • Knowledge interpretation (9) • Organizational memory (11)	Organization: 195 firms from the industrial and service sector	To analyze the relationship between organizational culture, OL and business performance
Templeton et al. (2002)	• Awareness (5) • Communications (3) • Performance assessment (4) • Intellectual cultivation (4) • Environmental adaptability(4) • Social learning (3) • Intellectual capital management (3) • Organizational grafting (2)	Organization: 119 knowledge-based firms	To develop a measure for the organizational learning construct
Tippins & Sohi (2003)	• Information acquisition (6) • Information dissemination (6) • Share interpretation (5) • Declarative memory (7) • Procedural memory (5)	Organization: 271 manufacturing firms	To examine the mediating role of OL in the linkage between information technology competency and firm performance

Systems thinking allows the bringing together of learning results from previous disciplines and allows its extension to the rest of the organization.

Concerning OL definitions, most academics agree that OL is a process which starts from acquisition and creation of knowledge on behalf of individuals, and continues with its interchange and integration until reaching a body of collective knowledge. This idea, represented in Table 3, is proposed by the second group of works, such as Pérez López, Montes Peón, and Vázquez Ordás (2004), Templeton, Lewis, and Snyder (2002), and Tippins and Sohi (2003). These authors consider OL as a dynamic process that, according to Huber (1991), develops in time via several stages.

Table 4 sums up these phases of subprocesses with the dimensions identified in several works. These will be discussed subsequently.

Knowledge acquisition is defined as a process followed by organizations in order to actively search for information and knowledge from both internal and external sources. Such knowledge can have its origin in a firm's founders, intellectual capital management, learned from other organizations, embodiment of new members in the firm who have previously unavailable knowledge, and environmental scanning and observation (Huber, 1991).

Information distribution represents the stage at which information obtained in the previous step is delivered intentionally or not among units and members of the organization, promoting learning of new knowledge or its understanding (Garvin, 1993).

Information interpretation implies that one or more meanings could be given to this information (Daft & Weick, 1984). This requires the existence of a consensus among organizational members concerning information meaning. They learn about organizational matters via social channels.

Organizational memory is the last stage of learning. It refers to the group of systems and structures implemented in an organization to store knowledge created in the entity for this knowledge to be able to be used later (Walsh & Ungson, 1991).

Finally, with a different approach (as shown in Table 5), there is a group of authors which presents a scale for measuring the organizational learning as a knowledge creation process in organizations. In this sense, Nonaka, Byosiere, Borucki, and Konno (1994) consider that the dimensions of the knowledge creation are the four modes of knowledge conversion (SECI) in the theoretical model defined by Nonaka (1994).

Bontis, Crossan, and Hulland (2002) present a macro perspective of OL in which it relates to the phenomenon of strategic renewal. These authors describe OL as a process through which stocks and flows of learning are managed to increase a firm's performance. In this way, according to Crossan Lane, and White (1999), OL is a dynamic process, via levels, producing a tension between the incremental or amplified logic that involves

Table 4. Basic aspects of organizational learning processes and their relationship with the organizational learning dimensions

Organizational learning process dimensions	Related factors according to authors revised
Knowledge acquisition	• Social learning, awareness, intellectual cultivation, performance assessment, intellectual capital management, organizational grafting (Templeton et al., 2002) • Knowledge external/internal acquisition (Pérez et al., 2004) • Information acquisition (Tippins & Sohi, 2003)
Information distribution	• Environmental adaptability, social learning, awareness, intellectual cultivation (Templeton et al., 2002) • Knowledge distribution (Pérez et al., 2004) • Information dissemination (Tippins & Sohi, 2003)
Information interpretation	• Environmental adaptability, social learning, communications, performance assessment (Templeton et al., 2002) • Knowledge interpretation (Pérez et al., 2004) • Share interpretation (Tippins & Sohi, 2003)
Organizational memory	• Environmental adaptability, communications, intellectual cultivation, performance assessment, intellectual capital management (Templeton et al., 2002) • Organizational memory (Pérez et al., 2004) • Declarative and procedural memory (Tippins & Sohi, 2003)

Table 5. The measurement of OL and its integration within the knowledge-based view

Author(s)	OL dimensions (items)	Unit of analysis	Research objective
Bontis et al. (2002)	• Individual level learning (10) • Group level learning (10) • Organization level learning (10) • Feedforward learning (10) • Feedback learning (10)	Individual: A survey instrument based on the strategic learning assessment map (SLAM) was administered to 15 individuals from 32 organizations	To analyze the relationship between the stocks and flows of learning and business performance
Nonaka et al. (1994)	Knowledge conversion phases (SECI): • Socialization (10) • Externalization (9) • Combination(10) • Interiorization (9)	Organization: 105 firms	To validate a scale for measuring the knowledge creation process

the scanning or new assimilation of knowledge (feed-forward), and the reductive logic that implies the exploitation or use of learnt knowledge (feedback). Through a feed-forward process, new ideas and actions flow from the individual to the group and from them to the organization. While learning, a feedback process from the organization to the group takes place, and from the group to the individual level, thus affecting the way people think and act. According to this social approach of OL, learning happens and knowledge is created by social interaction developed among the different levels proposed by the ontological dimension of knowledge (i.e., individual, group, and organization).

FUTURE TRENDS

Future works are needed that consider the necessity of carrying out longitudinal studies using the intermediate perspective that complete the existing cross-sectional studies, especially if we consider the continuous nature of OL. This is an accumulative process in time, implying that the amount of knowledge reached at a specific moment in time is the result of learning accumulated up to this moment. In any case, the existence of a measurement method of OL will allow us to go further in the comprehension of mechanisms that facilitate the transformation process of OL into an increase of business performance. In this sense, in the future, it would be interesting to develop works in line with the micro/interpretative perspective that allows us to obtain objective indicators via case studies.

The measurement of the OL can help to reveal different areas in which the managers act to develop this capability. Also, it can allow the establishment of standard values with which to initiate processes of benchmarking between organizations. Those that score above these standards may be considered as learning organizations. Without a doubt, the existence of OL measures will be useful for evaluating more complex models in which different connections with antecedent and consequent variables can be analyzed (Jerez-Gómez et al., 2004). All this is going to contribute to eliminating part of the existing controversy in significant questions, such as its impact on business performance.

CONCLUSION

This article has shown how the limited consensus on OL meaning has led to a confusion regarding its measurement. This issue has not been considered enough by the literature developed during decades of organizational thought. This has produced a lack of empirical works on the matter and, in particular, the almost absence of an elaboration of multi-item scales.

We have, despite this, focused on analyzing different scales from a macro/positivist approach that allows the undertaking of the measurement of OL as a multidimensional latent construct. Via this approach, a first group of analyzed works measures the organizational learning ability through a set of attributes that defines a learning organization. A second group establishes the learning measurement throughout several stages or phases in time, producing a collective knowledge. Finally, we have presented the OL measurement by the concept of learning stock and flow, aiming to show that OL and organizational knowledge represent both one and the same organizational reality.

REFERENCES

Abernathy, W.J., & Wayne, K. (1974). Limits of the learning curve. *Harvard Business Review, 52*(5), 56-72.

Bontis, N., Crossan, M.M., & Hulland, J. (2002). Managing an organizational learning systems by aligning stocks and flows. *Journal of Management Studies, 39*(4), 437-469.

Chaston, I., Badger, B., & Sadler-Smith, E. (1999). Organisational learning: Research issues and applications in SME sector firms. *International Journal of Entrepreneurial Behaviour & Research, 5*(4), 191-203.

Crossan, M., Lane, H.W., & White, R.E. (1999). An organizational learning framework: From intuition to institution. *Academy of Management Review, 24*(3), 522-537.

Crossan, M., Lane, H.W., White, R.E., & Djurfeldt, L. (1995). Organizational learning: Dimensions for a theory. *International Journal of Organizational Analysis, 3*(4), 337-360.

Daft, R.L., & Weick, K.E. (1984). Toward a model of organizations as interpretation systems. *Academy of Management Review, 9,* 284-295.

Day, G.S. (1994). The capabilities of market-driven organizations. *Journal of Marketing, 58*(3), 37-52.

Easterby-Smith, M., & Araujo L. (1999). Organizational learning: Current debates and opportunities. In M. Easterby-Smith, J. Burgoine, & L. Araujo (Eds.), *Organizational learning and the learning organization* (pp. 1-21). London: Sage.

Easterby-Smith, M., Crossan, M., & Nicolini, D. (2000). Organizational learning: Debates past, present and future. *Journal of Management Studies, 37*(6), 783-796.

Galer, G., & van der Heijden, K. (1992). The learning organization: How planners create organizational learning. *Marketing Intelligence and Planning, 10*(6), 5-12.

Garvin, D.A. (1993). Building a learning organization. *Harvard Business Review, July-August,* 78-91.

Goh, S.C. (2003). Improving organizational learning capability: Lessons from two case studies. *The Learning Organization, 10*(4), 216-227.

Goh, S.C., & Richards, G. (1997). Benchmarking the learning capacity of organizations. *European Management Journal, 15*(5), 575-583.

Huber, G.P. (1991). Organizational learning: The contributing processes and the literature. *Organization Science, 2*(1), 88-115.

Hult, G.T.M. (1998). Managing the international strategic sourcing process as a market-driven organizational learning system. *Decision Science, 29*(1), 193-216.

Hult, G.T.M., & Ferrell, O.C. (1997). Global organizational learning capacity in purchasing: Construct and measurement. *Journal of Business Research, 40*(2), 97-111.

Jerez-Gómez, P., Céspedes-Lorente, J., & Valle-Cabrera, R. (2004). Organizational learning capability: A proposal of measurement. *Journal of Business Research, 58*(6), 715-725.

Levitt B.G., & March, J.G. (1988). Organizational learning. *Annual Review of Sociology, 14*, 319-340.

Nonaka, I. (1994). A dinamyc theory of organizational knowledge creation. *Organization Science, 1*(1), 14-37.

Nonaka, I., Byosiere, P., Borucki, C.C., & Konno, N. (1994). Organizational knowledge creation theory: A first comprehensive test. *International Business Review, 3*(4), 337-351.

Pérez López, S., Montes Peón, J.M., & Vázquez Ordás, C. (2004). Managing knowledge: The link between culture and organizational learning. *Journal of Knowledge Management, 8*(6), 93-104.

Senge, P.M. (1990). *The fifth discipline.* New York: Currency Doubleday.

Sinkula, J.M., Baker, W.E., & Noordewier, T. (1997). A framework for market-based organizational learning: Linking values, knowledge, and behaviour. *Journal of the Academy of Marketing Science, 25*(4), 305-318.

Slater, S.F., & Narver, J.C. (1995). Market orientation and the learning organization. *Journal of Marketing, 59*(3), 63-74.

Swieringa, J., & Wierdsma, A.F. (1992). *Becoming a learning organization.* MA: Addison-Wesley.

Templeton, G.F., Lewis, B.R., & Snyder, C.A. (2002). Development of a measure for the organizational learning construct. *Journal of Management Information Systems, 19*(2), 175-218.

Tippins, M.J., & Sohi, R.S. (2003). IT competency and firm performance: Is organizational learning a missing link? *Strategic Management Journal, 24*(8), 745-761.

Vera, D., & Crossan, M. (2003). Organizational learning and knowledge management. In M. Easterby-Smith & M. Lyles (Eds.), *Handbook of organizational learning and knowledge management* (pp. 122-141). MA: Blackwell.

Walsh, J.P., & Ungson, G.R. (1991). Organizational memory. *Academy of Management Review, 16*(1), 57-91.

Yeung, A.K., Ulrich, D.O., Nason, S.W., & von Glinow, M.A. (1999). *Organizational learning capability. Generating and generalizing ideas with impact.* New York: Oxford University Press.

KEY TERMS

Construct: A not-directly-observable hypothetical concept whose existence must be inferred by actions, behaviour, or observable characteristics.

Learning Flow: Process by which knowledge is transferred and diffused between the different levels of the organization. It describes the new knowledge production process (feed-forward) and the use of the knowledge that has already been generated (feedback).

Learning Organization: Type or form of organization that continuously expands its capacity to create the wished-for results, using learning as an intentional and strategic tool for organizational and individual improvement, and facilitates the learning of all its members via the elimination of any kind of barrier.

Learning Orientation: Set of organizational values, such as the commitment to learning, the shared vision and open-mindeness that influence the propensity of the company to create and use knowledge.

Learning Stock: Knowledge store in a specific agent (i.e., individual, group, and organization) both in its technical dimensions or know-how and its cognitive dimension.

Organizational Learning Capability: Ability an organization has to learn or the capacity for increasing its own learning power via the putting into practice of the appropriate management activities, structures, and procedures which facilitate and stimulate the learning.

Organizational Learning: Dynamic process which is generated in the heart of the organization via its individuals and the groups they make up, aimed at the generation and development of knowledge that allows an organization to improve its performance and results.

Mentoring Knowledge Workers

M

Ciara Heavin
National University of Ireland, Cork, Ireland

Karen Neville
National Univeristy of Ireland, Cork, Ireland

INTRODUCTION

In an economic environment where organizations have been forced to take a step back and reevaluate their core competencies and ability to innovate, organizational knowledge has come to the forefront as a valuable strategic asset (Haghirian, 2003). While the concept of knowledge management (KM) is not new, the focus on knowledge management as a strategy has increased in recent times as organizations realize the importance of knowledge as an intangible asset contributing to the enhancement of competitive advantage (Bolloju, 2000). In the 21st century, it is believed that successful companies are those that effectively acquire, create, retain, deploy, and leverage knowledge (Cecez-Kecmanovic, 2000). Knowledge work is the ability to create an understanding of nature, organizations, and processes, and to apply this understanding as a means of generating wealth in the organization (Boland & Tenkasi, 1995). Evidently, the focus on knowledge management as a strategy has become central to organizations (Davenport & Prusak, 1998). Ichijo, Von Krogh, and Nonaka (1998) view knowledge as a resource that is unique and imperfectly imitable, allowing firms to sustain a competitive advantage. Additionally, knowledge management as a formalized organizational strategy is supported; it should not be left unintentional to become unsystematic and random (Ichijo et al.). This article provides an example of knowledge workers and experts collaborating to implement successful training and learning programmes to support knowledge-management activities in their organization. The authors hope that the case discussed will inform researchers of an appropriate model in designing an interactive learning environment that enables a positive knowledge-sharing environment and in turn contributes to the growth of an organization's memory.

BACKGROUND

The intensity of competition in the business market, advances in technology (Crossman, 1997), and a strong shift toward a knowledge-based economy have each contributed to the demand for Web-based mentoring systems (WBMSs). According to Emerson (1843), "There is no knowledge that is not power," and the organization (public or private) that can utilize its knowledge resources more effectively than its competitor will persevere (Laudon & Laudon, 1998). An effective mentoring system between knowledge workers and experts can provide an organization with a strategic advantage in the market (Benjamin & Blunt, 1993). Mentoring environments can help create and maintain skills and, therefore, the corporate knowledge base (Garvin, 1993). They both alleviate the strain on corporate resources and facilitate employees' changing training needs (Driscoll, 1998) through knowledge sharing. Therefore, the majority of organizations face the enormous challenge of supporting their employees' thirst for expanding their skill bases and corporate assets effectively as "[k]nowledge implies a knower; the rest is just information." In the case under consideration in this article, the organization implemented a successful mentoring system in order to develop employee skills and knowledge in both IT and managerial issues such as knowledge management. This article is focused on the development of a Web-based mentoring system to mentor workers and enhance learning (Neville, Adam, & McCormack, 2002). The case study indicates a strong requirement for the utilization of such an environment to both increase support for and collaboration between the knowledge workers.

MAIN FOCUS OF THE ARTICLE

Mentoring is a traditional method of teaching that strengthens the concept and objectives of learning and training (Benton, Elder, & Thornbury, 1995). The Oxford dictionary defines the word mentor as a "wise counselor, who tutors the learner in intellectual subjects..." When this model is applied to a learning network, the student is called a teleapprentice who studies using appropriate methods (Levin, 1990). The teleapprentice reads messages, answers questions, participates in discussions, and conducts research online to master his or her subject. Mentorship is a method of teaching that has been used for hundreds of years; this design is incorporated into learning and knowledge networks to develop more effective learning and collaborating practices (Eisenstadt & Vincent, 1998), and to provide additional support and mediation to the learners and workers (Alexander, 1995). Access to experts is one of the many advantages provided through learning networks (Harasim, 1995). Networks are, in fact, modeled on this method (Harasim, Hiltz, Teles, & Turoff, 1995). Therefore, WBMSs allow students and workers to communicate with experts in a field and collaborate with their peers (Crossman, 1997; Dick & Reiser, 1989). WBMSs can be described as learning delivery environments in which the World Wide Web (WWW) is its medium of delivery (Crossman, 1992; Driscoll, 1998; Neville et al., 2002). The possibilities of WBMSs are limited only by constraints imposed by the university or organization in question, such as technological or managerial support (Neville, 2000). Innovative companies and universities are using this implementation for a number of reasons, specifically to keep employees or students abreast of emerging technologies in their fields and to provide effective training to both staff and customers on new products and skills (Khan, 1997). Designing a WBMS requires a thorough investigation into the use of the Web as a medium for delivery (Driscoll; McCormack & Jones, 1997; Ritchie & Hoffman, 1996). The designer must be aware of the attributes of the WWW and the principles of instructional design to create a meaningful support environment (Driscoll; Gagne, Briggs, & Wagner, 1988). The Web-based training room is viewed as an innovative approach to teaching (Relan & Gillani, 1997). The virtual training room, like the traditional method, requires careful planning to be both effective and beneficial (Dick & Reiser). As stated by

McCormack and Jones, a Web-based classroom must do more than just distribute information. It should include resources such as discussion forums to support collaboration between learners and ultimately it should also support the needs of both the novice and advanced learner (Sherry, 1996; Willis, 1995). A WBMS is composed of a number of components that are integral to the effective operation of the environment (Banathy, 1992), for example, for the development of content and the use of multimedia, Internet tools, hardware, and software (Reeves, 1993). A developer must understand the capabilities of these components (search engines, feedback pages, and movie clips) as their use will determine the success or the failure of the learning environment (Driscoll). In this article, we provide an example of a WBMS to help illustrate the main elements, issues, components, and problems encountered through the implementation of learning systems to enhance knowledge management in organizations.

The WBMS (Figure 1) was constructed to support and develop knowledge sharing for personnel who seek to acquire and develop their knowledge-management skills. Training material is available online, but in addition, a discussion forum enables both learners and experts to exchange ideas and add to the environment. This allows learners to provide feedback (anonymously, if desired) to the experts. It also enables them to pose queries, which other participants or the experts can answer. All participants are able to see the initial queries and the discussion stream of answers from other participants and the instructors. This further extends the reach of the training material as employees can log on to the WBMS at home or at work and pose questions for which answers are available when they next log on. The facility also allows the learners to voice their satisfaction regarding the different elements of the environment. This provides the participants with the opportunity to

Figure 1. The Web-based mentoring system

Mentoring System (WBMS)

take part in the ongoing design of the WBMS, and therefore increases user acceptance.

Figure 1 illustrates the opportunities available to the participants of the case. The system provides professional training to a range of employees including full-time staff at all levels and senior management. Its core aim is to further develop the knowledge and abilities of personnel so that they are increasingly aware of IT and management issues within the organization with a particular focus on capturing, storing, disseminating, and creating knowledge. The course is designed on a distance learning basis and is supported by a tutorial system. The main purpose of the tutorials is to facilitate the learning process, assist in the completion of interactive assignments, and encourage team playing within the group. Learners are presented with written modules, which act as the lecture, and the expert plays the role of the facilitator, enabling the students to combine the written materials with their own experiences. Feedback from the students identified the need to provide additional learning support through an online environment. The WBMS has provided an improved learning process and has enabled enhanced collaboration among employees. This article focuses on the development of these requirements through an interactive learning environment for employees, and on the fact that the WBMS is designed or customized for the requirements of the individual learner. This approach accounts for the varying learning abilities of students and overcomes the limitations of traditional training environments that are restricted to rules in order to adequately facilitate the group. The educator or expert instructs a class, but the level of collaboration and the development of problem-solving skills can be directly correlated to class sizes. The greater the size of the group, the less attention individual learners gain or the more intimidated a student is to participate in discussions, thus reducing collaboration. The WBMS, when adequately designed, can reduce the limitations of the classroom and allow the learner to work at his or her own pace with structured support from both the educators and the other learners.

DESIGN CONSIDERATIONS

Web-based learning is regarded as a silver-bullet solution to training issues faced by organizations, therefore it is essential to define the characteristics of interactive education that can be achieved through the WWW and to expand the Web-based mentoring concept to promote learning. The identification of these characteristics is necessary to implement such a concept. Thus, this section reviews 10 dimensions proposed by Reeves and Reeves (1993) for interactive training and collaboration:

(a) the educational philosophy, (b) the learning theory, (c) the goal orientation, (d) the task orientation, (e) the source of motivation, (f) the role of the teacher, (g) metacognitive support, (h) collaborative learning, (i) cultural sensitivity, and (j) structural flexibility. The dimensions are proposed to describe the characteristics of a WBMS. Each of the dimensions identified is outlined in the following paragraphs:

1. Educational philosophy emphasizes the belief that learners build their cognitive strategies on previous knowledge and on the learning environment. Therefore, a rich and stimulating environment is required to train different adult learners. Thus, direct instruction is also replaced with challenging tasks.

2. The design of the environment should be based on researched learning theories. The two dominant theories identified in the design of training environments are behavioral and cognitive psychology. Behaviorists believe that the most important factors that should be taken into consideration are the arrangement of stimuli, responses, feedback, and reinforcement to shape the desirable behavior of the learners. By contrast, cognitive psychologists place more emphasis on internal mental states rather than on behavior. As a result, the WBMS design, using cognitive theory, will be based on direct instruction and practice exercises.

3. The goals for a WBMS can vary from being sharply focused, where a specific environment is required, to a having a more general approach.

4. The orientation of tasks can range from being academic to authentic. As an example, an authentic design for adult education would require the learners to tackle job-related exercises or cases (tacit knowledge). The design orientation of a WBMS should support the transfer of skills to the learners.

5. Motivation is the main factor for the success of any learning environment. The source of motivation ranges from two extremes: from the extrinsic (outside the learning environment) to the intrinsic (a part of the learning environment).

6. Lecturers and tutors fulfill different roles, from the traditional role of instructor (didactic) to the facilitative role.

7. Flavell (1979) described metacognition as the learner's ability to identify objectives, and plan and understand learning strategies. Thus, a WBMS can be designed to challenge the learner to solve course-related problems (Driscoll, 1998).

8. The collaborative learning dimension for a WBMS can also range from a lack of support to the inclusion of facilities to support it.

9. Reeves and Reeves (1993) argue that all training environments have cultural implications. However, the development of a WBMS cannot be designed to adjust to every rule. Therefore, a WBMS should be designed to be as culturally aware as possible.

10. Structural flexibility describes a WBMS as either asynchronous or synchronous (Driscoll, 1998). Open or asynchronous environments refer to the use of such an environment at any particular time or from any location. However, synchronous environments refer to fixed environments that can only be used in the training room of an organization. The WWW provides educators and students alike with the opportunity to avail of resources from more open environments through which students are supported or mentored in the acquisition of both tacit and explicit knowledge.

The dimensions were used as an aid in the production of the generic WBMS (see Figure 1). Both the study of the different dimensions and the factors necessary for the collaboration and structure of learning provide valuable information and steps for the analysis, and therefore the development, of the solutions.

FUTURE TRENDS

Knowledge workers have praised the hands-on approach provided through this expert-driven system. As knowledge sharing has increasingly become a key organizational objective, this type of environment provides an extensive communication channel leveraging technology to support a wide variety of knowledge-sharing activities. It also enables the experts and learners to collaborate, therefore providing 24-hour online support. This case is a prime example of a successful KM-support tool that can and will continue to avail of technological advances to ensure ongoing success. Further research exploring the various pedagogy and technology mixes to produce a set of options, which would identify the integration of a particular pedagogy with an appropriate technology, would prove beneficial if WBMSs are to meet their full potential. Additionally, the WBMS illustrated in this article is primarily concerned with the downstream development process that incorporates key design and development considerations. Therefore, further research exploring the upstream development process would be worthwhile. This would involve exploring some of the development options that were identified in the development of off-the-shelf packages, and exploring the open-source development option for WBMSs. These further studies may yield interesting results and therefore increase the level of understanding of the development of effective WBMSs.

CONCLUSION

After an in-depth analysis, it was apparent that learners lacked an efficient online support system that would complement alternative communication channels such as face-to-face encounters and traditional training classes as a means of knowledge sharing. An effective KM training-support system can provide an organization with a strategic advantage in the market. Learning environments can help create and maintain skills and therefore increase the corporate knowledge base. They both alleviate the strain on corporate resources and facilitate employees' changing training needs. This article focuses on the design of a suitable environment to support knowledge workers and encourage collaboration. The research outlines the factors necessary for the successful implementation and use of the system. It also highlights the potential of the system to overcome the physical barriers of traditional knowledge-sharing and learning channels. Interactive learning environments can, when properly mediated and structured, facilitate cooperation and enhanced learning practices, reduce conflict, and avail of all of the benefits that technology can provide.

REFERENCES

Alexander, S. (1995). *Teaching and learning on the World Wide Web.* Retrieved from *http://www.scu.edu.au/ausweb95/chapters/education2/alexnder/*

Banathy, B. H. (1992). *A systems view of education: A journey to create the future.* Englewood Cliffs, NJ: Educational Technology Publications.

Benjamin, R. I., & Blunt, J. (1992). Critical IT issues: The next ten years. *Sloan Management Review, Summer,* 7-19.

Benton, V., Elder, M., & Thornbury, H. (1995). *Early experiences of mentoring: Design and use of multimedia material for teaching OR/MS* (Working Paper No. 95/5). Department of Management Science, University of Strathcycle.

Bolland, R., & Tenkasi, R. (1995). Perspective making and perspective taking in communities of knowing. *Organizational Science, 2*, 40-57.

Bolloju, N., & Khalifa, M. (2000). A framework for integrating decision support and knowledge management in enterprise-wide decision making environments. *Proceedings of IFIP TC8/WG8.3 International Conference on Decision Support through Knowledge Management*, Stockholm, Sweden.

Cecez-Kecmanovic, D. (1999). Understanding knowledge sharing in organizational decision making supported by CMC. *Proceedings of IFIP TC8/WG8.3 International Conference on Decision Support through Knowledge Management*, Stockholm, Sweden.

Crossman, D.M. (1997). The evolution of the World Wide Web as an emerging instructional technology tool. In B.H. Khan (Ed.), *Web-based instruction* (pp. 19-23). Englewood Cliffs, NJ: Educational Technology Publications.

Davenport, T. H., & Prusak, L. (1998). *Working knowledge: How organizations manage what they know.* Boston: Harvard Business School Press.

Dick, W., & Reiser, R. (1989). *Planning effective instruction.* Englewood Cliffs, NJ: Prentice-Hall.

Driscoll, M. (1998). *Web-based training: Using technology to design adult learning experiences.* San Francisco, CA: Jossey-Bass/Pfeiffer.

Eisenstadt, M., & Vincent, T. (1998). *The knowledge Web: Learning and collaborating on the Net.* London: Kogan Page Ltd.

Emerson, R.W. (1843). Quotes by Ralph Waldo Emerson. Quotations Book. Retrieved 2004 from *http://www.quotationsbook.com/quotes/31653/view*

Flavell, J. H. (1979). Metacognition and cognitive monitoring: A new area of psychological inquiry. *American Psychologist, 34*, 906-911.

Gagne, R. M., Briggs, L. J., & Wagner, W. W. (1988). *Principles of instructional design* (3rd Ed.). New York: Holt Reinbank Winston.

Garvin, D. A. (1993). Building a learning organization. *Harvard Business Review.*

Haghirian, P. (2003). Does culture really matter? Cultural influences on the knowledge transfer process within multinational corporations. *European Journal of Information Systems.*

Harasim, L., Hiltz, S. R., Teles, L., & Turoff, M. (1995). *Learning networks: A field guide to teaching and learning online.* Cambridge, MA: The MIT Press.

Ichijo, K., Von Krogh, G., & Nonaka, I. (1998). *Knowledge enablers. Knowing firms: Understanding, managing and measuring knowledge.* London: Sage Publications.

Khan, B. (1997). *Web-based instruction.* Englewood Cliffs, NJ: Educational Technology Publications.

Laudon, K. C., & Laudon, J. P. (1998). *Management information systems: Organization and technology in the networked enterprise* (6th Ed.). Upper Saddle River, NJ: Prentice Hall International Editors.

Levin, J. (1990). Teleapprenticeships on globally distributed electronic networks. Paper presented at the *Meeting of the American Educational Research Association.*

McCormack, C., & Jones, D. (1997). *Building a Web-based education system.* New York: Wiley.

Neville, K. (2000). A Web-based training (WBT) system development framework: A case study. *Proceedings of Business Information Technology Management (BIT) 2000: 10th Annual Conference*, Manchester, UK.

Neville, K., Adam, F., & McCormack, C. (2002). Mentoring distance learners: An action research study. *Proceedings of the 10th European Conference on Information Systems*, Gdańsk, Poland.

Nonaka, I. (1991). The knowledge creating company. *Harvard Business Review, 69*, 96-104.

Oxford English Dictionary. (1989). Oxford: Oxford University Press.

Reeves, T. C. (1993). Research support for interactive multimedia: Existing foundations and future directions. In C. Latchem, J. Williamson, & L. Henderson-Lancett (Eds.), *Interactive multimedia: Practice and promise* (pp. 79-96). London: Kogan Page.

Reeves, T.C., & Reeves, P.M. (1997). Effective dimensions of interactive learning on the World Wide Web. In B.H. Khan (Ed.), Web-based instruction (pp. 59-66). Englewood Cliffs, NJ: Educational Technology Publications, Inc.

Relan, A., & Gillani, B. (1997). Web-based information and the traditional classroom. In C. M. Reigeluth & R. J. Garfinkle (Eds.), *Systemic change in education.* Englewood Cliffs, NJ: Educational Technology Publications.

Ritchie, D. C., & Hoffman, B. (1996). Incorporating instructional design principles with the World Wide Web. In B.H. Khan (Ed.), Web-based instruction (pp. 135-138). Englewood Cliffs, NJ: Educational Technology Publications.

M

Sherry, L. (1996). Raising the prestige of online articles. *Intercom, The Society for Technical Communication Magazine, 43*(7), 24-25, 43.

Von Krogh, G., Ichijo, K., & Nonaka, I. (2000). *Enabling knowledge creation: How to unlock the mystery of tacit knowledge and release the power of innovation.* Oxford: Oxford University Press.

Willis, J. (1995). A recursive, reflective, instructional design model based on constructivist-interpretivist theory. *Educational Technology, 35*(6), 5-23.

KEY TERMS

Explicit Knowledge: Information that has specific meaning and that can be easily and clearly understood.

Knowledge Management: The capture, storage, dissemination, and creation of organizational knowledge as a means of creating competitive advantage.

Knowledge Web: The use of electronic linkages among different teaching and learning communities to facilitate information acquisition and knowledge building.

Knowledge Work: The ability to create an understanding of nature, organizations, and processes, and to apply this understanding as a means of generating wealth in the organization

Mentoring: A method of teaching that has been used for hundreds of years; this design is incorporated into learning networks to develop more effective learning practices and to provide additional support to the learner.

Tacit Knowledge: That which refers to knowledge gained through an individual's own experiences.

Web-Based Mentoring System (WBMS): A Web-based technology that enables the interactive communication between students and mentors, supporting a collaborative learning environment.

Military Knowledge Management

M

R. William Maule
Naval Postgraduate School, USA

INTRODUCTION

Knowledge is a critical component of military operations, and the military has been an early adopter of knowledge management (KM) technologies. Significant events include a strategic use of tools to filter information into knowledge, the designation of knowledge officers in high-level strategic positions, and the implementation of knowledge systems as a means to support situational awareness and understanding. Following is a brief overview of knowledge management within the military and a review of knowledge theory and practice pertinent to military knowledge management.

MILITARY KNOWLEDGE MANAGEMENT

The military is extremely diverse in its knowledge systems and practices. In the collective, the military would be the equivalent of many large corporate conglomerates, each with multiple research and development (R & D) branches. Adding to the complexity is the secrecy of many of the systems. To attempt to summarize military knowledge management in its entirety would be presumptuous, if not impossible. Rather, this discussion will focus on some representative systems and approaches being advanced in military-sponsored KM research and practice. Included are comparisons to knowledge-management initiatives in the private sector. The discussion begins with an overview of private-sector and academic-research practices that have carried forward into the military.

Relevant Research

The importance of knowledge management has been equated to the importance of natural resources in previous generations wherein strategies that companies once devoted to optimizing capital and labor are now being applied to maximize the productivity of knowledge resources (Silver, 2001). A means to maximize productivity in the military is to integrate systems, technologies, and information resources. Such aggregations are increasingly under the umbrella of knowledge management.

At a technical level, military knowledge management is addressed within enterprise-systems engineering initiatives, with a current initiative force transformation through network-centric systems (MIT, 2002). Knowledge systems may be an adjunct to specialized computing systems or an umbrella under which information and communications technologies can be grouped. Similar to the private sector, military KM integrates disciplines addressing computer and communications technology, cognitive science and artificial intelligence (AI), and human-computer and human-systems integration. There is additional research addressing information synthesis or fusion, with XML (extensible markup language) as a categorization schema and ontology structure in support of semantic understanding. In addition are military-specific KM initiatives such as command and control, military intelligence, and sensors.

Common to both the military and private sector is research into mechanisms to consolidate data and information into knowledge, and once integrated, to understand strategic options and cause-effect relationships (Primix Solutions, 2000). The desired result is improved decision making, interorganizational communications, cooperation, and interaction (Schwartz, Divitini, & Brasethvik, 1999). An example at the macrolevel is Army knowledge management with its transformation mission toward a knowledge-based organization that integrates best practices into professional duties through active involvement with the knowledge infostructure (MIT, 2003).

At a microlevel are issues in knowledge design that address navigation and search mechanisms (Sherman, 2000), and knowledge structures to help achieve a goal or objective (Saward, 2000). In the military, a current focus is on context to help document knowledge flows (Nissen, 2001). Metrics are important for the assessment of knowledge initiatives, and means have been advanced to address the value of specific knowledge units (Gao & Sterling, 2000), to include relevance weightings for context-integration points, and to allow the knowledge value added (KVA) methodology to ascertain return on knowledge investments (Housel & Bell, 2001).

Both the military and private sector have an interest in cognitive understanding and research to encode process, procedural, and expert knowledge into software (Storey, Goldstein, & Ullrich, 2002); to find techniques to capture common-sense knowledge in a context-sensitive manner and extract expert-level specifics (Storey & Day, 2002); to derive metacognitive attributes to help define relationships between user cognitive needs and knowledge metadata (Maule, 1998, 2000, 2001); and to implement reasoning tools to identify patterns of behavior to resolve problems or identify opportunities (Fensel & Motta, 2001). All of these approaches are active in military research as a means to structure or derive knowledge for decision-support applications.

A next step is to make this processed knowledge readily available. Portals with collaborative tools are mechanisms to establish relevance (Silver, 2001); to personalize, sort, and filter information (Moore, 2001); and to enhance business intelligence with decision support (Ruber, 2000). A portal with real-time chat and messaging empowers users with collaborative abilities (Loria, 2001). In the Navy, portals have become a primary means for information, communications, collaboration, work-flow coordination, and decision support (Maule, Gallup, & Schacher, 2003).

Also notable is the trend toward communities of practice as a means to build knowledge expertise. Communities increase social capital or the economic value of relationships within an organization and therein lower the cost of knowledge. Workers find information more quickly and realize overall information efficiencies as a life cycle of involvement forms around the knowledge community (DoN CIO, 2000). In the military, knowledge communities support work-group collaboration around specific knowledge concepts or initiatives. They help extend and expedite the traditional reach of individuals to colleagues who can share knowledge in a just-in-time manner (Tate, 2001). For example, the Air Force Materiel Command is fielding an Air Force-wide knowledge management initiative using the community-of-practice methodology to support collaboration among a widely dispersed workforce to enable teamwork, communication, and sharing within a virtual environment (AFMC, 2003).

Warriors need specific data in a timely manner. As in the private sector, semantics, ontology, and XML are emerging techniques to support transparent, automated knowledge exchange. Research in semantics has established that (a) content can be embedded with meaning, (b) relationships between meanings are delineated, and (c) access methods are coordinated around those meanings (Grimes, 2002). Semantics can additionally characterize participant roles in an interaction to establish relationships between entities, context, and knowledge bases (Storey et al., 2002). XML provides the syntax and structure, and ontology provides the means to define

terms and relationships (Berners-Lee, Hendler, & Lassila, 2001). Value is added through classification and metadata (Chandrasekaran, Josephson, & Benjamins, 1999).

Military-specific ontology has been developed to aid in experimentation analysis and to contextualize problem scenarios in support of detailed situational assessment and understanding (Maule, Schacher, Gallup, Marachi, & McClain, 2000; Schacher, Maule, & Gallup, 2001). Military-specific ontology is being developed by agencies including DARPA (Defense Advanced Research Projects Agency) with its DAML (DARPA agent markup language), and the North Atlantic Treaty Organization (NATO) with its LC2IEDM (Land C2 information exchange data model; NATO, 2000).

MILITARY KNOWLEDGE SYSTEMS

Similar to KM private-sector research, there are many approaches to knowledge management in the military, each with its own set of tools, techniques, and methodologies. These range from AI-based techniques, to the statistical analysis of content, to ontology and metadata for categorization, to structural methodologies for cognitive profiling and user personalization, and to data mining for content pattern recognition. In complex environments, such as the military, an effective approach might involve several techniques, multiple tool sets in various combinations, and the integration of knowledge outputs with current situational data to help form an understanding for decision makers.

The services have taken somewhat different routes to KM. The Navy has its wide-reaching $6.9 billion Navy-Marine Corps intranet program that is converting 200 networks into the world's largest intranet while simultaneously consolidating date, information, and knowledge resources. The Army is using knowledge management as a way to centralize systems management at major commands under the CIO's (chief information officer's) office, and the Air Force portal will consolidate hundreds of disparate legacy data systems into a single decentralized point of access (Onley, 2001).

Current Practices

Joint-forces operations and cross-service integration is a current focus in the military. With this comes the challenge of data, information, and knowledge integration across the services. In response to such challenges are new techniques to evolve data into information, and information into knowledge and understanding. Figure 1 provides a Navy perspective to illustrate how knowledge is evolved from learning and training to address technol-

Figure 1. Evolution from information to knowledge (DoN CIO, 2000)

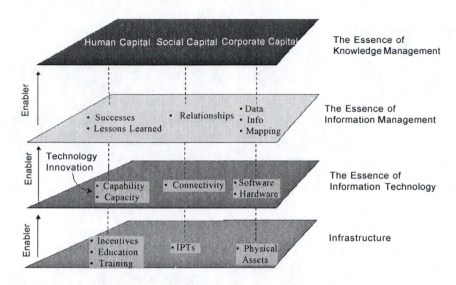

ogy, connectivity, and access. Then, information management is where data and information are mapped, relationships are explored, and lessons are derived. Finally, knowledge management is where human, social, and corporate capital are integrated.

Knowledge management in the military is often used in the broadest sense to include such variables as the management of numerical values obtained from automated collection systems, qualitative data from human subjective opinions, synthetic results from both human and machine simulation, and systems output or result sets tailored to address specific long-range plans or objectives (Maule, Schacher, & Gallup, 2002). Military knowledge applications are often designed to support specific strategic, operational, or tactical decision-making processes and related questions.

Many knowledge tools are adopted from the commercial sector, but there are some notable differences in application, especially for warfare. Of course, there are unique demands placed upon the military for just-in-time knowledge for the warriors.

For example, in corporate knowledge management, a dynamic situational assessment for a real-time attack is not a typical company objective. In the military, knowledge systems for such an objective would need to help convey understanding. The concept is modeled in Figure 2.

Military knowledge systems may be called upon to integrate information and knowledge output with current

Figure 2. Corporate vs. military knowledge management

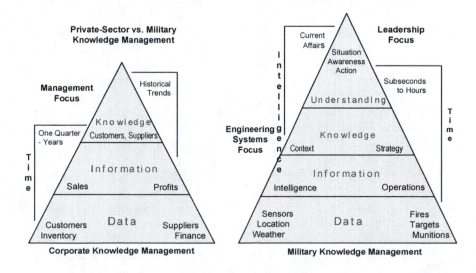

Figure 3. Army knowledge online and navy knowledge online knowledge portals

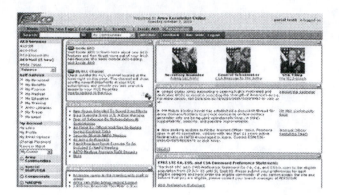 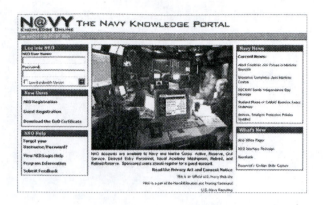

situational data to form an understanding in the mind of the decision maker. Understanding requires a real-time context. The idea is to develop real-time understanding faster than the enemy, and this cannot be achieved if decision makers are overloaded with too much information. Knowledge should enable a commander to develop an understanding of the situation, make good decisions, and implement them faster than the enemy (Harrigan, Jenkins, Winters, Mohs, & Hay, 2001). The Army is attacking information overload by developing knowledge ontology and infrastructure, evaluating existing knowledge-fusion algorithms, and developing computational models to address specific knowledge-management needs (MIT, 2002).

Collaborative tools are important in military knowledge systems because they can integrate resources to enhance situational awareness and understanding. Chat, instant messaging, online meetings, and shared application technologies are hallmarks of current knowledge-management initiatives (Donnelly, 2003). The integration of traditional knowledge technologies with collaborative capabilities has increased overall complexity, and knowledge officers have been assigned to monitor information flow, encourage the use of collaborative planning tools, and assist with knowledge-based communications. An example is the global war games in which the "knowledge warrior" has emerged as a facilitator of information for the Commander Joint Task Force with responsibilities for shaping knowledge in response to information requirements and therein speeding decision times within multitiered collaborative environments (Harrigan et al., 2001).

Portals are a popular means to provide access to information and knowledge repositories. Military portal initiatives focus on the aggregation of Web services, information sites, collaboration tools, and decision-support applications into centralized portals (Tate, 2001). Portals are often supported through communities of practice to ensure active participation by key decision

makers. Portals additionally offer a means to implement system-wide security policies through single sign-on and common-directory services for the authentication of specific information items on a need-to-know basis (MIT, 2003). Portals are often implemented to provide warriors with access to tacit or know-how knowledge from communities of practice and collaborative access to subject-matter experts (Donnelley, 2003).

Some examples include Army Knowledge Online and Navy Knowledge Online that, in addition to current events and operations, integrate e-mail, chat, personal Web portals, and communities (Onley, 2004; Figure 3). The Air Force portal gives people the ability to view information needed to do their job without regard to the system which manages that information such that a soldier anywhere in the world can log on to a computer, check e-mail, and get the status of an order or review a schedule.

The Army Knowledge Awards Program acknowledges initiatives, programs, and concepts that exploit knowledge-management tools and principles. The program recognizes KM-based reengineering enterprise initiatives that focus on major commands, functional areas, and process transformation (DOIM, 2004). The Center for Army Lessons Learned (CALL) (a) transforms raw data into knowledge that can be acted upon, (b) sends the knowledge out to the whole organization, and (c) produces rapid behavioral change based on the knowledge. Teams of experts observe missions firsthand, collect and analyze information, ask experts to validate it, and once the information is validated, produce lessons learned that are delivered as written reports, videos, or simulations to the troops (CALL, 2004).

The Knowledge-Centric Organization (KCO) is a Navy initiative wherein personnel organize virtually around knowledge needs such that the virtual organization becomes an overlay to existing command structures (Millward, 2000). Focus areas include preparation and issues of culture, leadership, relationships, and communications; knowledge-centric systems and the development of strategy, performance measures, and incentives; knowledge-centric organizations and the measurement of performance, assessment, validation, and strategy revision; knowledge creation and brokering to address learning styles and knowledge facilitation and instruction; and knowledge communities to aid in knowledge design, mobilization, and connection (DoN CIO, 2000). Sailors reporting to a new command would previously spend days acclimating to new processes and procedures, while with a KCO, learning time has been reduced up to 80% as sailors, marines, and civilians can immediately access lessons learned and command knowledge stored in the knowledge systems (Millward).

Knowledge Metrics

Metrics are an important component of military knowledge-management initiatives. In the private sector, requirements and specifications typically lead to product evaluations, demonstrations from vendors, selection, and implementation. The process is somewhat more complicated in the military where production selection often involves a rigorous test and evaluation cycle in live operational experiments, with a focus on systems interoperability and knowledge integration at both technical and organizational levels. It is in this context that metrics provide the basis for evaluation. A few prominent themes and categories of metrics are identified in Table 1.

The metrics are largely extracted from the research presented above, so the references will not be repeated. This categorization of knowledge metrics pertinent to the military will hopefully aid future researchers in military knowledge management.

Metrics addressing cognition consider knowledge needs of classes of decision makers. Initiatives may consider metadata and perception, visualization, or interpretation. Reasoning models specific to a given situation may assess concept formation and evolution, collaborative behavior, inference, case-based reasoning, problem solving, or adaptation and learning. The decomposition of interactions, and cause-effect relationships based on knowledge and resultant decisions help in reasoning about information flows. Artificial-intelligence tools may be tested as aids in the information-synthesis and -extraction process.

Knowledge fusion is a related area providing a basis for the integration of content, often addressing semantics and ontology as the knowledge infrastructure. Fusion research generally considers the processes involved in combining data and information to produce knowledge to make estimates and predictions. As previously discussed, in the military, the focus is on situation assessment and impact (threat) analysis. Other fusion areas address metadata, information interaction and integration, knowledge discovery and visualization, and knowledge and information flow. Process models are means to

Table 1. Military knowledge functions and metric categories

KM Function	Metric Categories
Discovery	Acquisition, query optimization, indexing, filtering, link analysis, ontology, agents, semantics, concurrency, domains, interfaces, visualization, AI tools, sequences, streams, temporal, spatial, clustering, mining, pattern matching
Management	Logs, interviews, surveys, observers, coverage, evolution, sustenance, reuse, domains, requirements, documentation, value added, scalability, planning, scheduling, agents, organization, cleansing, unification, maintenance, safety, migration
Performance	System, process, communications, events, flows, status, readiness, integration, latency, behavior, interoperability, optimization, maintenance, survivability, fault tolerance
Decision Support	Effectiveness, efficiency, prediction, integration, representation, reaction, concurrency, agents, optimization, disambiguation, categorization, summarization, filters, mining, pattern matching, cleansing, unification
Work Flow	Planning, scheduling, domains, interfaces, concurrency, agents, sequences, streams, constraints, optimization, organization, clustering, unification
Collaboration	Synergism, domains, media, interfaces, behavior, agents, temporal, spatial, constraints, organization, clustering, pattern matching, unification
Assurance	Security, privacy, trustworthiness, authentication, aggregation, nonrepudiation, reliability, survivability, validation, consistency, documentation, verification, concurrency, interoperability, constraints, maintenance, safety, survivability, fault tolerance
Metadata	Schemas, XML structures, objects, inheritance, temporal, spatial, optimization, organization, categorization, profiles, clustering, unification, migration
Fusion	Algorithms, inference, relationships, uncertainty, ambiguity, ambience, value added, incompleteness, concurrency, sequences, streams, temporal, spatial, constraints, optimization, organization, categorization, summarization, filters, clustering, pattern matching, cleansing, unification, maintenance, migration, ubiquity
Reasoning	Integration, multimodal, inconsistency, uncertainty, incompleteness, behavior, agents, AI tools, sequences, streams, temporal, spatial, constraints, optimization, organization, disambiguation, filters

capture organizational and system processes. Metrics may consider the impact of knowledge injects or fusions into specific processes.

Collaboration metrics address the results of human-human interchanges concerning generated information, and the impact of new variables introduced during the course of any given flow of events (ad hoc alliances, changed positions or objectives, etc.). Work-flow technologies in the military are increasingly grouped under collaborative technologies, which are in turn a driving force in military knowledge management. Metrics would stress integration between supporting technologies, systems, and organizational processes.

FUTURE TRENDS

Predicting new developments in knowledge management in the military is challenging given the size of the organizations and the complexity of the operations. Some trends that do seem certain involve the increase in interoperability of knowledge across the branches, likely occurring under joint-forces initiatives. Web services will continue to expand, integrate operations, and provide a means for knowledge sharing to increase situational awareness and understanding.

Of special interest are emerging opportunities to synthesize or fuse knowledge, and then supplement the collective with visualization or reasoning. This may be considered an area of research akin to artificial intelligence in the previous decade, but today it crosses into real-world military operations, with concerns in performance and decision support.

Virtualization and distributed knowledge through the Global Information Grid and grid computing architectures will offer many possibilities for the cross-pollination of knowledge and the integration of previously disparate knowledge operations and applications. The impact of peer-to-peer technologies for knowledge sharing will be an interesting area for future research. Experimentation is currently underway with many peer-peer technologies, however, security concerns are evident.

CONCLUSION

Knowledge management is a serious area of inquiry in the military. Given the life-threatening situations modern warriors confront and the new types of behaviors exhibited in conflict, knowledge systems have become a priority area. Many knowledge technologies and research approaches have come from the commercial

sector, while many others remain proprietary and classified. This discussion has attempted to provide a bridge between public KM technologies and research in current military R & D, highlighting common areas in each. Examples of military knowledge portals and management practices provide some insight on current thinking, and the areas synthesized in the metrics and future-trends sections above hopefully provide visibility in some of the areas in which the military seeks active research and development.

REFERENCES

AFMC. (2003). *AFMC finance team leads Air Force-wide knowledge management initiative* (Air Force Materiel Command News Service Release No. 0602). Retrieved from *http://www.afmc-pub.wpafb.af.mil/HQ-AFMC/PA/news/archive/2003/June/0602-03.htm*

Berners-Lee, T., Hendler, J., & Lassila, O. (2001). The semantic Web. *Scientific American.* Retrieved from *http://scientificamerican.com/2001/0501issue/0501berners-lee.html*

CALL. (2004). *Welcome to the center for army lessons learned public Web site.* Retrieved from *http://call.army.mil*

Chandrasekaran, B., Josephson, J., & Benjamins, V. (1999). What are ontologies, and why do we need them. *IEEE Intelligent Systems, 14*(1), 20-26.

DOIM. (2004). *Army knowledge awards winners list.* Retrieved from *http://www.doim.army.mil/Army_Awards_Dispatch.html*

DoN CIO. (2000). *Knowledge-centric organization toolkit.* Washington, DC: Department of the Navy, Chief Information Officer.

Donnelly, H. (2003). Capturing a community of knowledge. *Military Information Technology, 7*(5). Retrieved from *http://www.military-information techn ology.com/archive_article.cfm?DocID=147*

Fensel, D., & Motta, E. (2001). Structured development of problem solving methods. *IEEE Transactions on Knowledge and Data Engineering, 13*(6), 913-932.

Gao, X., & Sterling, L. (2000). Semi-structured data extraction from heterogeneous sources. In D. Schwartz, M. Divitini, & T. Brasethvik (Eds.), *Internet-based organizational memory and knowledge management* (pp. 83-102). Hershey, PA: Idea Group Publishing.

Grimes, S. (2002). The semantic Web. *Intelligent Enterprise, 5*(6), 16-52.

Harrigan, G., Jenkins, N., Winters, M., Mohs, S., & Hay, O. (2001). Knowledge management in global war games. *CHIPS.* Retrieved from *http://www.chips.navy.mil/archives/01_fall/knowledge _management_in_global_w.htm*

Housel, T., & Bell, A. (2001). *Measuring and managing knowledge.* New York: McGraw-Hill Irwin.

Loria, M. (2001). Knowledge management and collaboration. *KMWorld,* S8-S9.

Maule, R. (1998). Cognitive maps, AI agents and personalized virtual environments in Internet learning experiences. *Journal of Internet Research, 8*(4), 347-358.

Maule, R. (2000). Metacognitive research & development framework (MRDF) for Internet instructional science software. *Journal of Internet Research, 10*(4), 329-345.

Maule, R. (2001). Framework for metacognitive mapping to design metadata for intelligent hypermedia presentations. *Journal of Educational Multimedia and Hypermedia, 10*(1), 27-45.

Maule, R., Gallup, S., & Schacher, G. (2003). Broadband Internet applications for multi-organizational collaborative processes, workflow automation, and complexity analysis in multi-national experimentation. *Proceedings of the 2003 Pacific Telecommunications Conference,* Honolulu, Hawaii.

Maule, R., Schacher, G., & Gallup, S. (2002). Knowledge management for the analysis of complex experimentation. *Journal of Internet Research, 12*(5), 427-435.

Maule, R., Schacher, G., Gallup, S., Marachi, C., & McClain, B. (2000). *IJWA ethnographic qualitative knowledge management system.* Monterey, CA: Naval Postgraduate School, Institute for Joint Warfare Analysis.

Millward, B. (2000). Knowledge-centric organizations. *CHIPS. http://www.chips.navy.mil/archives/00_apr/kco.htm*

MIT. (2002). Communications and electronics technology for transformation: Interview with Major General William H. Russ. *Military Information Technology, 6*(9). Retrieved from *http://www.military-information-technology.com/archive_article.cfm?DocID=49*

MIT. (2003). Infostructure commander: Interview with Major General James C. Hylton. *Military Information Technology, 7*(8). Retrieved from *http://www.military-information-technology.com/archive_article.cfm?DocID=230*

Moore, A. (2001). Enterprise information portals: The power and the peril. *KMWorld,* S2-S3.

Nissen, M. (2001). *Facilitating naval knowledge flow.* Monterey, CA: Naval Postgraduate School.

North Atlantic Treaty Organization (NATO). (2000). *The land C2 information exchange data model. Internal report: ADatP-32 Edition 2.0.* Brussels, Belgium: Author.

Onley, D. (2001, September 24). Service branches take different routes to KM. *Government Computer News.* Retrieved from *http://www.gcn.com/20_29/news/17174-1.html*

Onley, D. (2004, June 7). Army knowledge online portal seeks one vendor, upgrades. *Government Computer News,* 30.

Primix Solutions. (2000). Customer knowledge management. *Knowledge Management,* 90-91.

Ruber, P. (2000). Opening doors to structured data. *Knowledge Management,* 81.

Saward, G. (2000). The challenge for customer service: Managing heterogeneous knowledge. In D. Schwartz, M. Divitini, & T. Brasethvik (Eds.), *Internet-based organizational memory and knowledge management* (pp. 57-81). Hershey, PA: Idea Group Publishing.

Schacher, G., Maule, R., & Gallup, S. (2001). Knowledge management system for joint experimentation. *Proceedings of the NATO OSLO Symposium. Building a Vision: NATO's Future Transformation,* Oslo, Norway.

Schwartz, D., Divitini, M., & Brasethvik, T. (2000). On knowledge management in the Internet age. In D. Schwartz, M. Divitini, & T. Brasethvik (Eds.), *Internet-based organizational memory and knowledge management* (pp. 1-19). Hershey, PA: Idea Group Publishing.

Sherman, L. (2000). Creating useful knowledge structures. *Knowledge Management,* 82-83.

Silver, B. (2001). The face of knowledge management: A status report. *KMWorld,* 14-15.

Storey, V., & Dey, D. (2002). A methodology for learning across application domains for database design systems. *IEEE Transactions on Knowledge and Data Engineering, 14*(1), 13-28.

Storey, V., Goldstein, R., & Ullrich, H. (2002). Naïve semantics to support automated database design. *IEEE*

Transactions on Knowledge and Data Engineering, 14(1), 1-12.

Tate, B. (2001). *DON enterprise portal initiative: Following the NMCI path to knowledge.* CHIPS. *Retrieved from http://www.chips.navy.mil/archives/01_nmci/portal.htm*

KEY TERMS

Collaborative Tools: Traditional chat, whiteboard, messaging, presentation, VoIP, and conferencing systems. They are a strong component of knowledge management in the military.

Communities of Practice: Collaborative means to build and share knowledge and expertise, increase social capital and the economic value of relationships within the military, and lower the cost of training.

Global Information Grid (GIG): The Department of Defense's next-generation network and future infrastructure for advanced data, information, and knowledge operations. Current GIG initiatives involve high-security systems.

Knowledge Officers: Military officers with varying levels of responsibilities depending on the service and operation. Navy experimentation has involved knowledge officers reporting to a chief knowledge officer with overall strategic responsibilities for information and communications.

Knowledge Warrior: A facilitator of information with responsibilities for shaping knowledge in response to information requirements to speed decision times.

Network-Centric Operations: Military focus on systems integration and interoperability to provide a common infrastructure for data, information, and knowledge applications, including the realization of those applications in operational settings.

Network-Centric Warfare: Combat based on network-centric operations and GIG-type infrastructures to provide just-in-time information, knowledge, situational assessment, and understanding.

Portals: Integrative site of sites to personalize, sort, and filter information; enhance knowledge with intelligence for decision support; and improve overall information, communications, collaboration, and workflow operations. In the military, it is a primary means to aggregate systems and information services.

Situational Assessment: Important military concept referencing a common operational picture that provides current conditions with supporting context, knowledge, information, and data.

Understanding: A layer above the traditional three-tier model of data, information, and knowledge to address the additional need of military personnel for knowledge systems capable of conveying understanding or expertise for the decision maker.

MNE Knowledge Management Across Borders and ICT

M

Jürgen Kai-Uwe Brock
University of Strathclyde, UK

Yu Josephine Zhou
International University of Applied Science, Bad Honnef-Bonn., Germany

INTRODUCTION

Firms are consumers, producers, managers, and distributors of information (Egelhoff, 1991; Casson, 1996) and as such a repository of productive knowledge (Winter, 1988). Consequently the ability to generate, access, and utilize relevant knowledge is an essential organizational activity in order both to reduce uncertainty about the firm's external environment and improve the efficiency of its internal operations.

Particularly for multinational enterprises (MNEs), efficient implementation of knowledge management processes is of competitive importance. In contrast to their set of indigenous competitors, MNEs face liabilities of foreignness (Zaheer, 1995) and a more complex organizational structure that transcends cultures and countries.

Advances in location insensitive information and communication technology (ICT), in particular the Internet's marketspace (Rayport & Sviokla, 1994), could significantly facilitate MNEs' knowledge management efforts. Ease of information gathering, communication, and knowledge management is no longer a strict function of geographical proximity. As a result of the Internet, the location specificity of knowledge (von Hayek, 1945) is becoming less location dependent, and thus less costly. Despite this, the role of the Internet in knowledge management has its limits due to its inherent media characteristics and the aforementioned liabilities particular to the operations of MNEs.

This article explores the possibilities and limitations of the Internet in supporting knowledge management in the specific context of MNEs. It is structured as follows. First we will provide a background to the article by discussing and defining the specifics of MNEs, MNEs' knowledge management challenges, and the specifics of the Internet. Subsequently the article will analyze and explore the potential impact of the Internet on MNEs' knowledge management processes. A discussion of future trends and an overall conclusion close the article.

BACKGROUND

Global trade has grown 16-fold since the 1950s, by far outstripping the growth in GDP (Economist, 1998). A key driving force behind this trend is foreign direct investment (FDI), whereas FDI is defined as an acquisition of an asset in a foreign country (host country) made by an investor in another country (home country) with the intention to manage this asset (WTO, 1996). MNEs are the main driver behind FDI. Although definitions vary, an MNE can be defined as a firm that is engaged in FDI in several countries outside its home country (for a more detailed discussion the reader might refer to, e.g., Vahlne & Nordström, 1993; Rugman & Verbeke, 2004).

Before discussing the specific knowledge management challenges of MNEs and the role of the Internet therein, it is vital to understand why MNEs exist at all. International business theory has addressed this. The core idea of international trade theory—the idea of market imperfections—was utilized by international business researchers to explain international activities at the firm level by projecting these imperfections into the firm. This helped to explain the emergence and existence of MNEs, as opposed to firms only trading with each other by means of importing and exporting. In 1960 (published in 1976), Hymer's market imperfections theory in essence postulated that firm specific advantages like technology and management skills are the core source enabling firms to successfully operate abroad, offsetting cost and information advantages enjoyed by indigenous firms. Hymer's idea was then further refined and developed by Buckley and Casson (1976) to become internalization theory. Buckley and Casson conceptualized the MNE as a firm that responds to pre-product or intermediate-product market imperfections by internalizing these markets (like components, semi processed goods, knowledge, skills, and technology) across national boundaries (via FDI). Internalization means that a firm makes use of its organizational hierarchy and in-house resources to manage a specific business transaction as opposed to buying it on the market. By internalizing the transfer of a firm's assets and capabilities, firms mitigate transfer problems and at the same time exploit their internal advantage(s) internationally.

At the heart of internalization is the management of knowledge-related imperfections (Kogut & Zander, 1993), which makes effective knowledge management a central task for MNEs. Knowledge management within MNEs is about two interrelated tasks:

1. Knowledge management within the MNE (intra-MNE) which focuses on continuous knowledge creation, transmission, use, and retention between and within headquarters and subsidiaries.
2. Interface knowledge management (extra-MNE) which is about the continuous identification of the MNEs' external knowledge environment, its scanning, the collection of relevant external knowledge, and synthesis with existing intra-MNE knowledge.

This categorization can be related to types of MNEs (see Figure 1). Intra-MNE knowledge management mainly relates to the integration dimension, and extra-MNE knowledge management mainly relates to the responsiveness dimension. Obviously, as an MNE moves from low to high on both dimensions, knowledge management (intra- and extra-MNE) requirements increase.

This article will focus on the first knowledge management task (intra-MNE knowledge; integration), because it is unique to MNEs.

The key challenge for intra-MNE knowledge management is knowledge transmission (Kogut & Zander, 1993). Transmitting knowledge is costly (Teece, 1977). The more tacit—or personal (Polanyi, 1958)—and complex the information, the more difficult and expensive it will be to transmit it. This is so because the codification and teaching costs in the transmission process increase as tacitness and complexity increases. Transmitting knowledge across different cultures and countries further increases the costs due to different norms, habits, languages, and interpersonal processes that can inhibit communication flows (Johanson & Vahlne, 1977). These differences operate at two levels, the intra-organizational level and the extra-organizational level, both defining the communication complexity in the knowledge transmission process (see Figure 2). While the former refers to differences between the different organizational cultures within MNEs (mainly headquarters to subsidiary/-ies), the latter refers to differences at the national level (home country to host country/-ies). However, the intra-MNE transfer of knowledge can be eased by the development of a common understanding and of capabilities—combinative capabilities according to Kogut and Zander (1993)—how to manage this transmission. Such development emerges—

Figure 1. Types of MNEs

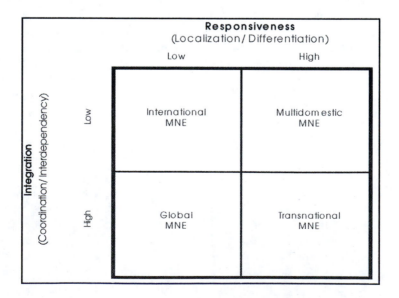

Source: Derived from Harzing's MNE typology synthesis (Harzing, 1997)

Figure 2. Intercultural MNE communication matrix

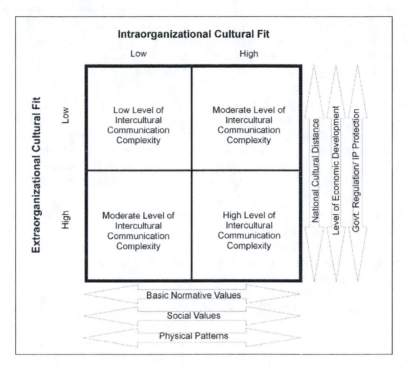

Source: Derived from Harvey and Griffith (2002)

via repeated interactions—over time in the form of organizational routines.

Before analyzing how the Internet's marketspace could impact the intra-MNE knowledge management process, an evaluation of the marketspace is required.

Whereas the *marketplace* represents the physical world of resources, the *marketspace* represents the virtual world of digitized information (Rayport & Sviokla, 1994). The most evident and widely known manifestation of the marketspace is the Internet. Following key elements of December's (1996) definition, the Internet can be defined as:

- Computer-mediated communication, including
- information dissemination and
- information retrieval that
- involves data (bits) exchanges taking place on the
- global collection of computer networks using
- the TCP/IP protocol suite for data transfer.

The information content can involve a broad range of data types (text, graphics, images, sound, video), and various forms of open and closed (in the case of intranets and extranets) information processes (one-to-one, one to many; asynchronous, synchronous) are possible. The Internet can thus be used by organizations such as MNEs to process, distribute, and retrieve codified knowledge, and it can be used to interact (communicate) with others. To express this, the terms "information pull," "information push," and "interaction" are introduced. Information pull refers to organizational activities related to synchronously or asynchronously pulling information from the Internet (or intranet, extranet). Information pull can be active or passive, with, for example, searching the Web referring to the former and subscribing to mailing lists referring to the latter. Subscribing to corporate mailing lists is a passive, non-specific information pull activity, because the subscriber does not know exactly what specific kind of information he or she receives prior to subscribing.

On the other hand, information push refers to organizational activities related to pushing information onto the Internet (or intranet, extranet). Active information push refers to organizations actively marketing their information push activities. In contrast, passive information push refers to organizations setting up Web sites without any internal or external promotions.

Interaction is the Internet's third potential use for organizations. The main difference between information push/pull and interaction is that interaction involves non anonymous, asynchronous or synchronous personal exchange of information between known communication parties. Both information pull and information push is at least partially anonymous. Interaction as understood here means mediated personal interaction between known users or parties. When an organization pushes corporate information onto the Internet, it does not know ex ante who might actually retrieve and read its content. The same applies for posting non personalized messages to newsgroups or mailing lists, because the sender does not know in advance who will read his message and who will not. In addition, the sender does not know the identity of all the receivers, unless he is the initiator and owner of the mailing list requiring subscribers to reveal their identity during the subscription process. The same applies in the case of information pull. Although users accessing a Web page or Internet-based databases leave "digital fingerprints" (Drèze & Zufryden, 1997) and Web sites can send so-called "cookies" to users accessing a Web page, users pulling information from the Internet can remain anonymous if they wish to by refusing cookies or by using anonymizer software. In contrast, interaction as defined here involves the one-to-one or one to many exchange of information between pre-specified and known parties. The defining element of interaction is value exchange between known parties.

All of the aforementioned three use categories are interrelated, with information pull activities potentially being influenced by and leading to information push activities and interaction activities, and vice versa. Also, the three uses relate to similarly interrelated activities taking place in the non mediated marketplace.

MAIN FOCUS OF THE ARTICLE

Although the role of ICT in organizations in general has been the focus of studies since the 1970s (e.g., Pfeffer & Leblebici, 1977), little is known about the specific role of ICT in cross-cultural contexts (e.g., St.Amant, 2002; Weisinger & Trauth, 2002) and MNE operations (e.g., Petersen & Welch, 2003). With the background provided in the previous section, it is possible to explore possible effects of the Internet's marketspace on intra-MNE knowledge management.

Knowledge management scholars have identified four dynamically interacting processes how organizational knowledge is created and transmitted (Nonaka, 1991). The first process—termed "socialization"—is about tacit-to-tacit knowledge transfers. The traditional German apprenticeship system is an example of such a transfer. An apprentice learns via observation, imitation, and practice. In this process he or she "imports" the tacit knowledge base of the master which becomes his or her own tacit knowledge. The second knowledge transfer process is "articulation," whereby explicit or codified knowledge is directly transferred to become explicit knowledge elsewhere. An example of such a process would be an indi-

vidual recombining a set of coded knowledge such as a financial report into a different document. The third and fourth processes are about transformative transfers, whereby explicit knowledge in turned into tacit knowledge or vice versa. The tacit-to-explicit transfer is called "combination." Combination takes place when an individual articulates his or her tacit knowledge base, thereby converting it into explicit knowledge that can be shared with others. Finally, "internalization"—a technical term in the knowledge management literature that has a different meaning to the one in the international business context—is the explicit-to-tacit process of knowledge transfer. This process takes place when employees use the explicit organizational knowledge available, for example in the form of a database, to extend their own tacit knowledge.

How could the Internet support or enhance these four processes in the case of intra-MNE knowledge management?

On the one hand, the answer lies in an understanding of the differences between mediated and unmediated communication. On the other, an appreciation of cultural differences in communication is required. With regards to the former, rational media choice theories, such as social presence theory (Short, Williams, & Christie, 1976) and media richness theory (Daft & Lengel, 1986) postulate that an individual determines his or her choice of media by rationally assessing the requirements of a communication task and selecting an appropriate medium matching these requirements. Media is categorized along a continuum based on the channel's information richness, which depends on the medium's ability for immediate feedback, the number of carried cues, the number of channels utilized, its language variety, and its level of personalization capable of reducing equivocality. This set of theories postulates that the higher the perceived need for social cues and equivocality reduction in a communication situation, the higher the likelihood of face-to-face communication, the richest mode of information exchange with the highest degree of social presence. This would, for example, be the case in tacit-to-tacit knowledge transfers ("socialization"). In contrast, the Internet is considered less information rich. It follows that the reduction in channel capacity on the Internet compared to face to face communications makes knowledge transfers more difficult despite its cost-reducing properties in general.

Mixed empirical findings regarding the predictive validity of the rational media choice theories (e.g., Markus, 1994; Walther, 1996; Ngwenyama & Lee, 1997) have led to the development of social influence models of communication technology use (e.g., Ngwenyama & Lee, 1997). The social influence models of communication technology use all regard information richness or leanness in communications not as attributable to the properties of the communication medium alone, but as emerging from the interaction between people and contexts. According to this school of thought, media choice is influenced by the attitudes and behaviors of others, as well as norms that have developed within a group, within organizations, or across organizations. Hence, media perception is not fixed, but it varies across people, organizations, situations, tasks, time, and user experience with the medium. Because these models make no a priori assumption about any direct relationships between communication richness and the quantity of social cues (Ngwenyama & Lee, 1997), they in essence detach the message from the medium. Any message can be rich (or lean) relatively independent of the medium, more dependent upon the users' experience with the medium, their experience with the communication topic, and their experience with the communication partner or the communication context (Carlson & Zmud, 1999). Communication richness is therefore an outcome of social behavior, not solely an outcome of the nominal, rationally determined media richness of the communication channel. All this implies that although the amount of social information per communication act via the Internet is lower compared to face to face communication, it is more the *rate* of social information exchange than the *amount* of social cues exchanged that constitutes the key difference between the two forms of communication (Walther, 1996). Compared to non mediated communication, the exchange of social cues is "just" temporally retarded. Hence, informal, interpersonal communication can take place over computer-mediated communication channels, as user experience with the medium, the topic, the communication partner, and the communication context accumulates and increases. This phenomenon has been termed the "channel expansion effect" (Carlson & Zmud, 1999). But when first exposed to new media such as the Internet, it is likely that people's need for unmediated, face-to-face interactions increases (Nohria & Eccles, 1992).

A similar, albeit media-independent expansion effect can be observed within the organizational context of the MNE. As described by Kogut and Zander (1993), the personnel of the MNE must share a similar background and organizational culture in order to be able to encode and decode messages—in any of the four processes described above—correctly, otherwise misunderstandings will arise. Such capability, constituting the MNEs' transactional ownership-advantage (Dunning & Rugman, 1985), is MNE specific and only emerges over time through repeated interactions.

Considering communication differences across cultures is the second aspect that requires attention to understand how the Internet could support or enhance the four processes of intra-MNE knowledge management (see Figure 2). Hall's work on intercultural communication

(Hall, 1976, 1983) provides a suitable framework that has been applied widely in similar research contexts, especially its contextual dimension (e.g., St.Aman, 2002; Zakaria, Stanton, & Sarker-Barney, 2003; Matveev & Nelson, 2004). The contextual dimension in Hall's framework represents the ways in which information is perceived, exchanged, and used by people from different cultures. Hall categorized cultures on a high- to low-context continuum. Low-context cultures such as those in the United States, Germany, and Scandinavian countries tend to present and exchange information in an explicit and direct manner. The implicit assumption is that little or no contextual overlap with the receiver is required, because all necessary information is vested in the explicit code (i.e., words) used. In contrast, high-context cultures such as those in Japan, China, Russia, and Latin America tend to rely less on coded, explicit communication. In such cultures most of the actual information content resides within the physical and situational context, as well as inside the communication parties. Less explicit information exchange is the natural consequence. Research has shown that such cultural differences also impact the way people go about their information pull, push, and interaction tasks, whether ICT mediated or unmediated (e.g., Straub, Keil, & Brenner, 1997; Pook & Füstös, 1999; Kersten et al., 2003; Pauleen, 2003; Zakaria et al., 2003).

Considering these different aspects, it becomes evident that it is likely that the relative role of Internet versus face-to-face-based knowledge management processes depends on the type of knowledge transfer process; the MNEs employees' experience with the Internet and its three generic uses; the employees' experience in transferring, absorbing, and using intra-MNE knowledge; and the intercultural communication complexity. Table 1 provides an overview.

For tacit-to-tacit transfers, the role of the Internet is the most limited, and only one of the three generic uses apply. Unmediated face-to-face interactions will play the dominant role with the highest base level, particularly in complex communication situations that require very personal communication strategies (Harvey & Griffith, 2002). Only over time, as the previously mentioned expansion effects occur and the emergence of an organizational communication culture reduces communication complexity, will the interaction use of the Internet increase and the role of unmediated interactions decrease. An exception to this trajectory is a surmised initial increase in face-to-face interaction (Nohria & Eccles, 1992). The overall shift over time will be of a complementary rather than fully substitutive nature (Kraut, Steinfield, Chan, Butler, & Hoag, 1998), especially in high-context cultures (Zakaria et al., 2003). A video conference over the Internet with an instructor practically demonstrating procedural knowledge is an example of a tacit-to-tacit knowledge transfer.

Table 1. Knowledge management aspects, culture, ICT, and MNEs*

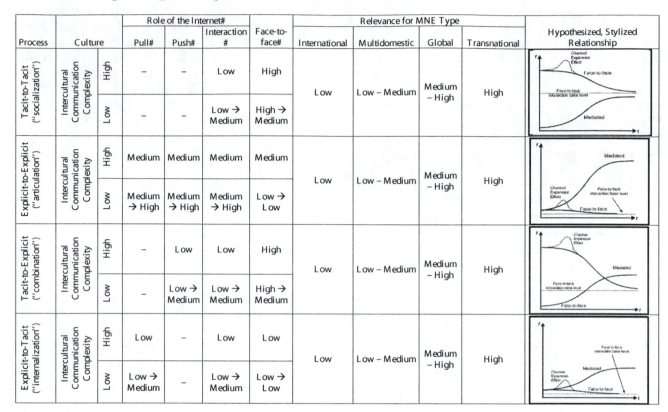

Process	Culture		Role of the Internet#				Relevance for MNE Type				Hypothesized, Stylized Relationship
			Pull#	Push#	Interaction #	Face-to-face#	International	Multidomestic	Global	Transnational	
Tacit-to-Tacit ("socialization")	Intercultural Communication Complexity	High	–	–	Low	High	Low	Low – Medium	Medium – High	High	
		Low	–	–	Low → Medium	High → Medium					
Explicit-to-Explicit ("articulation")	Intercultural Communication Complexity	High	Medium	Medium	Medium	Medium	Low	Low – Medium	Medium – High	High	
		Low	Medium → High	Medium → High	Medium → High	Low → Low					
Tacit-to-Explicit ("combination")	Intercultural Communication Complexity	High	–	Low	Low	High	Low	Low – Medium	Medium – High	High	
		Low	–	Low → Medium	Low → Medium	High → Medium					
Explicit-to-Tacit ("internalization")	Intercultural Communication Complexity	High	Low	–	Low	Low	Low	Low – Medium	Medium – High	High	
		Low	Low → Medium	–	Low → Medium	Low → Low					

* Focus Intra-MNE; # Over time ($t_1 \rightarrow t_{1+n}$)

Explicit-to-explicit transfers are the stronghold of the Internet. All three generic uses apply, the frequency of use is the highest, and the face-to-face base level is the lowest. Codified organizational knowledge such as a blueprint stored in an Internet-enabled database is an example. Here, the need for unmediated communication is rather low, with the exception of complex intercultural communication situations. In addition, the need for unmediated communication might increase initially to achieve source credibility and trust.

For tacit-to-explicit transfers, only the push and inter-action use of the Internet applies and its relative role lies somewhere between the two processes previously discussed. Turning uncodified, personal knowledge into codified knowledge requires richer, unmediated communication, particularly initially and in culturally dissimilar contexts. However, similar to tacit-to-tacit transfers, expansion effects might reduce the relative importance of unmediated interactions over time. As previously mentioned, an initial increase in face-to-face interactions (Nohria & Eccles, 1992) might be an exception to this. An example of such a transfer over the Internet would be an employee who publishes (pushes) an installation guide that incorporates his experience in installing the described piece of machinery on an MNE's best practice intranet site.

In the case of explicit-to-tacit transfers, both media play a limited role, with the influence of the Internet's pull and interaction use likely to increase over time as users gain expertise in pulling the right set of information from the medium and in interacting with colleagues from different countries. Here the relative role of the Internet for the MNE is similar to its role in the tacit-to-explicit transfer. The two differences are that the pull use of the Internet applies while the push use does not and that the overall use frequency of both media is lower. Internalization is more of a media-independent internal human learning process where mainly the source—face-to-face or mediated—matters. An example would be an employee in a subsidiary who downloads a new manual containing work rules that he or she will subsequently use in the daily work. Over time the explicit, codified knowledge is absorbed and becomes part of the employee's personal, tacit knowledge base.

As indicated in Table 1, the importance of these effects depends on the MNE type and the associated importance of intra-MNE knowledge management (see Figure 1 and Table 1). If integration is low, the relevance and role of the Internet is limited. If integration is high, the Internet can facilitate intra-MNE knowledge management as described above. In addition, the MNE's overall strategic intent regarding knowledge management matters. If a personalization strategy rather than a codification strategy is followed (Hansen, Nohria, & Tierney, 1999), the role of the Internet will be more limited.

FUTURE TRENDS

The importance of knowledge management in MNEs will increase in the future. As economies' value add shifts to services and knowledge becomes the key asset for firms, productive use of organizational knowledge becomes the main challenge (Drucker, 1999). Moreover, as the international integration of economies increases, cross-cultural communication competence becomes an increasingly important aspect in knowledge management. Research has demonstrated its positive impact on performance (Matveev & Nelson, 2004). What is less clear is how the role of the Internet will change in the future and how this relates to knowledge management within MNEs. Even its present role in knowledge management processes is not well understood. The Internet is a very dynamic and innovative medium, and its capabilities have significantly improved over time, including faster network connections. Therefore one could speculate that the role of the Internet will expand further. As mobile access to the Internet improves, individuals' and organization's skills in using it improve, and its bandwidth further expands richer information can be transmitted. This will reduce—albeit not completely substituting—the need for unmediated communication in the knowledge transmission process. Real time, virtual reality conferencing between headquarters and subsidiaries is but one example. Additionally, as global Internet diffusion further increases, cultural differences might matter less and lead to the emergence of a meta-culture that transcends location-bound aspects of culture in communication.

Yet it is important to understand that the Internet is "only" an infrastructure technology available to every MNE. In other words, it is a competitive necessity, not a source of competitive advantage per se. Only if the MNE integrates the Internet seamlessly into its culturally sensitive knowledge management processes, leveraging its resource-related and transaction-related advantages, will the Internet enable MNEs to sustain their competitive advantage. An understanding of the Internet's limitations and strengths as discussed above will help.

CONCLUSION

This article explored the possibilities and limitations of the Internet in supporting intra-MNE knowledge management. As was shown theoretically, the Internet can support such management tasks, assuming that personal relationships among employees and a joint understanding of the organizational context and culture have developed. Over time, as experience with the medium, the exchange partner, and the exchange context increases, this role becomes more prominent. Despite this, unmediated communication remains of importance. Especially in complex intercultural communication situations, in the early phases of knowledge transmission processes, and in cases where tacit knowledge is dominant, the Internet's current role is more limited. In addition, the nature of the MNE matters. Especially for MNEs that manage a highly interdependent network of subsidiaries with a high level of integration, efficient use of the Internet is imperative to stay competitive. With this in mind, a more differentiated role of the Internet in intra-MNE knowledge management processes emerges. Neither will it completely obsolete distance and the location-dependency of knowledge, nor will it play no role in knowledge management (for the latter argument see, for example, McDermott, 1999).

Although this middle-of-the-road position might be logically appealing, future research should test these conclusions. Thus far, empirical evidence in this area is scant and mainly anecdotal. Can the hypothesized relationship be found in MNEs? What are the antecedents and consequences of face-to-face versus Internet-mediated knowledge management processes? Does intercultural complexity moderate or mediate antecedents and consequences of media use in knowledge management processes? What overall organizational impact could be expected? Will it lead to—or be the result of—smaller MNEs and/or more decentralized MNEs and/or more integrated MNEs (for such findings in general, see Brynjolfsson, Malone, Gurbaxani, & Kambil, 1994; Dewan, Michael, & Min, 1998)? So far, these questions have not been answered.

REFERENCES

Brynjolfsson, E., Malone, T.W., Gurbaxani, V., & Kambil, A. (1994). Does information technology lead to smaller firms? *Management Science, 40*(12), 1628-1644.

Buckley, P.J., & Casson, M.C. (1976). *The future of the multinational enterprise.* New York: Holmes & Meier.

Carlson, J.R., & Zmud, R.W. (1994). Channel expansion theory: A dynamic view of media and information richness perceptions. *Academy of Management, Best Papers* (pp. 280-284).

Casson, M.C. (1996). The nature of the firm reconsidered: Information synthesis and entrepreneurial organization. *Management International Review, 36*(Special Issue I), 55-94.

Daft, R.L., & Lengel, R.H. (1986). Organizational information requirement, media richness and structural design. *Management Science, 32*(5), 554-571.

December, J. (1996). Units of analysis for Internet communication. *Journal of Communication, 46*(1), 14-38.

Dewan, S., Michael, S.C., & Min, C.-K. (1998). Firm characteristics and investments in information technology: Scale and scope effects. *Information Systems Research, 9*(3), 219-232.

Drèze, X., & Zufryden, F. (1997). Testing Web site design and promotional content. *Journal of Advertising Research, 37*(2), 77-91.

Drucker, P.F. (1999). Knowledge-worker productivity: The biggest challenge. *California Management Review, 41*(2), 79-94.

Dunning, J.H., & Rugman, A.M. (1985). The influence of Hymer's dissertation on the theory of foreign direct investment. *American Economic Review, 75*(2), 228-236.

Economist. (1998). Survey world trade—time for another round. *The Economist,* (October 3).

Egelhoff, W.G. (1991). Information processing theory and the multinational enterprise. *Journal of International Business Studies, 22*(3), 341-368.

Hall, E.T. (1976). *Beyond culture.* Garden City, NY: Anchor.

Hall, E.T. (1983). *The dance of life: The other dimension of time.* Garden City, NY: Anchor.

Hansen, M.T., Nohria, N., & Tierney, T. (1999). What's your strategy for managing knowledge? *Harvard Business Review,* (March-April), 106-116.

Harvey, M.G., & Griffith, D.A. (2002). Developing effective intercultural relationships: The importance of communication strategies. *Thunderbird International Business Review, 44*(4), 455-476.

Harzing, A.-W. (1997). An empirical analysis and extension of the Bartlett and Ghoshal typology of multinational companies. *Journal of International Business Studies, 31*(1), 101-120.

Hymer, S.H. (1960). *The international operations of national firms: A study of direct investment.* PhD thesis, Massachusetts Institute of Technology, USA.

Johanson, J., & Vahlne, J.-E. (1977). The internationalization process of the firm—a model of knowledge development and increasing foreign market commitments. *Journal of International Business Studies, 8*(1), 23-32.

Kersten, G.E., Koeszegi, S.T., Vetschera, R. (2003). The effects of culture in computer-mediated negotiations. *Journal of Information Technology Theory and Applications, 5*(2), 1-28.

Kogut, B., & Zander, U. (1993). Knowledge of the firm and the evolutionary theory of the multinational corporation. *Journal of International Business Studies, 24*(4), 625-645.

Kraut, R., Steinfield, C., Chan, A., Butler, B., & Hoag, A. (1998). Coordination and virtualization: The role of electronic networks and personal relationships. *Journal of Computer-Mediated Communication, 3*(4). Retrieved August 5, 2000, from *http://jcmc.huiji.ac.il/vol3/issue4/kraut.html*

Markus, M.L. (1994). Electronic mail as the medium of managerial choice. *Organization Science, 5*(4), 502-527.

Matveev, A.V., & Nelson, P.E. (2004). Cross cultural communication competence and multicultural team performance—perceptions of American and Russian managers. *International Journal of Cross Cultural Management, 4*(2), 253-270.

McDermott, R. (1999). Why information technology inspired but cannot deliver knowledge management. *California Management Review, 41*(4), 103-118.

Ngwenyama, O.K., & Lee, A.S. (1997). Communication richness in electronic mail: Critical social theory and the contextuality of meaning. *MIS Quarterly, 21*(2), 145-167.

Nohria, N., & Eccles, R.G. (1992). Face-to-face: Making network organizations work. In N. Nohria & R.G. Eccles (Eds.), *Networks and organizations: Structure, form, and action* (pp. 288-308). Boston: Harvard Business School Press.

Nonaka, I. (1991). The knowledge creating company. *Harvard Business Review,* (November-December), 96-104.

Pauleen, D.J. (2003). Lessons learned crossing boundaries in an ICT-supported distributed team. *Journal of Global Information Management, 11*(4), 1-19.

Pook, L., & Füstös, J. (1999). Information sharing by management: Some cross-cultural results. *Human Systems Management, 18,* 9-22.

Petersen, B., & Welch, L.S. (2003). International business development and the Internet, post-hype. *Management International Review, 43*(Special Issue I), 7-29.

Pfeffer, J., & Leblebici, H. (1977). Information technology and organizational structure. *Pacific Sociological Review, 20*(2), 241-261.

Polanyi, M. (1958). *Personal knowledge: Towards a post critical philosophy.* Chicago: Chicago University Press.

Rayport, J.F., & Sviokla, J.J. (1994). Managing in the marketspace. *Harvard Business Review,* (November-December), 141-150.

Rugman, A.M., & Verbeke, A. (2004). A perspective on regional and global strategies of multinational enterprises. *Journal of International Business Studies, 35*(1), 3-18.

Short, J., Williams, E., & Christie, B. (1976). *The social psychology of telecommunication.* London: John Wiley & Sons.

St.Amant, K. (2002). When cultures and computers collide—rethinking computer-mediated communication according to international and intercultural communication expectations. *Journal of Business & Technical Communication, 16*(2), 196-214.

Straub, D., Keil, M., & Brenner, W. (1997). Testing the technology acceptance model across cultures: A three country study. *Information and Management, 33,* 1-11.

Teece, D.J. (1977). Technology transfer by multinational firms: The resource cost of transferring technological know-how. *Economic Journal, 87,* 242-261.

Vahlne, J.-E., & Nordström, K.A. (1993). The internationalization process: Impact of competition and experience. *The International Trade Journal, 7*(5), 529-548.

Walther, J.B. (1996). Computer-mediated communication: Impersonal, interpersonal, and hyperpersonal interaction. *Communication Research, 23*(1), 3-43.

Weisinger, J.Y., & Trauth, E.M. (2002). Situating culture in the global information sector. *Information Technology & People, 15*(4), 306-320.

Winter, S.G. (1988). On Coase, competence, and the corporation. *Journal of Law, Economics and Organization, 4*(1), 163-180.

WTO. (1996, October 16). *Trade and foreign direct investment.* Report by the WTO Secretariat.

von Hayek, F.A. (1945). The use of knowledge in society. *American Economic Review, 35*(4), 519-530.

Zaheer, S. (1995). Overcoming the liabilities of foreignness. *Academy of Management Journal, 38*(2), 341-363.

Zakaria, N., Stanton, J.M., & Sarker-Barney, S.T.M. (2003). Designing and implementing culturally sensitive IT applications: The interaction of culture values and privacy issues in the Middle East. *Information Technology & People, 16*(1), 306-320.

KEY TERMS

Articulation: One of four knowledge transmission mechanisms according to Nonaka. Articulation is about explicit or codified knowledge being transferred to become explicit knowledge elsewhere by recombining two or more sets of coded knowledge.

Channel Expansion Effect: Communication over computer-mediated communication channels such as the Internet can increase in richness and social presence over time while keeping its nominal channel capacity. This effect occurs as user experience with the medium, the topic, the communication partner, and the communication context accumulates.

Combination: One of four knowledge transmission mechanisms according to Nonaka. It is a tacit-to-explicit knowledge transfer taking place when individuals articulate their tacit knowledge base, converting it into explicit knowledge that can be shared with others.

Foreign Direct Investment (FDI): An acquisition of an asset in a foreign country (host country) made by an investor in another country (home country) with the intention to manage this asset.

Internalization: In international business and organization science literature, internalization means that an organization makes use of its organizational hierarchy to manage a specific business transaction, as opposed to buying it on the market. In knowledge management literature, internalization is one of four knowledge transmission mechanisms according to Nonaka. It refers to the explicit-to-tacit process of knowledge transfer. This process takes place when individuals use explicit knowledge to extend their own tacit knowledge base.

Multinational Enterprise (MNE): A firm that is engaged in FDI in several countries outside its home country.

Socialization: One of four knowledge transmission mechanisms according to Nonaka. Socialization is about tacit-to-tacit knowledge transfers via observation, imitation, and practice.

Tacit Knowledge: Polanyi's statement "We know more than new can say" probably best explains what tacit knowledge is. In contrast to explicit knowledge, which is expressed in formal language systems (e.g., data, formulae, or any written document), tacit knowledge is personal and difficult to formalize. Personal insights, intuition, and sensing are examples of such knowledge. It is embodied in procedures, routines, activities, values, culture, and feelings.

Mobile Knowledge Management

Volker Derballa
University of Augsburg, Germany

Key Pousttchi
University of Augsburg, Germany

INTRODUCTION

Whereas knowledge management (KM) has gained much attention in the field of management science and practice as the eminent source of competitive advantage (e.g., Davenport & Prusak, 1998; Drucker, 1993; Nonaka & Takeuchi, 1995; Probst, Raub, & Romhardt, 2003), one issue has been largely neglected: The aspect of mobility.

Conventional solutions for knowledge management systems (KMSs) have in common that they are designed for stationary workplaces and consequently require the corresponding infrastructure—that is, personal computers and fixed-line network access. Thus, they do not cater for business processes in which workers move around in or outside the premises. The result is that knowledge support for mobile workers is often rather restricted, once a task has to be performed outside of the office. Organizations in which parts of the workforce belong to one of the following classifications are concerned in that context:

- Specialists, mobile on the premises (e.g., in-house technicians)
- Specialists, mobile outside the premises (e.g., members of the sales force)
- Specialists and executives in companies with mobile operations (e.g., organizations like contracting business, police, or armed forces)
- Decision makers (e.g., CEOs who are required to make timely and well-funded decisions disregarding their current position)

The need for mobile KM stems from one of the most prominent challenges in KM: ensuring the availability of knowledge in the moment of knowledge demand. Insufficient knowledge at "point-of-action" is the wording Wiig (1995) uses to describe that problem. There exist situations in the course of daily work that require particular knowledge that is not owned by the individual actor. As long as organization members are located at the same place, knowledge repositories can be easily accessed. In some cases it might for example be sufficient to walk down the office floor and ask colleagues for help in order to establish a basic form of knowledge exchange. Another example is the access of best practices databases using a stationary computer.

Analyzing business processes with mobile elements, it is obvious that the insufficient integration of many mobile workplaces leads to suboptimal processes. It is usually required to interrupt the actual task in order to feed knowledge into or retrieve it from repositories. A mobile worker can access his company's knowledge infrastructure not at all or only indirectly. This leads to a time-consuming process in which workers spend valuable working hours searching for knowledge instead of pursuing their actual job. That is exactly what has to be avoided, considering the imperative of making access to knowledge as simple as possible. Figure 1 illustrates the break existing in the process chain due to the insufficient integration of mobile workplaces: as the mobile worker is not integrated into the process chain, the information and knowledge flows in mobile business processes are equally disrupted.

As the aspect of mobility is underrepresented in KM literature, we aim at providing an evaluation framework for managing knowledge in mobile settings (i.e., mobile KM). In order to do that, we will resort to the insights gained in the discussion of mobile techniques. As both concepts have not been sufficiently put together, we think that substantial benefits can be derived by merging the ideas behind mobile techniques and KM.

Figure 1. Non-integration of mobile workplaces into the process chain

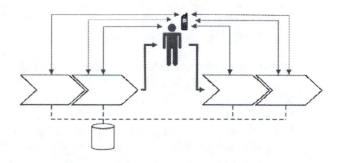

BACKGROUND

As a survey of KM literature shows, mobile KM has been largely neglected. The following section presents an overview of exemplary articles dealing with mobile KM.

The works of Fagrell (2000) can be regarded as some of the first valuable approaches to address the area of mobile KM. With NewsMate, Fagrell is presenting a KMS application that aims at supporting mobile knowledge workers. In this system KM is integrated with the relevant task that needs to be supported. A proof of concept is given by presenting a working prototype. This prototype allows journalists to access internal and external information. Further, NewsMate acts as an expert finder by automatically identifying colleagues who have worked on the same topic.

Grimm, Tazari, and Balfanz (2002) are discussing limitations of mobiles devices for the purposes of mobile KM and present a framework for the implementation of mobile KMSs. In the course of that, they address technological as well as human limitations and thus touch the area of human computer interaction (HCI). The authors aim at using the potential of mobile technology to deliver context-specific information by using the user's location to determine relevant context. Using a "virtually centralized" context manager to handle profiles of relevant objects, a situation recognition engine enables the context-specific provision of knowledge.

Martens and Gronau (2003) introduce the potentials of mobile KM by primarily referring to the dimension of ubiquity. They base their analysis on specific characteristics of mobile technology as discussed in literature dealing with the mobile economy. As a result, the reductions of spatial and temporal limitations, as well as persistent connectivity, are isolated as relevant factors. Further, the authors present short examples of how those potentials can be used in the area of KM.

Two areas can be pointed out as deficits in existing mobile KM literature. There is a lack of a holistic concept, as the focus is put either on specific technological or on KM-related issues. Additionally, it can be observed that the term "mobile KM" is used for a wide variety of cases (e.g., Lehner & Berger, 2001). That said, some of those cases do not deserve the term mobile KM, as they represent simple data integration processes. In order to structure the different applications termed mobile KM, the following three categories are developed:

1. **Mobile information exchange** includes the transfer of data and information using e-mail as well as the access to operational systems used in an organization to retrieve sales figures or market data.

2. **Mobile business intelligence** refers to the access of processed enterprise data using mobile devices. It involves the technologies introduced earlier (e.g., data mining and data warehouses).

3. **Mobile KM** describes that management process in the course of which mobile communication techniques in conjunction with mobile devices are employed for the creation, validation, presentation, distribution, or application of knowledge.

The basis for those categories is the knowledge versus information view (Holsapple, 2003). One of the authors representing this point of view is North (1999). He argues that information—derived from signs and data—is the basis for knowledge as soon as it is associated with context or other information (North, 2001). Starting with signs (e.g., "0123") and structuring them with a certain syntax will result in data (e.g., "10,23"). Data plus semantic becomes information (e.g., "10.23 refers to the percent improvement in sales figures"). This information is relatively useless, because up to that point it cannot be assessed whether—in this example—the increase can be judged as being sufficient enough. Only in context with other information and experiences is one able to determine that an increase of 10.23% is positive indeed for a company that operates in a shrinking or stable market, whereas it would considered below average for a company in booming business. Included in the knowledge stair is the idea that knowledge is a direct precursor of competence, because it enables competent action. Information on the other hand is relatively useless (Sveiby, 1997), as long as it is not processed and linked with other information, judgments, or personal opinions.

Talking about mobile KM in the narrower sense, we think that only those processes dealing with representations that have been to some degree mentally processed by human actors can be considered mobile KM. Additionally, mobile KM must be integrated into a holistic KM concept. Mobile data access as well as mobile business intelligence serve as supporting techniques in the context of mobile KM as they provide the input for human knowledge creation and thus can be referred to as mobile KM in the broader sense.

MAIN FOCUS OF THE ARTICLE

We state that for the success of mobile KM, it is not sufficient to merely make a conventional KM application available with new media. Instead, the use of mobile communication technology is only remunerative if it results in obtaining distinct supplementary added value. In order to verify the contribution mobile technology can make to KM, we are referring to the theory of informational added values (IAVs) which has been augmented with electronic added values (EAVs) and mobile added values (MAVs) (Bazijanec, Pousttchi, & Turowski, 2004).

In his theory of informational added values, Kuhlen (1996) discusses the impacts of information work in information markets. In this context we will introduce the categories of the supplementary gains of utility. Kuhlen terms resulting gains as informational added values and classifies them into eight main types: organizational, strategic, innovative, macroeconomic, efficiency, effectiveness, aesthetic-emotional, and flexible added values.

Efficiency added values cover the increase of operating efficiency and cost effectiveness. Effectiveness added values cover an augmentation in output quality. Aesthetic-emotional added values cover increase of subjective factors as wellbeing, job satisfaction, or acceptance of performance. Flexible added values cover a shift to a higher level of flexibility. Organizational added values cover the opportunity to build new forms of organization through the use of information and communication systems. Innovative added values cover the creation of an entirely new product or service (or combination of both) through the usage of new means of communication. Strategic added values qualify advantages that go beyond the operational and tactical level by creation of a significant competitive edge. Macroeconomic added values qualify advantages that go beyond the level of single companies and result in impacts on occupational images, economy, or society as a whole. IAV can be described as the resulting benefit of electronic or mobile solutions.

EAV refers to typical characteristics of electronic solutions leading to supplementary IAV. EAV results from the advantages of the utilization of fixed-line Internet access. Four EAVs can be differentiated: reduction of spatio-temporal restrictions, multimediality and interaction, equality of access, and reduction of technical restrictions. As the focus of this article is on mobile KM, we are not going to discuss EAV further. Interested readers can find further information in Turowski and Pousttchi (2003).

MAV refers to properties of mobile technology and its utilization leading to supplementary IAV like gains in efficiency or effectiveness in comparison to the use of fixed networks. MAV however only represents a potential, and a mobile solution does not have to take advantage of any MAV. But in order to gain supplementary IAV, at least one MAV has to be employed. Otherwise, the use of mobile technology is not remunerative. In the following we introduce the MAV ubiquity, context-sensitivity, identifying functions, and command and control functions.

Ubiquity

Ubiquity is the possibility to send and receive data anytime and anywhere, and thus eliminate any spatiotemporal restriction. It is originated not only in the technical possibility, but also in the typical usage of mobile devices, which accompany their user nearly anytime and anywhere. It permits the reception of time-critical and private information. Ubiquity effects in accessibility of mobile services anytime, anywhere for the user which affects reaction time and convenience aspects of services. But it affects also in reachability of users. This means primarily to reach a single user anytime, anywhere.

Context-Sensitivity

Another typical attribute is context-sensitivity, which describes the delivery of customized products or services fitting the particular needs of the user in his current situation. This is particularly enabled by three features.

Personalization allows creating specific services through preference profiles. These may be generated by information the user provides about him, but also by applications tracking his attitude. As on one hand a mobile device is typically used only by a single user and on the other hand one user typically uses only one mobile device, resulting data is of high quality. *Interactivity* enables specific services through direct information exchange. Both sides can react without any delay on actions or requests of the other. *Location determination* allows specific products and services for the user to be created, in the context of his current location or by referencing on the location of other users. In particular, combinations of these concepts allow determining a user's context. Typical applications based on the MAV of context-sensitivity are location-based services.

Identifying Functions

The ability to authenticate the user as well as the device is already immanent to a mobile network. Together with the aforementioned typical 1:1-attribution of a mobile device to its user (which is perhaps not true for any other technical device except a wristwatch), this provides a capability to authenticate the actual user with a feasibility already sufficient for most applications. In case it may be necessary, it is also easily possible to apply further means of authentication on the device, from a personal identification number to biometric identification or mobile signatures. This allows much easier than conventional Internet techniques to use mobile devices for critical processes.

Command and Control Functions

The last properties to present are command and control functions of mobile devices. Mobile devices can be used as remote control for almost any application or device. For this purpose they use networking capabilities of any range, from the personal or local area network up to the wide area network. If the target is an application, it has just to be connected to the Internet. If the target is a device (which can be almost any electrical device), control may be realized, for example using networking capabilities via ubiquitous computing technology or embedded mobile devices.

MAV-BASED ANALYSIS

For analytical purposes it was necessary to choose a KM process model that serves as a framework for the evaluation of the potential mobile techniques can contribute towards KM. In the next section the process model according to Bhatt (2001)—consisting of the elements knowledge creation, validation, presentation, distribution, and application—is introduced, before the results of the MAV-based analysis are discussed (examples for mobile KM use cases demonstrating the effect on KM processes can be found in Derballa & Pousttchi, 2004).

Knowledge creation refers to a process in which new knowledge is created by combining and integrating different modes of knowledge. Knowledge validation describes controlling activities like testing new and removing old knowledge. Knowledge presentation refers to the display of knowledge—that is, different formats, data standards, and so forth. Knowledge distribution deals with sharing and distributing knowledge between organization members. Knowledge application is the term for the use of knowledge in a particular context. Taking into account two approaches—the technical as well as the social strategy—we have examined each KM sub-process regarding the mobile added values that can be generated through the use of mobile technology. Table 1 presents an overview of the results.

Knowledge creation is supported through the mobile added value of ubiquity, as this aspect allows the creation of knowledge regardless of spatial and temporal restrictions. This refers to the enabler function; mobile technology is inherent when it comes to virtual teamwork and the mobile access to knowledge repositories. Context-sensi-

tivity and identifying functions act as supporting factors in that context. They facilitate the documentation of the knowledge creation process. Using those values, it becomes possible to gather information in which that knowledge was created as well as on the participating users.

Knowledge validation benefits from the aspect of ubiquity as the verification of knowledge becomes possible immediately in that moment an event has occurred that leads to a new judgment of existing knowledge. Furthermore, the MAV identification function enables an accurate documentation of the user responsible for the validation.

Knowledge presentation is only supported to a very low degree regarding all four MAVs.

Knowledge distribution is improved by the ability of mobile technology to deliver knowledge everywhere (MAV ubiquity), adjusted/aligned to the relevant context (MAV context-sensitivity), and appropriate for the individual user (MAV identification functions). Taking that into account, it becomes possible to employ push approach and deliver the knowledge to the user, instead of requiring the user actively to retrieve knowledge. Thus the overall KM process is considerably improved as it is no longer necessary for knowledge seekers to be actively involved in the process of determining what knowledge is relevant for them. Instead, the relevancy of knowledge for a particular actor can to some degree be determined by the context. Thus the knowledge seeker is relieved from that burden. Further, to retrieve knowledge, the knowledge seeker has to have a certain understanding of what he is looking for. Without that, it is almost impossible to find that knowledge, which is relevant in a particular context. By switching from pull to push, this problem can be attenuated. In addition the MAV control and command functions enable the control of KMS using mobile devices.

Knowledge application is enhanced indirectly by the fact that mobile technologies make it possible to have relevant knowledge delivered to the individual user regardless of spatial and temporal restrictions and thus ensure that "insufficient knowledge in time-of-action" is avoided.

Table 1. Results of MAV-based analysis

KM Process	Mobile Added Values			
	Ubiquity	Context-Sensitivity	Identifying Functions	C&C Functions
Creation	X	X	X	
Validation	X		X	
Presentation				
Distribution	X	X	X	X
Application	X	X	X	

The results of the MAV-based analysis demonstrates the substantial impact of mobile techniques on the process of knowledge distribution. Considering the different roles of individual MAVs in the context of mobile KM, an order of relevancy can be identified. The primary MAV is ubiquity as it extends the reach of KM. Due to that MAV, KM solutions become available in situations that otherwise could not have been included in the KM process. The other MAVs act as supporting factors, with context-sensitivity and identifying functions coming second and control and command functions ranking third. Those MAVs improve the quality as well as the effectiveness of KM solutions.

FUTURE TRENDS

Current research projects (e.g., the EU-funded project MUMMY) demonstrate the relevancy of mobile KM. As mobile KM is no isolated application, further research is necessary to determine how KM can be fully integrated into a holistic KM concept. In the technological domain this includes questions of data and application integration. Regarding the process perspective the integration of knowledge flows into mobile business processes needs to be analyzed.

Mobile techniques offer a great potential to KM. The impact on organizations and its actors however is not clear. The Adaptive Structuration Theory as presented in DeSanctis and Poole (1994) can be used to assess possible effects. Further, empirical studies need to be conducted to investigate the usability of mobile technology in the conjunction with different KM techniques.

Two major trends can be identified as factors that influence future developments in the area of mobile KM. In the field of KM, a stream of research with focus on process orientation of KM is evolving (e.g., Becker, Hinkelmann, & Maus, 2002). On the other hand, enterprises are increasingly considering mobile business processes and aim at integrating the necessary applications into their business information systems (Gruhn & Book, 2003). If those trends can successfully be integrated, mobile KM is on the way to establish itself as an integral part of KM.

CONCLUSION

As more and more business processes are conducted by organization members who are locally and temporally dispersed, it is obvious that KM restricted to stationary workplaces alone can not cater for knowledge support requirements of mobile workers. The gaps existing due to the insufficient integration of mobile actors can be filled using MAV. With the MAV ubiquity, context-sensitivity, identifying functions, and command and control functions, serious KM deficits can be reduced, and thus the overall KM scope and effectiveness can be improved.

This article contributes to the area of mobile KM by introducing the relevant values a mobile KM solution has to provide in order to be remunerative. By doing so, the basis for an evaluation of mobile KM is laid. Further, the ideas presented in this article can be used to support the development of a holistic mobile KM framework.

REFERENCES

Bazijanec, B., Pousttchi, K., & Turowski, K. (2004). *An approach for assessment of electronic offers. Proceedings of FORTE 2004,* Toledo, OH.

Becker, A., Hinkelmann, K., & Maus, H. (2002). Integrationspotenziale für Geschäftsprozesse und Wissensmanagement. In A. Becker, K. Hinkelmann, & H. Maus (Eds.), *Geschäftsprozessorientiertes Wissensmanagement: Effektive wissensnutzung bei der Planung und Umsetzung von Geschäftsprozessen.* Berlin.

Bhatt, G.D. (2001). Knowledge management in organizations: Examining the interaction between technologies, techniques, and people. *Journal of Knowledge Management, 5*(1), 68-75.

Davenport, T.H., & Prusak, L. (1998). *Working knowledge: How organizations manage what they know.* Boston.

Derballa, V., & Pousttchi, K. (2004). Extending knowledge management to mobile workplaces. *Proceedings of the 6th International Conference of Electronic Commerce,* Delft, The Netherlands.

DeSanctis, G., & Poole, M.S. (1994). Capturing the complexity in advanced technology use: Adaptive Structuration Theory. *Organization Science, 5*(2), 121-145.

Drucker, P.F. (1993). *Post-capitalist society.* New York.

Fagrell, H. (2000). *Mobile knowledge (no. 18): Gothenburg studies in informatics.*

Grimm, M., Tazari, M.-R., & Balfanz, D. (2002). Towards a framework for mobile knowledge management. *Proceedings of the PAKM,* Vienna.

Gruhn, V., & Book, M. (2003). Mobile business processes. *Proceedings of the Innovative Internet Community Systems, 3rd International Workshop* (IICS 2003), Leipzig.

M

Holsapple, C.W. (2003). Knowledge and its attributes. In C.W. Holsapple (Ed.), *Handbook on knowledge management* (Vol. 1, pp. 165-188). Berlin.

Kuhlen, R. (1996). *Informationsmarkt: Chancen und Risiken der Kommerzialisierung von Wissen.* Konstanz.

Lehner, F., & Berger, S. (2001). *Mobile knowledge management.* Regensburg: Universität Regensburg, Lehrstuhl für Wirtschaftsinformatik III.

Martens, S., & Gronau, N. (2003). Erschließung neuer Potentiale im Wissensmanagement über den mobilen Kanal. *Proceedings der GI,* Bonn.

Nonaka, I., & Takeuchi, H. (1995). *The knowledge creating-company: How Japanese companies create the dynamics of innovation.* New York.

North, K. (1999). *Wissensorientierte Unternehmensführung: Wertschöpfung durch Wissen.* Wiesbaden.

Probst, G., Raub, S., & Romhardt, K. (2003). *Wissen managen: Wie Unternehmen ihre wertvollste Ressource optimal nutzen.* Wiesbaden.

Sveiby, K.E. (1997). *The new organizational wealth.* San Francisco.

Turowski, K., & Pousttchi, K. (2003). *Mobile commerce.* Heidelberg.

Wiig, K.M. (1995). *Knowledge management methods: Practical approaches to managing knowledge.* Arlington.

KEY TERMS

Electronic (EC) and Mobile Commerce (MC): EC is defined as any kind of business transaction, in the course of which transaction partners employ electronic means of communication, may it be for initiation, arrangement, or realization of performance. MC is a subset of these, on the condition that at least one side uses mobile communication techniques (in conjunction with mobile devices).

Mobile Added Values (MAVs): Those properties (ubiquity, context-sensitivity, identifying functions, and command and control functions) of mobile technology and its utilization which are responsible for gaining supplementary IAV in comparison to EC solutions.

Mobile Business Intelligence: Refers to the access of processed enterprise data using mobile devices. Involves different technologies (e.g., data mining and data warehouses).

Mobile Information Exchange: Includes the transfer of data and information using e-mail as well as the access to operational systems used in an organization to retrieve data or information (e.g., sales figures or market data).

Mobile Knowledge Management: Describes that management process in the course of which mobile communication techniques in conjunction with mobile devices are employed for the creation, validation, presentation, distribution, or application of knowledge. An important issue is the integration of knowledge flows and mobile business processes to ensure knowledge support for mobile workers.

Theory of Informational Added Values (IAVs): Concept discussing the impacts of information work in information markets comprising the following eight types: organizational, strategic, innovative, macroeconomic, efficiency, effectiveness, aesthetic-emotional, and flexible added values. IAVs may represent the resulting benefit of an EC solution as well as of an MC solution.

Mobile Technology for Knowledge Management

Volker Derballa
University of Augsburg, Germany

Key Pousttchi
University of Augsburg, Germany

INTRODUCTION

IT support for knowledge management (KM) is a widely discussed issue. Whereas an overemphasis on technology is often criticized, the general consensus is that a well-balanced combination of technical and social approaches can be a rewarding departure (Alavi & Leidner, 1999). The usage of knowledge management systems (KMSs) (i.e., information systems including for example data warehouse techniques and artificial intelligence tools) is seen as a factor that can beneficially support different KM processes (Frank, 2001; Wiig, 1995). Due to the fact that an increasingly large proportion of work is not conducted in the context of stationary workplaces anymore, it becomes necessary to make KMSs available to those mobile workers (Rao, 2002; Sherman, 1999). Considering the different technological infrastructure in the stationary, as well as the mobile context, a KMS that so far is only available at a stationary workplace cannot simply become mobile without any changes. Further, the aspect of mobility implies specific design requirements for KMS. Taking together the rapid developments in the field of technology, allowing more and more mobile processes to be potentially supported through mobile KMS, as well as the current social and occupational developments, resulting in more mobile workplaces and business processes (Gruhn & Book, 2003), the relevance of mobile KM can be expected to increase in the future.

Once the focus is shifted away from the superordinate process perspective and addresses the design and development of applications to support mobile knowledge workers, technology and its use by human actors turns out as a major factor that has to be considered. The multiplicity of devices as well as the variety of KM applications, combined with technological and human limitations, all affect the development of mobile KMS. This article aims at addressing important design requirements pointing to different directions that need further research. By doing so, the goal is to put not too much emphasis on technological issues, but rather to introduce the relevant mobile technology and provide a basis for the further discussion of mobile technology usage in the context of KM.

BACKGROUND

Taking into account the wide range of literature available in the field of KM, the aspect of mobility as such is comparably under-researched so far. The same is true for the use of mobile information and communication devices in the context of KM. Studies on workplaces usually focus on stationary characteristics (Churchill & Munro, 2001). To approach the issue of mobile technology in the context of KM, input has to be taken from several different disciplines, including the area of computer-supported cooperative work (CSCW), which has been dealing for some time with the potential of mobile devices to support human decision-making and interaction processes is a comprehensive source. Further, literature dealing with mobile commerce can deliver some input as well. Finally, organization and work studies can contribute insights, especially when it comes to the wider context of mobile KM. In the following, relevant trends concerning the aspects of knowledge work and mobility are presented, and by doing so the basis for the further discussion is laid.

Knowledge Work

Knowledge work is, like many other types of work, influenced by development of an increasingly mobile workforce. Due to changes in work processes and structures as well as the adoption of information and communication technology (ICT), workplaces become increasingly mobile. In this context, not only dependent workers but also independent knowledge workers—freelancers—have to be considered, as their number is dramatically increasing (Kakihara & Soerensen, 2002b). This new form of worker is backed by ICT, allowing mobile workers to coordinate their interactions and communicate with other parties involved. This group of knowledge workers is also referred to as (digital) "nomads" (Soerensen, 2002; Hardless,

Lundin, & Nuldén, 2001) or "post-modern professionals" (Kakihara & Soerensen, 2002b). The first term conveys the two characteristic properties of those workers. Firstly, they use ICT to connect and coordinate; secondly, they are on the move for a considerable amount of their working time.

Mobility

The concept of mobility can be seen from different points of view, which have to be addressed in order to develop a common understanding of mobile knowledge work. Literature is providing several different perspectives of mobility. Traditionally, mobility is considered as being geographically without constraints. Kakihara and Soerensen (2002a) however extend that view by focusing on the aspect of human interaction and provide a differentiation between three aspects of mobility. *Spatial* mobility refers not only to the geographical mobility of humans, but also to the mobility of objects and symbols. With the Internet they are no longer bound to a certain space, but are available regardless of their location. *Temporal* mobility pertains to the opportunities of ICT to enable asynchronous communication and thus frees the user from the restrictions of time. *Contextual* mobility serves next to spatial and temporal mobility as a major factor influencing human action. For the purpose of this article, we are focusing on that aspect of mobility that can be considered as spatial mobility, as this factor is most relevant for the perspective we are pursuing. Depending on the mode of spatial mobility, different requirements for the evaluation of mobile technology in the context of KM have to be considered.

Taking a closer look at the idea of spatial mobility can provide insights regarding the particular requirements during the period of being mobile. Kristoffersen and Ljungberg (2000) classify the following types of spatial mobility. *Traveling* refers to the process of changing from one location to another location usually using some kind of vehicle. *Visiting* describes the process of spending time in one particular location before traveling to another location. Visitors can either bring their ICT equipment with them or use the ICT that is already there. However, if visiting involves a certain degree of wandering (see below) between different offices and meeting rooms, the possibility to use existing ICT equipment is usually not a realistic option. *Wandering* refers to restricted spatial mobility in a building or a restricted area. This form of mobility is usually conducted by support workers or knowledge workers interacting with several other mobile workers. Due to the high degree of physical movement, the use of easily portable devices is feasible. Taking into account the fact that some forms of spatial mobility allow certain devices to be used and others not, stresses the

importance of a detailed analysis for determining design requirements for mobile KM. While traveling in an airplane, it might for example be possible to use an laptop PC, although that is not always realistic, considering the fact that power supply is usually restricted to business class passengers. Thus, in that context it might for example be feasible to use a mobile device with less power demand, enabling longer running time.

MAIN FOCUS OF THE ARTICLE

After having addressed the issues of mobility and knowledge work, this section provides an overview of relevant mobile technologies and introduces certain mobility-specific requirements.

Mobile Devices

We use the term *mobile devices* for information and communication devices that have been developed for mobile use. Thus the category of mobile devices encompasses a wide spectrum of appliances. Although the laptop is often included in the definition of mobile devices, we have reservations to include it here without precincts due to its special characteristics: It can be moved easily, but it is usually not used during that process. For that reason we argue that the laptop can only be seen to some extent as a mobile device. In the following the devices are differentiated according to their relevant interfaces, functionality, as well as their possibilities for user interaction. In particular, the following four characteristics can be introduced enabling the realization of certain KMSs (Turowski & Pousttchi, 2003):

- Voice functionality, usage of IVR (Interactive Voice Response)
- Capability to send and receive short messages (Short Message Service, or SMS)
- Internet-enabled
- Capability of executing applications

Mobile phones are mobile devices that are primarily geared at the use of the telephone functionality. 2G mobile phones are usually Internet enabled and support Short Message Service. With Java support, even complex applications can be implemented. *Smartphone* is a device that can only be roughly defined as there is no clear delineation. Typical characteristics of a *Smartphone* include mobile phone functionality and an operating system that is similar to that of a *personal digital assistant* (PDA). A PDA is a handheld computer with core functionality similar to a personal information manager. Current models include the possibility to establish an Internet connection using modem-supported mobile phone, GSM cards, or integrated mobile phone technology. Operating systems are similar to that of conventional PCs. *Tablet PC* describes a modification of the laptop PC which can be used in stationary as well as mobile settings. *Wearable computing* is the term for miniature devices that can be integrated for example into clothing and thus have the characteristic to be immediately available. Additionally, proprietary devices that have been designed according to the specific needs of an organization have to be considered as well. However, as those devices are usually derived from the types introduced above, we are not going to specify them further.

Communication Standards

Where the communication standards are concerned, there are currently with 2G (e.g., GSM, IS-136, IS-95) and 3G (Universal Mobile Telecommunications System, or UMTS) two main standards available for the transmission of data. Whereas the 2G networks are generally capable for transmitting data, they are optimized for voice transmission. With 2.5 technologies like General Packet Radio Service (GPRS) and Enhanced Data Rate for Global Evolution (EDGE), however, packet transmission is possible, enabling always-on operation. Using up to 8 time slots, data speeds of a maximum of 171.2 kbps are theoretically possible.

Due to the restricted capacity of current mobiles devices and networks, a realistic downlink speed of approximately of 40.2 kbps to 62.4 kbps can be expected. The advent of UMTS will make bandwidth concerns increasingly negligible, enabling transfer rates up to 384 kbps (using UMTS FDD) respectively 2 mbps (using UMTS TDD), although the realistic speed—depending on network capacity—will be in the area of 128 kbps. For some KM applications, UMTS will act as an enabler; for example, videoconferencing will become possible.

For mobile devices used within the premises, the bandwidth problem can be neglected, considering the application of wireless LAN technologies. Handheld devices with WLAN connectivity are already in rapid advance in industrial production management, which provides a promising base for in-premises mobile KM. As the restricted range of wireless LAN cannot fulfill the requirement of ubiquitous access, this technology has to be treated with some reservations in this context.

Concept and Design Requirements

In contrast to mobile commerce, mobile KM aims almost exclusively at the intraorganizational or interorganizational use. That enables the particular organization to choose the most appropriate technology for the desired KM solution and regulate its use. The same is true at an intraorganizational level, where the employed technology can be determined by an agreement with the respective business partners. Compared with mobile commerce, that results in a considerable advantage, because that way an optimal fit between the type of mobile devices and the employed KM solution is ensured. Thus certain problems arising due to the heterogeneity of devices can be avoided. Further, the employment of devices can be intentionally managed in order to ensure the fit of individual users' KM needs and the particular features of the different mobile devices. But as stated above, the different modes of spatial mobility require the use of different mobile devices. That results in the fact that although in the organizational context the use of mobile devices can be regulated to some extent,

Figure 1: Functionality of mobile devices

Type of Mobile Device	Available Functionality			
	IVR	SMS	Internet	Programm Code executable
Mobile Phone (speech functionality only)	X			
Mobile Phone (SMS-enabled)	X	X		
Mobile Phone (Internet-enabled)	X	X	X	
Mobile Phone (Java-enabled)	X	X	X	X
Smart Phone	X	X	X	X
PDA	(x)	(x)	(x)	X
Tablet PC	X	X	X	X
Wearable Computing	Depending on the combination with other mobile devices			X

there still exists a considerable amount of heterogeneity. Heterogeneity implies special requirements for the design process of mobile KMS solutions. As the different mobile devices possess diverse technological characteristics, there is no one-size-fits-it-all solution. For that reason it is recommended to choose a platform-independent approach for the implementation (Grimm, Tazari, & Balfanz, 2002).

Taking KM mobile has to account for further special requirements that are associated with mobile technology. Limitations for the use in the mobile KM context arise above all due to displays and input possibilities, as well as bandwidth and transfer modes. With the exception of tablet PCs, the display sizes range from a few lines only (mobile phone) to 240x320 or larger (PDA). Regarding the input methods, the possibilities vary from a restricted number of pushbuttons that enable operating simple menus to more sophisticated solutions like handwriting recognition or virtual keyboards. Further, design requirements for common user interfaces need to be adjusted, as they are developed for stationary use, assuming that all concentration is focused on the display. That is naturally not the case if the device is used on the move.

Where the employment of mobile devices is concerned, every type of device introduced earlier can be used in the KM process. Categorizing mobile KM into the following different groups enables delineation of the effectual technological requirements (Derballa & Pousttchi, 2004):

1. **Mobile Information Exchange** includes the transfer of data and information using e-mail, as well as the access to operational systems used in an organization to retrieve sales figures or market data.
2. **Mobile Business Intelligence** refers to the access of processed enterprise data using mobile devices. It involves the technologies introduced earlier (e.g., data mining and data warehouses).
3. **Mobile KM** describes that management process in the course of which mobile communication techniques in conjunction with mobile devices are employed for the creation, validation, presentation, distribution, or application of knowledge.

Mobile Information Access

For the retrieval of data and information, all mobiles devices can be used that feature the basic capability of displaying text. It has to be taken into account though that in reading longer textual information like e-mails, the use of small display devices is not very feasible. Mobile phones thus are suited best for the display of a small amount of data and information.

Mobile Business Intelligence

The display of processed enterprise data requires the mobile devices used to be able to display complex tables and maybe graphical visualization of the processed data. Thus more processing power is needed, which disqualifies simple mobile phones from being used in that context. Consequently, Smartphones as well as PDAs meet the minimum requirements for that mobile KM stage.

Mobile KM

In this context we are referring to the definition of KM in the narrower sense introduced above. The specific requirements for mobile devices used results from the type of KM technique that is taken mobile. For low-technology KM solutions like expert finder—as long as there is no graphical visualization—even mobile phones can be considered. However, with the richness of the KM solution, the requirements regarding display, processing power and entering methods, and required bandwidth increase dramatically. That is for example the case when a lessons learned database includes complex graphics for visualization purposes.

FUTURE TRENDS

Considering the fact that research for IT support for mobile business processes in general and mobile KM in particular is still in its early days, a considerable amount of work has to be done to catch up with the state of research in other areas of KM. The questions to be answered are manifold, but the following issues, without claiming to be exhaustive, are introduced as possible research topics.

We consider a KMS as a socio-technical system, according to Ropohl (1979), comprising the elements human actors, tasks, and technology. Based on that perspective, possible research questions are grouped into the following categories.

Human Actor-Related Questions

Apart from the potential to greatly improve mobile business and knowledge processes, the wide use of mobile devices might lead to some undesirable effects. A current example for this problem can be observed in the United States with the increasing popularity of the Blackberry. Its owner is always connected, always on, has the possibility to interact, and is never cut off from the information flow. According to recent reports, that results in an excessive overuse of the device, including derogatory effects on the mental condition of its user, which resulted in the fact that the Blackberry is ironically called "Crackberry" (e.g., Pilcher, 2004). Two main problems can be addressed in this area and need further empirical research: information overload and interaction overload. Certain types of (knowledge)work require outmost concentration. Considering the possibility to provide the user with information on a push basis, these moments of concentration might be interrupted, leading to unwanted performance loss of the individual user (Davis, 2002). It might however be possible to fight information overload with the possibility to deliver context-relevant information only, which is enabled through the aspect of context-specifity. Until today, it has however not been fully evaluated whether the delivery of context-specific information can be conducted with enough feasible practicability. With an accretive amount of interaction shifting towards the space of mobility, there is further the problem of too much interaction, of interaction overload. Similar to information overload, the possibility to interact continuously might reach dimensions in which the amount of interaction is detrimental to the productivity of individual workers.

Task-Related Questions

Mobile knowledge work can be considered as work that includes a considerable amount of self-management. The introduction of mobile KM might reduce this amount of freedom in exchange for more structured processes and greater control. It needs to be tested how this development might influence worker's productivity. A basic precondition for the adoption of new technology, in this case mobile technology, assumes that the prospective users are willing to use new technology. That however might not always be the case. Further, organizational effects can be expected due to the extensive effect mobile technology can have on business processes. Adaptive Structuration Theory can provide a framework for the evaluation of the possible effects on work processes and organizational changes (DeSanctis & Poole, 1994).

Technology-Related Questions

With the focus on technology, it needs to be empirically tested which type of mobile device can be feasibly used during different types of spatial mobility. Krogstie (2003) cites a case study dealing with an electronic newspaper delivery guide, demonstrating that the usage of mobile devices to support workers with the task of route planning and scheduling of activities, is potentially remunerative compared to the earlier paper-based solution. As potential benefits he identified for example the optimized scheduling and planning process. Practice however showed that the mobile devices used were not robust enough to withstand snow, rain, and other environmental influences.

CONCLUSION

According to the general technological and social trends introduced above, mobile technology in the context of KM will become an increasingly relevant topic. Technology will act as an enabler in this field, with increasingly powerful mobile devices as well as higher data transmission speeds allowing significant KMSs to be taken mobile. Designing mobile KM solutions, however, has to cater for several different requirements that are still subject to further research. This article addresses important design issues in order to provide some leads for the further discussion of mobile KM, and presents an introduction to the relevant mobile technologies.

REFERENCES

Alavi, M., & Leidner, D.E. (1999). *Knowledge management systems: Issues, challenges, and benefits.*

Churchill, E.F., & Munro, A.J. (2001). WORK/PLACE: Mobile technologies and arenas of activity. *SIGGROUP Bulletin, 22,* 3-9.

Davis, G.B. (2002). Anytime/anyplace computing and the future of knowledge work. *Communications of the ACM, 45*(12), 67-73.

Derballa, V., & Pousttchi, K. (2004). Extending knowledge management to mobile workplaces. *Proceedings of the 6th International Conference of Electronic Commerce,* Delft, The Netherlands.

DeSanctis, G., & Poole, M.S. (1994). Capturing the complexity in advanced technology use: Adaptive Structuration Theory. *Organization Science, 5*(2), 121-145.

Frank, U. (2001). Knowledge management systems: Essential requirements and generic design patterns. *Proceedings of the International Symposium on Information Systems and Engineering* (ISE), Las Vegas, NV.

Grimm, M., Tazari, M.-R., & Balfanz, D. (2002). Towards a framework for mobile knowledge management. *Proceedings of the PAKM,* Vienna.

Gruhn, V., & Book, M. (2003). Mobile business processes. *Proceedings of the Innovative Internet Community Systems 3rd International Workshop* (IICS 2003), Leipzig.

Hardless, C., Lundin, J., & Nuldén, U. (2001). Mobile competence development for nomads. *Proceedings of the International Conference on System Sciences* (HICSS), Hawaii.

Kakihara, M., & Soerensen, C. (2002a). Mobility: An extended perspective. *Proceedings of the International Conference on System Sciences* (HICSS), Hawaii.

Kakihara, M., & Soerensen, C. (2002b). 'Post-modern' professionals' work and mobile technology. *Proceedings of the New Ways of Working in IS: The 25th Information Systems Research Seminar in Scandinavia* (IRIS25), Copenhagen.

Kristoffersen, S., & Ljungberg, F. (2000). Mobility: From stationary to mobile work. In K. Braa (Ed.), *Planet Internet* (pp. 137-156). Lund.

Krogstie, J. (2003). Mobile process support systems—myths and misconceptions. *Proceedings of the Workshop on Ubiquitous Computing Environment,* Cleveland, OH.

Pilcher, J. (2004). Blackberry or Crackberry? *The Detroit News,* (October 8).

Rao, M. (2002). Mobilizing knowledge workers with wireless solutions. Retrieved October 5, 2004, from *http://www.destinationkm.com/articles/default.asp?ArticleID=973*

Ropohl, G. (1979). *Eine Systemtheorie der Technik: Zur Grundlegung der Allgemeinen Technologie.* Munich.

Sherman, L. (1999). The knowledge worker unplugged. Retrieved February 5, 2004, from *www.destinationkm.com/articles/default.asp?ArticleID=973*

Soerensen, C. (2002). Digital nomads and mobile services. Retrieved June 9, 2004, from *http://www.receiver.vodafone.com /archive/inner.html*

Turowski, K., & Pousttchi, K. (2003). *Mobile commerce.* Heidelberg.

Wiig, K.M. (1995). *Knowledge management methods: Practical approaches to managing knowledge.* Arlington.

KEY TERMS

Knowledge Work: Refers to work conducted by knowledge workers. That is, work that comprises to a large extend the tasks of retrieving, evaluating, integrating, and creating knowledge.

Knowledge Management Systems (KMSs): Information systems designed to support certain KM processes like the dissemination or application of knowledge.

Mobility: Traditionally refers to the aspect of being geographically independent. Different types of mobility can be discerned: spatial, temporal, and contextual mobility. Regarding spatial mobility, three distinct categories are relevant: traveling, visiting, and wandering.

Mobile Commerce (MC): A subset of electronic commerce (EC), on the condition that at least one side uses mobile communication techniques (in conjunction with mobile devices). EC is any kind of business transaction, in the course of which transaction partners employ electronic means of communication, may it be for initiation, arrangement, or realization of performance.

Mobile Devices: Term used for information and communication devices that have been developed for mobile use and can be employed in the context of mobile KM. A wide variety of devices is relevant: mobile phones, Smartphones, PDAs, tablet PCs, and wearable computing.

Mobile Knowledge Management: The management process in the course of which mobile communication techniques in conjunction with mobile devices are employed for the creation, validation, presentation, distribution, or application of knowledge.

Motivation for Knowledge Work

M

Paul H.J. Hendriks
Radboud University Nijmegen, The Netherlands

Célio A.A. Sousa
Radboud University Nijmegen, The Netherlands

INTRODUCTION

The importance of motivation in knowledge work is generally acknowledged. With lacking motivation, the quality of the products of knowledge work is bound to drop dramatically. Without work motivation, individual knowledge workers may direct their efforts to their individual needs at the expense of organization goals or decide to leave the firm. Creativity, knowledge teamwork, knowledge sharing, and other knowledge processes depend on the motivation of knowledge workers. Lacking sustained motivation in association with an insufficiently knowledge-friendly culture has often been mentioned as the principal culprit for failed knowledge management (KM) initiatives and programs (Davenport, DeLong, & Beers, 1998; McKenzie, Truc, & Winkelen, 2001). Several traits of knowledge workers explain, so it is argued, why prevailing work motivation programs will not work when applied to knowledge workers: they have high needs for autonomy, their career formation is external to the organization, they are loyal to their networks of peers and to their profession rather than to the organization that employs them, and the exact form and sequence of their work processes cannot be fully predicted (Despres & Hiltrop, 1996).

BACKGROUND

Motivation is a big issue in KM debates. Notwithstanding its recognized relevance to KM, knowledge about motivation issues in the KM arena is scarce and scattered. Huber (2001, p. 72) argues that "the management practice literature is replete with reports of practices being used to motivate a firm's knowledge workers…to participate with commitment in the firms' knowledge management system." Empirical research on the effectiveness of such practices, however, is in short supply. With respect to the connection between KM practice and motivation for knowledge work, our ignorance exceeds our knowledge (Huber, 2001). Whereas empirical research on the impact of KM practices on motivation is lacking, research does exist that addresses how motivation affects aspects of knowledge work. This research can be divided into two classes. Firstly, several studies link motivation issues to the broad categories of knowledge work and knowledge workers. Questions addressed in these studies are how motivation explains knowledge worker turnover or which role career development plays in knowledge work motivation (e.g., Kubo & Saka, 2002; Tampoe, 1993). Secondly, studies address how motivation is linked to knowledge aspects of work, such as creativity and other facets of knowledge exploration, and cooperation and knowledge transfer in knowledge teams. Questions addressed in such studies are how motivation plays a role in the establishment of key mechanisms that will lead to knowledge becoming organizationally valuable (e.g., Amabile, 1997; Janz, Colquitt, & Noe, 1997; Osterloh & Frey, 2000).

In this article, we argue that understanding the effect of KM practices on motivation presumes an understanding of how motivation plays a role in knowledge work. We also argue that the second class of studies specified above deserves more attention than the first, as it aims to glance into the black box of what constitutes the knowledge elements in work. It will provide better guidance for drafting KM practices and evaluating their effectiveness than studies in the first class can. Any work is knowledge based, unless performed by an automated machine. Therefore the terms *knowledge work* and *knowledge worker* are container concepts that are low in meaning without a specification of how knowledge defines them. Themes such as creativity and knowledge transfer provide exactly those specifications. The logical sequence for addressing the connections between motivation and the placeholder of knowledge work, therefore, is first to define work motivation and specify work motivation theories, next to link them to knowledge themes, and finally to derive inspiration from that connection for KM programs aimed at furthering motivation for knowledge work. This sequence defines the structure of this article.

THE MOTIVATION FOR KNOWLEDGE-RELATED ASPECTS OF WORK

The Concept of Work Motivation and Work Motivation Theories

Motivation concerns the question: "What is in it for me?" Motivation is about what makes people's clocks tick. That is, it concerns how behavior is instigated and inspired by the expected outcomes of that behavior defined as goals, aspects of success, performance, or in other ways. What involves restricting the motivation concept to the work situation is succinctly expressed by the title of Maccoby's (1988) monograph on work motivation: "Why Work?" Work motivation concerns the individual's degree of willingness to exert and maintain an effort towards aligning individual goals with organizational goals, organizational success, organizational performance, and so forth. Such goals, success, and performance refer to what is commonly called group motivation. The concept of work motivation is closely related to such concepts as work commitment, attachment, involvement, and engagement. These concepts refer to the degree and different aspects of emotional binding to the job. Therefore, they can serve as indicators of motivation. Work motivation is also related to job satisfaction or personal assessment of work revenues. Job satisfaction simultaneously plays the role of a cause and an effect of work motivation.

Drawing from the plethora of motivation theories that such disciplines as psychology and sociology have brought forth, organization studies have had their share in adding to the smorgasbord of motivation-related concepts, ideas, and frameworks (for an excellent overview, see Ambrose & Kulik, 1999). Some work motivation theories appear more popular than others for addressing motivation issues with respect to knowledge work. Below we give an outline of these theories.

Two-Factor Theory and Self-Determination Theory

Probably the most used distinction in motivation discussions is that between intrinsic and extrinsic motivation. These concepts are the basic concepts of Deci and Ryan's (1985, 2004) Self-Determination Theory (SDT). They are closely related to what Herzberg (1968, 1987) in his Two-Factor Theory calls motivators and hygiene factors. Intrinsic motivation works through immediate need satisfaction. A person is intrinsically motivated to perform an activity when the goal of the action is thematically identical with the action itself, that is, when it is carried out for the sake of its own objectives. Extrinsic motivation works through indirect need satisfaction, for example, through monetary and symbolic compensation. Intrinsic motivation and extrinsic motivation represent positions on a continuum describing where the locus of causality or degree of self-determination lays in particular behavior. In intrinsically motivated behavior, that locus is fully internal. It moves to external and impersonal to the extent that individuals fully assimilate outside regulations or ignore these (with several intermediate positions identified; see Deci & Ryan, 2004).

Goal-Setting Theory

Goal-Setting Theory (Locke, 1968; Locke & Latham, 1990) states that higher performance results from specifying goals, depending on how and by whom that specification is given. Once individuals determine the goals they intend to achieve, these goals and intentions direct and motivate efforts to attain them. Studies based upon goal-setting theory indicate that levels of goal specification are related to level of success in goal attainment (see Ambrose & Kulik, 1999). Individuals must be aware of the goal and accept it. Specific and difficult objectives lead to better achievement than vague or easy ones (Durham, Knight, & Locke, 1997). Goals should involve a challenge; to boost motivation, they should entail an extra effort. Research has also demonstrated that participation in goal setting is critical to commitment to the goal (e.g., O'Leary-Kelly, Martocchio, & Frink, 1994). Receiving feedback on goal achievement is also essential for motivation. If an employee does not get timely and accurate feedback on performance, it is impossible to know what behaviors to continue in order to achieve similar goals in the future (e.g., Carson & Carson, 1993; Gambill, Clark, & Wilkes, 2000).

Job Characteristics Theory

Job Characteristics Theory (JCT; Hackman & Oldham, 1980) involves a three-stage model, specifying a set of core job characteristics that impact critical psychological states (meaningfulness, responsibility, knowledge of results). These influence a set of affective and motivational outcomes. The five job characteristics are: (1) skill variety, which describes the degree to which a job requires the exercise of a number of different skills, abilities, or talents; (2) task identity, defined as the extent to which a job requires completion of a whole and identifiable piece of work; (3) task significance, referring to the degree to which the job has an impact on the lives of other people; (4) autonomy, or the extent to which the jobholder is free to determine work procedures; and (5) feedback, or the information an individual obtains about performance effectiveness.

Self-Efficacy Theory

Bandura's (1986, 1997) Self-Efficacy Theory links elements of expected or desired outcomes of work behavior to the perception of what feasible outcomes are, given one's capabilities and competencies. The theory is based on the premise that people are more likely to engage in certain behaviors when they believe they are capable of executing those behaviors successfully. Critical factors in the development of self-efficacy are self-regulation, setting standards and goals, self-observation, self-judgment, and self-reaction. Much empirical evidence supports Bandura's contention that self-efficacy beliefs affect how well individuals motivate themselves and persevere in the face of adversities (e.g., Gibson, 2001; Gibson, Randel, & Earley, 2000; Pajares, 1996; Tierney & Farmer, 2002).

Main Themes of Knowledge Work Motivation

Motivation plays a key role in knowledge work in many respects. In the literature discussing motivation issues related to knowledge aspects of work, four key themes emerge, including the overall motivation: (1) for knowledge work, (2) for knowledge creation, (3) for knowledge sharing, and (4) for the adoption of KM. The bulk of motivation studies of knowledge work address themes 2 and 3. Table 1 shows how different studies addressing these themes use the work motivation theories presented above.

Overall Motivation for Knowledge Work

Some studies link motivation to the broad class of knowledge workers. Knowledge-intensive firms show up in statistics with high turnover rates, which is partly explained by the fact that individual knowledge workers identify with their profession rather than their employer, and that they need 'job hopping' to keep abreast of developments. Highly motivated employees may therefore experience a drive to change jobs on a regular basis. An intriguing object for the study of knowledge worker motivation is that high workforce turnover may also show lacking motivation (Horwitz, Heng, & Quazi, 2003). When knowledge workers experience their work as a source of frustration, workforce turnover along with high absence rates are signs of low motivation. Tampoe (1993) shows that three key motivators for knowledge workers are personal growth, operational autonomy, and task achievement. His research shows that salary and bonuses on personal effort are not a principal motivator for knowledge workers. Research by Kubo and Saka (2002) partly contradicts this finding in that it shows the relevance of monetary incentives as a principal motivator for Japanese knowledge workers, next to such factors as personal growth and human resource development. Studies addressing motivation issues as described above treat the class of knowledge workers as a black box. As we argued in the Background section, the findings of these studies have a limited value for KM discussions because they do not specify whether the motivation mechanisms they address concern the knowledge-intensive facets of the knowledge work involved or not.

Knowledge Development and Creativity

Creativity is the first step in knowledge development and innovation. The connection between motivation and creativity has attracted much research attention for decades (e.g., Ambrose & Kulik, 1999). Amabile (1997), a

Table 1. Motivation theories and knowledge themes: Sample studies

	Knowledge development, creativity	Knowledge sharing, cooperation, participation in communities, knowledge teams
Self-Determination Theory (Deci & Ryan), Two-Factor Theory (Herzberg)	Amabile, 1997; Amabile et al., 2004; Wilkesmann & Rascher, 2002	Hendriks, 1999; Huber, 2001; Wilkesmann & Rascher, 2002
Job Characteristics Theory (Hackman & Oldham)	Amabile, 1988, 1997	Janz, 1999; Janz et al., 1997; Wilkesmann & Rascher, 2002
Goal-Setting Theory (Locke & Latham)	Carson & Carson, 1993; Gambill et al., 2000	Durham et al., 1997; Reinig, 2003
Self-Efficacy Theory (Bandura)	Janssen, 2000; Shalley & Gilson, 2004; Spreitzer, 1995; Tierney & Farmer, 2002, 2004	Cheng, 2000; McClough & Rogelberg, 2003

leading researcher on what motivates creativity, is one of many researchers who stress that a particularly strong connection exists between creativity and intrinsic motivation. She summarizes this core research finding in the Intrinsic Motivation Principle: "Intrinsic motivation is conducive to creativity. Controlling extrinsic motivation is detrimental to creativity, but informational or enabling extrinsic motivation can be conducive, particularly if initial levels of intrinsic motivation are high" (Amabile, 1997, p. 46). A person's social environment can have a significant effect on that person's level of intrinsic motivation, and therefore affects that person's creativity in an indirect way. Job characteristics have been shown to play a critical role in creativity (Amabile, 1988). Research supports the idea that specific job characteristics, most notably skill variety, task identity, and autonomy, are associated with greater intrinsic motivation, especially for growth-oriented people (Smith & Rupp, 2002). Challenging and complex jobs for which employees have the autonomy to plan their work are crucial for creativity (Shalley, Gilson, & Blum, 2000). The effect of goal setting in creative work has been shown to be positive: research confirms that clearly stated missions, clear organizational goals, and the assignment of creativity goals are critical factors for high creativity (e.g., Carson, 2001; Carson & Carson, 1993; Gambill et al., 2000). Elements of the work environment have also been shown to be correlated with the motivation for creativity (Amabile, 1997; Shalley & Gilson, 2004): supervisory encouragement, workgroup supports, adequate availability of resources, absence of undue workload pressure, and other work contextual variables have been shown to have a positive impact on creativity. Most empirical studies show that working for reward can be damaging to both intrinsic motivation and creativity (see Hennessey & Amabile, 1998). Nonetheless, rewards may support intrinsic motivation and creativity if presented carefully (Carson, 2001).

Knowledge Sharing, Knowledge Teams, and Communities

As regards knowledge transfer and knowledge sharing, which are key topics in KM debates, research stresses and shows the fundamental importance of intrinsic motivation. Knowledge sharing and associated motivation is related to a variety of subjects, such as knowledge-intensive collaboration, the formation of knowledge teams, and so forth. Several studies support the idea that intrinsic motivation for knowledge sharing is an important element in team motivation that will improve team performance (e.g., Janz, 1999; Janz et al., 1997). Osterloh and Frey (2000) argue that intrinsic motivation is particularly important for the transfer of tacit knowledge. Intrinsic

motivation and extrinsic motivation are not independent. The most extensively researched phenomenon showing this is the fact that the introduction of extrinsic motivators (e.g., money) may reduce intrinsic motivation, which is discussed under the label of the 'hidden cost of reward' or the crowding-out effect (Osterloh & Frey, 2000). Market arrangements, which only provide extrinsic motivations, are problematic when the transfer of tacit knowledge is at stake, because of this crowding-out effect. In addition, Wilkesmann and Rascher (2002) show that the importance of intrinsic motivation in knowledge transfer also derives from the fact that without it, the team element in learning will not be established, and groups cannot solve the free-rider problem. Several studies show that the context in which knowledge transfer takes place (its purpose, the support mechanisms in place, the roles played by transfer partners) lead to different motivators being important (Hendriks, 1999; Janz et al., 1997; Wasko & Faraj, 2000). A factor such as 'challenge of work' shows to be relevant when knowledge sharing concerns the team element in learning, but not when the transfer of best practices is at stake. A sense of achievement and responsibility appear important motivators for the role of conveying to others what one has learnt. Operational autonomy appears a key motivator for acquiring knowledge from others (Hendriks, 1999; Janz et al., 1997). However, in a team setting, high task interdependence with other teams reduces the importance of autonomy as a motivator. Also, when knowledge transfer concerns communities, as a more organic form of knowledge sharing than knowledge transfer in teams, moral obligation and generalized reciprocity (that is defined as reciprocity at the level of the community rather than individuals) have been shown to define intrinsic motivation rather than motivation factors that focus on self-interest, along with the more 'selfish' motivator of keeping abreast of innovations (Wasko & Faraj, 2000).

Acceptance of KM Interventions

Motivation is among the factors that explain whether or not KM programs and practices are successfully adopted by an organization (Bailey & Clarke, 2001; Davenport et al., 1998; Malhotra & Galletta, 2003; McKenzie et al., 2001). Empirical research in this domain is scarce and inconclusive. In a small-scale survey, McKenzie et al. (2001) found, perhaps not surprisingly, that an understanding and recognition of the value of a KM initiative by the end users is the best guarantee that these will be motivated to adopt the initiative. This finding suggests that a close connection between intrinsic motivation and the KM program is essential. Exploratory research by Malhotra and Galletta (2003) suggests that, next to intrinsic motivation, also introjected regulation (taking in a regulation for reasons of anxiety and guilt without fully accepting it; this is an extrinsic motivator) and external regulation (adopted behavior to satisfy an external demand or reward contingency; this too is an extrinsic motivator) explain for the motivation whether or not to participate in a KM initiative.

Motivating Knowledge Workers

KM as knowledge-directed intervention in organizations offers several strategies, means, and practices aimed at affecting an individual's motivation, most of which stem from organization design theories and from the HRM arena. Much research shows that work design is a key factor in the motivation of knowledge workers and that work design forms the backdrop against which additional interventions such as HRM practices gain relevance (e.g., Hackman & Oldham, 1980; Osterloh & Frey, 2000). Winning motivation strategies have been shown to include allowing individuals and teams the freedom to define their work, the design of challenging jobs, and ensuring the support from top management for knowledge-related initiatives (McKenzie et al., 2001). Flexibility in work practices, cash rewards for knowledge products, and recruitment practices aimed at hiring people that fit existing culture prove to be less successful motivation strategies (Despres & Hiltrop, 1996; Horwitz et al., 2003). In line with these findings, Horwitz et al. (2003) show the strong motivational importance of what they describe as 'job crafting', or the degree of freedom for individuals to adapt the physical and cognitive elements in the task and relationship boundaries of their work. Within the broad spectrum of motivational measures for knowledge work, the class of incentive and reward systems has received special attention (e.g., Amabile, Conti, Coon, Lazenby, & Herron, 1996; Carson, 2001; Despres & Hiltrop, 1996; Hennessey & Amabile, 1998; Krönig, 2001; Kubo & Saka, 2002; McKenzie et al., 2001; Salo, 2001). Prescriptions for knowledge-friendly reward systems, which are partly backed by research, include that reward systems should be perceived as rational by the individual and the team, that they should focus on insights rather than status and hierarchical position, that they put challenge before monetary compensation, that they should involve an appropriate degree of flexibility and adaptability, and that the drafters of such systems should be aware that rewards can also demotivate because of crowding-out effects.

FUTURE TRENDS

KM researchers and practitioners show a sustained high level of interest in matters of motivation. Simultaneously, there is a growing awareness of lacking insight as to how motivation plays a role in the knowledge arena, and how and when KM may improve or decrease motivation. Therefore, a rise in research efforts in this domain may be expected. Prevailing research plans, programs, and calls for research show at least three trends in motivation research. Firstly, future research aims at establishing a conceptually more rich connection between motivation and organizational knowledge. This concerns using our growing understanding of what does and does not constitute organizational knowledge to guide inspections of motivation elements for knowledge work, instead of looking for knowledge elements in extant motivation theories. For instance, if knowledge work is not defined by knowledgeability but by ambiguity, as Alvesson (2000) argues, what does this then tell us about motivation? It also concerns an increased attention for the question how different cultures, and other situational factors, imply different motivators. In addition, an exploration of the broader landscape of motivation theories and the possible combinations between elements of existing theories in light of the discussions of organizational knowledge is necessary. Secondly, a trend can be noted toward broadening the scope of motivation research in KM. Currently, most motivation research is geared toward knowledge exploration, knowledge transfer, and their constituent themes. Also other knowledge processes, including knowledge combination, application, and retention, plus a broader set of constituent themes (e.g., aspects from learning theories) deserve attention in motivation research. Thirdly, there is a clear need of qualitative and quantitative empirical research both on the intricate relationships between motivation and knowledge aspects of work and on the effectiveness of KM programs and practices.

CONCLUSION

The motivation for knowledge work appears as an intriguing phenomenon that we are only beginning to understand. Its relevance for KM derives from the fact that it connects the content side of knowledge work with the associated aspects of knowledge work processes and knowledge-friendly organization structures to the people side of KM with its attention for talents and competences. How work is organized appears crucial for motivated knowledge workers. Their individual talents, dispositions, and intrinsic motivation are the other side of the medal that decide whether the promises of a knowledge-friendly work environment are fulfilled. Furthering our understanding of what to do and what not to do in attempts to boost knowledge work motivation requires a deepened understanding of how motivation relates to the various themes, such as creativity and knowledge sharing, that define what is commonly described as knowledge work. Only by lifting the veil of such container concepts as knowledge work and knowledge worker may we hope to unravel the motivation aspects involved.

REFERENCES

Alvesson, M. (2000). Social identity and the problem of loyalty in knowledge-intensive companies. *Journal of Management Studies, 37*(8), 1101-1123.

Amabile, T.M. (1988). A model of creativity and innovation in organizations. In B.M. Staw & L.L. Cummings (Eds.), *Research in organizational behavior* (Vol. 10, pp. 123-167). Greenwich, CT: JAI Press.

Amabile, T.M. (1997). Motivating creativity in organizations: On doing what you love and loving what you do. *California Management Review, 40*(1), 39-58.

Amabile, T.M., Conti, R., Coon, H., Lazenby, J., & Herron, M. (1996). Assessing the work environment for creativity. *Academy of Management Journal, 39*(5), 1154-1184.

Amabile, T.M., Schatzel, E.A., Moneta, G.B., & Kramer, S.J. (2004). Leader behaviors and the work environment for creativity: Perceived leader support. *Leadership Quarterly, 15*(1), 5-32.

Ambrose, M.L., & Kulik, C.T. (1999). Old friends, new faces: Motivation research in the 1990s. *Journal of Management, 25*(3), 231-292.

Bailey, C., & Clarke, M. (2001). Managing knowledge for personal and organizational benefit. *Journal of Knowledge Management, 5*(1), 58-68.

Bandura, A. (1986). *Social foundations of thought and action: A social cognitive theory.* Englewood Cliffs, NJ: Prentice-Hall.

Bandura, A. (1997). *Self-efficacy: The exercise of control.* New York: Freeman.

Carson, P.P. (2001). Rewarding excellence: Pay strategies for the new economy. *Organizational Dynamics, 29*(3), 228-229.

Carson, P.P., & Carson, K.D. (1993). Managing creativity enhancement through goal-setting and feedback. *Journal of Creative Behavior, 27*(1), 36-45.

Cheng, E.W.L. (2000). Test of the MBA knowledge and skills transfer. *International Journal of Human Resource Management, 11*(4), 837-852.

Davenport, T., DeLong, D., & Beers, M. (1998). Successful knowledge management projects. *Sloan Management Review, 39*(2), 43-57.

Deci, E.L., & Ryan, R.M. (1985). *Intrinsic motivation and self-determination in human behavior.* London: Plenum.

Deci, E.L., & Ryan, R.M. (2004). *Handbook of self-determination research.* Rochester, NY: University of Rochester Press.

Despres, C., & Hiltrop, J.-M. (1996). Compensation for technical professionals in the knowledge age. *Research Technology Management, 39*(5), 48-55.

Durham, C.C., Knight, D., & Locke, E.A. (1997). Effects of leader role, team-set goal difficulty, efficacy, and tactics on team effectiveness. *Organizational Behavior and Human Decision Processes, 72*(2), 203-231.

Gambill, S.E., Clark, W.J., & Wilkes, R.B. (2000). Toward a holistic model of task design for IS professionals. *Information & Management, 37*(5), 217-228.

Gibson, C.B. (2001). Me and us: Differential relationships among goal-setting training, efficacy and effectiveness at the individual and team level. *Journal of Organizational Behavior, 22*(7), 789-808.

Gibson, C.B., Randel, A.E., & Earley, P.C. (2000). Understanding group efficacy—an empirical test of multiple assessment methods. *Group & Organization Management, 25*(1), 67-97.

Hackman, J.R., & Oldham, G.R. (1980). *Work redesign.* Reading, MA: Addison-Wesley.

Hendriks, P.H.J. (1999). Why share knowledge? The influence of ICT on the motivation for knowledge sharing. *Knowledge and Process Management, 6*(2), 91-100.

Hennessey, B.A., & Amabile, T.M. (1998). Reward, intrinsic motivation, and creativity. *American Psychologist, 53*(6), 674-675.

Herzberg, F. (1968). *Work and the nature of man.* London: Granada Publishing.

Herzberg, F. (1987). One more time—how do you motivate employees? *Harvard Business Review, 65*(5), 109-120.

Horwitz, F.M., Heng, C.T., & Quazi, H.A. (2003). Finders, keepers? Attracting, motivating and retaining knowledge workers. *Human Resource Management Journal, 13*(4), 23-44.

Huber, G.P. (2001). Transfer of knowledge in knowledge management systems: Unexplored issues and suggested studies. *European Journal of Information Systems, 10*(2), 72-79.

Janssen, O. (2000). Job demands, perceptions of effort-reward fairness and innovative work behavior. *Journal of*

Occupational and Organizational Psychology, 73(3), 287-302.

Janz, B.D. (1999). Self-directed teams in IS: Correlates for improved systems development work outcomes. *Information & Management, 35*(3), 171-192.

Janz, B.D., Colquitt, J.A., & Noe, R.A. (1997). Knowledge worker team effectiveness: The role of autonomy, interdependence, team development, and contextual support variables. *Personnel Psychology, 50*(4), 877-904.

Krönig, J. (2001). *Do incentive systems for knowledge management work? An empirical study on the design and influence of incentive systems of knowledge creation and transfer in manufacturing-based industry.* Bern: Lang.

Kubo, I., & Saka, A. (2002). An inquiry into the motivations of knowledge workers in the Japanese financial industry. *Journal of Knowledge Management, 6*(3), 262-271.

Locke, E.A. (1968). Toward a theory of task motivation and incentives. *Organizational Behavior and Human Performance, 3*, 157-189.

Locke, E.A., & Latham. (1990). *A theory of goal setting and task performance.* Englewood Cliffs, NJ: Prentice-Hall.

Maccoby, M. (1988). *Why work: Leading the new generation.* New York: Simon & Schuster.

Malhotra, Y., & Galletta, D. (2003, January). Role of commitment and motivation in knowledge management systems implementation: Theory, conceptualization, and measurement of antecedents of success. *Proceedings of the Hawaii International Conference on Systems Science,* Hawaii.

McClough, A.C., & Rogelberg, S.G. (2003). Selection in teams: An exploration of the teamwork knowledge, skills, and ability test. *International Journal of Selection and Assessment, 11*(1), 56-66.

McKenzie, J., Truc, A., & Winkelen, C.V. (2001). Winning commitment for knowledge management initiatives. *Journal of Change Management, 2*(2), 115-127.

O'Leary-Kelly, A.M., Martocchio, J.J., & Frink, D.D. (1994). A review of the influence of group goals on group-performance. *Academy of Management Journal, 37*(5), 1285-1301.

Osterloh, M., & Frey, B.S. (2000). Motivation, knowledge transfer, and organizational forms. *Organization Science, 11*(5), 538-550.

Pajares, F. (1996). Self-efficacy beliefs in academic settings. *Review of Educational Research, 66*(4), 543-578.

Reinig, B.A. (2003). Toward an understanding of satisfaction with the process and outcomes of teamwork. *Journal of Management Information Systems, 19*(4), 65-83.

Salo, A.A. (2001). Incentives in technology foresight. *International Journal of Technology Management, 21*(7-8), 694-710.

Shalley, C.E., & Gilson, L.L. (2004). What leaders need to know: A review of social and contextual factors that can foster or hinder creativity. *Leadership Quarterly, 15*(1), 33-53.

Shalley, C.E., Gilson, L.L., & Blum, T.C. (2000). Matching creativity requirements and the work environment: Effects on satisfaction and intentions to leave. *Academy of Management Journal, 43*(2), 215-223.

Smith, A.D., & Rupp, W.T. (2002). Communication and loyalty among knowledge workers: A resource of the firm theory view. *Journal of Knowledge Management, 6*(3), 250-261.

Spreitzer, G.M. (1995). Psychological empowerment in the workplace—dimensions, measurement, and validation. *Academy of Management Journal, 38*(5), 1442-1465.

Tampoe, M. (1993). Motivating knowledge workers—the challenge for the 1990s. *Long Range Planning, 26*(3), 49-55.

Tierney, P., & Farmer, S.M. (2002). Creative self-efficacy: Its potential antecedents and relationship to creative performance. *Academy of Management Journal, 45*(6), 1137-1148.

Tierney, P., & Farmer, S.M. (2004). The Pygmalion process and employee creativity. *Journal of Management, 30*(3), 413-432.

Wasko, M.M., & Faraj, S. (2000). "It is what one does": Why people participate and help others in electronic communities of practice. *Journal of Strategic Information Systems, 9*(2-3), 155-173.

Wilkesmann, U., & Rascher, I. (2002). *Motivational and structural prerequisites of knowledge management* (No. 02-2). Bochum: Fakultät für Sozialwissenschaft, Ruhr-Universität Bochum.

KEY TERMS

Extrinsic Motivation: The motivation to engage in an activity as a means to an end, based on the belief that participation will result in desirable outcomes such as a reward or avoidance of punishment.

Goal-Setting Theory: This theory, developed by Locke and Latham, states that individuals make calculated decisions about their desired goals, and that these goals and intentions, once established, direct and motivate efforts to attain them.

Intrinsic Motivation: The motivation to engage in an activity for its own sake, because the activity is considered enjoyable, worthwhile, or important.

Job Characteristics Theory: This motivation theory, which stems from Hackman and Oldham, identifies several characteristics of jobs, such as skill variety and autonomy, that influence the experienced meaningfulness of work, and therefore the internal motivation and job satisfaction of workers.

Motivation: An energizing force directed toward a specific target considered to explain behavior.

Self-Determination Theory: A motivation theory, developed by Deci and Ryan, which suggests that individuals have three innate psychological needs: autonomy, competence, and relatedness. It distinguishes between intrinsically motivated, or autonomous, self-determined activity, and extrinsically motivated activity, which is more controlled (i.e., less autonomous).

Self-Efficacy Theory: This motivation theory, developed by Bandura, posits that motivation is the combined product of beliefs about whether one is capable of performing (or learning) some task, and beliefs about whether such performance will lead to desirable outcomes.

Work Motivation: Involves the restriction to those motivation elements that relate to the work situation; concerns the individual's degree of willingness to work towards organizational targets.

Multidisciplinary Project Teams

Patrick S.W. Fong
The Hong Kong Polytechnic University, Hong Kong

INTRODUCTION

Knowledge in designing a product or rendering a service does not form a complete and coherent body of knowledge that can be precisely documented or even articulated by a single individual. Rather, it is a form of knowing that exists only through the interaction among various collective actors (Gherardi & Nicolini, 2000). Existing literature (Kanter, 1988; Nonaka, 1994; Spender, 1998; Starbuck, 1992) has highlighted a need for the development of a diverse workforce if knowledge creation is to be promoted and sustained within organisations. This literature suggests that a diverse set of resources (experts with different backgrounds and abilities) provides a broad knowledge base at the individual level, offering greater potential for knowledge creation.

Conceptually, a team can be viewed as a socially constructed phenomenon or linking mechanism that integrates individuals and organisations (Horvath, Callahan, Croswell, & Mukri, 1996). A multidisciplinary team is defined by Nonaka and Takeuchi (1995, p. 85) as "a self-managed, self-organised team in which members from various functional departments, and/or areas of expertise work together to accomplish a common goal." The primary goal of the multidisciplinary composition is to marry diverse bodies of knowledge in a way that produces a synergistic knowledge outcome that is innovative, contextualised, and, as such, has strategic value. For the most part, project team tasks are nonrepetitive in nature and involve considerable application of knowledge, judgement, and expertise.

The advantage of adopting multidisciplinary project teams is that they are quicker in integrating the expert knowledge of different functions, for example, design, construction, marketing, maintenance, and accounting. Cross-functional project teams with mutual accountability and collective work products have been found to decrease development time and increase product quality (Ancona & Caldwell, 1992; Dougherty, 1992; Van de Ven, 1986; Wheelwright & Clark, 1992). Multidisciplinary project teams create a "task culture," facilitating the necessary close linkages and direct personal contacts between different functions (Cohen & Levinthal, 1990). These close connections are necessary, as new product development by its very nature includes uncertainty about potential market response and about new technology (Henke, Krachenberg, & Lyons, 1993). This transformation process is a team-level phenomenon. It emerges through "heedful interrelationships" (Weick & Roberts, 1993) and interdependencies between team members, their actions and interactions, and the enmeshment of their individual knowledge paradigms. If creating new collective knowledge is indeed a team-level phenomenon, then the multidisciplinary team is considered the greenhouse where such a phenomenon can be best cultivated.

This article views the multidisciplinary project team as an unusual team arrangement, primarily because it is composed of professionals from various disciplines who take pride in their fields of expertise. They are committed to the basic assumptions of their paradigms and they perceive their roles in the team as representing their knowledge bases in the best possible way. In addition, a project on which a multidisciplinary team works can metaphorically be seen as an experiment, a vehicle for knowledge creation, with knowledge being created through the process of executing the project.

Examining knowledge creation from a microscopic view, it can be further subdivided into knowledge development and knowledge acquisition. The former develops knowledge that is made available through internal resources, whereas the latter acquires required knowledge by external means. Knowledge development involves the development of knowledge through internal effort after identifying the difference between required and available knowledge. Developing knowledge internally can be achieved via personnel in-house, or through research and development efforts, education and training, creativity techniques like brainstorming, or customer satisfaction surveys. Knowledge acquisition entails the acquisition of knowledge from external sources if developing knowledge internally is not possible. This is done through employing specifically qualified personnel, by merging or acquiring firms, by purchasing e-learning training, by forming joint-venture companies, or by employing an external company to conduct market research.

The relationship between knowledge creation and knowledge management is like the metaphor of the chicken and the egg, that is, it is hard to say which one should come first. If we imagine just managing existing knowledge without creating new knowledge, we can foresee what kind of world we would be living in—probably just a highly effective society without much technological advancement or improvement in living standards. Alternatively, if we kept on creating new knowledge or innovating without properly managing our existing knowledge, we would end up going round and round in circles and repeating the same mistakes time after time. In order for a society to flourish or a new product to be successful when it is launched, knowledge should not simply be managed: The creation of new knowledge also should be possible. In essence, knowledge creation should go hand in hand with knowledge management, as without one or the other, our knowledge journey will be futile.

BACKGROUND

The issue of knowledge has been debated for several centuries. Knowledge has only recently been viewed as a collective phenomenon in organisational contexts. Two conflicting theoretical perspectives about knowledge emerge. The first, as highlighted by Prahalad and Hamel (1990) and Wernerfelt (1984), focuses on the resource-based view where knowledge is considered to be a set of strategically important commodities that exist independent of their creators and are context-independent (i.e., the firm's primary role is as knowledge applicator). The second perspective, from Berger and Luckmann (1966) and Nonaka and Takeuchi (1995), perceives knowledge as a set of shared beliefs that are constructed through social interactions and embedded within the social contexts in which knowledge is created (i.e., the firm's primary role is as knowledge creator). This view of knowledge embodies the social construction perspective held by this article of trying to understand knowledge creation processes in multidisciplinary project teams.

The present framework for examining the knowledge creation processes within multidisciplinary project teams is based on Nonaka and Takeuchi's (1995) organisational knowledge creation theory. Nonaka and Takeuchi's theory is utilised because it is one of the few knowledge creation theories available that examines the interrelationships between explicit and tacit knowledge. Further, Nonaka and Takeuchi's (1995) theory was inductively developed using case studies of product development projects, so the focus on technical knowledge creation is appropriate for this study. However, Nonaka and Takeuchi's (1995) knowledge creation model has some limitations that lessen the model's suitability for the study of knowledge creation in multidisciplinary

project teams. Their primary distinction between tacit and explicit knowledge is problematic as tacit or unarticulated knowledge is always a precondition for explicit knowledge (Engeström, 1999). Tuomi (1999) also criticises the model for taking culture and language for granted. The difficulty of discussing the role of language as a "repository of culturally shared meaning" (Tuomi, 1999, p. 340), critical for any knowledge creation theory, may make its use difficult for multidisciplinary project teams. It also is not clear what happens when the knowledge-creating spiral expands outside a team: Is knowledge still created in the same way (Tuomi, 1999)? As pointed out by Tuomi (1999, p. 328), "There is no model of social activity within the [knowledge creation] model—the motives for knowledge creation, and their relations to individual or organisational needs, remain obscure. Why some knowledge is created, and why some knowledge is not, remains an open question." Furthermore, Tuomi (1999) finds that though Nonaka and Takeuchi (1995) stress that the process of knowledge creation is "social", their underlying focus is on individual and intrapersonal knowledge. He adds that "as their concept of knowledge is intrapersonal, truth becomes a necessary aspect of knowledge, grounding intrapersonal knowledge into interpersonal reality" (Tuomi, 1999, p. 333).

In order to overcome some of the shortcomings in Nonaka and Takeuchi's knowledge creation model, if one accepts the social construction perspective of knowledge as a set of shared beliefs constructed through social interaction amidst certain social circumstances, then both individual and social levels require acknowledgement and integration.

Two multidisciplinary project teams, working on two different construction projects at the design stage, were selected for study. In this article, a construction project also can be treated as a product because at the end of construction a facility will exist, with consumers using it to fulfill their needs. The selection of a residential development project recognises the large reservoir of idiosyncratic knowledge developed by the owner company over the years. It also recognises the crucial innovating dynamics behind the need to compete on the market with other residential developments. The infrastructure project presented alternative opportunities for knowledge creation and learning, unique in several respects. First, it was a complex operation, distinguished by an extraordinary multiplicity of consultants employed. Second, it is rare to find such a project, usually managed by government, in private hands. Finally, the technical challenges presented in this project made it an interesting arena for knowledge creation and absorption within the team.

MAIN FOCUS OF THE ARTICLE

Beyond modifying Nonaka and Takeuchi's (1995) model of knowledge conversion processes, a major and significant finding is that the collaborative nature of multidisciplinary project teams is essential in creating new knowledge. With a traditional focus on professional specialisation, many new development projects may be managed with tasks being executed in parallel or in sequence, or by certain project team members in isolation. This is often counter-productive when projects are so designed that the success of creating new knowledge among diverse disciplines may suffer, with optimal value possibly not being achieved.

The first process in knowledge creation involves boundary crossing, with two types of boundaries identified as affecting the progress and success of multidisciplinary knowledge creation. The importance of boundary crossing is reflected in solving the "boundary paradox" (Quintas, Lefrere, & Jones, 1997), where team members are able to exchange and combine knowledge (Nahapiet & Ghoshal, 1998). The interactions across these boundaries can either foster or hinder knowledge creation. The first boundary identified was between team members of different disciplines. The second existed between different stakeholders. The expertise boundaries could be crossed, not only through knowledge redundancy among team members, but also through boundary objects. The most prominent project boundary objects were drawings and personal conversations among team members. The second hierarchical boundaries could be crossed through team members consciously breaking down any barriers by valuing the expertise of others. It must be stressed that crossing boundaries does not necessarily guarantee the creation of knowledge. It is seen, however, as a prerequisite for the four remaining processes to occur.

The second process relates to knowledge sharing, with project team members of differing knowledge domains more likely to discuss their uniquely distinct information and knowledge than those who possess information in common. It seemed to be an advantage to have a diverse pool of knowledge for team members to access and share in discussion. Despite the existence of little competition among team members, external competition could act as a double-edged sword in the knowledge sharing process. Sharing important market or design knowledge could lead to imitation by competitors, possibly even resulting in project poaching. In addition, the type of communication appeared more influential in the transfer of tacit rather than explicit knowledge. For tacit knowledge to be effectively transmitted, interpersonal communication seemed of the utmost importance.

The third process to be considered is that of knowledge generation, in which teams create knowledge by generating new or "emergent" knowledge through interaction and communication. New or emergent knowledge, not possessed before discussion, can develop through group discussion and interaction (Kogut & Zander, 1992). The development of emergent knowledge is vital for creativity and innovation. It is generated through various means, including those of social networks, printed sources, and customer and competitor feedback.

Social networks were identified as the most important vehicle for information and knowledge exchange, with team members heavily reliant upon colleagues, friends, and ex-colleagues as rich resources for generating design knowledge. The use of printed data in the design process appeared to be limited: It was viewed as time-consuming and used mainly to cross-check the solutions offered. Social networks tended to recommend published materials, helping to reduce research time and enhance usability. Comprehension of customer needs, insight into competitor products, and an inspection of completed facilities all seemed to stimulate knowledge generation. Time and motivation were identified as two very significant influences, and it is interesting to note that both of these impacted on the sharing of knowledge, as well as the generation of new knowledge.

Fourth is knowledge integration, realised by marrying the differing perspectives and knowledge of various disciplines in the design decision-making process. This enables different stakeholder views to be incorporated so that they can be considered and integrated. New product design requires multidisciplinary skills and knowledge input. Various team members brought different sets of assumptions about optimal ways to proceed, prioritising different values and perspectives to ultimately best meet stakeholder requirements as well as arrive at satisfactory design solutions. Project documentation as well as various design objects were used as tools to integrate the range of knowledge input from project participants.

The fifth process involves collective project learning, in which professionals with extensive experience in self-directed learning learn from the projects they are engaged in. Project team members had to constantly absorb new technology and techniques in order to remain competitive. Experts in self-directed learning, they created an environment maximising opportunities for individual inquiry and learning. Problem-solving being central to their work, they also recognised that failure was an opportunity for learning and understanding. Understanding failure is a primary mechanism in learning how new technology and systems operate, optimally avoiding repetitive mistakes. Therefore, considerable effort should be made to support an individual's critical problem-solving and reflection processes. Individuals then develop personal strategies based on their own thinking and learning preferences.

The project teams themselves encouraged team learning activities, independent of any directives. Small subteams typically pooled their resources for learning, acquiring the necessary skills and knowledge to solve problems in an open and permissive environment. Individuals shared their information seeking strategies so that the sub-team might learn in as many different ways as possible. The larger project teams followed more formal processes and procedures for sharing and interacting. The smaller teams contributed directly to the work of the larger project teams, but they were not formally recognised in the organisational structure of the projects. They spontaneously grouped and regrouped, navigated by the team members themselves. Most formations were temporary, lasting only until the immediate goals were accomplished.

Inter-project learning can be seen as gaining knowledge from a project and transferring it directly or indirectly to other subsequent or concurrent projects. Interproject learning can happen both concurrently or sequentially. In concurrent transfer, a new project begins to transfer knowledge from a base project before it has completed its task. Sequential transfer happens when knowledge and experience are transferred from an initial project to a new one upon the original's completion. A central prerequisite for interproject learning is a certain degree of repetitiveness between projects, with the similarity of aspects enabling construction and refinement of

procedures, whereas the total uniqueness of a project can slow learning, possibly hindering immediate progress. The most widely observed strategy in interproject learning involved personalisation rather than codification.

Through studying two multidisciplinary project teams working on two facilities projects during their design phase, this article has arrived at a new model of knowledge creation within multidisciplinary project teams, differing from the organisational knowledge creation theory developed by Nonaka and Takeuchi (1995). The new model of knowledge creation within multidisciplinary project teams is proposed and illustrated in Figure 1, with the interrelationships among different processes highlighted. It is emphasised that these processes are not linear in nature but intertwined with one another.

FUTURE TRENDS

As more organisations employ multidisciplinary teams to sustain or improve their competitive advantage through innovative products or services, more attention should be directed to highlighting their unique features and understanding how to turn such teams into an effective knowledge creation force.

Though project teams with diverse workforces can be seen as essential units in promoting and sustaining knowledge creation within organisations (Kanter, 1988;

Figure 1. The interrelationships between multidisciplinary knowledge creation processes

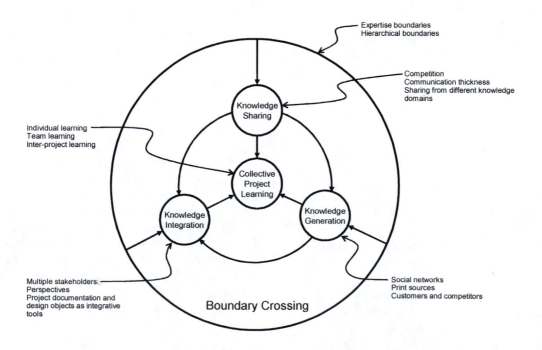

Nonaka, 1994; Spender, 1998; Starbuck, 1992), the diversity of team members can be problematic, placing demands on the team to manage divergent thinking paradigms and basic assumptions, as well as the "professional egos" of team members (Dougherty, 1992). This would suggest a need for proper management before the benefits of knowledge creation can be harvested. This would require the joint effort of teams and their management. Four key lessons for multidisciplinary project teams and management are suggested here:

- The support of intra- and interorganisational social networks
- The enhancement of cooperative teamwork
- Mechanisms for easing tension among project team members
- Concentration on project value maximisation

Although this article has made some theoretical and practical contributions, it has limitations that call for further research. Several research agendas emanating from this model are:

First, only a specific type of team was included in the research data. The research site provided an excellent opportunity to explore the processes, interrelationships, and contributory factors to knowledge creation within a multidisciplinary setting. However, the experience of these teams cannot be extrapolated to all teams. It is suggested that future research could attempt to conduct similar studies in more diverse settings. Since different team structures and cultures could influence the knowledge creation processes in different ways, future research could contribute to the development of a pluralistic, rather than normative, view of team knowledge-creation capability. This might include comparative studies of information-intensive teams vs. production-oriented teams, and research- vs. product-oriented teams. Future studies could examine teams in more complex interdisciplinary circumstances (e.g., biotechnology, genomics, etc.) where teams are brought together, even from quite different fields and industries. These teams might work on complex problems, pooling their diverse backgrounds and training, possibly to solve a complex business problem, design a new system, product or service, or to reorganise a company.

Second, the research on knowledge creation extends across multiple theoretical boundaries. However, this study emphasised primarily the areas of knowledge creation and team processes. Though other related literature has been discussed, their review was not the main thrust. The ample information management and information systems literature, devoted to knowledge management or organisational knowledge, was not in-

corporated into the study. This limitation can be explained by the study's focus on the processes of knowledge creation within multidisciplinary project teams, rather than the effects of information systems on these processes. Such a limitation represents a major research opportunity through exploring the impact of information systems on knowledge creation.

Finally, the study did not measure the effectiveness or quality of the knowledge created by the multidisciplinary project teams. Such a measurement could facilitate a clearer understanding of any organisational competitive advantage that might result from knowledge creation. Clearly, future research aiming to tackle these issues might enable project teams and management to better understand and evaluate the potential impact of multidisciplinary project teams on knowledge creation.

CONCLUSION

This article has arrived at a new model of knowledge creation within multidisciplinary project teams, differing from the organisational knowledge creation theory developed by Nonaka and Takeuchi (1995). It places primary emphasis on the processes rather than the outcomes of multidisciplinary knowledge creation as put forward by previous researchers.

The underlying processes of knowledge creation in multidisciplinary project teams are different to those proposed in the organisational knowledge creation theories. A new model of knowledge creation within multidisciplinary project teams is proposed. In the model, the five processes of knowledge creation are identified, including the processes of boundary crossing, knowledge sharing, knowledge generation, knowledge integration, and collective project learning. The interrelationships of these five processes are elaborated to enable their thorough understanding. It must be stressed that that these knowledge creation processes within multidisciplinary teams are not linear. Instead they are interwoven, occurring throughout the projects. In addition, there is a need for proper management of multidisciplinary project teams before the benefits of knowledge creation can be harvested and recognised.

REFERENCES

Ancona, D.G., & Caldwell, D.F. (1992). Demography and design: Predictors of new product team performance. *Organization Science, 3*(3), 321-341.

Berger, P.L., & Luckmann, T. (1966). *The social construction of reality: A treatise in the sociology of knowledge.* Garden City, NY: Doubleday.

Cohen, W.M., & Levinthal, D.A. (1990). Absorptive capacity: A new perspective on learning and innovation. *Administrative Science Quarterly, 35*(1), 128-152.

Dougherty, D. (1992). Interpretive barriers to successful product innovation in large firms. *Organization Science, 3*(2), 179-202.

Engeström, Y. (1999). Innovative learning in work teams: Analyzing cycles of knowledge creation in practice. In Y. Engeström, R. Miettinen, & R.-L. Punamäki-Gitai (Eds.), *Perspectives on activity theory* (pp. 377-404). Cambridge: Cambridge University Press.

Gherardi, S., & Nicolini, D. (2000). The organizational learning of safety in communities of practice. *Journal of Management Inquiry, 9*(1), 7-18.

Henke, J., Krachenberg, R., & Lyons, T. (1993). Perspective: Cross-functional teams: Good concept, poor implementation! *Journal of Product Innovation Management, 10*(3), 216-229.

Horvath, L., Callahan, J.L., Croswell, C., & Mukri, G. (1996, February 29-March 3). Team sensemaking: An imperative for individual and organizational learning. In E.F. Holton (Ed.), *Proceedings of the Academy of Human Resource Development,* Minneapolis, MN (pp. 415-421).

Kanter, R.M. (1988). When a thousand flowers bloom: Structural, collective, and conditions for innovation in organizations. In B. Staw & L.L. Cummings (Eds.), *Research in organizational behavior* (pp. 169-212). Greenwich, CT: JAI Press.

Kogut, B., & Zander, U. (1992). Knowledge of the firm, combinative capabilities, and the replication of technology. *Organization Science, 3*(3), 383-397.

Nahapiet, J., & Ghoshal, S. (1998). Social capital, intellectual capital, and the organizational advantage. *Academy of Management Review, 23*(2), 242-266.

Nonaka, I., & Takeuchi, H. (1995). *The knowledge-creating company: How Japanese companies create the dynamics of innovation.* Oxford: Oxford University Press.

Nonaka, I. (1994). A dynamic theory of organizational knowledge creation. *Organization Science, 5*(1), 14-37.

Prahalad, C.K., & Hamel, G. (1990). The core competence of the corporation. *Harvard Business Review, 68*(3), 79-91.

Quintas, P., Lefrere, P., & Jones, G. (1997). Knowledge management: A strategic agenda. *Long Range Planning, 30*(3), 385-391.

Spender, J.C. (1998). Pluralist epistemology and the knowledge-based theory of the firm. *Organization, 5*(2), 233-256.

Starbuck, W.H. (1992). Learning by knowledge intensive firms. *Journal of Management Studies, 29*(6), 713-740.

Tuomi, I. (1999). Corporate *knowledge: Theory and practice of intelligent organizations.* Helsinki: Metaxis.

Van de Ven, A.H. (1986). Central problems in the management of innovation. *Management Science, 32*(5), 590-607.

Weick, K.E., & Roberts, K.H. (1993). Collective mind in organizations: Heedful interrelating on flight decks. *Administrative Science Quarterly, 38,* 357-381.

Wernerfelt, B. (1984). A resource-based view of the firm. *Strategic Management Journal, 5*(2), 171-180.

Wheelwright, S.C., & Clark, K.B. (1992). *Revolutionizing product development: Quantum leaps in speed, efficiency, and quality.* New York: Free Press.

KEY TERMS

Boundary Crossing: The crossing of one's own professional, disciplinary, or expertise boundaries (i.e., knowledge zones), and venturing into others. This is required when people work in situations that require multifaceted input, where no one possesses all the different types of knowledge necessary (e.g., a medical doctor working with a structural engineer on an artificial limb project).

Innovation: The creation of something new. This involves a radical step of making something different from before or creating something that has not existed before.

Interproject Learning: In project-based industries, people are organised around projects rather than on a functional basis. Learning rarely happens in a project, as people will disband upon its completion, and all the successes or failures are easily forgotten or not learnt by those who are not involved. This concept involves trying to leverage knowledge and experience from other projects which may benefit the current one.

Knowledge Creation: The creation of new knowledge or the combination of existing knowledge to achieve an outcome, which can be in terms of innovation or problem-solving.

Multidisciplinary Project Team: A group of team members with diverse educational backgrounds, training, skill sets, experience, and professional identities working together in a team situation in order to tackle a task or project. They will be disbanded upon the completion of the temporary assignment. They can come from different functional departments or organisations.

New Product Development (NPD): The development of a new product, such as a car or a facility, in order to fulfill the needs of its customers. It involves the whole product life cycle from initial design to the production of the product.

Problem–Solving: The application of new knowledge to existing problems, which results in an improvement in efficiency or lowering of the production cost. Usually, a problem exists that requires resolving. Alternatively, we can apply knowledge from another arena to an existing problem, which results in a different way of doing things.

M

Musical Metadata and Knowledge Management

François Pachet
Sony CSL - Paris, France

INTRODUCTION

Is music a form of knowledge? Probably not, even if music is undoubtedly an important part of our cultural heritage. Music is not a type of knowledge, at least in first approximation, because music has no consensual, shared *meaning*. One of the main reasons why music has no meaning, as opposed to text or even pictures, is that music is not *referential*: music is made of elements (notes, chords, sounds) which do not refer to any objects or concepts outside the musical world (Meyer, 1956). Being without meaning, music is not a type of knowledge.

However, our heavily digitized society continuously produces and exploits an increasing amount of *knowledge about* music. This knowledge, also called *metadata*, has taken a growing importance in the music industry and deserves a special treatment in this encyclopedia because of the specificities of music. On one hand, music is ubiquitous and pervasive: there are about 10 million music titles produced by the major music labels in the Western world. Adding the music produced in the non-Western world probably doubles this figure. The music industry is one of the prevalent industries in the Western world today. On the other hand, music is elusive, in that it is difficult to define exactly what music is (for instance, distinguishing music from ambient sounds is not always trivial). To make all this music easily accessible to listeners, it is important to describe music in ways that machines can understand. Music knowledge management is precisely about this issue: (1) building meaningful *descriptions* of music that are easy to maintain, and (2) exploiting these descriptions to build efficient music access systems that help users find music in large music collections.

BACKGROUND

The issue of building music description is the subject matter of the audio part of the Mpeg-7 standard (Nack & Lindsay, 1999). Mpeg-7 focuses only on the notion of metadata, as opposed to its predecessors (Mpeg-1, 2, and 4), and proposes schemes to represent arbitrary symbolic and numeric information about multimedia objects, such as music or movies. However, Mpeg-7 deals only with the syntax of these descriptions, and not with the way these descriptions are to be produced. Here is, for instance, an extract of an Mpeg-7 description of the music title "Blowin' in the Wind" by Bob Dylan. This extract declares the name of the artist, the name of the song, and its genre (here, "Folk," according to a genre classification indicated in the extract itself).

The first step toward music knowledge management is probably music identification. Robust audio fingerprinting techniques have been developed recently to identify music titles from the analysis of possibly distorted sources, such as radio broadcasts, or direct recordings from cell phone microphones (Cano, Batlle, Kalker, & Haitsma, 2002). Audio fingerprinting is not a knowledge management technique *per se*, but is a prerequisite to build music collections. This technique has received considerable attention in the last few years, and today very robust solutions have been designed and implemented in real-world systems, such as the MoodLogic Music Browser.

To give a concrete idea of typical music descriptions used in musical knowledge management systems, let us give here three examples and their related use.

Several companies produce and exploit so-called *editorial* musical metadata—for instance, AllMusicGuide (Datta, 2002) or MusicBrainz (*http://www. musicbrainz. org*). This information typically relates to songs and albums (e.g., track listings of albums), but also includes information on artists (biographies, periods of activities) and genres. A typical scenario of use is the display in a popular music player of an artist's biography and genre when a title is played. When a title is played, an identification mechanism produces the identity of the title and artist, and a query is made to AllMusicGuide to retrieve more information, for example, the biography of the artist or the photograph of the album the title comes from.

Another popular application of musical metadata is *query-by-humming*. Query-by-humming consists of letting users sing or hum a melody, and retrieves the songs whose melodies match the input (Birmingham et al., 2002). Technically, query-by-humming is one instance of music information retrieval systems. In terms of knowledge management, this application makes use of the analysis of melodies from the audio signal and the sung inputs, so they fall in the category of acoustic descriptors as described below.

Finally a popular view on music knowledge management is *collaborative filtering*, as used in music portals such as Amazon. Collaborative filtering makes intensive

Figure 1. An Mpeg-7 extract for describing information about a music title

```
<?xml version="1.0" encoding="UTF-8"?>
<Mpeg7
  xmlns="urn:mpeg:mpeg7:schema:2001"
  xmlns:xsi="http://www.w3.org/2001/XMLSchema-instance"
  xmlns:mpeg7="urn:mpeg:mpeg7:schema:2001"
  xsi:schemaLocation="urn:mpeg:mpeg7:schema:2001 mpeg7-smp-2004.xsd">
    <Description xsi:type="CreationDescriptionType">
      <!-- ID3 Track number -->
      <CreationInformation id="track-01">
        <Creation>
          <!-- ID3 Song Title -->
          <Title type="songTitle">Blowin' in the wind</Title>
          <!-- ID3 Album Title -->
          <Title type="albumTitle">The Freewheelin'</Title>
          <!-- ID3 Artist -->
          <Creator>
            <Role href="urn:mpeg:mpeg7:RoleCS:2001:PERFORMER"/>
            <Agent xsi:type="PersonType">
              <Name>
                <FamilyName>Dylan</FamilyName>
                <GivenName>Bob</GivenName>
              </Name>
            </Agent>
          </Creator>
          <!-- ID3 Genre  -->
          <Classification>
            <Genre href=" urn:id3:cs:ID3genreCS:v1:80"><Name>Folk</Name></Genre>
          </Classification>
        </CreationInformation>
    </Description>
</Mpeg7>
```

use of user profiles, and exploits similarity or patterns in large databases of profiles. Technically, collaborative filtering is one instance of so-called *cultural descriptors*, as we will see below.

The three examples are deliberately chosen to represent three types of information: editorial, cultural, and acoustic. These three types of information actually cover the whole range of techniques for music knowledge management. The next section reviews in more detail each of these types of information and highlights the main technical issues related to each of them.

THREE TYPES OF MUSICAL METADATA

Although there is a virtually infinite number of musical metadata that can be thought of concerning the description of music, we propose here to classify all of them in only three categories: editorial, cultural, and acoustic. This classification is based on the nature of the process that leads to the elaboration of the metadata.

Editorial Metadata

Editorial metadata refers to metadata obtained, literally, by the editor. Practically, this means that the information is provided manually, by authoritative experts. Examples of editorial metadata in music range from album information (e.g., the song "Yellow Submarine" by the Beatles appears on the Album "Revolver" issued in the UK) to administrative information such as the dates of recording, the composers or performers. Because editorial metadata covers a wide range of information, from *adminstratrivia* to historical facts, it is difficult to define precisely its scope other than by stating how it was produced.

Editorial metadata is not necessarily objective. For instance, the AllMusicGuide editorial metadata portal (Datta, 2002) provides information about artist biographies, which may be biased by cultural factors. In particular, genre information—seen as editorial metadata (i.e., entered by human experts)—is known to be particularly subjective.

Technically, the tasks of organizing editorial metadata raises specific challenges, such as:

- **Providing a consensual view on subjective editorial information.** For instance, agreeing on a taxonomy of musical genres.
- **Coping with the evolving nature of music.** New artists, new genres, new events occur all the time in music. The organization of an editorial information system must be able to cope with these changes efficiently.
- **Organizing the human effort into clear and distinct roles.** For example, as editorial management and data enterers.

There is another distinction one can make concerning editorial metadata which concerns the nature of the human source: editorial metadata as produced in AllMusicGuide is prescriptive: the information is decided by one well-defined expert or pool of experts.

Editorial metadata can also be produced in a non-prescriptive manner, using a collaborative scheme—that is, by a community of users. In this case, both the nature of the information provided and the management techniques differ.

A typical example of this "collaborative editorial" information is the CDDB effort (www.cddb.com). CDDB is a database of "track listing" (i.e., the information, for each music album produced, of the songs contained in the album). Surprisingly, this track listing information is not systematically present in CD albums, and it is precisely the role of CDDB to fill this gap. The identification technique used is very simple and relies on a hashing code produced by the number of tracks and their exact durations. This signature uniquely identifies most of the albums. To the signature is associated the track listing information. Such editorial information is, however, not prescriptive, and is on the contrary produced by a collaborative effort. When a user fetches a track listing information for a given album, it is retrieved automatically from the CDDB database (provided the media player used has a license with CDDB). If the album is not recognized, then the user can input the information himself, and thus contribute to the database content.

Another example of such an approach is MoodLogic (www.moodlogic.com). The MoodLogic approach consists of building a database of song "profiles" from ratings of users. This database is used to classify and recommend music, and is integrated in various music management tools such as music browsers. When a song is added to a user's collection, a fingerprinting technique identifies the song and fetches the corresponding metadata in the MoodLogic database. If the song is not present in the database, the user is asked to rate the song. This approach has proven to be scalable, as the MoodLogic database now contains profiles for about one million titles. The nature of the information entered is quite different, however, than the information present in prescriptive systems such as AllMusicGuide: MoodLogic includes information such as genres, mood, perceived energy, and so forth.

It is important to stress again here that this information is considered in our context as editorial—more precisely as collaborative editorial—because of the way the information is provided. However, we will see that this kind of information can be used in a totally different context, in particular to produce acoustic metadata.

Cultural Metadata

Cultural information or knowledge is produced by the environment or culture. Contrarily to editorial information, cultural information is not prescribed or even explicitly entered in some information system. Cultural information results from an analysis of emerging patterns, categories, or associations from a source of documents.

A common method of obtaining cultural information is collaborative filtering (Cohen & Fan, 2000). In this case, the source of information is a collection of user profiles.

However, user profiles are a relatively poor source of information, and there are many other cultural information schemes applicable to music. The most used sources of information are Web search engines like Google, music radio programs, or purely textual sources such as books or encyclopedias. The main techniques used borrow from natural language processing and are mostly based on co-occurrence analysis: for a given item of interest (say an artist or a genre), co-occurrence techniques allow one to associate to this item other items which are "close," in the sense that they often appear close to each other. Co-occurrence can be based on closeness of items in a Web page or by neighboring relations in music playlists. The main difficulty in this approach is to derive a meaningful similarity relation from the co-occurrence information. Approaches such as Pachet, Westerman, and Laigre (2001) or Whitmann and Lawrence (2002) give details on the actual language processing techniques used and the evaluation of results. The typical information that can be obtained from these analysis are:

- Similarity distance between musical items such as artists or songs. Such similarities can be used in music management systems such as music browser, or music recommendation systems.
- Word associations between different word categories. For instance, a co-occurrence technique described in Whitmann and Lawrence (2002) indicates which most common terms are associated with a given artist. The same technique can also be used to infer genre information; by computing the

co-occurrence between an artist name (say, "the Beatles") and different genre names (say "Pop," "Rock," "Jazz," etc.). In this case, the resulting information may also be called *genre*, as in the editorial case, but editorial genre and cultural genre will most of the time not coincide (see the section titled "Discussion").

Acoustic Metadata

The last category of music information is acoustic metadata. Acoustic here refers to the fact that this information is obtained by an analysis of the audio file, without any reference to a textual or prescribed information. It is intended to be purely objective information, pertaining to the "content" of the music.

A typical example of musical acoustic information is the tempo, that is, the number of beats per second. Beat and Tempo extraction have long been addressed in the community of audio signal processing, and current systems achieve excellent performances (Sheirer, 1998). Other, more complex rhythmic information can also be extracted, such as the metric structure (is it a ternary rhythm, like a waltz, or binary rhythm?) or the rhythm structure itself.

Besides rhythm, virtually all dimensions of music perception are subject to such extraction investigation: percussivity (is a sound percussive or pitched?), instrument *recognition* (Herrera, Peeters, & Dubnov, 2002), perceived energy (Zils & Pachet, 2003), or even mood (Liu, Lu, & Zhang, 2003). The results of these extractions are very disparate, and today no commercial application exploits these descriptors. But the robustness of these descriptors will likely greatly improve in the coming years, due to the increase of attention these subjects have attracted recently.

These preceding examples are *unary* descriptors: they consist of one particular value for a whole title and do not depend on other parameters such as the position in the music title. Non-unary descriptors are also very useful to describe music and manage large music collections. Melodic contour or pitch extraction can be used, for instance, for query-by-humming applications (Birmingham et al., 2001). At a yet higher level, music *structure* can be inferred from the analysis of repetitions in the audio signal (Peeters, La Burthe, & Rodet, 2002), leading to applications such as automatic music summaries.

The issue of representing in a standardized manner all these metadata is addressed by the audio part of the Mpeg-7 standard (Nack & Lindsay, 1999). However, Mpeg-7 focuses on the syntax of the representation of these descriptors, and it is quite obvious that the success of the standard heavily depends on the robustness of the corresponding extractors.

One major problem this endeavor has to deal with is that there is rarely any "music grounded facts," except for trivial information. Building a grounded facts database is therefore one of the main difficulties in acoustic descriptor design. Information obtained from collaborative editorial sources, such as MoodLogic, can paradoxically prove very valuable in this context.

Another issue is that although there is a lot of formal knowledge about music structure (tonal music in particular), this knowledge is rarely adapted to perceptive problems. For instance, taxonomies of genres or taxonomies of instruments are not directly usable for building ground truth databases, because they are not based on perceptive models: depending on the playing mode, context, and so forth, a clarinet can sound very close to a guitar and very different from another clarinet.

DISCUSSION

Because of the wide diversity of music knowledge types, there is a growing concern about the evaluation and comparison of these metadata. Indeed, the exploitation of large-scale music collections is possible only if these metadata are robust. But what does it mean exactly to be robust?

There are different types of evaluations in our context, some of which do not raise any particular problems. For instance, the evaluation of acoustic descriptors targeting consensual, well-defined music dimensions (such as tempo or instrument recognition on monophonic sources) do not usually raise any particular issues. The evaluation of acoustic similarities is more problematic, as the elaboration of a ground truth reference is itself a hard task (Aucouturier & Pachet, 2004).

However, the most complex evaluation task is probably the comparison of metadata across different categories. For instance, comparing acoustic similarity with cultural similarity is not a well-defined problem. Indeed, cultural metadata can be used to train machine-learning algorithms to produce acoustic metadata or similarities. In this case, the comparison is simple to do, but misleading, since the cultural similarities are known to be based not only on acoustic features. On the other hand, comparing two similarity measures obtained from different sources (e.g., Berenzweig, Ellis, Logan, & Whitman, 2003) produces results that are hard to interpret or exploit.

Another important consequence of this diversity of sources of metadata is that complex information dependency loops can be created which eventually produce meaningless musical knowledge, at least to non-informed users. The example of genre is, to this respect, emblematic, as genre can be produced by any of our three categories of approaches:

- **Editorial genre** is a genre prescribed by an expert, say, the manager of a label, or the team of AllMusicGuide. In this case, the Beatles can be described as "Pop-Sixties."
- **Cultural genre** is extracted from an analysis of textual information such as the Web. Depending on the source used, the Beatles can be described, culturally, as, say "Pop" (versus "Jazz" and "Classical").
- Finally, **acoustic genre** can be extracted too, using audio signal processing techniques (see, e.g., Tzanetakis, Essl, & Cook, 2001). It is important to note that acoustic genre will entirely depend on the learning database used for building the extractor. This database usually comes either from editorial or cultural information sources.

These intricate dependencies of information call for a better realization, by users, of the implications and meanings of the metadata they are provided with for managing their collections. Instead of trying to artificially compare or fit these different sources of knowledge about music, a simpler and more efficient strategy is probably to find simple ways to explain to users what each of them is doing.

FUTURE TRENDS

The representation of musical knowledge, as represented by metadata, is a blooming field. From the early experiments in beat tracking to the industries of metadata, many results have been obtained and problems solved. More are being addressed with promising results, such as the separation of sources in polyphonic recordings, which will bring new descriptions to music management systems.

Important directions concerning the future of music knowledge in this context are:

- **The invention of new music access modes.** So far, the main use of music metadata has been for implementing efficient music query systems. Metadata can also be used to create new music access modes, for instance integrating performance and music access. Preliminary works have been proposed, such as concatenative synthesis (*musaicing*) (Zils & Pachet, 2001), which exploits metadata to create new music and not only to listen to songs.
- **More subjective measures of user interests.** So far, work on evaluation has focused on objective measures. However, users accessing large-scale music collections are often animated by desires such as the quest for discovery or the pleasure of partially

controlled browsing. Music access systems would clearly benefit from measures of interestingness combining possibly contradictory similarity relations together.

CONCLUSION

While music itself is not a form of knowledge, musical knowledge is needed to manage large-scale music collections. We have discussed a classification of musical metadata into three basic categories, based on the nature of the process leading to the creation of the metadata and their potential uses. These three categories may intersect, at least superficially, and it is important to understand the possibilities and limits of each of these categories to make full use of them. It is very likely that future applications of music content management will make increasing use of such metadata, and conversely will exert pressure for the creation of new music metadata types.

REFERENCES

Aucouturier, J.-J., & Pachet, F. (2004). Improving timbre similarity: How high is the sky? *Journal of Negative Results in Speech and Audio Sciences, 1*(1).

Berenzweig, A., Ellis, D., Logan, B., & Whitman, B. (2003, October 26-30). A large-scale evaluation of acoustic and subjective music similarity measures. *Proceedings of the 2003 International Symposium on Music Information Retrieval*, Baltimore, MD.

Birmingham, Dannenberg, Wakefield, Bartsch, Bykowski, Mazzoni, Meek, Mellody, & Rand. (2001). MUSART: Music retrieval via aural queries. *Proceedings of ISMIR 2001, the 2nd Annual International Symposium on Music Information Retrieval* (pp. 73-82). Bloomington, IN: Indiana University.

Cano, P. Batlle, E. Kalker, T., & Haitsma, J. (2002, December). A review of algorithms for audio fingerprinting. *Proceedings of the International Workshop on Multimedia Signal Processing,* U.S. Virgin Islands. Retrieved from *http://www.iua.upf.es/mtg*

Cohen, W., & Fan, W. (2000). Web-collaborative filtering: Recommending music by crawling the Web computer networks. *The International Journal of Computer and Telecommunications Networking, 33*(1-6).

Datta, D. (2002). Managing metadata. *Proceedings of the International Symposium on Music Information Retrieval 2002,* Paris.

Herrera, P., Peeters, G., & Dubnov, S. (2002). Automatic classification of musical instrument sounds. *Journal of New Music Research, 31*(3).

Liu, D., Lu, L., & Zhang, H.-J. (2003). Automatic mood detection form acoustic music data. *Proceedings of ISMIR 2003,* Washington.

Meyer, L. (1956). *Emotions and meaning in music.* Chicago: University of Chicago Press.

Nack, F., & Lindsay, A. (1999). Everything you wanted to know about Mpeg-7: Part 2. *IEEE Multimedia, 6*(4).

Pachet, F., Westerman, G., & Laigre, D. (2001). Musical data mining for electronic music distribution. *Proceedings of the 1st WedelMusic Conference.*

Peeters, G., La Burthe, A., & Rodet, X. (2002). Towards automatic music audio summary generation from signal analysis. *Proceedings of the International Conference on Music Information Retrieval* (ISMIR02), Ircam.

Scheirer, E. (1998). Tempo and beat analysis of acoustic musical signals. *JASA, 103*(1), 588-601.

Sheirer, E. (2002). About this business of metadata. *Proceedings of the International Symposium on Music Information Retrieval 2002,* Paris.

Tzanetakis, G., Essl, G., & Cook, P. (2001). Automatic musical genre classification of audio signals. *Proceedings of ISMIR 2001,* Bloomington, IN.

Whitman, B., & Lawrence, S. (2002, September 16-21). Inferring descriptions and similarity for music from community metadata. *Voices of Nature: Proceedings of the 2002 International Computer Music Conference* (pp. 591-598), Göteborg, Sweden.

Zils, A., & Pachet, F. (2003, September). extracting automatically the perceived intensity of music titles. *Proceedings of the 6th COST-G6 Conference on Digital Audio Effects* (DAFX03), Queen Mary University, London.

Zils, A., & Pachet, F. (2001, December). Musical mosaicing. *Proceedings of DAFX 01,* University of Limerick, Ireland.

KEY TERMS

Acoustic Metadata: Metadata obtained from an analysis of the audio signal.

Fingerprinting: Technique to associate a single—and small—representation of an audio signal that is robust to usual audio deformations. Used for identification.

Cultural Metadata: Metadata obtained from the analysis of corpora of textual information, usually from the Internet or other public sources (radio programs, encyclopedias, etc.).

Editorial Metadata: Metadata obtained manually, by a pool of experts. Typically AMG.

Prescriptive Metadata: Produced by a single expert or group of experts.

Tonal Music: Music following the rules of tonality (i.e., based on scales). Usually opposed to atonal music such as serial music (based on the principle that all notes must be used with the same frequencies), spectral music (based on the nature of sounds rather than on pitches), minimalism, and so forth.

Timbre: A dimension of music which is defined by negation: timbre is not pitch nor dynamics, and is everything else. Timbre defines the texture of the sound, and allows to differentiate between different instruments playing the same note (pitch) at the same volume.

Narrative

Dave Snowden
The Cynefin Centre, UK

INTRODUCTION

Narrative or the use of stories is an ancient discipline. Our ancestors evolved the ability to see the world through a set of abstractions, and thereby enabled the development of sophisticated language and the ability to use stories as a primary mechanism for knowledge transfer. The oral-history tradition was the only method of knowledge transfer for many eons and persists into the current day despite the prevalence of the written word. First Nation elders in Canada passing on their wisdom to young people facing the conflicts of old and new, a Seanachie (the Irish word that means far more than storyteller) ensconced with an enraptured audience around a peat fire, the Liars bench of the Midwest in the USA where old timers sit to swap tall tales, and the ubiquitous watercooler conversations of the modern organisation: all evidence the persistence of story. The archetypal story form of the myths of the Greek gods and the trickster stories of Native Americans find modern expression and use in Dilbert cartoons, and the old fairy stories of Europe find new expression in Hollywood. Good teachers always tell stories to provide context and life to otherwise dull material. Anyone joining an organisation will take months or years to hear and reexpress the key stories of past success and failure that form a key part of the organisation's deep culture. Executives who abandon the tyranny of PowerPoint and instead tell a story rooted in their own experience nearly always discover the power of story to move people; to quote Steve Denning (2000), one of the early pioneers with his work in the World Bank—"Nothing else would do."

However, for a period at the end of the last century, business forgot about the value of stories; perhaps the form was too familiar or maybe too ambiguous for the process-driven focus on cost reduction and efficiency that dominated management thinking in the 1980s and '90s. Maybe with our newfound discovery and neo-fetishist use of technology, we simply lost the space that story had occupied in our lives: The television remote control that provides multiple choices and short attention spans simply muscled out the attention span necessary for a good story. However, story has persisted, and when J. K. Rowling had the courage to write a 766-page story of a boy wizard, children across the world queued up overnight and then sat down and read it from cover to cover within hours. The author's own 12-year-old son sat down with the full director's cut of *The Lord of the Rings* during Christmas 2004 and watched it from opening scene to closing scene with only brief interruptions for food and sleep.

Story is remarkably persistent and the narrative form surprisingly effective, if not efficient, in both communicating and storing knowledge. As such, it is not surprising that it was rediscovered rapidly by some knowledge management (KM) practitioners who had to deal with the postprocess reengineering need to manage uncodified and often unstructured human knowledge. Indeed, we have now reached the point where narrative may have outgrown knowledge management and become a management discipline in its own right.

WHAT IS NARRATIVE KNOWLEDGE?

Figure 1 is adapted from Boisot's (1998) I-Space, which looks at three aspects of knowledge-information flow, namely, abstraction, codification, and diffusion. At the bottom left-hand extreme of the model we have the uncodified and deeply concrete knowledge of the person who just knows: the Zen archer who is so in tune with his or her bow, the arrow, and the environment that he or she draws, shoots, and hits the target without opening his or her eyes; the modern equivalent is the London taxi driver whose two plus years of training involves driving the streets of London on a motor scooter until the patterns of navigation are so imprinted on the brain that a part of his or her hypothalamus is larger than that in other humans. The taxi driver, like the Zen archer, *just knows*. In contrast, at the top right we have the abstracted knowledge of the corporate database, or the novice reading the manual. The

Figure 1. The necessary ambiguity of narrative (adapted from Boisot's [1998] I-Space)

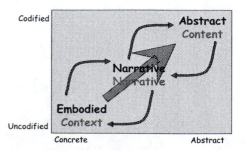

knowledge exists and has value, but the user lacks direct experience.

One key insight from I-Space is that the more abstracted and codified the knowledge, the easier it is for that knowledge to diffuse to a large population: It is independent of the knowledge holder. This fact was the driving force behind much early KM effort supported by the emphasis on tacit to explicit knowledge conversion that followed the widespread adoption of Nonaka and Takeuchi's (1995) SECI model. The goal of knowledge management was to render an organisation's knowledge into as abstract and codified a form as possible: the corporate database of best practices, a yellow-pages directory of skills, or a community of practice confined to the input capabilities of a QWERTY keyboard. The argument was that knowledge was not an organisational asset until it existed independently of the knowledge owner.

In a world separated into tacit and explicit knowledge, it is obviously undesirable for key knowledge to be solely tacit or concrete. The sharing of knowledge, enabling rapid diffusion, and the deployment of knowledge are sensible goals, and the conversion of tacit to explicit, or concrete to abstract, knowledge has thus driven knowledge management for the past eight years. However, early practice in knowledge management started to identify the weaknesses of this bipolar view. While much knowledge could and was codified, much failed to survive the translation. Rather like taking a message in one language and translating it into another using software, something was always lost in the process; just as translating the translated text back to the original language using the same software produces nonsense, so the conversion of codified knowledge back to its tacit or concrete form proved problematic. To use an example, very few of us learned to ride a bicycle by reading a manual and looking up a best-practice database on bicycle riding. For most of us, our parents held on to the saddle and ran behind us until one day they let go and we discovered we knew how to ride a bike: Theory came later if ever. The most basic rule of knowledge management is that we always know more than we can say, and we can always say more than we can write down. The process of going from head to mouth to hands involves a loss of content and to a greater extent, loss of context.

That rule also points to the role of narrative, which represents a halfway house between concrete and abstract knowledge. The way that the Zen archer teaches is to tell stories. In fact, any master will normally provide rights of observation to their practice, and multiple stories of failure and success together with some direct coaching and training. As the apprentice experiments, he or she in turn creates his or her own stories that stabilise into new knowledge. As aspects of a discipline's knowledge become universal, then the knowledge can be codified: The

book or the manual can be written. However, to translate that knowledge, it is not enough just to read the material. One must both hear the stories of others and create one's own stories if context is to be established and progress made. Narrative then sits between the two extremes of knowledge; it is experienced based and builds the context critical to knowledge creation and flow. As such, it has a necessary ambiguity of expression that allows translation into different contexts over time, wherein rests its resilience.

BACKGROUND

Most writers at some stage or other reference back to Aristotle's *Poetics* with its formulation of plot, character in the various forms of tragedy comedy, and so forth; the schools of rhetoric in the Greco-Roman tradition provided much of the formal method that informs modern practice. In the modern era, gathering stories and interpreting stories is a fundamental aspect of anthropology. Levi-Strauss used anthropology and linguistics to systematically analyze myth as a cultural artifact and a variety of academic disciplines, particularly in the postmodern tradition that emphasises the gathering and interpretation of narrative material. Boje (2001) and Gabriel (2000) are amongst the most frequently cited authors. There is also a strong artificial-intelligence tradition that seeks to use computing power to identify deep structures (following from Chomsky, 1975) in narrative. A common characteristic of what we can term the academic school is an emphasis on the expert analysis of naturally occurring stories to identify meaning and cultural signifiers.

The use of story in knowledge management can be traced to three early pioneers: Denning (2000) with the use of springboard stories in the World Bank, Ward (2000) in a variety of applications in Spark Knowledge, and Snowden (1997), then at IBM and now in the Cynefin Centre. Each represents a compatible but distinct approach to the use of story. Denning focuses on telling stories to convey a distinct message determined in advance and focused on a particular audience. Ward brings an academic tradition of interpretation and strong facilitation skills to gather meaning from people's stores. Snowden enters the field with a focus on narrative capture to enable more effective mapping of knowledge, but moves into narrative as a means of creating cultural indicators (utilising complexity science), creating narrative databases to store knowledge, and using metaphor and the social constructions of narrative and narrative interpretation.

The increasing acceptance of narrative produces a plethora of practitioners from the late 1990s mainly focused on the process of creating and telling stories. Some of these come from a vigorous background in film and others from journalism or the storytelling movement. The latter is significant with the Jonesborough Story Telling Festival (http://www.storytellingcenter.net) starting to talk actively about storytelling in organisations, not just storytelling as a folk art, by the turn of the century. We also see a strong strand of thought emerging from counseling and "soft" facilitation backgrounds, of which the most noticeable is appreciative enquiry, which focuses on redirecting stories to a positive focus. The latter approach is sometimes opposed by narrative practitioners (in particular, Snowden) who see the prevalence for negative storytelling in organisations as a key aspect of learning. A lot of narrative practice is frequently confused with neurolinguistic programming (NLP), which has a particular take on predictability in human systems that is not generally shared by narrative practitioners in the KM space, although it does have a quasicultist following in some areas.

By the turn of the century, the use of story, primarily storytelling, was widely accepted in knowledge management, and several of the mainstream KM authors and speakers (for example, Prusak and Seeley-Brown) started to reorientate their material to include aspects of storytelling building on the prior decade of academic and practitioner experimentation.

So in 2005, we see a series of distinct schools emerging in the field. Oliver and Snowden (2005), in a comprehensive review of academic and practitioner background, summarise the main divide as follows:

Since narrative enquiry moves people into the foreground it has appeal to art-Luddites and the techno-fabulists. The art-Luddites are individuals who believe in giving primacy to human creativity and interaction on a personal basis. They may reject mechanical metaphors in favour of organic approaches or humanist values. In particular, the art-Luddites see storytelling replacing mass forms of entertainment with personal accounts that potentially offer a spiritually enriching experience as well as new opportunities to communicate with others. In some cases, they also have a tendency to take on the worst aspects of counseling and psychological manipulation. The techno-fabulists are believers in technology who seek opportunities to improve efficiency in the mediation processes through advocating the benefits available when technology is removed from its shrink-wrap. Techno-fabulists may suggest the technology has economic benefits however its intrinsic features are championed.

At a simpler level, we may summarise the schools (with a main protagonist) as follows:

1. The academic school, building a long tradition of narrative use and interpretation, uses its expertise to interpret and represent the meaning of peoples' stories. This is best represented by the contrasting view of Gabriel (2000) and Boje (2001).

2. The "nothing else would do" school represented by Denning (2000), which focuses on purposeful stories, enhances naturally occurring material to create stories with specific business purpose.

3. The narrative patterning school (Snowden; http://www.cynefin.net), which places more emphasis on mass anecdote capture than story construction, and focuses heavily on removing an expert from the gathering or interpretation stage, prefers to focus on processes to enable the self-interpretation of material. This school is increasingly linked with the growing interest in complexity science and is focused on marketing as much as organisational change.

4. The "sideways" school, variously comprising traditional storytellers (Jonesborough Story Telling Festival; see previous comment), scriptwriters (McKee, 1999), journalists (many and various), and others, seek to take their existing skills sideways into industry and knowledge management in particular

5. The unscrupulous school (the only negative here), consisting of some otherwise respectable consultancy firms, realising there is a demand for story work, throws together a few recipes from existing books and materials and offers its capability to pliant clients

Generally, with the exception of the narrative patterning school, the focus is on storytelling and the power of stories.

KEY ISSUES

One of the important aspects of narrative and one of the reasons it works is that it creates a higher resonance of new concepts of ideas with existing patterns than exist in the human mind. Stories can provide context to interpret otherwise difficult data. They can, through metaphor and example, enable someone to see the application of an otherwise abstract concept. So, resonance is a key word in narrative.

Another key word is displacement; one of the traditional uses of the story form is to allow the confession of failure without the attribution of success. Archetypal story forms allow failure to be spread using stories about the archetypes. This is an old and new tradition: Both Dilbert cartoons and the Sufi stories of the Mullah Nasrudin provide this function. Urban myths enable the rapid dissemination of warnings.

There is also a series (and this is not complete) list of issues on the use of story in organisations. These include the following:

1. What is the relationship between the narrator and the collector of narration? To what extent does the collector influence and direct his or her subject? To see the power of this issue, look at a supposedly neutral oral history from, say, 50 years ago, and with modern eyes you will see the deep cultural bias of the collectors showing forth: The assumption is that the same happens today, but we are not aware of it.

2. What are the artifacts of narrative? Is it the narrator and his or her story, or can stories be abstracted and codified? Can enhanced stories on Web sites linked to corporate goals have the same effect as naturally occurring anecdotes loosely captured with abstracted indexes in a narrative database?

3. To what extent is the narrative form culturally determined and contextual? Are their universal aspects as Campbell and NLP would maintain?

4. Does truth and falsity matter in stories? Some practitioners argue the paradox of story: If you ask people to tell the truth, they will lie, and if you tell them to lie, they will tell the truth. For some, truth and falsity do not matter (unless a specific claim is made). However, for those focusing on best practice or formal illustration through a story of a corporate objective, not only actual truth but perceived truthfulness becomes critical.

5. What are the ethics of narrative work? Ethnographic study has long had rigid standards on narrative work that do not often see the light of day in organisational uses of story. Can there be a standard for the use of narrative? What is the boundary between legitimate uses of narrative and propaganda?

CONCLUSION

The first and most obvious conclusion is that story has arrived; it is an established discipline and as Figure 1 shows, it is a critical aspect of human-knowledge flow. The different schools all coexist with occasional context, but they have different purposes and are therefore probably all valuable (although the author has a particular dislike for NLP techniques). However, there is a strong danger of abuse, backlash, and faddism that is ever present in any new management technique. But story is particularly vulnerable as it appeals to many aspects of society, not least to the art-Luddites and technofabulists.

It is worth going back to Aristotle (McKeon, 1973), who saw three types of rhetorical proof.

1. **Logos:** The use of language to create a coherent argument
2. **Pathos:** consisting of emotional appeal
3. **Ethos:** representing the character and believability of the storyteller

He also separates the forensic (what was) from the deliberative (what should be) and epideictic (elegance or beauty) as three types of rhetoric.

In a corporate world that is dominated by logos and forensic rhetoric, story steps back in to correct the balance. Character, emotion, and beauty need to be a part of out corporate rhetoric, and the narrative movement is opening up that possibility.

REFERENCES

Boisot, M. H. (1998). *Knowledge assets: Securing competitive advantage in the information economy.* Oxford: Oxford University Press.

Boje, D. (2001). *Narrative methods for organizational & communication research.* Thousand Oaks, CA: Sage Publications.

Campbell, J. (1949). *The hero with a thousand faces.* Princeton, NJ: Princeton University Press.

Chomsky, N. (1972). *Language and the mind.* New York: Hardcourt Brace Jovanovich.

Chomsky, N. (1975). *The Logical structure of linguistic theory.* Chicago: University of Chicago Press.

Denning, S. (2000). *The springboard.* Butterworth Heinemann.

Gabriel, Y. (2000). *Story telling in organisations: Facts, fictions, and fantasies.* Oxford: Oxford University Press.

http://en.wikipedia.org

McKee, R. (2003). Storytelling that moves people: A conversation with screen writing coach Robert McKee. *Harvard Business Review,* June, 51-55.

McKeon, R. (1973). *Introduction to Aristotle.* Chicago: University of Chicago Press.

Nonaka, I., & Takeuchi, H. (1995). *The knowledge-creating company.* London: Oxford University Press.

Oliver, G., & Snowden, D. J. (2005). Patterns of narrative in organisations: Refolding the envelope of art-Luddism and techno-fabulism in Schreyögg. In G. Schreyögg & J. Koch (Eds.), *Narratives and knowledge management: Exploring the links between organizational storytelling and knowledge management.* Berlin, Germany: Erich Schmidt.

Snowden, D. J. (1999). Story telling: An old skill in a new context. *Business Information Review, 16*(1), 30-37.

Snowden, D. J. (2004). Narrative patterns: The perils and possibilities of using story in organistions. In Eric Lesser and Laurence Prusak (Eds). *Creating value with knowledge.* Oxford: Oxford University Press.

KEY TERMS

This is a difficult area as there is not yet, and probably will never be, any agreed use of language in this field. For example, the words narrative and story are often used interchangeably. The following is thus advisory rather than mandatory.

Anecdote: A naturally occurring story or the recounting of an experience in conversation or when prompted. Anecdotes are in effect a response to some form of stimulus and recount real or imagined experience.

Antistory: A specialized form of anecdote that occurs naturally in organisations as a counter to some official message. Generally, it is opposite in value and, if negative, is often cynical in a form such as, "Well, they would say that wouldn't they," or variants. Often involving black humour and challenge, these are the natural responses to authority that is not present when they are told. They can be a safety valve—a certain amount of negative storytelling is a sign of learning—but if taken to excess, can drag an organisation down.

Archetype: A naturally occurring constituent and output of a story tradition in which characters emerge from a body of anecdotes and stories that over time become more extreme until each archetype represents one aspects of that society. In a true archetype, all members of a community would recognise some aspect of themselves in each archetype. Archetypes are often associated with the work of Jung and Campbell who, in different contexts, argue for the existence of universal archetypes. This is not the only interpretation; many authors (including this one) argue from experience that archetypes across cultures may appear similar, but are in fact very different. For example, the trickster archetype of Norse legend is Loki, whose primary purpose if any seems at times destructive, whereas in many Native American stories the trickster is the coyote, whose function is to teach and advance humans to greater understanding.

Myth: There are many different definitions of the word, some with pejorative overtones. However, all organisations create myths and mythology, an underpinning, common set of stories or story types that can be used to interpret and understand the culture of that organisation and are used to induct new members. To quote Wikipedia, "A myth is often thought to be a lesson in story form which has deep explanatory or symbolic resonance for preliterate cultures, who preserve and cherish the wisdom of their elders through oral traditions by the use of skilled story tellers." This is a good summary, but a myth is as much a part of the modern organisation as it was of "preliterate cultures." Creation myths (accounts of how the world came to be) and trickster myths (culturally specific stories of human ingenuity) are omnipresent in all story traditions and also persist in the modern organisation. They are particularly revealing once gathered and interpreted.

Script: Where all the stories in an organisation follow a certain form with common messages, this indicates that the members of that organisation are in effect reading a script. A certain type of story is the only legitimate one, and anyone telling stories that contradict the script will be eliminated. Expert communities are prone to rejecting new or novel stories that do not confirm with the establishment.

Stereotype: This is used in contrast to an archetype in that a stereotype is a way of labeling someone or something and may be positive or negative. Stereotypes are frequently stock characters or are clichéd and lack depth or sympathy. Racial and culture stereotypes are common and nearly always negative. In organisational work, stereotypes often occur in respect to employees, bosses, competition, and/or the customer.

Story: Generally a collection of anecdotes, but sometimes a single one that has been refined and purposefully constructed to make a point, communicate an idea or value, or share key knowledge. Anecdotes occur, but stories are designed.

Urban Myths: A specialized type of story, often starting with "This happened to a friend of a friend…," or "I don't know if it's true, but..." Urban myths appear to occupy a special place in learning in that while nearly always fictional, they carry some form of lesson that is considered essential to the society that gives them life. In organisational uses of narrative, searching for an interpreting urban myth is one way to reveal deep-seated concerns, attitudes, and beliefs.

Object–Process Methodology

Dov Dori

Technion, Israel Institute of Technology, Israel and Massachusetts Institute of Technology, USA

INTRODUCTION

Capturing the knowledge about existing systems and analysis and design of conceived systems requires an adequate methodology, which should be both formal and intuitive. Formality is required to maintain a coherent representation of the system under study, while the requirement that the methodology be intuitive stems from the fact that humans are the ultimate consumers of the knowledge. Object-Process Methodology (OPM) is a vehicle for knowledge representation and management that perfectly meets the formality and intuition requirements through a unique combination of graphics and natural language.

Function, structure, and behavior are the three main aspects that systems exhibit. Function is the top-level utility that the system provides its beneficiaries who use it or are affected by it, either directly or indirectly. The system's function is enabled by its architecture—the combination of structure and behavior. The system's architecture is what enables it to function so as to benefit its users.

Most interesting, useful, and challenging systems are those in which structure and behavior are highly intertwined and hard to separate. For example, in a manufacturing system, the manufacturing process cannot be contemplated in isolation from its inputs—raw materials, model, machines, and operators—and its outputs—the resulting product. The inputs and the output are objects, some of which are transformed by the manufacturing process, while others just enable it.

Modeling of complex systems should conveniently combine structure and behavior in a single model. Motivated by this observation, OPM (Dori, 1995, 2002) is a comprehensive, holistic approach to modeling, study, development, engineering, evolution, and lifecycle support of systems. Employing a combination of graphics and a subset of English, the OPM paradigm integrates the object-oriented, process-oriented, and state transition approaches into a single frame of reference. Structure and behavior coexist in the same OPM model without highlighting one at the expense of suppressing the other to enhance the comprehension of the system as a whole.

Rather than requiring that the modeler views each of the system's aspects in isolation and struggle to mentally integrate the various views, OPM offers an approach that is orthogonal to customary practices. According to this approach, various system aspects can be inspected in tandem for better comprehension. Complexity is managed via the ability to create and navigate across possibly multiple detail levels, which are generated and traversed through by several abstraction/refinement mechanisms.

Due to its structure-behavior integration, OPM provides a solid basis for representing and managing knowledge about complex systems, regardless of their domain. This chapter provides an overview of OPM, its ontology, semantics, and symbols. It then describes applications of OPM in various domains.

THE OPM ONTOLOGY

The elements of the OPM ontology, shown in Figure 1, are divided into three groups: entities, structural relations, and procedural links.

Entities

Entities, the basic building blocks of any system modeled in OPM, are of three types: stateful objects, namely *objects* with *states*, and *processes*. As defined below, processes transform objects by (1) creating them, (2) destroying them, or (3) changing their state. The symbols for these three entities are respectively shown as the first group of symbols at the left-hand side of Figure 1, which are the symbols in the toolset available as part of the GUI of OPCAT 2 (Dori, Reinhartz-Berger et al., 2003).

Figure 1. The three groups of OPM symbols in the toolset of OPCAT 2

entities   structural relations   procedural links

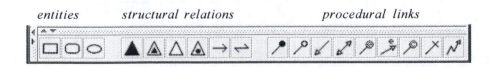

OPM Things: Objects and Processes

Objects are (physical or informatical) things that exist, while *processes* are things that transform (create, destroy, or change the state of) objects. Following is a set of basic definitions that build upon each other.

An object is a thing that exists.

Objects are the things that are being transformed in the system.

Transformation is generation (creation) or consumption (destruction) of an object, or a change of its state.

Processes are the things that transform objects in the system.

A process is a thing that represents a pattern of object transformation.

Table 1 shows the OPM things and their basic attributes. The third column on Table 1 contains a description of each thing or attribute and below it the syntax of the corresponding sentence in Object-Process Language (OPL)—a subset of English that reflects the graphical representation. In OPL, bold Arial font denotes non-reserved phrases, while non-bold Arial font denotes reserved phrases. In OPCAT, various OPM elements are colored with the same color as their graphic counterparts

(by default, objects are green, processes are blue, and states are brown).

Objects and processes are collectively called *things*.

The first two lines of Table 1 show the symbol and a description of the two types of OPM things. The next two lines show two basic attributes that things can have: essence and affiliation.

Essence is an attribute that determines whether the thing is physical or informational.

The default essence is informational. A thing whose essence is physical is symbolized by a shaded shape.

Affiliation is an attribute that determines whether the thing is environmental (external to the system) or systemic.

The default affiliation is systemic. A thing whose affiliation is environmental is symbolized by a dashed contour.

OPM States

Objects can be stateful, that is, they may have one or more states.

A state is a situation at which an object can exist at certain points during its lifetime or a value it can assume.

Table 1. Things of the OPM ontology and their basic attributes

Thing / Attribute	Symbol	Description / OPL sentence
Object	Object Name	A thing (entity) that has the potential of stable, unconditional physical or mental existence.
		Object Name is an object.
Process	Processing	A thing representing a pattern of transformation that objects undergo.
		Processing is a process.
Essence	Object / Processing	An attribute that determines whether the thing (object or process) is physical (shaded) or informational.
		Processing is physical.
Affiliation	Object / Processing	An attribute that determines whether the thing is environmental (external to the system, dashed contour) or systemic.
		Processing is environmental.

Table 2. States and values

	Symbol	Description / OPL sentence
Stateful object with two states	**Website** [reachable] [unreachable]	A situation at which an object can exist. **Web site** can be **reachable** or **unreachable.**
Value	**Temperature** [15]	A value that an object can assume. **Temperature** is **15.**
Stateful object with three states: initial, default, and final	**Car** [new] → [used] [junk]	A state can be initial, default, or final. **Car** can be **new**, which is **initial, used**, which is **default**, or **junk**, which is **final.**

Stateful objects can be affected, that is, their states can change.

Effect is a change in the state of an object.

OPM STRUCTURE MODELING

Structural relations express static, time-independent relations between pairs of entities, most often between two objects. Structural relations, shown as the middle group of six symbols in Figure 1, are of two types: fundamental and tagged.

The Four Fundamental Structural Relations

Fundamental structural relations are a set of four structural relations that are used frequently to denote relations between things in the system. Due to their prevalence and usefulness, and in order to prevent too much text from cluttering the diagram, these relations are designated by the four distinct triangular symbols shown in Figure 1.

The four fundamental structural relations are:

1. **Aggregation-participation:** A solid triangle, ▲, which denotes the relation between a whole thing and its parts

Table 3. The fundamental structural relation names, OPD symbols, and OPL sentences

Structural Relation Name		Root Refineables	OPD with 3 refineables	OPL Sentences with 1, 2, and 3 refineables
Forward	Backward			
Aggregation	Participation	Whole Parts		A consists of **B.** A consists of **B** and **C.** A consists of **B, C,** and **D.**
Exhibition	Characterization	Exhibitor Features		A exhibits **B.** A exhibits **B** and **C.** A exhibits **B, C,** and **D.**
Generalization	Specialization	General Specializations		**B** is an **A.** **B** and **C** are **As.** **B, C,** and **D** are **As.**
Classification	Instantiation	Class Instances		**B** is an instance of **A.** **B** and **C** are instances of **A.** **B, C,** and **D** are instances of **A.**

2. **Generalization-specialization:** A blank triangle, △, which denotes the relation between a general thing and its specializations, giving rise to inheritance;

3. **Exhibition-characterization:** A solid inside blank triangle, ▲, which denotes the relation between an exhibitor—a thing exhibiting one or more features (attributes and/or operations)—and the things that characterize the exhibitor; and

4. **Classification-instantiation:** A solid circle inside a blank triangle, ▲, which denotes the relation between a class of things and an instance of that class.

Table 3 lists the four fundamental structural relations and their respective OPDs and OPL sentences. The name of each such relation consists of a pair of dash-separated words. The first word is the forward relation name, i.e., the name of the relation as seen from the viewpoint of the thing up in the hierarchy. The second word is the backward (or reverse) relation name, i.e., the name of the relation as seen from the viewpoint of the thing down in the hierarchy of that relation.

Each fundamental structural relation has a default, preferred direction, which was determined by how natural the sentence sounds. In Table 3, the preferred shorthand name for each relation is underlined. As Table 3 shows, each one of the four fundamental structural relations is characterized by the hierarchy it induces between the *root*—the thing attached to the tip of the triangle, and the *leaves*—the thing(s) attached to the base of the triangle, as follows.

1. In aggregation-participation, the tip of the solid triangle, ▲, is attached to the whole thing, while the base is attached to the parts.

2. In generalization-specialization, the tip of the blank triangle, △, is attached to the general thing, while the base is attached to the specializations.

3. In exhibition-characterization, the tip of the solid inside blank triangle, ▲, is attached to the exhibitor (the thing which exhibits the features), while the base is attached to the features (attributes and operations).

4. In classification-instantiation, the tip of the solid circle inside a blank triangle, ▲, is attached to the thing class, while the base is attached to the thing instances.

The things which are the leaves of the hierarchy tree, namely the parts, features, specializations, and instances, are collectively referred to as *refineables*, since they refine the ancestor, the root of the tree.

Refineable is a generalization of part, feature, specialization, and instance.

Figure 2. OPD of the sentence "RDF statement consists of subject, predicate, and object"

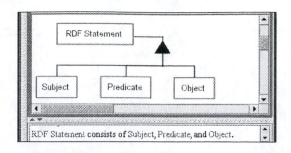

The third column in Table 3 lists for each fundamental structural relation the name of the root (whole, exhibitor, general, class) and the corresponding refineables (parts, features, specializations, and instances). The next column contains an OPD with three refineables, while the rightmost column lists the syntax of three OPL sentences for each fundamental structural relation, with one, two, and three refineables, respectively.

Having presented the common features of the four fundamental structural relations, in the next four subsections we provide a small example for each one of them separately.

Aggregation-Participation

Aggregation-participation denotes the relation between a whole and it comprising parts or components. Consider, for example, the excerpt taken from Section 2.2 of the RDF Primer (Manola & Miller, 2003):

…each statement consists of a subject, a predicate, and an object.

This is a clear case of whole-part, or aggregation-participation relation. The OPM model of this statement, which consists of both the OPD and the corresponding OPL, is shown in Figure 2. Note that the OPL sentence, "RDF Statement consists of Subject, Predicate, and Object," which was generated by OPCAT automatically from the graphic input, is almost identical to the one cited from the RDF Primer. The same OPD exactly (disregarding the graphical layout) can be produced by inputting the text of the OPL sentence above. This is a manifestation of the OPM graphics-text equivalence principle.

Generalization-Specialization

Generalization-specialization is a fundamental structural relationship between a general thing and one or more of its specializations. Continuing our example from the RDF

Figure 3. The OPD obtained by inputting into OPCAT the OPL sentence "RDF is a Language"

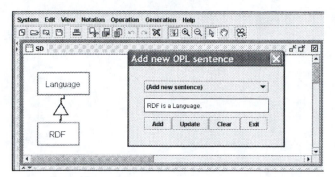

Figure 5. The OPM model of XMLLiteral, an instance of a Datatype of RDF

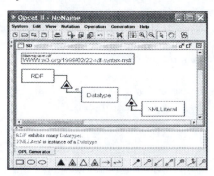

Primer (Manola & Miller 2003), consider the very first sentence from the abstract:

The Resource Description Framework RDF is a Language for representing information about resources in the World Wide Web.

Let us take the main message of this sentence, which is that *RDF is a language*. This is exactly in line with the OPL syntax, so we can input the OPL sentence "RDF is a Language" into OPCAT and see what we get.

The result, without any diagram editing, is shown in Figure 3, along with the conversation window titled "Add new OPL sentence," in which this sentence was typed prior to the OPD creation.

Exhibition-Characterization

Continuing to scan the RDF Primer (Manola & Miller 2003), in Section 2.2.1 we find the sentence:

RDF has a simple data model.

Figure 4. The OPD representing the sentence "RDF has a simple data model"

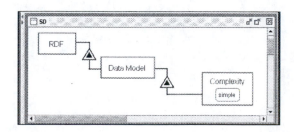

To model this statement, we need to rephrase this sentence into the following three sentences:

1. RDF is characterized by a data model.
2. The data model of RDF is characterized by a complexity attribute.
3. The value of this complexity attribute is "simple."

These three sentences are further rephrased to conform to the OPL syntax as follows:

1. RDF exhibits Data Model.
2. Data Model exhibits Complexity.
3. Complexity is simple.

Classification-Instantiation

Reading through the RDF Primer, we find:

Datatypes are used by RDF in the representation of values, such as integers, floating point numbers, and dates.

...

RDF predefines just one datatype, <u>rdf:XMLLiteral</u>, used for embedding XML in RDF.

An OPL interpretation of these two sentences, respectively, is:

1. **RDF** exhibits many **Datatypes**.
2. **XMLLiteral** is an instance of **Datatype**.

Figure 5 is the OPM model of **XMLLiteral**, an instance of a **Datatype** of **RDF**.

OPM BEHAVIOR MODELING

Procedural links connect entities (objects, processes, and states) to express dynamic, time-dependent behavior of the system. Behavior, the dynamic aspect of a system, can be manifested in OPM in three ways:

1. A process can *transform* (generate, consume, or change the state of) objects
2. An object can *enable* a process without being transformed by it
3. An object or a process can *trigger* an event that might, in turn, invoke a process if some conditions are met

Accordingly, a procedural link can be a transformation link, an enabling link, or an event link.

In order to be able to talk about object transformation, we need to first define state and demonstrate how states are used.

Object States

In Figure 6 we added to the object **Check** two states: the initial state **uncashed** and the final state **cashed**. This causes the addition of the following OPL sentence to the OPL paragraph:

Check can be **uncashed**, which is initial, or **cashed**, which is final.

Table 4 shows the OPD and OPL syntax for objects with one, two, and three or more states, and optional time designator attributes: initial, final, and default.

Transformation Links

A *transformation link* expresses how a process transforms one or more objects. The transformation of an object can be its consumption, generation, or state change. The transforming process is the *transformer,* while the object being transformed is called *transformee.*

Figure 6. Adding states to Check

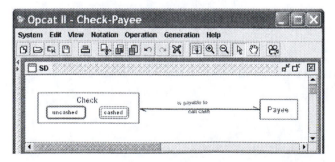

Figure 7. The **Cashing** *process changes the state of* **Check** *from* **uncashed** *to* **cashed**

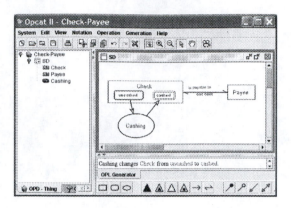

Input and Output Links

Having added the states to the object **Check** , we can now show how the process **Cashing** affects **Check** by changing its state. In Figure 7, **Cashing** was added and linked to the two states of **Check**: an input link leads from the initial **uncashed** state to **Cashing**, while an output link leads from **Cashing** to the final state cashed.

The OPL sentence generated automatically by OPCAT as a result of adding these input and output links is:

Cashing changes **Check** from uncased to **cashed**.

Effect Link

Sometimes we may not be interested in specifying the states of an object, but still show that a process does

Figure 8. Suppressing the input and output states of **Check** *causes the two link edges to migrate to the contour of* **Check** *and coincide, yielding the single bidirectional effect link between* **Check** *and* **Cashing**

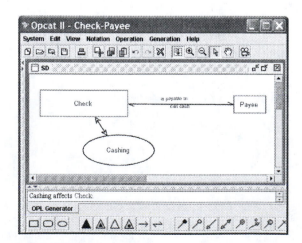

Table 4. OPD and OPL syntax for objects with one, two, and three or more states, and optional time designator attributes

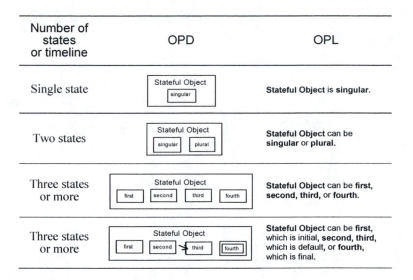

Number of states or timeline	OPD	OPL
Single state	Stateful Object — singular	**Stateful Object** is **singular**.
Two states	Stateful Object — singular | plural	**Stateful Object** can be **singular** or **plural**.
Three states or more	Stateful Object — first | second | third | fourth	**Stateful Object** can be **first**, **second**, **third**, or **fourth**.
Three states or more	Stateful Object — first | second → third | fourth	**Stateful Object** can be **first**, which is initial, **second**, **third**, which is default, or **fourth**, which is final.

affect an object by changing its state from some unspecified input state to another unspecified output state. To express this, we suppress (hide) the input and output states of the object, so the edges of the input and output links "migrate" to the contour of the object and coincide, yielding the effect link shown in Figure 8.

The OPL sentence that represents this graphic construct is:

Cashing affects **Check**.

Result and Consumption Links

We have seen that one type of object transformation is effect, in which a process changes the state of an object

from some input state to another output state. When these two states are expressed (i.e., explicitly shown), then we can use the pair of input and output links to specify the source and destination states of the transformation. When the states are suppressed, we express the state change by the effect link, a more general and less informative transformation link.

State change is the least drastic transformation that an object can undergo. Two more extreme transformations are generation and consumption, denoted respectively by the result and consumption links.

Generation is a transformation that causes an object, which had not existed prior to the process execution, to become existent. For example, **Check** is born as a result of a **Check Making** process.

*Figure 9. The object **Check** is generated as a result of executing the **Check Making** process.*

*Figure 10. The object **Check** is consumed as a result of executing the **Destroying** process.*

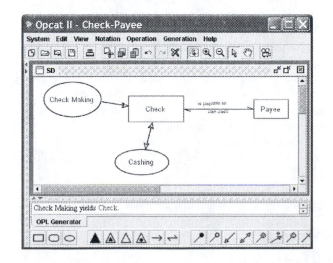

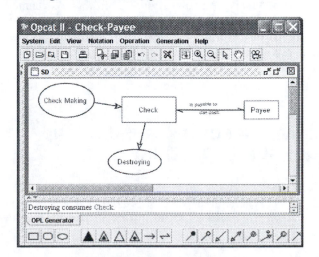

Figure 11. The object **Check** *is generated in its* **unendorsed** *state as a result of executing the* **Check Making** *process*

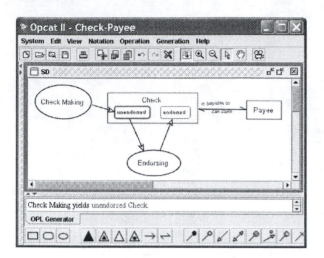

Figure 12. The object **Check** *is consumed in its* **cashed** *state as a result of executing the* **Destroying** *process*

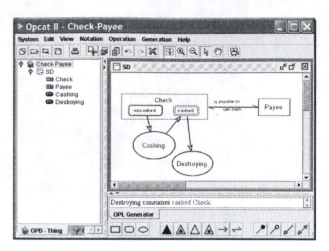

As Figure 9 shows, the object **Check** is generated as a result of executing the process **Check Making**. The result link is the arrow originating from the generating process and leading to the generated object. The OPL sentence that represents this graphic construct (shown also in Figure 9) is:

Check Making yields **Check**.

In contrast to generation, consumption is a transformation which causes an object, which had existed prior to the process execution, to become non-existent. For example, **Check** is consumed as a result of a **Destroying** process.

As Figure 10 shows, the object **Check** is consumed as a result of executing the process **Destroying**. The consumption link is the arrow originating from the consumed object and leading to the consuming process. The OPL sentence that represents this graphic construct (shown also in Figure 10) is:

Destroying consumes **Check**.

STATE-SPECIFIED RESULT AND CONSUMPTION LINKS

We sometimes wish to be specific and state not only that an object is generated by a process, but also at what state that object is generated. Some other times, we might wish

to be able to state not only that an object is consumed by a process, but also at what state that object has to be in order for it to be consumed by the process. As Figure 9 shows, the object **Check** is generated in its unendorsed state as a result of executing the process **Check Making**.

The OPL sentence that represents this state-specified result link graphic construct (shown also in Figure 11) is:

Check Making yields unendorsed **Check**.

In comparison, the "regular," non-state-specified result link is the same, except that the (initial) state is not specified:

Check Making yields **Check**.

The difference is the addition of the state name (unendorsed in our case) before the name of the object (**Check**) that owns that state.

Analogously, a state-specified consumption link leads from a (final) state to the consuming process. For example, assuming a check can only be destroyed if it is cashed, Figure 12 shows the state-specified consumption link leading from the final state cashed of **Check** to the consuming process **Destroying**.

The OPL sentence that represents this state-specified consumption link graphic construct (shown also in Figure 12) is:

Destroying consumes cashed **Check**.

Table 5. Summary of the procedural links between a process and an object or its state

Transformation Link Type	Source Entity	Destination Entity	OPD	OPL
Input link	Input state	Affecting process		**Affecting Process** changes **Object** from **input state** to **output state**.
Output link	Affecting process	Output state		
Consumption link	Consumed object	Consuming process		**Consuming Process** consumes **Consumed Object**.
Result link	Generating process	Resulting object		**Generating Process** yields **Generated Object**.
State-specified Consumption link	Final state of the consumed object	Consuming process		**Consuming Process** consumes **terminal Consumed Object**.
State-specified Result link	Generating process	Initial state of the resulting object		**Generating Process** yields **initial Generated Object**.

Summary of Procedural Links Between Processes and Objects

Table 5 provides a summary of the six procedural links between a process and a (possibly stateful) object. They are divided into three pairs: input and output links, which always come as a pair; consumption and result links; and state-specified consumption and result links.

Enablers and Enabling Links

An *enabler* is an object that is required for a process to happen, but is not transformed by the process. An *enabling link* expresses the need for a (possibly state-specified) object to be present in order for the enabled process to occur. The enabled process does not transform the enabling object. Enablers are divided into instruments and conditioners, each of which can be stateless or stateful.

APPLICATIONS OF OPM AND SUMMARY

OPM has been applied in many domains, including education (Dori & Dori, 1996), computer integrated manufac-

turing (Dori, 1996a; Dori, Gal, & Etzion, 1996), the R&D universe and its feedback cycles (Myersdorf & Dori, 1997), real-time systems (Peleg & Dori, 2000), banking (Dori, 2001), requirements engineering (Soffer, Golany, Dori, & Wand, 2001), Web applications development (Reinhartz-Berger, Dori, & Katz, 2002a), ERP modeling (Soffer, Golany, & Dori, 2003), axiomatic design (Soderborg, Crawley, & Dori, 2002), computational synthesis (Dori & Crawley, 2003), software reuse (Reinhartz-Berger, Dori, & Katz, 2002b), systems architecture (Soderborg, Crawley, & Dori, 2003), and Web Service Composition (Yin, Wenyin, & Chan. 2004).

This article has presented an overview of Object-Process Methodology and its applications in a variety of domains. There are a number of important OPM-related issues that could not be discussed in detail in this article due to space limitations. One such topic is complexity management. Complexity is managed in OPM via in-zooming, unfolding, and state-expression, which provide for looking at any complex system at any desired level of granularity without losing the context and the "big picture." Another issue is the systems development and evolution methodology with OPM, for which a comprehensive reflective metamodel (which uses OPM) has been developed. These issues and others are treated in detail in the book, *Object-Process Methodology: A Holistic Systems Paradigm* (Dori, 2002).

The domain-independent nature of OPM makes it suitable as a general, comprehensive, and multidisciplinary framework for knowledge representation and reasoning that emerge from conceptual modeling, analysis, design, implementation, and lifecycle management. The ability of OPM to provide comprehensive lifecycle support for systems of all kinds and complexity levels is due to its foundational ontology that builds on a most minimal set of stateful objects and processes that transform them. Another significant uniqueness of OPM is its unification of system knowledge from both the structural and behavioral aspects in a single diagram—OPD. It is hard to think of a significant domain of discourse and a system in it, in which structure and behavior are not interdependent and intertwined. A third unique feature of OPM is its dual knowledge representation in graphics and text, and the capability to automatically switch between these two modalities. Due to its single model, expressed in both graphics and text, OPM lends itself naturally for representing and managing knowledge, as it is uniquely poised to cater to the tight interconnections between structure and behavior that are so hard to separate.

OPM and its supporting tool OPCAT continue to evolve. The site www.ObjectProcess.org is a rich, continuously updated resource of OPM-related articles, free software downloads, and more.

REFERENCES

Dori, D. (1994). Automated understanding of engineering drawings: An object-oriented analysis. *Journal of Object-Oriented Programming,* (September), 35-43.

Dori, D. (1995). Object-process analysis: Maintaining the balance between system structure and behavior. *Journal of Logic and Computation, 5*(2), 227-249.

Dori, D. (1996A). Object-process analysis of computer integrated manufacturing documentation and inspection. *International Journal of Computer Integrated Manufacturing, 9*(5), 39-353.

Dori, D. (2001). Object-process Methodology applied to modeling credit card transactions. *Journal of Database Management, 12*(1), 2-12.

Dori, D. (2002). *Object-process methodology: A holistic systems paradigm.* Berlin, Heidelberg, New York: Springer Verlag.

Dori, D., & Crawley, E. (2003). Towards a common computational synthesis framework with Object-Process Methodology. *Proceedings of the 2003 AAAI Spring Symposium Series: Computational Synthesis: From Basic Building Blocks to High Level Functionality,* Stanford University, USA. Technical Report SS-03-02.

Dori, D., Gal, A., & Etzion, O. (1996). A temporal database with data dependencies: A key to computer integrated manufacturing. *International Journal of Computer Integrated Manufacturing, 9*(2), 89-104.

Dori, D., & Dori, Y.J. (1996). Object-process analysis of a hypertext organic chemistry module. *Journal of Computers in Mathematics and Science Teaching, 15*(1/2), 65-84.

Myersdorf, D., & Dori, D. (1997). The R&D universe and its feedback cycles: An object-process analysis. *R&D Management, 27*(4), 333-344.

Peleg, M., & Dori, D. (2000). The model multiplicity problem: Experimenting with real-time specification methods. *IEEE Transaction on Software Engineering, 26*(8), 742-759.

Reinhartz-Berger, I., Dori, D., & Katz, S. (2002a). OPM/Web: Object-process methodology for developing Web applications. *Annals of Software Engineering, 13,* 141-161.

Reinhartz-Berger, I., Dori, D., & Katz, S. (2002b). Open reuse of component designs in OPM/Web. *Proceedings of the IEEE 26th Annual International Computer Software and Applications Conference* (pp. 19-26).

Soderborg, N., Crawley E., & Dori D. (2002). System definition for axiomatic design aided by Object-Process Methodology. *Proceedings of the 2nd International Conference on Axiomatic Design* (pp. 134-140), Cambridge, MA.

Soderborg, N., Crawley E., & Dori D. (2003). OPM-based system function and architecture: Definitions and operational templates. *Communications of the ACM, 46*(10), 67-72.

Soffer, P., Golany, B., & Dori, D. (2003). ERP modeling: A comprehensive approach. *Information Systems, 28*(6), 673-690.

Soffer, P., Golany, B., Dori, D., & Wand Y. (2001). Modeling off-the-shelf information systems requirements: An ontological approach. *Requirements Engineering, 6,* 183-199.

Wenyin, L., & Dori, D. (1998). A generic integrated line detection algorithm and its object-process specification. *Computer Vision: Image Understanding (CVIU), 70*(3), 420-437.

Wenyin, L., & Dori, D. (1998A). Genericity in graphics recognition algorithms. In K. Tombre & A.K. Chhabra

(Eds.), Graphics recognition: algorithms and systems. *Lecture Notes in Computer Science, 1389,* 9-18.

Wenyin, L., & Dori, D. (1999). Object-process based graphics recognition class library: Principles and applications. *Software: Practice and Experience, 29*(15), 1355-1378.

Yin, L., Wenyin, L., & Changjun, J. (2004). Object-process diagrams as explicit graphic tool for Web service composition. *Journal of Integrated Design & Process Science: Transactions of the SDPS, 8*(1), 113-127.

KEY TERMS

Effect: A change in the state of an object.

Object: A thing that exists.

Procedural Link: A link between an object and a process expressing the behavior of the system.

Process: A thing that represents a pattern of object transformation.

Refineable: A generalization of part, feature, specialization, and instance.

State: A situation at which an object can exist at certain points during its lifetime or a value it can assume.

Structural Link: A link between two objects expressing the structure of the system.

Transformation: Generation (creation) or consumption (destruction) of an object, or a change of its state.

Ontology

William Buchholz
Bentley College, USA

INTRODUCTION

An ontology comprises the explicitly articulated and shared concepts of a knowledge community or domain. These concepts are arranged formally in a taxonomy and are governed by specifically defined rules and axioms. Ontologies often play an important role in *knowledge management information technology* (KMIT). An enterprise knowledge management IT system, for example, may use an ontology "to facilitate communication, search, storage, and [knowledge] representation" (O'Leary, 1998, p. 58). A general survey of the literature suggests that ontologies are capable of improving performance in a large variety of knowledge management IT functions, especially relative to knowledgebases for best practices, lessons learned, human resource skills, Help Desks, FAQs, document collections, standards and regulations, products, services, proposals, and the like. In addition, as we look to the future, ontologies will function centrally in agent-mediated knowledge management (AMKM), distributed knowledge management (DKM), and the Semantic Web (Daconta, Obrst, & Smith, 2003; Fensel, 2001; Heflin, Volz, & Dale, 2002; McGuiness, 2002), as these technologies become pervasive in a global economy that distributes KM knowledgebases across companies and cultures.

The term *ontology* is rarely used in knowledge management circles. In fact, after researching "the KM literature both in print and online" and visiting KM Europe for "two consecutive years," Mika and Akkermans (2004) only "found prototypes of ontology-based KM applications in the ontology literature, [and] very few of the KM sources even mentioned the use of ontologies." When ontologies were mentioned, they were termed "future KM technologies." In the opinion of Mika and Akkermans, "The relation between KM and technology is only superficially developed in the business-oriented side of KM" (p. 6). Holsapple and Joshi (2004) are in the process of remedying this situation by developing a high-level, general knowledge management ontology that "provides a unifying view of KM phenomena" that will help researchers, educators, and practitioners (p. 593) "to characterize KM technologies,…structure KM case studies, and…develop a KM model for competitive analysis" (p. 594). To provide a deeper understanding of just such an ontology, and to offer a general sense of the ontological aspect of IT in KM, this article defines the history, purpose, scope, and function of the term *ontology*.

Ontology has its origins in philosophy, and to this day informs a vital approach to philosophical inquiry. Philosophical ontology deals with metaphysical aspects of the nature of existence, touching upon the various meanings, relationships, and instances of the abstract, the concrete, the general, and the specific. It could be said that historically much of philosophy has been devoted to constructing a high-level ontology, an abstract model of reality, its primary constituents, their essential/accidental characteristics, and the various relationships that pertain among them.

Ontological philosophers often examine existence by delineating its parts categorically in accordance with an explicit theory. Aristotle's categories, syllogisms, definitions, and axioms, for example, form the basis of identifying, classifying, and theorizing about existence in just this way. So too have modern philosophers such as Kant, Peirce, Husserl, Whitehead, and Heidegger (Sowa, 2000, pp. 56-77) attempted to understand reality through categorization and logic. Much of their philosophical groundwork, in fact, forms the basis of *ontology* as it is presently understood in practical applications for computerized systems of information. Additionally, the mathematician and logician Stanislaw Lesniewski supplied a key component of the computerized sense of *ontology* when he used "an artificial formal language to represent his formal theory of parts (mereology)." He thereby "inaugurated philosophy's use of artificial languages and formal logic in expressing ontologies" (Mayhew & Siebert, 2004, pp. 1-2). Thus, the philosophical sense of the word *ontology*, with its long and rich history, forms much of the theoretical and logical base of the computer sense of the word. The relatively modern use of *ontology*, as applied to computerized information systems, appears first in 1967 in G.H. Mealy's "Another Look at Data," a paper dealing with "the foundations of data modeling" (Smith, 2004, p. 22).

Today's computerized ontologies attempt to capture some aspect of the explicit knowledge of a specific domain, such as medicine, accounting, finance, or engineering. With this knowledge, the ontology helps a computer agent or program function in some practical way to operationalize the key concepts made explicit and constrained by highly specified rules. An agent operating on the Semantic Web, for example, could theoretically consult various ontologies distributed on the Web to gather the meaning of key terms, assertions, processes, and actions that would allow the agent to shop for your dinner, buy your favorite wine, get the best price available for both, make sure that everything is delivered at a specified time, charge your credit card, and have your garage door open when you arrive home for dinner. Only an agent with a brain could perform all these activities. But computerized agents do not have brains. They have ontologies—ontologies to consult in carrying out your instructions for dinner. Computers cannot understand as humans do; but ontologies help to create the illusion that they can.

Within the last 40 years, *ontology* has become a central component in computerized information processing, especially in constructing large databases (sometimes termed knowledgebases). Ontologies have also figured predominantly in software application development, Artificial Intelligence initiatives, Web services, e-business, information and document retrieval, e-commerce, decision-support, medical informatics, the Semantic Web technologies, and, of course, in various IT applications of knowledge management. Within all these areas, the highly theoretical (philosophical) view of the term *ontology* undergirds the very pragmatic outcomes sought in computerized knowledge systems. Ontologies, formal and informal, will continue to be major functional elements in the design, maintenance, handling, and implementation of the large-scale information stores at the heart of knowledge management initiatives.

BACKGROUND: ONTOLOGY DEFINED

While never pretending to duplicate exactly the workings of the human imagination or experience, ontologies attempt to capture conceptually the rational building blocks of the mind by modeling our knowledge of reality. The whole purpose of this is to give the computer humanlike, albeit modest, thinking ability, by providing an explicit vocabulary for things, ideas, actions, relations, and approved behaviors. Ontologies with the expressive power that provides these capabilities are generally termed *formal ontologies*.

FORMAL ONTOLOGY

A formal ontology seeks to capture the essence of selected aspects of existence by stating explicitly and formulaically the concepts of the various constituents of the domain being modeled and the relationships that pertain among them. Ontologies are said to be "formal" or "formalized" when they are capable of being rendered into a computer programming language. Probably the single most famous definition of *ontology* is offered by Gruber (1993), who defines ontology simply as "an explicit specification of a conceptualization." Concepts, Gruber notes, are abstract, "simplified view[s] of the world" (p. 1) that become the models for the objects and ideas of some part of the world as we know it. Guarino and Giaretta (1995), emphasizing that purpose determines how these concepts are specified, note that an ontology can give only a "partial account of a conceptualization" (p. 7). Knowledge, after all, is in the mind of the beholder, and an ontology will necessarily represent only the point of view of the ontology builder. An ontology, in short, will never be omniscient nor all-encompassing.

What follows examines two inherent aspects of Gruber's classic ontology definition: *explicitly specified concepts* and the *relationships* among them.

Explicitly Specified Concepts

The concepts, which represent selected aspects of reality in a formal ontology, are variously termed *entities*, *objects*, or *elements*. Concepts can represent concrete entities (books, cameras, toads, clouds), abstract notions (fictional places, ideas, theories), beliefs, processes, tasks, goals, events, states, or methods—in short, anything that needs to be modeled in the knowledge domain (the universe of discourse). Entities can further be specified to make explicit some chosen characteristics or attributes, such as color, size, price, manufacturer, location, name, and the like. Ontologists thus work with *declarative representations*, also termed *declarative knowledge* or *declarative formalisms*, because they are using descriptive logic to represent symbolically a selected set of real-world objects and events in their abstract models or knowledge representations.

Ontologies formally express concepts, not just words. For example, the word "cell" in an ontology must clearly represent its concept; ambiguity is not allowed. To *disambiguate* "cell," a *polyseme* or word with multiple meanings, the ontologist needs to create an unequivocal nomenclature that reflects accurately the usage context and the purpose of the ontology. The nomenclature must also be formalized, that is, rendered to allow the ontology to be set into formal notations used in first-order predicate logic that can be translated into any suitable programming language. Thus, the various possible meanings of cell, from biological (AnimalCell, PlantCell), to jail (JailCell), to phone (CellPhone), to electronic engineering (BatteryCell), must be indicated overtly and succinctly in the nomenclature of the concept itself. In addition, the ontology should supply concept definitions in Natural Language sentences, and if appropriate declare the physical attributes of the elements being modeled. Thus, a communication ontology could focus on CellPhone attributes such as Manufacturer, UnitPrice, BatteryLife, Color, HasVideoCamera, ServiceProvider, CountryOfOrigin, and the like.

Relationships Among Concepts

The semantic relationships of the concepts must be clearly determined, and the antecedents or parents, as well as the children, of each concept must be established. Ontologies establish concept relationships primarily as *is-a* or *part-of*. Some further possible relationships could include isMemberOf, subscribesTo, overseesJointly, isAuthorOf, isCausedBy, and the like. This article focuses on the two primary relationships, *is-a* and *part-of*, as they form the core hierarchy of the ontology.

Is-a

In a truly *formal ontology*, the categories (classes) of aggregated concepts are related hierarchically in a *specialization* taxonomy: lower categories fall under higher categories in *subsumption relationships*. The backbone of an ontology is its taxonomy (Guarino & Welty, 2002; Daconta et al., 2003, p. 150), as that ineluctably establishes the concept relationships which must be rigorously enforced.

Historically, the epitome of practical categorization is the 18th century taxonomy of Linnaeus. The Linnaean principles of organization, relationship, and inheritance today inform our use of ontologies. Linnaeus classified plants and animals in *taxa* (groups or classes) with various delineated properties inherited by the organisms residing (instantiated) in the lowest taxa. The eight major categories proceed from the most general down to the instance of a species (instantiation): Kingdom, Phylum, Class, Subclass, Order, Family, Genus, and Species. Each category in the taxonomy inherits the qualities or attributes of its parent category (*inheritance* through *nesting*). For example, a human being (Genus: Homo, Species: Sapiens) inherits all the characteristics of its *superordinate* category "mammal," which inherits all the characteristics of its ultimate superordinate category "animal" (Daconta et al., 2003, p. 148). This process of going from the particular to the general is known as traversing a *specialization hierarchy*, going from the *species* to the *genera*, from the special case to the general case. A specialization hierarchy, then, is nothing more than a collection of carefully arranged *is-a* relationships. Thus, *homo sapiens* **is a** (belongs to the category) primate; a primate **is a** (belongs to the category) mammal; and a mammal **is a(n)** (belongs to the category) animal.

The same kind of taxonomy can be constructed using the concept *vehicle*, where instances of *vehicle* can be grouped a number of ways relevant to the domain of discussion. For example, vehicles could be classified as operating on land, sea, in the air, or in outer space. Land vehicles could be classified as trains, trucks, trolleys, automobiles, bicycles, scooters, and the like. Automobiles could be classified by make, model, year, and country of origin. What is happening in this classification process is that a concept or model is being explicitly "realized" as the classification becomes less abstract and more concrete. Ambiguity is eliminated by deriving explicit attributes that allow us to articulate clearly exclusive differences. Once these mutually exclusive differences are made explicit, various objects can be appropriately categorized. When categorized, the objects can be further defined to the point where a human being, computer program, or agent could perform simple or complex logical operations on the categorized instances. For example, if it is known that a Toyota Celica is a type of automobile, it is also known by inference that a Toyota Celica is a land vehicle and that land vehicles do not float or fly. Thus, it is categorically illogical—indeed silly—to express the hope to land a man on the moon using a Renaissance Red 1997 Toyota Celica GT Convertible.

Formal ontologies seeking rigor must be composed of concepts whose instances exist exclusively in their class location in the hierarchy. In defining a class, the ontologist seeks the *necessary and sufficient* characteristics or exclusive *differentia* that define the set of members in that class. An instance of one class should never reside simultaneously in other classes at the same level in the hierarchy (*sibling* classes). Often in fact, out of desperation, taxonomists will opt for this kind of *polyhierarchy* (placing a single instance in numerous sibling classes), but the purist tries always to avoid polyhierarchy, as the power of the specification is weakened. For example, in a taxonomy of fruits and vegetables, a truly rigorous ontology would classify the entity "tomato" as either a fruit or a vegetable, but not both. In defining the classes fruit and vegetable, the ontologist would be careful to articulate a definition, supply attributes, and provide constraints that would unequivocally differentiate fruits from vegetables. Then all members of each class would inherit these characteristics. If too many individual members of the class sets can live in either class (tomato is a fruit, tomato is a vegetable), then the ontology is ambiguous—less rigorous and less useful in describing the domain. A computer agent, forced to make a single choice, would not know how to proceed, simply because the agent cannot tolerate ambiguity. You might get a scoop of ice cream plopped on your tomato if the computer agent infers that tomatoes are fruits.

Part-of

Besides the *is-a* relationship, hierarchies can also express *part-of* relationships. This type of hierarchy is sometimes called an *aggregation taxonomy* (Daconta et al., 2003, p. 149), but more strictly speaking it should be termed a *partonomy* or *composition hierarchy*. Here is how an ontology of geography could represent hierarchically the *part-of* relationships of concepts.

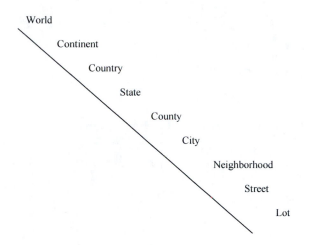

The relationships in this partonomy are known as *part-of* relationships because lower elements in the hierarchy are part of higher elements; that is, a lot is *part of* a street, which is *part of* a neighborhood, which is *part of* a city, and so forth. In formal notation, this could be expressed as (is Part Of Street Lake Neighborhood 10) which in Natural Language is saying that Lake Street is located in neighborhood 10. This *monocline subsumption* of named concepts moves from the largest and most general term (World) in a progression that becomes increasingly and logically narrower until the smallest conceptual unit is reached (Lot). Note that every larger concept preceding a given concept must have characteristics or attributes that allow it to contain properly every concept lower and to the right. Thus, **streets** have as their direct parents **neighborhoods** and as their direct children **lots**. A **city** is subsumed under a **county** which is subsumed under a **state**.

What makes all of these relationships work ineluctably is the agreement among the ontology engineers about nomenclature (class names), lexicon (explicit definitions for what to include and exclude in each class—the differentia, based upon various qualities or attributes), and mereology (establishing a whole-part relationship from parent to child that pertains in the formalized partonomy). *Partonomical hierarchies* or *mereologies* (Simons, 1987) are used extensively in ontologies for medical informatics, bioinformatics, genetics, chemistry, and physics—any domain that must aggregate concepts according to their parts and constituents.

Other Key Elements of a Formal Ontology

As we have seen thus far, formal ontologies are characterized by their rigorous use of explicit definition and logical structure, which makes it possible for them to be shared and reused in various computer applications that need accurate and succinct information models for processing. To make computer processing possible, terms and their relationships in a formal ontology are often expressed in a first-order logic predicate calculus language such as Knowledge Interchange Format (KIF) or related languages such as LOOM, CycL, Classic, Flogic, KRIS, Ontolingua, or OWL. The ontology is encoded in such a way that computerized agents can access its knowledge representations to carry out some specified practical action. Figure 1 shows how an axiom stated in natural language might be encoded in KIF.

Sowa (2000) has further delineated formal ontologies into two subgroups: *axiomatized* and *prototype based*. The axiomatized ontology is characterized by its logical definitions and axioms (assumed truths) that ultimately have great power because they "can support more complex inferences and computations" (p. 493). As examples, Sowa cites "formal theories in science and mathematics, the collections of rules and frames in an expert system, and specifications of conceptual schemas in languages like SQL." In modeling a concept of reality, the axiomatized ontology carefully presents well-named concepts (the nomenclature) and well-defined concepts (the lexicon) arranged hierarchically to expose the ineluctable relationships of the concepts. Rules in the ontology allow for inferences to be drawn from the explicitly defined terms and relationships (Perez & Benjamins, 1999, p. 2).

The axiomatized ontology, as a "statement of a logical theory" (Gruber, 1993, p. 2), also contains some number of assertions, axioms (Figure 1), rules, constraints, theorems, functions, explanations in Natural Language, instances, or anything else that expresses descriptively what is allowed and disallowed to obtain in the ontology of the domain being specified.

Sowa's prototype-based ontology tends, unfortunately, to complicate the definition of formality. The prototype-based ontology does not contain axioms nor does it rely necessarily on logical definitions or theories. It is by and large simply a hierarchical arrangement of categories with sets of "typical instances or prototypes" (Sowa, 2000, p. 495). Prototype-based ontologies are commonly devoted to categorizing (cataloging) products, books, computer files, music, and the like. They fulfill an important function in e-business, e-commerce,

Figure 1. Example of an axiom in KIF

This natural language statement:

If any two animals are siblings, then there exists someone who is the mother of both of them.

When axiomatized in KIF looks like this:

```
(=> (sibling ?sib1 ?sib2)
    (exists (?mom) (and (has-mother ?sib1 ?mom)
        (has-mother ?sib2 ?mom)))
```

Source of KIF: Knowledge Systems Laboratory (KSL), Stanford University. *A Glossary of Ontology Terminology,* http://www-ksl-svc.stanford.edu:5915/doc/frame-editor/glossary-of-terms.html

---

the Internet, and the Semantic Web. Helping to clarify a specific distinction between formal and informal ontology, Gruber (1993) maintains more strictly than Sowa that all formal ontologies claiming "to specify a conceptualization" must have "axioms that do constrain the possible interpretations for the defined terms" (p. 2, note 1).

Much confusion about ontologies can be avoided if Gruber's distinctions are maintained. This strict definition of a formal ontology is depicted in Figure 2, a simplified schematic of a formal (axiomatized) ontology that specifies a universe of discourse (anything one chooses to model). The conceptualization of this domain is being specified through explicit assertion of the truths of the universe. Specification of a conceptualization in a formal ontology usually consists of all the bulleted items (and even more, if desired).

Sample Formal Ontologies

Formal ontologies are often divided into two basic types: *foundational* (also known as upper-level or top-level) and *applied*.

Foundational (upper- or top-level) ontologies specify conceptualizations that are more general and have universal applicability. They may focus on defining logical concepts, relationships, human understanding, and the like. Good examples of foundational ontologies include:

Figure 2. The conceptualization of a knowledge domain (Universe of Discourse)

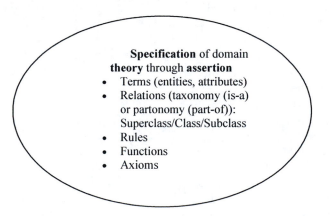

Specification of domain theory through assertion
- Terms (entities, attributes)
- Relations (taxonomy (is-a) or partonomy (part-of)): Superclass/Class/Subclass
- Rules
- Functions
- Axioms

- **CYC top-level ontology:** http://www.cyc.com/
- **DOLCE (Descriptive Ontology for Linguistic and Cognitive Engineering):** http://www.loa-cnr.it/DOLCE.html
- **Generalized Upper Model (GUM):** http://www.darmstadt.gmd.de/publish/komet/gen-um/newUM.html
- **GOLD (General Ontology for Linguistic Description):** http://emeld.douglass.arizona.edu:8080/index.html

- **PhysSys (The Physical Systems Ontology):** http://ksi.cpsc.ucalgary.ca/KAW/KAW96/borst/node2.html
- **IEEE SUMO (Suggested Upper Merged Ontology):** http://ontology.teknowledge.com/

Applied ontologies, which are domain specific, more strictly focus on a functional application related to a particular domain, such as enterprise modeling, knowledge management, chemistry, law, e-commerce, medicine, botany, and zoology. A few representative application fields and their actual ontologies include:

- **Biology:** Ontologies for Ethology—http://www.mesquiteproject.org/ontology/
- **Business:** The Open Source Business Process Management Ontology, BPMO—http://www.bpiresearch. com/Resources/RE_OSSOnt/re_ossont. htm
- **Knowledge Management:** KM Ontology (under development), which "provides researchers with a relatively comprehensive, organized foundation and common language for studying KM. It gives practitioners a frame of reference for assessing KM practices and recognizing KM opportunities. It points toward a structure and content for developing a formal KM curriculum." (Holsapple & Joshi, 2004, p. 2)
- **Manufacturing:** The Process Specification Language Ontology, PSL—http://www.mel.nist.gov/psl/ontology.html
- **Math:** An Ontology for Engineering Mathematics—http://www.ksl.stanford.edu/knowledge-sharing/papers/engmath.html
- **Medicine:** Systematized Nomenclature of Medicine, SNOMED—http://www.snomed.org/

The vast majority of applied ontologies are proprietary and unavailable to the general public.

INFORMAL ONTOLOGY

"Informal ontologies" (Sowa 2000, p. 493), to a greater or lesser degree, have some of the characteristics of formal ontologies, particularly selected groups of terms or labels relevant to some topic or area of interest (a document collection, Web site, product catalog, or business area). When the components of the informal ontology are arranged hierarchically, they are often termed **taxonomies** (Verity's Classifier, http:// www.ultraseek.com /products /vcc/; Inmagic Classifer, http://www.esprit soutronpartnership . com /Products /Classifier. asp), **directories** (Yahoo, http://www.yahoo.com; DMOZ, http:/

/www.dmoz.com), **subject-heading lists** (Library of Congress Subject Headings, http://www.loc.gov/), or **thesauri** (Medical Subject Headings, MeSH®, http://www.nlm.nih.gov/mesh/). When including definitions, they may be called **lexicons** (WordNet, http://www.cogsci.princeton.edu/~wn/) or **glossaries** (Information Architecture Glossary, http://argus-acia.com/white_papers/iaglossary.html). If they are simply computer files containing sets of controlled terms, they may be called **controlled vocabularies** or **synonym rings**.

Informal ontologies, because of their weak semantics (term meanings), are incapable of rich expression (McGuiness, 2002; Daconta et al., 2003, pp. 157-167); they simply do not provide enough significant meaning about a knowledge domain. Compare the semantic richness, for example, of a well-explained scientific theory to the semantic poverty of a mere listing of chemistry terms.

While offering some control over the knowledge domain, informal ontologies cannot by themselves be used for automated purposes. Computer programs, agents, and applications may refer to them for various reasons, but the informal ontology itself does not have the power of a formal ontology. Informal ontologies are not driven overtly by logical constraints, are not formalized in a knowledge representation language, are not axiomatized—in short, they do not have the expressive power that may need to be harnessed for sophisticated purposes in academia, business, medicine, law, or government.

ISSUES, CONTROVERSIES, AND PROBLEMS

The literature has tried for years to define exactly what constitutes an ontology (Chandrasekaran, Josephson, & Benjamins, 1999; Daconta et al., 2003; Gruber, 1993; Gruber, 2003; Guarino & Welty, 1995; Heflin et al., 2002; McGuiness, 2002; Noy & McGuinness, 2001; Sheth & Ramakrishnan, 2003; Smith, 2004; Sowa, 2000). While this article has presented the consensus view as depicted in the literature, the concept of ontology is still very slippery. For example, vendors, IT professionals, knowledge management experts, and technicians often erroneously equate simple taxonomies with formal ontologies. While a formal ontology contains a taxonomy or partonomy in expressing the relationships of the concepts, a taxonomy or partonomy is only a part of the formal ontology. A formal ontology also includes community-shared definitions, rules, and axioms.

Ontology has also been equated with Web directories such as DMOZ and Yahoo, neither of which is, strictly speaking, a formal ontology. Both employ rough classification schemes (loose aggregations) to order groups and subgroups of Internet resources, but again they do not provide concept definitions, rules, or axioms. Thus, to see those very rough schemes as formal ontologies is to abuse the term. They are simply directories. Lists of controlled words, glossaries, and thesauri are also often erroneously termed formal ontologies, but should be seen more properly only as potential parts of formal ontologies.

People often confuse terminological ontologies (Sowa, 2000) with formal ontologies. Thus, WordNet and Sensus are lexicons, not strictly formal ontologies. They contain words, their definitions, their relationship to other words in the hierarchy (in WordNet these are synonym sets), and part-whole (mereological) distinctions, but the definitions are not always complete, the taxonomic structure is faulty at many points (Guarino & Welty, 2002), and the collections are usually not axiomatized. Terminological ontologies have their uses, certainly, but primarily as starting points for more rigorous and limited formal ontological applications.

Formal ontological rigor is not easy to establish. One of the main stumbling blocks in establishing rigor is modeling the formal ontology to reflect strict and mutually exclusive *is-a* relationships in a specification hierarchy and not confusing *is-a* relationships with *part-of* relationships. The work of Guarino and Welty (2002) is dedicated to exposing these kinds of identity and subsumption weaknesses in formal ontologies. The less rigor a formal ontology has, the less value it has in accurately and unambiguously depicting a knowledge domain. This is not to say, however, that informal or semi-formal ontologies have no value; indeed, they may well meet many general and large-scale information needs, especially as we look forward to increasing numbers of ontology applications on the Semantic Web (Sheth & Ramakrishnan, 2003; Gruber, 2003).

Because so much of formal ontology building is still an art rather than a science (Abou-Zeid 2003; Gruber 1993; Gruninger & Fox, 1995; Guarino & Giaretta, 1995; Perez & Benjamins, 1999), even formal ontologies are selectively based on subjective choices. Ontologies, therefore, are capable only of representing the knowledge (specifying the concepts) that humans provide. If the ontology builders are not domain experts; if they make knowledge representation choices for political, organizational, or personal reasons rather than sound ontological reasons; if they omit important elements, attributes, or axioms because they rush to publication; if they construct the ontology based on the limitations of the programming language with which they are familiar (encoding bias); if they do not adequately understand the purpose and the audience for the ontology; if they fail to standardize their nomenclature; if they choose to model too much or model too little, their ontology is very likely doomed to fail.

How might these issues be avoided and these problems be solved? Only by establishing and following clear guidelines and standards in constructing ontologies will we ever hope to realize the full potential of the major initiatives in which ontologies play such a fundamental role. Much work remains to be done in standardization and implementation technologies, but much is at stake. If the Semantic Web, distributed global knowledge management initiatives, and the various application projects underway in areas such as e-business, government, publishing, Artificial Intelligence, and medical informatics are to be successful on a large scale, they will have to be buttressed by well-designed ontologies.

CONCLUSION

This article discusses the philosophical origins and modern practical implementations of *ontology*. For easier understanding, approaches to ontology building were divided into formal and informal. Formal ontologies were explained, focusing in particular on specifying concepts by establishing relationships through *is-a* and *part-of* approaches. The other components of a formal ontology were briefly mentioned. Informal ontologies were defined and contrasted with formal ontologies. Finally, issues, controversies, and problems in the implementation of ontologies were briefly explored.

Ontologies will continue to play an important role in the development of large-scale, computer mediated, and global knowledge management projects. Communicating knowledge within an organization, and among organizations worldwide, will be facilitated by ontologies, as they create a knowledge layer critical to the automated sharing and reuse of essential explicit knowledge.

The research agenda in ontologies includes solving many of the technical problems that bedevil organizations at the application level, developing stable and standard methodologies and tools to move ontology construction out of the area of art and into that of science (ontological engineering), and continuing to hone the theoretical insights that will allow construction and implementation of rigorous high-level and application-level ontologies.

REFERENCES

Abou-Zeid, E. (2003). What can ontologists learn from knowledge management? *The Journal of Computer Information Systems, 43*(3), 109-118.

Chandrasekaran, B., Josephson, J.R., & Benjamins, V.R. (1999). What are ontologies, and why do we need them? *IEEE Intelligent Systems & Their Applications, 14*(1), 20-26.

Daconta, M.J., Obrst, L.J., & Smith, K.T. (2003). *The Semantic Web: A guide to the future of XML, Web services, and knowledge management.* Indianapolis: John Wiley & Sons.

Fensel, D. (2001). *Ontologies: A silver bullet for knowledge management and electronic commerce.* Berlin: Springer-Verlag.

Gruber, T. (1993). Toward principles for the design of ontologies used for knowledge sharing. In N. Guarino & R. Poli (Eds.), *Formal ontology in conceptual analysis and knowledge representation.* Dordrecht: Kluwer Academic. Retrieved November 24, 2004, from *http://www-ksl.stanford.edu/kst/what-is-an-ontology.html*

Gruber, T. (2003). It is what it does: The pragmatics of ontology. *Proceedings of Sharing Knowledge—International CIDOC CRM Symposium,* Washington, DC. Retrieved November 24, 2004, from *http://cidoc.ics.forth.gr/docs/symposium_presentations/gruber_cidoc-ontology-2003.pdf*

Gruninger, M., & Fox, M.S. (1995). Methodology for the design and evaluation of ontologies. Retrieved November 24, 2004, from *http://www.eil.utoronto.ca/enterprise-modelling/papers/gruninger-ijcai95.pdf*

Guarino, N., & Giaretta, P. (1995). Ontologies and knowledge bases: Towards a terminological clarification. "Slightly amended version of a paper" published in N. Mars (Ed.), *Towards very large knowledge bases.* Amsterdam: IOS Press. Retrieved November 24, 2004, from *http://www.loa-cnr.it/Papers/KBKS95.pdf*

Guarino, N., & Welty, C. (2002). Evaluating ontological decisions with Ontoclean. *Communications of the ACM, 45*(2), 61-65.

Heflin, J., Volz, R., & Dale, J. (2004, February 10). OWL Web Ontology Language use cases and requirements: W3C recommendation. Retrieved November 24, 2004, from *http://www.w3.org/TR/webont-req/*

Holsapple, C.W., & Joshi, K.D. (2004). A formal knowledge management ontology: Conduct, activities, resources, and influences. *Journal of the American Society for Information Science and Technology, 55*(7), 593-612.

Knowledge Systems Laboratory (KSL). (n.d.). A glossary of ontology terminology. Retrieved November 24, 2004, from *http://www-ksl-svc.stanford.edu:5915/doc/frame-editor/glossary-of-terms.html*

Mayhew, D., & Siebert, D. (2004). Ontology: The discipline and the tool. In G. Büchel, B. Klein, & T. Roth-Berghofer (Eds.), *Proceedings of the First Workshop on Philosophy and Informatics* (pp. 57-64). Deutsches Forschungszentrum für künstliche Intelligenz, Cologne. Retrieved November 24, 2004 from *http://www.ifomis.de/Research/Publications/Mayhew_Siebert__OntologyDisciplineAndTool.pdf*

McGuiness, D. (2002). Ontologies come of age. In D. Fensel, J. Hendler, H. Lieberman, & W. Wahlster (Eds.), *Spinning the Semantic Web: Bringing the World Wide Web to its full potential.* Cambridge, MA: MIT Press. Retrieved November 24, 2004, from *http://www.ksl.stanford.edu/people/dlm/papers/ontologies-come-of-age-mit-press-(with-citation).htm*

Mika, P., & Akkermans, H. (2004). Towards a new synthesis of ontology technology and knowledge management. Submitted to *Knowledge Engineering Review,* (April). Retrieved November 24, 2004, from *http://www.cs.vu.nl/~pmika/research/papers/IR-BI-001.pdf*

Noy, N.F., & McGuinness, D. (2001). Ontology development 101: A guide to creating your first ontology. Retrieved November 24, 2004, from *http://www-smi.stanford.edu/pubs/SMI_Reports/SMI-2001-0880.pdf*

O'Leary, D. (1998). Enterprise knowledge management. *IEEE Computer, 31*(3), 54-61.

Sheth, A., & Ramakrishnan, C. (2003). Semantic (Web) technology in action: Ontology driven information systems for search, integration and analysis. *Making the Semantic Web Real* in *IEEE Data Engineering Bulletin, 26*(4), 40-48. Retrieved November 24, 2004, from *http://wwwt.semagix.com/documents/SemanticWebTechinAction.pdf*

Simons, P. (1987). *Parts: A study in ontology.* Oxford: Oxford University Press.

Smith, B. (2004). Ontology and information systems. Retrieved November 24, 2004, from *http://ontology.buffalo.edu/ontology.doc*

Sowa, J. (2000). *Knowledge representation: Logical, philosophical, and computational foundations.* Pacific Grove, CA: Brooks/Cole Thomson Learning.

Van der Vet, P.E., & Mars, N.J.I. (1998). Bottom-up construction of ontologies. *IEEE Transactions on Knowledge and Data Engineering, 10*(4), 513-526.

KEY TERMS

Assertion: A statement (entity definition, attribute value, constraint, rule, function, and the like) assumed to be true and therefore supporting the theory of the ontology. *Example*: Gravity is an attracting force in nature.

Axiom: A rule or maxim accepted as a truth in the ontology. Axioms provide the inferencing or logical power of the ontology. *Example*: "If and only if a wine is red, then it is derived from a grape that is red."

Conceptualization: A model of reality, a generalized abstraction of particular items. *Example*: A radio exists physically, but when conceptualized it exists symbolically as some form of knowledge representation: a word, picture, diagram, graph, or formula.

Mereology: An ontology that examines part-whole relationships and the composition of various levels of matter itself. Mereologies employ part-of relationships in examining essence, process, occurrence, and the like. *Example*: An ontology on the structure of atoms would examine all constituent parts and their relationships.

Partonomy (part-of): A realization of mereology that specifies in a subsumption hierarchy the relationship of parts to the whole. *Example*: A whole wooden pencil consists of these parts: wooden shaft, paint, embossed logo, graphite core, eraser, and the like.

Subsumption: An entity exists in a subsumption relationship to another entity when it falls in a directly lower class in the taxonomy. The subsumed entity inherits the characteristics of the classes above it. *Example*: The term *dog* exists in a subsumption relationship to the family Canidae, and inherits canine characteristics; *dog* does not, however, exist in a subsumption relationship to the family Felidae, so logically cannot inherit feline or cat-like characteristics.

Taxonomy (is-a): An ordered list of taxa or categories. A subordinate taxon (category) inherits the defining characteristics of its superordinate (parent) taxon. *Example*: An *automobile* has all the characteristics of its superclass, *vehicle*, but not of its sibling class, *truck*.

Operational Knowledge Management

Fons Wijnhoven
University of Twente, The Netherlands

INTRODUCTION

The differences between the paradigms of knowledge management (KM) and operations management are huge. Whereas KM is rooted in the disciplines of human relations, sociology, organization analysis, and strategic management, the operations management paradigm finds its roots in industrial engineering, business economics, and information systems. These differences result in poor acceptance of KM ideas in operations management and vice versa. Several approaches to this problem are possible. For instance, one may state that the operations management paradigm is irrelevant for knowledge management. This is incorrect, because besides of the traditional person-oriented knowledge management processes, modern knowledge intensive firms use reengineered knowledge processes intensively (e.g., Hansen, Nohria, & Tierney, 1999). An alternative approach may be to forget about the KM paradigm and only use the operations management paradigm. This is wrong again, because most industrial enterprises compete on the development and exploitation of their expertise and human capabilities (Hamel & Prahalad, 1994; Quinn, 1992). Consequently, if knowledge management is relevant and if operations management is not irrelevant, then the main question is how to translate knowledge management issues into an operations management framework. I provide a conceptual framework for such a knowledge operations management (KOM) perspective.

BACKGROUND

Operations management studies the handling or transformation of inputs to outputs (the operations function), and the consequent realization of organizational goals via certain means (management of operations) (Hill,

1983). Operations management thus distinguishes objects, which are the inputs and outputs of operations, related support tasks, and the setting of goals and application of means. In the operations, I distinguish logistics as the delivery of the input to a client without changing this input (Ballou, 1992) from transformation as the change of the input object to something different (see Figure 1).

Given the wide paradigmatic differences between operations management and KM, not many attempts have been made to apply operations management on KM. One of the scarce attempts is from Armistead (1999), who distinguishes knowledge inputs and outputs and four related operations processes, that is,. two transformation processes (knowledge creation and knowledge embedding) and two knowledge logistics or transfer processes (exchange of knowledgeable people and the exchange of knowledge representations). The KM literature sees knowledge creation and embedding as related organizational learning processes (Nonaka, 1994), therefore, the term *learning* better covers what we mean by knowledge transformation. Finally, Armistead also defines metrics to control and feedback to improve these processes. This article continues the attempt made by Armistead with a further specification of a knowledge operations management model. Such a model does not only structure the KM field, but at the end of the article I also will explain some of its heuristic value.

MAIN FOCUS: THE KOM MODEL

In the context of KOM, the input-output objects are different types of knowledge. The input objects may be handled in operations without fundamentally changing them. This is what I call knowledge logistics and includes the storing and distributing of knowledge and its related

Figure 1. The operations function (based on Hill, 1983, p. 25)

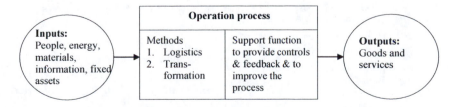

Figure 2. The KOM framework

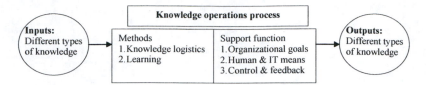

representations. Alternatively, in learning processes, the knowledge inputs are transformed to new or different knowledge objects. The logistic process is an important support for learning, especially when done in organizations where learning is essentially a group process. Authors in the artificial intelligence discipline (e.g., Turban, Aronson, & Bolloju, 2001) have stated that besides people, machines also can learn. Although this is basically correct, the artificial intelligence field mainly regards learning at the behavioral and statistical level and not at the level of understanding and human skills formation, which is the focus of the KM literature. Thus, I exclude machine learning from KOM. In the knowledge operations management framework, the operation methods are supported by human and information technological means for specific goals, and metrics are used to control and deliver feedback on process performance as presented in Figure 2.

I first treat the input-output knowledge objects, then I discuss the knowledge operation methods. After that, a description of the support function, by a typology of possible organizational goals, means, and metrics for knowledge logistics and learning is given.

Knowledge Objects

Scientists often restrict the term knowledge for explicit understanding, which consists of explanations, predictions, and methodologies (Hempel, 1965). In information management, the term information is mostly reserved for representations of thoughts (e.g., explicit understandings), or the representation of objects and events, which may be stored or communicated (Stamper, 1973). Much of what popularly is called knowledge is neither an explicit understanding, nor a representation, but refers to effective behavior or skills (Spender, 1998). Especially in the arts and professions, people do not express (represent) how they do the job, and they also may not be successful in explaining their success. Thus, effective behavior is "what walks out the organization each day and hopefully returns the next morning" (Senge, 1990), and it is personally owned human capital. Some personal or individual knowledge consists of explicit knowledge that is not shared, while other individual knowledge consists of personal values. Much of a person's effectiveness, though, is based on individual

knowledge and the social setting in which the work is done. More precisely, groups have norms and values, based on an underlying (sub)culture, that explain much of a group's effectiveness. For instance, decision-making norms and values that are well shared may speed up decision-making. These norms and values are often tacit knowledge (Leonard-Barton, 1992; Nonaka & Takeuchi, 1995). Their abilities of being shared require longer term and complex organizational change processes (Leonard-Barton, 1992).

The dimensions of sharedness (individual vs. group) and codification (explicitness vs. tacitness) make up four ideal types of knowledge (Spender, 1998; see Figure 3). Besides these types of knowledge, organizations use representations of knowledge to store, reuse, and distribute knowledge (Markus, 2001). Organizations also use representations of objects in reality as part of potential knowledge (Earl, 1994). Knowledge and information, which both form the content aspects of an organizational memory, are both needed in effective decision-making (Stein & Zwass, 1995).

Knowledge Management Operation Methods

The KM literature often defines the following knowledge operation methods: knowledge generation, distribution and sharing, usage, maintenance, and storage (Alavi & Leidner, 2001; Stein & Zwass, 1995). Generation and maintenance are knowledge transformation processes (i.e., learning). The other knowledge operations are knowledge logistics. The next two subsections describe the activities of these operations in relation to the input-output objects.

Learning

Following Nonaka (1994), learning consists of interactions between tacit and explicit knowledge. The interaction of knowledge as input and output relations is given in Table 1.

Socialization transfers individual tacit knowledge to other people, such that these others adopt these tacit insights and collective knowledge is created. Externalization changes tacit knowledge to explicit knowl-

Figure 3. Organizational memory, classes of knowledge, information, and objects in reality

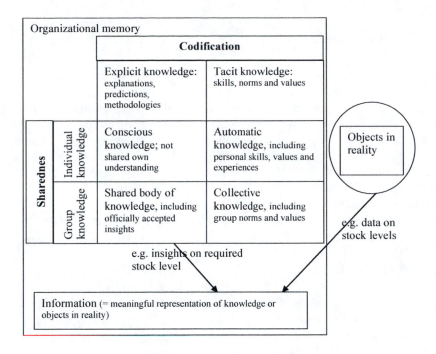

edge, so that the knowledge becomes person-independent. Internalization is the reverse process of externalization and implies that the shared body of knowledge is personally accepted as automatic knowledge and integrated with existing individual norms and values. Finally, combination merges different kinds of individual conscious knowledge to a larger body of shared knowledge. When defining the support function later on, I will explain how goals, means, and metrics can be selected to improve these learning processes.

Knowledge Logistics

As I stated, knowledge logistics is about the sharing, distribution, storage, and retrieval of knowledge and its representations. The sharing and distribution of knowledge can be more or less formal and planned, and the sharing and distribution of information occurs in different reuse contexts. The storage and retrieval of knowledge and information is done by human and person-independent media (see Table 2).

Formality of Knowledge Logistics

Distribution of knowledge objects might vary from very formal and organized to ad hoc. Standard reporting is most organized, by automatic dissemination of knowledge and information. This may be extremely efficient, though often insufficiently flexible. Less organized is a knowledge communication with a predefined procedure of starts and finish. Even less formalized is the case when a potential user can retrieve specific knowledge objects from a larger resource. For instance, this is the case of libraries, which use an information pull logistic model.

Table 1. Learning modes and knowledge objects

Learning mode	Knowledge object inputs	Knowledge object outputs
Socialization	Individual norms and values	Collective knowledge
Externalization	Automatic and collective knowledge	Shared body of knowledge and related representations
Internalization	Shared body of knowledge	Automatic knowledge and accepted collective and shared body of knowledge
Combination	Conscious knowledge and individual owned information	Shared body of knowledge and information

Table 2. Characteristics of knowledge and information logistics

	Knowledge	Information (representations)
Logistic procedures	More or less formal	Different reuse contexts
Storage	Individual, group and cultural media	Ecology and information systems

Even more informal are research and development activities. However these might be planned, it is mostly unclear what answers they should deliver and the moment of delivery is often unpredictable. These research activities share an organization and the people involved are recognizable, which is not the case in ad hoc search. Ad hoc searching can be done actively (by action of individual's with specific knowledge needs) or passively (by knowledge provision). The message might contain information about knowledge or knowledge itself.

Knowledge Reuse Contexts

According to Markus (2001), knowledge reuse processes can be described in the stages of capturing or documenting knowledge, packaging knowledge for reuse, distributing or disseminating knowledge, and reusing knowledge. A fundamental point here is that after the documenting and packaging of knowledge, only the knowledge representations (and not the knowledge itself) is distributed and reused. Consequently, the receivers and reusers have to interpret the messages. Interpretation errors can easily happen if the distance between the knowledge producer and the knowledge representation user is large (Ackerman & Halverson, 2000). The context of reuse can vary in terms of the cognitive distance of knowledge producers and knowledge (representation) reusers, which supports Markus's (2001) classification of reuse contexts as (1) reuse by shared knowledge producers, (2) reuse by shared work practitioners, (3) reuse by expertise-seeking novices, and (4) reuse by secondary knowledge miners.

Storage and Media

Walsh and Ungson (1991) and Wijnhoven (1998) have listed a number of storage media and related knowledge types. Each medium has different potentials for the handling of different knowledge objects. Table 3 gives a list of the potentially best combinations.

The *knowledge logistics* can be subject to evaluation with the same criteria as any other *logistic* process (Wijnhoven, 1998). I will describe these criteria in the next section.

The Support Function for Knowledge Logistics and Learning

This section first presents a typology of goals that the support function may have. Next, I describe some of the human and information technological means for the knowledge logistics and learning processes. Finally, I mention a few metrics for control and feedback of these processes.

Support Function and Organizational Goals

Operations knowledge management may contribute to several organizational goals. These organizational goals may be categorized as follows: (1) organizational integration, (2) adaptation, (3) goal attainment, and (4) pattern maintenance (Quinn & Rohrbaugh, 1984; Stein & Zwass, 1995). The integrative goal aims at multi-local and instantaneous access to shared knowledge and the sharing of knowledge over time and space. The adaptive goal aims at boundary-spanning activities to recognize, capture, organize, and distribute knowledge about the environment to the appropriate organizational actors. Goal attainment aims at assisting organizational actors in planning and control. The emphasis of the pattern maintenance goal is on human resources. "Pattern" pertains to attitudes, values, norms, personal routines, and personal

Table 3. Knowledge media and related knowledge objects

Knowledge media	Possible effective media for the following knowledge objects
Individual	Professional skills; personal ethics and beliefs; individual routines
Culture	Schemes; stories; external communications; cultural routines
Transformation	Tasks; experiences; rules, procedures and technology; patents
Structure	Task divisions; hierarchy; social structure; formal structure
Ecology	Layout of work place; building architecture
External	Client and market characteristics; list of knowledgeable people and organizations
Systems	Process control systems; GroupWare, computer aided design systems, knowledge based-systems; administrative systems

Table 4. KM objectives and KM process requirements

Organizational goal	Requirements for KM process
Integration	Knowledge logistics investments to realize temporal and spatial integration of knowledge resources, for instance by temporally indexed databases.
Adaptation	Investments in knowledge logistics and learning to realize the retention of cross-linked historical information on stakeholders, memory bases of user preferences, links to external sources of information (Stein & Zwass, 1995), and availability of software and people for interpretation of acquired data (Daft & Weick, 1986).
Goal attainment	Investments in learning through the development of templates of the context-plan-result nature, expert planning knowledge, evaluation models, company performance data, past and current performance forecasts (Stein & Zwass, 1995).
Pattern maintenance	At the individual level: knowledge logistic like the creation and dissemination of work history of individuals. At the organizational level: knowledge logistics and learning through the preservation and communication of organizational protocols (Stein & Zwass, 1995).

knowledge. Effective organizations "maintain" values, attitudes, and norms that contribute to corporate cohesion and morale. Some of the requirements for the learning and logistic processes are listed in Table 4.

Support for Knowledge Logistic Processes

Knowledge logistics may be parsed into acquisition, retention, maintenance, search, and retrieval of knowledge objects. Knowledge acquisition is the gathering and placing of knowledge into knowledge stores. This necessitates a knowledge directory giving a storage location for knowledge objects and an index with retrieval keys. The seven storage media mentioned before (individuals, culture, transformation, structure, ecology, external environment, and information systems) all differ on their opportunities and limitations for storing knowledge, as well as in speed, reliability, physical degeneration, and availability. Knowledge maintenance is the management of the integrity of retained knowledge. An inherent problem is the integration of new knowledge with existing knowledge, and applying an effective method of removing obsolete knowledge. Search is the process by which retained information is selected as relevant to particular problems or goals on the part of the user. Retrieval is the reconstruction of the selected information in order to satisfy the user's request. Sometimes the retrievable knowledge permits satisfactory formal definition and the knowledge management system is able to deliver standard reports with interpretations. Often, however, the retrieval demands are unpredictable and the required knowledge is difficult to describe. Consequently, much knowledge may best be kept tacit, which means that only the location of knowledge will be retrieved. Table 5 summarizes several human and IT means to realize the objectives of logistics.

Metric for Knowledge Logistics Control and Feedback

I propose distinguishing at least two classes of knowledge logistic metrics: (1) measures related to the logistic processes and (2) measures related to the customer satisfaction of the outcome of the logistic process. Armistead (1999) and Wijnhoven (1998) mention the following logistic process measures:

- **Timeliness:** This involves speed and compliance with agreed schedules.
- **Reliability:** This is the number of deliveries that are according the agreement.
- **Completeness:** This is the amount of information and knowledge delivered in relation to what is needed; thus, a delivery may be incomplete or over-complete.
- **Accessibility:** This is the ease of getting a knowledgeable person or entering a system that has the knowledge or information.
- **Costs and efficiency:** Cost is what people have to pay for the service. Efficiency is what costs and other efforts are involved as objects that should be measured to control and feedback the logistics processes.

Measures related to customer satisfaction have been studied intensively in the information systems literature under the heading of information systems end-user satisfaction. Doll and Torkzadeh (1988) have found five main constructs, which have been empirically replicated several times and are relevant for knowledge satisfaction as well:

- *Content* is the perceived level in which the information (and knowledge) precisely meets the receivers'

Table 5. Knowledge logistic process and means

Knowledge logistics	IT means	Human means
Acquisition	Business intelligence system, Internet resources	Researchers, library collection service, data collection activities
Storage	Databases, library systems, data warehouses, document management systems	Archiving professionals, database administrators, indexing experts
Maintenance	Content management systems, databases	Content maintenance procedures and quality circles
Search & retrieval	Search engines, retrieval technology	Search and retrieval experts, social networks to find people, information service suppliers
Dissemination	Content publishing software, Internet facilities	Publication procedures, public relations policies, publishing expertise

needs and in which the information and knowledge is regarded as relevant and sufficient.

- *Accuracy* is the level in which people regard the information and knowledge as reliable and the level in which people feel they can depend on the information and knowledge.
- *Format* is the level in which people regard that the information and knowledge is well presented, clear, understandable, and, with respect to the information, has a good layout.
- *Ease of use* is about the user friendliness of the system and the ease of interactions with the knowledge owner.
- *Up-to-dateness* of the information and knowledge received. Doll and Torkazadeh (1988) use timeliness as the fifth factor, which includes delivery on time, but this is more a logistic feature and not an end-user satisfaction measure. Therefore, I propose up-to-dateness instead of timeliness here.

Support for Learning

The learning processes transform knowledge objects from rather explicit to rather tacit and reverse. These transformations are further analyzed here to define means for the learning support function.

- **Socialization:** The creation of new tacit knowledge from old tacit knowledge is highly inter-personal. Socialization requires a strong personal commitment of each of the participants and is obstructed from the negative attitude, which is often placed on the communication of uncertain and incomplete knowledge. Possible solutions for these knowledge-sharing obstructions are the creation of reward structures (Lawler & Rhodes, 1976), creation

of synergy among knowledge owners (Quinn, 1992; Senge, 1990), and the development of an IT knowledge infrastructure.

- **Externalization:** The transformation of tacit knowledge to explicit knowledge—requires the coding of experiences, personal and group skills, norms, and values, and thus needs highly motivated experts to give away an important source of personal success. It also requires high communication skills of the system engineer in understanding experts from another discipline. Some methods for knowledge representation are (1) proposition and predicate logic, (2) production rules, (3) scripts, and (4) semantic nets. Besides the quality of the externalization, the importance of maintenance of the knowledge base is high. Particularly in complex knowledge bases, this is hard to realize.
- **Combination:** The putting together of pieces of explicit knowledge requires configuration or synthesis (Galunic & Rodan, 1998). Configuration puts together the owners of different objects of explicit knowledge in workgroups, teams, or departments, or just letting each other know each other or refer to each other's knowledge objects (Liebeskind, Oliver, Zucker, & Brewer, 1996). Configuration also can be enabled by information technology, through the creation of Web links between different knowledge objects, the creation of Semantic Webs (Berners-Lee, Hendler, & Lassila, 2001) or ontologies (Borst, Akkermans, & Top, 1997), and the detection of patterns among data in data mining (Singh, 1998). Synthesis is the integration of different knowledge objects to one or more new knowledge objects.
- **Internalization:** The process by which externalized knowledge is merged with personal existing frames of reference assumes that knowledge is only

Table 6. Learning processes and possible means

	Means	
	IT	*Human*
Learning processes		
Socialization		
Quickly find people with specific skills.	Skills database	Motivated individuals who submit content, but knowledge delivery pay is likely ineffective.
Development of mutual interests and collaboration among experts.	Communication infrastructure	Requires additional reward structure and reinforcements by management.
Externalization		
Machine processing of knowledge. Reduction of errors in routine processes.	Knowledge-based systems	Knowledge representation. This is difficult in unstable domains and experts sometimes are not willing to participate.
Standardization of work and decision-making.	Electronic manuals	Maintenance of knowledge is especially complex in larger domains.
Combination		
Combination of distributed and formalized knowledge.	Ontologies, Semantic Webs, Internet links	Complex, only applicable on static knowledge. Requires engineers who manage the complexity.
Brings together experts.	Communication infrastructure	May lead to insufficient commitments and poor goal achievement.
Analyzing databases to find explicit understanding.	Data mining and knowledge discovery	Human interpretation needed by adding tacit and explicit knowledge to the data patterns.
Explicit knowledge distribution in an organization.	Word-of-mouth emulator	May lead to poor utilization of insights gained. Need a knowledge coordinator.
Internalization		
Feedback on repertory of action and improves efficiency in routines	Computer aided instruction and decision support	The model needs validation and usability improvements, thus the role of the trainer is not obsolete.

truly adopted when it leads to changes of existing tacit knowledge (Senge, 1990). This will be manifested in changes of people's repertory of action.

Table 6 summarizes some human and IT means to realize the objectives of the learning processes. Though information technology (IT) is not a necessary component of KM means, in KOM information technology is often indispensable.

Metrics for Learning

Armistead (1999) gives a list of possible measures for learning (what he calls knowledge creation and knowledge embedding). These are presented here with a short explanation:

- **Reliability of learning:** This implies that we should know if the learning has been done well
- **Completeness of learning**
- **Acceptability of learning:** True knowledge needs (organizational) justification before it can be used (Nonaka, 1994)

- **Readiness for learning:** This is especially a problem when people lack sufficient knowledge to understand the new knowledge, or when people do not recognize the importance of the lessons gained
- **Economics of learning:** This is about the costs and expected economic benefits.
- **Number of new ideas and patents**
- **Contribution on individual knowledge:** It is not always clear how this benefits the organization, because it may raise the power and prestige of individuals and lower the access and control of the organization over this knowledge
- **Organizational learning:** This is a contribution to collective knowledge and the shared body of knowledge
- **Knowledge productivity:** This is the speed in which people are able to create new knowledge and the level to which they are able to embed this new knowledge in new products and business processes
- **Evidence of best practices**

FUTURE TRENDS

The KOM framework distinguishes knowledge objects, operations methods, and the aspect of the support function. Of course, all the distinctions and insights mentioned are more aiming at explaining the KOM framework than pretending that this would be the final word about KOM. I will discuss some of the challenges related to each topic.

In the KM literature, the differences in knowledge objects and their related representations is mentioned many times, but the consequences of these differences is seldom explicitly studied. This omission of the KM literature can be understood from KM research's emphasis on holistic insights instead of a study of a specific type of knowledge. The KOM model indicates the need to more seriously study the consequences of these differences for the development and management of related operations. Such an approach also helps to avoid misfits of knowledge and operation types. For instance, such research could help avoid an over-reliance or underutilization of IT means for the management of specific types of knowledge.

I proposed four types of learning, based on Nonaka's work and knowledge input transformations. There is substantial evidence that these four explain most learning processes in and between organizations, though lack of space also prevented me from mentioning Argyris and Schön's (1978) classification of single loop and double loop learning (which emphasize the organizational adoption of innovations), and the different levels of abstraction (Bohn, 1994) that an organization can realize (e.g., changes from elementary observations to complex explanatory models). These different theoretical approaches require the definition of different inputs and outputs, and different operation methods.

I described knowledge logistics in terms of formality, reuse contexts, and storage and media. These are suggestions from the literature, but neither much descriptive nor explanatory research in these fields has been done at the moment.

With respect to the selection of means, goals, and metrics, I have been able to collect several examples, some better and some less based on empirical evidence, but also this can be studied further. The current KM movement seems more rooted in human relations, organization studies, economics, or computer science, which results in less priority for rigorous studies in the mentioned support function. The KOM framework more or less logically indicates the need for such studies. A research topic here could be the study of effective goal specification in KM. Also the tradeoff and balance of human vs. IT means may be a fruitful research topic. The development of KM metrics and their effective use for feedback in the KM context is another topic to study.

Finally, I want to note that the KOM framework is independent of the question if we study KM in an intraorganizational or interorganizational perspective. Though for KOM this probably is true, for the practical implementation of KOM, the context matters a lot. I believe much fruitful research can be done on comparing KOM in intraorganizational contexts (e.g., knowledge management in a department) and an interorganizational context (e.g., KM in interfirm codesign projects and KM by optimally using the Internet; cf. Schwartz, Divitini, & Brasethwik, 2000).

CONCLUSION

This article started from the idea to apply concepts from the operations management field to knowledge management. I gave an elaboration of a knowledge operations management framework (KOM). The framework states that KOM wants to operate on four types of knowledge objects and related representations (of knowledge and of objects in reality). These objects may be transformed by learning and handled without transformation to clients via knowledge logistics. The support function has to manage these knowledge operation methods by selecting specific organizational goals, selecting the best set of human and IT means, and applying metrics for control and feedback. These concepts may be used for the innovation and design of KM, and they (as the Future Trends sections demonstrated) are a fruitful heuristic model for further KM research.

REFERENCES

Ackerman, M., & Halverson, C. (2000). Reexamining organizational memory. *Communications of the ACM, 43*(1), 59-64.

Alavi, M., & Leidner, D. (2001). Knowledge management and knowledge management systems: Conceptual foundations and research issues. *Management Information Systems Quarterly, 25(*1), 107-136.

Argyris, C., & Schön, D. (1978). *Organizational learning: A theory of action perspective.* Reading, MA: Addison-Wesley.

Armistead, C. (1999). Knowledge management and process performance. *Journal of Knowledge Management, 3*(2), 143-154.

Ballou, R.H. (1992). *Business logistics management.* Englewood Cliffs, NJ: Prentice-Hall.

Bell, D. (1979). The social framework of the information society. In M. Dertouzos & J. Moses (Eds.), *The computer age: A twenty year view* (pp. 163-211). Cambridge, MA: The MIT Press.

Berners-Lee T., Hendler J., & Lassila O. (2001). The semantic Web. *Scientific American, 284*(5), 34-43.

Bohn, R.E. (1994). Measuring and managing technological knowledge. *Sloan Management Review, 36*(1), 61-73.

Boisot, M.H. (1998). *Knowledge assets: Securing competitive advantage in the information economy*. Oxford, UK: Oxford University Press.

Borst P., Akkermans H., & Top J. (1997). Engineering ontologies. *International Journal Human-Computer Studies, 46*(2-3), 365-406.

Daft, R.L., & Weick, K.E. (1984). Toward a model of organizations as interpretation systems. *Academy of Management Review, 9,* 284-295.

Damsgaard J., & Scheepers, R. (1999). A stage model of Intranet technology implementation and management. *Proceedings of the European Conference in Information Systems* (pp. 100-116).

Davenport, T.A., & Prusak, L. (1997). *Working knowledge: How organizations manage what they know*. Cambridge, MA: Harvard Business School Press.

Doll, W., & Torkzadeh, G. (1988). The measurement of end-user satisfaction. *Management Information Systems Quarterly, 12*(2), 259-274.

Earl, M. (1994). Knowledge as strategy. Reflections on Skandia International and Shorko Films. In C. Ciborra & T. Jelassi (Eds.), *Strategic information systems: A European perspective* (pp. 53-69). Chichester, UK: John Wiley.

Galunic, D.C., & Rodan, S. (1998). Resource recombinations in the firm: Knowledge structures and the potential for Schumpeterian innovation. *Strategic Management Journal, 19,* 1193-1201.

Hamel, G., & Prahalad, C.K. (1994). *Competing for the future*. Boston: Harvard Business School Press.

Hansen, M., Nohria, N., & Tierney, T. (1999). What's your strategy for managing knowledge? *Harvard Business Review, 77*(2), 106-116.

Hempel, C.G. (1965). *Aspects of scientific explanation and other essays in the philosophy of science*. New York: The Free Press.

Hill, T. (1983). *Production/operations management*. Englewood Cliffs, NJ: Prentice-Hall.

Lawler, E.E., & Rhode, J.G. (1976). *Information and control in organizations*. Beverly Hills, CA: Goodyear.

Leonard-Barton, D. (1992). The factory as a learning lab. *Sloan Management Review, 34*(1), 23-38.

Liebeskind, J.L., Oliver, A.L., Zucker, L., & Brewer, M. (1996). Social networks, learning, and flexibility: Sourcing scientific knowledge in new biotechnology firms. *Organization Science, 7*(4), 428-443.

Markus, M.L. (2001). Toward a theory of knowledge reuse: Types of knowledge reuse situations and factors in reuse success. *Journal of Management Information Systems, 18*(1), 57-93.

Nonaka, I. (1994). A dynamic theory of organizational knowledge creation. *Organizational Science, 5*(1), 14-37.

Nonaka, I., & Takeuchi, H. (1995). *The knowledge-creating company: How Japanese companies create the dynamics of innovation*. New York: Oxford University Press.

Polanyi, M. (1967). *The Tacit dimension*. London: Routledge and Kegan Paul.

Quinn, J.B. (1992). *Intelligent enterprise: A knowledge and service based paradigm for industry*. New York: The Free Press.

Quinn, R.E., & Rohrbaugh, J. (1983). A spatial model of effectiveness criteria: Towards a competing values approach to organizational analysis. *Management Science, 29*(3), 363-377.

Schwartz, D.G., Divitini, M., & Brasethwik, T. (2000). On knowledge management in the Internet age. In D.G. Schwartz, M. Divitini, & T. Brasethwik (Eds.), *Internet-based knowledge management and organizational memory* (pp. 1-23). Hershey, PA: Idea Group Publishing.

Senge, P. (1990). *The fifth discipline: The art and practice of the learning organization*. New York: Doubleday Currency.

Singh, H.S. (1998). *Data warehousing concepts, technologies, implementations, and management*. Englewood Cliffs, NJ: Prentice-Hall.

Spender, J.-C. (1998). Pluralistic epistemology and the knowledge-based theory of the firm. *Organisation, 5*(2), 233-256.

Stamper, R.K. (1973). *Information in business and administrative systems*. New York: John Wiley.

Stein, E.W., & Zwass, V. (1995). Actualizing organizational memory with information systems. *Information Systems Research, 6*(2), 85-117.

Turban, E., Aronson, J., & Bolloju, N. (2001). *Decision support systems and intelligent systems*. Upper Saddle River, NJ: Prentice-Hall.

Walsh, J.P., & Ungson, G. (1991). Organizational memory. *Academy of Management Review, 16,* 57-91.

Wijnhoven, F. (1998). Knowledge logistics in business contexts: Analyzing and diagnosing knowledge sharing by logistics concepts. *Knowledge and Process Management, 5*(3), 143-157.

KEY TERMS

Knowledge Logistics: The distribution and storage of knowledge.

Knowledge Objects: These are the inputs and outputs of KOM. There are at least four types of knowledge (conscious knowledge, automatic knowledge, shared body of knowledge, and collective knowledge), on the basis of the dimensions codification (explicit vs. tacit) and sharedness (individual vs. group) of knowledge. Additionally, information is a representation of knowledge or a representation of objects from the real world.

Knowledge Operations Management: In the context of KOM, the operations management input-output objects are knowledge. The input objects may be handled in operations without fundamentally changing them. This process is named knowledge logistics, and includes the storing and distributing of knowledge. In other operation processes, the knowledge inputs are transformed to new or different knowledge objects. This operation method is called learning. These operation methods are realized by certain human and information technological means for specific goals.

KOM Goals: Integration, adaptation, goals attainment, and pattern maintenance.

KOM Means: Information technological and human means, which support knowledge logistic processes (acquisition, storage, maintenance, search and retrieval, and dissemination).

Learning: The transformation of knowledge by socialization, externalization, internalization, or combination.

Operations Management: The operations management approach studies the handling or transformation of certain inputs to outputs (the operations function), and the consequent realization of organizational goals via certain means (management of operations) (Hill, 1983). Operations management distinguishes objects, which are the inputs and outputs of operations, related support tasks, and the setting of goals and creation of means.

Support Function for KOM: The development and management of goals, means, and metrics for KOM.

Operational Knowledge Management in the Military

Gil Ariely
University of Westminster, UK and Interdisciplinary Center Herzliya, Israel

INTRODUCTION

This article intends to cover operational-knowledge management (KM) as implemented in the military. In particular, it is based on experience and published examples from the U.S. Army and the IDF (Israeli Defense Forces). It concentrates on the characteristics of operational knowledge as the core type of interest for the military due to the nature of the mission. The proxy of human lives and mission success are used vs. the more common currencies in the business industry.

The article covers common vehicles in KM through examples implemented in the military (such as communities of practice in the U.S. Navy, storytelling, and scenario planning), with special attention given to a detailed description of the AAR (after-action review). This is a military-originated KM process now widely adopted by industry. Although all these are familiar KM methods and concepts in industry, their value and uniqueness for military applicability are illustrated.

In the current and future battlefield, knowledge and information are critical resources (both of the enemy and of our forces). Through innovative and dispersed IT systems, KM has transformed the modern battlefield situational awareness, both for the individual soldier and the very core of command and control.

A section is devoted to KM in low-intensity conflicts (LICs) that emphasizes learning throughout fighting due to the unique and asymmetric nature of LIC as the contemporary and most common modern form of warfare. In LIC, the learning cycles are short as opposed to those of classic wars where the main learning is done before and after conflicts. In LIC, as a prolonged process (of varying intensities), learning must be conducted throughout the fighting.

BACKGROUND

Liddell Hart (1991) stressed that throughout history, militaries that should have been organizations of the highest adaptability capabilities (due to the nature of their mission) have been the least flexible, harming their own functioning. This has promoted the adoption, for more than a decade in the military, of the learning-organization concept aimed at transforming the military into a dynamic organization that continuously implements organizational learning. Indeed the learning-organization concept (Senge, 1990) is closely entwined with, and is one of the drivers of, the KM movement.

The concentration of knowledge management is derived from the military's mission and vision. The U.S. Army, in its "knowledge vision" (2004), defines "a transformed Army, with agile capabilities and adaptive processes, powered by world class network-centric access to knowledge, systems and services, interoperable with joint environment." Indeed, a continuum strategy to such vision transforms the Army into "a network-centric, knowledge-based force."

Why Operational-Knowledge Management?

Operational has two different meanings in the military context: a knowledge type, and a level of fighting forces and warfare. This article refers to the first.

As a knowledge type, operational knowledge has meaning in industry as well. Although operational research (OR) started in the British Military during WWII, it evolved as a discipline into industry and different domains and areas (Keys, 1995).

However, operations are entwined in most organizations on their way to achieve organizational goals. In the military, the operations (in the sense of military operations) are the very core and essence of the organization. A military organization is established and trained toward operations, be it peacekeeping, defense preparedness, or wartime operations. Hence, operational knowledge is a salient.

The characteristics of operational knowledge demand exploration as the core type of interest for the military (due to the nature of the mission). Indeed, this supports the usage of proxy indicators, such as human lives and mission success vs. the more common currencies in industry.

Although various knowledge types exist in the military (e.g., professional or procedural knowledge in different domains), most of these may be differentiated in their

Figure 1. A simplification of a firm's operations compared to the nature of military operations

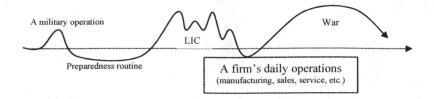

connection to operations, hence to operational knowledge. Whether knowledge is entwined with the conduct of military operations, or indirectly connected merely due to the eventual goals of a military, makes a difference in the way it is referred to.

The military is a competencies-based, mission-oriented organization, which is operational in nature. Hence, operational knowledge is the very essence of the military. So, we need to focus on managing it first, for more reasons than one.

- It is the best testing ground for KM in the military, rendering the fastest ROI.
- Every operational KM implementation is principally applicable toward other knowledge types in the military (once the methodologies are familiar).
- Since commanders' and sponsors' attention are scarce (as are other resources), it is aimed at the operational goals of the military.

Since operational in this context refers to knowledge type, the discrimination from the analogous military term for a level must be determined. Operational refers in the army command also to levels of forces and warfare (i.e., strategic, operational, tactical levels). However, KM can be implemented at all these levels, aimed at operational goals.

Although presumably KM is more applicable at organizational levels, tactical implementation yields a higher mission success rate. Exploring new operational paradigms is especially crucial for special-operations success (Gagnon 2002), where a clear delineation between essentially tactical missions and possible operational or strategic effects does not exist.

FIRST FOCUS: ADAPTING KM VEHICLES FROM (AND TO) INDUSTRY

Most common KM vehicles implemented in industry are applicable to the military with appropriate adaptation.

Furthermore, some KM practices that originated from the military have been adopted by industry. However, the military might have called it by a different name, or did not consider it a KM process. The scope of this article allows a sample of only a few such prominent vehicles, but many more exist, entwined in the daily operations of the military. Even regular officers' gatherings, from the battalion level to divisions, account for such KM processes that aim to create a knowledge-sharing culture as well as sharing specific knowledge.

Since even the titles of these KM processes may differ from those familiar in industry, it is essential to describe their military reembodiment and value. Furthermore, KM in the military context requires adaptations to operational settings, for instance, to "match the pace of operations" (McIntyre, Gauvin, & Waruszynski, 2003, p. 38): "Knowledge management and the knowledge cycle within the context of military operational environments, therefore, require emphasis on these additional requirements of robustness, content and speed."

The current synergy of the military, the academic community, and industry practitioners and researchers promises to benefit the military from the progress of KM.

The After-Action Review

One of the fundamental tools of KM in the Army is the after-action review process. It was developed by the U.S. Army, although it is in use by other militaries as well, sometimes under different titles and a slightly different process (e.g., debriefing). Due to the intense nature of events in the Army, it allows for almost real-time learning in a brief session.

There are four distinct phases in the after-action review.

1. What was supposed to happen? What was the action plan, and what did we aim to do?
2. What actually happened? There is a reviewing and establishing of the facts of the events.
3. What was the gap? What went wrong, causing the gap between 1 and 2?

4. What can we learn? What are the lessons learned that could be implemented in future circumstances (vs. just erroneous judgments)?

Furthermore, a fifth phase may be added.

5. How can we disseminate the lessons learned and to whom should we communicate them?

Higher resolution AAR requires a more detailed prescription, but the principal phases are kept, and so are some cultural principles.

- The AAR is a learning event and not an inquiry aimed at blaming.
- The AAR should be conducted as soon as possible after the action or event, when facts are clear and memory is fresh. In some cases, it can also be conducted throughout events.
- The action itself may be a mission, a training exercise, a project phase, or any clearly defined event.
- Participants should be inclusive of all those in the action reviewed.
- The climate should be open and nonhierarchical, contrary to military culture.

The product of the after-action review is an after-action report detailing the lessons learned. The terms might differ slightly; for example, the Australian Army refers to PAR and POR (post-action review and post-operation report) templates for similar purposes.

Since the U.S. Army's after-action reviews are "probably the best known example of leveraging knowledge within a team" (Dixon Nancy, 2000, p. 37), they are widely adopted by industry. For instance, "British Petroleum has made it the middle step of its three-part knowledge management process" (p. 38) since the AAR is so intuitive and appropriate to the "serial transfer" of knowledge and of lessons learned in the organization.

Sullivan and Harper (1997) observed the direct, immediate personal benefits and usefulness to participants in action and in AAR as its success rationale. Indeed, AARs produce *local value*: knowledge to be used at the decision-making point (Sullivan & Harper). What the basic AAR process lacks is a system to transform and disseminate it beyond local knowledge and value to the organizational level, and to permeate it throughout the Army. That system is the Center for Army Lessons Learned (CALL).

The CALL

Since the disadvantage of AAR is that it is conducted locally and produces local value, the CALL aims to disseminate AARs and lessons learned organizationally throughout the Army while validating their content in a wider context.

Military knowledge management is far from secretive (although the knowledge itself might be). Voluminous unclassified material exists (methodological and core) on the Web site of the CALL (http://call.army.mil/).

Similar examples are the Australian Army's CAL (http://www.defence.gov.au/army/cal/) and the IDF Central-Command Operational-KM Site on the internal intranet.

The CALL may also assign *learning observers* to specific units or training exercises. Their role is to accompany a unit on its duties, bring lessons learned through AARs back to the CALL, and disseminate them to the forces. An excellent example of such conduct was with the U.S. Army's 10th Mountain Division on the naval aircraft carrier Eisenhower during the 1994 Haitian peacekeeping efforts (Baird & Henderson, 2001).

Organizational Knowledge Portal

One of the first steps to the implementation of a dispersed IT-enabled organization like the Army is the creation of accessible knowledge centers containing codified, explicit knowledge and information. An effective infrastructure vehicle for such knowledge centers are organizational portals, which the military as a whole (or specific units) implement extensively on internally accessible networks.

The collaborative IT infrastructure is the foundation for many KM and knowledge-sharing vehicles, especially for a geographically dispersed organization. Some (like CoPs [communities of practice]) are elaborated upon in this article.

The U.S. Army Knowledge Online (AKO) is the Army's intranet portal, which "features content-management software, e-mail, instant messaging, chat rooms, knowledge centers, a people locator and white pages" (U.S. Army, 2004, p. 374). "AKO, the army's knowledge portal has grown to over one million soldier and civilian registered users."

Communities of Practice

IT collaboration tools and environments, like organizational portals, are crucial for the establishment of geographically dispersed communities of practice, a common vehicle in KM.

Indeed, the Army has long acknowledged the role of communities of practice in the creation, sharing, and leveraging of tacit knowledge. CoPs cross units and domains since they may share a professional interest or practice, or rather an operational one. They may be active (as is usually the case) during routine times, but should aim at maintaining, and if possible, implementing, the support networks of relationships and knowledge where and when needed operationally in real time.

An example of implementation guidelines can be found in the U.S. Navy's CoPs manual (http://www.hq.usace.army.mil/cecc/PG/StarterKit.doc).

Indeed, CoPs are implemented widely in the military and yield high operational results: "Communities of Practice (CoPs) are the cornerstone of NAVSEA's strategy for evolving a knowledge enterprise. CoPs offer a collaboration structure that facilitates the creation and transfer of knowledge" (Department of the Navy's Knowledge-Centric Organization).

The ultimate implementation goal of CoPs in a network-centric military should be operational (due to the nature of the mission). It is improved operational ability resulting from real-time support amongst combating units (geographically or task tangential). Such collaboration is based on acquaintance and common language, values, and knowledge nurtured in routine times in these communities of practice.

Storytelling

Nothing is more common and familiar in the Army than war stories. However, besides being just good stories, they also act as a key learning vehicle. They are perhaps even the most ancient and intuitive learning vehicle to human nature as recent research of narration and storytelling proves and promotes.

From the minute a unit returns from mission activity, even before formal AAR or debriefing, storytelling takes form at all levels: from a personal level to a group. This ontological re-creation of events in memory allows for the screening of events through learning binoculars on different levels, formal or nonformal.

Once researched and made explicit through KM processes such as AAR, stories become a formal military learning apparatus—as battle stories are taught not only in military colleges, but are also communicated in other surroundings many times as heritage and history.

KM supports the transition of such processes toward the organizationally cognitive by entwining storytelling beyond heritage: the dissemination of currently relevant or emphasized lessons learned from past occurrences.

For example, a history quiz prepared in the Counter-Terrorism School of IDF was aimed to disseminate contemporarily validated lessons learned from past hostage-rescue events to instructors.

Scenario Planning, War Games, and Simulations

Scenarios are of instrumental core use in the military. They detail contingency plans for a range of eventualities from which the action plan is chosen and formed.

In a similar manner, throughout the process of intelligence analysis, the enemy's possible scenarios are created and analyzed in light of probability and perilousness to our forces. This is done not merely as a risk analysis, but is entwined into the force's own scenarios.

In industry, scenarios are used in different contexts. Ringland (2002, p. 2) says, "In the creative media, it may mean a storyline…strategists, policy makers and planners use scenarios in a 'future-oriented' sense." Indeed, in the field of knowledge management, the usage of scenarios has been researched and promoted as a vehicle for the creation and dissemination of common knowledge and vision through the creation of common future scenarios. This allows for the creation of a unified organizational paradigm. According to Ringland, "Scenarios have been in use at Royal Dutch Shell since the 1960s," and they "help us to understand today better by imagining tomorrow, increasing the breadth of vision and enabling us to spot change earlier" (http://www.shell.com).

The synergy between the KM scenarios approach and the common one in the military allows for a step further in other knowledge and KM military implementations—when using simulations for training.

In the '70s, an experiment with two groups of flight controllers showed that the learning of one group a priori was much less effective than the other group, which was in control towers in a real-life context. Indeed, critical-incidents professions emphasize this notion, which I refer to as *context-dependent learning*, most applicable in the Army.

Context-dependent learning uses familiar methodologies in the Army like war games and simulations that are implemented for various tasks and enhances them.

The U.S. Army prairie-warrior simulation, for instance, tested the effects of digitizing the battlefield, allowing the consideration of possible changes before actual combat deployment (Baird and Henderson, 2001).

Such war games and simulations are also the most effective learning vehicle for soldiers and commanders at all levels of the systems they operate in (social or technological). Furthermore, they allow participants to learn about themselves in a unique context, and they trigger the most inherent level of learning that comes only from doing.

War games were always used by military organizations on strategic and operational levels. However, recent research shows (Ariely, 2004) that even the learning of a terrain cell becomes more effective through context-dependent learning when taken to tactical levels (e.g., a tactical war game played on that terrain cell).

Further goals of scenarios, war games, and simulations include the following (Ariely & Fighel, 2004).

- Testing different scenarios as they develop, including accordance with enemy scenarios
- Testing of specific subjects (e.g., battlefield digitization in the prairie-warrior simulation)
- Context-dependent learning for new commanders and decision makers
- Rehearsal and repetitive knowledge aimed at testing and maintaining readiness
- Dissemination of lessons learned (either through other simulations or AARs)

As illustrated, the blend of KM methods and concepts used in industry are of critical value when adapted and implemented in the military. Experience from KM in industry promoted the cognitive and explicit implementation of KM and KM managerial education, which leads to the appointment of KM-related roles to leverage knowledge as a resource. Hence, it is requisite in a modern military. According to Kaplinski (2004), in the IDF's Central Command, for instance, operational CKOs were appointed up to battalion level (as cited in Lubetzki, 2004).

It is the duty of operational knowledge officers to disseminate methodologically and to implement the KM vehicles proven to be so effective operationally (such as the AAR, which leverages local knowledge, and the lessons-learned repositories that complement it organizationally). The ability of a unit arriving at a unique terrain cell to learn from the past experience of other units operating in the same place before is crucial for maintaining human life and mission success.

SECOND FOCUS: KM AND MODERN WARFARE

KM Transforming the Modern Battlefield

Information technology and the network-centric approach are transforming the nature of the modern battlefield. It is not the existence of voluminous, immediate information from multiple sources that makes the transformation the application in fighting. Tactical knowledge has become a major resource for fighting from the individual level to command and control at all levels. Anyone with combat experience is familiar with the battlefield "information fog" during chaotic events.

Combat KM and IT systems aim at minimizing this fog while not overloading with unnecessary information. Such an example is the Blue Force Tracker system, which Col. Mike Linnington of the 101st Airborne's Third Brigade in Iraq described, dealing with one of the biggest problems of "situational awareness and the ability to battle track blue force, or friendly units" (as cited in Chilcote, 2003). It allows locating units (through GPS [Global Positioning System]) and friend or foe identification that prevent friendly fire (or "blue-on-blue") incidents. Other systems allow intelligence to be transmitted to the battlefield in real time, for example, visual digital aerial imagery of enemy locations and status.

Today, the field commander manages a battle picture loaded with information and knowledge through a variety of supporting measures. These measures are supportive in managing and integrating (mainly technologically) the knowledge and information both of our forces and of the enemy. However, they demand a cultural adaptation of command and control as strategic commanders must reject the temptation to micromanage the battlefield.

Furthermore, knowledge and information that were conveyed to field commanders (and back) are now dispersed to the individual level, allowing a whole new concept of the "knowledge warrior."

KM and Information Warfare

Information warfare stands as a military domain of its own. Clearly, where the ammunitions are information and knowledge, managing both becomes a core military competency, both offensively and defensively (protecting information, infrastructure, and knowledge risk analysis). The scope of this article does not allow full coverage of the relationship between KM and information warfare (e.g., Hall, 2003), however, it suffices to posture knowledge warfare as the next evolutionary phase in information warfare. The fight is not only for information superiority, but rather the way it is implemented toward action and the widening effect of knowledge (e.g., on public opinion and consciousness in low-intensity conflicts, directly affecting military stakeholders).

Learning throughout Fighting: KM in Low-Intensity Conflicts

In his book *Low Intensity Operations* (1971), Frank Kitson claimed that during the quarter of the century since WWII, the British Army participated in only four conflicts classified as "limited war," while at the same time it was

717

active in about 30 other low-intensity operations, not confronting regular forces of enemy nations.

The elusive nature of such warfare (even more than other forms of modern urban warfare that is fought amongst civilians) is asymmetric by definition. The advantages of conventional military force cannot be expressed vs. the full implementation of the opponent's advantages. The LIC is a very demanding form of warfare for the Army (challenging Clausewitz's focus on decisive battle (Clausewitz, 1956)) since it is a prolonged process of varying intensities. It demands the extraction of resources including knowledge, and managing them skillfully.

In the LIC, learning cycles are short, and contrary to classic wars when the main learning is done before and after, the learning must be conducted throughout the fighting. It can be compared to two learning sinus waves adapting one to the other, where every event obliges the opponent to quickly adapt through a short learning cycle and vise versa (Nir, Or, Bareket, & Ariely, 2002). Such an example is the IRA vs. the British detonation-devices learning cycles, or the equivalent learning cycles relating to detonation devices between Hizbulla and the IDF in Lebanon (Gordon, 2002). Hence, in LIC, operational KM is crucial not only amongst the Army's forces, but also in learning from the enemy's activities. Confronting the asymmetric nature of the LIC is achieved through the replication of the opponent's advantages (e.g., through special forces), only implementing that knowledge better. Such an example is the replication of guerilla warfare tactics from Hizbulla in Lebanon to the EGOZ IDF unit (Gordon).

One of the main tasks of the military today is the global war on terrorism. In the current global era of state-sponsored and postmodern terrorism, no clear delineation can be drawn between LIC involving terrorist organizations or guerilla forces and other forms of global terrorism. This is greatly due to the lack of an agreed-on definition of terrorism (Ganor, 2001). Hence, further attention is needed on the synergy between military KM in LIC and other organizations countering terrorism.

Brig. Gen. Kochavi of the IDF referred to the main insight from LIC as the need for having a learning mechanism: "Victory in a changing reality = the ability to learn" (as cited in Yair, et al., 2004).

The Transformation of KM toward Intellectual Capital

Intellectual capital (IC) is briefly defined as intangible assets, and since there is no clear delineation between IC and KM, the relationship clearly deserves further attention (see in this publication "Intellectual Capital and its Relationship with KM" by the same author).

In fact, much of the resources used in the military are intangible: Within the soldiers exist their knowledge and training, there are the weapon systems required for implementation and planning, and so forth. For all these, the IC paradigm developed in the last decade is useful.

The U.S. Army (2004, p. 367) KM strategy defines intellectual capital as "[i]ndividual, team, and enterprise knowledge, systems, and services, and workforce strategies that are necessary to improve operations and decision making."

What forms does IC take in the military? As opposed to the more common currencies in industry (that transform to "hard capital"), proxies in the military for IC differ.

Human casualties within the military and between civilians seems to be the ultimate cost, both the trivial and the critical one when considering the mission of the Army.

However, in the current economically oriented militaries, we may find interesting examples of how military KM becomes through intellectual capital hard currency. In a recent example, the Israeli Army chief of staff offered training knowledge and facilities (part of IDF's intellectual capital) to be marketed to foreign armies (Shapiro, 2003). Some of that intellectual capital relates directly to KM since the Army's tactical training center includes sophisticated debriefing and AAR technological systems that allow 3D images of the conducted training.

Recent research in the military (Ariely, 2004) proposes that internal stakeholders perceive operational KM as a core competency in itself, and that various proxy indicators exist to common industry financial indicators for valuing IC and knowledge assets. In many cases, these may be achieving the mission objectives or minimizing casualties (e.g., reducing cases of friendly fire on soldiers' own forces). Nevertheless, a particular unit's IC is perceived as its ability to be assigned the mission vs. other competing units being assigned. Hence, many concepts relevant to competitive edge and the intellectual-capital paradigm may be very relevant indeed for the military (internally or amongst units).

FUTURE TRENDS

KM is prominent for the future of the military. In the short and medium run, KM promises to continue revolutionizing the battlefield, not just technologically but culturally (as seen in the past and in the present with embedded reporters in fighting). Every soldier and vehicle should arrive at full real-time knowledge autonomy, free to engage in fighting. The network-centric approach requires new operational paradigms to be revisited at all levels.

In the long run, the combination of technology, IT, and the human factor (the soldier as a knowledge worker) is of consequences beyond any imagination.

Forecasts predict unmanned vehicles and even possibly (with progress in research) brain-machine interfaces (BMIs; Shran, Hauptman, & Marcus-Kalish, 2003). Parallel progress in the research of knowledge management, cognitive science, and artificial intelligence may bring a whole new era of knowledge-based warfare aiming at a lower rate of casualties. The U.S. DARPA (Defense Advanced Research Projects Agency) predicts the future warrior to wear clothing that will include processors and sensors, allowing more information to be available at the individual level and thus requiring less (scarce) attention.

Since knowledge is humane and knowledge management is societal, the real transformation is expected in the essence of modern warfare through trends like transparency to the public, casualty sensitivity, and wider global trends.

The result is only greater dependencies on knowledge, and hence, on managing it best.

Subsequently, the explicit understanding of knowledge as a resource renders it vulnerable and as such a target in itself. KM might support further development in the field of information warfare toward a whole new concept of knowledge warfare.

CONCLUSION

Nowhere is the transformation from the industrial age to the information age more evident than in the modern battlefield. Knowledge has become a major resource for fighting from the individual level to strategic command. The skills of managing and implementing methodologies relating to knowledge (like learning throughout fighting) are now critical fighting skills. Thus, knowledge management may become not only a mission-improving and life-saving vehicle, but the very difference between defeat and victory.

REFERENCES

Ariely, G. (2005). *Knowledge management as a methodology towards intellectual capital.* PhD thesis, University of Westminster, London.

Ariely, G., & Fighel, J. (2004). *"Unilateral cooperation" in response to terrorist attacks.* Retrieved from *http://www.ict.org.il/articles/articledet.cfm?articleid=521*

Baird, L., & Henderson, J. C. (2001). *The knowledge engine.* San Francisco: BK.

Chilcote, R. (2003). Technology links 101st on the battlefield. *Behind the Scenes.* CNN.

Clausewitz, C.v. (1956). *On war.* (New and revised ed). New York: Barnes & Noble.

Dixon Nancy, M. (2000). *Common knowledge: How companies thrive by sharing what they know.* Boston: Harvard Business School Press.

Gagnon, G. (2002). Network-centric special operations: Exploring new operational paradigms. *Air & Space Power Chronicles.*

Ganor, B. (2001). *Defining terrorism: Is one man's terrorist another man's freedom fighter?* Retrieved from *http://www.ict.org.il/*

Gordon, S. L. (2002). *Israel against terror: A national assessment.* Efi Meltzer.

Hall, W. M. (2003). *Stray voltage: War in the information age.* Annapolis, MD: Naval Institute Press.

Hart, B. H. L. (1991). *Strategy* (2nd ed.). Meridian Books.

Keys, P. (Ed.). (1995). *Understanding the process of operational research.* John Wiley & Sons.

Kitson, F. (1971). *Low intensity operations: Subversion, insurgency, peace-keeping* (1st ed.). Harrisburg, PA: Stackpole Books.

Lubetzki, G. (2004, August 20). Knowledge management in central command. *Bamahane—IDF Weekly* Newspaper.

McIntyre, S. G., Gauvin, M., & Waruszynski, B. (2003). Knowledge management in the military context. *Canadian Military Journal,* 35-40.

Nir, S., Or, S., Bareket, Y., & Ariely, G. (2002). *Implications of characteristics of low intensity conflict on the issue of learning and operational knowledge management.* Learning throughout Fighting Conference, School of Command.

Ringland, G. (2002). *Scenarios in business.* John Wiley & Sons.

Senge, P. M. (1990). *The fifth discipline* (1st ed.). New York: Doubleday/Currency.

Shapiro, M. (2003, October 14). For rent: New base, first hand. *Bamahane: IDF Weekly Newspaper.*

Shran, Y., Hauptman, A., & Marcus-Kalish, M. (2003). *Future technologies and effect on defence R&D presentation.* Paper presented at Future Technologies and Effect on Defence R&D, Tel Aviv, Israel.

Sullivan, G., & Harper, M. (1997). *Hope is not a method.* New York: Broadway Books.

U.S. Army. (2004). Army knowledge management. In *How the army runs* (2003/2004 ed.). Carlisle: U.S. Army War College.

Yair, Y., Ariely, G., Fighel, J., Kochavi, A., Pratt, A.N., & Tamic, D. (2004). *Panel on military aspects of terrorism.* Paper presented at the Terrorism's Global Impact Conference, Herzliya, September 2004.

KEY TERMS

After-Action Review (AAR): The AAR process, developed mainly in the U.S. Army, is a central building block of KM in the military, conducted immediately (or as soon as possible) after every mission, training exercise, or project. It is a nonhierarchical knowledge event that allows debriefing, understanding, and realizing the value of tacit knowledge on the local level.

Blue-on-Blue Incidents: Also referred to as friendly fire, these are the accidents of one side's forces firing on the same side's forces due to misidentification. Friendly fire is one of the acute challenges for KM in the modern battlefield. In the 1991 Persian Gulf War, these accounted for almost a quarter of the U.S. fatalities.

Context-Dependent Learning: The learning both of knowledge and of the way one behaves in specific scenarios in a realistic life context (preferably one that relates directly to past and future experiences of the learner). It allows the learning of terrain, procedures and processes, events, and almost anything else by doing rather than a priori.

Low-Intensity Conflict (LIC): A military confrontation in which at least one side is either not a regular army (e.g., guerilla forces, insurgents) or not deployed in full scale. Hence, it is usually characterized by asymmetric forces, with contradictious symmetry in the ability to implement force advantages on a prolonged time axis.

Military Intellectual Capital: The U.S. Army (2004) defines intellectual capital as "[i]ndividual, team, and enterprise knowledge, systems, and services, and workforce strategies that are necessary to improve operations and decision making," but it is further perceived through the proxy indicators of reducing casualties, supporting mission success, and "getting the mission" amongst competing units (Yair, 2004).

Modern Battlefield: A holistic concept implementing network-centric operations that allows the real-time connectivity of fighting units, with the availability of combat-supportive information and knowledge on demand of friendly forces and of the enemy.

Operational-Knowledge Management: KM processes that directly affect or relate to core military operations or operational activities.

War Games: Learning events that allow simulating the battlefield in advance, either in order to test various scenarios or to train decision makers at all levels.

Organisational Storytelling

N.A.D. Connell
University of Southampton, UK

INTRODUCTION

In this article we consider some of the ways in which narrative approaches might contribute towards a better understanding of organisational knowledge management. The telling of stories has a long, rich, and varied tradition, stretching back hundreds of years. In the study of organisations, storytelling can be seen as part of a wider field of enquiry, Organisational Discourse, which seeks to ascribe meaning to social exchanges within organisations (Grant, Hardy, Oswick, & Putnam, 2004; Grant & Hardy, 2003). Narratives have been explicitly identified (Wensley, 1998; Denning, 2000; Ward & Sbarcea, 2001) as one of the ways in which knowledge might be exchanged in organisational settings, but only limited consideration has been given to the ways in which storytelling approaches can increase our understanding of the creation and dissemination of knowledge in organisations. In this article we reflect on what we might learn from the application of narrative processes, particularly organisational storytelling, and from narrative content, particularly organisational narrative knowledge, to assess the place of such storytelling in KM.

WHAT IS AN ORGANISATIONAL STORY?

Many of us are actors, and sometimes narrators, in organisational stories that are potentially rich in knowledge. We all think we can recognise a story when we see one, perhaps by recognising the story's content, or by recognising the process by which certain knowledge is being exchanged. In this section we consider definitions surrounding the relationship between what we see as "organisational storytelling" and organisational knowledge.

The first broad issue to consider is the distinction between *narrative* and *story*. This article will treat both terms synonymously within the context of KM, but the reader should be aware that some authors' definitions offer subtle and interesting distinctions (for example, Polkinhorne, 1988; Czarniawska, 1998; Boje, 2001; Gabriel, 2004).

Stories can be seen as one of the ways in which we can encode data about our environment, both personal and organisational. A particular strength of storytelling for KM lies in its capacity not only to represent such sets of data, but also to offer some insights into the complex interrelationships between such data elements. In an organisational context, these interrelationships might help us to *make sense* of the organisation (e.g., Weick, 1995).

We may define these stories according to the form that they take (content definitions), or the way in which we recognise their use (process definitions).

Narrative Defined by Content

If we define stories (including organisational stories) according to their content, we can recognise that they have certain characteristics (Pentland, 1999):

- **a plot** (for example, the employee who has made a mistake, but is forgiven by the boss, who praises and rewards her honesty)
- **actors** in the story (the employee, her boss, an important client, etc.)
- **a sequence of events** (the mistake, her discovery of the mistake, how she attempts to rectify the situation, her boss's discovery of the mistake, etc.)
- **an outcome or closure** (the boss rewards her honesty rather than firing her)—which is often embedded within some sort of "moral context"(for example, honest behaviour is rewarded)
- **a wider recognisable context** within which the story operates (for example, a multinational company with a fierce reputation).

The balance of these properties is not always equal, but might shift as the circumstances (either of the narrative or its purpose) might demand.

Narrative Defined by Process

In process definitions, the situational characteristics of the performance of the story are considered by some authors (e.g., Boje, 1991) to be as insightful as its content. From a KM perspective, such performances might be rich in tacit knowledge, only some of which will be evident from a story's transcript. Boje's operational definition of a story performance—*"an exchange between two or more persons during which past or anticipated experi-*

ence was being referenced, recounted, interpreted, or challenged" (p. 111)—is typical of such definitions. A more general definition might view stories, within an organisational context, as the socially constructed accounts of past events that are considered important or significant to members of an organisation (Feldman, 1990). Within such a definition, stories need not be factual; some argue that they are seldom so (Hansen & Kahnweiler, 1993), reflecting instead what those involved in the storytelling process believe *should* be true. Although some stories purport to convey "facts," such facts are not always straightforward to identify or interpret (Gabriel, 2004).

Within both classes of definition, it is clear that organisational stories are often extraordinarily rich in tacit knowledge (see, for example, Orr, 1990; Hernandez-Serrano, Stefanou, Hood, & Zoumas, 2002; Hoopes & Postrel, 1999; Meyer, Connell, & Klein, 2003). Such knowledge has the potential to be stored (and perhaps through constant retelling, even archived) within the "package" of a story, and transferred in a succinct yet rich way. In this respect, a better understanding of organisational storytelling can contribute some useful insights into the ways in which knowledge exchange, in particular informal knowledge exchange, might be effected within organisations.

A number of authors have acknowledged this potential. In one of the earliest descriptions of the use of organisational storytelling and KM, Denning (2000) describes his experiences within the World Bank, illustrating the use of storytelling as an enabler of organisational change. Snowden (2002) has demonstrated ways in which knowledge might be exchanged, using examples drawn from a number of large organisations. Yet it is clear that many questions are not fully answered within this literature. What sort of knowledge particularly lends itself to being encoded and transferred in stories? Why use stories in preference to other media? What are the organisational processes that might be implemented to encourage the use of stories? In the following section we address these questions in the context of three significant aspects of organisational KM—the creation, storage, and transfer of knowledge.

KNOWLEDGE CREATION AND STORYTELLING

Much of the existing literature has concentrated on viewing stories primarily, sometimes even solely, as a way of storing existing knowledge. Can stories also be seen as a way of creating new knowledge? If so, where do such stories originate? Boje (2001) offers the view that stories begin as what he describes as "ante-narratives," which contain the fragments or seeds of a story that might then be used to create the story. Whilst such fragments might be based on organisational events, this need not necessarily be the case. Although an organisational story, in the context of KM, is rarely an invented story, in the sense of a work of pure fiction, we are not always looking at a precise telling (or retelling) of some aspects of "organisational history." Instead, we are hearing a subjective interpretation.

This lack of objective accuracy in the creation of organisational "knowledge" makes the study and utility of stories interesting when considering knowledge creation in practice; most managers would probably consider accuracy to be a key desirable characteristic of organisational information, yet as we have seen above, some authors have questioned the importance of this aspect, whilst others have instead stressed the "performative" aspects of the storytelling. For such authors, the question of "an objective truth" appears secondary to the reader's or listener's appreciation of the narrative. In essence, the story is in some sense "well told," in a way which evokes understanding and interpretation in the listener or reader, and as a consequence "*the 'truth' of these stories ... is not the issue*" (Rayment-Pickard, 2000, p. 280). The knowledge we are creating is not necessarily a telling or reretelling of "what actually happened," but is instead a structuralist interpretation. "Facts," such as they are, will be woven into each story (by the teller) and interpreted (by both the teller and the listener), sometimes in a selective way to serve the purpose of the story.

This selectivity in the creation (and subsequent transfer) of knowledge is referred to as *glossing* (Weick, 1981; Boje, 1991) or "*colouring*" (Hansen & Khanweiler, 1993), and is often intended to emphasise or sell a particular point of view: "*A gloss is akin to marginal notes or digression that can exaggerate, simplify, or shift the meaning of the experience*" (Boje, 1991, p 117). Although we have already noted that the "truth" of the story may be secondary to its intended use, we might reflect on whether this emphasis on, or deliberate exclusion of, particular aspects of the story is consistent with the typical organisational aspiration for the management of knowledge. Although the notion of "literary licence" appears to be a common feature of storytelling—such that we might reflect, for instance, that "we're not getting the whole story here"—some might argue that such licence is not restricted to storytelling, and that it is ubiquitous across other knowledge-bearing media.

Lastly, a feature of storytelling that might help to explain its potential as a knowledge-creating medium is its receptiveness to casual or informal use in the organisation. Most organisational knowledge is created continuously, yet only stored and reported upon (or transferred) periodically, typically in some formal or semi-formal way. The informal nature of some organisational storytelling allows these episodes not only to occur more frequently, but also in more flexible organisational contexts. This aspect will be returned to when we consider knowledge exchange.

KNOWLEDGE STORAGE AND STORYTELLING

In looking at the definitional characteristics of stories in an earlier section of this article, we noted the importance of context to both process and content definitions. Stories require a cultural context within which their knowledge content can be embedded and stored, and can sometimes provide the listener with a shortcut to knowledge about an organisation's cultural climate, particularly for new members of the organisation (Martin, 1982).

In their work on the different types of stories commonly found in organisations, Martin, Feldman, Hatch, and Sitkin (1983) identify seven types of story, each of which might be viewed as representing unique yet recurring organisational themes, such as rule-breaking, intolerance, or a "them and us" culture. Each theme can be told with a positive or negative story outcome. She suggests three reasons for the ubiquity of these themes.

First is the dualities of behaviour inherent in all organisations, for instance the tension between the firm's values and those of its employees, or whether the same rules apply equally to all, or how those in control behave towards those with less power. "*Organisational stories*," argues Martin, "*express tension created by dualities, perhaps reducing that tension by expressing it*" (p. 448). In considering the story as a knowledge storage medium, it might encode hope (or denial) for resolution of the duality, as well as some predictive knowledge about past organisational behaviour.

Martin's second reason suggests that these themes occur as illustrations of self-preserving rationalisations of past organisational events. Drawing on attribution theory, in which individuals attribute success to their own actions, and failures to external forces beyond their control, she argues that this helps to explain both positive and negative versions of each story theme, as each provides an appropriate vehicle for either version. The acquisition of such knowledge also helps the listener position him/herself about appropriate behaviour to adopt in certain situations, for example, when "to look the other way" or "to keep your head down."

Lastly, she maintains that the stories endow each organisation with a certain "uniqueness," either uniquely good—"*a sanctuary in an otherwise difficult world*" (p. 451), or uniquely bad—"*uniquely unworthy of its employees*" (p. 452). As stories change, or endure, so they store important knowledge for the teller and listener about the prevailing culture of the organisation.

Gabriel (1991) views content themed not in terms of organisational cultural characteristics, but of more generically recognisable story themes—for example, epic, tragic, and comic—each having familiar narrative themes, whilst operating within an organisational context. In the *epic*, the hero struggles against an unfair or weak boss; in the *tragic* story, the hero is a victim, powerless in the face of the organisation; and in the *comic* story, there is an ambiguity, where the characters are shown enjoying, or suffering, an uneasy mix of pleasure and anxiety. Gabriel (1998) identifies a further seven story types, each centred around emotions such as injustice, humour, or romance. The knowledge stored within such stories therefore focuses more on the emotional characteristics of the organisation, and although he cautions against the interpretive difficulties in gauging the precise emotional content of each story, it seems reasonable to conclude that the emotional climate of the organisation might be stored in such stories, and indicated by their use.

A further aspect of knowledge storage associated with stories lies in their plots. Much of the tacit knowledge is held in a story's plot, such that we "know" what aspects of the story are sad, what constitutes a "happy" ending, even what signals an "ending" to the story. Czarniawska (2004) refers to the strength of plots, and that this strength is derived from the repetition of a few "strong plots":

...some plots are strong—or stronger than others—because they have been institutionalised, repeated through the centuries, and are well rehearsed...One should therefore speak of conventional rather than traditional plots, and of dominant rather than strong plots; they are 'strong' in a given time and place. (p. 3)

This emphasis on the contextual aspect of the strong plot appears very resonant with the concept of tacit knowledge, embedded within a familiar story. If each story contains a recognisable "package" of knowledge, so each plot helps to anchor the relevance of that package within an organisational and cultural context.

There appears to be some agreement in the literature that stories provide a valuable way in which organisational knowledge, particularly tacit knowledge, might be encoded. The following section considers how this knowledge might be transferred.

KNOWLEDGE TRANSFER AND STORYTELLING

In this section, we consider how knowledge that has been created and stored in stories could be effectively transferred through storytelling.

Storytelling might be viewed as a process in which an individual shares his or her knowledge with others, typically in a face-to-face spoken encounter, during which the story is told and listened to rather than, say, written or read. Such storytelling might be formal, perhaps as part of a formal presentation that might be organisation-specific or to a wider audience (Clark & Salaman 1998), or informal, perhaps arising from a chance meeting or prompted by events. The nature of such encounters, particularly but not exclusively informal encounters, means that the listener role can be more active—s/he can interrupt, ask for clarification, and express emotions such as approval, disbelief, and so forth about the knowledge being transferred. Such interaction might change the behaviour of the teller, who might modify the story and its knowledge content, in light of such feedback. In this way, the story and its content are less rigidly defined, more dynamic, and perhaps more informal. In some circumstances, the story might be deliberately designed to elicit a response, which may have political or otherwise charged meanings. Informal stories may be counter-cultural or sub-cultural, and their political dimension should not be underestimated, both as a means of reacting to dominant organisational control, and of making sense of the storyteller's and/or listener's place within it. For both formal and informal telling, there will be a selectivity (and, by implication, exclusion) in the process, either deliberate (for example in informal telling) or perhaps as a by-product of organisational structure, culture, or politics (for example, "this story is not to leave the fifth floor").

So far we have considered informal or formal *processes* of organisational storytelling. What motivates the storyteller to choose stories to transfer knowledge, and will such motivation be influenced by or influence the choice of formal or informal organisational story use?

The literature on this question presents two opposing views; on the one hand a willingness of knowledge sharers to exchange knowledge to their mutual benefit (e.g., Orr, 1990), and on the other a reluctance of knowledge carriers to deposit their knowledge due either to its "stickiness" (von Hippel, 1994) or to absence of incentive (Huber, 2000). Much of the motivational literature seems to have less relevance in the context of informal storytelling; organisational storytelling is an optional activity, with willingness on the part of teller and listener to be involved, and therefore little need for incentives in the "management" sense. The "stickiness" of the knowledge, often seen as an inhibitor of effective knowledge

transfer, is much less problematic in storytelling; in some respects it might be regarded as an enabler of more efficient transfer of tacit knowledge, as stories are a "sticky" medium (Connell, Klein, & Meyer, 2004).

Although stories have an inherent capability to capture rich tacit knowledge, it is by no means certain that it is this characteristic that makes them the "medium of choice" among their users. Such tacit knowledge is often exchanged unconsciously, in a taken-for-granted way, during storytelling. Because the teller and listener share the context, the story can often be abbreviated into a particular type of informal story that Boje (1991) refers to as a "terse story."

I call this filling-in-the-blanks form terse storytelling. Much of the story that is told is not actually uttered. A terse telling is an abbreviated and succinct simplification of the story in which parts of the plot, some of the characters, and segments of the sequence of events are left to the hearer's imagination. (p. 115)

The knowledge exchange taking place makes efficient use of this tacit dimension:

...the terser the telling, the more the shared understanding of the social context, since insiders know what to leave to the imagination...The terser the telling, the less sharing of understanding of the social context can be detected by outsiders. (p. 116)

Most of the preceding observations about knowledge transfer and storytelling relate to informal stories. Formal stories, for example those used in presentations or sales pitches, are also used to exchange knowledge, and in these cases the motivation is often easier to discern. Drawing on the work of Bowen (1978), Connell et al. (2004) describe four motives for story use, based on two criteria: *control of story content* and *selection of audience* (see Table 1).

Educational stories are those directed to meet the needs of particular people, with content directed towards a specific meaning or message. If there is no specific meaning or message, the story is intended to *enrich* the understanding of the audience. If a story has a specific meaning or message, but its audience is not identified until after the story has been created, such stories are designed to achieve a particular *effect*. Finally, a story carrying no specific meaning or message, whose audience is selected to hear it after it has been created, is probably being told for *entertainment*, as when one selects an audience who would enjoy or appreciate hearing about some experience one has recently had. The intention of this "four Es" categorisation is to help practitioners reflect on how and why a story might be an effective

Table 1. Motives for organisational story use (Connell et al., 2004)

		Selection of story audience	
		Story directed at the needs of particular people	People selected who would benefit from story
Control of story content	Specific meaning or message	EDUCATION	EFFECT
	No specific meaning or message	ENRICHMENT	ENTERTAINMENT

knowledge transfer medium in a particular situation, rather than an attempt to "pigeon-hole" stories, which might span two categories or might be used in different ways in different situations. Clearly, such reflections will be more relevant in addressing the deliberate use of stories, where the intention is to manage the story content and recipient reaction.

Both formal and informal stories appear to take advantage of a palatable contextual framework for knowledge transfer. This distinction is not dependant on the "truth" of a story, as we have noted above; formal and informal stories can be equally "untrue." The *structure* of stories appears to be supportive of their use as a knowledge *exchange* medium, in particular because stories appear to encourage, or perhaps even invite, retelling.

FUTURE TRENDS

There is a sparseness of empirical support for many of the assertions claimed for narrative approaches to KM. Both "descriptive" and "prescriptive" studies, within different organisational structures, would help to shed more light upon the knowledge processes within organisational storytelling, and if such encounters could, or should, be "managed." Evidence is available from communities of practice such as those identified by Orr (1990) and Shaw, Brown, and Bromiley (1998). Snowden (2002) describes a "private collaboration space" within IBM, containing stories recording "significant mistakes and associated learning that would only be shared by a small trusted community" (Snowden, 2002, p. 20). There is also some limited empirical evidence of story use from voluntary organisations such as Alcoholics Anonymous (Steffen, 1995; Swora, 2001), and caregiving environments (Kirkpatrick, Ford, & Castelloe, 1997; Meyer et al., 2003), where stories may perform a unique or special knowledge-sharing role. It has yet to be seen if the potential for the use of ICT-enabled knowledge exchanges (Meyer et al., 2003; van der Hoof & de Leeuw van Weenen, 2004) will act as an inhibitor or accelerator of organisational storytelling.

If we consider stories as knowledge-flow facilitation devices, and if we seek to explore the ways in which they might be used as effective knowledge transfer devices, then we may need to consider occasions when organisations might be particularly receptive, perhaps even vulnerable, to stories, and also to consider physical locations which might promote, formally or informally, their use.

CONCLUSION

In this article, we have examined both "process" issues—why, when, where, and how stories might be used to create, store, and exchange knowledge—and also "content" issues—the nature of the knowledge, its potency, and its perceived validity. Organisational knowledge is inextricably bound up within the context of the story, and for such knowledge exchanges to be "managed" we need to reflect on ways in which organisations can influence or encourage (or perhaps even inhibit) a storytelling culture through both formal and informal mechanisms; such conscious and deliberate organisational action might be termed "*narrative engineering*" (Connell et al., 2004).

Organisational stories have significant potential to shed light upon the characteristics of the organisations in which they exist, not least because of the tacit knowledge which is often inextricably bound up within them. We have noted how the stickiness of this knowledge is a valuable characteristic of stories when transferring knowledge, but that the dynamic and unpredictable nature of storytelling offers a challenge to the manager attempting to harness its power.

REFERENCES

Boje, D.M. (1991). The storytelling organization: A study of story performance in an office supply firm. *Administrative Science Quarterly, 36*, 106-126.

Boje, D.M. (2001). *Narrative methods for organisational and communication research.* London: Sage Publications.

Clark, T., & Salaman, G. (1998). Telling tales: Management gurus' narratives and the construction of managerial identity. *Journal of Management Studies*, 35(2), 137-161.

Connell, N.A.D., Klein, J.H., & Meyer, E. (2003, September). Narrative, knowledge and communities of practice: What sort of stories do practitioners listen to, and tell? In S. Parkinson & J. Shutt (Eds.), *Proceedings of the British Academy of Management Conference* (pp. 1-8). Harrogate.

Connell, N.A.D., Klein, J.H., & Meyer, E. (2004). Narrative approaches to the transfer of organisational knowledge. *Knowledge Management Research and Practice, 2*(3), 184-193.

Czarniawska, B. (1998). *A narrative approach to organizational studies.* London: Sage Publications.

Czarniawska, B. (2004, June). Femmes fatales in finance, or women and the city. *Proceedings of "The End of Stories and the Limits of Storytelling" Conference* (pp. 1-36). University of Exeter, UK.

Denning, S. (2000). *The springboard: How storytelling ignites action in knowledge-era organizations.* Boston: Butterworth Heinemann.

Feldman, S.P. (1990). Stories as cultural creativity: On the relation between symbolism and politics in organisational change. *Human Relations, 43,* 809-928.

Gabriel, Y. (2000). *Storytelling in organizations: Facts, fictions and fantasies.* London: Sage Publications.

Gabriel, Y. (2004). The narrative veil: Truth and untruths in storytelling. In Y. Gabriel (Ed.), *Myths, stories and organizations.* Oxford: Oxford University Press.

Grant, D., & Hardy, C. (2003). Struggles with organizational discourse (introduction to special issue on OD). *Organization Studies, 25*(1), 5-13.

Grant, D., Hardy, C., Oswick, C., & Putnam, L. (2004). *The Sage handbook of organizational discourse.* London: Sage Publications.

Hansen, C.D., & Kahnweiler, W.M. (1993). Storytelling: An instrument for understanding the dynamics of corporate relationships. *Human Relations, 46,* 1391-1409.

Hernandez-Serrano, J., Stefanou, S.E., Hood, L.F., & Zoumas, B.L. (2002). Using experts' experiences through stories in teaching new product development. *Journal of Product Innovation Management, 19*(1), 54-68.

Hoopes, D.G., & Postrel, S. (1999). Shared knowledge, 'glitches' and product development performance. *Strategic Management Journal, 20,* 837-865.

Huber, G.P. (2000, July). Transferring soft knowledge: Suggested solutions and needed studies. In J. Edwards & J. Kidd (Eds.), *Proceedings of the KMAC 2000 Knowledge Management Conference* (pp. 12-22). Birmingham.

Kirkpatrick, M.K., Ford, S., & Castelloe, B.P. (1997). Storytelling: An approach to client-centred care. *Nurse Educator, 22*(2), 38-40.

Martin, J. (1982). Stories and scripts in organisational settings. In A. Hasdorf & A. Isen (Eds.), *Cognitive social psychology* (pp. 255-305). New York: Elsevier-North Holland.

Martin, J., Feldman, M.S., Hatch, M.J., & Sitkin, S.B. (1983). The uniqueness paradox in organisational stories. *Administrative Science Quarterly, 28*(3), 438-453.

Meyer, E., Connell, N., & Klein, J.H. (2003). Knowledge exchange within small teams, some preliminary empirical findings from two contrasting environments. In J.S. Edwards (Ed.), *Proceedings of KMAC 2003, Knowledge Management Aston Conference 2003* (pp. 272-283).

Orr, J. (1990). Sharing knowledge and celebrating identity: War stories in a community culture. In D.S. Middleton & D. Edwards (Eds.), *Collective remembering: Memory in society* (pp. 169-189). Beverly Hills, CA: Sage Publications.

Pentland, B.T. (1999). Building process theory with narrative: From description to explanation. *Academy of Management Review, 24*(4), 711-724.

Polkinghorne, D.E. (1988). *Narrative knowing and the human sciences.* Albany, NY: State University of New York Press.

Rayment-Pickard, H. (2000). Narrativism. In R.M. Burns & H, Rayment-Pickard (Eds.), *Philosophies of history: From enlightenment to postmodernity.* Oxford: Blackwell.

Shaw, G., Brown, R., & Bromiley, P. (1998). Strategic stories: How 3M is re-writing business planning. *Harvard Business Review,* (May).

Snowden, D. (2002). Complex acts of knowing—paradox and descriptive self-awareness. *Journal of Knowledge Management, 6*(2).

Steffen, V. (1995). Stories as therapy. Life stories and myth in Alcoholics Anonymous. *Nordisk Alkohol Tidskrift, 12*(6), 273-281.

Swora, M.G. (2001). Narrating community: The creation of social structure in Alcoholics Anonymous through the performance of autobiography. *Narrative Inquiry, 11*(2).

van der Hoof, B., & de Leeuw van Weenen, F. (2004). Committed to share: Commitment and CMC use as antecedents of knowledge sharing. *Knowledge and Process Management, 11*(1), 13-24.

Ward, V., & Sbarcea, K. (2001). Voice: Storytelling is knowledge management. In J. Ranyard (Ed.), *OR43 Keynote Papers, Proceedings of the OR Society Annual Conference* (pp. 129-143). Bath, UK.

Weick, K. (1995). *Sensemaking in organizations.* Thousand Oaks, CA: Sage Publications.

Wensley, A. (1998). The value of storytelling. *Knowledge and Process Management, 5*(1), 1-2.

KEY TERMS

Glossing: The telling or retelling of a story in a way which emphasises or excludes particular points of view.

Narrative: A social exchange, within an organisational context, in which events, either actual or imagined, unfold over time.

Narrative Engineering: The deliberate use of stories and storytelling to bring about some organisational outcome.

Organisational Discourse: Collections of organisational texts, such as conversations, stories, dialogues, meetings, and other socially constructed exchanges, of which storytelling represents an example of a unit of analysis.

Stickiness of Knowledge: A characteristic of some types of knowledge is to only "make sense" in a particular or specific context; attempts to disentangle or isolate such knowledge are thought to be made more difficult because the knowledge "sticks" to its context, making its transfer more challenging.

Story: A form of narrative in which certain characteristics, such as a plot, actors, a sequence of events over time, and an implicit evaluative framework, are described or presented by the storyteller to the listener.

Organizational Attention

Eyal Yaniv
Bar-Ilan University, Israel

David G. Schwartz
Bar-Ilan University, Israel

INTRODUCTION

Attention is a term commonly used in education, psychiatry, and psychology. Attention can be defined as an internal cognitive process by which one actively selects environmental information (i.e., sensation) or actively processes information from internal sources (i.e., stored memories and thoughts; Sternberg, 1996). In more general terms, attention can be defined as an ability to focus and maintain interest in a given task or idea, including managing distractions. Attention is selective by its nature. According to Pashler (1998, p. 37), "The process of selecting from among the many potentially available stimuli is the clearest manifestation of selective attention."

Why do firms respond to certain events or stimuli in their environment while neglecting others? It seems that organizations, just like individuals, have limited attention capacity. Hence, they must select from among the many potentially available stimuli and respond to these selected stimuli only. Organizational attention is defined as the socially structured pattern of attention by decision makers within the organization (Ocasio, 1997). Organizational attention, like human attention, is a limited resource: "Attentional limits filter or screen incoming information such that a great deal of data pertinent to strategic decision may never get processed" (Corner, Kinicki, & Keats, 1994, p. 296). Garg, Walters, and Priem (2003) show that the extent to which CEOs (chief executive officers) are selective in their attention to sectors of the environment is a significant predictor of performance.

Knowledge management (KM) models and process theories, almost without exception, incorporate a stage or phase in which a given knowledge item is brought to bear on a current decision or action. This stage, referred to alternatively as externalization (Nonaka, 1994) or awareness (Schwartz, Divitini, & Brasethvik, 2000), is of crucial importance in any knowledge-management cycle. The flow of knowledge in and out of an awareness stage is not merely a function of the universe of available organizational memory or the technological tools available to filter and identify such knowledge. It is influenced to a large degree by organizational attention.

The second area in which organizational attention is key is knowledge acquisition and creation as discussed by Ocasio (1997), and Yaniv and Elizur (2003).

Successful knowledge management requires attention. Davenport and Volpel (2001) argues that attention is the currency of the information age. Knowledge consumers must pay attention to knowledge and become actively involved in the knowledge-transfer processes. This is particularly important when the knowledge to be received is tacit (Nonaka, 1994). Knowledge can be part of the organization's repository, however, if it does not get the attention of decision makers or other knowledge workers, it is not effective. This knowledge can be very important and relevant to the organization, but since it does not get attention, it does not become useful. Organizational attention is crucial in the context of knowledge management as it lays the infrastructure for knowledge acquisition and transfer.

Like human attention, organizational attention is limited in its capacity. Davenport and Volpel (2001) terms this as the attention-deficit principle: "Before you can manage attention, you need to understand just how depleted this resource is for organizations and individuals." Organizational attention limits the ability of organizations to process knowledge and thus it should be of major concern when knowledge management is discussed.

The limited organizational attention span reduces the number of sources that the organization can use as knowledge sources. The organization has to pay attention to some sources while ignoring or paying less attention to others. An increased likelihood of missing key information when making decisions is the direct result of this selective attention. In this article, organizational attention is discussed in the context of organizational knowledge flow and processing.

BACKGROUND: ORGANIZATIONAL ATTENTION AND KNOWLEDGE PROCESSING

The fact that a situation demands information to fill cognitive gaps, to support values and beliefs, or to influence affective states, and that sources of information are available and accessible to the decision maker is no guarantee that the information will be processed (that is, incorporated into the users' framework of knowledge, beliefs, or values) or used (that is, lead to changes in behavior, values, or beliefs).

Mintzberg's (1973) model of the managerial use of information includes information acquired from the external environment. In his conceptualization of top managers as information-processing systems, the managers' interpersonal roles provide access and exposure to information from a large number of external and internal information sources. The manager in the informational role of monitor "continually seeks and receives information from a variety of sources in order to develop a thorough understanding of the organization and its environment" (p. 97).

Ocasio (1997) developed a framework for an attention-based view of the firm. He defines corporate strategy as "a pattern of organizational attention, the distinct focus of time and efforts by the firm on a particular set of issues, problems, opportunities, and threats, and on a particular set of skills, routines, programs, projects and procedures" (p. 188). Simon (1947) describes organizational behavior as a complex network of attentional processes. Ocasio argues that since the environment of a firm's decision is of infinite complexity and firms are bounded in their capacity to attend to all environmental stimuli, decision makers are selective in those aspects of the environments of the decisions that they attend to. Different environmental stimuli are noticed, interpreted, and brought into conscious consideration. According to this view, attention is the noticing, encoding, interpreting, and focusing of time and effort by organizational decision makers on both issues and answers. Issues are problems, opportunities, and threats, and answers are action alternatives, such as proposals, routines, projects, programs, and procedures.

A basic example of organizational attention in action is as follows. Consider a cellular service provider in a very dynamic, competitive environment. Decision makers are faced with an overwhelming number of problems to deal with: competitive rivalry, customers' demands, technological innovation, and so forth. Their sources of information about these issues are diverse. Competitors' behavior and expected moves can be determined to a certain degree from public sources, such as newspapers and conferences, or by business intelligence activities. Different evaluations of the future behavior of competitors are available. Customers' demands are also based on different sources of information. Technological news come both from internal and external sources. Decision makers are bombarded with more information than they can effectively attend to and assimilate as their attention capacity is bounded. They have to select which problems, issues, and inputs they can deal with among the infinite available sources. Organizational attention is the pattern that is derived from decision makers' selections. The organization as a whole responds, according to this pattern, to certain issues while paying less attention to others. In our cellular example, the firm might ignore signals about the intention of a competitor to launch a new technology if the source that provides this information is not in the attention focus of the firm.

Durand (in press) investigates organizational attention in terms of the firms' investment in internal and external information, and finds that higher relative investments in market information appear to reduce errors and bias in forecasting.

Organizational attention affects both the forward and backward search for information in order to solve organizational problems and acquire new knowledge (Cyert & March, 1963), and to perceive opportunities or threats in the environment (Gavetti & Levinthal, 2000).

Decision makers differ in their knowledge of alternatives and consequences (March & Simon, 1958), their values, and their cognitive styles (Hambrick & Mason, 1984). These factors may contribute significantly to managers' focus of attention.

Ocasio (1997, p. 204) stresses that "the focusing of attention by organizational decision makers allows for enhanced accuracy, speed, and maintenance of information-processing activities, facilitating perception and action for those activities attended to." As stated by Cockburn, Henderson, and Stern (2000, p. 1142):

Ex post, it is clear that some firms actively identify, interpret, and act upon early signals from their external and internal environment, and so position themselves to effectively exploit these opportunities well in advance of others' demonstration of the pay-off from the strategies which emerge later on as best practices.

Two major aspects of human attention are capacity and selection. These aspects are adaptable and applicable to the discussion of organizational attention. Contemporary research discusses attention within the framework of the information-processing approach (Pashler, 1998). At the individual level, capacity is the amount of stimuli that can be noticed and processed in a given time. Kahneman (1973) suggests that the allocation of finite resources might account for a broad range of limitations people have in doing different activities at the same time. Due to these limitations, the individual has to select from the available stimuli those she or he will focus on and process. According to Kahneman focused attention facilitates perception and actions toward issues and activities being attended to, while inhibiting perception and action toward those that are not.

MAIN FOCUS: THE IMPORTANCE AND IMPACT OF ORGANIZATIONAL ATTENTION IN A KNOWLEDGE-MANAGEMENT SETTING

In the organizational context, capacity can be defined as the amount of issues that can be processed by decision makers, and selection refers to the specific issues that were selected and are being processed by the firm and its decision makers. These two dimensions complement each other. According to Ocasio (1997), "The environment of decisions is of infinite complexity and firms are bounded in their capacity to attend to all (or even most) environmental stimuli that impinge, directly or indirectly, upon any particular situation." Within the constraint of limited capacity, organizations have to select the issues that they can attend to while filtering the rest. Organizations differ in both factors. They differ in attention capacity and they select different issues or stimuli to deal with (Yaniv, 2004; Yaniv & Elizur, 2003). As organizational attention is the socially structured pattern of attention by decision makers, the attention capacity of the organization is a function of the decision makers' attention capacity and the organizational knowledge-flow structure.

The organizational knowledge-flow structure is an intangible resource that is part of the organizational tacit knowledge that embodies strategic advantage (Baumard, 1999; Eisenhardt & Santos, 2002). The knowledge-flow structure is a major factor in creating new knowledge (Corner et al., 1994). This structure creates differences between firms when they absorb and create new knowledge. Even more interesting is how this structure hinders the exploitation of available knowledge that might be very valuable.

In the context of knowledge processing, organizational attention is a filter mechanism that enables focusing on some of the available inputs while suppressing the rest. While organizational attention is rarely discussed in the literature, some related terms depict organizational limits. Absorptive capacity and bounded rationality can be mapped to the above attention-related constructs selection and attention capacity, respectively.

Absorptive Capacity

Cohen and Levinthal (1990) describe the ability of the firm to evaluate and utilize new knowledge to the evolving knowledge base already accumulated by the firm. They define absorptive capacity as the idea that prior related knowledge confers an ability to recognize the value of new information, assimilate it, and apply it to commercial ends. Cohen and Levinthal argue that when a firm wishes to acquire knowledge that is unrelated to its ongoing activity, the firm must dedicate efforts to creating or increasing absorptive capacity.

Since absorptive capacity affects the ability of the firm to recognize the value of new knowledge, it acts as a knowledge filter. The firm's existing knowledge influences the absorption of new knowledge and filters unrelated knowledge. In other words, the existing knowledge directs the firm's attention to new related knowledge. Absorptive capacity is an organizational situational feature that determines which knowledge sources the firm will choose to focus on. In terms of organizational attention, absorptive capacity is akin to selection. Absorptive capacity explains some aspects of accumulating new knowledge by the organization and considerably influences selection, yet it does not fully explain selection behavior. There are more factors to be considered.

Bounded Rationality

The limited attentional capability of humans results in their bounded capacity to be rational (Simon, 1947). The bounded-rationality problem (Simon, 1955) is the inability of firms to maximize over the set of all conceived alternatives when dealing with real-life decision problems. These problems are often too complex to comprehend. Based on the bounded-rationality problem, Nelson and Winter (1982) focus on the evolution of simple, stable routines that are used to guide action. Because of the bounded-rationality problem, these routines cannot be too complicated and cannot be characterized as optimal since they are taking into account only partial information. However, Nelson and Winter claim that "they may be quite satisfactory for the purposes of the firm given the problems the firm faces" (p. 35).

The bounded rationality of the individual is parallel in many ways to organizational attention. It is based on the limited ability of decision makers to pay attention to all aspects of the problems they deal with. Their attention capacity is limited, and they therefore make shortcuts. Bounded rationality is akin to attention capacity. What causes decision makers to choose certain knowledge to focus on and ignore other knowledge? They do have a limited capacity, but they still could choose to use this capacity in different ways and focus on different sets of knowledge.

The two filters discussed here—bounded rationality and absorptive capacity—are closely related to organi-

Figure 1. Knowledge creation (Gavetti & Levithal, 2000)

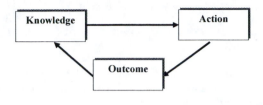

zational attention. Bounded rationality is the result of attention's limited capacity, while absorptive capacity is a major factor that affects attention selection. The following section discusses the affect of attention selection on the creation of new knowledge.

Organizational Attention and Knowledge Creation

Gavetti and Levinthal (2000) present an iterative process of knowledge creation, illustrated in Figure 1. The influence of the outcome on knowledge is mediated by the reinforcement of routinized patterns of action.

Building on this model, organizational attention can be incorporated into the process of new knowledge creation. The new knowledge is not derived automatically from the outcomes, but filtered and directed by organizational attention. The process is illustrated in Figure 2.

Organizational attention mediates knowledge and actions. Since not all the available knowledge can be noticed and used by the firm for its actions, organizational attention affects the creation of new knowledge. In other words, the creation of new knowledge depends on the knowledge that penetrates the organizational attention filter.

Neisser (1976) describes the human perceptual cycle. He suggests that perceptual processes produce a preliminary and temporary representation of input features that act as cues to activate knowledge-schema representations, which in turn can direct attention to a

Figure 3. The perceptual cycle (Neisser, 1976)

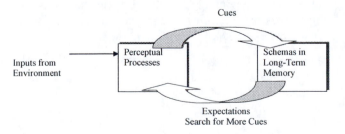

Figure 2. Knowledge creation mediated by organizational attention

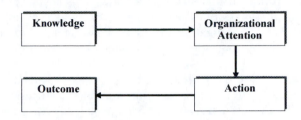

more detailed analysis of cue features. The perceptual process is depicted in Figure 3.

The organizational processes of acquiring and accumulating knowledge can be characterized by a similar cycle. These knowledge-transfer processes are cyclic, thereby the existing knowledge directs the organizational attention to certain knowledge and ignores others. The organization receives inputs from its environment, both internal and external, and processes them according to its existing knowledge. The organizational existing knowledge is stored in organizational memory (Ackerman, 1996; Tuomi, 1999; Walsh & Ungson, 1991). Knowledge is stored in several physical locations (Simon, 1947), individuals (Argyris & Schon, 1978), procedures (Cyert & March, 1963), and culture (Ackerman; Barney, 1986). Walsh and Ungson posit the existence of five storage bins that compose the structure of organizational memory and one external source. The storage bins include individuals, culture, transformations (procedures), structures (roles), and the ecology (physical plant). By external source, they refer to external archives.

FUTURE DIRECTIONS

The knowledge-seeking behavior of an organization is not simply the sum of the parts of its individual members. In order to better understand how organizational attention influences the knowledge-management cycle, there are two main areas that require additional research and development.

First is the development of analysis techniques that can effectively identify and quantify organizational attention. By understanding the detailed elements within an organization that impact and influence attention, we can begin to harness it.

Second is the use of models of organizational attention as an intervention tool to help modify and steer the direction of KM in an organization. Viewing organizational attention as a systemic part of a firm's KM processes opens the door to focusing that attention in more effective ways.

SUMMARY

Organizational attention is an important concept that can explain organizations' knowledge-seeking and -awareness behavior. Organizational attention affects a firm's behavior by controlling organizational knowledge flow and knowledge processing. Explaining firms' behavior is a basic issue of strategic management (Rumelt, Schendel, & Teece, 1994), and strategy formulation is a process of guided evolution (Lovas & Ghoshal, 2000). The firm can be viewed as a collection of discrete organizational activities (Porter, 1985; Sigglekow, 2002), and the mechanism that guides the evolution of the strategy within the firm is organizational attention. Organizational attention is guided by the selective attention to organizational issues and initiatives (March & Olsen, 1976; Ocasio, 1997).

Like individual attention, the capacity of organizational attention is bounded. Nevertheless, organizational attention capacity is varied as a function of the organizational decision structure. Efficiency of decision processes and knowledge flow in the organization can result in the extended attention capacity of the organization. This limited capacity determines the amount of information inputs that can be effectively handled by the firm's decision makers.

The selection of inputs to be considered in knowledge-intensive tasks depends, of course, on the available attention capacity. Since the capacity is limited, this process must be economical, and being economical in the context of knowledge processing means optimizing the use of processing resources. One way of doing so is to select inputs that are easier to deal with: often inputs that are related to existing knowledge as they are easier to perceive and process. This notion is compatible with Cohen and Levinthal's (1990) definition of absorptive capacity, where existing knowledge plays a critical role in the ability of the organization to absorb new knowledge. Both attention capacity and existing knowledge predispose the organization's selection of knowledge inputs from available sources, and an improved understanding of the factors that affect organizational attention will lead to better use of these scarce resources.

REFERENCES

Ackerman, M. S. (1996). Definitional and contextual issues in organizational and group memories. *Information Technology and People, 9*, 10-24.

Argyris, C., & Schon, D. A. (1978). *Organizational learning: A theory of action perspective.* Reading, MA: Addison-Wesley.

Barney, J. B. (1986). Organizational culture: Can it be a source of sustained competitive advantage? *Academy of Management Review, 11*, 656-665.

Baumard, P. (1999). *Tacit knowledge in organizations.* London: SAGE.

Bettis, R. A., & Prahalad, C. K. (1995). The dominant logic: Retrospective and extension. *Strategic Management Journal, 16*, 5-14.

Cockburn, I. M., Henderson, R. M., & Stern, S. (2000). Untangling the origins of competitive advantage. *Strategic Management Journal, 21*, 1123-1145.

Cohen, W. M., & Levinthal, D. A. (1990). Absorptive capacity: A new perspective on learning and innovation. *Administrative Science Quarterly, 35*, 128-152.

Conner, K. R., & Prahalad, C. K. (1996). A resource-based theory of the firm: Knowledge versus opportunism. *Organization Science, 7*, 477-501.

Corner, P. D., Kinicki, A. J., & Keats, B. W. (1994). Integrating organizational and individual information perspectives on choice. *Organization Science, 5*, 294-308.

Cyert, R. M., & March, J. G. (1963). *A behavioral theory of the firm.* Englewood Cliffs, NJ: Prentice-Hall.

Davenport, T. H., & Volpel, S. C. (2001). The rise of knowledge towards attention management. *Journal of Knowledge Management, 5*, 212-221.

Durand, R. (2003). Predicting a firm's forecasting ability: The roles of organizational illusion of control and organizational attention. *Strategic Management Journal, 24*(9), 821-838.

Eisenhardt, K. M., & Santos, F. M. (2002). Knowledge-based view: A new theory of strategy? In A. Pettigrew, H. Thomas, & R. Whittington (Eds.), *Handbook of strategy and management* (pp. 139-164). London: Sage Publications.

Garg, V. K., Walters, B. A., & Priem, R. L. (2003). Chief executive scanning emphases, environmental dynamism, and manufacturing firm performance. *Strategic Management Journal, 24*, 725-744.

Gavetti, G., & Levinthal, D. (2000). Looking forward looking backward: Cognitive and experimental search. *Administrative Science Quarterly, 45*, 113-137.

Hambrick, D. C., & Mason, P. A. (1984). Upper echelons: The organization as a reflection of its top management. *Academy of Management Review, 9*, 193-206.

Kahneman, D. (1973). *Attention and effort*. Englewood Cliffs, NJ: Prentice Hall.

Lovas, B., & Ghoshal, S. (2000). Strategy as guided evolution. *Strategic Management Journal, 21*, 875-896.

March, J. G. (1991). Exploration and exploitation in organizational learning. *Organization Science, 2*, 71-78.

March, J. G., & Olsen, J. P. (1976). *Ambiguity and choice in organizations*. Bergen: Universitetsforlaget.

March, J. G., & Simon, H. A. (1958). Organization. New York: Wiley.

Mintzberg, H. (1973). *The nature of managerial work*. New York: Harper and Row.

Neisser, U. (1976). *Cognition and reality*. San Francisco: Freeman.

Nelson, R. R., & Winter, S. G. (1982). *An evolutionary theory of economic change*. Cambridge, MA: Harvard University Press.

Nonaka, I. (1994). A dynamic theory of organizational knowledge creation. *Organization Science, 5*, 14-37.

Ocasio, W. (1997). Towards an attention-based theory of the firm. *Strategic Management Journal, 18*, 187-206.

Pashler, H. E. (1998). *The psychology of attention*. Cambridge, MA: The MIT Press.

Porter, M. E. (1985). *Competitive advantage*. New York: Free Press.

Rumelt, R. P., Schendel, D., & Teece, D. (1994). *Fundamental issues in strategy*. Cambridge, MA: Harvard Business School Press.

Schwartz, D. G., Divitini, M., & Brasethvik, T. (2000). On knowledge management in the Internet age. In D. G. Schwartz, M. Divitini, & T. Brasethvik (Eds.), *Internet-based organizational memory and knowledge management* (pp. 1-23). Hershey, PA: Idea Group Publishing.

Sigglekow, N. (2002). Evolution toward fit. *Administrative Science Quarterly, 47*, 125-159.

Simon, H. A. (1947). *Administrative behavior: A study of decision-making processes in administrative organizations*. Chicago: Macmillan.

Simon, H. A. (1955). A behavioral model of rational choice. *Quarterly Journal of Economics, 69*, 99-118.

Stehr, N. (1992). *Practical knowledge*. London: Sage Publications, Inc.

Sternberg, R. J. (1996). *Cognitive Psychology*. Harcourt Brace College Publishers.

Tuomi, I. (1999). Data is more than knowledge: Implication of the reversed knowledge hierarchy for knowledge management and organizational memory. *Journal of Management Information Systems, 16*, 103-117.

Walsh, J. P., & Ungson, G. R. (1991). Organizational memory. *Academy of Management Review, 16*, 57-91.

Yaniv, E. (2004). *Organizational attention as a knowledge filter: The influence of organizational attention on exploiting knowledge as a strategic resource*. Unpublished PhD dissertation, Bar Ilan University, Israel.

Yaniv, E., & Elizur, D. (2003). The structure of organizational attention: A Radex representation of multiple knowledge sources. In S. Levi & D. Elizur (Eds.), *Facet theory: Towards cumulative social science*. Ljubljana: University of Ljubljana.

KEY TERMS

Absorptive Capacity: The ability of an organization to recognize the value of new knowledge, assimilate it, and apply it to commercial ends.

Attention-Deficit Principle: Recognizes that organizations have limited attention capacity, and attention should be treated as a resource that needs to be managed.

Awareness: A stage in the knowledge-management cycle in which a decision maker is made aware of the potential application of organizational memory to a current issue.

Bounded Rationality: According to Simon (1947), it is the limited attentional capability of humans resulting in their bounded capacity to be rational.

Capacity: The amount of stimuli that can be noticed and processed in a given time period, or the number of concurrent issues that can be processed by a decision maker.

Organizational Attention: The socially structured pattern of attention by decision makers in an organization guiding how they select from and respond to available stimuli.

Selection: The choice of which stimuli should be considered and which issues should be addressed when presented with a set of stimuli and issues beyond the available capacity.

Organizational Communication

Dov Te'eni
Tel-Aviv University, Israel

INTRODUCTION

All organizations depend on communication. Communication is the exchange of information between two or more people with the intent that the sender's message be understood and considered by the receivers in their cognition, affect, and behavior. As organizations are designed for action, most organizational communication eventually leads to action and to working relationships between actors. Indeed, communication plays a pivotal role in organizations and may even be seen as the foundation for most organizational action (Galbraith, 1977; Weick, 1979).

KM and communication go hand in hand. On the one hand, communication is the basis for knowledge sharing, which is a necessary component of successful knowledge management. On the other hand, knowledge is crucial for effective communication, and KM is therefore potentially central in facilitating communication. This article concentrates only on the latter direction, namely, the role of KM in promoting effective communication, although as we shall see, the two directions are interrelated. (For literature on the former, i.e., the role of communication in knowledge sharing, see numerous resources in Alavi & Liedner, 2001). Furthermore, our discussion is restricted to computer-based knowledge management, as well as computer mediated communication. Therefore, the terms KM and communication, whenever used here, imply that these functions involve computer support.

Despite the central role of communication in organizations, organizational communication is unfortunately susceptible to numerous obstacles and barriers to effective communication. Barriers to communication occur at the individual and organizational level. At the individual level, interpersonal dynamics interfere with communication, individuals choose inappropriate channels and media, the sender and receiver use different semantics, making it difficult to communicate, and people send conflicting cues in different messages and channels. At the organizational level, different functions and departments see things differently, power and politics interfere with open and sincere exchanges, and organizational norms or policies dictate ineffective channels and inappropriate forms of messages. KM can help overcome these barriers and improve organizational communication, and, in particular, KM can enhance computerized communication support systems such as structured e-mail, video conferencing, listservs, and so forth. However, to do so, designs of KM systems must be based on an understanding of communication.

BACKGROUND

Our understanding of communication, and particularly computer-mediated communication in the organizational context, has developed dramatically in the last few decades. The classical information-transmission model introduced by Shannon and Weaver (1949) has transformed into more active, psychological, and social models of communication (Axley, 1984). See, for example, Riva and Galimberti (1998) for an overview of these transformations in theories and metaphors of communication. In the interest of brevity and in order to identify the role of KM in enhancing communication, we select one model of organizational communication (Te'eni, 2001) that helps to define the link between KM and communication. The model has three main factors, each of which includes several attributes:

1. Inputs to the communication process include (a) distance between sender and receiver, (b) values and norms of communication, and (c) attributes of the task that is the object of the communication;
2. A cognitive-affective communication process of exchanging a message that describes the choice and implementation of (a) one or more communication strategies used to transmit the message, (b) the form of the message and (c) the medium through which it is transmitted; and
3. The communication impact: (a) the mutual understanding and (b) the relationship between the sender and receiver.

Consider the following example. A product designer in an industrial plant may send a message to the marketing director about a new product under development, explaining the bill of materials expected for the product. This information is useful to the marketing director when pricing the product. The communication (semantic) distance between the communicators may be large due to their different background disciplines (engineering and marketing). However, working for the same company, they accept the same communication norms by which information in the organization is always openly shared as early as possible. The sender may choose to communicate the message by a typed letter (choice of medium) and using the formal template for internal budgeting (choice of message form). Additionally, the sender sends an informal memo in the form of a story describing how this product has been developed at home by one of the engineers. This story provides contextual information about the product and explains the rather expensive list of required materials (this is an example of a communication strategy). Finally, the impact of the communication is essentially that the marketing director understands the message and prices the product accordingly. This example demonstrates how organizational communication can take on different forms and media and how the communication situation and people involved adapt these communication parameters to ensure effective communication. This article explores how KM can help communicators achieve this goal.

KM FOR SUPPORTING COMMUNICATION: A FRAMEWORK

Four concepts in this model are especially relevant to the link with KM: context, levels of abstraction, adaptation, and organizational memory. The idea of context is central to the model. We assume that in any communication there is a core message that the sender wishes to convey to the receiver. Senders add contextual information to the core message to increase the likelihood that the receiver will understand their intentions. Whatever information receivers choose to use (from the information available to them) in reasoning about the core message can be regarded as context. Part of this context is in the receivers' heads or in other available sources and part needs to be provided to the receivers by the senders as contextual information to ensure mutual understanding. Some first steps toward a formal treatment of context can be found in Ghidini and Giunchiglia, 2001.

Contextual information refers to several possible aspects of the core message: the situation in which the message was produced, the situation in which it is anticipated to be received, an explanation about a statement, an explanation how to go about executing a request for action, or the underlying assumptions about an argument. Providing the contextual information to explain the core message is a common communication strategy called *contextualization*. Contextual information can be seen as layers of information around the core

message and contextualization can be seen as the act of adding more coats of information. KM techniques capable of determining and identifying context, retrieving or generating the information, providing the information in effective message forms and through effective media, and testing its impact may play a crucial role in enriching communication with appropriate contextual information.

The second idea involves levels of abstraction in the core and contextual information communicated. In thinking and communicating, people represent action at multiple levels of abstraction, and at any one moment, one of these levels is their focal level (Vallacher & Wegner, 1987; Berger, 1998). Moreover, people tend to remain on higher rather than lower levels of abstraction, but shift their attention to a lower level of abstraction when communication complexity increases and breakdowns occur. The lowest levels of abstraction in communication concern the lexicon and syntax (i.e., the terminology and grammar of the language). A higher level is the semantics (i.e., meaning of the message). Finally, the highest levels concern the task or pragmatic aspects of the message (i.e., the impact of the message on thought and action). A failure of communication at any level will hinder mutual understanding. KM techniques capable of identifying communication breakdowns and correcting them must rely on knowledge of communication at all levels of abstraction (such knowledge may be modeled as a multi-level model of communication analogous to the Open Systems Interconnect seven-layered protocol model). These KM techniques would be essential for ensuring effective communication and correcting lower levels of communication in order to enable communicators to concentrate on higher levels.

Another concept is that of adaptation in communication. Effective communicators match the medium, the message form, and the communication strategies to the communication situation, and the dynamics of the dialog. For example, communication between heterogeneous communicators should include more contextual information and may be more effective when richer, rather than leaner, media is selected. Knowledge of the communication situation (e.g., the relationships between communicators) as well as knowledge of how to communicate can be used to generate more effective communication. Communication complexity can be seen as a systemic measure of the communication situation and its susceptibility to communication breakdowns (Te'eni, 2001). It can therefore act as a sensor to trigger adaptation. KM techniques capable of detecting the need to adapt and also capable of adapting the system parameters can play an important role in facilitating communication support systems that provide tailored communication.

The last concept is the role of organizational memory (OM) in communication (Anand, Manz, & Glick, 1998). OM is a general term for the collection of information and knowledge "known" to the organization, as well as the KM necessary to acquire, store, and utilize this knowledge. Therefore, OM is essential for communication not only because it is a source of contextual information but also because it embodies the knowledge of how to communicate effectively in the organization (e.g., who knows, or should know, what). Furthermore, the information known to the organization is, in a substantial part, represented in organization communication on digital media such as e-mail and bulletin boards. It follows that computer-mediated communication can be a major source of the information stored in the OM. In other words, communication is a major provider of knowledge as well as being an essential enabler of KM. Referring to Figure 1, while the focus of this article is the arrow flowing from the OM to communication; we also see how communication injects knowledge into the OM. The relationship between communication and KM is bidirectional. Indeed, KM techniques are needed to store, organize, and make the information embodied in the communication available, via the OM, for distribution in future communication. Very often the core message of today becomes the context of tomorrow.

These four concepts (context, levels of abstraction, adaptation, and OM) are interrelated. In particular, OM should be modeled to enable effective contextualization, comprehensive support for all levels of abstraction and a basis for adaptation. OM will need to encompass a wide range of message forms (e.g., formal as well as informal materials and structured as well as unstructured information) and utilize a mix of media such as text, voice and video. Without such a mix, computer-supported communication will fall short of the flexible and adaptive nature of effective organizational communication. Moreover, OM will need to include information organized along levels of abstraction in order to support communication that fluctuates between levels, for instance, design OM to store and retrieve episodic memories (e.g., in the form of stories) as well as abstract rules generalizing the episodes. We return to the design of OM later on.

The three factors of the communication model, along with the four concepts discussed, create a framework for analyzing the role of KM in communication (see Figure 1). One can conceive of KM technologies that: (1) identify the inputs (e.g., the initial distances between communicators); (2) support the formulation of goals and the choice of communication strategies, choose and provide medium and message form, and gauge the complexity of communication in order to adapt it; and (3) provide the user with feedback on impact. Organizational memory is a key resource in supporting each of these types of functionality, but it also builds on the information and feedback from the communication.

APPLICATIONS AND FUTURE TRENDS

Following Figure 1, we examine several demonstrations of the potential roles of KM in the support of computer-mediated communication. First is the identification of the communication situation as well as the partners to communication. Groupware that helps the user identify "who knows what" and "who knows whom" in the workplace are examples of systems that employ KM techniques to identify whom to communicate with

Figure 1. Communication enhanced by organizational memory (adapted from Te'eni, 2001)

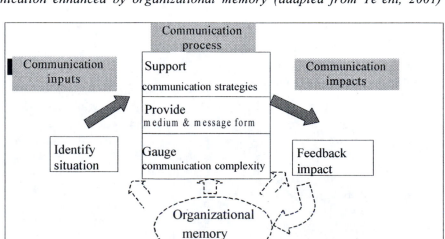

(e.g., Moreland, 1999). For example, IKNOW (Contractor, Zink, & Chan, 1998) is a program that organizes information about a network of colleagues and what knowledge each one has. In other words, the software attempts to answer the question: "Who knows who knows what?"

Given that two communicators are about to communicate, the relation between them can be characterized using organizational and personal knowledge. For example, knowledge of the organizational structure or of personal ontologies is the basis for computing the linguistic distance between the communicators (Maedche & Staab, 2001). Similarly, systems that employ collaborative filtering based on user profiles can compute a measure of similarity between profiles to decide what information to provide. For example, electronic media is personalized on the basis of user profiles (e.g., www.crayon.net), and similarly Intranet-based communication can be personalized according to internal employee profiles.

Finally, the information included in senders' signature files also can be used to define work relations between communicators (e.g., levels of expertise). As users may use different signatures, depending on the role they wish to assume in a particular communication, knowledge of the organizational structure combined with the user's choice of signature is particularly informative. When a sender from one department communicates with a colleague from the same department, a communication support system based on an OM that includes the organizational structure will be able to recognize the communicators as presumably sharing the same terminology. When the receiver is from a different organization, the signature could provide some clues on the semantic distance between the communicators. On the basis of such information, the communication support system can adapt the communication process to provide more or less contextual information.

KM can enhance the communication process in several ways. First, the initiation and control of the communication process relies on knowledge. For example, organizational maps can determine who should be contacted on what occasion. LiveMaps (Cohen, Jacovi, Maarek, & Soroka, 2002) tracks and analyzes colleagues using the same information. Another example is the early work on *Coordinator* (Winograd & Flores, 1986), which shows it is possible to assign to each message its purpose. A related communication support system is CHAOS (De Cindio, Simone, Vassallo, & Zanaboni, 1986), which organizes communications as a bank of conversations that serves as the basis for supporting communication and action. It includes a knowledge builder that observes messages and updates the bank of conversations accordingly.

Contextualization is perhaps the prime meeting point between communication and KM. First, the smart organization of messages (e.g., intelligent categorization of messages into folders and keywords) and then the advanced retrieval of information (e.g., text mining techniques) are crucial for effective contextualization. A knowledge-based mailer called kMail is an example of contextualization in communication support systems (Schwartz & Te'eni, 2000). The system builds links to relevant information automatically by parsing outgoing messages to detect possible information that elaborates the message. Indeed, contextualization highlights the role of knowledge management techniques in computer mediated communication. Such techniques are essential for detecting relevant knowledge, linking it to the core message and delivering it in context and in time.

Moreover, different people hold different views of context for the same core message. For instance, a production manager will think of a particular product, such as men's trunks, in terms of a production specification and the resulting product. In contrast, the marketing manager's mental model of the same product may be a packaged set of 10 pairs of colored trunks, with its associated sales and customer information. In kMail, the different views, owned by different communicators, are indexed so that people can see a message in light of alternative perspectives (see Figure 2). While the current picture of the trunks is part of the marketing view (mental model), an alternative view may depict a sketch with dimensions and other production specifications such as color options. Being able to depict the different views of the same product so that the communicators can appreciate the different context held by their partners requires advanced KM. Another communication support system is *Spider* (Boland, Tenkasi, & Te'eni, 1994), which is designed to present context in a variety of forms so that it can lead more efficiently to better and richer communication. The system displays the different rationales behind an issue in the form of cognitive maps that highlight the similarities and differences in the communicators' perspectives. This requires KM that is not only capable of maintaining individuals' ownership over their own perspectives but also KM techniques that can compare and contrast perspectives (e.g., by comparing cognitive maps).

Contextualization can very quickly overload and needs to be prioritized according to the communicators, task, norms, and situation (see Figure 1). Prioritizing contextual information found in the OM so as to show only the most relevant information or enable the user to select, say, the 10 most relevant items requires advanced KM techniques such as those employed in search engines. For example, if knowledge in the OM is organized according to levels of abstraction, context can be presented at higher levels and expanded to lower levels only when needed. In kMail, knowledge items in the OM

Figure 2. Contextualization based on organizational memory, showing on the right hand side different perspectives of different communicators

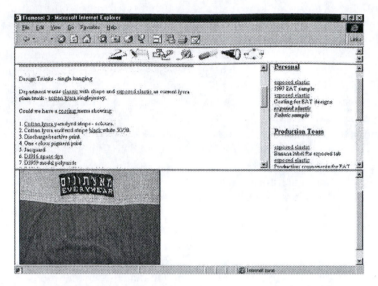

were classified as either a definition or a related item. A definition of a term (such as "BOM-bill of materials") can be shown at the highest priority, while lower abstraction levels of context can provide guidelines and templates for preparing a BOM and also may include examples of previous cases. KM is needed to organize the knowledge and provide it according to a hierarchy of levels. kMail also relies on the organization's communication maps to determine the likelihood of the communicators using the same or different terminologies, and accordingly recommending high or low levels of contextualization. A more recent system based on a Formal Language for Conversations, which also relies on previous messages in organizational memory, builds threads of associated messages and provides them as the context of the message sent (Takkinen, 2002).

Organizational knowledge can be managed so as to preserve the progression of information items from low to high formality (e.g., stories, facts, and abstract principles). Cleverly designed KM could be used to enable communication systems to supply the right level at the right time. Clearly, some knowledge sharing involves close human-to-human interaction and cannot rely on automatic processes for storing and retrieving data via structured databases. KM must therefore not only maintain knowledge in different forms but also enable their exchange through different media to support rather than replace human-to-human communication. Some messages such as stories are best sent as texts but accompanied by voice messages highlighting or interpreting some complex or sensitive point. In other words, human knowledgeability combines with predefined rules embodied in the KM systems to provide more effective communi-

nication. Furthermore, complex, tentative, and fuzzy ideas are often communicated informally and safely between colleagues (friends) in the form of conversations or ongoing dialog. Communities of practice (Wegner, 1998) are an essential enabler of meaningful conversations, and knowledge-based software (sometimes called "communityware") helps organize such conversations (Wellman, 2001).

Ultimately, feedback on the impact of communication must come from the user's own reaction, but future systems may effectively channel this feedback back to the sender. The OM can be designed to include results of successes and failures of communication that are provided to the sender at the appropriate time. For example, in a multinational organization, a history of poor communication between certain departments in two different nations should be fed back to these communicators in order to take the necessary precautions such as a higher level of information redundancy and more detailed feedback. Little research has been carried out in this area but as communication support systems become more common, the importance of informing senders of the communication impact will grow. Some form of feed-forward may be possible, for example, a simulation of probable errors due to a high semantic distance between communicators (e.g., communicators speaking different languages.) Furthermore, advanced computer support may be able to dynamically sense fluctuations in communication complexity and adapt the communication accordingly to ensure effective communication. Clearly, there is still much to do in terms of developing ways of identifying and reporting on communication failures.

CONCLUSION

In conclusion, KM is becoming a crucial element in the design and enhancement of organizational communication. The model shown in Figure 1 provides a framework for understanding the different types of enhancement to computer-mediated communication contribution that can build on knowledge (stored in OM) and KM. The knowledge is of two types: knowledge about the issue communicated and knowledge about how and with whom to communicate. KM must be designed to utilize both types of knowledge to enhance communication. It does so through techniques such as content and document management, contextualization, profiling people in the organization, finding contextual information through text and data mining, categorizing information, and more. Several of the systems described use these techniques to capitalize on organizational knowledge for enhancing communication.

Not all knowledge, however, can be communicated explicitly. Some forms of knowledge sharing are inherently tacit. KM techniques that rely on explicit information are therefore necessarily limited to part of organizational communication. Nevertheless, as computer-mediated communication accounts for a growing part of organizational communication, KM is rapidly becoming a necessary component of computer-supported communication systems. Moreover, our discussion has focused on cognitive aspects of communication and KM. Future research will need to expand to include cultural and political aspects as well as affective aspects of organizational communication. Future communication systems will learn to adapt to the communicators' emotions as well as their genres of communication. KM will undoubtedly be called on again.

As computer support for organizational communication expands within organizations, including dispersed organizations, and extends to different forms of knowledge (data, stories, policies, best practices, etc.) and different media (synchronous and asynchronous text, voice, multimedia, etc.), KM will have to invent new ways to organize and integrate the multiple sources of knowledge available in the organization. Communication relies on knowledge regardless of its form and medium and KM will have to rise to the occasion.

REFERENCES

Alavi, M., & Liedner, D. (2001). Knowledge management and knowledge management systems: Conceptual foundations and research issues. *MIS Quarterly, 25*(1), 107-136.

Anand, V., Manz, C.C., & Glick, W.H. (1998). An organizational memory approach to information management. *Academy of Management Review, 23*(4), 796-809.

Axley, S.R. (1984). Managerial and organizational communication in terms of the conduit metaphor. *Academy of Management Review, 9*(3), 428-437.

Berger C.R. (1998). Message plans, communication failure and mutual adaptation during social interaction. In M.T. Palmer & G.A. Barnett, *Progress in Communication Sciences*, Volume XIV, mutual influence in interpersonal communication: Theory and research in cognition, affect and behavior (Chapter 5, 1998, pp. 91-111), Stamford, CO, Ablex Publishing,

Boland, R., Tenkasi, R., & Te'eni, D. (1994). Designing information technology to support distributed cognition. *Organization Science, 5*(3), 456-475.

Cohen, D., Jacovi, M., Maarek, YS., & Soroka, V. (2002). LiveMaps for collection awareness. *International Journal of Human-Computer Studies, 56*(1), 7-23.

Contractor N., Zink D., & Chan M. (1998). Community computing and support systems. In T. Ishida (Ed.), *Lecture notes in computer science,* (pp. 201-217). Berlin: Springer-Verlag.

De Cindio, F., Simone, C, Vassallo, R., & Zanaboni, A. (1986, December 3-5). CHAOS as a coordination technology. *Proceedings of the Conference on Computer-Supported Cooperative Work (CSCW' 86),* 325-342, ACM Press.

Galbraith, J.R. (1977). *Organization design.* Reading, MA: Addison-Wesley.

Ghidini, C., & Giunchiglia, F. (2001). Local models semantics, or contextual reasoning – locality + compatibility. *Artificial Intelligence, 127*(2), 221-259.

Maedche, A., & Staab, S. (2002). Ontology learning for the Semantic Web. *IEEE Intelligent Systems, 16*(2), 72-79.

Moreland, R.L. (1999). Transactive memory: Learning who knows what in work groups and organizations. In L. Thompson, D. Messick, and J. Levine (Eds.). *Sharing knowledge in organizations* (pp. 3-31). Mahwah, NJ: Lawrence Erlbaum.

Riva, G., & Galimberti C. (1998). Computer-mediated communication: Identity and social interaction in an electronic environment. *Genetic, Social and General Psychology Monographs, 124,* 434-464.

Schwartz, D.G., & Te'eni, D. (2000). Tying knowledge to action with kMail. *IEEE Intelligent Systems, 15*(3), 33-39.

O

Shannon, C.E., & Weaver, W. (1949). *The mathematical theory of communication.* Urbana, IL: University of Illinois Press.

Takkinen, J. (2002). *From information management to task management in electronic mail.* Dissertation No. 732, Institute of Technology, Linkopings University, Sweden.

Te'eni, D. (2001). A cognitive-affective model of organizational communication for designing IT. *MISQ (Review) 25*(2), 251-312.

Vallacher, R.R., & Wegner D.M. (1987). What do people think they're doing? Action identification and human behavior. *Psychological Review, (94)*1, 3-15.

Weick, K.E. (1979). *The social psychology of organizing.* Reading, MA: Addison-Wesley.

Wenger, E. (1998). *Communities of practice.* Cambridge University Press.

Wellman, B. (2001). Computer networks as social networks. *Science, 293,* 2031-2034.

Winograd, T., & Flores, F. (1986). *Understanding computers and cognition: A new foundation for design.* Reading, MA: Addison Wesley.

KEY TERMS

Cognitive Maps: Cognitive maps are structured representations of decision depicted in graphical format (variations of cognitive maps are cause maps, influence diagrams, or belief nets). Basic cognitive maps include nodes connected by arcs, where the nodes represent constructs (or states) and the arcs represent relationships. Cognitive maps have been used to understand decision situations, to analyze complex cause-effect representations and to support communication.

Communication: Communication is the exchange of information between two or more people with the intent that the sender's message be understood and considered by the receiver.

Contextual Information: Contextual information refers to several possible aspects of the core message: the situation in which the message was produced, the situation in which it is anticipated to be received, an explanation about a statement, an explanation how to go about executing a request for action, or the underlying assumptions about an argument.

Organizational Memory: OM is a general term for the collection of information and knowledge "known" to the organization, as well as the KM necessary to acquire, store, and utilize this knowledge.

Organizational Semantic Webs

Jean-Yves Fortier
University of Picardie Jules Verne, France

Gilles Kassel
University of Picardie Jules Verne, France

INTRODUCTION

The main subject tackled in this article is the use of knowledge technologies to develop corporate memories or (stated more generally) "organizational memories" (OMs) (Dieng, Corby, Giboin, & Ribière, 1999).

At the end of the 1990s, AI technologies, in general, and knowledge technologies, in particular, were recognized as pertinent and promising tools (in addition to information technologies) for the design of OMs (Buckingham Shum, 1997; O'Leary, 1998; Milton, Shadbolt, Cottam, & Hammersley, 1999). These very diverse technologies (concepts, methods, and tools) have been conceived to assist knowledge acquisition, modeling, and discovery, as well as the development of knowledge-based systems (Studer, Benjamins, & Fensel, 1998). In this article, we focus on knowledge modeling and formalization techniques, since our prime interest is the preservation of knowledge within OMs and its impact on the exploitation of this knowledge.

In practice, the use of these technologies generates two complementary proposals: (1) the formalization of a part of knowledge to be preserved, which means considering hybrid memories in terms of specification modes (formal, semi-formal, and informal); and (2) the introduction of a formal ontology of the domain in question, in order to facilitate the expression, comprehension, and access to capitalized knowledge. Formalization thus relates to both (1) *knowledge* (as propositional knowledge) and (2) *meaning* (as conceptual knowledge).

Regarding the balance between formal and informal specification, a broad spectrum of OM architectures have been proposed, ranging from informal annotation of formal knowledge bases (Euzénat, 1996) to the formal annotation of informal documents (Buckingham Shum, Motta, & Domingue, 2000). It should be noted that these extremes (i.e., the development of a text-documented knowledge base and the publication of scientific articles on the Web, respectively) correspond to atypical OM applications.

The knowledge technologies used in 2004 to develop OMs are generally those of the Semantic Web, where languages like OWL (Antoniou & van Harmelen, 2004) allow us to exchange knowledge bases on the Web. One particular asset of OWL is its ability to offering several dialects with different expressive powers—the choice of the dialect depending on the specific application in question.

A review of the state of the art (cf. section 2) shows that current OM architectures rely on "lightweight" knowledge models, corresponding to formal annotations of textual resources. These approaches focus on document "enrichment" (Motta, Buckingham Shum, & Domingue, 2000), since the knowledge models and ontologies are used to facilitate access to textual resources and the dissemination of the latter to interested users.

In contrast to these initiatives (or rather by extending them), we recommend giving more importance to formalization, by going back to Buckingham Shum's original proposal (1997) of formalizing a part of the knowledge to be capitalized. Such an approach requires us to improve the knowledge technologies used, in order to make it possible to apprehend and reason on the contents of the resources independently of the specification modes (cf. sections 3, 4, and 5).

BACKGROUND

Our current work concerns the conception and development of organizational Semantic Webs (OSWs), that is, OMs whose implementation exploits Semantic Web technologies. The evolution of the Web into a Semantic Web is currently the subject of numerous research programs (Berners-Lee, Hendler, & Lasilla, 2001). The principal aim is to enable software agents to exploit the contents of textual resources present on the Web so that users can ultimately be relieved of certain information searching and combination tasks (Fensel, Wahlster, Lieberman, & Hendler, 2003). The developed technologies apply as much to the Web as a whole as to OSWs in particular.

Current OSW architectures rely on the coupling of a collection of textual resources with formal resources, the latter also being qualified as "semantic" resources. Of these, one can distinguish *annotations* of textual resources or "metadata" (which express knowledge about textual resources) (Handschuh & Staab, 2003) on one hand, and *ontologies* (which stipulate the meaning of the terms used to express the textual resources and the metadata) (Davies, Fensel, & van Harmelen, 2003; Abecker & van Elst, 2004) on the other hand. Again, one finds a distinction between knowledge and meaning. In terms of the contribution of these semantic resources, various approaches are being explored. They may thus be used for:

- navigating within a network of annotations, in order to help discover documents and apprehend their contents (Buckingham Shum et al., 2000)
- furnishing the user with the documents likely to interest him or her, by taking into account his or her centers of interest expressed in terms of ontological concepts (Davies, Duke, & Sure, 2003; Middleton, De Roure, & Shadbolt, 2004; Uschold et al., 2003)
- ranking answers to queries by taking into account the annotations' contents (Stojanovic, Studer, & Stojanovic, 2003) and/or the memory's uses such as previous consultations

The study of these architectures shows that they force formal resources into a precise role: constituting an index for textual resources. This type of coupling can be qualified as "weak," to the extent that the only aim of these formal resources is to facilitate the exploitation (access, dissemination) of the textual resources – the capitalized knowledge being only present in the latter. When a user sends a query to this type of OSW, the answer he or she receives is a list (ranked by estimated relevance) of textual resources likely to contain the desired information. This user must then still locate information within these documents.

In order to increase the assistance provided by OSWs, we recommend carrying out "strong" coupling by modeling a part of knowledge to be capitalized, which amounts to distributing the capitalized knowledge between the textual resources and the formal resources. It is necessary to choose which knowledge to model. Several dimensions must be taken into account: the value of knowledge for the organization and its degree of consensuality and stability. In this respect, our priority is to model the organization to which the OSW is dedicated, resulting to some extent in the maintenance of a modeled management report on the organization. This choice appears to us to offer a good return on investment if one compares the assistance provided

with information searching on one hand, and the cost of modeling this knowledge on the other hand.

The principal utility of knowledge modeling is to enable an OSW to reason on this knowledge. For example, by reasoning on the organization model, the OSW can build views of the organization suited to the user profile—this profile itself being modeled—thus, facilitating access to the organization's documentation.

At the same time, however, knowledge modeling raises difficulties. First, the distribution of capitalized knowledge across several information sources (according to their specification modes) complicates localization of (and thus access to) this knowledge. In addition, another problem relates to the dissemination of modeled knowledge, which is specified in a formal language not easily understood by a user. One can draw a parallel with the Semantic Web's "metadata": these formal annotations are interpretable by machines but not by humans. Lastly, modeling some pieces of knowledge does not solve the problem of access to information contained within textual resources.

To overcome these difficulties, we recently proposed (1) splitting up the textual resources (in order to reveal information relating to targeted subjects) and introducing a metamodel of knowledge and information contained into the OSW, independently of the way the knowledge/information is specified and located (Fortier & Kassel, 2003a); (2) combining this metamodel with a mechanism for dynamic document generation, created on demand and meeting user expectations (Fortier & Kassel, 2003b).

▢STRONG▢ COUPLING AT WORK

In this section, we present a general view of our proposal by illustrating it with a simple example: the memory of a R&D project. This is inspired by a real application currently conceived within the K^2M^3 environment (Knowledge Management through Meta-Knowledge Modeling) developed on a multi-agent platform and encapsulating DefOnto as a knowledge representation language (Cormier, Fortier, Kassel, & Barry, 2003).

Example of an OSW consultation

Consultation of an OSW consists of a series of exchanges during which (1) the user expresses a need for information on a given subject and (2) the OSW answers him or her by dynamically generating a document which gathers together relevant information.

Thus, if a participant in a R&D project requests information on a particular project task, the OSW will provide a document similar to that shown in Figure 1. This

Figure 1. Information presentation generated for a participant in an R&D project

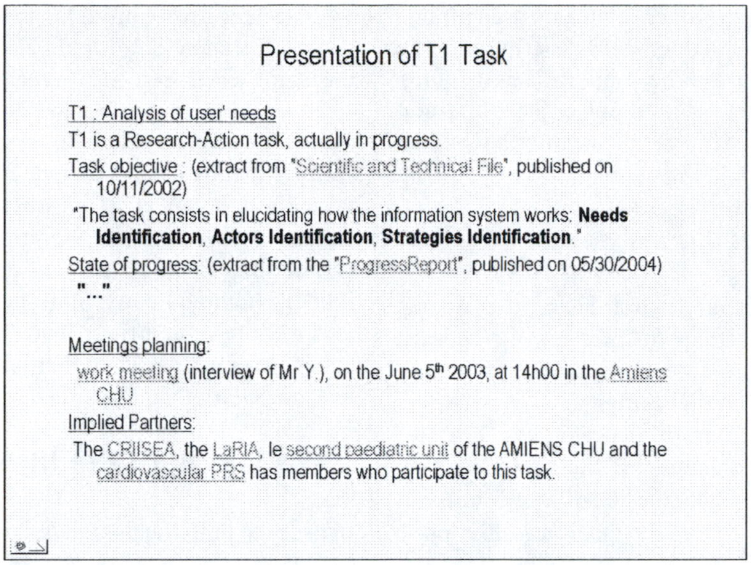

> ### Presentation of T1 Task
>
> T1 : Analysis of user' needs
> T1 is a Research-Action task, actually in progress.
> Task objective : (extract from "Scientific and Technical File", published on 10/11/2002)
> "The task consists in elucidating how the information system works: **Needs Identification, Actors Identification, Strategies Identification**."
> State of progress: (extract from the "ProgressReport", published on 05/30/2004)
> "..."
>
> Meetings planning:
> work meeting (interview of Mr Y.), on the June 5th 2003, at 14h00 in the Amiens CHU
> Implied Partners:
> The CRIISEA, the LaRIA, le second paediatric unit of the AMIENS CHU and the cardiovascular PRS has members who participate to this task.

document contains information about the task, organized by the OSW into a certain order so as to constitute a coherent whole. The text begins with an acronym, followed by the task's full title and category. It continues with the presentation of the general objective as well as the task's current state of progress, before introducing the work meeting schedule and the partners involved in performance of the task.

Certain pieces of information stem from the organizational model, whereas others are extracted from documents. In our example, the acronym, the heading, the category, the meeting dates, and the involved partners are modeled information, whereas the general objective of the task, its progress report, and the agenda of the meetings of work are extracted from various documents (the project's scientific and technical file, the last progress report, e-mail messages about forthcoming meetings, and meeting reports for previous meetings, respectively).

The generated document comprises moreover two types of links added by the OSW. The first is placed whenever the OSW cites elements for which it is possible to present further information. The activation of this link leads to a new information presentation (document). In our example, these links correspond to the work meeting on June 5, 2003 and the various partners involved in performance of the task. The second type of link appears during the introduction of the document fragments whenever it is possible to consult the corresponding document. It is placed so as to allow the user to consult the entire document if he or she so desires.

The Organization Model

The *organization model* (with which the OSW is equipped) corresponds to the description of an organization (here a R&D project) according to different viewpoints and at different levels of abstraction. Just like an organization (i.e., a group of people carrying out a project together), a project itself comprises participants (who may be affiliated to various organizations considered as partners) and generally has a leader. As a complex process, a project can be decomposed into tasks, giving rise to the performance of a variety of activities (e.g., work meetings, document writing, software development, etc.). Finally, a project produces results, some of which are material (e.g., software, documents, and other artefacts) and others of which are immaterial (e.g., a conceptual methodology).

Hence, one finds different kinds of objects in such a model. The *organization ontology* makes the meaning of these different object types explicit, and contains a specification of notions such as "*Partner,*" "*SteeringCommittee,*" "*FinalReport,*" "*Task,*" and so forth. Such an ontology plays two roles: During the OSW development phase, it helps express the organizational model and thus corresponds to populating the ontology; later, at runtime, the implemented version is used to infer facts which are implicit within the organization model. In our approach, these two roles are exploited in turn.

According to the definition, the *organization model* includes a description of the organization's textual resources. Therefore, we can consider that describing an organization according to different viewpoints amounts to extending the metadata approach generally used for the Semantic Web: In addition to document descriptions, we have descriptions relating to other objects. Let us note, however, that this is knowledge about objects and not knowledge about knowledge, which is the aim of the content model.

The Content Model

The content model corresponds to a description of the content of an OSW, according to different viewpoints and at different levels of abstraction. Such a model supposes the reification of the contents so as to make the latter the subject matter of descriptions. For instance, after reifying the content of the sentence "the person in charge of the project is G. Kassel" into an object (called *InfoResponsible,* for example), it is possible to describe this object by expressing (for example) that "*InfoResponsible* was made public by the project Steering Committee." The content model thus contains meta-knowledge.

As a starting point for working out such a model, we consider that content consists of *Propositions* relating to *Subjects* and that these *Subjects* are conceptual in nature. Concepts playing the role of *Subjects* can be generic (if they classify a set of objects, *e.g.: ScanningTask, TechnicalNote*) or individual (when they classify only one object, *e.g.: SteeringCommittee, ProjectTechnicalFile*). This starting point applies indiscriminately to *Assertions* constituting the organizational model (in terms of *Propositions* considered as true by the OSW) and *Information* conveyed in the textual resources (in terms of *Propositions* stated by an author and intended for another agent). We supplement it by considering that these *Propositions* may or may not be *confidential* and that the organizational concepts

playing the role of a *Subject* also can constitute a *CentreOfInterest* for OSW users.

The *Assertion* model and the *Information* model rely on the same ontology, being expressed by means of the same concepts. However, the expressed *Propositions* are not comparable in nature: On one hand, *Assertions* are simple *Propositions* because they are formalized by means of a knowledge representation language with limited power of expression; on the other hand, pieces of *Information* are complex *Propositions* corresponding to the content of a text. To render the two models homogeneous, it is necessary to describe the text's content on a finer level of detail. This is why we split up such texts into elementary contents relating to a *MainSubject*.

Expression of the Information Need

In order to help the user in his or her information search, the OSW generates an index of the different classes of information it is able to provide.

These classes of information are organized as a taxonomy of subjects. A semantic dependency between *Concepts* playing the role of *Subject* is to that end calculated. Such a classification allows us to consider, for instance, that information about a car's engine constitutes information about the car itself. Let us note, however, that there is no subsumption link between the concepts *CarEngine* and *Car*. Following the same principle for a given project task, the OSW will suggest (see Figure 2) information about the task manager, the schedule for future work meetings, and the progress report.

Taking into account the high density of this taxonomy of information, we introduce a complementary index containing concepts of the organization model. This serves as an entrance point to the taxonomy of information by selecting a privileged view of the organization, since each index entry constitutes a partial

Figure 2. Excerpt of a content index

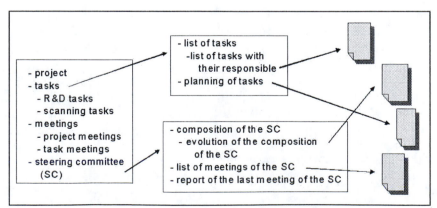

view of the organization. In our "project memory" example, the OSW enables us to consult information about project partners, tasks, or participants. In the case of generic concepts, the index can be developed according to the subsumption hierarchy and by presenting explicitly the various semantic axis (if they exist) used to define the ontology. For example, the project tasks can be derived into tasks in progress or finished tasks on the "progress stage" axis and into survey, R&D, or management tasks on the "task category" axis. These semantic axes allow better comprehension of the distinctions made between concepts during the ontology design and also help the user refine his or her need for information.

This whole content index (i.e., made up of the two indices presented) appears to us to be more useful than the expression of requests in a dedicated language because it avoids the need to know a query language and furthermore allows the user to find unanticipated information. It is generated for each user group, taking into account its access rights and centres of interest. To that end, the OSW exploits the content model in order to be aware of the users' centres of interest as well as the information subjects.

The Generation of Personalized Virtual Documents

We introduced a mechanism for generation of information presentations by taking what has been developed in the Customized Virtual Document field as a starting point for producing the information presentations. This mechanism allows us to customize the generated presentations according to users' access rights and centres of interests. The mechanism is composed of four steps:

- **Relevant information retrieval:** The OSW uses an inference engine to deduce all the propositions which deal with the required subject, being formalized or expressed in natural language in textual resources.
- **Selection:** The OSW carries out an initial sorting by only retaining those propositions which are transmissible to the user. For example, a person outside the project will only obtain general information about the project, whereas a project participant has access to more precise information, such as a task's progress report.
- **Scheduling:** The OSW must present the propositions in a logical order to the user. This is achieved by using presentation methods which specify order of ranking for different concept categories. Thus, for information in documents, the OSW will add a link to this document and will notably specify the author, the publication date, and the reason for drafting the document: This allows the user to contextualize a document, more easily evaluate its relevance, and only activate the link to consult the full document if it proves to be of interest.
- **Composition:** Once the presentation's logical structure has been defined, the OSW must generate the physical document. When the presentation mentions other elements on which the OSW is able to give further information, the OSW adds a link which leads to an index of available information on the subject.

FUTURE TRENDS

The approach presented concerning—the implementation of "strong" coupling between textual and formal resources—builds on the modeling of meta-knowledge. The taking into account of such meta-knowledge—on both the conceptual level (via ontologies) and the formal level (via knowledge representation languages)—is now recognized as an important issue for the future of the Semantic Web, and is subject of much research from which OSWs will benefit.

On the conceptual level, there is a need to introduce (meta-)concepts such as *Subject, Centre of interest* (denoting concepts), or *Assertion, Definition, Confidential Information, Hypothesis* (denoting propositions) into ontologies. Fox and Huang (2003) thus proposed an ontology of propositions to deal with the origin and validity of information contained in Web pages. Gangemi and Mika (2003) have, for their part, defined an ontology of Description and Situation to allow software agents to exchange information on the Web. Recently, we proposed a synthesis of these efforts with the Information and Discourse Acts (I&DA) ontology, which proposes a set of generic concepts allowing simultaneous definition of contents, the expression of contents, and the discourse acts which create and/or interpret these contents (Fortier & Kassel, 2004).

On the formal level, the issue is one of being able to simultaneously represent the content of propositions (e.g.: "current architectures of OSWs are based on weak coupling between textual and formal resources") and meta-knowledge relating to propositions (e.g.: "this information is a thesis defended by J.-Y. Fortier and G. Kassel") or concepts (e.g.: "the OSW concept is the subject of recent articles by J.-Y. Fortier and G. Kassel"). The OWL-Full language reuses the RDFS primitive "meta-class" and enables representation of certain pieces of meta-knowledge but does not enable one to perform inferences on the latter (Antoniou & van Harmelen, 2004). One of the objectives of our ongoing work on the definition of the DefOnto language is to equip Semantic Web languages with a semantic which enable representation and reasoning on meta-knowledge (Cormier et al., 2003).

CONCLUSION

In this article, we have situated our work within the context of the Semantic Web (a subject that it is impossible to ignore these days), considered the design of "Organizational Semantic Webs" and proposed an approach for the development of a new generation of OSWs—strong coupling between textual and formal resources.

The objective underlying this approach amounts to putting on an equal footing texts and knowledge models for capitalizing knowledge and thus exceeding the simple formal annotation of textual resources. We emphasized the fact that if the scientific community is to reach this objective, it must make progress with Semantic Web technologies, in particular in terms of representing meta-knowledge related to formal or informal contents.

The key issue of this proposal is to confer OSWs with better capacities to exploit their contents. It is a matter of transforming these knowledge and information "repertories"—currently OSWs—into agents which assist users with their work in general and with knowledge management tasks in particular (Baek, Liebowitz, Prasad, & Grangier, 1999).

REFERENCES

Abecker, A., & van Elst, L. (2004). Ontologies for knowledge management. In S. Staab & R. Studer (Eds.), *Handbook on ontologies* (pp. 435-454) Springer-Verlag.

Antoniou, G., & van Harmelen, F. (2004). Web ontology language: OWL. In S. Staab & R. Studer (Eds.), *Handbook on ontologies* (pp. 67-92) Springer-Verlag.

Baek, S., Liebowitz, J., Prasad, S.Y., & Grangier, M. (1999). Intelligent agents for knowledge management: Towards intelligent Web-based collaboration within virtual teams. In J. Liebowitz (Ed.), *Knowledge management handbook* (pp. 11-1, 11-23). CRC Press.

Berners-Lee, T., Hendler, J., & Lasilla, O. (2001). The semantic Web. *Scientific American*, *279*(5), 34-43.

Buckingham Shum, S. (1997). Balancing formality with informality: User-centred requirements for knowledge management technologies. In B.R. Gaines & R. Uthurusamy (Eds.), *Proceedings of the AAAI'97 Spring Symposium on Artificial Intelligence in Knowledge Management*, Stanford University, Palo Alto, AAAI Press. Retrieved June 20, 2005, from *http://ksi.cpsc.ucalgary.ca/AIKM97/sbs/sbs-paper1.html*

Buckingham Shum, S., Motta, E., & Domingue, J. (2000). ScholOnto: An ontology-based digital library server for research documents and discourse. *International Journal on Digital Libraries*, *3*(3), 237-248.

Cormier, C., Fortier, J.-Y., Kassel, G., & Barry, C. (2003). Representation of metaknowledge for the development of organizational Semantic Webs. In *Proceedings of the K-CAP'2003 Workshop on Knowledge Management and the Semantic Web*, Sanibel Island, FL.

Davies, J., Duke, A., & Sure, Y. (2003). OntoShare: A knowledge management environment for virtual communities of practice. In *Proceedings of the 2nd International Conference on Knowledge Capture (K-CAP 2003)*, Sanibel Island, FL, 20-27.

Davies, J., Fensel, D., & van Harmelen, F. (Eds.) (2003). *Towards the semantic Web: Ontology-driven knowledge management*. John Wiley & Sons.

Dieng, R., Corby, O., Giboin, A., & Ribière, M. (1999). Methods and tools for corporate knowledge management. *International Journal of Human-Computer Studies*, *51*(3), 567-598.

Euzénat, J. (1996). Corporate memory through cooperative creation of knowledge bases and hyperdocuments. In *Proceedings of the 10th Knowledge Acquisition for Knowledge-Based Systems Workshop*, Banff, Canada. Retrieved June 20, 2005, from *http://ksi.cpsc.ucalgary.ca/KAW/KAW96/euzenat/euzenat96b.html*

Fensel, D., Wahlster, W., Lieberman, H., & Hendler, J., (Eds.) (2003). *Spinning the semantic Web*. Cambridge, MA: MIT Press.

Fortier, J.-Y., & Kassel, G. (2003a). Modeling the information contained in an organizational memory to facilitate its access. In *Proceedings of the 10th International Conference on Human-Computer Interaction (HCI-2003)*, Crete, Greece (vol. 4, pp. 715-719).

Fortier, J.-Y., & Kassel, G. (2003b). Building adaptive information retrieval systems for organizational memories: A case study. In *Proceedings of the 12th International Conference on Intelligent and Adaptive Systems and Software Engineering (IASSE-2003)*, San Francisco, (pp. 50-53).

Fortier, J.-Y., & Kassel, G. (2004). Managing knowledge at the information level: An ontological approach. In *Proceedings of the ECAI'2004 Workshop on Knowledge Management and Organizational Memories*, Valencia, Spain, (pp. 39-45).

Fox, M.S., & Huang, J. (2003). *Knowledge provenance: An approach to modeling and maintaining the evolution and validity of knowledge.* EIL Technical Report, Univ. of Toronto. Retrieved June 20, 2005, from *www.eil.utoronto.ca/km/papers/fox-kp1.pdf*

Gangemi, A., & Mika, P. (2003). *Understanding the semantic Web through descriptions and situations.* In R. Meersman et al. (Eds.), *Proceedings of the International Conference ODBASE03*, Berlin, Germany.

Handschuh, S., & Staab, S. (Eds.) (2003). *Annotation for the semantic Web*. IOS Press.

Middleton, S., De Roure, D., & Shadbolt, N. (2004). Ontology-based recommender systems. In S. Staab & R. Studer (Eds.), *Handbook on ontologies* (pp. 477-498), Springer-Verlag.

Milton N., Shadbolt N., Cottam, H., & Hammersley, M. (1999). Towards a knowledge technology for knowledge management. *International Journal of Human-Computer Studies, 51*, 615-641.

Motta, E., Buckingham Shum, S., & Domingue, J. (2000). Ontology-driven document enrichment: Principles, tools and applications. *International Journal of Human Computer Studies, 52*(5), 1071-1109.

O'Leary, D.E. (1998). Using AI in knowledge management: Knowledge bases and ontologies. *IEEE Intelligent Systems, May-June*, 34-39.

Stojanovic, N., Studer, R., & Stojanovic, L. (2003). An approach for the ranking of query results in the Semantic Web. In *Proceedings of the 2nd International Semantic Web Conference (ISWC 2003)*, Sanibel Island, FL, (pp. 500-516).

Studer, R., Benjamins, V.R., & Fensel, D. (1998). Knowledge engineering: Principles and methods. *Data & Knowledge Engineering, 25*, 161-197.

Uschold, M., Clark, P., Dickey, F., Fung, C., Smith, S., Uczekaj, S., Wilke, M., Bechhofer, S., & Horrocks, I. (2003). A semantic infosphere. In *Proceedings of the 2nd International Semantic Web Conference (ISWC 2003)*, Sanibel Island, FL 882-898.

KEY TERMS

Annotation: An annotation (also referred to as "metadata") is a document containing knowledge about another document--hence the "meta" prefix. According to the specification language used, one distinguishes informal annotations (interpreted by humans) and formal annotations (intended to be interpreted by machines). Concerning the content of these annotations, knowledge can relate either to the contents of an annotated document (e.g., by means of a collection of concepts expressed in the document) or to a document's overall properties (e.g., author, publication date, language used, etc).

Hybrid Organizational Memory: A Hybrid Organizational Memory is an organizational memory whose contents are expressed by means of languages presenting different levels of formality (formal, semi-formal, informal). Such memories contain textual resources (be they structured or not, and either mono- or multimedia) as well as formal semantic resources (annotations and ontologies).

Meta-Knowledge: Meta-knowledge is knowledge which, instead of relating to objects or events, is about knowledge. There are several categories of meta-knowledge: Some are knowledge properties (e.g.: "Pythagorus' theorem was known to the Babylonians"), others are knowledge about the state of knowledge of an individual (e.g.: "Mr. Brown does not know Pythagorus' theorem"), and lastly others are knowledge about ways in which knowledge is used (e.g.: "in these circumstances, it is useful to use Pythagorus' theorem").

Ontology: An ontology is an explicit specification of a shared conceptualization for a domain of interest. Although in theory, an ontology can be specified in different languages (either formal or natural), the utility of the Semantic Web relates primarily to formal ontologies which are machine-interpretable.

Organizational Semantic Web: An Organizational Semantic Web is an organizational memory, that is, an information system dedicated to the knowledge management of an organization, which uses Semantic Web technologies for its deployment. The aim of these technologies is to allow software agents to exploit the content of the textual resources published on the Web.

Personalized Virtual Document: A virtual document is a document for which no persistent state exists and for which some or all instances are generated at runtime. It becomes personalized when one specifies that the document is composed of both information and the mechanisms required for generation of the real document, that is, that to be consulted by the reader. Thus, having been introduced with the goal of reusing resources available on the Web, the personalized virtual document inherits its dynamic generation and user adaptation abilities from Adaptive Hypermedia work.

Representation Language: A knowledge representation language is a set of structures expressed by means of symbols, that is, sequences of symbols obeying structural formation rules. Some symbols are interpreted as logical operators whereas others are treated like objects in a world model.

Organizational Structure

Paul H.J. Hendriks
Radboud University Nijmegen, The Netherlands

INTRODUCTION

For many decades, organization scientists have paid considerable attention to the link between knowledge and organization structure. An early contributor to these discussions was Max Weber (1922), who elaborated his concepts of professional bureaucracy. History shows a multitude of other descriptions and propositions which depict knowledge-friendly organization structures such as the 'organic form' for knowledge-intensive innovation promoted by Burns and Stalker (1961), professional bureaucracies and adhocracies described by Mintzberg (1983), and the brain metaphor for organization structure (Morgan, 1986). Discussions on such knowledge-friendly organization structures led to many neologisms including the flexible, intelligent, smart, hypertext, N-form, inverted, network, cellular, or modular organization.

This article discusses the fundamental importance of organization structure for a knowledge perspective on organizations. This discussion involves two classes of questions. Organization structure can be studied as the backdrop against which the knowledge aspects of organizations take shape. Key questions then are how different structural configurations involve stimuli and barriers to the generation and embedding of organizational knowledge through such processes as knowledge exploration and knowledge sharing. Organization structure can also be studied from the perspective of organization design, which is the premeditated construction or change of organization structure (see Bowditch & Buono, 1985). Questions that appear then include: what are possible design interventions and how does one assess their knowledge-friendliness? The article addresses both classes of questions. Its objective therefore is: (1) to look at what defines a knowledge-friendly organization structure, and (2) to explore which interventions organizations have at their disposal when trying to achieve such a structure.

BACKGROUND

The importance of organization structure is well established in the discussions that address matters of organizational knowledge and associated concepts such as creativity, learning, or R&D activities in organization design (e.g., Myers, 1996). Yet, in the stricter circle of studies that explicitly present themselves as knowledge management (KM) studies, organization structure plays second fiddle to issues of ICT and HRM. Organization structure concerns patterns of work relationships (a more elaborate definition of organization structure is given below). Such work relationships can be predefined (formal organization structure) or organically evolving (informal organization structure). There is a general recognition that relationships among individuals in collectives are centrally important in the organizational production of knowledge and its organizational embedding (e.g., Blackler, 1995). Several trends lend support to the idea that the perspective of knowledge workers and their work relationships should guide discussions of organization design. These trends include the increased complexity in the competitive environment, the greater pressure on innovation and proactive manipulation of markets, and the emergence of provisional structural arrangements such as in network organizations and organizational networks.

A common undertow in these discussions is that knowledge workers need the freedom or autonomy to decide for themselves when to establish work relationships. Such accounts stress that the formal organization structure can be a burden to knowledge aspects of work. They argue that organizational knowledge shows up much better in the informal organization structure (such as communities of practice, e.g., Brown & Duguid, 2001). As Teece (2000, pp. 39-40) puts it: "The migration of competitive advantage away from tangible assets towards intangible ones [forces organizations to] focus on generating, acquiring, transferring and combining such assets to meet customer needs. In order to be successful in these activities, firms and their managements must be entrepreneurial." This implies, according to Teece, that knowledge-intensive, entrepreneurial firms must have:

- flexible boundaries,
- high-powered incentives,
- non-bureaucratic structures,
- shallow hierarchies, and
- an innovative and entrepreneurial culture.

In short, the following suggestions are made for the design of knowledge-intensive forms: reduce hierarchy, only provide the basic outline of production structure, and transfer decisions to connect knowledge worker tasks from the formal to the informal organization structure. Note, however, that loosening control for knowledge work is a disputed issue (e.g., Butler, Price, Coates, & Pike, 1998).

Many of the proposed prescriptions for building knowledge-friendly organization structures (e.g., Quinn, 1992; Sanchez & Mahoney, 1996; Miles, Snow, Mathews, Miles, & Coleman, 1997) share with Teece's prescription a 'one-size-fits-all' character. The assertion that no single organization structure can be a panacea for all management ills, which underlies several organization theories (e.g., the contingency and configurational approaches; see Donaldson, 2001), seems to be fairly broadly accepted. Nevertheless, it appears to be weakly developed where organization structures for knowledge work are concerned. When authors do introduce contingencies (e.g., Nonaka & Takeuchi, 1997; Hobday, 2000), these are usually of a general nature (e.g., complexity or turbulence of the environment, analyzability of the task, size of the firm, type of technology), and not specifically knowledge related. The characteristics of an organization's knowledge base can also serve as contingency variables, as Birkinshaw, Nobel, and Ridderstrale (2002) show in a study of international R&D. Particularly the importance of system embeddedness, which is the extent to which knowledge is a function of the social and physical system in which it exists (Winter, 1987; Zander & Kogut, 1995), emerges from their study as an important contextual variable.

ORGANIZATIONAL STRUCTURE AND ORGANIZATIONAL KNOWLEDGE

Defining Organization Structure

In order to be able to assess the suitability of specific design advice for organizations from a knowledge perspective, we need to understand the denotation of the twin concepts of organization structure and organization design. The division of labor is the key concept underlying organization structure and design. When labor is divided among people and machines, the need also arises to integrate the tasks involved. These two elements, which Lawrence and Lorsch (Lawrence, Lorsch, & Garrison, 1967; Lawrence & Lorsch, 1969) identify as differentiation and integration, are generally recognized as the building blocks of organization structure. For instance, the definition of organization structure that Bowditch and Buono (1985, p. 258) give, which combines Mintzberg's (1979, 1983) well-known definition with the approach taken by Lawrence and Lorsch, states:

Organization structure can be broadly defined as the sum total of ways in which an organization divides its tasks and then coordinates them, in essence balancing job-related specialization (differentiation) with group-, intergroup, and organization-based coordination (integration) as appropriate.

Implied in any system of job definition are the relationships among the totality of tasks. Work relationships therefore define organization structure. A work relationship exists if and when the output of one task is used as part of the input of another task. Work relationships may be distinguished by their content or form. Regarding their content, two types of relationships are commonly discerned. Firstly, relationships exist within the production process (e.g., knowledge workers using the ideas or products of others as inspiration, or input, for their work). The pattern of these relationships defines what is commonly called 'the production structure'. Secondly, relationships can be discerned which affect the definition and realization of work relationships (e.g., knowledge workers deciding for themselves or being directed by a manager to use specific outputs as inputs). The pattern of these relationships is usually referred to as the control structure. As to their form, Thompson (1967) distinguishes three types of input-output connections or—as he calls them—three types of interdependencies: pooled (one actor receives input from multiple others), sequential (one actor transforms the output of an actor before passing it on as input for a third actor), and reciprocal interdependencies (two actors use each other's outputs as input).

The organization structure seen as patterns of work relationships concerns the content side of these relationships. Addressing issues of organization structure implies an abstraction from the personal elements in these relationships, such as individual preferences for work contacts, motivation, trust, and so forth. Obviously, such factors are important in the sense that they are affected by existing organization structures. They are also critical in the sense that they codetermine the success of organizational design choices. Therefore, fully understanding issues of organization structure is not possible when these are addressed in isolation.

From this account it follows that decisions of organization design fall into two basic categories. They concern: (1) either splitting or integrating tasks within production, and (2) either separating production from control or integrating production and control. Four archetypes of organization structures then appear situated on a continuum (see Table 1). The archetype of maximal splitting within production, combined with maximal separation of production from control, defines one end of the continuum (this describes the classical Tayloristic bureaucracy with its focus on specialization within production and elaborate

Table 1. Effects of separation, splitting, and integration of tasks on knowledge processes

	Separation of production from control	Integration of production and control
Splitting of tasks within production	Tayloristic bureaucracy: knowledge application and retention via formal routines, knowledge transfer via the hierarchy, improved retention and exploitation of explicit knowledge, possible specialization in knowledge development, problems of tacit knowledge sharing.	Professional bureaucracy designed around small cells with specialized task elements within a larger task that manage their own work and connections to other cells within their production chain (e.g., in health services): possible specialization in knowledge development, advantages of tacit knowledge sharing within the cells, but across-cell transfer limited to explicit knowledge.
Integration within production	E.g., the hypertext organization with integral tasks but separate control structures: flexible knowledge exploration within teams and exploitation within the hierarchically organized layer, but possible conflicts of transferring and connecting ideas and plans developed in the project team layer and the application of these in new business (possible clashes between innovatism and conservatism).	The integrated team-based organization: more flexible knowledge development in connected knowledge domains, advantages of within team transfer of tacit knowledge, possible problems of reinventing the wheel by teams, barriers to inter-team cooperation and knowledge sharing.

control hierarchies). Full integration on both aspects defines the other end of the continuum (here one finds the team-based or project-based organization in which autonomous, multi-skilled work teams are responsible for their own work; e.g., Sitter, Hertog, & Dankbaar, 1997; Hobday, 2000). Intermediate positions are taken by the two remaining archetypes that combine splitting in production with integration in control and vice versa. A team-based organization becomes a network organization when decisions as to integration within production and control are not specified beforehand, but are left to individual team or network members.

An important question for KM is how different organization structures affect knowledge aspects of work. A basic way of addressing this question is to inspect how splitting or integrating in production and separating or integrating in control affect the knowledge processes within an organization (see Table 1). Splitting production into sub-functions, leading to specialization in the production of knowledge, has both positive and negative impacts on all knowledge processes (knowledge exploration, knowledge exploitation, knowledge sharing, and knowledge retention; see Hendriks & Vriens, 1999). What the effects will be depends on the criteria used for splitting. For instance, splitting according to knowledge domains or areas of expertise will stimulate knowledge exploration within these domains, but it will hinder knowledge sharing across domains. Splitting according to market knowledge, on the other hand, puts more emphasis on individual, tacit elements in knowledge. It comes with the boons of improved customer presence in knowledge exploitation and knowledge exploration. However, it also brings the risks of

impaired knowledge sharing and knowledge retention within domains.

The Tayloristic machine bureaucracy is the archetype of an organization that combines maximal splitting in production with maximal separation of production from control. This organizational form is characterized by advantages of possible specialization in knowledge exploration, by the fact that knowledge sharing takes the form of formalized knowledge transfer, and by the fact that procedures mainly address explicit knowledge, which is an important vehicle in knowledge retention.

Combining sub-functions in production, which leads to integrated knowledge in production, may in turn involve problems of knowledge retention associated with the risk of reinventing the wheel by different integrated units. Conversely, it implies combination benefits of knowledge from different knowledge domains in knowledge exploration and knowledge exploitation. An example of the archetype that combines maximal integration in production with maximal integration of production and control is that of the team-based project organization. This organizational form does not stimulate specialization in knowledge exploration, as it aims at broad employability. It focuses on mostly informal knowledge sharing via communication in teams and retains knowledge mainly through the team members. This organization type also aims to facilitate the exchange of tacit, implicit knowledge.

Blackler (1995; Blackler, Crump, & McDonald, 2000) and Lam (2000) provide examples of an alternative way to link organization structure to knowledge. They identify contingencies for organizational effectiveness as dimen-

Table 2. Structural configurations and knowledge types (Blackler, 1995; Lam, 2000)

	Focus on problems with low complexity and variability, and high analyzability	Focus on problems with high complexity and variability, and low analyzability
Focus on individual knowledge agents	- *typical organization structure*: professional bureaucracy, which is individualistic, functionally segmented, hierarchical; experts have a high degree of autonomy - *key knowledge type*: embrained knowledge, or knowledge of generalizations and abstract concepts - *learning*: organizations have a narrow learning focus facing problems of innovation; power and status of experts inhibit knowledge sharing	- *typical organization structure*: adhocracy with its diverse, varied, and organic knowledge base, or other knowledge-intensive form - *key knowledge type*: embodied knowledge, or the tacit skills of key members - *learning*: fast and fluid learning and unlearning, but has problems of widely diffusing knowledge
Focus on collective knowledge agents	- *typical organization structure*: machine bureaucracy, which is characterized by specialization, standardization, control, functionally segmentation, hierarchy, seeking to minimize role of tacit knowledge - *key knowledge type*: encoded knowledge, or knowledge in documents and other registrations; a clear dichotomy exists between application and generation of knowledge - *learning*: learns by correction, through performance monitoring; unable to cope with novelty or change	- *typical organization structure*: communication-intensive organization organized as an adhocracy or other knowledge-intensive form; communication and collaboration are key processes; empowerment through integration; expertise is pervasive - *key knowledge type*: encultured knowledge, shared sense-making - *learning*: the organization is adaptive and innovative, but may find it difficult to innovate radically (learning is potentially conservative)

sions of a matrix, and enter a combined description of design choices and knowledge types of individual organizations or classes of organizations in the cells of the resulting matrix. Table 2 presents the approaches of these authors condensed into a two-by-two matrix. The arguments presented above calling for openness in the production structure and flat hierarchies imply calls to elaborate the right-hand column of the table.

Designing Knowledge-Friendly Organizational Structures

We now turn to the second theme of this article, which is designing knowledge-friendly organization structures. This theme involves looking at the interventions available for defining or changing organization structures. Two different types of such interventions, or KM practices, exist with respect to the organization structure: (1) practices that involve (re)designing the basic production structure from a knowledge standpoint, adjusting the control structure to the resulting production layout; and (2) practices that involve adapting existing production and control structures to knowledge-related demands with additional interventions of organization design. The following two sections will address both types of KM

practices in more detail, under the labels of 'basic structures' and 'support structures', respectively.

Knowledge-Friendly Basic Structures

The literature describes several knowledge-friendly organization structures. Among these, the three that appear to have received the most attention are: the team-based organization, the network structure, and the hypertext organization.

Team-Based Structure

A team is generally defined as a group of people working together towards a common goal. The team concept and the associated project structure (Hobday, 2000) have a rich history in organization studies, which also includes references to knowledge work (e.g., Mohrman, Mohrman, & Cohen, 1995). Two traditions provide the most extensive exploration of team concepts (Benders & Van Hootegem, 1999). The first of these is the sociotechnical system design approach, which focuses on self-managing teams (e.g., Sitter et al., 1997). Team concepts also play a central role in Japanese management studies, which focus on such concepts as 'lean teams' and 'just-in-time' teams. From a knowledge perspective, the team structure involves both pros and cons. The main advantage of a team structure is that teams can be designed to integrate the knowledge needed for a particular task (e.g., a team of experts from various specialties that share the goal of serving a particular regional market). This may lead to improvements in all of the knowledge processes within the team. The main disadvantage of teams is that the cohesion they need for success erects barriers for establishing lateral linkages with other teams. This will impair cross-team cooperation in knowledge exploration and knowledge exploitation. Several authors describe structural configurations that show resemblance to the team concept, but are at best less-developed accounts of elements of team concepts. These include the cellular structure (e.g., Miles & Creed, 1995; Miles et al., 1997) and the inverted organization (Quinn, 1992; Quinn, Anderson, & Finkelstein, 1996).

Network Structure

The network structure involves the largest degree of freedom for knowledge workers to establish work relationships. The term 'network structure' is not a neatly delineated concept in organization studies, but it serves as an umbrella for several organizational forms that show similarities with or are elaborations of the adhocracy structure described above (see Thompson, 2003). The network organization comes under several names: Hedlund (1994) labels it the N-form organization ('N' for 'new'), and Quinn (1992, 1996) uses the term 'spider-web organization'. At least three elements connect the various network concepts of organizations (Hedlund, 1994, p. 83ff.). First, they promote temporary constellations that use the pool of people and their competencies as a touchstone for design. Second, they stress the importance of lateral communication networks within and among production units. Third, they see top management as catalysts, architects, and protectors. Several different variants of the network structure exist. These range from an organization which adopts a web structure to connect its own semi-permanent parts via a network organization that consists as a network of semi-autonomous organizations, to an organizational network that is built around the semi-permanent relationships between autonomous organizations.

Hypertext Organization

Nonaka (1994; Nonaka & Takeuchi, 1995, 1997; Nonaka, Takeuchi, & Umemoto, 1996) describes a structural form that combines the traditional functional structure that is associated with efficiency gains with a project-based organization, that comes with the benefits of flexibility needed for a knowledge-creating company. It is grounded in a business system layer, which is the central layer for normal, routine operations organized as a hierarchical pyramid. On top of that layer, Nonaka identifies a project team layer for knowledge-creation activities. This layer involves the exclusive assignment of team members from different units across the business system to a project team until the project has been completed. These two layers are complementary rather than mutually exclusive. A strong corporate culture is therefore needed to combine the team-based project part of the organization with the hierarchical, bureaucratic part. This connecting culture Nonaka calls the organization's knowledge base. It involves the recategorization and recontextualization of knowledge newly generated in the other two layers. Nonaka uses the term 'hypertext' to indicate that combining knowledge contents more flexibly across layers and over time calls for the existence of dormant links between various parts and layers of the organization that can be activated when needed. This resembles the hypertext links connecting Web sites.

Knowledge-Focused Support Structures

Several mechanisms are described in the literature for improving existing organization structures from the perspective of knowledge processes. These include:

1. **Knowledge centers:** An organization may decide to assign tasks aimed at furthering the flow of knowledge processes to dedicated departments (e.g., Moore & Birkinshaw, 1998; Hertog & Huizenga, 2000). As an example, consider a library that adopts an active role of offering knowledge mapping services to further possibly fruitful cooperation based on the documents it stores. Thus, it facilitates the processes of knowledge transfer.

2. **Knowledge-centered roles and functions**, such as chief knowledge officer (CKO), knowledge manager, and knowledge broker (see Davenport & Prusak, 1998; Earl & Scott, 1999; Snyman, 2001; McKeen & Staples, 2003). The tasks involved are typically control tasks at strategic or operational levels that aim at providing knowledge workers with the appropriate infrastructure required for task completion.

3. Den Hertog and Huizenga (2000) describe several forms of **lateral knowledge linkages** between organizational units that aim to transcend the boundaries involved in the basic structure. These include the establishment of 'expertise circles' that bring together the domain specialists of several teams or other organizational units to discuss developments in that domain and exchange best practices. Pro-

grams of job rotation may also be appropriate tools to install lateral linkages.

4. Communities of practice (CoPs) and communities of interest (CoIs) are elements of the informal organization structure that, because of their organic nature, are generally recognized as important to knowledge flows. Within the domain of formal organizational design, an organization may want to use instruments that aim at *facilitating existing communities* and stimulating the emergence of new ones. As an example, consider an organization that uses project evaluation procedures as a vehicle to stimulate individuals to explore possibilities for community formation.

FUTURE TRENDS

In the discussions of organization structure, the links to knowledge have played an important role for many decades. Some of these discussions have presented themselves as KM studies, but most of them do not adopt that label. The contribution of KM studies in organization structure usually comes from two areas. The first area concerns the recognition of organization structure as a contextual factor influencing the choice and success rates of KM programs (Bennett & Gabriel, 1999; Gold, Malhotra, & Segars, 2001). The second area involves the design and implementation of concrete measures, management practices, and the like, which all involve an adaptation of the existing organization structure. KM may serve as an integrating umbrella to connect disparate thinking around knowledge aspects of organization structure. One form this integration is likely to take is through a further development of the knowledge element in the contingency theory of organizations. Many discussions of knowledge-friendly organization structures are contemplative in nature, and lack a firm basis in empirical research. Therefore, one would anticipate an increase of empirical studies which address how organizations choose among the alternatives available for making their organization structures knowledge friendly. A final trend that has become more apparent is the trend in which KM research on organization structure has increasingly turned to existing analysis models that allow focusing on relationships, such as social network theory or actor network theory (e.g., Benassi, Greve, & Harkola, 1999; Nelson, 2001; Chang & Harrington, 2003; Sorenson, 2003).

CONCLUSION

Organization structure is an important aspect of knowledge work as it concerns the establishment of work relationships. Any organization structure will stimulate the establishment of certain relationships at the expense of others. It is important to note that flatter, fuzzier, or less structure is by no means inherently superior to crisper or more structure. Too much openness in organization structures not identifying possible work relationships may well result in limited identification and exploitation of such relationships. Too much closure introduces the risk of virtually making it impossible for specific classes of possibly productive relationships to come about. The challenge for knowledge management is to come up with the appropriate mix of design interventions which will guide individuals when they try to establish work contacts, without depriving them of the freedom they need to be knowledgeable and to continue learning. This involves a threefold challenge: (1) choosing a basic structure that honors the key elements of knowledge exploration and knowledge exploitation; (2) identifying the drawbacks of the basic structure for the flow of knowledge processes, and correcting these with the appropriate support structures; and (3) addressing the limitations of organization design with interventions from other management realms, such as human resource management.

REFERENCES

Benassi, M., Greve, A., & Harkola, J. (1999). Looking for a network organization: The case of GESTO. *Journal of Market-Focused Management, 4*(3), 205-229.

Benders, J., & Van Hootegem, G. (1999). Teams and their context: Moving the team discussion beyond existing dichotomies. *Journal of Management Studies, 36*(5), 609-628.

Bennett, R., & Gabriel, H. (1999). Organizational factors and knowledge management within large marketing departments: An empirical study. *Journal of Knowledge Management, 3*(3), 212-225.

Birkinshaw, J., Nobel, R., & Ridderstrale, J. (2002). Knowledge as a contingency variable: Do the characteristics of knowledge predict organization structure? *Organization Science, 13*(3), 274-289.

Blackler, F. (1995). Knowledge, knowledge work and organizations: An overview and interpretation. *Organization Studies, 16*(6), 1021-1046.

Blackler, F., Crump, N., & McDonald, S. (2000). Organizing processes in complex activity networks. *Organization, 7*(2), 277-300.

Bowditch, J.L., & Buono, A.F. (1985). *A primer on organizational behavior*. New York: John Wiley & Sons.

Brown, J.S., & Duguid, P. (2001). Knowledge and organization: A social-practice perspective. *Organization Science, 12*(2), 198-213.

Burns, T.R., & Stalker, G.M. (1961). *The management of innovation*. London: Tavistock.

Butler, R.J., Price, D.H.R., Coates, P.D., & Pike, R.H. (1998). Organizing for innovation: Loose or tight control? *Long Range Planning, 31*(5), 775-782.

Chang, M.H., & Harrington, J.E. (2003). Multimarket competition, consumer search, and the organizational structure of multiunit firms. *Management Science, 49*(4), 541-552.

Davenport, T.H., & Prusak, L. (1998). *Working knowledge. How organizations manage what they know*. Boston: Harvard Business School Press.

Donaldson, L. (2001). *The contingency theory of organizations*. Thousand Oaks, CA: Sage Publications.

Earl, M.J., & Scott, I.A. (1999). Opinion—what is a chief knowledge officer? *Sloan Management Review, 40*(2), 29-38.

Gold, A.H., Malhotra, A., & Segars, A.H. (2001). Knowledge management: An organizational capabilities perspective. *Journal of Management Information Systems, 18*(1), 185-214.

Hedlund, G. (1994). A model of knowledge management and the N-Form Corporation. *Strategic Management Journal, 15*(Special Issue, Summer), 73-90.

Hendriks, P.H.J., & Vriens, D.J. (1999). Knowledge-based systems and knowledge management: Friends or foes? *Information and Management, 35*(2), 113-125.

Hertog, J.F.D., & Huizenga, E.I. (2000). *The knowledge enterprise: Implementation of intelligent business strategies*. London: Imperial College Press.

Hobday, M. (2000). The project-based organization: An ideal form for managing complex products and systems? *Research Policy, 29*(7-8), 871-893.

Lam, A. (2000). Tacit knowledge, organizational learning and societal institutions: An integrated framework. *Organization Studies, 21*(3), 487-513.

Lawrence, P.R., & Lorsch, J.W. (1969). *Developing organizations: Diagnosis and action*. Reading, MA: Addison-Wesley.

Lawrence, P.R., Lorsch, J.W., & Garrison, J.S. (1967). *Organization and environment: Managing differentiation and integration*. Boston: Division of Research, Graduate School of Business Administration, Harvard University.

McKeen, J., & Staples, S. (2003). Knowledge managers: Who are they and what do they do? In C.W. Holsapple (Ed.), *Handbook on knowledge management* (Vol. 1, pp. 21-42). Berlin: Springer-Verlag.

Miles, R.E., & Creed, W.E.D. (1995). Organizational forms and managerial philosophies—a descriptive and analytical review. *Research in Organizational Behavior: An Annual Series of Analytical Essays and Critical Reviews, 17*, 333-372. Greenwich, CT: JAI Press.

Miles, R.E., Snow, C.C., Mathews, J.A., Miles, G., & Coleman, H.J. (1997). Organizing in the knowledge age: Anticipating the cellular form. *Academy of Management Executive, 11*(4), 7-24.

Mintzberg, H. (1979). *The structuring of organizations: A synthesis of the research*. Englewood Cliffs, NJ: Prentice-Hall.

Mintzberg, H. (1983). *Structure in fives: Designing effective organizations*. Englewood Cliffs, NJ: Prentice-Hall.

Mohrman, S.A., Mohrman, A.M., & Cohen, S.G. (1995). Organizing knowledge work systems. In M.M. Beyerlein, D.A. Johnson, & S.T. Beyerlein (Eds.), *Knowledge work in teams* (vol. 2, pp. 61-91). Greenwich, CT: JAI Press.

Moore, K., & Birkinshaw, J. (1998). Managing knowledge in global service firms: Centers of excellence. *Academy of Management Executive, 12*(4), 81-92.

Morgan, G. (1986). *Images of organization*. Beverly Hills, CA: Sage Publications.

Myers, P.S. (1996). *Knowledge management and organizational design*. Boston: Butterworth-Heinemann.

Nelson, R.E. (2001). On the shape of verbal networks in organizations. *Organization Studies, 22*(5), 797.

Nonaka, I. (1994). A dynamic theory of organizational knowledge creation. *Organization Science, 5*(1), 14-37.

Nonaka, I., & Takeuchi, H. (1995). *The knowledge-creating company*. New York: Oxford University Press.

Nonaka, I., & Takeuchi, H. (1997). A new organizational structure. In L. Prusak (Ed.), *Knowledge in organizations; resources for the knowledge-based economy* (pp. 99-103). Boston: Butterworth-Heinemann.

Nonaka, I., Takeuchi, H., & Umemoto, K. (1996). A theory of organizational knowledge creation. *International Journal of Technology Management, 11*(7-8), 833-845.

Quinn, J.B. (1992). *Intelligent enterprise: A knowledge and service based paradigm for industry*. New York: The Free Press.

Quinn, J.B., Anderson, P., & Finkelstein, S. (1996). Managing professional intellect: Making the most of the best. *Harvard Business Review, 74*(2), 71-80.

Sanchez, R., & Mahoney, J.T. (1996). Modularity, flexibility, and knowledge management in product and organization design. *Strategic Management Journal, 17*, 63-76.

Sitter, L.U.D., Hertog, J.F.D., & Dankbaar, B. (1997). From complex organizations with simple jobs to simple organizations with complex jobs. *Human Relations, 50*(5), 497-534.

Snyman, R.M.M. (2001). Do employers really know what they want? An analysis of job advertisements for information and knowledge managers. *ASLIB Proceedings, 53*(7), 273-281.

Sorenson, O. (2003). Interdependence and adaptability: Organizational learning and the long-term effect of integration. *Management Science, 49*(4), 446-463.

Teece, D.J. (2000). Strategies for managing knowledge assets: The role of firm structure and industrial context. *Long Range Planning, 33*(1), 35-54.

Thompson, G.F. (2003). *Between hierarchies and markets: The logic and limits of network forms of organization*. Oxford: Oxford University Press.

Thompson, J.D. (1967). *Organizations in action: Social science bases of administrative theory*. New York: McGraw-Hill.

Weber, M. (1922). *Wirtschaft und Gesellschaft*. Tübingen: Mohr.

Winter, S.G. (1987). Knowledge and competence as strategic assets. In D. Teece (Ed.), *The competitive challenge* (pp. 159-184). New York: HarperCollins.

Zander, U., & Kogut, B. (1995). Knowledge and the speed of the transfer and imitation of organizational capabilities—an empirical test. *Organization Science, 6*(1), 76-92.

KEY TERMS

Hypertext Structure: Organization structure described by Nonaka, distinguishing a functionally organized, hierarchical, and bureaucratic business system layer for regular knowledge exploitation, a project layer for development work, and a knowledge base layer connecting the first two layers.

Knowledge Centers: Support structure that assigns a distinct set of knowledge-related tasks, usually within the coordination domain, to a separate department.

Knowledge-Friendly Organization Structures: Organization structures that, in the combination of their basic structures and support structures, provide an appropriate infrastructure for knowledge to gain organizational value.

Knowledge Managers: Support structure that assigns a distinct set of knowledge-related tasks, usually within the coordination domain, to an individual person.

Network Organization: Relatively loose organization form, which does not predefine all possible work relationships, but establishes these when needed.

Organization Structure: Patterns of work relationships (or task interdependencies). Production structure refers to work relationships among production tasks. Control structure refers to the hierarchical work relationships involved in coordinating production work. Informal organization structure concerns organically developing work relationships, whereas formal organization structure concerns predefined work relationships.

Team-Based Organization: Organization structure that gives a group of people responsibility for a coherent part of production, and assigns the associated control responsibilities to that group (self-managing teams).

Work Relationships: The task connections or interdependencies involved in input-output combinations: output of one task gets used as input for another. The concept of work relationships focuses on the content side to these combinations, and involves an abstraction from the personal elements in work-related cooperations.

Postmortem Reviews

P

Torgeir Dingsøyr
SINTEF Information and Communication Technology, Norway

INTRODUCTION

Postmortem reviews are collective learning activities which can be organized for projects either when they end a phase or are terminated. The main motivation is to reflect on what happened in the project in order to improve future practice—for the individuals that have participated in the project and for the organization as a whole. Projects are the typical way of working in most knowledge-intensive organizations, and postmortems provide a possibility to learn from the projects with little effort, which makes it ideal as an initial knowledge management activity in a company.

This type of process has also been referred to as "after action reviews," "project retrospectives," "postmortem analysis," "post-project review," "project analysis review," "quality improvement review," "autopsy review," "Santayana review," and "touch-down meetings."

Researchers in organizational learning sometimes use the term "reflective practice," which can be defined as "the practice of periodically stepping back to ponder on the meaning to self and others in one's immediate environment about what has recently transpired. It illuminates what has been experienced by both self and others, providing a basis for future action" (Raelin, 2001). This involves uncovering and making explicit results of planning, observation, and achieved practice. It can lead to understanding of experiences that have been overlooked in practice.

There are a number of methods to conduct postmortems which we will describe in more detail in the following. The methods rely on collecting information from project participants either through interviews, group processes, or a meeting (preferably where participants meet physically). The outcome of a meeting is a postmortem report.

BACKGROUND

In the knowledge creation model of Nonaka and Takeuchi (1995), postmortems are a combination of learning through socialization and through externalization. In listening to others you employ socialization, and in reflecting and sharing your own experience you externalize your tacit knowledge. Postmortems are also a method for leveraging knowledge from the individual level to the organizational level.

In a survey on essential practices in research and development-companies, "learning from post-project audits" are seen as one of the most promising practices that could yield competitive advantage (Menke, 1997).

A survey on post-project reviews in research and development companies show that only one out of five projects received a post-project review (Zedtwitz, 2002). Also, the reviews tend to focus on technical output and bureaucratic measurements. Process-related factors are rarely discussed.

As a knowledge management tool, postmortem reviews are simple to organize. The process focuses on dialogue and discussion, which is a central element in knowledge transfer. Von Krogh, Ichijo, and Nonaka (2000) write:

It is quite ironic that while executives and knowledge officers persist in focusing on expensive information-technology systems, quantifiable databases, and measurement tools, one of the best means for knowledge sharing and creating knowledge already exists within their companies. We cannot emphasize enough the important part conversations play.

An example of postmortem reviews are "after action reviews" conducted by the U.S. army since after the Vietnam war, focusing on a "professional discussion of an event" to provide insight, feedback, and details about the event (Townsend & Gebhart, 1999).

Conducting Postmortem Reviews

There are several ways to perform postmortem reviews. Apple has used a method (Collier, DeMarco, & Fearey, 1996) which includes designing a project survey, collecting objective project information, conducting a debriefing meeting and a "project history day," and finally publishing the results. At Microsoft they also put much effort into writing "postmortem reports." These contain discussion on "what worked well in the last project, what did not work well, and what the group should do to improve in the next project" (Cusomano & Selby, 1995). The size of the resulting document is quite large: "Groups generally take three to six months to put a postmortem document together. The documents have ranged from under 10 to more than 100 pages, and have tended to grow in length."

Kerth (2001) lists a total of 19 techniques to be used in postmortems, many focusing on creating an atmosphere for discussion in the project. Kerth recommends taking three days to discuss projects in detail. (For a more complete overview of methods and purpose of postmortem reviews, see Dingsøyr, 2005)

METHODS FOR CONDUCTING POSTMORTEM REVIEWS

Postmortems can differ in length from activities that takes weeks, to an activity that can be done as a half-day group process. In the following, we present two methods for conducting postmortems, and also present example results from one type of postmortem.

Two techniques are used in both types of postmortems: For a focused brainstorm on what happened in the project, a technique called the "KJ Method," named after Japanese Ethnologist Jiro Kawakita (Scupin, 1997), is used. For each of these sessions, the participants are given a set of Post-It notes and asked to write one "issue" on each note. Five notes are handed out to each person. After a few minutes, the participants are asked to attach one note to a whiteboard and say why this issue is important. Then the next person presents a note and so on until all the notes are on the whiteboard. The notes are then grouped, and each group is given a new name.

Root cause analysis, also called Ishikawa or fishbone-diagrams, are used to analyze the causes of important issues. A process leader draws an arrow on a whiteboard, indicating the issue being discussed, and attaches other arrows to this one like in a fishbone, with issues the participants think are causing the first issue. Sometimes, underlying reasons for some of the main causes are attached as well.

Postmortem Review as a Large-Scale Process

Collier et al. (1996) describe postmortem reviews through five activities:

1. **Project Survey:** Define a set of questions you would like project participants to answer, such as "Did schedule changes and related issues involve the right people?" and "Were the right tradeoffs between features, quality, resources, and schedule done for the product developed in the project?" Analyze the results of such a survey, and complement with gathering objective data.
2. **Collect Objective Information:** Objective information related to resources spent, products devel-

oped, and other objective information that is valuable for a project.
3. **Debriefing Meeting:** Give project participants the opportunity to give direct feedback about the project. Use survey results to guide the topics to be covered in the meeting. Organize a series of meetings if more than 30 people participated in the project. Use a facilitator for the meetings in order to ensure a balanced discussion.
4. **Project History Day:** Formulate a problem statement to focus activities based on findings from the previous steps. An example is: "What are the root causes that determined or affected resources, schedule, and quality?" Invite key project participants, use a facilitator to discuss the problem statement, and use techniques such as root-cause-analysis. Limit participation to six or eight people. Ask participants to read the information gathered from the project, discuss deviations from the project schedule, and perform root-cause analysis on major deviations. Take note of the top 20 "root causes," and categorize using the KJ process.
5. **Publish the Results:** The leadership summarizes its findings and publishes it in an "open letter to project teams," which should be readable for project management and participants in the organization. It consists of four parts: (1) a description of the project, (2) a summary of positive findings ("the good"), (3) a summary of negative findings ("the bad"), and (4) issues that need to be improved ("the ugly").

Postmortem Review as a Half-Day Group Process

Birk, Dingsøyr, and Stålhane have used postmortem reviews as a group process (Birk, Dingsøyr, & Stålhane, 2002; Dingsøyr, Moe, & Nytrø, 2001; Stålhane, Dingsøyr, Moe, & Hanssen, 2003), where most of the work is done in one meeting lasting half a day. They try to get as many of the persons working in the project as possible to participate, together with two process consultants—one in charge of the postmortem process, the other acting as a secretary. The goal of this meeting is to collect information from the participants, make them discuss the way the project was carried out, and also analyze causes for why things worked out well or did not work out.

The "requirements" for this process include that the project should not take much time for the project team to participate, and it should provide a forum for discussing and analyzing the most important experience from the project. The main findings are documented in a report.

The postmortem meeting has following steps:

1. **Introduction:** First, the consultants introduced the agenda of the day and the purpose of the postmortem review.
2. **KJ Session 1:** Consultants hand out Post-It notes and ask people to write down what went well in the project, hear presentations, group the issues on the whiteboard, and give them priorities.
3. **KJ Session 2:** Consultants hand out Post-It notes and ask people to write down problems that appeared in the project, hear presentations, group the issues on the whiteboard, and give them priorities.
4. **Root Cause Analysis:** The process consultant leading the meeting draws fishbone diagrams for the main issues, both from the things that went well and the things that were problematic.

Birk et al. use a Dictaphone during the presentations and transcribe everything that is said. The consultants write a postmortem report about the project; the report contains an introduction, a short description of the project analyzed, how the analysis was carried out, and the results of the analysis. The result is a prioritized list of problems and successes in the project. Statements from the meeting are used to present what was said about the issues with highest priority, together with a fishbone diagram to show their causes. In an appendix, everything that was written down on Post-It notes during the KJ session is included, as well as a transcription of the presentation of the issues that were used on the Post-It notes. Such reports are usually between 10 and 15 pages in length.

The day after the meeting, the consultants present the report to the people involved in the project to gather feedback and do minor corrections.

Example Results from a Postmortem

We now present results from one review. First, we present the company, then the project where the review was carried out, and finally extracts from the postmortem report (see Dingsøyr et al., 2001, for more information).

The company makes software and hardware for stations receiving data from meteorological and Earth observation satellites.

The postmortem was organized for a project which had developed a software system for a satellite that was recording environmental data. The project had developed a module that was to analyze data from this satellite from European Space Agency specifications. The project lasted for approximately one year, and employed six people full time and two people part-time—a total of eight man-years. Five people participated in the postmortem review including the project manager.

One result from the KJ session was two Post-It notes grouped together and named "changing requirements." They are shown in the upper left corner of (some of) the results from the KJ process in Figure 1.

Participants made the following statements about "changing requirements":

Another thing was changes of requirements during the project: from my point of view—who implemented things, it was difficult to decide: when are the requirements changed so much that things have to be made from scratch? Some wrong decisions were taken that reduced the quality of the software.

Figure 1. Post-It notes showing some of the problems in a software development project

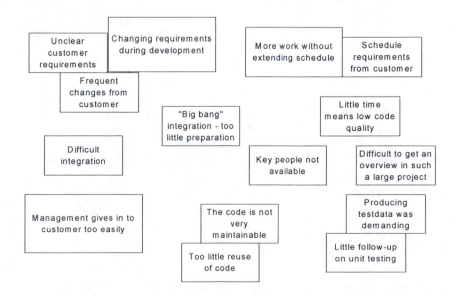

Figure 2. Ishikawa diagram for "changing requirements"

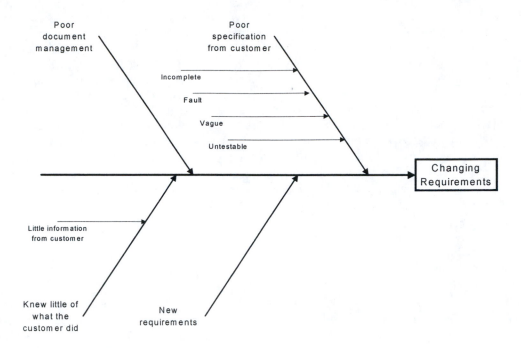

Unclear customer requirements—which made us use a lot of time in discussions and meetings with the customer to get things right, which made us spend a lot of time because the customer did not do good enough work.

When we later brought this up again and tried to find some of the root causes for "changing requirements," we ended up with the fishbone diagram in Figure 2.

The root causes for the changing requirements, as the people participating in the analysis saw it, was that the requirements were poorly specified by the customer, there were "new requirements" during the project, and the company knew little of what the customer was doing. Another reason for this problem was that documents related to requirements were managed poorly within the company. In Figure 2, we have also listed some sub-causes.

The postmortem helped surface problems and successes that people were already aware of, but was not systematically presented in any way. It helped to focus on some important issues to improve and to sustain in future projects. The report was readable for people who were working on other projects in the company.

FUTURE TRENDS

In a study of 19 companies across Europe on project-based learning practices, Keegan and Turner (2001) found that "project team members frequently do not have the time for meetings, or for sessions to review lessons learned. Often, project team members are immediately reassigned to new projects before they have had time for lessons learned sessions or after action reviews." They did not find a single company where employees expressed satisfaction with the postmortem process.

We think there is a need for simple and practical descriptions of how to conduct postmortems, in order to stimulate knowledge-intensive companies to do it more often. The benefit of conducting postmortem reviews is mainly that it provides a learning forum where discussions are relevant to the project and to the company. It can also be a way for management to show that they listen to what the employees say, and are willing to discuss improvement efforts.

CONCLUSION

We have described postmortem reviews as a simple knowledge management technique, along with two particular methods to conduct postmortem reviews as a group process. We have also presented example results from a postmortem report.

REFERENCES

Birk, A., Dingsøyr, T., & Stålhane, T. (2002). Postmortem: Never leave a project without it. *IEEE Software, 3*(19), 43-45.

Collier, B. DeMarco, T., & Fearey, P. (1996). A defined process for project postmortem review. *IEEE Software, 4*(13), 65-72.

Cusomano, M.A., & Selby, R.W. (1995). *Microsoft secrets—how the world's most powerful software company creates technology, shapes markets, and manages people.* New York: The Free Press.

Dingsøyr, T. (2005). Postmortem: Purpose and approaches in software engineering. *Information and Software Technology, 5*(47), 293-303.

Dingsøyr, T., Moe, N.B., & Nytrø, Ø. (2001). Augmenting experience reports with lightweight postmortem reviews. In F. Bomarius & S. Komi-Sirviö (Eds.), *Proceedings of the 3rd International Conference on Product Focused Software Process Improvement* (pp. 167-181). Kaiserslautern, Germany: Springer-Verlag (LNCS2188).

Keegan, A., & Turner, J.R. (2001). Quantity versus quality in project-based learning practices. *Management Learning, 1*(32), 77-98.

Kerth, N.L. (2001). *Project retrospectives: A handbook for team reviews.* Dorset House.

Menke, M.M. (1997). Managing R&D for competitive advantage. *Research Technology Management, 40*(6), 40-42.

Nonaka, I., & Takeuchi, H. (1995). *The knowledge-creating company.* Oxford: Oxford University Press.

Raelin, J.A. (2001). Public reflection as the basis of learning. *Management Learning, 32*(1), 11-30.

Stålhane, T., Dingsøyr, T., Moe, N.B., & Hanssen, G.K. (2003). Postmortem—an assessment of two approaches. In R. Conradi & A.I. Wang (Eds.), *Empirical methods and studies in software engineering: Experiences from ESERNET* (pp. 129-141). Heidelberg: Springer-Verlag (LNCS2765).

Scupin, R. (1997). The KJ method: A technique for analyzing data derived from Japanese ethnology. *Human Organization, 56*(2), 233-237.

Townsend, P.L., & Gebhart, J.E. (1999). *How organizations learn.* Crisp Publications.

Tiedeman, M.J. (1990). Postmortems—methodology and experiences. *IEEE Journal of on Selected Areas in Communications, 8*(2).

von Krogh, G., Ichijo, K., & Nonaka, I. (2000). *Enabling knowledge creation.* New York: Oxford University Press.

Zedtwitz, M. (2002). Organizational learning through post-project reviews in R&D. *R&D Management, 32*(3), 255-268.

KEY TERMS

Ishikawa Diagrams: See Root Cause Analysis.

KJ: A technique to structure information, typically after a brainstorm. Keywords are written on stickers and organized according to group. The technique is named after Japanese Ethnologist Jiro Kawakita.

Postmortem Review: A collective learning activity which can be organized for projects either when they end a phase or are terminated. The main motivation is to reflect on what happened in the project in order to improve future practice—for the individuals that have participated in the project and for the organization as a whole.

Reflective Practices: Analyzing events that have happened, usually in a group setting, so that events are seen from different perspectives.

Root Cause Analysis: Also called Ishikawa or fishbone diagrams; used to structure discussions on the causes of important issues by drawing a line for an issue, and arrows for causes and sub-causes.

Practice–Based Knowledge Integration

Glenn Munkvold
Norwegian University of Science and Technology, Norway

INTRODUCTION

For organisations, the tension between integration and specialisation has become a key issue as the knowledge of work is becoming increasingly fragmented through specialisation (Becker, 2002; Grant, 1996; Kogut & Zander, 1992). Specialisation, as knowing more about less, distributes the overall accomplishment of work on several entities (Aanestad, Mørk, Grisot, Hanseth, & Syvertsen, 2003; Becker; Berg, 1997; Hutchins, 1995) with the consequent need for the integration of different competencies and types of expertise. Becker (p. 3) provides the following definition of knowledge integration:

By knowledge integration we mean solving problems raised by specialisation: Specialisation leads to a dispersion of specialised bodies of knowledge that are held by different specialists...Knowledge integration refers to how this drawing on different bodies of specialised knowledge is organised.

The capability of relying upon specialisation and the ability to integrate specialised knowledge have been identified as critical factors in the competitiveness of an organisation (Grant, 1996; Kogut & Zander, 1992). Because of this, integration has become a theme for numerous research efforts.

A first line of research looks at knowledge integration as the transferring of knowledge to where it is supposed to be used (Berends, Debackere, Garud, & Weggeman, 2004). By transferring knowledge to someone who is able to use it and combine it with his or her own work practice, knowledge is integrated. If we are able to capture and model the content of knowledge, we can disseminate it and make it usable across contexts. As an integration mechanism, transfer is problematic because "it is costly and counters the necessary specialisation of organisation members" (Berends et al., p. 4). Moreover, the notion of knowledge as something that can be externalised and combined is problematic in itself (Blackler, 1995; Walsham 2001, 2004).

Current discourse on knowledge is filled with ambiguities and varying conceptualisations (see, e.g., Alvesson, 2001; Blackler; Boland & Tenkasi, 1995; Carlsen, Klev, & von Krogh, 2004; Cook & Brown, 1999; Davenport & Prusak, 1998; Fitzpatrick, 2003; Gherardi, 2000; Walsham, 2001), and a detailed discussion of this issue is beyond the scope of this article. For this article, we will recall that the underlying tenet grounding most of the existing views is a distinction between explicit and tacit knowledge. Explicit knowledge refers to knowledge that is movable and easy to convey, while tacit knowledge is intimately connected to our identity and is thus hard to formalize (Polanyi, 1966). Nonaka and Takeuchi (1995, p. 61) claim that the conversion between tacit and explicit knowledge is "a 'social' process between individuals and not confined within an individual." While popular, their view on tacit knowledge as something to be externalised and combined has been criticized (see, e.g., Blackler, 1995; Walsham 2001, 2004). As human interaction is always mediated by representations, our experiences and the way we perceive the world can never be replicated perfectly. Hence, Walsham (2001) argues that the knowledge-management discourse in general, and knowledge-management systems in particular, should pay closer attention to the contextual sides of knowledge.

This different understanding of knowledge leads to a second line of research on knowledge integration: one that is first and foremost paying attention to the relational and situated nature of knowledge (Brown & Duguid, 1991; Lave & Wenger, 1991; Suchman, 1987). Rather than trying to single out the knowledge entities and how they could merge, the focus is on understanding how knowledge is deeply embedded in situated practices and closely connected to people's ability to act (see, e.g., Carlsen et al., 2004; Cook & Brown, 1999). In this article, we discuss research in this direction. In particular, we elaborate on the practice-based perspective on knowledge integration to understand better the role of artefacts. In our opinion, it is not enough to look at the practice in terms of human interaction; we also need to look at the overall system where integration takes place. Our perspective is illustrated with an example from the health care domain. We will look in particular at the patient list, an A4 format template created by nurses to support their everyday activities and used in different settings in the hospital ward. We illustrate how the patient list serves various functions within the ward and how it, along with other actors, helps the integration of different aspects of work. For the ongoing efforts of introducing information technology in health care, understanding the implicit roles of existing material arrangements is essential as it helps us identify how technology might be better designed.

The article is organised as follows. In the next section we discuss research on knowledge integration and the relevance of adopting a practice-based perspective, paying attention to the artefacts used within practices. The section after introduces health care as a relevant domain to study integration and presents a concrete example on how the patient list integrates different aspects of work. The last section sums up the contribution of this article.

KNOWLEDGE INTEGRATION

While the literature abounds in diverse classifications on how to coordinate the efforts of specialists (see, e.g., Becker, 2002; Berends et al., 2004; Ditillo, 2002; Willem & Scarbrough, 2002), we remain at their common reference point: the work of Grant (1996). Grant identifies four different organising mechanisms for integrating knowledge: (a) rules and directives, (b) sequencing, (c) routines, and (d) group problem solving. Rules and directives are standards that regulate interaction between workers (e.g., policies and rules). These standards or artefacts can be said to accumulate knowledge. In health care, for example, the transition from paper-based to electronic health records (EPR) has imposed new rules and directives on how to handle EPRs (e.g., security and privacy). Sequencing is a mechanism for coordinating efforts across time and space. For instance, a procedure is a sequence of actions that should be undertaken to do a certain task. In terms of work, sequencing can be said to be a mechanism for minimising communication and maximising specialisation. In health care there are diverse types of procedures ranging from clinical (e.g., how to perform an operation) to administrative (e.g., how to refer a patient to a specialist). Routines are habitual procedures embedded in work practices. They are beneficial in that they enable complex interaction in the absence of other coordinating mechanisms. For example, experienced surgeons do not search for a procedure before performing a standard operation as it has become an embodied routine. Group problem solving is different from the previous three mechanisms in that it requires personal and communication-intensive forms of integration. In this sense, group work in itself is a mechanism for integrating knowledge.

Of the four mechanisms, the latter (group) has been recognised as fundamental for knowledge creation (see, e.g., Becker, 2002; Ditillo, 2002). Ditillo (p. 11), claiming that "knowledge integration is best achieved through direct involvement," suggests a group-based approach to knowledge integration. In a similar vein, Fitzpatrick (2003, p. 106) contends that "strategies to supporting knowledge sharing, even in large scale communities cannot discount for the interactional human-to-human processes through which it is nurtured in local settings or across settings." The fundamental view grounding these perspectives is that no individual can possess all knowledge, and thus a group or community, where knowledge is naturally distributed, becomes an effective mechanism for integration. In this sense, knowledge is not treated as a transferable entity, but rather knowledge integration is considered to be a collective and interactive process. Understanding integration thus implies unfolding human interaction.

A Practice-Based Perspective on Knowledge Integration

Based on the assumption that we know more than we can express, Polanyi (1966) points out that we sometimes act according to our feelings without being able to give rational explanations for our conduct. In this sense, the notion of tacit knowledge has become an important aspect of the way we understand work (Levin & Klev, 2002). Empirically assessing knowledge thus implies attending to the everyday practices constituting organisational performances. Practice implies doing and is the situation of all human action (Suchman, 1987).

In a practice-based perspective, emphasis is on the active and productive processes of knowledge (see, e.g., Carlsen et al., 2004; Cook & Brown, 1999). Practices are driven by, but not limited to, tacit knowledge; they are improvised, spontaneous, and hallmarked by responses to changing and unpredictable environments (Brown & Duguid, 2000). Emphasis is on communities of practice (CoPs) in which knowledge sharing and integration takes place rather than on individuals, methods, or particular systems. In this sense, the traditional view on knowledge integration needs elaboration. Boland and Tenkasi (1995, p. 359) provide an interesting perspective:

...the problem of integration of knowledge...is not a problem of simply combining, sharing or making data commonly available. It is a problem of perspective taking in which the unique thought worlds of different communities of knowing are made visible and accessible to others.

Our experiences and the way we perceive the world can never be replicated perfectly, but to be able to make visible different world views, we need common denominators: that is, entities that are interpreted differently in different social worlds, but still remain common enough to be recognisable (Star & Griesemer, 1989). These entities are what Star and Griesemer call boundary objects. In a practice perspective, these boundary objects are means of representing, learning about, and transforming knowledge (Carlile, 2002). They enable collaborative work across social worlds (i.e., different CoPs).

We would like to emphasise that these social worlds consist of both people and artefacts. Knowledge is distributed among actors, and no actor has the complete picture of the collaborative work process (Berg, 1997; Hutchins, 1995).

Activating the Artefacts

Practice, then, as knowing in action, implies unfolding the joint activity performed by interrelated elements. In this perspective, activity does not take place solely in people's heads. Hutchins (1995) would contend that it is the system that knows. Looking at the practice of navigating ships, Hutchins develops a methodological and analytical framework for understanding how cognitive achievements can be conceptualised as a joint accomplishment. Hutchins maintains equality between people and artefacts in structuring practice. One expects to find a system that can dynamically configure itself to bring subsystems into coordination to accomplish various functions (Hollan, Hutchins, & Kirsh, 2000). Thus, the centre of attention in work activities is the interdependencies between people, and between people and artefacts.

In the same way, Berg (1996, 1997) illustrates each minute part of a work process aiming at documenting a hospital patient's fluid balance, which is a sum of what fluid goes in and what comes out. In observing and recording each minute detail of a particular process, the separate elements are identified. This hybrid comprises everything that is needed for the activity to proceed including several people, various artefacts, routines, and experiences. The formal tools come to life only as part of the real-life activity. In Berg's (1996) and Hutchins' (1995) terminology, integration implies looking at how work is distributed, delegated, coordinated, and communicated across time and space (Ellingsen & Monteiro, 2003).

In this article, artefacts are provided an active role in integrating knowledge. Artefacts not only mediate human action, but rather, they play an active role in shaping that same action. Furthermore, there is a relational interaction between artefacts and humans. Knowledge, then, is not a group of entities that can be merged, but rather a distributed system of cognitive elements whose integrative potential lies in the collective ability to perform.

INTEGRATION IN PRACTICE: AN EXAMPLE FROM HEALTH CARE

Below we provide a short example on how an artefact, the patient list, is produced and used in a hospital ward. By going beyond the concrete representational aspects of the list, other aspects of work become visible, for instance, the informal and implicit coordination and interaction among the people that populate the ward. The description and analysis of the patient list described below is based on observations from a 4-week stay at a hospital ward working as a nursing assistant.

The Patient List

Medical records take many forms. Information from the electronic patient record, clinical-specific systems, and other systems are often printed out on paper and copied to become usable in everyday work. Representations of patients are found on walls, in circulation, in copies, in annotated copies, on computers, in people's heads, in letters, on Post-It notes, in pockets, and so forth. In this article, we analyse one of these artefacts: the patient list. The patient list is a sheet of A4 paper listing all admitted patients, arranged after which room they are lying in. Every nurse on watch carries a copy of the list. The patient list summarizes information about the patient's diagnosis, type of treatment, and report, that is, recent information that might be relevant for nurses (as shown in Figure 1). It is a tool for planning, coordinating, distributing, delegating, and communicating.

A new list is assembled during each night watch. A fresh copy of the patient list is given to all nurses starting a new watch. During their watch, the nurses use the patient list to record information regarding things that happen. Upon change of watch, in order to hand over tasks and information, a briefing meeting is held with the nurses ending their watch and those starting a new watch. Nurses actively use the patient list during these meetings (sometimes supported by other documents). Nurses finishing the watch use their personal patient list as a reference. Nurses starting their watch take notes on their own blank copy while listening to the brief. All the patients at the ward are reported on, and at the end of the brief, all nurses have information about the patients. Moreover, they all have written down the distribution of responsibility on the patient list. Afterward, they go about doing their duties in the ward with the patient list nicely folded into their pockets. Frequently during the watch, they pick up the list to make sure that they are on schedule. Furthermore, the list is used as a reference point during discussions, meetings, and so on.

Figure 1. A section of the patient list (fabricated for visualisation purposes only)

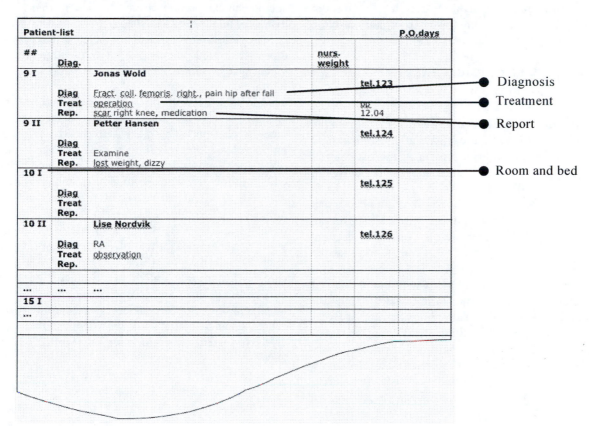

Constructing Knowledge by Interplaying, Tinkering, and Enacting

The patient list itself seems like a rather poor representation of patients. It is assembled from a myriad of different, richer representations. What, then, makes its way from these richer representations into the patient list? During the night watch, a software program assembles the list. This program delegates the task of providing information to the nurses. It determines what information the nurses are expected to provide. Still, it presents a limited number of fields to fill. Once the nurses have provided the software with the required information, the patient list is assembled. Knowledge is in this sense distributed between the nurses, the software, and the patient list. What is it then that decides what information is extracted from the different representations? Is it the fields provided by the software? Is it the nurses who determine what goes into these fields? There is an interplay between the nurses and the software: in effect, an integration process. In deciding what should go into the different fields, the nurses fluctuate between glimpsing into the patient record, asking colleagues, and memorising. In this sense, filling out the form is a process of tinkering (searching, combining, reducing, and writing down). Furthermore, what eventually becomes engraved into the patient list is based on a process of enactment based on different knowledge representations. According to Ellingsen and Monteiro (2003), in rendering knowledge credible, relevant, and trustworthy, knowledge representations have to be enacted.

Reconstructing Meaning by Telling Stories and Circulating

In the briefing meeting, the reporting nurses (accompanied by the patient list) are themselves highlighting certain parts of what has happened during their watch. The report takes form as a story, structured by the list and told by the nurse. Stories, the patient lists remade by the nurse, act as repositories of accumulated wisdom, and it allows people to keep track of the sequence of behaviour and their wisdom (Brown & Duguid, 1991; Orr, 1996). Storytelling thus serves as a mechanism for integrating knowledge. Furthermore, the stories are not only shared in the briefing meeting, but they circulate, partly by means of the patient list, partly by means of nurses' encounters and so forth.

Circulation can also be seen as the way the patient list travels as a template among the nurses. The list is easy to replicate and thus easy to circulate. In this way, knowledge about nursing, as manifested in the patient list, can circulate and spread. Furthermore, the list has an organising effect, having the power to organise a large number of workers (see Turnbull, 1993).

Knowing as a Sociotechnical Interaction

In the latter part of this analysis, we look closer into the details of the list (see Figure 1). What does the patient list know? By taking a brief look at it, the list can tell nurses which rooms and bed are available. In the figure, the list tells us that Bed 1 in Room Number 10 is available. Furthermore, the list does not give Petter any diagnosis, but tells us that the he is waiting for an examination. For Lise Nordvik, the situation is more clear-cut: The list tells us of a diagnosis and that the patient is admitted to the hospital for observation.

The way that the nurse interacts with the patient list regulates and coordinates the action that can be taken. For example, a new patient should be admitted to Bed 1 in Room 10. The list tells nothing about Petter's diagnosis. The nurse might want to consult a physician before giving him any medication. The patient list tells nurses that Lise has been here before and that this patient knows her way around, but that the nurses must keep an eye on her regularly. All three cases illustrate that interaction does not solely take place between people mediated by artefacts. Rather, interaction can often be identified as something happening between humans and artefacts. Artefacts and humans have knowledge about different aspects of the ward and its patients, and it is in the interaction that this knowledge becomes usable. Action is the result between the social and the material, and the integration is not observable in itself, only the resulting practice.

CONCLUSION

This article has addressed the concept of knowledge integration. We have described how a practice-based perspective provides an extension of the seminal work on knowledge integration by Grant (1996). In our practice-based approach, we have emphasised the role of artefacts not only as mediators of human action, but as active participants in shaping that same action. By providing an example from health care—the patient list, an A 4-format template created by nurses and used in different settings at a hospital ward—we have highlighted the relational interplay between artefacts and humans in work perfor-

mance. Tinkering, enacting, storytelling, circulation, and sociotechnical interaction have been identified as mechanisms for integrating knowledge.

The main contribution of this article is the proposal for a practice-based perspective on knowledge integration where specialisation, as traditionally being located only within humans, is challenged. We have emphasised the need to look beyond the pure representational aspects and also attend to the interactive roles of tangible arrangements (e.g., paper). This makes it imperative to be explicit on the role of artefacts in work performance because it plays such an important part in our understanding of collaboration and work. As we have demonstrated, the patient list plays an active role in structuring and coordinating work (see also Fitzpatrick, 2000). Furthermore, paper in itself provides rich support for collaborative work: It can help us gain knowledge of how technology might be better designed (Sellen & Harper, 2002). In health care, for instance, any move to introduce IT impacts the very nature of that care, so if we do not have a profound understanding of the richness and complexity in the accomplishment of that work, we will not be able to design effective systems that will fit with the work (Fitzpatrick, 2000).

Traditionally, when specifying requirements for knowledge management systems, conventional interview techniques are employed to portray existing work arrangements. In other words, work is specified as presented by the human workers. The problem then is that they (the human workers) are not consciously aware of the interactive role artefacts play in performing work. As artefacts do not talk back, conventional interview techniques need to be supplemented with additional ethnographic techniques to enable technology designers to look beyond the pure representational aspects of tangible arrangements. However, technology designers do not have the professional competence of ethnographers, so there is a need to provide them with guidelines to simplify the effort needed.

Another issue that naturally comes out of this article is the understanding of how users themselves actually design their own work practices in the usage of artefacts. For instance, in health care, organisational decisions on what kind of general types of information systems to implement have already been made (e.g., the electronic patient record, picture archive and communication system, etc.). Thus, future research needs to attend to the domestication of technology, that is, how to effectively integrate it into different work environments. This implies not only an understanding of how technology needs to be designed, but also of how existing work arrangements need to be adjusted.

REFERENCES

Aanestad, M., Mørk, B. E., Grisot, M., Hanseth, O., & Syvertsen, C. M. (2003). Knowledge as a barrier to learning: A case study from medical R&D. *Proceedings of the 4th European Conference on Organisational Knowledge, Learning and Capabilities*, Barcelona, Spain.

Alvesson, M. (2001). Knowledge work: Ambiguity, image and identity. *Human Relations, 54*(7), 863-886.

Becker, M. C. (2002). Towards a consistent analytical framework for studying knowledge integration: Communities of practice, interaction, and recurrent interaction patterns. Paper presented at the *3rd European Conference on Organizational Learning, Knowledge and Capabilities*, Athens, Greece.

Berends, J. J., Debackere, K., Garud, R., & Weggeman, M. C. D. P. (2004). *Knowledge integration by thinking along* (Working Paper No. 04.05). Netherlands: Eindhoven Centre for Innovation Studies.

Berg, M. (1996). Practices of reading and writing: The constitutive role of the patient record in medical work. *Sociology of Health and Illness, 18*, 499-524.

Berg, M. (1997). On distribution, drift and the electronic medical record: Some tools for a sociology of the formal. *Proceedings of the 5th European Conference on Computer-Supported Cooperative Work, ECSCW'97*, 141-156.

Blackler, F. (1995). Knowledge, knowledge work and organizations: An overview and interpretation. *Organization Studies, 16*(6), 1021-1046.

Boland, R. J., Jr., & Tenkasi, R. V. (1995). Perspective making and perspective taking in communities of knowing. *Organization Science, 6*(4), 350-372.

Brown, J. S., & Duguid, P. (1991). Organizational learning and communities-of-practice: Toward a unified view of working, learning, and innovation. *Organization Science, 2*(1), 40-57.

Brown, J. S., & Duguid, P. (2000). *The social life of information*. Boston: Harvard Business School Publishing.

Carlile, P. R. (2002). A pragmatic view of knowledge and boundaries: Boundary objects in new product development. *Organization Science, 13*(4), 442-455.

Carlsen, A., Klev, R., & von Krogh, G. (2004). *Living knowledge: The dynamics of professional service work*. New York: Palgrave Macmillan.

Cook, S. D. N., & Brown, J. S. (1999). Bridging epistemologies: The generative dance between organisational knowledge and organisational knowing. *Organization Science, 10*(4), 381-400.

Davenport, T. H., & Prusak, L. (1998). *Working knowledge*. Boston: Harvard Business School Press.

Ditillo, A. (2002). *The relevance of information flows in knowledge-intensive firms* (Working Paper No. 74). SDA Bocconi.

Ellingsen, G., & Monteiro, E. (2003). Mechanisms for producing a working knowledge: Enacting, orchestrating and organizing. *Information and Organization, 13*, 203-229.

Fitzpatrick, G. (2000). Understanding the paper health record in practice: Implications for EHRs. *Proceedings of HIC: Integrated Information for Health Care*.

Fitzpatrick, G. (2003). Emergent expertise sharing in a community. In M. Ackerman, V. Pipek, & V. Wulf (Eds.), *Sharing expertise: Beyond knowledge management* (pp. 81-110). Cambridge, MA: MIT Press.

Gherardi, S. (2000). Practice-based theorizing on learning and knowing in organisations. *Organization, 7*(2), 211-223.

Grant, R. M. (1996). Toward a knowledge-based theory of the firm. *Strategic Management Journal, 17*, 109-122.

Hollan, J., Hutchins, E., & Kirsh, D. (2000). Distributed cognition: Toward a new foundation of human-computer interaction research. *ACM Transactions on Computer-Human Interaction, 7*(2), 174-196.

Hutchins, E. (1995). *Cognition in the wild*. Cambridge, MA: MIT Press.

Kogut, B., & Zander, U. (1992). Knowledge of the firm, combinative capabilities, and the replication of technology. *Organization Science, 3*(3), 383-397.

Lave, J., & Wenger, E. (1991). *Situated learning: Legitimate peripheral participation*. Cambridge, MA: Cambridge University Press.

Levin, M., & Klev, R. (2002). *Forandring som praksis: Læring og utvikling i organisasjoner*. Bergen, Norway: Fagbokforlaget

Nonaka, I., & Takeuchi, H. (1995). *The knowledge-creating company*. Oxford, UK: Oxford University Press.

Orr, J. (1996). *Talking about machines: An ethnography of a modern job*. Cornell, CA: Cornell University Press.

Polanyi, M. (1966). *The tacit dimension.* London: Routledge & Kegan Paul.

Sellen, A. J., & Harper, R. H. R. (2002). *The myth of the paperless office.* Cambridge, MA: MIT Press.

Star, S. L., & Griesemer, J. R. (1989). Institutional ecology, translations, and boundary objects: Amateurs and professionals in Berkeley's Museum of Vertebrate Zoology. *Social Studies of Science, 19,* 1907-1939.

Suchman, L. A. (1987). *Plans and situated actions: The problem of human-computer communication.* Cambridge, MA: Cambridge University Press.

Turnbull, D. (1993). The ad hoc collective work of building Gothic cathedrals with templates, string and geometry. *Science, Technology and Human Values, 18*(3), 315-340.

Walsham, G. (2001). Knowledge management: The benefits and limitations of computer systems. *European Management Journal, 19*(6), 599-608.

Walsham, G. (2004). Knowledge management systems: Action and representation. *Proceedings of Action in Language, Organisations and Information Systems (ALOIS2004).*

Willem, A., & Scarbrough, H. (2002). Structural effects on inter-unit knowledge sharing: The role of coordination under different knowledge sharing needs. *Proceedings of the 3rd European Conference on Organisational Knowledge, Learning and Capabilities,* Athens, Greece.

KEY TERMS

Artefact: Any human-made object. It can be physical (e.g., paper, application) or conceptual (e.g., norm, convention, habit).

Distributed Cognition: Cognition is understood as being derived from the environment. It is based on an assumption of equality between people and artefacts in structuring practice.

Integration: Integration refers to how work is performed. Knowledge entities cannot be merged but should be looked upon as a distributed system of cognitive elements whose integrative potential lies in the collective ability to perform.

Knowledge Integration: By knowledge integration, we mean solving problems raised by specialisation. Specialisation leads to a dispersion of specialised bodies of knowledge that are held by different specialists. Knowledge integration refers to how this drawing on different bodies of specialised knowledge is organised.

Knowledge-Integration Mechanism: The mechanism from where knowledge integration is performed (becomes visible). Examples here are tinkering, enacting, storytelling, circulating, and interplaying.

Practice: The relational interplay between humans and artefacts that enables work performance.

Sociotechnical: The interactive interplay between humans and artefacts in work performances.

RDF and OWL

Gian Piero Zarri
University of Paris IV/Sorbonne, France

INTRODUCTION

As Web-based content becomes an increasingly important knowledge management resource, Web-based technologies are developing to help harness that resource in a more effective way.

The current state of these Web-based technology—the "first generation" or "syntactic" Web—gives rise to well-known, serious problems when trying to accomplish in a non-trivial way essential management tasks like indexing, searching, extracting, maintaining, and generating information. These tasks would, in fact, require some sort of "deep understanding" of the information dealt with: In a "syntactic" Web context, on the contrary, computers are only used as tools for posting and rendering information by brute force. Faced with this situation, Berners-Lee first proposed a sort of "Semantic Web" where the access to information is based mainly on the processing of the *semantic properties* of this information: "… the Semantic Web is an extension of the current Web in which information is given well-defined *meaning* [emphasis added], better enabling computers and people to work in co-operation" (Berners-Lee, Hendler, & Lassila, 2001, p. 35). The Semantic Web's challenge consists then in being able to manage information on the Web by "understanding" its proper semantic content (its meaning), and not simply by matching some keywords.

BACKGROUND

The architecture proposed by Berners-Lee for the Semantic Web is reproduced in Figure 1. "Unicode" and "URI" make up the basis of this hierarchy. The Unicode Standard provides a unique numerical code for every character that can be found in documents produced according to any possible language, no matter what the hardware and software used to deal with such documents. Uniform Resource Identifier (URI) represents a generalization of the well-known Uniform Resource Locator (URL) that is used to identify a "Web resource" (e.g., a particular page) by denoting its primary access mechanism (essentially, its "location" on the network). URI has been created to allow recording information about all those "notions" that, unlike Web pages, do not

Figure 1. Semantic Web architecture according to Tim Berners-Lee

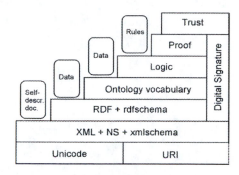

have network locations or URLs, but that need to be referred to in an RDF statement. These notions include network-accessible things, such as an electronic document or an image, things that are not network-accessible, such as human beings, corporations, and bound books in a library, or abstract concepts like the concept of a "creator."

XML (eXtensible markup language) (see Bray, Paoli, Sperberg-McQueen, Maler, & Yergeau, 2004) has been created to overcome some difficulties proper to hypertext markup language (HTML); this last suffers from a number of limitations, from its lack of efficiency in handling the complex client/server communication of today's applications to the impossibility of defining new tags to customize exactly the user's needs. XML is called "extensible" because, at the difference of HTML, it is not characterized by a fixed format, but it lets the user design its own customized markup languages (a specific DTD, document type description) for limitless different types of documents; XML is a "content-oriented" markup tool. Basically, the syntactic structure of XML is very simple. Its markup elements are normally identified by an opening and a closing tag, like <**employees**> and </**employees**>, and may contain other elements or text; the elements must be properly nested and every XML document must have exactly one root element. Markup elements can be specialized by adding attribute/value pairs inside the opening tag of the element, like <**person name**="Jane">; taking into account the nesting constraint, a very simple fragment of XML document could then be represented as: "<**employees**> <**person name**="Jane"> <**id**>99276</**id**> </**person**> </**employees**>". To allow a computer inter-

Figure 2. RDF statements represented in graph format

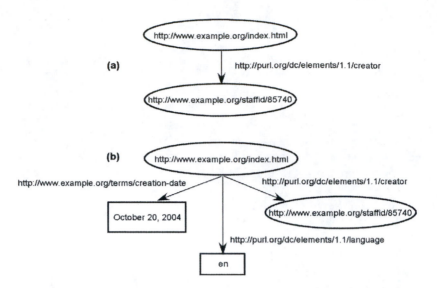

preting correctly a fragment like this, it is necessary, however, to specify the semantics of the markup elements and tags used to make it; a simple way of doing this is to make use of a DTD. A DTD is a formal description in XML Declaration Syntax of a particular type of document: for example, a DTD may specify that every **person** markup element must have a **name** attribute, and that it can have an offspring element called **id** whose content must be text. There are many sorts of DTDs ready to be used in all kinds of areas (e.g., www.w3.org/QA/2002/04/valid-dtd-list.html#full) that can be downloaded and used freely: some of them are MathML (for mathematical expressions), Sync Multimedia Integration Language (SMIL), Chemical Markup Language (CML), Open Software Description (OSD), Electronic Data Interchange (EDI) , Platform for Internet Content Selection (PICS), and so forth. A more complete way of specifying the semantics of a set of XML markup elements is to make use of XML Schema (as mentioned in Figure 1): XML Schema (Thompson, Beech, Maloney, & Mendelsohn, 2001; Biron & Malhotra, 2001) supplies a more complete grammar for specifying the structure of the elements allowing, for example, to define the cardinality of the offspring elements, default values, and so forth.

MAIN FOCUS OF THE ARTICLE: RDF AND OWL

Moving up in the structure of Figure 1, we find now Resource Description Framework (RDF), an example of "metadata" language (metadata = data about data) used

to describe generic "things" ("resources," according to the RDF jargon) on the Web. An RDF document is basically a list of statements under the form of triples having the classical format: <**object, property, value**>, where the elements of the triples can be Universal Resource Identifiers (URIs), literals (mainly, free text), and variables. To follow a well-known RDF example (Manola & Miller, 2004), let us suppose we want to represent a situation where someone named John Smith has created a particular Web page. We will then make use of the RDF triple: <**http://www.example.org/index.html** (*object*), **creator** (*property*), **john_smith** (*value*)>. Adding additional information about the situation, by stating, for example, that the Web page was created October 20, 2004, and that the language in which the page is written is English, amounts to add two additional statements: <**http://www.example.org/index.html** (*object*), **creation_date** (*property*), **October 20, 2004** (*value*)> and <**http://www.example.org/index.html** (*object*), **language** (*property*), **English** (*value*)>. Note that RDF uses a particular terminology for denoting the three elements of the triples, calling then "subject," "predicate," and "object," respectively, the "object," "property," and "value" elements of the triples; this decision is really questionable because it introduces an undue confusion with well-defined and totally different linguistic categories.

RDF triples can be represented as directed labeled graphs, by denoting resources as ovals, properties (predicates) as arrows, and literal values like **October 20, 2004** or **English** within boxes. Figure 2a represents under graph form the original statement: "John Smith has created a Web page"; the addition of information about date and

Table 1. The RDF/XML syntax

```
<?xml version="1.0"?>
<rdf:RDF xmlns:rdf="http://www.w3.org/1999/02/22-rdf-syntax-ns#"
    xmlns:dc="http://purl.org/dc/elements/1.1/"
    xmlns:exterms="http://www.example.org/terms/">
  <rdf:Description rdf:about="http://www.example.org/index.html">
    <exterms:creation-date>October 20, 2004</exterms:creation-date>
    <dc:language>en</dc:language>
    <dc:creator rdf:resource="http://www.example.org/staffid/85740"/>
  </rdf:Description>
</rdf:RDF>
```

language gives rise to the graph of Figure 2b, given that groups of statements are represented by corresponding groups of nodes and arcs. Note that, to simulate the actual conditions of utilization of RDF, the properties **creator**, **creation_date** and **language** in Figure 2 have been replaced, respectively, by **http://purl.org/dc/elements/1.1/creator**, **http://www.example.org/terms/creation-date**, and **http://purl.org/dc/elements/1.1/language**; analogously, **john_smith** has been replaced by **http://www.example.org/staffid/85740**. All these "**http://...**" terms are URIs that identify in an unambiguous way specific RDF entities; more exactly, they refer to the ontologies/metadata repositories/lists of reserved domain names where these entities are defined. For example, "**http://purl.org/dc/...**" refers to the collection of metadata terms maintained by the Dublin Core Metadata Initiative (Dekkers & Weibel, 2003); in this collection, **http://purl.org/dc/elements/1.1/creator** is defined as: "An entity primarily responsible for making the content of the resource." The literal **en** (Unicode characters) is an international standard two-letter code for English, see **http://purl.org/dc/elements/1.1/language**; the **example.org** Internet domain name is reserved for documentation purposes.

From what expounded until now, RDF seems to be nothing more than a Internet-oriented, downgraded form of Semantic Networks as they were used in the artificial intelligence domain at the beginning of the 1970s. Its significance in a Semantic Web context becomes more evident when we examine the way of writing RDF statement into XML format – the so-called "RDF/XML syntax" (Beckett, 2004), that is, when RDF is seen as a sort of additional DTD of XML. Table 1 reproduces then the simple example of Figure 2b making use of the RDF/XML syntax.

The first line of the code, <?xml version="1.0"?> is the "XML declaration," which states that what follows consists of XML, and which specifies the version used. In the second line, we find an XML markup element that starts with the tag <rdf:RDF – this tag specifies that all the following XML code, until the </rdf:RDF> tag of the last line, is intended to represent RDF statements – and ends with the '>' symbol at the right limit of line 4. Within this markup element we find three "XML attributes" of the opening <rdf:RDF tag; all these attributes (xmlns attributes) have as values the declarations of the namespaces to be used within the RDF/XML code. An attribute like xmlns:rdf means that, according to the "value" associated with this attribute (after the '=' symbol), all the terms/tags included in this RDF/XML content and prefixed with rdf: are part of the namespace identified with the URI: http://www.w3.org/1999/02/22-rdf-syntax-ns#; analogously for the xmlns:dc (Dublin Core terms) and xmlns:exterms (example terms) attributes.

After these preliminary, "housekeeping" declarations, lines 5 to 9 represent the core of the RDF/XML representation of the example. The rdf:Description start-tag of line 5 indicates that we are now introducing the "description" of a resource; this resource, http://www.example.org/index.html, is identified as the value of the rdf:about attribute of the start-tag. The three following lines, 6 to 8, are examples of use of "property element" constructions. In these lines, the tags are built up according to the XML Qname (Qname = Qualified name) convention, which allows shortening the writing of full RDF triples by introducing abbreviations for the URI references. A Qname tag contains, in fact, a "prefix" that denotes a given namespace (e.g., exterms in line 6) followed, after a "colon," by a "local name" (creation-date, i.e., the name of the property); a full URI reference is then created by appending the local name to the URI of the namespace identified by the first part of the Qname. For lines 6 to 8, the full URIs become then http://www.example.org/terms/creation-date, http://purl.org/dc/elements/1.1/Language, and http://purl.org/dc/elements/1.1/creator. Note that the values of the properties corresponding to literals (lines 6 to 7) are directly included within opening and closing Qname tags; for the property of line 8, which corresponds to a resource, the value corresponds to the value of the rdf:resource attribute of the dc:creator Qname tag. The description of the resource introduced in line 5 ends with the closing tag of line 9.

To conclude about RDF, we will note that RDF Schema (RDFS) (Brickley & Guha, 2004) provides a mechanism for constructing specialized RDF vocabularies through the description of domain-specific properties. This is obtained mainly by describing the properties in terms of the classes of resource to which they apply: for example, we could define the **creator** property saying that it has the resource **document** as "domain" (**document** is the value or "object" of this property) and the resource **person** as "range" (this property must always be associated with a resource **person**, its "subject"). Other basic modeling primitives of RDFS are used to set up hierarchies, both *hierarchies of concepts* (i.e., ontologies) thanks to the use of "class" and "subclass-of" statements, and *hierarchies of properties* thanks to the use of "property" and "subproperty-of" statements. Instances of a specific class (of a specific concept) can be declared making use of the "type" statement.

Passing to the next stage of the structure of Figure 1, "ontologies," we can make three general remarks:

- the basic "nature" of ontologies as described in the article "Knowledge Representation" in this encyclopedia does not change fundamentally in a Semantic Web context: They are still formed by hierarchies (DAGs) of concepts defined through properties and values;
- for their practical implementation, however, these Semantic Web ontologies make a large use of the RDF/XML syntactic/semantic constructs;
- taking also into account that the level that follows "Ontology vocabulary" in the pyramid of Figure 1 is "Logic," the Semantic Web ontologies evidence a very strong logic influence.

On February 10, 2004, the W3C published an official "recommendation" concerning OWL, the Web Ontology Language (Bechhofer et al., 2004); W3C—the World Wide Web Consortium, coordinated by MIT (USA), ERCIM, the European Research Consortium for Informatics and Mathematics, and the Keio University (Japan)—includes all the main bodies on earth interested in the developments of Internet and the Web. At the beginning of this document is stated that: "The Web Ontology Language (OWL) is a semantic markup language for publishing and sharing ontologies on the World Wide Web. OWL is developed as a vocabulary extension of the Resource Description Framework (RDF) and is derived from the DAML+OIL Web Ontology Language…An OWL ontology is an RDF graph, which is in turn a set of RDF triples." The mention of

DAML+OIL (McGuinness, Fikes, Hendler, & Stein, 2002) explains the strong logic orientation of OWL, given that Ontology Inference Layer (OIL), the "European" component of DAML+OIL (DAML is the Darpa Agent Markup Language) was implemented in Description Logics (DL) terms—DL (Baader, Calvanese, McGuinness, Nardi, & Patel-Schneider, 2002) have been created to offer, among other things, a formal foundation for frame-based systems.

OWL consists of three subsets (three specific sub-languages) characterized by an increasing level of complexity and expressiveness, OWL Lite, OWL DL (DL stands for Description Logics), and OWL Full.

OWL Lite is the syntactically simplest sub-language; it includes only a reduced subset of the OWL language constructors and has a lower formal complexity than the other OWL versions. It is meant mainly to allow: (1) the implementation of simple classification hierarchies; (2) the familiarization with the OWL approach; (3) the possibility of a quick migration path for existing thesauri/taxonomies and other conceptually simple hierarchies. It employs all the features already introduced by RDFS, making use of the same tags—like **rdfs:subclassOf, rdfs:subPropertyOf, rdfs:domain, rdfs:range**—with the same semantics. Note that **rdfs:subclassOf** is the fundamental constructor that is used to set up taxonomies/ontologies in OWL. It relates, in fact, a more specific class (concept) to a more general one; if X is a sub-class of Y, then every instance of X is also an instance of Y. The relation **rdfs:subclassOf** is transitive: If X is a sub-class of Y and Y is a sub-class of Z, then X is a sub-class of Z. With respect to RDFS, OWL Lite includes several new features:

- Constructors for equality and inequality, for example, **owl:equivalentClass, owl: equivalent Property, owl:sameAs** (two individuals may be stated to be the same), **owl:differentFrom, owl:AllDifferent.**
- Constructors used to provide specific information about properties and their values, like **owl:inverseOf**—for example, stating that the property **hasChild** is the inverse of the property **hasParent**, and stating that Mary is endowed with the property (**hasParent** Lucy), allows then an OWL reasoner to deduce that Lucy is endowed with the property (**hasChild** Mary)—**owl:TransitiveProperty** and **owl:Symmetric Property.**
- Constructors used to impose constraints on the way properties can be used by the instances of a class (concept). They are **owl:allValuesFrom** and **owl:someValuesFrom.** For example, **owl:allValuesFrom** introduces a range restriction,

imposing, for example, that the property **hasDaughter** of the class Person is restricted to obtaining all its values (**allValuesFrom**) from the class Woman. This allows a reasoner to deduce that, if an individual Lucy is related by the property **hasDaughter** with the individual Mary, Mary must be an instance of the class Woman.

- Constructors, for example, **owl:minCardinality** and **owl:maxCardinality**, used to introduce a limited form of cardinality restrictions, stated on the properties of a particular class, and to be intended as constraints on the cardinality of that property when used in the instances of that class. Note that, for algorithmic efficiency reasons, OWL Lite allows using only the integers 0 and 1 to express the cardinality constraints; this restriction is removed in OWL DL.

- OWL Lite includes a (restricted form) of intersection constructor, **owl:intersectionOf**, allowing, for example, to state that the class EmployedPerson is the **intersectionOf** the classes Person and EmployedThings.

OWL DL is much more expressive than OWL Lite and is totally based on Description Logics—this is denoted by the suffix DL. OWL DL makes use of the full set of the OWL constructors, but it also introduces some constraints on their use to give rise to systems that are "complete" (all the possible deductions are computable) and "decidable" (all the computations will be executed in finite time). Mainly, OWL DL implements what is called "type separation," which means that a class (concept) also cannot be an individual or a property, and that a property also cannot be an individual or a class. This restriction is removed in OWL Full. OWL DL adds to the OWL Lite list of constructors some new constructors like **owl:oneOf** (classes may be described by enumeration of the individuals that make up the class), **owl:hasValue** (a property is required to have a given individual as value), **owl:disjointWith** (classes can be described as disjoint from each other, see the classes Man and Woman), **owl:unionOf, owl:complementOf, owl:intersectionOf** (Boolean combinations of classes), and so forth.

OWL Full is the most expressive of the OWL sublanguages, and should be used in situations where very high expressiveness is particularly important. It is similar to OWL DL but, in the OWL Full case, all the constraints have been suppressed—for example, a class (concept) can be simultaneously treated as a collection of instances (individuals) and as an individual in itself. This can lead to the implementation of systems that are, at least partly, "incomplete" and/or "undecidable": this means that it is not possible to perform automated reasoning on OWL Full hierarchies. Currently, no complete implementation of OWL Full exists.

To give at least a partial picture of the representation of an ontology in OWL format, we reproduce in Table 2 a small fragment of the OWL version of the "wine" ontology, an ontology often used for exemplification's purposes in the Semantic Web milieus (see McGuinness, Fikes, Hendler, & Sten, 2002; Smith, Welty, & McGuinness, 2004). The code in this table can be considered indifferently as OWL Lite, OWL DL, or OWL Full. Note that for simplicity's sake, we have not reproduced in Table 2 and the following the "housekeeping" declarations (see Table 1) that are necessary to identify all the XML namespaces associated with the wine ontology.

In the first line of Table 2, the class Wine is introduced making use of an rdf:ID attribute. At the difference of the rdf:about attribute used in Table 1, rdf:ID introduces as its value only a "fragment identifier" (here Wine) that represents an abbreviation of the complete reference to the URI of the resource being described. The full URI reference is formed by taking the base URI of the wine ontology, for example, http://www.w3.org/TR/2004/REC-owl-guide-20040210/wine, and appending the character # (to indicate that what follows is a fragment identifier) and then Wine to it, giving then the absolute URI reference: http://www.w3.org/TR/2004/REC-owl-guide-

Table 2. A fragment of the OWL wine ontology

```
<owl:Class rdf:ID="Wine">
 <rdfs:subClassOf rdf:resource="#PotableLiquid"/>
 <rdfs:subClassOf>
   <owl:Restriction>
     <owl:onProperty rdf:resource="#madeFromGrape"/>
     <owl:minCardinality rdf:datatype="&xsd;nonNegativeInteger">1</owl:minCardinality>
   </owl:Restriction>
 </rdfs:subClassOf>
 ...
</owl:Class>
```

Table 3. Vintage class and vintageOf property

```
<owl:Class rdf:ID="Vintage">
 <rdfs:subClassOf>
   <owl:Restriction>
     <owl:onProperty rdf:resource="#vintageOf"/>
     <owl:minCardinality rdf:datatype="&xsd;nonNegativeInteger">1</owl:minCardinality>
   </owl:Restriction>
 </rdfs:subClassOf>
</owl:Class>


<owl:ObjectProperty rdf:ID="vintageOf">
 <rdfs:domain rdf:resource="#Vintage" />
 <rdfs:range rdf:resource="#Wine" />>
</owl:ObjectProperty>
```

20040210/wine#Wine. Note that the Wine class can now be referred to by using #Wine; for example, rdf:resource="#Wine" is a well-formed OWL statement. As already stated, the fundamental taxonomic constructor is rdfs:subClassOf; the second line of the code of Table 2 allows the insertion of the class Wine into the global ontology by asserting that it is a specialisation of the class (concept) PotableLiquid (liquid suitable for drinking)—which can be defined, in turn, as a specialisation of the class ConsumableThing.

The third line of the code warns that the class Wine is also a specialisation of a second class: This last is an "anonymous" class, whose definition is included within the opening owl:Restriction markup element in line 4 and ends with the closing /owl:Restriction markup element in line 7. In OWL, in fact, a property restriction on a class is a special kind of class description, that of the anonymous class including all the individuals that satisfy the given restriction. In line 5, the owl:onProperty constructor introduces the name of the property, madeFromGrape, to associate with the class Wine; line 6 specifies that the cardinality of this property is 1. The insertion of this restriction in the definition of Wine states, globally, that every specific wine also must be characterized by at least one madeFromGrape relation. Note that (1) the &xsd;nonNegativeInteger datatype used to introduce the literal 1 in the owl:minCardinality restriction of line 6 is part of the built-in XML Schema datatypes (Biron and Malhotra, 2001): Their use is strongly recommended in an OWL context; (2) the value 1 conforms to the OWL Lite restrictions.

Following (Smith et al., 2004, pp. 11-13), we can now supply, in the upper part of Table 3, the definition of the Vintage class—vintage is a particular wine made in a specific year. The lower part of Table 3 shows how the property vintageOf ties a Vintage to a Wine; the rdfs:domain and rdfs:range features indicate, respectively, that the property vintageOf can only be associated with terms of the Vintage type (e.g., RomaneeConti1998), and that the

values of this property can only be specific terms of the Wine hierarchy (e.g., RomaneeConti).

To conclude about OWL, we reproduce in Table 4 another fragment of the wine ontology that makes use of constructors proper to the DL version of the language. The code fragment of Table 4 defines the class RedWine as the precise intersection (logical conjunction, "and") of the class Wine and the set of things that are red in color (anonymous class). The presence of the attribute rdf:parseType="Collection" is mandatory for this type of construction. Note the use of the DL constructor owl:hasValue to impose the value "Red" on the property hasColor of the anonymous class.

FUTURE TRENDS, AND THE IMPLICATIONS FOR KNOWLEDGE MANAGEMENT

Rules—self-contained knowledge units that entail some form of reasoning—are explicitly mentioned in the upper level of the architecture of Figure 1 and are, obviously, an essential prerequisite for a practical utilization of the RDF/OWL data structures. However, rules have not been included in the OWL standard, and they are still a hot topic of discussion in the Semantic Web and W3C milieus.

In RuleML (see Boley, Tabet, & Wagner, 2001), the inferential properties of Prolog/Datalog are associated with an XML/RDF-based rule format—for an introduction to Prolog/Datalog and to their logical support, Horn clauses, see, e.g., Bertino, Catania, and (Zarri, 2001, pp. 112-121, 170-207). The main categories of rules considered in RuleML are the "derivation rules" (i.e., rules used to automatically defining derived concepts), "integrity rules" (constraints on the state space), "reaction rules" (for specifying the reactive behavior of a given system in response to specific events), "production rules" (if-then

Table 4. Use of OWL DL constructors in the context of the wine ontology

```
<owl:Class rdf:about="#RedWine">
 <owl:intersectionOf rdf:parseType="Collection">
  <owl:Class rdf:about="#Wine" />
  <owl:Restriction>
   <owl:onProperty rdf:resource="#hasColor" />
   <owl:hasValue rdf:resource="#Red" />
  </owl:Restriction>
 </owl:intersectionOf>
</owl:Class>
```

rules according to the classical expert systems paradigm) and "transformation rules" (used to implement translators between different versions of RuleML, and between RuleML and other rule languages like Jess).

TRIPLE, see (Sintek & Decker, 2002), is a rule language that also follows the logic programming paradigm; its core is based on Horn logic clauses, and it has been syntactically extended to support RDF primitives like namespaces, resources, and RDF triples—these last have given TRIPLE its name. Rules expressed in this core language can be compiled into Horn logic programs and then executed by Prolog inference engines like XSB.

SWRL is a proposal (see Horrocks et al., 2004) based on a combination of OWL DL with the Datalog sublanguage of RuleML. Concretely, the proposal extends the set of the OWL axioms to include Horn-like rules, enabling then these rules to be combined with an OWL knowledge base. The rules have the form of an implication between an antecedent (body) and a consequent (head); their meaning corresponds to say that, whenever the conditions specified in the antecedent hold, then the conditions specified in the consequent also hold. Both the antecedent and the consequent consist of zero or more atoms; atoms can be in the form of $C(x)$, $P(x, y)$, sameAs(x, y) or differentFrom(x, y), where C is an OWL description, P is an OWL property, and x, y are either variables, OWL individuals or OWL data values. An XML- and an RDF-based syntax for the rules also have been defined.

Another "hot topic" in a Semantic Web context concerns Semantic Web services. A "normal" Web service can be defined as a Web site that does not simply supply static information, but that also allows the automatic execution of some "actions" (services), like the sale of a product or the control of a physical device; an increasing number of Web services are accessible on the Web, developed by independent operators or large companies such as Amazon and Google. To carry out their tasks, Web services must provide interoperability among diverse applications, using platform and language independent interfaces for a smooth integration of heterogeneous systems. This has led to a standardization of the Web service descriptions, discovery, and invocation, making use of XML-based standards like WSDL (Christensen, Curbera, Meredith, & Weerawarana, 2001), a description protocol, and SOAP (Mitra, 2003), a messaging protocol. However, these standards, in their present form, are characterized by a low level of semantic expressiveness: For example, WSDL can be used to describe the interface of the different services, and how these services are deployed via SOAP, but it is very limited in its ability to express what the overall competences of this service are. Semantic Web services are then Web services that can specify not only their interfaces, but also describe in full their capabilities and the prerequisites and consequences of their use.

OWL-S (Semantic Markup for Web Services) (Ankolekar et al., 2002)—formerly DAML-S—is a specification, in the form of an OWL-based ontology, that describes different Semantic Web services features. It should enable Web users and software agents to automatically discover, invoke, select, compose, and monitor Web-based services. The ontology is structured into three main parts: (1) The "profile" component supplies a general description of a particular Web service by specifying the input and output types, the preconditions, and (3) the effects. (2) The "process model" component describes how the Web service works and the Web service interaction protocol; each service is either an atomic process that can be executed directly or a combination of several processes. An example of atomic process can be a service that returns a postal code, or the longitude and latitude when supplied with an address. A complex service often requires some form of interaction with the user, who can make choices and provide information conditionally: an example can be that of a personal shopping agent, that can assist the user in finding and buying many different sorts of items, requiring, in case, credit card and mailing information. (3) The "grounding" component specifies how the atomic processes defined in the process model can be mapped into

WSDL descriptions, able to directly call up the described (atomic) service.

The ODE SWS framework, (see Gómez-Pérez, González-Cabrero, & Lama, 2004) proposes both an ontology to describe Semantic Web services and an environment to support their graphical development. A characteristic of this framework is the use of Problem-Solving Methods to describe these services at the "knowledge level" (see the "Knowledge Representation" article in this encyclopedia), that is, independently of the language in which they will be actually expressed. The ODE SWS ontology reproduces the upper level concepts of OWL-S, with the exception of the concepts associated with the "process model" component that are substituted by method descriptions. The ODE SWS environment is composed of three main layers: (1) The "data source" layer is devoted to the integration of external applications; (2) the "domain" layer includes the main modules of the environment, as the SWSOntologiesManager, the SWSInstanceCreator—this module creates, from the graphical description of a particular service, the corresponding instance of a concept pertaining to the OWL-S ontology—and the SWSTranslator, which translates the general model of the service into a Semantic Web language description; (3) the "presentation" layer consists of a SWSDesigner module, that is, a user-friendly graphical interface that the user employs to describe a service – according to the authors, this graphically oriented process is more simple and less error prone than manipulating directly instance of the internal OWL-S ontology.

Implications for knowledge management of what expounded in this section and in the previous ones could be very important. There is general agreement that, from a very concrete point of view, the notion of knowledge management amounts, practically, to the set up and management of large corporate memories. These last can be defined (van Heijst, 1966) as the indexing and persistent storing of strategic knowledge about a given organization to facilitate its access, sharing, and reuse by the members of the organization in their individual and collective work. Taking into account the fact that ontologies provide a *shared* and *common understanding* of a domain, which can be communicated across people and application systems, corporate memories can, in turn, be materialized as a "Corporate Semantic Web," this last consisting both of ontologies and of Web-stored documents annotated with ontological tools. In this context, all the Semantic Web conceptual tools mentioned in this article, from XML to Semantic Web services, can then contribute—at least in principle, see the next section—to make knowledge management a tangible reality.

CONCLUSION

In spite of the heavy W3C support, the Semantic Web vision outlined in this article has not fully reached the status of "inescapable" standard.

First of all, the intrinsic "binary" nature—based on an "attribute value" approach—of tools like RDF and OWL makes it extremely difficult to use them for dealing with complex "narrative" documents particularly important from a knowledge management point of view, like memos, policy statements, reports, minutes, news stories, normative and legal texts, medical records, many intelligence messages, and so forth. This point is developed in depth in the "Representation Languages for Narrative Documents" article in this encyclopedia.

Moreover, Berners-Lee's architecture has been criticized from the beginning, in particular because it ignores some fundamental components of computer science today, from database technology (the whole world economy runs on SQL) to Unified Modeling Language (UML): UML is the standard modeling language in software engineering and, at the difference of RDF, OWL, and so forth, has received wide attention not only in academia but also in the professional milieus. Note, however, that some researchers are actually investigating the possibility of defining a mapping between UML and OWL-like languages. UML has, in fact, a type hierarchy comparable with OWL and a class diagrams facility that can be compared to a frame-based language (see, in this context, the comparison between UML and DAML in Baclawski et al., 2001). A general discussion about the proposals for defining transformations between UML and the Semantic Web ontology languages can be found in Falkovych, Sabou, and Stuckenschmidt, (2003).

In the context of the Semantic Web architecture, the choice of OWL as paradigmatic language to be used for ontological work also has raised some criticisms, and several knowledge representation specialists have challenged as hastily the endorsement of OWL by the W3C—for the relationships between Semantic Web, artificial intelligence and knowledge representation (see Schwartz, 2003). Apart from the "binary flaw" already mentioned before, criticisms range from the use of a particularly cumbersome syntax, inherited from RDF/XML, to the availability of an expressive power that, from a strict knowledge representation point of view, does not seem to improve so much with respect to "traditional" frame systems like Protégé-2000 (see the article "Knowledge Representation" in this encyclopedia). We can, however, remark, in this context, that an "OWL plugin" for Protégé has been recently implemented (see Horridge, 2004 and http://protege.stanford.edu/

plugins/owl/); it allows loading and saving OWL and RDF ontologies, editing and visualizing OWL classes and their properties and, mainly, supporting reasoners such as the description logics classifiers.

Note that, according to OWL's supporters, it is precisely this last characteristic that "makes all the difference" between a simple frame system that utilize pragmatically based inference procedures, and an OWL-based reasoning tool—see, for example, RACER (Haarslev & Möller, 2003)—that employs sound and complete inferencing algorithms supported by the description logics theory. Unfortunately, description logics have been, in turn, criticized in spite (or because) their (too) rigorous formal framework, associated, *inter alia*, with a reduced expressiveness of their main reasoning component, the automatic classification mechanism. To give only an example, nearly a printed page is needed in McGuinness et al. (2002) to demonstrate that, using the DAML+OIL definitions (DAML+OIL is the ancestor of OWL), we can infer that "Red" can be considered as a sort of "WineColor." A plea for the use, in a Semantic Web context, of knowledge representation languages more "meaningful" than those based on a description logics approach can be found in Zarri (2002).

In spite of all the criticisms, Semantic Web techniques have really represented a quantum leap in the "knowledge management" domain, in the widest meaning of these words, and are surely here to stay.

REFERENCES

Ankolekar, A., Burstein, M., Hobbs, J., Lassila, O., Martin, D., McDermott, D., McIlraith, S., Narayanan, S., Paolucci, M., Payne, T., & Sycara, K. (2002). DAML-S: Web service description for the Semantic Web. In *Proceedings of the 1st International Semantic Web Conference—ISWC 2002* (LNCS 2342). Heidelberg: Springer-Verlag.

Baader, F., Calvanese, D., McGuinness, D., Nardi, D., & Patel-Schneider, P.F. (Eds.) (2002). *The description logic handbook: Theory, implementation and applications*. Cambridge, MA: University Press.

Baclawski, K., Kokar, M.K., Kogut, P.A., Hart, L., Smith, J., Holmes, W.S., Letkowski, J., & Aronson, M.L. (2001). Extending UML to support ontology engineering for the Semantic Web. In *Proceedings of the 4th International Conference on the Unified Modeling Language—UML 2001* (LNCS vol. 2185). Heidelberg: Springer-Verlag.

Bechhofer, S., van Harmelen, F., Hendler, J., Horrocks, I., McGuinness, D.L., Patel-Schneider, P.F., & Stein, L.A.

(Eds.) (2004). *OWL Web ontology language reference—W3C recommendation—W3C. Retrieved February 10, 2004, from www.w3.org/TR/owl-ref/*

Beckett, D. (Ed.) (2004). *RDF/XML syntax specification (Revised)—W3C recommendation.* Retrieved February 10, 2004, from *www.w3.org/TR/rdf-syntax-grammar/*

Berners-Lee, T., Hendler, J., & Lassila, O. (2001). The semantic Web. *Scientific American, 284*(5), 34-43.

Bertino, E., Catania, B., & Zarri, G.P. (2001). *Intelligent database systems*. London: Addison-Wesley and ACM Press.

Biron, P.V., & Malhotra, A. (Eds.) (2001). *XML schema part 2: Datatypes—W3C recommendation. Retrieved May 2, 2001*, from *www.w3.org/TR/xmlschema-2/*

Boley, H., Tabet, S., & Wagner, G. (2001). Design rationale of RuleML: A markup language for Semantic Web rules. In *Proceedings of SWWS'01—The 1st Semantic Web Working Symposium.* Stanford: Stanford University.

Bray, T., Paoli, J., Sperberg-McQueen, C.M., Maler, E., & Yergeau, F. (Eds.) (2004). *Extensible markup language (XML) 1.0 (3rd ed.)—W3C recommendation.* Retrieved February 4, 2004, from *www.w3.org/TR/REC-xml/*

Brickley, D., & Guha, R.V. (Eds.) (2004). *RDF vocabulary description language 1.0: RDF Schema—W3C recommendation.* Retrieved February 10, 2004, from *www.w3.org/TR/rdf-schema/*

Christensen, E., Curbera, F., Meredith, G., & Weerawarana, S. (2001). *Web services description language (WSDL) 1.1—W3C Note.* Retrieved March 15, 2001, from *www.w3.org/TR/wsdl*

Dekkers, M., & Weibel, S. (2003). State of the Dublin Core Initiative, April 2003. *D-Lib Magazine 9*(4). Retrieved from *www.dlib.org/dlib/april03/weibel/04weibel.html*

Falkovych, K., Sabou, & Stuckenschmidt, H. (2003). UML for the Semantic Web: Transformation-based approaches. In B. Omelayenko & M. Klein (Eds.), *Knowledge transformation for the Semantic Web.* Amsterdam: IOS Press.

Gómez-Pérez, A., González-Cabrero, R., & Lama, M. (2004). ODE SWS: A framework for designing and composing Semantic Web services. *IEEE Intelligent Systems 19*(4), 24-31.

Haarslev, V., & Möller, R. (2003). Racer: A core inference engine for the Semantic Web. In *Proceedings of the 2nd International Workshop on Evaluation of Ontology Tools (EON2003)*, October 20, Sanibel Island, FL.

Horridge, M. (2004). *A practical guide to building OWL ontologies with the Protégé-OWL Plugin* (Edition 1.0). Manchester: The University of Manchester.

Horrocks, I., Patel-Schneider, P.F., Boley, H., Tabet, S., Grosof, B., & Dean, M. (2004). *SWRL: A Semantic Web rule language combining OWL and RuleML—W3C member submission.* Retrieved May 21, 2004, from *www.w3.org/Submission/SWRL/*

Manola, F., & Miller, E. (2004). *RDF primer—W3C recommendation.* Retrieved February 10, 2004, from *www.w3.org/TR/rdf-primer/*

McGuinness, D.L., Fikes, R., Hendler, J., & Stein, L.A. (2002). DAML+OIL: An ontology language for the Semantic Web. *IEEE Intelligent Systems, 17*(5), 72-80.

Mitra, N. (Ed.) (2003). *SOAP version 1.2 Part 0: Primer—W3C recommendation.* Retrieved June 24, 2003, from *www.w3.org/TR/soap12-part0*

Schwartz, D.G. (2003). From open IS semantics to the semantic Web: The road ahead. *IEEE Intelligent Systems, 18*(3), 52-58.

Sintek, M., & Decker, S. (2002). TRIPLE: A query, inference, and transformation language for the semantic Web. In *Proceedings of the 1st International Semantic Web Conference—ISWC 2002* (LNCS 2342). Heidelberg: Springer-Verlag.

Smith, M.K., Welty, C., & McGuinness, D.L. (Eds.) (2004). *OWL Web ontology language guide—W3C recommendation.* Retrieved February 10, 2004, from *www.w3.org/TR/owl-guide*

Thompson, H.S., Beech, D., Maloney, M., & Mendelsohn, N. (Eds.) (2001). *XML schema part 1: Structures—W3C recommendation.* Retrieved May 2, 2001, from *www.w3.org/TR/xmlschema-1/*

van Heijst, G., van der Spek, R., & Kruizinga, E. (1996). Organizing corporate memories. In B.R. Gaines & M. Musen (Eds.), *Proceedings of the 10th Banff Knowledge Acquisition for Knowledge-Based Systems Workshop*, Calgary: Department of Computer Science of the University.

Zarri, G.P. (2002). Semantic Web and knowledge representation. *Database and expert systems applications.* In *Proceedings of the 13th International Conference, DEXA'02.* Los Alamitos, CA: IEEE Computer Society Press.

KEY TERMS

eXtensible Markup Language (XML): Has been created to overcome some difficulties proper to Hypertext Markup Language (HTML) that—developed as a means for instructing the Web browsers how to display a given Web page—is a "presentation-oriented" markup tool. XML is called "extensible" because, at the difference of HTML, it is not characterized by a fixed format but lets the user design its own customized markup languages (a specific DTD, Document Type Description) for limitless different types of documents; XML is then a "content-oriented" markup tool.

OWL: The Web Ontology Language (OWL) is a semantic markup language for publishing and sharing ontologies on the World Wide Web. OWL is developed as a vocabulary extension of RDF and is derived from the DAML+OIL Web Ontology Language. An OWL ontology is an RDF graph, which is in turn a set of RDF triples. OWL includes three specific sub-languages, characterized by an increasing level of complexity and expressiveness: OWL Lite, OWL DL (DL stands for Description Logics, a particular, logic-oriented, knowledge representation language introduced to supply a formal foundation for frame-based systems), and OWL Full.

RDF Schema (RDFS): Provides a mechanism for constructing specialized RDF vocabularies through the description of domain-specific properties. This is obtained mainly by describing the properties in terms of the classes of resource to which they apply: For example, we could define the **creator** property saying that it has the resource **document** as "domain" (**document** is the value or "object" of this property) and the resource **person** as "range" (this property must always be associated with a resource **person**, its "subject"). Other basic modeling primitives of RDFS allow setting up hierarchies (taxonomies), both *hierarchies of concepts* thanks to the use of "class" and "subclass-of" statements, and *hierarchies of properties* thanks to the use of "property" and "subproperty-of" statements. Instances of a specific class (concept) can be declared making use of the "type" statement.

Resource Description Framework (RDF): An example of "metadata" language (metadata = data about data) used to describe generic "things" ("resources," according to the RDF jargon) on the Web. An RDF document is a list of statements under the form of triples having the classical format: <object, property, value>, where the elements of the triples can be Universal Resource Identifiers (URIs), literals (mainly free text). and variables. RDF statements are normally written into XML format (the so-called "RDF/XML syntax").

Semantic Web Architecture: A layered architecture proposed by Berners-Lee for the Semantic Web applications. In this architecture, ontologies occupy a central place: They are built on the top of the Resource Description Framework (RDF) layer, which is in turn built on the top of the XML layer. The XML/RDF base constraints the particular format ontologies assume in a Semantic Web context, inheriting, for example, all the well-known XML "verbosity."

Semantic Web Rules: Still a "hot" topic in a Semantic Web context. The present proposals (like RuleML, TRIPLE, or SWRL) are based on an expansion of the classical "logic programming" paradigm where the inferential properties of Prolog/Datalog are extended to deal with RDF/OWL knowledge bases. Examples of Semantic Web rules in RuleML are the "derivation rules" (i.e., rules used to automatically defining derived concepts), the "reaction rules" (for specifying the reactive behavior of a given system in response to specific events), the "transformation rules" (used to implement translators between different versions of RuleML, and between RuleML and other rule languages like Jess), and so forth.

Semantic Web Services: A Web service is a Web site that does not simply supply static information, but that also allows automatic execution of some "actions" (services), like the sale of a product or the control of a physical device. To do this, Web services make use of XML-based standards like WSDL, a description protocol, and SOAP, a messaging protocol, characterized by a low level of semantic expressiveness. For example, WSDL can describe the interface of the different services, and how these services are deployed via SOAP, but it is very limited in its ability to express what the overall competences of this service are. Semantic Web services are Web services that can specify not only their interfaces, but also describe in full, under the form of OWL-based ontologies, their capabilities and the prerequisites and consequences of their use. For example, OWL-S is a specification, in the form of an ontology, intended to describe different Semantic Web services features, enabling Web users and software agents to automatically discover, invoke, select, compose, and monitor Web-based services.

XML Schema: A more complete way of specifying the semantics of a set of XML markup elements. XML Schema supplies a complete grammar for specifying the structure of the elements allowing, for example, to define the cardinality of the offspring elements, default values, and so forth.

Representation Languages for Narrative Documents

Gian Piero Zarri
University of Paris IV/Sorbonne, France

INTRODUCTION

A big amount of important, "economically relevant" information, is buried into unstructured "narrative" information resources: This is true, for example, for most of the corporate knowledge documents (memos, policy statements, reports, minutes, etc.), for the news stories, the normative and legal texts, the medical records, many intelligence messages as well as for a huge fraction of the information stored on the Web. In these "narrative documents," or "narratives," the main part of the information content consists in the description of "events" that relate the real or intended behavior of some "actors" (characters, personages, etc.)—the term "event" is taken here in its more general meaning, also covering strictly related notions like fact, action, state, and situation. These actors try to attain a specific result, experience particular situations, manipulate some (concrete or abstract) materials, send or receive messages, buy, sell, deliver, and so forth. Note that in these narratives, the actors or personages are not necessarily human beings; we can have narrative documents concerning, for example, the vicissitudes in the journey of a nuclear submarine (the "actor," "subject," or "personage") or the various avatars in the life of a commercial product. Note also that even if a large amount of narrative documents concerns natural language (NL) texts, this is not necessarily true. A photo representing a situation that verbalized could be expressed as "Three nice girls are lying on the beach" is not of course an NL text, yet it is still a narrative document.

Because of the ubiquity of these "narrative" resources, being able to represent in a general, accurate, and effective way their semantic content—that is, their key "meaning"—is then both conceptually relevant and economically important: Narratives form, in fact, a huge underutilized component of organizational knowledge. This type of explicit yet unstructured knowledge can be, of course, indexed and searched in a variety of ways, but it requires, however, an approach for formal analysis and effective utilization that is neatly different from the "traditional" ones.

BACKGROUND

Usual ontologies—both in their "traditional" and "Semantic Web" versions (see the "Knowledge Representation" and "RDF and OWL" articles in this Encyclopedia)—are not very suitable for dealing with narratives. Basically, ontologies organize the "concepts"—that we can identify here with the important notions to be represented in a given application domain – into a hierarchical structure, able to supply an elementary form of definition of these concepts through their mutual generic/specific relationships ("IsA" links). A more detailed definition of the concepts is obtained by associating them with a set of binary relationships of the "property/value" type (e.g., a "frame"). The combination of these two representational principles is largely sufficient to provide a *static*, *a priori* definition of the concepts and of their properties.

Unfortunately, this is no more true when we consider the *dynamic behavior* of the concepts, that is, we want to describe their mutual relationships when they take part in some concrete action or situation ("events"). First of all, representing an event implies that the notion of *"role"* must be added to the traditional generic/specific and property/value representational principles. If we want to represent adequately a narrative fragment like "NMTV (an European media company) ... will develop a lap top computer system...," besides asserting that NMTV_ is an instance of the concept *company_* and that we also must introduce an instance of a concept like *lap_top_pc*, we have to create a sort of "threefold" relationship; this relationship includes a "predicate" (like DEVELOP or PRODUCE), the two instances, and a third fundamental component, the "roles" (like SUBJECT or AGENT for NMTV_ and OBJECT or PATIENT for the new lap top system) used to specify the exact function of these two instances within the formal description of the event. Moreover, in an event context, we also must deal with those *"connectivity phenomena"* like causality, goal, indirect speech, co-ordination, and subordination that link together the basic "elementary events." It is very likely, in fact, that dealing with the sale of a company, the global information to represent is something like: "Company X has sold its subsidiary Y to Z *because* the profits of Y have fallen dangerously these last years *due to* a lack of investments," or, returning to our previous example, that "NMTV will develop a lap top computer system *to put* controlled circulation magazines out of business," or, that dealing with the relationships between companies in the biotechnology domain, "X made a milestone payment to Y *because* they decided to pursue an in vivo evaluation of the candidate compound identified by X." In computational linguistics terms, we are here in the domain of the "Discourse Analysis" which deals, in short, with the two following problems: (1) determining the nature of the information that in a sequence of statements goes beyond the simple addition of the information conveyed by a single statement; (2) determining the influence of the context in which a statement is used on the meaning of this individual statement or part of it.

It is now easy to imagine the awkward proliferation of binary relationships that sticking to the traditional ontological paradigm it would be necessary to introduce to approximate high-level notions like those of "role" and "connectivity phenomena."

Solutions for representing narratives in computer-usable ways that could move beyond a strict "binary" framework have, therefore, already been proposed in the past. In the context of his work—between the mid 1950s and mid 1960s—on the set up of a mechanical translation process based on the simulation of the thought processes of the translator, Silvio Ceccato (Ceccato, 1961, 1967), proposed a representation of narrative-like sentences as a network of triadic structures ("correlations") organized around specific "correlators" (a sort of roles). The correlators (100 or 200 in all, according to the different natural languages) included conjunctions and prepositions, punctuation marks, and syntactic/semantic relationships like subject-predicate, substance-accident, apposition, development-modality, comparison, and so forth. Ceccato also is credited to be one of the pioneers of the semantic network studies, even if the "official" beginning of this discipline is traditionally associated with the first publication, in 1966, of the Ross Quillian's thesis on "Semantic Memories" (Quillian, 1968). Basically, semantic networks are directed graphs (digraphs) where the nodes represent concepts, and the arcs represent different kinds of associative links, not only the "classical" IsA and property-value links, but also "ternary" relationships derived from Case Grammar in Linguistics (see Fillmore, 1966), and labeled as Actor, Object, Recipient, Instrument, and so forth. A panorama of the different conceptual solutions proposed in a semantic network context can be found in Lehmann (1992). In the 1970s, a sort of particularly popular semantic network approach was repre-

sented by the Conceptual Dependency theory of Roger Schank (1972). In this theory, the underlying meaning ("conceptualization") of narrative-like utterances is expressed as combinations of "semantic predicates" chosen from a set of 12 "primitive actions" (like INGEST, MOVE, ATRANS, the transfer of an abstract relationship like possession, ownership and control, PTRANS, physical transfer, etc.) plus states and changes of states, and seven role relationships ("conceptual case") in the Case Grammar style. Conceptual Graphs (CGs) is the representation system developed by Sowa (1984, 1999) and derived from Schank's work and other early work in the Semantic Networks domain. CGs make use of a graph-based notation for representing "concept-types" (organized into a type-hierarchy), "concepts" (which are instantiations of concept types) and "conceptual relations" that relate one concept to another. CGs can be used to represent narratives in a formal way, like "A pretty lady is dancing gracefully," and more complex, second-order constructions like contexts, wishes, and beliefs. CYC (see Lenat, Guha, Pittman, Pratt, & Shepherd, 1990) concerns one of the most controversial endeavors in the history of artificial intelligence. Started in the early 1980s as a MCC (Microelectronics and Computer Technology Corporation, TX) project, it ended about 15 years later with the set up of an enormous knowledge base containing about a million of hand-entered "logical assertions" including both simple statements of facts and rules about what conclusion can be inferred if certain statements of facts are satisfied. The "upper level" of the ontology that structures the CYC knowledge base is now freely accessible on the Web (*www.cyc.com/cyc/opencyc*). A detailed analysis of the origins, developments and motivations of CYC can be found in Bertino, Catania, and Zarri (2001, pp. 275-316).

NARRATIVE KNOWLEDGE REPRESENTATION LANGUAGE (NKRL)

With the exception of CYC and (very partially) of the Conceptual Graphs, the greater part of the solutions evoked in the last section concern mainly pure academic work, implying very sketchy forms of implementation. Narrative Knowledge Representation Language (NKRL) (Zarri, 1997, 2003) represents an up-to-date, fully implemented, and relatively complete solution to the problem of representing narratives without a too important loss of the original "meaning." NKRL innovates with respect to the usual ontology paradigm by associating with the traditional ontologies of concepts an "ontology of events," that is, a new sort of hierarchical organization

Table 1. Deriving a predicative occurrence from a template

```
name: Move:TransferOfService
father: Move:TransferToSomeone
position: 4.24
NL description: "Transfer or Supply a Service to Someone"

MOVE    SUBJ        var1: [var2]
        OBJ         var3
        [SOURCE     var4: [var5]]
        BENF        var6: [var7]
        [MODAL      var8]
        [TOPIC      var9]
        [CONTEXT    var10]
        {[modulators]}

var1  =    <human_being_or_social_body>
var3  =    <service_>
var4  =    <human_being_or_social_body>
var6  =    <human_being_or_social_body>
var8  =    <process_>    <sector_specific_activity>
var9  =    <sortal_concept>
var10 =    <situation_>
var2, var5, var7 = <geographical_location>

c1)     MOVE    SUBJ    british_telecom
        OBJ     payg_internet_service
        BENF    (SPECIF customer_ british_telecom)
        date-1: after-1-september-1998
        date-2:
```

where the nodes correspond to N-ary structures called "templates."

Instead of using the traditional *object (class, concept)—attribute—value* organization, templates are generated from the combination of quadruples connecting together the *symbolic name* of the template, a *predicate*, and the *arguments* of the predicate introduced by named relations, the *roles*. The quadruples have in common the "name" and "predicate" components. If we denote then with L_i the generic symbolic label identifying a given template, with P_j the predicate used in the template, with R_k the generic role and with a_k the corresponding argument, the NKRL core data structure for templates has the following general format:

$$(L_i \ (P_j \ (R_1 \ a_1) \ (R_2 \ a_2) \ ... \ (R_n \ a_n)))$$ (1)

See the example in Table 1. Predicates pertain to the set {BEHAVE, EXIST, EXPERIENCE, MOVE, OWN, PRODUCE, RECEIVE}, and roles pertain to the set {SUBJ(ect), OBJ(ect), SOURCE, BEN(e)F(iciary), MODAL(ity), TOPIC, CONTEXT}. An argument of the predicate can consist of a simple "concept" (according to the traditional, "ontological" meaning of this word) or of a structured association ("expansion") of several concepts.

In turn, templates are included in an inheritance hierarchy, HTemp(lates), which implements the new "ontology of events," (see Figure 1); they represent then formally generic classes of elementary events like "move a physical object," "be present in a place," "produce a service,"

"send/receive a message," and "build up an Internet site." When a particular event pertaining to one of these general classes must be represented, the corresponding template is "instantiated" to produce what, in the NKRL's jargon, is called a "predicative occurrence."

To represent then a simple narrative like "British Telecom will offer its customers a pay-as-you-go (payg) Internet service in autumn 1998," we must first select in the HTemp hierarchy the template corresponding to "supply a service to someone," represented in the upper part of Table 1.

This template is a specialization (see the "father" code) of the particular MOVE template of HTemp corresponding to "transfer of resources to someone" (see Figure 1). In a template, the arguments of the predicate (the a_k terms in (1)) are represented by variables with associated constraints—which are expressed as concepts or combinations of concepts, that is, using the terms of the NKRL standard "ontology of concepts" (HClass, "hierarchy of classes"). The constituents (as SOURCE in Table 1) included in square brackets are optional. When deriving a predicative occurrence (an instance of a template) like c1 in Table 1, the role fillers in this occurrence must conform to the constraints of the father-template. For example, in occurrence c1, british_telecom is an individual instance of the concept *company_*: this last is, in turn, a specialization of *human_being_or_social_body*. *payg_internet_service* is a specialization of *service*, a specific term of *social_activity*, and so forth.

The meaning of the expression "BENF (SPECIF *customer_british_telecom*)" in c1 is self-evident: The beneficiaries (role BENF) of the service are the customers of—SPECIF(ication)—British Telecom. The "attributive operator," SPECIF(ication), is one of the four operators that make up the AECS sub-language, used for the set up of the structured arguments (expansions); apart from (SPECIFication = S), AECS also includes the disjunctive operator (ALTERNative = A), the distributive operator (ENUMeration = E), and the collective operator (COORDination = C). The interweaving of the four operators within an expansion is controlled by the so-called "precedence rule" (see Zarri, 1997, 2003).

In the occurrences, the two operators date-1, date-2 materialize the temporal interval normally associated with narrative events; a detailed description of the methodology for representing temporal data in NKRL can be found in Zarri (1998).

About 150 templates are permanently inserted into HTemp; Figure 1 reproduces the "external" organization of the actual state of the MOVE branch in HTemp; this branch includes the Move:TransferOfService template used in Table 1. HTemp, the NKRL ontology of events, corresponds then to a sort of "catalogue" of narrative formal structures that are very easy to "customize" in order to derive the new templates that could be needed for a particular application. This approach is particularly advantageous for practical applications, and it implies, in particular, that: (1) a system-builder does not have to create himself the structural knowledge needed to describe the events properly to a (sufficiently) large class of narrative documents; (2) it becomes easier to secure the reproduction or the sharing of previous results.

What we have expounded until now illustrates the NKRL solutions to the problem of providing a coherent and complete representation of elementary (simple) events. To deal now with those "connectivity phenomena" that arise when several elementary events are connected through causality, goal, indirect speech etc. links, the basic NKRL knowledge representation tools have been complemented by more complex mechanisms that make use of second order structures created through *reification* of the predicative occurrences' conceptual labels (see Zarri, 1998, 2003). For example, the "binding occurrences" are NKRL structures consisting of lists of symbolic labels (c_i) of predicative occurrences; the lists are differentiated making use of specific binding operators like GOAL and CAUSE. Let us suppose that in Table 1 we would now state that: "British Telecom *intends* to offer to its customers a pay-as-you-go (payg) Internet service...," where the elementary event corresponding to "British Telecom ... (will) offer to its customers a pay-as-you-go (payg) Internet service..." is represented by the occurrence c1 in Table 1. We must first introduce an additional predicative occurrence labeled as c2 that we will represent here, in a very simplified way, as: "c2) BEHAVE SUBJ british_telecom." c2 means: "at the date (date-1) associated with c2, it can be noticed that British Telecom is (mentally) acting in some way." We will then add a *binding occurrence* c3 to link together the conceptual labels c2 (the intention) and c1 (the intended result); c3 will have the following form: "c3) (GOAL c2 c1)." The

Figure 1. 'MOVE' branch of the HTemp hierarchy

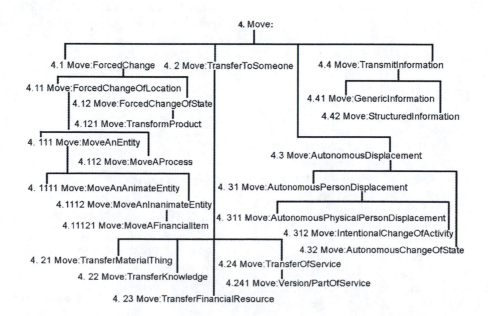

global meaning of c3 is: "the activity described in c2 is focalized toward (GOAL) the realization of c1"—c1 is represented in Table 1.

Reasoning in NKRL ranges from the direct questioning of an NKRL knowledge base making use of "search patterns" (the formal NKRL equivalents of natural language queries) that try to unify the predicative occurrences of the base, to high-level inference procedures employing complex inference engines.

For example, the "transformation rules" try to "adapt," from a semantic point of view, the original query/queries (search patterns) that failed to the real contents of the system knowledge base. The principle employed consists in using rules to automatically "transform" the original query (i.e., the original search pattern) into one or more different queries (search patterns) that are not strictly "equivalent" but only "semantically close" to the original one. In this way, an original query posed, for example, in terms of "searching for evidence of having lived in a given country" will be replied in terms of "searching for evidence of an original school/university diploma delivered in that country."

"Hypothesis rules" allow building up "reasonable" answers according to a number of predefined reasoning schemata, such as "causal" schemata. For example, after having directly retrieved information like "Pharmacopeia, an USA biotechnology company, has received $64,000,000 from the German company Schering in connection with an R&D activity," we could be able to automatically construct a sort of "causal explanation" of this information by retrieving in the knowledge base information like (1) "Pharmacopeia and Schering have signed an agreement concerning the production by Pharmacopeia of a new compound" and (2) "in the framework of the agreement previously mentioned, Pharmacopeia has actually produced the new compound."

FUTURE TRENDS AND THE IMPORTANCE OF NKRL IN KNOWLEDGE MANAGEMENT

In these last years, knowledge has been recognized as one of the most important assets of an enterprise and a possible success factor for any industrial organization, on the condition that it could be controlled, shared, and reused in an effective way. Accordingly, the core of the organization can then be conceived the form of a general and shared "corporate memory," (see van Heijst, van der Spek, & Kruizinga, 1996; Brooking, 1998; Beckett, 2000), that is, of an online, computer-based storehouse of expertise, experience, and documentation about all the strategic aspects of the organization. The construction and practical use of corporate memories then becomes the main activity in the knowledge management of a company. As already stated, this corporate knowledge is mainly represented under the from of narrative documents; the possibility of having at one's disposal a tool in the NKRL style becomes then an essential condition for the concrete setup and for the "intelligent" exploitation of non-trivial corporate memories.

In this context, we can remark that the different working groups managed by the W3C are not, apparently, very interested in the problem of dealing in an appropriate way with everyday life and complex narratives. W3C (the World Wide Web Consortium) is coordinated by MIT (USA), ERCIM, the European Research Consortium for Informatics and Mathematics, and the Keio University (Japan), and includes all the main bodies on earth interested in the developments of Internet and the Web. As an at least partial exception to this attitude, we can mention a recent paper from the W3C Semantic Web Best Practices and Deployment Working Group (SWBPD WG) about defining N-ary relations on the Semantic Web (Noy & Rector, 2005). After having recognized that the Semantic Web languages promoted by the W3C, like RDF and OWL, can only support binary relations (properties) between individuals (see the "RDF and OWL" article in this encyclopedia) the authors try to propose some extensions to these languages that could be able to deal with narratives like: "Christine has breast tumor with high probability," "Steve has temperature, which is high, but failing," or "John buys a *Lenny the Lion* book from *books.Example.com* for $15 as a birthday gift," which, obviously, cannot be represented, making use only of IsA and property-value relationships. The solutions proposed range from the introduction of fictitious individuals to represent the n-ary relations to the rediscovery of some semantic networks solutions of the 1970s. Interestingly enough, the authors state that "The SWBDP WG does not expect this document to become a Recommendation (i.e., a W3C Recommendation)" (Noy & Rector, 2005, p. 2). In NKRL, the two first examples—"Christine has breast tumor…" and "Steve has temperature…"—are translated as simple instantiations of the template Experience:NegativeHuman/SocialSituation (3.211), and the example about "John buys…" as an instantiation of the template Produce:Buy (6.361).

CONCLUSION

In this article, we have recalled first the importance, from an economic point of view, that "narratives" have in the context of the corporate knowledge. We have then shown that the usual ontological tools, both the "traditional" (frame-based) ones and the new ones proposed in a Semantic Web context, are unable to offer complete and reliable solutions to the problem of a non-trivial representation and exploitation of narratives. After having recalled the existence of early proposals in this field, we have supplied some details about NKRL (Narrative Knowledge Representation Language), a fully implemented, up-to-date knowledge representation and inferencing system especially created for an "intelligent" exploitation of narrative knowledge. The main innovation of NKRL consists in associating with the traditional ontologies of concepts an "ontology of events," that is, a new sort of hierarchical organization where the nodes correspond to N-ary structures called "templates." Templates—150 at present, but new templates can be easily created on the model of the existing ones—represent formally generic classes of elementary events like "move a physical object," "be present in a place," "produce a service," "send/receive a message," and "build up an Internet site." More complex, second order tools based on the "reification" principle allow to encode narratives characterized by the presence of elementary events linked by relationships like causality, goal, indirect speech, co-ordination, and subordination. After having evoked the query/answering and inferencing tools associated with NKRL, the article ends by mentioning the importance of having at one's disposal tools in the NKRL style for the actual setup of non-toy corporate memories.

REFERENCES

Beckett, R.C. (2000). A characterization of corporate memory as a knowledge system. *Journal of Knowledge Management, 4*(4), 311-319.

Bertino, E., Catania, B., & Zarri, G.P. (2001). *Intelligent database systems*. London: Addison-Wesley and ACM Press.

Brooking, A. (1998). *Corporate memory: Strategies for knowledge management*. London: Thomson Business Press.

Ceccato, S. (1961). *Linguistic analysis and programming for mechanical translation*. Milan: Feltrinelli.

Ceccato, S. (1967). Correlational analysis and mechanical translation. In A.D. Booth (Ed.), *Machine translation*. Amsterdam: North-Holland.

Fillmore, C.J. (1966). Toward a modern theory of case. In D.A. Reibel & S.A. Schane (Eds.), *Modern studies of English: Readings in transformational grammar*. Englewood Cliffs, NJ: Prentice Hall.

Lehmann, F. (Ed.) (1992). *Semantic networks in artificial intelligence*. Oxford: Pergamon Press.

Lenat, D.B., Guha, R.V., Pittman, K., Pratt, D., & Shepherd, M. (1990). CYC: Toward programs with common sense. *Communications of the ACM, 33*(8), 30-49.

Noy, N., & Rector, A. (2005). *Defining n-ary relations on the Semantic Web—Editor's draft*. Retrieved June 20, 2005, from *www.w3.org/TR/swbp-n-aryRelations#ref-1*.

Quillian, M.R. (1966). Semantic memory. In M. Minsky (Ed.), *Semantic information processing*. Cambridge, MA: MIT Press.

Schank, R.C. (1973). Identification of conceptualisations underlying natural language. In R.C. Schank & K.M. Colby (Eds.), *Computer models of thought and language*. San Francisco: Freeman and Co.

Sowa, J.F. (1984). *Conceptual structures: Information processing in minds and machines*. Reading, MA: Addison-Wesley.

Sowa, J.F. (1999). *Knowledge representation: Logical, philosophical, and computational Foundations*. Pacific Grove, CA: Brooks Cole Publishing Co.

van Heijst, G., van der Spek, R., & Kruizinga, E. (1996). Organizing corporate memories. In Gaines, B.R., and Musen, M., (Eds.) *Proceedings of the 10th Banff Knowledge Acquisition for Knowledge-Based Systems Workshop*, Calgary: Department of Computer Science of the University.

Zarri, G.P. (1997). NKRL, a knowledge representation tool for encoding the 'meaning' of complex narrative texts. *Natural Language Engineering: Special Issue on Knowledge Representation for Natural Language Processing in Implemented Systems, 3*, 231-253.

Zarri, G.P. (1998). Representation of temporal knowledge in events: The formalism, and its potential for legal narratives. *Information and Communications Technology Law: Special Issue on Models of Time, Action, and Situations, 7*, 213-241.

Zarri, G.P. (2003). A conceptual model for representing narratives. In R. Jain, A. Abraham, C. Faucher, & van der Zwaag (Eds.), *Innovations in knowledge engineering*. Adelaide, Australia: Advanced Knowledge International.

KEY TERMS

Connectivity Phenomena: A term drawn from computational linguistics. In the presence of several, logically linked elementary events, it denotes the existence of a global information content that goes beyond the simple addition of the information conveyed by the single events. The connectivity phenomena are linked with the presence of logico-semantic relationships like causality, goal, indirect speech, co-ordination, and subordination, as in a sequence like: "Company X has sold its subsidiary Y to Z *because* the profits of Y have fallen dangerously these last years *due to* a lack of investments." These phenomena cannot be managed by the usual ontological tools; in NKRL, they are dealt with using second order tools based on reification.

Corporate Memories and Narrative Documents: Knowledge is one of the most important assets of an enterprise, on the condition that it could be controlled, shared and reused in an effective way. The core of any commercial/industrial organization can then be conceived under the form of a general and shared "corporate memory," that is, of an online, computer-based storehouse of expertise, experience, and documentation about all the strategic aspects of the organization. Given that this corporate knowledge is mainly represented under the form of narrative documents, the possibility of having at one's disposal tools for an effective management of these documents becomes an essential condition for the concrete setup and for the "intelligent" exploitation of non-trivial corporate memories.

Narrative Documents or "Narratives": Multimedia documents (very often, unstructured, natural language documents like memos, policy statements, reports, minutes, news stories, normative and legal texts, etc.) that constitute a huge underutilized component of corporate knowledge. In these "narratives," the main part of the information content consists in the description of "events" that relate the real or intended behavior of some "actors" (characters, personages, etc.); these try to attain a specific result, experience particular situations, manipulate some (concrete or abstract) materials, send or receive messages, buy, sell, deliver, and so forth. "Classical" ontologies are inadequate for representing and exploiting narrative knowledge in a non-trivial way.

NKRL: The Narrative Knowledge Representation Language. "Classical" ontologies are largely sufficient to provide a *static, a priori* definition of the concepts and of their properties. This is no more true when we consider the *dynamic behavior* of the concepts, that is, we want to describe their mutual relationships when they take part in some concrete action or situation ("events"). NKRL deals with this problem by adding to the usual ontology of concept an "ontology of events," a new sort of hierarchical organization where the nodes, called "templates," represent general classes of events like "move a physical object," "be present in a place," "produce a service," "send/receive a message," and so forth.

Predicative Occurrences: In NKRL, these are conceptual structures obtained from the instantiation of templates and used to represent particular elementary events. To take into account the "connectivity phenomena" (see the corresponding defining term), conceptual labels denoting predicative occurrences can be associated within second order structures making use of operators like CAUSE, GOAL, and COORD(ination).

Semantic Networks: Basically, directed graphs (digraphs) where the nodes represent concepts, and the arcs represent different kinds of associative links, not only the "classical" IsA and property-value links, but also, "ternary" relationships derived from Case Grammar in Linguistics and labeled as Actor, Object, Recipient, Instrument, and so forth. Representational solutions that can be reduced in some way to a Semantic Network framework include, among (many) other things, Ceccato's Correlational Grammar which goes back to the 1950s, Quillian's Semantic Memory, Schank's Conceptual Dependency theory, Sowa's Conceptual Graphs, Lenat's CYC, and Zarri's NKRL (Narrative Knowledge Representation Language). Semantic Network solutions have been often used/proposed to represent different kinds of narrative phenomena.

Templates: In NKRL, templates take the form of combinations of quadruples connecting together the "symbolic name" of the template, a "predicate" – as BEHAVE, MOVE, OWN, PRODUCE...—and the "arguments" of the predicate (concepts or combinations of concepts) introduced by named relations, the "roles" (like SUBJ(ect), OBJ(ect), SOURCE, BEN(e)F(iciary), etc.). The quadruples have in common the "name" and "predicate" components. If we denote with L_i the generic symbolic label identifying a given template, with P_j the predicate used in the template, with R_k the generic role, and with a_k the corresponding argument, the NKRL core data structure for templates has the following general format:

$$(L_i(P_j(R_1 a_1)(R_2 a_2) \dots (R_n a_n))).$$

Templates are included in an inheritance hierarchy, HTemp(lates), which implements NKRL's "ontology of events."

Secure Knowledge Discovery in Databases

S

Rick L. Wilson
Oklahoma State University, USA

Peter A. Rosen
University of Evansville, USA

Mohammad Saad Al-Ahmadi
Oklahoma State University, USA

INTRODUCTION AND BACKGROUND

Knowledge management (KM) systems are quite diverse, but all provide increased access to organizational knowledge, which helps the enterprise to be more connected, agile, and effective. The dilemma faced when using a KM system is to balance the goal of being knowledge-enabled while being knowledge-secure (Cohen, 2003; Lee & Rosenbaum, 2003).

A recent survey of IT security professions found that over 50% of respondents indicated an increase in the security budgets of their organizations since September 11, 2001, and projected that 2004 IT security budgets would be larger than ever (Briney & Prince, 2003).

The need for increased security is driven by both monetary concerns and legal/regulatory requirements. The goal of any security architecture, and specifically for KM systems, is to reduce the potential loss caused by intrusion, system misuse, privilege abuse, tampering, and so forth. Protection must be provided against external threats and from internal abuse and must include components that address the requirements for preserving the confidentiality of data where appropriate.

A 2002 Jupiter Research Consumer Survey estimates that as much as $24.5 billion in online sales will be lost by 2006 due to consumers' lack of confidence in the privacy of online transactions (*E-Compliance Advisor*, 2002). While lack of trust is an opportunity cost, security breaches can causes real losses. One study found firms with publicly announced security breaches lose an average of 2% of market capitalization within two days of attack, for an average of $1.65 billion dollars per breach (Cavusoglu, Mishra, & Raghunathan, 2002). On the regulatory side, legislation like the Health Insurance Portability & Accountability Act (HIPAA) and the Gramm-Leach-Bliley Act (GLBA) have forced companies in health care and financial services fields to improve their security measures (Briney & Prince, 2003; Ingrian Networks, 2004). Table 1 summarizes some common security threats.

While most of the major news stories about security breaches involve hackers who steal or access confidential information, infect systems with viruses, and cause trouble with worms or spam, an equally important threat comes from inside organizations. A report from Ingrian Networks (2004) indicated that 50% of security breaches are perpetrated by internal staff (see Lee & Rosenbaum, 2004). Internal threats represent a bigger risk than those from outsiders due to the difficulty in quantifying and counteracting the attacks. But while the risk of insider intrusions looms large, many IT security professionals still seem to be externally focused (Briney & Prince, 2003).

With the increased focus on security, both internally and externally, a method that seems to be gaining popularity is a layered security approach (e.g., Kolluru & Meredith, 2001; Clark, Croson, & Schiano, 2001). The layered approach proposes using multiple, overlapping forms of security measures. A representative list of such security measures is summarized in Table 2. The layered security approach is a good way to prevent breaches, because if one measure fails, it is possible that other measures employed can stop the attack.

While many network security texts discuss network related hardware and software that are relevant for protecting the IT and KM system infrastructure (e.g., Panko, 2004) from external threats, this article illustrates a complimentary approach. *Data perturbation* focuses on protecting confidential data primarily from unauthorized internal data snoopers. This approach can be used alone or in conjunction with other methods.

Data perturbation involves modifying confidential attributes using random noise, with the objective being to prevent disclosure while maximizing access to accurate information (Muralidhar, Parsa, & Sarathy, 1999). Thus, a KM system can maintain and allow access to masked representative confidential data while preventing exact data disclosure.

To illustrate the different ways that perturbation techniques can be utilized, consider an example scenario

Table 1. Security threats

Information Source	Ingrian, 2004	Briney, 2000	Boren, 2003
General	Poor security policies, human error, dishonesty, abuse of privileges, introduction of unauthorized software	Viruses, malicious code, executables, electronic theft, disclosure of proprietary data, use of resources for illegal / illicit activities	Storage threats: theft of servers, desktops, hard drives, tape backups, information, malicious software installed on server
Identification / Authorization	Internal / external attackers posing as valid users / customers		
Reliability of Service	Natural disasters, equipment failures, denial of service	Denial of service, buffer overflows	
Privacy	Eavesdropping, unauthorized monitoring of sensitive data		
Integrity / Accuracy	Modification or damaging of information		
Access Control	Password cracking, backdoors, security holes	Protocol weakness, insecure passwords, attacks on bugs in servers	Authentication credentials stolen / not properly managed, users given access to unnecessary information

Table 2. Selected security measures

Information Source	Ingrian, 2004	Briney, 2000	Boren, 2003
Security Policies / Security Education Programs	X	X	X
Identification/ Classification of Sensitive Data	X		
Determination of acceptable threat level	X		X
Passwords	X	X	X
Firewalls	X	X	X
Encryption	X	X	X
Backup / Recovery	X		X

where two divisions of a company are sharing information, some of which is considered confidential, and the sharing of data is done electronically. A layered approach to security would be the use of both data perturbation and encryption to secure the data. Data perturbation can be done before the transfer to mask or hide confidential attributes. During the transfer of data, encryption can be used to prevent attackers from accessing the data. By using the layered approach, the sending division protects its confidential data, obtains security during the transfer, and gives the receiving division full access to the perturbed data on the back end.

Data perturbation also can be used as a stand-alone technique to prevent unauthorized access from snoopers and hackers. If the data that users have access to is masked, then the impact of either an internal or external security breach is minimized. All attributes that are confidential (and numerical) can be masked, so their true values are hidden. In this way, even if there is a breach of security, no confidential information will be exposed.

Of all the different hardware and software security measures that are well documented for use in all information systems, data perturbation techniques are uniquely equipped to be one of the most useful and specifically applicable security techniques for knowledge management systems due to their focus on the data (and, therefore, on knowledge contained in the data). Thus, understanding how such perturbation techniques work and the implications on knowledge workers in the organization is extraordinarily applicable and very important for today's knowledge worker. Since this area is relatively new, organizations that learn about perturbation could gain considerably from increased protection of confidential data. Thus, the article's focus on perturbation techniques, rather than a general discussion of all possible (well-documented) hardware and software techniques that "might" be applicable to KM, is definitely warranted.

SECURITY AND ACCURACY USING DATA PERTURBATION

Data Perturbation Techniques

Database, security, and KM administrators face a problematic balancing act regarding access to shared organizational data. Confidentiality might be a requirement for some data elements due to legal or competitive reasons, but using KM tools (such as data mining and knowledge discovery algorithms) to find patterns in data can lead to increased profits or improved processes for the organization. Thus, limiting access to data will hamper these important organizational efforts. Nonetheless, the need to protect individual confidential data elements in databases from improper disclosure is critical.

Data perturbation techniques are sophisticated, yet easily implemented, statistically based methods that protect confidential data by adding random noise to original data values. These approaches prevent exact disclosure of confidential data, add a degree of inferential security, and, most importantly from a KM perspective, allow complete data access and analysis flexibility. This flexibility provides significant benefits to the organization using the database in their KM activities. These techniques mask individual confidential data elements while maintaining underlying aggregate relationships of the database.

Note that these techniques are not encryption techniques, where the data is modified, transmitted, and then returned back to its original form. Once data is perturbed, it stays (and is accessed) in its perturbed form.

The Generalized Additive Perturbation Process (GADP) has emerged as the de facto standard in the data protection research area. Thus, we focus on it exclusively. Past studies have shown that today it is the best way to protect confidential data in this manner. No doubt, future research will find additional techniques that will improve upon GADP. But for now, it serves as the most appropriate example.

GADP possesses no statistical biases and preserves statistical relationships in a dataset (Sarathy & Muralidhar, 2002). The GADP process is briefly explained next, and Table 3 compliments the discussion by showing the differences between a dataset with confidential attributes and its perturbed compliment.

In a database, the confidential attributes that data administrators want hidden will be called set **X**, and all other non-confidential attributes set **S**. A database **U** has i instances with attributes **X+S**. The GADP process creates a perturbed database **P**, based on **U**, also with i instances and attributes **X+S**.

For all attributes in **S**, the attribute value for instance i in database **P** will equal the corresponding value of that instance. Thus, GADP does not alter non-confidential attributes. However, for all **X**, the attribute values for instance i in database **P** will be perturbed, making it different from the value in the corresponding instance i in database **U**.

The perturbation process preserves the original statistical relationships of database **U**. These relationships include the mean values for attributes **X**, the measures of covariance between attribute sets **X** and **S** (i.e., a measure of how the two sets of attributes are related), and the canonical correlation between the attribute sets **X** and **S**, which is how well the actual values of attribute set **X** can be predicted by knowing the actual values of attribute set **S**.

Table 3. GADP method details

Original Data Set				Perturbed Data Set		
Confidential Attributes	Non-Confidential Attributes	Class Variable		Confidential Attributes	Non-Confidential Attributes	Class Variable
Original values	Original values	Original values		Values are perturbed (masked) here	Same as original values	Same as original values

Mean (x) COV (xx)   Mean (x) COV (xx)

Statistical relationships unchanged

Given these statistical properties of **U**, a multivariate normal distribution function is constructed for each instance i. Then, a multivariate random number generator generates the new **X** attribute values for the ith entry in the perturbed database P. This is repeated for all i instances.

Illustrating Data Perturbation

To illustrate the method and its analysis implications, a 50,000 record fictitious bank customer database was used. The data has five numerical attributes (Home Equity, Stock/Bonds, Liabilities, Savings/Checking, and CDs) and a sixth binary categorical class variable indicating whether a customer has been granted special service privileges or not (1 if yes, 0 if no). The means, standard deviations and correlation among these variables are shown in Table 4.

When the dataset was constructed, a decision tree format relating the five numeric attributes to the one class variable was used to assign the 50,000 records to the two classes equally (25,000 cases to each class). The choice of this format is arbitrary and just one of many structures that could represent the database's knowledge. The database was created with different degrees of "noise" in the assignment of class variables, representing different degrees of knowledge "crispness" (i.e., how well the five variables truly differentiate among the two classes of bank customers). We report the results for the 0% noise case, even though knowledge in practice would typically not be this easily defined. Nonetheless, the results will remain representative for the sake of our example.

Additionally, for example's sake, the variables representing Stock/Bonds, Liabilities, and Savings/Checking were deemed confidential, and the others, non-confidential. Thus, the perturbation process will mask the actual

Table 4. Original database information

Descriptive Statistics	Home Equity	Stocks/Bonds	Liabilities	Savings/Checking	CDs	Class Variable
Mean	20.000	50.000	100.000	50.000	80.000	0.500
Standard Deviation	5.000	10.000	20.000	10.005	19.981	0.500
Correlation Matrix	Home Equity	Stocks/Bonds	Liabilities	Savings/Checking	CDs	Class Variable
Home Equity	1.000					
Stocks/Bonds	0.440	1.000				
Liabilities	0.501	0.218	1.000			
Savings/Checking	0.357	0.137	0.631	1.000		
CDs	0.237	0.112	0.756	0.723	1.000	
Class Variable	0.353	0.129	0.018	0.068	-0.161	1.000

Table 5. Perturbed database information

Descriptive Statistics	Home Equity	Stocks/Bonds	Liabilities	Savings/Checking	CDs	Class Variable
Mean	20.000	49.906	100.011	49.966	80.000	0.500
Standard Deviation	5.000	9.995	20.046	10.031	19.981	0.500
Correlation Matrix	Home Equity	Stocks/Bonds	Liabilities	Savings/Checking	CDs	Class Variable
Home Equity	1.000					
Stocks/Bonds	0.435	1.000				
Liabilities	0.498	0.000	1.000			
Savings/Checking	0.355	0.132	0.633	1.000		
CDs	0.237	0.106	0.758	0.724	1.000	
Class Variable	0.353	0.124	0.018	0.067	-0.161	1.000

values of these three variables but will still preserve the linear relationships between the six variables.

Statistical Relationship Preservation

To check for the proper implementation of perturbation, the means, standard deviations, and variable correlations of the dataset before and after perturbation can be examined (see Tables 4 and 5). We see that the GADP process does preserve these important statistical relationships while masking or hiding the confidential data.

Thus, the knowledge worker can perform analyses on the protected database, and in terms of aggregate statistical measures, suffer no loss of accuracy. Given the confidential attributes have been masked, there is also no chance for the specific confidential data fields to be discovered by a data snooper or unauthorized user.

Knowledge Discovery Preservation

Using only simple statistical measures (means, variances, covariances, etc.) to measure the retained information and/or knowledge in a perturbed database is certainly a limited view of the usefulness of data. Knowledge discovery (KD) techniques (i.e., data mining) can identify underlying patterns in a database, which provide decision-makers deeper knowledge about that database, and, therefore, the organization. In this continuing example, we explore how perturbation impacts the ability for KM tools to discover the relationships (if any) between the five quantitative variables and the special services classification designation.

There are innumerable knowledge discovery tools. We choose two basic tools from two "common" families of knowledge discovery approaches. Multiple discriminant analysis (MDA) and logistic regression (LR) are the two traditional parametric approaches utilized, while an inductive learning approach—Classification and Regression Tree (CART)—and a feed-forward neural network (NN) approach were the two non-parametric tools utilized. All four approaches are readily available in software packages like SPSS, and our implementation was performed with SPSS using default values.

Classification accuracy of the knowledge discovery tools was measured to provide a measure of knowledge retention. Ten-fold cross-validation was used to ensure a robust measure of tool classification accuracy (Weiss & Kulikowski, 1991). An instance was labeled correctly classified when the tool classification matched the actual class value of the database instance. The correct number of classifications was assessed both for the training (development) and testing partitions. Because of the large size of the database, the accuracy of the tools for the training and testing sets were nearly identical. For simplicity, the results of only the testing sets are reported.

Table 6 shows the results of the analysis. Not surprisingly, CART, an inductive learning algorithm that discovers database knowledge in the format of a decision tree, correctly classified 100% of the cases in the original database. One would expect this approach to discover database knowledge in a precise manner because its structure matches the method in which the original knowledge was artificially created.

Table 6. Classification accuracy

	Tool	Mean	Standard Deviation
Original Dataset	Decision Tree	100.000	0.000
	Artificial Neural Network	98.640	0.237
	Logistic Regression	72.850	0.836
	Multiple Discriminant Analysis	72.550	0.759
Perturbed Dataset	Decision Tree	90.240	0.470
	Artificial Neural Network	90.010	0.438
	Logistic Regression	71.800	0.978
	Multiple Discriminant Analysis	71.740	0.956

The level of performance of the other three approaches on the original data is also interesting. The NN performs almost as well as CART (98.6% accuracy), while the two parametric approaches, MDA and LR, perform quite poorly (72.55% and 72.85%, respectively). This suggests that the relative performance of knowledge discovery tools is a function of matching the underlying structure of the knowledge in the database. Unfortunately, this structure is not known until the data is analyzed. This example also indicates the potential utility of NN's as a general-purpose knowledge tool regardless of the knowledge structure.

When using our decision-making tools with the perturbed data, we can see a "loss" in classification accuracy for all tools used. CART and ANN correctly classify about 90% of the cases, a loss in accuracy of about 8 to 10%. The parametric tools had classification accuracy rates that were statistically similar between the original and perturbed data. This was due primarily to their relative inability to differentiate among the two customer classes in the original database.

This loss of accuracy stems from the perturbation process changing the values of the confidential data. While it preserves the statistical relationships, the masking of confidential data does destroy some of the crispness of the underlying knowledge.

Summarizing the results, the use of perturbation to mask confidential data in a KM-enabled database provides good inferential disclosure security and perfectly preserves aggregate statistical relationships, but appears to cause a loss in accuracy in discovering deeper relationships (knowledge) in the database.

Decision-Maker Implications

The results in the previous section have shown that using data perturbation as a means to secure confidential data shows promise. However, the GADP method could not perfectly preserve underlying knowledge in the database as it did the aggregate statistical relationships. A database administrator, or security policy maker, would need to assess whether a small reduction in predictive accuracy from a representative knowledge discovery tool is tolerable given the inferential disclosure security provided in the perturbation procedure.

There may be other measures of successful knowledge discovery beyond classification accuracy. Even with an 8 to 10% drop in accuracy, the rules discovered from the perturbed database might be the same or similar to the rules for the original data. If that were true, the accuracy loss would be irrelevant because the knowledge discovered would be equivalent.

Some practical implementation issues also are worthy of mentioning. The manner in which updates are made to the database is important. Most, if not all, organizational databases are dynamic (not static), and data would need to be perturbed on an ongoing basis. Certainly, coordination of this update would be an important implementation issue.

The costs to implement data perturbation techniques appear to be minimal, so from an economic standpoint, a database administrator would have no trouble justifying its use. In this article, for example, the authors used Microsoft Excel and a free spreadsheet add-in to accomplish the perturbation. For larger databases, similar libraries of code could be utilized to automatically update the databases appropriately. Since frequent updates to databases cause the need for ongoing perturbation, procedures would need to be put into place so that perturbation would occur on a regular (daily) basis and not interfere with employee use of the data. An automated routine can be written such that the perturbation process could occur nightly with little need for human supervision, so the only implementation costs would be in the form of computing time. It is our estimation that the additional cost that would accrue to an organization implementing this as part of their KM security process would be well worth the increase in confidential data protection.

As organizations continue to increase the degree of KM system sophistication, the difficult tradeoffs between data access, protection, and confidentiality must be considered. There are many security issues involved, and a layered, multi-faceted approach has obvious merit.

FUTURE TRENDS

This article has shown how data protection techniques can be used to help mask confidential attributes in an organization's database, which is a part of the overall KM system. The GADP method, a standard in the data protection literature, was used to illustrate the impact on the database attributes of the perturbation (very little) and the impact on the ability of knowledge discovery tools to accurately find important knowledge (somewhat impacted).

The findings indicated that GADP-protected databases have desirable characteristics but cannot perfectly maintain knowledge relationships to the same level as the statistical relationships are preserved. Therefore, some loss of knowledge accuracy is sacrificed when organizations employ this form of data protection technique. The benefits, though, are reduced disclosure risk and full access to data for analysis. These benefits are not found in any query reduction technique or other methods in which access to confidential data is restricted.

Future research will no doubt continue to look at techniques that go beyond GADP in their sophistication and ability to preserve additional relationships (such as knowledge) in databases. There also will be increased emphasis on sharing data between organizations in the future, and the promise of data perturbation will play a key role in dealing with the dilemma of protecting the unauthorized sharing of confidential data.

The focus of this article on one specific technique should not be viewed as myopic. Present research has shown that this technique cannot be matched. Of course, future modifications and variations will occur and these techniques will further mitigate "knowledge lost" that the example application in this article showed could occur. The future is promising for the use of perturbation as part of the layered security techniques in data-centric organizations.

CONCLUSION

The use of data perturbation techniques as a component of KM system security shows great promise, even as a stand-alone approach to protecting confidential data. Future research will continue to enhance our ability to simultaneously keep confidential data secure while making it available and useful to our KM systems. The continued importance of data and knowledge in business will spur further advances in this new innovative, effective, and economical area of data perturbation.

REFERENCES

Boren, S. (2003). *IT security cookbook*. Retrieved June 11, 2004, from *http://boran.linuxsecurity.com/security/IT1x-2.html*

Briney, A. (2000). *Security focused: industry survey 2000*. Retrieved June 11, 2004, from *http://infosecuritymag.techtarget.com/articles/september00/pdfs/Survey1_9.00.pdf*

Briney, A., & Prince, F. (2003). *Security survey: Disciplined security*. Retrieved June 11, 2004, from *http://infosecuritymag.techtarget.com/ss/0,295796,sid6_iss143_art294,00.html*

Cavusoglu, H., Mishra, B., & Raghunathan, S. (2002). *The effect of Internet security breach announcements on market value: Capital market reactions for breached firms and Internet security developers*. Retrieved June 11, 2004, from *www.utdallas.edu/~huseyin/eventstudy.PDF*

Cohen, A. (2003). *Security vs. accessibility: A fine balance*. Retrieved June 16, 2004, from *http://zdnet.com.com/2100-1107_2-1018121.html*

Clark, T.H., Croson, D.C., & Schiano, W.T. (2001). A hierarchical model of supply-chain integration: Information sharing and operational interdependence in the U.S. grocery channel. *Information Technology and Management, 2*, 261-288.

E-Compliance advisor: Use online privacy as a marketing initiative. (2002). Retrieved June 11, 2004, from *http://crm-advisor.com/doc/09873*

Ingrian Networks (2004). *Achieving data privacy in the enterprise*. Retrieved June 14, 2004, from *www.itsecurity.com/papers/ingrian1.htm*

Kolluru, R., & Meredith, P.H. (2001). Security and trust management in supply chains. *Information Management and Computer Security, 9*(5), 233-236.

Lee, J.B., & Rosenbaum, A.D. (2004). Knowledge management: Portal for corporate espionage? Part 2. *KM World, 13*(1), 10.

Lee, J.B., & Rosenbaum, A.D. (2003). Knowledge management: Portal for corporate espionage? Part 1. *KM World, 12*(10), 14.

Muralidhar, K., Parsa, R., & Sarathy, R. (1999). A general additive data perturbation method for database security. *Management Science, 45*(10), 1399-1415.

Panko, R. (2004). *Corporate computer and network security* (1st ed.). New York: Prentice Hall.

Sarathy, R., & Muralidhar, K. (2002). The security of confidential numerical data in databases. *Information Systems Research, 13*(4), 389-403.

Sarathy, R., Muralidhar, K., & Parsa, R. (2002). Perturbing non-confidential attributes: The copula approach. *Management Science, 48*(12), 1613-1627.

Shirley, R. (2000). Internet Security Glossary. Retrieved June 14, 2004, from *www.ietf.org/rfc/rfc2828.txt*

Weiss, S., & Kulikowski, C. (1991). *Computer systems that learn*. San Mateo, CA: Morgan Kauffman.

KEY TERMS

Confidential Information: Sensitive organizational information that should be disclosed only to authorized users. Usually stored in the database, or data warehouse, this information needs to kept secure from hackers and snoopers.

Data Perturbation: Involves modifying confidential attributes using random statistical noise. The objective of data perturbation is to prevent disclosure of confidential attributes while maximizing access to both confidential and non-confidential attributes within a database.

General Additive Data Perturbation (GADP): A general form of Additive Data Perturbation techniques. This method is based on the idea that the relationships between the confidential and non-confidential attributes should be the same before and after perturbation of the confidential attributes has occurred. Designed both to eliminate all forms of statistical bias found in other additive methods and to provide for the highest level of security of all data perturbation techniques.

Hacker: An entity outside of an organization that gains or attempts to gain access to a system or system resource without having authorization to do so.

Layered Security Approach: The use of multiple, overlapping security technologies and applications to protect an organization's information assets.

Noise: In this article, it can be viewed in two similar ways. Noise is a statistical concept that represents some form of variation in a database. In the context of using a perturbation approach to protect confidential data, noise is added to mask the confidential data item. From the perspective of using a knowledge discovery tool, noise represents the ease or difficulty in classifying individual records correctly (i.e., relative ease in defining or finding the knowledge). The noisier a database is, the more difficult it is to gain insight into knowledge present.

Snoopers: An entity within the organization (vs. a hacker who is from the outside) that gains or attempts to gain access to a system or system resource without having the authorization to do so.

Secure Knowledge Management

S. Upadhyaya
University at Buffalo, USA

H. Raghav Rao
University at Buffalo, USA

G. Padmanabhan
GE Transportation Systems, USA

INTRODUCTION

As the world is getting more and more technology savvy, the collection and distribution of information and knowledge need special attention. Progress has been made on the languages and tools needed for effective knowledge management and on the legal issues concerning the consumption and dissemination of critical knowledge. From a business perspective, a knowledge-management system (KMS) within a firm generally strives to maximize the human-capital utilization and profitability of the firm. However, security is becoming a major issue revolving around KMS; for instance, the KMS must incorporate adequate security features to prevent any unauthorized access or unauthorized dissemination of information. Acquiring the information that one needs to remain competitive while safeguarding the information one already has is a complicated task. Firms must balance the advantages of openness against its inevitable risks, and maximize the efficiency of electronic communication without making it a magnet for intruders. One must integrate offense and defense into a comprehensive strategy, and scholars have suggested that it is time to integrate intelligence and security imperatives with other knowledge-management strategies and processes (Barth, 2001).

Since the widely reported attacks on knowledge repositories in 2001 (e.g., Amazon was hit by denial-of-service attacks and the NIMDA virus hit financial markets), many organizations, especially the U.S. government, have increased their concern about KMSs. With the advent of intranets and Web access, it is even more crucial to protect critical corporate knowledge as numerous individuals now have access to the assets of a corporation. Therefore, we need effective mechanisms for securing data, information, and knowledge as well as the applications (Thuraisingham, 2003, 2004).

Security methods for knowledge-management systems may include authentication or passwords, cryptography programs, intrusion-detection systems, or access-control systems. Issues include insider threat (protecting from malicious insiders), infrastructure protection (securing against subversion attacks), and establishing correct policies, refinement, and enforcement. KMS content is much more sensitive than raw data stored in databases, and issues of privacy also become important (Thuraisingham, Chadwick, Olivier, Samarati, & Sharpston, 2002).

Asllani and Luthans (2003) surveyed over 300 knowledge managers about their job roles and found little or no evidence of security issues being considered in their jobs; their primary role was focused on communication within the organization. This article about secure knowledge management raises a number of issues in this critical area of research that need to be tackled by knowledge-management practitioners. The following sections focus on three important aspects of secure knowledge management: secure languages, digital-rights management (DRM), and secure content management (SCM).

BACKGROUND

A firm exists as a repository of knowledge over time (Zander & Kogut, 1995). Knowledge management is the methodology for systematically gathering, organizing, and disseminating information (Morey, Maybury, & Thuraisingham, 2003) in a firm. It essentially consists of processes and tools to effectively capture and share data, as well as use the knowledge of individuals within a firm. Knowledge management is about sharing information more freely such that firms derive benefit from such openness.

Secure knowledge-management (SKM) systems can be described in terms of the three *C*s: communication, collaboration, and content. SKM systems act as a gateway to the repository of intellectual content that resides within an organization. SKM systems need to source and/or provide access to knowledge that resides in multiple machines across an organization or multiple organizations for collaborative efforts. Secure languages are uti-

Figure 1. A framework for secure knowledge-management systems

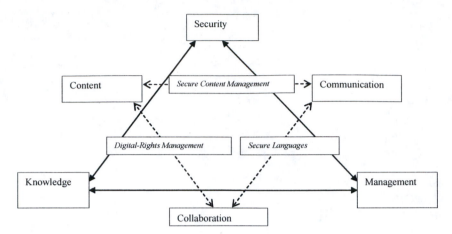

lized to transfer information safely. At the same time, digital-rights management becomes critical in cross-organizational transfers of knowledge, while access control and identity management play an important role in securing the knowledge-management system. A framework for secure knowledge management is shown in Figure 1 as two interlinked, triangular chains: The larger chain focuses on security, knowledge, and management, while the smaller triangular chain (with dotted links) focuses on content, communication, and collaboration. Different aspects within the smaller chain include secure content management, digital-rights management, and secure languages. This article focuses on the interarticulation of the different concepts in the triangles.

SECURE LANGUAGES

In order to communicate securely and collaborate with one another, organizations need to use secure languages. These languages can be implemented to enhance the security of knowledge-management systems. Some of these are detailed in the following sections.

Security-Assertion Markup Language

The security-assertion markup language (SAML) can secure the KMS from insider or outsider threat by managing access control and identity. SAML is an extensible-markup-language- (XML) based framework (Cohen, 2003) for exchanging security information. In SAML, the expression of security is in the form of assertions about subjects. Most other security approaches use a central authority to authenticate the identity or the data. However, SAML does not use a central authority that authen-

ticates the identity; it is up to the receiving application to accept if it trusts the assertion. The security-assertion markup domain model is depicted in Figure 2.

SAML shows how to represent users, identifies what data need to be transferred, and defines the process for sending and receiving authorization data (Cohen, 2003). SAML also has extensive applications in automated business-to-business (B2B) transactions that require secure transactions between the two parties. The increased collaboration among the various businesses has necessitated the need for such a technology (Patrizio, 2003). A case in point is that of Southwest Airlines (Wagner & Witty, 2003)—one of the first to use SAML-enabled identity management on a large scale to perform cross-domain trust. This implementation also marks an early step in the movement toward federated identity management.

SAML does not provide a complete security solution, but it does provide the identity-management functionality. In addition, it provides password management and access control, and a framework for implementing the "single sign-on" mechanism where authentication needs to be shared across multiple systems. Single sign-on becomes an absolute necessity when implementing complex KMSs that need to source or access data from multiple machines.

A number of commercial and open-source products provide SAML, including the following:

- Entegrity Solutions AssureAccess (http://www.entegrity.com/products/aa/aa.shtml)
- Internet2 OpenSAML (http://www.opensaml.org/)
- Netegrity SiteMinder (http://h71028.www7.hp.com/enterprise/cache/8258-0-0-225-121.aspx)

Figure 2. Security-assertion markup model

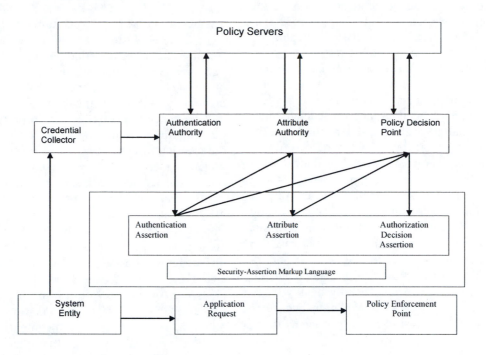

(Adapted from http://www.fawcette.com/xmlmag/2002_03/magazine/departments/marketscan/SAML/)

- RSA Security ClearTrust (http://www. rsasecurity.com/node.asp?id=1186)
- VeriSign Trust Integration Toolkit (http:// www.xmltrustcenter.org/developer/verisign/tsik/ download.htm)

Secure Knowledge-Query and Manipulation Language

KQML or the knowledge-query and -manipulation language is a language for exchanging information and knowledge. KQML focuses on an extensible set of performatives that defines the permissible operations that agents may attempt on each other's knowledge and goal stores. The performatives comprise a layer on which to develop higher level models of interagent interaction such as contract nets and negotiation. In addition, KQML provides a basic architecture for knowledge sharing through a special class of agents called communication facilitators, which coordinate the interactions of other agents. The ideas that underlie the evolving design of KQML are currently being explored through experimental prototype systems that are being used to support several test beds in such areas as concurrent engineering, intelligent design, and intelligent planning and scheduling (Lebrou, Finin, Sherman, & Rabi, 1997).

An extension of KQML is secure KQML, which is being developed to take into account security and privacy concerns that agents could encounter whenever they cross multiple administrative domains. Since traditional agent communication-language standards lack the necessary constructs that enable secure cooperation among software agents, SKQML enables KQML-speaking agents to authenticate one another, implement specific security policies based on authorization schemes, and, whenever needed, ensure the privacy of the messages exchanged. SKQML employs public-key cryptographic standards and it provides security mechanisms as an integral part of the communication language. In summary, SKQML incorporates a synthesis of public-key certificate standards and agent communication languages to achieve an infrastructure that meets the security needs of cooperating agents.

B2B Circles of Trust

As can be seen from the discussion above, while the secure languages do allow secure communication to an extent, they are not complete solutions. An alternate mechanism for enhancing secure communication and collaboration across organizations in the knowledge-management environment has been termed "circles of trust."

Circles of trust involve two or more organizations sharing supplier or customer authentication information among themselves via a common interface or single sign-on capability. XML provides the basis for operating circles of trust (Varney, 2003).

One of the premier organizations espousing the concept of circles of trust is the Liberty Alliance—a consortium of more than 150 organizations working worldwide to create open, technical specifications for federated network identity. The alliance outlines the specifications for simplified sign-on capabilities using federated network-identity architecture. Permission-based attribute sharing is utilized to enable organizations to provide users with choice and control over the use and disclosure of personal information. A commonly accepted platform and mechanism for building and managing identity-based Web services is based on open industry standards. The Liberty Alliance specification addresses privacy and security concerns, and enables the participating organization to build more secure, privacy–friendly identity-based services that can comply with local regulations and create a trusted relationship with customers and partners (Varney, 2003).

DIGITAL-RIGHTS MANAGEMENT

The confluence of content and collaboration across organizations has brought up the concept of digital-rights management. DRM has traditionally focused on security and encryption to alleviate copyright-infringement and unauthorized-use problems. In order to do so, DRM techniques have implemented a mechanism to lock content and limit distribution to subscribed customers. Current DRM solutions include the description, identification, trading, protection, monitoring, and tracking of all forms of rights usages over both tangible and intangible assets including the management of rights holders' relationships (Iannella, 2001).

DRM systems are supposed to serve markets in which the participants have conflicting goals and cannot be fully trusted, yet need to collaborate and share knowledge content with each other. This adversarial situation introduces interesting new twists on classical problems studied in cryptology and security research, such as key management and access control (Feigenbaum, Freedman, Sander, & Shostack, 2002). Furthermore, novel business models and applications often require novel security mechanisms. Recent research has also proposed new primitives for DRM that make it possible to identify content in an adversarial setting.

Functional Architecture

The overall DRM framework suited to building digital-rights-enabled systems is illustrated in Figure 3. The functional architecture stipulates the roles and behavior of a number of cooperating and interoperating modules under the three areas of intellectual property (IP): asset creation, management, and usage (Figure 3).

The concept of intellectual-property asset creation and capture refers to the key question of how to manage the creation of content so it can be easily traded. This includes asserting rights when content is first created (or reused and extended with appropriate rights to do so) by various content creators or providers. The IP asset-creation and -capture module supports (a) rights validation to ensure that content being created from existing content includes the rights to do so, (b) rights creation to allow rights to be assigned to new content, such as specifying the rights owners and allowable usage permissions, and (c) a rights workflow to allow for content to be processed through a series of work-flow steps for review and/or approval of rights (and content).

IP asset management involves the management and enabling of the trade of content. This includes accepting content from creators into an asset-management system. The trading systems need to manage the descriptive metadata and rights metadata (e.g., parties, usages, payments, etc.).

The IP asset-management module supports repository functions to enable the access or retrieval of content in potentially distributed databases and the access or retrieval of metadata. The metadata cover information regarding parties, rights, and descriptions of the work. The module also supports trading functions that enable the assignment of licenses to parties who have traded agreements for rights over content, including payments from licensees to rights holders (e.g., royalty payments). In some cases, the content may need to go through fulfillment operations to satisfy the license agreement. For example, the content may be encrypted, protected, or packaged for a particular type of desktop usage environment.

Once the IP asset has been traded, this module focuses on how to manage the usage of content. This includes supporting constraints over traded content in specific desktop systems or software.

The IP asset-usage module supports permissions management to enable the usage environment to honor the rights associated with the content. For example, if the user only has the right to view the document, then printing will not be allowed. It also allows tracking management to

Figure 3. Digital-rights-management architecture

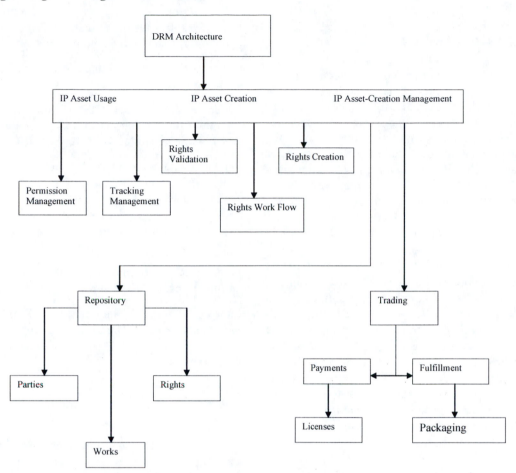

enable the monitoring of the usage of content where such tracking is part of the agreed-to license conditions (e.g., the user has a license to play a video 10 times; Iannella, 2001).

SECURE CONTENT MANAGEMENT

The final link in the secure knowledge-management chain is the one that links content and communication, that is, secure content management. The Internet is a tremendous tool for enterprises to share intellectual property with customers, partners, and suppliers. It is an instant distribution network any corporation can use to improve communications while lowering operating costs (Ogren, 2003). The Yankee Group estimates that the market for secure content-delivery products and services amounted to $302 million in 2002 and will grow to $580 million by 2007. It is widely believed that more destructive and harder-to-detect threats, spam, legal liability, employee productivity, and compliance with privacy regulations will continue

to fuel the growth of the secure content-management market over the next several years (http://www.csoonline.com/analyst/report1490.html).

The Internet, instant messaging, and the availability of Web content have transformed everyday business activities (Robb, 2003). As a result, CIOs (chief information officers) and IT management are increasingly looking for solutions to help enforce corporate policy, comply with privacy regulations, limit legal liability, increase employee productivity, and reduce network bandwidth consumption. All this is made possible by secure content-management solutions.

Secure content-management tools help to correctly label business-related content. The first generation of SCM products is now beginning to appear on the market. Generally, they consist of the following features: antivirus capabilities, proactive identification to block only malicious code, smart filtering of spam and URLs (uniform resource locators), keyword identification to safeguard against the transmission of proprietary and confidential information via e-mail, and centralized management of all facets to bring simplicity to the task of security administration (Robb, 2003).

Secure Content Delivery

With the advent of the Internet, content that enterprises once closely guarded in private databases is now being placed on the Internet to save distribution costs throughout the supply chain and to increase customer satisfaction. A Web initiative can take multiple forms: for example, an employee portal or Web-enabled self-service partner extranet. Each such initiative involves delivering business value. The Web has been instrumental in expanding communication channels and providing endless opportunities. Globalization has led to increased collaboration among trading partners that require the sharing of confidential information. The quest for cost-effective solutions for secure content delivery is intense since it must not only ensure the privacy of the electronic customers, but also reliably deliver important information only to designated recipients.

The trend has been to centralize identity management and documents in secure server repositories and portals accessed by browsers, and to avoid the complexities of client-side software installations. Content in transit has traditionally been protected by secure-sockets-layer (SSL) communications for browsers, and virtual private networks (VPNs) for application access, encrypted e-mail, and proprietary application solutions.

CONCLUSION

We are moving into a knowledge-based economy in the 21st century. Knowledge-based assets are gaining in importance, and it is becoming extremely important to protect these assets. In the area of national security, the knowledge that must be shared comes from many fields including homeland-defense activities, tactical intelligence missions, diplomatic channels, and direct military support. A range of KMS approaches and technologies and their security features need to be examined to enable critical intelligence gathering. Critical issues in secure knowledge management include content, communication, and collaboration. In this context, SAML, SKQML, circles of trust, DRM, secure content management, and secure content-delivery mechanisms would ensure the security and privacy of knowledge repositories.

REFERENCES

Barth, S. (2001). Open yet guarded: Protecting the knowledge enterprise. *Knowledge Management Magazine*.

Cohen, F. (2003). Debunking SAML myths and misunderstandings. *IBM Developer Works*.

Esllani, B., & Luthans, F. (2003). What knowledge managers really do: An empirical and comparative analysis. *Journal of Knowledge Management, 7*(3), 53-66.

Feigenbaum, J., Freedman, M., Sander, T., & Shostack, A. (2002). Privacy engineering in digital rights management systems. In *Lecture notes in computer science: Vol. 2320. Proceedings of the 2001 ACM Workshop on Security and Privacy in Digital Rights Management*. Berlin, Germany: Springer.

Iannella, R. (2001). Digital rights management (DRM) architectures. *D-Lib Magazine, 7*(6).

Labrou, Y., Finin, T., Sherman, A., & Rabi, M. (1997). *A proposal for a new KQML specification*. Baltimore, MD: Computer Science and Electrical Engineering Department, University of Maryland.

Morey, D., Maybury, M., & Thuraisingham, B. (2003). *Knowledge management: Classic and contemporary works*. MIT Press.

Ogren, E. (2003). Secure content delivery protects shared, transmitted and post-delivery digital assets. *CSO*.

Patrizio, A. (2003). *SAML advances single sign-on prospects*. Fawcette Technical Publications.

Robb, D. (2003). The emergence of secure content management. *IT Management*.

Thuraisingham, B. (2003). Data mining and cyber security. *Proceedings of the Third International Conference on Quality Software (QSIC'03)*.

Thuraisingham, B. (2004). Cybertrust, data and applications security. *Proceedings of the Secure Knowledge Management Workshop*, Buffalo, NY.

Thuraisingham, B., Chadwick, D., Olivier, S. M., Samarati, P., & Sharpston, E. (2002). Privacy and civil liberties. In *IFIP Conference Proceedings* (256). Kluwer.

Varney, C. (Ed.). (2003). *Privacy and security best practices*. Liberty Alliance Project.

Wagner, R., & Witty, R. (2003). *Southwest Airlines shows SAML's promise.* Gartner Research.

Zander, U., & Kogut, B. (1995). Knowledge and the speed of the transfer and limitation of organizational capabilities: An empirical test. *Organization Science, 6.*

KEY TERMS

Digital-Rights Management: DRM is a platform to protect and securely deliver content on a computer.

IP Asset Management: This involves management and enabling the trade of content, and includes accepting content from creators into an asset-management system.

Knowledge Management: Knowledge management is the methodology for systematically gathering, organizing, and disseminating information. It essentially consists of processes and tools to effectively capture and share data as well as use the knowledge of individuals within a firm.

Secure Content-Delivery Space: Content that enterprises once closely guarded in private databases is now being placed on the Internet to save distribution costs. Hence, content has to be delivered securely. The mechanisms that allow this form the secure content-delivery space.

Secure Knowledge Management: The management of knowledge while adhering to principles of security and privacy. Enterprises must find cost-effective solutions to ensure the privacy of electronic customers, reliably deliver important information only to designated recipients, and offer revenue-generating services based on access profiles.

Secure Knowledge-Management Trends: The trend has been to centralize identity management and documents in secure server repositories and portals accessed by browsers.

Security-Assertion Markup Language: SAML is an XML-based framework for exchanging security information. This security information is expressed in the form of assertions about subjects (either human or computer) that have an identity in some security domain. Assertions can convey information about authentication acts and authorization decisions about whether subjects are allowed to access certain resources.

S

Sketching in Knowledge Creation and Management

Fernando Ferri
Istituto di Ricerche sulla Popolazione e le Politiche Sociali - CNR, Italy

Patrizia Grifoni
Istituto di Ricerche sulla Popolazione e le Politiche Sociali - CNR, Italy

INTRODUCTION

A sketch is a schematic representation of an image containing a set of objects or concepts. When people need to express and communicate a new idea, they often sketch a rough picture to represent it. Drawing a sketch helps to develop and explore new ideas and enables useful reflection on an idea, elaborating possible alternatives and promoting its evolution. The development of different interaction and communication tools has produced new attention to more natural interaction and communication modalities, including sketching. Hand-drawn sketching is easy and intuitive to use to communicate with others, and human-computer interaction is also simplified.

Because the knowledge to be represented and managed in human-computer interaction is typically multidimensional, for example, spatial and temporal data, images, video, and so forth, it can be managed by a representation having the same dimensions. A sketch can be very useful for representing concepts and complex information because it is typically multidimensional and people naturally use sketching as a medium for concisely representing the reality of interest.

Sketches are characterized by vagueness, incompleteness, and ambiguity. It is therefore essential to solve ambiguities caused by hand-drawn sketching. These may be produced by various factors, such as the variability of hand-drawn input and different interpretations for the same input. In addition, the drawing tools used may introduce noise.

This article considers sketch interpretation based on drawing behaviour in different contexts. One behaviour type is characterized by the objectives and features common to all the users, while another is related to the specific context in which the sketch was designed, taking into account complex information on the application domain, the interaction tool, and the user's skill in drawing sketches.

BACKGROUND

Some cognitive scientists highlight the relevance of sketching for the external representation of ideas and problems. In particular, some works (Verstijnen, 1997) have studied the importance of sketching for expressing new ideas in the creative process. Drawing a sketch does not require a high level of precision. However, simple corrections or drawing the sketch from a different point of view can entail its complete redesign. Familiar objects are most frequently drawn using a part-by-part strategy: this in accordance with the user preference to complete one object before drawing a second one. This analysis confirms the results of studies carried out by Kavakli, Scrivener, and Ball (1998). In fact, sketches are drawn using a part-by-part approach 73% to 90% of the time. They observed the connection between the functional aspect of each part of an object and its drawing. In particular, drawing multifunctional parts of objects implies a non-part-by-part drawing. Another work (Scrivener, Tseng, & Ball, 2002) considers a particular context: (a) when the user draws an object from memory, and (b) when the user draws an object by copying it. In the first case, the drawing strategy is part by part if the object's geometry is identified. If its geometry is confused, and consequently the function of each part is also confused, then the object is drawn using a non-part-by-part strategy.

Some applications manage only a few types of graphical objects, such as sketch-based geographical query languages (Blaser & Egenhofer, 2000), a sketch-based user interface editor like SILK (Landay & Myers, 2001), or sketch-based diagrammatic systems and query languages. Several systems have been designed to recognize formal sketches in a specific diagrammatic notation. These were specifically designed for UML, finite-state machines, flowcharts, networks, program class structures, and others (Blostein, Lank, & Zanibbi, 2000; Kanungo, Haralick, & Dori, 1995; Lank, Thorley, Chen, & Blostein, 2001; Zanibbi, Blostein, & Cordy, 2002). In this type of applica-

Figure 1. Some examples of sketches in different application domains

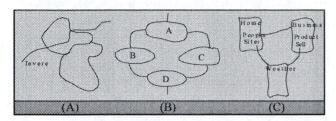

Figure 2. A sketch and some possible interpretations

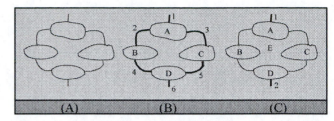

tion, it is usually necessary to manage several types of graphical objects describing the diagrams and their spatial relationships. Other applications need to manage very complex objects. This is the case of languages for image retrieval and tools for computer-aided design (CAD; Lin, Thomsen, & Landay, 2002).

The developed applications are usually not sufficiently general. They normally involve specific sketches (i.e., one kind of diagram only) and do not consider the possibility of deletion or modification. Some other applications enable these operations, but they must be performed by the user through a graphical command or symbol.

Sometimes, one kind of information lacking in an image can be associated to the sketching process: the sequence of drawing actions defining the sketch. This is because a sketch contains both static and dynamic information. The first refers to the image produced by the sketching process, while the second refers to the drawing actions. Techniques and methodologies defined for image interpretation can also be used effectively to interpret sketches (Mussio, Bruno, & Esposito, 1994). The drawing actions provide further suggestions to correctly interpret the sketch and solve its ambiguities. Ferri and Grifoni (2003), Kavakli et al. (1998), Scrivener, Ball, and Tseng (2000), and Scrivener et al. (2002) have carried out studies on this subject.

It is also possible to consider another aspect of sketching: the drawing behaviour of different users. One behaviour type is characterized by objectives and features common to all users, while another is related to the specific context in which the sketch was designed. The context takes account of complex information on the application domain, the interaction tool, the user's skill in drawing sketches, and so on. The first kind of behaviour (context independent) produces a sketch interpretation independent of the user. The second (context dependent) produces a sketch interpretation according to the user characteristics. This is why some sketching behaviours are connected with user categories.

MAIN FOCUS OF THE ARTICLE

The ambiguity of sketches can determine a mismatching with a single corresponding interpretation. Sketches can therefore have multiple interpretations. This occurs because, on one hand, a unique space is used to express different kinds of information, and on the other, signs on the sketch may not completely represent the semantics of the information relating to them. The information provided by the sketch may thus be insufficient to identify a unique interpretation. Ambiguities may also be caused by noise from tools and sensors, or by cotermination failure (where pen strokes do not meet at their end points; Mahoney & Fromherz, 2002). The context is often very useful to correctly interpret and disambiguate the sketch.

The context may consider a set of operative variables that influence users' drawing strategies and behaviour (application domain, information devices, interaction tools, user goals, etc.). The system's ability to identify the context could be useful for the sketch's correct interpretation. Such information can be used to interpret the user's drawing strategy and behaviour.

In the following section, sketch ambiguity is presented and discussed using one of the operative variables influencing the user's drawing strategy and behaviour: the application domain.

The Sketch and Different Application Domains

Depending on the application domain, sketches can have different characteristics and needs in representing concepts, objects, and relationships. Figure 1 shows three sketches concerning the related domains: geographical (Figure 1A), diagram representation (Figure 1B), and hypertext representation (Figure 1C).

The sketch in Figure 2A representing a diagram has various interpretations, two of which are shown in Figures 2B and 2C. Figure 2B considers the sketch as formed by 10 graphical components: four closed shapes (A, B, C,

803

Figure 3. Another sketch and some possible interpretations

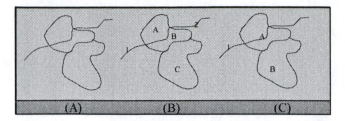

- Each sequence of strokes represents a closed shape or a polyline.
- Each closed shape, polyline, and point is part of the sketch's simple or complex objects.
- The user generally completes the drawing of one object before beginning a second one.
- The user draws a complex object starting from the external parts and continues by specifying its particulars.
- The user draws different objects of a sketch in accordance with a spatial contiguity (tending to begin a new object near the previous one).

In addition to these previous behaviours related to spatial and temporal concepts, bad sketch drawing must be considered as a context-independent spatial factor. In fact, it is impossible for a user to completely represent his or her goal through a sketch because even the most precise and expert user makes a schematic representation of objects and concepts and adds noise to the sketch (e.g., line cotermination failure, etc.).

However, some sketching tools can increase imprecision. This second type of imprecision (related to the interaction tool) can also be considered dependent from the context.

The interpretations of the sketch's spatial aspects consider the sketch's spatial information in order to list its elementary components, distinguishing among types of components: closed shapes, polylines, and points. They identify spatial relationships existing between elementary components. However, temporal aspects play an important role for the correct interpretation of a sketch. In this article, temporal aspects concern both the analysis from the temporal point of view of the sequence of the strokes drawn, and remake (cancellation and eventual redrawing of a part of the sketch). In fact, analogously to spatial relationships, for the correct interpretation of the sketch, it is important to consider temporal relationships in the sketching process between strokes and components.

The information derived allows the identification of graphical components that are closely related from a temporal point of view. These components are obtained by composing the elementary components obtained considering spatial aspects, and are thus more complex than these elements. They could be considered as the graphical components the user wants to draw, however, they are not the simple or complex objects of the sketch.

Each component can be characterized temporally by a set of time intervals: that is, the intervals during which the component was drawn. For example, in the sketch of Figure 4A consisting of two strokes, represented in Figure 4B, the two closed shapes (Figure 4A) can be characterized by the time intervals of Figures 4C and 4D.

D) and six polylines (1-6). Figure 2C considers the sketch as formed by 7 graphical components: five closed shapes (A, B, C, D, E) and just two polylines (1-2). Obviously, because the sketch is a diagram, the correct interpretation is Figure 2B. However, changing the application domain can lead to changes in determining the correct interpretation. So, if the sketch in Figure 2A is not a diagram but a map, Figure 2C is probably the correct interpretation.

In Figure 3A another example of ambiguity is presented. The sketch has at least two interpretations as shown in Figures 3B and 3C. Obviously, if the goal of the user is to sketch a river passing through a region, the correct interpretation is that of Figure 3C.

A sketch cannot be correctly interpreted through consideration of the application domain alone. For instance, the interaction tool must also be considered as a context variable because its type can influence the introduction of some noise and errors in the sketch. Consequently, user drawing strategies and behaviours can only be correctly interpreted by using all the significant context variables for a given application.

Context-Independent Behaviours and Their Interpretation

Context-independent behaviours and drawing strategies are usually related to spatial and temporal concepts such as contiguity, inclusion, part-of, consequence, and so forth. In fact, space and time are concepts that can be considered common to all, and their related drawing behaviours are therefore generally applicable for sketch interpretation. A nonexhaustive set of behaviours and drawing strategies (related to spatial and temporal concepts) follows:

- The user draws strokes.
- Each stroke represents a closed shape (triangle, rectangle, regular and irregular polygons), polyline, or point.

Figure 4. Temporal information related to the sketch

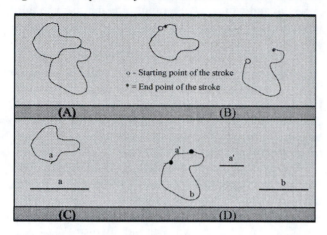

Temporal information can be very useful in identifying the user's goals. In fact, people tend to draw all of a component or graphic object before moving on to a new one. This important criterion can be used in two ways to approach the sketch's correct interpretation:

• Minimizing the total number of breaks between intervals for all components; that is, each component is drawn as a stroke (preferably) without interruption.

• Minimizing the total waiting time (of breaks) between intervals for all components; that is, each series of strokes refers to only one component. This is very important if the user prefers to draw a component through a series of strokes. This minimization can also be applied for recognizing complex objects.

Context-Dependent Behaviours and Their Interpretation

The interpretation of context-dependent behaviours provides the semantic of the sketch using context information. Automatic sketch recognition, as discussed in the previous sections, is a very complex task because ambiguous situations must be interpreted. Ambiguity is produced by the lack of one-to-one correspondence between the user's elementary drawing actions (strokes) and the objects to be represented. In fact, ambiguity is produced by the need to define a more specific correspondence between sketching actions and objects. However, the user can draw each object with a meaning in the specific application context using different drawing sequences. Ambiguity can also be produced by a bad sketch or by noise caused by the sketching tools.

Some ambiguities can be correctly interpreted only by considering the sketch in its context of drawing. This can

be characterized specifying the admissible objects only, the set of admissible relationships existing between them, the behaviours, and/or the drawing strategies of the users in the context.

A sketch interpretation is therefore correct if each drawing action is part of the sketch of one or more admissible objects, the relationships between objects have a sense in the context, and the behaviours and/or drawing strategies and given interpretations correspond to the goals of the users' drawing activities.

The introduction highlighted that user behaviour during sketching can be described from as many different points of view as there are different contexts represented. For this reason, a set of contexts must be considered in order to describe user behaviour. For instance, the application domain, interaction tool, and user's skill may be necessary for a complete description. This approach implies two different problems. The first is due to the fact that sets of behaviours referring to two different contexts may be inconsistent as there may be contradictory behaviours between them. For this reason, a priority must be given to activated contexts in order to interpret user behaviour. The second problem is related to the identification of the context where the user begins to interact. It can be solved using three different approaches. In the first, the context is defined by the user selecting (for example) the application domain and specifying the interaction tool used and his or her skill. In the second, the system captures this information from the sketch and the drawing process. The third approach is a combination of the first two.

The first approach obviously simplifies interpretation. In fact, the set of elements of the language and their relationships are defined in the context identified by the user. However, this approach cannot manage possible changes to the operational situation (for instance, change of the interaction tool or an incorrect user-skill evaluation). The second approach is more complex as it requires the identification of a set of candidate contexts from the sketch, which may not always be possible. For example, a query of a database of images could be incorrectly interpreted as a query of a geographical database or vice versa, or the skill for similar user activities could be erroneously interpreted. The third approach has the advantage of flexibility but also the difficulties of the second, especially when the user does not provide a description at the beginning of interaction.

In order to introduce some considerations about the context-dependent interpretation, two application domains are considered: query languages for geographical information systems (GISs), and the data-flow diagram (DFD; De Marco, 1979). Problems of sketching recognition connected with drawing inaccuracy (nonclosed polygon) are not considered.

Figure 5. Three configurations representing typical ambiguous situations

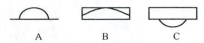

In visual query languages for GIS, users can use graphical objects to draw their queries, expressing in the query semantics by simply juxtaposing graphical objects on the screen. This allows easier and more intuitive specification of query constraints. Simple graphical objects are used to emphasize the aspects that are topologically relevant in representing the properties of more complex geographic objects. These graphical objects represent the generic instances of geographic objects or classes stored in the GIS database.

Visual query languages for GIS can be usually characterized considering three elements represented by three kinds of graphical objects: polygons, polylines, and points, which allow the modeling of geometric entities in space. Geographical information systems represent both geometric characteristics of the geographical elements and the relationships among them.

Visual query languages for GIS also consider topological relationships among the elements of the language, which are the most significant of the spatial relationships introduced in literature.

The three configurations presented in Figure 5 represent some typical ambiguous situations that can be solved using this context.

For Figure 5A, two possible interpretations can be given. The first considers the sketch as being formed by two polylines, where one of them has its boundary intersecting the other. The second considers the sketch as a polygon with a polyline touching the polygon. Some tests with users have demonstrated that they tend to draw the polygon before the polyline when defining a spatial relationship between the two, and thus this interpretation can be excluded.

Three interpretations are possible for Figure 5B. The first considers the sketch as being formed by a polygon containing a polyline whose boundaries and one internal point touch the polygon's boundaries. The second considers the sketch as formed by a polygon and two touch-ing polylines whose boundaries are the boundaries of the polygon, and which have a point in common. The third interpretation considers the sketch as formed by three polygons.

In this case, too, the last interpretation can be excluded. In fact, two polygons are not usually drawn by splitting a polygon in this context (the user focuses on two different areas instead of splitting one area into two of them). However, choosing between the first and second interpretation is very complex, and the use of temporal information is not very effective.

Figure 5C can be interpreted as (a) a polygon and a polyline whose boundaries touch the polygon boundaries, or (b) formed by two polygons. In this case, temporal information is not relevant for the interpretation; in fact, the sketch could be drawn with only two strokes.

To solve the ambiguities for Figures 5B and 5C, the context could be used not to consider the user's behaviour during the drawing of the sequence for querying geographical databases, but to consider the frequency of the configuration in the context of a geographical query. According to this approach, for Figure 5C, the frequency of the configuration with the two touching polygons is greater than the other and it must thus be considered the most probable interpretation.

In visual query languages for GIS users, combining the three considered elements can obtain a significant number of possible and valid configurations. Sometimes a configuration can have more than one interpretation. In all these cases, there is an ambiguity problem to solve using temporal information and context-dependent information.

A Data Flow Diagram (DFD) is a tool for modeling information flow and producing a functional analysis of system information and incoming and outgoing data. It provides a graphical description of the data in a system and how the process transforms such data. This context can be characterized considering four kinds of graphical objects: data flows, processes, data stores, and external entities. Each has its own representation, given in Figure 6.

In DFD, the elements of the graph must satisfy the following constraints.

1. A process
   • must be linked to at least an input data flow and an output data flow.

Figure 6. Elements of the language in the data-flow-diagram context

| Data flow | ⟶ | Data store | |
| Process | | External entity | |

Figure 7. The different configurations considered in the DFD context

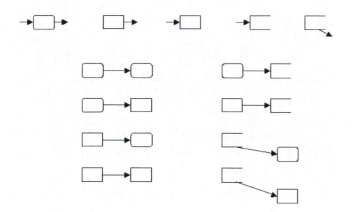

2. A data flow
    *   has a direction.
    *   has a process (or an external entity) at one or both of the two extremes, producing or acquiring the data flow.
3. A data store can have one or more data flows as input and output.
4. An external entity has data flows as input and output.

The system considers only the correct configurations (represented in Figure 7). The others might be approximated to the nearest correct configuration. When the user draws a sketch of a DFD, the system must recognize the closed shapes representing the four different elements and verify the DFD constraints. The use of constraints can resolve ambiguities persisting after the context-independent interpretation. In fact, the limited number of language elements and admissible configurations among them helps automatic interpretation of the sketch.

Different from visual query languages for GIS, the DFD rules define a limited number of possible configurations. For this reason, the ambiguity management in DFD is simpler than in visual query languages for GIS.

FUTURE TRENDS

The amount, intensity, and accuracy of information that is communicated from computer to user are typically far greater than the amount, intensity, and accuracy of information from user to computer. Graphics, animations, audio, and other media can furnish large amounts of information rapidly, but the user does not yet have the means of inputting comparably large amounts of information.

This asymmetry is caused by three main factors. The first factor is the inadequacy of input devices; they are tools conceived specifically for human-computer interaction and they do not represent a natural interaction manner to communicate for humans. The second factor is the inadequacy in modeling the complexity of information and knowledge to manage and recognize. The third factor is the inadequacy in integrating different input modalities.

Future input mechanisms may continue the actual trend toward naturalness and expressivity by allowing users to perform natural gestures or operations and translating them for computer input. These input devices will improve the amount of information from user to computer and represent a part of the complexity of human communication, typically multimodal. In this context, there is very promising research concerning the integration of sketches and other input modalities such as voice.

CONCLUSION

Drawing a sketch is a good approach for expressing ideas spontaneously and improving communication and cooperation among different users. As the Internet and multimodality develop, this area is becoming a very intense research goal for human-computer interaction. However, using sketches to interact requires the interpretation and resolution of their ambiguities. This article proposed some considerations on sketch interpretation based on user behaviours and drawing strategies, both context independent and context dependent. In particular, context-independent sketch interpretation uses spatial and temporal information related to the sketch and the drawing process. Context-dependent sketch interpretation uses context information to provide the correct interpretation. Context information concerns elements of the language, relationships, behaviours, and drawing strategies of the user in the specific context.

REFERENCES

Blaser, A. D., & Egenhofer, M. J. (2000). A visual tool for querying geographic databases. *Proceedings of ACM AVI 2000* (pp. 211-216).

Blostein, D., Lank, E., & Zanibbi, R. (2000). Treatment of diagrams in document image. In M. Anderson, P. Cheng, & V. Haarslev (Eds.), *Lecture notes in computer science, 1889. Theory and application of diagrams* (pp. 330-344). Berlin: Springer Verlag.

De Marco, T. (1979). *Structured analysis and system specification.* Prentice Hall.

Ferri, F., & Grifoni, P. (2003). Vectorization of graphical components in sketch-based interfaces. In *Lecture notes in computer science: Vol. 2822. Databases in networked information systems* (pp. 231-244). Berlin: Springer Verlag.

Kanungo, T., Haralick, R., & Dori, D. (1995). Understanding engineering drawings: A survey. *Proceedings of International Workshop on Graphic Recognition* (pp. 119-130).

Kavakli, M., Scrivener, S.A.R., & Ball, L. J. (1998). Structure in idea sketching behaviour. *Design Studies, 19*(4), 485-518.

Landay, J.A., & Myers, B.A. (2001). Sketching interfaces: Toward more human interface design. *IEEE Computer, 34*(3), 56-64.

Lank, E., Thorley, J., Chen, S., & Blostein, D. (2001). An on-line system for recognizing hand drawn UML diagrams. *Proceedings of the International Conference on Document Analysis and Recognition* (pp. 356-360).

Lin, C., Thomsen, M., & Landay, J.A. (2002). A visual language for sketching large and complex interactive designs. *Proceedings of ACM CHI 2002* (pp. 307-314).

Mahoney, J.V., & Fromherz, M.P.J. (2002). Three main concerns in sketch recognition and an approach to addressing them. *AAAI Spring Symposium on Sketch Understanding* (pp. 105-112).

Mussio, P., Bruno, N., & Esposito, F. (1994). Image interpretation and ambiguities. In V. Cantoni (Ed.), *Human and machine vision: Analogies and divergencies* (pp. 319-338). Plenum Press.

Scrivener, S. A. R, Ball, L.J., & Tseng, W. (2000). Uncertainty and sketching behaviour. *Design Studies, 21*(5), 465-481.

Scrivener, S.A.R., Tseng, W. S.-W., & Ball, L. J. (2002). The impact of functional knowledge on sketching. *Proceedings of the Fourth International Conference on Creativity and Cognition* (pp. 57-64). ACM Press.

Verstijnen, I.M. (1997). *Sketches of creative discovery: A psychological inquiry into the role of imagery and sketching in creative discovery.* PhD thesis, Delft University of Technology. ACM Press.

Zanibbi, R., Blostein, D., & Cordy, J. (2002). Recognizing mathematical expressions using tree transformation. *IEEE Transactions on Pattern Analysis and Machine Intelligence, 24*(11), 1455-1467.

KEY TERMS

Closed Shape: A closed shape is represented by the ordered set of points and the ordered set of lines connecting points. The start point and the end point are coincident in closed shapes.

Computer-Aided Design: Software used in art, architecture, engineering, and manufacturing to assist in precision drawing.

Data-Flow Diagram: A graphical model describing data in a system and how the process transforms such data. It is a tool for modeling information flow and producing a functional analysis.

Diagrammatic Systems: A computerized system that adopts different diagrammatic representation forms. Many different systems are currently used in a wide variety of contexts: logic teaching, automated reasoning, specifying computer programs, reasoning about situations in physics, graphical user interfaces to computer programs, and so on.

Geographical Information System (GIS): A computerized database system used for the capture, conversion, storage, retrieval, analysis, and display of spatial objects.

Pictorial Query Language: A specialized query language devoted to querying a database by a picture. These kinds of languages focus on spatial relationships existing among the elements of the database.

Polyline: A polyline is represented by the ordered set of points and the ordered set of lines connecting consecutive points. The direction of a polyline is from the start point to the end point.

Stroke: A stroke is represented by the set of points starting from the point at which a designer presses the pen (or another drawing tool) to the point at which the pen is lifted.

Visual Query Language: A specialized language for requesting information that allows the user to specify his or her goals in a two- (or more) dimensional way with visual expressions: spatial arrangements of textual and graphical symbols.

Social Capital Knowledge

Daniel L. Davenport
University of Kentucky Chandler Medical Center, USA

Clyde W. Holsapple
University of Kentucky, USA

INTRODUCTION

Organizations have capabilities for creating and sharing knowledge (intellectual capital) that give them their distinctive advantage over other institutional arrangements, such as markets (Ghoshal & Nahapiet, 1998). But, what is the basis of a firm's knowledge development capabilities? At least in part, the answer is that these capabilities stem from the social capital that an organization possesses as a result of bringing people together for extended periods of time, creating interdependence through specialization and integration, forcing interaction, and providing boundaries and directions. Following the resource-based theory of the firm (Conner & Prahalad, 1996), enterprises that cultivate particular forms of social capital are likely to realize competitive advantages (Ghoshal & Nahapiet, 1998).

This article traces the connections between an organization's social capital and the organization's development of knowledge. Understanding these connections is important for leaders of knowledge management initiatives, particularly if they seek to leverage knowledge production into enhanced competitiveness. We begin with a background discussion of the nature of social capital including its structural, cognitive, and relational dimensions. This is followed by a consideration of intellectual capital (i.e., knowledge that can be used to achieve an organization's purpose) and an explanation of the supportive role of social capital in furnishing conditions necessary for developing this knowledge. We describe a model of knowledge conversion processes whereby intellectual capital is developed within a social capital context known as Ba. Some future trends in socially-based processes of knowing by people and organizations are outlined, followed by concluding remarks.

BACKGROUND

Social capital is the "sum of actual and potential resources embedded within, available through, and derived from the network of relationships possessed by an individual or social unit. Social capital thus comprises both the network and the assets that may be mobilized through that network" (Nahapiet & Ghoshal, 1998, p. 243). All social capital constitutes some aspect of social structure and facilitates the actions of individuals within that structure (Coleman, 1990). Social capital is inherent in relationships among persons and is a productive asset facilitating some forms of social action while inhibiting others. It has three dimensions: (1) structural, (2) relational, and (3) cognitive.

The *structural dimension* of social capital includes three "properties of the social system and of the network of relations as a whole" (Nahapiet & Ghoshal, 1998, p. 244): appropriable organization structure, network ties, and network configuration within a set of relationships. Appropriable organization structure refers to structure created for one purpose which provides a valuable source of resources for another purpose. Network ties are social relations that provide information benefits in the form of access, timing, and referrals. Network configuration refers to the structure of network ties that influence the range of information and the cost in accessing it.

The *cognitive dimension* of social capital includes those resources providing shared representations, interpretations, and systems of meaning among parties (Cicourel, 1973). Examples are shared language and codes, ontologies, and shared narratives.

- **Shared language and codes:** The means by which people discuss and exchange information, ask questions, and conduct business. Language and codes organize sensory data into perceptual categories and provide a frame of reference for observing and interpreting our environment. Language and codes filter our awareness. A common language enhances the capacities for sharing knowledge and for combining knowledge.
- **Ontologies:** Simplified, abstract views of a domain adopted by participants in an organization that characterizes key concepts and offers axioms about them and their relationships (Gruber, 1995). Commitment by participants to an ontology promotes sharing and reuse of knowledge, collabora-

tive exploration of the domain, and development of new knowledge about the domain.

- **Shared narratives:** Myths, stories, and metaphors that provide powerful means in communities for creating, exchanging, and preserving rich sets of meanings (Denning, 2000).

The *relational dimension* of social capital includes the kinds of personal relationships that people have developed with each other through a history of interactions (Granovetter, 1992). This dimension stems from, or is conditioned by, an organization's culture and subcultures. It includes the trust, norms, obligations, and identification within a set of relationships.

Trust is a belief that results of an entity's intended action will be beneficial (or at least not harmful) to our interests (Miztal, 1996). Factors that promote trust include open communication, participation in decision-making, sharing valuable knowledge, and sharing viewpoints and attitudes (Mishra & Morrisey, 1990). Where relationships are high in trust, people are more willing to engage in social exchange, in general, and cooperative interaction, in particular (Nahapiet & Ghoshal, 1998). A norm exists when the socially-defined right to control an action is held not by the actor but by others; norms are expectations that bind (Kramer & Goldman, 1995). Norms may have a significant influence on exchange processes involved in knowledge development, opening up access to parties for the exchange of knowledge and ensuring the motivation to engage in such exchange (Nahapiet & Ghoshal, 1998).

Obligations and expectations refer to commitments or responsibilities to undertake some activity in the future. They differ from norms in that they are developed within the context of a particular relationship (Coleman, 1990). Obligations and expectations are likely to influence both access to parties for exchanging and combining knowledge and the motivation to combine and exchange such knowledge (Nahapiet & Ghoshal, 1998). Identification refers to a self perception of belonging within a social group or network, carrying with it an adherence to its culture and an understanding of characteristics or boundaries of that group that distinguish it from other groups.

INTELLECTUAL CAPITAL CREATION AND SOCIAL CAPITAL

Intellectual capital (IC) has been defined in many ways. Relative to social capital, IC is defined as the knowledge of an organization's participants that results in a competitive advantage for that organization (Stewart, 1991), or as knowledge and knowing capability belonging to a social collective (Nahapiet & Ghoshal, 1998). Moran and Ghoshal (1996) maintain that all resources, including intellectual capital, are created primarily through the generic processes of combination and exchange of existing resources. (We note that it is unclear whether creation involving discovery, insight, or imagination can be fully described in terms of combination and exchange.) Intellectual capital, then, is developed through processes that combine knowledge and experience of different parties and is therefore dependent on exchange, which implies that knowledge development in an organization is influenced by the organization's social capital.

Because exchange often occurs through social interaction and coactivity permitted by a firm's social capital, firms provide the necessities for creating new intellectual capital through opportunities for the sustained interaction, conversations, and sociability (Nahapiet & Ghoshal, 1998). Thus, a firm can be defined as a "social community specializing in the speed and efficiency in the creation and transfer of knowledge" (Kogut & Zander, 1996, p. 503).

Through their purpose and organizational structure, firms develop social closure and interdependence. Closure is a feature of social relationships that is conducive to the development of high levels of relational and cognitive social capital. Formal organizations such as firms, by definition, imply a measure of closure through the creation of explicit legal, financial, and social boundaries (Kogut & Zander, 1996). Because they promote specialization and integration (i.e., interdependence), firms encourage development of social capital and, hence, intellectual capital as well.

There are four conditions that must exist for the creation of new intellectual capital through exchange to take place: (1) opportunity, (2) expectation of the creation of value, (3) motivation (expectation of realizing and benefiting from some of the newly created value), and (4) capability (Nahapiet & Ghoshal, 1998). The links between the elements and dimensions of social capital and these four conditions are shown in Figure 1. The structural elements of social capital are shown promoting access to participants and anticipation of value. The cognitive elements support access to participants, anticipation of value, and combination capability. The relational dimension elements support access, anticipation of value, and motivation for exchange.

Social Knowledge

In addition to supporting the creation of new intellectual capital through combination and exchange, social relationships become the locus for their own type of intel-

Figure 1. Social capital in the creation of intellectual capital (Nahapiet & Ghoshal, 1998)

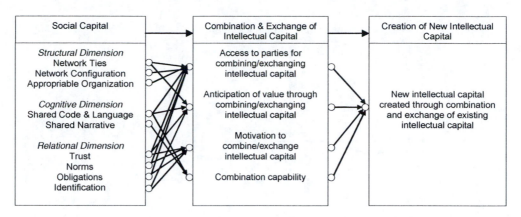

lectual capital, called social knowledge. Social knowledge is knowledge inextricably embedded in complex, collaborative social practices, separate from individual knowledge. This is consistent with the notion of schematic knowledge resources (Holsapple & Joshi, 2004), which exist independent of any organizational participant and include an organization's purpose/vision, strategy, culture, and infrastructure (i.e., roles, relationships, regulations).

Nahapiet and Ghoshal (1998) have identified two modes of social knowledge: explicit and tacit. They define the former as "objectified" knowledge shared across the organization. Social tacit knowledge, on the other hand, is fundamentally embedded in the forms of social and institutional practice; it resides in the tacit experiences and enactment of the collective (Brown & Duguid, 1991). Such knowledge and knowing capacity may remain relatively hidden from individual actors but manifests and is sustained through their interactions (Spender, 1994). The notions of tacit and explicit knowledge play a central role in the SECI model.

The SECI Model and Ba

The SECI model is a conceptualization of how new intellectual capital is developed via processes of socialization, externalization, combination, and internalization (SECI). The SECI model focuses on the perspective of knowledge as existing in two modes: tacit and explicit. Value creation by an organization emerges from using the four processes to convert knowledge between tacit and explicit modes. This conversion happens within Ba, "a shared space for emerging relationships" (Nonaka & Konno, 1998, p. 40). The concept of Ba is a perspective on the idea of social capital as discussed.

Tacit and Explicit Knowledge

One of the many attributes for characterizing knowledge is its mode (Holsapple, 2003). Two modes of knowledge are tacit and explicit. Sometimes, a third mode, called implicit knowledge, also is considered. "Tacit knowledge is highly personal and hard to formalize, making it difficult to communicate or share with others. Subjective insights, intuitions, and hunches fall into this category of knowledge. It is deeply rooted in an individual's actions and experience as well as in the ideals, values, or emotions he/she embraces." (Nonaka & Konno, 1998, p. 42) They go on to contend that there are two dimensions of the tacit mode:

- **Technical dimension of tacit knowledge:** "The informal personal skills or crafts often referred to as 'know-how.'"
- **Cognitive dimension of tacit knowledge:** "Beliefs, ideals, values, schemata, and mental models which are deeply ingrained in us and which we often take for granted. It shapes the way we view the world."

Explicit knowledge is knowledge that can be codified into symbolic representations such as words and numbers. As such, it can be readily transferred among persons in formal, systematic ways.

THE SECI SPIRAL OF KNOWLEDGE CREATION

In the SECI model, knowledge creation is a spiraling process of conversions between explicit and tacit

Figure 2. Spiral evolution of knowledge conversion and self-transcending process (Nonaka & Konno, 1998)

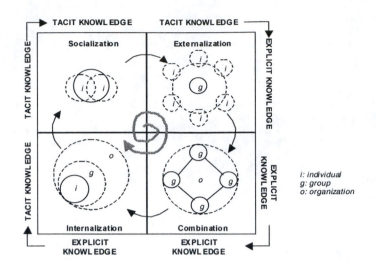

knowledge. The combinations of possible interactions between the two modes lead to four conversion patterns called socialization, externalization, combination, and internalization. These are illustrated in Figure 2 and characterized by Nonaka and Konno (1998) as follows:

- Socialization is the process of individuals sharing tacit knowledge. It is shared through interaction over time, rather than through written or verbal instructions. It involves transcending oneself and empathizing with another.
- Externalization is the articulation into explicit knowledge of previously held tacit knowledge to others within a group setting. In externalization, the individual fuses with the group and transcends their inner and outer boundaries of self.
- Combination is the process of synthesizing explicit knowledge into new, more complex explicit knowledge.
- Internalization is the process whereby new knowledge is shared throughout the organization and various participants convert it to their own tacit knowledge through using it to broaden, extend, and reframe their own tacit knowledge.

The Shared Space of Ba

The four conversion processes for developing knowledge take place in Ba: "a shared space for emerging relationships....This space can be physical, mental, virtual, or any combination....It is the platform for the "resource concentration" of the organization's knowledge assets and the intellectualizing capabilities within the knowledge-creation process" (Nonaka & Konno, 1998,

p. 40). Organizations manage knowledge creation through nurturing the Ba (i.e., social capital) that provides its context. The four aspects of Ba illustrated in Figure 3 correspond with the four stages of the SECI model: originating, interacting, exercising, and cyber Ba. Each is especially suited to the knowledge conversion process that it supports. Nonaka and Konno (1998, pp. 46-47) describe the four social capital spaces as follows:

- Originating Ba is the "space where individuals share feelings, experiences, and mental models. An individual sympathizes or further empathizes with others, removing the barrier between self and others." Originating Ba produces care, love, trust, and commitment leading to self-transcendence and therefore sharing and new knowledge. It is the primary Ba from which the knowledge creating process begins.
- Interacting Ba is the "shared space where people's mental models and skills are converted into common terms and concepts through dialogue. It is the place where tacit knowledge is made explicit and represents the externalization process."
- Cyber Ba is a "place of interaction in a virtual world instead of real space and time; and it represents the combination phase. Here the combining of new explicit knowledge with existing information and knowledge generates and systematizes explicit knowledge throughout the organization." Cyber Ba supports the combination process.
- Exercising Ba is the space that supports the internalization process. It facilitates the conversion of explicit knowledge to tacit knowledge in the individual. "Rather than learning from teaching

Figure 3. Four characteristics of Ba (Nonaka & Konno, 1998)

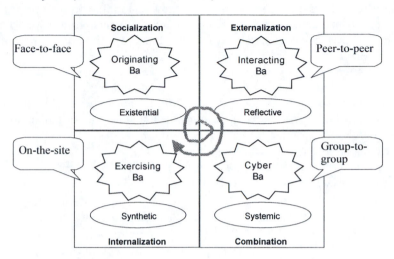

based on analysis, it stresses learning through continuous self-refinement via on-the-job training or peripheral and active participation."

Thus, the SECI model identifies four social capital spaces that an organization needs to cultivate as a basis for developing knowledge by way of the four conversion processes. Further information about the SECI model and Ba can be found in Nonaka and Takeuchi (1995, 1996) and Nonaka (1991, 1994). For instance, Nonaka and Takeuchi (1995) indicate that even when there is social capital conducive to knowledge creation, further conditions need to be met: vision, autonomy, fluctuations, redundancy, and variety. The organization needs a clear vision that allows it to evaluate the utility of developed knowledge relative to the organization's purpose and strategy. The condition of autonomy means that participants in the organization should be self-motivated in their quests for new knowledge. Fluctuation refers to the introduction of breakdowns in rigid, stale processes as a means for fostering creative chaos. The redundancy condition refers to having knowledge available beyond what is necessary for supporting short-run operations. Finally, variety is concerned with ensuring sufficient internal diversity to deal with the dynamics and complexity of situations imposed by external circumstances.

The Knowing Organization

Extending the work of Nonaka and colleagues, Choo (1998) advances the notion of a knowing organization as one in which knowledge is developed not only by knowledge conversion processes of the SECI model, but also by knowledge building and knowledge linking. Like knowledge conversion, both knowledge building and knowl-

edge linking are rooted in an organization's social capital, in the social networks that shape an organization's potential for creating knowledge.

The idea of knowledge building comes from Leonard-Barton's (1995) observation that organizations can engage in such activities as experimentation, prototyping, joint problem-solving, adopting new techniques/tools, acquiring knowledge, and acquiring special processing skills (e.g., new participants with some special expertise). These kinds of activities are both enabled and constrained by the structural, relational, and cognitive dimensions of an organization's social capital. They build on an organization's current knowledge base in the sense of expanding its scope and quality, and leave the organization poised to better cope with its future knowledge needs.

The idea of knowledge linking holds that knowledge is developed not only by networks of participants within an organization but also by forming networks of links to external entities (e.g., customers, suppliers, partners) to encourage inter-organizational knowledge flows (Badaracco, 1991; Wikstrom & Normann, 1994). That is, the social capital of an organization can be seen as having two components: internal and external. The internal orientation of social capital is concerned with internal networks among core participants in an organization (Tsai & Ghosal, 1998). The external orientation of social capital involves networking across organization boundaries, encompassing knowledge-intensive interactions between core participants and virtual or ancillary participants from outside the organization. As in the internal case, externally- oriented social capital needs to be cultivated to furnish a healthy context for fostering knowledge development.

Thus, knowledge creation can be seen as being developed from other knowledge via processes of knowledge conversion, knowledge building, or knowledge linking, each of which is conditioned by extant social capital. Choo (1998) goes on to point out that there are three kinds of organization knowing: Knowledge is used not only for knowledge creation, but also for sensemaking and decision-making. Here, we contend that both sensemaking and decision-making are knowledge creation processes that are conditioned by social capital.

Sensemaking occurs in situations that are open to multiple interpretations (Weick, 1995). It involves (1) the production or selection of an interpretive scheme to apply to the situation so as to grasp its meaning, thereby giving a basis for determining appropriate responses, and (2) the assimilation of helpful interpretive schemas to be reused or adapted for making sense of future ambiguous situations (Boland & Yoo, 2003). The immediate goal of sensemaking is for the organization's participants to share a common understanding of what the organization is and what it is doing; the longer-term goal is to ensure that the organization adapts and therefore continues to thrive in a dynamic environment (Choo, 1998).

The outcome of sensemaking is shared meanings and intents for the organization. Such sharing implies the pre-existence of social capital, a network of social relationships in which the meanings and intents can incubate and propagate. The meanings and intents are, in essence, knowledge about what is and what is should be. These did not exist before the sensemaking exercise, but rather are the result of it. Thus, sensemaking is a process of developing new knowledge, just as knowledge conversion, knowledge building, and knowledge linking are processes for developing new knowledge.

Results of sensemaking can be important ingredients for decision-making. "All organizational actions are initiated by decisions, and all decisions are commitments to action. In theory decision-making is rational, based upon complete information about the organization's goals, feasible alternatives, probable outcomes of these alternatives, and the values of these outcomes to the organization. In practice choicemaking is muddled by the jostling of interests among stakeholders, idiosyncrasies of personal choice making and lack of information" (Choo, 1996, p. 329). In other words, decision-making processes happen within the context of social networks which have the property of either facilitating/enhancing the process or muddling/obstructing it. This is certainly the case for multi-participant decision-making (i.e., multiple entities participate in the making of a decision). It is also the case, albeit indirectly, for individual decision-making (i.e., the individual's deliberations are affected by the organization's social capital).

Decision-making has long been recognized as a knowledge-intensive activity (Bonczek, Holsapple, & Whinston, 1981; Holsapple, 1995). Knowledge is the raw material, work-in-process, byproduct, and final outcome of decision-making. That is, a decision is knowledge that indicates a commitment to action. Thus, decision-making processes are knowledge creation processes, just as sensemaking, knowledge conversions, knowledge building, and knowledge linking. All five of these approaches to developing knowledge unfold in and as a result of an organization's social capital.

FUTURE TRENDS

Understanding knowledge development and its antecedents, particularly those related to social capital, is an important issue for KM practitioners and remains an area for continuing investigation by researchers. For instance, is there a difference in how social capital manifests in large enterprises vs. small firms? Characterizations of social capital are often made from the standpoint of the large enterprise. Davenport, Graham, Kennedy, and Taylor (2003) are studying how social capital manifests in small firm networks that rely on rapid turnover of projects, as a basis for devising prescriptions about building, maintaining, and refreshing social capital. As another example, consider the constructs that contribute to social capital. One of these is trust. Ford (2003) analyzes trust implications for knowledge processes such as knowledge creation. She poses a series of propositions that give a starting point for future research into the connections between trust and the development of knowledge. Similar analyses and detailed proposition statements wait to be performed for the connections between other social constructs and knowledge development.

At a more macro level, social capital connections to knowledge development are related to several broad topic areas within the KM field. Advances in these topic areas will impact our understanding of better creating the social capital needed for effective knowledge development, and vice versa. One of these topics is communities of practice (Brown & Duguid, 1991; Wenger, 2000). These are social networks (often technologically supported or enabled) that are dedicated to knowledge sharing and development pertaining to some domain of interest/expertise that is common to participants in the community. Another topic area is organizational learning (Bennet & Bennet, 2003) which is concerned with the means whereby organizations learn (i.e., develop greater intellectual capital) and the impacts of that learning. All five of the knowledge development approaches identified in this article can be regarded as variants of organizational learning. For organizational learning to happen, there must be sufficient social capital in terms of communication, interaction, and flexibility (Allard, 2003).

The knowledge management ontology (Holsapple & Joshi, 2004) suggests that we need to better understand techniques and technologies that can foster knowledge development episodes in an organization; specifically how do we lead, coordinate, control, and measure such episodes relative to the organization's present resources and environing situation? These and other questions remain for practitioners and researchers to resolve.

CONCLUSION

An organization's intellectual capital includes the knowledge that it can apply to enhance performance through increased productivity, agility, innovation, and/or reputation. Given the challenges of a dynamic, global, hypercompetitive environment, it is imperative that organizations be actively and consciously engaged in developing knowledge. One prerequisite for doing so is social capital. This article has outlined basic considerations important for cultivation of social capital and described its connections with the development of intellectual capital. It has identified five kinds of knowledge creation: knowledge conversions, knowledge building, knowledge linking, sensemaking, and decision-making. All of these deserve and can benefit from attention by leaders of KM initiatives and by the cultivation of appropriate networks of social relationships. The result is a more competitive organization.

REFERENCES

Allard, S. (2003). Knowledge creation. In C.W. Holsapple (Ed.), *Handbook of knowledge management*: *Knowledge matters* (pp. 367-379). Berlin: Springer-Verlag.

Badaracco, J.L. (1991). *The knowledge link: How firms compete through strategic alliances*. Boston: Harvard Business School Press.

Bennet, A., & Bennet, D. (2003). The partnership between organizational learning and knowledge management. In C.W. Holsapple (Ed.), *Handbook of knowledge management: Knowledge matters* (pp. 439-455). Berlin: Springer-Verlag.

Bonczek, R.H.,, Holsapple, C.W., & Whinston, A.B. (1981). *Foundations of decision support systems*. New York: Academic Press.

Brown, J.S., & Duguid, P. (1991). Organizational learning and communities of practice: Toward a unified view of working, learning and innovation. *Organization Science, 2*(1), 40-57.

Choo, C.W. (1996). The knowing organization: How organizations use information to construct meaning, create knowledge, and make decisions. *International Journal of Information Management, 16*(5), 329-340.

Choo, C.W. (1998). *The knowing organization: How organizations use information to construct meaning, create knowledge, and make Decisions*. New York: Oxford University Press.

Cicourel, A.V. (1973). *Cognitive sociology*. Harmondsworth, UK: Penguin Books.

Coleman, J. (1990). *Foundations of social theory*. Cambridge, MA: Harvard University Press.

Conner K, & Prahalad, C.K. (1996). A resource-based theory of the firm: Knowledge versus opportunism. *Organization Science, 7*(5) 477-501.

Davenport, E., Graham, M., Kennedy, J., & Taylor, K. (2003, October 20-23). *Managing social capital as knowledge management: Some specification and representation issues*. American Society of Information Science and Technology Annual Meeting, Long Beach, CA.

Denning, S. (2000). *The springboard: How storytelling ignites action in knowledge-era organizations*. Amsterdam: Butterworth-Heinemann.

Ford, D. (2003). Trust and knowledge management: The seeds of success. In C.W. Holsapple (Ed.), *Handbook of knowledge management: Knowledge matters* (pp. 553-575). Berlin: Springer-Verlag.

Granovetter, M.S. (1992). Problems of explanation in economic sociology. In N. Nohria & R. Eccles (Eds.), *Networks and organizations: Structure, form and actions* (pp. 25-26). Boston: Harvard Business School.

Gruber, T.R. (1995). Toward principles for the design of ontologies used for knowledge sharing. *International Journal of Human and Computer Studies, 43*(5/6) 907-928.

Holsapple, C.W. (1995). Knowledge management in decision making and decision support. *Knowledge and Policy, 8*(1) 5-22.

Holsapple, C.W. (2003). Knowledge and its attributes. In C.W. Holsapple (Ed.), *Handbook of knowledge man-*

agement: Knowledge matters (pp. 165-188). Berlin: Springer-Verlag.

Holsapple, C.W., & Joshi, K. (2004). A formal knowledge management ontology: Conduct, activities, resources, and influences. *Journal of the American Society for Information Science and Technology, 55*(7), 593-612.

Kogut, B., & Zander, U. (1996). What firms do? Coordination, identity, and learning. *Organization Science, 7*(5), 502-518.

Kramer, R.M., & Goldman, L. (1995). Helping the group or helping yourself? Social motives and group identity in resource dilemmas. In D. A. Schroeder (Ed.), *Social dilemmas*. New York: Praeger.

Leonard-Barton, D. (1995). *Wellsprings of knowledge: Building and sustaining the sources of innovation*. Boston, MA: Harvard Business School Press.

Moran, P., & Ghoshal, S. (1996). Bad for practice: A critique of the transaction cost theory. *Academy of Management Review, 21*(1), 13-47.

Mishra, J., & Morrisey, M. (1990). Trust in employer/ employee relationships: A survey of West Michigan Managers. *Public Personnel Management, 19*(4), 443-463.

Misztal, B. (1996). *Trust in modern societies*. Cambridge, UK: Polity Press.

Nahapiet, J., & Ghoshal, S. (1998). Social capital, intellectual capital, and the organizational advantage. *Academy of Management Review, 23*(2), 242-266.

Nonaka, I. (1991). The knowledge creating company. *Harvard Business Review, 69*(6), 96-105.

Nonaka, I. (1994). A dynamic theory of organizational knowledge creation. *Organization Science, 5*(1), 14-37.

Nonaka, I., & Konno, N. (1998). The concept of "Ba": Building a foundation for knowledge creation. *California Management Review, 40*(3), 40-54.

Nonaka, I., & Takeuchi, H. (1996). A theory of organizational knowledge creation. *International Journal of Technology Management, 11*(7/8), 833-845.

Nonaka, I., & Takeuchi, H. (1995). *The knowledge creating company*. New York: Oxford University Press.

Polanyi, M. (1974). *Personal knowledge: Towards a post-critical philosophy* (2nd Ed). Chicago: University of Chicago Press.

Schein, E. (1985). *Organizational culture and leadership*. Washington, DC: Jossey-Bass.

Spender, J.C. (1996). Knowing, managing and learning: A dynamic managerial epistemology. *Management Learning, 25,* 387-412.

Stewart, T.A. (1991). Brain power: How intellectual capital is becoming America's most valuable asset. *Fortune,* June 3.

Tsai, W., & Ghoshal, S. (1998). Social capital and value creation: The role of intrafirm networks. *Academy of Management Journal, 41*(4), 464-476.

Weick, K.E. (1995). *Sensemaking in organizations*. Thousand Oaks, CA: Sage Publication

Wenger, E. (2000). Communities of practice and social learning systems. *Organization Articles, 7*(2), 225-246.

Wikstrom, S., & Normann, R. (1994). *Knowledge and value: A new perspective on corporate transformation*. London, UK: Routledge.

KEY TERMS

Ba: "A shared space for emerging relationships." (Nonaka & Konno, 1998, p. 40).

Decision-Making: Theoretically, a selection among alternative choices based on complete information of the one which maximizes probable achievement of goals in light of established values. Practically, the process is constrained by limited information and competing interests among participants in the organization.

Explicit Knowledge: Knowledge that "can be expressed in words and numbers and shared in the form of data, scientific formulae, specification, manuals, and the like. This kind of knowledge can be readily transmitted between individuals formally and systematically." (Nonaka & Konno, 1998, p. 42).

Intellectual Capital: "The knowledge and the knowing capability of a social collectivity, such as an organization, intellectual community, or professional practice." (Nahapiet and& Ghoshal, 1998, p. 245).

Knowledge Creation: A process whereby new knowledge results from the conversion of knowledge between its tacit and explicit modes within the organization through the action of socialization, externalization, combination, and internalization. (Nonaka and& Takeuchi, 1996).

Sensemaking: Interpreting changes in the environment through a connected sequence of enactment, selection, and retention. (Weick, 1995).

Social Capital: "The sum of actual and potential resources embedded within, available through, and derived from the network of relationships possessed by an individual or social unit." (Nahapiet and& Ghoshal, 1998, p. 243).

Social Knowledge: Knowledge inextricably embedded in complex, collaborative social practices, separate from individual knowledge. (Nahapiet and& Ghoshal, 1998).

Tacit Knowledge: "Tacit knowledge is highly personal and hard to formalize, making it difficult to communicate or share with others. Subjective insights, intuitions, and hunches fall into this category of knowledge. It is deeply rooted in an individual''s actions and experience as well as in the ideals, values, or emotions he/she embraces." (Nonaka & Konno, 1998, p. 42).

Social Network Analysis

David J. Dekker
Radboud University Nijmegen, The Netherlands

Paul H.J. Hendriks
Radboud University Nijmegen, The Netherlands

INTRODUCTION

In knowledge management (KM), one perspective is that knowledge resides in individuals who interact in groups. Concepts as communities-of-practice, knowledge networks, and "encultured knowledge" as the outcome of shared sense-making (Blackler, 1995) are built upon this perspective. Social network analysis focuses on the patterns of people's interactions. This adds to KM theory a dimension that considers the effects of social structure on for example, knowledge creation, retention and dissemination. This article provides a short overview of consequences of social network structure on knowledge processes and explores how the insights generated by social network analysis are valuable to KM as diagnostic elements for drafting KM interventions. Relevance is apparent for management areas such as R&D alliances, product development, project management, and so forth.

BACKGROUND

Social network analysis (SNA) offers a combination of concepts, formal (mathematical) language, statistical, and other methods of analysis for unraveling properties of social networks. Social networks have two building blocks: nodes and ties among the nodes. Nodes may represent people, groups, organizations, and so forth, while the ties represent different types of relationships for example communication flows, collaboration, friendships, and/or trust. As illustration, Figures 1a and 1b represent graphs of the business and marriage network of Florentine families in 15th century (see Padgett & Ansell, 1993). The graphs are created with Netdraw (Borgatti, 2002).

SNA has its origins in the early decades of the 20th century. It draws on insights from a variety of disciplines, most notably social psychology, structural anthropology, sociology, and particularly the sociometric

Figure 1a. Florentine families business network

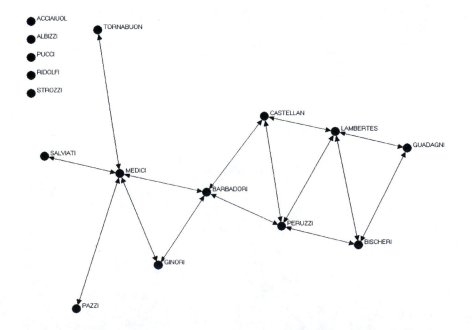

Figure 1b. Florentine families marriage network

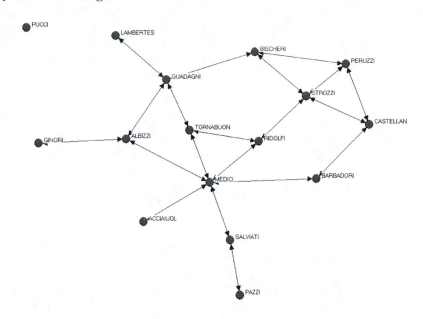

traditions (Scott, 2000). The formal language of SNA is based in the mathematical branch of graph-theory (e.g., Harary, Norman, & Cartwright, 1965).

Network statistics describe characteristics of a network and include network size, density, centrality, and so forth. Social network thinking has produced many such statistics (see Wasserman & Faust, 1994). However, only a limited number have been studied and have known consequences for knowledge management. To analyze and characterize networks, SNA provides statistics of the whole network, groups within the network, individuals, and relationships. The substantive meaning of these statistics often depends on the contents of the ties in the network.

Granovetter's (1973) seminal paper, titled "The Strength of Weak Ties," heralds the central place of social networks in knowledge management and shows the importance of relationship characteristics for knowledge transfer. Others show that social relationships and structures also are important for other knowledge processes, such as creation and retention (e.g., Burt, 2004; Hansen, 2002; Hargadon & Sutton, 1997; Reagans & McEvily, 2003). Granovetter's (1973) title may be a bit misleading. It suggests that "weak ties" will help individuals to get unique beneficial information. However, the paper demonstrates that it is the quality of "bridging ties" that brings this advantage. Bridging ties are relationships in a network that, when they would be removed, would leave the network in two unconnected

components. These relationships are often weak in the sense that contacts are less frequent and affect is low. However, as Burt (1992) points out, this is a mere correlation. "Strong bridging ties" would offer the same or even more advantages than weak bridging ties. The advantage of bridging ties Granovetter refers to lies in the structure of all relationships, not the strength of the relationship.

This leads us to focus here on the structural characteristics of networks and their impact on KM goals. This allows tapping into accumulating insights in the KM domain generated by SNA applications. Several recent studies in network literature focus on the (contingent) effects of such dyadic qualities as tie strength, level of trust, and power on knowledge transfer and retention (e.g., Hansen, 1999; McEvily, Perrone, & Zaheer, 2003; Uzzi, 1997).

SNA AND KM GOALS

Many SNA concepts bear relevance for KM research. Recent studies show that four SNA concepts in particular affect KM. These are:

1. **Brokerage:** Affects creativity, the generation of ideas and knowledge exploration
2. **Centrality:** Shapes knowledge transfer
3. **Cohesion:** Influences both knowledge transfer and retention

Figure 2. Node 'A' is a broker between nodes 'B' and 'C'

4. **Equivalence:** Reflects knowledge retention through common knowledge

Elaborating how the inspection of organizations through the lens of these four concepts is relevant for KM debates presumes an understanding of KM. KM is about an organization selecting appropriate goals with regard to knowledge, selecting a management model, and executing interventions, also called KM practices. Commonly, three KM domains and sets of KM goals are discerned:

1. The domain of knowledge processes that constitute valuable knowledge for an organization, most notably knowledge exploration, knowledge exploitation, knowledge sharing or transfer, and knowledge retention (see Alavi & Leidner, 2001; Argote, McEvily, & Reagans, 2003; Hendriks & Vriens, 1999)
2. The domain of a knowledge infrastructure as the organization setting in which knowledge processes evolve
3. The domain of a knowledge strategy as the set of goals that refer to how knowledge may give an organization its specific competitive position

These three KM domains and the goals they involve are interconnected. The domain of a knowledge infrastructure concerns setting the appropriate conditions for knowledge processes to evolve in such a way that they fit strategic KM goals. Focusing on aspects of social network structure, as this article does, involves paying special attention to the KM domain of knowledge infrastructure and its link to the first domain, that of knowledge processes.

Knowledge managers may benefit from insights in the four SNA concepts that will be presented in more detail in the remainder of this article. As elaborated next, insights into the domain of knowledge infrastructure and knowledge processes may form the basis for an informed selection of interventions for reaching KM goals.

These interventions may target individuals (nodes) and/ or their ties. Such KM interventions directly change the way knowledge processes develop. As such, the efforts of KM target the level of the individual knowledge worker. For example, SNA may prove useful:

1. in helping these individuals review their personal networks
2. in showing the necessity for them to develop their networking skills (e.g., Baker, 2000)
3. for their career planning

Furthermore, the insights that SNA generates also may allow KM to facilitate conditions for establishing network relationships and affect the resources used in networks. Note that both concern KM at the level of the knowledge infrastructure.

BROKERAGE

The first concept discussed here is that of knowledge brokerage. A broker is defined as someone who holds a position in a network that connects two or more unconnected parts of that network (see Figure 2). It is closely related to the idea of bridging ties because bridging ties imply brokerage. To emphasize that it is not the bridge itself, but the gap it closes that reflects value, Burt coined the term "Structural Hole" (Burt, 1992). A structural holes reflects the opportunity to connect two or more unconnected others.

Several authors suggest the value of brokerage for the creation of innovative ideas (Burt, 2004; Dekker, 2001; Hargadon & Sutton, 1997). Burt (2004) shows that there is strong evidence that brokerage generates good ideas. He states: "People with connections across structural holes have early access to diverse, often contradictory information and interpretations which gives them a competitive advantage in seeing and developing good ideas." They derive their value by enabling the flow of resources between otherwise unconnected subgroups within a larger network. This induces innovation (Hargadon & Sutton, 1997). Hansen (2002) shows that brokers work best when they use their own contacts and do not depend on other intermediaries. Dealing with fewer intermediaries who serve as boundary spanners provides search advantages, which leads to better knowledge acquisition.

The result that brokers may hold value is not without controversy. It has been shown that the value of brokers depends very much on the content of relationships (Podolny & Baron, 1997). Some relationship contents such as trust or tacit knowledge flow better through nonbridging relationships (Dekker, 2001; Gargiulo & Benassi, 2000).

In short, SNA identifies brokers and shows the conditions under which broker positions become valuable.

KM Interventions

The insights from knowledge brokerage analyses inspire, for example, the following KM interventions:

- Retention of key knowledge brokers in the organization. This could be done by aligning the reward systems with the recognition that informal reputation is central. Formal peer reviews should tap into those mechanisms
- Knowledge brokers need to be managed (or manage themselves) in such a way that they need as little other intermediaries as possible to acquire knowledge. Ideally, every team needs to organize its own "intelligence"
- The structure of work should confront some members of the workforce with a continuous flow of new problems, discourage them to overspecialize, and rotate them between projects on a regular basis. Only then is an "organic emergence of brokerage skills" conceivable
- Management style and the basic management model should reflect norms for collaboration. This could be implemented by avoiding management through normative control and by teaching newcomers the "attitude of wisdom" through brainstorming routines and regular meetings (e.g., Monday Morning meetings as described by Hargadon & Sutton, 1997)
- Recruitment and employee selection policies should respect the work and management styles and practices described. Peers should play a key role in those policies. Hargadon and Sutton (1997) describe how the product design firm IDEO only hires new personnel when at least 10 peers support these

Another KM intervention would be to find potential brokers to fill structural holes as starting points for idea generation. Other possible interventions include:

- The introduction of programs for team building and the development of networking skills and collaborative exercises may increase the chances that structural holes disappear
- Individuals' motivation to become knowledge brokers may be stimulated, through the reward system, career management, the selection of topics addressed in their development interviews, and personal commitment statements.

- Exit interviews and outplacement procedures may be considered for individuals who prove unfit for any boundary spanning activities

CENTRALITY

Centrality is a network structural characteristic of an individual or a whole network (for an overview, see Wasserman & Faust, 1994). The definition of various forms of centrality we will give focuses on individual centrality or point centrality. On a network level, similar measures have been developed (see Freeman, 1979). Several different types of centrality have been defined. Three well-known measures defined by Freeman (1979) are degree centrality, betweenness centrality, and closeness centrality. Degree centrality is measured as the number of ties an individual has in a network. This measure indicates the potential for communication activity that individual has. Betweenness centrality is based on the number of times that an individual stands between two others. Standing between two others here means being on the shortest path (geodesic) that connects two others. The more often an individual is on the shortest paths between any two others in the network, the higher that individual's "betweenness centrality." This form of centrality says something about control of communication within the network. Closeness centrality measures how close an individual is to the others in a network. Having relationships with everybody implies being closest, while having to depend on others to reach someone implies a greater distance toward that individual. Closeness centrality indicates independence. The higher the closeness centrality the more an individual can avoid the potential control of others (Freeman, 1979).

Centrality of networks has a close relationship to coordination in teams and particularly has an impact on knowledge transfer. For instance, Rulke and Galaskiewicz (2000) show that generalist teams do better than specialist teams in centralized networks. In decentralized networks, generalist and specialist teams perform equally well. Tsai (2002) shows that hierarchy has a negative impact on knowledge sharing, particularly in situations of inter-unit competition for market share. In such situations, informal lateral relations show a positive impact on knowledge sharing. Furthermore, Tsai (2002) shows that the drawbacks of hierarchy for knowledge transfer are less severe when competition among teams concerns usage of internal resources.

KM Interventions

Insights in the centrality of networks provide specific guidance for drafting control structures within project-

Figure 3. The group of nodes 'A,' 'B,' 'C,' and 'D' form a clique. In the group of nodes 'A,' 'B,' and 'C,' a fourth node 'D' can be added that has ties with all three others. Node 'E' doesn't belong to the clique because 'E' does not have ties with all clique members.

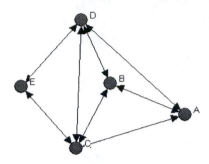

based or team-based organizations:

- Especially among specialists, if knowledge sharing is important, centralized, hierarchical control structures as coordination mechanisms in teams should be avoided
- Particularly in situations of inter-unit competition for market share, it may be wise to reexamine the degree of hierarchy in the prevailing control structures
- SNA research also has implications for staffing policies of teams: developing generalist teams puts less pressure on adequacy of existing control structures

COHESIVENESS

Cohesiveness in a network implies that all individuals or subgroups of individuals in that network have strong, direct, intense, frequent, and positive ties (Wasserman & Faust, 1994, p. 249). Several measures to detect cohesiveness have been developed. Probably the most well-known is the clique. Cliques are formally defined as maximal complete subgraphs of three or more nodes (Luce & Perry, 1949). This means a group is a clique if no individual in the network can be added to that group such that all those in the group have a direct tie with each other (see Figure 3). Ties in cliques are sometimes referred to as "Simmelian ties" after the renowned German sociologist Georg Simmel (Krackhardt & Kilduff, 1999). Simmel was the first to discuss the properties of triads, which are the smallest possible cliques. Simmelian ties are super strong, according to Krackhardt (1998), because they create opportunity for norms to arise and the means to enforce these norms (see also Coleman, 1990).

For knowledge management, this means that cohesiveness in networks allows the development, transfer, and retention of routines. Reagens and McEvily (2003) show that cohesion improves knowledge transfers. Hansen (2002) shows that cohesiveness between units may prove counterproductive under circumstances. He argues that the direct relations that produce cohesiveness are most effective for the transfer of complex knowledge. His research shows that the higher the number of direct relations, the longer the completion time of projects that employ codified knowledge. As to the cost involved in maintaining strong ties, research by Borgatti and Cross (2003) shows that its negative impact on knowledge transfer cannot be substantiated. They do show that awareness of competent knowledge transfer partners and easy access to their knowledge furthers knowledge transfer.

KM Interventions

SNA research shows that stimulating cohesiveness within teams is crucial for the broad spectrum of knowledge processes. If there is a lack of cohesiveness in parts of the organizational network, concrete interventions to help achieve such objectives include:

- The introduction of programs for developing networking capabilities not just for team members but particularly for managers (Baker, 2000). Other research has shown that heavyweight project leaders are needed for successful projects. SNA research shows that networking capabilities skills are crucial in addition to other managerial competencies
- As research suggests that successful teams have both weak and strong ties with other units, recruitment and selection procedures for team composition should ensure an adequate balance between both types of ties
- The introduction of programs for team building including collaborative exercises
- SNA may identify those nodes in the network, for example, team members that contribute most to low cohesiveness scores. These insights may inspire exit interviews with such team members and starting outplacement procedures for them
- The identification and adoption of key tasks and deliverables of teams and subgroups, as these may provide a focus for cohesion
- The introduction of elements of networking by team members in personal commitment statements, career management, and development interviews

- All aforementioned KM interventions should not just focus on intra-unit communication, but also address inter-unit communication. However, it should be considered that cohesiveness based on direct relations across units may only be worth the cost of maintaining for noncodified knowledge

EQUIVALENCE

A fourth SNA concept is equivalence. Equivalence of two individuals in a network indicates that they are embedded in equal or very similar network structures. Note that this does not mean that both need to have a direct contact. Rather, equivalence measures indicate the extent to which two individuals have the same role in a network. Equivalence measures have been developed for sociometric positional and role analyses. These analyses group people on the bases of their similarity in relational patterns. For an overview of different equivalence measures, see Wasserman and Faust (1994). In their study, Reagens and McEvily (2003) suggest that knowledge flows more easily between two equivalent individuals, because they have more common knowledge. More research is needed to show the effects of equivalence on knowledge management outcomes.

KM Interventions

- To the extent that inter-team knowledge transfer is important, staffing policies of teams need to tap into the insights that the existence of common knowledge among team members of different teams is an important precondition for the ease of knowledge transfer between teams, particularly for complex, noncodified knowledge. One way to achieve this is to gather data on the networks of individuals and to use these data to maximize structural equivalence of teams, an insight that may be provided by SNA
- Installing a system of job rotation makes sense because experience at one task is shown to help in performing a related activity
- Dedicated network ability training programs also may help in expanding the capacities of individuals and teams to achieve equivalence with other individuals and teams

FUTURE TRENDS

The increasing attention for knowledge aspects in organizations is likely to boost the interest in SNA research and may be expected to influence the direction that re-

search takes. The KM community may be expected to strengthen its embrace of SNA as a solid basis for diagnosis. As to the development of a knowledge-based SNA, a multitude of suggested research directions, ideas, and developments appear on the horizon. Two of these deserve special attention.

First, we anticipate SNA researchers that show an interest in the knowledge-based view of organizations to expand their focus that is currently mainly on the process of knowledge transfer. Other knowledge processes, particularly knowledge exploration and knowledge retention, have attracted the attention of SNA researchers, but not so much as knowledge transfer. The process of knowledge exploration, for instance, has been approached mainly via related concepts as creativity and idea generation. The process itself and the variety of learning and knowledge development models circulating in KM debates that involve elements of networks still remain largely outside the scope of SNA research. Also, an understanding of the core knowledge processes of knowledge exploitation and knowledge retention may greatly benefit from an inspection from a SNA standpoint. The same goes for the broad spectrum of supporting knowledge processes including knowledge acquisition, knowledge evaluation, knowledge identification, and knowledge combination.

Second, the further integration of SNA can be foreseen with qualitative studies that provide an in-depth examination of the intricacies surrounding the knowledge aspects of work. Hargadon and Sutton (1997) give an outstanding example of combining SNA with an extensive qualitative study of the mechanisms that shape the amalgamation of idea generation and knowledge retention. SNA addresses the crucial structural conditions for knowledge processes to develop. However, the intricate workings of the knowledge component in these processes remain a black box in a SNA. This is indicated by the fact that in much SNA research the term knowledge is easily substituted with the term information. Development of both knowledge-based SNA and qualitative inspections of organizational knowledge will advance due to their mutual connection.

CONCLUSION

Concepts from SNA strike a chord among adherents of a knowledge-based view of organizations. They recognize that knowledge, and especially organizational knowledge, is essentially situated on the fringes of connecting individuals with collectives. These concepts have inspired researchers from different origins and led to elaborations of network thinking into different directions, such as the economic theories of networks as governance modes and organizational theories around concepts of organization structure (Wijk, Bosch, & Volbeda, 2003). Both in the domain of knowledge management research and in the domain of individual organizations drafting their knowledge management diagnosis and design efforts, SNA has great potential to further develop the knowledge-based view of organizations.

REFERENCES

Alavi, M., & Leidner, D.E. (2001). Review: Knowledge management and knowledge management systems: Conceptual foundations and research issues. *MIS Quarterly 25*, 107-136.

Argote, L., McEvily, B., & Reagans, R. (2003). *Managing knowledge in organizations: An integrative framework and review of emerging themes. Management Science, 49*(4), (571-582).

Baker, W.E. (2000). *Achieving success through social capital: Tapping the hidden resources in your personal and business networks.* University of Michigan Business School management series (pp. XVII, 238). San Francisco: Jossey-Bass.

Blackler, F. (1995). Knowledge, knowledge work and organizations: An overview and interpretation. *Organization Studies 16*, 1021-1046.

Borgatti, S.P. (2002). *NetDraw: Graph visualization software.* Harvard: Analytic Technologies.

Borgatti, S.P., & Cross, R. (2003). A relational view of information seeking and learning in social networks. *Management Science, 49*(4), 432-445.

Burt, R S. (1992). *Structural holes: The social structure of competition* (p. 313). Cambridge, MA: Harvard University Press.

Burt, R.S. (2004). Structural holes and good ideas. *American Journal of Sociology* (in press).

Coleman, J.S. (1990). *Foundations of social theory.* Cambridge, MA: Harvard University Press.

Dekker, D.J. (2001). *Network perspectives on tasks in account management.* Erasmus University: Rotterdam.

Freeman, L.C. (1979). Centrality in social networks conceptual clarification. *Social Networks, 1*, 215-239.

Gargiulo, M., & Benassi, M. (2000). Trapped in your own net? Network cohesion structural holes, and the adaptation of social capital. *Organization Science, 11*(2), 183-196.

Granovetter, M.S. (1973). The strength of weak ties. *American Journal of Sociology, 78,* 1360-1380.

Hansen, M.T. (Ed.) (1999). The search-transfer problem: The role of weak ties in sharing knowledge across organization subunits. *Administrative Science Quarterly, 44*(1), 82-111.

Hansen, M.T. (Ed.) 2002. Knowledge networks: Explaining effective knowledge sharing in multiunit companies. *Oraganization Science, 13*(3), 232-248.

Harary, F., Norman, R.Z., & Cartwright, D. (1965). *Structural models: An introduction to the theory of directed graphs.* New York: Wiley.

Hargadon, A., & Sutton, R.I. (1997). Technology brokering and innovation in a product development firm. *Administrative Science Quarterly, 42,* 716-749.

Hendriks, P.H.J., & Vriens, D.J. (1999). Knowledge-based systems and knowledge management: friends or foes?, *Information and Management, 35,* 113-125.

Krackhardt, D. (1998). Simmelian tie: Super strong and sticky. In M. Neale (Ed.), *Power and influence in organizations* (pp. 21-38). Thousand Oaks, CA: Sage.

Krackhardt, D., & Kilduff, M. (1999). Whether close or far: Social distance effects on perceived balance in friendship networks. *Journal of Personality and Social Psychology, 76,* 770-782.

Luce, R.D., & Perry, A.D. (1949). A method of matrix analysis of group structure. *Psychometrika, 14,* 95-116.

McEvily, B., Perrone, V., & Zaheer, A. (2003). Trust as an organizing principle. *Organization Science, 14,* 91-103.

Padgett, J., & Ansell, C. (1993). Robust action and the rise of the Medici, 1400-1434. *American Journal of Sociology, 98*(6), 1259-1330.

Podolny, J.M., & Baron, J.N. (1997). Resources and relationships: Social networks and mobility in the workplace. *American Sociological Review, 62*(5), 673-693.

Reagans, R., & McEvily, B. (2003). Network structure and knowledge transfer: The effects of cohesion and range. *Administrative Science Quarterly, 48,* 240-267.

Rulke, D.L., & Galaskiewicz, J. (2000). Distribution of knowledge, group network structure, and group performance. *Management Science, 46,* 612-625.

Scott, J. (2000). *Social network analysis: A handbook* (2nd Ed.). London: Sage.

Tsai, W.P. (2002). *Social structure of "coopetition" within a multiunit organization: Coordination, competition, and intraorganizational knowledge sharing.* Unpublished manuscript.

Uzzi, B. (1997). Social structure and competition in interfirm networks: The paradox of embeddedness. *Administrative Science Quarterly, 42,* 35-67.

Wasserman, S., & Faust, K. (1994). *Social network analysis: Methods and applications.* New York: Cambridge University Press.

Wijk, R.v., Bosch, F.A.J.v.d., & Volbeda, H.W. (2003). Knowledge and networks. In M. Easterby-Smith & M.A. Lyles (Eds.), *The Blackwell handbook of organizational learning and knowledge management* (pp. 428-453). Malden, MA: Blackwell.

KEY TERMS

Brokerage: The activity of connecting two or more unconnected nodes in a network.

Centrality: The extent to which ties give an individual or subgroup a central position in a network.

Cohesion: The extent to which nodes form a group such that all members have mutual strong ties.

Network Structure: The overall configuration of the network, as reflected in the patterns of ties among nodes.

Social Network: A set of nodes (that represent actors, groups, etc.) and the ties that connect these nodes.

Social Network Analysis: The systematic analysis of empirical data describing social networks, guided by formal, mathematical, and statistical theory.

Structural Equivalence: The extent to which the tie patterns of two or more nodes of the network are equal.

A Social Network Perspective on Knowledge Management

Reed E. Nelson
Southern Illinois University, USA

HY Sonya Hsu
Southern Illinois University, USA

INTRODUCTION

Social networks—the sets of relations that link individuals and collectives—have implications for the speed and effectiveness with which knowledge is created and disseminated in organizations Both social networks and knowledge management (KM) are complex, multifaceted phenomena that are as yet imperfectly understood. Not unsurprisingly, our understanding of the interface between the two is similarly imperfect and evolving. There are, however, a number of foundational concepts upon which existing thought converges as well as a body of emerging research that offers practical and conceptual guidance for developing the kind of network best suited for managing different kinds of knowledge. In this article, we introduce rudimentary network concepts, briefly recapitulate KM and organizational learning concepts related to networks, and then explore some of the interfaces between social networks and KM.

RUDIMENTS OF SOCIAL NETWORK ANALYSIS

There are two fundamental dimensions of social networks: transactional content and configuration. These in turn have both direct and indirect interactions on each other and on knowledge dissemination if not on both creation and transfer of knowledge. Configuration refers to "shape" of a network (Nelson, 2001). For instance, some networks look like stars, with actors connected only to a central person. Some look like spider webs, with a dense center, but with some connections between peripheral actors (Handy, 1995). Other networks, such as those typified by unrestricted markets, exhibit more random patterns.

Important for an individual within a network is the degree to which he or she fills a "structural hole" between members of the network. A structural hole refers to a gap in a network which isolates one set of actors from another. Individuals whose personal ties bridge such gaps can exercise a "brokerage" role which

benefits them personally and facilitates the flow of information and resources through the network. There are at least two other important configurational aspects of an individuals networks; centrality and structural equivalence. Together they constitute what Galaskiewicz and Wasserman (1993) identified as the core constructs defining of social structure:

1. Actor centrality is the degree to which the ties in a network converge upon an individual actor. Thus, if actor A is connected to everyone in a network and no other actors entertain ties to each other, actor A has maximum centrality. Centrality has been measured in various ways from simple counts of sociometric nominations to measures based on the number of geodesics linking each actor, but space will not permit a discussion of these nuances. Common to all measures is the idea that central actors can reach or directly contact other members of the network more easily than less central actors.

2. Structural equivalence is the degree to which the patterns of individual networks are similar. People who are tied to the same people are said to be structurally equivalent. For instance, two professors who team teach the same course would have rather similar patterns of ties, at least with their students. Supervisors on a day and night shift in the same factory also would have somewhat similar network patterns. Because strict equivalence is quite rare, scholars have sought to develop less constraining definitions of equivalence. Actors with similar network structures but with connections to different actors are said to have "regular equivalence" for instance. An example would be quarterbacks on opposing football teams. In practice, equivalence is usually measured using clustering algorithms which group similar network patterns together.

3. Bridging relationships are idiosyncratic relationships that link otherwise unconnected groups or individuals. This concept is very similar to both

Burt's brokerage and Freeman's "betweenness" constructs.

To Glaskiewicz and Wasserman's constructs must be added a fourth—the concept of density. Density refers to the overall number of contacts in a network compared to the number of ties possible. In a "sparse" network, there are few connections between people. In a "dense" network everyone is connected. Density is expressed as a ratio of realized to possible ties. The network of four people sharing six ties has a density of 1. One containing three ties has a density of .5. The overall density of a network or a network's subregion is closely related to virtually every other network dimension.

Transactional content refers to the kind of relationship that exists between two actors rather than the shape of the network or the actor's position within the network. Many types of relationship are possible, including influence, information exchange, advice, emotional support, antagonism, and exchange of goods and services. However, to date, the most commonly used way to classify the transactional content of a network is the concept of "tie strength" developed by Grannovetter (1973). In addition to formalizing the concept of tie strength, Grannovetter was perhaps the first to recognize the relationship between tie strength, network configuration, and the dissemination of information.

The strength of a tie is a combination of the amount of time, the emotional intensity, and the extent of reciprocal services which characterize the tie. In general, the stronger the tie the more easy it is for one actor to influence and convey complex, multifaceted information to another. At the same time, strong ties tend to be resistant to change and stifle innovation. They also tend to clump together into incestuous cliques, creating many structural holes in a network that are difficult to bridge and that create conflict in social systems (Nelson, 1989; Uzzi, 1997). The relationship between tie strength, network configuration, and information transfer is probably the single most important network finding and its implications for KM and surfaces in one way or another in almost all studies of networks and KM.

DIMENSIONS OF KNOWLEDGE AND KM

Although most readers will be acquainted with KM and related concepts, it will be useful here to summarize a few central constructs so that our discussion of the relationship between networks and KM will be based on common understandings and definitions. We briefly restate commonly used definitions of knowledge and knowledge management. Nonoka (1994) defines knowledge as "a justified belief that increases an entity's capacity for effective action." He also affirms that knowledge is created and organized by the flow of information, anchored on the commitment and beliefs of its holder (Nonoka, 2002).

It is important to distinguish between data, information, and knowledge. The primary distinction between the three lies in the degree to which they are organized and useful. Data are raw stimuli with little organization or ready utility (Avali & Leidner, 2001). Data become information when they are processed and organized in a systematic way. Information becomes knowledge when it is ready to be used to orient action. In Davenport, Long, and Beers' terms, "Knowledge is a high value form of information that is ready to apply to decisions and actions (Davenport et al., 1998, p. 43). An important type of knowledge is tacit knowledge, which, while it is useful, is difficult to codify, transmit, and convey (Schön, 1983). Tacit knowledge contains data that are processed, organized, and useful, but the underlying logics of their organization are frequently complex, implicit, and ambiguous. Tacit knowledge is important to the solution of problems that are intractable, complex, extremely variable, or all of the above. As phenomena become better understood and solutions more routine, the knowledge necessary for their processing becomes more explicit, and solution procedures more codified, so that producing information from data becomes simpler and more routine.

Generating knowledge, be it tacit or explicit, is a complex task. Nonoka (1994) identifies four interrelated related processes leading to knowledge creation: knowledge socialization, knowledge internalization, knowledge externalization, and knowledge combination. Almost by definition, the processes of knowledge socialization and externalization if not combination and internalization will be influenced by the nature and distribution of individual and collective networks. Most views of KM recognize that it has both social and technological dimensions which need to be integrated, and that KM has broad aims involving organizational culture, transparency, and agility of processes, and the development of infrastructure that is harmonious with individual needs and organizational context.

For Davenport and Prusak (1998), most KM projects have one of three aims: (1) to make knowledge visible and show the role of knowledge in an organization; (2) to develop a knowledge-intensive culture by encouraging and aggregating behaviors (e.g., knowledge sharing); and (3) to build a knowledge infrastructure—not only a technical system, but a web of connections to encourage interaction and collaboration. Again, social networks would logically limit or enhance visibility, culture, and infrastructure.

Alavi (1997) believes that KM includes both technology and social-cultural factors. This view is supported by Tiwana (2001) who adds that: (1) KM should focus on the flow of information; (2) it is a foremost a management issue—and technology is only an enhancer driven "by the right people in the right place to support knowledge management." A similar but more individualistic perspective is expressed by Alavi and Leidner (2001). For them, KM involves enhancing individual's learning and understanding through provision of information. They also see the role of IT as providing the access to sources of knowledge rather than knowledge itself. Sources of knowledge are the nodes of a social network that create, acquire, or transfer the majority of information/knowledge.

From this brief overview, it would seem clear that: (1) Networks are an important part of the knowledge creation, acquisition, and transmission process; and (2) different network properties will come into prominence at different stages of this process. In the next section, we attempt to identify some of the likely specifics of this relationship.

NETWORKS AND KNOWLEDGE MANAGEMENT

The relation between networks and KM has been recognized and explored by several researchers, some of whom have made extensive use of formal network theory and methods, others who have made fairly little use of the existing network literature. It is generally recognized that early KM initiatives focused too heavily on IT, missing opportunities to improve performance through the knowledge and enhancement of employee networks (Parker, Cross, & Walsh, 2001). Practicing managers especially recognize that human relationships, their deployment, and configuration are critical to KM. For instance, the manager of the technical information center at Xerox emphasized that KM is not technology-driven but "people-driven" (Hickins, 1999). A case study of Xerox affirmed that 80% of KM systems involved adapting to the social dynamics of the workplace.

Beyond this general admission of the importance of human factors, literature on KM has frequently noted that formal vertical relations are not as effective at disseminating knowledge, as are lateral contacts. A number of studies suggest that hierarchical contacts (frequently, equated with "formal structure") are not as effective for knowledge sharing as "lateral" or informal contacts. Knowledge organizations are characterized by weak hierarchies, dense lateral connections, low departmental walls, and openness to the environment (Achrol & Philip, 1999). These studies, however, have made little or no use

of network theories, which would help to explain the effectiveness of lateral ties.

Perhaps the most sophisticated work on KM and networks is that of Cross, Parker, Prusak, and Borgatti (2001). They identify four dimensions of network ties which influence a firm's KM capability: (1) Knowledge: "knowing what someone else knows" when managers face a problem or opportunity; (2) Access: being able to contact and secure useful information for an actor in a timely fashion; (3) Engagement: the expert understands the problem as experienced by the seeker and then adapts his or her knowledge to the needs of the person information; and (4) Safety: ease in admitting a lack of knowledge.

Although the work on networks and KM clearly establishes the importance of networks to KM, we as yet have found no integrative statements about the general contours of the relationship between network attributes and knowledge creation and dissemination. In an effort to move toward such a statement, we juxtapose the tacit/explicit knowledge distinction with the various network properties to offer the beginnings of a contingency perspective on networks and KM.

Knowledge creation generally begins with isolated and unintegrated insights, which are brought to bear on a practical problem until a desired result is achieved. At this point, the practitioner has a working ability which we defined above as tacit knowledge. Over time, this tacit knowledge may or may not be distilled into codified information, which is more easily conveyed through written or other transportable means. The degree to which knowledge is tacit is closely related to the kind of network that will best be able to convey and disseminate it.

When knowledge is at the tacit stage, it is only transferable (if at all) through very rich channels requiring frequent face to face interaction. When physical artifacts are involved, the artifact or physical setting must simultaneously be available to all parties. This demands both strong ties and a dense network configuration, which can be quite expensive to develop in terms of time and resources. Although relations in the network may be hierarchical (mentor and apprenticeship relations are prominent), little brokerage occurs because all members of the network know each other and relate on a face to face basis.

As tacit knowledge gives way to at least partial codification, formerly isolated communities of practice trafficking in tacit knowledge come into contact with one another. Brokers then emerge who retain a stake in their original community but who acquire the insights of rival groups or of other disciplines or crafts. These brokers often face ostracism from their own group and suspicion from other groups, but if they succeed in forging connections, they are often richly rewarded. The great tinker-inventors of the 19th century tended to build networks of this type, Edison and his famous Menlo Park facility being the most prominent example. These networks are characterized by tight cliques of strong ties connected by brokers with somewhat weaker ties to other communities. This tradition is carried on today and the organizational mechanisms used to manage such networks are lucidly portrayed in Hargadon and Sutton's (1997) pioneering work on Ebsco, the famed Silicon Valley design firm. Work of this type has generally been ignored by both network analysts and KM scholars and needs to be acknowledged by and integrated into both literatures.

As knowledge becomes codified but still somewhat volatile, networks with weaker ties, less density, and more brokerage are needed. These use channels with less richness and more agility, although even these networks ordinarily build associations and cartels to provide a forum for face-to-face contact and deal-making. Frequently, actors who develop high centrality may drive out other brokers and become dominant in managing and controlling information at this stage. Many of the incidental contacts of the general managers described by Kotter (1982) are with brokers of information which is largely codified but not routine or widely disseminated.

Finally, highly codified and relatively stable information is found in market-like networks which rely heavily on public mechanisms such as publications, bulletin boards, and wire services. These networks are low in density and weak in tie strength and require relatively little conscious understanding or management. Even these networks, however, can only be navigated by people who have been introduced to the conventions and protocols used by someone already initiated in the system. In these situations, information is more prominent than knowledge, but even in these settings, it may take a knowledgeable, initiated person to orient newcomers.

Understanding the continuum of tacit to explicit knowledge and its implications for social network strength and configuration may enhance current thinking and practice in knowledge management as well as the study of social networks. As an example, we return to Cross et al.'s categories of *knowledge, access, engagement,* and *safety*. When we examine their typology in the light of tacit knowledge, it seems reasonable to predict that the different dimensions and their configuration will vary by the state of knowledge being developed.

The *knowledge* (i.e., knowing what someone else knows) dimension will be relatively unimportant during the tacit phase if only because engagement will be almost impossible. When information is more trans-portable however, knowledge will be very important and will benefit by high density and connectivity with many brokerage relationships. *Engagement* (expert understands the problem of the seeker) becomes important during the intermediate stages when the ability to find the exact person who can "speak the language" of the information seeker becomes critical. Brokerage relationships become critical here and much time will be dedicated to forging brokerage relations and developing strong ties to diverse actors in a sparse network. When knowledge is generally codified and diffused, *safety* (ease in admitting lack of knowledge) becomes an issue because of the expectation that people should already know certain information or where to find it. Thus, strong mentoring relationships in otherwise sparse networks composed of weak ties become important when information is explicit rather than tacit.

Cross et al. describe a situation in one firm in which one executive provided the only bridge between two cliques. Their intervention established other brokerage contacts, generally taking pressure off the sole broker and speeding coordination and communication in the workgroup. It is our expectation that in situations high in tacit knowledge, such change in the network might not be practical. In one knowledge-intensive organization to which we consulted, the top executives of the company also occupied important bridging roles in a field high in tacit knowledge. Rather than making their networks denser and more egalitarian, we found it was best to buffer the most knowledgeable executives from administrative duties so they could devote more energy to a brokerage role that was harder to compensate for than their administrative role.

TIE STRENGTH AND KM

In our discussion, we mentioned tie strength, but our focus was chiefly on network configuration and knowledge generation and transmission. Before closing, we turn to a few more detailed predictions about tie strength and knowledge management. The presence of strong ties provides a rich communication channel, which facilitates the accurate transmittal of complex information, tacit knowledge, and development of trust. They also promote commitment and solidarity between actors which is necessary for communication and coordination of large projects that require intensive sharing of knowledge across many actors (Fukayama, 1995).

At the same time, the presence of strong ties requires large amounts of time and psychological energy to develop and maintain, generally reducing the efficiency of the system. They also reduce variability in thought and perspectives at the same time they stifle undesirable deviance and build loyalty. Thus, at the same time, they help convey tacit knowledge, they stifle the "reflection in action" that Schön deems necessary to perfect tacit knowledge. This, in turn, limits that ability to adapt to new circumstances and novel situations. The benefits of strong ties are most evident when producing knowledge for the incremental perfection or improvement of an existing system or technology—in sum, for exploitation rather than exploration.

When competence-destroying innovations are expected or intended, the strength of ties becomes a weight that renders the knowledge system less agile. Tacit knowledge tends to carry with it "irrelevant content" (Nelson, 1997) and superstitions that prevent the system from understanding or recognizing the value of competence destroying innovations. The literature on KM glimpses aspects of this paradox but generally does not see both horns of the dilemma at the same time and tends to be more aware of the value of weak ties than of strong ties. From a network perspective, then, the observation of the KM community that lateral ties are better for information diffusion may be because they are likely weak rather than strong. KM observations of the benefits of laterial ties should include caveats. Lateral ties are more likely to be more adaptable and flexible than contacts with hierarchical content. Lateral ties also would be desirable because they would bridge a number of structural holes in the organization, facilitating information flow. However, they do not convey the solidarity and coercive power of strong and/or hierarchical ties.

CONCLUSION

As the KM field continues to mature, we expect that the social network perspective will play a more prominent role in our understanding of knowledge in organizations. In closing, we suggest a few measures that may be taken to speed up this process. We suspect first that tighter theoretical linkages between social network theory, theories of knowledge, and theories of organizational learning would be useful. Students of organizational learning are generating ever more sophisticated studies using large archival data sets. These studies (Chuang & Baum, 2003; McDonald & Westphal, 2003) contain insights that could be exploited by students of knowledge management who have a basic grasp of network concepts. Second, more complete use of the sophisticated social network techniques available would be useful, especially those methods that consider multiple types of tie simultaneously. The techniques used in the KM literature to date tend to be quite rudimentary

and therefore best for case-based research rather than comparative studies which yield higher generalizability. The normative orientation of KM could stimulate network analysts to be less coy about developing prescriptions for managing networks. Much is known about networks' content and morphology but not about how they are actually formed and what specific network properties are efficacious in what settings.

Early network analysts discussed the benefits and drawbacks of highly central networks but turned away from practical concerns in search of ever more esoteric theory. Very little thought at all has been given to the practical impacts of structural equivalence between actors, which would be a natural next step in terms of practical analyses. We suspect that different degrees and types of equivalence may have implications for KM, and research in this area by the KM community is likely to push network theory in interesting directions.

Granovetter's (1973) original formulation of strong and weak has been thoroughly exploited for its practical and theoretical value, and it is time to look at more fine-grained characterizations of relations. The KM community can be of considerable value in taking the notion of "transaction content" from network analysis and giving back a more practical and sophisticated view of the kinds of relations that people develop, how they develop them, and how these relations are mobilized to generate and distribute knowledge.

As is the case with most social endeavors, the different possible configurations of network attributes present contrasting implications for knowledge management, reflecting the tensions and tradeoffs that are inherent in almost any social setting in which goal-oriented performance is sought. Continued integration of these two bodies of thought should ultimately benefit both but also might contribute to the more general debates of our time about solidarity, innovation, change, and the fundamental nature of human systems.

REFERENCES

Achrol, S.R., & Philip K. (1999). Marketing in the networked economy. *Journal of Marketing, 63,* 146-163.

Alavi, M., & Leidner, D. (2001). Review: Knowledge management and knowledge management systems: Conceptual foundations and research issues. *MIS Quarterly, 25*(1), 107-136.

Alavi, M. (1997). *KPMG Peat Marwick U.S.: One giant brain.* Harvard Business School, Case 9-397-108.

Chuang, Y., & *Baum*, J.A. (2003). It's all in the name: Failure-induced learning by multiunit chains. Administrative Science Quarterly, *48*(1), 33-60.

Cross, R., Parker, A., Prusak, L., & Borgatti, S.P. (2001). Supporting knowledge creation and sharing in social networks. *Organizational Dynamics, 30*(2), 100-121.

Davenport, T.H., De Long, D.W., & Beers, M.C. (1998). Successful knowledge management projects. *Sloan Management Review, 39*(2), 43-57.

Davenport, T.H., & Prusak, L. (1998). *Working knowledge.* MA: Harvard Business School Press.

Fukayama, F. (1995). *Trust: The social virtues and the creation of prosperity.* New York: Free Press.

Galaskiewicz, J., & Wasserman, S. (1993). Social network analysis: Concepts, methodology and directions for the nineties. *Sociological Methods and Research, 22,* 3-22.

Granovetter, M.S. (1973). The strength of weak ties. *The American Journal of Sociology, 78*(6), 1360-1380.

Handy, C.B. (1995). *Gods of management: The changing work of organizations.* New York: Oxford University Press.

Hargadon, A., & Sutton, R.I. (1997). Technology brokering and innovation in a product development. *Administrative Science Quarterly, 42*(4), 716-750.

Hickins, M. (1999). Xerox shares its knowledge. *Management Review*, 40-45.

Kotter, J.P. (1982). *The general managers.* New York: Free Press.

Levitt, B., & March, J.G. (1988). Organizational learning. *Annual Review Sociology, 14,* 319-340.

McDonald, M.L., & Westphal, J.D. (2003). Getting by with the advice of their friends: CEOs' advice networks and firms' strategic responses to poor performance. *Administrative Science Quarterly, 48*(1), 1-33.

Nelson, R.E. (2001). On the shape of verbal networks in organizations. *Organization Studies, 22*(5), 797-823.

Nelson, R.E. (1997). *Organizational troubleshooting: Asking the right questions, finding the right answers.* CT: Quorum Books.

Nelson, R.E. (1989). The strength of strong ties: Social networks and intergroup conflict in organizations. *Academy of Management Journal, 32,* 327-401.

Nonaka, I. (2002). A dynamic theory of organizational knowledge creation. In C.W. Choo & N. Bontis (Eds.), *The strategic management of intellectual capital and organizational knowledge.* New York: Oxford University Press.

Nonaka, I. (1994). A dynamic theory of organizational knowledge creation. *Organization Science, 5*(1), 14-37.

Parker, A., Cross, R., & Walsh, D. (2001). Improving collaboration with social network analysis. *Knowledge Management Review, 4*(2), 24-29.

Schön, D.A. (1983). *The reflective practitioner: How professionals think in action.* New York: Basic Books.

Tiwana, A. (2001). *The essential guide to knowledge management: e-business and CRM applications.* Upper Saddle River, NJ: Prentice Hall.

Uzi, B. (1997). Social structure and competition in interfirm networks: The paradox of embeddedness. *Administrative Science Quarterly, 41,* 373-391.

KEY TERMS

Density: Density is the ratio of realized to possible ties. In a network with a density of one, every member of a network is connected to every other. In a "sparse" network, there are few connections between people. The overall density of a network or a network's subregion is closely related to every other network dimension.

Knowledge Organizations: Knowledge organizations are characterized by weak hierarchies, dense lateral connections, low departmental walls, and openness to the environment. A number of studies suggest that use of hierarchical contacts (frequently, equated with "formal structure") are not as effective for knowledge sharing as "lateral" or informal contacts.

Organization Learning: Organizational learning involves encoding inferences from history into routines that guide behavior. It is routine-based, history dependent, and target-oriented. Organization learning may be facilitated by knowledge management, which presumably can decrease eliminate structural and cultural barriers to organization learning.

Social Network Analysis: The social network perspective views organizations as consisting of social units with relatively stable patterns of relationships over time. There are two fundamental dimensions of social networks: transactional content and configuration.

Structural Hole: A structural hole refers to a gap in a network, which isolates one set of actors from another. Individuals whose personal ties bridge such gaps can exercise a "brokerage" role, which benefits them personally and facilitates the flow of information and resources through the network.

Tie Strength: The strength of a tie is a function of frequency of contact, affect, and reciprocity. The stronger the tie, the more easy it is for one actor to influence and convey complex, multifaceted information to another.

Transactional Content: Transactional content refers to the kind of relationship that exists between two actors rather than the shape of the network or the actor's position within the network. Many types of relationship are possible including influence, information exchange, advice, emotional support, antagonism, and exchange of goods and services.

Tacit Knowledge Sharing

Syed Z. Shariq
Stanford University, USA

Morten Thanning Vendelø
Copenhagen Business School, Denmark

INTRODUCTION

When people solve complex problems, they bring knowledge and experience to the situation, and as they engage in problem solving they create, use, and share tacit knowledge. Knowing how context emerges and transforms is central if we want to understand how people create, use, and share tacit knowledge. Consequently, this article focuses on the three questions: What is context? How does context emerge and transform? What is the relationship between context and tacit knowledge sharing?

Initially the article describes how context is conceptualized in the theory of the firm as a knowledge-creating entity, and it argues that this theory lacks a detailed account for how context emerges and transforms. Thereafter, we define context, and based on the writings by the Austrian sociologist Alfred Schütz, a theory of how context emerges and transforms is put forward. This theory is illustrated with an empirical case describing the Carbon Dioxide filtering problem, which occurred during the ill-fated Apollo 13 mission. The article concludes by explaining how a theory of context helps us to understand the role of context in tacit knowledge sharing.

BACKGROUND: CONTEXT IN THE THEORY OF THE FIRM AS A KNOWLEDGE-CREATING ENTITY

Knowledge management scholars have put forward ideas for a theory of the firm as a knowledge-creating entity, and suggest that the firm can be conceptualized as a dynamic configuration of 'ba' (roughly means place) (Nonaka, Toyama, & Nagata, 2000a). More precisely, 'ba' is defined as the context shared by those who interact with each other, and 'ba' is the place where they create, share, and use knowledge.

Putting knowledge in context is important as "knowledge creating processes are necessarily context-specific, in terms of who participates and how they participate in the process. The context here does not mean "a fixed set of surrounding conditions but a wider dynamical process of which the cognition of an individual is only a part" (Hutchins, 1995, p. xiii). Hence, knowledge needs a physical context to be created, as "there is no creation without place" (Casey, 1997, p. 160; Nonaka et al., 2000a, p. 8).

The initial step towards a theory of the firm as a knowledge-creating entity (Nonaka et al., 2000a) has given many insights to knowledge creation in organizations, and with the introduction of the 'ba'-concept, a step towards a conception of context has been taken. However, it remains unclear what exactly 'ba' is, how 'ba' emerges, and what exactly happens inside 'ba'. The definition of 'ba' offered by Nonaka et al. (2000a) is unclear or ambiguous at best. On the one hand they note: "Knowledge needs a physical context to be created, as 'there is no creation without place'" (p. 8). On the other hand they note that "'Ba' does not necessarily mean a physical space. Rather, it is a specific time and space" (p. 9). Furthermore, 'ba' seems to be a very inclusive concept. According to Nonaka and Konno (1998, p. 40), "'Ba' can be thought of as a shared space for emerging relationships. This space can be physical, virtual, mental, or a combination of them." We therefore think it is fair to ask: What is not included in 'ba'?

Concerning the emergence of 'ba' then it seems that on the one hand 'ba' is created spontaneously. "'Ba' is constantly in motion. 'Ba' is fluid, and can be born and disappear quickly" (p. 9). On the other hand 'ba' can be built intentionally (Nonaka, Toyama, & Konno, 2000b). According to Nonaka et al. (2000a, p. 12): "…building 'ba' such as project teams or functional departments, and determining how such 'ba' should be connected to each other, is an important factor in determining the firm's knowledge creation rate." In addition, it is worth noting that "the boundary for 'ba' is fluid and can be changed quickly as it is set by the participants. Instead of being constrained by history, 'ba' has a 'here and now' quality. It is constantly moving; it is created, functions and disappears according to need" (Nonaka et al., 2000b, pp. 15-16).

Finally, regarding the question: What exactly happens inside 'ba'? The closest we get to an answer to this question is provided by Nonaka and Toyama (2000, p. 3) who write "…'ba' is…an open space where participants with their own contexts can come and go and the shared context (that is, 'ba') can continuously develop." Therefore, although the concept of 'ba' (Nonaka & Konno, 1998; Nonaka et al., 2000a) represents an attempt to define context, we are still far from an explanation of how context emerges and transforms, and thus, we have yet to understand what happens inside 'ba'.

MAJOR FOCUS I: DEFINING CONTEXT

We maintain that contexts are not 'just there' as static entities, but that they are emerging phenomena. A similar perception is put forward by Erickson and Schultz (1997), who describe context as a mutually constituted, constantly shifting, situation definition emerging through the interaction of the involved individuals. "Contexts are not simply given in the physical setting…nor in combinations of personnel…Rather, contexts are constituted by what people [do and where and when they do it]. As McDermott puts it succinctly (1976), "People in interaction become environments for each other" (p. 22), and Dilley agrees (1999): "Context is both constitutive of social action and itself the outcome of social action, it is both a generative principle and a resulting outcome" (p. 19). Yet, neither of these authors make clear if they perceive context as an collective or individual construct. Based on Polanyi's (1962) statement that all knowledge is personal knowledge, we suggest that context is an individual construct. Furthermore, we propose that context emerges as an individual encounters a situation, including others and artifacts, as it is the individual's interpretation of a situation that results in a context. After its emergence the context transforms as the situation evolves, for example, as a result of the acting of the individual and the others involved.

By claiming that the individual interpretation of a situation results in a context, we imply that the context emerging for an individual in a specific situation is based on that individual's previous experiences. As two individuals never have fully similar experiences, the contexts emerging for two individuals can never be similar, yet similarities among individual experiences might result in contexts with many similarities. Another important implication of our context definition is that if individual X encounters situation Y in both t=1 and t=2, then the contexts emerging for individual X at these two points in time will differ as individual X brings a different set of experiences to the two instances of the situation Y.

By defining context as an emergent and individualistic construct, we are in agreement with Rapport (1999, p. 190) who writes:

Context is determined by the questions which people ask of events…Just as many questions can be asked of events,

so there will be many contexts; just as different people can ask different questions of events, so different people will determine different contexts; just as people can ask a number of different questions of events at the same time, questions of which other people may or may not be aware, so different people can simultaneously create and inhabit multiple contexts, contexts whose commonality is questionable.

Further, Ackerman and Halverson (1998) emphasize that "To reuse a memory, the user must then recontextualize that information. The information, if not supplied by the same individual, must be reunderstood for the user's current purpose" (p. 47). Hence, assuming that the questions individuals ask of events are determined by their experience, then there can be little doubt that contexts emerge and transform during acts of interpretations. In the following section we therefore take a closer look at acts of interpretations.

MAJOR FOCUS II: INTER-SUBJECTIVITY, TYPICALITY, IDEAL TYPES, AND CONTEXT

We recognize Schütz (1962, 1964, 1967), as a major focus in his research was on how cooperation evolves among actors who are more or less anonymous to each other (Ebeling, 1987). Thereby, his research can be used to provide insight into the emergence of contexts for sets of individuals with different degrees of similarities among their experiences. Schütz explains (Augier, 1999, pp. 158-159):

…that our 'life world' consists of a multitude of others, with whom we live and interact, although our knowledge about them is scarce. That is, we are more or less 'anonyme' to each other, despite the fact that the life world in which we are both is full of structures containing inter-subjective knowledge (see Schütz & Luckmann, 1973, 1989). This knowledge is used by imputing 'typical' 'course of action-types' and 'personal ideal types' to the individuals to analyze what happen if he/she follow[s] particular 'roles' (personal ideal types) or pursue[s] certain ends ('course of action-type').

Ideal types are used when we act and interpret events in the social world, and ideal types are abstractions from the particulars and the idiosyncrasies of the world; thus, they produce statements of general validity. Ideal types can be:

…arranged according to the degree of increasing anonymity of the relationship among contemporaries

involved and therewith of the context needed to grasp the other and his behavior. It becomes apparent that an increase in anonymity involves a decrease in fullness of content. The more anonymous the [ideal type] is the more detached is it from the uniqueness of [other individuals involved] ... If we distinguish between (subjective) personal ideal types and (objective) course-of-action types we may say that increasing [anonymity] of the construct leads to the superseding of the former by the latter. (Schütz, 1962, pp. 17-18)

In addition to our ideal typical knowledge, we possess more specialized information about particular kinds and groups of others. If we formerly had direct experience of the particular other facing us now, we can use the specialized information extracted in these experiences (Schütz, 1964, p. 30).

The individual brings ideal typical knowledge and more specialized information about others, artifacts, and situations, to a situation. Here they constitute the basis for the individual's interpretation of the situation, including others and artifacts, and thereby for the individual's conception of context. Consequently, specialized information and ideal types are the basic elements from which context emerges.

We, Thou, and They Relations

When we encounter others in the social world, they do not appear to us in identical perspectives, and our relations with them have different degrees of intimacy and anonymity (Schütz, 1964, p. 22). It is possible to distinguish among three types of relations: *they, thou,* and *we relations* (Schütz, 1967). In *we* relations individuals are aware of each other and of the awareness, and they are able to obtain understanding of each other's motives. In *thou* relations no such reciprocal awareness exists, and understanding involves more anonymous types of meaning. Finally, in *they* relations individuals use ideal types in order to impute 'typical' motives into each other and thereby understand each other's actions.

In *we* relations we experience others directly, we and they share a common sector of time and space, and thus we and they age together. The sharing of a common sector of space implies that we and others appear to one another in person as ourselves and nobody else (Schütz, 1964). "In the ongoing experiences of the *we* relation I check and revise my previous knowledge about my partner and accumulate new [specialized] knowledge about him. Thereby my general stock of knowledge also undergoes a continuous modification" (p. 30).

In *they* relations our partners are not concrete and unique individuals, but types, and "the experiences of

contemporaries appear to [us] more or less anonymous processes" (p. 43). As a result we obtain relatively little specialized information about their motives and actions. Also, in *they* relations my experience of my contemporaries is not continuously modified and enriched. "Each new experience of contemporaries adds, of course, to my stock of knowledge; and the ideal types by which I am oriented to others in a *they* relation do, indeed, undergo modifications...But these modifications remain minimal as long as a given situation and my interests in it—which have determined the original application of a given typifying scheme—remain constant" (p. 55).

Even if the ideal typical knowledge and the more specialized information that we obtain in our relations with others enable us to interpret and give meaning to the behavior by others, then these meanings may not correspond to the meanings of the others, as "...the subjective meaning of another person's behavior need not to be identical with the meaning which his perceived external behavior has for...an observer" (Schütz, 1967, p. 20).

In *we* relations we can assign our meaning to others with greater confidence, as the world within their reach coincides with ours. In *they* relations this reciprocity of experiences is replaced by acts of reflection on the typifying scheme which presumably orients the conduct of both they and us. The validity of our assumption that they share a given typifying scheme with us cannot be verified, since they are not present (Schütz, 1964, p. 54). "I cannot presuppose, for example, that my partner in a *they* relation will grasp a nuance of a word or that he will place a statement of mine in the proper context unless I explicitly and 'objectively' refer to that context. The direct evidence that I have been understood, which I have if my partner is present in the community of space and time, is lacking in a they relation" (Schütz, 1964, pp. 55-56).

From above it follows that individuals who have prior experience from a range of *we* relations with each other are likely to establish contexts with many similarities. In contrast, individuals who have little prior experience from *we* relations with each other are likely to establish contexts with few similarities. Therefore, as a group begins problem solving, the members of the group are not necessarily in the position to understand one another. Yet, as individuals we assume that everybody takes the world around us for granted in essentially the same way as we do ourselves, and thus we orient our actions towards other people, assuming that they will behave in a 'typical' manner. Consequently, it might take time before we register that this is not the case, and thereby register that little common understanding has emerged.

MAJOR FOCUS II: PEOPLE SOLVING COMPLEX PROBLEMS

We illustrate the emergence and transformation of context with a case where a complex problem is solved within a constrained timeframe, as we believe it is in such problem-solving processes that emergence and transformation of context are most visible. We build this belief on Ciborra, who some years ago suggested that "people improvise when they are overwhelmed by the world, and thus, is forced to read the world in a different way."[1] Improvisation "is purposeful human behavior which seems to be ruled at the same time by intuition, competence, design, and chance" (Ciborra, 1999, p. 78). Thus, it is the lack of time to solve complex problems that leads people to improvise. Furthermore, improvisation is grounded in memory of the past (Weick, 1998, p. 547), and thereby, in the ideal typical knowledge and more specialized information that individuals bring to the process.

Complex Problem Solving During the Ill-Fated Apollo 13 Mission

The Apollo 13 mission was on schedule when the message *"Okay, Houston, we've got a problem here..."* came from the Apollo 13 Command Module. An oxygen tank had exploded, damaged the Service Module, and left the Command Module without power and air. After a health assessment of the spacecraft, it was decided to abandon the mission, move the three astronauts to the Lunar Module, and attempt a loop around the moon in order to get the spacecraft back to the planet earth.

Soon after the explosion, the assessment of life-support systems determined that although oxygen supplies were adequate, the system for removing Carbon Dioxide in the Lunar Module was not. The Lunar Module was designed to support two men for two days and was being asked to care for three men nearly four days. Thus, removal of Carbon Dioxide in the Lunar Module became a concern. The system in the Lunar Module used canisters filled with Lithium Hydroxide to absorb Carbon Dioxide as did the system in the Command Module. Unfortunately the canisters were not interchangeable between the two systems, so the astronauts were faced with plenty of capacity for removing Carbon Dioxide but no way of using it.

Facing this potentially fatal problem, a ground crew team at NASA Mission Control in Houston brought into a room all the items available on board the spacecraft, including the space suits originally planned for use during the visit to the moon. Using these items the team worked on a solution and constructed a device it believed could be implemented by the astronauts. After a test in the spacecraft simulator, the solution was verified and the instructions were transmitted to the astronauts on board the spacecraft. The astronauts succeeded in assembling the two carbon dioxide removal devices:

There was, of course, a fix; and it came in the form of an ingenious combination of suit hoses, cardboard, plastic stowage bags, and Command Module canisters—all held together with a liberal application of gray duct tape. As was usual whenever the Apollo team had to improvise, engineers and astronauts on the ground got busy devising ways around the problem and then checked out the new procedures. A day and a half after the Apollo 13 accident, the ground team had designed and built a filtering device that worked to their satisfaction. They promptly radioed instructions to the crew, carefully leading them through about an hour's worth of steps. As Lovell wrote later: 'the contraption wasn't very handsome, but it worked.'

Emergence and Transformation of Context in the Apollo 13 Case

We draw three inferences about the emergence and transformation of context in the Apollo 13 case. We show how the need for problem solving by improvisation emerged, we interpret how the ground crew responded to the problem, and finally, we discuss the conditions for their success with problem solving.

The explosion on board the spacecraft created a novel problem and forced the NASA Mission Control Team into action. The team was overwhelmed by the urgency of the crisis, as the challenge was to create a solution that could be implemented by using the items available on board the spacecraft. Hence, the ground crew had to move beyond their ex ante knowledge, and include and create knowledge useful in the present situation.

In our interpretation of the ground crews' response, we claim that as soon as the Carbon Dioxide filtering problem was known, each of them produced a personal interpretation of what it meant and how it could be solved. As a result a context emerged for each of them, with their individual contexts including their knowledge about how each of the other ground crews could contribute. This knowledge was based both on ideal types of these others and on more intimate experiences from past *we* relations with them.

Realizing that the solution could not be found within the potential solutions available on ground, but should be created from the items available on board the spacecraft, the ground crew experienced a transformation of their contexts, as now they had to perceive their knowledge about Carbon Dioxide filtering within the permutations of possibilities that existed within the scope of items available on board the spacecraft. By acknowledging this as a constraint, they adapted their contexts to the complexity of the problem situation. We assert that when adapting their contexts, they took into account what they knew about the fellow team members' knowledge about Carbon Dioxide filtering and the possibility of applying it within the constraints imposed by the situation. Consequently, they experienced that knowledge previously irrelevant to the Carbon Dioxide filtering problem might be relevant in this particular situation.

Reviewing the Carbon Dioxide filtering problem-solving process, we suggest that the ground crew experienced that none of them held sufficient knowledge to solve the problem on their own. Hence, they realized that knowledge sharing was necessary for creating a solution. It is our assertion that knowledge sharing required that the problem solvers took on *we* orientations towards each other, and thereby established *we* relations in the problem-solving process, as otherwise they could not obtain verifications of similarities in typifying schemes among themselves and their partners, and had not been able to solve the problem.

Establishment of *we* relations in problem solving is however not sufficient to give way for effective knowledge sharing. Also, the intimacy of *we* relations is important—that is, how easy problem solvers experience it to follow each other's lines of thoughts. We suggest that the intimacy of *we* relations is a result of the extent to which the context emerging and transforming for each of the problem solvers exhibits similarities with the contexts emerging and transforming for the other problem solvers. In turn the emergence of contexts with many similarities requires that problem solvers have shared many common sectors of time and space prior to the problem solving in situ. Consequently, the less anonymous problem solvers are to each other, the fewer obstacles to tacit knowledge sharing they will experience. These preconditions existed in the Apollo 13 case where the ground crew and the astronauts held similar experiences from prior training and collaboration. Had this not been the case, then we assert that the ground crew had experienced difficulties in following each other's line of thought and in gaining a common ground for problem solving.

In sum, we find that problem solving in the Apollo 13 case was conditioned on: (a) the ability of the ground crew to register the world and form novel views of the available resources (the suit hoses, cardboard, plastic bags, tape, etc.) as possible components of a new Carbon Dioxide filtering devices; and (b) the establishment of *we* relations, which allowed for the emergence of contexts with many similarities and thereby for tacit knowledge sharing. Accordingly, it is the ability to create contexts with many

similarities as well as the possession of in-depth knowledge about the items available for the creation of a solution that enables people to solve complex problems.

CONCLUSION AND FUTURE TRENDS

In the introduction we asked: What is context? How does context emerge and transform? What is the relationship between context and tacit knowledge sharing?

First, using Polanyi (1962) as our point of departure, we defined context as an individual construct, which emerges as an individual encounters and interprets a situation, and therefore contexts are not "just there" as static entities.

Second, building on the theories of Schütz (1962, 1964, 1967), we argued that an individual's interpretation of a situation happens as that individual brings his experience in the form of ideal typical knowledge and more specialized information to the situation. Subsequently, his context transforms over time, as he is confronted with other problem solvers and constraints imposed on the problem-solving process.

Third, we argued that sharing of tacit knowledge in complex problem solving requires the emergence of contexts with many similarities, as otherwise the problem solvers cannot obtain verifications of similarities in understandings. We also argued that contexts with many similarities solely emerge if problem solvers have shared many common sectors of time and space prior to the problem solving in situ.

Having established the relationship between context and tacit knowledge sharing, we argue that the salience of context will become increasingly important to problem solvers as they face compressed timeframes for problem solving, while at the same time the complexity of problems to be solved requires bringing together knowledge from experts in several specialized domains. For success with such problem solving, the possibility of establishing intimate *we* relations is of paramount significance, and therefore, organizations must consider if there are areas for which it makes sense for them to invest in preparation for emergence of contexts with many similarities, as only such contexts allow for tacit knowledge sharing. For these areas, *we* relations among experts should be fertilized as only these, and for example not *they* relations, will breed the ground tacit knowledge sharing.

In this article we have showed that contexts are not just there, and even more important we have moved beyond the highly general conceptions of context and provided insight into the processes that result in the emergence of contexts, which allow for tacit knowledge sharing. Now returning to the initial discussion of the

837

context concept 'ba' provided by Nonaka and peers, we remember that they acknowledged the importance of context, because knowledge-creating processes are necessarily context specific. Yet, from their writings, for example Nonaka and Konno (1998) and Nonaka and Toyama (2000), it was unclear what context is and how it emerges. In this article these two questions were addressed and answered, and thus the article provided new insights of significance to future knowledge management research. Our definition of context, its emergence and transformation do not go against Nonaka et al. (2000b), as for example they note that "... 'ba' has a here and now quality, and that it is constantly moving, it is created, functions and disappear according to need" (pp. 15-16). However, a verification of our theory of context calls for more empirical studies of complex problem solving, and thus, such studies must be the next step in the research focusing on context and its implication for tacit knowledge sharing.

REFERENCES

Ackerman, M.S., & Halverson, C. (1998, November). Considering an organization's memory. *Proceedings of the ACM Conference on Computer Supported Cooperative Work* (CSCW '98) (pp. 39-48).

Augier, M. (1999). Some notes on Alfred Schütz and the Austrian School of Economics: Review of Alfred Schütz's collected papers (vol. IV). In H. Wagner, G. Psathas, & F. Kersten (Eds.). (1996), *Review of Austrian Economics, 11*, 145-162.

Casey, E.S. (1997). *The fate of place: A philosophical history*. Berkeley, CA: University of California Press.

Ciborra, C.U. (1999). Notes on improvisation and time in organizations. *Accounting, Management and Information Technology, 9*(1), 77-94.

Dilley, R. (Ed.). (1999). *The problem of context*. New York: Berghahn Books.

Ebeling, R. (1987). Cooperation in anonymity. *Critical Review, 1*, 50-59.

Erickson, F., & Schultz, J. (1997). When is a context? Some issues and methods in the analysis of social competence. In M. Cole, Y. Engeström, & O. Vasquez (Eds.), *Mind, culture and activity—seminal papers from the Laboratory of Comparative Human Cognition* (pp. 22-31). Cambridge, UK. Cambridge University Press.

Hutchins, E. (1995). *Cognition in the wild*. Cambridge, MA: MIT Press.

McDermott, R.P. (1976). *Kids make sense: An ethnographic account of the interactional management of success and failure in one first-grade classroom*. Unpublished dissertation, Stanford University, USA.

Nonala, I. (1994). A dynamic theory of organizational knowledge creation. *Organization Science, 5*(1), 14-37.

Nonaka, I., & Konno, N. (1998). The concept of "ba": Building foundation for knowledge creation. *California Management Review, 40*(3), 40-54.

Nonaka, I., & Toyama, R. (2000, May 25-26). What is a good ba? Providing shared context-in-motion for organizational knowledge creation. *Proceedings of the Conference on Knowledge and Innovation* (pp. 1-20), Helsinki, Finland.

Nonaka, I., Toyama, R., & Nagata, A. (2000a). A firm as a knowledge creating entity: A new perspective on the theory of the firm. *Industrial and Corporate Change, 9*(1), 1-20.

Nonaka, I., Toyama, R., & Konno, N. (2000b). SECI, ba, and leadership: A unified model of dynamic knowledge creation. *Long Range Planning, 33*(1), 5-34.

Polanyi, M. (1962). *Personal knowledge: Towards a post-critical philosophy*. Chicago: Chicago University Press.

Polanyi, M. (1966). *The tacit dimension*. London: Routledge & Kegan Paul.

Rapport, N. (1999). Context as an act of personal externalization. In R. Dilley (Ed.), *The problem of context* (pp. 187-211). New York: Berghahn Books.

Schütz, A. (1962). Common sense and scientific interpretation of human action. In M. Natanson (Ed.), *Collected papers I—the problem of social reality* (pp. 3-47). Dordrect, The Netherlands: Kluwer Academic Publishers.

Schütz, A. (1964). The dimensions of the social world. In A. Brodersen (Ed.), *Collected papers II—studies in social theory* (pp. 20-63). The Hague, The Netherlands: Martinus Nijhoff.

Schütz, A. (1967). *The phenomenology of the social world*. Evanston, IL: Northwestern University Press.

Schütz, A., & Luckmann, T. (1973). *The structures of the life-world* (vol. 1). London, UK: Heinemann.

Schütz, A., & Luckmann, T. (1989). *The structures of the life-world* (vol. 2). Evanstone, IL: Northwestern University Press.

Weick, K.E. (1998). Improvisation as a mindset for organizational analysis. *Organization Science, 9*(5), 543-555.

KEY TERMS

Ba: Nonaka and peers concept for context. Yet, they lack a concise definition of what 'ba' is, and therefore, it remains unclear what exactly 'ba' is, how it emerges, and what happens inside it.

Context: An individual construct that emerges as an individual encounters a situation, including others and artifacts, as it is the individual's interpretation of a situation that results in context.

Ideal Types: Abstractions from the particulars and the idiosyncrasies of the world which produce statements of general validity, and we know some part of the world because of its character as ideal typical knowledge.

Tacit Knowledge: Based on Polanyi (1966), Nonaka (1994) defines tacit knowledge as knowledge that has a personal quality, which makes it difficult to formalize and communicate. Tacit knowledge may be embedded in routines and mental models.

They **Relations:** Relations where our partners are types, and not concrete and unique individuals. We experience then in more or less anonymous processes, and thus we obtain relatively little specialized information about their motives and actions.

Thou **Relations:** Relations where no reciprocal awareness exists among us and our partners, and therefore, understanding involves more anonymous types of meaning.

We **Relations:** Relations where we experience others directly, we and they share a common sector of time and space, and thus we and they age together.

ENDNOTE

[1]   From a talk given by Claudio Ciborra at the Academy of Management Meetings in Toronto, 2000.

Task-Based Knowledge Management

Frada Burstein
Monash University, Australia

Henry Linger
Monash University, Australia

INTRODUCTION

In modern organizations, the major role of knowledge management is supporting knowledge work. The concept of knowledge work assumes not only task performance, but also the review and evaluation of the work done in order to understand and learn from the experience. Knowledge work relies on a body of knowledge to support processes that address both the performance of work and the intellective aspects of the work activity (Zuboff, 1988). In this sense knowledge management becomes one of the most important mechanisms in implementing such support. In this article we present task-based knowledge management (TbKM) as an alternative approach to knowledge management (KM).

BACKGROUND

Most KM approaches focus on organizational knowledge and/or organizational processes and their management (e.g., Davenport & Prusak, 1998; Tiwana, 2000; Awad & Ghaziri, 2003). The TbKM approach addresses the management of knowledge work rather than knowledge. It is a bottom-up approach that focuses on the practicalities of work activities, as performed by individuals and groups. Thus TbKM is directed to supporting both:

- task performance to achieve organizationally defined outcomes; and
- work practices of actors including the generation and collection of experiential knowledge associated with task performance, as well as single- and double-loop learning (Argyris & Schön, 1978).

The focus of TbKM is not directed towards automating any work practice. Task-oriented methods for knowledge-based systems were proposed in artificial intelligence projects to automate problem solving and reasoning by representing knowledge in a computable form (Chandrasekaran & Johnson, 1993). These approaches relied on capturing all organizational knowledge related to the task and creating a formally defined knowledge repository (Schreiber, Welinger & Breuker, 1993).

The TbKM approach provides an infrastructure for knowledge work where knowledge is a by-product of task performance. This infrastructure allows the knowledge worker to document the task instances in a way that is shareable with other actors performing that task. Thus TbKM is essentially an implementation of a *knowledge work support system (KWSS)* that systemically preserves knowledge of each instance of the task in a dynamic memory system. In order to support knowledge work, this memory includes the pragmatic outcomes as well as the knowledge created through task performance. Effective utilisation of this memory is facilitated by TbKM functionality such as reasoning, memory aids, explanation facilities, and learning capability. Moreover, the TbKM approach is consistent with reflective practice in that actors are encouraged to reuse and create knowledge through learning as an integral part of the task (Schön, 1991).

The task-based approach has been formalised as a theoretical framework that underpins our research. This approach has been used as an evolving framework analytically to diagnose research settings and determine the aspects of focus. Additionally, the framework has also been the core of the conceptual design for prototyping KM systems and KM development programs.

The task-based approach to knowledge management has evolved from a wide range of projects that have been undertaken and the practical requirements imposed by industry collaborators (Burstein & Linger, 2003, 2002; Linger & Burstein, 2001; Linger, Burstein, Zaslavsky & Crofts, 1999; Linger, Burstein, Ryan & Kelly, 2000; Fennessy & Burstein, 2000).

MAJOR ELEMENTS OF THE TASK-BASED APPROACH TO KNOWLEDGE MANAGEMENT

The TbKM approach focuses on *knowledge work*, not *knowledge* as the object of knowledge management. Thus the major elements of this approach are:

- a task focus
- a task-based model of knowledge work
- a community of practice
- an organizational memory
- task outcome
- knowledge work support

Task Focus

Underlying the TbKM approach is the focus on work practice. The approach aims to explore how the work is actually done, not how it is meant to be done or what individuals say they do. In this context, a *task:*

is a substantially invariant organizational activity with outcomes that include tangible outputs that are central to the organization's viability and the internal outcomes that are potential drivers of organizational change. (Burstein & Linger, 2003, p. 290)

In terms of this article, no distinction is made between an (organizational) *activity* and *task,* and the terms are used interchangeably unless indicated otherwise. Organizational activity, as used here, derives from Situated Activity Theory proposed by Iivari and Linger (1999, 2000) to characterize knowledge work. Such activity differs from the actions of individual actors, as the scope of the activity requires a number of actors for its completion.

For example, weather forecasting is organised around shifts that involve a number of forecasters. Each forecaster is given responsibility for particular forecast products, but each product needs to be consistent with the forecast policy that is set collectively by the shift. This example also highlights that such activity is socially situated in that all actors collectively engage in processes that enable them to gain a shared understanding of the activity. It is this understanding that enables each actor to intentionally complete their activity. Since the activity outcomes are organizationally determined, the actors' shared understanding of the activity also includes their understanding of the organizational imperatives that underlie the activity.

Task-Based Model of Knowledge Work

Task models produced for knowledge-based systems (KBS) development (see for example, Duursma, 1993) mapped the task into a generic task category (Chandrasekaran, Johnson & Smith, 1992). The intention was to generate a computational procedure based on Generic Task model represented as a hierarchical or tree model, including tasks, methods, and subtasks (Chandrasekaran & Johnson, 1993), that intended to mimic an expert's performance.

Such formal problem-solving methods are based on task structures that attempt to fully represent the problem-space and produce fully computable knowledge-level descriptions. For example, KADS and KADS-II European projects came up with a four-layered model of problem-domain knowledge (Schreiber et al., 1993). Although such knowledge-level descriptions made a major contribution in their analysis of task-oriented approaches to knowledge modelling, in many practical contexts the normative algorithms for solving real problems are "less useful than they seem" (Chandrasekaran & Johnson, 1993, p. 52).

The TbKM approach departs from the idea of generic representation of the task and its context. Organizational work, the task, is represented as two nested layers. The *pragmatic* represents actual work practice and the work that needs to be done. It is associated with the performance of the task, and is concerned with the efficient and effective execution of the task. The *conceptual* layer views the task from a more generalised, abstract perspective, expressed in terms of the overall goals and objectives of the task and related concepts and structures. The conceptual layer represents some aspects of the actors' understanding of the task in terms of models representing the structure of their knowledge and their knowledge of the process required to perform the task.

In a context of knowledge work, these layers correspond to *doing* (pragmatic) and *thinking* (conceptual) components of the activity as represented in Figure 1. From the point of view of knowledge management, we concentrate on the conceptual layer since the actors are knowledge workers who have the expertise to perform the task.

The model represents a generalisation of the task. We recognise two conceptual components associated with the task: a Structure and a Process. These two components come from the understanding of *what* concepts are involved in performing the task and *how* these concepts need to be applied. Task performance involves instantiating, and where necessary modifying, these generic components in a way that accommodates the current situation, and then executing the procedure. Reflection on and learning from task performance contributes to changes or improvements to the generic structure and process. In the context of knowledge work, specialising the structure and process, as well as reflecting on the instances of the task, is a fundamental feature of TbKM.

Each time a task is performed in a specific work context, the Structure and Process models are instantiated to reflect the specific work situation. Each instantiation then becomes a record of the task and cumulatively represents a task-based organizational memory (Ackerman & Mandel, 1995). The importance of this interpretation of the framework is that this memory is an essential part of the learning process. The historical evolution of these models is a

Figure 1. A task-based model of knowledge work (adapted from Linger & Burstein, 1997)

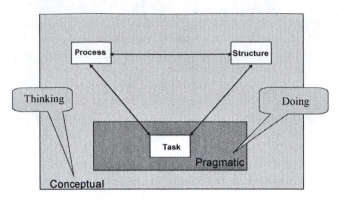

representation of learning and a component of organizational memory (Spender, 1996).

A Community of Practice: CoP

Actors engaged in the task can be collectively termed a community, as they all have a professional interest in that work (Wenger, 1998; Brown & Duguid, 1991). In the TbKM approach, a community of practice is defined as a group of actors who are engaged directly in performing some aspects of the task. This conceptualisation of community is more restrictive than the commonly used definitions in the literature (e.g., Wenger, 1998). It is used deliberately to distinguish between members of the community and others who are potential stakeholders in the task or its outputs. However, actors are not restricted from participating in other communities within an organization through their engagement in other activities and tasks.

Restricting the community to actors engaged in task performance enables the community to establish and maintain the body of knowledge and shared meanings associated with the task. These are necessary elements to ensure the reliability and validity of each actor's contribution to the task. Moreover, each actor brings to the community contextual knowledge based on their other involvements within the organization. This enables computer-based knowledge management systems to be constructed as closed systems without the need for extensive contextual information to be included (Schatz, 1992).

Since the community is engaged in knowledge work, the actors have considerable autonomy in performing the task. However, as a community, working with other actors requires a degree of common understanding of the object of their work, the task, to ensure task outcomes meet organizational requirements. TbKM accommodates the idiosyncratic work practices of individual actors, but also

provides the tools for the community to maintain its shared understanding of the task. Thus knowledge sharing is acknowledged as an integral part of work practices that still tolerates individual differences.

Organizational Memory

Each time the task is performed, it generates a collection of outcomes, related processes, and "stories" or narratives shared by the community (Czarniawska-Joerges, 1992). There is a potential of recording and preserving aspects of this experience in an organizational memory as instances and episodes of the task including the conceptual models that represent the individual and collective understanding of the task. As TbKM supports knowledge work, it needs to provide actors with the necessary tools to perform both the *doing* and *thinking* aspects of the task.

Instantiation of the whole range of tools to perform the task allows memory to be constructed as a by-product of task performance. Moreover, the more menial aspects of the task (*doing*) can be articulated and automated, the more time and space is left for the actor to be more involved with the tools for the intellective aspects of the task (*thinking*) without a punitive overhead. An example of this approach is in weather forecasting, where the forecast (and the rationale for the forecast) forms part of the memory that is used as input to future forecast preparation, as well as the basis for learning from past forecast performance.

Task Outcomes

Task performance must result in the organizationally defined outcomes that contribute to the organization's viability. In terms of TbKM, task performance also results in outcomes that relate the intellectual assets of the organization. These can be considered at two levels: individual and organizational. At the organizational level the outcomes contribute to the organizational productivity, through improved work practices, and knowledge assets in terms of contributions to organizational memory. Organizational outcomes also relate to effectiveness in terms of the organization's ability to deploy and exploit knowledge through knowledge sharing, reuse, and creation. At the individual level, task outcomes relate to the actor's ability to learn, use the knowledge assets productively, and contribute to and sustain the community of practice. TbKM is a heterogeneous approach in that it adopts a cognitive perspective when focussed on individual outcomes, but it has a social perspective when community or organizational aspects are in focus.

Knowledge Work Support System

We view technology as a very important enabler for knowledge management. This is consistent with the view expressed in mainstream KM research and practice (e.g., Alavi & Leidner, 2001; Davenport & Prusak, 2000). Task performance needs to be supported by a technological system that enables actors to produce tangible outputs. Much of IT development effort is directed to support the *doing* aspects of knowledge work. Less common is support for the *thinking* aspects. These support systems allow actors to engage in a joint cognitive process to evaluate, review, and reflect on task performance, as well as access and reuse past knowledge stored in memory. Memory can be deployed in processes that allow actors to understand and make sense of the task, as well as explore, innovate, and learn.

THE TbKM FRAMEWORK FOR ORGANIZATIONAL KNOWLEDGE MANAGEMENT

The TbKM approach to task performance is based on integrating production with knowledge processes. In this respect, technology, in the form of a knowledge work support system, mediates task performance by the community of practice. Figure 2 represents a TbKM system for organizational knowledge work.

In this framework the Knowledge Work Support (KWS) system is in the centre of two dimensions referred to as

"*doing*" and "*thinking*" as in Figure 1. Thus in the vertical axis (Task, KWS, Outcomes) the KWS supports production, while in the horizontal axis (KWS, Memory) it supports knowledge processes.

The outcome of production is goods and/or delivery of services. By including the KWS system in the KMS, the task outcomes also potentially include improvement in the means of production of goods and delivery of services. Put differently, the functioning of the KWS system is concerned with organizational efficiency, its ability to supply market demands, as well as the organization's internal effectiveness including its ability to learn and create, share and reuse knowledge.

In the context of task-based KMS, the organizational memory system (OMS) needs to be a dynamic and multi-dimensional source of useful organizational knowledge. It needs to support learning and other organizational knowledge processes, as well as accommodate individual perspectives. This contrasts with the more static view of OMS as a repository. We see it rather as an active component of an intelligent system supporting knowledge processes. The OMS contains the necessary information to perform the task, artefacts that express the actors' and CoP knowledge, and understanding of the task at the individual as well as collective and organizational levels. This material enables the OMS to support learning based on feedback, review, and evaluation. The diversity of the content of the OMS does not mandate any specific technology. In fact our approach is strengthened if different technologies are combined as it allows actors to express their understanding by constructing artefacts using inscriptions (Latour, 1990) that represent the task in

Figure 2. A model of a task-based knowledge management system (adopted from Burstein & Linger, 2003)

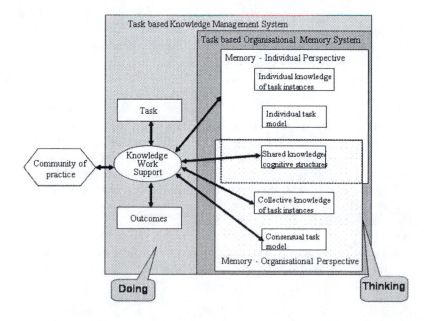

a way that is consistent with the knowledge that under-pins task performance.

FUTURE TRENDS

The TbKM framework explicitly supports knowledge work in the *thinking* and *doing* dimensions. Implicit in this formulation is the temporal dimension. The formulation of organizational memory in the *thinking* dimension allows the TbKM framework to represent temporal aspects of knowledge management in the form of past experiences. Moreover, this memory is a fundamental aspect of the *thinking* dimension and explicitly facilitates knowledge processes including double-loop learning (Argyris & Schön, 1978) to review work practices and for knowledge creation.

However, knowledge work is by definition a socially situated activity and implicitly assumes all actors, in the community defined by the task, interact and communicate. The challenge therefore is to explicitly extend the TbKM framework to incorporate another dimension—*communicating*. This would define knowledge management as existing within the three dimensions of *thinking, doing,* and *communicating*.

The TbKM framework currently assumes an organizational or enterprise context. This context is essential to situate the activities, the work practices, that are its focus. This bottom-up approach differentiates task-based knowledge management from the mainstream literature, but needs to be extended to explicitly incorporate the organizational perspective. To accommodate this perspective, we intend to extend the framework by adopting a three-level approach that deals with knowledge management at the micro, meso, and macro levels, as foreshadowed in Linger and Burstein (2001) and Linger and Warne (2001). The suggested approach accommodates the integration of organizational (macro), group (meso), and individual (micro) perspectives, as well as identifying capability (macro), collaboration (meso), and action (micro) as the discourse of these perspectives.

The TbKM framework as currently presented is grounded with the context of a specific organization. However, the imperative of the new (information or knowl-edge) economies requires consideration of inter-organizational as well as intra-organizational knowledge management strategies. This will require consideration of issues beyond work practices such as governance, collaborative arrangements, and the legal framework. In this context, the TbKM framework can be considered as a foundational structure for an inter-organizational knowl-edge management architecture.

CONCLUSION

The TbKM framework is general and applicable in any domain, as demonstrated by the diversity of the case studies we have undertaken (Linger et al., 1999; Linger et al., 2000; Fennessy & Burstein, 2000; Linger & Burstein, 2001; Linger & Warne, 2001). Moreover, the generality of the framework is enhanced, as it does not prescribe any modelling formalism for any element of the framework. Rather, as the case studies illustrate, it is the task, and its underlying body of knowledge, that influences how elements are represented and modelled.

The framework provides a practical means for organizations to implement knowledge management regimes as it is applicable to any task that involves knowledge work. This flexibility derives from the fact that the framework is based on a theoretical understanding of knowledge work that allows TbKM to:

- add value to knowledge that the organization already has by explicitly recognising knowledge work;
- support actors performing the task, rather than automating it, in order to exploit knowledge processes;
- apply knowledge management on a scale that can be operationalised within a time scale that meets organizational imperatives;
- focus on knowledge creation and organizational learning rather than the self-limiting goal of organizational efficiency;
- produce outputs, in terms of products and services, while supporting the continuous improvements to these outputs and the means of their production;
- focus on work activities rather than modelling the organization; and
- integrate and support dynamic knowledge and production processes rather than view knowledge management in terms of a static knowledge repository.

In the literature there is a remarkable number of definitions of knowledge management, not least because of its currency and because of its perceived importance (Davenport & Prusak, 1998; Tiwana, 2000; Awad & Ghaziri, 2003). Our working definition is:

Knowledge management is a broad concept that addresses the full range of processes by which the organization deploys knowledge.

This definition is consistent with our premise that KM is about the management of knowledge work. This entails a conception of the actor as a professional (knowledge worker) working in a community of practice defined by the task. Each actor makes autonomous professional/ethical/moral judgements that are consistent with the task and its organizational context. Such judgements are an intrinsic part of the understanding of the task shared by the community.

The TbKM framework addresses all aspects of this definition. Moreover, TbKM reveals actual work practices in a way that allows organizations to integrate their production functions with learning. Thus the framework can be used diagnostically, to identify implicit knowledge management practices, and as an architecture to design the informational and technological infrastructure to support the organizational changes that underpin a knowledge management strategy.

REFERENCES

Ackerman, M.S., & Mandel, E. (1995). Memory in the small: An application to provide task-based organizational memory for a scientific community. *Proceedings of the 28ᵗʰ Hawaii International Conference on Systems Science* (pp. 323-332). IEEE Press.

Alavi, M., & Leidner, D.E. (2001). Knowledge management and knowledge management systems: Conceptual foundations and research issues. *MIS Quarterly, 25*(1), 107-136.

Angehrn, A., & Luthi, S. (1990). Intelligent decision support systems: A visual interactive approach. *Interfaces, 20*(6), 17-28.

Argyris, C., & Schön, D.A. (1978). *Organizational learning: A theory of action perspective*. Reading, MA: Addison-Wesley.

Awad, E.M., & Ghaziri, H.M. (2003). *Knowledge management*. Pearson International.

Brown, J.S., & Duguid, P. (1991). Organizational learning and communities-of-practice: Toward a unified view of working, learning, and innovation. *Organization Science, 2*(1), 40-57.

Burstein, F., & Linger, H. (2002, September 24-25). A task-based framework for supporting knowledge work practices. *Proceedings of the 3ʳᵈ European Conference on Knowledge Management* (ECKM2002) (pp. 100-112), Trinity College Dublin, Ireland.

Burstein, F., & Linger, H. (2003). Supporting post-Fordist work practices: A knowledge management framework for dynamic intelligent decision support. *Journal of IT&P* (Special Issue on KM), *16*(3), 289-305.

Chandrasekaran, B., Johnson, T.R., & Smith, J.W. (1992). Task structure analysis for knowledge modelling. *Communications of the ACM, 35*(9), 124-137.

Chandrasekaran, B., & Johnson, T.R. (1993). Generic tasks and task structures: History, critique and new directions. In J.-M. David, J.-P. Krivine, & R. Simmons (Eds.), *Second generation expert systems* (pp. 232-272). Berlin: Springer-Verlag.

Czarniawska-Joerges, B. (1992). Exploring complex organizations: A cultural perspective. Newbury Park, CA: Sage Publications.

Davenport, T., & Prusak, L. (1998). *Working knowledge: How organizations manage what they know*. Boston: Harvard Business School Press.

Duursma. (1993). *Task model definition for task analysis process*. KADS-II Report, VUB AI Lab.

Fennessy, G., & Burstein, F. (2000). Developing a knowledge management system to support intermediaries in health care decision making. *Proceedings of the IFIP WG 8.3 Conference: Decision Support Through Knowledge Management* (pp. 122-136).

Iivari, J., & Linger, H. (2000, August). The characteristics of knowledge work: A theoretical perspective. *Proceedings of the Americas Conference on Information Systems* (AMCIS'2000), Long Beach, CA.

Iivari, J., & Linger, H. (1999). Knowledge work as collaborative work: A situated activity theory view. *Proceedings of Hawaiian International Conference on Systems Science* (HICSS'32). IEEE Press.

Latour, B. (1990). Drawing things together. In M. Lynch & S. Woolgar (Eds.), *Representation in scientific activity* (pp. 19-68). Cambridge, MA: MIT Press.

Linger, H., & Bustein, F. (2001). From computation to knowledge management: The changing paradigm of decision support for meteorological forecasting. *Journal of Decision Systems* (Special Issue on Decision Systems in Action), *10*(2), 195-216.

Linger, H., Burstein, F., Ryan, C., & Kelly, J. (2000, December). Implementing a knowledge management system: The case of meteorological forecasting. *Australian Conference on Knowledge Management and Decision Support* (ACKMIDS'2000) (pp. 139-153). Melbourne: Australian Scholarly Publishers.

Linger, H., & Warne, L. (2001). Making the invisible visible: Modelling social learning in a knowledge management context. *Australian Journal of Information Systems* (Special Issue on Knowledge Management), (December), 56-66.

Linger, H., & Burstein, F. (1998). Learning in organizational memory systems: An intelligent decision support perspective. *Proceedings of the Hawaiian International Conference on Systems Science* (HICSS'31). IEEE Press.

Linger, H., & Burstein, F. (1997). Intelligent decision support in the context of the modern organization. *Proceedings of the 5th ISDSS International Conference*, Laussane.

Linger, H., Burstein, F., Zaslavsky, A., & Crofts, N. (1999). A framework for a dynamic organizational memory information system. *Journal of Organizational Computing and Electronic Commerce, 9*(2&3), 189-204.

Schatz, B.R. (1992). Building an electronic community system. *Journal of Management Information Systems, 8*(3).

Schön, D.A. (1991). *The reflective practitioner: How professionals think in action.* Aldershot, UK: Arena Ashgate Publishing.

Schreiber, G., Welinger, B., & Breuker, J. (Eds.). (1993). *KADS : A principled approach to knowledge-based system development.* London: Academic Press.

Spender, J.C. (1996). Organizational knowledge, learning and memory: Three concepts in search of a theory. *Journal of Organizational Change Management, 9*(1), 63-78.

Stein, E.W., & Zwass, V. (1995). Actualizing organizational memory with information systems. *Information Systems Research, 6*(2), 85-117.

Tiwana, A. (2000). *The knowledge management toolkit: Practical techniques for building a knowledge management system.* Englewood Cliffs, NJ: Prentice-Hall International.

Walsh, J.P., & Ungson, G.R. (1991). Organizational memory. *Academy of Management Review, 16*(1), 57-91.

Wenger, E. (1998). *Communities of practice: Learning, meaning and identity.* Cambridge: Cambridge University Press.

Zuboff, S. (1988). *In the age of the smart machine, the future of work and power.* Oxford: Heineman.

KEY TERMS

Collaboration: Involves multiple actors who participate in an action that shares a common object of work. Within that action, actors maintain their individual perceptions of the objective of that action, as their participation and contribution is directed to promoting individual goals. Thus the individual objectives of the actors are not necessarily positively linked. This formulation explains cooperation between competitive actors (Iivari & Linger, 1999).

Community of Practice: In TbKM, a community of practice shares the characteristics of a community described by Wenger (1998), but is limited to those actors who are actively engaged in all aspects of task performance. This definition excludes other stakeholders who have a potential interest or involvement with the task (Burstein & Linger, 2002).

Intelligent Decision Support (IDS): A term used in an epistemological sense in relation to its role in the workplace in the sense that "[IDS] behave(s) like human consultants supporting decision makers in understanding, expressing, and structuring their problems" (Angehrn & Luthi, 1990). Intelligence in this context stems from the active role played by the system in supporting task performance, knowledge processing, and experiential learning. In this role it incorporates functionality absent from traditional DSS—learning, memory, and reasoning. Thus actors engage with an IDS in a joint cognitive process to achieve the task outcomes (Linger & Burstein, 1997).

Knowledge Work: Work that

- is based on a body of knowledge;
- is focused on an object of work, usually defined through negotiation;
- usually entails working on representations of the object of work;
- typically assumes a deep understanding of the object of work; and
- entails knowledge as an essential ingredient of its outputs.

Knowledge work thus involves both knowledge-applying and knowledge-producing activities, but significantly it also includes activities that have outputs other than knowledge or information (Iivari & Linger, 2000).

Organizational Memory: A historical repository whose purpose is to support organizational effectiveness (Walsh & Ungson, 1991; Schatz, 1992). Stein and Zwass (1995) define a two-layered framework consisting of mnemonic functions (knowledge acquisition, storage, maintenance, search, and retrieval) supporting subsystems that address knowledge sharing, environmental scanning, planning and control, and the evolution of the cultural and social environment of the organization.

Organizational Memory System: A system that uses organizational memory to support post-Fordist work practices through processes of remembering and forgetting.

These processes involve the interaction of internal images, cognitive representation of the activity with external inscriptions, and explicitly recorded material. In this sense the memory system is an cognitive process that involves an actor, engaged in purposeful activity, interacting with stored material that is generally computer based (Linger & Burstein, 1998)

Post-Fordism: A description of the changing nature of work practices that address an organization's dynamic environment and its internal needs to adapt to the changing environment. Post-Fordist work practices involve workers taking responsibility for analysing, reflecting, and innovatively changing their work tasks. Post-Fordism is characterised by work teams, increased skill levels of the actors, time for reflection and learning incorporated into work tasks, longer cycle times or work units, and devolution to work teams of decisions relating to product quality, production planning, process improvements, and general self-management. (Linger & Burstein, 1997).

Task: A substantially invariant organizational activity with outcomes that include tangible outputs that are central to the organization's viability and the internal outcomes that are potential drivers of organizational change. The size of the activity defined by the task requires a number of actors for its completion. Although each instance of the task deals with different content, the structure and function of the task, its nature and character, is unchanged. However the task within its organizational context can evolve as a consequence of reflective practice. (Burstein & Linger, 2003).

Taxonomies of Knowledge

Phillip Ein-Dor
Tel-Aviv University, Israel

INTRODUCTION

Knowledge management has become a major application of information technology (IT) and a major focus of IT research. Thus, it becomes increasingly important to understand the nature of the knowledge object and knowledge engineering processes. The assumption underlying this article is that in order for knowledge to be managed by technological means, it must first be represented in the relevant technology. As Sowa (1999) puts it:

Knowledge engineering can...be defined as the branch of engineering that analyzes knowledge about some subject and transforms it to a computable form for some purpose.

The purpose assumed here is the management of knowledge for organizational aims. The other key term is "analyzes knowledge"; to analyze an object, one must first describe it, and taxonomies are intended to facilitate description and analysis. A useful analogy is that of taxonomies of living creatures which employ multiple characteristics such as size, number of legs, blood temperature, and many more to assign specimens to categories.

As different kinds of knowledge require different modes of representation, taxonomy becomes the central link between knowledge engineering and knowledge management. For example, accounting data are represented as data records; routine manipulation of the data is performed employing accounting knowledge embedded in programs. Organizational use of accounting data may be mediated by expert systems, which are generally realized as a special form of rule-based programs. Thus, in order to effectively design a knowledge management system, one must first classify the types of knowledge to be embedded in it. Hence the importance of a taxonomy of knowledge. A definition of knowledge is itself knowledge; thus, this article deals essentially with knowledge about knowledge—that is, meta-knowledge.

Knowledge is a highly multidimensional phenomenon and can be studied from many points of view. Thus, Sowa's (1999) book titled *Knowledge Representation* is subtitled *Logical, Philosophical, and Computational Foundations*. The approach taken here is largely a computational one, since knowledge management is generally discussed, though not necessarily in the context of computer-based systems. Given a computerized knowledge management system, questions also arise of eliciting the knowledge to be embedded in the system; some of these are also addressed here.

BACKGROUND

Attempting to understand the nature of knowledge has been a major theme of philosophical enquiry for thousands of years. Thus, Aristotle (384-322 BC) argued that knowledge objects are made accessible to thought by assigning them to categories. This approach still underlies much of knowledge management in specific areas. It applies especially to library classification systems—for example, The Dewey Decimal Classification (Dewey et al., 2003) for organizing all published knowledge. The classic Yahoo search engine was based on the same principle.

However, not all knowledge management relates to knowledge by content area; many other classifications are possible, and it is the purpose of this article to elaborate those. Because of the multidimensionality of knowledge, many taxonomies are possible. A well-known attempt to survey taxonomies of knowledge in the context of knowledge management systems is that of Alavi and Leidner (2001); they present 10 categories of knowledge gleaned from the knowledge management literature; their summary is cited as Table 1. This article uses the Alavi and Leidner (2001) categories as a basis, while extending and rationalizing them.

In general, taxonomies of knowledge may be ordered by their degree of generality; one may deal with knowledge at the highest level of abstraction, as Sowa (2000) does, while at the other extreme there are taxonomies of knowledge within specific fields (i.e., subsets of the general scheme of classification by content). The approach taken here is something of an amalgam of these two extremes. As it is impossible within the confines of an encyclopedia article to cover the entire gamut of types of knowledge, the emphasis here is on some higher level categories that we consider most relevant to practical knowledge management.

Table 1. Knowledge taxonomies and examples (Alavi & Leidner, 2001)

Knowledge Types	Definitions	Examples
Tacit	Knowledge is rooted in actions, experience, and involvement in specific context	Best means of dealing with specific customer
Cognitive tacit:	Mental models	Individual's belief on cause-effect relationships
Technical tacit:	Know-how applicable to specific work	Surgery skills
Explicit	Articulated, generalized knowledge	Knowledge of major customers in a region
Individual	Created by and inherent in the individual	Insights gained from completed project
Social	Created by and inherent in collective actions of a group	Norms for inter-group communication
Declarative	Know-about	What drug is appropriate for an illness
Procedural	Know-how	How to administer a particular drug
Causal	Know-why	Understanding why the drug works
Conditional	Know-when	Understanding when to prescribe the drug
Relational	Know-with	Understanding how the drug interacts with other drugs
Pragmatic	Useful knowledge for an organization	Best practices, business frameworks, project experiences, engineering drawings, market reports

THE FOCUS: DIMENSIONS OF KNOWLEDGE

In discussing types of knowledge, one can think of the characteristics of knowledge items as unique points, each representing a class of knowledge. In this approach, for example, tacit and explicit knowledge are two different types. Most taxonomies to date have adopted this view. However, these two categories are also opposite poles of a single dimension along which there may well be types of knowledge that are combinations of the extreme points: for example, a given item of knowledge may be partly tacit and partly explicit. It therefore seems useful to think of the dimensions as having two extremes and to juxtapose those to depict characteristics of any given knowledge object.

The dimensions of knowledge discussed here are the tacit-explicit, individual-social, procedural-declarative, commonsense-expert, and task-contextual; three additional dimensions—true-false, certain-uncertain, and private-public are also briefly introduced. As the reader will

note, there is considerable, but not complete, overlap with the Alavi and Leidner (2001) typology. The dimensions are also consistent with, but broader than, Nichols' (2000) identification of tacit, explicit, declarative, and procedural knowledge.

Given the multidimensional nature of knowledge, the ontology of an item of knowledge must refer to its location on all relevant dimensions in order to provide a complete specification. Such a specification should provide guidance in building systems to manage knowledge.

The Tacit-Explicit Knowledge Dimension

Tacit knowledge is knowledge that is possessed by an individual, but which he or she is unable to express verbally. At the other extreme of this dimension is explicit knowledge—knowledge that can be fully verbalized and so is available to any enquirer. An extreme statement of the tacit knowledge problem is that of Wittgenstein (1922): "The limits of my language are the limits of my mind. All

I know is what I have words for." This might seem to imply that there can be no tacit knowledge. If we cannot put things into words, we cannot know them. "Whereof one cannot speak, thereof one must be silent" (Wittgenstein, 1922). This position, however, does not consider the possibility of assistance to explicate tacit knowledge, and it seems likely that there are varying degrees on the tacit/ explicit dimension.

One of the best known philosophical treatments of tacit knowledge is that of Polanyi (1983), who distinguishes between tacit and "focal" knowledge. Polanyi characterizes tacit knowledge in the statement, similar to Wittgenstein's, that "...we can know more than we can tell." But knowledge that "we cannot tell" can sometimes be elucidated with appropriate help; for example, Police Identikits aid witnesses to crimes to concretely describe physiognomies of persons glimpsed under poor conditions and which they cannot describe verbally. However, some deeper level still remains unfathomable. This might derive from the fact that words cannot express all the detail of a physical entity or concept—a problem of granularity of language.

We may regard Polanyi's tacit knowledge as inchoate cognitive sensations for which we have not yet found words. In that case, this is knowledge about "whereof one cannot speak." However, with assistance, one may be able to find the words and so make the knowledge explicit. That would render much tacit knowledge potentially explicable. Thus, in principle, there is nothing we know that we cannot tell; practically, however, there may be things we know that we have not yet developed the ability to tell.

Tacit knowledge is, among other things, the knowledge of experts who intuitively know what to do in performing their duties, but find it difficult to express. Such knowledge is frequently based on intuitive evaluations of sensory inputs or *gestalts* of smell, taste, feel, sound, or appearance. Eliciting such knowledge was a major problem in early attempts to automate production processes such as brewing beer, manufacturing paper, or making wine, which were traditionally managed by master craftsmen who acquired their knowledge from long apprenticeship and experience. Eliciting such knowledge can be a major obstacle in attempts to build expert systems, as will be elaborated in discussing the commonsense-expert dimension.

The Individual-Social Knowledge Dimension

The process of converting tacit knowledge into explicit knowledge has been dealt with in great depth by Nonaka (1995). The emphasis there is on explicating tacit individual knowledge and converting it into social knowledge at ever higher levels. Alavi and Leidner (2001) include individual and social knowledge as separate categories in

their list of taxonomies; Nonaka, however, sees a continuum from individual knowledge through group, organizational, and inter-organizational levels. He envisions the process as a spiral in which the expansion of explicit knowledge permits the creation of knowledge at higher levels of organization: "A spiral emerges when the interaction between tacit and explicit knowledge is elevated dynamically from a lower ontological level to higher levels" (Nonaka, 1995, p. 57).

This dimension is well nigh synonymous with what has also been referred to as the objective artifact-socially constructed perception (Davenport & Prusac 1998): this view relates to the manner in which knowledge is attained—whether through personal experience or by social interaction.

The Procedural-Declarative Knowledge Dimension

Declarative knowledge consists of facts and figures. Procedural knowledge is knowledge about means for achieving goals. At first blush, it might not seem clear why the two are considered poles of a single dimension. There are, however, a number of reasons for this juxtaposition.

Psychologists have studied the interaction in humans between declarative and procedural knowledge for some time. There is disagreement over whether procedural knowledge develops from declarative knowledge (Anderson, 1996), or whether declarative knowledge plays a role in the development of procedural knowledge but does not evolve into procedures (Nichols, 2000). In any case, some procedures (e.g., facial recognition) are developed without recourse to declarative intervention.

Beginning with human knowledge, in many cases there is a tradeoff between knowing facts and knowing how to compute those facts. Thus, one may learn the multiplication table by heart, or one may compute a multiplication when needed. In fact, most people know the multiplication table for relatively small numbers, but must compute the outcomes for larger numbers. One may remember telephone numbers as facts, or one may have a procedure for recovering them from a repository of such numbers.

From the computer point of view, declarative knowledge (data) and procedures (programs) are indistinguishable. Both reside in digital memory in the same format and possibly intermingled. In some programming languages (e.g., LISP), programs are themselves data that can be manipulated by the program itself. As with humans, computer resident knowledge may be stored as the facts themselves, or as procedures for computing the facts. However, the degree of flexibility in deciding which form of representation to adopt is much greater for machine resident knowledge because of the far greater computing power of the machine. For example, it would be impractical to re-compute account balances for every access required to manually maintained bank records. However, a strategy of re-computation might be adopted in machine maintained accounts if the tradeoff between maintaining balances digitally and re-computing them is in favor of the latter.

Furthermore, declarative and procedural knowledge are increasingly intertwined in modern information systems. Thus, markup documents (HTML, XML, etc.) contain both declarative knowledge (the content) and procedural knowledge (the controls) that dictate the presentation of the declaratives. Spreadsheet cells may contain declarative knowledge or procedures that compute and display the declarative values.

The conclusion from this discussion is that design of a knowledge management system must take into consideration whether any knowledge item is optimally represented declaratively, procedurally, or both.

The Commonsense-Expert Knowledge Dimension

Commonsense knowledge is what every member of a society is expected to know. This includes socially approved behavior, how to conduct simple commercial transactions (Ein-Dor & Ginzberg 1989), and naïve physics (Hayes, 1978, 1979). Expert knowledge is that which imbues recognized experts with their status. Implicit in the recognition of experts is the understanding that their number is severely limited. When experts' knowledge is diffused to the population at large, it becomes commonsense knowledge. One example of this is driving automobiles; when they first appeared, automobiles were driven by professional drivers who were considered experts. Eventually, the majority of people in advanced economies learned to drive and that knowledge is now close to commonsense. Another example is writing, once the domain of expert scribes; with the advent of universal education, knowing how to write has become commonsense. The examples of driving and writing also exemplify the existence of a continuum between commonsense and expert knowledge.

This dimension of knowledge is one which poses severe problems for knowledge management (Buchanan et al., 1983; Feigenbaum, 1993), often related to the fact that expert knowledge is frequently tacit in nature. Expert systems are embodiments of expert knowledge. One of the reasons that expert systems have not realized the potential once projected for them is that it has proven extremely difficult, in many cases, to elicit the requisite knowledge from the relevant experts. Feigenbaum (1993) gives this as one of the reasons for the delay in expert systems achiev-ing the expectations from them. Furthermore, once the knowledge has been elicited, it may be difficult to represent in digital form. The representation is usually as a set of rules determining the action to be taken for a given input set.

As for commonsense knowledge, one might first ask why is it necessary to represent such knowledge, given that it is possessed by all? There are several reasons to digitally represent commonsense knowledge. First, if it is desired to automatically process natural language texts—for example, newspaper items, professional reports, or voice recordings—commonsense knowledge is necessary in order to interpret the texts. Second, commonsense knowledge is common to a culture, but not necessarily outside that culture; much has been written, for example, concerning the different negotiating styles of Western and Asian businessmen and the difficulties this can cause. Such problems increase in intensity with the spread of globalization. Formal representation of the commonsense of cultures might help alleviate these problems.

Unfortunately, representing commonsense knowledge is an extremely difficult undertaking. There are numerous reasons for this (see Ein-Dor & Ginzberg, 1989). In spite of great efforts, much work still remains to compile a general commonsense knowledge base. One consolation is the presumption that once such a knowledge base has been compiled, it should be useable by all, with adaptation required perhaps to specific cases. A large project, known as Cyc, with the objective of building a commonsense knowledge base has been underway since 1984 (see Cycorp, 2004; Guha, Lenat, Pittman, Pratt, & Shepherd, 1990; Lenat & Guha, 1990; Lenat, 1995).

The Task-Context Knowledge Dimension

Organizational knowledge is generally utilized to perform tasks of various kinds from the most routine to the highest level strategic decision making. Many of these tasks, however, require some context for their performance (Pomerol & Brézillon, 2001). That context may be intra-organizational or external. Building on this definition, what we refer to here as "task knowledge" is also called "organizational knowledge."

The knowledge to perform a given organizational task may be exclusively internal to the organization (e.g., where to store inventory items) or it may require much contextual knowledge (e.g., devising a marketing program). Note however that while the low-level task of storing inventory may be dictated by organizational procedures, those procedures may themselves be influenced by contextual knowledge concerning the frequency of and size of requests for items.

Thus, the knowledge for performing a given task may vary from high to low task-context combinations. The import of this fact for knowledge management is that task information is internal to the organization and is relatively easier to acquire and maintain. But note the discussion of expert knowledge above, which suggests that even internal knowledge may be difficult to manage, partly because of the contextualization required. Van Leijen and Baets (2004) discuss the way business processes are affected by the contextual knowledge patterns of the individuals responsible for their execution.

Contextual knowledge external to the organization poses severe acquisition problems, as sources need to be identified and the organization's environment changes constantly, requiring that the knowledge be constantly updated. Such contextual knowledge is either commonsense or expert in nature and is consequently subject to the problems discussed for the commonsense-expert dimension.

Additional Dimensions of Knowledge

As noted, the dimensions of knowledge outlined above are those considered particularly relevant to knowledge management. However, some additional dimensions of knowledge have been identified, beyond those discussed above. These may be relevant to some knowledge management systems and are here noted very briefly.

- **True-False:** Certain things we know are true; others things we think we know are probably false. Much knowledge lies between the extremes of truth and untruth and may be closer to one extreme or the other. Thus, in recording knowledge, knowledge items will be of varying degrees of veracity. For example, respondents to a survey may give their exact years of experience, slightly overstate or understate it, or exaggerate wildly. A computerized knowledge management system cannot evaluate veracity, except perhaps by triangulation of different representations of the same knowledge item or by logical inference from a number of items. Thus, evaluating veracity is a function primarily of those who collect and use the knowledge.

- **Certain-Uncertain:** Things can be known with different degrees of certainty from accurately measured physical properties to estimations of an opponent's intentions based on evaluation of relevant facts, which may themselves be subject to high uncertainty and low veracity. Again, a computerized knowledge management system cannot evaluate degrees of certainty unless programmed to do so, with the quality of the determination depending both on the accuracy of the data and the correctness of the evaluation parameters. Thus, controlling for certainty is again the responsibility of the knowledge collector and user.

- **Private and Individual-Public and Shared Dimension (Aarons, 2005):** This dimension is linked to the objective artifact-socially constructed perception above. The latter deals with the way in which knowledge is constructed, the former with the current state of construction.

FUTURE TRENDS

Managing knowledge efficiently and effectively requires a deep understanding of the nature of knowledge and its embedding in computerized systems. Thus, it is reasonable to assume that greater efforts will be invested in research to improve our understanding of knowledge. In the context of this article, that presumes a full mapping of all the dimensions of knowledge and establishing relationships between knowledge, as mapped on these dimensions, and the technological implications for the management of that knowledge. Understanding knowledge, studied in the past primarily by philosophers and psychologists, is an area in which the Information Systems field might make a profound contribution.

CONCLUSION

Knowledge is a multidimensional artifact, and cognizance of the various dimensions is useful for understanding the

Figure 1. Example of dimensions of knowledge for a hypothetical knowledge item

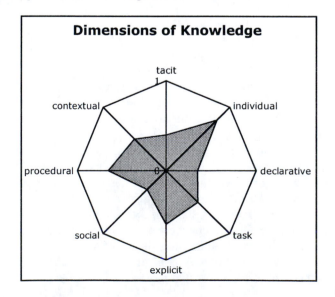

nature of a body of knowledge and is required in order to completely specify an item of knowledge. The principal dimensions of knowledge recognized here are tacit/explicit, individual/social, declarative/procedural, and task/context. The categorizations of a knowledge item may be graphically displayed as in the example in Figure 1.

Additional dimensions have been suggested—for example, the categories recognized in Alavi and Leidner (2001) as *conditional, relational,* and *pragmatic*; these are not included here because, while they may describe certain aspects of knowledge items, they are not generally recognized as basic dimensions of knowledge. The specification of knowledge to be represented computationally is important in choosing the computational solution to be employed.

A major conclusion from the multidimensional view of knowledge presented here is that the distinctions usually made in the IS literature between data, information, and knowledge are largely irrelevant (Ein-Dor, 1986). A data item in an organization's information systems is simply a piece of knowledge that is generally explicit, declarative, social, and organizational. A manager's knowledge of an aspect of the marketplace is probably to a large extent implicit, individual, declaratively and procedurally mixed, and contextual. Any knowledge item may be classified on these dimensions as a basis for analysis and implementation. This view can lead to greater integration of the various kinds of knowledge embedded in information systems.

REFERENCES

Aarons, J. (2005). The relationship between epistemology and knowledge management. In D.G. Schwartz (Ed.), *Encyclopedia of knowledge management.* Hershey, PA: Idea Group Publishing.

Anderson, JR. (1996). ACT: A simple theory of complex cognition. *American Psychologist, 51,* 355-365. Retrieved July 14, 2004, from *http://act-r.psy.cmu.edu/publications/pubinfo?id=97*

Alavi, M., & Leidner, D.E. (2001). Review: Knowledge management and knowledge management systems: Conceptual foundations and research issues. *MIS Quarterly, 25*(1), 107-136.

Buchanan, B.G., Barstow, D., Bechtal, R., Bennett, J., Clancey, W., Kulikowski, C., Mitchell, T., & Waterman, D.A. (1983). Constructing an expert system. Chapter 5 in F. Hayes-Roth, D.A. Waterman, & D.B. Lenat (Eds.), *Building expert systems* (pp. 127-167). Reading, MA: Addison-Wesley.

Cycorp. (2004). Retrieved July 14, 2004, from *http://www.cyc.com/cyc*

Davenport, T., & Prusac, L. (1998). *Working knowledge: How organizations manage what they know.* Boston: Harvard Business School Press.

Dewey, M., Mitchell, J.S., Beall, J., Martin, G., Matthews, W.E., & New, G.R. (2003). *Dewey Decimal Classification and Relative Index* (22nd ed.). Retrieved October 4, 2004, from *http://www.oclc.org/dewey/*

Ein-Dor, P., & Ginzberg, Y. (1989). Representing commonsense business: An initial implementation. In L.F. Pau, J. Motiwalla, J.Y.H. Pao, & H.H. Teh (Eds.), *Expert systems in economics, banking, and management* (pp. 417-426). Amsterdam: North-Holland.

Ein-Dor, P. (1986). An epistemological approach to the theory of information systems. *Proceedings of the 18th Annual Meeting Proceedings of the Decision Sciences Institute* (pp. 563-363), Honolulu, Hawaii.

Feigenbaum, E.A. (1993). *Tiger in a cage: Applications of knowledge-based systems.* Stanford: University Video Communications.

Guha, R.V., Lenat, D.B., Pittman, K., Pratt, D., & Shepherd, M. (1990). Cyc: Toward programs with common sense. *Communications of the ACM, 33*(8), 30-49.

Hayes, P.J. (1978). *Naïve physics 1: Ontology for liquids.* Working Paper, University of Essex, UK.

Hayes, P.J. (1979). The naïve physics manifesto. In D. Michie (Ed.), *Expert systems in the micro electronic age* (pp. 242-270). Edinburgh: Edinburgh University Press.

Lenat, D.B., & Guha, R.V. (1990). *Building large knowledge-based systems.* Reading, MA: Addison Wesley.

Lenat, D.B. (1995). Cyc: A large-scale investment in knowledge infrastructure. *Communications of the ACM, 38*(11), 33-38.

Nichols, F.W. (2000). The knowledge in knowledge management. In J.W. Cortada & J.A. Woods (Eds.), *The knowledge management yearbook 2000-2001* (pp. 12-21). Boston: Butterworth-Heinemann. Retrieved July 11, 2004, from *http://home.att.net/~OPSINC/knowledge_in_KM.pdf*

Nonaka, I. (1995). *The knowledge-creating company: How Japanese companies create the dynamics of innovation.* Oxford: Oxford University Press.

Polanyi, M. (1983). *The tacit dimension.* Gloucester, MA: Peter Smith reprint.

T

Pomerol, J.-C., & Brézillon, P. (2001, July 27-30). About some relationships between knowledge and context. *Proceedings of the 3rd International and Interdisciplinary Conference* (CONTEXT), Dundee, UK.

Sowa, J.F. (2000). *Knowledge representation: Logical, philosophical, and computational foundations.* Pacific Grove, CA: Brooks Cole. Actual publication date: August 16, 1999.

van Leijen, H., & Baets, W. (2004). Process standardization and contextual knowledge. *Proceedings of the 5th European Conference on Organizational Learning, Knowledge, and Capabilities* (OLKC), Innsbruck, Austria. Retrieved July 13, 2004, from *http://www.ofenhandwerk.com/oklc/menu.html*

Wittgenstein, L. (1922). *Tractatus logico philosophicus.* New York.

KEY TERMS

Commonsense Knowledge: This is the knowledge expected of every individual in a society. It includes acquaintance with the physical world and the laws governing it, social behaviors, and procedures for everyday tasks, such as simple business transactions. It lies on the commonsense-expert knowledge dimension.

Contextual Knowledge: Knowledge of the contexts in which organizational tasks are performed. Depending on the task, this knowledge may be entirely internal to the organization or it may require acquaintance with many extra-organizational contexts—for example, markets, legal contexts, and legislative contexts.

Declarative Knowledge: Knowledge of basic facts, generally referred to in computerized systems as data. Examples are the number of items in an storage bin, the balance of the account of a customer, or the date of birth of a person. It is one pole of the factual-procedural dimension.

Expert Knowledge: That possessed by individuals who have acquired deep knowledge in some particular field by training and experience. Examples are the specialized knowledge of physicians, vintners, or architects.

Expert knowledge is opposite commonsense knowledge on their shared dimension.

Explicit Knowledge: Knowledge that can be externally verbalized and recorded. This distinguishes it from tacit knowledge, which is at the opposite end of the same dimension.

Individual Knowledge: Knowledge possessed by persons rather than social entities. It is frequently tacit in nature, rendering it absolutely personal. When tacit knowledge is made explicit, it moves toward the other end of its dimension—social knowledge.

Knowledge Dimensions: Any knowledge object comprises numerous characteristics. Pairs of these characteristics represent opposite ends of dimensions, and an item of knowledge may display combinations of the two characteristics on any dimension. This concept of knowledge dimensions is the basis for the taxonomy presented here.

Procedural Knowledge: The knowledge to perform tasks. It shares a dimension with declarative knowledge. The latter may be the result of processing (i.e., the application of procedural knowledge), or it may exist as stored data, requiring no further processing.

Social Knowledge: Knowledge that is available to members of a social entity or organization. Thus, it is in contradistinction to individual knowledge, which is known only to a particular person. Thus, individual and social knowledge are opposite poles of a single dimension.

Tacit Knowledge: Knowledge possessed by an individual, who is unable to formulate and communicate it verbally. Such knowledge is frequently the product of intuition, emotions, and fleeting impressions, which form inchoate or incomplete memories. Tacit knowledge is the partner of explicit knowledge on the dimension they share.

Task Knowledge: Knowledge required to perform a task in an organizational or extra-organizational context. Examples are storing inventory items, updating accounts, or delivering goods. The extent to which the task is performed solely within the organization or externally determines the nature of the knowledge on the task-context dimension.

Theoretical and Practical Aspects of Knowledge Management

Frank Land
London School of Economics and Political Science, UK

Sevasti-Melissa Nolas
London School of Economics and Political Science, UK

Urooj Amjad
London School of Economics and Political Science, UK

INTRODUCTION AND BACKGROUND

The last decade of the 20th century saw the emergence of a new discipline within the realm of information systems, which became known as *knowledge management* (KM). As such, it has become one of the most discussed issues amongst academics and practitioners working in the information systems and human resource management arenas (Prusack, 2001). Amongst academics it has become an area of specialisation with research projects, journals, conferences, books, encyclopaedias, and numerous papers devoted to the topic. Businesses are investing heavily in buying or developing KM supportive systems. However, predominately researchers and practitioners in this area have tended to see (see for example, Alavi & Leidner, 2001; Baskerville, 1998):

1. consider the context in which knowledge management takes place as teams of knowledge workers in communities of practice, whose performance and the performance of their organisation, can be enhanced by knowledge sharing;

2. focus on the process—the creation and application of knowledge management programmes and systems as an organisational *resource*—neglecting, with some exceptions (Alvesson & Karreman, 2001; Swan & Scarborough, 2001; Schultze, 1999), the wider context in which knowledge management takes place and the fact that resources can be used in ways that can be both creative and destructive, facilitating and manipulative; and

3. stress the role of technology as the enabling agent for KM.

OBJECTIVES AND FOCUS

This article proposes to broaden the KM discourse by re-examining some of the foundations of knowledge manage-

ment in order to show that much of the current discussion—including by those who are critical of the conceptual basis of KM—neglects or underplays some otherwise well-known aspects of the topic. Two aspects in particular need to be considered:

a. the notion that knowledge is managed for a purpose—it is used as an instrument to achieve some objective, sometimes explicit, but often hidden or tacit. We note that the purpose is not necessarily benign, and that this, the darker side of knowledge management, includes knowledge and information manipulation.

b. that knowledge has been managed since mankind invented speech, and that few purposeful activities do not include some elements of knowledge management. Examples are provided to illustrate the point.

The article is presented from the perspectives of the IS scholar in particular, and organisational studies in general, as both face KM as a new area of study. The article is intended to act as a warning to both scholars and practitioners interested in KM, and suggests that the rhetoric emerging from the KM field should be treated with caution.

The article concludes with some reflections on the ethical dimensions stemming from KM practices.

Outline Argument

The argument presented in the article may be briefly summarised as follows: knowledge is not some benign resource which is only managed for the good of the individual, the team, and the organisation. Knowledge can be, and is, used instrumentally to achieve a range of objectives, ranging from the criminal, the mischievous, to the constructive and benign. The argument focuses on the *relationship* between the provision, acquisition, and dissemination of information, and the formation and creation of knowledge. It is argued that information, as a building block of knowledge, can be, and in practice is, guided, managed, controlled, or manipulated for a desired outcome. The practice of research is cited in order to demonstrate the argument. Finally, by drawing on some familiar institutional canons of our culture such as education, marketing, (scientific) management, and law, the article takes the first steps in broadening the KM discourse looking at control, instrumentality, and power relations.

The Argument Expanded

There is almost complete unanimity in the academic literature that KM is an essential activity for a modern enterprise to flourish in a global competitive economy, and many practicing managers share this view. Two assumptions underlie the KM literature:

- that there is a positive relationship between knowledge and truth; and
- that knowledge is the sum of beliefs, values, insights, and experiences.

Both assumptions serve to hide the instrumentality of knowledge. The article notes that underlying the management of knowledge are the notions of purpose and control. One purpose of providing software to facilitate knowledge sharing may be to improve the productivity of the group. But a second purpose may be to control the way the group works, for example, by determining who can share in the knowledge. Again the purpose of a marketing campaign may ostensively be to provide knowledge for the consumer, but also to mislead the consumer and ultimately to control the consumer's behaviour.

Both assumptions raise questions about the ethical implications and the power dynamics of knowledge management. How do these assumptions work and what are their implications?

Assumptions

KM, as a concept, is a good example of "reification" (Thompson, 1990)—the use of various ideological strategies for the purpose of maintaining a particular order of things—of what is essentially a very old idea, that we can work/live together much more harmoniously and productively, if only we communicate better (and more) with each other. Naturalisation takes place by supporting that it is always *good* and desirable to communicate and *exchange knowledge* with each other. The notion has been provided with an agenda: that through technological development, we can create an infrastructure that enables us to

communicate and *exchange* (share) knowledge more effectively. Finally, the ideas are given a label—KM—and presented as a natural development of historical events, such as the emphasis on knowledge work and the capabilities provided by ICT.

Nevertheless, it is well known that the above does not completely capture reality. The tools provided by the technology and by organisational architecture are as much used to manipulate or hide knowledge, as to reveal and share it. The activity of exclusion and inclusion, of amplification and distortion of *data,* can be strategic, and no amount of technical sophistication can prevent that. Indeed, the technology can be harnessed to assist in these activities. White-collar crime is a good case in point. The literature on white-collar crime does not use the terms 'knowledge management' or 'knowledge manipulation' in describing the various manifestations of the crime, but it is clear that these activities are central to the expansion taking place in that type of crime and ICT can play major role in facilitating criminal activity.

In the process of reifying knowledge as something to be harnessed and exploited, there is also a tendency in the literature to reify the organisation, and therefore to think about *organisational knowledge* in terms of the benefit derived by the organisation, where organisation usually refers to top management. The ensuing power dynamics and the politics of knowledge production and use are all too clear. Knowledge and organising are not the privilege of the few, but the "processes" (Hosking & Morley, 1991) that occur in spaces where individuals form and un-form social relations, and carry out formal and informal practices across the organisation. Entering into this space, whether as a researcher or as a KM "manager," or indeed any other stakeholder, has implications for the dynamics of that space.

Implications

The implications are explored by examining the practice of research looking at the notions of bias, involvement, and lay/expert knowledge.

An individual approaching anything will be doing so from a particular position, be that theoretical, methodological, historical, or political, consciously or unconsciously. Past experiences tend to inform future actions by constraining as well as enabling one's movements. As such, the assumption about the positive relationship between knowledge and truth is unfounded because of the natural *bias*—by virtue of our unique experiences—that we all have. For example, in the context of organisational research, the study may be intended to gain understanding (knowledge) of some aspect of the organisation's activity. The choice of research methodology, a facet of knowledge management, guides and constrains the researcher.

Exactly the same applies to the design, implementation, and development of any organisational system or project. For example, the choice of development tool, as Actor Network Theory suggests (Nijland, 2004), plays a key role in determining both what knowledge is utilised and the way that knowledge is used. Furthermore, ignoring the 'power' dimensions of the situation being studied gives the impression that organisational space is neutral, and that the action of entering the space is also neutral. For example, in the case of 'resistance to change' to new technology, it may not be so much an instance of resisting the technology, *per se*, but a form of protest against those (usually superiors) who implement new technology for the benefit of the organisation as a whole, with little knowledge or understanding of the actuality at subordinate levels of the organisation (Land, 1992).

Lessons drawn from different forms of research—from observational to action research—teach us that the moment of interaction or engagement with our subject of research is never without its power dynamics. Access to the organisation and acceptance of the research in the first place is dependent on some form of hierarchical 'buy-in'—that is, the support of people who are senior enough in the organisation and who have the power to 'open doors' for the researchers. But problems arise, particularly if a researcher is forced to choose between access and compromise in research design; following the management's agenda does not necessarily reflect the organisation's concerns. The knowledge that is produced is likely to benefit the particular group in question and the organisation as a whole, but only in so far as management (or the subclass of management involved) represents the organisation. As such, one of the most obvious dangers involved in working with pre-selected groups in an organisation is perpetuation of a *hierarchy of knowledge*. Similarly, it may be said that KM initiatives and systems are yet another management tool designed to enhance the working of the management; the old "panopticon" (Foucault, 1979) in a new packaging.

Lessons from research demonstrate that the processes of knowledge production are far from neutral. This can be explored with respect to the so-called 'lay/expert' knowledge debate. According to Shenav's analysis (1999), scientific management was introduced into the organisation as a way of neutralising the political/power dimensions of organisational life. Furthermore, when this was done, engineers had a special role of "redefining industrial conflict as a mechanical problem rather than as a result of political struggles" (p.3; cited in Grint, 2002, p. 173). It would seem that in the case of KM, the 'K' neatly replaces the 'scientific' and the role of the KM system designer or manager is taking over from the engineer. In both the case of the engineer and the knowledge manager, the problem is one of manipulation of 'expert' knowledge.

The problem is manifest at both internal and external levels. At the internal level the assumption is that managers *know*—in other words, managers are experts, and subordinates follow. Stories from senior management are more likely to be taken as authoritative and representative of the organisation than stories told by lower-level employees. Yet experience suggests that on important issues, knowledge is more evenly distributed than the authority structure implies (Land, 1992), and that at the micro level those at the coal face have more knowledge than those in positions of authority. At the external level, the 'expert' problem is manifest in the form of the consultants' guides which are often based on a pre-designed, standardised formula. Expert knowledge uses "formal theories [that] are often developed by powerful and/or socially elite individuals who use the theory to influence and control others. Some elements of formal theory may be based on scientific research, but others are based upon unsupported assumptions" (Whyte, 1990. p. 13). The problem arises when 'unsupported assumptions' become equated with being 'objective' knowledge in order to uphold positions of control. So long as the KM literature continues to refer to knowledge in terms of beliefs, values, and experience, the 'knowledge' will be susceptible to control and manipulation.

In the following section we will give examples of other areas, beyond the research context, which can help us to broaden the discourse on knowledge management.

Examples

The introduction to this article suggested that manipulation of knowledge takes place at the interface between information and knowledge. Information can be guided, managed, controlled, or manipulated for a desired outcome. The following examples have been selected in that they illustrate both the instrumental use of information and knowledge, and the wide variety of human activity in which knowledge is an indispensable component subject to management and manipulation. They are given from a non-expert position and are intended as triggers for thinking about how the knowledge management discourse could be broadened.

EDUCATION

Education, a major institutional force in the socialisation of the individual, is at least in part about managing the transfer of information for the creation of knowledge between teacher and pupil(s). Let us consider the teacher-pupil interaction for a moment. A teacher is a trained expert in a particular field and uses different resources (books, articles) in order to teach a, usually, national curriculum. The different resources form the link between what the teacher needs to convey and what the pupils need to learn. This is an informational link on the one level. On another level, however, it intends to 'form' the pupil's knowledge of a particular subject. We know that education—whether at the level of the curriculum, school, or individual teacher—is not objective, and the information intended to form pupils' knowledge can be managed for a desired effect. The subject of history is a case in point. There are good criticisms of this form of education. The Socratic dialogue is probably the oldest form of criticism; more recent, and widely cited, is the work of Brazilian educator Paolo Freire (1970). The criticism is against individuals as "repositories" of information, and instead encourages the active questioning and dialogue between teacher, pupil, curriculum. Control is a central theme in this questioning.

MARKETING

Marketing, embracing advertising and public relations, is another area redolent of KM. Marketing, widely taught as a core discipline in business schools, epitomises the use of knowledge management to provide consumers with product or service knowledge in order to enable them to make informed choices on what to buy. In the domain of marketing, the manipulative aspect of KM is widely recognised—its use to manipulate information in an instrumental way designed to provide consumers with a very partial or even distorted picture of the goods or service on offer and those offered by the competition. Advertising and public relations are constrained to some extent by regulations, in recognition that left unregulated organisations will manage knowledge in an unprincipled way for competitive advantage and maximum profit. Organisations like the Consumer Association exist to redress the balance between vendor and consumer, and try to offset the sometimes tacit, but often explicit knowledge management of the vendor.

(SCIENTIFIC) MANAGEMENT

Taylor's (1911) "scientific management" provides a further source of ideas with regards to the control aspect of KM. The advocates of scientific management believe firmly in the need to manage knowledge in order not to clutter up the minds of employees and to distract them from the limited tasks they are assigned to. Hence someone of higher authority always determines, on the principle of providing knowledge on a strict 'need-to-know' basis, what information and knowledge is to be provided for the employee. Whilst the KM movement espouses the

reverse view, in reality Taylorism is deeply embedded in managerial practices, for example so called modern ideas of industrial reorganisation such as Business Process Reengineering (Hammer, 1990; Hammer & Champy, 1993; Davenport, 1993, 1996). Practical implementations of KM suffer a similar fate by carefully defining what knowledge can be shared and with whom sharing is permitted.

LAW

The law itself, and its study, provides another perspective on KM. The law relating to intellectual property rights, for example, defines and limits the way knowledge about intellectual property can be shared. The controversy about the human genome illustrates the relationship of intellectual property rights to KM. One group of scientists working on the human genome project took their discoveries to be knowledge that they were entitled to treat as a commodity not available to anyone except as they determined and for a price. Another group of scientists working on a human genome project reached a very different conclusion. They held that their discoveries were not an 'invention', but merely knowledge derived from the decoding of a natural phenomenon and as such could not be regarded as a commodity, and hence freely available to all (Sulston & Ferry, 2002; Wickelgren, 2002). Debates about intellectual property rights, data retention, and privacy (Hosein, 2001; Tsiavos & Hosein, 2003; Drahos & Braithwaite, 2003) provide concrete examples around the discourse of ownership and control of information and knowledge.

The instruments that support KM in its benign or destructive forms are varied. They include organisational architectures such as the authority structure, organisational provisions such as social clubs, technology-based provisions such as data warehouses, expert systems, case-based reasoning, web facilities, the intranet, and many others and, as ENRON demonstrated, the humble shredder as a potent weapon of KM.

FUTURE TRENDS

Given the argument presented in this article, two trends are noted in particular. The first is the growing realisation that technological developments provide ever widening opportunities for the dark side of knowledge management to flourish, and hence that there is a need to develop both awareness of the potential problems and defence mechanisms. Such mechanisms will need to emerge out of critical research that no longer relies on linear, fixed representations of reality, but which allows for the representation of uncertainty and the unexpected. For an example, see Land,

Amjad, and Nolas's approach (in another article in this encyclopedia, titled "Knowledge Management Processes").

The second is the growing awareness of the political aspects of organisational processes driving the use of information and knowledge. There is a need to take an ethical stance both in the design of KM systems, as well as in research about the KM systems and their relationship with and effects on organisational processes. This requires a more interdisciplinary approach that permits the researcher and practitioner to both learn from the past and critically engage with the future.

CONCLUSION

The article has shown that it is possible and insightful to trace notions that might be interpreted as knowledge management to a broad range of older disciplines, and that a study of these provides us with a richer picture and deeper understanding of KM. It is as if—to use a metaphor—the study of KM in the literature of the subject has focused a light on an iceberg so that we can see it in its full glory, but omits to note that there is more under the water than above it. What this article has set out to do is to expose some of the underside of the iceberg.

It is clear from studies in KM that whilst management can create the conditions for the beneficial aspects of KM—for example, knowledge sharing by the provision of tools, or by providing the conditions for relationships to develop, or both—the outcomes are dependent on a range of other factors such as organisational culture (Ackerman, Pipek, & Wulf, 2003). On the other hand, knowledge sharing can and does take place without any management intervention at all—without a conscious KM.

Despite its eminence and the notion of KM as a subject of study, critiques around the notion do exist and have evolved around the definition of knowledge and the choice of tools to support KM, those being either technological or human. But neither the technology, nor the relationship-oriented models have specially noted that KM involves power dynamics, as well as ethical issues. We need to look elsewhere for the discourse with which to address power dynamics and ethical issues (Foucault, 1980; Sussman, Adams, & Raho, 2002).

Knowledge management is not a chimera. KM has been helpful in drawing attention to the value of knowledge and how it can be utilised for the benefit of organisations, individuals, and society. But much of the work currently defined as being about KM takes a one-eyed stance. The Mafia principle of 'omerta' is also a form of knowledge management, albeit at its most malign, and

companies like ENRON prompt us to question the ethical problems for society as a whole, but also for the individual, whether in the role of employee, outside observer (for example, journalist), or researcher, in the management of knowledge.

If the study of KM is to have an enduring future, it must take a more dynamic and contextual approach, recognising that its antecedents come from many more disciplines than those which are cited in the literature. Of course, research into the part of the iceberg above water is easier, in the sense that the stories that are told about it reflect the views of those who want to extol its beauty. Diving into the cold water below the iceberg and explaining what is there is more difficult. The dark side of KM is protected against exposure. It is perhaps not surprising that it requires more than auditors or academic researchers to reveal what lies under the iceberg. But students, researchers, and practitioners alike have to recognise the instrumentality of which drives action and the problems it gives rise to in terms of values, truth, and ethics.

In presenting these arguments we have followed the advice of two very distinct views of scientific progress. On the one hand we follow Popper (1972) in believing that one function of the researcher is to provide warnings about the fallibility of current orthodoxies. The evidence provided by the examples goes some way to throw doubt on the interpretation of KM as set out in much of the current literature. The second source of advice comes from Foucault (1980) and critical theory, which alerts us to power and politics implicit in the process of knowledge creation and utilisation.

ACKNOWLEDGMENTS

An earlier version of this article appears in the proceedings of the *Seventh ETHICOMP International Conference on the Social and Ethical Impacts of Information and Communication Technologies* (2004), Syros, Greece.

We would like to acknowledge the LSE Complexity Group for providing the space in which the present collaboration could develop. The LSE Complexity Group's work has been enabled by the support of our academic advisors, business partners, and EPSRC (Engineering and Physical Science Research Council) awards, including a three-year collaborative action research project, Integrating Complex Social Systems (ICoSS) under the Systems Integration Initiative entitled *Enabling the Integration of Diverse Socio-Cultural and Technical Systems within a Turbulent Social Ecosystem* (GR/R37753). Details of the LSE Complexity Research Programme and the ICoSS Project can be found at http://www.lse.ac.uk/complexity.

REFERENCES

Ackerman, M., Pipek, V., & Wulf, V. (Eds.). (2003). *Sharing expertise: Beyond knowledge management.* Cambridge, MA: MIT Press.

Alvani, M., & Leidner, D. (2001). Knowledge management and knowledge management systems: Conceptual foundations and research issues. *MIS Quarterly, 25*(1), 107-136.

Alvesson, M., & Karreman, D. (2001). Odd couple: Making sense of the curious concept of knowledge management. *Journal of Management Studies, 38*(7), 995-1018.

Baskerville, R.L. (1998). *A survey and analysis of the theoretical diversity in knowledge management.* Georgia State University Computer Information Systems Department Working Paper No. CIS98-1.

Davenport, T.H. (1993). *Process innovation, reengineering work through information technology.* Boston: Harvard Business Press.

Davenport, T.H. (1996). Why reengineering failed: The fad that forgot people, fast company. *Premier Issue,* 70-74.

Drahos, P., & Braithwaite, I. (2003). *Information feudalism.* New Press.

Foucault, M. (1979). *Discipline and punish: The birth of the prison.* Harmondsworth: Penguin

Foucault, M. (1980). *Power/knowledge.* New York: Pantheon.

Friere, P. (1970). *Pedagogy of the oppressed.* London: Penguin.

Hammer, M. (1990). Don't automate—obliterate. *Harvard Business Review,* (July-August), 104-112.

Hammer, M., & Champy, J. (1993). Reengineering the corporation: A manifesto for business revolution. *Insights Quarterly,* (Summer), 3-19.

Hosein, I. (2001). The collision of regulatory convergence and divergence: Updating policies of surveillance and information technology. *The South African Journal of Information and Communications, 2*(1), 18-33.

Hosking, D.M., & Morley, I.E. (1991). *A social psychology of organizing: People, processes and contexts.* New York: Harvester

Land, F., Amjad, U., & Nolas, S.M. (2005). Introducing knowledge management as both desirable and undesirable processes. In D.G. Schwartz (Ed), *The encyclopaedia of knowledge management.* Hershey, PA: Idea Group, Reference.

Land, F.F. (1992). The management of change: Guidelines for the successful implementation of information systems. In A. Brown (Ed.), *Creating a business-based IT strategy.* Chapman & Hall (and UNICOM).

Nijland, M.H-J. (2004). *Understanding the use of IT evaluation methods in organisations.* Unpublished PhD thesis, University of London, UK.

Popper, K.R. (1972). *Conjectures and refutations: The growth of scientific knowledge* (5th ed.). London: Routledge, an imprint of Taylor & Francis Books Ltd.

Prusack, L. (2001). Where did knowledge management come from? *IBM Systems Journal, 40*(4), 1002-1007.

Schultze, U. (1999). Investigating the contradictions in knowledge management. In T.J. Larsen, L. Levine, & J.I. DeGross (Eds.), *Information systems: Current issues and future changes* (pp. 155-174). Austria: Laxenberg.

Shevav, Y. (1999). *Manufacturing rationality: The engineering foundations of managerial rationality.* Reviewed by Grint, K. (2002). *Organization, 9*(1),173-175.

Sulston, J., & Ferry, G. (2002). *The common thread: A story of science, politics, ethics and the human genome.* Joseph Henry Press.

Sussman, L., Adams, A.J., & Raho, L.E., (2002). Organizational politics: Tactics, channel, and hierarchical roles. *Journal of Business Ethics, 40,* 313-329.

Swan, J., & Scarborough, H. (2001). Knowledge management: Concepts and controversies. *Journal of Management Studies, 38*(7), 913-991.

Taylor, F. (1911/1998). *The principles of scientific management.* Dover Publications.

Thompson, J.B. (1990). *Ideology and modern culture: A critical social theory in the era of mass communication.* Cambridge, UK: Polity.

Tsiavos, P., & Hosein, I., (2003, June 18-21). Beyond good and evil: Why open source development for peer-to-peer networks does not necessarily equate to an open society. *Proceedings of the 11th European Conference on Information Systems: New Paradigms in Organization, Markets and Society,* Naples.

Whyte, W.F. (1990). *Social theory for action.* CA: Sage Publications.

Wickelgren, I. (2002). *The gene masters: How a new breed of scientific entrepreneurs raced for the biggest prize in biology.* Times Books.

KEY TERMS

Belief: A conceptual construct that guides and organises one's actions, identity, and knowledge. Knowledge is what the individual *believes* to be true. But that belief is socially constructed and reflects the individual's perceptions, memories, and experiences. To the extent that belief lends itself to manipulation, knowledge too is subject to manipulation.

Critical Thinking: Encompasses the belief that the function of the researcher is to provide warnings about the fallibility of current orthodoxies by pointing to the power and politics implicit in the process of knowledge creation and utilisation.

Ethics of Knowledge Management: The study of the impact of knowledge management on society, the organisation, and the individual, with a particular emphasis on the damaging effects knowledge management can have.

Instrumentality: The notion that action, including knowledge management, is carried out for a purpose, and that the purpose underlying the action can be maligning as well as beneficial.

Knowledge Dissemination: The act of making information as a component of knowledge available to others. As a purposeful act, knowledge dissemination can be manipulated to withhold, amplify, or distort information in order to deceive the recipient.

Knowledge Manipulation: The abuse of knowledge management; when information is hidden, distorted, withheld for a particular purpose.

Reification: The use of various ideological strategies for the purpose of maintaining a particular (social/ organisational) order.

Research Practice/Research Design: Research is conducted to acquire knowledge about a topic. Research design defines the way that knowledge is to be acquired. Hence research involves knowledge management.

T

Understanding Innovation Processes

Sue Newell
Bentley College, USA

INTRODUCTION

Knowledge integration is a process whereby several individuals share and combine their information to collectively create new knowledge (Okhuysen & Eisenhardt, 2002). Here we are interested in knowledge integration in the context of innovation project teams tasked with developing a new product or organizational practice. Knowledge integration is crucial in relation to innovation, since innovation depends on the generation of new ideas (new knowledge) that leads to the development of new products or organizational practices. Knowledge integration, rather than simply knowledge per se, is important for innovation because it is not simply the possession of new knowledge that will create success in terms of improved practice or new products, but rather, the ability to *integrate* knowledge across groups and organizations (Gibbons et al., 1994). This is especially the case in relation to radical innovation, which depends on involvement of an increasingly dispersed range of professional groups and organizations (Powell, Koput, & Smith-Doerr, 1996). For example, in the medical domain there are an increasing number of breakthroughs in scientific and technical knowledge that could drastically change medical practice. Achieving such breakthroughs, however, does not necessarily result in performance improvements in medical practice. Major pharmaceutical companies take, on average, 11 years and a minimum of one-third of $1 billion to bring a drug to market, and over 90% of development processes fail (CMR International, 2000). Similarly, in relation to major transformational IT innovation projects in organizations, many do not just fall short of meeting cost, functionality, and scheduling targets, but actually fail outright (Johnson, 1995).

While there are many reasons for such failure, one important reason relates to the problem of integrating knowledge, because breakthroughs leading to radical innovation are highly disruptive (Christensen, Bohmer, & Kenagy, 2000) and potentially "competency destroying" (Henderson, Orsenigo, & Pisano, 1999). For example, the development of the new drug or the new IT system will often cut across established institutionalized domains and structures for the production of knowledge, and therefore require radical shifts in relationships among professional and functional groups. New developments made possible by breakthroughs in science may not align well, for example, with existing professional regimes and medical practices (Christensen et al., 2000).

In this article then, we consider the issue of knowledge integration in the context of innovation projects and relate it to social capital, since understanding the process of knowledge integration involves exploring the "micro-social interactions among individuals" (Okhuysen & Eisenhardt, 2002). It is helpful to explore these micro-social interactions through the lens of social capital since social capital refers to the social networks and the assets that can be mobilized through these networks that enable social action generally and knowledge sharing more specifically (Nahapiet & Ghoshal, 1998). In other words, given that the development of new products and practices typically involves teams of people from different backgrounds (i.e., multi-disciplinary project teams) working together, exploring how individual team members share and combine their respective knowledge in order to generate new ideas to support innovation is important. Specifically, we will consider how different approaches to creating and using social capital leads to different levels of knowledge integration, which in turn influence the innovation achieved, which can be either incremental or radical.

BACKGROUND

The Concept of Knowledge Integration

To reiterate, in this article we are interested in how a project team, tasked with developing a new product or practice, shares and combines the information of the different team members and of other stakeholders who have relevant information in order to create new knowledge that supports innovation. While the Okhuysen and Eisenhardt definition (above) suggests that knowledge integration is a simple process, the reality is that sharing and combining information is often very difficult. This is because knowledge is dispersed (Tsoukas, 1996) and ambiguous (Dougherty, 1992), as well as being potentially competency destroying (Henderson et al., 1999) in the sense that new products or practices may make obsolete the knowledge of particular groups who may then resist involvement in the knowledge integration process and so limit progress.

Teams will differ in terms of what they achieve in relation to knowledge integration. To simplify this we can identify two extremes in the way that knowledge can be taken to be integrated in the context of a project team tasked with developing a new product or service—"mechanistic pooling" (Knights & Wilmott, 1997) versus "generative" (Cook & Brown, 1999) knowledge integration. Mechanistic pooling occurs when each project member works independently on a set of clearly defined tasks or processes with which he/she is familiar and uses his/her existing knowledge to consider the potential of the new scientific/technological breakthrough on the particular problem domain, be this a new drug to help treat cancer or a new IT system to support information integration within an organization. In such circumstances, the new drug or IT system is perceived as simply fitting independent pieces together, like a jigsaw puzzle. This mechanistic pooling of knowledge is likely to result in a new product or service that may have higher performance than current products or services, in which case it may replace what currently exists. However, the innovation is likely to be incremental and is unlikely to lead to any radical change in practice, because radical change is likely to require a more generative and interactive approach to knowledge integration (Newell, Huang, & Tansley, 2004).

Generative knowledge integration occurs when there is joint knowledge production achieved through the combination and exchange of knowledge (Nahapiet & Ghoshal, 1998) and experimentation (Rosenberg, 1982) between individuals from diverse backgrounds (Grant, 1996; Hitt, Nixon, Hoskisson, & Kochhar, 1999). Through this exchange and experimentation, new and novel ways of doing things are identified that could not have been predetermined by the independent parts (Cook & Brown, 1999). In other words, generative knowledge integration occurs when communication and exchange within a group or a team evokes novel associations, connections, and hunches such that new meanings and insights are generated. In this case, knowledge integration involves a process of social construction in which organizational members negotiate, achieve, and refine a shared understanding through interaction, sense-making, and collective learning (Ayas & Zeniuk, 2001; Boland & Tenkasi, 1995). It is this process that provides the basis for creativity, and it is precisely such creative, generative knowledge integration that is much more likely to lead to radical change—for example, radical changes in medicine that many declare is possible with new scientific/technological breakthroughs.

As indicated, exploring knowledge integration processes involves understanding the network relationships and social interactions within and across communities that support this activity (Okhuysen & Eisenhardt, 2002; Grant, 1996). Grant (1996) points out that there is a dearth of empirical research exploring these networking processes supporting knowledge integration. In the next section we consider how these micro-social processes are viewed through the lens of social capital.

The Concept of Social Capital

Effective knowledge integration during an innovation project depends on selecting project team members with an appropriate mix of knowledge, skills, and expertise (Teram, 1999). This will include both organizational and technical/scientific knowledge. This intellectual capital of the team comprises both human and social capital. The human capital of the team refers to the "knowledge and knowing capability of the collectivity" (Nahapiet & Ghoshal, 1998). While important, it is unlikely that team members will have all the relevant knowledge and expertise necessary. Thus, the development of a new drug or a new IT system requires the integration of an extremely broad base of knowledge, but the number of individuals that can be directly involved in the project is necessarily small because of communication and resource constraints (Grant, 1996). So the project team will need to network with others. In doing this they will be drawing upon their collective *social capital*. Social capital is derived from the network of relationships that connect people together and refers to the "goodwill that is engendered by the fabric of social relations and that can be mobilized to facilitate action" (Adler & Kwon, 2002, p. 17), here to access and integrate knowledge needed for innovation. Social capital would, therefore, appear to be highly relevant in understanding these processes of knowledge integration.

The concept of social capital has become very popular in Management literature, based on the recognition that social networks are useful in a variety of contexts (Coleman, 1988) and can influence a wide range of outcomes (Burt, 1997). Here, we are interested in the ways in which social capital influences knowledge integration during innovation projects. We focus on the antecedent conditions for social capital in such projects (Adler & Kwon, 2002). Thus, networks will vary in their quality and configuration. For example, networks will differ in terms of the extent to which actors' contacts are also connected (Coleman, 1988). They will also differ in the content of the network ties (Uzzi, 1996, 1999), for example the extent to which the connected actors share common knowledge (Nonaka, 1994) and/or beliefs and norms (Portes, 1998). This will influence the development of social relationships and influence the strength of the ties (Granovetter, 1973). As individuals interact with each other, social relationships are built, and goodwill develops (Dore, 1983). This can be drawn upon to gain benefits at some later point in time. While the terms of exchange are not clearly specified, there is a tacit understanding that a 'favor' will be repaid at some time and in some way. This repayment (the outcome of social capital) may be in the form of information, influence, and/or solidarity (Sandefur & Laumann, 1998).

While the concept of social capital is widely used, Adler and Kwon (2002) highlight one central distinction in the way the concept is defined, contrasting the "bridging" from the "bonding" view of social capital. The "bridging" view is focused externally, seeing social capital as a resource inhering in a social network that can be appropriated by a focal actor, based on relations with others in the network (Burt, 1997). Individuals who provide a "bridge" across divided communities are important, since they play a brokerage role. For example, Burt (1997) identifies how there are structural gaps within any given network—individuals and groups who are relatively disconnected from each other. He suggests that people who bridge across these gaps are particularly important to ensure that individuals and groups are not isolated from the larger network. The "bonding" view, by contrast, focuses on the collective relations between a defined group (Coleman, 1988). Social capital relates to the internal structure and relations within this collective. It ensures an internal cohesiveness that allows the collective to pursue shared goals. The source and effects of social capital are, therefore, viewed differently, depending on whether the focus is on bonding or bridging.

Adler and Kwon (2002) note that some definitions of social capital do not distinguish whether the focus is internal (bonding) or external (bridging). They argue that this is preferable because, in practice, both bridging and bonding will influence behavior in all situations, and because bridging and bonding are essentially interchangeable depending upon the unit of analysis considered. They argue against "bifurcating our social capital research into a strand focused on external, bridging social capital and a strand focused on internal, bonding, social capital" (Adler & Kwon, 2002, p. 35). They develop a definition of social capital that does indeed include both internal and external ties. Thus, social capital is "the goodwill available to individuals or groups. Its source lies in the structure and content of the actor's social relations. Its effects flow from the information, influence, and solidarity it makes available to the actor" (Adler & Kwon, 2002, p. 23).

However, given that in this article we are considering the project team as the unit of analysis, we can differentiate between internal bonding within the project team itself, as members collaborate and share and combine knowledge, and external bridging, as team members seek out or are provided with knowledge and information from others outside the project team. Thus, while we agree that in practice both forms of social capital are involved simultaneously in any social activity system and, therefore, adopt Adler and Kwon's definition, we argue that, in relation to

innovation projects, it is helpful to maintain the distinction (Newell et al., 2004). This is because while project teams engage in both external bridging and internal bonding activities, they differ in how they undertake these two activities and this influences the way they approach knowledge integration. This article, then, explores how social capital, considered in terms of the bridging and bonding components, is an antecedent to knowledge integration within innovation project teams.

In summary, it is argued that knowledge integration is a key issue during an innovation project. The level of knowledge integration achieved will influence the extent to which the innovation is incremental and simply reinforces the status quo (mechanistic pooling) or is radical, with the potential to create transformational change in a product or a practice (generative knowledge integration). The level of knowledge integration actually achieved depends upon how social capital is used by the project team tasked with designing and implementing the new product or service.

MAIN FOCUS: THE LINK BETWEEN SOCIAL CAPITAL AND KNOWLEDGE INTEGRATION

Table 1 presents a summary of the suggested link between social capital and knowledge integration.

Starting with generative knowledge integration, it is argued that this is necessary for radical innovation, and requires the establishment of strong bonds within the team plus access to diverse stakeholders beyond the team (through bridging relationships). First, developing strong bonds within a project team appears to be critical to facilitate generative knowledge integration. Encouraging the development of strong ties (Granovetter, 1973) increases the closeness and reciprocity between project members who develop strong common or "consummatory" norms (Portes, 1998). Moreover, building a project team where members participate because they are interested in and knowledgeable about the project helps to ensure some 'knowledge redundancy' (Nonaka, 1994)—that is, overlapping knowledge within the team. The development of strong links, common understanding, and norms of trust and reciprocity (i.e., the structural, cognitive, and relational aspects of social capital; Nahapiet & Ghoshal, 1998) leads to high levels of cooperation (Gulati, 1998) that facilitates knowledge sharing and creativity. Team building to enhance the bonding aspect of social capital within the project team is, therefore, crucial for generative knowledge integration. The effect of this bonding is that it allows the team to subsequently share and integrate the dispersed knowledge that they gather during their bridging activities.

Table 1. The link between social capital and knowledge integration

Knowledge Integration	Social Capital	
	Bonding	**Bridging**
Generative knowledge integration	Establishment of trust and redundant knowledge allows team to synergistically share and integrate unique knowledge and expertise	Involvement of multiple stakeholders with diverse and conflicting views—resolving conflicts and evaluating different views provides source of new ideas
Mechanistic pooling	Each team member works independently to design his or her part of the new product or service based on existing knowledge and expertise	Minimal involvement of stakeholders, thus restricting access to different views

In relation to this bridging activity, as already discussed, a project team is unlikely to have all the knowledge necessary for developing the new product or service so that bridging activity with a wider stakeholder community is also important (Coleman, 1988). The ties between the project team members and the wider stakeholder community are likely to be much looser or weaker (Granovetter, 1973) than those ties developed within the project team itself. This is necessary since it will not be possible to develop the dense network, based on a strong sense of common purpose, across so many people. Thus, the network will be open and loose, with others getting involved with the project team for instrumental reasons—to ensure that they had some influence on the new product or service. Such weak ties are sufficient for such information access (Hansen, 1999, 2002). The effect of encouraging this wider involvement is that the team will have access to broader knowledge from across the stakeholder community, which will mean that different perspectives will be surfaced. These differences will need to be discussed in order to develop new products or practices that people will buy-in to. Radical innovation, based on generative knowledge integration, depends on cultivating extensive social networking between the project team and other stakeholders, in order to foster opportunities for the transformation of a product or a practice.

To achieve mechanistic pooling of knowledge, adequate for more incremental innovation, is simpler so that bonding within the team can be weaker and bridging to other stakeholders more limited. This is because incremental innovation does not depend on breakthrough knowledge but rather builds on existing knowledge. For incremental innovation, team members can work independently of each other, and knowledge sharing can be limited because the interfaces between the knowledge domains are already established. Moreover, there is less need to bridge extensively to a diversity of stakeholders because there is no need to identify new knowledge trajectories that may be relevant, nor will stakeholders be

required to radically change their existing practices. They do not, therefore, need to be involved in the innovation project in order to ensure that their commitment is built. This mechanistic approach to knowledge integration is therefore more economical and facilitates the introduction of a new product or practice more quickly with limited disruptive change, albeit the new product or practice only improves what currently exists.

The point of making this distinction is that there are some contexts in which a mechanistic approach to knowledge integration to support innovation is likely to be more effective, while there are other contexts in which a more generative approach will be more beneficial. For example, mechanistic pooling will be most efficient where a new product or practice, for example a new medical treatment or a new IT system, simply replaces an existing product or practice. Similarly, mechanistic pooling will be more efficient where there is little need for interaction across professional or functional domains in developing the new product or practice. On the other hand, generative knowledge integration will be necessary where the development of the new product or practice depends upon interactions between professional groups who have not worked together previously or where the innovation results in radical changes to a product or a practice so that the buy-in of stakeholders requires cultivation. In other words, a contingency approach is suggested, which specifies that for incremental innovation, where a mechanistic approach is appropriate, social networking both within the project team and between the project team and the wider stakeholder community can be minimized. Under conditions where a generative approach to knowledge integration is necessary, team bonding and bridging will need to be more intensive and extensive because of the need to engage in the "generative dance" (Cook & Brown, 1999) of sharing and integrating knowledge that underpins innovation processes that lead to radical changes in products or practices.

FUTURE TRENDS

It is likely that radical innovation, requiring a lot of interactivity across professional and disciplinary groups, will become more important as competition intensifies in most industries (Gibbons et al., 1994). This suggests that the need for generative knowledge integration will increase in the future. Below we consider the implications of this for the management and organization of project teams tasked with creating radical new products and practices. More specifically we consider a number of aspects of a project team that will be differentially affected depending upon whether the focus is radical or incremental innovation. It is likely that the aspects that foster radical innovation through generative knowledge integration will become more important:

1. **Team Building:** Where generative knowledge integration is necessary to foster radical innovation, it will be important to nurture a strong and cohesive project team through, for example, team-building exercises. Where mechanistic pooling is sufficient, there is less need for such team building.

2. **Division of Tasks:** Where mechanistic pooling is adequate, tasks can be divided up into independent activities that are assigned to different people, since as Becker (2001) identifies, one strategy for dealing with the dispersion of knowledge is to decompose organizational units into smaller ones so that each unit (in this case each individual) is responsible for one part of the larger problem. As Becker notes, this strategy of specialization reduces the opaqueness of complex problems. Where the resulting 'pieces' of work can be put together easily because interfaces between the 'pieces' are pre-established, this is very efficient. For generative knowledge integration, however, this is problematic because these interfaces are not pre-established, since different groups are involved, which have not previously worked together. In this case, tasks are more effectively divided up so that there is considerable overlap and inter-dependency built in.

3. **Allocation of Tasks:** Where the mechanistic pooling of knowledge is sufficient, it is most efficient to allocate only specialists to tasks. However, where generative knowledge integration is required, the allocation of specialists may not be appropriate because these specialists are likely to have preconceived ideas about how activities should be completed and so will not think about alternative processes that could be supported by the new scientific/technological breakthroughs. As Meacham (1983) states:

Each new domain of knowledge appears simple from the distance of ignorance. The more we learn about a particular domain, the greater the number of uncertainties, doubts, questions, and complexities. Each bit of knowledge serves as the thesis from which additional questions or antithesis arise. (p. 120)

The point is that specialists may not get past their "distance of ignorance" because they believe that they already have the solution. Involving non-expert individuals may therefore help in generative knowledge integration because such individuals are more likely to ask the questions that could identify the complexities of the situation and the alternative opportunities afforded by the breakthroughs.

4. **Knowledge Redundancy:** Generative knowledge integration also requires significant common understanding within the project team where mechanistic pooling does not require this to the same extent because, as already indicated, the interfaces between the different parts of the project are already well established. Bruner (1983) described creativity as "figuring out how to use what you already know in order to go beyond what you currently think" (p. 183). This implies that an important impetus to creativity is knowledge about the issue you are dealing with. So, while existing knowledge can be a barrier to creative thinking, it is also the case that without knowledge there can be no creativity. Without this effort to understand broader issues across different disciplines, individuals will rely on their existing knowledge and so a more mechanistic orientation to knowledge integration is likely to result. In the future it will be increasingly important for those involved in radical innovation projects to have a broad inter-disciplinary understanding.

5. **Stakeholder Involvement:** Another important issue relates to the extent of bridging activity. Limiting bridging activity means that the diversity of opinion that exists across the wider stakeholder community will not be voiced. This may be efficient in contexts where incremental innovation is the goal. Yet, as Leonard-Barton (1995) reminds us, bringing together individuals with different views and backgrounds can lead to "creative abrasion" that results in new and innovative approaches being considered. Creative abrasion is necessary to achieve generative knowledge integration. User involvement is likely to be especially important in this respect. Involving users can help to encourage commitment to the project. Additionally, users can be a source of creativity if they are given the opportunity to voice their ideas about alternative processes and prac-

tices. Discussion with users may lead to conflicting suggestions, as expected in such novel situations; nevertheless they can also provide a significant source of ideas.

CONCLUSION

In conclusion, there are significant differences in the knowledge integration challenge of a project team that is tasked with developing a radical innovation compared to a team tasked with some kind of incremental innovation. These differences in the knowledge integration challenge have implications for the way the team will need to create and use its social capital. It is suggested that where the focus is on radical innovation, it is important for project teams to develop strong internal ties and develop a sense of a shared purpose to foster generative knowledge integration. The focus is thus on team bonding and the development of a closed network. This allows team members to develop some common or redundant knowledge that is crucial for generative knowledge integration. This team building creates a sense of shared destiny and understanding among the project members, which leads to a normative commitment to the project. However, where the focus is on more incremental innovation, knowledge integration within the team can be more mechanistic. The social capital bonding requirements for the team are then much simpler because within the team, bonds do not need to be as strong since individuals can work more independently.

For generative knowledge integration, once the core project team has developed a shared sense of purpose—a "collective mind" (Weick & Roberts, 1993)—they can begin to bring in ideas and information from individuals across the wider network of stakeholders who will be affected by the innovation. In doing this they are using their bridging social capital to gather information needed for the project. External parties provide the needed information because they can see an instrumental return in doing this. The provision of this information gives the project team an understanding of the likely sources of resistance to the change in practice and so can begin the process of building user commitment to the change. The network focus is on bridging activity, and it is helpful if the network structure is more open to facilitate wider information flow. However, for more incremental innovation projects, the project team can work in a more isolated way from potential users and other stakeholders, with a more restricted network, since there is less need to capture the diversity of views and ideas. Working in this way, the project team will probably be unchallenged by creative abrasion, but this is efficient where the goal is incremental innovation.

Where project teams work towards a common goal in a very mechanistic way, the extent of transformational change that they can anticipate from the new product or practice they develop is likely to be limited. But there are situations in which this is highly appropriate. Where project teams work more collaboratively, this will encourage interaction and the sharing of knowledge more synergistically and creatively so that they are more likely to be able to generate products and practices that can encourage more transformational change. Which approach to knowledge integration is appropriate will depend on the unique circumstances of each innovation project.

REFERENCES

Adler, P., & Kwon, S.-W. (2002) Social capital: Prospects for a new concept. *Academy of Management Review, 27*(1), 17-40.

Ayas, K., & Zeniuk, N. (2001). Project-based learning: Building communities of reflective practitioners. *Management Learning, 32*(1), 61-76.

Becker, M. (2001). Managing dispersed knowledge: Organizational problems, managerial strategies and their effectiveness. *Journal of Management Studies, 38*(7), 1037-1051.

Boland, R.J., & Tenkasi, R.V. (1995). Perspective making and perspective taking in communities of knowing. *Organization Science, 6*(4), 350-372.

Burt, R. (1997). The contingent value of social capital. *Administrative Science Quarterly, 42,* 339-365.

Bruner, J. (1983). *In search of mind.* New York: Harper.

Christensen, C., Bohmer, R., & Kenagy, J. (2000). Will disruptive innovations cure health care? *Harvard Business Review,* (September/October), 102-112.

CMR International. (2000). *R&D Briefing,* (26).

Coleman, J. (1988). Social capital in the creation of human capital. *American Journal of Sociology, 94,* S95-S120.

Cook, S.D.N., & Brown, J.S. (1999). Bridging epistemologies: The generative dance between organizational knowledge and organizational knowing. *Organization Science, 190,* 381-400.

Dore, R. (1983). Goodwill and the spirit of market capitalism. *British Journal of Sociology, 34,* 459-482.

Dougherty, D. (1992). Interpretive barriers to successful product innovation in large firms. *Organization Science, 3,* 179-202

Gibbons, M., Limoges, C., Nowotny, H., Schwartzman, S., Scott, P., & Trow, M. (1994). *The new production of knowledge: The dynamics of science and research in contemporary societies*. London: Sage Publications.

Granovetter, M. (1973). The strength of weak ties. *American Journal of Sociology, 78,* 1360-1380.

Grant, R. (1996). Prospering in dynamically competitive environment: Organizational capability as knowledge integration. *Organization Science, 7,* 375-387.

Gulati, R. (1998). Alliances and networks. *Strategic Management Journal, 19*(April), 293-317.

Hansen, M. (1999). The search-transfer problem: The role of weak ties in sharing knowledge across organizational subunits. *Administrative Science Quarterly, 44,* 82-111.

Hansen, M. (2002). Knowledge networks: Explaining effective knowledge sharing in multiunit companies. *Organization Science, 13*(3), 232-248.

Henderson, R., Orsenigo, L., & Pisano, G. (1999). The pharmaceutical industry and the revolution in molecular biology: Interactions among scientific, institutional, and organizational change. In D. Mowery & R. Nelson (Eds.), *Sources of industrial leadership* (pp. 267-311). Cambridge, MA: Cambridge University Press.

Hitt, M., Nixon, R., Hoskisson, R., & Kochhar, R. (1999). Corporate entrepreneurship and cross-functional fertilization: Activation, process and disintegration of a new product design team. *Entrepreneurship Theory and Practice, 24,* 145-167.

Johnson, J. (1995). Chaos: The dollar drain of IT project failures. *Application Development Trends,* (January), 41-47.

Knights, D., & Wilmott, H. (1997). The hype and hope of interdisciplinary management studies. *British Journal of Management, 8*(9), 9-22.

Leonard Barton, D. (1995). *The wellsprings of knowledge: Building and sustaining the sources of innovation.* Boston: Harvard Business School Press.

Meacham, J. (1983). Wisdom and the context of knowledge. In D. Kuhn & J. Meacham (Eds.), *Contributions in human development* (vol. 8, pp. 111-134). Basel: Karger.

Nahapiet, J., & Ghoshal, S. (1998). Social capital, intellectual capital, and the organizational advantage. *Academy of Management Review, 23,* 242-266.

Newell, S., Huang, J., & Tansley, C. (2004). Social capital and knowledge integration in an ERP project team: The importance of bridging AND bonding. *British Journal of Management, 15,* 43-57.

Nonaka, I. (1994). A dynamic theory of organizational knowledge creation. *Organization Science, 5,* 14-37.

Okhuysen, G., & Eisenhardt, K. (2002). Integrating knowledge in groups: How formal interventions enable flexibility. *Organization Science, 13*(4), 370-386.

Portes, A. (1998). Social capital: Its origins and applications in modern sociology. *Annual Review of Sociology, 24,* 1-24.

Powell, W., Koput, W., & Smith-Doerr, L. (1996). Interorganizational collaboration and the locus of innovation: Networks of learning in biotechnology. *Administrative Science Quarterly, 41*(1), 116-130.

Rosenberg, N. (1982). *Inside the black box.* Cambridge, MA: Cambridge University Press.

Sandefur, R., & Laumann, E. (1998). A paradigm for social capital. *Rationality and Society, 10,* 481-501.

Teram, E. (1999). A case against making the control of clients a negotiable contingency for interdisciplinary teams. *Human Relations, 52,* 263-278.

Tsoukas, H. (1996). The firm as a distributed knowledge system: A constructionist approach. *Strategic Management Journal, 17,* 11-25.

Uzzi, B. (1996). The sources and consequences of embeddedness for the economic performance of organizations: The network effect. *American Sociological Review, 61,* 674-698.

Uzzi, B. (1999). Embeddedness in the making of financial capital: How social relations and networks benefit firms seeking finance. *American Sociological Review, 64*(4), 481-505.

Weick, K., & Roberts, K. (1993). Collective mind in organizations: Heedful interrelating on flight decks. *Administrative Science Quarterly, 38*(3), 357-282.

KEY TERMS

Generative Knowledge Integration: Occurs when communication and exchange of knowledge within a group or a team evokes novel associations, connections, and hunches such that new meanings and insights are generated.

Human Capital: The knowledge and knowing that exists within a particular unit, which could be a team, an organization, an industry, or even a society.

Incremental Innovation: The generation of new ideas (new knowledge) that leads to the incremental development of new products or services that build on existing practices.

Innovation: The generation of new ideas (new knowledge) that leads to the development of new products or organizational practices.

Knowledge Integration: The process whereby several individuals share and combine their information to collectively create new knowledge.

Mechanistic Pooling of Knowledge: Occurs when each team member works independently on a set of clearly defined tasks or processes with which he or she is familiar and uses his or her existing knowledge to consider the potential of the new scientific/technological breakthrough on the particular problem domain.

Radical Innovation: The generation of new ideas (new knowledge) that leads to the development of radically new products or services that lead to transformations in practices.

Social Capital: The social networks and the assets that can be mobilized through these networks that enable social action generally and knowledge sharing more specifically.

Understanding Organizational Memory

Sajjad M. Jasimuddin
University of Dhaka, Bangladesh and University of Southampton, UK

N.A.D. Connell
University of Southampton, UK

Jonathan H. Klein
University of Southampton, UK

INTRODUCTION

It is generally recognized that Walsh and Ungson (1991) "provided the first integrative framework for thinking about organizational memory" (Olivera, 2000, p. 813). Within the field of knowledge management (KM), there has been interest in a variety of issues surrounding organizational memory (OM), which is understood to involve processes of storage and retrieval of organizational knowledge of the past for use in both the present and the future. The recognition of the importance of OM has implications for practice. For example, Argote, Beckman, and Epple (1990) suggest that the effective use of OM can protect an organization from some of the negative effects of staff loss, while Stein (1995, p. 19) asserts that an appreciation of OM can facilitate the solution of problems associated with the retention and utilization of knowledge within organizations.

Although the need to preserve knowledge in organizations is now recognized, organizational theorists still disagree on a number of issues relating to OM. Existing literature exhibits contradictory arguments regarding OM which can make the relevance and application of OM concepts to KM difficult to understand. This article describes some of the disagreements surrounding OM in order to provide a deeper understanding of how OM might help to manage knowledge.

BACKGROUND

The topic of OM has received a great deal of attention from researchers across a wide range of disciplines, most notably organization theory, psychology, sociology, communication theory, and information systems. In a detailed exploration of OM, Stein (1995, p. 17) suggests that "there are three major reasons to explore this concept in more detail: (1) memory is a rich metaphor that provides insight into organizational life; (2)

OM is embedded in other management theories; (3) OM is relevant to management practice."

Most of the literature on OM tends to focus on definitions of the term, the content and types of OM, its location, and the processes associated with the acquisition, storage, retrieval, and maintenance of memory (Walsh & Ungson, 1991; Stein & Zwass, 1995; Casey, 1997). Walsh and Ungson (1991, p. 61) provide an overall definition of OM as "stored information from an organization's history that can be brought to bear on present decisions." This corresponds closely with the definition given by Stein (1995), who regards OM as the way in which organizational knowledge from the past is brought to bear on present activities.

Some studies have addressed the role of information technology in developing OM systems (OMS) which support OM processes (Sherif, 2002). Several researchers have highlighted the barriers to the implementation of OMS, the ways in which they might be overcome (Sherif, 2002), and the influence of OM on organizational effectiveness (Olivera, 2000).

OM occupies a significant place within management literature. However, Walsh and Ungson (1991, p. 57) argue that "the extant representations of the concept of OM are fragmented and underdeveloped." Examination of the existing literature reveals frequent divergence of understanding of the notion of OM (Corbett, 1997). Indeed, earlier researchers (most notably Ungson, Braunstein, & Hall, 1981; Argyris & Schon, 1978) denied the existence of OM. Generally, organizational theorists disagree about a variety of issues surrounding OM. Ackerman and Halverson (1998, cited by Schwartz, Divitini, & Brasethvik, 2000, p. 3) are concerned that a clear and universally accepted definition of what an OM should do appears to be lacking:

After nearly 10 years of research, the term organizational memory has become overworked and confused. It is time for a re-examination. The term is burdened with the practical wish to reuse organizational experience, leading researchers to ignore critical functions of an organization's memory and consider only some forms of augmenting memory.

CONTROVERSIES IN OM

The field of OM exhibits many controversies in which researchers seem unable to agree about fairly fundamental features. The literature regarding these issues tends to be somewhat sparse and inconclusive. Some of the most notable of these issues, on which we focus in subsequent sections, are:

- Can organizations be said to have memories, or is OM essentially anthropomorphism?
- What is the relationship between the research fields of OM and KM?
- Does OM reside in the minds of individual organizational members, or elsewhere?
- Is OM appropriately modeled in terms of static storage bins, or should it be treated as a dynamic socially constructed process?
- How are OM systems operationalized?
- Is OM functional or dysfunctional in terms of organizational performance and effectiveness?

IS OM ANTHROPOMORPHISM?

Some researchers question whether OM can truly exist at all. They argue that, unlike an individual human being, an organization cannot be said to have a memory. Walsh and Ungson (1991) suggest that the idea of OM raises possible problems of anthropomorphism: Attributing characteristics that may be uniquely human to organizations may be an everyday convenience, but may obscure rather than clarify research issues. Argyris and Schon (1978), for example, contend that organizations cannot memorize knowledge of the past. Others, however, argue the contrary. Weick (1979, p. 206), for instance, asserts that organizational memory is implicated in the production of organizational personality, and that organizations must accept and live with their memories.

WHAT IS THE RELATIONSHIP BETWEEN OM AND KM?

The relationship between OM and KM is another issue of contention. Knowledge management encompasses the management of organizational knowledge to en-

hance competitive advantage and implies an integrated approach to identifying, capturing, preserving, and retrieving the knowledge associated with the activities of an organization. Davenport and Prusak (1998), for example, define KM as the process of capturing, preserving, and distributing organizational knowledge. But are OM and KM fundamentally distinct fields of enquiry, or do they possess substantial commonality? This question is unresolved. Recent KM literature has either identified OM as an element of KM or appears to have used the terms, whether by accident or design, interchangeably. Unfortunately, however, there has been little attempt to systematically address the nature of the differences and similarities between them. There is little agreement as to what, if indeed anything, distinguishes OM from KM.

OM and KM seem to have evolved, at least, into close partners (Schwartz et al., 2000). Most researchers, including Kuhn and Abecker (1998), view OM as an important component of the KM perspective. The argument is that OM, being concerned with the preservation of knowledge for present and future use, must be integrated with KM. Similarly, Randall, Hughes, O'Brien, Rounefield, and Tomie (2001) consider OM to be a sister concept to KM, and the two are in practice used interchangeably. Hoog and Spek (1997, p. v) acknowledge the close relationship between OM and KM when they state that an important problem in KM is "insufficient use of knowledge possibly stored in badly organised corporate memories."

However, some researchers hold the view that OM and KM are not the same and should not be confused. Marsh and Morris (2001), for example, draw attention to temporality, arguing that KM is of the present, while OM is of the past. They regard KM as relating to the management of knowledge that is currently in use, while OM is concerned with the storage of past knowledge for future use.

Given that a central aspect of KM is the preservation and retrieval of organizational knowledge and that OM is the mechanism by which knowledge from the past is brought to bear on the present and future, it seems legitimate to regard OM as a constituent of KM. The two terms are not synonymous: KM, which addresses the entire issue of managing organizational knowledge, is a far broader area than OM. The storage and retrieval of organizational knowledge is just a part, albeit a crucial part, of the whole job.

WHERE DOES MEMORY RESIDE?

The memories held by an organization constitute a record of its past that may contain a vast amount of knowledge.

Table 1. Knowledge storage devices

Knowledge storage devices
Formal and informal behavioral routines, procedures, and scripts (Nelson & Winter, 1982)
Standard routine procedures (Stein, 1995)
Managerial technical systems and capabilities (Leonard-Barton, 1992)
Individuals (El Sawy et al., 1986)
Culture (Cook & Yanov, 1992)
Products (Olivera & Argote, 1999)
Physical artifacts of an organization (Campbell-Kelly, 1996)
Computer-based information systems (Stein & Zwass, 1995)

The literature recognizes a variety of types of devices that may store knowledge (Table 1).

Where organizational memory resides, however, is controversial. The traditional view is that organizational knowledge is brought into being by people within the organization, and that it is located within the human mind (El Sawy, Gomes, & Gonzalez, 1986; Olivera, 2000). Others place it in the organization itself (Galbraith, 1977). Walsh and Ungson (1991) suggest that memory resides in many different organizational locations, and adopt a "storage bin" analogy, in which OM is structured in six bins which underpin processes of knowledge acquisition and retention (Table 2).

SHOULD OM BE VIEWED AS A SOCIALLY CONSTRUCTED PROCESS?

The storage bin model of OM is typical of a perspective that regards OM as centered around "sets of knowledge retention devices, such as people and documents, that collect, store, and provide access to the organization's experience" (Olivera, 2000, p. 815). However, this is not a universal perspective. The typology of OM constructed by Nissley and Casey (2002) contrasts the storage bin view with that of OM as a socially constructed process, and this is an approach adopted by many researchers (Conklin & Star, 1991; Randall, O'Brien, Rounefield, & Hughes, 1996; Casey, 1997; Randall et al., 2001; Nissley & Casey, 2002; Ackermann & Halveson, 1998). For example, Nissley and Casey (2001) regard collective memory as a socially constructed shared interpretation of the past, and Randall et al. (1996) suggest that considerations of memory should acknowledge "social context," which is relevant not only to retention and transfer of knowledge but also to how it becomes useful to people in the course of their work.

Similarly, Conklin and Star (1991) regard OM as a facilitator of organizational learning. OM is more than the aggregate of the memories of the members of the organization—it is a social phenomenon. Randall et al. (1996, p. 29) emphasize that:

OM should be seen as a collection of socially organized activities done by persons in organizations; that is, remembering as a feasible achievement verb. To put it another way, the 'organizational memory' metaphor fails to distinguish the kinds of social remembering that

Table 2. A storage bin model of organizational memory (Walsh & Ungson, 1991)

Storage bins
Internal retention bins:
1. Individuals (and their own memory aids, such as files);
2. Culture;
3. Transformations (procedures, rules, and systems that guide the transformations of inputs into outputs);
4. Structures (in particular, organizational roles);
5. Ecology (the physical structure of the workplace); and
External bin:
6. External bin (external archives).

might take place in organizational life, and provides few examples of the 'remembering how,' 'remembering who,' and 'remembering what' that we are interested in.

HOW ARE OM SYSTEMS OPERATIONALIZED?

Existing literature tends to either neglect the operationalization of OM systems, taking them for granted, or describe it in the context of a technology-based or a people-focused approach. Technologies do indeed play an important role in how organizations preserve their knowledge. Anand, Manz, and Glick (1998) consider technology-based OM systems to fully acknowledge technologies as forms of OM, and several researchers (e.g., El Sawy et al., 1986; Te'eni & Weinberger, 2003) conceptualize IT-supported OM.

Computer-mediated IT, such as Lotus Notes, databases, and Intranets, provide mechanisms for retaining and accessing electronic archives. Stein and Zwass (1995) stress the role of technology in actualizing OM and provide a model for an OM system, of which information systems are a vital component. Meanwhile, some researchers recognize the importance of non-IT-based processes in operationalization of OMS (Walsh & Ungson, 1991). Organizational members may be the most effective means to operationalize storage and retrieval of knowledge.

IS OM FUNCTIONAL OR DYSFUNCTIONAL?

It is perhaps surprising that there are arguments not only for, but also against, the desirability of making the knowledge of the past available in knowledge storage repositories (Paper & Johnson, 1996). Some do indeed argue that OM is functional (Walsh & Ungson, 1991; Stein 1995). Walsh and Ungson (1991, pp. 73-74), for instance, identify three important organizational roles occupied by OM: (1) an informational role; (2) a control function; and (3) a political role. Other benefits that have been identified include increased organizational learning (Te'eni & Weinberger, 2003), improved coordination (Yates, 1989), rapid product development (Moorman & Miner, 1997), and the facilitation of knowledge sharing (Te'eni & Weinberger, 2003). Stein (1995, pp. 31-32) contends that OM can benefit organizations in several ways, including strengthening its identity and providing new personnel with access to the expertise of their predecessors.

However, some authorities (e.g., Walsh & Ungson, 1991; Stein & Zwass, 1995) have pointed to dysfunctionalities. In their view, organizations should discard old practices and develop new ones. Argote (1999) provides evidence which indicates the significance of such policies. Stein (1995) argues that organizational memory is not necessarily a good thing for individuals or organizations, and that, at the other extreme, it can become a constraint that threatens organizational viability.

FUTURE TRENDS

This discussion of OM has focused on a number of key controversies in the field. The contention of the authors of this article is that exploration of these controversies will be valuable to the development of OM theory and practice, and that resolving and accommodating the disagreements will lead to substantial advance. Some research has been directed at such resolution and accommodation, and it is in this direction, the authors consider, that the future lies.

OM, as currently depicted, describes the ways in which organizations can learn and memorize knowledge of their past, through their members, by means of both mental and structural artefacts. As such, OM may be seen as a significant element of KM (Schwartz et al., 2000): KM addresses organizational knowledge holistically, while OM focuses on the storage of past or current knowledge for present and future use. The article presents divergent perspectives—static storage bin or dynamic socially constructed process—on an appropriate model of OM, with the bulk of the literature apparently favoring the former. In the future, we may expect to see some integration of these perspectives, perhaps moving toward a "dynamic socially-constructed storage bin" model which captures valuable aspects of both.

In parallel to this, the technological view of OM that many adopt has been challenged by some researchers. Anand et al. (1998) argue that in order to implement KM initiatives and to manage OM in particular, it will be crucial to understand the nature of the relationships between technology and other organizational features and, in particular, people. We can expect to see more even-handed approaches to human and technical elements in future OM developments.

Although the arguments pointing to the dysfunctionality of OM, potential or otherwise, should not be ignored, we would suggest that the Markovian organization—the organization with no memory—is a foolhardy goal. Indeed, we suggest it might be an impossible one and that organizations need to address the issue of OM, if for no other reason than managed memory is likely to be more functional (or, to put it more pessimistically, less dysfunctional) than unmanaged memory. The functionality of OM lies in the contribution it can make to the effective management of the future of the organization—to organizational decision-making. However, it is essential to ensure that the knowledge available in the repositories of OM is relevant to that activity.

CONCLUSION

Organizational memory is the function of the organization in which organizational knowledge is stored and retrieved for present and future use, and thus contributes importantly to the processes of designing and creating the future of the organization. Although it has interested researchers for several years, many aspects remain unclear and contradictory. The authors hope that this article has provided insight into these aspects and recommend a pluralistic stance to them.

REFERENCES

Ackerman, M.S., & Halverson, C. (1998). Considering an organization's memory. *Proceedings of CSCW '98.* Washington, (pp. 39-48).

Anand, V., Manz, C., & Glick. W.H. (1998). An organizational memory approach to information management. *Academy of Management Review, 23*(4), 796-809.

Argote, L. (1999). *Organizational learning: Creating, retaining and transferring knowledge.* Norwell, MA: Kluwer Academic Publishers.

Argote, L., Beckman, S.L., & Epple, D. (1990). The persistence and transfer of learning in industrial settings. *Management Science, 36*(2), 140-154.

Argyris, C., & Schon, D. (1978). *Organizational learning: A theory of action perspective.* Reading, MA: Addison-Wesley.

Campbell-Kelly, M. (1996). Information technology and organizational change in the British census, 1981-1911. *Information Research Systems, 7*(1), 22-36.

Casey, A. (1997). Collective memory in organizations. *Advances in Strategic Management, 14,* 111-146.

Conklin, E.J., & Star, S. (1991). *Panel on organization memory.* ECSCW'91.

Cook, S.D.N., & Yanov, D. (1993). Culture and organizational learning. *Journal of Management Inquiry, 2,* 373-90.

Corbett, J.M. (1997). Towards a sociological model of organizational memory. *Proceedings of the 30th Annual Hawaii International Conference on System Sciences,* 2, (pp. 252-261).

Davenport, T.H., & Prusak L. (1998). *Working knowledge: How organizations manage what they know.* Boston: Harvard Business School Press.

El Sawy, O.A., Gomes, G.M., & Gonzalez, M.V. (1986). Preserving institutional memory: The management of history as an organizational resource. *Academy of Management Best Paper Proceedings, 37,* 118-122.

Galbraith, J.R. (1977). *Organizational design.* Reading, MA: Addison-Wesley.

Hoog, R.D., & Spek, R.v.d. (1997). Knowledge management: Hope or hype? *Expert Systems with Applications, 13*(1), v-vi.

Kuhn, O., & Abecker, A. (1998). In U.M. Borghoff & R. Pareschi (Eds.), *Corporate memories for knowledge management in industrial practice: Prospects and challenges* (pp. 183-206). Berlin: Springer.

Leonard-Barton, D. (1992). Core capabilities and core rigidities: A paradox in managing new product development. *Strategic Management Journal, 13*(Summer), 111-125.

Marsh, C.H., & Morris E.C. (2001, October 24-27). Corporate memory and technical communicators: A relationship with a new urgency. *IEEE on Communication Dimensions Proceedings.* IEEE International.

Moorman, C., & Miner, A.S. (1997). The impact of organizational memory on new product performance and creativity. *Journal of Marketing Research, 34* (February), 91-106.

Nelson, R.R., & Winter, S.G.. (1982). *An evolutionary theory of economic change.* Cambridge, MA: The Belkman Press.

Nissley, N., & Casey, A. (2001). The politics of the exhibition: Viewing corporate museums through the paradigmatic lens of organizational memory. *British Journal of Management, 13,* 35-45.

Olivera, F. (2000). Memory systems in organizations: An empirical investigation of mechanisms for knowledge collection, storage and access. *Journal of Management Studies, 37*(6), 811-32.

Olivera, F., & Argote, L. (1999). *Organizational learning and CORE processes in new product development.* In L. Thompson, L. Levine, & D. Messick (Eds.) (pp. 297-326). NJ: Laurence Erlbaum Associates.

Paper, D.J., & Johnson J.J. (1996). A theoretical framework linking creativity, empowerment, and organizational memory. *Proceedings of the 29th Annual Hawaii International Conference on System Sciences* (pp. 20-29).

Randall, D., Hughes, J., O'Brien, J., Rounefield, M., & Tomie, P. (2001) Memories are made of this: Explicating organisational knowledge and memory. *European Journal of Information Systems, 10,* 113-21.

Randall, D., O'Brien, J., Rounefield, M., & Hughes, J.A. (1996). Organizational memory and CSCW: Supporting the "Mavis Phenomenon." *Proceedings of 6th Australian Conference on Computer-Human Interaction.*

Schwartz, D.G., Divitini, M., & Brasethvik, T. (2000). *Internet-based organizational memory and knowledge management.* Hershey, PA: Idea Group Publishing.

Sherif, K. (2002). *Barriers to adoption of organizational memories: Lessons from industry.* In Stuart Barnes (Ed.) (pp. 210-221). London: Thompson Learning.

Stein, E.W., & Zwass, V. (1995). Analyzing organizational memory with information systems. *Information Systems Research, 6,* 285-314.

Stein, E.W. (1995). Organizational memory: Review of concepts and recommendations for management. *International Journal of Information Management, 15*(2), 17-32.

Te'eni, D., & Weinberger, H. (2003). *Systems development of organizational memory: A literature survey.* Center for Global Knowledge Management, Bar-Ilan University. Retrieved from *www.Biu.ac.il*

Ungson, G.R., Braunstein, D.N., & Hall, P.D. (1981). Managerial information processing: A research review. *Administrative Science Quarterly, 26,* 116-134.

Walsh, J.P., & Ungson, G.R. (1991) Organizational memory. *Academy of Management Review, 16*(1), 57-91.

Weick, K.E. (1979). *The social psychology of organizing.* Reading, MA: Addison-Wesley.

Yates, J. (1989) *Control through communications: The rise of system in American management.* Baltimore: John Hopkins Press.

KEY WORDS

Anthropomorphism: To ascribe human characteristics to things not human. Some authors argue that, unlike a human being, an organization can have no memory. Walsh and Ungson (1991) argue that the idea of organizational memory raises problems of anthropomorphism.

Computer-Mediated Information Technology: An effective means of storing and retrieving knowledge. IT tools such as Lotus Notes and Intranets are designed to provide a means for retaining and accessing electronic archives.

Knowledge Management (KM): Efforts made by an organization to manage knowledge. Knowledge management is a discipline that promotes an integrated approach to identifying, capturing, storing, retrieving, and transferring an organization's knowledge so as to enhance its competitive advantage.

Organizational Memory (OM): The processes of storing and retrieving knowledge of the past for present and future use. OM draws from a wide variety of disciplines including organization theory and information systems. A better understanding of OM can assist managers in solving problems regarding the retention of knowledge within their organizations.

Socially Constructed Process: Socially organized activities undertaken by people in organizations. Socially constructed processes may be examined to achieve a greater understanding of social phenomena by exploring the situated experiences of the persons involved in the social situations. OM can be viewed as a socially constructed process.

Socio-Technical Approach: A paradigm in which both social and technical elements are integrated to give a holistic view of a phenomenon. There is a strong argument for an integrated socio-technical approach to KM (particularly OM) which recognizes the active participation of each organizational member in line with the use of technology.

Storage Bin: A generic knowledge retention device in which memory is stored. The storage bin concept as generally presented implies a static conceptualization of OM. The memory's retention facility can be structured in terms of five internal retention "bins" (individuals, culture, transformations, structures, ecology) and one external "bin" (external archives).

Virtue–Nets

David Croasdell
University of Nevada, Reno, USA

Y. Ken Wang
Washington State University, USA

INTRODUCTION

David Skyrme (1999) has observed that knowledge workers exploit knowledge generated from business activities and turn it into business opportunities. Technical infrastructures enable knowledge workers and improve knowledge processes (Von Krogh, Ichijo, & Nonaka, 2000). Improving knowledge awareness requires creating a dynamic and generative environment for organizational workers (Senge, 1990). Organizations are faced with developing communication strategies that maintain centralized and fully accessible knowledge bases while at the same time trying to compete in a highly decentralized marketplace. Technological solutions for enabling and enhancing communication among knowledge workers are used for activities such as scheduling, negotiating, checking e-mail, revising documents, making reservations, connecting laptops remotely to the Net, problem solving, and decision making. There are numerous electronic devices for communicating between knowledge workers. These networked devices serve the purpose of connecting human-knowledge capital. For many companies, human-knowledge capital is a significant source of competitive advantage, and the dispersion of this capital without effective communication networks can greatly hinder the decision makers and the overall corporate decision-making process. One place to start examining the practices of knowledge workers is to study the networks in which they work.

This article explores knowledge networks and their advantage in grouping data based on qualitative attributes to support knowledge work. Such networks support and enable individual interactions with knowledge systems to enrich understanding. The next section provides a survey of communication technologies and theories to support the need to develop a network infrastructure to enable intelligent business practices. The next section on knowledge sharing proposes a virtue-net network architecture to support network connectivity using qualitative measures as a method for leveraging knowledge networks. The article concludes with a brief discussion and ideas for future research in this area. A glossary of terms for the virtue net is provided as an appendix to the article.

BACKGROUND

Knowledge management (KM) was popularized in the 1990s at a time when the dominant organizational metaphor was "organizations as computers" (Nonaka & Takeuchi, 1995). Knowledge management can be defined as "the process of identifying, capturing, and leveraging knowledge to help the company compete" (O'Dell & Grayson, 1998). Knowledge is key to organizations learning from and about customers, competitors, business partners, and staffs. Skyrme (1999) lists creating, identifying, gathering, organizing, sharing, learning, applying, exploiting, protecting, and evaluating in his representative sample of KM practices reported as key elements of knowledge-management programs.

One basic assumption of knowledge management contends that resource constraints such as time, capital, and understanding limit the ability to reasonably expect that all necessary and relevant knowledge can be captured and disseminated throughout an organization. Nonetheless, mechanisms to capture, encode, and store process knowledge in organizations provide (a) a starting point for future projects, and (b) a basis for avoiding similar mistakes in future projects. Knowing the how and why (i.e., process knowledge) behind the what (i.e., factual knowledge) leads to greater abilities to generate insight and better understanding.

Knowledge-Sharing Networks

Individuals seek information for both normative and informational reasons. Normative-influence theory suggests that human beings usually seek approval, a sense of belonging, and communality, which in some cases could account for the individual decision maker's drive for knowledge and for his or her communication with other knowledge stakeholders (Huang & Wei, 2000). Shared understanding is a relatively strong component that binds individuals in organizational and group settings. Informational-influence theory suggests the search for factual information and task truth can also act as a driver for decision makers seeking knowledge, including those seeking knowledge confirmation (Guenther & Braun, 2001).

This sort of environment requires highly efficient, responsive, and self-adaptive information systems. Ideally, the systems are designed to be able to collect and classify information automatically and keep the system updated promptly. Interconnective knowledge-sharing structures are better ways for today's companies to construct their internal knowledge-sharing mechanism. Interconnective knowledge-sharing structures establish a two-way communication pathway across the intranet. The nodes in the system include individuals as well as aggregates of individuals, such as work groups, departments, and organizations within a company.

There are numerous challenges to overcome to effectively share knowledge among organizational members. Many organizations are faced with their own sets of unique challenges. Literature in knowledge management has shown that studies on knowledge reuse need to consider both the knowledge search and transfer processes simultaneously in order to get a full understanding of how knowledge is reused within an organization (Kraemer, 1998). Locating relevant knowledge sources for reuse during problem solving incorporates two separate processes: locating relevant experts and locating relevant expert knowledge (Housel & Skopec, 2001).

Ackerman and Mandel (1995) suggest that decision makers seek expert knowledge either in the form of knowledge artifacts or connections to known experts. Thus, decision makers require access to a set of knowledge stakeholders. In turn, those stakeholders are part of other networks allowing for further access to additional knowledge resources. Among knowledge-sharing methods, personal networks are the most predominate and convenient way for people to locate relevant expertise (e.g., Faniel & Majchrzak, 2003). Unfortunately, key knowledge stakeholders or decision makers are not always readily available for consultation. Knowledge networks provide a virtual network of key knowledge stakeholders and knowledge artifacts regardless of location or time (Skyrme, 1999). The network exists in *n* dimensions enabling potential benefits through connections along knowledge pathways. This full-time access to relevant knowledge across time and space provides an environment in which knowledge seekers can gain confidence that their decisions consider the most correct and most appropriate inputs (Festinger, 1957).

Knowledge-sharing networks support and enhance communications by integrating knowledge artifacts from different sources and domains across space and time. Research in knowledge networks endeavors to achieve new levels of knowledge integration, information flow, and interactivity among people, organizations, and communities, and to deepen our understanding of the ethical, legal, and social implications of knowledge networking (Skyrme, 1999). The successful implementation of knowledge networks creates rich communication environments for sharing knowledge and reducing decision uncertainty. Knowledge networks can be used to examine the life cycle of ideas in organizations and the role and characteristics of the people who introduce and diffuse new ideas. Tracking and supporting such life cycles will allow organizations to better understand how innovation and knowledge spreads. Effective knowledge networks increase innovation and improve organizational efficiency, and they can have even greater benefits if they are structured to receive management guidance.

SUPPORTING KNOWLEDGE-SHARING NETWORKS IN ORGANIZATIONS

Beyond individual-driven knowledge-sharing methods, businesses are able to organize in-house networks to deliver value by reusing existing company knowledge. The pace of business is speeding up as customer demands become more intense, and competitors move more quickly to meet their needs. Network nodes and network bandwidth need to be improved and expanded to enable the information-carrying capacity of the network. Combining elements of business intelligence and network performance enable real-time business for activity monitoring, process value measurement, and enterprise performance indicators (Huang & Wei, 2000).

A knowledge-content view has demonstrated the importance of relatedness in the skill base, but it does not shed much light on the integrative mechanisms that would allow one business unit to obtain knowledge from another (Kraemer, 1998). Scholars have demonstrated the importance of having lateral linkages among organization subunits for effective knowledge sharing to occur. Research has shown that a subunit's information-processing capacity is enhanced by lateral interunit integration mechanisms (Keen, 1986). Tiwana (2003) has indicated that individuals began to share information, expertise, best practices, and content in a peer-to-peer network created by affinity, while businesses created organization-spanning affinity that expanded such networks, thus facilitating the exchange and sharing of know-how and tacit expertise. Advanced technology, pervasive computing power, ubiquitous wireless communications, and distributed vast storage are triggering effective business knowledge-sharing platforms based on modern networking technologies.

Jarvenpaa and Ives (1994) indicate that the sharing of knowledge requires a "highly adaptive information architecture that can provide anytime-anyplace, multimedia interconnectivity across a constantly changing network of nodes…and must be independent of any organizational structure." The discussion presented in the previous sections suggests it is necessary to develop communication networks capable of supporting and sharing communication and collaboration among knowledge workers. Implementing these types of networks could provide an infrastructure for determining the most important business processes and value-creation measures. In addition, they could establish a working environment to assemble data warehouses, operational data stores, and enterprise applications to get a real-time view of required data elements. Such systems are able to continuously monitor for anomalies and exceptions, and proactively alert key personnel when performance falls outside expected ranges. Finally, these environments allow teams to collaborate and react to perform analysis and take action on detected anomalies and exceptions.

Connecting Knowledge

Associative relationships are defined as those that describe associations. They can be one-to-one or one-to-many relationships. Guided tours and indexes describe navigation between and among entities. Slices group one or more attributes of an object. Associative relationships are then built on the contents of varying attribute slices. This methodology provides for multiple attribute groupings to be associated with a single object. In this way, it may provide for a way to create dynamic links simply by selecting search criteria based on varying sets of object attributes (i.e., different slices). Traversing associative links differs depending upon what slices of information have been specified. The model allows knowledge workers to view knowledge objects in a specific context.

Berryman and Hockenhull (1996) describe associative relationships using interactive media works. Based on a nonhierarchical graph with multiple connections, data elements (i.e., association objects) contain one or more pointers that viewers can follow to reach other related data elements. The authors' vision differs from others by its shift in paradigms. They argue that hypermedia systems are based on a hunting paradigm in which users arbitrarily navigate space to find information. In contrast, an associative paradigm allows for the gathering of information in global contexts and subsequent arrangements to form local contexts. Association is described as a relational activity in which the viewer builds contexts through interaction with the work. Mixed-initiative searching is introduced as a way in which gathering choices are made jointly by the viewer and the system. The system intelligently builds associations from previous searches. As a viewer builds up his or her work space, successive searches tend to find objects that work, thus the system could support continuity and style. The artifacts of the searches may

then be preserved and shared as searchable contexts. This model requires the design of the appropriate database structures to support the required collaborative relationships.

Virtue-Nets

Managers invest in telecommunication technology that "increases direct, flexible contact between people" and that "provide simple access to information, simply organized" (Galbraith, 1973). Knowledge networks can be implemented on network infrastructures that have the potential of giving firms instant communication infrastructure with the ability to engage in direct, flexible, anytime, anyplace information exchange and access. The immediate, systematic, and reciprocal nature of discussing new and novel approaches and confirming understanding and clarity has been shown by Kepner and Tregoe (1965) to increase decision efficiency and decision outcomes.

A virtue net describes a knowledge network where nodes are linked using a set of qualitative and dynamic attributes. There are four principle structures: data structures, nodes, communication links, and representation. A discussion of the various elements along with approaches to the four principles is provided in the following paragraphs. The glossary to this article reviews the elements of the virtue net.

Virtue nets provide an alternative mechanism for creating a distributed architecture for handling data attributes. Each data item would exist as an individual node. This data node would reside in a plane of existence of identical determined attributes. Each node is self-aware such that it can "realize" its own set of attributes or virtues. This self-awareness operation replaces the metadata traditionally used to describe the node. Data nodes automatically realize their place in the virtue net, enabling and enhancing search operations and connections to similar nodes. Planes of existence are created by specialized virtue links of dynamically connected data nodes with multiple connections, each of which is specific to an attribute or virtue. Similar to a virtual private network (VPN), these virtue links exist within the total bandwidth allotted to the virtue net. The virtue net is a set of weighted pathways between data nodes based on various attributes, effectively creating a bond between the data nodes with the same virtues: The stronger the similarity of a given virtue, the stronger the bond between the data nodes in a particular plane of existence. The key to the virtue net is the virtue manager, the decision-making heart of the system that makes decisions as if it were a real person.

Each data node has many bonds to many other data nodes. This nth dimensionality is the power of the virtue network, enabling data nodes to connect with numerous other data nodes based on the level of similarity they have with respect to each other. Since each dimension portrays a certain virtue, the need for querying the information is eliminated. By tapping into the virtue plane, every instance of that virtue is simultaneously available since, by definition, this plane would be the sum links of all data nodes with the given virtue. A table is used to associate files with virtues. That table establishes a virtue map used to track a particular virtue's plane of existence.

Virtue planes are dynamic since the virtues can be tapped from multiple dimensions. The dynamic nature of these virtue planes suggests network bandwidth must be able to accommodate multiple perspectives. As individuals gain experience with a device or with other entities using a similar device, their total utility with that given device will increase (Carlson & Zmud, 1999). Knowledge networks provide a taxonomy of bandwidth through which the users' manipulation of the bandwidth's attributes yield utility expansion. As people learn to utilize the knowledge bandwidth, or k-band, they learn how to expand their knowledge-accessing capabilities to use a given device by manipulating the k-band attributes.

Naturally, differences in opinion and interpretation will cause conflicts within the system. As such, differences in preference between different users must be managed in some way. One solution is derived from the availability of the fundamental hardware and the more flexible software nature of the system. A virtue map exists in the virtue chip, but it is the virtue manager that manages the links and plane-of-existence assignments. This manager also learns the preferences and habits of the user(s) in a similar way that voice-recognition software learns the nuances of a user's speech. Node managers control files housed within the cognitive node. Owners of each file impose their preferences on their data, so in a file server, the owner—not the server—dictates the preferences. The cognitive node is the computer in which the virtue manager is running. Cognitive nodes are responsible for the management of the files belonging to a user. Servers, SANs, or disk arrays are merely vessels for containing the data. This insures low impact on the server. Cognitive nodes perform the calculations and general housekeeping for the maintenance of the data nodes and their virtue links.

Figure 1. Color code depicts different virtues within each data-node. Each data-node that contains the color of a certain virtue, resides in the plane of existence of that virtue (virtue-plane). The data-nodes existing within the same virtue-plane are linked to each other through that virtue-plane by the virtue-link. The virtue links take advantage of multiple channels that form the knowledge bandwidth.

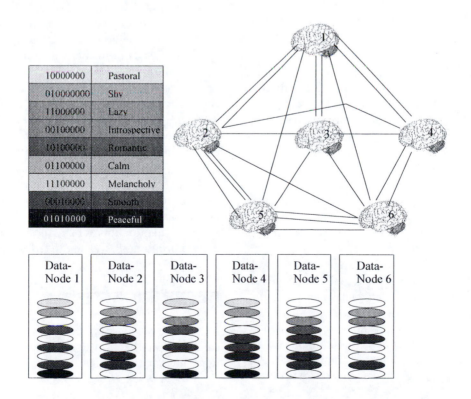

For the purposes of illustration, consider an example in which the virtue links could be color coded (Figure 1).

A table of virtues specifies color-coded virtues. The table is used as an analog for the different paths represented in binary notation readable by the machine. Each data node is connected to other data nodes that have common virtues, thereby creating a web of connections. Connections for a particular color between all the data nodes create a virtue plane for that attribute. For example, in the case of qualifying audio files, sad or happy music types could be recognized by different color codes. Melancholy, contemplative, heartwarming, and funny might be some of the attributes in this group. Once these pathways are in place, the applicable pathways can be connected to all the files they pertain to. So, when searching for performances that contain political humor, the logical intersection of the funny virtue plane and political virtue plane is viewed, which will result in every type of political comedy in all file types. This is of especial value to mobile handheld devices that tend to be more cumbersome to search databases with. Instead of entering all the query, the user can click on the virtue button on the desktop and select one of the primary emotion types (resulting in a specific virtue path) followed by a virtue link, which results in access to the virtue plane for the selected virtue. To widen or narrow the search, the previous steps can be repeated using the logical *and* to narrow the search, or the logical *or* to widen the search. The virtue paths have the ability to narrow the number of virtues by grouping virtues that are related to one of the fundamental primary emotions.

Virtue-Net Exemplars

There are no examples of systems currently implemented that exhibit all of the characteristics of the virtue net described in this article. However, there are examples of systems that exhibit some of the characteristics. This section compares some of those tools and systems in the context of virtue nets.

ACT-R 5.0 is a cognitive modeling architecture developed at Carnegie Mellon University based on John Anderson's Adaptive Character of Thought: Revised (ACT-R; Anderson & Lebière, 1998). This software is evolving to simulate human thought, knowledge organization, and intelligent behavior.

Lotus Notes and Microsoft Exchange are groupware programs that help people work together collectively even when located remotely from each other. They provide sharing services such as e-mail, calendars, task management, database access, and electronic conferences so that each person is able to communicate and work with others. The groupware programs provide data and information sharing. The links between data or relationships between information must be preset by program or human instruction.

A new generation of search engines has the ability of acquiring, analyzing, and articulating knowledge without the involvement of human intelligence. KartOO.com represents the application of visualized knowledge representation in the practice of virtue nets. Alltheweb.com represents a trend in which language analysis and common-phrase identification technologies are being applied into virtue nets.

CONCLUSION

Virtue nets represent a new way of thinking about managing and utilizing knowledge within organizations. This article has outlined some of the characteristics of such systems. The next step is to design and develop a virtue net that combines the best features of systems described in the previous section. Part of the effort will be to analyze and test prototype systems to determine the effective mechanisms for performing the relevant tasks throughout the knowledge-value life cycle.

Computer and telecommunication networks offer powerful, expressive, and efficient information-access, search, and data-exchange capabilities. Intranet technology dramatically changed the way people are connected within an organization. New technologies built a new way for knowledge-based networks to be perceived, operated, and utilized by their users. However, representing and acquiring knowledge is still a difficult and time-consuming task having to be done by humans. Problem-formulating methods and knowledge-organization approaches are two important issues in further research.

This article has provided a conceptual view of collaborative communication networks to support knowledge processes in organizations. Inherent in such networks are dynamic capabilities for recognizing the value of knowledge elements extant in the network. Virtue nets enhance and support dynamic interactions in organizations by providing necessary knowledge artifacts from different sources and domains across time and space. It has been told that advances in technology will change the way organizations are organized. Knowledge networks and the dynamic support of virtue nets will go a long way toward bringing that vision to fruition.

REFERENCES

Ackerman, M. S., & Mandel, E. (1995). Memory in the small: An application to provide task-based organizational memory for a scientific community. *Proceedings of the 28th Annual Hawaii International Conference of System Sciences,* (vol. 4, pp. 323-332).

Anderson, J. R., & Lebière, C. (1998). *The atomic components of thought.* Lawrence Erlbaum Associates.

Berryman, J., & Hockenhull, O. (1996). *Towards a furious philosophy of the discrete mediabase.* Retrieved February 28, 2004, from *http://english.ttu.edu/acw/essay/o.hockenhull.html.done/mediabasediscussiondoc.html*

Carlson, J., & Zmud, R. (1999). Channel expansion theory. *Academy of Management Journal, 42*(2), 153-170.

Davis, R., Shrobe, H.E., & Szolovits, P. (1993). What is a knowledge representation? *AI Magazine, 14,* 17-33.

Faniel, I. M., & Majchrzak, A. (2003). *Designing IT for knowledge reuse in a complex uncertain environment.*

Festinger, L. (1957). *A theory of cognitive dissonance.* Evanston, IL: Row, Peterson.

Galbraith, J. (1973). *Designing complex organizations.* Reading, MA: Addison-Wesley.

Gray, P.M.D., Preece, A., Fiddian, N.J., & Gray, W. (1997). KRAFT: Knowledge fusion from distributed databases and knowledge bases. *Proceedings of the 8ᵗʰ International Workshop on Database and Expert Systems Applications (DEXA)* (pp. 682-691). IEEE Computer Society.

Guenther, K., & Braun, E. (2001). Knowledge management benefits of intranets. *Online, 25*(3), 17-22.

Housel, T. J., & Skopec, E. (2001). *Global telecommunications revolution.* McGraw-Hill.

Huang, W. W., & Wei, K. K. (2000). An empirical investigation of the effects of group support systems (GSS) and task type on group interaction from an influence perspective. *Journal of Management Information Systems, 17*(2), 181-206.

Jarvenpaa, S., & Ives, B. (1994). The global network organization of the future: Information management opportunities and challenges. *Journal of Management Information Systems, 10*(4), 25-57.

Keen, P. G. W. (1986). *Competing in time: Using telecommunications for competitive advantage.* Cambridge, MA: Ballinger.

Kepner, C. H., & Tregoe, B. B. (1965). *The rational manager: A systematic approach to problem solving and decision-making.* New York: McGraw-Hill.

Kraemer, R. (1998). Visual languages for knowledge representation. *KAW'98: Eleventh Workshop on Knowledge Acquisition, Modeling and Management,* 18-23.

Nonaka, I., & Takeuchi, H. (1995). *The knowledge-creating company: How Japanese companies create the dynamics of innovation.* New York: Oxford University Press.

O'Dell, C., & Grayson, C. J. (1998). If only we knew what we know: Identification and transfer of internal best practices. *California Management Review, 40*(3), 144-174.

Schultz, T., & Lepper, M. (1996). Cognitive dissonance reduction as constraint satisfaction. *Psychological Review, 2,* 219-240.

Senge, P. (1990). *The fifth discipline: The art and practice of the learning organization.* New York: Doubleday.

Simons, G.L. (1984). *Introducing artificial intelligence.* Manchester: NCC Publications.

Skyrme, D. (1999). *Knowledge networking: Creating the collaborative enterprise.* Oxford: Butterworth Heinemann.

Tiwana, A. (2003). Affinity to infinity in peer-to-peer knowledge platforms. *Communications of the ACM, 46*(5), 77-80.

Von Krogh, G., Ichijo, K., & Nonaka, I. (2000). *Enabling knowledge creation.* Oxford University Press.

KEY TERMS

Cognitive Node: Scalable access point for augmenting knowledge and facilitating communication in knowledge networks. Nodes manage virtue maps and data relevant to knowledge workers.

Communication: The exchange of thoughts, messages, or information as by speech, signals, writing, or behavior. Communication generally includes a sender, a receiver, a message, and a medium used to carry the message.

Data Node: An entity containing virtue attributes used to describe and aggregate knowledge in a knowledge network.

Directory Resources: Individuals who can get you in touch with other immediately unknown knowledge stakeholders or experts.

Knowledge: Personal interpretation of facts and processes.

Knowledge Artifact: Anything that helps illustrate or answer how, why, when, what, where, and so forth.

Knowledge Provider: Stakeholder who supplies relevant knowledge to the network.

Knowledge Stakeholder: Someone with critical knowledge specific to current problems, opportunities, and prior consulting engagements, and who can act as a human directory resource.

Network: A system of lines or channels that cross or interconnect; an extended group of people with similar interests or concerns who interact and remain in informal contact for mutual assistance or support. Networks provide methods and mechanisms enabling communication between sender and receiver.

Utility: The quality or condition of being useful (usefulness).

Virtue: An attribute or nonquantitative quality for data nodes.

Virtue Chip: The hardware chip that contains the standard table for the virtue nets (virtue map).

Virtue Link: The connection or bond between data nodes dictated by the types of virtues they posses.

Virtue Manager: A module within the operating system that manages the virtue net and learns the preferences of the user(s).

Virtue Map: A table used to store virtue-net pathways. Table values reflect attributes in the table. It is dynamically updated in programmable virtue chips.

Virtue Net: A set of weighted pathways between data nodes based on various attributes they have in common within a cognitive node's control.

Virtue Path: A set of virtue links grouped by their relationship to fundamental primary emotions.

Virtue Plane: A virtual plane of existence for each virtue or attribute.

ADDITIONAL TERMS

Channel Expansion: A theory introduced by Carlson and Zmud (1999) that posits that as communication participants acquire experience with the communication (channel, topic, context, coparticipants), they increase the richness of their message encoding and message decoding. Technology leads to increasingly rich communication as users increase their ability to communicate effectively using the given technology. In addition, when individual decision makers have a shared knowledge base, they obtain richer results with leaner media. The channel-expansion theory helps to support the notion that decision makers, especially remote decision makers, may use a knowledge network for solving equivocal tasks and for sharing tacit knowledge.

Cognitive Dissonance: A psychological state of tension that accounts for people rationalizing their decisions in an attempt to reduce the tension invoked by their decision (Festinger, 1957). Schultz and Lepper (1996) extend the notion of cognitive dissonance to what they call a free-choice paradigm. In part, the paradigm points out that choosing between alternatives creates cognitive dissonance because the decision maker knows that the rejected alternatives have additional valuable features that are forgone once the decision is made. By involving other key knowledge stakeholders into the decision process, it may be possible to reduce the perceived burden of being the main decision maker, thus reducing the decision maker's postdecision dissonance. Virtue nets would help establish such an environment by enabling one to consider a variety of perspectives in making decisions.

Equivocality: An expression or term liable to more than one interpretation. Equivocality refers to ambiguity, confusion, a lack of understanding, or the existence of multiple and conflicting interpretations about a particular situation. Equivocality is addressed by the exchange of existing views among individuals to define problems and resolve conflicts through the enactment of shared interpretations that can direct future activities. It is used to decide which questions to ask to reach agreement and gain commitment.

Knowledge Access: A process that allows authorized information users to read, update, duplicate, and transfer data in a convenient and prompt way. Based on Internet searching algorithms, database technology, and modern communication technology, people are able to access knowledge networks at anytime, anywhere, and from any terminal on the Internet.

Knowledge Codification: The process of converting information into explicit knowledge that can be accessed, stored, and transferred by the validation of content, codification, classification, organization, and integration. An intranet is a repository for information as well as it provides a set of associated services. Yet, information is not knowledge, and bridging the gap to knowledge requires an understanding of the processes that create value within an organization (Guenther & Braun, 2001).

Knowledge Control: A process that provides data safeguards against invasion, corruption, and knowledge theft. It also provides statistics to network administrators for monitoring the operating status of the network.

Knowledge Generation: A process to capture or create new knowledge. Contents can be purchased, leased, or created through research and development. Another source of new knowledge is "fusion" or shared problem solving. Fusion brings together people with different backgrounds and cognitive styles to work on the same problem. This approach is popular in technology companies where scientists and engineers share their knowledge via developmental databases, client service logs, and personal Web pages (Gray, Preece, Fiddian & Gray, 1997).

Knowledge Network: A virtual network of key knowledge stakeholders and knowledge artifacts independent of location or time (Skyrme, 1999) providing a communication infrastructure that focuses on the integration of knowledge artifacts from different sources to enable and enhance communication. Knowledge networks achieve new levels of knowledge integration, information flow, and interactivity among people, organizations, and communities. The network exists in *n* dimensions, enabling potential benefits through connections along knowledge pathways. This full-time access to relevant knowledge across time and space provides an environment in which knowledge seekers can gain confidence that their decisions consider the most correct and most appropriate inputs.

Knowledge Representation (KR): The study of how knowledge about the world can be represented and what

kinds of reasoning can be done with that knowledge. The representation of knowledge is a combination of data structures and interpretive procedures that can enable a program to exhibit knowledgeable behavior (Simons, 1984). Davis, Shrobe and Szolovits (1993) indicate that knowledge representations serve as surrogates for real-world representations, provide a set of ontological commitments about how to think about the world, establish a partial theory of intelligent reasoning, establish a medium for efficient reasoning, and create media for human expression. The goal of knowledge representation is to encode human knowledge—in all its various forms—in such a way that the knowledge can be used.

Knowledge Sharing: A cross-functional and collaborative information-distribution and learning activity. Advantages of knowledge sharing include its commonsense comprehensibility, along with a certain degree of interactivity implicit in any sharing. Drawbacks include the possibility that even sharing is insufficiently interactive, and that it implies that the existence of knowledge precedes the sharing process, thereby separating knowledge management from innovation and research.

Work and Knowledge

Tom Butler
University College Cork, Ireland

Ciaran Murphy
University College Cork, Ireland

INTRODUCTION

It is widely believed that knowledge work is a relatively new phenomenon and that it constitutes the main form of activity in post-industrial organizations. While the term remains undefined, *knowledge work* is taken to refer to the knowledge that individuals apply in performing role-related business activities in "knowledge-intensive" organizations. In this scheme of things, the conventional wisdom holds that the subjective knowledge of individual social actors is applied to "objectified" organizational knowledge (i.e., data held in various paper and electronic repositories) as the raw material of the production process. Thus, knowledge is considered to be both an input to, and an output of, business processes: It also is argued to underpin the process by which knowledge inputs are transformed to outputs.

Cooley (1975) was one of the first to employ the term "knowledge worker," however, his conception encompasses both white and blue-collar workers, professionals, and craftspeople alike. This is to be contrasted with Drucker's (1999) perspective on knowledge work, which focuses primarily on the upper echelons of management. This article echoes Cooley's perspective in many respects, however, it seeks to strengthen, extend, and apply it in a contemporary context. The following section provides the rationale and context for this article's thesis by illustrating the socially distributed and collective nature of knowledge. It also helps illustrate certain deficiencies in the conventional understanding of this important topic; these are then addressed in the third section's exploration of the social construction of knowledge. The third section also deconstructs commonly held beliefs on knowledge by examining its relationship to data and information. The fourth section then presents this article's main contribution by presenting a conceptual model and taxonomy of knowledge in organizational contexts. It is hoped that this will help researchers and practitioners better understand the relationship between knowledge and work going forward.

In sum, the article's motivation is to eliminate the misunderstandings that surround the concept of knowledge work and to propose an understanding of the phenomenon that is more in tune with the "reality" of organizational life. The article's marriage of philosophy (Aristotle, 1945; Gadamer, 1975; Heidegger, 1976) and institutional theory (e.g., Berger & Luckmann,1967, from sociology, and Nordhaug, 1994, from economics) acts to "inform" researchers who seek to understand the know-how, -why, and -what of social action in organizational settings. For practitioners, it highlights areas where experiential and skill-based knowledge are of value in organizations and illustrates for them the relative importance of task- and firm-specific knowledge.

BACKGROUND: EVERYBODY KNOWS☐ BUT ONLY COLLECTIVELY

Aristotle argues that no one individual can know or possess all of the available knowledge, rather, knowledge is dispersed among individuals in society (Aristotle, 1945; Hayek, 1945; Berger & Luckmann, 1967). However, Grant (1996) maintains that knowledge creation is an individual activity, and that the extant emphasis on "organizational knowledge" is misplaced—he argues that organizational knowledge does not exist as a distinct phenomenon (see Stata, 1989; Taylor, 1993; Pfeffer, 1994). Therefore, what Hayek says about society also may be applied to organizations, viz knowledge of and about an organization and its activities will be dispersed among organizational actors and the "communities-of-practice" which they constitute (cf. Tsoukas, 1996). The problem facing social groupings such as organizations, societies, and cultures is therefore "a problem of the utilization of knowledge not given to anyone in its totality" (Hayek, 1945, p. 450). A portion of this dispersed knowledge may, and particularly in more formal institutions will, be codified as information in documents, manuals, books of operating procedures, and so forth, which may be paper-based, electronic, or both (Bruner, 1990; Davenport & Prusak, 1998). Berger and Luckmann (1967) consider this as pretheoretical recipe knowledge and, as such, it forms an operational backdrop for organizations by supplying institutionally appropriate rules of conduct, by placing boundaries on acceptable actions and by defining and enumerating activities to be performed by social actors (see Taylor, 1993; Tsoukas, 1996). Therefore, it acts as both a controlling and predictive mechanism for such conduct.

Thus, institutions are akin to "collective minds" (Weick & Roberts, 1993) whose cultures become a learned product of group experiences, particularly those of the organization's founders (Schein, 1985). Over time, the cognitive dispositions and dispersed knowledge of individual social actors, who actively participate in the dialogic process of institutional reality construction within the aforementioned unarticulated background of wider social and institutional contexts, come to populate this metaphorical "collective mind," which emerges as the unarticulated background of organizational experience. Hence, it is an individual's Heideggerian "fore-knowledge" of the type of actions required of him or her by other actors in the relevant "community-of-practice" and in the wider organization that shapes his or her ongoing actions and utterances (Heidegger, 1976); in turn, these actions once taken and linguistic expressions uttered influence the actions and cognitive dispositions of others (Lincoln & Guba, 1985). Thus, it is the existence of previously acquired knowledge of social convention, in the form of what may be described as a Gadamerian "effective-historical consciousness" (Gadamer, 1975), that guides the self-reinforcing, reciprocal "typification of habitualized" action and dialogue among social actors and which enables individuals to share knowledge relevant to their social grouping or organization (Berger & Luckmann, 1967; cf. Latour, 1993).

This shared corpus of social, communal, or organizational knowledge manifests itself in the form of relatively fixed repertoires of highly reproducible routines, recipes, reciprocal social action, and intersubjective cognitive arrangements (e.g., Nelson & Winter, 1982; Hannan & Freeman, 1984; Spender, 1989; Weick & Roberts, 1993). Alternatively put, an organization's "collective mind" is manifested in the actions and linguistic expressions/narratives of social actors as they commit to and engage in a network of communal and organizational activities (see Bruner, 1990; Law & Callon, 1992). This "collective mind" is, in as much as it represents a collective knowledge of the social groupings concerned, also sedimented in the products of these activities, in the "fused horizons of understanding" of participating actors (Gadamer, 1975), and also in a community's or organization's texts, electronic documents, and databases (Bruner, 1990; Hall, 1994; Boland & Tenkasi, 1995; Kusunoki, Nonaka, & Nagata, 1998). Therefore, it must be emphasized that an organization's "collective mind" is not the property of a single actor, neither is it contained in its entirety in the Gadamerian "horizons" (fused or otherwise) of all actors; rather, it is distributed among all participating actors as a knowledge of and about communal and/or organizational activities (Weick & Roberts, 1993).

The logical conclusion of this argument is that all work in organizations is "knowledge work," as knowledge about organizational activities is dispersed either within "communities-of-practice" or across them. The next section further elaborates on this and explores how knowledge is socially constructed; it also differentiates between practical wisdom or experiential knowledge and technical or skills-based knowledge. This helps put knowledge in context and points toward a more inclusive appreciation of knowledge work.

AN ONTOLOGICAL PERSPECTIVE ON THE SOCIAL CONSTRUCTION OF KNOWLEDGE

Boland (1987) gives an account of five misguided fantasies that surround the concept of information, viz that it is structured data, that an organization is information, and that information is power, is intelligence, or is perfectible. This observation could be extended to the concept of knowledge. For example, conventional wisdom dictates that knowledge is processed information and as such is capable of objective representation. In order to dispel such notions, the ontological basis of knowledge is explored. This fosters an understanding of how people come to know what they know and provides insights into the constitution of knowledge.

It is clear from Gadamer's (1975) hermeneutics that data, information, and knowledge are loosely coupled: Depending on the "worldview," "lived experience," and "tradition" of the recipient, the same data can yield different knowledge and understanding. Consider, for example, Heidegger's (1976) argument that Dasein's "'Being-in-the-world" is characterised by a "pre-understanding" or "fore-knowledge" of the nature of being and its constituent phenomenon. Consider also Heidegger's argument that Dasein, as the mode of being characteristic of all humans, always understands itself in terms of its existence and the possibilities it presents. Any "breakdown" in Dasein's understanding of phenomena results in the search for data that will enable phenomena to be interpreted in a new light and thereby repair the "breakdown" by developing an enhanced understanding. Thus, as Brown and Lightfoot (1998) argue, "knowledge occurs in the wake of the breakdown. It proceeds slowly, perhaps without clear direction" (p. 293).

In Gadamerian terms, the process of acquiring new knowledge-informing data on a phenomenon is governed by the hermeneutic "circle of understanding," which involves the cycling back and forth between the actor's existing "horizon of understanding" and that suggested by the phenomenon of interest. A dialectic of question and answer, of thesis, antithesis, and synthesis, operates to help the actor interpret new data in light of the old. Hence, a new understanding is arrived at when a "fusion of horizons" occurs between the interpreter's horizon of understanding and that of the phenomenon under consideration (Butler, 1998). Thus, knowledge is, first and foremost, an enigmatic and personal phenomenon in that it arises from the practical experience of social actors. In order to delineate the dimensions of such experience, the work of Aristotle is presently explored.

Phronesis and Techne as the Core Constituents of Practical Knowledge

Gadamer (1975) and Dunne (1993) drew on Aristotle's *Nicomachean Ethics* to extend further our understanding of individual knowledge. Aristotle presents what he considered to be the core components of practical knowledge in social contexts—*phronesis* as experiential self-knowledge (practical wisdom) and *techne* as skills-based technical knowledge. The conduct of social affairs involves the application of *phronesis* in a thoughtful and competent manner, this Aristotle refers to as praxis. The social activity that has as its concern the "making" or "production" of social artefacts is called *poiesis* and involves the application of *techne*. A techne is knowledge of how to perform task-based activities in pursuit of some practical end: This end may be tangible or intangible. Thus, techne provides managers, professionals, craftsmen, labourers, and scientists with an understanding of the why and the wherefore, the how and with-what of their concerns. The skills of qualified craftsmen, artists, musicians, surgeons, computer programmers, physicists, accountants, and so on, all fall into this category—as indeed does the oft-ignored skills of ordinary "unskilled" workers. On the other hand, a social actor's "self-knowledge" (phronesis) is a synthesis of his temporal experience of social phenomena and his ability to take or perform practical action in relation to such phenomena—and this clearly applies to every class of worker. All this has important implications for the way in which knowledge is viewed in research and practice, as will be seen in the concluding sections. However, it is clear from Aristotle that *phronesis* and *techne* possess a social nature, accordingly, the social context of knowledge construction is now explored.

The Social Construction of Knowledge Work

Researchers point out that social action is the dominant means of knowledge diffusion in organizations (Berger & Luckmann, 1967). However, it must be noted that individual knowledge is inseparable from the social context and practices that help construct it and which shape and influence its acquisition (Berger & Luckmann, 1967; Bruner, 1990; Brown & Duguid, 1991). Following this line of argument, Tsoukas (1996) argues that a social actor's knowledge lies, first and foremost, in the social and occupational practices in which he or she engages and, in effect, knowledge is socially constructed (Berger & Luckmann, 1967). It is clear, however, that while knowledge is embodied in the social actors that comprise the various "communities-of-practice" that constitute organizations, no one actor or group of actors possesses all the knowledge required to effect social action. This gives rise to the notion that knowledge in organizations is dispersed (Hayek, 1945), as actors may not be in a position to observe, at first hand, the knowledge embedded in the actions of others or communicate linguistically with them (Kogut & Zander, 1992). Therefore, social actors resort to texts and other media, such as IT, to augment their limited cognitive capacities (Bruner, 1990); these mechanisms provide conduits or repositories for the spatial and temporal transfer of knowledge-informing data between actors (Boland & Tenkasi, 1995). They are not, as this article argues, knowledge repositories and therefore cannot be managed as such. It is clear, however, that social narrative is the dominant mechanism for understanding acts of meaning in social contexts, hence, this issue is next explored.

The cultural psychologist Jerome Bruner (1990) illustrated the role of narrative in all human understanding (see Brown & Duguid, 1991). Accordingly, Gadamer argues that language is an essential component of communication and understanding. Nevertheless, Heidegger (1976) maintains that:

Communication is never anything like a conveying of Experiences, such as opinions or wishes, from the interior of one subject into the interior of another... In discourse Being-with becomes "explicitly" shared, that is to say, it is already, but it is unshared as something that has not been taken hold off and appropriated. (p. 205)

Thus, strictly speaking, language is not normally used for the exchange of information, as is commonly assumed; instead, it merely calls attention to some aspect of the shared existence of social actors. As Taylor (1993) argues, human knowledge and understanding are based upon the unarticulated background of the "ready-to-hand," that is, the taken-for-granted understandings that constitute the web of human relationships (Heidegger, 1976). This has profound implications for the commonly held conception of knowledge. Accordingly, Winograd and Flores (1986) point out that "knowledge lies in the being that situated us in the world, but not in a reflective representation" (p. 74). Thus, individual knowledge is possible because of the social practices actors engage in. However, it is clear that social practices are not an aggregation of individual experiences; rather, they constitute the set of background distinctions that underpin individual action. In addition, actors are socialized into institutional practices which involves internalizing the set of background distinctions that constitute such practices (see Brown & Duguid, 1991; Taylor, 1993). Knowledge is therefore open-ended and its creation goes far beyond the mere processing of knowledge-informing data.

Working on Data, Not Knowledge

Von Foerester (1984) states "information is the process by which knowledge is acquired" (p. 193). However, texts, documents, computer files, databases, and so forth merely provide data. Why? Individuals become informed through the process of interpretation and the application of individual "fore-knowledge" (Introna, 1997). Therefore, as a text (social action is included here) is read and interpreted, it informs. So, from a hermeneutic perspective, texts and narratives contain data that when interpreted inform the reader. Hence, information is abstract and ambiguous in its depiction, and data is all that can be represented, stored, transferred, and manipulated by information and communication technologies (ICT) (Galliers & Newell, 2001). Ulti-

mately, all that can be said of knowledge then is that it is always in a process of becoming, extending beyond itself (Fransman, 1998). This "becoming" refers to different interpretations or meanings attributed to data derived from the multi-voiced dialectic that takes place within and between social actors who are embedded in cultural contexts that are historical, on the one hand, and that are oriented toward the future, on the other (Bruner, 1990).

FUTURE TRENDS: TOWARD A CONCEPTUAL MODEL AND TAXONOMY OF KNOWLEDGE IN ORGANIZATIONS

It has already been established that the two basic components of social actors' knowledge are *phronesis* and *techne*. When coupled with the tacit knowledge that arises from the unarticulated web of social activities and relationships, these types of knowledge combine to provide social actors with a unique stock of knowledge and a "worldview." There is, however, a need for an extended conceptualization that incorporates a pragmatic, taxonomic perspective on knowledge in organizational and institutional contexts. Nordhaug's (1994) taxonomy of organizational competencies is of particular interest here, as it indicates the focus and application of individual phronesis and techne in organizational and institutional "communities-of-practice." Therefore, it is of particular relevance to this article's thesis as it contributes to the formulation of a conceptual model and taxonomy of knowledge within organizational settings (see Figure 1). It is hoped that this will inform the future deliberations of practitioners and researchers in the area.

By way of representing the various dimensions of *phronesis* and *techne* in finer granularity, the taxonomy of

Figure 1. A conceptual model and taxonomy of knowledge in organizational contexts (adapted from Nordhaug, 1994)

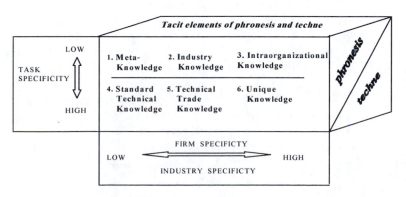

knowledge presented captures what is regarded as organizational knowledge from an individual perspective. In Figure 1, the term specificity refers to the degree to which an individual's knowledge is general or specific[1] to (a) the execution of organizational tasks, (b) the organization itself, and (c) the industry the organization competes in. For example, *meta-knowledge*, which is general background knowledge and which possesses a significant tacit component, can be used in the performance of a range of organizational activities—social and technical. Examples of meta-knowledge are individual literacy, knowledge of a foreign language, and so on. This type of knowledge also is generally available within the firm and the industry as a whole; nevertheless, the widespread possession of such knowledge by individual actors is important for an organization's general "stock of knowledge."

Industry-based knowledge also is a general type of knowledge, widely available to individuals in their role-related organizational activities, across both firms and industry. It is not specific to either organizations or any individual organizational tasks as such, but it is, however, highly industry specific. Examples of this type of knowledge are knowledge of the industry structure, its current state of development, and of the key individuals, networks, and alliances in an industry.

Intraorganizational knowledge is highly firm and industry specific but is not specific to organizational activities or tasks. In effect, this component of social actors' knowledge is firm-specific meta-knowledge. Examples are knowledge about colleagues, knowledge about elements of the organizational culture, communication channels, informal networks, knowledge of a firm's strategy and goals, and so on.

Standard technical knowledge is task specific, industry and firm non-specific, and involves a wide range of technical, operationally oriented knowledge that is generally available to all actors. Examples are knowledge of financial and management accounting practices, knowledge of computer programming and standard software packages, and knowledge of craft and engineering principles and methods.

Technical trade knowledge is task specific, industry specific, and is generally available among firms in an industry. Examples of such knowledge are knowledge of automobile construction methods, knowledge of the techniques of computer hardware construction, and so on.

Finally, *unique knowledge* is specific across all dimensions and applies to the possession by social actors of knowledge—self-knowledge and skills-based knowledge—of unique organizational routines, production processes, and IT infrastructures, to mention a few.

This section of the article explored the socially constructed nature of individual/collective knowledge in organizations. In order to provide insights into the type of knowledge relevant to social actors in organizational contexts, a taxonomy of individual knowledge in organizational contexts was then offered. The strands of the arguments made are now woven together in the concluding section.

CONCLUSION

An understanding of phronesis and techne is, we believe, essential to an understanding of knowledge work. If the observation that phronesis and techne constitute the practical components of individual knowledge in social contexts is accepted, then those who apply experiential self-knowledge and/or skills-based technical knowledge in institutional settings can be considered knowledge workers. It is clear that this definition applies to workers in pre-industrial and industrial settings, as well as IT-enabled post-industrial organizations. Certainly, the appearance of ICT in the post-industrial age has led to the development of IT-related knowledge and skills by many workers. One example is professional workers who employ personal productivity tools, such as spreadsheets and DSS, while another is scientists and practitioners who develop skills in the use of sophisticated technologies to develop new understandings of natural or social phenomena. But this in itself does not make these individuals any more or less knowledge workers than their industrial or pre-industrial predecessors. What does, then?

Many clearly feel that the quantity and quality of data that can be stored, accessed, communicated, analyzed, and processed by contemporary workers using ICT renders the work they perform a special status (i.e., knowledge work). Maybe it does. And maybe this is why academics and practitioners now accord to data the status of knowledge. In contrast, the argument presented in the second section of this article illustrates that knowledge, unlike data, cannot exist outside the heads of knowers, and that such knowledge has an explicit social context. In the context of ICT, this article posits that "so-called" knowledge workers work on data, not knowledge. In addition, the all-pervasive Taylorist prejudice against workers has led to a focus by decision-makers on the management of what has been described as "objective knowledge" in and by ICT, rather than attempting to leverage the "subjective knowledge" of workers, which is the real and only source of organizational knowledge. Thus, like the emperor in the fairytale, practitioners have been duped by consultants and some well-meaning academics into believing that there is something special in the "knowledge management paradigm." What can and should be managed are workers and the data they create, collate, and disseminate, but stating the obvious would not make many consultancy dollars or help have papers accepted for publication. How then can researchers begin to understand what is happening in organizations where workers employ ICT in innovative ways? Taken in the context of the theoretical argument articulated in the foregoing sections, the model and knowledge taxonomy presented in the fourth section should act to "inform" researchers who seek to understand the know-how, -why, and -what of knowledge and social action in organizational settings. Accordingly, it highlights areas where experiential and skill-based knowledge are of value in organizations and recognizes the relative importance of task and firm specific knowledge.

REFERENCES

Aristotle (1945). *Nicomachean ethics*. Translated by H. Rackham. Cambridge, MA: Harvard University Press.

Berger, P., & Luckmann, T. (1967). *The social construction of reality: A treatise in the sociology of knowledge*. Garden City, NY: Doubleday and Company, Inc.

Boland, R.J. (1987). The in-formation of information systems. In R.J. Boland & R.A. Hirschheim (Eds.), *Critical issues in information systems research* (pp. 362-379), Chichester, UK: John Wiley.

Boland, R.J., & Tenkasi, R.V. (1995). Perspective making and perspective taking in communities of knowing. *Organization Science*, *6*(4), 350-372.

Brown, J.S., & Duguid, P. (1991). Organisational learning and communities-of-practice: Toward a unified view of working, learning and innovation. *Organisation Science*, *2*, 40-57.

Brown, S.D., & Lightfoot, G.M. (1998). Insistent emplacement: Heidegger on the technologies of informing. *Information Technology and People*, *11*(4), 290-304.

Bruner, J. (1990) *Acts of meaning*. Cambridge, MA: Harvard University Press.

Butler T. (1998). Towards a Hermeneutic method for interpretive research in information systems. *Journal of Information Technology*, *13*(4), 285-300.

Butler T., & Murphy, C. (1999, December 13-15). Shaping information and communication technologies infrastructures in the newspaper industry: Cases on the role of IT competencies. In Prabuddha De and J. I. DeGross (Eds.), *The Proceedings of the 20ᵗʰ International Conference on Information Systems* (pp. 364-377), Charlotte, NC.

Cooley, M. (1975). *The knowledge worker in the 1980s*. Doc. EC35, Diebold Research Programme, Amsterdam.

Cooley, M. (1987). *Architect or bee? The human price of technology*. London: The Hogarth Press.

Davenport, T.H., & Prusak, L. (1998). *Working knowledge: How organisations manage what they know*. Boston: Harvard Business School Press.

Drucker P.F. (1999). *Management challenges for the 21ˢᵗ Century*. New York: Harper Business.

Dunne, J. (1993). *Back to the rough ground: 'Phronesis' and 'techne' in modern philosophy and in Aristotle*. Notre Dame, IN: University of Notre Dame Press.

Fransman, M. (1998). Information, knowledge, vision, and theories of the firm. In G. Dosi, D.J. Teece, and J. Chytry (Eds.), *Technology, organisation, and competitiveness: Perspectives on industrial and corporate change* (pp. 147-192). New York: Oxford University Press Inc.

Gadamer, H.G. (1975). *Truth and method*. New York: The Seabury Press.

Galliers, R.D., & Newell, S. (2001, June 27-29). Back to the future: From knowledge management to data management. In *Global Co-Operation in the New Millennium, The 9tʰ European Conference on Information Systems* (pp. 609-615). Bled, Slovenia.

Grant, R.M. (1996). Toward a knowledge-based theory of the firm. *Strategic Management Journal*, *17*, Winter Special Issue, 109-122.

Hall R. (1994). A framework for identifying the intangible sources of sustainable competitive advantage. In G. Hamel and A. Heene (Eds.), *Competence based competition* (pp. 149-170). Chichester, UK: Wiley & Sons Ltd.

Hannan, M.T., & Freeman, J. (1984). Structural inertia and organizational change. *American Sociological Review*, *49*, 149-164.

Hayek, F.A. (1945). The use of knowledge in society. *American Economic Review*, *35*, 519-532.

Heidegger, M. (1976). *Being and time*. New York: Harper and Row.

Introna, L.D. (1997). *Management, information and power: A narrative for the involved manager*. London: MacMillan Press Ltd.

Kogut, B., & Zander, U. (1992). Knowledge of the firm, combinative capabilities and the replication of technologies. *Organisation Studies, 3,* 383-397.

Kusunoki, K., Nonaka, I., & Nagata, A. (1998). Organizational capabilities in product development of Japanese firms: A conceptual framework and empirical findings. *Organization Science, 9*(6), 699-718.

Latour, B. (1993). *We have never been modern.* Cambridge, MA: Harvard University Press.

Law, J., & Callon, M. (1992). The life and death of the aircraft: A network analysis of technical change. In W.E. Bijker & J. Law (Eds.), *Shaping technology/building society: Studies in sociotechnical change* (pp. 21-52). Cambridge, MA: MIT Press.

Lincoln, Y.S., & Guba, E.G. (1985). *Naturalistic inquiry.* Beverly Hills, CA: Sage.

Nelson, R.R., & Winter S.G. (1982). *An evolutionary theory of economic change.* Cambridge, MA: The Belknap Press of Harvard University Press.

Nordhaug, O. (1994). *Human capital in organisations: Competence, training and learning.* New York: Oxford University Press.

Pfeffer, J. (1995). *New directions for organization theory.* New York: Oxford University Press.

Schein, E.H. (1985). *Organizational culture and leadership: A dynamic view.* San Francisco: Jossey Bass.

Spender J.C., & Grant, R.M. (1996). Knowledge and the firm. *Strategic Management Journal, 17,* Winter Special Issue, 5-9.

Spender, J.C. (1989). *Industry recipes.* Oxford: Blackwell.

Stata, R. (1989). Organizational learning: The key to management innovation. *Sloan Management Review, 30*(3), Spring, 63 74.

Taylor, C. (1993). To follow a rule… In C. Calhoun, E. LiPuma, & M. Postone (Eds.), *Bourdieu: Critical perspectives* (pp. 45-59). Cambridge, UK: Polity Press.

Tsoukas, H. (1996). The firm as a distributed knowledge system: A constructionist approach. *Strategic Management Journal, 17,* Winter Special Issue, 11-25.

Von Foerster, H. (1984). Principles of self-organization in socio-managerial context. In H. Ulrich & G.J.B. Probst (Eds.), *Self-organization and management of social systems* (pp. 2-24). Berlin, Germany: Springer.

Weick, K.E., & Roberts, K.H. (1993). Collective mind in organisations: Heedful interrelating on flight decks. *Administrative Science Quarterly, 38,* 357-381.

Winograd T., & Flores, F. (1986). *Understanding computers and cognition: A new foundation for design.* Norwood, NJ: Ablex Publishing Corporation.

KEY TERMS

Industry-Based Knowledge: Industry-based knowledge is a general type of knowledge, widely available to individuals in their role-related organizational activities, across both firms and industry. It is not specific to either organizations or any individual organizational tasks as such; it is, however, highly industry specific. Examples of this type of knowledge are knowledge of the industry structure, its current state of development, and of the key individuals, networks, and alliances in an industry.

Intraorganizational Knowledge: Intraorganizational knowledge is highly firm and industry specific but is not specific to organizational activities or tasks. In effect, this component of social actors' knowledge is firm-specific meta-knowledge. Examples are knowledge about colleagues, knowledge about elements of the organizational culture, communication channels, informal networks, knowledge of the firm's strategy and goals, and so on.

Meta-Knowledge: Meta-knowledge is general background knowledge, which possesses a significant tacit component. It can be used in the performance of a range of organizational activities—social and technical. Examples of meta-knowledge are individual literacy, knowledge of a foreign language, and so on. This type of knowledge also is generally available within the firm and the industry as a whole; nevertheless, the widespread possession of such knowledge by individual actors is important for an organization's general "stock of knowledge."

Phronesis: Phronesis is experiential self-knowledge or practical wisdom. A social actor's "self-knowledge" is a synthesis of his temporal experience of social phenomena and his ability to take or perform practical action in relation to such phenomena.

Standard Technical Knowledge: Standard technical knowledge is task specific, industry and firm non-specific, and involves a wide range of technical, operationally oriented knowledge that is generally available to all actors.

Examples are knowledge of financial and management accounting practices, knowledge of computer programming and standard software packages, and knowledge of craft and engineering principles and methods.

Techne: Techne is skills-based technical knowledge. The social activity that has as its concern the "making" or "production" of social artefacts is called poiesis and involves the application of techne. A techne is knowledge of how to perform task-based activities in pursuit of some practical end: This end may be tangible or intangible. Thus, techne provides managers, professionals, craftsmen, labourers, and scientists with an understanding of the why and the wherefore, the how and with-what of their concerns. The skills of qualified craftsmen, artists, musicians, surgeons, computer programmers, physicists, accountants, and so on all fall into this category—as indeed does the oft-ignored skills of ordinary "unskilled" workers.

Technical Trade Knowledge: Technical trade knowledge is task specific, industry specific, and is generally available among firms in an industry. Examples of such knowledge are knowledge of automobile construction methods, knowledge of the techniques of computer hardware construction, and so on.

Unique Knowledge: Unique knowledge is firm specific and applies to the possession by social actors of knowledge—self-knowledge and skills-based knowledge—of unique organizational routines, production processes, and IT infrastructures, to mention a few.

ENDNOTE

[1] The classification of knowledge into general and firm specific categories is a fundamental tenet of human capital theory (see Nordhaug, 1994).

Workflow Systems and Knowledge Management

Alfs T. Berztiss
University of Pittsburgh, USA

INTRODUCTION

The business reengineering movement has left two lasting benefits: One is the identification of an organization as a set of processes (Davenport, 1993); the other is an emphasis on knowledge management (Davenport, 1997). The process orientation finds an expression in workflow systems. Processes have to be supported by knowledge management. Our purpose here is to provide an outline of how knowledge management relates to workflow systems.

The main source of information on workflow systems is the Workflow Management Coalition (WfMC). In 1994, the coalition published a 55-page *Workflow Reference Model* (available from its Web site *www.wfmc.org*), which establishes a common vocabulary, a description of key software components of a workflow management system, and interfaces between these components. The WfMC has been publishing an annual workflow handbook, an example being Fischer (2004). This volume contains an evaluation of the Workflow Reference Model (Hollingsworth, 2004). For a textbook with exercises refer to van der Aalst and van Hee (2002). Important pioneering work in this area was done by Schael (1998). A somewhat dated bibliography has been compiled by the ISYS group of the University of Klagenfurt (ISYS, 2000).

We start with a few definitions, based in part on the 65-page *WfMC Terminology and Glossary* document (also available from the WfMC Web site *www.wfmc.org*), and on van der Aalst and van Hee (2002). A *business process* is a set of linked activities that collectively realize a business objective or policy goal, and *workflow* is the result of automation of this process, in whole or part. A workflow comprises cases and resources. Cases are instances of the business process, and resources support the process. For example, the set of resources of an automated process that provides information about flight arrivals has to include a constantly updated database of flight data and a set of telephones. Every enquiry submitted to this system is a case.

A workflow system (WfS) manages the routing of cases through a workflow: A case "flows" from one station to another, and at each a task is performed on it. The task can be manual, automatic, or semiautomatic, but the definition of workflow as given suggests that the tasks of an *ideal* WfS should be automatic. It is important to realize that the ideal will not be achieved in the foreseeable future. Most WfSs of today are semiautomatic because they have to deal with unanticipated situations that only a human operator can handle. Moreover, software, the platforms on which it is implemented, and communication links can break down, requiring transfer of control to people. It is therefore important that the skills of these people be maintained by occasionally switching to a totally manual mode of operation.

The term "workflow," which we take to be a way of writing "flow of work," is appropriate because the cases move between workstations connected in a network. Indeed, implementation of workflows would have been difficult before computer networks became commonplace. A *workflow management system* (WMS) is a software package for the implementation of a WfS; adaptation of the generic WMS to the needs of a specific application turns it into a WfS for this application. This means that the WfS is also a software package. A distinction has to be made between the movement of cases between stations and the tasks performed at the stations. The movement, which is what the WfS controls, is normally fully automated: After a case has arrived at a station, the task is started automatically, or the system prompts a person to start the task; the task is then started at once, or after a delay. The delay may be due to a backup of cases or because the task is to be performed within a specified time window.

In the next section, we present a background survey, namely a discussion of processes that relate to workflows, and a discussion of information and knowledge. Then, we consider the management of knowledge in the context of workflow systems. We look to the future and offer a conclusion.

BACKGROUND SURVEY

Software Processes

In our view, the key concept of workflows is the use of software. With any software system, one has to consider: (a) the processes that create the software; (b) the software being created, which also defines a process; (c) the capabilities needed to implement and manage these processes; and (d) the knowledge resources involved throughout. As regards (a), the software development process can be regarded as a workflow system—this follows from the insight that the software development process is itself software (Osterweil, 1987).

Having established that a WfS is essentially a software system, we need to take a closer look at software development. The software process is made up of people, tools, and procedures. The people have to possess a set of capabilities that are to allow them to understand and make full use of the tools and procedures. For software development, such capabilities are defined by the Capability Maturity Model (CMM-SW) of the Software Engineering Institute (1995), and the more recent CMMI-SW (CMMI Product Team, 2002).

Under CMM-SW there are three types of processes: (1) a generic software development process; (2) processes derived from the generic process for the development of specific applications; and (3) these application processes. In addition, there is a process that assists in the conversion of process (1) into an instance of processes (2). In our context, the WMS would correspond to type (2): a process adapted from a generic software process that takes into account the specialized needs of WfSs. However, the workflow community has been understandably more concerned with business processes than with principles of software development. As a result, WMS is an abstraction of the features of application processes. Nevertheless, the capabilities of the CMM-SW can be of great value in the determination of how best to allocate the resources of an organization in the setting up of a workflow system, and how to modify the system to deal with changing business conditions.

We should also note that an application software system may in principle be developed by a WfS, which is itself an application software system. Rus and Lindvall (2002) and Dingsøyr and Conradi (2002) discuss knowledge management in this context, but software engineering shows that it is difficult to automate all tasks. Although some business processes have been fully automated (e.g., responses to enquiries by telephone), in the software development process not much more can be automated than the transfer of the software system under development from one work group to the next, help with extraction of components from a software reuse library, and prompts that tell developers what they should be doing next.

Information and Knowledge

Three kinds of knowledge are associated with a WfS. The first assists in the setting up of the system. The second is to be accessed by the system in its regular mode of operation. The third allows the system to be adapted in response to changing business conditions. In other words, the first and third kinds relate, respectively, to the implementation and maintenance of the WfS. Since the WfS is a software system, these components are in fact knowledge about the software process. The second kind is specific to a WfS. Its management is to be our primary concern. Note that Davenport (1997) prefers the term information management. In his view, knowledge exists in the human mind and is very difficult to embed in machines. This view is shared by Nonaka and Takeuchi (1995). Based on the seminal work of Polanyi (1958), they distinguish between tacit knowledge, which is personal and hard to formalize, and explicit knowledge that can be expressed in a formal language. We agree in principle. However, the driving force for workflows is the *automation* of business processes. Hence, we prefer to make the following distinction between information and knowledge: Information for our purposes is embedded in machines and is interpreted (i.e., it is data provided with meaning), and knowledge is information that is being put to use. This implies that we shall refer to information bases rather than knowledge bases, but what is extracted from an information base will be referred to as knowledge. According to Levesque and Lakemeyer (2000), a knowledge base is a collection of symbolic structures representing what a knowledge-based system believes and reasons with during the operation of the system. This view strengthens our distinction between information and knowledge. For Nonaka and Takeuchi (1995), "information is a flow of messages, while knowledge is created by that very flow of information, anchored in the beliefs and commitment of its holder." Fernandes (2000) makes this distinction: Information is obtained by deduction, knowledge by induction. As these examples show, it is difficult to make a clear distinction between information and knowledge, and sometimes we will use the terms interchangeably.

The knowledge that is to support the operation of a WfS can be grouped into five classes: databases, data warehouses, business rules, libraries of cases for case-based reasoning, and external sources. Databases have been extensively studied, and they are well understood.

Data warehouses are repositories of archival data. Data mining (Hand, Mannila, & Smyth, 2001) looks for interesting relationships between these data, particularly for cause-effect relationships, with the aim of using these relationships for the improvement of business practices, which in our context means improvement of WfSs. Some WfSs operate on data streams. Thus, data from points of sale in a supermarket can determine policy. Research on mining from data streams is an active research area. A bibliography on this topic (Gaber, 2004) has 63 entries.

Business rules are of the form "if condition, then action." An example: "If the credit rating of the customer is of grade C or below, then demand payment before the order is shipped." Such uncertainty can be intrinsic to any WfS. For example, if the customer is of very long standing, we would be justified to assume some risk, and ship the order even though the credit worthiness may be questionable. To take a broader view, a rule is a trigger for a decision to be made, as it is in our example, or it is an operational definition, for example, "an *age* is obtained from *date-of-birth* by applying procedure *get-age*," or it is a terminological definition, such as "the grandfather of *x* is the male parent of a parent of *x*," or it is explanatory as in "the countries that have the euro for their currency are …" We are now in a position to define *capability* more precisely: It is the potential that an organization or an individual possesses for collecting and making effective use of information, rules, and process definitions.

Case-based reasoning (CBR) allows a system to respond to a situation by modifying a response made to a similar situation in the past (for surveys, see Watson, 1997; Shiu & Pal, 2004). In any software system the most difficult design problem is the treatment of exceptions. Consider a WfS that implements a loan approval process. Most applications can be handled routinely, but in borderline cases, approval or rejection could depend on some exceptional condition that is normally not taken into account. The information base of CBR is a case library of past decisions with the reasons for the decisions. By extracting loan applications similar to the application under consideration, the decisions made in those cases allow a decision to be made for the case being considered, and this decision will be reasonably consistent with the earlier decisions. Note that British law has been for centuries grounded in CBR.

FOCUS: KNOWLEDGE MANAGEMENT AND WORKFLOW SYSTEMS

Information has to be put to use in the operation of a WfS. The structure of the information base is to facilitate access to information, and this is a pragmatic concern. Pragmatics relate signs to their users. These are the people who gather, organize, manipulate, and use the information base. In terms of the distinction between information and knowledge that we made earlier, they convert information into knowledge. A WfS implements a process in a particular domain, and for the implementation to succeed, there has to be adequate knowledge about the domain. Ontologies and design patterns are pragmatic tools for managing domain knowledge.

A widely accepted definition of an ontology is that it is an explicit specification of a conceptualization of a domain. It is important to note that concepts are the basis for the interpretation of data. An ontology makes explicit the set of concepts that characterize a domain. It also indicates how the concepts are related. For example, an ontology for banking would include the concepts of account, account owner, and balance, and would tell that an account has an account owner and that balance is an attribute of an account. Kalfoglou (2001) surveys ontologies and includes a useful list of Web sites.

Software patterns represent general solutions to recurring problems. A pattern has five main components: the problem addressed, the context in which it arises, the solution, several known uses, and related patterns. The known-uses component indicates that patterns are not invented, but are the codification of experience with real projects. Devedzic (2002) surveys software patterns and provides a very useful list of Web addresses to libraries of patterns. There is a similarity to CBR. Under CBR, a search is made in a library of cases for a solution to a similar problem, and this solution is modified to suit present conditions. A pattern is an abstraction that has to be refined to make it correspond to the new situation. This means that a library of cases could be reduced to a limited number of patterns by merging similar cases. However, the advantage of CBR is precisely the details that would be lost in a pattern: The details help to achieve consistency in decision-making.

Most of the patterns to be found in libraries of patterns are very general, for example, requirements gathering, finding and defining domain objects, and user interface requirements. At this level of abstraction workflow itself is a pattern. What we need is a set of templates for the tasks of a WfS. This is investigated in Berztiss (1997) for the general class of rentals. Rentals relate to cars, formal wear, and library books. Even restaurant visits and airline flights have the characteristics of rentals: You "rent" a restaurant table or a seat on a flight. The rental processes for different types of rentals differ, and the different varieties of the process are obtained by refinement of the templates. Some of the templates for rentals include reservation, cancellation, handover, return, damage assessment, overdue item, payment, and inventory management. As a first step, each task is described as natural language text. Our example is the reservation template:

- **Reservation:** A customer makes a reservation of a rental object for a length of time starting at an indicated date and/or time. Variants of the basic task include (a) group reservations, (b) indication of just the starting point and not the duration, (c) no indication of a starting time, as in the case of a library book currently out on loan, (d) confirming of the reservation, (e) overbooking in anticipation of cancellations, (f) return site differs from rental site.

The description of a task of a specific rental WfS has to follow a definite format, but it is still expressed in natural language. From these refinement templates a decision can be reached regarding what is to be automated, and what is to be done by people. The format of the specialization templates includes:

- **"Triggered by"** establishes how the task is initiated.
- **"Activities"** gives an outline of all the activities that are part of the task, an indication under what conditions an activity is to be performed, and the order in which they are to be performed.
- **"Information base changes"** indicates those parts of the information base supporting the WfS that are to be affected.
- **"Affects"** identifies all tasks that can be affected by this task and states the conditions under which this task would interact with other tasks. This establishes flow patterns for a WfS.
- **"Notes"** contains any information thought to be relevant by the author of the template, for example, an explicit indication of what is not to be part of this task.

The *Triggered by* and *Affects* components define the flowlines of a workflow. Thus, specialization templates define both the tasks and the flow structure of a WfS.

A LOOK TO THE FUTURE

The biggest challenge to the manager of a WfS is keeping the system up-to-date. The business world of today is very volatile, and managers of WfSs that are interacting with the world have to adapt their systems in response to changes taking place in this world. It is not enough merely to react to changes that have already taken place. There also has to be proactive adaptation of a WfS in response to analysis of business process data, such as the extrapolation of trends. We regard the determination of what existing and anticipated changes should lead to a modification of a WfS, what form the modification should take, and how the modification is to be implemented as very important research topics in knowledge management as it relates to WfSs. Totally new knowledge management problems arise when a workflow spans more than one organization (Schmidt, 2004).

The updating of a WfS is to be triggered by information that can come in various guises. But this creates a problem: How reliable is a particular item of information? Techniques such as data quality control (Tayi & Ballou, 1998), computing with words (Wang, 2001), and fuzzy techniques (Klir & Yuan, 1995) can be used to deal with data that are not crisp or reliable; Berztiss (2002) is a general survey. Methods have to be found for the determination of the level of unreliability of knowledge used in the estimation of business risks, and for the configuring a WfS in a way that reduces the risk associated with business process changes based on such knowledge.

A fairly recent development is the view that knowledge management can be purchased as a service (Woitsch, 2003). Workflow systems have become products, marketed by companies such as SAP. It remains to be seen to what extent the knowledge required to support these systems can become a service.

CONCLUSION

Workflow is a representation of a business process as software, but with the understanding that exceptional situations, and even some normal ones, require human intervention. Both the software system and human operators base their decisions on knowledge. Our main focus has been on the use of templates for the representation of this knowledge.

REFERENCES

Aalst, W.v.d., & Hee, K.v. (2002). *Workflow management: Models, methods, and systems.* Cambridge, MA: MIT Press.

Berztiss, A.T. (1997). Domains and patterns in conceptual modeling. In *Information Modelling and Knowledge Bases VIII* (pp. 213-223). Amsterdam: IOS Press.

Berztiss, A.T. (2002). Uncertainty management. In S.K. Chang (Ed.), *Handbook of software engineering and knowledge engineering* (Vol. 2, pp. 389-417). Singapore: World Scientific.

CMMI Product Team (2002). Capability Maturity Model Integration, Version 1.1 (CMMI-SW, V1.1) Staged Representation. CMU/SEI-2002-TR-029. Retrieved from *www.cmu.edu/sei*

Davenport, T.H. (1993). *Process innovation: Reengineering work through technology.* Cambridge, MA: Harvard Business School Press.

Davenport, T.H. (1997). *Information ecology.* New York: Oxford University Press.

Devedzic, V. (2002). Software patterns. In S.K. Chang (Ed.), *Handbook of software engineering and knowledge engineering* (Vol. 2, pp. 645-671). Singapore: World Scientific.

Dingsøyr, T., & Conradi, R. (2002). A survey of case studies of the use of knowledge management in software engineering. *International Journal of Software Engineering and Knowledge Engineering, 12,* 391-414.

Fernandes, A.A.A. (2000). Combining inductive and deductive inference in knowledge management tasks. In *Proceedings of the 11th International Workshop on Database and Expert Systems Applications (DEXA'00)* (pp. 1109-1114). Los Alamitos, CA: IEEE CS Press.

Fischer, L. (Ed.) (2004). *The workflow handbook 2004.* Mississauga, Ontario: Future Strategies, Inc.

Gaber, M.M. (2004). Mining data streams bibliography. Retrieved from *www.csse.monash.edu.au/~mgaber/WResources.htm*

Hand, D., Mannila, H., & Smyth, P. (2001). *Principles of data mining.* Cambridge, MA: MIT Press.

Hollingsworth, D. (2004). The workflow reference model: 10 years on. In (Fischer, 2004) (pp. 295-312).

ISYS (2000). Workflows technology bibliography. Retrieved from *www.isys.uni-klu.ac.at/ISYS/JE/Projects/Workflow/bibliobis2k.doc*

Kalfoglou, Y. (2001). Exploring ontologies. In S.K. Chang (Ed.), *Handbook of software engineering and knowledge engineering* (Vol. 1, pp. 863-887). Singapore: World Scientific.

Klir, G.J., & Yuan, B. (1995). *Fuzzy sets and fuzzy logic: Theory and applications.* Englewood Cliffs, NJ: Prentice Hall.

Levesque, H.J., & Lakemeyer, G. (2000). *The logic of knowledge bases.* Cambridge, MA: MIT Press.

Nonaka, I., & Takeuchi, H. (1995). *The knowledge creating company: How Japanese companies create the dynamics of innovation.* Oxford University Press.

Osterweil, L. (1987). Software processes are software too. In *Proceedings of the 9th International Conference of Software Engineering* (pp. 2-12). Los Alamitos, CA: IEEE CS Press.

Polanyi, M. (1958). *Personal knowledge.* London: Routledge & Kegan Paul.

Rus, I., & Lindvall, M. (2002). Knowledge management in software engineering. *IEEE Software 19*(3), 26-38.

Schael, T. (1998). *Workflow management systems for process organizations,* (2nd Ed.) Berlin: Springer.

Schmidt, R. (2004). Enactment of inter-organizational workflows using aspect-element-oriented Web services. In *Proceedings of the 15th International Workshop on Database and Expert Systems Applications (DEXA'04)* (pp. 254-258). Los Alamitos, CA: IEEE CS Press.

Shiu, S., & Pal, S.K. (2004). *Foundations of soft case-based reasoning.* New York: Wiley.

Software Engineering Institute (1995). *The capability maturity model: Guidelines for improving the software process.* Reading, MA: Addison-Wesley.

Tayi, G.K., & Ballou, D.P. (1998). Examining data quality (editorial introduction). *Communications of the Association for Computing Machinery 41*(2), 54-73.

Wang, P.P. (Ed.) (2001). *Computing with words.* New York: Wiley.

Watson, I. (1997). *Applying case-based reasoning: Techniques for enterprise systems.* San Francisco: Morgan Kaufmann.

Woitsch, R. (2003). Knowledge management services as a basic concept for enterprise knowledge management systems. In *Proceedings of the 3rd International Conference on Knowledge Management (I-Know03)* (pp. 523-531).

KEY TERMS

Business Process: A set of linked activities that collectively realize a business objective or policy goal.

Domain Model: Codified information about an application domain, specifically a domain for which a business process is being developed.

Ontology: An explicit specification of the concepts that characterize a domain, and of their interrelation.

Pattern: A generic solution to a recurring general problem.

Template: A solution to a recurring problem that is more specialized than problems handled by patterns.

Workflow: The result of automation, in whole or part, of a business process.

Workflow System: A software system that manages workflows.

Index of Key Terms

A

B

C

Index